Dictionary of Literary Biography

1. *The American Renaissance in New England,* edited by Joel Myerson (1978)
2. *American Novelists Since World War II,* edited by Jeffrey Helterman and Richard Layman (1978)
3. *Antebellum Writers in New York and the South,* edited by Joel Myerson (1979)
4. *American Writers in Paris, 1920-1939,* edited by Karen Lane Rood (1980)
5. *American Poets Since World War II,* 2 parts, edited by Donald J. Greiner (1980)
6. *American Novelists Since World War II, Second Series,* edited by James E. Kibler Jr. (1980)
7. *Twentieth-Century American Dramatists,* 2 parts, edited by John MacNicholas (1981)
8. *Twentieth-Century American Science-Fiction Writers,* 2 parts, edited by David Cowart and Thomas L. Wymer (1981)
9. *American Novelists, 1910-1945,* 3 parts, edited by James J. Martine (1981)
10. *Modern British Dramatists, 1900-1945,* 2 parts, edited by Stanley Weintraub (1982)
11. *American Humorists, 1800-1950,* 2 parts, edited by Stanley Trachtenberg (1982)
12. *American Realists and Naturalists,* edited by Donald Pizer and Earl N. Harbert (1982)
13. *British Dramatists Since World War II,* 2 parts, edited by Stanley Weintraub (1982)
14. *British Novelists Since 1960,* 2 parts, edited by Jay L. Halio (1983)
15. *British Novelists, 1930-1959,* 2 parts, edited by Bernard Oldsey (1983)
16. *The Beats: Literary Bohemians in Postwar America,* 2 parts, edited by Ann Charters (1983)
17. *Twentieth-Century American Historians,* edited by Clyde N. Wilson (1983)
18. *Victorian Novelists After 1885,* edited by Ira B. Nadel and William E. Fredeman (1983)
19. *British Poets, 1880-1914,* edited by Donald E. Stanford (1983)
20. *British Poets, 1914-1945,* edited by Donald E. Stanford (1983)
21. *Victorian Novelists Before 1885,* edited by Ira B. Nadel and William E. Fredeman (1983)
22. *American Writers for Children, 1900-1960,* edited by John Cech (1983)
23. *American Newspaper Journalists, 1873-1900,* edited by Perry J. Ashley (1983)
24. *American Colonial Writers, 1606-1734,* edited by Emory Elliott (1984)
25. *American Newspaper Journalists, 1901-1925,* edited by Perry J. Ashley (1984)
26. *American Screenwriters,* edited by Robert E. Morsberger, Stephen O. Lesser, and Randall Clark (1984)
27. *Poets of Great Britain and Ireland, 1945-1960,* edited by Vincent B. Sherry Jr. (1984)
28. *Twentieth-Century American-Jewish Fiction Writers,* edited by Daniel Walden (1984)
29. *American Newspaper Journalists, 1926-1950,* edited by Perry J. Ashley (1984)
30. *American Historians, 1607-1865,* edited by Clyde N. Wilson (1984)
31. *American Colonial Writers, 1735-1781,* edited by Emory Elliott (1984)
32. *Victorian Poets Before 1850,* edited by William E. Fredeman and Ira B. Nadel (1984)
33. *Afro-American Fiction Writers After 1955,* edited by Thadious M. Davis and Trudier Harris (1984)
34. *British Novelists, 1890-1929: Traditionalists,* edited by Thomas F. Staley (1985)
35. *Victorian Poets After 1850,* edited by William E. Fredeman and Ira B. Nadel (1985)
36. *British Novelists, 1890-1929: Modernists,* edited by Thomas F. Staley (1985)
37. *American Writers of the Early Republic,* edited by Emory Elliott (1985)
38. *Afro-American Writers After 1955: Dramatists and Prose Writers,* edited by Thadious M. Davis and Trudier Harris (1985)
39. *British Novelists, 1660-1800,* 2 parts, edited by Martin C. Battestin (1985)
40. *Poets of Great Britain and Ireland Since 1960,* 2 parts, edited by Vincent B. Sherry Jr. (1985)
41. *Afro-American Poets Since 1955,* edited by Trudier Harris and Thadious M. Davis (1985)
42. *American Writers for Children Before 1900,* edited by Glenn E. Estes (1985)
43. *American Newspaper Journalists, 1690-1872,* edited by Perry J. Ashley (1986)
44. *American Screenwriters, Second Series,* edited by Randall Clark, Robert E. Morsberger, and Stephen O. Lesser (1986)
45. *American Poets, 1880-1945, First Series,* edited by Peter Quartermain (1986)
46. *American Literary Publishing Houses, 1900-1980: Trade and Paperback,* edited by Peter Dzwonkoski (1986)
47. *American Historians, 1866-1912,* edited by Clyde N. Wilson (1986)
48. *American Poets, 1880-1945, Second Series,* edited by Peter Quartermain (1986)
49. *American Literary Publishing Houses, 1638-1899,* 2 parts, edited by Peter Dzwonkoski (1986)
50. *Afro-American Writers Before the Harlem Renaissance,* edited by Trudier Harris (1986)
51. *Afro-American Writers from the Harlem Renaissance to 1940,* edited by Trudier Harris (1987)
52. *American Writers for Children Since 1960: Fiction,* edited by Glenn E. Estes (1986)
53. *Canadian Writers Since 1960, First Series,* edited by W. H. New (1986)
54. *American Poets, 1880-1945, Third Series,* 2 parts, edited by Peter Quartermain (1987)
55. *Victorian Prose Writers Before 1867,* edited by William B. Thesing (1987)
56. *German Fiction Writers, 1914-1945,* edited by James Hardin (1987)
57. *Victorian Prose Writers After 1867,* edited by William B. Thesing (1987)
58. *Jacobean and Caroline Dramatists,* edited by Fredson Bowers (1987)
59. *American Literary Critics and Scholars, 1800-1850,* edited by John W. Rathbun and Monica M. Grecu (1987)
60. *Canadian Writers Since 1960, Second Series,* edited by W. H. New (1987)
61. *American Writers for Children Since 1960: Poets, Illustrators, and Nonfiction Authors,* edited by Glenn E. Estes (1987)
62. *Elizabethan Dramatists,* edited by Fredson Bowers (1987)
63. *Modern American Critics, 1920-1955,* edited by Gregory S. Jay (1988)
64. *American Literary Critics and Scholars, 1850-1880,* edited by John W. Rathbun and Monica M. Grecu (1988)

65 *French Novelists, 1900-1930*, edited by Catharine Savage Brosman (1988)
66 *German Fiction Writers, 1885-1913*, 2 parts, edited by James Hardin (1988)
67 *Modern American Critics Since 1955*, edited by Gregory S. Jay (1988)
68 *Canadian Writers, 1920-1959, First Series*, edited by W. H. New (1988)
69 *Contemporary German Fiction Writers, First Series*, edited by Wolfgang D. Elfe and James Hardin (1988)
70 *British Mystery Writers, 1860-1919*, edited by Bernard Benstock and Thomas F. Staley (1988)
71 *American Literary Critics and Scholars, 1880-1900*, edited by John W. Rathbun and Monica M. Grecu (1988)
72 *French Novelists, 1930-1960*, edited by Catharine Savage Brosman (1988)
73 *American Magazine Journalists, 1741-1850*, edited by Sam G. Riley (1988)
74 *American Short-Story Writers Before 1880*, edited by Bobby Ellen Kimbel, with the assistance of William E. Grant (1988)
75 *Contemporary German Fiction Writers, Second Series*, edited by Wolfgang D. Elfe and James Hardin (1988)
76 *Afro-American Writers, 1940-1955*, edited by Trudier Harris (1988)
77 *British Mystery Writers, 1920-1939*, edited by Bernard Benstock and Thomas F. Staley (1988)
78 *American Short-Story Writers, 1880-1910*, edited by Bobby Ellen Kimbel, with the assistance of William E. Grant (1988)
79 *American Magazine Journalists, 1850-1900*, edited by Sam G. Riley (1988)
80 *Restoration and Eighteenth-Century Dramatists, First Series*, edited by Paula R. Backscheider (1989)
81 *Austrian Fiction Writers, 1875-1913*, edited by James Hardin and Donald G. Daviau (1989)
82 *Chicano Writers, First Series*, edited by Francisco A. Lomelí and Carl R. Shirley (1989)
83 *French Novelists Since 1960*, edited by Catharine Savage Brosman (1989)
84 *Restoration and Eighteenth-Century Dramatists, Second Series*, edited by Paula R. Backscheider (1989)
85 *Austrian Fiction Writers After 1914*, edited by James Hardin and Donald G. Daviau (1989)
86 *American Short-Story Writers, 1910-1945, First Series*, edited by Bobby Ellen Kimbel (1989)
87 *British Mystery and Thriller Writers Since 1940, First Series*, edited by Bernard Benstock and Thomas F. Staley (1989)
88 *Canadian Writers, 1920-1959, Second Series*, edited by W. H. New (1989)
89 *Restoration and Eighteenth-Century Dramatists, Third Series*, edited by Paula R. Backscheider (1989)
90 *German Writers in the Age of Goethe, 1789-1832*, edited by James Hardin and Christoph E. Schweitzer (1989)
91 *American Magazine Journalists, 1900-1960, First Series*, edited by Sam G. Riley (1990)
92 *Canadian Writers, 1890-1920*, edited by W. H. New (1990)
93 *British Romantic Poets, 1789-1832, First Series*, edited by John R. Greenfield (1990)
94 *German Writers in the Age of Goethe: Sturm und Drang to Classicism*, edited by James Hardin and Christoph E. Schweitzer (1990)
95 *Eighteenth-Century British Poets, First Series*, edited by John Sitter (1990)
96 *British Romantic Poets, 1789-1832, Second Series*, edited by John R. Greenfield (1990)
97 *German Writers from the Enlightenment to Sturm und Drang, 1720-1764*, edited by James Hardin and Christoph E. Schweitzer (1990)
98 *Modern British Essayists, First Series*, edited by Robert Beum (1990)
99 *Canadian Writers Before 1890*, edited by W. H. New (1990)
100 *Modern British Essayists, Second Series*, edited by Robert Beum (1990)
101 *British Prose Writers, 1660-1800, First Series*, edited by Donald T. Siebert (1991)
102 *American Short-Story Writers, 1910-1945, Second Series*, edited by Bobby Ellen Kimbel (1991)
103 *American Literary Biographers, First Series*, edited by Steven Serafin (1991)
104 *British Prose Writers, 1660-1800, Second Series*, edited by Donald T. Siebert (1991)
105 *American Poets Since World War II, Second Series*, edited by R. S. Gwynn (1991)
106 *British Literary Publishing Houses, 1820-1880*, edited by Patricia J. Anderson and Jonathan Rose (1991)
107 *British Romantic Prose Writers, 1789-1832, First Series*, edited by John R. Greenfield (1991)
108 *Twentieth-Century Spanish Poets, First Series*, edited by Michael L. Perna (1991)
109 *Eighteenth-Century British Poets, Second Series*, edited by John Sitter (1991)
110 *British Romantic Prose Writers, 1789-1832, Second Series*, edited by John R. Greenfield (1991)
111 *American Literary Biographers, Second Series*, edited by Steven Serafin (1991)
112 *British Literary Publishing Houses, 1881-1965*, edited by Jonathan Rose and Patricia J. Anderson (1991)
113 *Modern Latin-American Fiction Writers, First Series*, edited by William Luis (1992)
114 *Twentieth-Century Italian Poets, First Series*, edited by Giovanna Wedel De Stasio, Glauco Cambon, and Antonio Illiano (1992)
115 *Medieval Philosophers*, edited by Jeremiah Hackett (1992)
116 *British Romantic Novelists, 1789-1832*, edited by Bradford K. Mudge (1992)
117 *Twentieth-Century Caribbean and Black African Writers, First Series*, edited by Bernth Lindfors and Reinhard Sander (1992)
118 *Twentieth-Century German Dramatists, 1889-1918*, edited by Wolfgang D. Elfe and James Hardin (1992)
119 *Nineteenth-Century French Fiction Writers: Romanticism and Realism, 1800-1860*, edited by Catharine Savage Brosman (1992)
120 *American Poets Since World War II, Third Series*, edited by R. S. Gwynn (1992)
121 *Seventeenth-Century British Nondramatic Poets, First Series*, edited by M. Thomas Hester (1992)
122 *Chicano Writers, Second Series*, edited by Francisco A. Lomelí and Carl R. Shirley (1992)
123 *Nineteenth-Century French Fiction Writers: Naturalism and Beyond, 1860-1900*, edited by Catharine Savage Brosman (1992)
124 *Twentieth-Century German Dramatists, 1919-1992*, edited by Wolfgang D. Elfe and James Hardin (1992)
125 *Twentieth-Century Caribbean and Black African Writers, Second Series*, edited by Bernth Lindfors and Reinhard Sander (1993)
126 *Seventeenth-Century British Nondramatic Poets, Second Series*, edited by M. Thomas Hester (1993)
127 *American Newspaper Publishers, 1950-1990*, edited by Perry J. Ashley (1993)
128 *Twentieth-Century Italian Poets, Second Series*, edited by Giovanna Wedel De Stasio, Glauco Cambon, and Antonio Illiano (1993)
129 *Nineteenth-Century German Writers, 1841-1900*, edited by James Hardin and Siegfried Mews (1993)
130 *American Short-Story Writers Since World War II*, edited by Patrick Meanor (1993)
131 *Seventeenth-Century British Nondramatic Poets, Third Series*, edited by M. Thomas Hester (1993)

132 *Sixteenth-Century British Nondramatic Writers, First Series,* edited by David A. Richardson (1993)

133 *Nineteenth-Century German Writers to 1840,* edited by James Hardin and Siegfried Mews (1993)

134 *Twentieth-Century Spanish Poets, Second Series,* edited by Jerry Phillips Winfield (1994)

135 *British Short-Fiction Writers, 1880-1914: The Realist Tradition,* edited by William B. Thesing (1994)

136 *Sixteenth-Century British Nondramatic Writers, Second Series,* edited by David A. Richardson (1994)

137 *American Magazine Journalists, 1900-1960, Second Series,* edited by Sam G. Riley (1994)

138 *German Writers and Works of the High Middle Ages: 1170-1280,* edited by James Hardin and Will Hasty (1994)

139 *British Short-Fiction Writers, 1945-1980,* edited by Dean Baldwin (1994)

140 *American Book-Collectors and Bibliographers, First Series,* edited by Joseph Rosenblum (1994)

141 *British Children's Writers, 1880-1914,* edited by Laura M. Zaidman (1994)

142 *Eighteenth-Century British Literary Biographers,* edited by Steven Serafin (1994)

143 *American Novelists Since World War II, Third Series,* edited by James R. Giles and Wanda H. Giles (1994)

144 *Nineteenth-Century British Literary Biographers,* edited by Steven Serafin (1994)

145 *Modern Latin-American Fiction Writers, Second Series,* edited by William Luis and Ann González (1994)

146 *Old and Middle English Literature,* edited by Jeffrey Helterman and Jerome Mitchell (1994)

147 *South Slavic Writers Before World War II,* edited by Vasa D. Mihailovich (1994)

148 *German Writers and Works of the Early Middle Ages: 800-1170,* edited by Will Hasty and James Hardin (1994)

149 *Late Nineteenth- and Early Twentieth-Century British Literary Biographers,* edited by Steven Serafin (1995)

150 *Early Modern Russian Writers, Late Seventeenth and Eighteenth Centuries,* edited by Marcus C. Levitt (1995)

151 *British Prose Writers of the Early Seventeenth Century,* edited by Clayton D. Lein (1995)

152 *American Novelists Since World War II, Fourth Series,* edited by James and Wanda Giles (1995)

153 *Late-Victorian and Edwardian British Novelists, First Series,* edited by George M. Johnson (1995)

154 *The British Literary Book Trade, 1700-1820,* edited by James K. Bracken and Joel Silver (1995)

155 *Twentieth-Century British Literary Biographers,* edited by Steven Serafin (1995)

156 *British Short-Fiction Writers, 1880-1914: The Romantic Tradition,* edited by William F. Naufftus (1995)

157 *Twentieth-Century Caribbean and Black African Writers, Third Series,* edited by Bernth Lindfors and Reinhard Sander (1995)

158 *British Reform Writers, 1789-1832,* edited by Gary Kelly and Edd Applegate (1995)

159 *British Short-Fiction Writers, 1800-1880,* edited by John R. Greenfield (1996)

160 *British Children's Writers, 1914-1960,* edited by Donald R. Hettinga and Gary D. Schmidt (1996)

161 *British Children's Writers Since 1960, First Series,* edited by Caroline Hunt (1996)

162 *British Short-Fiction Writers, 1915-1945,* edited by John H. Rogers (1996)

163 *British Children's Writers, 1800-1880,* edited by Meena Khorana (1996)

164 *German Baroque Writers, 1580-1660,* edited by James Hardin (1996)

165 *American Poets Since World War II, Fourth Series,* edited by Joseph Conte (1996)

166 *British Travel Writers, 1837-1875,* edited by Barbara Brothers and Julia Gergits (1996)

167 *Sixteenth-Century British Nondramatic Writers, Third Series,* edited by David A. Richardson (1996)

168 *German Baroque Writers, 1661-1730,* edited by James Hardin (1996)

169 *American Poets Since World War II, Fifth Series,* edited by Joseph Conte (1996)

170 *The British Literary Book Trade, 1475-1700,* edited by James K. Bracken and Joel Silver (1996)

171 *Twentieth-Century American Sportswriters,* edited by Richard Orodenker (1996)

172 *Sixteenth-Century British Nondramatic Writers, Fourth Series,* edited by David A. Richardson (1996)

173 *American Novelists Since World War II, Fifth Series,* edited by James R. Giles and Wanda H. Giles (1996)

174 *British Travel Writers, 1876-1909,* edited by Barbara Brothers and Julia Gergits (1997)

175 *Native American Writers of the United States,* edited by Kenneth M. Roemer (1997)

176 *Ancient Greek Authors,* edited by Ward W. Briggs (1997)

177 *Italian Novelists Since World War II, 1945-1965* edited by Augustus Pallotta (1997)

178 *British Fantasy and Science-Fiction Writers Before World War I,* edited by Darren Harris-Fain (1997)

179 *German Writers of the Renaissance and Reformation, 1280-1580,* edited by James Hardin and Max Reinhart (1997)

180 *Japanese Fiction Writers, 1868-1945,* edited by Van C. Gessel (1997)

181 *South Slavic Writers Since World War II,* edited by Vasa D. Mihailovich (1997)

182 *Japanese Fiction Writers Since World War II,* edited by Van C. Gessel (1997)

183 *American Travel Writers, 1776-1864,* edited by James J. Schramer and Donald Ross (1997)

184 *Nineteenth-Century British Book-Collectors and Bibliographers,* edited by William Baker and Kenneth Womack (1997)

185 *American Literary Journalists, 1945-1995, First Series,* edited by Arthur J. Kaul (1998)

186 *Nineteenth-Century American Western Writers,* edited by Robert L. Gale (1998)

187 *American Book Collectors and Bibliographers, Second Series,* edited by Joseph Rosenblum (1998)

188 *American Book and Magazine Illustrators to 1920,* edited by Steven E. Smith, Catherine A. Hastedt, and Donald H. Dyal (1998)

189 *American Travel Writers, 1850–1915,* edited by Donald Ross and James J. Schramer (1998)

190 *British Reform Writers, 1832–1914,* edited by Gary Kelly and Edd Applegate (1998)

Documentary Series

1 *Sherwood Anderson, Willa Cather, John Dos Passos, Theodore Dreiser, F. Scott Fitzgerald, Ernest Hemingway, Sinclair Lewis,* edited by Margaret A. Van Antwerp (1982)

2 *James Gould Cozzens, James T. Farrell, William Faulkner, John O'Hara, John Steinbeck, Thomas Wolfe, Richard*

Wright, edited by Margaret A. Van Antwerp (1982)

3 *Saul Bellow, Jack Kerouac, Norman Mailer, Vladimir Nabokov, John Updike, Kurt Vonnegut*, edited by Mary Bruccoli (1983)

4 *Tennessee Williams*, edited by Margaret A. Van Antwerp and Sally Johns (1984)

5 *American Transcendentalists*, edited by Joel Myerson (1988)

6 *Hardboiled Mystery Writers: Raymond Chandler, Dashiell Hammett, Ross Macdonald*, edited by Matthew J. Bruccoli and Richard Layman (1989)

7 *Modern American Poets: James Dickey, Robert Frost, Marianne Moore*, edited by Karen L. Rood (1989)

8 *The Black Aesthetic Movement*, edited by Jeffrey Louis Decker (1991)

9 *American Writers of the Vietnam War: W. D. Ehrhart, Larry Heinemann, Tim O'Brien, Walter McDonald, John M. Del Vecchio*, edited by Ronald Baughman (1991)

10 *The Bloomsbury Group*, edited by Edward L. Bishop (1992)

11 *American Proletarian Culture: The Twenties and The Thirties*, edited by Jon Christian Suggs (1993)

12 *Southern Women Writers: Flannery O'Connor, Katherine Anne Porter, Eudora Welty*, edited by Mary Ann Wimsatt and Karen L. Rood (1994)

13 *The House of Scribner, 1846-1904*, edited by John Delaney (1996)

14 *Four Women Writers for Children, 1868-1918*, edited by Caroline C. Hunt (1996)

15 *American Expatriate Writers: Paris in the Twenties*, edited by Matthew J. Bruccoli and Robert W. Trogdon (1997)

16 *The House of Scribner, 1905-1930*, edited by John Delaney (1997)

Yearbooks

1980 edited by Karen L. Rood, Jean W. Ross, and Richard Ziegfeld (1981)

1981 edited by Karen L. Rood, Jean W. Ross, and Richard Ziegfeld (1982)

1982 edited by Richard Ziegfeld; associate editors: Jean W. Ross and Lynne C. Zeigler (1983)

1983 edited by Mary Bruccoli and Jean W. Ross; associate editor: Richard Ziegfeld (1984)

1984 edited by Jean W. Ross (1985)

1985 edited by Jean W. Ross (1986)

1986 edited by J. M. Brook (1987)

1987 edited by J. M. Brook (1988)

1988 edited by J. M. Brook (1989)

1989 edited by J. M. Brook (1990)

1990 edited by James W. Hipp (1991)

1991 edited by James W. Hipp (1992)

1992 edited by James W. Hipp (1993)

1993 edited by James W. Hipp, contributing editor George Garrett (1994)

1994 edited by James W. Hipp, contributing editor George Garrett (1995)

1995 edited by James W. Hipp, contributing editor George Garrett (1996)

1996 edited by Samuel W. Bruce and L. Kay Webster, contributing editor George Garrett (1997)

Concise Series

Concise Dictionary of American Literary Biography, 6 volumes (1988-1989): *The New Consciousness, 1941-1968; Colonization to the American Renaissance, 1640-1865; Realism, Naturalism, and Local Color, 1865-1917; The Twenties, 1917-1929; The Age of Maturity, 1929-1941; Broadening Views, 1968-1988.*

Concise Dictionary of British Literary Biography, 8 volumes (1991-1992): *Writers of the Middle Ages and Renaissance Before 1660; Writers of the Restoration and Eighteenth Century, 1660-1789; Writers of the Romantic Period, 1789-1832; Victorian Writers, 1832-1890; Late Victorian and Edwardian Writers, 1890-1914; Modern Writers, 1914-1945; Writers After World War II, 1945-1960; Contemporary Writers, 1960 to Present.*

Dictionary of Literary Biography® • Volume One Hundred Ninety

British Reform Writers, 1832–1914

Dictionary of Literary Biography® • Volume One Hundred Ninety

British Reform Writers, 1832–1914

Edited by
Gary Kelly
University of Alberta
and
Edd Applegate
Middle Tennessee State University

A Bruccoli Clark Layman Book
Gale Research
Detroit, Washington, D.C., London

Advisory Board for
DICTIONARY OF LITERARY BIOGRAPHY

John Baker
William Cagle
Patrick O'Connor
George Garrett
Trudier Harris

Matthew J. Bruccoli and Richard Layman, Editorial Directors
C. E. Frazer Clark Jr., Managing Editor
Karen Rood, Senior Editor

Printed in the United States of America

The paper used in this publication meets the minimum requirements of American National Standard for Information Sciences–Permanence Paper for Printed Library Materials, ANSI Z39.48-1984.∞ ™

This publication is a creative work fully protected by all applicable copyright laws, as well as by misappropriation, trade secret, unfair competition, and other applicable laws. The authors and editors of this work have added value to the underlying factual material herein through one or more of the following: unique and original selection, coordination, expression, arrangement, and classification of the information.

All rights to this publication will be vigorously defended.

Copyright © 1998 by Gale Research
835 Penobscot Building
Detroit, MI 48226

All rights reserved including the right of reproduction in
whole or in part in any form.

Library of Congress Cataloging-in-Publication Data

British reform writers, 1832–1914 / edited by Gary Kelly and Edd Applegate.
    p. cm.–(Dictionary of literary biography; v. 190)
"A Bruccoli Clark Layman book."
Includes bibliographical references and index.
ISBN 0-7876-1845-4 (alk. paper)
1. English literature–19th century–Bio-bibliography–Dictionaries. 2. Literature and society–Great Britain–Bio-bibliography–Dictionaries. 3. English literature–20th century–Bio-bibliography–Dictionaries. 4. Social reformers–Great Britain–Biography–Dictionaries. 5. Authors, English–19th century–Biography–Dictionaries. 6. Authors, English–20th century–Biography–Dictionaries. 7. Reformers–Great Britain–Biography–Dictionaries. 8. Social problems in literature–Dictionaries. I. Kelly, Gary. II. Applegate, Edd. III. Series.
PR468.S6B76 1998
820.9'008'03   98-4950
[B]–DC21   CIP

---

10 9 8 7 6 5 4 3 2 1

For Vera and Albert Levine

Contents

Plan of the Series xiii
Introduction xv

Arthur James Balfour (1848-1930) 3
   Timothy J. Evans

Samuel Bamford (1788-1872) 13
   Ronald Tetreault

Sabine Baring-Gould (1834-1924) 18
   Max Keith Sutton

Sir Walter Besant (1836-1901) 32
   Kirsten Escobar

William Booth (1829-1912) 43
   Donald S. Armentrout

James Bryce, Viscount Bryce (1838-1922) 52
   Hayden Ward

Josephine Elizabeth Butler (1828-1906) 64
   Susan Mumm

Sir George Tomkyns Chesney (1830-1895) 73
   Pamela Shorrocks

Frances Power Cobbe (1822-1904) 78
   Susan Hamilton

John Doherty (1798?-1854) 87
   Timothy Randall

Ebenezer Elliott (1781-1849) 93
   Timothy Randall

Havelock Ellis (1859-1939) 101
   Terrie M. Romano

Millicent Garrett Fawcett (1847-1929) 111
   Sandra den Otter

Katharine Bruce Glasier (1867-1950) 120
   Erika Rothwell

Thomas Hill Green (1836-1882) 127
   John Ferns

Frederic Harrison (1831-1923) 132
   Timothy J. Evans

Ellice Hopkins (1836-1904) 139
   Susan Mumm

Charles Kingsley (1819-1875) 145
   Isobel M. Findlay

Samuel Lover (1797-1868) 160
   Paul G. Ashdown

Harriet Martineau (1802-1876) 167
   Alison Winter

Henry Mayhew (1812-1887) 180
   Lynn MacKay

John Stuart Mill (1806-1873) 189
   Eugene R. August

Hugh Miller (1802-1856) 200
   Douglas S. Campbell

John Morley (1838-1923) 207
   Christopher A. Kent

Frederic W. H. Myers (1843-1901) 216
   Barbara Frey Waxman

Francis William Newman (1805-1897) 224
   Sidney Coulling

Margaret Oliphant (1828-1897) 232
   Rhonda Batchelor

Sir Arthur Quiller-Couch (1863-1944) 245
   John Ferns

John Ruskin (1819-1900) 253
   Gregory Claeys

Olive Schreiner (1855-1920) 266
   Sylvia Vance

Bernard Shaw (1856-1950) 273
   Sos Eltis

Edith Jemima Simcox (1844-1901) 289
   James Diedrick

Sir Leslie Stephen (1932-1904) 298
   Kathryn Harvey

Contents

Hesba Stretton (Sarah Smith) (1832–1911).........310
   Patricia Demers

Charlotte Maria Tucker (A.L.O.E.)
   (1821–1893) 316
   Erika Rothwell

Alfred Russel Wallace (1823–1913) 325
   Charles Blinderman

Samuel Warren (1807–1877) 334
   Bege K. Bowers

Beatrice Webb (1858–1943) and
   Sidney Webb (1859–1947) 339
   Sylvia Vance

Richard Whately (1787–1863) 347
   William Naufftus

Oscar Wilde (1854–1900) 360
   Jennifer Kelly

Books for Further Reading 371

Contributors 374

Cumulative Index 377

Plan of the Series

... Almost the most prodigious asset of a country, and perhaps its most precious possession, is its native literary product — when that product is fine and noble and enduring.

Mark Twain*

The advisory board, the editors, and the publisher of the *Dictionary of Literary Biography* are joined in endorsing Mark Twain's declaration. The literature of a nation provides an inexhaustible resource of permanent worth. We intend to make literature and its creators better understood and more accessible to students and the reading public, while satisfying the standards of teachers and scholars.

To meet these requirements, *literary biography* has been construed in terms of the author's achievement. The most important thing about a writer is his writing. Accordingly, the entries in *DLB* are career biographies, tracing the development of the author's canon and the evolution of his reputation.

The purpose of *DLB* is not only to provide reliable information in a convenient format but also to place the figures in the larger perspective of literary history and to offer appraisals of their accomplishments by qualified scholars.

The publication plan for *DLB* resulted from two years of preparation. The project was proposed to Bruccoli Clark by Frederick C. Ruffner, president of the Gale Research Company, in November 1975. After specimen entries were prepared and typeset, an advisory board was formed to refine the entry format and develop the series rationale. In meetings held during 1976, the publisher, series editors, and advisory board approved the scheme for a comprehensive biographical dictionary of persons who contributed to North American literature. Editorial work on the first volume began in January 1977, and it was published in 1978. In order to make *DLB* more than a reference tool and to compile volumes that individually have claim to status as literary history, it was decided to organize volumes by topic, period, or genre. Each of these freestanding volumes provides a biographical-bibliographical guide and overview for a particular area of literature. We are convinced that this organization—as opposed to a single alphabet method—constitutes a valuable innovation in the presentation of reference material. The volume plan necessarily requires many decisions for the placement and treatment of authors who might properly be included in two or three volumes. In some instances a major figure will be included in separate volumes, but with different entries emphasizing the aspect of his career appropriate to each volume. Ernest Hemingway, for example, is represented in *American Writers in Paris, 1920-1939* by an entry focusing on his expatriate apprenticeship; he is also in *American Novelists, 1910-1945* with an entry surveying his entire career, as well as in *American Short-Story Writers, 1910-1945, Second Series* with an entry concentrating on his short stories. Each volume includes a cumulative index of the subject authors and articles. Comprehensive indexes to the entire series are planned.

The series has been further augmented by the *DLB Yearbooks* (since 1981) which update published entries and add new entries to keep the *DLB* current with contemporary activity. There have also been *DLB Documentary Series* volumes which provide biographical and critical source materials for figures whose work is judged to have particular interest for students. One of these companion volumes is entirely devoted to Tennessee Williams.

We define literature as the *intellectual commerce of a nation:* not merely as belles lettres but as that ample and complex process by which ideas are generated, shaped, and transmitted. *DLB* entries are not limited to "creative writers" but extend to other figures who in their time and in their way influenced the mind of a people. Thus the series encompasses historians, journalists, publishers, book collectors, and screenwriters. By this means readers of *DLB* may be aided to perceive literature not as cult scripture in the keeping of intellectual high priests but firmly positioned at the center of a nation's life.

*From an unpublished section of Mark Twain's autobiography, copyright by the Mark Twain Company

DLB includes the major writers appropriate to each volume and those standing in the ranks behind them. Scholarly and critical counsel has been sought in deciding which minor figures to include and how full their entries should be. Wherever possible, useful references are made to figures who do not warrant separate entries.

Each *DLB* volume has an expert volume editor responsible for planning the volume, selecting the figures for inclusion, and assigning the entries. Volume editors are also responsible for preparing, where appropriate, appendices surveying the major periodicals and literary and intellectual movements for their volumes, as well as lists of further readings. Work on the series as a whole is coordinated at the Bruccoli Clark Layman editorial center in Columbia, South Carolina, where the editorial staff is responsible for accuracy and utility of the published volumes.

One feature that distinguishes *DLB* is the illustration policy–its concern with the iconography of literature. Just as an author is influenced by his surroundings, so is the reader's understanding of the author enhanced by a knowledge of his environment. Therefore *DLB* volumes include not only drawings, paintings, and photographs of authors, often depicting them at various stages in their careers, but also illustrations of their families and places where they lived. Title pages are regularly reproduced in facsimile along with dust jackets for modern authors. The dust jackets are a special feature of *DLB* because they often document better than anything else the way in which an author's work was perceived in its own time. Specimens of the writers' manuscripts and letters are included when feasible.

Samuel Johnson rightly decreed that "The chief glory of every people arises from its authors." The purpose of the *Dictionary of Literary Biography* is to compile literary history in the surest way available to us–by accurate and comprehensive treatment of the lives and work of those who contributed to it.

The *DLB* Advisory Board

Introduction

This volume of the *Dictionary of Literary Biography* follows *DLB 158: British Reform Writers, 1789–1832,* which covers the period of crisis in Britain caused by the French Revolution, the Napoleonic Wars, and the aftermath of that crisis, as Britain struggled to establish a new and stable political, social, and economic order. Reform issues during that earlier period were usually clear-cut; the options were usually presented forcefully and with an urgency arising from a sense of crisis. The present volume covers a longer period, one of greater changes and more momentous reforms than those of the earlier period, and one in which the sense of crisis and urgency was, for most people, usually less pressing. The reforming impulse moved in many more directions, engaged many more issues, and consequently may appear more diffuse. For that reason the kinds and quality of writing that promoted reform were also more varied from 1832 to 1914, the period of reforms covered in this volume and extending from the Reform Act of 1832 to World War I.

The importance of these events is indicated by the appellation "great" conventionally accorded to them by both historians and ordinary people. This importance can be exaggerated, but these events demarcate a period of unquestionably great change in Britain, its empire, and indeed the world. Change is not to be equated with reform, yet desire for reform is at least part of and an important motive for change—for better or worse. If reform is instrumental in change, then even a cursory study of nineteenth-century Britain and its empire suggests that reform was a leading and pervasive characteristic of the age. As in the times that preceded and followed this period, however, *reform* is not easy to define precisely. Yet this should not deter one from attempting to survey or explore a representative selection of reforms, or more particularly of reform writing.

The period from 1832 to 1914 was characterized by reform ideas, movements, and legislation of many kinds. These last include the great political Reform Acts in 1832, 1867, 1868, 1884, and 1885. Such reforms of the electoral system, parliamentary representation, and the franchise were followed by further reforms in 1918, 1928, 1948, and 1969, but the "Great" Reform Act of 1832 has been seen as the watershed in British political history. Hotly contested at the time, this piece of legislation democratized the political process, but one can attribute its significance as a watershed to the fact that many thought that the reforms it enacted, or something like them, were necessary in order to avoid reform through violent revolution. Whether this was true or not, from the passing of the Reform Act of 1832 and throughout the period covered by this volume, reforms of the political process were often seen as important, if not crucial, to achieving reforms of other kinds, however remote they may seem from the political and parliamentary process. Accordingly, the year 1832 marks one boundary point for this volume.

The other boundary is the beginning of World War I, an event and experience that to many seemed to have come about because the world had failed to be sufficiently reformed. This event also seemed to many to precipitate additional and more radical political, economic, and social reforms. The Russian Revolution in 1917 was one example, and the extension of the franchise to women—partly as a consequence of their contribution to the war effort—was another.

Although some political reform writers are included, and to some extent all reform writers were engaged in some kind of political action, this volume does not focus on political reform. In fact, political reform—especially legislative reform—may be regarded as only one part of a wider transformation, a massive if uneven and often contradictory process that historians call modernization, or the transition from a society, culture, and economy based on hierarchical and "traditional" social relations of mutual obligation to a society based on more or less freely applying capitalist principles and practices to economic relations and thereby radically altering social relations and cultural life. Such modernization effected drastic changes, often represented as reforms, in almost every aspect of British life.

Raising the reform issues explored in the previous volume of reform writers, modernization can be seen as the cause of revolutionary crises of the late eighteenth and early nineteenth centuries. In the period from 1832 to 1914 reform issues proliferated to include dimensions of culture such as religion, the economy, medicine and science, education, public colonial administration, local and national government, the legal system, the property and civil rights of women and other oppressed groups, public sanitation and hygiene, working conditions, the treatment of children, the condition of enslaved or otherwise bound labor, the treatment of animals, ecology (as it is now called), treatment of the poor, the armed forces, international relations, warfare, sexuality and birth control, professional training and organization, social values and attitudes, literature and the humanities—the list could go on.

Not all kinds of reform promoted between the passage of the Great Reform Act and the beginning of the "Great" War appear progressive when they are viewed from the present time. Most reformers of the period claimed to speak for a future that would be better in some way—materially, socially, morally, spiritually, or culturally. Many reformers were therefore concerned to address what they found to be current evils and abuses, which they often represented, accurately or not, as the legacy of the past. In addressing such evils, reformers tried to seize the public imagination with images of a better future, a reality that did not yet exist. The broad movement that historians refer to as modernization was relentlessly forward-looking and inclined to disregard or dismiss the past as the source of continuing evils and present abuses.

Some reformers claimed, however, that the past had much of value to offer as a source of and inspiration for reforms of the present. Consequently, one of the preoccupations of nineteenth-century intellectual and cultural life was with the problem of history, the character and continuity of the past in relation to the present and future. The period from 1832 through 1914 was a golden age of history, of grand narratives in historiography ranging from fictional representations of British national history, identity, culture, and imperial destiny to the subtly racist celebrations of the history and destiny of English-speaking peoples and the radically reformist, indeed revolutionary, economy interpretations of history made by Karl Marx and his followers.

Some reformers used history in yet another way: as a model to which the present ought to return. To late twentieth-century readers, such reformers may seem to deserve the title of reactionaries. As Mark Girouard has shown, a powerful cultural movement in the nineteenth-century embraced precisely such a social transformation or "return"—the "return to Camelot," or an idealized, stable, cultured, noble, and conflict-free hierarchical society of the Middle Ages. This return was clearly aimed to ameliorate or reform what many felt was a society that had become too materialistic, oppressive, beset with conflict, brutalizing, and simply ugly. Readers who remember the Camelot of another reform-oriented period of American history, that of the John Fitzgerald Kennedy presidency of the early 1960s, must recognize that such returns to the past in the name of a better future can powerfully shape the political imagination of the public, whatever the actual reforms born of such a movement may be.

Inevitably a retrospective view of reform from 1832 to 1914 seems to include many paradoxes and contradictions. Readers looking for a coherent, consistent pattern to reform in this or any period will be disappointed by the perplexing and apparently confusing varieties of reform ideas, movements, and writing. Disappointed, too, will be those who try to apply to the past their own definitions of reform, or their understanding of what reform might have achieved in the past. Such disappointments may dispose readers to regard reform movements and writers of the past as largely irrelevant to the present. On the other hand, taking the view that history is relentlessly particular can make the past seem to be a rich mine of ideas for the present instead of either an obsolete or an idealized version of the present. This is the view that partly shapes the selection of reform writers included in this volume.

Rather than applying a strict, present-centered definition of reform to the past, it may be useful to adopt a looser criterion and occasionally to try to view the present from the past. Some surveys of reform ideas and movements and biographical dictionaries of reformers take a strict approach and usually focus on reform dedicated to social, economic, and political change. This kind of approach reflects important concerns of the past, but it also powerfully reflects interests, often unstated or unexamined, of the present conflict-laden, violent time. Furthermore, such a survey, if attempting to be comprehensive and based on what those who lived in the past understood as reform, might prove impossibly voluminous and confusingly diverse. This volume is deliberately based on a broad understanding of reform and includes both reformers who seemed important in their own time and reformers who seem to be of interest now. The conception of reform understood in this volume is exploratory and permissive rather than monolithic or definitive.

Another important criterion informs the selection in this volume and distinguishes it from other collections of biographies of reformers. This collection appears in a series of literary biography and thus considers those reformers who were also writers in some substantial, influential, or interesting and unusual ways. Not all reformers were writers, and the writing of many reformers was a minor part of their reform work. Indeed, it might seem that the fully engaged, activist reformer would have had little time for writing, or at least for writing that would have more than merely ephemeral importance as writing, especially the kind of work usually designated as "literature." It will be obvious, too, that not all writers considered important to literature were reformers. Nevertheless, most nineteenth-century writers who are still part of the literary canon or are considered to have produced literature of enduring value seem to have had reform interests and to have promoted such interests in their writing. Some literary critics today may argue that the reform interests of these writers are inextricable from their artistic achievements. Most surveys of reform, even when they include writers in addition to activists and focus on reform as it is represented in writing, do not consider genre, style, and other "literary" features as rhetorically significant to the reformative aim of the writing.

Another important point should be made about the relation between reform and writing from 1832 to 1914. Literacy and printed works of all kinds—from newspapers to scholarly books, religious tracts, fashionable novels, learned and literary magazines, and cheap, ephemeral street literature—expanded enormously throughout this period. A growing social, cultural, and political awareness of a new and, to many people, worrisome phenomenon—often referred to as "the rise of reading public" or the spread of reading among all social classes—had begun in the period immediately before 1832, and the number of people who made up this reading public enormously expanded in the years between 1832 and 1914. Social and cultural expectations, lack of access to education, and the sheer cost of books had virtually excluded many lower-class readers from the information and imaginative breadth that literacy and reading habits afforded such new readers. Public education became a major interest throughout the British Empire, and writing thus became an important focus of reform interest. Reformers of many kinds initiated grand schemes to spread books "of the right kind" to this new lower-class reading public, and to furnish a volume on reform as such activities were embodied and disseminated through writing of various (and not merely literary) kinds should enhance our understanding and appreciation of some consequences of those cultural developments.

Even with these criteria in mind one must recognize that a volume such as this can only begin to reflect the diversity of reform writing throughout this period. This volume aims to be as representative as possible, given the resources of available space and informed contributors able to assess both the reform ideas and the writings appropriate for each entry. Inevitably, many reform writers who might have been included in the volume are not discussed in it. The aim has been to include some major as well as minor figures, many being remembered primarily as writers and secondarily as reformers, in addition to writers known primarily as reformers whose writing also comprised some part of their reform activism. Some writers are included who have appeared mainly as literary artists of one kind or another in earlier volumes of the *Dictionary of Literary Biography*. In this volume these writers are considered in terms of their reform interests or influence. An attempt has also been made to include representative writers from as many fields as possible, although it is again inevitable that some arenas of reform activity and writing have had to be left out.

The editors hope, however, that the variety of writing and writers included in this volume may stimulate readers who refer to it for one purpose to think about other aspects of reform and writing in the period. The volume aims to present a cross-section, however partial, of reform writing between two major turning points in the history of reform, and consequently in reform writing, in Britain.

Among the major literary figures included are the art critic, historian, and cultural campaigner John Ruskin; the playwright and social provocateur Oscar Wilde; and the playwright and socialist Bernard Shaw—three different characters and writers whose influence extended from the beginning to well beyond the end of the period covered by this volume. Many lesser literary figures have been included, and such writers have been receiving increasing attention as part of continuing academic debate on and revision of ideas about the nature and function of literature in education and society.

The distinction between literature and other forms of writing, including supposedly "higher" forms of journalism, was not as clear in the nineteenth century as it may be today. In the nineteenth century many writers moved easily from the writing of what were recognized as "high" literary forms to the writing of what were then considered lesser ones such as the novel, essays, biographies, popular treatises, and other varieties of writing done by professional men and women of letters. Among these writers included in this volume are Olive Schreiner, Margaret Oliphant, Charles Kingsley, Thomas Hill Green, Frederic Harrison, Harriet Martineau, and Leslie Stephen.

Stephen, for example, is known to students of literature mainly as the father of Virginia Woolf and is a man whose works are rarely read, even more rarely read for their own sake. Like many of the other "obscure" writers of this period, however, Stephen was a prominent figure in his time and deserves notice in his own right. If many of these "lesser" writers now receiving attention are women, this reflects the contribution of feminist scholarship and criticism to a changing understanding of the past roles of women in literature and society. Also included have been a few literary writers such as Sir Walter Besant, Oliphant, and Sabine Baring-Gould, who are even less well known than such women or are known mainly as prolific hacks or gentrified amateurs. These lesser-known literary writers have been included partly to suggest the dimensions of what was regarded as literature at the time and the relation of literature to reform issues—and also to show that neither belletrism nor commercialism necessarily prevented writers from expressing reform interests, however sharply or diffusely.

Much nineteenth-century writing was designed for children, and much of it was designed to effect reform through appeals directed toward the younger generation. Writing specifically published for children, rather than as works normally read by adults, began in the late eighteenth century and was clearly associated with the process of modernization. Books for children were designed to instill a particular intellectual and moral discipline in the youth of the middle classes—at that time the revolutionary classes—and to defend children against ideological and moral corruption by both upper-class culture and plebeian consciousness and culture. Writers in the nineteenth century found an enormous opportunity, and an enormous audience, in writing such literature specifically for middle-class children. Although most of these books seem, from a late twentieth-century perspective, to be moralistic and even reactionary, they were part of a broad movement to transform and reform society, and such writing may legitimately be considered in a volume such as this. Because women were conventionally and historically associated with child-rearing and with early childhood education, women were tolerated and even encouraged as writers of children's books. Many such writers might have been considered in this volume, but this host must be represented by Sarah Smith, better known as Hesba Stretton, and Charlotte Maria Tucker, better known as A.L.O.E. ("A Lady of England").

Other late eighteenth-century events also shaped nineteenth-century reform and reform writing, as the dramatic and violent appearance of the lower classes in historical events and in the writing about such events reveals. So dramatic and violent was this appearance that the state was traumatized, and middle- and upper-class reformers in the nineteenth century were much concerned for these working classes or common people. This concern is expressed in a wide range of reform writing, from social investigation and journalism to historical fiction. Members of the lower classes increasingly spoke and wrote for themselves, however. As David Vincent and others have shown, many lower-class writers, both men and women, began to write and publish their work in the nineteenth century, and their personal experience and firsthand social observation made reformers of many of them.

In earlier times the poor and oppressed had been more often spoken for than prepared to speak for themselves, but in the nineteenth century they were determined to speak for themselves—in political writing, in prose and verse, and especially in the genre of autobiography. For this reason some working-class writers have also been included, such as the reform activist and autobiographer Samuel Bamford, the popular poet Ebenezer Elliott, the radical journalist John Doherty, and the essayist, folk historian, and autobiographer Hugh Miller. Associated with these writers in giving voice to the common people and thus indirectly encouraging reforms designed for their benefit is another range of writers who quickly developed new methods and techniques, scientific as well as literary, for representing the life of the common people. Such writers represented in this volume include fiction writers Samuel Lover and Sir Walter Besant and journalist Henry Mayhew.

Forms of writing now considered the preserve of the academic specialist were often not, in the Victorian period, so specialized. Much writing in many fields, from science to historiography, was pursued in such a way as to make information in those fields accessible to a wide reading public and thus to mobilize public opinion on behalf of general or particular reforms. Historiography was a highly respected, widely read, and influential form of writing in the nineteenth century, and many writers used accounts of the past to argue for general or particular reforms in the present. Among such writers included in this volume is James Bryce, Viscount Bryce. Science was another domain from which information was available that could often serve reform purposes, and the figure and influence of Charles Darwin are known to all students of the nineteenth century. However, many other lesser-known writers also contributed to making science a central part of ideological, social, and cultural transformation. The study of science, like that of history, was not as strictly defined and professionalized in the nineteenth century as it has become, and many scientific writers such as Alfred Russel Wallace, as well as many readers in their broadening audience, followed interests that today seem pseudoscientific.

Among the major figures included in this volume are others who are now known mainly as sociopolitical thinkers and reformers, such as John Stuart Mill, Sidney Webb, and Beatrice Webb. Many readers today associate the idea of reform particularly with a left-wing, socialist, or social-democratic tradition. Writers included who could be associated with this tradition and are included in this volume are Edith Jemima Simcox (better known to literary history as a disciple of novelist George Eliot) and Bernard Shaw. Other social campaigners whose writings were influential include William Booth, the founder of the Salvation Army, and Henry Mayhew, a journalist who investigated the lives of the wretched at the lowest end of Victorian society and published a remarkable account of those people. Feminist writers whose interests include a range of additional reform subjects include Josephine Elizabeth Butler, Millicent Garrett Fawcett, Ellice Hopkins, and Katherine Bruce Glasier.

The nineteenth century was a period of great growth in the professions and in public and state institutions. This growth was attended by constant criticism and calls for reforms in professions such as the law or education and institutions such as the Church. Among the writers with active reform interests in such fields was Samuel Warren, the legal reformer. It is significant that Warren, like many other reformers, not only published expository reform writing but also embodied his reform ideas in the popular genre of prose fiction. The period from 1832 to 1914 was one of great change in religious beliefs and in the influence churches held in social, cultural, and political life. Among the writers whose work reflects their active interests in religious matters are Richard Whateley and Francis William Newman. In addition, given the importance of literature in disseminating reform ideas and in presenting debate over the role of writing and the study of literature in public culture and education, it is important to include in a volume such as this some reform-oriented literary critics and educators such as John Morley and Sir Arthur Quiller-Couch.

Beyond the shores of England the British Empire and the armed forces necessary to maintain and extend it were matters of prominent and continuing concern throughout this period. Although many who wrote about these concerns are today almost forgotten, one writer included among the entries in this volume is Sir George Tomkyns Chesney, a British army officer in India during the Indian Mutiny of 1857. Chesney returned to Britain to campaign for reform in military and colonial administration, but, like so many other writers who sought to gain a wider readership for their work, he turned to the novel as a genre to convey his ideas.

The broad reform movement known as liberalism, which became organized as a distinct Liberal Party and was broad enough to include a "liberal" wing of the Conservative Party in Britain, grew and consolidated throughout the nineteenth century. An important figure representing several strands of liberalism as well as Liberalism was Arthur James Balfour, a critic of nineteenth-century materialism in science. A politician who rose to become prime minister, he supported free trade, opposed Irish independence, supported Zionism, and wrote on philosophy and aesthetics. Clearly his positions mark him as a reformer in some social and political respects, and even his "conservative" views favored social amelioration and change in Britain and its empire. His importance in this volume is in demonstrating that during this period even people who were fully engaged in public political life were expected to be, as they often were in their work as writers, engaged intellectually with the leading issues, especially the reform issues, of their times.

–*Gary Kelly*

Acknowledgments

This book was produced by Bruccoli Clark Layman, Inc. Karen L. Rood is senior editor for the *Dictionary of Literary Biography* series. Denis Thomas was the in-house editor. He was assisted by Karen L. Rood, George P. Anderson, and Tracy S. Bitonti.

Administrative support was provided by Ann M. Cheschi and Brenda A. Gillie.

Bookkeeper is Joyce Fowler.

Copyediting supervisor is Jeff Miller. The copyediting staff includes Phyllis A. Avant, Patricia Coate, Christine Copeland, Thom Harman, and William L. Thomas Jr. Freelance copyeditor is Rebecca Mayo.

Editorial associate is L. Kay Webster.

Layout and graphics staff includes Janet E. Hill and Mark McEwan.

Office manager is Kathy Lawler Merlette.

Photography editors are Margaret Meriwether and Paul Talbot. Photographic copy work was performed by Joseph M. Bruccoli.

Production manager is Samuel W. Bruce.

Systems manager is Marie L. Parker.

Typesetting supervisor is Kathleen M. Flanagan. The typesetting staff includes Pamela D. Norton and Patricia Flanagan Salisbury. Freelance typesetters include Melody W. Clegg and Delores Plastow.

Walter W. Ross, Steven Gross, and Ronald Aikman did library research. They were assisted by the following librarians at the Thomas Cooper Library of the University of South Carolina: Linda Holderfield and the interlibrary-loan staff; reference-department head Virginia Weathers; reference librarians Marilee Birchfield, Stefanie Buck, Stefanie DuBose, Rebecca Feind, Karen Joseph, Donna Lehman, Charlene Loope, Anthony McKissick, Jean Rhyne, and Kwamine Simpson; circulation-department head Caroline Taylor; and acquisitions-searching supervisor David Haggard.

Dictionary of Literary Biography® • Volume One Hundred Ninety

British Reform Writers, 1832–1914

Dictionary of Literary Biography

Arthur James Balfour
(25 July 1848 – 19 March 1930)

Timothy J. Evans
Richard Bland College of the College of William and Mary

BOOKS: *A Defence of Philosophic Doubt: Being an Essay on the Foundations of Belief* (London: Macmillan, 1879);

Reminiscences of Golf on St. Andrews Links (Edinburgh: Douglas, 1887);

The Pleasures of Reading: An Address Delivered at St. Andrews University, December 10, 1887 (Edinburgh & London: Blackwood, 1888);

The Religion of Humanity: An Address Delivered at the Church Congress, Manchester, October 1888 (Edinburgh: Douglas, 1888);

British Industries and International Bimetallism (London: Wilson, 1892);

A Fragment on Progress: Inaugural Address Delivered on His Installation as Lord Rector of the University of Glasgow, November, 1891 (Edinburgh: Douglas, 1892);

Lies and Replies: An Exposure of Some of the Commoner Gladstonian Fallacies: Being a Reprint of Forty Letters from A. J. Balfour and from George Wyndham in Reply to Various False Charges Made by Members of the Gladstonian-Parnellite Party (Westminster: Liberal Unionist Association, 1892);

The Currency Question (London: Wilson / Manchester: Cornish, 1893);

Essays and Addresses (Edinburgh: Douglas, 1893; enlarged, 1905);

The Foundations of Belief: Being Notes Introductory to the Study of Theology (New York & London: Longmans, Green, 1895; revised, New York & London: Longmans, 1901);

International Bimetallism: Speech . . . in the House of Commons, March 17, 1896, on Mr. Herbert Whiteley's Resolution (London: Bimetallic League, 1896?);

Arthur James Balfour, 1892

Briton and Boer: An Address (Malden, Mass.: "Topics for Today" Publishing, 1900);

"The Nineteenth Century": Inaugural Address, August 2, 1900 (Cambridge: Cambridge University Press, 1900);

3

The Education Bill, 1902 (London: Eyre & Spottiswoode, 1902);
Letter on the Criticisms of an Opponent of the Education Bill, 1902 (London, 1902);
Economic Notes on Insular Free Trade (New York & London: Longmans, Green, 1903);
The Right Hon. A. J. Balfour, M.P., and Fiscal Reform: Economic Notes on Insular Free Trade . . . and Speech at Sheffield, October 1, 1903 (London: Conservative Central Office, 1903);
Tariff Reform (London: Longmans, Green, 1903);
Reflections Suggested by the New Theory of Matter: Being the Presidential Address before the British Association for the Advancement of Science, Cambridge, August 17, 1904 (London, New York & Bombay: Longmans, Green, 1904);
The Defence of the Empire (London, 1905);
Imperial Defence: A Speech Delivered in the House of Commons, May 11, 1905 (London & New York: Longmans, Green, 1905);
Fiscal Reform: Speeches Delivered . . . from June 1880 to December 1905 (London, New York & Bombay: Longmans, Green, 1906);
Decadence: Henry Sidgwick Memorial Lecture (Cambridge: Cambridge University Press, 1908);
Questionings on Criticism and Beauty (Oxford: Clarendon Press / London: Frowde, 1909); revised as *Criticism and Beauty* (Oxford: Clarendon Press, 1910);
Mr. Balfour on Imperial Preference: Speech in the House of Commons on the Consolidated Fund (Appropriation) Bill, July 21st, 1910 (London: Truscott, 1910);
Arthur James Balfour as Philosopher and Thinker: A Collection of the More Important and Interesting Passages in His Non-Political Writings, Speeches, and Addresses, 1879–1912 (London & New York: Longmans, Green, 1912);
Against Home Rule: The Case for the Union, by Balfour, J. Austen Chamberlain, and others, edited by Simon Rosenbaum (London & New York: Warne, 1912);
Arthur James Balfour as Philosopher and Thinker: A Collection of the More Important and Interesting Passages in His Non-political Writings, Speeches, and Addresses, 1879–1912, edited by Wilfrid M. Short (London & New York: Longmans, Green, 1912); republished as *The Mind of Arthur James Balfour: Selections from His Non-political Writings, Speeches, and Addresses, 1879–1917, Including Special Sections on America and Germany* (New York: Doran, 1918);
Aspects of Home Rule (London: Routledge, 1912; London: Kegan Paul, Trench & Trübner / New York: Dutton, 1913);
Nationality and Home Rule (London & New York: Longmans, Green, 1913);
After a Year: Speech Delivered . . . at the London Opera House, 4th August, 1915 (London: Darling, 1915);
The British Blockade (London: Darling, 1915);
The Navy and the War, August 1914 to August 1915 (London: Darling, 1915);
Theism and Humanism (London & New York: Hodder & Stoughton, 1915; New York: Hodder & Stoughton/Doran, 1915);
The Freedom of the Seas (London: Unwin, 1916);
The Fourth of July in London (London: Darling, 1917);
Balfour, Viviani and Joffre: Their Speeches and Other Public Utterances in America, and Those of Italian, Belgian and Russian Commissioners during the Great War, with an Account of the Arrival of Our Warships and Soldiers in England and France under Admiral Sims and General Pershing, April 21, 1917–July 4, 1917, edited by Francis W. Halsey (New York & London: Funk & Wagnalls, 1917);
The Obstacles to Peace (London: National War Aims Committee, 1918);
Mr. Balfour on a League of Nations and the German Attitude of Mind (N.p., 1918?);
Zionism and Jewish Rights (New York: Zionist Organization of America, 1919);
Speech in the House of Commons on Women's Suffrage (London: Central Society for Women's Suffrage, 191–?);
The League of Nations: Statement . . . in the House of Commons, June 17, 1920 (London: Harrison, 1920);
Essays, Speculative and Political (London: Hodder & Stoughton, 1920; New York: Doran, 1921);
League of Nations: Return to an Order of the Honourable the House of Commons, Dated 19 July, 1921, anonymous (London: His Majesty's Stationery Office, 1921);
Relief of Children in Countries Affected by the War (Geneva, 1921);
America and England: Addresses by the Rt. Hon. Earl Balfour and Chief Justice Taft at a Dinner in London, June, 19, 1922, Given by the Pilgrims (New York & Greenwich, Conn.: American Association for International Conciliation, 1922);
Theism and Thought: A Study in Familiar Beliefs (London: Hodder & Stoughton, 1923; New York: Doran, 1924);
Familiar Beliefs and Transcendent Reason (London: Oxford University Press, 1926);
Opinions and Arguments from Speeches and Addresses of the Earl of Balfour, 1910–1927 (London: Hodder & Stoughton, 1927; Garden City, N.Y.: Doubleday, Doran, 1928);
Speeches on Zionism (London: Arrowsmith, 1928);

Chapters of Autobiography, edited by Blanche Dugdale (London & Toronto: Cassell, 1930);

Retrospect: An Unfinished Autobiography, 1848-1886 (Boston & New York: Houghton Mifflin, 1930).

OTHER: George Berkeley, *The Works of George Berkeley, D.D., Bishop of Cloyne,* biographical introduction by Balfour, edited by George Sampson (London: Bell, 1897-1898);

Morris R. Jones, *The Education Act, 1902, Together with Copious Notes and the Principal Explanatory Remarks of the Right Hon. A. J. Balfour* (London, 1903);

Sir Clement K. Cooke, *Chinese Labour in the Transvaal: Being a Study of Its Moral, Economic, and Imperial Aspects,* letter of introduction by Balfour (London: Macmillan, 1906);

The Case against Socialism: A Handbook for Speakers and Candidates, prefatory letter by Balfour (London: George Allen, 1908);

"Race and Nationality," in *Transactions of the Honourable Society of Cymmrodorion* (London: Cymmrodorion Society, 1910);

Society for Psychical Research, *Presidential Addresses to the Society for Psychical Research, 1882-1911,* by Balfour and others (Glasgow: Society for Psychical Research, 1912);

"Francis Bacon," in *Francis Bacon: The Commemoration of His Tercentenary at Gray's Inn* (London: Chiswick, 1913);

Herbert Henry Asquith, Lord Oxford and Asquith, *"To a Victorious Conclusion!" The Prime Minister's Appeal to the Nation: Speeches Delivered at the Guildhall, London, on September 4th, 1914,* by Balfour, Asquith, Bonar Law, and Winston Churchill (London: Parliamentary Recruiting Committee, 1914);

Gottfried Heinrich von Treitschke, *Politics,* introduction by Balfour, 2 volumes (London: Constable, 1916);

The Case of the Allies: Being the Replies to President Wilson, and Mr. Balfour's Despatch (London: Hayman, Christy & Lilly, 1917);

"Eugenics: Birthrate; Destitution," in *The Mind of Arthur James Balfour, 1912,* edited by Wilfrid M. Short (New York: Doran, 1918), pp. 126-132;

Nahum Sokolov, *History of Zionism, 1600-1918,* introduction by Balfour, 2 volumes (London: Longmans, 1919);

Jean V. Bates, *Sir Edward Carson, Ulster Leader,* introduction by Balfour (London: John Murray, 1921);

Noël J. T. M. Needham, ed., *Science, Religion and Reality,* introduction by Balfour (London: Sheldon / New York & Toronto: Macmillan, 1925);

Walter Bagehot, *The English Constitution,* introduction by Balfour (London: Oxford University Press, 1928).

Arthur James Balfour, philosopher and statesman, came to epitomize conservative thought in England while serving in Parliament for more than half a century. Originally elected in 1874 to represent Hertford, he served in several government posts, most notably under his uncle, Lord Robert Cecil, third Marquess of Salisbury, and later in the coalition government of David Lloyd George. Balfour was prime minister in 1902-1905.

Born 25 July 1848 in East Lothian, Scotland, Balfour was the eldest son of James Maitland Balfour and Lady Blanche Mary Harriett Gascoigne Cecil. His father, who made a fortune as director of the North British Railway and also served in Parliament, died in 1856. Balfour notes in *Retrospect* (1930), his autobiography, that his mother played an active and influential role in his upbringing, and contemporary accounts agree that she was a remarkable woman.

Before Balfour was eleven years old he was sent to the Grange, a boarding school located at Hoddesdon, Hertfordshire. At age thirteen he entered Eton, where he studied for five years before he began attending Trinity College, Cambridge, in late 1866. At the latter institution a special boarding arrangement allowed him to dine with the faculty, a privilege that he appreciated and used to his advantage. Two of his tutors became not just friends but his brothers-in-law: Henry Sidgwick, later founder of the British Academy of Sciences, and John Strutt, later the third Lord Rayleigh and Nobel prize-winning physicist. Balfour's lifelong interest in science and technological innovations developed partially through these early friendships.

In summer 1870 Balfour was introduced to May Lyttleton, the sister of Spencer Lyttleton, his college friend. Although Balfour's youth, his career, and his mother's death in 1872 initially prevented him from becoming more intimate with May, by 1875 he apparently intended to propose. In February, however, she contracted typhoid fever and died a few weeks later. Balfour was devastated and remained a bachelor for the rest of his life.

Encouraged by his uncle and mentor, Lord Salisbury, Balfour stood for Parliament in 1874. Balfour notes in *Retrospect* that he believed a parliamentary career would allow him to fulfill what he saw as his civic duties while leaving him time for the philo-

Whittingehame House in East Lothian, Balfour's birthplace

sophical pursuits he had begun at Cambridge. Lord Salisbury continued his patronage by asking his nephew to serve as his personal secretary at the Congress of Berlin in June 1878. During that two-month affair Balfour fulfilled his obligations to his uncle, took an active part in Berlin society, and finished his first book, *A Defence of Philosophic Doubt: Being an Essay on the Foundations of Belief* (1879).

This first work was originally to be titled "A Defence of Philosophic Scepticism," but Balfour explains in his preface that he changed the title after he became convinced that people "would assume that by Scepticism was meant scepticism in matters of religion." The chief concern of Balfour's book instead is conveyed in his argument that many writers of his day were judging science and metaphysics by different standards—at the expense of the latter. Theology, because it begins with certain a priori arguments and assumptions, is dismissed by writers willing to accept scientific knowledge that begins with similar theoretical foundations.

Balfour did not intend, of course, to dismiss scientific knowledge. He was an avid reader of current scientific and scholarly writers and was familiar with and untroubled by Charles Darwin, Charles Lyell, David Friedrich Strauss, and Ernest Renan. What he was defending was his own ability to balance apparently contradictory beliefs while working toward a resolution. As Balfour noted,

> The discord between Science and Religion has reference chiefly, if not entirely, to the interference by the supernatural with the natural, which Religion requires us to believe in; and the amount of the discord may be measured by the importance of the scientific doctrines which such a belief would require us to give up, if we were determined at all hazards to make the two systems consistent with each other.

Balfour's argument is with writers who approach this discord by assuming that one side or the other is necessarily false and who ignore the similarity between logical structures supporting both scientific and metaphysical conclusions.

During the next fourteen years Balfour continued to develop his ideas concerning metaphysics, but official duties demanded increasing amounts of his time. In 1880 he helped found the "Fourth Party" to protest what he believed was the ineffective leadership of the Conservatives. This "party," whose aim was to distract and delay the opposition, consisted of only four members of Parliament: Balfour, Sir Henry Drummond Wolff, John Eldon Gorst, and Lord Randolph Churchill. This group

Caricature of Balfour as Saint Patrick (from Punch, *1903)*

catapulted Churchill into the political forefront. Lord Salisbury became prime minister in 1886, and in 1887 he appointed Balfour as chief secretary to Ireland. In 1891 Balfour became first lord of the treasury and leader of the House of Commons.

During this period he collected and published seven essays in *Essays and Addresses* (1893). Perhaps the best known of these essays is "Handel," an extended analysis of Balfour's favorite composer. Indicating his continuing interests in science and theology are the essays "A Fragment of Progress" and "The Religion of Humanity." The former answers writers who, on the basis of Darwin's theories, predict continued evolution of mankind as a species. If Darwin is correct, Balfour argues, man's evolution has ended. In a civilized society the weak and disadvantaged are protected by their fellows, and this defuses any potential evolutionary pressures, leaving the human gene pool with no net change. In the latter essay Balfour discusses positivism and concludes that Christianity remains a better and more logical "religion of humanity."

When Salisbury returned as prime minister in 1895, Balfour resumed his duties as first lord of the treasury and leader of the House of Commons and published another book, *The Foundations of Belief: Being Notes Introductory to the Study of Theology* (1895), which begins where *A Defence of Philosophic Doubt* left off. Following the same philosophical approach taken in the earlier work, Balfour examines how people come to believe certain things and how those beliefs are then explained. In *Foundations of Belief,* however, he focuses on Christianity. In the preface he states that he does not intend to address any specific, current controversy involving Christianity, that every age has had and will have controversies reflecting the times in which they arise. His purpose, rather, is to suggest "a certain attitude of mind" appropriate for discussing questions involving belief and faith, and he concludes that science, ethics, and aesthetics all grow from a fundamental assumption of the divine.

While Balfour's interest in the relationship between science and metaphysics continued throughout his life, during the next two decades his writing turned largely toward political topics. He became prime minister in 1902 when Lord Salisbury stepped down. Two essays written while he was prime minister have received particular attention because they concern Free Trade and religious education, the issues that eventually toppled his ministry in 1906.

The essay *Economic Notes on Insular Free Trade*, published as a monograph in 1903, addresses the issue that eventually split Balfour's cabinet. The Free Traders were a minority within the Conservative ranks, and Balfour favored retaliatory tariffs against countries with trade practices that placed England at a disadvantage. He argued that England could not remain insular and ignore the economic disadvantages that would come if Britain would refuse to raise tariffs in retaliation. The Free Traders in his cabinet, however, refused to allow Balfour to declare tariffs an "open issue," not bound by party loyalties. The resulting tumult led to resignations by several key cabinet members.

The second essay, "Dr. Clifford on Religious Education," was republished in the enlarged edition of *Essays and Addresses* (1905). It defended the Education Act of 1902, one provision of which allowed parents to choose the type of religious education their children would receive. Conservatives opposed the act because it did not require instruction in the Anglican Church, and the act proved to be unpopular among both Conservatives and Liberals. Balfour, a lifelong communicant of both the Church of England and the Scottish Presbyterian Church, miscalculated the willingness of members of Parliament to accept religious diversity. Although the act was the cornerstone for all later developments in British education, the controversy it raised contributed to the downfall of the Conservatives.

Two significant events in January 1906 modified the direction of Balfour's career. In the Liberal landslide during the election, the Conservatives lost the majority that Balfour had directed as prime minister, and even Balfour lost his seat. A new seat representing the City of London was found for him, and three weeks later he won a by-election. Balfour continued to lead the Conservatives in opposition, but many party members blamed him for their staggering loss at the polls. He remained the party leader until 1911 when he resigned, discovering in the process that this change of position actually enhanced his effectiveness. No longer perceived as a partisan leader, he assumed a role of elder statesman whose views commanded attention from all members of Parliament.

The second event of January 1906 occurred while Balfour was waiting in Manchester for the election results. He received word that Dr. Chaim Weizmann, a lecturer in chemistry at Manchester University, wished to speak with him. Weizmann, a Zionist, desired Balfour's support for establishing a homeland for the Jews in Palestine. Balfour as prime minister had been developing a proposal for forming a Jewish national state in what became Uganda, and he had been seeking leaders of the Zionist movement to solicit their response. He believed that European civilization owed a debt to Jewish culture and that the treatment of Jews in Europe was a disgrace. He hoped that establishing such a national state would prove to be a first step toward ending that disgrace.

Yet Wiezmann told Balfour that the Jews could not be happy with Uganda rather than Palestine. To illustrate his point Weizmann asked if, after centuries of wandering, the British people were offered Paris, could they be happy with that rather than with London. Balfour, an ardent British nationalist, sympathized with this view and began actively supporting the Zionist movement. The most visible result came in 1917, while Balfour was foreign secretary in the second coalition government of Lloyd George. In August 1917 Balfour wrote a charter of Jewish national rights that became known as the Balfour Declaration. The charter declared British support for the formation of a Jewish national state in Palestine, and both the "Declaration" and Balfour's speeches defending it are collected in *Speeches on Zionism* (1928).

From 1906 until the outbreak of World War I, Balfour pursued his familiar variety of interests. His essays of this period reflect this diversity, beginning with his address on "Decadence," the Sidgwick Memorial Lecture in 1908. This essay was followed the next year by "Beauty: And the Criticism of Beauty," which was the Romanes Memorial Lecture in 1909. They were published in *Essays, Speculative and Political* (1920). These two essays begin Balfour's discussion of aesthetics, which he expanded in *Theism and Humanism* (1915) and *Theism and Thought: A Study in Familiar Beliefs* (1923).

His political interests during this period often concerned the increased tension between Germany and England. In 1912 at the request of the editor of

> Foreign Office,
> November 2nd, 1917.
>
> Dear Lord Rothschild,
>
> I have much pleasure in conveying to you, on behalf of His Majesty's Government, the following declaration of sympathy with Jewish Zionist aspirations which has been submitted to, and approved by, the Cabinet.
>
> "His Majesty's Government view with favour the establishment in Palestine of a national home for the Jewish people, and will use their best endeavours to facilitate the achievement of this object, it being clearly understood that nothing shall be done which may prejudice the civil and religious rights of existing non-Jewish communities in Palestine, or the rights and political status enjoyed by Jews in any other country".
>
> I should be grateful if you would bring this declaration to the knowledge of the Zionist Federation.

The Balfour Declaration, aimed at encouraging Zionists without arousing Arab fears about the establishment of an independent Jewish state in Palestine (from Kenneth Young, Arthur James Balfour, 1963)

Nord und Süd Balfour wrote "Anglo-German Relations," which was published in the June 1912 issue and reprinted in *Essays, Speculative and Political*. Later criticized by English readers who thought he had been too restrained in the article, Balfour replies in the preface to *Essays, Speculative and Political* that he was writing to a German audience and was seeking to improve relations, not to increase the strain. He begins the essay by praising German culture, science, and scholarship, and he notes that since 1688 England and the German states had generally fought on the same side. He states that current English anxiety about the relations between the countries arises not from the massive buildup of arms in Germany but rather from the ambiguous explanations that German leaders offer for why such increases are necessary. In such a situation, Balfour notes, it is difficult for England to see the armaments as merely defensive, and he suggests that Germany could indicate more clearly by word and deed that its intentions are not hostile.

In 1912 Balfour also gave two addresses that describe his perception of the difference between Scottish and Irish nationalism. The first address, "On Nationalism, Chiefly Scottish," is collected in *Opinions and Arguments from Speeches and Addresses of the Earl of Balfour, 1910–1927* (1927), and it notes that the early history of England and Scotland is marked by wars and disagreements about both land and authority. Eventually, though, the people of Scotland learned that they could be loyal to both, that a feeling of patriotism for Scotland and England could coexist. Balfour tells his Saint Andrew's Day Festival audience that Scotland has "set an example how to reconcile naturally and completely, and without effort, two things which at first do not seem easily reconciled. I mean the intense and ardent patriotism for a part, which yet only reinforces and strengthens the larger patriotism for the whole."

Less than a year later he addressed an audience in Nottingham on this subject in *Nationality and Home Rule* (1913), in which he compares the Scotsman to the Irishman and examines their attitudes toward national identity. He notes that the Irish complain about being oppressed while they are represented in Parliament in greater proportion than either Scotsmen or even Englishmen. Ireland "is in the position, singular among 'oppressed' nationalities, of enjoying more than her fair proportion of representation in the Imperial Parliament, and paying less than her fair proportion of taxation to Imperial objects." The Irish Nationalists, however, insist that

> Ireland, on the ground of her separate nationality, possesses inherent rights which cannot be satisfied by the fairest and fullest share in the parliamentary institutions of the United Kingdom. What is enough for Scotsmen and Englishmen can never be enough for them. To think so would be treason to Ireland.

Parliament eventually passed a Home Rule bill in 1917, while Balfour was on a diplomatic mission in the United States, and his views on nationality were again prominent at the Imperial Conference of 1926, when he wrestled to define the relationship between England and the countries that once had been her colonies.

When war broke out in 1914, Balfour joined Prime Minister Herbert Henry Asquith's coalition government as secretary of the Admiralty, and when Lloyd George formed his coalition government in 1916, Balfour became foreign secretary. Perhaps his most important responsibility in this latter post was his leadership of the Balfour Mission to the United States in April 1917. On April 2 President Woodrow Wilson asked Congress for a declaration of war, and within a week a delegation headed by Balfour was organized to go to the United States to help coordinate British and American war efforts. Balfour was already a recognized statesman in the United States following an interview conducted by the American press in 1916 and reprinted the same year as *The Freedom of the Seas*. In this interview he had argued that the unrestricted submarine warfare conducted by Germany was a threat to all civilized countries, not just to those immediately engaged in the conflict, and this was a position that American leaders eventually came to accept. During his 1917 mission Balfour was invited to address Congress; he was the first British member of Parliament to be so invited since Charles Stewart Parnell in 1880.

After the war Balfour was involved first in drafting the peace treaty and then in negotiating its acceptance. The stability of Europe, and in particular the independence of Austria, was threatened by the economic burdens that the war had caused. Balfour negotiated what was referred to as the Balfour Note, a proposal that canceled the war debts of Austria and allowed it to begin its economic recovery.

Prior to the war Balfour had been invited to deliver the Gifford Lectures on natural theology at the University of Glasgow. His invitation was for two series of lectures, and in the winter of 1913-1914 he delivered the first series of ten, which he later collected in *Theism and Humanism*. The second series had to be postponed because of the outbreak of the war, and not until 1922 was he was able to begin this series. These lectures became the basis for *Theism and Thought*.

In the first series of lectures Balfour returns to the themes of *A Defence of Philosophic Doubt* and *The Foundations of Belief*. This series, however, is aimed at a more general audience and attempts to define what he calls the "creed of common sense." The "most important formulas" of this creed "represent beliefs which, whether true or false, whether proved or unproved, are at least inevitable. All men accept them in fact. Even those who criticize them in theory live by them in practice." Balfour again separates belief into three types—factual, ethical, and aesthetic—and describes how the latter two types of belief are formulated, defended, and accepted in a fashion identical to that of beliefs involving factual data. Theism, then, is belief in "a God whom men can love, a God to whom men can pray, who takes sides, who has purposes and preferences, whose attributes, however conceived, leave unimpaired the possibility of a personal relation between Himself and those whom He has created." Naturalism and humanism, Balfour argues, are often suggested as alternatives to theism, but naturalism accepts only factual beliefs. Humanism accepts certain beliefs in ethics and aesthetics but without any system of value linking them, and Balfour concludes, "Humanism without Theism loses more than half its value."

When Balfour began his second series of lectures more than eight years later, he noted that "The object of the two courses is the same—namely, to determine on what theory of the universe the highest values of ethics, aesthetics, and knowledge—the good, the beautiful, and the true—could be most effectively maintained." He asserts that his purpose is not to prove the existence of God or to es-

George V and Balfour at Bognor, 11 May 1929 (photograph by H. R. H. Princess Victoria)

tablish reasons for belief in God but rather to argue that without belief in the divine, other human thoughts and aspirations become meaningless. Naturalism, the acceptance of factual knowledge alone, may show the parts of the universe, but theism shows the relationship and purpose of those parts. He begins with the assumption that "some part of the alleged 'conflict between theology and science' is not a collision of doctrine, but a rivalry of appeal."

One position that he discusses at length concerns theism in relation to evolution and natural selection. He had written that he believed human evolution had ceased because civilization promoted survival of both the fit and the unfit. In this series of lectures he suggests that natural selection could not be used to explain how life first appeared because too many phenomena—beginning with variables such as the distance of the planet from the sun—had nothing to do with selection. Because a belief in naturalism as the sole explanation of man's existence and essence demands belief in such an extraordinary series of coincidences, Balfour concludes that belief in evolution without belief in a guiding divine purpose cannot claim to be scientific.

In 1922 Balfour was made a peer, becoming the earl of Balfour and viscount Traprain, and moved into the House of Lords. Although he was in his mid seventies, he continued to serve in several governmental posts, most notably as lord president of the council beginning in 1925. In this position he was able to become chairman of the Inter-Imperial Relations Committee and to serve at the Imperial Conference of 1926 when England and the other countries of the Commonwealth attempted to establish bases for their future relationship. The conference eventually adopted what was called the Balfour Definition: these countries were to declare allegiance to the English monarchy yet govern themselves independently. Balfour received some criticism after the conference from those members of Parliament who thought that he had given up too much. Balfour, on the other hand, believed that no other relationship between England and these countries was possible or even desirable. He pointed out that by demanding compliance England had driven the United States from colonial status in the eighteenth century, and he noted how well dual patriotism worked in his native Scotland. "A common interest in loyalty, in freedom, in ideals—that is the bond of Empire. If that is not enough, nothing else is enough," he concluded.

At the age of eighty Balfour resigned his last government post in 1929 and began devoting much of his time to writing the first volume of his autobiography. *Retrospect* covers events only up to 1886 and ends with a rough draft of a chapter on the Balfour Mission. His niece, Blanche Dugdale, edited *Retrospect* and, in collaboration with Balfour, prepared a two-volume biography, *Arthur James Balfour*, published in 1936.

Balfour died on 19 March 1930. He is remembered by his contemporaries as a man of great charm, wit, and intelligence. Several of his biographers attribute much of his success to the "Balfour Charm" and to his decades of experience. During and after World War I, at an age when most men have retired from active life, Balfour made many of his most significant contributions.

Biographies:

E. T. Raymond Thompson, *A Life of Arthur James Balfour* (Boston: Little, Brown, 1920);

Blanche E. C. Dugdale, *Arthur James Balfour,* 2 volumes (London: Hutchinson, 1936; New York: Putnam, 1937).

References:

Denis Judd, *Balfour and the British Empire: A Study in Imperial Evolution, 1874–1932* (London & Melbourne: Macmillan / New York: St. Martin's Press, 1968);

Ruddock R. Mackay, *Balfour: Intellectual Statesman* (Oxford & New York: Oxford University Press, 1985);

Catherine B. Shannon, *Arthur J. Balfour and Ireland, 1874–1922* (Washington, D.C.: Catholic University of America Press, 1988);

Sydney H. Zabel, *Balfour, a Political Biography* (Cambridge: Cambridge University Press, 1973).

Papers:

Much of Balfour's correspondence fills 280 volumes in the British Library.

Samuel Bamford
(28 February 1788 – 13 April 1872)

Ronald Tetreault
Dalhousie University

BOOKS: *An Account of the Arrest and Imprisonment of Samuel Bamford, Middleton, on Suspicion of High Treason* (Manchester: Cave, 1817);

The Weaver Boy; or, Miscellaneous Poetry (Manchester: Observer, 1819); republished as *Miscellaneous Poetry by Samuel Bamford, Weaver, of Middleton, Lancashire, Lately Imprisoned in the Castle of Lincoln* (London, 1821);

Hours in the Bowers: Poems (Manchester: Printed for the author, 1834);

Passages in the Life of a Radical (published in parts, 1839–1841; 2 volumes, Heywood: Printed for the author, 1841, 1843; 1 volume, revised and corrected, London: Simpkin, Marshall / Manchester: Heywood, 1859);

Poems (Manchester: Printed for the author, 1843); revised and enlarged as *Homely Rhymes, Poems and Reminiscences* (Manchester: Ireland / London: Simpkin, Marshall, 1864);

Walks in South Lancashire and on Its Borders, with Letters, Descriptions, Narratives, and Observations, Current and Incidental (Blackley: Printed for the author, 1844);

Early Days (published in parts, 1848; 1 volume, London: Simpkin, Marshall, 1849; revised edition, London: Simpkin, Marshall / Manchester: Heywood, 1859);

The Lord of the Manor, and The Lord of the Mill; or, Scenes in Lancashire (Manchester & Liverpool: Sold by all Booksellers, 1851).

Collection: *Passages in the Life of a Radical, and Early Days*, 2 volumes, edited by Henry Dunckley (London: Unwin, 1893);

OTHER: John Collier, *Dialect of South Lancashire; or, Tim Bobbin's Tummus and Meary; Revised and Corrected with His Rhymes, and an Enlarged and Amended Glossary of Words and Phrases, Chiefly Used by the Rural Population of the Manufacturing Districts of South Lancashire*, edited by Bamford (Manchester, 1850).

Through the economic upheaval caused by the Industrial Revolution and his experience in the movement for political reform in and around Manchester, Samuel Bamford witnessed the transformation of working-class life during the first half of the nineteenth century. His renown as a writer rests less on his commonplace though popular poetry than on his prose chronicles, closely observed and finely detailed records of everyday existence and cataclysmic events. E. P. Thompson declares *Passages in the Life of a Radical* (1841, 1843), Bamford's two-volume autobiography recounting his tumultuous career as a reformer during the years from 1816 to 1821, to be "essential reading for any Englishman." Of no less value is Bamford's account of social conditions in his diary-like collection, *Walks in South Lancashire and on Its Borders, with Letters, Descriptions, Narratives, and Observations, Current and Incidental* (1844), and in *Early Days* (1848-1849), his charming and informative account of growing up in a changing world.

"I was born a Radical," he avows in *Early Days*, which he calls as much "a history of a time, and of a district" as a record of his youth. His maternal grandfather was held in Lancaster Castle on a charge of high treason for having assisted "Bonnie Prince Charlie" (Prince Charles Stuart) in 1745, and Bamford's father, Daniel, who studied closely Thomas Paine's *The Rights of Man* (1795), formed a political discussion circle whose members were dubbed Jacobins by some residents of the Lancaster area. Daniel Bamford was a muscular man six feet tall and reputed to be a formidable opponent in a tavern brawl, but he was learned and accomplished in ways typical of skilled artisans in his time. A musician and occasional composer of hymns as well as topical verses, the elder Bamford became a cotton spinner, a schoolmaster, and eventually a handloom weaver of fine muslin as his family grew. His wife, Hannah Battersby, daughter of a master maker of boots and shoes, assisted in the home-weaving operation and tended the children. Samuel, their fourth child, was born in Middleton, a village just north of Manchester.

By the time Bamford was six years old his father became superintendent of the cotton weavers in the new workhouse for the township of Manchester at Strangeways and soon thereafter became governor of the institution. During the smallpox epidemic of 1795 Bamford's uncle, a brother, a sister, and his mother, who was only forty years old, succumbed to the disease. To recover his own health Bamford was sent to Middleton, where he lived with relatives whose strict Methodist principles influenced him morally and encouraged his disposition to dissent. As a strong young man with broad shoulders and a pugnacious temper, Bamford writes in *Early Days,* he shunned "the dominance of mere muscle and bone . . . except when exercised in the repression of other brute forces employed in the perpetration of wrong, or in the maltreatment of right." Having been forbidden to learn Latin because his father, who remarried and went on to become governor of the Salford workhouse until his death sometime after 1813, decreed that studying it would not befit the young boy's social station, Bamford attended the Manchester Grammar School.

As a youth he worked variously as a handloom weaver and as a warehouseman in the cotton trade. Seeking adventure at the age of nineteen, he went away to sea aboard the *Aeneas*, a brig that hauled coal between South Shields and London. He soon jumped ship and narrowly evaded His Majesty's press-gangs, and the tale of his journey back to Manchester by foot is one of the more vivid episodes in the first volume of his autobiography. Resuming his post as a warehouse porter, he found that his employment afforded ample opportunity for reading, and he accordingly began a period of intense self-education. He had read the works of Homer and Virgil and the plays of William Shakespeare, and the writing of John Milton was an old favorite; between 1808 and 1812 he began reading eighteenth-century literature, beginning with Samuel Johnson's *Prefaces, Biographical and Critical, to the Works of the English Poets* (1779, 1781) and turning to works by Thomas Chatterton and Robert Burns. Reading Burns inspired him to write poems of his own, but a gruff editor of the *Manchester Gazette* rebuffed Bamford's attempts to publish. Besides Burns, another formative influence was William Cobbett, whose *Political Register* he read weekly. On 24 June 1810 Bamford married Jemima Shepherd, the mother of his daughter, Ann, probably born in 1809.

The war with France brought hard times to England, and Manchester became a site of considerable unrest. A riot there gave Bamford his first taste of a popular rising, and although he sympathized with the populace, he was shocked by the violence: during Luddite disturbances in the area in 1812 power looms were wrecked, and four rioters were shot and killed. Concerned for the safety of his wife and child, Bamford shortly afterward resumed working as a weaver and moved to Middleton.

These experiences sharply focused Bamford's political views. In 1816 he joined a committee of parliamentary reformers and soon became secretary to the Hampden Club of Middleton. Modeled on the reform society founded in London, Hampden Clubs advocated direct-taxation suffrage, equal electoral districts, and annual Parliaments, and they undertook a program of mass petitioning to achieve their aims. Early in 1817 Bamford attended the first Hampden Club convention in London, the so-called Crown and Anchor Meeting, at which delegates with petitions that held half a million signatures gathered from more than 150 provincial centers. *Passages in the Life of a Radical* opens with his account of this meeting, and Bamford memorably sketches leaders such as Cobbett, Sir Francis Burdett, and Henry "Orator" Hunt as well as firebrands such as William Benbow and James Watson. Bamford allied himself with the radicals among this group when he supported Hunt's proposal in favor of universal suffrage.

Shortly after he returned to the North, Bamford was rounded up, arrested with other reformers, and held in the New Bailey Prison, Salford, on suspicion of high treason. Although he had distanced himself from plans for a hunger march that he felt could be subverted to violence and that involved the Blanketeers in March 1817, he was chained and taken to London on a warrant to appear before the home secretary, Lord Henry Sidmouth. Bamford's first publication, the 1817 pamphlet *An Account of the Arrest and Imprisonment of Samuel Bamford, Middleton, on Suspicion of High Treason,* takes an oddly comic turn, as he recounts an almost Pickwickian expedition in which he and his fellow prisoners, although in irons on remand, enjoy sumptuous dinners, much drink, and mirth, all at state expense: "we lived more like gentlemen than prisoners," he writes. Even the feared Sidmouth, after holding four interviews with Bamford, proves patient and forgiving in discharging the prisoner on a bond of good behavior.

State power was not so benevolent two years later at Saint Peter's Field in Manchester, where Bamford returned to his political activities and became an influential reform figure. A measure of his influence was his proposal in spring 1818 that women be allowed the right to vote at reform meetings. As a logical extension of his commitment to universal suffrage, votes for women became an established practice at radical meetings, and, as Bamford writes in *Passages in the Life of a Radical,* encouraged the formation of independent political unions of women. Thus women as well as men were mustered to march on Manchester for the great reform meeting set for 16 August 1819. Bamford organized the Middleton contingent and assembled a party of three thousand marchers who joined other similar columns converging on the city. "We would disarm the bitterness of our political opponents by a display of cleanliness, sobriety, and decorum," he writes in *Passages in the Life of a Radical,* in one of the most important eyewitness accounts of the infamous Peterloo Massacre, the centerpiece of the book.

The carnage of Peterloo confirmed Bamford's opinion about the futility of violent confrontation. He had mistrusted the dynamics of insurrection, and the scars left by the cavalry at Peterloo fixed his commitment to moral force that endured through the years of the Chartist struggles. Published more than two decades after these events, *Passages in the Life of a Radical* expresses his faith in gradualism: "The industrious and patient man will sooner arrive at his ends by a beaten and legalized path though he advances slowly, than will he who, breaking down all barriers, is himself broken down.... Neverthe-

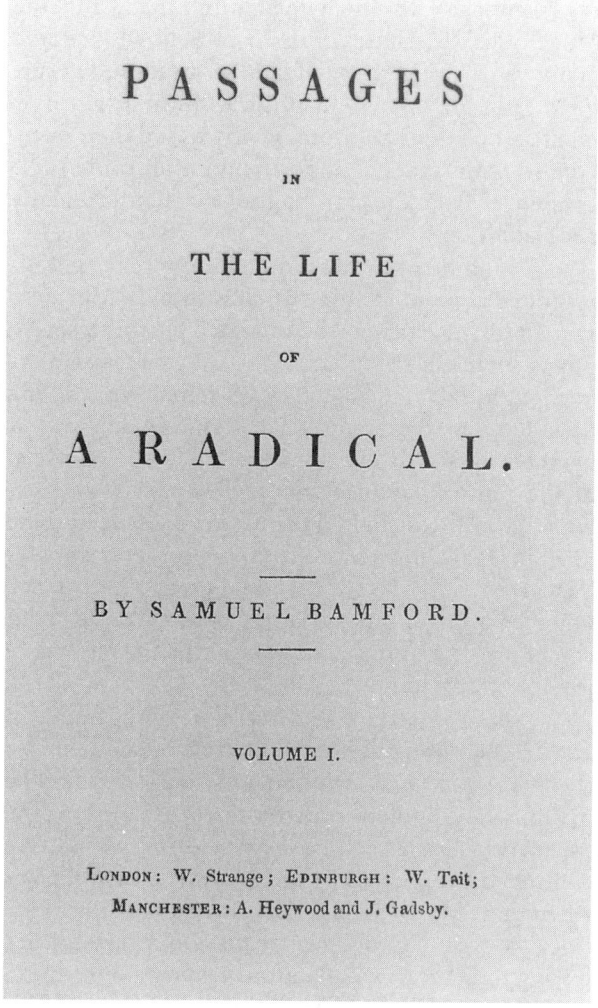

Title page for Bamford's autobiographical account of his years as a radical labor reformer

less, the immediate result of Bamford's participation in the Peterloo demonstration was his arrest, trial, and imprisonment for twelve months in Lincoln Castle. On his release in 1821 he published *Miscellaneous Poetry by Samuel Bamford, Weaver, of Middleton, Lancashire, Lately Imprisoned in the Castle of Lincoln* (1821), a second edition of the poems he had first published as *The Weaver Boy; or, Miscellaneous Poetry* in 1819.

Bamford returned to his trade as silk weaver following his release, and he faded from leadership of the reform movement. He maintained his allegiance to his class and his goal of securing the vote for working people, but he had lost faith in mass action, and in his subsequent political involvements he appears as an ambiguous figure in the history of Victorian radicalism. Perhaps his later career is best understood in light of the claim he makes in *Passages* that "our educators, are, after all, the best reformers." From the time he helped found the Middleton Mechanics' Institute in 1825, Bamford devoted many years to the cause of adult education. He supported the development of local mutual-improvement associations and consistently urged their members to maintain an "honest and honourable independence" from the patronage of the middle and upper classes.

Yet some reformers increasingly regarded his positions as alien to working-class interests. In summer 1826, for example, he thwarted a plan to smash power looms in East Lancashire. As he recounts the incident in *Walks in South Lancashire,* mobs of starving hand-loom weavers who were breaking machinery in neighboring towns threatened to "make a clear sweep of the obnoxious machinery, all around by Heywood, Middleton and Oldham." He convinced some local delegates to refrain from the riot, and the plot miscarried. Afterward he lamented, "I was denounced as a spy and a traitor," but he treated "with contempt" a rumor that he was marked as "a fit subject for assassination."

About this time he left the weaving trade. In 1826 he became the Manchester correspondent for the *Morning Herald* of London, and soon afterward he became the Middleton district correspondent for the *Manchester Guardian,* a post he held until 1833. He continued to make his living as a journalist and news agent until 1839, and his efforts to contain violent political protest clouded his reputation as a reformer during these years. As Bamford remarks in his introduction to *Homely Rhymes, Poems and Reminiscences* (1864), he "was compelled to undertake the office of Constable" in Middleton in 1832. Even though he tried to avoid taking the oath for that office, giving in only when he was threatened with prosecution, the rising new radicals never forgave him. He recounts that "a faction was at that time appearing in Middleton which afterwards became the Chartist party . . . and ever afterwards the Chartists of Middleton omitted but few opportunities of acting towards him as if he had been their enemy" as he conducted his duties. This occasion was not the only one on which local radicals were dismayed to see their former leader enforcing law and order. In 1839 he became a special constable during the first Chartist agitations, and he wrote in *Homely Rhymes* that his service in this capacity "was again a cause of enmity on the part of the Chartists." Never a friend of parties committed to the use of physical force, Bamford disliked the Chartists' all-or-nothing pursuit of their six points and distrusted the new generation of working-class leaders represented by Feargus O'Connor.

From 1839 to 1848 Bamford reviewed the lessons of his political career and sought to apply them to the current time. Living in a small cottage at Blackley, he engaged in literary activity throughout the Chartist era. In 1839 he began writing *Passages in the Life of a Radical,* which he published privately in parts until 1841. Some of these installments came to the attention of Thomas Carlyle, who helped him find a London publisher. Bamford also published *Poems,* another collection, in 1843, and in *Walks in South Lancashire,* which he collected and published in 1844, he presents snapshots of life in the age of industrialization. In 1848 he began to publish *Early Days* in parts.

Carlyle had brought attention to "the condition of England" in his *Past and Present* (1843), bewailing the plight of two million unemployed who were locked up in "Poor Law Bastilles," but Bamford's writings depict the situation in human terms. In his "Walks amongst the Workers" series in *Walks in South Lancashire* he makes "an actual survey of the present condition of labouring persons," inhabitants of the villages of his youth, who dwell in "a vast city scattered amongst meads and pastures, and belts of woodland; over which, at times, volumes of black furnace clouds go trailing their long wreaths on the wind." He describes the lives of Heathershaw coal miners, "compelled to work 'short' time" with a consequent decline in wages: "The cause is want of sale. . . . it is only about two-thirds of what it used to be, and the falling off in employment is proportionate." The hand-loom weavers of Narrowhead Brow are hardly better off, as their wages are barely enough to cover the rent on a cottage housing four looms. "Several houses were unoccupied," he reports; "others [were] in a state of partial delapidation; garden fences were broken down, and the gardens had become glass plats." The weavers still in residence "were not by any means uncleanly or slovenly, but they seemed to be contending against necessities, which left them small leisure for thinking of niceties in dress or furniture."

On every page Bamford provides details of work and wages, diet and housing, astute observations that reveal his sympathies. Though he was deeply moved by the conditions he found, he took pride in the dignity and endurance of his class. "Let us then cherish our workers," he wrote in 1848 as the Chartists marshaled their last march, "Let them be anxiously cared for. . . . For all in all, with their faults and depreciations, the wide world has not, in this our day, such another race as that which guards the shores, and labours on the fields and in the manufactories of Old England."

During the economic prosperity of the 1850s Bamford found an opportunity to better his own condition. In 1851 he secured through government patronage a minor clerical post at Somerset House in the office of inland revenue, but he was never comfortable in London, "the great Babylon" that he had derided in his autobiographical writings. By 1858 he had risen to the post of superintendent of books and papers under the accountant-general, but he resigned in order to return to his native Lancashire. He was drawn to political discussions in local pubs, where he confided to his diary that he could hear "more real thoughtful expression in the course of half an hour, than I had done among the working men of London for seven years." He had long thought that the country Sunday schools "had produced many working-men of sufficient talent to become readers, writers, and speakers in the village meetings for Parliamentary Reform," and he rededicated himself to promoting adult literacy.

Bamford and his wife settled in Moston Vale at Harpurhey, near Middleton, where they lived a poverty-stricken existence. Between 1859 and 1861 he eked out a living by giving public readings in emulation of Charles Dickens, but Bamford was a dull, ineffectual stage performer. Yet he remained active as a lecturer in the cause of parliamentary reform and regularly contributed articles on reform issues to the Manchester newspapers. He had by this time accepted all six points of the Charter, and he continued to stress universal suffrage and the secret ballot. In 1859 he helped organize the Manchester Parliamentary Reform Association and dedicated himself to preserving its independence from the middle-class Reform Union. People who "seek the pecuniary aid of persons who are of a more wealthy class than workers," he warned, "are like a ship sailing under false colours."

After fifty years of married life his beloved wife died in 1861. Living alone at Moston, Bamford grew deaf and his eyesight began to fail, so that by 1865 he could no longer see well enough to read. Well-wishers established an annuity for him in 1864, and in 1872 the old man finally died. On the day of his funeral, according to the *Manchester City News*, crowds gathered to line the route of the procession despite driving rain and a bitter April wind, and Bamford was buried in the parish churchyard of Saint Leonard's, Middleton.

Bamford's reputation as a reformer suffered because middle-class interests seized upon him as an articulate workingman whose moderate views could be used to combat the growing influence of Chartism. Having learned the harsh lesson of the state's repressive power at Peterloo, Bamford certainly disagreed with the tactics of mass protest and consequently thought the Chartist leadership to be "deluded," an opinion he took no pains to hide in *Walks in South Lancashire*. Yet he persisted in advocating universal suffrage; he preferred, however, to achieve it through education and debate.

At his death the *Manchester Guardian* hailed him as one who knew "the provocation of injustice, yet invariably denounced in unmeasured terms the suggestions of physical force, and never lost sight of the truth that all permanent reforms result from moral suasion alone." He cannot be simply dismissed as a traitor to his class. His writings indicate the diversity of radical opinion among working people during the formative years of the labor movement, and he is of great significance as an author whose works present the daily lives of an otherwise voiceless class. He is at his best when recording those annals of customs and conditions among the people, a legacy that those interested in social history and cultural studies should not overlook.

Bibliographies:

John Albert Green, *Bibliography of the Town of Heywood* (Heywood: Advertiser Officer, 1902), pp. 6–9;

W. H. Chaloner, "Chronological List of the Published Works of Samuel Bamford," in *The Autobiography of Samuel Bamford,* 2 volumes, edited by Chaloner (London: Cass, 1967; New York: Kelly, 1967), I: 43–45.

Biographies:

James Dronsfield, *Incidents and Anecdotes of the Late Samuel Bamford* (Oldham: Hirst & Rennie, 1872);

W. H. Chaloner, ed., *The Autobiography of Samuel Bamford,* 2 volumes (London: Cass, 1967; New York: Kelly, 1967);

Terence A. Lockett, *Three Lives–Samuel Bamford, Alfred Derbyshire, Ellen Wilkinson* (London: University of London Press, 1968).

Reference:

Martin Hewitt, "Radicalism and the Victorian Working Class: The Case of Samuel Bamford," *Historical Journal,* 34 (1991): 873–892.

Papers:

The Manchester Public Reference Library has a collection of Bamford's letters and four volumes of his manuscript diary for 1858–1861; the Middleton Public Library has a collection of his letters; Chetham's Library, Manchester, also has some Bamford materials.

Sabine Baring-Gould
(28 January 1834 - 2 January 1924)

Max Keith Sutton
University of Kansas

See also the Baring-Gould entry in *DLB 156: British Short-Fiction Writers, 1880-1914: The Romantic Tradition.*

BOOKS: *An Account of an English Camp near Bayonne* (Cambridge, 1851);

The Chorister: A Tale of King's College Chapel in the Civil Wars (Cambridge: Meadows, 1856; revised edition, Cambridge: Ladds, 1869);

The Path of the Just: Tales of Holy Men and Children (London: Masters, 1857);

Iceland: Its Scenes and Sagas (London: Smith, Elder, 1863);

The Book of Were-Wolves: Being an Account of a Terrible Superstition (London: Smith, Elder, 1865);

Post-Mediæval Preachers: Some Account of the Most Celebrated Preachers of the 15th, 16th, & 17th Centuries, with Outlines of Their Sermons, and Specimens of Their Style (London: Rivingtons, 1865);

Curious Myths of the Middle Ages (London: Rivingtons, 1866; Boston: Roberts, 1867); second series (London: Rivingtons, 1868; Philadelphia: Lippincott, 1868);

The Silver Store: Collected from Mediæval Christian and Jewish Mines (London: Longmans, Green, 1868; New York: Young, 1882; expanded edition, London: Skeffington, 1887);

Through Flood and Flame: A Novel, anonymous, 3 volumes (London: Bentley, 1868);

Curiosities of Olden Times (London: Hayes / New York: Pott & Amery, 1869; revised and enlarged edition, Edinburgh: Grant, 1895; New York: Whittaker, 1896);

The Origin and Development of Religious Belief, 2 volumes (London, Oxford & Cambridge: Rivingtons, 1869, 1870; New York: Appleton, 1871);

The Golden Gate: A Complete Manual of Instructions, Devotions, and Preparations, 3 parts (London: Simpkin, Marshall, 1869-1870); revised as *The Golden Gate: A Manual of Church Doctrine and Devotions* (London: Skeffington, 1896);

Sabine Baring-Gould

In Exitu Israel: An Historical Novel, 2 volumes (London: Macmillan, 1870; New York: Macmillan, 1870);

"Organization": A Sermon Preached at St. Michael's Church, Wakefield (London: Hayes, 1870);

Legends of Old Testament Characters, from the Talmud and Other Sources, 2 volumes (London & New York: Macmillan, 1871); republished as *Legends of the Patriarchs and Prophets and Other Old Testament Characters from Various Sources* (New York: Holt & Williams, 1872);

One Hundred Sermon Sketches for Extempore Preachers (London: Masters, 1871);

Protestant or Catholic? A Lecture (London: Hayes, 1872);

Secular v. Religious Education: A Sermon (London: Hodges, 1872);

The Lives of the Saints (17 volumes, London: Hodges, 1872-1889; revised and expanded edition, 16 volumes, London: Nimmo, 1897-1898; revised again, Edinburgh: Grant, 1914);

Village Conferences on the Creed (London: Masters, 1873; New York: Gorham, 1901);

How to Save Fuel (London: Chapman & Hall, 1874);

The Lost and Hostile Gospels: An Essay on the Toledoth Jeschu, and the Petrine and Pauline Gospels of the First Three Centuries of Which Fragments Remain (London & Edinburgh: Williams & Norgate, 1874);

Yorkshire Oddities, Incidents and Strange Events, 2 volumes (London: Hodges, 1874; revised edition, London: Methuen, 1890);

Some Modern Difficulties: Nine Lectures (London: Skeffington, 1875);

Village Preaching for a Year, 3 parts (London: Skeffington, 1875-1876); second series, 2 volumes (London: Skeffington, 1884);

The Vicar of Morwenstow: A Life of Robert Stephen Hawker (London: King, 1876; revised, 1876; New York: Whittaker, 1879);

The Mystery of Suffering: Six Lectures (London: Skeffington, 1877);

Germany, Present and Past, 2 volumes (London: Kegan Paul, Trench, 1879; New York: Holt, 1882);

Sermons to Children, first series (London: Skeffington, 1879); second series (London: Skeffington, 1907);

Mehalah: A Story of the Salt Marshes, anonymous, 3 volumes (London: Smith, Elder, 1880; New York: Lovell, 1889);

The Preacher's Pocket: A Packet of Sermons (London: Skeffington, 1880; New York: Pott, 1880);

Village Preaching for Saints' Days (London: Skeffington, 1881);

The Village Pulpit: A Complete Course of 66 Short Sermons, or Full Sermon Outlines for Each Sunday and Some Chief Holy Days of the Christian Year, 2 volumes (London: Skeffington, 1881, 1887);

Germany (London: Sampson Low, Marston, Searle & Rivington, 1883);

John Herring: A West of England Romance (3 volumes, London: Smith, Elder, 1883; 1 volume, New York: Lovell, 1889);

Church Songs, by Baring-Gould with music edited by Henry Fleetwood Sheppard, 2 series (London: Skeffington, 1884; New York: Pott, 1884);

The Seven Last Words: A Course of Sermons (London: Skeffington, 1884);

The Birth of Jesus: Eight Discourses for Advent, Christmas and Epiphany (London: Skeffington, 1885);

Our Parish Church: Twenty Addresses to Children on Great Truths of the Christian Faith (London: Skeffington, 1885; New York: Young, 1885);

The Passion of Jesus. First Series: Seven Discourses for Lent (London: Skeffington, 1885);

Germany, by Baring-Gould and Arthur Gilman (London: Unwin, 1886; New York: Putnam, 1886); republished as *The Story of Germany* (New York & London: Putnam, 1886); expanded again as *Germany,* by Baring-Gould and Wilfrid C. Lay (New York: Collier, 1898); revised and enlarged by Baring-Gould and Gilman (London: Unwin, 1905; New York: Putnam, 1906);

The Trials of Jesus: Seven Discourses for Lent (London: Skeffington, 1886);

Court Royal: A Story of Cross Currents, anonymous, 3 volumes (London: Smith, Elder, 1886; New York: Munro, 1886);

Nazareth and Capernaum: Ten Lectures on the Beginning of Our Lord's Ministry (London: Skeffington, 1886);

Little Tu'penny (London: Ward & Downey, 1887);

The Gaverocks: A Tale of the Cornish Coast (3 volumes, London: Smith, Elder, 1887; 1 volume, Philadelphia: Lippincott, 1888);

Red Spider (2 volumes, London: Chatto & Windus, 1887; 1 volume, New York: Lovell, 1888);

The Way of Sorrows: Seven Discourses for Lent (London: Skeffington, 1887);

The Death and Resurrection of Jesus: Ten Lectures for Holy Week and Easter (London: Skeffington, 1888; New York: Pott, 1888);

Our Inheritance: An Account of the Eucharistic Service in the First Three Centuries (London: Skeffington, 1888; New York: Pott, 1888);

Eve: A Novel, 2 volumes (London: Chatto & Windus, 1888; New York: Munro, 1888);

Richard Cable, the Lightshipman, 3 volumes (London: Smith, Elder, 1888; Philadelphia: Lippincott, 1888);

Historic Oddities and Strange Events: First Series (London: Methuen, 1889);

The Pennycomequicks: A Novel, 3 volumes (London: Blackett, 1889; New York: Lovell, 1889);

Conscience and Sin: Daily Meditations for Lent Including Week-Days and Sundays (London: Skeffington, 1890);

Arminell: A Social Romance, 3 volumes (London: Methuen, 1890; New York: Lovell, 1890);

Jacquetta and Other Stories (London: Methuen, 1890);

Grettir the Outlaw: A Story of Iceland (London: Blackie, 1890; New York: Scribner & Welford, 1890);

My Prague Pig, and Other Stories for Children (London: Skeffington, 1890);

Old Country Life (London: Methuen, 1890);

The Church in Germany (London: Gardner, Darton, 1891; New York: Pott, 1891);

Historic Oddities and Strange Events: Second Series (London: Methuen, 1891); also published as *Freaks of Fanaticism and Other Strange Events* (London: Methuen, 1891);

In Troubadour-Land: A Ramble in Provence and Languedoc (London: W. H. Allen, 1891; New York: Pott, 1891);

Margery of Quether, and Other Stories (London: Methuen, 1891; New York: Lovell, 1892);

Urith: A Tale of Dartmoor (3 volumes, London: Methuen, 1891; 1 volume, New York: United States Book Company, 1891);

In the Roar of the Sea (3 volumes, London: Methuen, 1892; 1 volume, New York: Lovell, Coryell, 1892);

Strange Survivals: Some Chapters in the History of Man (London: Methuen, 1892);

Through All the Changing Scenes of Life (London: Christian Knowledge Society, 1892);

Wagner's Parsifal at Baireuth (London: Skeffington, 1892);

The Tragedy of the Caesars: A Study of the Characters of the Caesars of the Julian and Claudian Houses, 2 volumes (London: Methuen, 1892; New York: Scribners, 1892);

Cheap Jack Zita, 3 volumes (London: Methuen, 1893; New York: Tait, 1894);

Mrs. Curgenven of Curgenven, 3 volumes (London: Methuen, 1893; New York: Lovell, Coryell, 1893);

A Book of Fairy Tales (London: Methuen, 1894; New York: Gaskin, 1894);

The Deserts of Southern France: An Introduction to the Limestone and Chalk Plateaux of Ancient Aquitaine, 2 volumes (London: Methuen, 1894; New York: Dodd, Mead, 1894);

The Icelander's Sword; or, The Story of Oraefa-Dal (London: Methuen, 1894);

Kitty Alone: A Story of Three Fires, 3 volumes (London: Methuen, 1894; New York: Dodd, Mead, 1894);

Noémi: A Story of Rock-Dwellers (New York: Appleton, 1894; London: Methuen, 1895);

The Queen of Love: A Novel, 3 volumes (London: Methuen, 1894; Philadelphia: Lippincott, 1894);

Evening Communions: A Letter to the Lord Bishop of Exeter (Oxford: Mowbray, 1895);

The Broom-Squire (London: Methuen, 1896; New York & London: Stokes, 1896);

Dartmoor Idylls (London: Methuen, 1896);

Guavas, the Tinner (London: Methuen, 1897; Philadelphia: Lippincott, 1897);

The Life of Napoleon Bonaparte (London: Methuen, 1897; New York: Truslove, 1897; abridged edition, London: Methuen, 1908; New York: Stokes, 1908);

Perpetua: A Story of Nimes in A.D. 213 (London: Isbister, 1897; New York: Dutton, 1897);

A Study of St. Paul: His Character and Opinions (London: Isbister, 1897);

Bladys of the Stewponey (London: Methuen, 1897; New York: Stokes, 1898);

An Armory of the Western Counties, Devon and Cornwall, from Unpublished Manuscripts of the XVI Century, by Baring-Gould and Robert Twigge (Exeter: Commin, 1898);

Domitia (London: Methuen, 1898; New York: Stokes, 1898);

An Old English Home and Its Dependencies (London: Methuen, 1898);

Romances of the West Country, edited by William Henry Kearley Wright (Plymouth: Doidge, 1898);

The Sunday Round: Plain Village Sermons for the Sundays of the Christian Year, 4 volumes (London: Skeffington, 1898-1899);

A Book of the West: Being an Introduction to Devon and Cornwall, 2 volumes (London: Methuen, 1899; New York: New Amsterdam Book, 1900);

The Crock of Gold (London: Methuen, 1899; Boston: Page, 1899);

Furze Bloom: Tales of the Western Moors (London: Methuen, 1899);

Pabo the Priest (London: Methuen, 1899; New York: Stokes, 1899);

The Present Crisis: A Letter to the Bishop of Exeter (London: Skeffington, 1899);

A Book of Dartmoor (London: Methuen, 1900);

In a Quiet Village (London: Isbister, 1900; New York & London: John Lane, 1900);

Virgin Saints and Martyrs (London: Hutchinson, 1900; New York: Crowell, 1901);

Winefred: A Story of the Chalk Cliffs (London: Methuen, 1900; Boston: Page, 1900);

The Frobishers: A Story of the Staffordshire Potteries (London: Methuen, 1901);

A Book of Brittany (London: Methuen, 1901);

Royal Georgie (London: Methuen, 1901);

Brittany (London: Methuen, 1902);

A Coronation Souvenir (London: Skeffington, 1902);

Miss Quillet (London: Methuen, 1902);

Nebo the Nailer (London & New York: Cassell, 1902);

Amazing Adventures (London: Skeffington, 1903);

A Book of North Wales (London: Methuen, 1903);

Chris of All-Sorts (London: Methuen, 1903);

In Dewisland (London: Methuen, 1904);

Siegfried: A Romance Founded on Wagner's Operas, "Rheingold," "Siegfried," and "Götterdämmerung" (London: Dean, 1904; Boston: Page, 1905);

A Book of Ghosts (London: Methuen, 1904; New York: Putnam, 1904);

A Book of the Riviera (London: Methuen, 1905; New York: Dutton, 1905; revised edition, London: Methuen, 1928);

A Memorial of Horatio, Lord Nelson (London: Skeffington, 1905);

Monsieur Pichelmère, and Other Stories (London: Digby, Long, 1905);

A Book of South Wales (London: Methuen, 1905);

A Book of Cornwall (London: Methuen, 1906);

A Book of Devon (London: Methuen, 1906);

A Book of the Rhine from Cleve to Mainz (London: Methuen, 1906; New York: Macmillan, 1906);

A Book of the Cevennes (London: Long, 1907);

A Book of the Pyrenees (London: Methuen, 1907; New York: Dutton, 1907);

Devon (London: Methuen, 1907; New York: McBride, 1928);

The Restitution of All Things; or, "The Hope That Is Set before Us" (London: Skeffington, 1907);

The Lives of the British Saints: The Saints of Wales and Cornwall and Such Irish Saints as Have Dedications in Britain, by Baring-Gould and John Fisher, 4 volumes (London: Cymmrodorion Society, 1907-1913);

The Baring-Gould Continuous Reader, edited by G. H. Rose (London: Methuen, 1908); revised as *The Baring-Gould Selection Reader* (London: Methuen, 1908);

Devonshire Characters and Strange Events (London: John Lane, 1908);

Cornish Characters and Strange Events (London & New York: John Lane, 1909);

A History of Sarawak under Its Two White Rajahs, 1839-1908, by Baring-Gould and Charles Agar Bampfylde (London: Sotheran, 1909);

Cornwall (Cambridge: Cambridge University Press, 1910);

Family Names and Their Story (London: Seeley, 1910);

Cliff Castles and Cave Dwellings of Europe (London: Seeley, 1911; Philadelphia: Lippincott, 1911);

A Coronation Souvenir (London: Skeffington, 1911);

The Land of Teck and Its Neighbourhood (London & New York: John Lane, 1911);

Two Sermons for the Coronation of King George V, by Baring-Gould and the Reverend Canon Duncan (London: Skeffington, 1911);

Sheepstor (Plymouth, U.K.: Hoyten & Cole, 1912);

Village Sermons to Simple Souls (London: Skeffington, 1912);

A Book of Folk-Lore (London & Glasgow: Collins' Clear-Type Press, 1913);

The Church Revival: Thoughts Thereon and Reminiscences (London: Methuen, 1914; New York: Dutton, 1914);

Thoughts from S. Baring-Gould, edited by H. B. Elliott (London: Holden & Hardingham, 1917);

The Evangelical Revival (London: Methuen, 1920);

Early Reminiscences, 1834-1864 (London: John Lane, 1923);

My Last Few Words (London: Skeffington, 1924);

Further Reminiscences, 1864-1894 (London: John Lane, 1925; New York: Dutton, 1925).

PLAY PRODUCTION: *Red Spider*, libretto by Baring-Gould, music by Learmont Drysdale, Lowestoft, Suffolk, The Marina, 25 July 1898.

OTHER: "Household Tales," in *Notes on the Folk-Lore of the Northern Counties of England*, by William Henderson (London: Folk Lore Society, 1866), pp. 299-344;

Hanna Olava Winsnes, *Norwegian Stories; or, Evenings at Oakwood*, translated by E. White, preface by Baring-Gould (London, 1868);

Cecilia Anne Jones, *Footprints of Our Fathers*, preface by Baring-Gould (London, 1876);

Wilhelmine von Hillern, *Ernestine: A Novel*, translated by Baring-Gould, 2 volumes (London: De la Rue, 1879; New York: Gottsberger, 1881);

Please Tell Me a Tale: A Collection of Short Original Stories for Children, edited by Baring-Gould and Charlotte M. Yonge (London: Skeffington, 1886);

Just One More Tale: A Second Collection of Short Original Stories for Children, edited by Baring-Gould and Yonge (London: Skeffington, 1886);

John Ashton, *The Legendary History of the Cross*, preface by Baring-Gould (London: Unwin, 1887);

Sophia Frances Anne Caulfeild, *The Lives of the Apostles, Their Contemporaries and Successors*, introduction by Baring-Gould (London: Hatchards, 1887);

John Bickley Hughes, *Deans Rural: The History of Their Office and Duties*, introduction by Baring-Gould (London: Skeffington, 1889);

Songs and Ballads of the West: A Collection, edited by Baring-Gould and Henry Fleetwood Sheppard, 4 parts (London: Methuen, 1891; revised, 1892); revised again as *Songs of the West: Folk Songs of Devon & Cornwall, Collected from the*

Mouths of the People, edited by Baring-Gould, Sheppard, and F. W. Bussell (London: Methuen, 1905);

A Book of Nursery Songs and Rhymes, edited by Baring-Gould (London: Methuen / Philadelphia: Lippincott, 1895);

English Minstrelsie: A National Monument of English Song, edited by Baring-Gould, 8 volumes (London: Cowan, 1895);

A Garland of Country Song: English Folk Songs with Their Traditional Melodies, edited by Baring-Gould and Sheppard (London: Methuen, 1895);

Jacob Grimm and Wilhelm Grimm, *Fairy Tales from Grimm,* introduction by Baring-Gould (London: Gardner, 1895);

Old English Fairy Tales, edited by Baring-Gould (London: Methuen / Chicago: Way & Williams, 1895);

Preston King, *Bath Waters: A Rational Account of Their Nature and Use,* historical sketch by Baring-Gould (Bristol: Arrowsmith, 1901);

English Folk-Songs for Schools, edited by Baring-Gould and Cecil J. Sharp (London: Curwen, 1906?);

Saint Frances de Sales, *Saint Frances de Sales,* edited by Baring-Gould (London & Edinburgh: Jack, 1907);

James Matcham Gatrill, *Echoes: Some Words Pertaining to the Kingdom of God,* preface by Baring-Gould (London: Skeffington, 1912).

SELECTED PERIODICAL PUBLICATIONS–UNCOLLECTED: "Early Christian Greek Romances," *Contemporary Review,* 30 (1887): 858–876;

"What Is a Gentleman?," *Cornhill Magazine,* 56, new series 9 (1887): 552–560;

"Breton Fishermen's Distress Fund," *Times* (London), 2 February 1903, p. 10;

"The New Rich: Their Influence in Country Life," *Times* (London), 7 August 1922, p. 9; 14 August 1922, p. 13.

If magnitude and variety of production were all that counted, the Reverend Sabine Baring-Gould would rank among the world's greatest authors. He wrote or contributed to well over one hundred books. These include his *The Lives of the Saints* (1872–1889) in seventeen volumes, biographies of Nero and Napoleon, collections of folklore and folk songs, around twenty travel books, and more than forty works of fiction. He was the only popular novelist of his era who was also a theologian and the only theologian who wrote a book on werewolves. Barely known today as the composer of the words for the hymns "Onward, Christian Soldiers" and "Now the Day Is Over," he once received a letter from a lady who admired his hymns but hoped that he was unrelated to "the wicked novelist of the same name."

Wicked or not, Baring-Gould as a novelist wrote some of the most graphic scenes of men and women fighting in Victorian literature, and his tone offended the playwright and novelist J. M. Barrie, who accused him of cruelty and misogyny. Yet Baring-Gould's fiction often shows women acting in boldly independent and unconventional ways; it reflects his concern for social and ecclesiastical reform and his sympathy for the poor, whom he tried to help as a curate in Yorkshire and later as parson and squire of a remote parish in Devon. He did more than write about bridging the gap between the privileged and the working classes: he married a Yorkshire mill girl, and instead of sending his sons to the universities at Oxford or Cambridge he had them work for a while in an arsenic mine and on the Bristol docks. His novels were produced by the same mind that designed new cottages for his tenants, challenged Victorian bishops, tried to reconcile theology and Darwinism, and pondered the mystery of suffering. Seen in the context of his deepest concerns, his fiction can reveal neglected facets of his imperfect but amazingly prolific genius.

The first son of Edward and Sophia Charlotte Baring-Gould, Sabine was born in Exeter in 1834. His father, a former cavalry officer, was heir to the estate of Lew Trenchard near the western slopes of Dartmoor; his mother was a daughter of Adm. Francis Godolphin Bond. The boy's odd Christian name honored his great-uncle, Gen. Sir Edward Sabine. Because of Baring-Gould's weak lungs and the restlessness of his father, all but three of the boy's first sixteen years were spent on the Continent. In *The Pennycomequicks* (1889) Baring-Gould recalls how his father, before each new journey, would search through their carriage for the boy's collection of crystals, dried flowers, butterflies, and books: "Nothing escaped his eye, nothing melted his heart. The author came to the place bringing nothing with him and left it carrying nothing with him away.... It was an excellent discipline for life, yet hardly attained; even to this day he finds that he clings to trifles."

Taught mainly by his parents, Sabine had no regular schooling until he was enrolled at King's College School, London, where he was ill most of the winter, and at Warwick Grammar School, where further signs of delicate lungs gave his father an excuse to return to France. While the boy never played any outdoor sport, he learned to speak five languages fluently on the Continent, and at age fif-

Lew Trenchard, the Baring-Gould estate near Dartmoor

The gallery at Lew Trenchard

teen he supervised his first dig after he discovered the floor of a Roman villa at Pau in southern France. Already launched on his career as an antiquarian, he was gaining the experience that went into writing many travel books. Most important, his exposure to the contrasts between Protestant and Catholic sections of Europe gave him the strong leaning toward Catholicism that informed his ministry and his writing.

By 1853 when he entered Clare Hall, Cambridge, he was drawn to the Tractarian movement to restore the Catholic heritage of the English Church. The tall, quietly eccentric undergraduate, at first considered mad because of his piety, became a member of the Society of the Holy Cross, commonly known as the Holy Club, but he showed sufficient mischief to perpetrate a literary hoax by publishing a story purportedly based on a "very rare" book that turned out to be nonexistent. To Baring-Gould's subsequent embarrassment, many Cambridge editions of *The Chorister: A Tale of King's College Chapel in the Civil Wars* (1856) were printed. After he left Cambridge in 1857, his developing sense of a religious vocation put him at odds with his parents, who wanted their eldest son to become the squire and not the rector of Lew Trenchard.

Without venturing to become ordained, he taught in the choir school of Saint Barnabas, Pimlico, a center for the Tractarians in London. Later in 1857 he taught chemistry, Latin, French, German, and drawing at Hurstpierpoint College in Sussex, where he acquired the nickname Snout and a pet bat that sometimes perched on his shoulder. During 1859–1860 he witnessed the anti-Tractarian riots at St. George's Mission in the slums of London's East End. Judging from his account of these events in *The Church Revival: Thoughts Thereon and Reminiscences* (1914), what embittered him most was not the profanity of the mob but the hostility of the Low-Church bishop of London toward Charles Lowder and the other Tractarian clergy who had to endure the threats of violence and the shouted hoots and curses.

At Hurstpierpoint, Baring-Gould developed his powers of storytelling by giving his pupils installments of "The Sagas of Grettir the Strong," which he was trying to translate from Icelandic. In pursuing this project he took a summer tour of Iceland in 1861, an experience that resulted in his first important book, *Iceland: Its Scenes and Sagas* (1863), a large and expensive volume with engravings, some in color, from his own drawings. Dedicated to Sir Edward Sabine, president of the Royal Society, the book reveals Baring-Gould's scientific interest in geysers, volcanoes, birds, and plants as well as his concern with religion, history, legends, music, folkways, and human character. The travel book has novelistic features—characters, dialogue, and narratives of his quest to find the scenes of Grettir's exploits. Anecdotes abound in this early work, just as they do in the elderly Baring-Gould's *Early Reminiscences, 1834–1864* (1923) and *Further Reminiscences, 1864–1894* (1925).

One anecdote rounds off his description of the puffin, "a pretty, gay little fellow" who "makes a capital dish, stuffed with raisin pudding, and baked. I tasted it in the Faroe isles when I dined with the Catholic missionary on a Friday. 'It is not fish, you know,' said he, 'but it feeds on fish!'" Humor brightens the travel narrative, as when the sulky native guide, a theology student fictitiously named Grímr, boils a ptarmigan without cleaning it or tells how he protested to the Danish governor against being assigned as a pastor to a remote island:

> "I think, Mr. Governor, that if you banish me to the island, you are bound to provide me with a wife."
>
> "How is that possible?" asked his Excellency in amazement.
>
> "You have a very charming daughter, who—"
>
> Grímr never finished the sentence, and ever after showed an invincible repugnance to setting his foot within the Governor's door.

Sometimes the humor is self-directed, notably when the modest English narrator, preparing to go to bed, hears the housemaid say, "Do let me pull your breeches off!" Not appreciating Icelandic hospitality, he takes a "flying leap," buries himself under the feather bed, and cries, "Grímr, save me!"

Set against the bits of human comedy are the awed, if somewhat stilted, descriptions of the landscape and the vivid retellings of "The Saga of Grettir." Baring-Gould was obsessed with volcanoes and hot springs, which provided him with a recurring image of the self: "We are all volcanoes with fire in our hearts," he writes in *Arminell* (1890). The savage deeds in the accounts of Grettir dramatize this belief, and Baring-Gould brings descriptions of the landscape and renderings of the saga into odd correspondence.

Knowing how his storytelling affected the fascinated schoolboys at Hurstpierpoint, he warns all readers who have "weak nerves" to skip the nightmarish telling of Grettir's battle with the vampire, the animated and bloated corpse whose nails claw the flesh off the hero's back. Violence reigns in nature, he asserts in *The Mystery of Suffering: Six Lectures* (1877), and life is a "torture-chamber." The saga suggests that view and helps confirm what the twelve-year-old Baring-Gould had begun to believe at night in Warwick when he lay awake listening to the moans of a woman dying of cancer in a nearby house. In Baring-Gould's novels one hears echoes of the violence and cruelty in Grettir's adventures long before the novelist finally published his "free translation" of the saga as *Grettir the Outlaw: A Story of Iceland* in 1890, but in his first travel book the young author recounts something that transcended or transmuted the pain that these old stories present. An impoverished farmer who sold Baring-Gould his last manuscript copies of the sagas called them "our joy; without them our long winters would be blanks." Baring-Gould saw the tears in the man's eyes, but he took the manuscripts away and gave them to the British Museum.

After finally being ordained in 1864, he left Hurstpierpoint to become a curate in the small Yorkshire mill town of Horbury. His first task was to start a mission and night school at Horbury Brig among the colliers and the workers from the woolen mills. Directing the mission choir, he sometimes rushed out to seize an urchin harassing the performers and turn him into a chorister on the spot. Here "Onward, Christian Soldiers" was first sung not to Arthur Sullivan's tune but to one that Baring-Gould adapted from a symphony by Franz Joseph Haydn. Sitting on the laps of the curate's frock coat to keep him prisoner after choir practice or lessons, the boys and girls demanded stories. While living at Horbury, Baring-Gould had published *The Book of Were-Wolves: Being an Account of a Terrible Superstition* (1865), which an anonymous modern editor calls a "horrifying book," so the children must have had plenty to think about while trudging home to bed.

His first novel did not appear until 1868, the year of his marriage to Grace Taylor, who had gone to work in a woolen mill at the age of ten and was only sixteen when the new curate, more than thirty years old, first saw her and fell in love with her. According to Bickford H. D. Dickinson, Baring-Gould's grandson, the story of their courtship would have appeared in *Further Reminiscences,* but the chapter recounting it was cut after being shown to Baring-Gould's daughter, Mary, in 1923. Yet his forgotten novel of 1868, *Through Flood and Flame,* gives a fictional version of their improbable romance. William Purcell's biography, *Onward Christian Soldier: A Life of Sabine Baring-Gould; Parson, Squire, Novelist, Antiquary, 1834–1924* (1957), suggests that Baring-Gould, like the young middle-class protagonist of the novel, felt the imprudence of the match but overcame his social biases and realized that members of the working class in the "manufacturing counties" were neither "low" nor "de-

Grace Taylor, the young Yorkshire mill worker whom Baring-Gould married in 1868

graded." Yet the mill girl in the novel must be educated, and she goes away to York for two years, as Grace Taylor did, to learn genteel conduct before her marriage. From all accounts, by the time Baring-Gould's wife became lady of the manor at Lew Trenchard she had lost every trace of her Yorkshire accent.

While the marriage proved to be mutually rewarding, it brought almost immediate complications. After taking his bride to his boyhood haunts on the Continent and thus furthering her education, Baring-Gould tried to repaper the moldering vicarage at Dalton i' t' Muck, as the place was known in that part of Yorkshire. According to his grandson, Baring-Gould fell into such a raging fury at the wallpaper that his young wife fled back to Horbury and asked the kindly vicar to "unmarry them." Reunited, the couple had three children in the next three years and then moved to a roomier vicarage in East Mersea on the Essex coast in 1871. They had seven children by 1881 when they moved to Lew Trenchard in Devon; eventually they had fourteen, after one died in infancy. Although Baring-Gould had only half that total when he presented a curate with fourteen children in *Mehalah: A Story of the Salt Marshes* (1880), he sensed danger: Mr. Rabbit in that novel "was a crushed man, his ideas stunned in his head by the uproar in which he dwelt." At Dalton, Baring-Gould had considered buying a van in which to retire for the night. The time needed for writing must have distanced the father from his many children; at any rate, his grandson vouches for the story that at a party at Lew Manor when Baring-Gould asked a child, "And whose little girl are you, my dear?" she answered, "I'm yours, Papa." Dickinson, however, attributes Baring-Gould's mistake to dim lighting and poor eyesight.

Despite distractions the young vicar found enough time at Dalton to complete his major theological work, the two-volume *Origin and Development of Religious Belief* (1869, 1870), in which he claims that "mental activity is directly antagonistic to reproductiveness," and vice versa. As an attempt to ground theology on a scientific understanding of man, the work invited attacks from Protestants, Roman Catholics, and even the High Anglican party to which he belonged. Yet this daring effort to synthesize Darwinian science, Hegelian philosophy, and traditional Christian theology was published in at least five editions and still deserves notice in the history of Victorian thought. Implicit in its assumptions are the views, fully articulated in *Some Modern Difficulties: Nine Lectures* (1875), that "the Gospel of Science is as Divine as any of the historical Gospels of Christ," that both can be reconciled, and that the "law of the world is evolution." Yet *freedom*, not *law*, is the key term in this theology. "God wills man to be free, but the emancipation of himself is in man's own hands." For individuals and for societies, developing life is a struggle for liberation. This struggle of the individual provides the central action for his novels, in which despotic antagonists—usually Dissenters—deny love, the free and freeing act exemplified in God's making of free creatures.

This concern with freedom came naturally to a man who had faced his father's opposition and as a clergyman chafed under the authority of unapostolic bishops who let the Church of England be subservient to the state. His second novel, *In Exitu Israel* (1870), pursues the concern for freedom that distinguishes his theology by treating the struggle for liberty in the first year of the French Revolution. The title, from Psalm 114 ("When Israel came out of Egypt"), is both sadly ironic and boldly optimistic: the struggle for freedom leads to new forms of tyranny, yet something is gained: "The Revolution was a severe surgical operation, but it was the salvation of France." It need not have led to the Reign of Terror and Napoleon Bonaparte, according to the narrator, whose belief in human freedom of choice underlies his claim that following the advice of Jacques Necker, the finance minister, would have turned France into a constitutional monarchy such as England. Using the radical priest Thomas Lindet as his spokesman, Baring-Gould voices his dismay with the bishops of his own church, "for bishops were then, as they frequently are now, champions of abuses." His preface warns the English bishops against trying to suppress the reviving Catholicism within the Anglican Church. Rather than letting the state try to regulate public worship, the Tractarian "liberation party" would welcome disestablishment of the Church.

The novel becomes swamped in history, yet it offers impressive versions of the great events of 1789—the opening of the Estates-General, the fall of the Bastille, and the women's march to Versailles. The big scenes have more coherence than Thomas Carlyle's accounts in *The French Revolution: A History* (1837), and by developing the characters of the hated Parisian officials Joseph François Foulon and his son-in-law, Louis Bénigne François Bertier de Sauvigny, Baring-Gould makes their deaths more dramatic than does either Carlyle's history or Charles Dickens's *A Tale of Two Cities* (1859). The characterization of the deranged, lead-colored Madame Bertier with Gabriel, the saffron-dyed cat who is both her pet and her angel, shows Baring-Gould's debt to Dickens or Wilkie Collins, but it has its own grotesque distinction.

A tragic struggle for liberty of the individual appears in *Mehalah*, Baring-Gould's best-known novel. Living on the Essex coast near the time of the French Revolution, Mehalah, the bold heroine of this novel, wears the *bonnet rouge* but comes to see herself as the fallen Goddess of Liberty who has been proclaimed in Paris. She first appears as one of the most liberated women in Victorian fiction: full of gypsy blood, she carries a pistol, wears a sailor's blue outfit, rows out at night to find her sweetheart, and throws an insulting blonde rival off a boathouse and into the sea. But challenging her freedom is Elijah Rebow, a powerful Heathcliffian antagonist who has just enough Calvinism to believe in predestination and who claims to be her predetermined partner. Although his early schemes to force her to seek refuge in his house and then to marry him smack of crude melodrama, he starts sounding less like a villain than a crazed prophet of liberated passion. The destiny that he envisions for himself and Mehalah is sexual; their union is to be their salvation, their heaven in the heart of the "consuming fire" that is his god. A. C. Swinburne admired the novel, which he likened to Emily Brontë's *Wuthering Heights* (1847). As a character Mehalah has no clear counterpart in a major Victorian novel, and Rebow, for John Fowles, is the most memorable character of his type—"after Heathcliff"—in English fiction. The novel—with its bleak marshland setting; its stark symbols of bondage, freedom, and passion; and its moments of aptly grim humor—marks the height of Baring-Gould's artistic achievement. It went through seven editions by 1897 and was still being republished nearly a century later.

The novels that Baring-Gould began to produce after his move to Lew Trenchard in 1881 were bound to suffer from being composed so rapidly. The new squire was pressed for money, not only because of his growing family but also because of his ambitions for improving the estate. He began designing and building cottages, restoring the church to something like its pre-Reformation beauty, and rebuilding the manor. These projects revitalized the parish economy and created opportunities for local workers to learn skills in carving stone and wood. (Two Devonshire women carved the church's intricate rood screen.) To pay for everything, Baring-Gould began writing novels, which he often turned out at a rate of two a year after 1886, while publishing devotional books almost yearly throughout this decade.

Trying to avoid bankruptcy, Baring-Gould maintained this frantic pace until 1905, when he switched from writing novels to writing travel books. As a mass-producer of fiction he soon showed signs of discontent, particularly in asides to his readers, whom he refers to as the multitude of do-nothings "whose whole aim is distraction." "Shall I lay myself out for such as they?" he asks rhetorically in *Richard Cable, the Lightshipman* (1888), and he defiantly answers: "I would tear myself to pieces with my own hands rather than stoop to such baseness." He insisted on his right to put hard moral problems before the reader and to end a story unhappily. Yet he kept on contriving novels with suspenseful, improbable plots, swift action, thin but often vivid characterization, stiff dialogue, and generally happy endings.

Many were serialized in popular magazines, and some were published in five or more Victorian editions and printings, so he had learned to please the public. But in his view the greatest accomplishment of his career was his collection of folk songs, *Songs and Ballads of the West* (1891), gathered from the remaining "song men" in scattered cottages of Devon and Cornwall. Although criticized for bowdlerizing the lyrics or substituting new ones, Baring-Gould, Henry Fleetwood Sheppard, and Cecil J. Sharp, his collaborators on several editions of these volumes, preserved the original words and music in manuscript for the Plymouth City Library.

The interests that made him a pioneer collector of folk songs and folklore appear in many of his novels, particularly in *Red Spider* (1887), which he turned into the libretto for a light opera, with music

Title page for the American edition of Baring-Gould's last volume of reminiscences, from which the story of his courtship of Grace Taylor was removed by one of his daughters before it was published in 1925

by Learmont Drysdale. It opened in Lowestoft, Suffolk, in 1898 and toured the provinces for one hundred performances. Set in Bratton Clovelly, the parish just north of Lew Trenchard, the novel concerns an alleged witch who spouts Devonshire lore and, with the other rustics, makes this a significant work of regional fiction. The heroine's incompetent father and at least one of her family's misfortunes anticipate those of Tess Durbeyfield in Thomas Hardy's *Tess of the D'Urbervilles: A Pure Woman* (1891), although this story has a happy ending for everyone but the witch, who dies of rat poison.

As in *Mehalah*, the heroine's poverty and responsibilities restrict her freedom, and she barely escapes being trapped into a marriage to an elderly farmer, a despotic Dissenter like Rebow but without one spark of Rebow's passion. The focus on rustic life in a single parish makes *Red Spider* one of the few West Country novels of the period that can stand comparison with Hardy's lighter fiction. The dialogue may be stilted at times, as Baring-Gould's critics often complained; he never succeeds as well as Richard Dodderidge Blackmore or Eden Phillpotts in rendering the Devonshire dialect. Yet Baring-Gould compensates in his handling of the setting, which he treats almost as artfully as he does in *Mehalah*. Though not quite as popular as *The Vicar of Morwenstow: A Life of Robert Stephen Hawker* (1876), Baring-Gould's biography of an eccentric Cornish clergyman and poet, *Red Spider* offers as much local color as anyone could expect to find in the best regional fiction.

Many of his later novels explore the West Country. *John Herring: A West of England Romance*, a success of 1883, is set in Devon and Cornwall; in *The Gaverocks: A Tale of the Cornish Coast* (1887) and his popular adventure novel, *In the Roar of the Sea* (1892), the action occurs along the Cornish coast; in *Richard Cable* the setting shifts from Essex to Cornwall. *Kitty Alone: A Story of Three Fires* (1894) is set in South Devon, while *Eve* (1888) and *Urith* (1891) are Dartmoor novels, the latter of which was published in five editions and is set, like Blackmore's best-selling *Lorna Doone: A Romance of Exmoor* (1869), in the time of Monmouth's Rebellion. Baring-Gould's regionalism extends even beyond the West Country: to Yorkshire in *Through Flood and Flame, The Pennycomequicks,* and *Arminell*; to Cheshire in *The Queen of Love* (1894); to Essex in *Cheap Jack Zita* (1893); to the Devil's Punch Bowl in Surrey in the grim but popular *Broom-Squire* (1896); to Staffordshire in *The Frobishers: A Story of the Staffordshire Potteries* (1901); and to southwest Wales in *In Dewisland* (1904).

Baring-Gould's fictional work does not always focus on the rural folk. Several late novels treat social concerns in presenting some effort to bridge the gap between the upper classes and the barely educated masses. With increasing didacticism his later novels raise issues evident in his first novel, as aristocrats leave their places to live and work among the poor. Some of the cultured follow Baring-Gould's example and marry beneath their stations. The troubled heroine of *Richard Cable,* for instance, seeks salvation by marrying a good-natured, common lightship keeper and soon destroys his happiness by her scorn for his rustic ways. After they separate she lives first as a serving maid and then as a seamstress before, as a better woman, she finally rejoins her husband, who recovers his good nature and refines his manners under her influence.

In *Arminell* a lord's daughter commits social suicide by giving up her rank to live among the lower classes in London. After marrying a man to save him from poverty, she settles for a quiet life and gives up her dream of regenerating society by some "revolutionary method." Her goal becomes that of teaching her daughters to become "humdrum women": dutiful members of the lower middle class, young women who do good in their immediate circle without aspiring to the aristocratic role of a Lady Bountiful. Despite this rather flat conclusion *Arminell* fulfills what its subtitle promises as a "social romance," as it explores questions of class inequality from several different angles. A neighborhood witch awakens the heroine's social conscience by telling her a story to support the thesis that "the world is governed by injustice." When Arminell's noble father says that he is content with the "providential ordering of the world," she can reply, "Of course you are, papa, on fifty thousand a year." A religious fanatic prophesies an end to the "age of privilege" and shoots the noble lord, but his death betokens no sense of good riddance. In Baring-Gould's fiction aristocrats can fill a social function by displaying the discipline of self-restraint and courtesy that the working classes lack.

Precisely how seriously he regards the aristocratic virtue of self-restraint is hard to determine. In *The Pennycomequicks* the narrator asserts that what most distinguishes the upper from the lower classes is the "restraint of the facial muscles" that characterizes the former. Then with real or ironic approval he tells how Lady Beaconsfield, the wife of Benjamin Disraeli, "endured her finger to be jammed in the carriage-door without wince or cry, and continued listening or pretending to listen to her husband's conversation whilst driving to the House." In *The Frobishers,* a late novel, any uncertainty about the narrator's regard for aristocratic self-restraint vanishes before the earnestness of his heroine. She loses her fortune, goes to work in a Staffordshire pottery, and lives among girls who apply lead paint to the ware and often suffer from lead poisoning. She discovers that by working alongside the poor an aristocrat can learn to be honest, useful, and caring while the poor in return can profit from knowing models of courtesy and self-control. By their examples, members of the upper classes can teach others the virtue of "self-rule."

These ideas occur to her as she recognizes the possibility of a workers' revolution that may "wreck modern civilization and destroy culture past recovery." But when her aristocratic suitor asks if her plan to bring cultured people into the slums and factories is a scheme to ward off such a revolution, she denies it in saying: "I would not have you ... go down among the artisans and work, merely to save your class." Instead, the prevailing motive must be "love of God and our fellow man," for no other motive is great enough to bring about a good society. The heroine has no faith in socialism or the "half truth" of any *-ism:* "The socialist's heart aches, and he cries out at the suffering which everywhere surrounds him; but his suggested remedies would make existence insufferable, and, if carried out, could not last a generation." She also has no faith in public education: the new technical and primary schools teach knowledge and skills but not values, not "self control," and the result of relying on such a resolution to problems of class differences will be the creation of "intellectual monsters"–"very clever, very cunning, entirely selfish, and absolutely unscrupulous." She adds that not even organized religion can teach self-control to the masses, for to leaven the whole lump the yeast must be worked in, not applied to the surface. So members of the upper classes, "in whom self-rule has become a habit," must come to the lower classes and "infuse" this virtue into the social mass. Convinced of this truth, her suitor agrees to work with her in the potteries for five months during each of the first five years of their marriage. Afterward he may use the knowledge he has gained to muster support for more-enlightened laws in the House of Commons.

Yet Baring-Gould treats this idea differently in other narratives. At the end of *Cheap Jack Zita,* published eight years before *The Frobishers,* a wealthy farmer's son insists on leaving in his mother's old van and selling damaged or dubious goods to the "General Public," characterized as an ass that brays constantly for thistles. The farmer objects, but the mother recalls her youthful experience and supports the boy's pleas: "let him go. Cheap-jacking is an edication. It teaches a chap to know the General Public, what to lay on his back, how to tickle his ears, what you can make him swallow. If you think of making Jim a mimber of Parliament, there is no school, no college more suitable than the Cheap Jack's van." The good-humored cynicism here reveals an attitude that goes oddly with the earnestness at the end of *The Frobishers,* but that idealistic novel offers no preparation for Baring-Gould's later comment on those bits of aristocratic yeast that are supposed to leaven the social lump. In *The Church Revival,* published on the eve of World War I, he virtually gives up on the upper classes–"the nobility, the gentry, the plutocrats"–by saying that "they are pretty well left to stew in their own fat." By 1914 he sees the future of the English Church and the hope of a better society in the hands of the workers, and he sounds optimistic about those new "masters."

What hopes he had for society depended on his hopes for the Church and for the spiritual re-

Baring-Gould in 1923

generation that would direct unselfish actions such as those he envisioned in *The Frobishers.* In that novel and *The Queen of Love* he details the symptoms of a diseased industrial society by describing the pollution and the physical hazards it creates for workers. Elsewhere he examines the anger that could arouse a workers' rebellion, which he treats on a small scale in his chapters on the Fen Riots of the early nineteenth century in *Cheap Jack Zita* and in his unsympathetic accounts of the disturbances of Rebeccaite followers at roughly the same time in Wales, as shown in his novel *In Dewisland.* On a large scale Baring-Gould had presented this anger in *In Exitu Israel,* his early novel on the French Revolution, but he could not imagine any positive change in the social order without some reform of the human spirit.

Accordingly, his late fiction often puts the main characters through an earthly purgatory, in which a crucial part of the ordeal is for those characters to see themselves in a new and threatening light. In *Arminell* he cites the experience of Saint Theresa, who sees herself in this way and can never "recall the vision without a shudder." Both

Arminell and the man whom she marries pass through "purgatorial flame" as they face their own folly; the selfish young husband in *The Pennycomequicks* must suffer the breaking of the "pillar of self-esteem" that constitutes his wonted identity. This comes with a fall down an alpine rockslide and a still more painful psychological ordeal when a free-speaking American woman tells him just what she thinks of his manhood. A battered youth has to overhear similar unwelcome news about himself in *Red Spider*. The title character in *Eve* becomes crippled from her ordeals yet transformed into a better person: the "great and solemn priest Pain" has laid his hands on her, broken her, and held her up to Heaven as if she were the bread that becomes the body of Christ in the Eucharist. In another analogy for such transformations Baring-Gould writes in *Arminell* that after the larva stage of childhood comes the period "when the human conscience, glutted with as much knowledge and experience as it deems sufficient, encases itself in a chrysalis of conceit, and falls asleep in self-sufficiency." Then through suffering and a "shock of awakening life" the individual may emerge as a true "spiritual character," although some insects "never escape out of their chrysalis."

The novels are full of these hardened, encased characters who never emerge. These are often the antagonists, the iron-willed Dissenters such as Elijah Rebow, who enchains Mehalah, or Jabez Grice, the hardened Puritan in *The Queen of Love*. After falling into a pan of boiling brine at the salt works, he lies dying, and, as it crystallizes over his scalded body, he envisions Heaven as a "'blessed land of Total Abstinence . . . where there are no public houses, no skipping ropes, no butterflies nor vanities, no spangles, no tight-rope dancing and no circuses, where'—he tore his hair from the bags, as he forcibly raised his head and glared at his daughter-in-law—'and where there are no Ada Buttons.'" (Ada was her father-in-law's particular bête noire.) Instead of passing into such a Heaven, Grice is moved "into the World of Great Surprises, where the first and greatest surprise that awaits man is the vision of himself, not as he supposed, believed himself to be, but as he REALLY IS."

In creating characters such as Jabez Grice, Baring-Gould shows flashes of a grotesque, caustic vision that distinguishes Flannery O'Connor's fiction. Yet by the time of his death in 1924, his novels were being forgotten along with most of his other writing. During World War I he had not been able to publish any new books, and his last major work before the war had been *The Church Revival*, a lively, opinionated survey of the origins and influence of the Tractarian movement and a rogues' gallery of privileged, politically appointed Victorian bishops who had failed to support the Anglo-Catholic cause.

His wife had died in 1916, leaving him alone at Lew Trenchard. Although he was no longer able to write while standing at his special desk, he published *The Evangelical Revival* (1920), a second survey of recent church history that readers also regarded with disfavor, and his *Early Reminiscences* and *Further Reminiscences*. If parts of a projected third volume survived in manuscript, they were lost in the fire that destroyed his papers in 1967. These two published volumes give a wryly indirect self-portrait of a man surveying his life and work as he neared the age of ninety.

The portrait is engagingly modest: recalling his mother's handbag full of silk threads, he notes that *Early Reminiscences* is like his head—"a collection, nay, a very jumble of scraps." He acknowledges in *Further Reminiscences* the relatively small dimensions of his main ambition and accomplishment: "I had a work to do, not like that of [Cardinal John Henry] Newman in England at large, but at Lew Trenchard, the small." He shows that he has no rancor at perhaps having been listed in the bishops' "Black Book," for by not receiving any important church appointment he was able to concentrate on his own parish. If the bishops never rewarded him, he never showed much deference to them, and in the latter of his *Reminiscences* he cannot resist recalling, an old enemy, Archbishop Archibald Campbell Tait, whose face at a dinner party suddenly

> became ghastly. Laying down his knife and fork by the plate, he said to himself in a suppressed voice: "It has come to pass at last as I feared. I have been dreading, expecting, a stroke."
> "Console yourself, your Grace," said the Duchess of Sutherland, who sat beside him. "It is not *your* leg but *mine* that you have been pinching."

Baring-Gould received few honors for all his labors, although he was elected president of the Devonshire Association in 1895 and president of the Royal Institution of Cornwall in 1897. In 1918 he received an honorary fellowship from Clare Hall, Cambridge. He was not officially honored by the Church of England until after his death on 2 January 1924, when two bishops came to Lew Trenchard to conduct his funeral and join in the singing of "Onward, Christian Soldiers" and "Now the Day Is Over."

Interview:

Frederick Dolman, "Novel-Writing and Novel-Reading: A Chat with the Rev. S. Baring-Gould," *Cassell's Family Magazine,* new series (1 December 1894): 17–24.

Bibliography:

Samuel J. Rogal, "Sabine Baring-Gould (1834–1924): A Checklist," *Serif,* 9 (1972): 22–35.

Biographies:

William Purcell, *Onward Christian Soldier: A Life of Sabine Baring-Gould; Parson, Squire, Novelist, Antiquary, 1834–1924* (London: Longmans, Green, 1957);

Bickford H. D. Dickinson, *Sabine Baring-Gould: Squarson, Writer and Folklorist, 1834–1924* (Newton Abbot: David & Charles, 1970).

References:

William Addison, *The English Country Parson* (London: Dent, 1947);

J. M. Barrie, "Novels of Sabine Baring-Gould," *Contemporary Review,* 57 (1890): 206–226;

John Fowles, Introduction to Baring-Gould's *Mehalah: A Story of the Salt Marshes* (London: Chatto & Windus, 1969);

William J. Hyde, "The Stature of Baring-Gould as a Novelist," *Nineteenth-Century Fiction,* 15 (1960): 1–16;

Introduction to *The Book of Were-Wolves: Being an Account of a Terrible Superstition* (New York: Causeway, 1973);

David Roberts, "If One Had to Pick the Strangest Victorian," *Smithsonian,* 24 (July 1993): 74–82;

Max Keith Sutton, "Baring-Gould's *Mehalah* and *Red Spider:* Sources for Hardy's *Tess?*," *English Literature in Transition: 1880–1920,* 24 (1981): 91–98;

Sutton, "Place, Folklore, and Hegelianism in Baring-Gould's *Red Spider,*" *Victorians Institute Journal,* 13 (1985): 111–125.

Sir Walter Besant
(14 August 1836 – 9 June 1901)

Kirsten Escobar
Baylor University

See also the Besant entry in *DLB 135: British Short-Fiction Writers, 1880–1914: The Realist Tradition.*

BOOKS: *Studies in Early French Poetry* (London & Cambridge: Macmillan, 1868; Boston: Roberts, 1877);

Philanthropy: An Original Comedy in Three Acts, by Besant (as Walter Maurice) and James Rice (London: French's Acting Edition, 186–?);

Jerusalem, the City of Herod and Saladin, by Besant and Edward Henry Palmer (London: Bentley, 1871; New York: Scribner & Welford, 1889);

Ready-Money Mortiboy: A Matter-of-Fact Story, by Besant and Rice (3 volumes, London: Tinsley, 1872; 1 volume, New York: Worthington, 1879);

When George the Third Was King, 2 volumes (London: Sampson Low, 1872);

The French Humourists from the Twelfth to the Nineteenth Century (London: Bentley, 1873; Boston: Roberts, 1874);

My Little Girl, by Besant and Rice (3 volumes, London: Chatto & Windus, 1873; 1 volume, Boston: Osgood, 1873);

Our Work in Palestine: Being an Account of the Different Expeditions Sent Out to the Holy Land by the Committee of the Palestine Exploration Fund since the Establishment of the Fund in 1865 (New York: Scribner, Welford & Armstrong, 1873; London: Bentley, 1875); revised as *Twenty-One Years' Work in the Holy Land: A Record and a Summary, June 22, 1865–June 22, 1886* (London: Bentley, 1887); revised again as *Thirty Years' Work in the Holy Land: (A Record and a Summary) 1865–1895* (London: Watt, 1895);

Ready-Money: A Drama in Four Acts, by Besant (as Walter Maurice) and Rice (London & New York: French's Acting Edition, 1875);

With Harp and Crown: A Novel, by Besant and Rice (3 volumes, London: Tinsley, 1875; 1 volume, Boston: Osgood, 1876);

This Son of Vulcan: A Novel, by Besant and Rice (3 volumes, London: Sampson Low, Marston, Searle & Rivington, 1876; 1 volume, New York: Dodd, Mead, 1888);

Sir Walter Besant, circa 1894

The Case of Mr. Lucraft, and Other Tales, by Besant and Rice (2 volumes, London: Sampson Low, Marston, Searle & Rivington, 1876; 1 volume, New York: Dodd, Mead, 1888);

The Golden Butterfly: A Novel, by Besant and Rice (3 volumes, London: Tinsley, 1876; 1 volume, New York: Allison, 1877);

Such a Good Man! A Tale Written for Christmas, by Besant and Rice (London, 1877);

When the Ship Comes Home, by Besant and Rice (New York: Harper, 1877);

The Monks of Thelema: A Novel, by Besant and Rice (3

volumes, London: Chatto & Windus, 1878; 1 volume, New York: Munro, 1883);

By Celia's Arbour: A Tale of Portsmouth Town, by Besant and Rice (3 volumes, London: Sampson Low, Marston, Searle & Rivington, 1878; 1 volume, New York: Harper, 1878);

Shepherds All and Maidens Fair, by Besant and Rice (New York: Harper, 1878);

Constantinople: A Sketch of Its History from Its Foundation to Its Conquest by the Turks in 1453, by Besant and William J. Brodribb (London: Seeley, Jackson & Halliday, 1879);

Gaspard de Coligny (Marquis de Châtillon), Admiral of France (London: Ward, 1879; New York: Harper, 1879);

Rabelais (Edinburgh & London: Blackwood, 1879; Philadelphia: Lippincott, 1879);

Sweet Nelly, My Heart's Delight: A Novel, by Besant and Rice (New York: Harper, 1879);

'Twas in Trafalgar's Bay, and Other Stories, by Besant and Rice (London: Chatto & Windus, 1879);

'Twas in Trafalgar's Bay: A Story, by Besant and Rice (New York: Harper, 1879);

Over the Sea with the Sailor, by Besant and Rice (London: Chapman & Hall, 1880; New York: Munro, 1880);

The Seamy Side: A Story, by Besant and Rice (3 volumes, London: Chatto & Windus, 1880; 1 volume, New York: Appleton, 1880);

The Captain's Room: A Novel (New York: Harper, 1881; 3 volumes, London: Chatto & Windus, 1883);

The Chaplain of the Fleet: A Novel, by Besant and Rice (3 volumes, London: Chatto & Windus, 1881; 1 volume, New York: Harper, 1881);

Sir Richard Whittington, Lord Mayor of London, by Besant and Rice (London: Ward, 1881; New York: Putnam, 1881);

The Ten Years' Tenant, and Other Stories, by Besant and Rice (3 volumes, London: Chatto & Windus, 1881; 1 volume, New York: Dodd, Mead, 1888);

All Sorts and Conditions of Men: An Impossible Story, by Besant and Rice (3 volumes, London: Chatto & Windus, 1882; 1 volume, New York: Harper, 1882);

The Revolt of Man (Edinburgh: Blackwood, 1882; New York: Holt, 1882);

"So They Were Married": A Novel, by Besant and Rice (New York: Harper, 1883);

All in a Garden Fair: The Simple Story of Three Boys and a Girl (3 volumes, London: Chatto & Windus, 1883; 1 volume, New York: Harper, 1883);

The Captain's Room, and Other Stories, 3 volumes (London: Chatto & Windus, 1883);

The Life and Achievements of Edward Henry Palmer (London: John Murray, 1883; New York: Dutton, 1883);

Let Nothing You Dismay (New York: Lovell, 1883);

Life in a Hospital, Being an East End Chapter (London: Fisher, 1883);

The Ten Years' Tenant, by Besant and Rice (New York: Munro, 1883);

Uncle Jack (New York: Munro, 1883);

Love Finds the Way, and Other Stories, by Besant and Rice (New York: Munro, 1884);

The Art of Fiction: A Lecture Delivered at the Royal Institution on Friday Evening, April 25, 1884 (London: Chatto & Windus, 1884; Boston: Cupples, Upham, 1884);

Dorothy Forster: A Novel (3 volumes, London: Chatto & Windus, 1884; 1 volume, New York: Munro, 1884);

A Glorious Fortune (New York: Munro, 1884);

In Luck at Last (New York: Munro, 1885);

Uncle Jack and Other Stories, by Besant and Walter H. Pollock (New York: Harper, 1885; London: Chatto & Windus, 1885);

Children of Gibeon (3 volumes, London: Chatto & Windus, 1886; 1 volume, New York: Harper, 1886);

The Holy Rose (London: Chapman & Hall, 1886; New York: Munro, 1886);

The World Went Very Well Then: A Novel (New York: Harper, 1886; 3 volumes, London: Chatto & Windus, 1887);

Katharine Regina (Bristol: Arrowsmith, 1887; New York: Harper, 1887);

To Call Her Mine: A Novel (New York: Harper, 1887; London: Chatto & Windus, 1889);

The Eulogy of Richard Jefferies (London: Chatto & Windus, 1888; New York: Longmans, Green, 1888);

Herr Paulus: His Rise, His Greatness, and His Fall (3 volumes, London: Chatto & Windus, 1888; 1 volume, New York: Harper, 1888);

Fifty Years Ago (A Picture of Society in This Country as It Was When the Queen Ascended the Throne) (London: Chatto & Windus, 1888; New York: Harper, 1888; revised edition, London: Chatto & Windus, 1892);

The Inner House (Bristol: Arrowsmith, 1888; New York: Harper, 1888);

For Faith and Freedom: A Novel (New York: Harper, 1888; 3 volumes, London: Chatto & Windus, 1889);

The Bell of St. Paul's (3 volumes, London: Chatto & Windus, 1889; 1 volume, New York: Harper, 1889);

The Doubts of Dives (Bristol: Arrowsmith, 1889);

To Call Her Mine and Other Stories (London: Chatto & Windus, 1889);

Armorel of Lyonesse: A Romance of To-day (3 volumes, London: Chatto & Windus, 1890; 1 volume, New York: Harper, 1890);

Captain Cook (London & New York: Macmillan, 1890);

The Demoniac (Bristol: Arrowsmith / London: Simpkin, Marshall, Hamilton, Kent, 1890; New York: Ivers, 1890);

The "Literary Handmaid of the Church": In Reply to an Invitation from the Publication Committee of the Society for the Promotion of Christian Knowledge (London: Glaisher, 1890);

St. Katherine's by the Tower: A Novel (3 volumes, London: Chatto & Windus, 1891; 1 volume, New York: Harper, 1891);

The Ivory Gate (3 volumes, London: Chatto & Windus, 1892; 1 volume, New York: Harper, 1892);

London (Chatto & Windus, 1892; New York: Harper, 1892);

Verbena Camellia Stephanotis, and Other Tales (London: Chatto & Windus, 1892); republished as *Verbena Camellia Stephanotis, and Other Stories* (New York: Harper, 1892);

The History of London (London: Longmans, Green, 1893);

The Rebel Queen (3 volumes, London: Chatto & Windus, 1893; 1 volume, New York: Harper, 1893);

The Society of Authors: A Record of Its Action from Its Foundation (London: Incorporated Society of Authors, 1893);

Beyond the Dreams of Avarice (London: Chatto & Windus, 1895; New York: Harper, 1895);

In Deacon's Orders, and Other Tales (London: Chatto & Windus, 1895; New York: Harper, 1895);

Westminster, by Besant and Geraldine Edith Mitton (London: Chatto & Windus, 1895; New York & London: Stokes, 1895);

The Master Craftsman (2 volumes, London: Chatto & Windus, 1896; 1 volume, New York: Stokes, 1896);

The Charm, and Other Drawing-Room Plays, by Besant and Pollock (London: Chatto & Windus, 1896; New York: Stokes, 1896);

The City of Refuge (3 volumes, London: Chatto & Windus, 1896; 1 volume, New York & London: Stokes, 1896);

A Fountain Sealed (London: Chatto & Windus, 1897; New York: Stokes, 1897);

The Queen's Reign and Its Commemoration: A Literary and Pictorial Review of the Period; the Story of the Victorian Transformation . . . 1837–1897 (London & Chicago: Werner, 1897);

The Rise of the Empire (London: Marshall, 1897; New York: Mansfield, 1897);

The Changeling (London: Chapman & Hall, 1898; New York: Stokes, 1898);

King Alfred the Great (London: Cox, 1898);

South London (New York: Stokes, 1898; London: Chatto & Windus, 1899);

The Orange Girl (London: Chatto & Windus, 1899; New York: Dodd, Mead, 1899);

The Pen and the Book (London: Burleigh, 1899);

The Fourth Generation (New York: Stokes, 1899; London: Chatto & Windus, 1900);

The Alabaster Box (London: Burleigh, 1900; New York: Dodd, Mead, 1900);

East London (London: Chatto & Windus, 1901; New York: Century, 1901);

The Lady of Lynn (London: Chatto & Windus, 1901; New York: Dodd, Mead, 1901);

The Story of King Alfred (London: Newnes, 1901; New York: Appleton, 1901);

Autobiography of Sir Walter Besant (London: Hutchinson, 1902; New York: Dodd, Mead, 1902);

A Five Years' Tryst, and Other Stories (London: Methuen, 1902);

London in the Eighteenth Century (London: Black, 1902; New York: Macmillan, 1903);

No Other Way (London: Chatto & Windus, 1902; New York: Dodd, Mead, 1902);

The Strand District, by Besant and Mitton (London: Black, 1902);

The Survey of London, by Besant and others, 10 volumes (London: Black, 1902–1912);

As We Are and As We May Be (London: Chatto & Windus, 1903);

Essays and Historiettes (London: Chatto & Windus, 1903);

Holborn and Bloomsbury, by Besant and Mitton (London: Black, 1903);

London in the Time of the Stuarts (London: Black, 1903);

The Thames (London: Black, 1903);

London in the Time of the Tudors (London: Black, 1904);

Mediaeval London, 2 volumes (London: Black, 1906);

Early London: Prehistoric, Roman, Saxon and Norman (London: Black, 1908);

Shoreditch and the East End, by Besant and others (London: Black, 1908);

London in the Nineteenth Century (London: Black, 1909);

London City (London: Black, 1910);

London, North of the Thames (London: Black, 1911);

London South of the Thames (London: Black, 1912);

Sir Walter Besant's "Bourbon" Journal, August 1863 (London: Besant, 1933).

PLAY PRODUCTIONS: *Ready-Money*, by Besant, as Walter Maurice, and James Rice, London, Court Theatre, 12 March 1874;

Such a Good Man, by Besant and Rice, London, Olympic Theatre, 18 December 1879;

The Charm, by Besant and W. H. Pollock, London, Saint George's Hall, 22 July 1884;

The Ballad Monger, by Besant and Pollock, Haymarket, Theatre Royal, 15 September 1887.

OTHER: Charles Frederick Tyrwhitt Drake, *The Literary Remains of the Late C. F. Tyrwhitt Drake*, edited, with a memoir, by Besant (London, 1877);

Stewart's Local Examination Series, edited by Besant and Robert Jones Griffiths, 17 parts (London: Stewart, 1877-1882);

Plutarch, *The New Plutarch: Lives of Men and Women of Action*, edited by Besant and William J. Brodribb, 10 volumes (London: Ward, 1879-1888);

Claude R. Conder, *The Survey of Western Palestine: Memoirs of the Topography, Orography, Hydrography, and Archaeology*, edited, with additions, by Besant and Edward Henry Palmer, 3 volumes (London: Palestine Exploration Fund, 1881-1883);

François Rabelais, *Readings in Rabelais*, edited by Besant (Edinburgh & London: Blackwood, 1883);

The Author, edited by Besant (1890-1901);

Wilkie Collins, *Blind Love*, preface by Besant, 3 volumes (London: Chatto & Windus, 1890);

Athenian Society, *"The Athenian Oracle": A Selection*, prefatory letter by Besant (London: Scott, 1892);

Alfred Egmont Hake, *Suffering London*, introduction by Besant (London: Scientific Press, 1892);

Palestine Exploration Fund, *The City and the Land: A Course of Seven Lectures on the Work of the Society, Delivered in Hanover Square in May and June, 1892*, lecture by Besant (London: Watt, 1892);

Dorothy Wallis, *Dorothy Wallis*, introduction by Besant (London: Longmans, 1892);

Charles Reade, *The Cloister and the Hearth*, introduction by Besant, 4 volumes (London: Chatto & Windus, 1893);

Alfred E. Haynes, *Man-Hunting in the Desert: Being a Narrative of the Palmer Search-Expedition*, introduction by Besant (London: Cox, 1894);

"A Riverside Parish," in *The Poor in Great Cities: Their Problems and What Is Being Done to Solve Them*, by R. A. Woods, W. T. Elsing, J. A. Riis, and others (London: Kegan Paul, 1896);

"On University Settlements," in *University and Social Settlements*, edited by Will Reason (London: Methuen, 1898), pp. 1-10;

Alfred Bowker, *Alfred the Great*, introduction by Besant (London: Black, 1899);

John H. Round, *The Commune of London*, prefatory letter by Besant (Westminster: Constable, 1899);

Daniel Defoe, *A Journal of the Plague Year*, introduction by Besant (New York: Century, 1900);

William G. Gates, *Illustrated History of Portsmouth*, introduction by Besant (Portsmouth: Charpentier, 1900);

"The Two Sophias," in *Royal Navy and Military Bazaar . . . in Aid of H. R. H. Princess Christian's Homes for Disabled Soldiers and Sailors: . . . Being a Collection of Sketches and Drawings*, by John Charlton and others (London: Dangerfield, 1900);

Geraldine Edith Mitton, *Chelsea*, edited by Besant (London: Black, 1902);

Walter A. Locks, *East London Antiquities*, introduction by Besant (London: East London Advertiser, 1902);

Mitton, *Hampstead and Marylebone*, edited by Besant (London: Black, 1903);

Mitton, *Kensington*, edited by Besant (London: Black, 1903);

Mitton and others, *Mayfair, Belgravia and Bayswater*, edited by Besant (London: Black, 1903);

Mitton and J. C. Geikie, *Hammersmith, Fulham and Putney*, edited by Besant (London: Black, 1903);

Mitton, *Clerkenwell and St. Luke's: Comprising the Borough of Finsbury*, edited by Besant (London: Black, 1906);

Mitton, *Hackney and Stoke Newington*, edited by Besant (London: Black, 1908).

SELECTED PERIODICAL PUBLICATIONS—UNCOLLECTED: "The People's Palace," *Contemporary Review*, 51 (1887): 226-233;

"Candour in English Fiction," *New Review*, 2 (1890): 6-21;

"The Doll's House—and After," *English Illustrated Magazine*, 7 (1890): 315-325;

"The Science of Fiction," *New Review*, 4 (1891): 304-319;

"The Future of the Anglo-Saxon Race," *North American Review,* 163 (1896): 129–143;

"One of Two Millions in East London," *Century,* 59 (1899): 225–243.

Walter Besant began publishing novels in the early 1870s, and when the death of Queen Victoria in 1901 ushered in a new century, his death that same year signaled the demise of his immense popularity as a preeminent Victorian novelist. In critical discussions of fiction Besant is remembered for "The Art of Fiction," the 1884 lecture that he published the same year as an essay and to which Henry James responded with his own theoretical paper having the same title. While scholars regard Besant as a writer of popular literature and elevate James to the status of a "serious" artist, Besant's enduring contribution to social reform in the 1880s and 1890s capitalizes on his recognition as a popular novelist. His stories and magazine contributions, like his studies of the London he loved, reflect his interests in improving the education, entertainment, and standard of living of the working classes; protecting laboring women and children; and supporting charitable institutions as well as the legal rights of novelists.

Describing his espousal of these causes throughout his life, Besant writes in *Autobiography of Sir Walter Besant* (1902) that "my philanthropic work, such as it has been, has been due entirely to two or three novels. I drew a picture as faithfully as I could and I was identified with the picture.... First I drew what I saw; then my sympathy went out towards my models; the next step was to write for them, to work for them, to speak for them." This sympathy for others shaped his career and inspired his readers. As his acclaimed working-class novel *All Sorts and Conditions of Men: An Impossible Story* (1882) continues to attract critical interest and has been republished by the Oxford Popular Fiction Series in 1997, his works and his efforts in social reform movements of the late nineteenth century continue to arouse the sympathies of readers.

Besant was born in Portsea, the fifth child of a large family of six sons and four daughters. His parents were William Besant, a merchant, and Sarah Ediss Besant, the daughter of a builder and architect. After a preliminary education at home during which young Besant read English classics from his father's library, he was sent to St. Paul's grammar school, Portsea, in 1848. When it closed he attended the Stockwell grammar school in 1851 and began the first of his three terms at King's College, London, in 1854. After a distinguished tenure at Christ's College, Cambridge, culminating with his graduation in 1859, Besant worked briefly as a journalist. Finding his attempts largely unsuccessful, he accepted a position with Leamington College as a teacher of mathematics. In 1861 an offer of a senior professorship at Royal College on the island of Mauritius induced him to abandon thoughts toward taking Anglican orders. Although he enjoyed success and an intense period of essay writing and study in French literature at the college, he refused an offer to become rector of the school because of the bouts of ill health that he suffered on the island and his new aspirations for a literary career, and he returned to England in 1867.

The year following his return Besant published his first book, *Studies in Early French Poetry* (1868), and articles on French literature and social topics in the *Daily News* (London), *Macmillan's Magazine,* and *British Quarterly Review.* Encouraged by his success, Besant continued to write while he supported himself and his family through his position as secretary of the Palestine Exploration Fund, a post he accepted in 1868 and kept until the extraordinary success of *All Sorts and Conditions of Men* established his literary career. In October 1874 he married Mary Forster Barham, with whom he eventually had four children—two sons and two daughters. He also formed the Rabelais Club, a literary group that was devoted to François Rabelais and continued to meet for a decade after its inception in 1879. Earlier in the decade Besant and James Rice, the editor of *Once a Week,* wrote and published *Ready-Money Mortiboy: A Matter-of-Fact Story* (1872), a popular tale of virtue triumphant over greed and selfishness. First serialized in Rice's magazine and then published in the standard three volumes, the novel secured both Besant's entry into the profession of fiction writing and his partnership with Rice.

From 1872 until Rice's death from throat cancer in 1882 the two published more than a dozen novels as well as collected editions of long stories that brought them commercial and critical success. In recognizing the popularity of their work the editors of *All the Year Round* asked Besant and Rice to write their Christmas number in 1876, and that year the two collaborated to publish *The Golden Butterfly,* the story of a crass American millionaire. With this work Rice and Besant earned reputations as bestselling novelists; accordingly, they published one and at times two novels every year afterward until Rice's death. Each Christmas they also wrote for *All the Year Round,* and Besant continued to do so alone until 1887. In assessing the collaboration of Besant and Rice in works such as *With Harp and Crown* (1875), set in the East End of London; *By Celia's Arbour: A Tale of Portsmouth Town* (1878), which records much of Besant's childhood in its Portsmouth scenes; *The Monks of Thelema* (1878), a tale sympathetic to agricultural workers; and *The Chaplain of the Fleet* (1881), which vividly re-creates an eighteenth-century London setting, reviewers noted the coauthors' adventurous moral stories and well-written dialogue but also criticized their improbable plots and their penchant for unnecessary digression.

Following Rice's death Besant continued writing alone the East End, working-class romances upon which his reputation was made. In his autobiography he describes his turning, "even unconsciously," to the "philanthropic work and effort" of a social-reform writer: "It all began with a novel. In 1880 and in 1881 I spent a great deal of time walking about the mean monotony of the East End of London." The product of these rambles, *All Sorts and Conditions of Men,* enjoyed great success, as did Besant's subsequent fiction of this period from 1882 to 1886: *All in a Garden Fair: The Simple Story of Three Boys and a Girl* (1883), a *Künstlerroman* of a young novelist; *Dorothy Forster* (1884), the best of his historical novels; and *Children of Gibeon* (1886), a second working-class romance that presents seamstresses prominently in its agenda for social reform.

By writing about dressmakers and other figures from the East End of London, Besant contributed to the resurgence of interest in the working class, poverty, and charity during the 1880s. His image of the masses trapped within the stagnant, limited culture of East London promoted a new social reform novel that replaced the midcentury Condition-of-England novels and their image of the Two Nations—the Rich and the Poor—propagated by Benjamin Disraeli's *Sybil* (1845), with a highly symbolic image of Two Londons: the impoverished East and the abundant West. Clearly influenced by Charles Dickens, Besant's working-class novels allow the working man and woman to rise through both individual philanthropy and self help but often avoid or discredit, as do the works of other middle-class writers attempting to represent East London, issues of legislative reform. Besant's works develop images of respectable and law-abiding working classes more fully than those of the penury of such people. Angela Messenger and Harry Goslett, the wealthy purveyors of charity who are the protagonists of *All Sorts and Conditions of Men,* discover that the great evil plaguing East Enders is not unbearable poverty or a lack of industry but a terrible absence of variety and stimulation in their culture, an absence that they call "monotony."

Messenger and Goslett abandon their lives of luxury to reside in the East End during the opening chapters of the novel. A new graduate of Newnham College, Cambridge, Messenger seeks to avoid having to assume her position in fashionable society as the heiress of the Messenger Brewery fortune. Speaking to Constance Woodcote, a gifted mathematician who is her close friend and a staunch New Woman, Messenger unveils her plan to escape a destiny of upper-class idleness in Whitechapel, where her grandfather founded Messenger, Marsden and Company. Flushed with the excitement of a life of purpose, she proclaims, "I belong to the People—with a great, big P, my dear—I cannot bear to go on living by their toil and giving nothing in return." Calling herself Miss Kennedy, she takes a room in the lodging house of Mrs. Bormalack, the landlady to a colorful host of figures such as the Davenants, a couple who are from New Hampshire and aspire to a peerage; Daniel Fagg, an Australian lay scholar attempting to publish his book on the origin of all biblical languages; Mr. Maliphant, a carver; a professor-conjurer; and Josephus Coppin, a junior clerk at the Messenger Brewery.

Also in residence is Goslett, who has moved to Whitechapel after learning of his humble origins on his twenty-third birthday. Raised as Harry Le Breton by Lord Jocelyn Le Breton, Goslett learns from his guardian that he is not a gentleman's son but is instead a commoner. Intending at first merely to visit the place, Goslett changes plans when he befriends Messenger and soon falls in love with her. A carpenter by trade, he advises her as she opens a dressmakers' cooperative that operates on principles quite different from those of other enterprises during the period. Her dressmakers such as Nelly Sorenson, the daughter of an aged sea captain; Rebekah Hermitage, a Seventh-Day Independent; and other young women share in the profits of their sewing and enjoy not simply humane but commodious working conditions. Messenger's workplace provides good meals and regular breaks for the girls; it has a gymnasium, a tennis court, and a recreation room for exercise and entertainment.

Yet the cooperative is only the beginning of Messenger's projects. She offers practical help to the lodgers at Mrs. Bormalack's by hosting meals and providing work for the boarders. Taking advantage of her double identity, she uses the goodwill of Miss Messenger, who "mysteriously" works through Miss Kennedy, to improve the lot of those around her in Stepney Green through means such as ordering many gowns from her own cooperative. Most marvelous of all, Messenger and Goslett conceive of a Palace of Delight for the enjoyment and betterment of people living in the East End, a place where culturally enriching experiences can be offered, taught, and encouraged. With free facilities for the

Besant's study at Frognal End, his country house in Hampstead

enjoyment of arts, sports, dancing, and hobbies the Palace of Delight would most especially inspire "the more delightful forms of literature—so that poets and novelists should arise, and the East End, hitherto a barren desert, should blossom with flowers." The love between Messenger and Goslett also blossoms when she learns of his story from Lord Le Breton and secures him a good position in her brewery. On the triumphant day when the Palace opens she marries Goslett, with her dressmakers in attendance, and reveals her identity to her new husband. Unaffected by her dissembling, Goslett rejoices with his wife as they decide to become permanent settlers of the East End, to continue the sewing cooperative, and to continue working for the welfare of others.

Throughout the book Messenger and Goslett strive to create working-class discontent through an imported West End culture that would persuade the people to better themselves. Besant likewise evokes sympathy for the cultural desert in the East End and offers his middle-class readers an appealing remedy for the ills of the slums. Within three weeks of the novel's publication laudatory reviews appeared. The *Athenaeum,* the *British Quarterly Review,* the *Westminster Review,* and the *Spectator* heralded the novel for its strong moral purpose (one of Besant's own tenets for fiction), its pragmatic approach to the problems of the East End, and its usefulness as an educational tool for readers. The magazines differed in judging how well Besant's story merges a realistic picture of East London with its grossly fantastic features, which Besant acknowledged in his subtitle.

Whether individual reviewers applauded Besant for a realistic portrayal of the East End or found his picture to depart wholly from the experience of slum living, however, the novel was a marvelous success. It was widely circulated through Mudie's and Smith's lending libraries, and Chatto and Windus published an extraordinary 6,000 volumes of the 3s. 6d. cheap edition intended for individual purchase. In three months between January and April 1883 these were sold out. A second cheap edition of 3,000 copies was sold out by June 1883, and another of 3,000 copies was sold out by October that year. By November 1884 another 7,000 volumes were published, and these were sold out by May 1886. Chatto and Windus published a final run of 1,000 copies in September 1886, and by the end of 1900 a total of 99,500 copies of *All Sorts and Conditions of Men* were produced.

Besant's second working-class romance, another great commercial success, was also published in 1886. About this novel, *Children of Gibeon,* he writes: "This book was the most truthful of anything that I have ever written. . . . It offered the daily life and the manners—so far as they can be offered without offensive and useless realism—of the girls who do the rougher and coarser work of sewing in their own lodgings." The novel uses the same masked identities, upper-class philanthropy, misguided radicals, and rascally villains that appear in *All Sorts and Conditions of Men*.

Like Harry Goslett's guardian Lord Jocelyn Le Breton, Lady Mildred Eldridge raises the child of a washerwoman with her own daughter and gives her the education, training, and advantages of an upper-class upbringing. The two girls are so alike that it is impossible to tell them apart although it is commonly known that only one is Lady Eldridge's child and heir. Even the two girls, Valentine and Violet, do not know their true parentage. Convinced that she is the child of Mrs. Monument, a resident of Hoxton, Valentine goes there to live among her people, and, like Angela Messenger, she transforms the lives of the seamstresses there. Melenda Monument, another child of Mrs. Monument, reveals the miserable life of girls who sew as she tries to stave off starvation and destitution.

Sam Monument, a fiery radical, clamors for socialism, but Valentine, an advocate of gradual change through unions, brings harmony and beauty to the lives of the dressmakers through means such as dressing them in pretty clothes and teaching them how to keep orderly houses. Satisfied with her work in Hoxton, Valentine learns that Violet, who despises the East End, is really Mrs. Monument's child. Although Valentine is therefore not a daughter of the working classes, she marries Claude, her beloved cousin from the East End, who has taken a degree from Cambridge University through Lady Eldridge's philanthropy and plans to pursue a career in law.

In trying to judge the novel by the standards that *All Sorts and Conditions of Men* set when the Palace of Delight was constructed in 1887 as the People's Palace, Besant was unable to assess the success of *Children of Gibeon* as a work that effects social changes in the East End. Essentially he desired to ameliorate the lives of working-class people, lives that he saw plagued by monotony rather than brutality, by presenting an East End without the widespread destitution prevalent at the time. Ultimately these novels infused their middle-class reader with a rejuvenated commitment to social reform, but they did so through upper- and middle-class acculturation. Without confronting, in its actuality, the desperation of slum living, the wealthy characters of the stories discover a purpose for their lives by helping the inhabitants of Stepney Green. These novels take it for granted that vast improvements will be made in the slums, and they herald with enthusiasm and energy the work of bringing delight through the egalitarian measures of education and culture.

Much of Besant's acclaim as a prominent Victorian reform writer has been attributed to the opening of the People's Palace at the end of Mile End Road, the exact site where Angela Messenger erects her Palace of Delight. In *Victorian Novelists* (1906) Lewis Saul Benjamin comments on the deficiencies of *All Sorts and Conditions of Men* but concludes that "the picture of the joyless life of the East-End workers is, even if not convincing in its realism, at least most effective. And certainly the author can claim that the book served its purpose." That purpose was the construction of the People's Palace. Although the novel is perhaps flawed by unnecessary detail and characters lacking in complexity and humanity, Besant could actually say that his vision of a Palace of Delight was realized. In May 1887 Queen Victoria traveled to Stepney to open the palace to the two million inhabitants of the East End, and although Besant received cheers from the crowd, his novel alone did not bring about the construction of the palace.

In 1841 John Thomas Barber Beaumont left £12,000 for the cultural benefit of residents of East London. For forty years the trustees of this bequest neglected to carry out his wishes, but in 1882 they placed the fund under the direction of Sir Edmund Hay Currie, who immediately set about trying to fulfill Beaumont's aim. Besant's novel, published in December that year, fired the imagination of the public, and his fictional Palace of Delight fused with Currie's plan for a People's Palace. Even if Besant's novel did not actually inspire the idea of the People's Palace, the publicity that the popularity of his novel brought to the idea helped attract the £75,000 needed to erect it.

Between the completion of these two great successes, *All Sorts and Conditions of Men* and the People's Palace, Besant rallied behind another group whom he believed needed aid: his fellow novelists. Although his efforts for the working classes seem to have been motivated through genuine charity, his boundless energy and love of both a good fight and its ensuing publicity also strongly induced him to assail the British publishing industry. In September 1883 a dozen or so men formed the Society of Authors, with Besant as their leader. Remembering his early years of French studies, Besant ignored the failed attempts that Dickens and others in England had made in trying to organize such a society and patterned his after the Société des gens de lettres.

Serving as chairman of the society three times, Besant was prepared to enact and sustain what he instigated. In *The Society of Authors: A Record of Its Ac-*

tion from Its Foundation (1893) Besant recounts the initial aims of the society, its achievements during its first ten years of existence (most of which were the results of Besant's efforts), and his proposals for new objectives. In addition to publishing *The Author*, founded in May 1890 and edited by Besant until his death, the society enlisted nine hundred members and pursued goals such as establishing the author's ownership of his or her "literary property," amending domestic copyright laws, and promoting international copyright agreements. In shaping his vision for the future of the society Besant was determined to increase membership, to give its journal "a more literary character," to establish an Author's House as a library and place of study, to institute a writers' Pension Fund (which Besant believed was "absolutely necessary for the completion of the Independence of Literature"), and to secure recognition for the craft of fiction writing by establishing a Royal Academy.

As he was launching the Society of Authors, Besant delivered "The Art of Fiction," a lecture in which he described his theories—albeit largely incoherent ones—on narrative form. In this piece Besant argues that the novel is an art form equal to the work of painters, poets, and musicians; he not only promulgates the role and craft of the novelist but also appropriates legitimacy for his fellow novelists and members of the Society of Authors. In his view the business of fiction is to record the stories of all humanity and to possess a moral aim that accurately represents some ill of the human condition and genuinely propose some amelioration of that ill. Although the novel is a form of high art, it seeks to increase the capacities for sympathy and social consciousness in both writer and reader. Despite espousing such an elevated social import of the novel, Besant considered himself merely to be one of the "novelists of the day," and Robert A. Colby writes that in the February–July 1898 issue of *The Idler* Besant requested, "Let it be written on my tomb" that "His generation read his stories."

The final period of his career from 1887 to 1901 illustrates this hope to be remembered as an entertaining writer whose fiction possessed immense popular appeal even if it lacks the genius of the works of a Thomas Hardy, Rudyard Kipling, or George Meredith. Literary historians typify Besant's work during these years as almost uniformly mediocre, and contemporary reviews of his novels—reviews that typically had filled one to two full columns—steadily shrank to the length of a one-paragraph notice. He coupled an indefatigable energy for his various causes with publishing a novel every year, and this intense output necessarily taxed Besant: the quality of his work suffered, with dubious plots and less originality than he had shown in his earlier work.

However, he continued to pursue his interests in various social reforms through the novels he wrote during this period. *The Rebel Queen* (1893) and *The Alabaster Box* (1900), for example, are set in the East End and address issues such as the "settlements," whereby wealthy men and women settled among laborers to work for their benefit, and other problems of the slums. Indeed, the East End remained Besant's consuming interest, and he established a settlement and gymnasium for boys in Shoreditch. During this time he also published a body of nonfiction that examines in detail life in East London. One work in particular, *Fifty Years Ago (A Picture of Society in This Country as It Was When the Queen Ascended the Throne)*, was published in 1888 as an historical retrospective of the year Queen Victoria began her reign. In substantial chapters Besant describes the standard of living for the working classes of England and makes several assertions about 1837 that reveal his attitudes toward the problems of social and cultural poverty in the 1880s.

Besant urges his reader to remember that in the past England was "wholly in the hands of the wealthier sort." He laments that the "workers, who contribute the whole that makes the prosperity of the country, were then excluded from any share in managing it." The extension of suffrage, he feels, rightfully acknowledges that the people should govern themselves. He was thus advocating the growing democratization of England to a middle-class readership that experienced anxiety and feelings of paranoia about the enfranchising of another segment of the population through the reforms that followed those of the 1867 Reform Bill. He also asserts that Parliament alone, through its factory acts and child-labor laws, is able to curtail the egregious abuse of working-class women and children.

Besant sketches a graphic picture of the deplorable working conditions for women and children during the early decades of industrialization—realities that he had minimized in the East London romances. He directs "In Factory and Mine," written in a heavily didactic tone, to "fellow-sinners and partakers in the crimes of slavery, torture, and robbery of light, life, youth, and joy," and he asserts that by remembering the cries of children in the mines, the public will champion the cries of seamstresses in the 1880s. Besant observes that laboring men had improved their positions through their "combination" into unions, but he expresses his fears for women and children because, as disfranchised members of society, they cannot combine—and he enjoins his reader to work for their protection.

Charity, the money needed to secure this protection, was of paramount importance to Besant. His lengthy introduction to *Suffering London* (1892), Alfred Egmont Hake's study of the voluntary hospitals of London conveys his belief that charitable support for such causes should be voluntary but was nonetheless one's proper civic duty. Apart from any engines of governmental relief Besant insisted that the individual act with personal responsibility for others. In this introduction he explains that when people of their own volition give to the beggar, they show "that the starving man may have a claim upon us." This giving from one's "own free will—a thing that is not a tax" recognizes a personal obligation for "an offering, a tribute, a recognition of Lazarus as our brother."

In short Besant insists on charitable action but leaves the motive of the giver, whether selfish or selfless, to the giver. This sentiment that charity was essential—a characteristic feature of the prosperous citizen providing for the destitute—appears in Besant's works as early as *Ready-Money Mortiboy* and *The Golden Butterfly* and continues through the East End romances. Even in his ambitious survey of London, begun in 1894 and intended to be exhaustive, Besant included "Charitable Work" as one section of *London in the Nineteenth Century* (1909). In "Slums," a chapter within that section, Besant catalogues the differences between the London slums of 1798 and 1898, and he notes the free education for children and marked improvement in sanitation that have occurred by the latter date. "Light and hope, in a word, have been brought into the slum," he observes; "Yet it must be owned there is still a great deal to be desired, and a great deal to be done."

For Besant in the 1890s much was to be done to protect women and children. "One of Two Millions in East London," published in December 1899 in *The Century Magazine,* has been called his best piece of nonfiction writing, and in it Besant compares East London to a hive, "a city of working bees." Denouncing the few irredeemable drones (whom he thinks should be allowed to sink into the mire that engulfs them), Besant also describes a productive mass of workers whose toil he likens to the murmur of a hymn. In Carlylean fashion he espouses a doctrine of compulsory, sanctifying work for the individual and concludes that "it is the necessity of work that makes him human" and allows him to "subdue the animal within him." Yet after Besant describes East London labor through the collective image of the hive, he invites the reader to consider as individuals those people whom he describes, and he asserts that their socioeconomic class membership is insignificant in contrast to their character and personalities as individuals. To Besant nobility and refinement of character are consequences of environment rather than of genetics.

In making such an assumption he devotes the remainder of the essay to the birth and maturation of Liz, a fictional woman from Ratcliffe, where the lower echelons of the working classes are housed. Besant explains that Liz's childhood, humble enough, is not cause for pity, for youngsters such as she "are happy in their ignorance," unaware of what they lack. As in his great survey of London, Besant describes East London of the late nineteenth century as spare but greatly improved over its situation in 1837. Liz goes to boarding school until the age of fourteen and then joins her elder sisters at work in a jam factory. Eventually she marries, has children, and thus perpetuates what Besant views as the life of a "commonplace, average girl of the lower working-class."

Although it seems inconsistent for Besant to argue for working-class individuality and then draw a lengthy picture of the "typical" working-class girl, what twentieth-century readers miss is the incredible ignorance of each other that characterized the different classes at this time. The essay describes Liz's life in detail: the restlessness of her youth, the monotony of factory work, her decisions between faggots and fried fish for dinners, her memberships in clubs for saving money and acquiring luxuries, a seafaring cousin's Christmas visit, her courtship, and so forth. When Besant recounts such details of her life in eighteen pages of the Christmas issue of *The Century Magazine,* he humanizes her and makes her an individual. He does not maneuver to arouse pity for Liz, but he does not allow his readers to disregard the meanness of her life nor the strength with which she meets it.

Besant emphatically demanded the protection of workingwomen and improvements in their treatment by employers, but his weekly contributions to *The Queen,* a "Ladies Newspaper and Court Chronicle," revealed the limits of his radicalism. He believed that women should enjoy the democratization of England but strictly within the bounds of respectable female experience. *The Queen* supported female education and suffrage, but its agenda extended no further than that of a social magazine on fashions, etiquette, and life at Court. Thus, Besant lobbied against using phosphorus in manufacturing matches because it caused a "phossy jaw" ailment among women workers and published *Katharine Regina* (1887) to argue for decent and affordable housing for gentlewomen who had to work—yet he remained stridently opposed to the late-nineteenth-century New

Woman, whom he called the "shrieking sisterhood," a label he borrowed from Eliza Lynn Lytton, a regular contributor to *The Queen*. Although he clearly preferred that women preserve their limited traditional roles, as Earl A. Knies has documented, Besant argued passionately for the just treatment of women who chose to work or were forced into joining the labor force. He helped found the Women's Bureau of Work, an association to help women locate employment. "It is satisfactory to find," he writes in his memoir, "that there is something practical and definite actually established for their benefit."

A zealot for the causes he advocated in his novels, articles, and addresses, Besant wrote his autobiography during the last year of his life, looking back on his career and life with more sentiment and nostalgia than judgment. Published posthumously with a prefatory note by S. Squire Sprigge, the autobiography downplays Besant's achievements: it neglects to mention, for example, his knighthood–bestowed on him in 1895 for his East End writings and his efforts on behalf of social reform and the People's Palace. Sprigge comments on Besant's humility in the preface: "The modesty in his autobiography is a fault that he would never have corrected, and throughout his record of his life he studiously underrates himself, hardly at any time assuming credit for aught but industry." In the chapter titled "Philanthropic Work" Besant recounts the different avenues into which his lifelong commitment to being his brother's keeper led him. As he records the social ills that he attempted to redress, he lapses into a lengthy account of the boys' and girls' clubs that a Mrs. Heckford and others ran in East London and places himself in the background of his own story. When he discusses the Home Arts Association that he and Charles G. Leland, an American friend, began in 1879, Besant gives Leland and Miss Annie Dymes, the secretary of the association, full credit for the establishment of more than five hundred schools instructing working-class people in the minor arts such as metallurgy, carpentry, and embroidery.

He acknowledges his support, through his pen and his voice, for the Ragged School Union, the London voluntary hospitals, and the Salvation Army. Yet he discusses the work of the Salvation Army in detail–pressing for public support, emphasizing and praising its work and sacrifice. Besant lauds the organization for being popular–for being, as he writes, "of the people, for the people, by the people"–and he summarizes his purpose in writing and speaking for the impoverished of England as his effort to call those younger than himself to their duty toward their fellow citizens by inspiring them to "self-sacrifice," "devotion," and "voluntary obscurity."

While Walter Besant did not lead a life of obscurity, he consistently sought to effect social change. As a novelist he reached the apex of his acclaim during his lifetime, and both his writing and his vision have been subsequently evaluated for their flaws. But Besant achieved an enduring excellence in his commitment to work, diligently and continuously, for the good of others.

References:

Fred W. Boege, "Sir Walter Besant: Novelist (Part One)," *Nineteenth-Century Fiction,* 10 (1956): 249–280;

Boege, "Sir Walter Besant: Novelist (Part Two)," *Nineteenth-Century Fiction,* 11 (1956): 32–60;

Robert A. Colby, "Harnessing Pegasus: Walter Besant, *The Author,* and the Profession of Authorship," *Victorian Periodicals Review,* 23 (1990): 111–120;

Michael P. Dean, "Henry James, Walter Besant, and 'The Art of Fiction,'" *Publication of the Arkansas Philological Association,* 10 (1984): 13–23;

Simon Eliot, "'His Generation Read His Stories': Walter Besant, Chatto and Windus and *All Sorts and Conditions of Men,*" *Publishing History,* 21 (1987): 25–67;

Eliot, "Unequal Partnerships: Besant, Rice and Chatto, 1876–82," *Publishing History,* 26 (1989): 73–109;

John Goode, "The Art of Fiction: Walter Besant and Henry James," in *Tradition and Tolerance in Nineteenth-Century Fiction,* edited by David Howard, John Lucas, and John Goode (London: Routledge & Kegan Paul, 1966), pp. 243–281;

P. J. Keating, *The Working Classes in Victorian Fiction* (New York: Barnes & Noble, 1971);

Earl A. Knies, "Sir Walter Besant and the 'Shrieking Sisterhood,'" in *Victorian Literature and Culture,* edited by John Maynard and Adrienne Auslander (New York: AMS Press, 1994), XXI: 211–232;

Lewis Melville [Lewis Saul Benjamin], "Sir Walter Besant," in his *Victorian Novelists* (London: Constable, 1906), pp. 291–307;

Wim Neetens, "Problems of a 'Democratic Text': Walter Besant's Impossible Story," *Novel: A Forum on Fiction,* 23 (1990): 247–264;

Mark Spilka, "Henry James and Walter Besant: 'The Art of Fiction' Controversy," *Novel: A Forum on Fiction,* 6 (1973): 101–119.

William Booth
(10 April 1829 – 20 August 1912)

Donald S. Armentrout
University of the South

BOOKS: *How to Reach the Masses with the Gospel: A Sketch of the Origin, History, and Present Position of the Christian Mission* (London: Morgan, Chase & Scott, 1870);

Salvation Soldiery: A Series of Addresses on the Requirements of Jesus Christ's Service (London: Partridge, 1882);

The Salvation War, 1882 (1883): Under the Generalship of W. Booth, 2 volumes (London: Salvation Army Book Stores, 1883, 1884);

Training of Children; or, How to Make the Children into Saints and Soldiers of Jesus Christ (London: Salvation Army, 1884);

The General's Letters, 1885 (London: Salvation Army, 1886);

The Future of Missions and the Mission of the Future (London: International Headquarters, 1889);

Holy Living; or, What the Salvation Army Teaches about Sanctification (London: Salvation Army, 1890);

In Darkest England and the Way Out (London: International Headquarters, 1890; Chicago: Sergel, 1890);

What Is General Booth's Scheme? A Short Summary for Busy Men (London: Burgess, 1890);

Fishing for Men (London: International Headquarters, 1894);

To My Field Officers throughout the World (London: International Headquarters, 1900);

Purity of Heart: Letters by General Booth to Salvationists and Others (London & New York: Salvation Army Book-Room, 1902);

Letters to Salvationists on Religion for Every Day (London, New York & Melbourne: Salvation Army Book Department, 1902);

Letters to Salvationists on Love, Marriage, and Home (London: Salvation Army, 1902);

The Warrior's Daily Portion (London: Salvation Army Book Department, 1902);

The Vagrant and the Unemployable: A Proposal for the Extension of the Land and Industrial Colony System (London: International Headquarters, 1904);

The Recurring Problem of the Unemployed, One Permanent

William Booth in 1890

Remedy: Emigration-Colonisation (London: International Headquarters, 1906);

Visions: The General's Dream and Its Lessons (London: Salvation Army Book Department, 1906);

The Seven Spirits; or, What I Teach My Officers (London: Salvation Army Book Department, 1907);

A Letter from the General to the Officers of the Salvation Army throughout the World on the Occasion of His Eightieth Birthday (London: International Headquarters, 1909);

The Vagrant and the Unemployable: A Proposal Whereby Vagrants May Be Detained under Suitable Conditions and Compelled to Work (London: Salvation Army, 1909);

The Founder's Messages to Soldiers during the Years 1907–1908 (London: Salvation Army Book Department, 1921).

OTHER: *The Salvation Soldier's Song Book,* compiled by Booth (London: Partridge, 1880; Philadelphia: Railton, 1880);

R., *Twenty-One Years: Salvation Army,* introduction by Booth (London: Salvation Army Book Depot, 1887);

John Law, *In Darkest London,* introduction by Booth (London: Reeves, 1891);

William Branwell Booth, *Social Reparation, or Personal Impressions of Work for Darkest England,* introduction by Gen. William Booth (London: International Headquarters, 1899);

Annie S. Smith, *The Outsiders: Being a Sketch of the Social Work of the Salvation Army,* introduction by Booth (London: Salvation Army Printing Works, 1905–1906);

George R. Sims, F. A. McKenzie, and others, *Sketches of the Salvation Army Social Work,* introduction by Booth (London: Salvation Army Printing Works, 1906);

Margaret S. E. Reed, *Henry Reed,* preface by Booth (London: Morgan & Scott, 1907);

Hulda Friederichs, *The Romance of the Salvation Army,* preface by Booth (London & New York: Cassell, 1907).

SELECTED PERIODICAL PUBLICATIONS–UNCOLLECTED: "What Is the Salvation Army?," *Contemporary Review,* 42 (1882): 175–182;

"Studies in Character (No. V.): Mrs. Booth," *New Review,* 3 (1890): 385–392;

"Social Problems in the Antipodes," *Contemporary Review,* 61 (1892): 422–423;

"Church Work in England–The Social Question," *Catholic World,* 61 (1895): 571;

"What Has Come Out of the Darkest England Scheme," *Sunday Strand,* 1 (1900): 82–93.

William Booth was a major reformer and reform writer of the last half of the nineteenth and early part of the twentieth centuries. From 1865–when he and his wife, Catherine, put up a tent at Whitechapel and began a mission to the "Heathen of our own Country"–until his death Booth urged social reform in his writings by encouraging the poor to battle against sin and vice. Using military language and organization, Booth wrote that people should be saints and soldiers for Jesus Christ. His writings stress holy living and sanctification, which he saw as the primary means of reforming England.

An ardent evangelist who devoted his life to helping the poor, Booth was the founder and first general of the Salvation Army. He combined a passion for social justice and righteousness with a genius for organization and leadership. During his lifetime the Salvation Army became one of the major social-action bodies of Christendom and spread from England to many other parts of the world.

Born at Sneinton, a suburb of Nottingham, on 10 April 1829, Booth was the son of Samuel and Mary Moss Booth. His father was first a nail manufacturer and then a speculative and unsuccessful builder, and his mother was of Jewish descent. William attended several different schools, and in 1842 at the age of thirteen he began to work as a pawnbroker's apprentice in a poor part of Nottingham. This early contact with urban human misery that pawnbroking gave him roused Booth to a lifelong passion against the poverty and degradation in which many nineteenth-century English people lived. He resolved to devote his life to waging war against sin and suffering.

Although a nominal Anglican, Booth showed little interest in religion before the death of his father in September 1842. Gradually he drifted away from the Church of England and into Wesleyan Methodist circles. He was impressed by the Chartists, those reformers who adopted the "People's Charter" of the Working Men's Association and called for electoral reform. He was outraged by seeing children beg for bread in the streets and by what he heard at the Chartist meetings he attended. He was impressed particularly by the oratory of Feargus O'Connor, the traveling dominant leader of the Chartist movement, but Booth, turning instead to religious solutions for humankind's problems, left Chartism before its influence as a reform organization died out.

In 1844 Booth experienced a religious conversion and publicly confessed his sins. He became a local preacher in the Wesleyan Methodist Church, the main channel of the descent of Methodism from John Wesley's day. In 1846 James Caughey, an American Methodist revivalist from Vermont and later a Holiness revivalist, preached throughout Nottingham, and Booth, inspired by Caughey's oratory, decided to become a revivalist preacher and began to preach in the open. From the beginning he stressed that all the suffering, sorrow, and poverty in the world came from sin. He preached that by the power of Christ any person can be converted and that after this experience temptation loses its power and the convert is impelled toward holiness. For the rest of Booth's life the center of his preaching was this dogma of the new birth. In those early years some of the pattern of his life became apparent when he resigned his position as a local preacher to give himself to open-air preaching and evangelistic work.

In autumn 1849 Booth moved to London to continue his evangelism. At Walworth he worked at a pawnbroker's shop, a job that he hated but was obliged to do in order to be able to send money home. His passion for open-air preaching brought him into conflict with the Wesleyan Methodist Church, and in 1851 he became associated with the Wesleyan Reformers, a movement of reformers uneasy about the lack of democracy in English Methodist polity. The Wesleyan Methodists hired Booth as a preacher in 1852, but, dissatisfied with the chaotic state of the new group, he joined the Methodist New Connexion as a probationer minister in 1854. This organization had formed in 1797 because the Wesleyan Methodists were unwilling to grant to the laity the rights to choose their own class leaders, to decide who should become and who should cease to be members of the society, and to send their own elected representatives to the annual conference to decide all business in conjunction with the itinerant preachers. Booth offered himself as a candidate for ministry in the New Connexion, and in 1854 he was appointed to the London circuit of the New Connexion and was instructed to reside near the new chapel near Stockwell.

In this chapel on 16 June 1855 Booth married Catherine Mumford, later known as the "Mother of the Salvation Army." She had been born at Ashbourne, Derbyshire, on 17 January 1829, and in 1844 her family had moved to London, where she joined the Wesleyan Methodist Church in Brixton. There she met Booth, and their joint ministry began.

In 1855 Booth was stationed in the Manchester north circuit; in 1857, in the Halifax south circuit. He did not like the circuit ministry; he preferred special evangelistic work, and his feelings caused conflict between Booth and church officials. After briefly attending a London seminary he was ordained a minister in the Methodist New Connexion in 1858, and from then to 1861 he continued his ministry as an evangelist at Gateshead, Durham. When Catherine Booth insisted that he not be restricted to performing circuit work, the conflict between Booth and church officials reached a crisis at the New Connexion Conference in 1861.

Meanwhile, Catherine Booth had been publicly assisting in her husband's pastoral work, and in

Booth's wife, Catherine Mumford Booth, the "Mother of the Salvation Army"

1859 she wrote *Female Ministry,* a booklet in which she argued for the right of women to preach the Gospel in public. She preached at Gateshead, and thus began the ministry of women that is so prominent in the work of the Salvation Army. Her outspokenness on the equality of the sexes and her insistence that her husband not be limited to doing circuit work became circumstances that contributed to his decisions to resign from the Methodists and to create the Salvation Army.

In 1861 Booth was appointed to the Newcastle-upon-Tyne circuit, and when the conference confirmed this assignment, Catherine Booth rose from her seat in the gallery and cried out "Never." The Booths left the Methodist New Connexion and spent the next several years as itinerant evangelists.

At the insistence of Catherine Booth they moved to London in 1865, and she and William began holding tent meetings in the East End. Their goal was to reach the unchurched masses with the Gospel and to ameliorate the living conditions of the destitute people of the eastern portion of London. To these ends they established in the Whitechapel district the East London Revival Society, which became the East London Christian Mission, later the Christian Mission, and in 1878 the Salvation Army.

Booth and his daughter, Evangeline, who became leader of the Salvation Army in the United States in 1904

By 1872 the Christian Mission was running five Food-for-the-Million shops that sold inexpensive meals.

In 1870 Booth published *How to Reach the Masses with the Gospel: A Sketch of the Origin, History, and Present Position of the Christian Mission.* In tracing why and how the mission had been established, he argued that evangelism was a matter of taking the Gospel where people lived, not of waiting for people to come to the church. He also urged that evangelism must be concerned with alleviating all forms of suffering. The Christian Mission was intended to remove poverty, hunger, and unemployment, which he saw as the social results of sin.

In 1878 Booth, then as leader of the Salvation Army organization, wrote the "Orders and Regulations of the Salvation Army," modeled on those of the British army. He saw this new organization as a quasi-military army, and he published its declaration of faith as Articles of War. The basic unit of the Salvation Army was the corps, which corresponded to the congregation or parish of other denominations, and several of these corps might exist in a community. Each corps had a commanding officer ranging in rank from lieutenant to brigadier. Members were called soldiers, and converts who desired to become soldiers had to sign the Articles of War. Evangelists were called officers, and Booth, who believed that it was just as valid to build an army of crusaders to save souls as it had been to send armies to recover the Holy Sepulchre in Jerusalem, was designated as general.

The "Foundation Deed" of the Salvation Army in 1878 consisted of eleven cardinal affirmations that constitute its principal doctrines. These eleven articles show a generally Arminian strain in their insistence on an unlimited atonement and the possibility of falling from grace as well as a Methodist influence in their emphasis on perfection and entire santification. These affirmations define the theology of Booth's Salvation Army.

His organization operated differently from most other nineteenth-century churches. He used outdoor meetings and processions to attract the attention of the urban poor. He and his soldiers visited prisons and the poor in their homes, and they held religious services in theaters, factories, and other unusual buildings. Rather than using traditional church music, they sang their hymns to popular song tunes and employed the language of everyday life in their discourse. Booth insisted that every convert must be a daily witness for Christ, both in private and in public, and in 1880 he and his wife introduced the use of uniforms. Both of them were opposed to the fashions of the day and urged simplicity of dress. The uniforms were plain and distinctive, to show that their wearers were separated from the world.

The work of the Salvation Army spread rapidly over England, Scotland, and Wales, and in 1880 it was officially established in the United States by a pioneer group under the direction of George Scott Railton, the first national commander overseas. Once committed to a policy of expansion, Booth spent much of his time traveling to, organizing, and addressing meetings. The Salvation Army invaded Australia and France in 1881; Switzerland, Sweden, India, and Canada in 1882; New Zealand and South Africa in 1883; and Germany in 1886.

Yet Booth was greatly concerned about the children of urban England. In 1884 he published *Training of Children; or, How to Make the Children into Saints and Soldiers of Jesus Christ*. Written in catechismal style with questions and answers, this work begins by outlining the duties of parents to govern, influence, and inspire children so that they love, serve, and enjoy God and grow up to be good, useful men and women. Using military ideas and procedures, Booth believed profoundly in training, and he taught that if children are rightly trained, they will become useful Christians.

The first condition of this training to make children true servants and good soldiers of Christ is that of being a godly parent. Being such a parent encourages young people to serve God early in life and then to marry only with other Salvationists. Parents, who are stewards before God, are responsible for this training because children have been entrusted to them by God. Another condition of this training is that children are to be dedicated, or set apart, to be servants and soldiers of Christ, and this dedication is to be enacted at a ceremony when the child is given up to God. This ceremony draws attention to the sacred claims that God has upon all children, impresses on the hearts of parents and others the important duties that they owe to their families, and encourages unsaved parents to dedicate themselves to serving as soldiers of Christ. The date of the dedication is to be celebrated each year.

Parental example and godly family government—characterized by firmness, righteousness, justice, and spirits of mercy and love—are also essential in training children. The end of such training is to shape the will of the children by enabling them to become accustomed to doing what they ought to do, by creating in them the habit of doing it. Booth found habit to be important: children were to be trained in habits favorable to their happiness, usefulness, and salvation. The greatest habit to be developed in children is that of obedience, that orientation through which they have learned to do exactly what they are told without hesitating and without considering any punishment or reward. Booth insisted, for example, that children should be taught to dress in such a way that they show contempt for the pride and pageantry of worldly fashion. They should also be instructed in the evil consequences of using intoxicating liquors, which they should never touch or taste, and they should not smoke because it harms the brain and consequently the entire nervous system.

In 1886 Booth's 1885 letters to *The War Cry*, the official journal of the Salvation Army, were collected in *The General's Letters, 1885*. Written from what Booth saw as the field of battle to soldiers and friends, the letters generally contain spiritual advice and religious instruction and are intended to encourage readers in their work and urge them to persevere in their mission.

Booth was deeply committed to the missionary task of the church. *The Future of Missions and the Mission of the Future* (1889) spelled out details of what he saw as the ideal missionary society that would realize the universal sway of the Messiah. This society would liberally finance missions and adapt to the indigenous habits, conditions, and circumstances of the different races it seeks to conquer for Christ. All of its missionary activity would be motivated by Christian love.

Booth and the Salvation Army believed in perfectionism, and in *Holy Living; or, What the Salvation Army Teaches about Sanctification* (1890) he taught that entire sanctification, or perfectionism, means that one may be delivered from all sin and enabled to do

Booth's last residence, Rookstone, Hadley Wood

the will of God continually. Sanctification, the separation of the soul from sin and the devotion of the whole being to the will and service of God, denotes not a state of complete sinlessness but one of perfect love. One of the fruits of sanctification is in the giving up of tobacco, worldly articles of dress or ornament, and all worldly companionships and associations.

Booth's major literary work was *In Darkest England and the Way Out* (1890), the title of which ironically recalls American adventurer Henry Morton Stanley's narrative, *In Darkest Africa* (1890). Booth argued that, like Stanley's Africa, London also had colonies of heathens and savages untouched by Christianity and civilization. England had temples and churches to save people from the perdition to come, but, although the nation possessed enough wealth to minister to social regeneration, it never offered a helping hand to save those same persons from the inferno of their present lives.

Booth begins his book by describing the social and moral darkness. Three million people in England are destitute. Many of these are homeless, the nomads of civilization; many are without work and food, on the verge of the abyss. What is needed is a lifeboat brigade, a social organization, and an effort to save the body in order to save the soul. Some English citizens are victims of ignorance; some are criminals; and some are children cursed from the cradle. The system of charity in England is chaotic and ineffectual.

After describing the problems Booth discusses his vision of deliverance from them, the way out of darkest England. Admitting that the problems require a stupendous undertaking, he proposes ten programs to remedy pauperism and vice. The first three programs involve establishing self-helping and self-sustaining communities, each of which is a co-operative society that he calls a colony.

The first community is the city colony that is to help the ragged, hungry, and penniless who come for shelter, food, and work. The city colony is to have inexpensive food depots, a shelter depot, and a factory, so that charity for those in need is replaced by work. The second community, the farm colony, provides work for the rural poor and raises food for the urban poor. The third, the overseas colony, trains people who want to come to England.

Another of Booth's programs is what he calls the household salvage brigade. London is divided into districts for the collection of waste food, paper, rags, and other discarded items. Households are requested to place these items in a receptacle, from which the poor can collect and use them. Food that the salvage brigade collects but which is unfit for human consumption is to be sent to the farm colony for the animals.

Booth's fifth proposal addresses the regeneration of criminals. While prisons are to be reforming institutions, in darkest England they usually make the incarcerated worse. In Booth's scheme the prison brigade provides homes for first offenders, works with prisoners during their imprisonment, meets criminals at the gate when they are released, and finds them suitable employment. A similar program, which is to be much cheaper than imprisonment, as-

Booth's funeral procession in London (top) and the stone commemorating his founding of the Salvation Army at Mile End Road in London

sists drunkards with their problems, and Booth is also concerned about prostitutes and poor girls in danger of becoming prostitutes. For prostitutes he proposes to establish rescue homes, where these women can be supported and initiated into a system of reformation. Homes for poor or unfortunate girls who are yet unfallen are to provide legitimate work and a modest income.

As Booth sees British society in 1890, he finds it organized to give to the rich and to take from the poor. He therefore proposes to organize a poor-man's bank to loan money to the poor at low interest rates. Since the poor also need legal counsel, a program to provide lawyers for the poor is to be established. A final proposal is to establish a recreation center for the poor. Whitechapel-by-the-Sea is to become a refuge for the London poor, who otherwise never escape the sunless alleys and grimy streets. It is to have a park, playground, music, and boats for the recreation of the poor. In these proposals Booth aimed to effect the spiritual regeneration of the poor through measures designed to bring about their material rehabilitation.

Many of Booth's books were collections of letters and articles he wrote for *The War Cry* and *The Social Gazette,* the latter of which was another of the weekly publications of the Salvation Army in England. In 1902 Booth published two of these collections: *Letters to Salvationists on Religion for Every Day* and *Letters to Salvationists on Love, Marriage, and Home.* The collection on everyday life gave advice especially about work and personal habits. In this collection Booth teaches that work is essential for full humanity, that human beings want and need to be employed. The Bible enjoins people to work, and work is one of the ways in which people express love for one another. These letters also give advice about clothes, food, sleep, personal cleanliness, and wholesome conversation. They urge Bible study and observance of the Sunday Sabbath, a time that for the Salvationist is to be a day of rest as well as a day for the worship and service of God.

The volume on love, marriage, and the home gives practical advice about choosing a proper partner, conducting courtship, making engagements, and conducting weddings. It also discusses the advantages and disadvantages of marriage, the husband's duties and responsibilities, the wife's duties and responsibilities, and the training of children.

Purity of Heart: Letters by General Booth to Salvationists and Others, also published in 1902, is a collection of ten letters urging people to purify their souls by renouncing practices such as drunkenness, gluttony, cheating, and disobedience and qualities such as dishonesty, falsehood, pride, malice, bad tempers, selfishness, and unbelief. For members of Booth's Salvation Army purity of heart was both a gift from God and a task to be accomplished by each soldier.

One of Booth's last major books is *The Seven Spirits; or, What I Teach My Officers* (1907), which consists of addresses he gave to Salvation Army officers at the International Congress held in London in June 1904. These addresses represent the culmination of his religious teaching in their presentation of what Booth sees as the seven important spirits: life, purity, devotion, holy warfare, truth, faith, and burning love. He believes that with these spirits or gifts the Salvation Army could conquer the world.

During his entire ministry Booth was concerned about vagrants, homeless persons who roamed the country and subsisted chiefly on what they could beg or steal. It was estimated that England had about sixty thousand vagrants by the end of the nineteenth century, and in 1909 he published *The Vagrant and the Unemployable: A Proposal Whereby Vagrants May Be Detained under Suitable Conditions and Compelled to Work.* In this book Booth proposes that vagrants, who are like nomads, be rounded up and placed in labor colonies, where they could work and have places to live. The establishment of these labor colonies requires that authorities regard vagrancy and begging not as crimes but as social dangers that need treatment.

On the occasion of his eightieth birthday Booth wrote *A Letter from the General to the Officers of the Salvation Army throughout the World* (1909). This was his last publication, basically an apologia for his life's work. He urged his officers to stand up more boldly and firmly than ever in the expulsion of all wrongdoing from the earth and in effecting the universal acceptance of Christ. After William Booth's death the Salvation Army in 1921 published *The Founder's Messages to Soldiers during the Years 1907–1908,* a collection of letters in which Booth urges his soldiers to carry their religious faith into their daily relationships and to save their neighbors.

Catherine Booth, who assisted him throughout the entire history of the Salvation Army and was especially active in behalf of women and children, had died of cancer at Clacton-on-Sea, Essex, on 4 October 1890. When Booth himself died on 20 August 1912 near London, he was succeeded by his son, William Bramwell Booth. General Booth died a national hero, who during his lifetime saw his small band of followers swell in size to an army of thousands. At the time of his death the Salvation Army had already become an international organization, and Booth, directing the movements of the Salvation Army at home and abroad from his headquarters in London, had been its controlling power.

Booth had a simple nineteenth-century evangelical theology coupled with a passionate social concern. The unique features of the Salvation Army included its military organization and its teaching on the sacraments. The organization broke most radically with its theological antecedents in its doctrine of the sacraments, the discussion of which is relegated to an appendix in *The Salvation Army Handbook of Doctrine* (1927). It teaches that baptism and the Lord's Supper are neither necessary to salvation nor essential to spiritual progress and that the Salvation Army does not observe them.

Booth was a social reformer as well as a religious leader. He was concerned about problems such as education, housing, employment, health, alcoholism, legal aid for the poor, rehabilitation for convicts, and poverty. He hated squalor and suffering and had profound pity for the poor and outcast. His life and ministry present one of the more significant social and religious revivals of modern times, and his writings were a major impetus to reform in England and the United States. While they are not profound, they encouraged people to live better lives, to strive to overcome their existing conditions, and to rise above limitations born of their circumstances. Booth's writings encouraged an attack on social evils and presented a program of intense religious evangelism. For Booth and members of his Salvation Army "the way out of darkest England" was through a massive program of social action and reform.

Biographies:

Frederick St. George de Lautour Booth Tucker, *William Booth, the General of the Salvation Army* (New York: Salvation Army, 1898);

Thomas F. G. Coates, *The Prophet of the Poor: The Life-Story of General Booth* (London: Hodder & Stoughton, 1905);

George S. Railton, *General Booth* (London: Hodder & Stoughton, 1912);

Edward Harold Begbie, *The Life of General William Booth: The Founder of the Salvation Army*, 2 volumes (New York: Macmillan, 1920);

William H. Nelson, *Blood & Fire: General William Booth* (New York: Century, 1929);

Saint John G. Ervine, *God's Soldier: General William Booth*, 2 volumes (London: Heinemann, 1934);

Minnie L. R. Carpenter, *William Booth, Founder of the Salvation Army* (London: Epworth, 1944);

Harold C. Steele, *I Was a Stranger: The Faith of William Booth* (New York: Exposition, 1954);

Richard H. Collier, *The General Next to God: The Story of William Booth and the Salvation Army* (New York: Dutton, 1965);

Cyril J. Barnes, *William Booth and His Army of Peace* (Amersham, U.K.: Hilton Educational, 1975).

References:

Cyril J. Barnes, *Army without Guns* (London: Salvationist Publishing and Supplies, 1969);

Barnes, *God's Army* (Berkhamsted: Lion, 1978; Elgin, Ill.: Cook, 1978);

Edward Bishop, *Blood and Fire! The Story of General William Booth and the Salvation Army* (London: Longmans, 1964);

William Bramwell Booth, *Echoes and Memories* (London: Hodder & Stoughton, 1925);

Owen Chadwick, *The Victorian Church,* part 2 (New York: Oxford University Press, 1970; London: Black, 1970);

Frederick Coutts, *No Discharge in This War: A One-Volume History of the Salvation Army* (London: Hodder & Stoughton, 1975);

Lawrence Fellows, *A Gentle War: The Story of the Salvation Army* (New York: Macmillan, 1979);

Clifford W. Kew, *The Salvation Army* (Elmsford, N.Y.: Pergamon, 1977);

Edward H. Neal, *The Hallelujah Army* (Philadelphia: Chilton, 1961);

George S. Railton, *Heathen England: Being a Description of the Utterly Godless Condition of the Vast Majority of the English Nation, and of the Establishment, Growth, System, and Success of an Army for Its Salvation, Consisting of Working People under the Generalship of William Booth* (London: Partridge, 1877);

Robert Sandall, Arch R. Wiggins, and Coutts, *The History of the Salvation Army,* 7 volumes (London & New York: Nelson, 1947–1986);

William T. Stead, *Mrs. Booth of the Salvation Army* (London: Nisbet, 1900);

Bernard Watson, *A Hundred Years' War: The Salvation Army, 1865–1965* (London: Hodder & Stoughton, 1964).

Papers:

Booth's papers are at the Salvation Army headquarters in London and the Salvation Army Archives and Research Center in New York City.

James Bryce, Viscount Bryce
(10 May 1838 - 22 January 1922)

Hayden Ward
West Virginia University

See also the Bryce entry in *DLB 166: British Travel Writers, 1837-1875: Victorian Period.*

BOOKS: *The Holy Roman Empire* (Oxford: Shrimpton / London & Cambridge: Macmillan, 1864; revised edition, London: Macmillan, 1871; revised and enlarged edition, London: Macmillan, 1873; New York: Macmillan, 1877; revised and enlarged again, London & New York: Macmillan, 1904);

The Academical Study of the Civil Law: An Inaugural Lecture Delivered at Oxford, February 25, 1871 (London & New York: Macmillan, 1871);

Transcaucasia and Ararat: Being Notes of a Vacation Tour in the Autumn of 1876 (London: Macmillan, 1877; revised and enlarged edition, London & New York: Macmillan, 1896);

The Trade Marks Registration Acts, 1875 & 1876 (London: Maxwell, 1877);

England and Ireland: An Introductory Statement (London: Committee on Irish Affairs, 1884);

The Predictions of Hamilton and De Tocqueville (Baltimore: Publication Agency of the Johns Hopkins University, 1887);

The American Commonwealth (3 volumes, London & New York: Macmillan, 1888; revised and enlarged, 2 volumes, 1889; revised again, London & New York: Macmillan, 1893, 1895);

Legal Studies in the University of Oxford: A Valedictory Lecture Delivered before the University, June 10, 1893 (London & New York: Macmillan, 1893);

Impressions of South Africa (London: Macmillan, 1897; New York: Century, 1897; revised and enlarged edition, London: Macmillan, 1899; New York: Macmillan, 1900);

William Ewart Gladstone: His Characteristics as Man and Statesman (London: Macmillan, 1898; New York: Century, 1898);

Studies in History and Jurisprudence, 2 volumes (London: Clarendon Press, 1901; New York: Oxford University Press, 1901);

James Bryce, 1905 (photograph by G. C. Beresford)

The Relations of the Advanced and Backward Races of Mankind (Oxford: Clarendon Press, 1902);

Studies in Contemporary Biography (London & New York: Macmillan, 1903);

The Hindrances to Good Citizenship (New Haven: Yale University Press, 1909);

South America: Observations and Impressions (London & New York: Macmillan, 1912; corrected and revised edition, New York: Macmillan, 1914);

University and Historical Addresses Delivered during a Residence in the United States as Ambassador of Great Britain (London & New York: Macmillan, 1913);

Neutral Nations and the War (London & New York: Macmillan, 1914);

The Attitude of Great Britain in the Present War (London: Macmillan, 1916);

Proposals for the Prevention of Future Wars (London: Allen & Unwin, 1917);

Essays and Addresses in War Time (London & New York: Macmillan, 1918);

Modern Democracies, 2 volumes (London & New York: Macmillan, 1921);

Canada: An Actual Democracy (Toronto: Macmillan of Canada, 1921);

The Study of American History (Cambridge: Cambridge University Press, 1921; New York: Macmillan, 1922);

International Relations: Eight Lectures Delivered in the United States in August, 1921 (New York: Macmillan, 1922);

Memories of Travel, edited by Lady Bryce (London & New York: Macmillan, 1923).

OTHER: "The Flora of the Island of Arran," in *Geology of Clydesdale and Arran,* by James Bryce (1806–1877) (London: R. Griffin, 1859);

Handbook of Home Rule: Being Articles on the Irish Question, edited by Bryce (London: Kegan Paul, Trench, 1887);

Two Centuries of Irish History, 1691–1870, edited, with an introduction, by Bryce (London: Kegan Paul, Trench, 1888);

Leonard Woolsey Bacon, *A History of American Christianity,* preface by Bryce (New York: Scribners, 1899; London: Clarke, 1899);

Leslie Stephen, *Essays on Freethinking and Plainspeaking,* introductions by Bryce and Herbert Paul (New York & London: Putnam, 1905);

Abraham Lincoln, *Speeches and Letters of Abraham Lincoln, 1832–1865,* introduction by Bryce (New York: Dutton, 1907; London: Dent, 1919);

William Archibald Dunning, *The British Empire and the United States: A Review of Their Relations during the Century of Peace Following the Treaty of Ghent,* introduction by Bryce (New York: Scribners, 1914);

Arnold J. Toynbee, ed., *The Treatment of Armenians in the Ottoman Empire, 1915–1916: Documents Presented to Viscount Grey of Fallodon, Secretary of State for Foreign Affairs,* preface by Bryce (London: His Majesty's Stationery Office, 1916).

After extended private discussions concerning British policy in the war with Germany in 1915, Edward House, an aide to President Woodrow Wilson, pronounced his partner in the talks, James Bryce, to be "one of the foremost living Englishmen." Bryce was an influential writer and lecturer on education and civil law; a Liberal member of Parliament for twenty-six years and, briefly, cabinet secretary for Ireland; British ambassador to the United States in the years before World War I; and author of several books and many speeches giving his impressions of the histories, political systems, and cultural values of the countries he visited. Through all his various activities he sought to promote the dignity of individual lives, the efficient and upright functioning of representative democracy in countries prepared to exercise it, and the harmony of nations in Europe and the Americas. In pursuing these aims Bryce systematically studied the past and empirically analyzed present societies. He joined the venerable discipline of history to the nascent field of sociology to become one of the precursors, in intention if not in method, of modern political science, especially in that branch called comparative government. In many respects he remains an eminent representative of intellectual liberalism in Britain between 1870 and 1920.

Born in Belfast, James Bryce was the son of James and Margaret Bryce. His father was the son of a Scottish Presbyterian minister, and his mother was the daughter of a Belfast merchant. In 1846 the elder James Bryce, a teacher, left Belfast Academy and took a position at the Glasgow High School, where young James eventually attended classes. During the summers he shared his father's amateur researches in botany and geology, fields of growing popular interest and controversy. Bryce's training in the classics and the natural sciences influenced his entire life and informed his various writings on political and educational topics.

At age sixteen Bryce entered Glasgow University, where he studied Latin and Greek under the eminent William Ramsay and Edmund Lushington (Alfred Tennyson's brother-in-law) as well as mathematics and logic. The special strengths of his Scottish education and his Presbyterian training played important roles in his introduction to Oxford University.

When Bryce was nineteen years old, his effort to obtain a scholarship to Balliol or to one of the other Oxford colleges was initially blocked because his Presbyterian's conscience would not allow him to assent to the Thirty-Nine Articles of Anglican belief, as was generally required for admission to the university. Yet because he performed brilliantly on the prescribed examination and agreed to attend chapel without assenting to the Articles, Bryce was admitted to Trinity College. By standing out against the religious tests Bryce helped to get the Test Acts abolished at the university and thus began a lifelong

Bryce during his undergraduate days at Trinity College, Oxford

commitment to enlarging the civil liberties of the individual.

During his time at Trinity between 1857 and 1862, Bryce witnessed the impact of the publication of Charles Darwin's *On the Origin of Species by Means of Natural Selection* (1859) and of *Essays and Reviews* (1860), the controversial response by liberal clergy. He was also exhilarated by the fervent political spirit of the Italian Risorgimento and almost left school to enlist as one of Giuseppe Garibaldi's volunteers. More conventionally, he served as president of the Oxford Union and as a member of the Old Mortality, a prestigious essay society to which he presented papers on history, education, and Greek literature. Most significantly, he experienced an awakening of historical studies under the influence of Goldwin Smith, the Regius Professor of Modern History, and Arthur Stanley, who held the Chair of Ecclesiastical History and was a disciple of the late Dr. Thomas Arnold, whose three-volume *History of Rome* (1838–1843) was an early source of inspiration for Bryce. It was appropriate that the crowning academic achievement of Bryce, having been elected a Fellow of Oriel College, was to win the Arnold Prize in 1863 for a long essay on the Holy Roman Empire. He revised and enlarged this essay for publication with the enthusiastic endorsement of his teacher, historian E. A. Freeman, who, according to H. A. L. Fisher, wrote in a review that Bryce had "by a single youthful effort placed himself on a level with men who have given their lives to historical study." *The Holy Roman Empire* (1864), greatly praised upon its publication and still widely regarded as an important work of historiography, was Bryce's first commercially published book and demonstrated his ability to marshal details in support of a thesis of vast historical and geographical scope.

Bryce begins by sketching the Roman Empire in decline, during the third and fourth centuries A.D., when it was ceasing to be a coherent political entity even as it remained a potent ideal of order and unity. By proclaiming Christianity to be the state religion in A.D. 395, Emperor Constantine made it possible, in succeeding centuries, for the various warring tribes of Europe to interfuse their political power with that of the church at Rome, reminiscent of the old imperium. The union of secular and religious power was symbolized by the coronation of Charlemagne as the first Holy Roman Emperor in the year 800. Through many conflicts between spiritual and temporal powers during the Middle Ages and the Renaissance, the Roman Empire survived as an essentially unified entity, Bryce argues, because the foundation of Roman law was common to its various territories and peoples. The importance of Roman law as a central principle of order and continuity in Western history is a point Bryce emphasizes not only in his first book but also in his subsequent lecturing and writing as Regius Professor of Civil Law at Oxford from 1870 to 1893. Throughout his long career this idea informs most of his important scholarly projects and diplomatic activities, central among which is his study of the government and society of the United States. Near the end of *The Holy Roman Empire* Bryce offers this summation of his thinking about the historical importance of the idea of Rome:

> It was imperishable because it was universal; and when its power had ceased, it was remembered with awe and love by the races whose separate existence it had destroyed, because it had spared the weak while it smote down the strong; because it had granted equal rights to all, and closed against none of its subjects the path of honourable ambition. When the military power of the conquering city had departed, her sway over the world of thought began. By her the Greek theory of a commonwealth of mankind had been reduced to practice; the magic of her name remained, and she held a sway over the imagination which the passing of century after century scarcely reduced. She had gathered up and embodied in her literature and institutions all the ideas and all the practical results of ancient thought. Embracing and organizing and propagating the new religion, she made it seem her own. Her language, her theology, her

laws, her architecture, made their way where the eagles of war had never winged their flight, and with the spread of civilization have found new homes on the Ganges and the Mississippi.

The gradual unification of small, squabbling states into larger, harmonious federations such as those formed in Italy and Germany during the mid nineteenth century is the larger, implicit theme of Bryce's work. He welcomed this unification, but in the case of Germany he increasingly qualified his approval in reaction to the militarism of Prince Otto von Bismarck's Prussian state, which dominated German foreign policy from the 1870s onward. During World War I Bryce argued that this militaristic inclination must be extirpated if Germany were to return to the European "family of nations." In *The Holy Roman Empire* Bryce's vivid account of and sympathetic attitudes toward the confederation of the Germanic peoples, particularly under Frederick Barbarossa, contrasts with his later apprehensions about the threat of German power.

In addition to his first book, Bryce's activities in the 1860s included the study of law in Lincoln's Inn and in Heidelberg; membership on the Taunton Commission (1864–1867), which examined education in England and Wales; and the founding of the Victoria University of Manchester and of Girton College, Oxford, for women. He contributed to *Essays on Reform,* a volume setting out the Liberal argument for the 1867 Reform Bill. In his essay Bryce defines the ideal state in terms that recall his description of Rome as the guarantor of good to all its subjects and anticipates his concern with the theory of commonwealth in the years ahead:

> Hence the ideal of a Christian state is Democracy; a Commonwealth in which wealth is no honour, nor labour any degradation; all whose members are worthy of equal regard, although there be among them a diversity of gifts and government be assigned to the most gifted; wherein there is no strife of classes, because no divergence of interests, nor any need of coercion, because the law is the expression of their common will, and their will is to seek not their own good, but the good of all.

In 1870, the same year he became Regius Professor of Civil Law at Oxford, Bryce made his first trip to the United States with a friend, Albert Venn Dicey. On this initial visit, mostly to Boston, New York, and Washington, D.C., Bryce found a close approximation to this democratic ideal in the United States, an impression that subsequent visits and wide travels in 1881 and 1883 deepened and qualified. He began to plan a large book on America.

But a journey to southern Russia and Turkish Armenia in 1876 inspired Bryce's first travel book, *Transcaucasia and Ararat,* published in September 1877, after the outbreak of war between Russia and Turkey over the "Bulgarian atrocities" committed by Moslems against Christians. In a supplementary chapter written in 1896 Bryce enlarged upon his description of how, after the Russian intervention, the Christian Armenians continued to suffer under the Turks because the British government, under the Conservative Benjamin Disraeli, fearing Russian expansion in the Balkans and Asia Minor, insisted that Turkey, not Russia, should control the Armenians.

In England the beginning of Bryce's long and influential advocacy for Armenian relief (in 1916 he chaired a national commission on the matter) was the most important result of his travels to the Near East. A personal highlight of the trip was his solitary climb of Mount Ararat, a feat that made him an international celebrity. Bryce describes the view from the summit:

> Below and around, included in this single view, seemed to lie the whole cradle of the human race, from Mesopotamia in the south to the great wall of the Caucasus that covered the northern horizon, Mount Kaf, the boundary for so many ages of the civilised world. If it was indeed here that man first set foot again on the unpeopled earth, one could imagine how the great dispersion went as races spread themselves from those sacred heights along the courses of the great rivers down to the Black and Caspian Seas, and over the Assyrian Plain to the shores of the Southern Ocean, whence they were wafted away to the other continents and isles. No more imposing centre of the world could be imagined.

This vision from the "centre of the world" as he gazes down on the "cradle of the human race" in the Tigris River valley seems suggestively consonant with Bryce's political vision of a national commonwealth and a federation of peoples. His central interest as a writer is in delineating the forces and institutions that give people their rights as individuals and a sense of the value of a community in which that individuality can flourish. In this book his vision from Mount Ararat gives way to the spectacle of the suffering Armenians: both seem of a piece with Bryce's later political concerns, including his ardent efforts during and after World War I to create a just and viable League of Nations.

Bryce's active political life was punctuated in January 1886 by his efforts with John Dalberg-Acton, Lord Acton, and others in founding the *English Historical Review,* which remains an influential scholarly journal. Although the Liberals were out of power from 1885 to 1892, Bryce also continued to

Bryce in the 1890s (photograph by Miss M. V. Bryce)

work for Irish Home Rule despite the failure of William Ewart Gladstone's policy in his last government (1892–1894). In 1906 Bryce became secretary for Ireland, and after a year in that frustrating post he was appointed British ambassador to the United States. His reputation as a "friend of America" at a period of tense relations between the countries rested primarily on *The American Commonwealth,* which he had published in 1888 and revised several times afterward to reflect changes he had seen during later visits.

Bryce divides *The American Commonwealth* into six parts. In the first he describes the national government, from its origins in the conflict between Hamiltonian federalism and Jeffersonian democracy, through its turbulent development in the age of Andrew Jackson and the crisis of the Civil War to its contemporary strengths and weaknesses in the Gilded Age. The second part treats the constitutions and workings of the state governments. Part 3, the most celebrated of the book, analyzes the two great political parties and the ways in which, through the spoils system and machine politics, they have contributed to political corruption. In part 4 Bryce defines the sovereign power of public opinion in America, partly with a view to qualifying Alexis de Tocqueville's assertion that the "tyranny of the majority" is a serious threat in American democracy. Part 5 contains several extended examples of political movements and issues that demonstrate some virtues but mostly liabilities of that democracy in order to show (as Bryce calls the final chapter of part 5) "how far American experience is available for Europe."

In part 6 he gives capsule assessments of some American institutions: for instance, Wall Street, higher education, the railroads, the distinctive "temper of the west," and the status of women. He concludes with chapters speculating on the political, social, and economic future of the United States, and his closing words are glowingly optimistic:

> America has still a long vista of years stretching before her in which she will enjoy conditions far more auspicious than any European country can count upon. And that America marks the highest level, not only of material well being, but of intelligence and happiness, which the race has yet attained, will be the judgment of those who look not at the favoured few for whose benefit the world seems hitherto to have formed its institutions, but at the whole body of the people.

In his introductory chapter Bryce acknowledges that comparison of his book with Tocqueville's *Democracy in America* (1838) is inevitable, although "what I have tried to accomplish is something different." Whereas Tocqueville has written an abstract, theoretical treatise on democracy with America as a test case, Bryce sees his own method as phenomenological rather than metaphysical: "to paint the institutions and people of America as they are," emphasizing the special conditions of American democracy rather than its ideal or typical features. Despite the greater empiricism that Bryce claims to use, and allowing for differences of time and place between his work and that of Tocqueville, much of what Bryce says about the origin of the Constitution and the functions of government, about the "will of the people" as the supreme political sanction and the "tyranny of the majority" that becomes a threat borne by that sanction, and about the customs and institutions other than political ones seems similar to the general purpose and method of Tocqueville.

Bryce's tone is generally more optimistic than Tocqueville's; he is seldom skeptical or ambivalent in judgment, as is his French predecessor. The one subject on which Bryce seems consistently pessimistic is the spoils system and machine politics of the Gilded Age, phenomena that, since they are endemic only to modern big cities, with their paper wealth and masses of inexperienced voters, both the Founding Fathers and Tocqueville hardly anticipated. Bryce's most distinctive and lasting contribution to American political literature, in part 3 of *The American Commonwealth,* is his analysis of the party system and its dependence on political machines. Among historians one hundred years later Bryce's high-toned indictment is still controversial, since he leaves out what subsequent scholars have seen as the benefits of the machines for immigrants not yet fully assimilated to the established patterns of American life. For Bryce political spoils and machines, rings and bosses, are understandable but thoroughly perverse components of the democratic process.

"The active life" was typically part of the ethos of late-Victorian writers, and a climactic moment of the political campaign is the national convention, which Bryce is the first to analyze in terms that seem still vivid in exemplifying him in his favorite role as a vigorous, traveling observer, not like the bookish scholar he makes of Tocqueville:

> The convention presents in sharp contrast and frequent alternation, the two most striking features of Americans in public—their orderliness and their excitability. Everything is done according to strict rule, with a scrupulous observance of small formalities which European meetings would ignore or despise. Points of order almost too fine for a parliament are taken, argued, decided on by the chair, to whom every one bows. Yet the passions that sway the multitude are constantly bursting forth in storms of cheering or hissing at an allusion to a favourite aspirant or an obnoxious name, and five or six speakers often take the floor together, shouting and gesticulating at each other till the chairman obtains a hearing for one of them.

Bryce claims that five-sixths of the "facts" in his book derive from his personal observations and casual conversations or from information provided by American specialists. One of the most important of these sources was E. L. Godkin, the Irish-born founding editor of *The Nation,* a New York political journal to which Bryce regularly contributed a "letter from England." Much of Bryce's informed indignation about "machines" and "rings" is borrowed from editorials written by Godkin, whose fiery and tenacious style complemented Bryce's poised detachment. Godkin was one of Bryce's closest transatlantic friends.

Another was Charles W. Eliot, who was president of Harvard University from 1869 to 1909 and contributed much to Bryce's thinking about America. Eliot first defined the Darwinian cast of Bryce's idea of American democracy, its institutions ever adaptable to changeful local conditions. The point is fundamental in Bryce's book and at odds with another of his basic themes: the essential continuity and unity of American and English politics, law, and culture. Among other contemporary sources of this latter idea were two of Bryce's teachers at Oxford, Goldwin Smith and, especially, E. A. Freeman. Hugh Tulloch, a modern scholar of Bryce and his work, writes that

> Freeman's writing was an extraordinary inversion of Whig history. It conceived of progress, but of progress through retrogression, and considered the postmedieval world as a declension from purity and unity to racial mix and diversity. For him, even more than for Goldwin Smith, America preserved England's primal racial qualities undiminished, frozen as it were, in time. Less sullied by the modern world, American colonists in 1776 once again exercised their Teutonic instincts and revolted to further the cause of future racial freedom. Shorn of its more extreme overtones, Bryce in his *American Commonwealth* conceived of the American revolution in similar terms. His *Holy Roman Empire* was written as an act of homage to illustrate Freeman's thesis of historical unity. Deeply embedded in *The American Commonwealth* lie two crucial assumptions inherited from his mentor: the first is the explicit concept of Anglo-American unity, and the second is the implicit understanding of the American as essentially an Englishman writ large on a new frontier. The imaginative limitations which Bryce failed to escape, despite his far wider experience of the United States and his more open mind, are ascribable in part to Freeman. This is the measure of his influence.

The influence of Freeman's thinking is to be found in Bryce's later writings as well—*Impressions of South Africa* (1897), *South America: Observations and Impressions* (1912), and *Modern Democracies* (1921), the massive survey he published at the age of eighty-three. In each work Bryce measures the prospects for progress toward democracy by the extent to which other peoples are able to emulate the pattern of "Anglo-American" constitutionalism.

Goldwin Smith had also used this approach in "On the Foundations of the American Colonies," a lecture delivered at Oxford when Bryce was an undergraduate. Bryce, as he had done with Freeman, kept up a friendship with Smith, who immigrated first to the United States and then to Canada. From Smith's increasingly pessimistic views Bryce in *The American Commonwealth* derived his own pervasive concern for the mediocrity of talents attracted to politics in a democratic society. Paradoxically, he also shared Smith's earlier optimism that, following the Civil War, the United States had emerged as a greater, more mature nation than it had been before

A meeting between Ambassador James Bryce and President Theodore Roosevelt, as imagined by American cartoonist John Tinney McCutcheon

the trial of its unity. Furthermore, when Bryce was British ambassador and became closely involved with efforts to resolve boundary and trade disputes between the United States and Canada, he drew on Smith's opinions for guidance, especially on Smith's belief that Canada would eventually be absorbed into the United States.

On both sides of the Atlantic Ocean, Bryce's *American Commonwealth* was hailed as a great contribution to an understanding of both the similarities and differences of the political systems of England and the United States. However, some reviewers, including Professor Woodrow Wilson, found the work somewhat lacking in a sense of the diversity and development of American political institutions. Although *The American Commonwealth* is still regarded as an early monument of political science, several writers, such as Graham Wallas in his *Human Nature in Politics* (1921), have criticized certain facets of Bryce's argument, notably his rationalistic belief in the viability of the democratic ideal in all cultures—a view fundamental to the liberal perspective of nineteenth-century Oxford historians.

Other commentators—some, such as Harold Laski and Carl Becker, who are hostile generally to the values of Victorian liberalism—have criticized Bryce for having little understanding of the way the working class relied on party politics and the machine to gain access to power denied them by the sort of high-minded professional and academic elite to which Bryce himself belonged. Bryce's reiterated assertion of the essential classlessness of American democracy especially has been attacked as naive and as being of a piece with his unsympathetic views of the newly cohesive and restive labor movement of the 1880s. In recent years Bryce's emphasis on the cultural basis of the sectional and ethnic conflicts within the American political process has caused *The American Commonwealth* to be viewed more favorably than it was by historians immediately before and after World War I.

Following publication of *The American Commonwealth* Bryce took a four-month trip to India; married Marion Ashton, daughter of a prominent Lancashire Liberal; and resigned his Oxford professorship. (His lectures were published in 1901 as *Studies in History and Jurisprudence*.) He served as chairman of a royal commission on secondary education and as president of the Board of Trade. When the Liberal government of Archibald Rosebery (who had succeeded Gladstone) fell in 1895, Bryce and his wife traveled to South Africa.

Their visit anticipated by a few weeks the notorious Jameson Raid in 29 December 1895 in the Transvaal, an event that aggravated the worsening relations between the English of the Cape Colony and their Boer neighbors. Two years later Bryce, hoping that his description of the country and analysis of its political and racial situation would help to reconcile the hostile parties, published *Impressions of South Africa*. When the Boer War broke out in 1899, he felt obliged to add a long prefatory chapter examining the causes.

Bryce's view was that the British government had the right to request or enforce certain changes in the practices of the Boer government at Pretoria, especially the granting of full political rights to the Uitlanders (non-Boer immigrants, mostly English, to the Transvaal), and in relations with the English at Cape Town. However, Bryce believed that the policies of British Foreign Secretary Joseph Chamberlain had pushed the resentful Boers into armed conflict with the vastly superior British army: "The real cause of war was the menacing language of Britain, coupled with her preparation for war." Bryce reiterates the argument of his original final chapter, calling for "reconcilement and fusion" of the Dutch and English in South Africa. Otherwise the future of English colonization in the Cape would be threatened because imperial retrenchment, including the ceding of the Transvaal to the Boers in 1852, had already diminished the colonizing effort.

One reason Bryce believed that colonization must continue and harmony with the Boers must be achieved was that British interests in Africa were threatened by the new imperial thrust on that continent from Germany. The other reason was that Bryce believed, like many other Liberals, that English rule alone ensured the progress of South Africa toward true democracy, an impossible goal if the black and colored peoples, who greatly outnumbered the whites, were left to their own devices. To explain why this should be so, Bryce devotes several chapters to the history of the Hottentots, Bushmen, and Bantu to show that their tribal cultures could not be expected to form the basis of a viable, modern nation. In other chapters he analyzes the history of and reasons for the disaffection of the Boers, and he suggests that proper diplomacy could bring about a rapprochement between them and the Cape English, whose history he also details.

Not all of *Impressions of South Africa* is devoted to political issues. Early chapters reveal Bryce still enthusiastic about geology, botany, zoology, and archaeology. He is especially sensitive to the ways in which man has altered, for better and worse, the natural environment of the region. To modern readers Bryce the ecologist seems more pertinent than Bryce the political theorist.

With his party still out of office after the Boer War, Bryce found time to produce *Studies in Contemporary Biography* (1903), a collection of career sketches of eminent men that was then very popular. Among his subjects are Disraeli, Gladstone, Cardinal Henry Manning, and Anthony Trollope. A passage on his fellow historian, Lord Acton, reveals Bryce's ability to summon up his remembrance of a dead acquaintance:

> Twenty years ago, late at night in his library at Cannes, he expounded to me his view of how such a history of Liberty (Lord Acton had in 1882 drawn out a comprehensive scheme for such a history) might be written and in what wise it might be made the central thread of all history. He spoke for six or seven minutes only; but he spoke like a man inspired, seeming as if, from some mountain summit high in air, he saw beneath him the far-winding path of human progress from dim Cimmerian shores of prehistoric shadow into the fuller yet broken and fitful light of modern time. The eloquence was splendid, but greater than the eloquence was the penetrating vision which discerned through all events and in all ages the play of those moral forces, now creating, now destroying, always transmuting, which had moulded and remoulded institutions and had given to the human spirit its ceaselessly-changing forms of energy. It was as if the whole landscape of history had been suddenly lit up by a burst of sunlight. I never heard from any other lips any discourse like this, nor from his did I ever hear the like again.

This portrait presents an epitome of the Liberal historian as *vates*, priest or prophet, a role that Bryce would never have claimed for himself but which surely inspired his own tireless efforts in one massive book after another to track the progress of democracy through almost ceaseless travel and study.

After the frustrations of opposition and of serving as secretary for Ireland under Sir Henry Campbell-Bannerman once the Liberals returned to power in 1905, Bryce became British ambassador to the United States in February 1907, and the period of his greatest fame commenced. He was the trusted friend of Presidents Theodore Roosevelt and William Howard Taft and, as British steward of the affairs of Canada, which still had dominion status, Bryce worked with Sir Wilfred Laurier, Dominion Prime Minister, and Earl Grey, Governor-General of Canada, to smooth frequently roiled relations with the United States. Bryce was a popular figure: he knew most of the prominent men in American politics, business, and higher education, and he was in demand as a speaker at association and university functions. In 1913 he published *University and Historical Addresses Delivered during a Residence in the United States as Ambassador of Great Britain,* a collection of his speeches on topics such as American colonial and constitutional history, the function of state universities, and the need for enhancing the national park system—all subjects on which he was an acknowledged expert.

Bryce's political labors and extensive public appearances during his six years as ambassador earned him much goodwill in the United States, and by continually emphasizing Anglo-American unity, the "special relation" between his host country and Great Britain, he was a most effective emissary for British foreign policy. A bust in his likeness remains in the hallway outside the chamber of the United States Senate.

With the Panama Canal project under way, Bryce was sent by his government on a fact-finding tour of South America. From October 1910 to January 1911 he visited Panama, Peru (where he traveled to the ruins of Cuzco, the ancient Inca capital), Bolivia, Chile, Argentina, Uruguay, and Brazil. By September 1912 he had produced *South America: Observations and Impressions,* a six-hundred-page book detailing his journey and reporting on the progress of democracy in the Latin American republics. In this volume, similar in purpose and method to his work on South Africa, he provided for nonspecialist readers a vivid journal of travels through spectacular landscapes and poignant history combined with a rather pessimistic analysis of the prospects for democratic development among a group of nations that he believed, even more than South Africa, were suffering from irremediable racial confusion and the lin-

Bryce in 1915 (portrait by William Rothenstein; courtesy of the Lilly Library, Indiana University)

gering repressive influence of the recently departed Spaniards.

The book again presents Bryce's familiar refrain: where there has been no English presence, democracy fails to take root. The idea that modern democracy is a "Teutonic," specifically English, graft of ancient Roman republican stock had been Bryce's unifying historical thesis since *The Holy Roman Empire.* The one bright spot is the Panama Canal, which he ambiguously calls "the greatest liberty Man has ever taken with Nature." His description of the huge Culebra Cut, perhaps recalling Rudyard Kipling's celebration of heroic British engineering in the poem "MacAndrew's Hymn," is a prose paean to the new international willpower and technological prowess of the United States:

> The interior of the Culebra Cut presented, during the period of excavation, a striking sight. Within the nine miles of the whole cutting, two hundred miles of railroad track had been laid down side by side, some of the lowest level on terraces along which the excavating shovels were at work. Within the deepest part

of the cutting, whose length is less than a mile, many hundreds of railroad construction cars and many thousands of men were at work, some busy in setting dynamite charges for blasting, some clearing away the rubbish scattered round by an explosion, some working the huge moving shovels which were digging into the softer parts of the fill or were removing the material loosened by explosions, the rest working the trains of cars that were perpetually being made up and run out of the cutting at each end to dump the excavated material wherever it was needed somewhere along the line of the Canal. Every here and there one saw little puffs of steam, some from the locomotives, some where the compressed air by which power was applied to the shovels was escaping from the pipes, and condensing the vapour-saturated atmosphere.

There is something in the magnitude and methods of this enterprise which a poet might take as his theme. Never before on our planet have so much labour, so much scientific knowledge, and so much executive skill been concentrated on a work designed to bring the nations nearer to one another and serve the interests of all mankind.

The Bryces continued traveling: in 1912 to Australia and New Zealand; in 1913 to China, Japan, and Russia on a long voyage home at the end of his ambassadorial term; and in 1914 to Palestine and Syria after Bryce had been given the title of viscount by King George V.

During World War I Bryce headed a commission to investigate reports of German atrocities in Belgium, an experience that called into question his longstanding faith in "Teutonic" civilization, and he also collected documents concerning the Turkish massacre of Armenians in 1915. He was one of the first Liberal statesmen to advocate the League of Nations, and his letters to American friends at the time express concern and later frustration at the failure of the United States to support or join the League. Increasingly he criticizes President Wilson for mishandling negotiations at the Versailles conference in 1919 and for his ineptitude in the war of words with isolationist senators, led by Henry Cabot Lodge, who eventually blocked the entry of the United States into the League. By 1918 Bryce had grave doubts about the values and durability of European civilization, especially in light of the harsh conditions imposed on Germany by the Allies and of the frightening developments following the Russian Bolshevik revolution.

His native optimism tempered by foreboding, Bryce wrote his last major work, *Modern Democracies,* a work praised in Europe and America as much for the undiminished vigor of its aging author as for its content. The book treats with broader scope the subject of his previous volumes: the history of democratic institutions and the extent to which comparative studies reveal that various nations claiming to function democratically do in truth uphold majority rule by constitutional law.

Omitting Great Britain from this work because he felt that his long involvement in its politics compromised his scholarly disinterestedness, Bryce studies France, Switzerland, Canada, the United States, Australia, and New Zealand as test cases for the democratic principles he outlines in its opening part. (In this respect Bryce follows the method he had years before described as that of Tocqueville.) Ancient Athenian democracy provides the matrix for Bryce's democratic ideal, and he regards the republics of "Spanish America," as he had in *South America,* as instances in which the democratic state has thus far failed to mature. Except for France, where republican government is still in a confused, formative condition, Bryce's broad cultural perspective finds the other successful examples all to be "Teutonic" states. (He omits Germany, as a recent betrayer of democracy under the rule of the Prussian military caste.) This assessment reinforces the conviction of Bryce and the men who taught him that modern democracy is of northern European origin, a product of the preservation of Roman civil law as the basis for constitutional government.

The chapters on the United States reiterate much that Bryce had originally said and revised in several editions of *The American Commonwealth* up to 1910. However, in *Modern Democracies* he includes a long chapter on political reforms of the previous thirty years, especially election reforms, the consequent decline of political machines, and the introduction of the referendum and the voter initiative, which increased emphasis on the popular origins of legislation. Bryce sees new dangers to American democracy in the rising influence of wealth in politics, the instability that results from increasing labor agitation, and the failure of masses of new immigrants to become assimilated into the predominant Anglo-American culture. However, he finds American democracy, on the whole, a healthy process.

Generally, however, the survival of the nineteenth-century Liberal's dream of a democratic, peaceable world order has become more clouded than it was. The horrors of World War I and, no doubt, the failure of the goals of the League of Nations send Bryce back imaginatively to the condition of Europe before the formation of the Holy Roman Empire began the shaping of modern Western civilization. Near the end of the

Hindleap, Bryce's home in Sussex

book he reflects rather gloomily, and typically for thinkers of his time and philosophy, on the failure of moral and political intelligence:

> There has probably been since the fifth century no moment in history which has struck mankind with such terror and dismay as have the world-wide disasters which began in 1914, and have not yet passed away. The explanations of the facts are no more cheering than the facts themselves. Human passions have been little softened and refined by the veneer of civilization that covers them: human intelligence has not increased, and shows no sign of increasing, in proportion to the growing magnitude and complexity of human affairs. Knowledge has been accumulated, the methods and instruments of research have been improved, a wonderful mastery over the forces of Nature has been obtained, the world has become a more comfortable place to live in and offers a far greater variety of pleasures; but the mental powers of the individual man have remained stationary, no stronger, no wider in their range, than they were thousands of years ago, and the supremely great who are fit to grapple with the vast problems which the growth of population and the advances of science have created come no more frequently, and may fail to appear just when they are most needed.

Although H. A. L. Fisher notes that "the two volumes on *Modern Democracies* are continually in the hands of academic students who occupy themselves with the problems of political science," this book and most of Bryce's other works continue to interest readers not as textbooks but as documentation of how the theories of Liberal historians and philosophers from John Stuart Mill and Thomas Arnold through E. A. Freeman, William Stubbs, and Lord Acton were applied to practical politics by a man capable of astute observation and efficient but principled action. Bryce's works are accurately understood more as examples of the culminating phase of nineteenth-century liberal historiography than as pioneering works of twentieth-century political science. In his opening statement to *Modern Democracies* Bryce writes that his works are the expressions of an age passing away more than they are volumes that speak to the future; his writing is tinged with a sense of relativism:

> Every generalization now made is only provisional, and will have to be some day qualified: every book that is written will before long be out of date, except as a record of what were deemed to be salient phenomena at the time when it was written. Each of us who writes de-

scribes the progress mankind was making with its experiments in government as he saw them; each hands on the torch to his successor, and the succession is infinite, for the experiments are never completed.

In June 1921 in London, Bryce gave the inaugural address for the Sir George Watson Chair of American History, Literature and Institutions, designed by its founders to promote Anglo-American relations. Later that summer he lectured for the last time in the United States, at Williams College in Massachusetts, on international law. At the end of the Watson lecture, "The Study of American History," two leading themes of Bryce's career, in their long historical context and as delineated initially by Freeman, come together:

> I have spoken of American history as a part of the history of the English-speaking community of peoples. It is the history of that branch which is now the largest, the richest and the least assailable from without, yet whose fortunes are indissolubly linked with those of all the others. Through its three centuries of life in the Western hemisphere it has retained that boldness and resourcefulness and tenacity of purpose which belonged to the ancient stock that came from the Elbe to the Thames and from the Thames to the Hudson and onward to the Mississippi. It has cherished high ideals and holds fast to them still. Will it not be in days to come the glory of the free English-speaking peoples, to whom Providence has given the widest influence, and therewith the greatest responsibility, that any group of peoples has ever received, if they should join in using that influence to guide the feet of all mankind in the way of peace.

The passage is an epitome of all Bryce had written in the previous fifty-seven years.

James Bryce died seven months later at Sidmouth, on the south coast of England. *The Times* (London) obituary on 23 January 1922 catches the prevailing tone of the major eulogies he received:

> Few men have had so long and so honourable a record of intellectual productivity. Nor have many men, certainly few of his generation, had more friends or been held in such high esteem by large circles in almost every country in the world. He spoke the principal European languages with ease, and to those who met him he appeared to have been everywhere, known everybody, and read everything.

Biography:
H. A. L. Fisher, *James Bryce (Viscount Bryce of Dechmont, O.M.)*, 2 volumes (New York: Macmillan, 1927).

References:
Louis Auchincloss, "Lord Bryce," *American Heritage*, 32 (1981): 98-104;

Robert C. Brooks, ed., *Bryce's American Commonwealth: Fiftieth Anniversary* (New York: Macmillan, 1939);

J. W. Burrow, *A Liberal Descent: Victorian Historians and the English Past* (Cambridge: Cambridge University Press, 1981);

Martin David Dubin, "Toward the Concept of Collective Security: The Bryce Group's 'Proposals for the Avoidance of War,' 1914-1917," *International Organization*, 24 (1970): 288-318;

Christopher Harvie, "Ideology and Home Rule: James Bryce, A. V. Dicey and Ireland, 1880-1887," *English Historical Review*, 91 (1976): 298-314;

Edmund Ions, *James Bryce and American Democracy* (New York: Humanities, 1970);

Rosemary Jahn, *The Art and Science of Victorian History* (Columbus: Ohio State University Press, 1985);

Justin McCarthy, *British Political Leaders* (London, 1903);

Daniel P. Moynihan, "The American Experiment," *Public Interest*, 41 (1975): 4-8;

Peter Neary, "Grey, Bryce, and the Settlement of Canadian-American Differences, 1905-1911," *Canadian Historical Review*, 49 (1968): 357-380;

K. G. Robbins, "Lord Bryce and the First World War," *History Journal*, 10 (1967): 255-278;

Keith Robbins, "History and Politics: The Career of James Bryce," *Journal of Contemporary History*, 7 (1972): 37-52;

R. T. Shannon, *Gladstone and the Bulgarian Agitation, 1876* (London: Nelson, 1963);

Margaret F. Stieg, "The Emergence of the *English Historical Review*," *Library Quarterly*, 46 (1976): 119-136;

Arnold J. Toynbee, *Acquaintances* (London: Oxford University Press, 1967);

Hugh Tulloch, *James Bryce's "American Commonwealth": The Anglo-American Background* (Woodbridge, Suffolk: Boydell & Brewer, 1988);

John Wilson, *CB: A Life of Sir Henry Campbell-Bannerman* (London: Constable, 1973).

Papers:
The Bryce Papers are located in the Bodleian Library, Oxford University.

Josephine Elizabeth Butler
(15 April 1828 – 30 December 1906)

Susan Mumm
York University

BOOKS: *The Education and Employment of Women* (London: Macmillan, 1868);

Memoir of John Grey of Dilston (Edinburgh: Edmonston & Douglas, 1869; revised edition, London: King, 1874);

An Appeal to the People of England, on the Recognition and Superintendence of Prostitution by Governments, as An English Mother (Nottingham: Banks, 1870);

On the Moral Reclaimability of Prostitutes (London, 1870);

Address Delivered in Craigie Hall, Edinburgh, February 24th, 1871 (Manchester: Ireland, 1871);

Address Delivered at Croydon, July 3, 1871 (London: National Association for the Repeal of the Contagious Diseases Acts, 1871);

The Constitution Violated: An Essay (Edinburgh: Edmonston & Douglas, 1871);

Sursum Corda: Annual Address to the Ladies' National Association (Liverpool: Brakell, 1871);

Vox Populi (Liverpool, 1871);

A Letter on the Subject of Mr. Bruce's Bill, Addressed to the Repealers of the Contagious Diseases Acts (Liverpool: Brakell, 1872);

New Era: Containing a Retrospect of the History of the Regulation System in Berlin of the Repeated Opposition Directed against the System There . . . and of the Source Whence Hope Arises for the Future (Liverpool: Brakell, 1872);

Some Thoughts on the Present Aspect of the Crusade against the State Regulation of Vice (Liverpool: Brakell, 1874);

Speech Delivered by Mrs. Josephine Butler at the Fourth Annual Meeting of the "Vigilance Association for the Defence of Personal Rights," Held at Bristol, October 15th, 1874 (London: Vigilance Association for the Defence of Personal Rights, 1874);

Legislative Restrictions on the Industry of Women, Considered from the Women's Point of View, by Butler and others (London: Mathews & Sons, 1874);

A Letter to the Members of the Ladies' National Association (Liverpool: Brakell, 1875);

Josephine Elizabeth Butler, circa 1866

Une voix dans le désert (Paris & Neuchatel: Sandoz, 1875); translated by Osmund Airy as *The Voice of One Crying in the Wilderness* (Bristol: Arrowsmith, 1913);

The Hour Before the Dawn: An Appeal to Men (London: Trübner, 1876);

The New Abolitionists: A Narrative of a Year's Work, by Butler and British Continental and General Federation for the Abolition of Government Regulation of Prostitution (London: Dyer, 1876);

Catherine of Siena: A Biography (London: Dyer, 1878);

Social Purity (London: Morgan & Scott, 1879);

Government by Police (London: Dyer, 1879);

The Life of Jean Frederic Oberlin, Pastor of the Ban de la Roche (London: Religious Tract Society, 1882);

Dangers of Constructive Legislation in Matters of Morality (Bristol, 1883);

The Salvation Army in Switzerland (London: Dyer, 1883);

Rebecca Jarrett (London: Morgan & Scott, 1885);

The Work of the Federation (London, 1885);

The Principles of the Abolitionists: An Address Delivered at Exeter Hall, Feb. 20th, 1885 (London: Dyer, 1885);

A Grave Question That Needs Answering by the Churches of Great Britain (London: Dyer, 1886);

Simple Words for Simple Folk, about the Repeal of the Contagious Diseases Acts (Bristol: Arrowsmith, 1886);

Our Christianity Tested by the Irish Question (London: Unwin, 1887);

The Revival and Extension of the Abolitionist Cause: A Letter (Winchester: Doswell, 1887);

Mrs. Butler's Appeal to the Women of America: Addressed to the International Council of Women (New York: Philanthropist, 1888);

Recollections of George Butler (Bristol: Arrowsmith, 1892);

The Present Aspect of the Abolitionist Cause in Relation to British India (London: Pewtress, 1893);

Saint Agnes (London: Cox, 1893);

The Lady of Shunem (London: Marshall, 1894);

Two Letters of Earnest Appeal and Warning (London, 1895);

A Doomed Iniquity (London, 1896);

Personal Reminiscences of a Great Crusade (London: Marshall, 1896);

Truth before Everything (London: Dyer, 1897);

Prophets and Prophetesses: Some Thoughts for the Present Time (Newcastle-on-Tyne: Mason, Swan & Morgan / London: Dyer, 1898);

Native Races and the War (London: Gay & Bird, 1900);

Silent Victories (London, 1900);

In Memoriam: Harriet Meuricoffre (London: Marshall, 1901);

The Morning Cometh: A Letter to My Children, as Philalethes (N.p., 1903);

Josephine Butler: An Autobiographical Memoir, edited by George W. Johnson and Lucy A. Johnson (Bristol: Arrowsmith, 1909).

OTHER: *Woman's Work and Woman's Culture: A Series of Essays,* edited, with an introduction, by Butler (London: Macmillan, 1869);

The Dawn, edited by Butler (London: Burfoot, 1888-1896);

Henry Elwyn [Thomas], *The Martyrs of Hell's Highway,* preface and appendix by Butler (London: Allenson, 1896);

The Storm Bell, edited by Butler (London: Burfoot, 1898-1900);

Elizabeth W. Andrew and Katharine C. Bushnell, *The Queen's Daughters in India,* prefatory letter by Butler and Henry J. Wilson (London: Morgan & Scott, 1899);

Sir James Marchant, *A Record of a Great Moral Crusade in Chatham,* introductory letter by Butler (Rochester: Parrett & Neves, 1904).

Born Josephine Elizabeth Grey in Northumberland, Josephine Butler was the fourth daughter in a family that was steeped in the Liberal tradition and that enjoyed influential political and social connections. She was educated, although not unusually well, by a governess and her mother and later spent two years at a school in Newcastle. The greatest influence on her during her early life was her father, whom she idolized. John Grey was involved in the great public movements of his day, including the First Reform Bill, Free Trade, and the agitation for the abolition of the slave trade.

Antislavery agitation first introduced the young woman to the sexual and social inequality of women. At the age of seventeen she learned of the sexual oppression of women enslaved by their masters, and she later wrote that what she learned "combined to break my young heart, and . . . awakened my feelings concerning injustice to women through this conspiracy of greed of gold and lust of the flesh." Like many other reformers, the young woman experienced a prolonged religious struggle that was renewed when she was in her seventies; during both these times she struggled with the problem of evil and the meaning of human suffering.

She came to emphasize the egalitarianism of Christianity and to apply this theology to oppressed social groups. For her, Christ was most often "the Liberator," and she saw the teachings of Christ as revolutionary: Christ was an emancipator of women and founder of a religion ultimately committed to freeing women and the oppressed from sexual and social degradation. Her *Memoir of John Grey of Dilston* (1869) contains much autobiographical information on her childhood and youth; additional information is available in her less interesting *In Memoriam: Harriet Meuricoffre* (1901), in which Butler simply adds some explanatory matter between her sister's letters.

In 1852 she married George Butler, a schoolmaster who later took Anglican orders. She saw his ordination as signaling also a consecration of her-

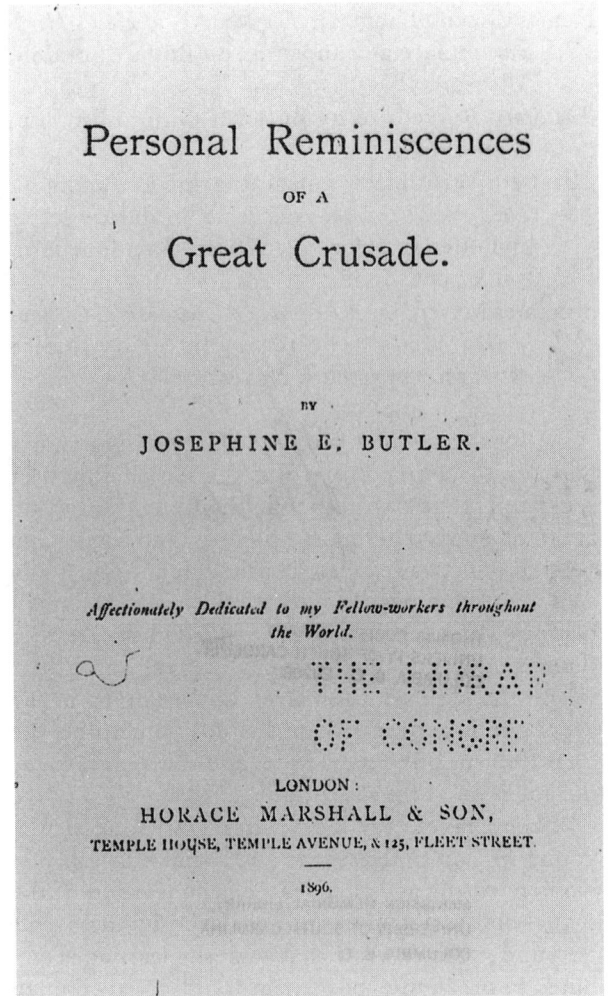

Title page for Butler's history of the movement to abolish the Contagious Diseases Acts

self, and the couple shared an evangelical faith that mixed great religious seriousness, tolerance of diverse opinions, and considerable personal exuberance. Three sons and one daughter were born in the course of their marriage, and during their early years together he lectured in geography at Oxford University, where she first publicly rebelled against the sexual double standard in taking into her home a female servant who had been imprisoned for murdering her infant, who had been illegitimately fathered by an Oxford academic. Despite the social and professional difficulties that Butler's act of kindness created for him, her husband adopted what became his pattern of constant support for her actions. Along with their strong and loving relationship, this support sustained Butler in her often-controversial public work.

In 1856 the Butlers left Oxford because the life there was affecting her health and because, given her refusal to remain in the shadows of domesticity, it had become clear that her husband could not expect to secure a permanent position at the university. In 1857 they moved to Cheltenham, where George Butler became assistant principal of Cheltenham College. There an event occurred that pushed Butler irrevocably into public affairs: her daughter, Eva, accidentally fell down a flight of stairs and died tragically in 1864. Devastated by the loss of her daughter, Butler was still struggling with depression when the family moved to Liverpool in 1866.

There she felt isolated and alone, with her husband and sons away many hours a day. Music, art, and reading failed to relieve her misery, and she turned to the work that shaped her public role for the rest of her life. Butler wrote in her autobiography that she

> became possessed with an irresistible desire to go forth and find some pain keener than my own, to meet with people more unhappy than myself.... I only knew that my heart ached night and day, and that the only solace possible would seem to be to find other hearts which ached night and day, and with more reason than mine. I had no clear idea beyond that, no plan for helping others; my sole wish was to plunge into the heart of some human misery.

Misery proved easy for Butler to find in Liverpool, and she attempted to relieve her suffering by identifying completely with that of other women. She went to Brownlow Hill workhouse, where she picked oakum with women tramps, petty criminals, homeless women, and prostitutes. Her experience in the oakum shed there was her first direct contact with prostitutes. Deciding that God was calling her to protect and defend prostitutes, Butler simply asked them, "Will you come with me to my home and live with me? I had a daughter once." In bringing them home to live with her family, Butler eventually recognized that it was impossible to accommodate penitent or dying prostitutes adequately there, so she rented another home to be a "House of Rest." This continued for many years and evolved into a hospital for the incurably ill. Finding alcoholism to be "the great, the hopeless obstacle" to the rehabilitation of prostitutes, Butler herself took the teetotal pledge. In the hope of forestalling the movement of working-class girls into prostitution by providing them with marketable domestic skills, she also started an industrial training school for them.

Along with these efforts to protect and train working-class girls, Butler actively campaigned for higher education for middle-class women and working-class men. She was president of the North of England Council for the Promotion of Higher

Education for Women from 1867 until 1873; the secretary of this organization was Ann Jemima Clough. Butler worked hard in petitioning Cambridge University to allow women the right to take entrance examinations, and in 1869 the university established such examinations for women. In this period she also campaigned to secure appropriation of public school endowments for the education of girls.

In 1868 Butler published her first pamphlet, *The Education and Employment of Women,* in which she argues that work for women is not a luxury but an economic necessity and that as long as women are not adequately educated for the workforce, they will be underpaid for their labor. In the following year she completed her first major literary project, the editing of *Woman's Work and Woman's Culture: A Series of Essays* (1869), for which she also wrote an introduction.

The range of essays in this volume accurately reflects the variety of reform movements in which she was involved during this period, and her introduction gives an intellectual and practical rationale for various reform proposals. First, she argues that the disabilities of women harm men as well as women because the oppressor suffers more spiritual and moral damage than the oppressed. She claims that decent work and wages will restore dignity to women and are necessary for social progress. According to Butler equality for women promises to bring advances in theological understanding, and she suggests that important theologians of the future may well be female. In returning to her preoccupation with the liberating effects of Christianity on the condition of women, she argues that the perfect equality of all human beings is the only Christian basis of society. Her *Memoir of John Grey of Dilston,* a reverential and doting biography of her deceased father, emphasizes how solidly within the Grey family tradition Butler was in her reform work; she presents the same theme in 1901 in her other family biography of her sister Harriet.

Near the end of the 1860s Butler's scattered reforming interests became focused on a single issue—the revocation of the Contagious Diseases Acts. These laws ensured that, under the plea of protecting military personnel from infection, women could be involuntarily subjected to medical examination for venereal diseases. If women refused to undergo such examination, they could be imprisoned and assigned to hard labor for six months. The first of the temporary Contagious Diseases Acts passed in 1864; it was renewed in 1866 and extended to eighteen towns in 1869. In 1866 Butler became aware of these laws, which immediately reminded her of a similar system that she had seen in France, and she was horrified that this system was being introduced in England.

Elizabeth Wolstenholme, a radical whose essay "The Education of Girls" is collected in Butler's *Woman's Work and Woman's Culture,* suggested to Butler that she lead the campaign to repeal these acts. Married and of good social position, Butler seemed less likely than other women to attract criticism for her stand on the issue. The National Association for the Repeal of the Contagious Diseases Acts was being organized, and she became head of the Ladies' National Association, which established regional branches throughout England, Scotland, and Ireland. "The Ladies Appeal and Protest," the first public protest against the acts, was written by Butler, published in the London *Daily News* on 31 December 1869, and included the names of Harriet Martineau and Florence Nightingale among its signatories. Butler and many other women got their first experiences of public life in giving speeches against the acts—behavior that offended many Victorians because such action was public and because the sexual focus of such lectures was regarded as unsavory.

The winter of 1869–1870 was a period of intense activity for Butler. In addition to addressing ninety-nine public meetings during the first year of agitation against the acts, she was writing a book and editing as well as contributing extensively to a new journal, *The Storm Bell.* In 1870 at Nottingham she published *An Appeal to the People of England, on the Recognition and Superintendence of Prostitution by Governments,* her first attack on the Contagious Diseases Acts. This work is a protest against plans by some activists who supported the acts and sought to extend jurisdiction of these laws by including the civilian population under them. Butler argues that the Contagious Diseases Acts violate the spirit of English justice through their bureaucratic use of paid spies and anonymous informants and through their punishing of only one sex (and only the poor of that sex). In her *Appeal* Butler examines prostitution as an economic rather than a moral issue: women sell themselves to earn bread and to support their families. Another concern she raises in the work is that doctors who treat venereal diseases in women must necessarily be women. The first edition of *The Shield,* a journal initiated by advocates for repeal of the acts, was published on 7 March 1870, and Butler had her first experience confronting mob violence that same year at the Colchester by-election.

In the following year Butler published *The Constitution Violated: An Essay* (1871), a book that puts the case against the Contagious Diseases Acts on consti-

Last page of a 1902 letter from Butler to Fanny Forsaith, closing with advice on tactics for women reformers (from A. S. G. Butler, Portrait of Josephine Butler, *1954)* tutional grounds. In it Butler claims that these acts contravene the two most important underpinnings of the English legal system—the Magna Carta and the right of habeas corpus. They also potentially deprive all women of the right to move about without impunity, make them liable to punishment for an offense that is not an offense in law, and allow them to be arrested and examined on suspicion alone.

Butler always insisted that the goal of the agitation was complete repeal of the Contagious Diseases Acts, not their modification. She alienated some supporters by continuing to insist that the acts be repealed when the government suggested that some revision of the law might be possible, but she remained extremely active and prominent in the repeal movement, speaking and writing on the subject throughout 1870 and 1871. Repeated repeal bills and petitions reached the legislature during the period of agitation, which ended with the suspension of the acts in 1883. In *Address Delivered at Croydon, July 3, 1871* (1871) Butler attacks the acts as legislation designed to oppress one class—the workers—and one gender—women. This impassioned piece also calls for the legislative protection of children. Published in the same year, *Sursum Corda: Annual Address to the Ladies' National Association* covers much of the same ground in an expanded form and, like *Address Delivered at Croydon*, compares state-sanctioned prostitution to American slavery. *A Few Words Addressed to True-hearted Women*, a broadsheet published in March 1872, is an attack on the Bruce amendment, which attempted to modify rather than abolish the act. Butler urged women to petition against it.

After the early 1870s Butler participated less actively in the public programs of the Ladies' National Association although she continued to write on their behalf. In *Speech Delivered by Mrs. Josephine Butler at the Fourth Annual Meeting of the "Vigilance Association for the Defence of Personal Rights," Held at Bristol, October 15th, 1874* (1874) she argues against protective factory legislation; Butler believed that in order to make prostitution less attractive to working-class women, they must have the right to earn their living in any legal occupation, regardless of how "unfeminine" such occupations may seem to middle-class legislators. She collaborated with others in publishing an expanded form of this protest against factory and shop-hours legislation in *Legislative Restrictions on the Industry of Women, Considered from the Women's Point of View* (1874). During the mid 1870s she wrote *The Hour Before the Dawn: An Appeal to Men* (1876), which argues for the moral equality of the sexes and is based on Christian teaching. In it Butler claims that because the equality of the sexes is based on a spiritual principle, it does not have to be proved, politically or biologically.

The Voice of One Crying In the Wilderness, one of her most impassioned and influential works, was first written in French as *Une voix dans le désert* (1875). As a collection of addresses given by Butler on the Continent, the book is an appeal for women to rebel against laws that men had created and that discriminated against women. In it Butler depicts herself as a female John the Baptist, the forerunner of Christ in the New Testament. She argues that women have been oppressed by the sexual double standard and that they must take moral responsibility for opposing sexual vice. The book discusses the problem of legally tolerated and state-supervised prostitution throughout Europe.

As always, one of her main concerns is what Butler termed "instrumental rape," the compulsory physical examination of women suspected of prostitution. *The Voice of One Crying in the Wilderness* persuasively argues that the examination fails the basic test of justice in that women alone, not their male sexual partners, are subject to it. These compulsory examinations not only degrade prostitutes but also dishonor every woman in the world, and Butler believes that those women who experience it are brutalized by the experience. She is convinced that it is impossible for men, whom she depicts as naturally having a moral code lower than that of women, to degrade some women and respect others; what is degradation to some women degrades all women. Butler repeatedly compares the experience of women in the vice trade to the experience of black slaves, and she argues how urgently prostitutes need emancipation. Wide-ranging in its concerns, the book also calls for the dissolution of standing armies, the establishment of courts of arbitration, and the abolition of war. *The Voice* lays out Butler's entire program of social and moral philosophy, and it was translated into Italian, German, Swedish, Danish, Spanish, Portuguese, and Russian before being translated into English by Osmund Airy.

In 1878 Butler published *Catherine of Siena: A Biography*, a study of the life of Saint Catherine that William Ewart Gladstone and other readers praised. This biography raises the same issues that she explores in her 1882 life of Jean Frederic Oberlin: the question of how one ought to live the Christian life and the difference that one courageous individual can make in his or her society. *Social Purity* (1879) argues that Christ was the only person who emphasized male sexual guilt. It presents Christianity as attacking the double standard by insisting that issues of right and wrong are independent of gender. This short work also attacks imperialism and the class

Butler in 1903

system, as does *A Grave Question That Needs Answering by the Churches of Great Britain* (1886).

Government by Police (1879) begins by insisting that men and women should work together for progress and that true liberalism contains a strong conservative spirit that preserves already established principles of liberty from those classes which, through clinging to privilege, would erode those principles. The central argument of the pamphlet is an attack on police rule, a problem that Butler believed was becoming endemic in many countries, especially France. In her view the vice police who monitored state-sanctioned prostitution in that country were educating the population through their inability to control their sexual impulses, their contempt for women, and their easy acceptance of the sexual double standard. Butler believed that such police rule also gives undue power in moral matters to the civil authorities, and she expresses her belief that the police will become corrupt and unjust in any state that relies on the police for order. To preclude this, police should be municipally controlled, decentralized, and severely restricted in powers. She displays the classic liberal suspicion of central government and bureaucracy and argues that the very existence of a police force may enfeeble the sense of responsibility in citizens. She also argues against ambitious legislative programs (even of reform), for their enforcement tends to expand police powers. Butler's suspicion of the police is so extreme that she concludes, "personal security against bodily violence . . . is itself purchased at too great a cost, if it be obtained at the price of personal liberty."

Following the suspension of the Contagious Diseases Acts in England in 1883, the acts were finally repealed in 1886. By this time Butler had turned much of her attention to repealing such legislation in Europe. As early as 1874 she had started to investigate the French system by which the state regulated brothels, and she followed this with a strenuous Continental tour. In 1877 Butler had been again in France, where in an investigation by the Paris Municipal Council she was called as a witness against the behavior of the vice police. Her *The New Abolitionists: A Narrative of a Year's Work* (1876) describes her efforts to repeal government regulation of prostitution on the Continent. In 1880 she published in *Le National*, a Brussels newspaper, an attack on the reputed traffic in women and children between England and Belgium. While many people in England received the report with incredulity, it resulted in the imprisonment of the chief of the morals police and his assistants in Belgium and the release of thirty-four English women from Belgian brothels. While it seems unlikely that few of these women were as innocent as Butler believed, the difficulty that registered prostitutes experienced in gaining permission to leave their brothels in Belgium was a genuine infringement on their civil liberties.

In 1883 Butler published *The Salvation Army in Switzerland,* a defense of the work of that organization in Switzerland, from which the Salvation Army had been expelled partly through pressure brought by the sex trade after the Salvation Army had denounced the brothels. The book contains another strong attack on the police and on the dangers that police control brings to the state and to individual liberties. Another work on Continental vice legislation and its opponents, *The Principles of the Abolitionists: An Address Delivered at Exeter Hall, Feb. 20th, 1885* (1885), states that work for the repeal of such acts has convinced Butler and her fellow workers that absolute moral equality between men and women is essential to human progress.

In 1885 Butler was also closely associated with W. T. Stead in the affair that became known as "The Maiden Tribute," his notorious exposé reported in the *Pall Mall Gazette.* Butler directed Stead to Rebecca Jarrett, a former prostitute who assisted him in procuring a twelve-year-old London girl whom her mother sold for immoral purposes. Stead was ultimately jailed for six months for criminal conspiracy, but his articles caused a sensation and resulted in the speedy passage of the Criminal Law Amendment Act of 1886, which raised the age of female consent to sixteen. Describing herself as a "revolutionist for God and for purity," Butler published a defense of Jarrett after the trial.

As she was approaching the age of sixty and had an ailing husband, Butler became less active in reform campaigns although she continued to write on behalf of women—especially those living under a version of the Contagious Diseases Acts in India. *The Revival and Extension of the Abolitionist Cause: A Letter* (1887) advocates the abolition of state-supervised prostitution throughout the British Empire and suggests that missionaries for justice and purity be sent around the world to combat such state-supervised legislation. While the Contagious Diseases Acts for India were repealed in 1888, they were replaced by the India Special Cantonment Acts, which allowed authorities to inspect brothels near military areas and even made it possible for the military to procure "sufficiently attractive" women. The Cantonment Acts were amended in 1895 after public outcry against them, but they were finally repealed only after Butler's death, during World War I.

Butler protested against imperial abuses close to home as well. In 1887 she published *Our Christianity Tested by the Irish Question,* which expresses her belief in the right of the Irish to govern themselves and sees the Coercion Acts violating the civil rights of individuals, much as the Contagious Diseases Acts had. She also founded *The Dawn,* a quarterly journal tracing the work of the abolitionists, in 1888.

After four years of illness George Butler died in 1890. Josephine Butler continued her preoccupation with the white-slave trade as she contributed the preface and appendix to Henry Elywn Thomas's *The Martyrs of Hell's Highway* (1896), a novel that recounts the purchase, abduction, forced rape, and murder of innocent preteen English girls by aristocratic roués and venal doctors with the ability to hypnotize their victims. As lurid as the tale appears, Butler writes that the novel is a fictionalized account of true events: "I have seen and known incidents and characters such as [these] and worse." Much of what appealed to Butler in the book probably resulted from its reinforcement of her hostility toward authority: the police, upper-class parliamentarians, and the medical profession are the villains of the novel, all of whom had defended the Contagious Diseases Acts she had opposed. She focused more and more on reform work outside England; she devoted much time and energy to the court-martial case of Capt. Alfred Dreyfus, the treatment of the Jews in Russia, and the Boer War.

Throughout her life Butler maintained her interest in the role of religious faith in the lives of women. Her *The Lady of Shunem* (1894) is a study of women in the Bible and is addressed to the women of England. It emphasizes the equality of men and women in marriage, reiterates Butler's theme that the fallen woman is not inferior to the respectable wife, and predicts that despite the history of women's lives all women will eventually be united.

Her last important book was *Personal Reminiscences of a Great Crusade* (1896), her attempt to write a personal history of the movement to abolish the Contagious Diseases Acts. Based on correspondence and her diaries, it traces the movement from the passage of the first of the Contagious Diseases Acts in 1864 until the 1870s. She hoped to publish a second volume, but her failing health made this impossible. Despite persecution and ostracism during her years of active agitation, Butler remembers these years as being less painful than her previous years of inaction. *Personal Reminiscences* makes clear that her underlying motive for social reform work was her belief that religion and justice were identical. Throughout her life she remained utterly contemptuous of religious sentiment that did not address social injustice. At the age of seventy-two Butler again suffered from religious doubt, but she in part resolved her doubts by repudiating the doctrine of eternal punishment, as she recounts in *The Morning Cometh: A Letter to My Children* (1903).

Josephine Butler has been raised to the equivalent of sainthood by the Church of England; in 1980 she was commemorated in the revised Anglican Book of Common Prayer, and her day of observance is 30 December, the day of her death in 1906. Butler might have seen this commemoration as fitting as she believed that her campaigns for the equality of the sexes were a God-given task, a holy crusade. As she had written years earlier in *The Constitution Violated,* "Eternal Justice has been, and will be again and again, as often as the conflict is renewed, a great force against the moral corruption of the people through the insidious force of the State proclamation of the necessity of vicious indulgence.... [We work with evil] without fear or danger, our eyes being fixed on the Light beyond."

References:

Enid Moberly Bell, *Josephine Butler: Flame of Fire* (London: Constable, 1962);

Nancy Boyd, *Three Victorian Women Who Changed Their World* (London: Macmillan, 1982);

Arthur S. G. Butler, *Portrait of Josephine Butler* (London: Faber & Faber, 1954);

Millicent G. Fawcett, *Josephine Butler* (London: The Association for Moral and Social Hygiene, 1927);

Glen Petrie, *A Singular Iniquity: The Campaigns of Josephine Butler* (London: Macmillan, 1971);

William T. Stead, *Josephine Butler: A Life Sketch* (London: Morgan & Scott, 1888).

Sir George Tomkyns Chesney

(30 April 1830 – 31 March 1895)

Pamela Shorrocks

BOOKS: *Indian Polity: A View of the System of Administration in India* (London: Longmans, Green, 1868; London & New York: Longmans, Green, 1894);

The Battle of Dorking: Reminiscences of a Volunteer, anonymous (Edinburgh & London: Blackwood, 1871); republished as *The Fall of England? The Battle of Dorking: Reminiscences of a Volunteer* (New York: Putnam, 1871); republished as *The German Conquest of England in 1875, and Battle of Dorking; or, Reminiscences of a Volunteer, Describing the Arrival of the German Armada—Destruction of the British Fleet—The Decisive Battle of Dorking—Capture of London—Downfall of the English Empire. By an Eye-witness, in 1925* (Philadelphia: Porter & Coates, 1871); republished as *The Second Armada: A Chapter of Future History* (Philadelphia: Porter & Coates, 1871);

A True Reformer, 3 volumes (Edinburgh & London: Blackwood, 1873);

The Dilemma (Edinburgh & London: Blackwood, 1876; New York: Harper, 1876);

The New Ordeal (Edinburgh & London: Blackwood, 1879);

The Private Secretary: A Novel (3 volumes, Edinburgh & London: Blackwood, 1881; 1 volume, New York: Munro, 1881);

The Lesters; or, A Capitalist's Labour, 3 volumes (London: Smith, Elder, 1893).

Sir George Tomkyns Chesney, a much-decorated army officer, government administrator, accomplished writer, and politician, was concerned for most of his professional life with military and administrative reform in both England and India. His commitment to such reform resulted from his having worked in various government departments in India and from his experiences as a front-line officer with the royal (late Bengal) engineers. He fought and was wounded in the Indian Mutiny of 1857, and this experience, which formed the colorful backdrop for the events presented in his most successful novel, enabled him to witness firsthand the inefficiencies of the British military establishment.

The youngest of four sons, Chesney was born on 30 April 1830 at Tiverton, Devon, into a highly regarded military family of Irish origin. His father, Capt. Charles Cornwallis Chesney of the Bengal artillery, died in 1830. Also involved in army reform was George Chesney's brother Col. Charles Cornwallis Chesney, a respected military historian and the first to attempt to write a nonpartisan account of the Battle of Waterloo that discussed mistakes by Gen. Arthur Wellesley, the Duke of Wellington, as well as by Napoléon Bonaparte. His interests were in educational improvements, and few officers did more to raise the intellectual standards among British army officers. The professional contributions of the brothers were merged in setting up an engineering college at Staines in 1868, and the writings of the two officers exerted wide influence in military circles in England and abroad.

Chesney attended Blundell's school at Tiverton, where his parents intended that he should prepare for a career in the medical profession. However, on receiving an Indian cadetship at the age of seventeen, he was admitted to the military college maintained by the East India Company for gunner and engineer officers at Addiscombe, and on 8 December 1848 he was made a second lieutenant in the Bengal engineers. This marked the beginning of a distinguished army life marked by his steady advancement through the ranks of lieutenant (1854), captain and then brevet major (1858), brevet lieutenant colonel (1869), colonel (1884), major general (1886), lieutenant general (1887), colonel commandant of royal engineers (1890), and general (1892). His military career, which during his active service in the Burmese War and the Indian Mutiny was as exciting and dramatic as that of the protagonist of his most popular novel, culminated with this last commission.

Following additional professional instruction at Chatham, Chesney was sent in 1850 to Calcutta, India, where he worked in the Public Works Depart-

Chesney (standing at left) and fellow military officers in January 1864

ment for seven years. During that time he met and in 1855 married Annie Louisa, daughter of George Palmer of Purneah, Bengal. The couple eventually had four sons and three daughters.

Chesney's involvement in the Indian Mutiny of 1857 helped him to formulate and focus his ideas on army reform. By May that year the mutiny involving Indian sepoys had spread to Delhi, and Chesney, whose specialized training at Addiscombe had prepared him as an expert on siege tactics and in breach fortifications, was ordered to join the column from Ambala. On 8 June, acting as Brigadier General Showers's field engineer, he participated in the battle of Badli-ke-Serai to regain the ridge in front of Delhi. As brigade major of royal engineers in the field force, he helped to plan the 11 June offensive that, by seizing the Kabul and Lahore gates, succeeded in driving the mutineers from the city. As staff officer to Maj. Richard Baird Smith, the chief engineer, Chesney distinguished himself during the ensuing months of siege and was severely wounded on 14 September when the final assault was launched. His outstanding conduct was mentioned in the *London Gazette* on 15 December 1857, and he was decorated for his service.

Chesney's experiences during these siege months convinced him of the need to reform some aspects of army management. Planning done at the convenience of bureaucrats in England rather than to ensure the availability of necessities in the field meant that severe shortages of food and ammunition occurred, and many officers, more used to civil service posts than battle-line duties, were totally unsuited for positions of high command, particularly in the unforgiving Indian climate. Such deficiencies in planning and training undermined military efficiency and discipline and resulted in high casualty rates among the ranks and their families both on and off the battlefield.

After recovering from his wounds, Chesney was appointed president of the engineering college in Calcutta, where he earned a reputation for sound decision making and respect for his communication skills in articulating issues of public interest. In 1859 he published an article in the *Calcutta Review* about the financing of public works and was invited to form a new department of accounts, of which he became head in 1860.

In 1867 he returned to England on leave, and in 1868 he published *Indian Polity: A View of the System of Administration in India,* a comprehensive and thoroughly researched policy study that, in both setting out what Chesney saw as the problems and suggesting solutions, expertly analyzed the administrative and military departments of the government of India. His program of social reform proposed improvements to transport networks such as roads, railways, and irrigation canals and monetary reforms of taxation and currency matters.

His ideas on army reform attacked the attachment that the military had for a promotion system based on ability to buy commissions rather than on merit to serve and for a centralized supply procedure that too often resulted in a scarcity of provisions and equipment. Military operations of both the British and Indian armies were impaired by the protocols Chesney attacked, and he proposed urgent and radical restructuring to promote individual officer responsibility and the awarding of commissions on the basis of merit. His study attracted attention as an authoritative, masterly textbook on the subject and was consulted as a source document when *The Indian Constitutional Law Guide in Catechetic Form* (1901) was compiled. Chesney's work became a valuable permanent guide for the civil service, and many of his suggestions for change were implemented.

Around 1868 Chesney helped to set up the Royal Indian Civil Engineering College at Cooper's Hill, Staines. He selected the site for the school, organized the teaching curriculum, outlined the standards of professional education there, and chose highly qualified tutors to ensure that those standards were met. The college was established as part of a government policy to improve the organization and education of the British military, an end to which one of Chesney's older brothers, Charles Cornwallis, was also committed following his appointment as a member of the royal commission on military education that same year. Chesney had returned to India when the college opened in 1871, but he was recalled to become its first president.

In addition to his duties as college president, Chesney published *The Battle of Dorking: Reminiscences of a Volunteer,* his first work of fiction, in 1871. Written anonymously as a serial in *Blackwood's Magazine* in May, it had both popular appeal and serious purpose as a means of criticizing army recruitment policy at home.

The imaginary tale concerns an invasion of England by a victorious German force and is told fifty years after these events by a member of the unprepared home volunteer defense that had been sent out to defend England. The account graphically sets out the tragic consequences of the loss of English liberties and ways of life under occupation, and its didactic tone contrasts the highly professional, well led and equipped German armies with the hastily assembled English forces, largely comprising untrained and inexperienced officers and men.

This narrative was Chesney's first attempt at what became a favorite literary method of using a fictional but credible context to express his disquiet over army recruitment, organization, and administration. *The Battle of Dorking* vividly exposes the risks to national security that are posed by a defense that is unable in times of crisis to call on a trained, disciplined, and well-equipped national reserve force led by competent officers. The anonymous article was the first pamphlet by a member of the British military establishment to criticize the British military openly. It was published in several editions; translated into many languages, including French, German, and Dutch; and inspired *Our Hero; or, Who Wrote "The Battle of Dorking"?* (1871), a satiric counterblast published under the pseudonyms of Sergeant Blower and Cheeks the Marine.

In 1873 Blackwood published, again serially, *A True Reformer,* the first of Chesney's semi-autobiographical novels in which he skillfully weaves his personal experience, aspirations, and frustrations into a work of popular fiction. Charles West, a high-ranking army officer who is the protagonist, gives up his commission to enter Parliament and is bent on introducing reform legislation. He becomes secretary of state, and after a dramatic all-night session in the House of Commons, he sees his bill become law before he returns home the next morning to his beautiful young wife, who collapses and dies in his arms. This typically winning Victorian mix of high romance and political drama was a popular success and provided an ideal vehicle for Chesney, using West as his mouthpiece, publicly to expose army mismanagement and to advance a coherent program for correcting its worst excesses.

In 1876 Chesney's best-known and openly autobiographical novel, *The Dilemma,* used the same fictional devices to reveal the incompetence of the British military in India and to analyze the character and organization of the native Indian soldiery. This novel, the most popular of his works, is an action-packed romance set amid the events of the Indian Mutiny. An incident in which British army officers and their families are attacked by mutinous Indian sepoys provides the situation for emotional entanglements and heroic deeds of passion and principle.

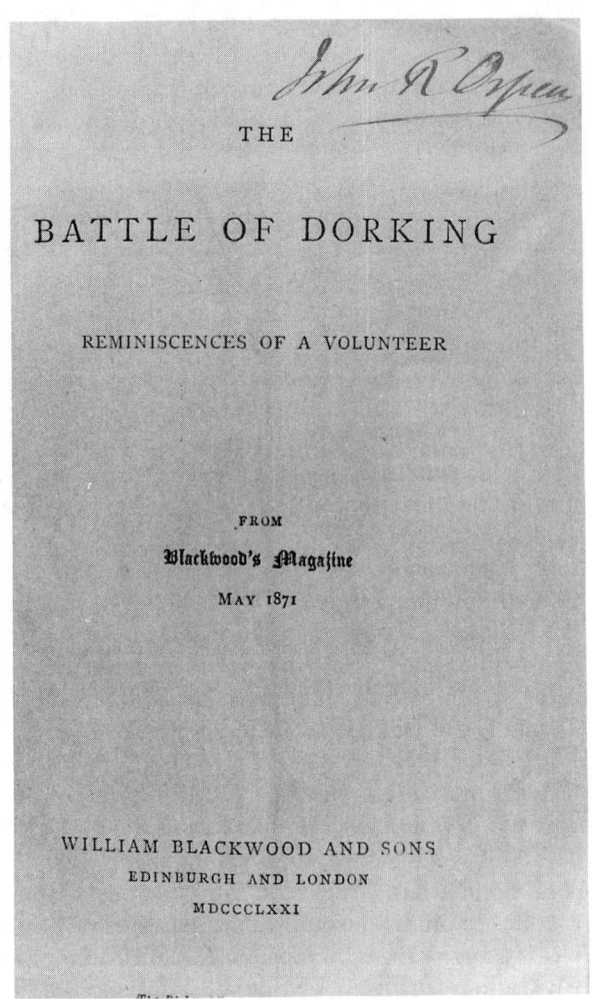

Title page for Chesney's first novel, the popularity of which convinced him that fiction was an excellent way to campaign for military reforms

The fictional events, in which a senior officer—aging, inept, and inexperienced—is relieved of his command by a dashing young low-ranking officer who is killed in an act of courage and self-sacrifice, could have been written from factual accounts of the siege of Delhi. Indeed, the fiction is eclipsed by the factual records of J. W. Fortescue's *History of the British Army* (volume 13, 1930), in which the high number of casualties during the final assault on Delhi on 14 September 1857 is blamed on ineffectual leadership. Nicholson, a low-ranking but much-respected officer, had assumed some duties of command and was killed in a near-impossible attempt to lead an assault down a narrow gully.

In 1879 Chesney published *The New Ordeal*, a novel which, like *The Dilemma*, contrasts wartime romance with the horror and barbarity of war. As a means of reducing conflict to a matter of parliamentary convenience, the government proposes that differences should be settled through a contemporary version of the medieval joust, in which chosen champions using the latest deadly weapons fight according to a formal set of rules under a winner-takes-all policy. This "new ordeal" was to be arranged by impartial international commissioners appointed by neutral powers. Chesney's self-mocking style and biting parody strip war of its illusions and grandeur and highlight the irony of pronouncing that waging war according to rules is "civilized" while not adhering to them is barbaric.

In 1880, after nine years as president of the Royal Indian Civil Engineering College, Chesney returned to India and took up the post of secretary to the military department of the government of India. Drawing on personal experience as bases for his romantic dramas that tend toward philosophic studies of the nature of morality, he continued to write successful works of fiction. The central character of *The Private Secretary* (1881) wishes to achieve an ambition no greater than marrying his poor but worthy secretary and dedicating his wealth to doing good.

Chesney also continued to accrue success and honors in his military career. On 24 May 1883 he was made a companion of the Order of the Star of India, and three years later, when his tenure as secretary of the military department ended, he became a companion of the Order of the Indian Empire on 30 July 1886. On 17 June of that year he had been appointed to be a military member of the governor-general's council, a position equivalent to that of secretary of state for war in England. On 21 June 1887 Chesney was made a companion of the Order of the Bath (military division), and on 1 January 1890 he became a knight commander.

During Chesney's five-year term as a member of the governor-general's council, Frederick Sleigh Roberts, later first Earl Roberts of Khandar, was commander in chief of all Indian forces. Roberts was a popular administrative and military reformer, and under his authority the efficiency of both the English army services in India and the loyal native troops greatly increased. Drunkenness among the British ranks was curbed; a higher standard of marksmanship was made obligatory; and better nursing and living accommodations became standard. When persuading Indian regiments to participate in a national defense scheme, account was taken of their traditions and culture, and a generally liberal attitude encouraged a style of life that was more humane and dignified than it had been for both British and Indian armies.

Roberts, who believed more strongly in strategic communications than in fortifications, began to implement the recommendations for improving road, rail, and telegraph networks that Chesney had proposed twenty years before in his Indian policy review. Defenses of the principal harbors and of the Indian frontier were nearly completed, and during this important time in the military administration of India, Roberts valued Chesney's services as military member of the governor-general's council. Roberts wrote of Chesney that "No commander-in-chief ever had so staunch a supporter."

In 1891 Chesney returned permanently to England and wrote a series of political articles for the July, August, and December numbers of *Nineteenth Century*. He was regarded as an expert on Indian affairs, and with the prospect of a successful parliamentary career ahead of him these articles applied the lessons of Chesney's Indian experience to reforms of the army at home. He wanted to see a military system that was professionally administered, with its political connections severed, and he knew that family wealth and privilege were the bases of both military and political influence. Those whose power of public speaking best fitted them to represent and maintain the position of the dominant party went into politics; the rest joined the class of military officers, their fitness to command being the least consideration. Chesney proposed that officers be appointed by merit only—no commissions would be purchased. Promotion also would not be automatic but according to ability, and an age of retirement would be enforced: colonels at age fifty-five, majors at fifty, and captains at forty-five. An additional mechanism would ensure the removal of incompetents, so that only fit, able, and professional officers could rise through the ranks.

Chesney's proposals to remedy his other long-standing complaints about central planning and the amateur status of national defense were similarly unequivocal. He proposed that the responsibility for supply decisions should belong to the individual officer in the field, and (forever mindful of the nightmare visions presented in *The Battle of Dorking*) he insisted that a permanent home militia should be established, trained, and led by battle-hardened officers. In 1892 he was elected as the Conservative member of Parliament for Oxford, and in the House of Commons he spoke occasionally on questions concerning India or army administration.

His final novel, *The Lesters; or, A Capitalist's Labour* (1893), is a moral tale of lost opportunity regained. Through the perspective of a penurious elderly man the novel presents a rather nostalgic portrait of the narrator as a young, wealthy, and well-married member of Parliament.

Just as Chesney was starting to impress parliamentary colleagues with his commonsense advice and sound knowledge, he died suddenly of angina pectoris at his house, 27 Inverness Terrace, London, on 31 March 1895. He was buried at Englefield Green, Surrey, on 5 April. He was survived by his wife and their four sons and three daughters. His friends presented a portrait of Chesney to his widow, and a Chesney gold medal was founded by the Royal United Service Institution in May 1900.

Sir George Tomkyns Chesney was both an accomplished, persuasive writer and a professional, successful soldier, and his obituary in the *Illustrated London News* on 16 April 1895 acknowledged his accomplishments in these dual careers by remarking, "He proved the pen to be as effective a weapon as the sword." He was a man of ideals, and his role as a military officer and administrator revealed the urgent need for army reorganization. As a writer of formal, meticulously detailed government reports and an author of popular fiction, he used his literary skills to direct his criticism of the military establishment toward a constructive program of reform.

His work as a novelist began late, when he was forty-three. He was no literary innovator and worked in the semi-autobiographical roman à clef tradition. His contribution to the genre was the extent to which he used fictional devices to criticize the military establishment or to provide a forum for discussion of political solutions.

Not all of his recommendations for improving the organization and administration of the British army were carried out at the time. As late as 1914, when an edition of *The Battle of Dorking* was published, G. H. Powell wrote in a dust-jacket blurb: "No book has ever touched the public conscience more strongly than this." Powell adds in his introduction that Chesney's criticisms were still relevant to the European political situation at the start of World War I.

Although the arguments for military reform had been thoroughly aired, Chesney's proposals urging the development of a volunteer movement to secure the national defense had remained largely unheeded. But his influence continued to be felt, and his recommendations, particularly about military government departments in India, were gradually implemented. His educational reforms, worked out when Chesney was president of the Royal Indian Civil Engineering College and his elder brother was a member of the royal commission, did much to raise the standards of army education not only in England but on the Continent and in America.

Reference:

G. H. Powell, Introduction to Chesney's *The Battle of Dorking: Reminiscences of a Volunteer* (London: Richards, 1914).

Frances Power Cobbe
(4 December 1822 – 5 April 1904)

Susan Hamilton
University of Alberta

BOOKS: *An Essay on Intuitive Morals, Being an Attempt to Popularise Ethical Science,* 2 volumes, anonymous (*Part I: Theory of Morals,* London: Longman, Brown, Green & Longmans, 1855; *Part II: Practice of Morals,* London: Chapman, 1857; revised and republished, 1 volume, Boston: Crosby, Nichols, 1859; London: Trübner, 1864); republished as *The Theory of Intuitive Morals, Being a Corrected Reprint of the Third Edition of An Essay on Intuitive Morals, with a New Preface and Appendices* (London: Swan Sonnenschein, 1902);

Friendless Girls, and How to Help Them: Being an Account of the Preventive Mission at Bristol (London: Emily Faithfull, 1861);

The Sick in Workhouses: Who They Are and How They Should Be Treated (London: J. Nisbet, 1861);

The Workhouse as an Hospital (London, 1861);

Female Education, and How It Would Be Affected by University Examinations: A Paper Read at the Social Science Congress, London, 1862 (London: Emily Faithfull, 1862);

Essays on the Pursuits of Women (London: Emily Faithfull, 1863);

The Red Flag in John Bull's Eyes (London: Emily Faithfull, 1863);

Rejoinder to Mrs. Stowe's Reply to the Address of Women of England (London: Emily Faithfull, 1863);

The Religious Demands of the Age: A Reprint of the Preface to the London Edition of the Collected Works of Theodore Parker (Boston: Walker, Wise, 1863);

Thanksgiving: A Chapter of Religious Duty (London: Trübner, 1863);

Broken Lights: An Inquiry into the Present Condition and Future Prospects of Religious Faith (London: Trübner, 1864; Boston: Tilton, 1864);

The Cities of the Past (London: Trübner, 1864);

Italics: Brief Notes on Politics, People, and Places in Italy, in 1864 (London: Trübner, 1864);

Religious Duty (London: Trübner, 1864; Boston: W. V. Spencer, 1864);

Studies New and Old of Ethical and Social Subjects (London: Trübner, 1865; Boston: W. V. Spencer, 1866);

The Confessions of a Lost Dog: Reported by Her Mistress F. P. Cobbe (London: Griffith & Farran, 1867);

Hours of Work and Play (London: Trübner, 1867);

Dawning Lights: An Inquiry Concerning the Secular Results of the New Reformation (London: Whitfield, 1868);

Why Women Desire the Franchise (London: London National Society for Women's Suffrage, 1869);

Our Policy: An Address to Women Concerning the Suffrage (London: London National Society for Women's Suffrage, 1870);

Darwinism in Morals, and Other Essays (London & Edinburgh: Williams & Norgate, 1872; Boston: G. H. Ellis, 1883);

Doomed To Be Saved (London: Williams & Norgate, 1874);

Essays on the Life and Death, and the Evolution of the Social Sentiment (London, 1874);

The Hopes of the Human Race, Hereafter and Here (London & Edinburgh: Williams & Norgate, 1874; New York: J. Miller, 1876);

False Beasts and True: Essays on Natural and Unnatural History (London: Ward, Lock & Tyler, 1876);

Re-Echoes (London & Edinburgh: Williams & Norgate, 1876; Leipzig: B. Tauchnitz, 1877);

The Age of Science: A Newspaper of the Twentieth Century, as Merlin Nostradamus (London: Ward, Lock & Tyler, 1877);

The British Medical Manifesto, by Cobbe and Ellen Elcum Rees (N.p., 1881);

The Duties of Women: A Course of Lectures (London: Williams & Norgate / Boston: G. H. Ellis, 1881);

The Higher Expediency: Address . . . to the Members of the Richmond Athenaeum, March 6th, 1882 (London: Victoria Street Society for the Protection of Animals from Vivisection, United with the International Association for the Total Suppression of Vivisection, 1882);

The Janus of Science (London: Victoria Street Society, 1882);

The Peak in Darien, with Some Other Inquiries Touching Concerns of the Soul and the Body (London: Williams & Norgate, 1882; Boston: G. H. Ellis, 1882);

Agnostic Morality (London & New York, 1883);

Light in Dark Places (London: Victoria Street Society, 1883);

The Study of Physiology as a Branch of Education (London: Victoria Street Society, 1883);

The New Benefactor of Humanity (Westminster, 1884);

A Faithless World (London: Williams & Norgate, 1885; Boston: G. H. Ellis, 1885);

Rest in the Lord, and Other Small Pieces (London: Pewtress, 1887);

Concerning Immortality (Chicago, 1888);

The Scientific Spirit of the Age, and Other Pleas and Discussions (London: Smith, Elder, 1888);

The Friend of Man: and His Friends,—the Poets (London: G. Bell, 1889);

The Modern Rack: Papers on Vivisection (London: Sonnenschein, 1889);

Vivisection in America: I. How It Is Taught; II. How It Is Practised, by Cobbe and Benjamin Bryan (London: Sonnenschein, 1889);

The Oubliettes of Science (Westminster: Victoria Street Society, 1890);

Health and Holiness (London: G. Bell, 1891);

Public Money: An Enquiry Concerning an Item of Its Expenditure (London: Victoria Street Society, 1892);

Life of Frances Power Cobbe, by Herself, 2 volumes (London: Richard Bently, 1894; Boston & New York: Houghton, Mifflin, 1894); revised edition, 1 volume (London: Sonnenschein, 1904);

The Divine Law of Love, in Its Application to the Relations of Man to the Lower Animals (London: National Antivivisection Society, 1895);

On Jesuit Doctrines Concerning the Rights of Animals (London, 1895).

SELECTED PERIODICAL PUBLICATIONS–
UNCOLLECTED: "The Rights of Man, Claims of Brutes," *Fraser's,* 68 (November 1863): 586-602;

"The Nineteenth-Century," *Fraser's,* 69 (April 1864): 481-494;

"The Morals of Literature," *Fraser's,* 70 (July 1864): 124-133;

"Philosophy of the Poor-Laws," *Fraser's,* 70 (September 1864): 373-394;

"Indigent Classes–Their Schools, and Dwellings," *Fraser's,* 73 (February 1866): 143-160;

"Conventional Laws of Society," *Fraser's,* 74 (November 1866): 667-673;

"Household Service," *Fraser's,* 77 (January 1868): 121-134;

"Criminals, Idiots, Women, and Minors: Is the Classification Sound?," *Fraser's,* 78 (December 1868): 777-794;

"The Defects of Women, and How to Remedy Them," *Putnam's,* 4 (1869): 226-233;

"Consciousness of Dogs," *Quarterly Review,* 133 (October 1872): 419-451;

"Life after Death," *Theological Review* (October 1872–July 1873);

"Dogs Whom I Have Met," *Cornhill,* 26 (December 1872): 662-678;

"Heteropathy, Aversion, Sympathy," *Theological Review* (January 1874);

"The Moral Aspects of Vivisection," *New Quarterly,* 4 (April 1875): 222-237;

"Sacrificial Medicine," *Cornhill,* 32 (October 1875): 427-438;

"Mr. Lowe and the Vivisection Act," *Contemporary Review,* 29 (February 1877): 335-347;

"The Little Health of Ladies," *Contemporary Review*, 31 (January 1878): 276-296;

"Wife-Torture in England," *Contemporary Review*, 32 (April 1878): 55-87;

"Tender Vivisection," *Scotsman*, 13 January 1881;

"The Medical Profession and Its Morality," *Modern Review* (April 1881);

"Vivisection: Four Replies," *Fortnightly Review*, new series 31 (January 1882): 88-104;

"Zoöphily," *Cornhill*, 45 (March 1882): 279-288;

"A Few Rabbits," *Manchester Guardian*, 14 December 1886;

"The Education of the Emotions," *Fortnightly Review*, new series 43 (February 1888): 223-236;

"The Scientific Spirit of the Age," *Contemporary Review*, 54 (July 1888): 126-139;

"The Ethics of Zoöphily," *Contemporary Review*, 68 (October 1895): 497-508;

"Lord Lister and Painless Vivisection," *Manchester Guardian*, 14 October 1898.

OTHER: Theodore Parker, *The Collected Works of Theodore Parker*, 14 volumes, edited by Cobbe (London: Trübner, 1863-1871);

"The Final Cause of Woman," in *Woman's Work and Woman's Culture*, edited by Josephine E. Butler (London: Macmillan, 1869);

Alone to the Alone: Prayers for Theists, by Several Contributors, edited by Cobbe (London & Edinburgh: Williams & Norgate, 1871);

Bernard's Martyrs: A Comment on Claude Bernard's Leçons de Physiologie Opératoire, edited by Cobbe (Westminster: Office of the Society for the Protection of Animals from Vivisection, 1879).

Frances Power Cobbe, journalist, workhouse philanthropist, activist, and antivivisectionist, was among the best-known feminist thinkers of her day. The "oldest New Woman now living on the planet," as the *Review of Reviews* called her in 1894, she was a prominent participant in the reform movements to improve poor relief; a spokeswoman for Victorian women's educational and employment opportunities; an indefatigable defender of so-called redundant women; a witty and formidable critic of the marriage contract; and a passionate advocate of woman suffrage and right to bodily integrity. She was also the leading figure in the British antivivisection movement, instrumental in the passage of the 1876 Vivisection Act and in establishing the Victorian Street Society, one of the first antivivisection societies in England. Though her work is now little known, and infrequently taught, she is a central figure in any assessment of the range and diversity of the aims, strategies, and philosophies of Victorian feminisms.

Frances Power Cobbe was born on 4 December 1822 at the family estate of Newbridge House, County Dublin, Ireland. Her father, Charles Cobbe, was an Anglo-Irish landowner whose remote interest in his only daughter influenced Cobbe's ideas on women's social duties, especially daughters' obligations to their parents. The youngest of five children, Cobbe was closest to her ailing mother, Frances Conway Cobbe, and cared for her until her death in 1847 when Cobbe was twenty-five. In her 1894 autobiography, *Life of Frances Power Cobbe, by Herself*, she calls her mother's death "the great sorrow" of her life; it was a key turning point. Frances Conway Cobbe had been "the one being in the world whom I truly loved through all the passionate years of youth and early womanhood; the only one who really loved me. . . . No relationship in all the world, I think, can ever be so perfect as that of mother and daughter under such circumstances."

Until her mother's death Cobbe had remained tied to the family home. A two-year sojourn at a fashionable school for young ladies in Brighton when she was fourteen was remarkable chiefly for its irrelevance: "a better system than theirs could scarcely have been devised had it been designed to attain the maximum of cost and labour and the minimum of solid results." Life on the family estate was spent studying history, astronomy, architecture, and heraldry, and avoiding the endless round of social visits that Cobbe found so tedious. Once her mother died, life at Newbridge House grew increasingly intolerable. Her father, a severe Evangelical, reacted strongly to Cobbe's revelation of religious doubt and her refusal to attend church or participate in family prayers. Her "confession"–prompted by her insistence on women's moral autonomy–was a clear sign that Cobbe would no longer bow to her father's authority.

Charles Cobbe threw his daughter out of the family home, threatening to disinherit her. She spent some ten months on her brother's farm in Donegal before being recalled by her father to take up the position of housekeeper. The arrangement was always a cold one, meeting the needs of the father for a household manager and the daughter for a roof over her head but never kindling an affection or confidence between them. Cobbe felt herself to be "all the time in a sort of moral Coventry, under a vague atmosphere of disapprobation wherein all I said was listened to cautiously as likely to conceal some poisonous heresy." Her final memorial to him in her autobiography illustrates the cool, reserved nature of their relationship: "His mistakes and errors, such as they were, arose solely from a fiery temper and a despotic will, nourished rather than checked by his ideas concerning the rights of parents, husbands, masters, and employers; and from his narrow religious creed. Such as he was, everyone honoured, some feared, and many loved him."

The first volume of Cobbe's first book, *An Essay on Intuitive Morals, Being an Attempt to Popularise Ethical Science,* was published anonymously in 1855 out of respect for her father's fears of public embarrassment. Her concern for his wishes indicates the balance Cobbe sought between the duty she owed Charles Cobbe as his daughter and her right to her own beliefs and moral values. The essay itself maps out Cobbe's religious and philosophical beliefs in a rational God to whom an individual's paramount duties belonged, taking necessary precedence over duties to family and friends. Cobbe's rationalist beliefs allowed her to claim an absolute moral autonomy for women, as for all individuals, that made them intellectually and spiritually equal with men while still stressing their relative duties to friends and family.

In later works Cobbe elaborated her understanding of women's moral autonomy, using the daughter's role as a kind of limit case. In papers such as "The Limits of Obedience of Daughters" (1865) and "Self-Development and Self-Abnegation" (1865) and in her widely read lectures, *The Duties of Women* (1881), the role of the daughter is both universal and inescapable. The need to blend care for parents, which Cobbe terms "primary benevolence," with the daughter's right to moral autonomy leads to a careful delineation in Cobbe's work of duties owed and responsibilities claimed. Cobbe insists that parents' needs for domestic companionship or care must be paramount in both a son's and a daughter's duties. On the other hand, daughters were within their rights to assess parental demands for their justness and rationality. Any parental demand rooted in selfishness, whimsy, or mere arbitrary power was to be rejected. As she explains in "Self-Development and Self-Abnegation" a child is "always free (and may be morally bound) to resist such a demand and to act to the best of his or her judgement independently thereof." On their side selfish parents were both morally reprehensible and simply wrong to insist on actions that limited their daughters' intellectual and moral development.

Charles Cobbe's death in 1857 left Cobbe free from family duties and able to pursue unencumbered the full range of her intellectual and moral interests. It also left her relatively impoverished. Newbridge House passed to her eldest brother and his wife, leaving Cobbe without a domestic role to play

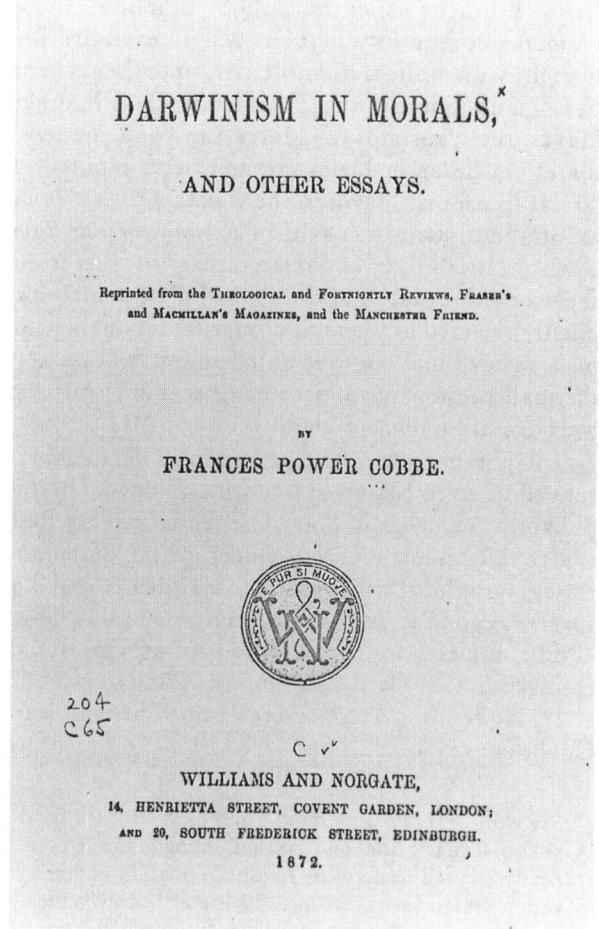

Title page for one of Cobbe's collections of essays

and effectively without a home. She was left only £200 per annum, a substantial sum by most estimations but far less than the £5,000 per annum her eldest brother received. The amount allowed her an independent life, only on a different scale from that she had so far enjoyed. Her first course of action was a lengthy trip. Cutting off her hair so she would not need a lady's maid, Cobbe made her way through Europe and "the East," visiting Egypt (before it was a regular stop on Cook's Tours for English tourists), Lebanon, Palestine, Syria, Italy, and Greece. She recorded some of her experiences and observations in an unpublished manuscript, "A Lady's Ride through Palestine, with a Journey to Baalbec in 1858."

In Italy, Cobbe met a group of independent, intellectual, and artistic women who were living the kind of emancipated life she was embarking upon for herself. These women—including the American actress Charlotte Cushman, sculptors Harriet Hosmer, Emma Stebbins, and Mary Lloyd, and painter

Rosa Bonheur–offered Cobbe a model of a women's community that she was to establish for herself, with some trial and error, upon her return to England. Some of these women, such as Matilda Hayes, the translator of George Sand and companion of Cushman and later Hosmer, were reputed to "dress like a man down to the waist." Others, such as Bonheur–who was said in *Reminiscences of Rosa Bonheur* (1910) to have declared that "the fact is, in the way of the male, I like only the bulls I paint"–explicitly rejected any sexual or marital relations with men, instead making substantial amounts of money through their work and causing scandals as they rode around unchaperoned.

Upon her return to England in 1858 Cobbe arranged to go to Bristol to live with and assist in the philanthropic work of Mary Carpenter and her Red Lodge reformatory for delinquent girls. Contemporary biographical notices state that Cobbe found the spartan regime at Red Lodge too trying to stay long. Cobbe appears to have insisted on an emotional connection that Carpenter was unwilling to give, as a 28 November 1859 letter from Carpenter to Cobbe suggests:

> My work and my cause require and must have the devotion of all my heart and soul and strength. I have not nearly enough to do what I wish; I could do nothing without the revelations which the Father has given me throughout . . . I thank you much for your love, and know that you think much better of me than I deserve.

Whatever the limits of her personal relationship with Carpenter may have been, Cobbe points to this time at the Red Lodge as definitive in her growing political consciousness. Years later, in her preface to *The Duties of Women,* Cobbe indicates that it was "only after I had laboured for some time with my honoured friend Mary Carpenter, at Bristol, and learned to feel intense interest in the legislation which might possibly mitigate the evils of crime and pauperism, that I seriously asked myself . . . *why* I should not seek for political representation as the direct and natural means of aiding every reform I had at heart." Deciding to leave Red Lodge, Cobbe moved to Durdham Down where she worked briefly visiting workhouses and published her first periodical article, "Workhouse Sketches," based on these experiences, with *Macmillan's Magazine* in April 1861. This piece was later included in *Essays on the Pursuits of Women* (1863).

In the early 1860s Cobbe was established as a regular front-page "leader" writer for the London daily newspaper the *Echo,* earning £300 per annum. These leaders, some of which were later collected in *Re-Echoes* (1876), were unsigned editorials on a range of current public issues, providing information and opinion in the form of personal commentary. Cobbe was a pioneer newspaperwoman; only one or two other women held regular staff positions on London papers at that time. Her leaders allowed her to bring a variety of women's issues to a wide audience, with the authority that came with the nongendered, unsigned persona she adopted.

The effect of Cobbe's *Echo* work is only beginning to be known. Although, for example, Cobbe is understood to have played a role in bringing domestic violence to public awareness with her April 1878 *Contemporary Review* article, "Wife-Torture in England," it now seems that she used her position as leader writer to bring this topic to the public as early as 1869. From that year the *Echo* carried second leaders on domestic violence, some of them readily identifiable as the work of Cobbe. Reports and one-paragraph news items from the *Echo* concerning domestic violence also found their way into feminist journals such as the *Women's Suffrage Journal* (whose editor, Lydia Becker, was a good friend of Cobbe's) and the *Englishwoman's Review,* which reprinted a long report of one case of domestic violence from the *Echo*. Cobbe's contribution to the domestic violence cause cannot then be limited to the effects of one periodical article, as some recent historians have claimed. Feminist contemporaries certainly recognized Cobbe as a central figure in the movement against marital assault, insisting that "Wife Torture in England" led directly to the drafting of the 1878 Matrimonial Causes Act. A reference in a 1 June 1878 *Women's Suffrage Journal* article to "the benefits conferred upon poor and suffering women through the political . . . influence of able . . . leaders of their own sex" also points to Cobbe and her work.

At the same time that Cobbe began regular newspaper writing she also began living with Mary Lloyd, who remained her lifetime domestic companion. Cobbe made few public statements about this relationship, saying in her autobiography, "Of a friendship like this, which has been to my later life as my mother's affection was to my youth, I shall not be expected to say more." But it is clear from Cobbe's correspondence with her close friends that the relationship was a "female marriage," an arrangement that gave Cobbe the domestic, emotional, and sexual life she wanted.

Cobbe also stepped boldly onto the national feminist stage in the early 1860s, moving confidently and with great authority in the key feminist circles of this period. Her 1862 presentation at the National Association for the Promotion of Social

Science Congress, *Female Education, and How It Would Be Affected by University Examinations,* brought her to the attention of Becker and Barbara Bodichon of the Langham Place Circle. She joined Emily Davies, who became a close friend, at the Kensington Discussion Society, a group dedicated to the discussion of women's issues. She also became a member of the Married Women's Property Committee chaired by Bodichon and was briefly a member of the Executive Committee of the London National Society for Woman's Suffrage.

Her writings for periodicals such as *Macmillan's, Fraser's Magazine,* the *Fortnightly Review,* and the *Theological Review* range over ethics, travel, and workhouse sketches. She makes the case for improved treatment of workhouse inmates, particularly infants and children, and argues for reform of the Poor Law. But the substantial bulk of her work focuses on women. Her articles for *Fraser's* and *Macmillan's* on women's issues—later collected and published with her Social Science Congress paper as *Essays on the Pursuits of Women*—inaugurated Cobbe's career as a feminist journalist, the only woman of her day to write regularly on women's issues from a feminist perspective in the mainstream press. It is important not to underestimate this achievement. While other Victorian feminists such as Becker and Bessie Raynor Parkes worked to found a specialist press, Cobbe's task was to make the case for feminism to a general, not specialist, public. That she did so in order to make a living is all the more remarkable. Certainly her £200 patrimony allowed Cobbe to pick her battles, to enter only into those debates that she felt were important. Nonetheless, the fact that Cobbe doubled her patrimony in most of her working years indicates that however selective she may have been in her topics, her feminist writing was effective and in demand.

Cobbe's writings of the 1860s establish for the most part the range and tenor of her feminism. Cobbe's periodical writing rarely focuses on the vote as its primary objective, although suffrage is not completely absent from her work. Such pieces as *Why Women Desire the Franchise* (1869) and *Our Policy: An Address to Women Concerning the Suffrage* (1870) indicate her strong support for the suffrage campaign. But Cobbe's periodical writings on marriage, charity work, and celibacy, for example, offer a different focus. In "Celibacy v. Marriage," published in the February 1862 *Fraser's* and included in *Essays on the Pursuits of Women,* Cobbe argues that economic pressures threaten to disrupt the moral work that marriage should perform, producing mercenary husbands who consider wives to be slaves and perverting women's "real political influence" by forcing them to be obsessed with superficial social polish. The single life is altogether preferable until such a time as marriage can be pursued in a disinterested way—that is, motivated only by love. Cobbe's apparent concern with the integrity of marriage allows her to argue for expanded educational and employment opportunities for all women. Marriage reform opens up a space for reforms in all areas of women's lives. Only when women need never marry in order to live a decent, satisfying, and complete life will marriage be truly disinterested and thus capable of performing its vital moral work.

Cobbe's argument here is repeated, expanded and much sharper in tone, in the November 1862 *Fraser's* and in *Essays on the Pursuits of Women* as "What Shall We Do with Our Old Maids?," a retort to W. R. Greg's "Why Are Women Redundant?" In response to a perceived "excess" of women, Greg's article had proposed making "the single life" as difficult as possible for women, advocating a regulated female emigration scheme and promoting the world of the "demi-monde" as a lesson in allure for middle-class women. In the name of the very ideal of marriage that Greg sees as threatened by improved social conditions for single women, Cobbe argues for expansion:

> for the very end of promoting marriage—that is, such marriage as it is alone desirable to promote—we should pursue a precisely opposite course to that suggested by the Reviewer or his party. Instead of leaving single women as helpless as possible, and their labour as ill rewarded—instead of dinning into their ears from childhood that marriage is their one vocation and concern in life, and securing afterwards if they miss it that they shall find no other vocation or concern;—instead of all this, we shall act on the reverse principle. We shall make single life so free and happy that they shall have not one temptation to change it save the only temptation which ought to determine them—namely, love.

Other essays use this idea to similar effect. "Criminals, Idiots, Women and Minors: Is the Classification Sound?" (*Fraser's,* December 1868) calls for changes to married women's property laws by arguing that such reforms would provide women with the material means and economic clout to formulate marriages that match the prevalent ideal. In an interesting twist Cobbe argues that in order to attain perfect marriage, women need financial and propertied autonomy: "Is perfect love to be called out by perfect dependence? Does an empty purse necessarily imply a full heart?" As in all of her writing, due deference to the idea of marriage as women's natural lot permits Cobbe to explore fully the better life that single women lead. For Cobbe, unmarried women

Hengwrt, the manor house where Cobbe lived with companion Mary Lloyd and wrote her autobiography

of independent means could lead lives of domestic comfort, emotional fulfillment, and intellectual reward. Unencumbered by men's domestic demands and expectations for devoted service, women made communities with each other. For Cobbe, celibacy was a radical opportunity for a kind of domestic comfort and fulfillment that no man could be part of.

By the end of the decade Cobbe was at the forefront of an increasingly confident, organized feminist movement. Her writings in this period, both in the mainstream and the specialist press, attest to Cobbe's importance. In "The Final Cause of Woman," her contribution to Josephine E. Butler's landmark collection of feminist essays, *Woman's Work and Woman's Culture* (1869), Cobbe argues against any conception of "woman as Adjective" or relative creature, insisting that "woman as Noun" has rights and duties of her own. Cobbe's contribution here, as elsewhere, points to the care with which contemporary assessments of Victorian feminisms should be made. In "The Final Cause of Woman" both equality and difference emerge as central to Cobbe's political thought. Like Davies, Bodichon, and Helen Taylor, Cobbe insisted on women's equal political, legal, and economic rights. But Cobbe also believed in profound differences between the sexes—differences that made women naturally more compassionate, nurturing, and pure than men. Her acceptance of those virtues assigned to women by Victorian domestic ideology formed the basis of what might be called her "woman's culture" perspective. She celebrated what she perceived to be the distinctiveness of women's views and the contributions that women could make to society when unobstructed by legal, social, and economic restrictions. Freed from such restrictions, women would be able to develop fully both their potential "equalities" with men and, as importantly, their real differences.

Cobbe's "difference feminism" means that her conception of women's social and political role is based on an understanding of "womanly nature" that we might now find overly prescriptive or politically debilitating. Indeed, by the time of her death Cobbe's difference feminism already seemed old-fashioned. In the 15 October 1905 issue of the feminist *Englishwoman's Review,* a critic rereading Cobbe's *Duties of Women* could already point to her work as a measure of "the enormous strides made [in the feminist movement] . . . since the lectures were delivered." For Cobbe, woman's difference, no matter how conservative or old-fashioned, was her political and social strength.

Cobbe's difference feminism also undergirds the terms of her engagement with the campaign against the use of live animals in scientific research, a cause that occupied most of Cobbe's attention from her initial involvement in the early 1870s until her death. By the time she looked back on her own life as she wrote her autobiography in 1894, she found she had written more than 320 books, articles, and pamphlets for the movement. Cobbe's antivivisection activism has often been seen as carrying her away from her feminist activities, and certainly she wrote more for the antivivisection cause than on women's issues from 1874 on. She gave up her work as regular staff writer on the *Echo* in mid 1875–the year of the passage of the Cruelty to Animals Act that she sought to repeal until her retirement from active politics, arguing as many did that it simply bureaucratized and so facilitated the very practice it was meant to limit. Indeed it is easy to see her involvement with antivivisection as threatening her feminist commitment. She insisted that the women's movement wholeheartedly support antivivisection, and she parted with feminist friends who did not, such as Davies, who advocated animal experiments at the new Girton College for women.

However, Cobbe's vehemency needs to be understood in terms of the connections that she, and the antivivisection movement more largely, made between animals' vulnerability and women's oppression. Like women, animals were vulnerable to the power of an increasingly materialist science, interested only in knowledge for its own sake and not in care for others. Middle-class women's health could also be understood as the product of a science more interested in technical proficiencies and rarefied medical knowledge than in care for a patient. Connections were made between the kind of experiments performed on animals and the emergence of new medical procedures, such as the ovariotomy, that were aimed at women.

Cobbe's antivivisectionist writings, like those of the larger movement, put forward the argument that because of their gender women were innately sympathetic to the plight of vulnerable animals and thus were the necessary guardians of a moral order threatened by the depraved medical science that the practice of vivisection revealed. Men, though always necessary political allies, were never the ethical center of antivivisection, having been shown in the figure of the medical scientist to be likely to become more cruel with exposure to pain and suffering. Instead, the women were targeted as the political activists able to make a difference by speaking on behalf of the endangered animal and taking up political arms in their quest. To argue for protection of the tortured animal, in antivivisectionist discourse, is to protect a domestic order vital to the well-being of civilized society. Though antivivisection focuses on animals as the suffering objects of humanitarian intervention, it is nonetheless a movement that produced, and drew upon, the political strengths of Victorian women.

As leader of the movement Cobbe oversaw innumerable petitions, protest letters, and memorials. For a decade she edited the *Zoöphilist,* the weekly journal of the Society for the Protection of Animals Liable to Vivisection (popularly known as the Victoria Street Society), which she had founded in 1875. As honorary secretary of the society Cobbe also combed the yearly Blue Books returns that recorded the granting of licences to physiologists and experiments undertaken in Great Britain, a painstaking and heart-wrenching search for any discrepancy that indicated a breach of the Cruelty to Animals Act and perhaps heralded the possibility of a successful prosecution. Her meticulous work occasionally yielded results, though the movement never did prosecute successfully under the terms of the act. In 1884 a weary but still fighting Cobbe finally left the Victoria Street Society, and in 1898 she established the British Union for the Abolition of Vivisection, having decided that total abolition of vivisection was ethically and legally necessary.

Throughout the last decade of Cobbe's active political life she continued to write, though less frequently, about women's issues. These late writings also mark a shift in Cobbe's thinking about women, away from questions of women's independence toward a pervasive concern with women's bodily integrity. This shift aligns Cobbe with feminists such as Butler, who campaigned against the Contagious Diseases Acts, and looks ahead to the agenda of the social-purity feminists at the turn of the century. Significantly, the shift also marks the integration of Cobbe's ethical thought, a feminist analysis that could now embrace the entire range of her interests in antivivisection, materialist medical science, and women's issues as related concerns.

For example, during this period she published "Wife-Torture in England," an essay that for many remains Cobbe's most vital legacy to the organized feminist movement. In the name of women's right to freedom from physical violence, Cobbe's article demands access to legal separations, protection and maintenance orders, and child custody for any woman whose husband was found guilty of assault against her. It was revolutionary. Focus hitherto had lingered on the appropriate punishment for the male offender, leaving unconsidered the position of the brutalized woman left to care for children. For Cobbe, "a husband is a beating animal" supported by an elaborate legal and social apparatus that required dismantling. In a strategy drawn from her antivivisectionist work, Cobbe somberly documents case after case of domestic assault, arguing that it was the social and legal status of wives as inferior to their husbands, as mere property to be handled or disposed of as men desired, that was the root cause of domestic violence: "The notion that a man's wife is his PROPERTY, in the sense in which a horse is his property . . . is the fatal root of incalculable evil and misery." Her proposed revisions to divorce law were presented as a necessary first step in changing the social role of all women, the only real answer to sexual violence.

Cobbe is careful in her article to acknowledge the classless nature of domestic violence, but she focuses on the working-class "kicking districts" of northern industrial towns where what she calls "the dangerous wife-beaters" reside. Drink, prostitution, and unbearably close living quarters are all listed as incitements to domestic violence, but Cobbe insists that it is the habitual depreciation of women in general that perpetuates violence: "How is a lad to learn to reverence a woman whom he sees daily scoffed at, beaten, and abused, and when he knows that the laws of his country forbid her, ever and under any circumstances, to exercise the rights of citzenship."

Other essays, including "The Little Health of Ladies" (*Contemporary Review,* January 1878) and "The Medical Profession and Its Morality" (*Modern Review,* April 1881), excoriate the medical profession as a system that enfeebles women, producing patients whose need for constant medical care incapacitates them for life. In "The Little Health of Ladies" Cobbe notes the timely correlation between feminist demands for access to the medical profession and the medical discovery of the debilitating effects of study on women: "the doctors grew earnest and made a grand discovery–namely, that mental labour is peculiarly injurious to the weaker sex–much worse, it would appear, for the feeble constitution, than any amount of ball-going and dissipation; and that, in short, a term at Girton was worse than five London seasons." Where Cobbe saw animal experimentation primarily as a way in which a newly emerging medical science sought to gain social authority, women's "little health" similarly benefited only medical practitioners. A medical science that believes "the normal condition of the female of the human species should be to have legs which walk not, and brains which can only work on pain of disturbing the rest of the ill-adjusted mechanism" is one Cobbe rejected in its entirety.

In 1884 Cobbe retired with Lloyd to Barmouth, Wales, where Lloyd had a life-interest in a family estate. An annuity of £100 raised by antivivisectionist friends allowed them to live in relative comfort. A second legacy of £25,000 in 1891 from a fellow antivivisectionist who admired Cobbe's work enabled Cobbe and Lloyd to move into the estate manor house, Hengwrt, from which Cobbe continued her antivivisectionist work at a slower rate, publishing corrected reprints of some of her earlier work and writing her autobiography. She died at Hengwrt on 5 April 1904, eight years after Lloyd; in her will she made provisions for her nieces and various single women, and left a substantial portion of her estate to the British Union for the Abolition of Vivisection.

References:

Carol Bauer and Lawrence Ritt, "'A Husband Is a Beating Animal': Frances Power Cobbe Confronts the Wife Abuse Problem in Victorian England," *International Journal of Women's Studies,* 6 (1983): 99–118;

Barbara Caine, "Frances Power Cobbe," in her *Victorian Feminists* (New York: Oxford University Press, 1992), pp. 102–149;

"Frances Power Cobbe," in *Criminals, Idiots, Women and Minors: Victorian Writing by Women on Women,* edited by Susan Hamilton (Peterborough, Ontario & Orchard Park, N.Y.: Broadview Press, 1995), pp. 74–171.

Papers:

Cobbes's papers are scattered; the primary archive is the Frances Power Cobbe Collection at the Huntington Library, San Marino, California. The manuscript of "A Lady's Ride through Palestine, with a Journey to Baalbec in 1858" is at the Cleveland Public Library.

John Doherty

(1798? - 14 April 1854)

Timothy Randall

PAMPHLETS: *A Letter to the Members of the National Association for the Protection of Labour* (Manchester, 1831);

The Quinquarticular System of Organisation (Manchester: Doherty, 1834);

A Letter to the Factory Operatives of Lancashire, on the Necessity of Petitioning Parliament in Favour of the Ten Hours' Bill (Manchester, 1845).

OTHER: *Returns of the Friendly Associated Cotton Spinners,* edited by Doherty (Manchester, circa August 1828-circa 30 December 1830);

The Conciliator, or Cotton Spinners' Weekly Journal, edited by Doherty (Manchester, 22 November 1828-20 December 1828);

The United Trades' Co-operative Journal, edited by Doherty (Manchester, 6 March 1830-2 October 1830);

The Voice of the People, edited by Doherty (Manchester & London, 1 January 1831-24 September 1831);

The Workman's Expositor, and Weekly Review of Literature, Science and the Arts, edited by Doherty (Manchester, 7 January 1832-14 January 1832); renamed *The Poor Man's Advocate, and People's Library* (Manchester, 21 January 1832-5 January 1833);

The Anti-Boroughmonger; or, The Poor Man's Key to the Elections, edited by Doherty (Manchester, circa May 1832);

The Herald of the Rights of Industry, and General Trades' Union Advocate, edited by Doherty (Manchester, 8 February 1834-24 May 1834).

In *What I Remember* (1888) Thomas Adolphus Trollope describes John Doherty as "a furious radical." Francis Place recalls him as "a very extraordinary, rigid, intolerant, wrong-headed, persevering man," while Major General Bouverie reported to the Home Office how "The minds of the operatives are worked up to a fresh state of excitement by the weekly Tracts ... written by a man of the name of Doherty.... [A] clever man and ... decidedly a very mischievous one." Doherty's mischief was achieved in several spheres. He was a trade-union activist and leader, a radical printer and bookseller, and a radical journalist who from 1828 through 1834 edited seven periodicals concerned primarily with factory reform and trade-union organization.

He was born in Buncrana, County Donegal, sometime in 1798 or close to that date. At the age of ten he started work in a cotton mill in Buncrana. He was a cotton spinner in Larne, near Belfast, before moving to Manchester around 1816 to continue his trade. There he was involved in the unsuccessful Lancashire spinners' strike of 1818, during which a Philanthropic Society, or union of all tradesmen, was briefly set up. Whether Doherty was involved in this is unknown, but the idea of a general union shaped his career as a reformer. He was arrested in 1819 for picketing and sentenced to two years at hard labor. Shortly after his release in 1821 he married a woman named Laura, a Manchester milliner with whom he was to have five children. Details of his personal life are scanty and ambiguous: for instance, he was charged in 1835 for assaulting his wife, but the case was dropped when she refused to press charges. How much this reveals of Doherty is unclear; certainly his political enemies publicized and embellished the episode with the intention of discrediting him.

During the 1820s he was variously involved in campaigns for electoral reform and in the 1824-1825 agitation to repeal the antiunion aims of the Combination Laws that had been passed in 1824. In March 1828 he was elected secretary to the Manchester Cotton Spinners' Union and thereby became a full-time union worker. In August he founded his first weekly paper, *Returns of the Friendly Associated Cotton Spinners,* a broadsheet that publicized union subscriptions and discussed union strategy. In protest at his election, and partly as a reflection of anti-Irish prejudice, a splinter group broke away from the Manchester Cotton Spinners' Union. Doherty was soon editing a second weekly, as in November 1828 he founded *The Conciliator, or Cotton Spinners' Weekly Journal.* This paper served not as his own mouthpiece but as a medium to "appeal to reason," to publish the viewpoints of both sides in order to achieve consensus. The faction shortly became reintegrated into the union, and Doherty's paper was discontinued after five numbers.

In *Returns* Doherty continued to publicize the union's activities. There were rather too many of them. In April 1829 the Manchester spinners came out on strike in support of other Lancashire spinners. At first Doherty welcomed this action and attempted to use it as an opportunity to foster working-class education. He announced the use of a room as a school for strikers, asked that literate workers volunteer to instruct those who could not read, and requested funds to establish a library. However, the union could not support twenty thousand unpaid strikers, let alone a library, and the union capitulated in October.

The failure of the Manchester spinners convinced Doherty that the workers' only prospect of attaining bargaining power lay in unions of trades across all regions. In "To the Operative Spinners of England," an address he presented on 22 September 1829, and in subsequent addresses in 1830 Doherty expounded his idea that the laboring man by himself was powerless against the wealthy and the manufacturers, who made the laws for their own benefit. He urged the creation of a union of labor, to which all workers would contribute a sum of money that was to comprise a central fund used for strikes and in times of distress.

Doherty was persuasive. In September 1829 he formed the Grand General Union of All the Operative Spinners of the United Kingdom (G.G.U.). He also worked toward forming a union of different trades, and on 28 June 1830 the National Association for the Protection of Labour (N.A.P.L.) was organized, with Doherty as secretary. The grandiosity of the names of these betokens their pioneering status and their considerable size: the N.A.P.L. had roughly one hundred thousand members in 1831. Neither region nor trade was comprehensively united, however: the membership of the G.G.U. was drawn largely from Lancashire, as was that of the N.A.P.L., which also consisted largely of spinners.

Doherty was also involved at this time with advocating protective legislation for factory children. The Factory Acts of 1802 and 1819 had legislated working hours and conditions for children, but authorities' reactions to the many abuses of the law were minimal. On 13 November 1828 Doherty formed the Society for the Protection of Children Employed in Cotton Factories, an organization that was intended to prosecute mill owners for breaking the law, but its efforts were obstructed by the use of legal technicalities, by intimidation of witnesses, and by abuse of Doherty in the press.

Despite these obstructions Doherty's approach was not confrontational. Instead, he appealed to the owners on common humanitarian grounds, and he was surprisingly successful in gaining public support from many factory owners. But a trade depression began, and, as this made it increasingly difficult for the society to operate effectively, it became inactive in autumn 1830. Although the society had secured only 40 convictions from the 185 cases it had brought, the real threat of conviction that this represented to mill owners must have curbed severe cases. In part Doherty was raising the issue of children's working hours in order to regulate adult working hours, and his progressive efforts toward this end also reflected a conservative attitude toward the family: the husband's status as primary wage earner had to be protected at a time when women and children, instead of men, were undertaking unskilled industrial labor. Yet his humanitarian appeal to the welfare of children in the face of the Industrial Revolution contributed to the profound shift in attitudes toward childhood that subsequently occurred.

Returns continued publication until at least December 1830, and even after its termination Doherty wished to speak for the wider union movement, so on 6 March 1830 he founded *The United Trades' Co-operative Journal,* a weekly published in Manchester by the N.A.P.L. and intended to be the collective voice of that organization. Doherty's use of the word *co-operative* referred to cooperation between the unions rather than to a cooperative movement. Doherty was becoming increasingly confident in workers' own powers to change their society. He urged self-help to the workers, but a collective, politicized self-help different from that which Samuel Smiles later popularized through his *Self-Help; with Illustrations of Character and Conduct* (1859). Doherty believed that the laboring classes

> have always been taught to look up to others, for any amelioration of their condition.... They have little or no idea of depending on their own resources and exertions. Like children, they expect everything to be done for them, and like fools they are always betrayed.... the people possess power, but they want the knowledge to use it.

Doherty increasingly saw the potential of the press as a means to gather and focus that power, as "an organ of communication for those whose whole power depends on their understanding of each other." The press was the means to forge a working-class con-

THE POOR MAN'S ADVOCATE,
And People's Library.

No. 1.   MANCHESTER, SATURDAY, JANUARY 21, 1832.   PRICE 1d.

"FOR TRUTH, THE POOR, AND JUSTICE!"

In compliance with the suggestions of numerous friends and correspondents we have this week changed the form of our little work; and as we have began the work of reform, we have carried it into every department—of name, form, and, though last not least, the price. The present, and all succeeding numbers, will be sold at ONE PENNY, instead of Two-pence. The name which we have given to the present number, we consider more appropriate than that which we had previously taken: especially as the change in the form rendered a change of name also necessary. In order to make the work complete, the present number will form No. 1 of the POOR MAN'S ADVOCATE.

BEAUTIES OF A COTTON FACTORY.

In the *Expositor*, we have endeavoured to convey to the public, some idea, though we know it is and must necessarily be a very imperfect one, of the system of physical as well as moral slavery to which the unhappy inmates of these "modern hells" are reduced, and of the haughty and dictatorial tone assumed by a long list of underlings in these establishments. Those who have done us the honour to read those observations will remember, that we charged Mr. Patrick with refusing to acquaint the hands with the rate by which they are paid, and in fact, that many of them are not paid at all. This charge we have promised to substantiate, and we are now about to do so.

We must now revert back to the principles which we laid down at the outset, of the perfect equality of masters and men. When we recollect that employer and employed are merely contracting parties, each giving the market rate of prices for what he receives, we shall be enabled to form some notion of the audacious insolence of the man who demands and receives a commodity from another without giving him an equivalent. The workmen in this establishment are compelled to give a stipulated quantity of labour, and of a quality sufficiently good to satisfy the receiver, and he who gets that labour not only refuses to give the workman the market rate of wages in exchange, but refuses to inform him how or by what rate he is paid. This is on a par with a person going into one of our shops to purchase a piece of cloth, and who, when he is told by the owner of the cloth the price at which it is to be obtained, gets the cloth cut from the piece, and then offers the owner of the cloth, not the price fixed upon it, but just what the purchaser's *conscience* will permit him to offer—perhaps not more than one-half or two-thirds of the market price. In such a case would any man call this payment, and the person capable of it a gentleman? Certainly not. On the contrary, the shopkeeper would instantly seize the impudent ruffian by the throat, and have him conveyed to the nearest prison, in order to secure him an introduction to the tread-mill.

Yet this is the conduct of Mr. Patrick, who, we suppose, passes for a gentleman all this while, instead of being punished as an audacious violator of established contracts. He engages men to perform certain work, and when it is done, he refuses to pay by any given rate or fixed price, but such as his caprice or whim may at the moment dictate. This is reducing the workmen to the condition of beggars who solicit something from the passing stranger, and are obliged to be content with whatever may be thrown them. Can this be justly dignified by the name of payment? We deny that it can or ought.

But our case does not rest here. We

First page of Doherty's third weekly newspaper, through which he waged war on "the authors of the factory system" sciousness; the trade-union movement would be its vehicle for action.

The United Trades' Co-operative Journal was unstamped, with initially little overt political content, but as Doherty recognized the potential influence of the press, he began to stake out a broader sociopolitical platform advocating factory legislation, abolition of the truck system, and repeal of the taxes on knowledge. As a result of carrying such political news, the paper was forced to close by the Stamp Offices on 2 October 1830, as the government began its suppression of the unstamped press.

Doherty, however, was not discouraged. On 1 January 1831 he founded a new weekly newspaper, *The Voice of the People,* this time stamped and costing seven pence. The next week Doherty gave up his position as secretary to the Manchester Spinners' Union to concentrate on editing the paper. The claim implicit in the title—that this paper was to be "the voice of the people"—was based on its being financed and printed by the N.A.P.L., which was increasing in size to nearly one hundred thousand members. Although Doherty achieved relatively high sales of thirty-five hundred copies, *The Voice* always struggled financially. Yet he reiterated his belief in the importance of the press: "We shall endeavour to collect their [the people's] scattered energies into a common focus, to give them importance and consequence, by acquainting them with their own strength; to consolidate their power, by uniting their exertions."

The Voice articulated a broader political and social platform than any of Doherty's previous papers. It was one of his greatest contributions to radical journalism and a direct challenge to various orthodoxies of the day. He engaged in an important debate with W. R. Greg, a master spinner, over the introduction of machinery. Doherty denied that he was against the introduction of machinery, but he was opposed to the selective use of it by employers and to employers appropriating all the profits gained by machinery. Workers needed to ensure "a full share of the produce of every machine."

In *The Voice* Doherty became increasingly concerned with the agitation over the Reform Bill, and he persuaded the N.A.P.L. to move its publication to London, which he characterized as both the "source of political intelligence and the hot-bed of corruption." There its circulation, he believed, would be greater. At the same time he broadened his social analysis and adopted the language, but not all the views, of Owenite socialism. He was confident that cooperative communities would usher in "the total renovation of the whole structure of society," but he insisted that this was a goal that was not immediately achievable.

The move to London and shift of focus provoked criticism from some unionists, who believed that the paper was diverting money and energy from trade strikes at a time when these were faring badly. By early 1831 the G.G.U. had virtually collapsed under the weight of too many strikes and too few workers' contributions. Criticized by committee members of the N. A. for the P. of L., Doherty published *A Letter to the Members of the National Association for the Protection of Labour* (1831), a pamphlet in which he defended himself. However, *The Voice* lost support when Doherty disagreed with Henry Hunt over strategy for the Reform Bill agitation, and the paper was discontinued after 24 September 1831.

During its short existence *The Voice* was an important seedbed of radical ideas. In its penultimate number on 17 September 1831 Doherty suggested that the workers unite to withdraw their labor until reform of the franchise was achieved: "Let a day be fixed upon," he urged; "let that day be well-known and fixed—say one month or six months hence; and when it arrives, let every workman in the United Kingdom REFUSE TO WORK ANOTHER STROKE until his class are permitted to exercise their due share of influence in the affairs of their country." He did not coherently argue what he expected such a strategy to achieve, however. William Benbow and, later, some Chartists such as George Julian Harney advocated a general strike in order to force a confrontation with the authorities that would provoke a people's revolution. Preferring instead to use the language of "moral force" rather than to incite a physical confrontation, Doherty had counseled caution in December 1830 during a long, ill-tempered strike in Ashton. As he advised workingmen,

> you would be as nothing when opposed to the power which the government of this country possesses. Let not your passions hurry you into contact with the force of government and the laws, but collect your moral force, that moral power which is of far more effect than any power which can oppress you. If you are only as united as the catholics of Ireland were, you will be blessed with similar success.

Doherty's conception of the strike probably derived from his view of the working classes as the creators of social wealth; a withdrawal of their labor would display their importance in society and validate their social and political rights. Having helped popularize the idea, however, he later argued against it. In 1833 he wrote "The Struggle for Existence—to the Workmen of Manchester," an address that was placarded throughout Manchester and that warned that a national strike might cause workers to starve or might provoke the authorities to massacre. His alternative, a passive resistance founded on moral force, remained willful optimism: "[R]ise in moral might, and STAND STILL, and you will immediately triumph against all foes."

At other times Doherty articulated a strong conviction that the workers were a single class holding shared interests, a class who opposed the interests of the state. In an article in the *Manchester & Salford Advertiser* on 9 November 1833 he proclaimed:

> The cause of the operatives is the same throughout the United Kingdom. Whatever evil injures one, if not successfully opposed, must eventually injure all. Every individual operative is therefore bound to support, by every means in his power, the whole body of his fellow-labourers. The war between "Capital" and Labour still rages with unabated fury.... "Capital" is supported by government and law. Labour has nothing to sustain it but the energies, wisdom, and virtue of its owners.

Karl Marx never wrote a clearer exposition of class war.

However, Doherty was unable to suggest a coherent strategy by which this war was to be fought, or even whether it should be declared. His thinking was fundamentally divided between his faith in the potential of the working classes to gain their social and political rights for themselves and his conviction that, for the present, the workers had to persuade the upper and middle classes to ameliorate the condition of the working classes for them. In December 1831 Doherty pointed out the limitations of the latter alternative: "legislative interference is at least but a negative good." Instead, he argued, "To require an act of parliament to protect men from evils which they can . . . annihilate by their own exertions, is to endeavour to perpetuate that state of slavish dependence from which we are just emerging." However, since trade unions, only partially united, had proven incapable of waging successful strike actions, from this time Doherty increasingly returned to the negative good of legislative interference, especially in the campaign for factory reform.

In January 1832, shortly after the demise of *The Voice,* Doherty founded *The Workman's Expositor, and Weekly Review of Literature, Science and the Arts,* a paper that failed after two numbers and was then relaunched on 21 January as *The Poor Man's Advocate, and People's Library.* In its pages he campaigned for the amelioration of factory conditions and carefully argued that "The facts must be authenticated, or they cannot be used." This weekly was first published by Abel Heywood and printed by A. Wilkinson, but according to Doherty they both became alarmed at its uncompromising stance, and after the sixth number he "had no alternative but to become printer and publisher himself." He set out on a tour of Lancashire in order to see the extent of factory abuses and "to discover and expose the authors of oppression and injustice to the poor defenceless operatives wherever I find them." His attitude toward factory reform seems to have become increasingly uncompromising at this time; in February 1832 he wrote, "[W]e must and shall make 'war to the knife,' upon the authors of the factory system."

On about 1 May, Doherty also founded *The Anti-Boroughmonger; or, The Poor Man's Key to the Elections,* with which he aimed "to promote the election of radical candidates at Manchester to the first reformed parliament." He publicly investigated the credentials of candidates in his paper and made recommendations to the electorate. However, in April 1832 he was accused of libeling a Mr. Gilpin, a Stockport clergyman, an offense for which he was twice placed in jail later that year. Doherty claimed that he was being victimized, and certainly his various campaigns were hindered. Only one issue of *The Anti-Boroughmonger* appeared, and Doherty continued to edit *The Poor Man's Advocate* until the start of 1833.

Doherty's final paper was *The Herald of the Rights of Industry, and General Trades' Union Advocate,* which was published for nearly four months in 1834. *The Herald* reported on union organization and the reform of working conditions, including a campaign for an eight-hour workday. In the same year Doherty published *The Quinquarticular System of Organisation,* in which he outlined a plan to restructure the Manchester Spinners' Union and to reform benefits such as unemployment pay, funeral allowances, and sick benefits. His scheme was too complex to be practicable, however, and it apparently had little influence.

Doherty's commitment to journalism had also led him to become a printer, and in March 1832 he registered as a bookseller, stationer, and printer at the offices of *The Poor Man's Advocate* in Manchester. The following year, concerned with disseminating political knowledge among the working classes, he opened a reading room. In 1832 he advertised the sale of "The People's Library of Cheap and Entertaining Knowledge," a series of penny pamphlets on subjects such as factory reform, trade unions, the condition of Ireland, local government reform, and temperance. Perhaps his most significant publication was the reprinting of John Brown's *A Memoir of Robert Blincoe, an Orphan Boy; Sent to Endure the Horrors of a Cotton-mill* (1832), first published in *The Lion,* Richard Carlile's periodical, in 1828. Doherty's edition, which included passages expurgated from the first edition, was intended "to give the most extensive publicity to the horrors of this infernal factory system." This narrative of the experiences of a child apprentice in the factories complemented Doherty's advocacy for the welfare of factory children.

Initially, Doherty sold unstamped as well as stamped newspapers, and on 21 January 1836 the government prosecuted him for selling *Cleave's Weekly Police Gazette*. For this offense he was fined five pounds and forced to assure the authorities that he would no longer sell unstamped papers. He appears to have abided by this policy, and from this time his business became less focused on political concerns. Although he did not abandon political causes, he published and sold an increasing number of romances, works of general fiction, and Catholic works. He became secretary of the Manchester Spinners' Union again from 1834 to 1836 and gave evidence before the Select Committee on Combinations of Workmen in 1838. He continued his membership in the Short-Time Committee, which campaigned for reduction of factory working hours, until the early 1840s. In 1845 he wrote *A Letter to the Factory Operatives of Lancashire, on the Necessity of Petitioning Parliament in Favour of the Ten Hours' Bill*. However, after 1841 his name was no longer listed among those in publishers' directories, and little is known about the last part of his life. Almost forgotten, he died of heart failure on 14 April 1854.

Much of his writing has been lost, and what remains is scattered as letters and pamphlets and other pieces published in various newspapers. Nevertheless, his importance as a writer of radical journalism should not be forgotten. Most of his newspapers were regional in circulation and had relatively small sales figures of around one thousand copies. However, these papers were probably read by thousands of readers, and his writing was national in orientation. His journalism was inspired by his position as trade-union leader and by his conviction that the working classes—as individual workers, as members of different trades, and as workingmen of different regions—needed to communicate with each other. His papers facilitated this communication, at first as an organ of a specific trade union and then as a "voice of the people." Many public figures have found it useful to claim to speak as the "voice of the people," and Doherty represented only one section of the working classes—within which there were internal disagreements. But he genuinely gave voice to thousands of working people who were politically excluded and legally abused.

Anyone who thinks that the importance of class has been overestimated in early-nineteenth-century Britain should read the work of John Doherty. His writings trenchantly express an awareness of class differences, even of class warfare, and this language serves a political strategy that operated at, and sometimes beyond, the boundaries of the law. (This is one reason why recovering his writings and records of his activities is so difficult.) Doherty never claimed that a single identity existed for a "working class." Indeed, no one could have been less likely than this practiced conciliator of differences to have underestimated the regional and occupational differences among members of the working classes. Yet Doherty constantly strove to bring the working classes together so that they could win their rights in society. Probably no one did more to make the English working class than this furious, wrongheaded, and mischievous man.

Bibliography:
Joel Wiener, *A Descriptive Finding List of Unstamped British Periodicals, 1830–1836,* new series (London: Bibliographical Society, 1970), items 19, 176, 398, 520, 556.

Biography:
R. G. Kirby and A. E. Musson, *The Voice of the People: John Doherty, 1798–1854; Trade Unionist, Radical and Factory Reformer* (Manchester: Manchester University Press, 1975).

References:
Eric Hopkins, *Working-Class Self-Help in Nineteenth-Century England* (New York: St. Martin's Press, 1995);

Sidney Webb and Beatrice Webb, *The History of Trade Unionism* (London: Longmans, 1920).

Papers:
Manchester Central Reference Library holds most of Doherty's journals. The Place Collection in the British Library contains correspondence with Doherty and some copies of his journals. None of Doherty's personal papers appear to have survived.

Ebenezer Elliott
(17 March 1781 - 1 December 1849)

Timothy Randall

See also the Elliott entry in *DLB 96: British Romantic Poets, 1789–1832, Second Series.*

BOOKS: *The Vernal Walk: A Poem* (Cambridge: Printed by & for B. Flower and sold by Crosby & Letterman, London, 1801); corrected and republished as *The Vernal Walk, a Descriptive Poem* (Cambridge: Printed by & sold by B. Flower, sold also by C. Sutton, Nottingham; T. Condor, Bucklersbury; Cosby & Company and E. Vidler, London, 1802);

The Soldier, and Other Poems, as Britannicus (Harlow: Printed by B. Flower for M. Jones, London, 1810);

Night, a Descriptive Poem (London: Printed for Baldwin, Cradock & Joy, 1818);

Peter Faultless to His Brother Simon, Tales of Night, in Rhyme, and Other Poems (Edinburgh: Printed for Archibald Constable and Hurst, Robinson, London, 1820);

Love, a Poem in Three Parts, to Which Is Added, The Giaour, a Satirical Poem (London: Charles Stocking, 1823);

Scotch Nationality: A Vision (London: Printed for Charles Stocking by J. & C. Adlard, 1824); republished as *A Vision* (Sheffield: Printed by W. Wilkinson, 1875);

The Village Patriarch: A Poem (London: Printed for the author & published by Edward Bull, 1829);

Corn Law Rhymes. The Ranter, Written and Published by Order of the Sheffield Mechanics' Anti-Bread-Tax Society (Sheffield: Printed for the author by Platt & Todd, 1830; enlarged edition, Sheffield: Printed for the author by Platt & Todd and sold by J. Pearce, Sheffield and B. Steill, London, 1831; enlarged again, London: Published by B. Steill & sold by J. Blackwell and J. Pearce, 1831);

The Splendid Village, Corn Law Rhymes, and Other Poems (London: B. Steill / Sheffield: J. Pearce, 1833);

An Address to the People of England, on the Corn-Laws, anonymous (London: Published by B. Steill, 1834);

Ebenezer Elliott (portrait by John Birch; Sheffield Corporation)

The Village Patriarch, Love, and Other Poems (London: B. Steill, 1834);

Kerhonah, The Vernal Walk, Win Hill, and Other Poems (London: B. Steill, 1835);

The Poetical Works of Ebenezer Elliott, the Corn-Law Rhymer (Edinburgh: William Tait / London: Simpkin, Marshall / Dublin: John Cumming, 1840);

More Verse and Prose by the Cornlaw Rhymer, 2 volumes (London: Charles Fox, 1850);

Blenham; or, What Came of Troubling the Waters: A Story Founded on Facts (London: Cash / Edinburgh: Menzies, 1855).

Collections: *The Poetical Works of Ebenezer Elliott,* 3 volumes (London: B. Steill, 1844);

The Poems of Ebenezer Elliott, edited, with an introduction, by Rufus W. Griswold (Philadelphia: J. Locken, 1844);

The Poetical Works of Ebenezer Elliott, revised, 2 volumes, edited by Edwin Elliott (London: Henry S. King, 1876).

OTHER: "Autobiographical Memoir," *Athenaeum,* no. 1159 (1850): 46–49.

Ebenezer Elliott was born at Masborough, near Rotherham, Yorkshire. His father, Ebenezer senior, was a clerk in an iron foundry, and although his mother, Ann, was an invalid, she worked as the mother of eleven children. Ebenezer junior had a modest education, and he records in his memoir that at school he was taught little more than how to write. He was sent to work in the foundry, where from age sixteen until twenty-three he weighed castings. His social and financial position improved when, probably in 1805, he married Fanny Gartside, who brought a considerable dowry to the marriage. The couple eventually had thirteen children together. Elliott invested his wife's fortune in an iron foundry, and, after this business went bankrupt in 1818, he moved to Sheffield the following year. In 1821 he was able to reopen his business with £100 that he received from his two sisters-in-law.

Elliott began writing verse as a teenager, and *The Vernal Walk: A Poem,* modeled on James Thomson's pastoral verse, was published in 1801. Elliott continued writing verse, in a more romantic and melodramatic mode, but for the next two decades he found it difficult to get his work published. In a letter to J. Warren on 13 April 1822 Elliott expressed concern that his low social status hindered his literary recognition: "No poem can succeed if the Reviewers do not notice it. I have few literary acquaintances." He published *The Soldier, and Other Poems* (1810) pseudonymously, and this collection also received little notice.

E. R. Seary finds that in 1809, when Elliott sent Robert Southey a portion of the work that Elliott later rewrote and published in *Night, a Descriptive Poem* (1818), the future poet laureate advised Elliott not to publish it. He accepted Southey's judgment, but he continued to feel that his social circumstances, rather than any lack of talent, were causing his failure: "I am a tradesman, at school I was not taught grammar." In *Love, a Poem in Three Parts, to Which Is Added, The Giaour, a Satirical Poem* (1823) he published a satirical attack on the popular work of the aristocratic George Gordon, Lord Byron; years later, in 1848, Elliott admitted in a letter to Richard Otley that he had "satirized Byron, in the hope that the noble poet might notice the satire, and so bring the satirist into notice!" Perhaps he had a similar motive in publishing *Peter Faultless to His Brother Simon, Tales of Night, in Rhyme, and Other Poems* (1820), which satirizes periodical reviewers in general.

From the mid 1820s Elliott increasingly focused his poetry on current social issues. In "Love," one of the poems published with "The Giaour" in his 1823 volume, he directs his invective against poverty rather than any poet. Byron may never have noticed Elliott, but those familiar with poverty certainly did. The publication of *The Village Patriarch: A Poem* in 1829 brought Elliott critical acclaim and wide popularity. A lengthy, discursive poem in ten books, *The Village Patriarch* centers on the figure of Enoch Wray, who is one hundred years old and therefore "the incarnation of a century." The narrator is a shadowy persona who walks with, and at times cannot keep up with, Enoch as they converse. The figure of Enoch offers Elliott opportunities to identify and deplore various social trends: the introduction of the bread-tax economy; the decline of the village; the unequal distribution of wealth; and the interfering, parsimonious treatment of the elderly and the poor by the State. The influence of George Crabbe on Elliott's poems is apparent in the character sketches, both affectionate and satirical, of many village figures.

Enoch's blindness contrasts with his extended vision of the past, his moral clear-sightedness, and his visionary glimpses of the future which his dreams provide and which he then renders into his verse. Book VII presents one such versified dream in the most impassioned social protest in the poem. Elliott distances himself from the poem's political radicalism, however, by filtering it through so many mediaries: the poetic narrator, the character of Enoch, the device of the dream, and the various figures who appear to Enoch. The language of Bradshaw, a ghost who appears to Enoch, expresses uninhibited scorn for "game-law'd, corn-law'd, war-worn, parish-paid / Rag-money'd, crawling wretches, reptile-flay'd!" Elliott uses such expressions but simultaneously disavows them, as Enoch condemns these "wild words."

Elliott's social denunciation is also expressed through embedded melodramatic and pathetic narratives, most dramatically in Book VIII, when Enoch's son, Joseph, is imprisoned for poaching and dies in jail. His widow, Hannah, is unable to meet the rent, and therefore Ezra, the landlord, evicts her. When Ezra later assaults her, he is murdered by Jane, Hannah's idiot child, and when Hannah takes the blame to protect her daughter, Hannah is executed. Jane, the voice of the poor and oppressed, is

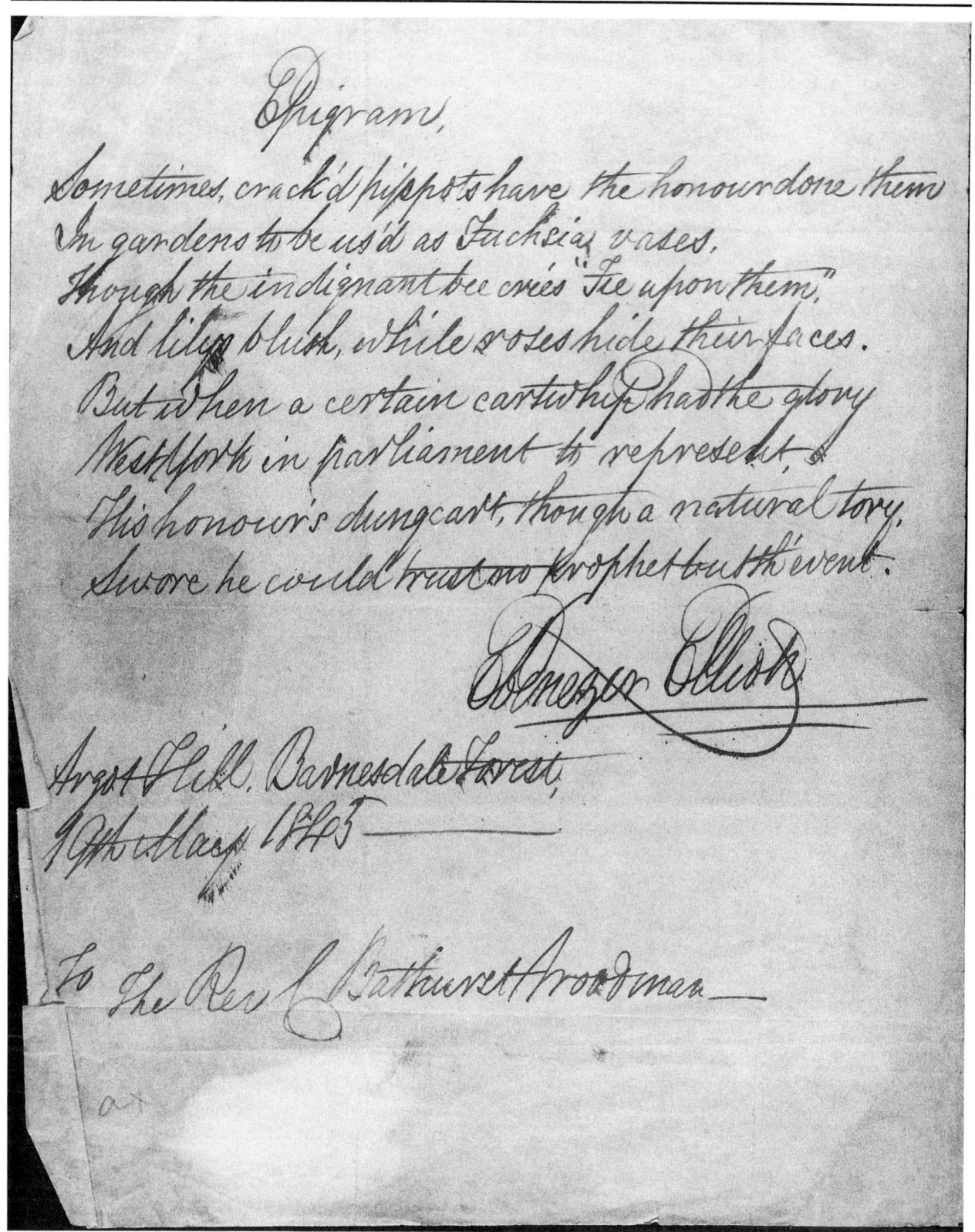

Manuscript for a lyric Elliott wrote in 1845, in response to the actions of a Tory M.P. for the West York region (Collection of William B. Thesing)

left to wander and bring down a curse upon the rich and unjust. But again Elliott disavows her language: Jane is "mad," after all.

The Village Patriarch is one of Elliott's more pessimistic poems. Everything is worse than it was in the past, and the only sources of optimism are found in the extent to which the past is able to survive and adapt to the present in new patterns of living, such as a country-born widow's struggle to grow a small garden in the town. Enoch's trade has been masonry, so the past of the village lives on not only in his mind but also in his works. Such monuments, however, are invariably in states of neglect and decay. When Enoch visits a sundial that he had constructed, it is covered with mold; the mill dam he had built is no longer working because the miller has gone bankrupt. Even science offers no hope for the future: "Triumphant Science! what avail thy deeds, / Thy sailless navy, and thy steam-drawn car, / If growing power to deeper misery leads?"

There are longueurs in *The Village Patriarch*, yet Elliott succeeds in this long poem: its solidity of detail accumulates through more than one hundred pages; images recur with effect in various forms through the poem; and the figure of the village centenarian provides a strong center to the many themes that concern Elliott. In the final section the unmitigated pessimism and the uninhibited sentimentality of the poet are both invoked, with sentiment perhaps the stronger of the two. Enoch reads with his fingers the gravestones of his wife and dead children, gravestones that he had carved, and the poem ends with the bailiffs coming to his daughter and grandson to seize their property. As they do so, Enoch "hears, in heav'n, his swooning daughter shriek."

Elliott uses similar subjects in "The Splendid Village," one of the title poems in *The Splendid Village, Corn Law Rhymes, and Other Poems* (1833). In this poem the narrator has returned to his home village from America (which Elliott frequently idealized) and describes the changes he observes. It is another narrative of social decline through the passing years: the village has become impoverished and demoralized; family members have died or been forced to emigrate; his lover has married someone unworthy who is suspected of having murdered her. The satirical portraits of "The Splendid Village" are darker than those of "The Village Patriarch," and the pessimism of "The Splendid Village" affords less relief through sentiment than does "The Village Patriarch." Elliott continually returns to the image of a patriarch: a tower "like a patriarch of the olden time, / Sees age around, but none like his sublime" and a five-hundred-year-old beech that the narrative

begs to "Speak in thy voice of bygone hopes and fears." Clearly Elliott was obsessed with how the past maintains a precarious, decayed presence in the present. As the present parasitically devours the past, Elliott voices also a fear of the future, especially of an apocalypse:

> The red-foam'd deluge, and the sea-wide tomb;
> The arm of vengeance, and the brow of doom;
> The grin of millions o'er the shock of all–
> A people's wreck, an empire's funeral!

From the early 1830s Elliott increasingly turned to writing the short lyric rather than the narrative poem, and his poetry changed from comprehensively depicting a particular community to actively advocating specific national issues. Around 1830 he helped organize the Sheffield Mechanics' Anti-Bread-Tax Society, and in 1830 his collection of short lyrics, *Corn Law Rhymes. The Ranter, Written and Published by Order of the Sheffield Mechanics' Anti-Bread-Tax Society,* was published. Elliott began writing very explicitly for a cause, and with the success of this volume and a subsequent collection, the "Corn-Law Hymns," he became identified as the "Corn-Law Rhymer." Southey viewed the Corn-Law rhymes as the work of a "Demon of Anarchy." But Elliott's opposition to the Corn Laws was partly motivated by his fear of anarchy, since these laws threatened to provoke the working class to a cataclysmic revolution: "Every man who would not welcome revolution, should oppose the Corn Law, or it will revolutionize the kingdom long before a reform can be effected. . . . [Thence] we shall become the prey of anarchy, and fall before the first invader." Elliott was a reformer, not a revolutionary, and his economic sympathies were explicitly with capitalists, in the conviction that capitalism was a profoundly progressive force: "It is false that I ever imputed the miseries of the poor to the accumulation of capital," he wrote; "No. I impute those miseries to the destruction of capital by the landed classes."

In these Corn-Law rhymes Elliott frequently expresses his sympathy for the poor by depicting a family in distress, as in "Song," which combines pathos with mordant satire. It begins:

> Child is thy father dead?
> Father is gone!
> Why did they tax his bread?
> God's will be done!

In other poems the husband's drunkenness contributes to the destruction of the family, as in one "Song" the opening line begins where "The Village Patriarch" had tragically concluded: "They sold the

Monument to Elliott in Weston Park, Sheffield (bronze statue by Nevill Bernard)

chairs, they took the bed. . . ." One child has died; another is dead but unburied "because they could not purchase earth and prayer"; and the pregnant mother murders her third child in a fit of insanity. At her public execution, "Drunk, in the crowd, her husband saw her die!" instead of pleading on her behalf. The mother's deed is a consequence of the husband's drunkenness, which is a symptom of the neglect of the poor by the government. In Elliott's hierarchical society those who possess authority are failing those to whom they are responsible. This spiraling chain of failure perpetuates itself from generation to generation.

Elliott supported political reform during the passage of the 1832 Reform Bill. He was a member of the Sheffield Working Men's Association, which by 1838 evolved into a Chartist association, and he was the Sheffield delegate to a national meeting for the charter on 17 September 1838. Probably from his involvement in Chartism and from witnessing his iron business founder in 1837 during a downturn in national trade, Elliott wrote perhaps his most avowedly militant poetry during the late 1830s. He soon became alarmed at some of the Chartist speeches, however, and on 23 September he wrote a letter "To the Chartists of Sheffield" to oppose the "physical force" wing which, infiltrated "by paid agents of the scoundrel Breadtaxery," he saw sabotaging the political cause of the working class. He formally withdrew his support from Chartism on 6 May 1839 and thereafter maintained that the movement had been irredeemably perverted.

Elliott always appeared to be less comfortable with national than with local politics, and he preferred to express his positions on the former in terms of a localized identity. During the 1830s and 1840s many of his lyrics are dedicated to the people of Sheffield or to workingmen's organizations in Sheffield or Rotherham. Many lyrics were songs and hymns intended to be sung at local demonstrations staged by reformists, Chartists, or the Anti–Corn Law Association. Such poems as "Hymn, Written for the Rotherham Political Union, and Sung There on the Celebration of the Passing of the Three Reform Bills" tend to be among Elliott's most celebratory and optimistic. He frequently appropriated popular idiom for a political cause, as in his many versions of national anthems. One Corn-Law rhyme, "When Freedom's Foes Mocked Labour's Groan," is set to the tune of "Rule Britannia," and Elliott eulogizes William IV as the safeguard of British freedom: "Rule, great William, rule the free! / William Britain's shield will be!" Written in 1832 for the Sheffield Political Union, "The Triumph of Reform" uses the same anthem tune, but the object of eulogy is the figure of political reform rather than the monarch: "Mind's great Charter! Europe saved! / Man *for ever* unenslaved!" "The People's Anthem," written in 1848, adapts music of the national anthem, but the words are "God, save the people!": "the people" are implicitly the sovereign body of the nation rather than the person of the monarch—although Elliott carefully restricts his definition of who the people are to those who are taxed, because "taxation and representation ought to be coextensive."

Elliott often celebrates locality in terms of its natural environs and effectively draws on dialect words to describe local flora, fauna, and topography. In some poems he takes a fresh, naive delight in nature itself; in others he politicizes nature by drawing from it images of the freedom that British society lacks. In "Hymn" ("Lord! To the rose . . . ") he writes:

> Streams trade with clouds, seas trade with heav'n,
> Air trades with light, and is forgiv'n;
> While man would make all climes his own,
> But chain'd by man, laments alone.

Nature serves also as an image of redemption, both as an escape from man's oppression and as a means to overthrow such oppression. In other poems such as "Win-Hill" Elliott's references to revolution are invariably negative, but when metaphorically linked to nature, revolution is benign and nurturing. In climbing a Derbyshire peak the poetic narrator of this poem describes the local flora and topography. An unidentified human skeleton had been discovered on these mountain slopes, and the narrator imaginatively reconstructs a story of woe and poverty. The peak is a fitting site for the death of an oppressed man because he is now at one with nature. For Elliott the peak is an emblem of true government, "Calling the feeble to thy sheltering breast," and the poem ends with the certainty that, acting through nature, God—"Thou whose whispering is the thunder!"—will restore social happiness.

Elliott also wrote many narrative poems set in far-distant times and places. In his memoir he lamented that he who "from his childhood has dreamed of visiting foreign countries . . . has never been twenty miles out of England . . . [or seen] Cumberland, Wales, and Scotland." Elliott was typical of working-class writers in choosing to write about foreign places despite having scant travel experience. Such writing was an imaginative escape from a circumscribed material existence, and it was often a utopian exploration of society. In "Etheline" the hero, Adwick, defies a tyrant priest with the words:

> Me thou canst rack, my blood canst spill;
> But there's a power thou canst not kill,
> The will and power To Think and Know.
> Sure is its march, however slow.

"Etheline" is a tale of ancient Britain; the march was slow indeed.

Elliott's sense of locality is intimately connected with his spiritual and political development. In "Don and Rother" the speaker addresses these local rivers, which have ensured the growth of the poet's mind: "For on your banks my infant thoughts were nursed; / Here from the bud the spirit's petals burst." Elliott's debt to William Wordsworth is obvious, but Elliott became radical as he grew older, and his later poems—even those which are similar in form and theme to the poet laureate's early works—are more radical than Wordsworth's. "The Year of Seeds: 1848" is a series of expressly "revolutionary sonnets" in contrast to the tradition of "the sonnet's slavish notes." He addresses Wordsworth in sonnet XIX, praising the poet laureate's intentions but criticizing him for succumbing to sycophancy and urging him to "hymn not thou pomp's pagan-priests and stalls."

Other evidence of Elliott's sense of local identity is in his writing on industry and science. In "Verses on the Opening of the Sheffield and Rotherham Railway," written in 1838, he combines local pride with a remarkable optimism not merely in technological progress but in science as an agent for social and political progress. The poem ends:

For Mind shall conquer time and space;
   Bids East and West shake hands!
Brings, over Ocean, face to face,
   Earth's ocean-sever'd strands;
And, on his path of iron, bear
Words that shall wither, in despair,
   The tyrants of all lands.

"Steam at Sheffield," written around the same time, seems to be Elliott's most remarkable poem. He explicitly affirms that industrial and scientific progress are appropriate subjects for poetry, and he refuses to make the conventional poetic division between the natural and the artificial. Man's industry is an integral part of nature and is its aesthetic pinnacle, as "there is nobler beauty in the form / That welds the hissing steel, with ponderous blow." It is significant that workingmen are responsible for the scientific innovations and are in control of such machinery:

No; there he moves, the thoughtful engineer,
The soul of all this motion; rule in hand,
And coarsely apron'd–simple, plain, sincere–
An honest man; self-taught to understand
The useful wonders which he built and plann'd.

The workers are the priests to this all-powerful, all-benevolent deity, science–"this metal god, that yet shall chase / The tyrant idols of remotest lands, / Preach science to the desert...."

That the owner of an iron foundry should be the writer who depicted and embraced the spirit of the Industrial Revolution is unsurprising. Yet even "Steam at Sheffield" asserts the presence of the past, for Andrew Turner, the central figure of the poem, is an *old* engineer who remembers the figures of James Watt and James Brindley and a phase of the Industrial Revolution that is already outmoded. Like the biblical Enoch, Turner is a patriarch who remembers and embodies the past (although it is an industrial past) and who welcomes and embodies the future. Elliott's ambivalences are creative ones; he was so far in the vanguard of the Industrial Revolution that he was the first writer to be capable of expressing nostalgia for it.

In the last two decades of his life Elliott was widely cited as the typical, and as the most important, working-class poet. Thomas Carlyle hailed him as "an intelligible voice from the hitherto Mute and Irrational," and Elliott, the poet, was almost obsessively analyzed as being also the "worker." George Gilfillan referred to "the savage power which taught him at one time to wield the hammer and the pen with little difference in degree of animal exertion and mental fury." Yet in many ways Elliott's work is not typical of working-class writing, which is too diverse to be represented adequately by that of one figure. As a manager and employer Elliott maintained an ambiguous class status in his maturity; his social position made him more independent than most working-class writers, but it also limited his radicalism. It is significant that he was known as the "Corn Law Rhymer" even though his verse concerned many social and political issues. Since opposition to the Corn Laws was primarily associated with the industrial merchant class, Elliott's radicalism was selectively packaged. He did not refuse this poetic identity, but he saw himself also as the poetic advocate for the poor: "Who is the poet of the poor, if I am not?"

Members of the working-class press admired him more than the middle class did. It was useful for the working classes to have a self-proclaiming "poet of the poor" and unnecessary to explore ideological differences where they existed. For instance, despite his criticism of the Chartist movement after 1839, Elliott's work was widely reprinted in Chartist newspapers such as *The Northern Star,* for the lack of specificity in some of his verse made it more broadly appealing than he may have wished. In "The Ranter" he specifically claims that "world-reforming Commerce" would henceforth be called "Liberty," but in his shorter lyrics he emotionally, rather than ideologically, deploys words such as "liberty," "slavery," "oppression," and "justice." Such works are therefore amenable to different readings informed by Chartists, socialists, or trade unionists, for example.

The subject matter of Elliott's poetry is heterogeneous. He was one of the first writers to celebrate the Industrial Revolution, yet he was often nostalgic. He proudly associated himself with the city of Sheffield, yet he lamented the decline of the village. For the most part these antitheses were creative and productive rather than stultifying, and Elliott evolved considerably in the course of his poetic career.

His creative ambivalence is apparent in the idea behind "The Year of Seeds," a work that finds hope in the political future just as Elliott knew that his own life was nearly ended. This poetic sequence, written in 1848, ends on a personal note, with sonnet XLV opening, "The morning of the last day of the year / Instructs me that my course is nearly run. / I thank Thee that I see another sun...." Elliott died during the next year, on 1 December 1849.

Bibliographies:

A. A. Eaglestone, E. R. Seary, and G. L. Phillips, *Ebenezer Elliott: (The Corn-Law Rhymer) 1781–1849: A Commemorative Brochure with . . . Bibliography* (Sheffield: Sheffield City Libraries & Rotherham Public Library, 1949);

Simon Brown, *Ebenezer Elliott: The Corn Law Rhymer. A Bibliography and List of Letters* (Leicester: University of Leicester Studies Centre, 1971).

Biographies:

January Searle (George Searle Phillips), *The Life, Character and Genius of Ebenezer Elliott, the Corn Law Rhymer* (London: Gilpin / Edinburgh: Black / Dublin: Gilpin, 1850);

John Watkins, *Life, Poetry, and Letters of Ebenezer Elliott, the Corn-law Rhymer; with an Abstract of His Politics* (London: Mortimer, 1850);

Searle, *Memoirs of Ebenezer Elliott, the Corn Law Rhymer, with Criticisms upon His Writings* (London: Whittaker, 1852);

J. W. King, *Ebenezer Elliott: A Sketch, with Copious Extracts from his Descriptive Poems* (Sheffield: Harrison, 1854);

K. Chandler, "Ebenezer Elliott," thesis, Sheffield Polytechnic University, 1984.

References:

Asa Briggs, "Ebenezer Elliott, the Corn Law Rhymer," *Cambridge Journal,* 3 (1950): 686–695;

Thomas Carlyle, "Corn Law Rhymes," *Edinburgh Review,* 55 (1832): 338–361;

George Gilfillan, "Ebenezer Elliott," in his *A Gallery of Literary Portraits* (Edinburgh: Tait, 1845);

John Guest, *Ebenezer Elliott* (Rotherham: Rotherham Literary & Scientific Society, 1880);

Louis James, *Fiction for the Working Man* (Harmondsworth: Penguin, 1974), pp. 201–211;

Charles Kingsley, "Burns and His School," *Miscellanies,* 2 volumes (London: Parker, 1859), I: 357–407;

Brian Maidment, *The Poorhouse Fugitives* (Manchester: Carcanet, 1987);

E. R. Seary, "Robert Southey and Ebenezer Elliott: Some New Southey Letters," *Review of English Studies,* 15 (1939): 412–421;

Samuel Smiles, *Autobiography* (London: John Murray, 1905).

Havelock Ellis

(2 February 1859 – 8 July 1939)

Terrie M. Romano
Queen's University

BOOKS: *The New Spirit* (London: Bell, 1890; revised edition, London: Scott, 1891; New York: Boni & Liveright, 1921);

The Criminal (London: Scott, 1890; New York: Scribner & Welford, 1890; revised and enlarged edition, London: Scott, 1901);

The Nationalisation of Health (London: Unwin, 1892);

Man and Woman: A Study of Human Secondary Sexual Characters (London: Scott, 1894; revised and enlarged edition, London: Scott / New York: Scribners, 1904; revised and enlarged again, 1914); revised as *Man and Woman: A Study of Secondary and Tertiary Sexual Characters* (Boston & New York: Houghton Mifflin, 1929; London: Heinemann, 1934);

Das konträre Geschlechtsgefühl, by Ellis and John Addington Symonds, German translation by Hans Kurella (Leipzig: Wigands, 1896); republished as *Sexual Inversion* [withdrawn from publication] (London: Wilson & Macmillan, 1897); rewritten by Ellis (London: University Press, Watford, 1897; Philadelphia: Davis, 1901; revised and enlarged edition, Philadelphia: Davis, 1915);

Affirmations (London: Scott, 1898; Boston: Houghton Mifflin, 1915);

A Note on the Bedborough Trial (London: University Press, 1898; New York: Privately printed, 1925);

The Evolution of Modesty; The Phenomena of Sexual Periodicity; Auto-Erotism (Leipzig: University Press / Philadelphia: Davis, 1900; revised and enlarged edition, Philadelphia: Davis, 1910);

The Nineteenth Century: A Dialogue in Utopia (London: Richards, 1900); republished as *The Nineteenth Century: An Utopian Retrospect* (Boston: Small, Maynard / London: Richards, 1901);

Analysis of the Sexual Impulse; Love and Pain; The Sexual Impulse in Women (Philadelphia: Davis, 1903; London: Printed for the Society of

Psychological Research, 1904; revised and enlarged edition, Philadelphia: Davis, 1913);

A Study of British Genius (London: Hurst & Blackett, 1904; revised and enlarged edition, Boston & New York: Houghton Mifflin, 1926; London: Constable, 1927);

Sexual Selection in Man: I. Touch. II. Smell. III. Hearing. IV. Vision (Philadelphia: Davis, 1905);

Erotic Symbolism; The Mechanism of Detumescence; The Psychic State in Pregnancy (Philadelphia: Davis, 1906);

The Soul of Spain (London: Constable, 1908; Boston & New York: Houghton Mifflin, 1908; revised edition, London: Constable, 1937; Boston & New York: Houghton Mifflin, 1937);

Sex in Relation to Society (Philadelphia: Davis, 1910; abridged and revised edition, London: Heinemann, 1937);

The Problem of Race-Regeneration (London & New York: Cassell, 1911);

The World of Dreams (London: Constable, 1911; Boston & New York: Houghton Mifflin, 1911);

The Task of Social Hygiene (Boston: Houghton Mifflin, 1912; London: Constable, 1912);

The Forces Warring against War (Boston: World Peace Foundation, 1913);

Impressions and Comments, First Series (London: Constable, 1914; Boston: Houghton Mifflin, 1914);

What to Do after the War Is Over (Boston: World Peace Foundation, 1915?);

Essays in War-Time (London: Constable, 1916; Boston: Houghton Mifflin, 1917);

The Erotic Rights of Women, and The Objects of Marriage: Two Essays (London: British Society for the Study of Sex Psychology, 1918);

The Love Rights of Women (New York: Birth Control Review, 1918);

The Philosophy of Conflict, and Other Essays in War-Time (London: Constable, 1919; Boston & New York: Houghton Mifflin, 1919);

Impressions and Comments, Second Series, 1914-1920 (London: Constable, 1921; Boston & New York: Houghton Mifflin, 1921);

The Play-Function of Sex (London: Francis, 1921);

Kanga Creek: An Australian Idyll (Waltham Saint Lawrence, U.K.: Golden Cockerel Press, 1922; New York: Black Hawk, 1935);

Little Essays of Love and Virtue (London: Black, 1922; New York: Doran, 1922);

The Dance of Life (London: Constable, 1923; Boston & New York: Houghton Mifflin, 1923);

Impressions and Comments, Third (and Final) Series, 1920-1923 (London: Constable, 1924; Boston & New York: Houghton Mifflin, 1924);

Sonnets, with Folk Songs from the Spanish (Waltham Saint Lawrence, U.K.: Golden Cockerel Press, 1925; Boston & New York: Houghton Mifflin, 1925);

Eonism and Other Supplementary Studies (Philadelphia: Davis, 1928);

The Art of Life: Gleanings from the Works of Havelock Ellis, edited by Mrs. S. Herbert (London: Constable, 1929); republished as *The Art of Life, from the Works of Havelock Ellis* (Boston & New York: Houghton Mifflin, 1929);

The Colour-Sense in Literature (London: Ulysses Book Shop, 1931);

Concerning Jude the Obscure (London: Ulysses Book Shop, 1931);

An Open Letter to Biographers (Berkeley Heights, N.J.: Oriole, 1931);

The Revaluation of Obscenity (Paris: Hours, 1931);

More Essays of Love and Virtue (London: Constable, 1931; Garden City, N.Y.: Doubleday, Doran, 1931);

Views and Reviews: A Selection of Uncollected Articles, 1884-1932, 2 volumes (London: Desmond, Harmsworth, 1932; Boston: Houghton Mifflin, 1932);

Psychology of Sex: A Manual for Students (New York: Long & Smith, 1933); republished as *Psychology of Sex: The Biology of Sex; The Sexual Impulse in Youth; Sexual Deviation; The Erotic Symbolisms; Homosexuality; Marriage; The Art of Love. A Manual for Students* (London: Heinemann, 1933);

Chapman (Bloomsbury: Nonesuch, 1934);

My Confessional: Questions of Our Day (Boston & New York: Houghton Mifflin, 1934; London: John Lane, 1934);

From Rousseau to Proust (Boston & New York: Houghton Mifflin, 1935; London: Constable, 1936);

Questions of Our Day (London: John Lane, 1936; New York: Vanguard, 1936);

Selected Essays (London: Dent, 1936; New York: Dutton, 1936);

Poems, selected by John Gawsworth (London: Richards, 1937);

Morals, Manners, and Men (London: Watts, 1939);

My Life: Autobiography of Havelock Ellis (Boston: Houghton Mifflin, 1939; London & Toronto: Heinemann, 1940);

From Marlowe to Shaw: The Studies, 1876-1936, in English Literature, edited by Gawsworth (London: Williams & Norgate, 1950);

The Genius of Europe (London: Williams & Norgate, 1950; New York: Rinehart, 1951);

Sex and Marriage: Eros in Contemporary Life, edited by Gawsworth (London: Williams & Norgate, 1951; New York: Random House, 1952).

Collection: *Studies in the Psychology of Sex,* 7 volumes (Philadelphia: Davis, 1900-1928)—includes *The Evolution of Modesty, The Phenomena of Sexual Periodicity, Auto-Eroticism; Sexual Inversion; Analysis of the Sexual Impulse, Love and Pain, The Sexual Impulse in Women; Sexual Selection in Man: Touch, Smell, Hearing, Vision; Erotic Symbolism, The Mechanism of Detumescence, The Psychic State in*

Pregnancy; Sex in Relation to Society; and *Eonism and Other Supplementary Studies.*

OTHER: James Hinton, *The Law-Breaker and the Coming of the Law,* introduction by Ellis (London: Kegan Paul, 1884);

Walter Savage Landor, *Imaginary Conversations,* introductory note by Ellis (London: Scott, 1886);

Heinrich Heine, *The Prose Writings of Heinrich Heine,* edited, with an introduction, by Ellis (London: Scott, 1887);

Thomas Middleton, *The Best Plays of the Old Dramatists: Thomas Middleton,* edited by Ellis (London: Unwin, 1887);

Henrik Ibsen, *The Pillars of Society, and Other Plays,* edited, with an introduction, by Ellis (London: Scott / New York: Whittaker, 1888);

The Best Plays of the Old Dramatists: John Ford, edited, with an introduction, by Ellis (London: Unwin, 1888); republished as *John Ford* (London: Unwin / New York: Scribners, 1903);

Landor, *The Pentameron and Other Imaginary Conversations,* edited by Ellis (London: Scott, 1889);

Landor, *Pericles and Aspasia,* preface by Ellis (London & New York: Scott, 1890);

Alexander Winter, *The New York State Reformatory in Elmira,* preface by Ellis (London: Sonnenschein, 1891);

Giorgio Vasari, *Vasari's Lives of Italian Painters,* selected, with a preface, by Ellis (London: Scott, 1895);

Christopher Marlowe, *Christopher Marlowe,* edited by Ellis (London: Unwin, 1903; New York: Wyn, 1948);

George Henry Lewes, *Lewes' Life of Goethe,* introduction by Ellis (London: Dent, 1908);

Ellen Karolina Sofia Key, *Love and Marriage,* introduction by Ellis (New York & London: Putnam, 1911);

Key, *The Woman Movement,* introduction by Ellis (New York & London: Putnam, 1912);

Key, *Rahel Varnhagen: A Portrait,* introduction by Ellis (New York & London: Putnam, 1913);

Louise Nyström, *Ellen Key: Her Life and Her Work,* introduction by Ellis (New York & London: Putnam, 1913);

Edith Mary Oldham Ellis, *James Hinton: A Sketch,* preface by Havelock Ellis (London: Paul, 1918);

Otto Braun, *The Diary of Otto Braun, with Selections from His Letters and Poems,* introduction by Ellis (London: Heinemann, 1924);

Pierre Victor de Besenval, *Spleen and Other Stories,* introduction by Ellis (London: Chapman & Hall, 1927);

William Shenstone, *Men & Manners,* edited, with an introduction, by Ellis (Boston & New York: Houghton Mifflin, 1927);

Henri Alain Fournier, *The Wanderer,* edited by Ellis (Boston & New York: Houghton Mifflin, 1928; London: Constable, 1929);

Victor Francis Calverton and Samuel Daniel Schmalhausen, eds., *Sex in Civilization,* introduction by Ellis (London: Allen & Unwin, 1929);

John William Lloyd, *Eneres; or, The Questions of Reksa,* introduction by Ellis (London: Allen & Unwin, 1929);

José Enrique Rodó, *The Motives of Proteus,* introduction by Ellis (London: Allen & Unwin, 1929);

Johann Peter Eckermann, *Conversations of Goethe with Eckermann,* introduction by Ellis (London & Toronto: Dent / New York: Dutton, 1930);

Pierre d'Exideuil, *The Human Pair in the Work of Thomas Hardy,* introduction by Ellis (London: Toulmin, 1930);

Hinton, *Life in Nature,* edited, with an introduction, by Ellis (New York: MacVeagh / Toronto: Longmans, Green, 1931; London: Allen & Unwin, 1932);

Joris Karl Huysmans, *Against the Grain,* introduction by Ellis (New York: Illustrated Editions, 1931);

Landor, *Imaginary Conversations and Poems: A Selection,* edited by Ellis (London & Toronto: Dent / New York: Dutton, 1933);

Jean Pierre Alexandre de Tilly, *Memoirs of the Comte Alexandre de Tilly,* introduction by Ellis (London: Gollancz, 1933);

The Song of Solomon as a Drama by Ernest Renan, translated, with an introduction, by Ellis (Birmingham, U.K.: Birmingham School of Printing, 1937);

Jean-Jacques Rousseau, *The Confessions of J. J. Rousseau in an Anonymous English Version First Published in Two Parts in 1783 & 1790,* introduction by Ellis, 2 volumes (London: Nonesuch, 1938);

Giacomo Girolamo Casanova di Seingalt, *The Memoirs of Jacques Casanova de Seingalt, 1725–1798,* introduction by Ellis, 8 volumes (Edinburgh: Limited Editions Club, 1940).

Although Havelock Ellis wrote on a variety of subjects, he was most famous, or notorious, as the preeminent sex theorist of his era in Britain. He discussed sex and promoted birth control at a time when neither of these activities was done openly. A

Manuscript for an early poem by Ellis (from Isaac Goldberg, Havelock Ellis, 1926)

pioneering sexologist, Ellis argued that women should enjoy their sex lives, and he was unusually tolerant of "deviant" sexuality. He was the first English-language writer to report sympathetically on homosexuality and lesbianism, or "sexual inversion." A self-described socialist, Ellis was also loosely connected to other progressive and radical movements of his time.

His interest in sexuality was rooted in his own sexual problems and his attempts to wrestle with them. It is believed that Ellis never completed sexual intercourse, either with a woman or a man, and Phyllis Grosskurth notes that the subjects of penetration and male orgasm are curiously missing from his sexual writings. A prominent feature of his own complex sexuality was "urolagnia," a term he defined in his *Psychology of Sex: A Manual for Students* (1933) as "sexual pleasure associated with urination."

Ellis, the only son and the eldest of the five children of Edward Ellis and Susannah Wheatley, was christened Henry Havelock after a distant relative, the hero of the Indian Mutiny; Ellis chose to use the name Havelock after he began his literary career. His family led a lower-middle-class existence in South London. His father was captain of a merchant ship and spent his fifty-year career mainly at sea; Susannah, a strong evangelical, was the predominant presence in her son's childhood, except during two long voyages that the boy took with his father. From an early age Ellis was a rather solitary, bookish child. At the age of seven his parents decided that he should accompany his father on a voyage around the world, and on his return home he returned to school. He was eventually sent to a boarding school, The Poplars at Mitcham, but he returned home every weekend because his mother wished to oversee his religious instruction.

In 1875 he accompanied his father on a second trip around the world. Upon arrival in Australia he abandoned the rest of the voyage when the ship's doctor suggested, and his father agreed, that the salubrious climate would be good for his weak constitution. He spent four years in Australia, including one year as a teacher in a remote settlement. There he read widely and became interested in the obscure mixture of scientific objectivity and mysticism he found in the philosophy of James Hinton. In what Ellis recalled as a conversion experience, his reading of Hinton's work led the young man to abandon his childhood religion and adopt Hinton's blend of medical and philosophical thinking.

Hinton had died in 1875, but in 1879 Ellis returned to England and contacted Hinton's surviving relatives, who became friends of the twenty-year-old disciple. After establishing a relationship with them Ellis in 1881 published his first essay, "James Hinton as Religious Thinker," in *The Modern Review,* a religious magazine. Assisted by a loan from Caroline Haddon, the sister of Hinton's widow, and a small inheritance from Ellis's mother, Ellis was able to enter medical school at St. Thomas's Hospital in London. Haddon died before Ellis could repay this loan. Even after he outgrew his fervor for Hinton, Ellis continued to feel indebted to him, both because of the unpaid loan and because Hinton had been so important to Ellis as a young man.

Ellis spent seven years studying in the medical program that students were expected to complete in five years. While he was in medical school he began his writing career, and through the contacts he made as a writer he met many radicals of the day. In the early 1880s he was a founding member of the Progressive Association and of the communal society the Fellowship of the New Life, from which the Fabian Society, which he did not join, emerged in 1884. An article Ellis wrote on Thomas Hardy brought him to the attention of the editor of *The Westminster Review,* Dr. John Chapman, who asked him in 1886 to become its theology editor.

In 1884 Ellis read *The Story of an African Farm* (1883) and wrote to Ralph Iron, the pseudonym of author Olive Schreiner, the daughter of a German missionary to South Africa. Schreiner became the first of a series of women with whom Ellis was sexually, emotionally, and intellectually involved during his lifetime. Initially through letters and later in person they discussed issues of the day, especially "the woman question" and the relations between the sexes.

Ellis in 1896

Schreiner introduced Ellis to her close friend Eleanor Marx, the daughter of Karl Marx, and to Karl Pearson, who later became Galton Professor of Eugenics at University College, London. For Ellis the most traumatic event of these years was the death of his mother in 1888 from scarlet fever, which she had caught while she was caring for him during an illness. In 1889 Schreiner returned to South Africa, and although she and Ellis continued to write to each other during their separation and to see each other when she returned to England for visits, their relationship never regained the intensity of its early years.

Continuing his literary career through the late 1880s, Ellis edited a series of unexpurgated reprints of works by Elizabethan dramatists. In 1890 he published his first book, *The New Spirit,* a collection of essays (most of which he had previously published) on Denis Diderot, Heinrich Heine, Walt Whitman, Henrik Ibsen, and Leo Tolstoy. In 1890 Ellis renewed his acquaintanceship with Edith Lees, and one year later they married, beginning a relationship that lasted for twenty-five years. Since neither believed in the institution of marriage, the two were determined to have an unconventional one: they

Edith and Havelock Ellis, circa 1895

planned to continue living separately, and Edith revealed her past affairs with women to Ellis. She was the main source of Ellis's views on lesbianism, and her case history is believed to be fully outlined in Ellis's *Sexual Inversion* (1897).

During the first years of his marriage Ellis worked on *Man and Woman: A Study of Human Secondary Sexual Characters* (1894), a study of the physical traits that differentiate men and women but are not directly involved in reproduction. In this book Ellis expounded his belief that women's chief purpose in life was reproduction and that all women were destined to become mothers. Since he and his own wife were determined to remain childless, this stance seems ironic although it is explicable in light of his eugenic beliefs. As a eugenicist Ellis believed that only the "fit" should reproduce so that the human race would improve with each succeeding generation, and he was probably unwilling to pass on his wife's mental instabilities and his own inadequacies.

Ellis's marriage soon became painful for both him and his wife. She began an intense affair with a woman, and then he began a relationship with Mneme Barker Smith, later Kirkland, the daughter of a friend, John Barker Smith. Smith and Ellis continued their relationship for fifteen years, even after Smith's marriage. Ellis's wife also continued her relationship with a woman known only as Claire, and when it ended, she began affairs with other women. Despite their advocacy of unconventional marriages the Ellises in fact each felt betrayed by the other.

In the early 1890s Ellis entirely abandoned his medical practice; he had established a scientific reputation as the author of *The Criminal* (1890) and *Man and Woman* and as the editor of the Contemporary Science series of up-to-date summaries for the nonspecialist reader. Originally planned as twelve volumes, the series was so successful that fifty were published, and Ellis earned the majority of his income from the series until it was ended in 1915. He began collecting information for his planned scientific, objective study of human sexuality. Although his work was in many ways progressive, it was also firmly rooted in nineteenth-century medical projects of categorizing the body and its pathologies, and Ellis was among those who, in expanding this study to sexuality, became pioneering sexologists. Despite the clear aim of such research to introduce human sexuality as a subject worthy of serious attention from the scientific and medical communities, medical authorities considered these sexologists to be marginal or unscientific because of the titillating nature of their studies.

In *Man and Woman* Ellis's scientific methodology was fully formulated. He depended on assembling data, both biometric (by measuring skulls, for example) and case histories, in a manner that some readers viewed as haphazard and biased. Karl Pearson criticized Ellis strongly for using what Pearson found to be unconvincing evidence for stating in *Man and Woman* that males were more variable than females, thereby implying that men were more fit than women for survival.

Inspired by his wife's affair, Ellis began collecting information on homosexuality, the subject of the first volume of his series, *Studies in the Psychology of Sex* (1900–1928). John Addington Symonds approached Ellis and asked to join him as a co-author of the book. Symonds, whose interest in the subject was rooted in his own homosexuality, was obsessed with the fact that British law, unlike that of other European countries, severely punished homosexual activity by men. Under the Criminal Law Amendment of 1885 any sexual act between men was punishable by two years of hard labor, and the penalty for anal intercourse was penal servitude for life.

Ellis and Symonds agreed to collaborate: Symonds collected case histories, and Ellis took charge of reviewing medical theories although he also contributed some case histories. With the cooperation of his wife Ellis obtained lesbian case histories from her and her friends, and he obtained some male homosexual histories from Edward Carpenter, a leading radical, sexologist, and open homosexual whom Ellis had known since his days in the Fellowship of the New Life. Yet the collaboration between Ellis and Symonds was uneasy. Symonds rejected all contemporary medical theories, which viewed homosexuality as an abnormal or deviant behavior; Ellis viewed it as an anomaly and was more sympathetic to the orthodox medical views.

The differences between the two writers became irrelevant when Symonds died suddenly in April 1893 in early stages of their work on the book. Ellis completed the manuscript, which was first published in 1896 in a German edition translated by Hans Kurella, the translator of *Man and Woman,* while Ellis searched for someone to publish the book in English. During this time Symonds's literary executor insisted that Symonds's name be removed from the book so Ellis rewrote the book, which was finally published as *Sexual Inversion* in November 1897. He later regretted that he had inaugurated the series with such a controversial subject and that this volume happened to appear soon after Oscar Wilde had served his sentence for homosexual crimes and was released from prison. In a later printing Ellis reorganized and renumbered the works in this series so that the first volume became *The Evolution of Modesty* (1900).

Sexual Inversion was the first of many works (such as Carpenter's *The Intermediate Sex,* 1908) to be published in English and to address homosexuality around the turn of the century. The writers of these works generally broke from contemporary medical dogma in presenting male homosexuality as congenital rather than as an acquired degeneration. They were also somewhat ambivalent about lesbians, whom Ellis saw as unnaturally mannish; many of his lesbian cases included histories of neurosis.

As Richard von Krafft-Ebing had done in addressing his influential *Psychopathia Sexualis* (1886) to doctors and lawyers, Ellis also addressed *Sexual Inversion* to an audience of professionals—physicians and psychologists. He did not intend the book to be regarded as salacious, but his message that inversion was congenital and therefore something to be tolerated was shocking to many readers. In fact, in 1898 George Bedborough—an anarchist bookseller and secretary of the Legitimation League, an organization that also advocated other shocking propositions such as free love and divorce by mutual consent—was arrested for selling copies of *Sexual Inversion.* Neither Ellis nor his publisher was charged with any offense, and Bedborough may have been prosecuted in an attempt to discredit anarchists and the Legitimation League rather than to ban the book. Yet Ellis was aware that the scientific credibility of his book was under attack, and he was also liable to prosecution. When Bedborough, in exchange for having other charges against him dropped, pleaded guilty to selling the book and thus assented to its obscenity, the affair left Ellis feeling betrayed and publicly humiliated.

During the next decade he underwent additional personal and professional problems. Edith, who had been writing novels under her name as Mrs. Havelock Ellis, increasingly suffered from physical and mental illness, and the Ellises never had enough income to meet their expenses. At this time Sigmund Freud was also emerging as the foremost theorist on the sexual basis of the human psyche, and while Ellis was one of the first in Britain to write about the Austrian researcher, Ellis resented Freud's ascendance. Ellis was prominent in his lifetime, but after both he and Freud died in 1939, the influence of Ellis was overshadowed by that of Freud, and Ellis's work was often trivialized—no doubt in part because of the eclectic nature of his publications. Although Ellis was careful never to dismiss Freud and his work entirely, many of Ellis's criticisms of Freud foreshadowed those that emerged in the 1970s and 1980s.

Sex in Relation to Society, the sixth volume of Ellis's series, was the most important to Ellis. In it he argued, on the basis of discussions he had held with Schreiner, that marriage was a fashionable form of prostitution in which wives were relatively ill paid. In the series as a whole Ellis demonstrated his modern—in opposition to Victorian—attitudes through two main opinions. The first was in his somewhat grudging acceptance of what were considered to be deviant or abnormal sexual practices; the second was in his belief that it was normal for women both to have sexual desires and to fulfill them. He contended that women did not have less sexual desire than men; they were merely the victims of bad lovers. Yet Ellis's positions were not unambiguously modern: he also believed that men were responsible for their female partners' lack of sexual interest because the men were responsible for initiating sex—women were naturally too modest and passive to do so. Thus he implied that aggressive women (lesbians, for example) were pathological. Ellis's emphasis on motherhood was also confining for many women who could not or would not have children, and although Ellis was sympathetic to homosexuality and considered masturbation or autoeroticism to be normal, he suggested that it was desirable and possible to cure homosexuality and curb masturbation.

The financial woes of the Ellises, who had been spending much of their time living in Cornwall, were exacerbated by Edith, who leased a cottage, Woodpecker Farm, nearer to London. Eventually in order

Moor Cottage, Carbis Bay, Cornwall, where in 1909 Ellis wrote part of his Studies in the Psychology of Sex *(1900–1928)*

to pay for their lease they had to rent rooms to guests at Woodpecker Farm, the last home that the two Ellises shared. Edith had a moderately successful career as a writer and was much in demand for her charismatic lectures, but in 1913 she was diagnosed as having diabetes, which was then a fatal disease. She refused to give in to the illness, however, and left for a lecture tour in the United States. Following her departure Ellis resumed his relationship with Smith. In 1914 Ellis's father died, and Smith became involved with a new man, whom she eventually married, and with nursing her sick mother.

Ellis, feeling alone after suffering these losses, then met thirty-year-old Margaret Sanger, a woman who had separated from her husband and children and come to England in order to evade prosecution for using the mail to disseminate birth-control literature in the United States. For the rest of Ellis's life the two remained close although he did not share Sanger's passion for promoting birth control. A firm eugenicist, he was acquainted with British birth-control advocate Marie Stopes, who tried unsuccessfully to draw him into her activities. For Ellis, birth control was but one means of pursuing the broader goal of eugenics—that of improving the inherited physical and mental characteristics of the human race. A member of the Eugenics Society from its beginning in 1908, he had contributed "The Sterilization of the Unfit" to the *Eugenics Review* in 1909, and near the end of his life in a 1939 edition of *Sex in Relation to Society* he wrote approvingly of Adolf Hitler's sterilization laws.

Sanger's position as a public figure made her friendship with Ellis a subject of gossip in the American press, and when he wrote to his wife about his intimate relationship with Sanger, Edith, who was quite ill, became further depressed and returned to England from Philadelphia. Suffering from a nervous breakdown, she was hospitalized in Cornwall, where her behavior became increasingly erratic, and she contracted many debts that Ellis eventually spent years paying off. She insisted on getting a legal separation from Ellis, and after she slipped into a diabetic coma following an attack of pleurisy, she died on 13 September 1916.

While Ellis was settling his wife's estate, he met Françoise Cyon, whom Edith had contracted to translate into French her *Three Modern Seers* (1910), a book about Hinton, Carpenter, and Friedrich Nietzsche. Cyon, separated from her husband, was in serious financial need and hoped to receive some money from Ellis. She first sought him out for counsel and then became enthralled by him. Their relationship was initially quite

Ellis in his Brixton apartment, circa 1912

erotic; Phyllis Grosskurth believes that they engaged mainly in mutual masturbation. Ellis disclosed his urolagnia in his posthumous autobiography, and Cyon's discussion of their sexual relationship in her memoir, *Friendship's Odyssey* (1946), offended many of his friends.

In 1919 Sanger, who had returned to the United States although she continued to visit Britain regularly, devoted an entire issue of her *Birth Control Review* to Ellis. She was largely responsible for bringing Ellis to the attention of readers in the United States. He eventually became more respected in the United States than he was in England, and his recognition in America provided a source of income that he needed badly. Ellis's prominence made him regularly sought out by other progressives, and he was increasingly approached by potential biographers, with whom he usually cooperated. While Cyon taught French to support herself and her children, Ellis had time to develop friendships with other women such as poet Hilda Doolittle (H. D.), Winifred Ellerman, and best-selling author Jane Burr. In 1920 he was saddened by the death of Olive Schreiner, whose husband, Samuel Cron Cronwright-Schreiner, subsequently asked Ellis to assist him in compiling an edition of her letters.

During the 1920s Ellis and Cyon were involved in a series of relationships involving novelist Hugh de Selincourt, an admirer of Ellis. Unknown to Ellis, Sanger and Selincourt had an affair, and later Sanger had an affair with Harold Child, the lover of Jane de Selincourt, Hugh's wife. Selincourt was also sexually involved with Cyon, an affair that gave Ellis pain when he learned of it. These relationships continued for years, through much correspondence between those involved.

The 1920s were also Ellis's last period of intense literary work. In 1923 he published *The Dance of Life,* his most popular book. In it he included revisions of previously published work and attempted to present a synthetic account of his philosophy of life, which emphasized that life was about change and development. He viewed this book as the final product of his lifetime of reading and contemplation. In 1928 he published *Eonism and Other Supplementary Studies,* his first major work on sexuality since 1910 and the seventh and final volume of his series, *Studies in the Psychology of Sex. Eonism and Other Supplementary Studies* was a collection of previously published essays on subjects such as eonism (transvestism), erogenous zones, narcissism, and what Ellis called "undinism," the love of urinating. He also contributed what he thought was a notice but became a commentary published with Radclyffe Hall's *The Well of Loneliness* (1928), a novel that incorporated lesbian themes and was banned by the British home secretary. An appeal against the ban failed in 1929, and in the controversy aroused by this book Ellis again became involved, albeit peripherally, with a celebrated "indecent" work.

As the 1920s ended, Cyon saw less of Selincourt, and their relationship finally ended in 1931. In 1929 Sanger gave Ellis a gift of enough money to employ Cyon as his secretary. Cyon was overjoyed, for the money allowed her to give up her uncongenial employment as a teacher and finally move in with Ellis. Ellis, who valued his privacy, was less enthusiastic than Cyon about this arrangement, but in the end he found it to be a success.

The Depression years were difficult for Ellis and Cyon, and Sanger had to reduce the amount that she contributed to maintaining them. Ellis made some money writing a column for William Randolph Hearst's *New York American.* After a long illness Ellis died at the age of eighty, leaving Cyon to publish posthumously *My Life: Autobiography of Havelock Ellis* (1939).

Letters:
The Unpublished Letters of Havelock Ellis to Joseph Ishill (Berkeley Heights, N.J.: Oriole, 1954).

Biographies:
Houston Peterston, *Havelock Ellis: Philosopher of Love* (Boston: Houghton Mifflin, 1928);

Arthur Calder-Marshall, *Havelock Ellis: A Biography* (London: Hart-Davis, 1959);

Françoise Delisle, *Friendship's Odyssey* (London: Delisle, 1964);

Delisle, *The Return of Havelock Ellis; or, Limbo or the Dove?* (London: Regency, 1968);

Vincent Brome, *Havelock Ellis: Philosopher of Love* (London: Routledge & Kegan Paul, 1979);

Phyllis Grosskurth, *Havelock Ellis: A Biography* (Toronto: McClelland & Stewart, 1980).

References:
Franz G. Alexander and Sheldon T. Selesnick, *The History of Psychiatry: An Evaluation of Psychiatric Thought and Practice from Prehistoric Times to the Present* (New York: Harper & Row, 1966);

Lucy Bland, *Banishing the Beast: English Feminism and Sexual Morality, 1885–1914* (Toronto: Penguin, 1995);

John Stewart Collis, *Havelock Ellis, Artist of Life: A Study of His Life and Work* (New York: Sloane, 1959);

Françoise Delisle, *Françoise, In Love with Love* (London: Delisle, 1962);

Michel Foucalt, *The History of Sexuality: An Introduction* (Markham: Penguin, 1987);

Isaac Goldberg, *Havelock Ellis: A Biographical and Critical Survey* (London: Constable, 1926);

Sheila Rowbotham, *Socialism and the New Life: The Personal and Sexual Politics of Edward Carpenter and Havelock Ellis* (London: Pluto, 1977).

Papers:
The letters exchanged by Ellis and Françoise Delisle (Cyon) are at the Mugar Library, Boston University. Ellis's letters to Margaret Sanger are in the Sanger Papers at the Library of Congress and in the Sanger Papers of the Sophia Smith Collection at Smith College. Ellis's letters to Radclyffe Hall are at the National Archives of Canada; those to Marguerite Agniel are in the Morris Library, Southern Illinois University; those to Josephine Walther are in the Lilly Library, Indiana University; and those to Thomas Davidson are in the Yale University Library.

Millicent Garrett Fawcett
(11 June 1847 – 5 August 1929)

Sandra den Otter
Queen's University

BOOKS: *Political Economy for Beginners* (London: Macmillan, 1870; revised and enlarged, 1876);

Representative Reform: Two Essays on Proportional Representation (London: Representative Reform Association, 1871);

Essays and Lectures on Social and Political Subjects, by Fawcett and Henry Fawcett (London: Macmillan, 1872);

Mrs. Fawcett on Women's Suffrage (Birmingham: Birmingham Morning News, 1872);

Mr. Fitzjames Stephen on the Position of Women (London: Macmillan, 1873);

Tales in Political Economy (London: Macmillan, 1874);

Janet Doncaster (London: Smith, Elder, 1875); republished as *Janet: A Novel* (New York: Munro, 1878); republished as *Friend or Lover: A Novel* (New York: Carleton, 1881);

The Martyrs of Turkish Misrule (London: Cassell, Petter & Galpin, 1877);

Some Eminent Women of Our Times: Short Biographical Sketches (London: Macmillan, 1889);

A Reply to the Letter of Mr. Samuel Smith, M.P., on Women's Suffrage (Westminster: National Society for Women's Suffrage, 1892);

Home and Politics: An Address Delivered at Toynbee Hall and Elsewhere (London: Women's Printing Society, 1894);

Life of Her Majesty Queen Victoria (London: W. H. Allen, 1895; Boston: Roberts, 1895);

Speech (Revised and Enlarged) Made at the Croyden Meeting of the General Committee of the National Union of Women Workers, October, 1897, . . . on the New Rules for Dealing with the Sanitary Condition of the British Army in India (London: Women's Printing Society, 1897);

International Congress. The White Slave Trade: Its Causes, and the Best Means of Preventing It (London, 1899);

Life of the Right Hon. Sir William Molesworth, Bart., M.P., F.R.S. (London: Macmillan / New York: Macmillan, 1901);

Five Famous French Women (London & New York: Cassell, 1905);

Millicent Garrett Fawcett, circa 1892

Women's Suffrage: A Short History of a Great Movement (London & Edinburgh: Jack, 1912; London: Jack / New York: Dodge, 1912?);

The Women's Victory—and After: Personal Reminiscences, 1911-1918 (London: Sidgwick & Jackson, 1920);

Six Weeks in Palestine, Spring, 1921 (London: Women's Printing Society, 1921);

Our Second Visit to Palestine, Spring, 1922 (London: Women's Printing Society, 1922);

What I Remember (London: Unwin, 1924; New York: Putnam, 1925);

Easter in Palestine, 1921–1922 (New York: Frank-Maurice, 1925; London: Unwin, 1926);

Josephine Butler: Her Work and Principles, and Their Meaning for the Twentieth Century, by Fawcett and E. M. Turner (London: Association for Moral and Social Hygiene, 1927).

OTHER: Mary Wollstonecraft, *A Vindication of the Rights of Woman,* introduction by Fawcett (London: Unwin, 1891);

Honnor Morten, *Questions for Women and Men,* introduction by Fawcett (London: Black, 1899);

Henry Fawcett, *Manual of Political Economy,* edited by Fawcett (London & New York: Macmillan, 1907);

John Stuart Mill, *The Subjection of Women,* introduction by Fawcett (London: World's Classics, 1912);

Helena M. Stanwick, *The Future of the Women's Movement,* introduction by Fawcett (London: Bell, 1913);

Elizabeth Blackwell, *Pioneer Work in Opening the Medical Profession to Women,* introduction by Fawcett (London: Everyman, 1914).

Millicent Garrett Fawcett presided over the suffrage movement in Great Britain for almost sixty years and therefore occupies a pivotal place in the history of British feminism. Although known for her robust leadership of the battle for suffrage, she was also engaged in reform of moral conduct, women's work, and women's education. Her life and writing afford an introduction to many reform questions about late-Victorian and Edwardian England.

Millicent Garrett was the seventh of the ten children of Newson Garrett and Louisa Dunnell. Her father ran a prominent business based on several profitable concerns: a gas works, maltings, shipyards, and a thriving merchant trade in coal and corn. The family spent summers at Alde House in the seaside resort town of Aldeburgh in East Anglia; in winter the Garretts lived at Snape, a nearby village dominated by the family's malting business.

In her autobiographical novel *Janet Doncaster* (1875) Fawcett recalls her mother's strong religious sentiments, but neither Millicent nor her protagonist shared the evangelical conscience of their mothers. It was not until she heard F. D. Maurice speak that she discovered a congenial form of spirituality. While her mother provided her with an affectionate and secure childhood, Millicent's autobiography recounts how actively her father encouraged his daughters in their unfeminine pursuits. Although he refused to be guided by the conventions of Aldeburgh society, Garrett was at the center of local public life. Taking care that the education of his daughters stretched beyond the feminine arts of needlework and music, Garrett arranged for them to be educated at a small academic school run by Miss Louisa Browning at Blackheath. Millicent remained there until a temporary crisis in her father's business affairs obliged her to leave the school at the age of sixteen. Garrett also shaped the unconventional paths of his daughters' lives by actively supporting one of Millicent's older sisters, Elizabeth, in her ultimately successful battle to study medicine at London University. Elizabeth also influenced the course of Millicent's life, for Elizabeth first introduced her to Emily Davies, the feminist reformer.

Upon leaving the school at Blackheath, Millicent spent much time in London with Louise, another sister who introduced her to the radical circles gathered around liberals such as John Stuart Mill, Sir Charles Dilke, and others. In 1866 she met Henry Fawcett, who, despite being blind, was a prominent radical Liberal politician and professor of political economy at Cambridge University. In view of their shared political convictions and commitment to public service, the Fawcett marriage in 1867 appeared to be a congenial one. "Between us there is such perfect intellectual sympathy," Henry Fawcett wrote, "that I am convinced we shall enjoy the most complete happiness."

Millicent's new responsibilities were substantial: she maintained a household in Cambridge and in London, and she was occupied with Philippa, their daughter, who was born two years after their marriage. Until 1871 her husband was entirely dependent on Millicent for secretarial assistance, and Fawcett worked closely with him on successive editions of his *Manual of Political Economy* (1863). This work provided her with a formidable grounding in the science, and she independently wrote *Political Economy for Beginners* (1870), which was published in many editions and translations, and *Tales in Political Economy* (1874). On the basis of this work the Political Economy Club was almost persuaded to offer membership to her, but this did not occur; no woman became a member until 1920.

While Fawcett gained much from her husband's knowledge of political economy, his interest in woman suffrage increased under her tutelage. In addition to collaborating with him on political economy and on social questions such as the Factory Acts, she began a long and productive career as an independent writer in the 1870s. She published vigorous pamphlets on woman suffrage; articles on education, the economy, and suffrage; and an entry on communism for the ninth edition of the *Encyclopaedia Britannica* (1877). In 1875 she published *Janet*

Doncaster, a narrative demonstrating the slavery of arranged marriage, the troubles wrought by drink, and the felicity of a companionate marriage. She also had begun to lecture on suffrage in the late 1860s, and by the early 1870s she became active in suffrage campaigns. After the unexpected death of her husband in 1884, Fawcett and her daughter took up residence with her sister Agnes and began to build a life devoted to transforming the place of women in British society.

Fawcett's first published article in *Macmillan's Magazine* addressed the issue of women's need for wider opportunities in higher education, and it was the first of many articles that she wrote, in addition to many speeches that she made, throughout her life on this subject. The matter was critical, she argued, because the lamentable state of women's education was so often used by opponents of suffrage to justify excluding women from the exercise of political power. Women were educated to lives of idleness rather than given a context in which to enlarge their intelligence. Fawcett acted to remedy this situation when she became involved in establishing a lecture scheme for women in Cambridge and, in 1874, in establishing Newnham Hall, the home of what became one of two pioneering educational institutions for women at Cambridge University. She remained on the governing body of Newnham from 1881 until 1901.

Fawcett's commitment to removing the barriers to advancement that poor education imposed on women was also reflected in the evidence that she forcefully presented to the Royal Commission on Education in 1886. She condemned the apprenticing of young children, a practice which, she argued, endangered young girls and provided them with only a low level of general education. Fawcett briefly taught political economy at Queen's College, Dublin, and at King's College Department for Ladies in the late 1880s and early 1890s.

Years later Fawcett's agitation for women's education in India strikingly demonstrated the close connection that nineteenth-century liberal thinking characteristically made between education and social progress. In 1916 she led a deputation on this issue to Austen Chamberlain, secretary of state for India, and she continued to lobby Chamberlain's successor, Edwin Montagu, about the education of women in India. Her interest in India began during her work with her husband on Indian matters, especially the Indian budget. She was also active in urging the British government to legislate against infant marriages in India, a social practice that she regarded as inimical to advancing the education of women. Pointing to the success of early-nineteenth-century prohibitions of infanticide, she argued forcefully against the inclination to do nothing.

Millicent and her sister Agnes, two of the ten Garrett children, in 1865

The protection of young girls and women generally was a concern that Fawcett raised in response to debate in the late 1860s and early 1870s around the Contagious Diseases Acts, legislation which permitted compulsory medical examination of any women in garrison towns and incarceration of them in lock hospitals. The London Suffrage Society was fiercely divided on this legislation, as was the Garrett family. Elizabeth Garrett supported the Contagious Diseases Acts on public-health grounds. Fawcett followed the direction of her husband in opposing the legislation but believing that silence was the most tactical response, in contrast to Josephine Butler, who loudly and publicly opposed the acts. Yet Fawcett's silence on this important issue was not entirely dictated by her husband's example. She felt

Henry and Millicent Fawcett, one year after their marriage in 1867

strongly that female suffrage was the most important political goal and that once this had been secured, the myriad of women's issues might be much more effectively treated.

Fawcett's silence in the controversy around the Contagious Diseases Acts contrasts to her public response to the "Maiden Tribute" scandal that broke in 1885. W. T. Stead–editor of the *Pall Mall Gazette,* which had earlier printed sensationalist accounts of poverty in the East End of London–published "The Maiden Tribute of Modern Babylon," a series of articles on child prostitution in London. When Stead demonstrated the extent of the white slave trade by purchasing a young girl, he was subsequently convicted and imprisoned on abduction charges in 1885. Fawcett, like Josephine Butler, was indefatigable in her public campaign not only to exonerate Stead but also to end the trade in young girls that he had exposed.

Overcoming her reticence, Fawcett wrote articles on the white slave trade and many letters on Stead's behalf. She argued that in exposing "a hideously perverted state of morals" Stead had helped to secure passage of the long-postponed Criminal Law Amendment Act, which was designed to lengthen the time that girls could bring charges in rape, seduction, or incest cases, and to increase the punishment for sexual assaults against children. Fawcett had energetically campaigned along with Butler in favor of this legislation, as she regarded the pervasive trade in young girls as an indisputable call for female suffrage. British reluctance to treat sexual crimes seriously could not characterize a government in which women were influential, and she argued that creating equality between men and women would help immeasurably to establish a higher moral standard in society. No longer would immorality be regarded as a necessity for men, and no longer would the state be expected to minister to male weakness by initiatives such as the Contagious Diseases Acts.

In the mid 1880s Fawcett assisted Butler in founding the National Vigilance Association; she headed the Preventative and Rescue Sub-committee, in which she pursued reforms in employment of children in theaters, medical homes for women, the protection of feebleminded girls from prostitution, and the "rescue" of individual girls and women from lives of prostitution. She remained active in this association until 1893, and she continued to attend annual meetings thereafter. The Travellers' Aid Society also provided Fawcett a conduit for her interest in working for social purity. This society protected girls arriving at large urban ports and railway terminals from what she described as the "class of fiends in human form who haunt railway stations especially for the purpose of entrapping ignorant and foolish girls, often little more than children, to their ruin." An implacable opponent of sexual impropriety, Fawcett crusaded in 1894 against Henry Cust, a parliamentary candidate whom she discovered had fathered illegitimate children. Her opposition derived in part from her outrage that male sexual exploits were tolerated while women were cast as immoral predators. In 1916 she spoke out again in opposition to the Criminal Law Amendment Bill, which would have permitted the detention of girls found soliciting on streets until they reached the age of nineteen; she also opposed another initiative made to protect servicemen under the guise of the Defence of the Realm Act by providing that women be examined for sexual diseases.

Another issue that engaged Fawcett throughout the 1880s and 1890s was Home Rule for Ireland. Throughout her life she remained an unyielding opponent to Irish Home Rule, as she regarded such schemes as rewards for political violence and as a betrayal of the loyalists. When the Liberal Party under Prime Minister William Ewart Gladstone became an advocate of Home Rule, she abandoned the Liberal Party in favor of the Liberal Unionists and became a vigorous and prominent campaigner against Home Rule at hustings with eminent Liberal Unionists. She went on many speaking tours in Ireland during the late 1880s and 1890s. Her prominent political activity in this cause lent support to her case for suffrage and an enlarged political role for women. The Liberal Unionist Party provided a rather odd home for Fawcett. She was unsympathetic with many currents in the party, especially with the opposition to female suffrage that most of its members maintained. Nonetheless, she became an active leader of the Women's Liberal Unionist Association.

Historians differ in their explanations of her affiliation with the Liberal Unionists. Some suggest that she was simply attempting to remain faithful to her husband's political convictions while others argue that her affiliation demonstrates her inherent conservatism, evident in the support that the party gave to the Boer War. Fawcett's move might best be explained by recalling the peculiarities of mid-nineteenth-century liberalism, for in many ways she remained an old-style liberal. Like most Liberal Unionists, she regarded free trade as essential to her political beliefs. Convinced that the impediments to women's advancement were entirely artificial, she favored abandoning such barriers to the free development of women's intellect. She remained a fierce critic of labor unionism, partly because she observed the reluctance of labor unionists to protect women's work and partly because she doubted the efficacy of limiting the freedom of contract between employer and laborer. Liberalism was, Fawcett averred in tones reminiscent of mid-nineteenth-century liberals, "the awakening of the democratic spirit, the rebellion against authority, the proclamation of the rights of man . . . a new ideal concerning the position of women." When the Liberal Unionists abandoned their free trade principles in 1903–1904, Fawcett severed her association with them and thereafter declined to be associated with any political party.

Although she also regretted the resistance to woman suffrage among Liberal Unionists, she sympathized with their endorsement of the Boer War, which broke out in 1899. Unlike those progressive Liberals who regarded British action as imperial belligerence, Fawcett firmly defended the war on the grounds that British settlers there required protection from Boer aggression. After Emily Hobhouse published a report condemning conditions in British

Fawcett in 1918

concentration camps for Boer women and children, Fawcett published in the *Westminster Gazette* her critical review of Hobhouse's report, and, partly as a result of Fawcett's prominence as an advocate of British policy in South Africa, she was asked to lead a government investigation of the camps. Composed entirely of women, this commission headed by an outspoken suffragist was an innovation.

Fawcett and the other commission members visited thirty-three concentration camps and painstakingly researched conditions in each. Reporting on 12 December 1901, they found much wanting in the camps: high mortality rates, polluted water supplies, and unsanitary conditions. Those who had concurred with Hobhouse's critique of the camps read this report as further evidence of mismanaged British endeavors while supporters of the government read it as a defense. Neither was entirely the case. Fawcett continued to endorse the conduct of the British government in South Africa, but she also called on the government to reform the camps. When she completed her work with this commission, she resumed her efforts for suffrage, a reform endeavor that dominated her life until World War I.

Garrett's long engagement with woman suffrage dated from 1867, when she was present in the House of Commons for Mill's proposal to include woman suffrage in the Reform Bill. When the Women's Suffrage Committee in London was formed in July 1867 to publicize suffrage arguments through pamphleteering and public meetings and to lobby for parliamentary support, she became an active member. In 1868 she addressed her first public suffrage meeting, at which she spoke with Mill, John Morley, and others. By the early 1870s she had become a persuasive public speaker.

In her early addresses and articles Fawcett grounded her suffrage arguments on the liberal position of the equality of all men and women and on the potential contributions that women could make to political life. While she continued to invoke this principle she increasingly appealed to essentialist arguments in which she contended that precisely because more women than men had been occupied with the domestic realm, women were peculiarly suited to political activity. They were especially well equipped to legislate about social issues such as child welfare, education, the poor law, temperance, health, and "moral" reform. When opponents to suffrage warned that womanliness would disappear with the advent of suffrage, Fawcett countered by emphasizing that feminine qualities would be enhanced in the political arena. In a pamphlet published in 1884 on the Franchise Bill, she answered fears that female suffrage would overthrow the social order by pointing out that the experience of municipal and school-board elections had not coarsened the femininity of enfranchised women: "the possession of a vote has not made women essentially different from what they were before; we still like needlework; we prefer pretty gowns to ugly ones; we are interested in domestic management and economy, and are not altogether indifferent to our friends and relations."

In another article in *The Fortnightly Review* in 1889 she assured readers that women would not be transformed by casting votes. She pointed to the reasonable and moderate conduct of the many women who worked in poor-law administration, the Primrose League, or the Women's Liberal Federation as evidence that women were capable of thoughtful citizenship that would enhance rather than compromise the honor of Great Britain. Dismissing anxieties that England would cease to be a "masculine" nation, she repeatedly appealed to patriotic arguments to buttress her claims for extending the franchise. In *A Reply to the Letter of Mr. Samuel Smith, M.P., on Women's Suffrage* (1892), her acerbic rejoinder to the member of Parliament who led the campaign against the 1892 Suffrage Bill, Fawcett again rejected the portrait of enfranchised women "destroying the Constitution," voting against their husbands, and neglecting their children and the suppers of their husbands. Although Queen Victoria did not support woman suffrage, Fawcett praises the queen in *Life of Her Majesty Queen Victoria* (1895) for exercising strong leadership, promoting the entrance of women into the medical profession, and generally fostering women's education. A central theme of Fawcett's portrait in this biography is of the queen as the mother of her children—and of the nation.

Historians have suggested that employing these essentialist arguments was tactical, for Fawcett repeatedly demonstrated her savvy political sense. Yet she certainly believed that women's political emancipation would genuinely enhance rather than undermine the femininity that she regarded as so critical to the national welfare, and her political judgment motivated her support for limited rather than universal suffrage. Since the majority of Englishmen believed that suffrage ought to be introduced in a slow, piecemeal fashion, Fawcett elected to endorse proposals to enfranchise women householders and property owners—about nine hundred thousand women. In response to the familiar argument that the worst abuses against women had already been remedied, she enumerated the inequities that still plagued women: the inequality of divorce laws, the inadequacy of laws protecting women and children from criminal immorality, the abysmal working conditions of many women, the exclusion of women as members of the professions and universities, and the precarious status of women's work in the trade unions.

When the National Union of Women's Suffrage Societies (NUWSS) was established in 1897, Fawcett was the unchallenged candidate for its leadership. The NUWSS sought to coordinate the various suffrage initiatives into one powerful pressure group; its principal task was to work toward ensuring support for a member's bill introducing woman suffrage. Much energy was spent to canvass candidates to determine their views on suffrage and to campaign for members who sympathized with the NUWSS. It also lobbied elected members of Parliament to vote for suffrage legislation. Most of this work was done within the Liberal Party, for most support was based there.

The task of piloting a multifarious union such as the NUWSS was a diplomatic quagmire.

One of the great difficulties lay in reconciling opposing strands within the union—advocates of moderate constitutional approaches and proponents of a more militant approach. The Women's Social and Political Union (WSPU), established by Emmeline Pankhurst and Christabel Pankhurst, advocated a militant approach characterized by public disturbances: interrupting the speeches of Liberal speakers or storming the London house of Home Secretary Herbert Henry Asquith.

While Fawcett unambiguously endorsed the constitutional and more-restrained methods, she was sympathetic to the militant approaches of the WSPU. She feared divisions within the suffrage movement, for she saw that these might destroy collective effort and postpone suffrage indefinitely. Recognizing that the new militancy was much more popular among laboring women than among others, she feared that to oppose militancy would arouse class divisions and wanted to present a united front that transcended class differences. In a letter to the *Times* (London) after Annie Kenney and others had been arrested following a WSPU demonstration at the House of Commons in fall 1906, Fawcett wrote:

> I hope the more old-fashioned suffragists will stand by them; and I take this opportunity of saying that in my opinion, far from having injured the movement, they have done more during the last twelve months to bring it within the region of practical politics than we have been able to accomplish in the same number of years.

The diplomacy in this statement illustrates why Fawcett dominated the suffrage campaign for such a long period. Although she could be implacable and inflexible, she was also capable of the delicacy that leadership of a potentially factional organization demanded.

The number of national union suffrage societies grew from thirty-one in 1906 to more than two hundred by 1910. In February 1907 Fawcett, as president under the new constitution of the NUWSS, participated in a large march in London, and in June 1908 the NUWSS and the WSPU held a joint rally. Under Fawcett's leadership the NUWSS decided against adopting the goal of universal suffrage and instead remained intent on securing the suffrage of women with the same qualifications as enfranchised men. Fawcett was reluctant to antagonize support. "To ask for adult suffrage now," she had cautioned in 1906, "is in reality to oppose Women's Suffrage."

As it became apparent that woman suffrage would not rank high among the many reforms of the new Liberal administration, members of the WSPU grew increasingly militant, and tensions between those in the WSPU and those in the NUWSS increased in late autumn 1908. Abandoning her reluctance to condemn militancy, Fawcett sanctioned several resolutions and initiatives distinguishing the tactics of the NUWSS from the militancy of the WSPU. By 1911 and 1912 she openly challenged militant suffragists. She attributed the failure of the Conciliation Bill in 1912 to militants who were "the chief obstacles in the way of the success of the suffrage movement in the House of Commons and far more formidable opponents of it than Mr. Asquith and Mr. [Lewis] Harcourt."

The defeat of the Conciliation Bill occasioned an important change in NUWSS lobbying. Recognizing that Asquith's Liberal government was unlikely ever to support woman suffrage and that, by contrast, every Labour member of Parliament supported the bill, Fawcett swung the support of the NUWSS behind the Labour Party. An Election Fighting Fund was set up to support Labour candidates, and the vigorous lobbying of the NUWSS on behalf of Liberal candidates was transferred to candidates of the Labour Party. While Fawcett insisted that the NUWSS had not become a partisan organization, this was a significant move, in view of her long-standing opposition to trade unionism and to its exclusionary treatment of women workers.

Under Fawcett's leadership the NUWSS weathered another storm less successfully. She publicly and energetically supported World War I and accordingly directed that the NUWSS suspend its suffrage campaign until hostilities ended. While her patriotic enthusiasms reflected the sentiments of the broad base of NUWSS members, there was also a strong pacifist strand within the organization. Yet Fawcett was genuinely persuaded that the war was a just conflict, and she feared that the identification of suffrage with pacifism would hurt the cause of the NUWSS. Her unyielding public endorsement of the war caused several prominent people—notably Kathleen Courtney and Catherine Marshall—to resign as members, and these different positions on suffrage during the war left a deep division within the NUWSS.

The campaign for suffrage in Britain was resumed only when it became apparent in 1916 that the franchise would be extended to soldiers and sailors. Drawing on her formidable powers of organization and persuasion, Fawcett led a large deputation of women suffragists from many suffrage organizations to lobby Prime Minister David

Fawcett and her sister Agnes, leading other feminists to lay flowers at a statue of John Stuart Mill in May 1927

Lloyd George. In June 1917 the House of Commons passed a bill enfranchising women more than thirty years old, and, having achieved limited suffrage for women, Fawcett chose to withdraw from leadership of the NUWSS in 1919. She remained an active member of the International Women's Suffrage Alliance, which she served as first vice president, and she continued to attend annual meetings of the NUWSS. She spent the 1920s delivering speeches, writing, and traveling to the Near East and Ceylon. She died on 5 August 1929 after a short illness.

Fawcett had become a venerable figure well before World War I. Granted an honorary doctorate of laws from the University of St. Andrews in 1905, she was the first woman to receive such an award. She was also made Dame of the Grand Cross Order of the British Empire in 1925. She had been at the forefront of the suffrage movement for almost sixty years, written scores of articles on the subject, led countless public meetings, and made many speaking tours. She had overseen attempts to guide suffrage legislation through Parliament, selected candidates, and lobbied members of Parliament. As president of the NUWSS for more than twenty years, she had minimized conflict within the potentially factious organization. She had quickly mastered political communications: she was successful not only in building contact with individual members of Parliament but also in mobilizing support effectively in large rallies.

The coherence of her activities reflects her abiding attachment to mid-nineteenth-century liberal principles. Unlike other late-Victorian or Edwardian reformers, Fawcett did not advocate a dramatic enlargement of the state's responsibilities; for example, she opposed family allowances. She remained loyal to the ethos of the individual, an orientation that characterized the liberalism of the radical circles in which she had moved during the 1860s and 1870s. Fawcett's espousal of woman suffrage was inseparable from the social and political reforms with which she had been engaged since the 1860s. In her ardent articles and speeches and in her persuasive leadership she used the essentialist view of the nobility of British womanhood to urge a transformation of the place of women. Because she regarded women as possessing such special moral authority, woman suffrage for Fawcett was the ultimate social reform.

Biographies:

Ray Strachey, *Millicent Garrett Fawcett* (London: John Murray, 1931);

David Rubinstein, *A Different World for Women: The Life of Millicent Garrett Fawcett* (London: Harvester Wheatsheaf, 1991).

References:

Barbara Caine, *Victorian Feminists* (Oxford: Oxford University Press, 1992);

Lawrence Goldman, *The Blind Victorian: Henry Fawcett and British Liberalism* (Cambridge: Cambridge University Press, 1989);

Brian Harrison, *Prudent Revolutionaries: Portraits of British Feminists between the Wars* (Oxford: Clarendon Press / New York: Oxford University Press, 1987);

Harrison, *Separate Spheres: The Opposition to Women's Suffrage in Britain* (London: Croom Helm, 1978);

Sandra Stanley Holton, *Feminism and Democracy: Women's Suffrage and Reform Politics in Britain, 1900–1918* (Cambridge: Cambridge University Press, 1986);

Leslie Parker Hume, *The National Union of Women's Suffrage Societies* (New York: Garland, 1982);

Susan Kingsley Kent, *Sex and Suffrage in Britain, 1860–1914* (Princeton: Princeton University Press, 1987);

Jane Lewis, ed., *Before the Vote Was Won: Arguments for and against Women's Suffrage* (London: Routledge, 1987);

Anne Oakley, "Millicent Garrett Fawcett: Duty and Determination," in *Feminist Theorists,* edited by Dale Spender (London: Women's Press, 1983);

Emmeline Sylvia Pankhurst, *The Suffragette Movement: An Intimate Account of Persons and Ideals* (London: Longmans, 1931).

Papers:

Fawcett's manuscripts are held at the Fawcett Library, London; Holborn Public Library, London; Manchester Public Library; and in other archives listed in David Rubinstein's *A Different World for Women.*

Katharine Bruce Glasier
(25 September 1867 – 14 June 1950)

Erika Rothwell
University of Alberta

BOOKS: *The Cry of the Children,* as Katharine St. John Conway (Manchester: Labour Press Society, n.d.; second edition, Manchester: Independent Labour Party, 1894);

Husband & Brother: A Few Chapters in a Woman's Life of To-day, and, From Key-Note to Dominant, as Katharine St. John Conway (Bristol: Arrowsmith, 1894);

The Road to Socialism, as Katharine St. John Conway (Manchester: Labour Press, 1894);

Aimée Furniss, Scholar, as Katharine St. John Conway (London: Clarion, 1896);

The Religion of Socialism: Two Aspects, by Katharine St. John Conway and J. Bruce Glasier, Labour Press Pamphlet no. 18 (Manchester: Labour Press Society, 189–?);

Socialism for Children, as Katharine Bruce Glasier (London: Independent Labour Party, 1902?);

Tales from the Derbyshire Hills: Pastorals from the Peak District, as Katharine Bruce Glasier (London: Independent Labour Party, 1907);

Socialism and the Home, as Katharine Bruce Glasier (London: Independent Labour Party, 1909);

Miners' Baths, by Katharine Bruce Glasier, Thomas Richardson, M.P., and others (London: Women's Labour League, n.d.); revised and enlarged, republished as *Baths at the Pithead and the Works* (London: Women's Labour League, 1912);

National Old-Age Homes, as Katharine Bruce Glasier (London, 1914);

The Price of War, edited by E. G. G. Evans (Boston, 1916);

Enid Stacy, A Commemoration Souvenir, as Katharine Bruce Glasier (Manchester: Independent Labour Party, 1924);

Dolly-Logues, as Katharine Bruce Glasier (London: Independent Labour Party, 1926);

Socialism for Beginners, as Katharine Bruce Glasier (London: Independent Labour Party, 1929);

The Glen Book, as Katharine Bruce Glasier (Manchester: Workers' Northern Publishing, n.d.; re-

Katharine Bruce Glasier

vised edition, London & New York: Hutchinson, 1947);

Eglantyne Jebb and the World's Children (Manchester, n.d.);

Margaret McMillan and Her Life Work (Manchester, n.d.);

National Homes for Disabled Soldiers and Sailors and the Aged (London, n.d.).

SELECTED PERIODICAL PUBLICATION–
UNCOLLECTED: "Margret: A Twentieth Century Novel," *Weekly Times and Echo,* 21 September 1902–1 March 1903.

As an early proponent of the socialist and labor reform movements in Great Britain, Katharine St. John Conway Bruce Glasier lived according to socialist principles and energetically attempted to popularize and defend socialism through her lectures and writings. Glasier received a feminist education at Cambridge, and her writing often addresses the difficulties and inadequacies of the contemporary woman's current social and political circumstances. She is also remembered as the only woman to be a founding member of the Independent Labour Party and as the first female member of its National Administrative Council.

Born on 25 September 1867 in Ongar, Essex, Katharine St. John Conway was the eldest of seven children. Her mother, Amy Curling Conway, was the daughter of an important Stoke Newington family, and her father, Samuel Conway, was a Congregational minister. Soon after her birth her father was called to the pulpit in Walthamstow, where Katharine spent her childhood and youth.

It was the norm for Victorian daughters to receive an education inferior to that given to sons, but Conway's parents gave her an education equal to that of her brother Seymour, who later became Hulme Professor of Latin at the University of Manchester. Amy Curling Conway had been educated alongside her own brother (an Oxford don) and gave her daughters their first instruction at home. At the age of ten Conway was enrolled in the local High School for Girls at Hackney Downs.

In 1881 Conway's mother died shortly after giving birth to her seventh child, a girl also named Amy. Conway, who was fourteen, seems to have been especially close to her mother and to have been deeply affected by her death. She left home for Newnham College, Cambridge, in 1886 and maintained silence on the intervening five years although she kept copious journals during all other periods of her life. Her final days at home were probably not happy ones as Samuel Conway remarried in 1885, and Conway apparently disliked and resented his second wife.

At the age of nineteen Conway obtained a scholarship and embarked upon the classics program at Newnham College. She excelled in both academics and athletics, particularly tennis. Laurence Thompson, Conway's biographer, writes that her classmates remembered her as earnest, outgoing, tactless, and overly talkative. While at Cambridge, Conway was influenced by Jemima Clough, an advocate of educational reform for women, and by Helen Gladstone, a militant feminist and High Church adherent. It seems likely that Conway chafed against the strict rules, regulations, and proprieties that governed the behavior of Newnham students at the insistence of Miss Clough. She long remembered the impact of meeting the more flamboyant feminist Olive Schreiner. In *The Labour Woman* (1 October 1929) she wrote:

> In the early starting days of my life, when I was only a Newnham student, determined to claim for women all the opportunities of education which men had won, I had the great privilege of meeting Olive Schreiner.... Eagerly she encouraged every bit of courageous aspiration or rebellion she found in us.

Conway completed her studies and left Cambridge in 1889. Cambridge did not yet grant degrees to women, but Conway often defiantly appended the initials B.A. to her name on the title pages of her novels and pamphlets. The initials B.A. were suggestive of status, education, and respectability, which aided Conway in her attempts to popularize socialism and effect reforms.

Conway secured an appointment as classics mistress at Redland High School in Bristol, a city plagued by considerable industrial unrest. One Sunday in November 1890 she was deeply impressed by the contrast a group of poorly dressed and workworn female protesters made with the richly decorated interior of the church where they had taken refuge from the rain. Soon afterward she joined the Bristol Socialist Society, formerly the Bristol branch of the Social Democratic Federation (SDF), and also affiliated herself with the Fabian Society in Bristol. However, Conway was repelled by what she perceived as the Fabians' intense intellectualism and unwillingness to mix with the common people. It is not clear whether she resigned from Redland or was let go due to her socialist views, but she soon took a job teaching seventy young children in a working-class school. She simultaneously gave up her comfortable lodgings, moved in with the socialist working-class family of SDF organizer Dan Irving, and took over the household chores for Mrs. Irving, who was an invalid. Conway was rumored to be romantically involved with Irving. She described herself as his wife in spirit, which does not clarify the exact nature of their relationship.

Conway's socialist activities and, no doubt, her possible relationship with Irving attracted the attention of W. S. De Mattos, the lecture secretary of the Fabian Society and a proponent of free love. De Mattos recruited Conway to join fellow member Enid Stacy on a Fabian lecture tour. As an outgrowth of her lectures Conway also became a regular contributor to the *Workman's Times*. Conway was an excellent orator who inspired, interested, and

John Bruce Glasier

motivated audiences. She found this new work both exciting and fulfilling, but it was not long before she and Stacy gave up their lecture tour due to rumors that linked both women sexually with De Mattos.

In 1893 Conway was appointed the only woman organizer to the committee that brought the Independent Labour Party (ILP) into being. Ironically, her presence was partly because the building had to be cleaned and decorated for the occasion. Her appointment to the National Administration Council (NAC) displays a more genuine appreciation of her talent for propagandizing through both the spoken and written word. Moving in various socialist circles, Conway met and interacted with all the celebrated socialists of the period, including George Bernard Shaw, with whom she began to correspond. In later years she claimed that he had proposed to her repeatedly.

Soon after the formation of the ILP, Conway and John Bruce Glasier were married on 21 June 1893 at Rough Firth according to the ancient Scottish custom of declaring vows before two witnesses without benefit of clergy. The couple had first become acquainted in the autumn of 1892 while attending the Trades Union Congress (TUC) meeting in Glasgow. Bruce Glasier was also a founding member of the ILP and NAC as well as being an ardent socialist and an agnostic poet. They determined to devote their lives to the socialist movement and did not plan to have children. Conway intended to retain her own name (though within a decade she started using her husband's) and to continue her lecturing and writing. Thompson quotes a letter Conway had written to Bruce Glasier prior to the marriage, in which she asked "what would a poet say to a woman who *liked* earning money and enjoyed the thought of being breadwinner as well as wife that the husband might *never* have to sell even a hair of himself?"

Neither Bruce nor Katharine Glasier are thought to have contributed any new ideas to socialist theory. Bruce Glasier's *The Meaning of Socialism* (1919) is at once a book of great breadth and humanity and a book of great vagueness characterized by a lack of specifics and focus. The Glasiers' socialism was rooted in ethics rather than in economics. Their interest and their influence lay in translating socialist theory into reality through regulating their lives and conduct according to socialist principles and in popularizing and disseminating socialism for the masses. They carried out these activities with intense, almost evangelical, fervor. Thompson's 1971 biography, *The Enthusiasts,* portrays the Glasiers as passionately dedicated and energetic but overly idealistic and somewhat naive. It may indeed seem true that Katharine Glasier supported a wide and unfocused variety of causes that favored anyone who was weak and disadvantaged for any reason; but in fact she also repeatedly focused upon the plight of working-class mothers and children and was instrumental in implementing specific reforms, such as the establishment of pithead baths for miners so they could clean up at work.

Glasier did not continue her membership in the NAC, refusing to stand for reelection after its inaugural year. She was content to leave the headaches of leadership to others, like Bruce and Keir Hardie. She preferred contact with the common people, whom she continued to reach out to through her writing and lectures. After her marriage Glasier continued to lecture and to write for various papers, but she also published novels and short stories. This may be because her marriage coincided with the creation of the ILP, whose presses were now available to print her works; or she may have had more time to write after her marriage; or she may have taken up her pen in an attempt to earn money for her family's support. She did not succeed terribly well in the last. *Husband & Brother: A Few Chapters in a Woman's Life of To-day, and, From Key-Note to Dominant*

The National Administrative Council of the Independent Labour Party, with Katharine Glasier seated at center, in 1893

(1894) and *Aimée Furniss, Scholar* (1896) were both well reviewed in socialist and radical papers to whom Glasier was well known, but they brought in little money. Both novels portray the need for reform in female education and social attitudes toward women.

Glasier's writing tends to have a semi-autobiographical strain. *Aimée Furniss,* for which Glasier received only five pounds against sales, deals with the struggles of a heroic classics mistress in an environment where prejudice against education for girls still has to be overcome. Glasier knew how to construct interesting characters and lively, humorous dialogue. The account of the stuttering vicar, who wishes the girls' characters to be carefully "m-m-molded," and the determined headmistress, Miss Mayfield, who wishes to break all molds, is entertaining and thought-provoking. "Margret: A Twentieth Century Novel," which was published serially in 1902–1903, focuses upon the middle-class woman's struggle to gain independence; it shows the fulfillment and happiness a woman can find in devoting herself to a cause in which she believes fervently. Glasier also dabbled in writing romances for periodicals such as *The Family Herald Supplement,* which paid thirty pounds for a serial. However, she found such writing, which did nothing to advance the cause of socialism, tiresome and hollow. In addition, a grueling lecture schedule and the birth of her children probably left little time for writing that Glasier did not see as immediately furthering a serious cause.

Glasier is said to have changed her mind about having children when she saw little Harry Pankhurst embrace his mother, Emmeline, upon her return from a court hearing. The Glasiers had three children: Jeannie Isabelle in 1897, Malcolm Bruce in 1903, and John Glendower Bruce (Glen) in 1910. The family does not seem to have interfered with Glasier's socialist activities. In 1900, when Jeannie was three, Glasier had more than thirty speaking engagements in various parts of the country. Glasier was certainly never a model wife or mother according to contemporary standards, caring little for appearances, housekeeping, or material possessions. She rarely owned more than one dress at a time; her housekeeping was haphazard; and her children remembered family friends as their primary caregivers and companions. Jeannie rejected her parents' politics, married, and moved to Australia, and Malcolm ran away to sea at the age of thirteen; nonetheless, relations between Glasier and her children always seemed warm and amicable. As an adult Malcolm often praised Glasier as a wonderful, warm, and cheerful mother.

However, in her writing Glasier repeatedly exalts the status of traditional family values and domestic virtues. She portrays close-knit and loving families living in clean, and scrupulously tidy residences that are described in convincing detail. Her mothers are brisk and intelligent and care devotedly for their bright, innocent children despite the odds that threaten to overwhelm them. Her dialogue is sharp, crisp, and energetic. Her plots are designed either to expose evils that can be cured by socialism or to show socialism and/or a specific socialist in the process of bringing about positive and healing change. Glasier often infuses a romantic subplot into her stories, and fairy-tale endings are the norm for her socialist heroes and heroines. No doubt such endings gave her work additional appeal for her readers. Her arguments are presented in simple terms and everyday language with the occasional learned reference, and her conclusions are shown to be obvious, natural, and easy solutions to social ills. Her tone varies between reasonable calm and tart indignation. Glasier's style is reminiscent of the tracts of the late eighteenth century, especially those written by Hannah More and her sisters. Her settings are both urban and rural but include the same plots, domestic scenes, and characters. The appreciation of nature and the outdoors is a constant theme, and characters may be evaluated based on their response to nature.

Tales from the Derbyshire Hills: Pastorals from the Peak District (1907) is a collection of Glasier's stories that had previously been published in various magazines or newspapers and are "given to the I.L.P. National Campaign Fund by the writer and publisher free of royalty or profits of kind, in the faith and comradeship of SOCIALISM, THE HOPE OF THE WORLD." The ten short stories in the collection are pastoral and romantic in theme and style, dealing mostly with the interactions of country people of different classes; the stories focus on the ways in which these people aid one another through personal sacrifices and on the transformation of old attitudes that helps to eradicate class barriers. A mistress and her maid, for example, come to see that they share the same emotions toward their respective beaus; in another tale a visiting artist is enchanted by a red and brown little country girl who reminds him of a robin, and he vows to help her impoverished family.

Glasier's fiction and nonfiction are both quite openly didactic and share much in terms of style and tone. The examples set forth as supporting evidence in her nonfiction are miniatures of the domestic verisimilitude and the simple but appealing characters in her fiction. *The Cry of the Children* (n.d., second edition 1894), which takes its title from Elizabeth Barrett Browning's poem of the same name, details the abuses of the poorest working-class children through various home industries, including box making, belt making, paper-bag making, and artificial-flower making. The families are neat, tidy, loving, and hardworking people who clearly deserve better. In one scene a mother energetically berates a well-meaning school inspector, who has no grasp of her difficulties, in inimitable style:

> What's good enough fur me is good enough for my kids an' when they goes to school they don't get no dinner an' no tea. . . . Yes, I thought yer'd say that, it's jest the sort o' thing bloomin' ole school inspector as knows no better *would* say. No, I don't starve 'em on puppus when they is forced to go to school. It's jest this. If the kids don't work there ain't no food to give 'em, cos there ain't the money to buy it. Put that in yer pipe an' smoke it.

Glasier was a strong supporter of educational reform, children's rights, and school meals.

From 1904 through 1909 Bruce Glasier edited the *Labour Leader* and Katharine Glasier wrote the women's column under the pseudonym Iona. While she upheld standard domestic values and traditions, in her column Glasier also attempted to provide the working-class woman with a place to discuss socialist and feminist issues that otherwise would have been unavailable. Glasier became a member of the Women's Labour League and a contributor to *The League Leaflet* and *The Labour Woman*.

As Iona, Glasier refused to endorse, or even discuss, the issue of woman suffrage although she seems to have been sympathetic to the goals of the movement, if not its means. During 1906–1907 the suffragettes became estranged from the Labour Party due to its failure to endorse a limited suffrage bill. The Glasiers also became estranged from the Pankhursts, whom they felt were growing increasingly radical and overly aware of their own importance. Like many "New Women" of the 1890s, Glasier capitalized upon the gains made for women by the more radical feminists of the 1880s but refused to countenance their methods and was sometimes uncomfortable calling herself a feminist. Bruce Glasier is also reported to have been affronted by Emmeline Pankhurst's fastidious taste in clothing and the makeup worn by her daughter, Christabel. However, other works by Glasier, such as *Socialism and the Home* (1909), include references to the suffragettes' cause that are decidedly sympathetic and supportive.

Glasier may not have supported suffrage openly due to the concern of the ILP over the bad publicity surrounding the perceived threat militant feminism posed to the institution of the family. *Socialism and the Home* was designed to combat the view that traditional domestic family life and socialism were incompatible. Glasier argues that the majority of socialists have become socialists because they believe in the home as the especial province of the poor and the worker. Capitalism, not socialism, is what undermines the status of the home. Socialism is seen as especially valuable to women because it will "remove every economic consideration that now practically forces women to submit to their degradation at the hands of men" and that does not allow for equal partnerships in marriage. State maintenance of children is not a socialist ideal but an evil necessity caused by the capitalist system. Socialism is shown to be the salvation, not the destruction, of the family.

In 1909 Glasier joined the Miners' Federation campaign to have pithead baths available for miners, a practice that had been pioneered in Germany. Her enthusiasm for this innovation seems to have sprung largely from a desire to lessen the labor of the working-class wife and mother. Pithead baths meant that dirt that came from the pit stayed at the pit. In her pamphlet *Miners' Baths* (n.d., revised 1912) she sets forth the domestic circumstances of the mining family in vivid, sympathetic, and indignant detail:

> A Welsh miner's wife has two elder sons working in the pit, as well as her husband. Under the Eight Hour Shift system her clean little home, where there were three other children still at school, would sometimes be invaded three times in the twenty-four hours by a miner covered in dirt and grime, his body soaked with perspiration, and an evil sulphurous smell from the workings hanging all about his clothes. The water for three baths had all to be heated over the fire. The kitchen or a small scullery were the only possible bath rooms, and the inevitable mess of dirty water, not to speak of the toil of drying and cleaning the miry clothes kept the wife incessantly employed merely to preserve decently cleanly conditions in her narrowly planned home.

The first pithead baths were opened in Britain in 1913, and the practice soon spread abroad. The pithead baths at Newcastle, New South Wales, Australia, were named for Glasier.

In 1909 Glasier's passionate devotion to socialist causes attracted the interest of a wealthy, philanthropic American widow, Elizabeth Glendower Evans, who was visiting Britain. Evans eventually established a trust fund to help pay the Glasiers' living expenses and further their work.

In 1916 Glasier assumed editorship of the *Labour Leader* after its previous editor, A. Fenner Brockway, was imprisoned as a conscientious objector. Her years as editor coincided with the emotionally exhausting years of Bruce Glasier's lengthy fi-

The Glasiers' son Glen at seven, the age at which he appeared on the cover of Socialism for Beginners *(1929)*

nal illness before his death in 1920. The Glasiers had been married for twenty-seven years and by all accounts were quite well suited and extremely happy together. Glasier was shattered by her husband's death. She had retained her position as editor for more than five years, even declining the "safe" Labour parliamentary seat offered to her. However, in 1921, when she was at open odds with the political adviser of the *Labour Leader,* Philip Snowden, and worn out by grief and exhaustion, Glasier suffered a nervous breakdown. Against her will she was replaced by the paper, who later refused to pay wages she felt were owed or to employ her in any meaningful capacity.

Her recovery from the heartache and loneliness caused by Bruce Glasier's death, from the shattered nerves and exhaustion caused by overwork, and from the sense of betrayal caused by the *Labour Leader* was largely due to her intense fusion of socialism and religious mysticism. She came to believe that her husband was constantly present spiritually to support her through life. By 1924 Glasier had returned to her life of social activism. She continued to give lectures and to write pamphlets; her passionate conviction earned her the nickname "Fighting Kate." She was also active in supporting the establishment of nursery schools for working-class children (a campaign begun by Margaret McMillan), Poor Law reform, old-age homes for working women, and the Save the Children fund founded by Eglantyne Jebb after World War I. *Dolly-Logues* (1926), a sprightly account of an upper-class socialist girl who transforms a dark and unhappy home into a dwelling full of sunshine and happy socialists, incorporates some elements of Glasier's new mysticism. Dolly possesses the ability to see into people's souls and perceive the animals that they used to be. Dolly explains that "in my nursery days, long before I had ever heard of Pythagorus, I knew that one of my nurses had been a hen. Dear old Nurse Jenkins was an Alderney cow. And, my goodness, she made life sweet for us!" Dolly's ability gives her a better understanding of personalities and characters. Dolly shared her gift with Glasier, who once saw Labour leader J. Ramsay MacDonald entering a room and immediately had a vision of him as a stag with his antlers entangled in the branches of a tree.

In 1928 Glasier was forced to cope with the tragic death of her younger son, Glen, who had just been awarded a scholarship to Oxford. Glen was killed when a ball struck him above the heart during a football match. Glasier eventually came to terms with her grief through *The Glen Book* (n.d., revised 1947). Shaw subtitled the book *Secrets of a Happy Life and Infinite Consolations*. The book is a mix of Bruce Glasier's socialist teaching, memories of Glen, and Katharine Glasier's evolving mysticism. Glasier writes that the work is not a biography of Glen but rather

> an endeavour to explain to fellow-mourners the triumphant certainty that has come to his mother there is no death. It is the outcome of an irresistible urge to share, while they are quick and warm, the experiences which have convinced his mother that those whom we call dead are not dead but gloriously living and working with us for the fulfilment of our highest dreams of human perfection.

Socialism for Beginners (1929) is dedicated to "Glen at age seven," and its cover features a cherublike photograph of the little boy, clearly designed to tug at the reader's heartstrings. In this pamphlet Glasier provides a simple but vivid introduction to socialism that focuses upon mothers and children and how their needs will be fulfilled by the new social order.

In the 1930s, following the near destruction of the Labour Party after the national election of 1931, Glasier worked long and hard to reestablish a party that had to be rebuilt from the ground up. Now something of an institution herself, Glasier was asked to be a goodwill ambassador for the party. It was in this capacity that she met Mahatma Gandhi during his visit to Britain in 1931. Glasier plunged eagerly into this work, which involved extensive traveling, lecturing, and writing a regular column for the Manchester Labour weekly, *Northern Voice*. She persisted in these activities until the onset of World War II, when advancing age and the needs of her invalid sister, Eva, brought an end to her travels. However, she continued to express her social concerns and her horror over the war in print.

Glasier died peacefully on 14 June 1950 at the age of eighty-two. Her last home in Earby, where she and Glen had moved in 1922, was preserved by British socialists and became a youth hostel.

Biography:

Laurence Thompson, *The Enthusiasts: A Biography of John and Katharine Bruce Glasier* (London: Gollancz, 1971).

References:

J. Bruce Glasier, *The Meaning of Socialism* (London: National Labour Press, 1919);

Glasier, *William Morris and the Early Days of Socialism* (London: Longmans, 1921).

Papers:

Malcolm Glasier presented his mother's and father's papers, including his mother's letters, to the Sydney Jones Library, University of Liverpool, in the 1970s. Glasier correspondence is also included in the George Bernard Shaw Papers in the British Library.

Thomas Hill Green
(7 April 1836 – 26 March 1882)

John Ferns
McMaster University

BOOKS: *An Estimate of the Value and Influence of Works of Fiction in Modern Times* (Oxford: Shrimpton, 1862; Ann Arbor, Mich.: Wahr, 1911);

Liberal Legislation and Freedom of Contract: A Lecture (Oxford: Slatter & Rose, 1881);

The Work To Be Done by the New Oxford High School: A Lecture (Oxford: Slatter & Rose / London: Simpkin, Marshall, 1882);

Prolegomena to Ethics, edited by A. C. Bradley (Oxford: Clarendon Press, 1883);

The Witness of God, and Faith: Two Lay Sermons, edited by Arnold Toynbee (London: Longmans, Green, 1883);

The Political Theory of T. H. Green: Selected Writings, edited by John R. Rodman (New York: Appleton-Century-Crofts, 1964);

T. H. Green: Lectures on the Principles of Political Obligation, and Other Writings, edited by Paul Harris and John Morrow (Cambridge & New York: Cambridge University Press, 1986).

Collection: *Works of Thomas Hill Green,* edited by R. L. Nettleship, 3 volumes (London: Longmans, Green, 1885).

OTHER: *The Philosophical Works of David Hume,* edited by Green and T. H. Grose, 4 volumes (London: Longmans, Green, 1874-1875).

Thomas Hill Green

Thomas Hill Green was an active reformer and reform writer on education, temperance, politics, religion, and philosophy. He worked to revise educational curricula and to increase educational opportunities for poor students from large towns, and he strove to achieve these objectives through his work with the Schools Commission (1864-1868) and at Balliol College, Oxford University, and the city of Oxford. "The Grading of Secondary Schools" and two lectures—"The Elementary School System of England" and "The Work To Be Done by the New Oxford High School for Boys"—constitute his principal reform writings on education, and these are all among the pieces in the "Miscellanies" collection published in volume three of his *Works of Thomas Hill Green* (1885).

His reform work in support of temperance was prompted by personal motives, for one member of his family proved to be an alcoholic, and Green made many addresses on behalf of temperance groups to which he belonged. In politics Green was a radical Liberal who spoke on party platforms and was active in local politics in Oxford. His principal reform writings in politics are "Liberal Legislation and Freedom of Contract" (1881) and his four other lectures on the English Commonwealth, which are also collected in "Miscellanies."

Green's religion was reformist in nature as he shifted his emphasis from doctrine to spirit in responding to Darwinism and the "Higher Criticism" of philosophers and historians in the years following publication of David Strauss's *Das Leben Jesu, kritisch bearbeitet* (The Life of Jesus, Critically Examined; 1835–1836). Many of his writings collected in "Miscellanies"–"Essay on Christian Dogma," "Justification by Faith," "The Incarnation," "The Witness of God," and "Faith"–reveal Green as a reform writer on religion. As a philosopher Green criticized the empiricism of David Hume in "Introduction to Hume" and the utilitarianism of Jeremy Bentham and James Mill in *Prolegomena to Ethics* (1883). For Green, reforming philosophy meant espousing a new idealism prompted by his readings in the works of Aristotle, Plato, Immanuel Kant, and Georg Wilhelm Friedrich Hegel.

Born in Birkin, Yorkshire, Green was the second son and youngest of the four children of the Reverend Valentine Green and his first wife. The boy's mother died when he was only a year old, and for the first fourteen years of his life Green was educated at home by his father, whose love of local people, interest in politics, and deep and undogmatic religious feeling influenced his son considerably.

From 1850 to 1855 Green attended Rugby, the public school that had been reformed by Dr. Thomas Arnold but that in Green's day was under the headmastership of E. M. Goulburn. Geoffrey Thomas writes that Green described Goulburn as "the most unsatisfactory personage I ever came across. He is surly, unfair, hasty and obstinate.... Besides this he teaches nothing." Goulburn found Green to be indolent and unimaginative but noted his clear mind.

One anecdote from Green's Rugby days reveals the independence of mind that Thomas notes; C. S. Parker, another teacher and friend, later remarked of Green: "His chief concern was to satisfy his own mind." Green found it unfair when he was placed second at Rugby in an English essay contest: "all the masters who looked it over liked mine best, but they gave it [the prize] to another fellow because his showed more labour, i.e. came out of thirteen books instead of his own head." This is the same Green of whom W. L. Newman, another friend, recalled, "I have sometimes seen him when something was said which called for reflection, walk to the common room fire from his seat in the circle, and after leaning his head against the mantlepiece for a moment, make some remark which went to the heart of the matter."

In October 1855 Green entered Balliol College, Oxford, and he maintained his connection with Balliol for the next twenty-seven years, until his death in 1882. Although Green gained only second-class standing in classical moderations (Greek and Latin literature) in 1857, he was inspired by the teaching of Benjamin Jowett and Parker and obtained a first in philosophy and ancient history in the summer of 1859. Then with only six months of study he gained a third in law and modern history that, as Richard Lewis Nettleship writes, "added to his knowledge." In 1860 he was appointed lecturer in ancient and modern history at Balliol and in the same year was elected to a Balliol fellowship that had been his "great hope" on entering Oxford. In 1862 he was awarded the Chancellor's Prize for his essay "The Value and Influence of Works of Fiction." Having told his father in January 1861 that he would not take orders in the Church of England, Green briefly considered becoming a Dissenting minister in June 1863. He spent the long vacations of 1862 and 1863 in Switzerland and Germany, and in May of that latter year he also turned down Sir Alexander Grant's offer of the editorship of *The Times of India*.

In the mid 1860s Green wondered whether he should continue in academic life, and in December 1864 he accepted the post of assistant commissioner in the Schools Inquiry Commission that had been appointed under Lord Taunton in 1864. This commission was to review endowed middle-class schools as the Newcastle Commission and the Clarendon Commission had reviewed elementary schools and the public schools, respectively. Green's principal responsibility was to inspect the independent schools of Staffordshire and Warwickshire, in particular King Edward's School in Birmingham. He had to examine curricula and standards in almost one hundred schools and to interview parents about their views of and wishes for the education of their children. Green's concern for educational reform grew from this experience.

His work with the commission also taught him that bureaucratic life did not suit him. Besides, the recommendation of a three-tier system of classical and scientific, commercial, and general education that Green and his commission approved was not endorsed by the Endowed Schools Act of 1869, which aimed only at improving the administration of endowments. Green's hopes for an improved secondary school system emerged from his wish to create opportunities for university education for all those who could benefit from it. As he noted in 1862, "Reforming and levelling are indeed more closely allied than we are commonly disposed to admit." University reform in Oxford had created scholarships for students unable to afford university educations, but without improved secondary educa-

Members of the Old Mortality Society at Oxford, circa 1858: Green is standing in the center, behind and between A. C. Swinburne and John Nichol (both seated); James Bryce is standing second from right, behind Nichol and A. V. Dicey.

tion those students would be unable to win the new scholarships.

In 1874 Green was elected to the Oxford School Board that had been established in 1871. Educational reform was one of his central concerns, for on improved and increased educational opportunities he pinned many of his hopes for the "reconstitution of society through that of education." Later in his life he supported the building of Oxford High School, and on his death Green left money for a school scholarship, a university essay prize, and the promotion of higher education in large towns. His disillusionment with the 1869 Endowed Schools Act is fully expressed in his "The Grading of Secondary Schools" and two lectures, "The Elementary School System of England" and "The Work to Be Done by the New Oxford High School for Boys." Green also did important work in launching the settlement which sought to assist students who had the intellectual ability to benefit from university education but were not able to pay for fees or accommodations without support from the movement.

Nettleship writes that next to popular education the social subject in which Green was most interested was temperance. His interest in temperance had a partly personal basis, for his older brother was an alcoholic. Beyond this, however, Green believed that no one could exercise his free will as a citizen when burdened by an addiction such as alcoholism, and his concern for temperance sprang from a keen sense of the need for this social reform. Prior to 1872 no age limit was imposed on those who purchased spirits outside London, and even the 1874 Licensing Act did not prohibit public houses from serving beer to children under the age of sixteen. He became vice president of the United Kingdom Alliance, an activist temperance group that petitioned Parliament to make the licensing laws more stringent. Joining the group in 1872, Green delivered at least a half-dozen speeches on temperance reform between 1873 and 1882, and these were often published in the *Alliance News*. He was also active in setting up a coffee tavern in St. Clement's, Oxford, in 1875, the year in which he became treasurer of the

Oxford Diocesan branch of the Church of England Temperance Society and a year before he became president of the Oxford Band of Hope Temperance Union.

The issue of temperance provided the only occasion that drew Green into direct political controversy when he objected to a speech by Sir William Harcourt, the Oxford M.P., in late 1872. On 4 January 1873 Green wrote to the *Oxford Chronicle* that "a politician who bids for the votes of the publicans cannot have ours." Thomas writes that Green proposed to resolve the social problems born of intemperance in a scheme that would have reduced the number of public houses in Oxford from three hundred to forty: "His solution was the scheme known as 'local option' by which local authorities were to be authorized to prohibit the sale of drink. He preferred this plan to an unconditional prohibition by central government since he believed first that prohibition would be ineffectual unless firmly rooted in local commitment and second that the elite of the working class would supply the basis of that commitment." From the time of Green's unsuccessful attempt to reform his alcoholic brother in 1862 until his own death Green remained firmly committed to temperance reform. In one of his last public acts he addressed an Oxford conference organized by the United Kingdom Alliance in February 1882, and this address was published in the *Oxford Chronicle* on 4 February 1882.

James Bryce, one of Green's Oxford contemporaries in the 1850s, characterized politics as "in a certain sense the strongest of his interests." In a letter from Rugby in 1852 Green told his sister that he was considered "a dreadful Radical, nay a Red Republican." Oliver Cromwell was Green's "favourite hero," and Green was deeply committed to the parliamentary cause in the English Civil War of the seventeenth century, as is clear from his "Four Lectures on the English Commonwealth." He also supported the North in the American Civil War; he admired Gen. Francis Barlow and was shocked by the assassination of President Abraham Lincoln. Green greatly admired other reformers such as John Bright, whom he enjoyed meeting in Oxford. For Jefferson Davis, Louis Napoleon, and Prime Ministers Henry Temple, Lord Palmerston, and Benjamin Disraeli he felt complete contempt.

To fulfill his liberal goals Green was committed as a writer and man of action to political reform. He was the first fellow of an Oxford college to be elected–by the ratepayers, not by the university–to the Oxford Town Council. His position on parliamentary reform was Liberal, and in making his first appearance on a political platform, that of the Oxford Reform League, he spoke in support of the 1867 Reform Bill. Green believed in the extension of the franchise and was so determined to block Disraeli's return to power as prime minister in 1880 that, despite poor health, he put off work on his *Prolegomena to Ethics* to support the Liberal election campaign. Even on his deathbed he maintained his keen interest in politics as he continued to discuss the Irish Land Bill and Bulgarian affairs.

His political writings have been the focus of the most sustained interest in Green's work. As early as 1895 his "Lectures on the Principles of Political Obligation" were excerpted from his *Works* for separate publication, and they have been republished by John R. Rodman in *The Political Theory of T. H. Green* (1964) and reedited by Paul Harris and John Morrow for Cambridge University Press in 1986. As a philosopher and political reform writer Green addresses the bankruptcy of empiricism and utilitarianism and offers a political theory based on the idea that individual citizens may exercise their will freely in participating in the common good.

Green's decision to commit himself to philosophy in the 1860s was partly in order to rethink empiricism and utilitarianism in light of the Greek and German thought in which Jowett had aroused his interest. In 1864 Green failed to obtain the professorship in moral philosophy at St. Andrews University, and in 1866 he failed to be appointed to the Waynflete professorship at Oxford before he was appointed as tutor at Balliol that year. Nettleship writes that after Edwin Palmer retired and Jowett became master in 1870, "practically the whole subordinate management of the College devolved" on Green when he became a kind of "senior dean" of the college.

On 1 July 1871 Green married Charlotte Symonds, the sister of John Addington Symonds, a friend of his undergraduate days. Although the Greens had no children, their marriage was happy. In April 1872 Green was reelected to a Balliol fellowship; he became more relaxed and completed his 380-page "Introduction to Hume," a destructive critique for the four-volume edition of Hume's works that Green and T. H. Grose edited and published in 1874–1875. In 1878 Green was appointed to the Whyte's Professorship of moral philosophy at Oxford, and his professorial lectures were posthumously published as *Prolegomena to Ethics*.

Philosophy and politics were Green's interests in these years; Charlotte ran their household and did good works among the poor. Until the late 1870s Green remained in good health, but in 1879 he began to suffer increasingly from sleeplessness that had plagued him throughout his life and also from giddiness that proved to be the early signs of congenital heart disease.

Green's completion of *Prolegomena to Ethics* involved a struggle against increasing ill health, and in the winter of 1881–1882 his health became worse. On 15 March 1882 his condition grew serious, and he died the following day. Nettleship records that Green asked on his deathbed to have someone read to him the eighth chapter of Saint Paul's epistle to the Romans—a selection that presents an emphasis on spirit which is surely important to understanding Green as a reform writer on religion and philosophy—but he was too ill to attend to it. Thomas writes that Charlotte Green recorded, "At 9 a.m. on Sunday 26th he [Green] passed away quietly, quite unconscious of the morning light which he had asked to see if he lived till then."

In an increasingly materialistic age Green believed that empiricism and utilitarianism had left British philosophy bankrupt. With the help of the writings of Aristotle and Plato, supplemented by Kant, Hegel, and Johann Gottlieb Fichte, Green devised a philosophy of self-awareness which perceived man's will as free and also posited an eternal consciousness. For Green, Darwinism said nothing against the existence of God, and Green perceived "the necessity of a philosophy of morals which no adaptation of natural science can supply." Nineteenth-century science and the Higher Criticism of the Bible did not undercut the fourth gospel or Saint Paul in Green's view. In political philosophy Green saw a clear need to provide a renewed sense of the importance of the individual as a freely acting citizen seeking the common good. This was the reforming burden of his religious and philosophical thinking from "Popular Philosophy in its Relation to Life" (1868), in which he writes that "man, above all modern man, must theorize his practice, and the failure adequately to do so, must cripple the practice itself," through *Liberal Legislation and Freedom of Contract: A Lecture* (1881); *The Witness of God, and Faith: Two Lay Sermons* (1883), edited by Arnold Toynbee; and *Prolegomena to Ethics*, edited by A. C. Bradley.

Biographies:

Richard Lewis Nettleship, ed., Memoir in *The Works of Thomas Hill Green* (London: Longmans, Green, 1885), III: xi–clxi;

Geoffrey Thomas, "T. H. Green: Life and Philosophy" in *The Moral Philosophy of T. H. Green* (Oxford: Clarendon Press, 1987), 6–71.

References:

Crane Brinton, *English Political Thought in the Nineteenth Century* (London: Benn, 1949);

Ann R. Cacoullos, *Thomas Hill Green: Philosopher of Rights* (New York: Twayne, 1974);

W. H. Fairbrother, *The Philosophy of T. H. Green* (London: Methuen, 1906);

P. Gordon and J. White, *Philosophers as Educational Reformers: The Influence of Idealism on British Educational Thought and Practice* (Boston & London: Routledge, 1979);

I. M. Greengarten, *Thomas Hill Green and the Development of Liberal-Democratic Thought* (Buffalo & Toronto: University of Toronto Press, 1981);

William D. Lamont, *Introduction to Green's Moral Philosophy* (London: Allen & Unwin, 1934);

H. N. Misra, *Moral Philosophy: Green and Gita* (Kanpur, India: Kitab Ghar, 1965);

A. K. Mukhopadhyay, *The Ethics of Obedience: A Study of the Philosophy of T. H. Green* (Calcutta: World, 1967);

Jean Pucelle, *La Nature et l'espirit dans la philosophie de T. H. Green* (Louvain & Paris: Nauwelaerts, 1965);

Melvin Richter, *The Politics of Conscience: T. H. Green and His Age* (London: Weidenfeld & Nicolson, 1964);

Henry Sidgwick, *Lectures on the Ethics of T. H. Green, Mr. Herbert Spencer, and J. Martineau* (London & New York: Macmillan, 1902);

A. Soper, *T. H. Green as Theologian: An Historical-Theological Study with Special Reference to the Sermon on Faith* (London: Pontifucium Athenaeum Anselmianum, 1972);

Geoffrey Thomas, *The Moral Philosophy of T. H. Green* (Oxford: Clarendon Press / New York: Oxford University Press, 1987);

Andrew Vincent, ed., *The Philosophy of T. H. Green* (Aldershot, Hampshire, U.K. & Brookfield, Vt.: Gower, 1986);

Vincent and R. Plant, *Philosophy, Politics and Citizenship* (New York & Oxford: Blackwell, 1984);

Ben Wempe, *Beyond Equality: A Study of T. H. Green's Theory of Positive Freedom* (Delft, Netherlands: Eburon, 1986);

Papers:

Balliol College Library and the Bodleian Library, Oxford, house the letters and papers of T. H. Green.

Frederic Harrison
(18 October 1831 - 14 January 1923)

Timothy J. Evans
*Richard Bland College
of the College of William and Mary*

See also the Harrison entry in *DLB 57: Victorian Prose Writers After 1867.*

BOOKS: *The Meaning of History* (London: Trübner, 1862); enlarged as *The Meaning of History, and Other Historical Pieces* (New York & London: Macmillan, 1894);

Order and Progress (London: Longmans, Green, 1875);

The Present and the Future: A Positivist Address (London: Reeves & Turner, 1880);

The Nature and Reality of Religion: A Controversy between Frederic Harrison and Herbert Spencer, by Harrison and Spencer (New York: Appleton, 1885); republished as *The Insuppressible Book: A Controversy between Herbert Spencer and Frederic Harrison* (Boston: Cassino, 1885);

The Choice of Books, and Other Literary Pieces (London: Macmillan, 1886; New York: Harper, 1886);

Oliver Cromwell (London & New York: Macmillan, 1888);

Annals of an Old Manor-House, Sutton Place, Guildford (London & New York: Macmillan, 1893; abridged edition, London: Macmillan, 1899);

Studies in Early Victorian Literature (London & New York: Arnold, 1895);

William the Silent (London & New York: Macmillan, 1897);

Tennyson, Ruskin, Mill and Other Literary Estimates (London & New York: Macmillan, 1899);

Byzantine History in the Early Middle Ages: The Rede Lecture Delivered in the Senate House, Cambridge, June 12, 1900 (London: Macmillan / New York: Macmillan, 1900);

George Washington, and Other American Addresses (London: Macmillan / New York: Macmillan, 1901);

John Ruskin (New York: Macmillan / London: Macmillan, 1902);

Theophano: The Crusade of the Tenth Century; a Romantic Monograph (London: Chapman & Hall, 1904; New York & London: Harper, 1904);

Frederic Harrison, circa 1885

Chatham (New York & London: Macmillan, 1905);

The Herbert Spencer Lecture Delivered at Oxford, March 9, 1905 (Oxford: Clarendon Press, 1905);

Nicephorus: A Tragedy of New Rome (London: Chapman & Hall, 1906; Buffalo, N.Y., 1906);

Memories and Thoughts: Men—Books—Cities—Art (New York: Macmillan / London: Macmillan, 1906);

The Creed of a Layman: Apologia pro fide mea (New York: Macmillan / London: Macmillan, 1907);

The Philosophy of Common Sense (London: Macmillan, 1907; New York: Macmillan, 1907);

My Alpine Jubilee, 1851-1907 (London: Smith, Elder, 1908);

National and Social Problems (London: Macmillan, 1908; New York: Macmillan, 1908);

Realities and Ideals: Social, Political, Literary, and Artistic (London: Macmillan, 1908; New York: Macmillan, 1908);

Autobiographic Memoirs, 2 volumes (London: Macmillan, 1911);

Among My Books: Centenaries, Reviews, Memoirs (London: Macmillan, 1912; New York: Ober, 1912);

The Positive Evolution of Religion: Its Moral and Social Reaction (London: Heinemann, 1913; New York: Putnam, 1913);

The German Peril: Forecasts, 1864-1914; Realities, 1915; Hopes, 191- (London: Unwin, 1915);

On Society (London: Macmillan, 1918);

Obiter scripta, 1918 (London: Chapman & Hall, 1919);

On Jurisprudence and the Conflict of Laws (Oxford: Clarendon Press, 1919);

Novissima verba: Last Words, 1920 (London: Unwin, 1921; New York: Holt, 1921);

De senectute: More Last Words (London: Unwin, 1923).

OTHER: "England and France," in *International Policy,* by Harrison, Edward Spencer Beesly, John Henry Bridges, and others (London: Chapman & Hall, 1866), pp. 51-152;

Auguste Comte, *Social Statics,* volume 2 of his *System of Positive Polity,* translated by Harrison (London: Longmans, Green, 1875);

Frederick Gard Fleay, *Three Lectures on Education,* preface by Harrison (London: Reeves & Turner, 1883);

Comte, *The Positivist Library of Auguste Comte,* translated by Harrison (London: Reeves & Turner, 1886);

The New Calendar of Great Men: Biographies of the 558 Worthies of All Ages and Nations in the Positivist Calendar of Auguste Comte, edited by Harrison (London & New York: Macmillan, 1892); republished as *The Positivist Calendar of 558 Worthies of All Ages and Nations* (London: Reeve, 1894); revised and enlarged as *The New Calendar of Great Men: Biographies of the 559 Worthies of All Ages & Nations in the Positivist Calendar of Auguste Comte,* edited by Harrison, S. H. Swinny, and F. S. Marvin (London: Macmillan, 1920);

"The Ethical View: The Duties of Man to the Lower Animals," in *The New Charter,* edited by Henry Stephens Salt (London, 1896), pp. 87-104;

Comte, *The Positive Philosophy of Auguste Comte,* introduction by Harrison (London: Bell, 1896);

Louisa C. Shore, *Poems,* appreciation by Harrison (London: John Lane, 1897);

Thomas Carlyle, *Past and Present,* introduction by Harrison (London: Ward, Lock & Bowden, 1897);

"Alfred as King," in *Alfred the Great: Containing Chapters on His Life and Times by Mr. Frederick [sic] Harrison, the Lord Bishop of Bristol, Professor Charles Oman, Sir Clements Markham, the Rev. Professor Earle, Sir Frederick Pollock and the Rev. W. J. Loftie,* edited, with a preface, by Alfred Bowker (London: Black, 1899), pp. 39-67;

"Positivism: Its Positions, Aims, and Ideals," in *Great Religions of the World,* by Herbert Allen Giles (New York & London: Harper, 1901), pp. 165-185;

Lucien Levy-Bruhl, *The Philosophy of Auguste Comte,* translated by Kathleen de Beaumont-Klein, introduction by Harrison (London: Sonnenschein, 1903);

Carlyle, *Essays,* introduction by Harrison (London: Blackie, 1904);

George Gissing, *Veranilda: A Romance,* preface by Harrison (London: Constable, 1904);

Francis Bacon, *Essays,* introduction by Harrison (London: Blackie, 1905);

Anthony Trollope, *The Barsetshire Novels,* introduction by Harrison, 8 volumes (London: Bell, 1906);

John Henry Bridges, *Essays and Addresses,* introduction by Harrison (London: Chapman & Hall, 1907);

Carlyle and the London Library, edited by Harrison (London: Chapman & Hall, 1907);

Comte, *A General View of Positivism,* introduction by Harrison (London: Routledge, 1908);

Trollope, *Phineas Finn, the Irish Member,* introduction by Harrison, 2 volumes (London: Bell, 1911);

Comte, *Early Essays on Social Philosophy,* introduction by Harrison (London: Routledge / New York: Dutton, 1911);

Mary Agatha Russell, *Golden Grain: Thoughts of Many Minds,* preface by Harrison (London: Nisbet, 1912);

"The Future of Woman," in *Representative Essays in Modern Thought,* edited by Harrison Ross Steeves and Frank Humphrey Ristine (New York & Cincinnati: American Book, 1913), pp. 502-518;

Matilda Barbara Betham Edwards, *The Lord of the Harvest,* introduction by Harrison (London & Edinburgh: Milford, 1913);

Austin Harrison, *The Kaiser's War,* introduction by Frederic Harrison (London: Austin & Unwin, 1914);

"The Romance of the Peerage," in *Modern English Essays,* edited by Ernest Rhys (London & Toronto: Dent / New York: Dutton, 1922), pp. 190-215.

SELECTED PERIODICAL PUBLICATIONS—UNCOLLECTED: "Historic London," *Macmillan's Magazine,* 49 (1884): 401-411;

"An Address Delivered November 15, 1894, on the Occasion of the Gibbon Centenary Commemoration," *Transactions* of the Royal Historical Society, new series 9 (1895): 31-48;

"A Proposal for a New Historical Bibliography," *Transactions* of the Royal Historical Society, new series 11 (1897): 19-30;

"The Bicentenary Commemoration of William Pitt, First Earl of Chatham (November 15, 1708-May 11, 1778)," *Transactions* of the Royal Historical Society, third series 3 (1909): 23-49;

"Charles Eliot Norton," *Cornhill Magazine,* third series 26 (1909): 65-72.

Frederic Harrison was the primary spokesman for the application of Positivist philosophy to social, historical, political, and literary questions of the late nineteenth and early twentieth centuries. As an essayist, novelist, translator, editor, and prolific contributor to the quarterly journals, he preached Positivism as a new religion and even founded a Church of Positivism in London.

Born in Muswell Hill, a rural area later engulfed by London, Harrison was the son of Frederick Harrison, a stockbroker, and Jane Brice Harrison. He attended King's College School until 1849, was graduated second in his class, and entered Wadham College, Oxford, on scholarship. He received his B.A. in 1853 and remained as a fellow of the college for two years. He was eventually admitted to the bar, but his activities followed his other interests, which ranged among art, literature, theology, politics, and philosophy. He later wrote about English law in *On Jurisprudence and the Conflict of Laws* (1919), but he seldom if ever practiced it.

At the end of his two-year fellowship Harrison's diverse interests became focused by an experience that gave purpose and direction to his studies and pursuits. Having been introduced to Positivism by a friend at Wadham, Harrison requested and was granted an interview with Auguste Comte in Paris. Comte stressed the importance of studying biology, chemistry, physics, and astronomy as keys to understanding the development of the human mind, a process that Comte felt followed three stages: theological, metaphysical, and positive. In the first two stages the mind of the subject develops from having an egocentric viewpoint to having one more ready to accept abstractions. In the third stage, a final stage that one could approach but never attain, the individual would become able to transcend a need for absolute answers. In his *Autobiographic Memoirs* (1911) Harrison stressed how profoundly the presence and ideas of the French philosopher had affected him. At Comte's suggestion Harrison returned to England and began studying mathematics and the sciences to "correct" the imbalance of his education.

In response to Comte's belief that intellectuals and workers needed to work together Harrison in 1857 began a long involvement with the Working Men's College, where he lectured on history, Positivism, and other subjects. He also began to write. His first effort, a letter to the London *Daily News* in 1859 on the Free Italy Question, was followed by his first extended essay, a critical review of *Essays and Reviews* that was published in 1860 in the *Westminster Review*. He became a prolific contributor of both essays to periodicals and letters to newspapers. His autobiography lists more than two hundred articles that he published in various journals, and he notes that this list of titles excludes essays that he reprinted in his books.

In 1862 Harrison met John Ruskin, with whom he was often to disagree in print. The two became close friends, however, and Harrison even weathered Ruskin's parody of him in *Fors Clavigera* (1871-1878). Harrison eventually wrote the entries on Ruskin that were published in the *Encyclopedia Britannica* (1902) and in Michael Bryan's *A Biographical and Critical Dictionary of Painters and Engravers* (1905).

Harrison's first book, *The Meaning of History* (1862), reveals the influence of Comte in the alliance Harrison proposes between intellectuals and workers. Harrison suggests that workingmen could benefit, personally and materially, from making a systematic study of history, and he offers a suggested reading list. The enlarged edition of 1894 includes lectures to the Positivist Society and essays from the *Fortnightly Review,* in which Harrison interprets several of those works on his suggested list of readings and presents a Positivist interpretation of several historical periods, particularly classical Greek and Roman.

The *Fortnightly Review,* which began publication in May 1865, provided Harrison with one of several ready outlets for his writing. Beginning with an article favoring trades unions for ironmasters in the inaugural issue, Harrison became a frequent contributor. By his own count he published sixty-

Elm Hill, Hawkhurst, Kent, Harrison's home from 1902 until 1912

four articles, all signed, in the *Fortnightly Review* between 1865 and 1904.

Between 1865 and 1875 Harrison was giving lectures and writing articles aimed at popularizing his understanding of Positivism. Most of these addresses and articles remain uncollected. In 1861 he had participated in the United Building Trades strike for a nine-hour workday, and he was appointed by Parliament to the Trades Union Commission, on which he served from 1862 through 1869.

In 1867 Harrison and others organized the Positivist Society. After helping the organization find suitable quarters, first in Chapel Street and later in Newton Hall, Harrison was one of the principal lecturers to address the society. Not including the annual address he gave to the society each New Year's Day from 1881 to 1904, his memoirs list titles for more than two hundred lectures he delivered, and in 1893 he became the founding editor of the *Positivist Review*. The goal of both the society and its *Review* was to increase political power and opportunities for working-class men. Harrison's lectures argued the needs for ensuring universal literacy, for extending voting rights (an aim achieved in 1884), and for increasing math and science instruction in the universities as well as other sociopolitical causes. The issues on which many of the *Positivist Review* essays focus were narrow, but all showed the influence of Comte's Positivism combined with Harrison's desire to improve the lot of the working classes.

In 1870 he married Ethel Harrison, his cousin, who shared his interest in Positivism. On several occasions he acknowledged her help and advice on his work, and following her death in 1916 he dedicated *On Society* (1918) to her. They had four sons and a daughter.

Order and Progress (1875), one of his works in which Harrison collected articles he had previously published in the *Fortnightly Review,* is divided into two sections, "Thoughts on Government" and "Studies of Political Crisis." The latter consists of such *Fortnightly* articles and largely expresses his opposition to British military involvements in the Crimea, Japan, and Abyssinia and his support for the policies of John Bright. The former section presents his belief that some form of executive government is needed to combat "the nearly unqualified autocracy of Parliament."

Inscription and title page in a copy of Harrison's most unified explanation and defense of Positivism (Thomas Cooper Library, University of South Carolina)

Seeking primarily to support Prime Minister William Ewart Gladstone on home rule for Ireland, Harrison ran unsuccessfully for Parliament in 1886. He was elected in 1889 to the London County Council, where he served as alderman until 1893. His history lectures at the Working Men's College convinced him that current approaches to teaching history were flawed, and, using a Positivist perspective, he began to reinterpret history, to emphasize leaders with backgrounds outside the existing aristocratic orders. His first attempt to incorporate this perspective in his writing was through *Oliver Cromwell* (1888), his biography of a politician whom Harrison greatly admired for having emerged as a leader through merit rather than birth. *William the Silent* (1897), on William I; *George Washington, and Other American Addresses* (1901); and *Chatham* (1905), on William Pitt, first Earl of Chatham, are later studies in which Harrison adopts the same perspective. He admired Washington more than any other American politician, and when Washington's privileged background was hard for Harrison to accommodate to his historical perspective, he sometimes overlooked that background by emphasizing what he saw as Washington's commitment to democratic equality for all men.

At the age of seventy-five Harrison began to gather materials for his autobiography and to collect his ideas and opinions to present his view of Positivism in a unified manner. With *The Creed of a Layman: Apologia pro fide mea* (1907) and *The Philosophy of Common Sense* (1907) he began to publish a four-volume explanation of Positivism and of how it could apply to current social and political issues. Part I of *Creed* recounts how his commitment to Positivism had begun and had been nurtured at Wadham through the influence of Charles Cookson, a close friend. Part II attempts to formulate creeds for use in a Positivist Church. Many of Harrison's contemporaries were turning to agnosticism, but he sought to create a

The Harrison family in 1907: Godfrey (seated on ground); Olive, Frederic, and Ethel (seated in chairs); and René, Austin, and Bernard (standing)

common ground for his Anglicanism and his new philosophical beliefs by adapting that Anglicanism to those new beliefs. *The Philosophy of Common Sense* presents his explanation of the philosophical bases of Positivism and discusses the flaws of other contemporary philosophies, particularly those of Thomas Henry Huxley, Herbert Spencer, and Arthur James Balfour. Harrison felt that the works of these writers demonstrate more style than substance, and he particularly objected to Balfour's extensive use of metaphor.

National and Social Problems (1908), the third of the four volumes in this series that Harrison published, collected various articles he had published in the *Fortnightly Review*. The subjects of these articles include antimilitarism, church disestablishment, and support for trades unions. The essays are not revised from their original publication in the *Fortnightly Review*, as Harrison believed that although specific events and social situations might no longer be current, the principles on which those essays had been based were unchanged.

The fourth volume, *Realities and Ideals: Social, Political, Literary, and Artistic* (1908), also consists primarily of reprinted articles, but these are collected from various periodicals. Of the forty-four essays included, twenty-four address social and political issues in calling for reforms to benefit the working classes. Some new essays are included, most notably four on women's rights. Harrison had early and often expressed his admiration for John Stuart Mill, of whom Harrison wrote in his *Autobiographic Memoirs*, "To have known such a man, as I believe, the most self-devoted and most scrupulous of all politicians of his age, is indeed the honour of a lifetime." Harrison felt obligated, however, to disagree with some of Mill's ideas on suffrage. While noting in *Realities and Ideals* that he agreed with Mill in supporting identical educational opportunities for men and women, Harrison adamantly opposed giving women the vote, for he feared that suffrage for women could lead them to desire to serve in Parliament, and he was opposed to this.

Autobiographic Memoirs was published as Harrison was reaching his eightieth birthday. His health continued to be excellent, and he supplemented this recounting of his long life in *Novissima verba: Last Words, 1920* (1921) and in *De senectute: More Last Words* (1923), the latter of which was published posthumously. In these four volumes Harrison augments the philosophy he expresses in other works while he examines the events that shaped that philosophy. Along with other familiar Positivist beliefs, improving education through increasing the study of mathematics and science continues to be the focus of these final essays.

Positivism and theology are the central subjects in *The Positive Evolution of Religion: Its Moral and Social Reaction* (1913). Of the fourteen essays included in this volume, the first four are new; the remainder are articles that had first appeared in the *Positivist Review* from June 1911 through June 1912. The essays, covering religious beliefs from Anglicanism and Catholicism to deism and polytheism, summarize Harrison's views on the state of religion at the beginning of the twentieth century. He concludes that people are seeking a religion of humanity, which he sees as Positivism. His final essay in this collection is a tribute to Comte, and it was written to commemorate the fiftieth anniversary of the philosopher's death.

Beginning with his opposition to the Crimean War, Harrison had publicly opposed all British military involvement in the political affairs of other countries. Like many writers of his time, however, Harrison was alarmed at the growing militarism throughout Europe at the beginning of the twentieth century. In *The German Peril: Forecasts, 1864–1914; Realities, 1915; Hopes, 191-* (1915) he studied German nationalism, which he called Bismarckism, as a threat to England. He had sounded this warning before, beginning with "Bismarckism: The Policy of Blood and Iron," which he had published in the *Fortnightly Review* in December 1870, and he had repeated this warning in other articles he had published before 1915. In *The German Peril* Harrison warns that "the greatest peril which Englishmen have known since they met the Norman at Hastings" is upon them.

In 1918 he published *On Society,* a series of twelve lectures through which Harrison aimed to summarize a half century of Positivist thought in England. He apparently thought that such a summary, from "the only survivor of those at home or abroad that had personal interviews with Auguste Comte," was necessary and that, as he was eighty-seven years old, this book would be his "last public utterance."

Contrary to his expectations, Harrison remained well and active. In the next four years he completed additional collections of his essays that had originally been published as monthly columns in the *Fortnightly Review* from January through December of 1918 and 1920. The first twelve of these are collected in *Obiter scripta, 1918* (1919), and they are primarily concerned with the course of events during World War I. One of Harrison's sons was killed in battle, and his other sons were also involved in the war effort, so the essays often display a personal tone.

Harrison attributed the growth of socialism to the belief held by the working classes that such a system would reduce nationalism. The results, he noted, had not supported this belief, and in the twelve essays of *Novissima verba: Last Words, 1920* Harrison examines politics in Europe and the United States following the war. He was particularly concerned with the lack of progress in establishing the League of Nations. While he supported the idea of such an organization, he accurately predicted that conflicting political interests would prevent any peacekeeping alliance.

On 13 January 1923 Harrison suffered a heart attack, and he died the next day. Appropriately "A Philosophic Synthesis," the final chapter of *De senectute* is about Comte and Positivism, the chief concerns throughout Harrison's life and writing. He concludes that Positivism is the only system he had found that "combines and gives equal consideration to man's energies, his mind, and his emotions."

As a reform writer Harrison was devoted to many causes. He was opposed to English militarism and political involvement in foreign conflict. He championed universal male suffrage and argued not only for educational reform to expand the study of mathematics and science in all schools but also for expanded educational opportunities for women and working-class men. In essays written throughout half a century he supported the growth of trades unions. He practiced his beliefs through teaching in the Working Men's College and forming the Positivist Church. During a long and active writing career he tirelessly sought to apply Positivist principles to social and political needs.

Biographies:

Austin Harrison, *Frederic Harrison* (New York & London: Putnam, 1927);

Harry R. Sullivan, *Frederic Harrison* (Boston: Twayne, 1983);

Martha S. Vogeler, *Frederic Harrison: The Vocation of a Positivist* (Oxford: Clarendon Press, 1984).

Papers:

Collections of Harrison's papers are in the British Library; the British Library of Political and Economic Science; the Huntington Library; the Library of Congress; the Musée d'Auguste Comte, Paris; and the libraries of Cornell University, Harvard University, Yale University, and the University of Texas at Austin.

Ellice Hopkins
(30 October 1836 – 21 August 1904)

Susan Mumm
York University

BOOKS: *English Idylls, and Other Poems,* as Jane Ellice (London & Cambridge: Macmillan, 1865);

Fred Williams: A Tale for Boys (London: Jarrold, 1866);

Home Thoughts for Mothers and Mothers' Meetings (London: Nisbet, 1869);

Sick-Bed Vows, and How to Keep Them: A Book for Convalescents (London: Nisbet, 1869);

Work among the Lost (London: Macintosh, 1870);

Active Service; or, Work among Our Soldiers (London, 1872);

Christ the Consoler: A Book of Comfort for the Sick (London: Longmans, 1872; New York: Randolph, 188-?);

Does It Answer? A Word for Soldiers (London: Hatchards, 1872);

The Visitation of Dens: An Appeal to the Women of England, anonymous (London: Hatchards, 1874);

An English Woman's Work among Workingmen (New Britain, Conn.: Williams, 1875); enlarged as *Work amongst Working-Men* (London: Strahan, 1879; New York: Whittaker, 1884);

Rose Turquand (2 volumes, London: Macmillan, 1876; 1 volume, New York: Harper, 1876);

Work in Brighton; or, Woman's Mission to Women, anonymous (London: Hatchards, 1877; enlarged, 1877);

Ladies' Associations for the Care of Friendless Girls: Being an Account of the Work in Brighton (London, 1878);

Notes on Penitentiary Work (London, 1879);

Occupation for the Sick; or, Practical Suggestions to Invalids and Those Who Have the Care of Them (London: Hatchards, 1879);

A Plea for the Wider Action of the Church of England in the Prevention of the Degradation of Women as Submitted to a Committee of Convocation (London: Hatchards, 1879);

Little Mary (London: Hatchards, 1881);

Preventive Work; or, The Care of Our Girls (London: Hatchards, 1881);

Grave Moral Questions Addressed to the Men and Women of England (London: Hatchards, 1882);

Ellice Hopkins

The Legal Protection of the Young (London: Strangeways, 1882);

Village Morality: A Letter Addressed to Clergymen's Wives and Christian Workers (London: Hatchards, 1882);

On the Early Training of Girls and Boys: An Appeal to Working Women, Especially Intended for Mothers' Meetings (London: Hatchards, 1882; New York: Hammett, 1884); republished as *The Early Training of Girls and Boys: An Appeal to Working Women, Especially Intended for Mothers' Unions* (London: King, n.d.); abridged as *On the Early Training of Girls and Boys: An Appeal to*

Working Women, Compiled Chiefly from the Writings of Ellice Hopkins (New York: Hammett, 1883);
Autumn Swallows: A Book of Lyrics (London: Macmillan, 1883);
England's Law for Women and Children (London: Hatchards, 1883);
The White Cross Army (London: Hatchards, 1883); expanded as *The White Cross Army: A Statement of the Bishop of Durham's Movement* (London: Hatchards, 1883); republished as *A Statement of the Bishop of Durham's Movement* (London: Hatchards, 1883);
Drawn unto Death: A Plea for the Children Coming under the Industrial Schools Act Amendment Act, 1880 (London: Hatchards, 1884);
How to Start Preventive Work; or, Hints on the Management of a Training Home and Free Registry Office on the Bristol Plan (London: Hatchards, 1884);
The Black Anchor (London: Hatchards, 1885);
The Defaced Image Restored (London: Hatchards, 1885);
"God's Little Girl": A Truthful Narrative of Facts Concerning a Poor "Waif" Admitted into "Dr. Barnardo's Village Home" (London: Shaw, 1885);
Is It Natural? (London: Hatchards, 1885);
Lost in Quicksand (London: Hatchards, 1885);
Moral Money-Clippers (London: Hatchards, 1885);
Power to Let (London: Hatchards, 1885);
The Purity Movement: Cannot We Use Existing Organizations? (London: Hatchards, 1885);
Rolling away the Stone (London: Hatchards, 1885);
Touching Pitch (London: Hatchards, 1885);
The White Cross: Ten Reasons Why I Should Join (London: Hatchards, 1885);
Who Holds the Rope? (London: Hatchards, 1885);
The Apocalypse of Evil (London: Hatchards, 1886);
Buried Seed (London: Hatchards, 1886);
The Crocodile and the Little Birds (London: Hatchards, 1886);
Little Kindnesses (London: Hatchards, 1886);
The Man with the Drawn Sword (London: Hatchards, 1886);
Man and Woman; or, The Christian Ideal (London: Hatchards, 1886);
Per angusta ad augusta (London: Hatchards, 1886);
The Standard of the White Cross: Do We Need It? An Appeal to Clergy and Laity (London: Hatchards, 1886);
What Can We Do? (London: Hatchards, 1886; Chicago: Gilbert, n.d.);
Conquering and to Conquer (London: Hatchards, 1886);
The Greeley Expedition (London: Hatchards, 1886);
A Homely Talk on the New Law for the Protection of Girls (London: Hatchards, 1886);
The Practical Working of the White Cross Movement (London: Hatchards, 1886);
The Present Moral Crisis: An Appeal to Women (London: Dyer, 1886);
Saved at Last (London: Hatchards, 1886);
The Secret and Method of Purity (London: Hatchards, 1886);
True Manliness (London: Hatchards, 1886);
Girls' Clubs and Recreative Evening Homes: How to Work Them (London: Hatchards, 1887);
Wild Oats, or Acorns? (London: Gardner, 1890);
The British Zulu (London: Hatchards, 1891);
God's Great Gift of Speech Abused (London: Gardner, 1892);
Damaged Pearls: An Appeal to Working Men (London: Gardner, 1892);
Purity, the Guard of Manhood: A Confirmation Paper (London: Gardner, 1892);
The Ride of Death (London: Gardner, 1892);
The Power of Womanhood; or, Mothers and Sons: A Book for Parents and Those in loco parentis (London: Gardner, Darton, 1899; New York: Dutton, 1899);
The Story of Life: For the Use of Mothers and Boys (London & Newcastle-on-Tyne: Scott, 1903);
The National Flag (London: White Cross League, 1915);
My Little Sister (London: Hatchards, n.d.).

OTHER: *Life and Letters of James Hinton*, edited by Hopkins (London: Kegan Paul, 1878);
I. L. Richmond, *Three Courses for Three-Pence: Ten Lessons in Cottage Cookery*, preface by Hopkins (London: Hatchards, 1885);
The National Purity Crusade, Its Origins and Results: A Brief Record, introduction by Hopkins (London: Morgan & Scott, 1904).

In the late nineteenth century three British women were notorious for their activism in the cause of social purity. The reputations of two of them–Josephine Butler and Dr. Elizabeth Blackwell–have survived in the twentieth century. The reputation of the third, Jane Ellice Hopkins, is forgotten although she was the founder of the White Cross Army, an international, nondenominational movement devoted to overthrowing the sexual double standard. By the mid 1880s this slight, middle-aged Victorian spinster was recognized as the foremost advocate of the sexual single standard and as a powerful advocate of legislative change furthering that end. In her own time Hopkins was one of the best-known women reform writers in England although she had more public detractors than apologists. Most of her writings address the issue of sexual purity in the context of women's needs for equal status in British society.

Born on 30 October 1836, Jane Ellice was the younger daughter of William Hopkins by his second wife, Caroline Boys. Hopkins began life as a farmer but abandoned this vocation to enter St. Peter's College, Cambridge, at the age of thirty. He became a celebrated lecturer in mathematics at Cambridge University and gave his younger daughter a rigorous education in the sciences and the classics. Profoundly attached to him, she began her public work only shortly before his death in 1866, when she started addressing large meetings of bricklayers and fossil diggers in a working-class suburb of Cambridge, experiences she recounts in *An English Woman's Work among Workingmen* (1875).

During this period Hopkins underwent a crisis of faith that forced her to abandon many of the traditional beliefs of Christian theology in favor of a single focus on what she described as the elements of belief, the Incarnation and Atonement. At the age of thirty she moved to Brighton, where she worked at the Albion Hill Home, a reformatory for prostitutes, from 1866 to 1870. Following a botched surgical procedure she underwent, Hopkins then spent seven years as an invalid before recovering her health and reentering public life. During this time she published most of her "literary" work, the more important of which are *Rose Turquand* (1876), a sensational novel, and *Autumn Swallows: A Book of Lyrics* (1883), her second book of poetry.

Rose Turquand is a two-volume romance with many Gothic features: it includes a bigamous marriage, an illegitimate orphan as the heroine, a long interpolated tale of doomed love between a monk and a woman pretending to be a monk, and a mysterious presence in the abandoned wing of a country house. The novel contains faint autobiographical parallels, such as a girl who is given a boy's education by a mathematician, and it gives a moving account of how the heroine transforms her stymied need to love someone into devotion to others whom society considers to be repulsive and unlovable. The London *Times* praised the "real power and no little originality" of the book.

Autumn Swallows deals explicitly with many of the issues on which Hopkins was to concentrate in her reform writing, especially the hypocrisy on which the sexual double standard was based. *Autumn Swallows*, like *Rose Turquand*, was also favorably reviewed, and both works indicate Hopkins's absorption in the problems of suffering, especially that caused by social or sexual inequality.

Title page for Hopkins's account of her early work as a social reformer

In 1876 she founded the Ladies' Association for the Care of Friendless Girls, which grew to have many branches and established more than two hundred refuges and domestic-service training homes for young women throughout Great Britain.

During the 1870s Hopkins was trained in medicine and reproductive physiology by James Hinton, a noted surgeon who was the founder of the altruistic school of philosophy in Britain. Hinton eventually lost much of his influence, although not Hopkins's loyalty, through his guarded defense of free love and his impassioned defense of the essential moral innocence of prostitutes. When Hinton was dying, Hopkins promised to devote herself to the cause of redressing women's wrongs, and she spent the next twelve years fulfilling this promise.

In preparing for her public work as lecturer and writer she studied the work of Puritan theologians and the writings of contemporary Evangelicals such as Charles Spurgeon. She scoured ancient and modern authors for racy anecdotes, telling examples, and memorable stories to convey the message of social purity to late-Victorian audiences. Hopkins disliked Latinate and what she called pulpit English, "the most vicious English in existence." She claimed that women made the best preachers and writers, for "women never wrong their thoughts with pulpit English, but preserve the strength and sweetness of their mother tongue.... [T]hey speak not from theological systems but from the heart and the life." Her writing contained little of the "water-gruel and brown sugar" that she felt constituted most religious writing.

In late 1882 Hopkins and Bishop Joseph Lightfoot of Durham founded the White Cross Army in the north of England. The structure of the organization was modeled on that of the temperance movement: up to three thousand men, mostly of the working class, attended mass meetings where they were urged by Hopkins to "take the pledge" of chastity until they were married. An important secondary goal of the organization was to raise the standing of women, from whom society demanded behavior that would ensure purity: educating their children about sexuality, demanding purity from men of their own class, developing a high standard of female courage, and devoting themselves to reversing the moral decay of the nation through loving and compassionate responses to their fallen sisters.

The White Cross Movement had considerable success, particularly in the industrial North and Midlands. In its first year alone more than two thousand men (mostly coal miners and industrial workers) signed the pledge. Branches of the movement were also active in the universities, especially at Cambridge, although university authorities at Oxford viewed the local branch with hostility. Overall, 102 branches of the White Cross Army were formed in Great Britain during the first year the movement operated, and other branches were formed in India, Canada, Australia, the United States, and Germany. In general it attracted the same people who also became involved in the temperance movement, the anti–Contagious Diseases Act program, and self-improvement organizations of many kinds. The White Cross Army was nondenominational: some branches were Anglican; some were Nonconformist; others contained a mixture of all faiths, including Jews, and of nonbelievers. Members were required only to promise to carry out the five aims of the society:

1. To treat all women with respect, and endeavor to protect them from wrong and degradation.
2. To endeavor to put down all indecent language and coarse jests.
3. To maintain the law of purity as equally binding upon men and women.
4. To endeavor to spread these principles among my companions, and to try and help my younger brothers.
5. To use every possible means to fulfill the command, "Keep THYSELF pure."

Hopkins used the White Cross Army as a means to spread her demand for social purity and social equality; especially important to her reform agenda was the White Cross Series, a series of pamphlets that Hatchards published in the mid 1880s and that enabled her to spread her ideas widely. Of thirty-two pamphlets in the series, twenty-six were written by Hopkins; of eleven shorter papers distributed by the White Cross, ten were her work. More than three hundred thousand copies of *True Manliness* (1886), her best-selling work, were sold within a year of its publication; published with only her initials, J. E. H., on the title page, it was popularly attributed to an eminent barrister. By the time of her death in 1904 more than two million copies of her works had been sold, and these were widely read. Publishing twenty to seventy-five editions of a single work was common, and some of these works remained in print until the 1940s. She did not profit financially from these enormous sales as she used the proceeds to further her work.

Having served as a rescue worker among women prostitutes in her early years, Hopkins wrote that while such work might occasionally save a woman, it did nothing to remedy the injustice inherent in the Victorian double standard of sexual behavior. She argued that moral cures for prostitution attacked the wrong problem: the reasons for prostitution were economic as it resulted from low wages and a general lack of alternatives for women. Throughout her life Hopkins ardently advocated all aspects of female emancipation, and she was angered by the familiar argument that prostitution provided a necessary safety valve for men. If prostitution were needed to ensure the purity of Victorian homes, she argued, then it should receive the sanction of both the state and the church: the parsonage should be built on one side of the parish church, for instance, and the brothel on the other. Hopkins also attacked the social-class assumptions of the double standard. In response to any Victorian doctor who claimed that regular intercourse was medically necessary for men, she suggested that such a physician should be asked if "his own daughter or sister was available for the carrying out of the prescription, since he so freely prescribed the degradation of other men's daughters and sisters."

Unlike most purity literature Hopkins's writings did not emphasize protecting one's own virtue; men and women were expected to remain virtuous while devoting their energies to caring for the weak and defenseless in their society. Hopkins poured her contempt on what she termed "mere passive purity, the purity of which the noblest utterance is, 'I know how to take care of myself,' and which is intent on saving its own alabaster skin." She worked with Thomas Barnardo, the founder of the Dr. Barnardo homes dedicated to caring for destitute children, but she adamantly opposed his sensationalist fund-raising techniques. She also opposed the work of self-appointed Vigilance Associations, the goal of which was the police suppression of vice. Hopkins was instrumental in the forming of the National Union of Women Workers in 1895, and although Edward J. Bristow incorrectly describes her as the editor of *Seeking and Saving,* a social-reform journal published from 1881 to 1890, she wrote much of what that journal published.

Hopkins's writings start from a premise that she had shaped from Hinton's "theology of others"—a premise that the purpose of Christian belief is not personal salvation but the service and protection of the weak and helpless. She saw working-class women as the most vulnerable, most exploited group in British society, and it followed naturally that this group produced the bulk of prostitutes and abused children. Hopkins argued that sexually exploited working-class women and children signified the suffering of Christ to the nineteenth century, that they actually as well as symbolically represented "the crucified body of your Redeemer." She claimed that the inequality of women, which she saw typified most vividly in the public depersonalization of the prostitute, thus violated the heart of the Gospel and constituted a second rejection of Christ. In her eyes the refusal of society to acknowledge the equality of the sexes meant that Britain was rejecting the work of God in the nineteenth century.

Hopkins complemented this theological position with a second premise based on a Victorian version of the ideals of chivalry. She argued that until men and women were able to become true equals in social and political life, men—as the stronger and more privileged sex—would have a chivalric responsibility for protecting women. Chivalric protection of women was thus necessary during a transitional state of society, but it was to be abandoned when women came to enjoy full equality with men. Until such equality was achieved, men should protect women rather than degrade them; furthermore, both sexes were obliged to ensure the innocence of children. Hopkins attacked the "pitiful meanness" as well as the unfairness of the premises inherent in the sexual double standard, and she worked closely with both Josephine Butler and W. T. Stead in their efforts to effect the social equality of the sexes.

In analyzing the White Cross Movement and other purity crusades for raising the age of consent one must acknowledge the social context of this sexual puritanism: these movements shared a concern over child prostitution and a desire to ensure that girls were old enough to be fully aware of what they were doing when they became sexually active. The nineteenth century was an era in which teenage girls were unlikely to have access to contraception, in which safe or legal abortion was unobtainable, in which effective cures for venereal disease were unknown, and in which the social consequences of premarital sexual activity could be serious. Hopkins's heated rhetoric dramatically warned the nineteenth-century man of

> the pitiful meanness of the bargain he makes, retaining his own social advantages, his friends, his refinements, all the bright prospects of his life, and leaving the curse of his wrong-doing to fall upon the woman, making her an outcast from God and man, cutting her off from the hope of wifehood and motherhood, exposing her to frightful disease, to live a degraded life.

To the Industrial Schools Amendment Act (1880) Hopkins proposed an amendment that made it a criminal offense to keep minor children in brothels. She also formulated and championed to its successful adoption another important piece of late-Victorian social legislation, the Criminal Law Amendment Act (1885), which allowed authorities to remove children working as prostitutes and which raised the age of consent to sixteen. In dramatic language many of her pamphlets explain the need for legislation such as these acts. A long series of Hopkins's pamphlets—the most important of which is *Damaged Pearls: An Appeal to Working Men* (1892)—emphasizes the class favoritism inherent in existing legislation, which removed all protection for working-class girls on their thirteenth birthday and yet protected heiresses until they reached the age of twenty-one.

As a consequence of her campaigns Hopkins became a social outcast. Many respectable organizations advocating moral reform, including several that she had helped to found, expelled her in the fear that her name might arouse prejudice toward the cause of social purity. In 1888 her health broke, and she became an invalid for the remainder of her life. Although she continued to publish until her death, she never wrote so prolifically as she had earlier in the 1880s.

Ellice Hopkins's notoriety resulted from her refusal to accept quietly the sexual double standard. As she wrote, "Nature made me a singing bird; man has made me a sewer rat." Her protest, expressed in more than seventy-five books and pamphlets, demanded equality for women—morally, economically, socially, and politically. She devoted her literary ability to unsavory causes, especially to reforming the double standard of morality and the sexual abuse of children. Hopkins promoted these causes through a torrent of publications that were sold in extraordinary numbers in the 1880s and that have been undeservedly forgotten by historians of social reform.

References:

Rosa M. Barrett, *Ellice Hopkins: A Memoir* (London: Wells Gardner, 1907);

Edward J. Bristow, *Vice and Vigilance: Social Purity Movements in Britain since 1700* (Dublin: Gill & Macmillan, 1977).

Charles Kingsley
(12 June 1819 - 23 January 1875)

Isobel M. Findlay
University of Saskatchewan

See also the Kingsley entries in *DLB 21: Victorian Novelists Before 1855; DLB 32: Victorian Poets Before 1850; DLB 163: British Children's Writers, 1800–1880;* and *DLB 178: British Fantasy and Science-Fiction Writers Before World War I.*

BOOKS: *A Sermon Preached at Eversley . . . on Sunday Morning, 18th April, 1847* (London: Roworth, 1847);

A Sermon Preached at Hawley Church, April 30, 1848, in Behalf of the New Church at York Town (Wokingham, U.K.: Gotelee, 1848);

The Saint's Tragedy; or, The True Story of Elizabeth of Hungary, Langravine of Thuringia, Saint of the Romish Calendar (London: Parker, 1848; New York: International Book, 1855);

Twenty-five Village Sermons (London: Parker, 1849; revised edition, 1852; Philadelphia: Hooker, 1854); republished as *Village Sermons* (London: Macmillan, 1913);

Cheap Clothes and Nasty, as Parson Lot (London: Pickering / Cambridge: Macmillan, 1850);

Alton Locke, Tailor and Poet: An Autobiography, anonymous (2 volumes, London: Chapman & Hall, 1850; 1 volume, New York: Harper, 1850);

The Application of Associative Principles and Methods to Agriculture: A Lecture (London: Bezer, 1851);

Yeast: A Problem, anonymous (London: Parker, 1851; New York: Harper, 1851);

The Message of the Church to Labouring Men: A Sermon (London: Parker, 1851);

Phaethon; or, Loose Thoughts for Loose Thinkers (Cambridge: Macmillan, 1852; Philadelphia: Hooker, 1854);

Sermons on National Subjects, Preached in a Village Church (London: Griffin, 1852); republished as *The King of the Earth, and Other Sermons on National Subjects Preached in a Village Church* (London: Macmillan, 1872);

Who Are the Friends of Order? A Reply to Certain Observations in a Late Number of Fraser's Magazine on the

Charles Kingsley (Gale International Portrait Gallery)

So-Called "Christian Socialists" (London: Lumley, 1852);

Hypatia; or, New Foes with an Old Face: A Novel (2 volumes, London: Parker, 1853; 1 volume, New York: Lowell, 1853);

Alexandria and Her Schools: Four Lectures Delivered at the Philosophical Institution, Edinburgh (Cambridge: Macmillan, 1854);

Sermons on National Subjects: Second Series (London & Glasgow: Griffin, 1854);

Who Causes Pestilence? Four Sermons (London & Glasgow: Griffin, 1854);

Brave Words for Brave Soldiers and Sailors, anonymous (Cambridge: Macmillan, 1855);

Westward Ho! or, The Voyages and Adventures of Sir Amyas Leigh, Knight, of Burrough, in the County of Devon, in the Reign of Her Most Glorious Majesty, Queen Elizabeth (3 volumes, Cambridge: Macmillan, 1855; 1 volume, Boston: Ticknor & Fields, 1855);

Glaucus; or, The Wonders of the Shore (Cambridge: Macmillan, 1855; Boston: Ticknor & Fields, 1855; corrected and enlarged edition, Cambridge: Macmillan, 1856; corrected and enlarged again, 1859);

Sermons for the Times (London: Parker, 1855; New York: Dana, 1856);

Sermons for Sailors (London, 1855); republished as *Sea Sermons* (London: Kegan Paul, 1885);

The Heroes; or, Greek Fairy Tales for My Children (London: Blackie, 1855; Boston: Ticknor & Fields, 1856);

Poems (Boston: Ticknor & Fields, 1856);

Two Years Ago (3 volumes, Cambridge: Macmillan, 1857; 1 volume, Boston: Ticknor & Fields, 1857);

Andromeda, and Other Poems (London: Parker, 1858; Boston: Ticknor & Fields, 1858);

Miscellanies, 2 volumes (London: Parker, 1859);

The Good News of God: Sermons (London: Parker, 1859; New York: Burt, Hutchinson & Abbey, 1859);

The Massacre of the Innocents (London: Jarrold, 1859);

The Limits of Exact Science as Applied to History: An Inaugural Lecture (Cambridge & London: Macmillan, 1860);

The Example of the Early Navigators: A Sermon (London: Parker, 1860);

Why Should We Pray for Fair Weather? A Sermon (London: Parker, 1860);

New Miscellanies (Boston: Ticknor & Fields, 1860);

Town and Country Sermons (London: Parker & Bourn, 1861);

Ode Performed in the Senate-House, Cambridge, on the Tenth of June, M.DCCC.LXII. Composed for the Installation of His Grace the Duke of Devonshire, Chancellor of the University (Cambridge & London: Macmillan, 1862);

Speech of Lord Dundreary in Section D on Friday Last, on the Great Hippocampus Question, anonymous (Cambridge & London: Macmillan, 1862);

A Sermon on the Death of His Royal Highness, the Prince Consort (London: Parker & Bourn, 1862);

The Water-Babies: A Fairy-Tale for a Land-Baby (London & Cambridge: Macmillan, 1863; Boston: Burnham, 1864);

The Gospel of the Pentateuch: A Set of Parish Sermons (London: Parker & Bourne, 1863; London & New York: Macmillan, 1890);

Mr. Kingsley and Dr. Newman: A Correspondence on the Question Whether Dr. Newman Teaches That Truth Is No Virtue? (London: Longman, Green, Longman, Roberts & Green, 1864);

"What, Then, Does Dr. Newman Mean?" A Reply to a Pamphlet Lately Published by Dr. Newman (London & Cambridge: Macmillan, 1864);

The Roman and the Teuton: A Series of Lectures Delivered before the University of Cambridge (Cambridge & London: Macmillan, 1864; London & New York: Macmillan, 1890);

Hints to Stammerers, by a Minute Philosopher, as C. K. (London: Longman, 1864); also published as *The Irrationale of Speech, by a Minute Philosopher* (London: Longman, 1864);

David: Four Sermons Preached before the University of Cambridge (London & Cambridge: Macmillan, 1865); enlarged as *David: Five Sermons* (London: Macmillan, 1874);

Hereward the Wake, "Last of the English" (2 volumes, London & Cambridge: Macmillan, 1866; 1 volume, Boston: Ticknor & Fields, 1866);

The Temple of Wisdom: A Sermon (London: Macmillan, 1866);

Three Lectures Delivered at the Royal Institution on the Ancien Regime as It Existed on the Continent before the French Revolution (London: Macmillan, 1867);

The Water of Life, and Other Sermons (London: Macmillan, 1867; Philadelphia: Lippincott, 1868);

The Hermits (London: Macmillan, 1868; Philadelphia: Lippincott, 1868);

Discipline, and Other Sermons (London: Macmillan, 1868; Philadelphia: Lippincott, 1868);

Women and Politics (London: National Society for Women's Suffrage, 1869);

God's Feast: A Sermon (London & Cambridge: Macmillan, 1869);

The Address on Education, Read before the National Association for the Promotion of Social Science (London: National Education League, 1869);

Madam How and Lady Why; or, First Lessons in Earth Lore for Children (London: Bell & Daldy, 1870; New York: Macmillan, 1885);

At Last: A Christmas in the West Indies, 2 volumes (London & New York: Macmillan, 1871; New York: Harper, 1871);

Town Geology (London: Strahan, 1872; New York, Appleton, 1873);

Poems: Including The Saint's Tragedy, Andromeda, Songs, Ballads, &c. (London: Macmillan, 1872; expanded, 1873; New York: Hurst, 1880);

Plays and Puritans, and Other Historical Essays (London: Macmillan, 1873; London & New York: Macmillan, 1889);

Prose Idylls, New and Old (London: Macmillan, 1873; London & New York: Macmillan, 1889);

Frederick Denison Maurice: A Sermon Preached in Aid of the Girls' Home (London: Macmillan, 1873);

Health and Education (London: Isbister, 1874; New York: Appleton, 1874);

The Study of Natural History: A Lecture Delivered at the R. A. Institution, Woolwich, Oct. 3, 1871 (Woolwich, 1874);

Westminster Sermons (London: Macmillan, 1874; London & New York: Macmillan, 1890);

Lectures Delivered in America in 1874 (London: Longmans, Green, 1875; Philadelphia: Coates, 1875);

Letters to Young Men on Betting and Gambling (London: King, 1877);

All Saints' Day, and Other Sermons, edited by W. Harrison (London: Kegan Paul, 1878; New York: Scribner, Armstrong, 1878);

True Words for Brave Men: A Book for Soldiers' and Sailors' Libraries (London: Kegan Paul, 1878; New York: Whittaker, 1886);

Sanitary and Social Lectures and Essays (London: Macmillan, 1880);

Scientific Lectures and Essays (London: Macmillan, 1880; London & New York: Macmillan, 1890);

Literary and General Lectures and Essays (London: Macmillan, 1880; London & New York: Macmillan, 1890);

Historical Lectures and Essays (London & New York: Macmillan, 1880);

Out of the Deep: Words for the Sorrowful, edited by Fanny Kingsley (New York: Macmillan, 1880; London & New York: Macmillan, 1883);

From Death to Life: Fragments of Teaching to a Village Congregation, with Letters on the Life after Death (London & New York: Macmillan, 1887);

Words of Advice to School-Boys, Collected from Hitherto Unpublished Notes and Letters, edited by E. F. Johns (London: Simpkin, 1912);

The Tutor's Story. An Unpublished Novel, revised and completed by Lucas Malet (Mary St. Leger Harrison) (London: Smith, Elder, 1916; New York: Dodd, Mead, 1916);

Charles Kingsley's Only Short Story, edited by Eric Verner Sandin (Urbana, Ill., 1937);

Charles Kingsley's American Notes, edited by Robert Bernard Martin (Princeton, N.J.: Princeton University Press, 1958).

Collections: *The Works of Charles Kingsley*, 28 volumes (London & New York: Macmillan, 1880-1885);

Novels, Poems & Letters of Charles Kingsley, 14 volumes (New York: Co-operative Publication Society, 1898-1899);

Novels and Poems, 14 volumes (New York: Taylor, 1898-1900);

The Life and Works of Charles Kingsley, 10 volumes (New York: Macmillan, 1901-1903);

The Novels, Poems, and Memories of Charles Kingsley, 14 volumes (New York: Taylor, 1903).

OTHER: "Why Should We Fear Romish Priests?," *Fraser's Magazine*, 37 (1848): 467-474;

"On English Composition" and "On English Literature," in *Introductory Lectures, Delivered at Queen's College, London, 1849,* by Kingsley and Frederick Denison Maurice (London: Parker, 1849);

Franz Pfeiffer, ed., *Theologia Germanica*, preface by Kingsley (London: Longman, Brown, Green & Longman, 1854);

"The Country Parish: A Lecture," in *Lectures to Ladies on Practical Subjects* (Cambridge & London: Macmillan, 1855);

"In Memoriam, C. B. M.," in *Paraguay, Brazil, and the Plate: Letters Written in 1852-1853,* by Charles Blachford Mansfield (Cambridge: Macmillan, 1856), pp. xi-xvi;

Johann Tauler, *The History and Life of the Reverend Doctor John Tauler, with Twenty-Five of His Sermons,* preface by Kingsley (London: Smith, Elder, 1857);

Henry Brooke, *The Fool of Quality; or, The History of Henry, Earl of Moreland*, preface by Kingsley, 2 volumes (London: Smith, Elder, 1859);

John Bunyan, *The Pilgrim's Progress*, preface by Kingsley (London: Longman, 1860);

Rose Georgina Kingsley, *South by West; or, Winter in the Rocky Mountains and Spring in Mexico*, edited, with a preface, by Kingsley (London & Edinburgh: Isbister, 1874).

Like other eminent Victorians, Charles Kingsley wrote in various genres, and his influence—specifically in the reforms in the fields of theology, history, and literature as well as in the cultivation and regulation of an educated citizenry—was far-reaching. The bulk of his writing was published between the First and Second Reform Bills of 1832 and 1867 and thus coincided with efforts to extend the privileges of citizenship across class and gender lines and to justify such extension culturally and politically. He collaborated with scientific researchers and legislators to reveal that diseases such as cholera were not the will of God but the results of unsanitary conditions. In his "First Sermon on the Cholera" he exposed links between cholera epidemics caused by "undrained stifling hovels, unfit for hogs," and economic interests: "To confess their sins in a general way cost them [the English people] a few words; to

Eversley Church, where Kingsley was rector from 1844 until his death in 1875

confess and repent of the real particular sins in themselves, was a very different matter; to amend them would have touched vested interests, would have cost money, the Englishman's god." Science, he felt, should be accessible to all and should transform industrial production as well as social life. Kingsley was an important contributor to various local and national reforms, not all of which were readily compatible with each other, and he expended his efforts at personal cost, as is evident in many attacks on his credibility and propriety that he suffered and in his history of breakdown, exhaustion, and illness.

Kingsley was born into a middle-class home at Holne in Devonshire and attended Clifton School, Bristol (where he witnessed the Bristol riots); Helston Grammar School, Cornwall; King's College, London; and Magdalene College, Cambridge. The son of a clergyman also named Charles and his wife, Mary Lucas Kingsley, the young Kingsley was ordained, after some struggle and doubt, and became curate of Eversley, Hampshire, in 1842. This was the beginning of a long ecclesiastical career that ended with Kingsley as chaplain to Queen Victoria and canon of Westminster Abbey, 1873–1875. He married Frances Eliza "Fanny" Grenfell in 1844, the year he became rector of Eversley, but he preferred to date their marriage from their "eye-wedlock" on 6 July 1839. Their offspring–Rose Georgiana, Mary St. Leger, Maurice, and Grenville Arthur–inspired Kingsley's writings and maintained with him a relationship much closer than the one that he had enjoyed with his own father.

As professor of English literature at Queen's College, London, in 1848, Kingsley promoted women's education, including their education for medical vocations. He was concerned always, as he advised his successor, Alfred Strettell, in an 1849 letter, that women not be subjected to "Elegant Extracts" but be educated to "read for themselves." "We want to train–not cupboards full of 'information' (vile misnomer), but real informed women," he stated. In 1857 he helped found the National Association for the Promotion of Social Science, which provided a platform for Florence Nightingale and others. In 1875 he had a hand in another important initiative: the Women's Protective and Provident League, a significant stage in developing a women's trade-union movement. He also contributed to workers' education through teaching at colleges, lecturing at mechanics' institutes, promoting libraries and museums, writing to workers, and agitating for sanitary living conditions. As Regius Professor of Modern History at Cambridge University from 1860 to 1869, Kingsley was also tutor to the Prince of Wales before becoming canon of Chester, 1869-1873.

Through his activities with the working classes Kingsley demonstrated how a Christian gentleman could be an advocate for working people and the poor. "What is the use," he would say, "of talking to hungry paupers about heaven?" In his second "Letter to Chartists" (*Politics for the People*, May 1848) he reproached his fellow parsons for derelictions of pastoral duty: "We have used the Bible as if it was a mere special constable's handbook—an opium dose for keeping beasts of burden patient while they were being overloaded—a mere book to keep the poor in order." His was a controversial departure from established ways, and controversy followed him all his life. Indeed, he seemed actively to seek it during several times in his career, as when he publicly declared his commitment to Chartism at an 1849 Christian Socialist meeting by insisting, "I am a Church of England Parson—and a Chartist," and when he challenged the efficacy of the Charter in his contribution to the second issue of *Politics for the People*, the Christian Socialist journal in which he declared that "my only quarrel with the charter is, that it does not go far enough *in reform*."

In *The Saint's Tragedy; or, The True Story of Elizabeth of Hungary, Langravine of Thuringia, Saint of the Romish Calendar* (1848) Kingsley tried to accommodate religious and social interests in a blank-verse drama that was set in the thirteenth century and was intended to comment on the Victorian present. The focus is on Catholic monasticism and celibacy, the dreadful costs of fashioning a saint, and the threat of revolt against Malthusian and laissez-faire thinking. Begun in 1842 as a prose life of Saint Elizabeth and wedding present for Fanny, the drama was revised and published with a preface by Kingsley's mentor, Frederick Denison Maurice. Neither as successful nor as forceful as Kingsley's later novels and pamphlets, *The Saint's Tragedy* presents through its interpretation of the historical and legendary record Kingsley's messages of moderation and muscular Christianity, of the sanctity of marriage, and of the value of service to the poor. If Kingsley's frank defense of the marital relationship proved to be "a little too bold" for some readers, as Maurice suggested, then Kingsley's questioning of the authority, coercive asceticism, and archaic iconography of the Church was unsettling for others. In a letter accompanying a copy of the drama that Kingsley sent to the Chartist Thomas Cooper, Kingsley, fearing that the work might be misread, directed Cooper: "At first sight it may seem to hanker after feudalism and the middle ages; I trust to you to see a deeper and somewhat more democratic moral in it." His concern was that English Protestants reexamine the grounds of their most cherished beliefs and of their assertion, as he said in his introduction, of "the purity and dignity of the offices of husband, wife, and parent." In "Why Should We Fear the Romish Priests?" in *Fraser's Magazine* Kingsley recapitulates arguments from *The Saint's Tragedy*.

Debates on the repeal of the Corn Laws in 1846 and the Chartist agitations of the Hungry Forties as well as growing fears of the potential for revolution among members of a society severely divided underlie the Condition of England Question and the social-problem novels of the period. For Kingsley the challenge was to identify concerns and movements that would alleviate those concerns without incurring the charge of Jacobinism. His Christian Socialism, shared with Maurice, chemist Charles Mansfield, and friends and barristers John Ludlow and Thomas Hughes, was offered as a viable alternative after they witnessed the collapse of Chartism in London on 10 April 1848. Situated between secular and conservative extremes, the Christian Socialists in 1850 offered reassurance by so naming themselves in the series Tracts on Christian Socialism, which, as Maurice explained to Ludlow, was "the only title which will define our object, and will commit us at once to the conflict we must engage in sooner or later with the unsocial Christians and the unchristian Socialists." Their form of intervention aimed to accommodate God-fearing profiteer as much as working-class aspirant. But efforts at self-designation are subject to reworking by opponents, as became clear in the mockery that Kingsley and his ilk received as "muscular Christians."

Muscular Christianity is a characterization from which Kingsley always sought to distance himself, but the concept reveals much about the nature of reform and resistance to it. Critics of the Christian Socialists deemed muscularity to be incompatible with true spirituality and social decorum because, in a kind of corporeal evangelism, those who gave primacy to social action rather than to contemplation were seen to be at odds with the sedate ways of the Church of England. Kingsley admired Thomas Arnold for the educational reforms Arnold had introduced at Rugby—*mens sana, in corpore sano* (a healthy mind in a healthy body). But a sociopolitical position connecting physical with mental activity, political with religious issues, and the interests of the clergyman with those of the common countryman was ridiculed by urban sophisticates as embodying the rural heartiness of the country sportsman who hunts and shoots and fishes—all of which Kingsley did, and did well.

Kingsley in the garden at Eversley Rectory

The first of Kingsley's reformist fictions is *Yeast: A Problem* (1851), which he intended to serialize in *Politics for the People,* the penny weekly edited by Maurice and Ludlow and first published in May 1848. Kingsley's contributions to *Politics for the People* included both literary essays and others on political and religious issues as well as those on national institutions such as the British Museum ("a truly equalizing place"), and he published these pieces under the pseudonym of Parson Lot. According to its prospectus *Politics for the People* was designed "to consider the questions which are most occupying our countrymen.... [P]olitics have been separated from household ties and affections, from art, and science, and literature.... Politics have been separated from Christianity.... But politics for the people cannot be separated from religion." After the demise of this journal in July 1848, *Yeast* was published anonymously in serial form in *Fraser's Magazine,* the subscribers to which included the country gentry that Kingsley wished to persuade of their responsibilities to the agricultural poor.

Although some critics stress the chief interest of *Yeast* as that of the self-portrait it provides of the young Kingsley and Fanny in the characters of Lancelot Smith and Argemone Lavington, whom he courts in the novel, the narrative presents religious debate as well as rural poverty and the condition of the agricultural laborer in southern England in striking contrast to sanitized versions of pastoral myth. Instead of the "expected ... Arcadia," there is a

> sad reality! the cool breath of those glittering water-meadows too often floats laden with poisonous miasma. Those picturesque villages are generally the perennial hotbeds of fever and ague, of squalid penury, sottish profligacy, dull discontent too stale for words. There is luxury in the park, wealth in the huge farm-steadings, knowledge in the parsonage: but the poor? those by whose dull labour all that luxury and wealth, ay, even that knowledge, is made possible, what are they? We shall see, please God, ere the story's end.

Yeast was much admired by George Meredith, who wrote to Kingsley about "the positive 'Education'" he had received from reading it: "It was the very book I was in want of and likely to do me more good than any that I know."

In his preface to the first edition Kingsley identifies pressing issues that need to be addressed if all is not to founder under "the combined influence of new truths which are fancied to be incompatible with it ["the faith of our forefathers"], and new mistakes as to its real essence." Kingsley's preface to the fourth edition in 1859 acknowledges the improved conditions "in those southern counties of England" during the intervening years, when "self-help and independence" were nourished in the laboring poor under the new Poor Law and free trade. These years, Kingsley suggests, mark the success of liberal principles, the consequent demise of the Whigs, and the failure of Neo-Anglicanism (represented most pointedly in *Yeast* by the portrait of Luke, Lancelot's cousin). Kingsley hoped that charity would not displace a continued effort to improve living conditions and sanitary reform, all of which continued "at a fearfully slow rate" because of "the apathy of the educated classes." Who might better influence such classes, he felt, than "men who share somewhat in their prejudices and superstitions, and doled out to them in such measure as will not terrify or disgust them."

In its efforts to alleviate misunderstanding and reassure readers that "Esau has a birthright," *Yeast* focuses on the conversion of Lancelot Smith, the upper-class hero. From being at times insouciant and discontented he becomes a concerned character committed to concerted action through his relationships with Argemone and the example of her sister Honoria; Paul Tregarva, the gamekeeper; and Barnakill, the prophetic figure. The novel draws on Kingsley's personal experience as well as on Blue Book accounts to represent harsh conditions and the class consequences of the Game Laws. In the process *Yeast* offers an image of division as powerful as Benjamin Disraeli's better-known image of two nations in *Sybil* (1845) when Smith surveys the scene in which Tregarva overlooks Crawy, the poacher:

> Tregarva stood over him and looked down at him, like some huge stately bloodhound on a trembling mangy cur. "Good heavens!" thought Lancelot, as his eye wandered from the sad stedfast dignity of the one, to the dogged helpless misery of the other—"can those two be really fellow-citizens? fellow-Christians?—even animals of the same species?"

Critics have made much of the exigencies under which Kingsley published *Yeast*—his economic incentives and his haste in completing it because of complaints from *Fraser's Magazine* about a dwindling and hostile audience that found his preaching and politics to be as inappropriate as his indulgence toward Lancelot's early lifestyle. The moral and political strictures of critics were grounded in claims about aesthetic worth and character consistency, and *Yeast* was found sorely lacking in the moral and artistic restraint appropriate to Victorian realism. Kingsley's prefatory note to the first part in *Fraser's Magazine* challenged the reader to reform reading as much as social practice and to recognize a form and method that were resolutely unconventional: "This work is composed according to no rules of art whatsoever, except the cardinal one,—That the artist knowing best what he wants to say, is also likely to know best how to say it." Kingsley eschews an aesthetic without an activist outcome even as he resists Tractarianism for ignoring the clamorous needs of the time. His epilogue addressed concerns about "the very mythical and mysterious denouement of a story which began by things so gross and palpable as fieldsports and pauperism." That denouement, he claimed, was a material sign of the times just as "the fragmentary and unconnected form of the book" represented the subject and challenged the traditional "stereotyped systems" unable to contain or comprehend a flood of heterogeneous "facts and notions" that betokened "a very Yeasty state of mind altogether."

The strain of political activity, writing and publishing, and professorial and parish duties brought on one of Kingsley's recurrent collapses in 1848. His recuperation was followed quickly by his support of James Anthony Froude, who had resigned his Oxford fellowship and whose *The Nemesis of Faith* (1849), revealing his religious doubts, had been burned at an Oxford lecture. Embroiled in the Froude controversy and pondering his next novel, Kingsley also responded to the challenges of cholera and poverty in England by touring areas beset by cholera, hauling fresh water, urging political and legislative action, and helping to establish the Sanitary League. In light of Henry Mayhew's *Morning Chronicle* disclosures about working conditions, early in 1850 the Christian Socialists developed under the management of Walter Cooper the first Co-operative Association of Tailors, an association that inspired such publications as *Cheap Clothes and Nasty* (1850), republished in 1851 for the Tracts by Christian Socialists series, and fueled Kingsley's new novel, *Alton Locke, Tailor and Poet: An Autobiography* (1850). The Christian Socialists also established the influential Society for the Promotion of Working Men's Associations, concerned to help working men "release themselves . . . from the thraldom of individual labour under the competitive system," according to a statement accompanying the constitution of the Society. Kingsley sat as a member of its council.

Alton Locke proved to be a hard sell to the publishers. It was rejected by John Parker, Kingsley's regular publisher, and Macmillan's before Chap-

Self-caricatures by Kingsley in an 1856 letter to his daughter Mary and an 1858 letter to his son Maurice
(British Library)

man and Hall accepted it for publication after Thomas Carlyle recommended it as a "salvo of red-hot shot against the Devil's Dung-heap." Its readers proved to be more receptive than publishers or reviewers. An *Athenaeum* reviewer, for example, regretted the "vulgar" characters in a work "to be read aloud in the family circle while the members are pursuing some graceful or fanciful work after the severer duties and studies of the day are closed." In the *Edinburgh Review* W. R. Greg was loud in his charges against *Alton Locke:* for an author to write with a purpose was a mistake, as was his confusion of the fourteenth and nineteenth centuries and of feudal socialism and Chartism in this example of "the absurd or violent language of a benevolent man whose understanding has been driven desperate by the sight of suffering which he cannot relieve." The *Quarterly Review* was no easier on the book, which it identified with injustice and misrepresentation. Nevertheless, Kingsley earned £150 from *Alton Locke* as well as "a name and a standing with many a one who would never have heard of me otherwise" as this novel reached a wider audience through three editions to 1852 than anything Kingsley had published hitherto. He directed his prefaces to the editions of 1856 and 1862 to "the Working Men of Great Britain" and "the Undergraduates of Cambridge," respectively; he acknowledged progress but also scolded the workers for inattention to cooperative ideals while he praised the undergraduates for the "noble change" their class was adopting in attending to the interests of the poor.

The first of Kingsley's novels to appear in volume form, *Alton Locke* is an important example of fiction pressed into the service of decency and concern. It was time for the established Church to earn some of its customary privileges by enlisting its moral authority and the university educations of its leaders to secure a peaceful solution to undeniable and urgent social problems while preserving the institutions of Church and State. This last concern was explicit in Kingsley's response to charges that he had revolutionary intentions in the Evangelical *Record* on 7 November 1850. The novel is as interesting for its deficiencies as it is for its accomplishments and for the revisions that Kingsley made in it between the first and second editions. These revisions reveal how important it was that Chartism outlive its usefulness as a movement in a reformed Britain where the excesses of the "great King Laissez-faire" were exposed and effectively countered. The novel has a nineteenth-century setting but a considerable historical reach, and Kingsley's heavy investment in historical and theological interpretation entitles him to speak for the working class through his eponymous hero and to speak to the middle and upper classes about the need for change and the dangers of resisting a modest program of reform.

The novel shows literary as well as literal solidarity with the self- and class-authenticating works of Francis Place, Cooper, and Carlyle. Alton Locke, the sweatshop tailor and aspiring poet, is radicalized by Orator Crosshwaite, the Chartist, and by Sandy Mackaye, the Scottish bookseller who transforms Locke's Romantic impulses into the activist work of the "People's Poet." As in *Yeast* Kingsley uses poetry while respecting the all-too-familiar territory of the

Charles and Fanny Kingsley

Blue Book and its exposé of oppressive authority in urban and rural settings. Locke is torn between his conflicting interests: his new political commitment; his love for Lillian Winnstay, the daughter of an upper-class clergyman; and his desire for literary and social respectability. As a result of his political actions Locke is imprisoned and abandoned by Lillian before he is nursed and converted by Eleanor, Lillian's cousin, to Christian Socialism.

Through 1850 and 1851 Kingsley contributed regularly to the weekly *Christian Socialist,* edited by Ludlow, and the *Journal of Association,* edited by Hughes. In 1852 the first of these two periodicals ceased publication, and Kingsley's active part in the Christian Socialist movement ended. Until then, however, in these publications and in the Bible Politics series (*Christian Socialist,* November 1850–April 1851) he continued to combine religion and politics and to engage in controversy, with the result that his rector publicly chastised him for propagating dangerous messages in "The Message of the Church to Labouring Men" before a huge congregation of workingmen at the Church of St. John the Evangelist in London on 22 June 1851. For Kingsley the business of the priest was "to preach and practise liberty, equality, and brotherhood, in the fullest, deepest, widest, simplest meaning of these three great words." As a result of his pursuit of this end the *Daily News* called for an investigation into his activities. He was widely denounced as the "Apostle of

Socialism," and his bishop barred him from preaching in London, although the bishop reversed this decision after reading Kingsley's published sermon. Kingsley practiced what he preached as he helped Maurice establish the Working Men's College and gave some lectures at this institution committed to liberal education and better relations between classes. Such activities were part of his "battle . . . against the shopkeepers and the Manchester school," as he wrote to Hughes in 1852.

In 1851 Kingsley began work on his next novel, *Hypatia; or, New Foes with an Old Face* (1853), in which he appropriated Roman and church history in order to unleash anti-Catholic comment on John Henry Newman's conversion to Rome in 1845 and on a restored Catholic hierarchy in England in 1850. The novel presents a typical muscular-Christian approach to the problem of celibacy and to what Kingsley termed Manichaeism in the figure of Philammon, the feisty monk who abandons Christianity when he is seduced by the Neoplatonism of Hypatia, a fifth-century Greek philosopher. After Hypatia is brutally murdered by a Christian mob, Philammon returns to his original community and becomes an abbot who remains faithful to his vows of celibacy even as he recognizes their limits. *Hypatia* prompted Cardinal Nicholas Wiseman to respond with a new series of works, the Catholic Popular Library, which he began with his own *Fabiola; or, The Church of the Catacombs* (1855), a work that presents an even more violent version of the past than Kingsley's. Newman responded with *Callista: A Sketch of the Third Century* (1856).

Attacks on *Hypatia* for its lurid depictions of sensuality and of Hypatia's dismemberment distressed Kingsley. Anxieties about Fanny's health after a miscarriage added to his cares, and she retreated to Torquay, Devon, for some months after autumn 1853. During this period Kingsley was able to indulge his enthusiasm for natural history, which is expressed in works such as *Glaucus; or, The Wonders of the Shore* (1855), a much revised and expanded version of "The Wonders of the Shore," an essay published in the *North British Review* in November 1854, and in *The Water-Babies: A Fairy-Tale for a Land-Baby* (1863). Kingsley had the respect of scientists such as Charles Darwin, Thomas Henry Huxley, Sir Charles Lyell, and Philip Henry Gosse; this scientific expertise qualified Kingsley to diversify his reviewing; and after he joined his wife in Torquay, his time there also brought him close to the heroic past of the Elizabethans.

In *Westward Ho! or, The Voyages and Adventures of Sir Amyas Leigh, Knight, of Burrough, in the County of Devon, in the Reign of Her Most Glorious Majesty, Queen Elizabeth* (1855), both Kingsley's hero and his antagonist, Amyas Leigh and Don Guzman, respectively, were designed, as he wrote in a letter of 22 July 1854, "to make others fight." The British needed support in this war, and the novel was distributed to English troops in the Crimea with the aim of encouraging them to keep up the good fight. Macmillan, as publisher, needed reassurances that this novel, securely located in Elizabethan times, was apolitical before it would accept this work for publication.

Once committed, Macmillan enthusiastically promoted *Westward Ho!* as a necessary spur to national pride, an appeal that ensured for it the greatest popularity Kingsley's work had enjoyed. Indeed, it proved to be one of the best-sellers of the century, going through five editions and being reprinted twenty-seven times before five hundred thousand copies of the cheap editions published after 1889 were sold. Kingsley proved to be open to input from his publisher as in a letter of 22 July 1854 he claimed to be "willing to alter or expunge wherever aught is likely to hurt the *sale* of the book." The entire book was produced in seven months, and again its presentation of violence–especially that of the Spanish colonizers–proved to be repellent to some readers; George Eliot in the *Westminster Review* regretted its "ferocious barbarism."

Kingsley's promotion of sanitary reform took fictional form in his narrative of the struggles of Tom Thurnall, the medical man and protagonist in *Two Years Ago* (1857). Set in 1854, this work is a strong expression of Christian Socialism under conditions of the Crimean War as that event precipitates both Thurnall's spiritual crisis and his union with Grace Harvey, the Nonconformist schoolmistress. Kingsley saw his concern with public-health issues as an important part of his life's work, for, as he explained in a letter to John Bullard on 26 November 1857, "Nature must be counteracted, lest she prove a curse and a destroyer, not a blessing and a mother." He had agitated for government control of water in London while preparing *Alton Locke,* had submitted evidence to Lord Palmerston, and was by 1857 a close collaborator of Edwin Chadwick, whose work at the Board of Health had done much to contain the cholera epidemic of 1848–1849. Thurnall's manly activism in the face of the cholera threat to his Cornish village contrasts sharply with the ineffectuality of Elsley Vavasour, the feminized, sentimental poet. Arguably more opportunistic than his earlier fictions, *Two Years Ago* proved to be another success; a review of it by T. C. Sandars in the *Saturday Review* is credited with coining the expression "muscular Christianity" that was popularly used to characterize Kingsley's work.

By 1860 Kingsley was being recognized not only by the reading public but also by royalty. Already chaplain to Queen Victoria, he became professor of modern history at Cambridge University and a favorite among students, if not among fellow historians. One student testified that for Kingsley's lectures, "We crowded him out of room after room till he had to have the largest of all the schools, and we crowded that—crammed it." The Prince of Wales was sent to Cambridge to have Kingsley as his tutor in history, and after the death of Albert, the Prince Consort, the Prince of Wales withdrew from Cambridge but maintained his relationship with Kingsley, whom he named as his chaplain.

The Water-Babies, first serialized in *Macmillan's Magazine* in 1862, is a fantasy that effectively brings together Kingsley's interests in natural history, politics, and religion while connecting physical evolution and sanitation to spiritual growth. Even as he satirizes features of contemporary society, he contributes to debates about science and religion and examines epistemological implications and the mystery of physical nature in this book. In the wake of the information presented before the Second Royal Commission on the Employment of Children (1862) Kingsley highlights the plight of climbing boys such as little Tom. Deprivation and abuse are so familiar that they seem to be "the way of the world," an apparently natural state of affairs rather than one maintained by social disciplinary mechanisms such as the law and education. In the wake of Robert Lowe's Revised Code of 1862 and open, competitive examinations for junior civil service appointments after 1860, Kingsley attacks the evils of the education and examination systems.

When Tom has become lost in one of the chimneys in which he is set to work and unwittingly emerges on the hearth of little Ellie's immaculately white bedroom, his escape from the consequences of his innocent actions in this upper-class home leads him to the river, to the Rabelaisian world of the water-baby—to the different social relations enforced by Mrs. Doasyouwouldbedoneby and Mrs. Bedonebyasyoudid. Thus, *The Water-Babies* presents a range of subject matter close to the "thirty-seven or thirty-nine" edifying elements Kingsley claims in the final chapter of his version of useful and entertaining knowledge. The book was so popular that the first edition was sold out within a year, and it has remained in print ever since. Following the report of the 1861 Children's Employment Commission, Parliament passed the Chimney Sweepers'

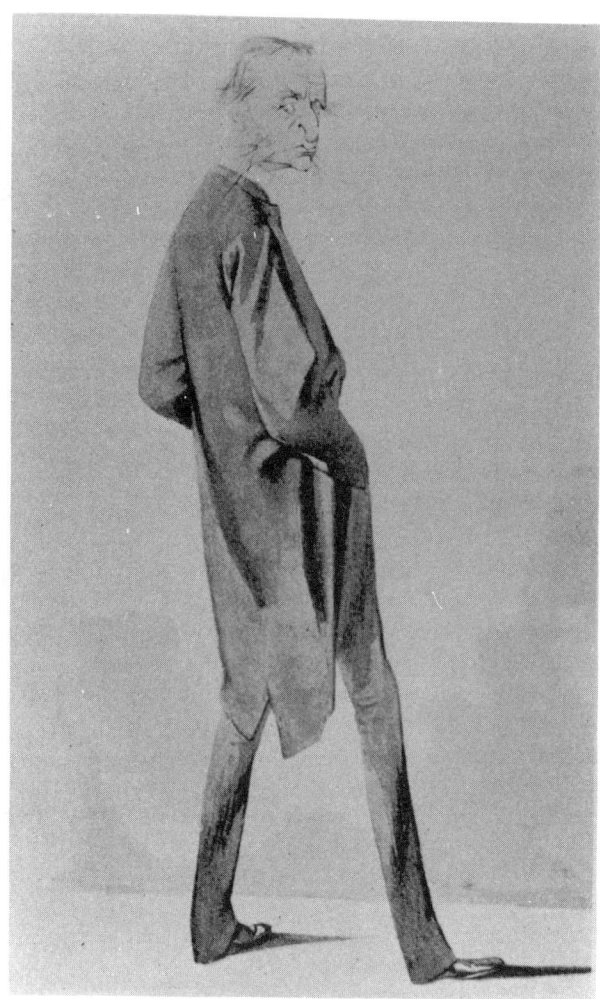

"Rev. Canon Kingsley, 'The Apostle of the Flesh,'" caricature by T. Gibson Bowles (Jehu Junior) for Vanity Fair (30 March 1872)

Regulation Act less than a year after the book was published.

Despite Kingsley's success and royal favor, controversy was never far away. In 1863 Edward Pusey, the well-known Tractarian who had long been one of Kingsley's opponents in clerical matters, remained so hostile toward Kingsley that he actively opposed a proposal that Kingsley be granted an Oxford honorary degree as doctor of civil laws. In the same year Kingsley became a fellow of the Royal Geological Society and also became embroiled in the dispute with Cardinal Newman, who embodied for Kingsley the iniquities of Roman Catholicism and who defended himself publicly in *Apologia pro Sua Vita* (1864).

When Kingsley published his history lectures as *The Roman and the Teuton* (1864), his views on the abolition of slavery had changed. In the continuing Civil War in the United States he had come to sup-

Kingsley's notes on the crossing from Liverpool to New York for his 1874 lecture tour in the United States (British Library) port the South as the best hope for the government of blacks, especially because he believed that a free South would be more likely to respond to English influence. His racial prejudice was also revealed in 1866 during the Eyre inquiry conducted after Gov. Edward John Eyre had responded to a Jamaican rebellion with unusual savagery. In defending Eyre, Kingsley found himself opposing old allies such as Ludlow and Hughes.

In 1865 Kingsley published serially in *Good Words* what was to be his last novel, "Hereward, the Last of the English," a retelling of a crucial stage in English history as England emerged from the Norman Conquest. Published in volume form in 1866 as *Hereward the Wake, "Last of the English,"* the novel strikes at Catholic and French forms of perfidy while bolstering English national identity and opposing threats to its core values of discipline and duty. Hereward is the outlaw figure whose valiant efforts keep the Normans at bay. The violent murder of Hereward, redeemed by the Darwinian fitness of Hereward's survival strategies but betrayed by a woman and monks, is a clear warning to Kingsley's contemporaries.

Feeling the pressure of continued attacks on his Cambridge professorship, Kingsley resigned in 1869, four months before his appointment as canon of Chester. In Chester he helped establish the Chester Natural History Society in 1870, and in 1872 he was named president of the Midland Institute in Birmingham. One of his lectures as president prompted a Birmingham manufacturer to provide a subvention of £2,500 for classes in physiology and hygiene. He resigned his post as canon at Chester in order to become canon at Westminster Abbey in 1873. Suffering from ill health early in 1874, he took his final trip overseas with his daughter Rose; however, what should have been a rest cure proved to be a taxing lecture tour that did little to improve his health.

Only months after his return Fanny became ill, and Kingsley cared for her at Eversley until he fell victim to pneumonia. He died on 23 January 1875, a year in which the Public Health Act was passed and many of his reforming endeavors reached fruition. His funeral service was attended by professors, publishers, parsons, scientists, socialists, laborers, legislators, gypsies, and regal representatives.

The personal success that Charles Kingsley enjoyed within the Church and other established social institutions throughout his life did not prevent him from making important contributions to the cause of reform in England. Although he has been often dismissed as a mere popularizer of the think-

Grave of Charles and Fanny Kingsley at Eversley

ing of others, especially of Maurice, Kingsley achieved much through his parochial duties and his activities involving political organization, print culture, and education. If he did not resolve contradictions at the heart of reform or reconstruct hierarchic notions of the healthy and unified social body, the power and particularity of his writing and public oratory nevertheless generated significant social change.

Letters:

Charles Kingsley: His Letters and Memories of His Life, edited by Frances Kingsley (2 volumes, London: King, 1877; abridged edition, New York: Scribner, Armstrong, 1877; London: Kegan Paul, 1879);

Charles Kingsley's American Notes: Letters from a Lecture Tour, 1874, edited by Robert Bernard Martin (Princeton: Princeton University Library, 1958).

Bibliographies:

Margaret Farrand Thorp, "Bibliography of Charles Kingsley's Works," in her *Charles Kingsley*

1819-1875 (Princeton: Princeton University Press, 1937; London: Oxford University Press, 1937), pp. 191-204;

James D. Barry, "Elizabeth Cleghorn Gaskell, Charles Kingsley," in *Victorian Fiction: A Guide to Research,* edited by Lionel Stevenson (Cambridge, Mass.: Harvard University Press, 1964), pp. 245-276;

Robert A. Campbell, "Charles Kingsley: A Bibliography of Secondary Studies," *Bulletin of Bibliography,* 33 (1976): 78-91, 104, 127-130;

Barry, "Charles Kingsley," in *Victorian Fiction: A Second Guide to Research,* edited by George H. Ford (New York: Modern Language Association, 1978), pp. 219-222;

Styron Harris, *Charles Kingsley: A Reference Guide* (Boston: G. K. Hall, 1981).

Biographies:

Stanley E. Baldwin, *Charles Kingsley* (Ithaca, N.Y.: Cornell University Press, 1934; London: Oxford University Press, 1934);

Margaret Farrand Thorp, *Charles Kingsley 1819-1875* (Princeton: Princeton University Press, 1937; London: Oxford University Press, 1937);

Una Pope-Hennessy, *Canon Charles Kingsley: A Biography* (London: Chatto & Windus, 1948; New York, Macmillan, 1949);

Robert B. Martin, *The Dust of Combat: A Life of Charles Kingsley* (London: Faber & Faber, 1959; New York: Norton, 1960);

Susan Chitty, *The Beast and the Monk: A Life of Charles Kingsley* (London: Hodder & Stoughton, 1974; New York: Mason, Charter, 1975);

Brenda Colloms, *Charles Kingsley: The Lion of Eversley* (London: Constable, 1975; New York: Barnes & Noble, 1975).

References:

Gillian Beer, "Charles Kingsley and the Literary Image of the Countryside," *Victorian Studies,* 8 (1965): 243-254;

Patrick Brantlinger, *The Spirit of Reform: British Literature and Politics, 1832-1867* (Cambridge, Mass.: Harvard University Press, 1977);

W. Henry Brown, *Charles Kingsley: The Work and Influence of Parson Lot* (London: Unwin, 1924);

Louis Cazamian, *The Social Novel in England 1830-1850,* translated by Martin Fido (London: Routledge & Kegan Paul, 1973);

Owen Chadwick, "Charles Kingsley at Cambridge," *Historical Journal,* 18 (1975): 303-324;

Valentine Cunningham, "Soiled Fairy: *The Water-Babies* in its Time," *Essays in Criticism,* 35 (1985): 121-148;

David Anthony Downes, *The Temper of Victorian Belief: Studies in the Religious Novels of Pater, Kingsley, and Newman* (New York: Twayne, 1972), pp. 48-81, 125-144;

G. R. Dunstan, ed., *Theology,* Charles Kingsley Centenary Number, 78 (1975);

George Eliot, "Westward Ho!," *Westminster Review,* 64 (1855): 288-294;

Catherine Gallagher, *The Industrial Reformation of English Fiction: Social Discourse and Narrative Form 1832-1867* (Chicago & London: University of Chicago Press, 1985);

W. R. Greg, "English Socialism, and Communist Associations," review of *Alton Locke, Edinburgh Review,* 93 (1851): 1-33;

Bruce A. Haley, *The Healthy Body and Victorian Culture* (Cambridge, Mass.: Harvard University Press, 1978), pp. 107-119, 180-188;

Donald E. Hall, ed., *Muscular Christianity: Embodying the Victorian Age* (Cambridge: Cambridge University Press, 1994);

Henry R. Harrington, "Charles Kingsley's Fallen Athlete," *Victorian Studies,* 21 (1977): 73-86;

Allan J. Hartley, *The Novels of Charles Kingsley: A Christian Social Interpretation* (Folkestone, U.K.: Hour-Glass, 1977);

Walter E. Houghton, "The Issue between Kingsley and Newman," *Theology Today,* 4 (1947): 80-101;

[Geraldine Jewsbury], "*Alton Locke,*" *Athenaeum* (7 September 1850): 944-946;

Arthur Johnston, "*The Water Babies:* Kingsley's Debt to Darwin," *English,* 12 (1959): 215-219;

Peter J. Keating, *The Working Classes in Victorian Fiction* (London: Routledge & Kegan Paul, 1971);

Guy Kendall, *Charles Kingsley and His Ideas* (London & New York: Hutchinson, 1947);

Arnold Kettle, "The Early Victorian Social-Problem Novel," in *From Dickens to Hardy,* edited by Boris Ford (Harmondsworth: Penguin, 1958), pp. 169-187;

Q. D. Leavis, "The Water-Babies," *Children's Literature in Education,* 23 (1976): 155-163;

Stephen Prickett, *Victorian Fantasy* (Hassocks, Sussex: Harvester Press, 1979; Bloomington: Indiana University Press, 1979), pp. 150-173;

Charles E. Raven, *Christian Socialism 1848-1854* (London: Macmillan, 1920);

Mark Reboul, *Charles Kingsley, La Formation d'une personnalité et son affirmation littéraire (1819-1850)* (Paris: Presses Universitaires de France, 1973);

Sheila M. Smith, "Blue Books and Victorian Novelists," *Review of English Studies,* new series 21 (1970): 23–40;

Smith, *The Other Nation: The Poor in English Novels of the 1840s and 1850s* (Oxford: Clarendon Press, 1980);

Charles William Stubbs, *Charles Kingsley and the Christian Social Movement* (New York: Stone, 1899);

John A. Sutherland, *Victorian Novelists and Their Publishers* (London: Athlone, 1976; Chicago: University of Chicago Press, 1976), pp. 117–132;

Larry K. Uffelman, *Charles Kingsley* (Boston: Twayne, 1979);

Uffelman and Patrick G. Scott, "Kingsley's Serial Novels: 'Yeast,'" *Victorian Periodicals Newsletter,* 9 (1976): 111–119;

Norman Vance, *The Sinews of the Spirit: The Ideal of Christian Manliness in Victorian Literature and Religious Thought* (Cambridge: Cambridge University Press, 1985);

Colwyn E. Vulliamy, *Charles Kingsley and Christian Socialism* (London: Fabian Society, 1914);

John O. Waller, "Charles Kingsley and the American Civil War," *Studies in Philology,* 60 (1963): 554–568;

Raymond Williams, *Culture and Society, 1780–1950* (London: Chatto & Windus, 1958; New York: Columbia University Press, 1958);

Stanley Williams, "*Yeast:* A Victorian Heresy," *North American Review,* 212 (1920): 697–704;

Robert Lee Wolff, *Gains and Losses: Novels of Faith and Doubt in Victorian England* (New York: Garland, 1977).

Papers:

Kingsley's papers can be found in the Kingsley, Gladstone, and Macmillan archives at the British Library; among the Ludlow papers at the Cambridge University Library; among the Thomas H. Huxley papers at the Imperial College, London; at the Tennyson Research Centre, Lincoln; at Dormy House, Pine Valley, N.J.; at the Henry E. Huntington Library, San Marino, Cal.; at the J. Pierpont Morgan Library, New York; among the Stapleton and Parrish collections at the Princeton University Library; and at the University of Illinois, Champaign-Urbana.

Samuel Lover
(24 February 1797 - 6 July 1868)

Paul G. Ashdown
University of Tennessee, Knoxville

See also the Lover entry in *DLB 159: British Short-Fiction Writers, 1800-1880.*

BOOKS: *Legends and Stories of Ireland* (Dublin: Wakeman, 1831; London: Baldwin & Cradock, 1834; 2 volumes, Philadelphia: Carey & Hart, 1835);

Rory O'More: A National Romance (3 volumes, London: Bentley, 1837; 2 volumes, Philadelphia: Carey, Blanchard & Lea, 1837; revised and corrected edition, 1 volume, London: Bentley, 1839);

Rory O'More (London: Dicks' Standard Plays, 1837; Philadelphia: Turner & Fisher, 1838);

The White Horse of the Peppers: A Comic Drama in Two Acts (London: Acting National Drama, 1838; New York: Berford, 1847);

The Happy Man: An Extravaganza in One Act (London: Chapman & Hall, 1839; Boston: Spencer, 1856?);

Songs and Ballads (London: Chapman & Hall, 1839; enlarged, 1844; Philadelphia: Lea & Blanchard, 1847; enlarged and corrected edition, New York: Wiley & Putnam, 1847);

The Hall Porter: A Comic Drama in Two Acts (London: Chapman & Hall, 1839?);

The Greek Boy: A Musical Drama in Two Acts (London: Sherwood, Gilbert & Piper, 1840?);

Il Paddy Whack in Italia: An Operetta in One Act (London: Duncombe, 1841);

Handy Andy: A Tale of Irish Life (London: F. Lover, 1842; Philadelphia: Coates, 1842);

Barny O'Reirdon, the Navigator, and Other Tales of Ireland (Philadelphia: Carey & Hart, 1844);

Mr. Lover's Irish Evenings: The Irish Brigade (London: Johnson, 1844);

Treasure Trove: The First of a Series of Accounts of Irish Heirs, Being a Romantic Irish Tale of the Last Century (London: F. Lover, 1844; New York & Philadelphia: Appleton, 1844); republished as *He Would Be a Gentleman; or, Treasure Trove* (London: Chapman & Hall, 1856; New York:

Samuel Lover

Sadlier, 1872); also published as *Irish Heirs* (New York: Dick & Fitzgerald, 1862);

Characteristic Sketches of Ireland and the Irish, by Lover, William Carleton, and Mrs. S. C. Hall (Dublin: Hardy, 1845);

Tom Crosbie and His Friends (Buffalo, N.Y.: Burke, 1855);

Metrical Tales and Other Poems (London: Houlston & Wright, 1860);

MacCarthy More; or, Possession Nine Points of the Law: A Comic Drama in Two Acts (London: Lacy, 1861);

Original Songs for the Rifle Volunteers, by Lover, Charles Mackay, and Thomas Miller (London: Clarke, 1861);

Barney the Baron: A Farce in One Act (London: Dicks' Standard Plays, 1883);

Further Stories of Ireland, edited by D. J. O'Donoghue (Westminster: Constable, 1899);

Miscellaneous Stories, Sketches, Etc., Now Chiefly Collected for the First Time, edited by O'Donoghue (Westminster: Constable, 1899).

Collections: *The Poetical Works of Samuel Lover* (London: Routledge, 1868; New York: Sadlier, 1869);

The Novels and Tales of Samuel Lover, 4 volumes (New York: Sadlier, 1880-1884);

Works, edited by D. J. O'Donoghue, 6 volumes (New York: Brentano's, 1900);

Works, 6 volumes (New York: Athenaeum Society, 1901);

Collected Writings, Treasure Trove Edition, 10 volumes, edited by James Jeffrey Roche (Boston: Little, Brown, 1901-1903).

PLAY PRODUCTIONS: *The Happy Man,* London, Theatre Royal, 20 May 1839;

The Hall Porter, London, Theatre Royal, 25 July 1839;

The Greek Boy, London, Covent Garden, 26 September 1840;

Il Paddy Whack in Italia, London, Theatre Royal, April 1841;

MacCarthy More; or, Possession Nine Points of the Law, London, Royal Lyceum Theatre, 1 April 1861.

OTHER: *The Parson's Horn-Book,* illustrated by Lover (Dublin: Comet Club, 1831);

Popular Tales and Legends of the Irish Peasantry, edited and illustrated by Lover (Dublin: Wakeman, 1834);

English Bijou Almanack for 1840, edited by Lover (London: Schloss, 1840);

Ireland Illustrated, Containing the Topographical History of the Principal Cities, Towns, Castles, Churches, and Monasteries in the Kingdom: Biographical Sketches, Tales and Legends, includes contributions by Lover (Dublin: Coldwell, 1844);

The Lyrics of Ireland, edited and annotated by Lover (London: Houlston & Wright, 1858); republished as *The Songs of Ireland* (New York: Dick & Fitzgerald, 1860?); republished as *Poems of Ireland* (London, New York & Perth: Ward, Lock, 1884);

Rival Rhymes, in Honour of Burns, with Curious Illustrative Matter, edited by Lover as Ben Trovato (London: Routledge, 1859);

Book of Irish Songs, compiled by Lover and others (Philadelphia: Winch, 1860).

As one of the first writers in Ireland to use folk stories and legends in satirical fiction, Samuel Lover helped change British and American attitudes toward the Irish peasantry during a period of political turmoil. His success and influence was considerable, not only in literary circles but also in music, painting, and the theater. Lover's best-known novel, *Handy Andy: A Tale of Irish Life* (1842), originated in 1837 as a series of sketches drawn from folktales published in *The Bentley Miscellany* under the editorship of Charles Dickens. Although the Irish Literary Revival that began in the 1880s and extended into the 1920s dismissed Lover as a mere entertainer who misrepresents Irish peasantry and perpetuates the stage Irishman, Maureen Waters finds Lover's characters "drawn with deft, comic strokes" in a manner reminiscent of Dickens and praises *Handy Andy* for unmasking political and social attitudes. Lover's grandson, the Irish American composer Victor Herbert, embellished Lover's reputation by enlisting his memory in the cause of Irish independence.

Born in Dublin, Lover was the eldest son of middle-class Protestant parents. His paternal family was probably of English origin. His father was a stockbroker who tried unsuccessfully to direct Lover into a career in commerce and to discourage the interest in art and music that the boy shared with his mother. As a child Lover was aware of the severity of British rule in Ireland following the rebellions of 1798 and 1803. After witnessing a British soldier force his way into the family home, insult his mother, and fight with his father, Lover said that every word he heard of "English oppression and Irish wrong I eagerly caught at and well remembered."

Sent to the Wicklow countryside for his health, he developed a sentimental attachment to nature and to Irish peasant life. He returned to Dublin in 1810, shortly after the death of his mother, to continue his schooling. Lover boasted that by the age of sixteen he "had become as staunch an assertor of national rights as ever trod my native soil." He left home in 1814 to prepare for a career in art, and by 1818 he had a reputation as a marine and miniature painter and as a writer of songs and ballads. In 1826 he became a member of the Royal Hibernian Academy. His portrait of Italian violinist Niccolò Paganini was exhibited in London, and it established his reputation in England. This attention earned Lover commissions from Arthur Wellesley, first Duke of Wellington, and his brother Richard, Marquess of Wellesley, and a suggestion from the duchess of Kent that Lover paint the portrait of Princess Victoria. His income and influence grew as he captured the countenances of the nobility.

Described as "a small man, with an intensely humorous and pleasant face, sparkling black eyes, and a delicious Dublin accent," Lover was celebrated as a raconteur, a charming and amusing guest at social gatherings. His work provided him with a widening circle of influential persons, and in 1827 he married Lucy Berrel, a Catholic and the daughter of a Dublin architect. The couple had two daughters.

His success did not make him forget the injustices he had witnessed as a child. In 1829 Lover joined the Comet Club, an association opposing a tithe that was levied on the tillage of Irish peasants for the support of the Protestant and Anglican Church of Ireland. The law required the peasants to pay the tithe before their crop was removed, but they were often too poor to use the crop for anything other than feeding their families. This requirement pitted the clergy against the peasants in the valuation of the crop, and Lover illustrated *The Parson's Horn-Book* (1831), a satirical attack against the system, published by the Comet Club. The book was said to have had a circulation greater than that of any book previously published in Ireland. Two of the leaders of the Comet Club were prosecuted and convicted following the publication of this book and others by the organization. Lover's identity as illustrator of the book was not generally known until later, and meanwhile he began collecting and writing stories about Irish peasants for the *Dublin National Magazine*. He published these pieces with his own illustrations as *Legends and Stories of Ireland* in 1831.

He also contributed stories and etchings to the *Dublin University Magazine,* the first two issues of which published Lover's "Barny O'Reirdon the Navigator." The title character, a blustering village hero, sets sail in his small hooker from Kinsale to fulfill a boast that he can find his way to Fingal. Although he doesn't know where Fingal is, he contrives to follow a British ship that he thinks is going there, and only when he is well out at sea does he learn that the ship is headed to India. The British captain offers to take Barny with him, and when Barny insists on trying to make his way home, the captain sets him on the proper course. Barny finally gets back to Ireland by bluffing the captain of an American ship into thinking that he is a harbor pilot. Lover adds praise for the buoyant spirits of the Irish: "How kindly have they been fortified by Nature against the assaults of adversity; and if they blindly rush into dangers, they cannot be denied the possession of gallant hearts to fight their way out of them."

Wayne Hall interprets "Barny O'Reirdon the Navigator" in terms of the precarious position of the magazine in which it was published. The Trinity College Tories who founded the *Dublin University Magazine* were firmly allied to the Protestant ascendancy but recognized that their cause was "simultaneously dependent upon and alienated from England, isolated within Ireland at the same time that it deeply loves and identifies with this country that no longer feels quite like home."

In 1837 Lover moved to London and published *Rory O'More,* a romance whose title character Lover had created in a popular ballad and whom Tyrone Power much later played in a drama at the Adelphi Theater, where it had a long engagement. The novel, which concerns the rebellion of 1798, was so popular that some of Lover's friends warned that he was too flattering toward the Irish. Lover's biographer Bayle Bernard describes Rory O'More as "the true ideal of the Irish peasant—the humble hero who embodies so much of the best of the national character, and almost lifts simple emotion to the same height as ripened mind. Lover has written nothing that affirms more worthily either his sympathies or talent."

Sally E. Foster, while noting Lover's sensitivity to the severe repression of the Irish and his desire to persuade British readers of the honorable intentions of at least a portion of the Irish people, argues that *Rory O'More* is nonetheless mired in stereotypical prejudices. She views the novel as a romantic apology for the feudal system, and she sees Lover's removal to London reflected in the novel through the unwillingness of O'More, the honorable peasant, and of De Lacy, the honorable aristocrat, to risk staying in Ireland to try to change anything.

D. J. O'Donoghue claims that by the time Lover's brother, Frederick, published *Handy Andy* in book form in 1842, following its serial publication in *The Bentley Miscellany,* Lover had joined Dickens "in the front rank of comic writers." Lover seems to have been uneasy about the popular appeal and the consequent "captiousness of overfastidious criticism" of *Handy Andy* because he says that it "was never meant to be a work of high pretension—only one of those easy trifles which afford a laugh."

Foster contends that, like *Rory O'More, Handy Andy* reveals Lover's prejudices and attempts "to prove to his audience that he has not biased his fiction in favor of Ireland." Foster writes that Lover reveals himself in the novel in the character of Edward O'Connor, an idealized Protestant gentleman-poet who regards himself as a patriot filled with noblesse oblige. In this view Lover portrays Irish peasants as childlike and unworthy of democracy; his stock characters "can only be found in an idealized, feudal society based on the notion that the good Protestant gentry enjoys a symbiotic relationship with what is called the stage-Irishman."

Foster faults Lover for literary pretentiousness and self-professed patriotism, and she sees in his work a pseudoscientific aura that masks the fatuity and inaccuracy of his portrayals of Irish life. She acknowledges that Lover may have modified the image of the Irishman as a violent savage, but she views the changeling he offers instead as something that justifies only a benign repression. In her view the social and economic system is never questioned, and the governmental system that oversees it is never unjust, merely misused: "One could conclude, from Lover, that the Irish need better caretakers, but certainly not independence."

Maureen Waters, in contrast, while agreeing that *Handy Andy* has some role in perpetuating the stage Irishman, praises the novel for accurately portraying social prejudices, richly using folklore, and demonstrating a comic vitality as well as Lover's excellent ear for dialogue. Waters believes Lover succeeds in both "exploiting the conventions of Irish character and background and at the same time challenging English and Anglo-Irish assumptions about the peasant." She links Andy to the folk tradition of the Fool, "who was considered lucky, who drew the blows of Fortune that might otherwise have landed on more normal heads." In Waters's view Lover draws from the *shanachie,* or bard tradition of Gaelic storytelling, and not only understands the Irish people but also offers a view of the emerging middle class. She explains that modern readers have difficulty understanding the buffooneries of Andy Rooney and other Irish peasants because Lover was trapped by his need to depict their humanity while catering to the ethnocentric prejudices of English readers. Those readers feared the growing resistance of the Irish peasantry and found Andy to be a welcome source of comic relief and security.

Waters suspects that Andy's moral progress in the novel reflects Lover's "ambivalence as an Anglo-Irishman, as well as his natural sympathies." Andy "begins to question the endless blows and the injustices that have been his lot, stating

Illustration by Lover in Legends and Stories of Ireland *(1831)*

what are obviously the author's long-standing sentiments as well. Hardship finally makes him witty and bolder. He observes that much of the behavior for which he is punished would be excused if he were a gentleman." Andy is redeemed by the literary device of the disclosed identity. Learning that he is the long-lost son of an aristocrat, Andy is taken to England to be groomed for a proper introduction to society. At the end of the novel he breaks bread with Edward O'Connor, whom Foster reads as Lover's ostensible alter ego, in a scene symbolizing the peaceful union of Catholic and Protestant.

Waters's reading of the novel seems truer to the purpose of the novel than does Foster's. Bernard insists that Lover was revolted by the received impression of the Irish peasantry and, especially in his songs, sought to "awaken in English circles a kindlier feeling towards a class which they had so little understood, and so imperfectly been pleased with." He writes that Lover could show the peasant only "as he felt and liked him, and as he believed others would like him also, if they could only grow familiar with his gayer and better nature."

Lover published one more novel: *Treasure Trove: The First of a Series of Accounts of Irish Heirs, Being a Romantic Irish Tale of the Last Century* (1844), an historically flawed account of the Irish Brigade in France. This novel was Lover's least successful work. Because of his failing eyesight, he gave up writing longer works of fiction and making etchings and turned to presenting evening recitals of his songs and stories. He gave the first of these "Irish Evenings" in London in March 1844 and followed its success with a British tour and performances in Dublin.

In 1846 Lover lost a large sum of money when a loan he had guaranteed for a friend was not repaid. Because his works were well known in North America, Lover took his act on a tour across the Atlantic Ocean for more than two years to restore his finances; he first appeared in New York at the Stuyvesant Institute on 28 September 1846. A newspaper account calls Lover's performance "a flow of polished witticisms, puns, songs, jokes and recitations, combined with touches of deep pathos." He rendered his recitation of a poem about the 1798 rebellion "in a vein of true, hearty, genuine Irish feeling, that proves the author to be a whole-souled Irishman," and his performance drew several minutes of applause. Lover had found a winning formula.

His success in the United States had much to do with the arrival of Irish immigrants fleeing the famine. By 1860 they comprised about a third of the population of New York City and Boston, and they endured middle-class prejudice wherever they settled. Some Irish American playwrights of the time were no longer producing melodramas that exploited mawkish tales of poverty; they were replacing these with stories of hard-working, honest, and sober Irishmen accommodating to middle-class American values through economic and political independence. Lover's sentimental ballads and stories of Irish peasants struggling against adversity appealed not only to working-class Irish but also "to audiences highly fashionable . . . and also numerous and applauding."

After this initial success Lover started gathering notes for a book about American society, but he abandoned the project when he became unexpectedly overwhelmed by social engagements along his route. These included meetings with Washington Irving, Nathaniel Hawthorne, William Cullen Bryant, Ralph Waldo Emerson, Henry Wadsworth Longfellow, and President James K. Polk. Nevertheless, his diary and letters provide vivid impressions of Canada and the United States. He thought that the great heroes of American civilization were the woodmen who cleared forests for cities and cultivation, and he quipped that the ax would be a better national symbol than the eagle: the latter suggests savageness and predation while the ax connotes industry and dominion. Always interested in technological advances that promised improved communication, Lover later wondered what effect a transatlantic telegraph cable might have on romantic attachments, as he wrote in these lines:

> Under the sea, under the sea,
> Some one in Europe is talking to me.
> Fondly I'm trusting to this lover of mine,
> In the depth of his love, by the depth of his line.

He incorporated some of these impressions into his act when he returned to England.

Lover showed little zeal for politics and had no tolerance for violence or revolt. While still in America in 1848, during the European revolutions and the Chartist disturbances (which he disparaged as "that bullying Chartist bravado") in England, he wrote a friend that "if anarchy were threatened in England, it would have been no place for me, who can only contribute to the refinements of life, and I would have sent for my girls and made out the cause here, for a time." Bernard claims that Lover manifests political opinion only in his satirical *Parson's Horn-Book* illustrations, but he always responded passionately to suffering and injustice.

While Lover was in the United States he was profoundly moved when he learned that Americans had stripped the armaments from a frigate and filled it with provisions for relieving the Irish famine. He spoke often of this charitable act during his travels and wrote a song about it for his stage performance. Of this frigate's mission to the Irish he wrote:

> Her thunder sleeps—'tis Mercy's breath
> That wafts her o'er the sea;
> She goes not forth to deal out death,
> But bears new life to thee!

Such lofty sentiments in a sentimental age resonated with audiences who came to see Lover seeking simple truths and compassionate amusement. Lover's political judgments were always charitable, viewing art as a sufficient means of effecting improvement and reform. Shortly before he died Lover wrote in a letter to a friend that although his politics were "utterly at variance" with the conservative views of Benjamin Disraeli, he applauded one of the prime minister's achievements because "my sympathy with a man of letters was stronger than my political bias."

The deaths of his wife and his older daughter, Meta, deeply shocked Lover, and for a time he lived in Wales with his other daughter, Fanny, who had recently married Edward Herbert. In 1852 Lover married Mary Wandby and resumed a more active professional life. He edited several volumes of verse, contributed short sketches to London periodicals, composed songs and poems, and even wrote opera libretti during the remainder of the decade. His grandson, Victor Herbert, was born in Dublin on 1 February 1859. Widowed soon after the birth of her son, Fanny often brought Victor to visit Lover and her stepmother in the village of Sevenoaks in Kent. Later in life Victor Herbert recalled watching Lover paint and draw, seeing him compose and play music, and listening to him tell stories about Ireland. Lover advised Fanny to take the boy to Germany, where Herbert studied at Stuttgart Conservatory. Lover was unable to visit them there because he became ill, and in an attempt to recover his health, he moved first to the Isle of Wight and then to Jersey. On 14 February 1868 he wrote a friend this account of his illness: "You know in our dear old native Ireland how every disease is called by the peasantry 'an impression of the heart,' and I really think that is the very disease I've got—that is, if I have any heart left at all." He died on 6 July 1868 at St. Helier.

At the end of the nineteenth century Lover remained one of the most widely known and admired Anglo-Irish novelists. His name and epitaph are engraved on a white Parian marble tablet placed on a wall near the north transept of St. Patrick's Cathedral in Dublin:

> In Memory of Samuel Lover, Poet, Painter, Novelist, and Composer, who in the exercise of a genius as distinguished in its versatility as in its power, by his pen and pencil illustrated so happily the characteristics of the Peasantry of his country that his name will ever be honourably identified with Ireland.

But Lover's literary work was reassessed during the Irish Literary Revival. William Butler Yeats believed that Lover, T. Crofton Croker, and other Irish writers had missed the spirit of Irish folklore and unwittingly perpetuated the stage Irishman:

> The impulse of the Irish literature of their time came from a class that did not—mainly for political reasons—take the populace seriously, and imagined the country as a humorist's Arcadia; its passion, its gloom, its tragedy, they knew nothing of. What they did was not wholly false; they merely magnified an irresponsible type, found oftenest among boatmen, carmen, and gentlemen's servants, into the type of the whole nation.

In the midst of this Irish Literary Revival, Lover's stories, lyrical ballads, and paintings were slowly forgotten, as were his achievements in moderating British attitudes toward the Irish peasantry by creating a sympathetic portrait of Irish life. Victor Herbert, a composer who arrived in the United States in 1886 and became a cello soloist with the Metropolitan Opera in New York City, restored Lover's popularity and turned him into a stage symbol of extreme Irish nationalism. The number of musical works that Herbert composed was prodigious. He produced fifty operettas in forty years and was the most popular light-opera composer in the United States. His songs remain familiar to millions. On 18 August 1918 Herbert played Lover's soulful melodies on the piano and cello at a successful Red Cross benefit for war relief at Lake Placid, New York, and through such work by Herbert, Lover's lyrics and melodies were revived. Herbert became something of a stage-Irish patriot, rabidly anti-British, and one of the leading apologists in the United States for Irish revolution.

A fair assessment of Lover's role as a reformer requires that he be seen apart from both accolades and criticisms and judged as a man of his time. As Lover's social class became supplanted by Irish nationalists who sought a political, cultural, and religious identity separate from Great Britain, the Irish Literary Revival attempted to displace the peasantry that had been invented. John Wilson Foster concludes, however, that the peasants of James Joyce, Yeats, John Millington Synge, and Isabella Augusta Persse, Lady Gregory—important figures of the revival period—are no less literary and cultural inventions than the peasants of Lover.

One must admire Lover as a reform writer for the variety of his achievements and for his subtly beneficial influence on social progress, understanding, and improvement. For Maureen Waters, Lover's criticism of British imperialism is most effective when he expresses it as satire or as gallows humor. While not as skillful a writer as Dickens, Lover uses humor and satire to give voice to an oppressed class in his own way, which may often perplex and amuse but also acknowledges suffering and strives for human dignity.

As Bernard suggested in 1874, "so far from gaining, he [Lover] had rather suffered by a diversity which diffusing public attention over a wide group of particulars, had necessarily placed some of them in a less distinct light than others." If, as O'Donoghue predicted, Lover is remembered "as a humorist long after he has been forgotten as an artist and musician," he then falls victim to the prejudice against what amuses and is accordingly not taken seriously. Yet a close examination of Lover's work shows a patient, careful, gentle man who knew how to broker opinion through media of popular expression such as oratory, drama, illustration, storytelling, comic and satiric prose, travelogue, song, and poetry—and among populations riven by class prejudice and exploitation. He knew that art, in whatever form proved most acceptable to changing tastes and political tides, ultimately could persuade as well as delight.

Bibliographies:

Steven J. Brown, S.J., *Ireland in Fiction: A Guide to Irish Novels, Tales, Romances, and Folk-Lore* (Dublin & London: Maunsel, 1919), pp. 176-177;

Brian McKenna, *Irish Literature, 1800-1875* (Detroit: Gale Research, 1978), pp. 236-239.

Biographies:

Bayle Bernard, *The Life of Samuel Lover,* 2 volumes (London: King, 1874);

Andrew James Symington, *Samuel Lover: A Biographical Sketch, with Selections from His Writings and Correspondence* (London: Blackie, 1880; New York: Harper, 1880).

References:

John Wilson Foster, *Fictions of the Irish Literary Revival* (Syracuse: Syracuse University Press, 1987);

Sally E. Foster, "Irish Wrong: Samuel Lover and the Stage-Irishman," *Eire-Ireland,* 13 (1978): 34-44;

Wayne Hall, "The First Year of the Dublin University Magazine (1833-1877)," *Eire-Ireland,* 12 (1987): 26-35;

Joseph Kaye, *Victor Herbert* (New York: Crown, 1931);

Bruce A. McConachie, "The Cultural Politics of 'Paddy' on the Midcentury American State," *Studies in Popular Culture,* 10 (1987): 1-13;

Russel Nye, *The Unembarrassed Muse: The Popular Arts in America* (New York: Dial, 1970);

Edward N. Waters, *Victor Herbert: A Life in Music* (New York: Macmillan, 1955);

Maureen Waters, *The Comic Irishman* (Albany: State University of New York Press, 1984);

Maureen Waters, "'No Divarshin': Samuel Lover's Handy Andy," *Eire-Ireland,* 14 (1979): 53-64;

William Butler Yeats, ed., *Fairy and Folk Tales of the Irish Peasantry* (London: Scott, 1888).

Harriet Martineau
(12 June 1802 - 27 June 1876)

Alison Winter
California Institute of Technology

See also the Martineau entries in *DLB 21: Victorian Novelists Before 1885; DLB 55: Victorian Prose Writers Before 1867; DLB 159: British Short-Fiction Writers, 1800–1880; DLB 163: British Children's Writers, 1800–1880;* and *DLB 166: British Travel Writers, 1837–1875.*

BOOKS: *Devotional Exercises, Consisting of Reflections and Prayers, for the Use of Young Persons, to Which Is Added a Treatise on the Lord's Supper,* anonymous (London: Hunter, 1823); enlarged as *Devotional Exercises, to Which Is Added a Guide to the Study of the Scriptures* (London: Hunter, 1832; Boston: Bowles, 1833); republished as *Devotional Exercises: Consisting of Reflections and Prayers for the Use of Young Persons, to Which Is Added a Guide to the Study of the Scripture* (Boston: Otis, Broaders, 1840);

Addresses with Prayers and Original Hymns for the Use of Families and Schools, anonymous (London: Hunter, 1826);

Principle and Practice; or, The Orphan Family, anonymous (London: Houlston, 1827; New York: Gilley, 1828);

The Rioters; or, A Tale of Bad Times, anonymous (London: Houlston, 1827);

Mary Campbell; or, The Affectionate Granddaughter, anonymous (London: Houlston, 1828);

The Turn Out; or, Patience the Best Policy, anonymous (London: Houlston, 1829);

The Essential Faith of the Universal Church Deduced from the Sacred Records (London: Unitarian Association, 1831; Boston: Bowles, 1833);

Five Years of Youth; or, Sense and Sentiment (London: Harvey & Darton, 1831; Boston: Bowles & Greene, 1832);

Sequel to Principle and Practice; or, The Orphan Family, anonymous (London: Houlston, 1831);

Brooke and Brooke Farm: A Tale (London: Fox, 1832);

Demerara (London: Fox, 1832);

The Faith as Unfolded by Many Prophets: An Essay ... Addressed to the Disciples of Mohammed (London:

Harriet Martineau, 1833

Unitarian Association, 1832; Boston: Bowles, 1833);

Providence as Manifested through Israel (London: Unitarian Association, 1832; Boston: Bowles, 1833);

Illustrations of Political Economy (9 volumes, London: Fox, 1832–1834; 8 volumes, Boston: Bowles, 1832–1834);

Poor Laws and Paupers, Illustrated (4 volumes, London: Fox, 1833–1834; 1 volume, Boston: Bowles, 1833);

Illustrations of Taxation, 5 volumes (London: Fox, 1834);

The Children Who Lived by the Jordan: A Story (Salem, Mass.: Landmark, 1835; London: Green, 1842);

The Hamlets (Boston: Munroe, 1836);

Miscellanies, 2 volumes (Boston: Hilliard, Gray, 1836);

Competition in Peril, by Martineau and Samuel Bower (Leeds: Hobson, 1837);

Society in America, 3 volumes (London: Saunders & Otley, 1837);

My Servant Rachel: A Tale (London: Houlston, 1838);

A Retrospect of Western Travel (3 volumes, London: Saunders & Otley, 1838; 2 volumes, New York: Lohman, 1838);

How to Observe: Morals and Manners (London: Knight, 1838; Philadelphia: Lea & Blanchard, 1838);

Deerbrook: A Novel, 3 volumes (London: Moxon, 1838; New York: Harper, 1839);

The Martyr Age of the United States (Boston: Weeks, Jordan / New York: Taylor, 1839; Newcastle upon Tyne: Finlay & Charlton, 1840);

The Hour and the Man: A Historical Romance (3 volumes, London: Moxon, 1841; 2 volumes, New York: Harper, 1841);

The Playfellow: A Series of Tales (4 volumes, London: Knight, 1841-1843; 1 volume, London & New York: Routledge, 1883);

Life in the Sick-Room: Essays, by an Invalid, anonymous (London: Moxon, 1844; Boston: Bowles & Crosby, 1844);

Dawn Island (Manchester: Gadsby, 1845);

Letters on Mesmerism (London: Moxon, 1845); republished as *Miss Martineau's Letters on Mesmerism* (New York: Harper, 1845);

Forest and Game Law Tales, 3 volumes (London: Moxon, 1845-1846);

The Billow and the Rock (London: Knight, 1846);

The Land We Live In: A Pictorial and Literary Sketchbook of the British Empire, 4 volumes, by Martineau, Charles Knight, and others (London: Knight, 1847-1850); republished as *The Land We Live In: A Pictorial, Historical, and Literary Sketch-Book of the British Islands,* 3 volumes (London: Orr, 1854-1856);

Eastern Life, Present and Past (3 volumes, London: Moxon, 1848; 1 volume, Philadelphia: Lea & Blanchard, 1848);

Household Education (London: Moxon, 1849; Philadelphia: Lea & Blanchard, 1849);

The History of England during the Thirty Years' Peace: 1816-1846, 2 volumes, by Martineau and Knight (London: Knight, 1849); revised and republished as *History of the Peace: Pictorial History of England during the Thirty Years' Peace, 1816-1846* (London: Chambers, 1858); republished as *The History of England from the Commencement of the XIXth Century to the Crimean War,* 4 volumes (Philadelphia: Porter & Coates, 1864); republished as *A History of the Thirty Years' Peace,* 4 volumes (London: Bell, 1877-1878);

Two Letters on Cow-Keeping, . . . Addressed to the Governor of the Guiltcross Union Workhouse (London: Gilpin / Edinburgh: Black / Dublin: Gilpin, 1850);

Half a Century of the British Empire: A History of the Kingdom and the People from 1800 to 1850 (London, 1851);

Introduction to the History of the Peace from 1800 to 1815 (London: Knight, 1851); republished as *History of England, A.D. 1800-1815: Being an Introduction to the History of the Peace* (London: Bell, 1878);

Letters on the Laws of Man's Nature and Development, by Martineau and Henry George Atkinson (London: Chapman, 1851; Boston: Mendum, 1851);

Letters from Ireland (London: Chapman, 1852);

Merdhen: The Manor and The Eyrie; and Old Landmarks and Old Laws (London: Routledge, 1852);

Guide to Windermere, with Tours to the Neighbouring Lakes and Other Interesting Places (Windermere: Garnett / London: Whittaker, 1854);

A Complete Guide to the English Lakes (Windermere: Garnett / London: Whittaker, 1855; expanded edition, Windermere: Garnett, 1858); republished as *A Complete Guide to the Lake District of England* (Windermere: Garnett, 1871); republished as *The English Lake District* (Windermere: Garnett, 1876);

The Factory Controversy: A Warning against Meddling Legislation (Manchester: National Association of Factory Occupiers, 1855);

A History of the American Compromises (London: Chapman, 1856);

Corporate Traditions and National Rights: Local Dues on Shipping (London & Windermere, 1857);

British Rule in India: An Historical Sketch (London: Smith, Elder, 1857);

Guide to Keswick and Its Environs (Windermere: Garnett / London: Whittaker, 1857);

Suggestions towards the Future Government of India (London: Smith, Elder, 1858);

England and Her Soldiers (London: Smith, Elder, 1859);

Endowed Schools of Ireland (London: Smith, Elder, 1859);

Health, Husbandry and Handicraft (London: Bradbury & Evans, 1861); republished in part as *Our Farm of Two Acres* (New York: Bunce & Huntingdon, 1865);

Biographical Sketches (London: Macmillan, 1869; New York: Leypoldt & Holt, 1869; enlarged edition, London: Macmillan, 1876);

Harriet Martineau's Autobiography, with Memorials by Maria Westman Chapman (3 volumes, London: Smith, Elder, 1877; 2 volumes, Boston: Osgood, 1877);

The Hampdens: An Historiette (London: Routledge, 1880).

OTHER: *Traditions of Palestine,* edited by Martineau (London: Longman, Rees, Orme, Brown & Green, 1830); revised as *The Times of the Saviour* (Boston: Bowles, 1831);

John Anderson Collins, *Right and Wrong among the Abolitionists of the United States; or, The Objects, Principles and Measures of the Original American Anti-Slavery Society, Unchanged: Being a Defence against the Assaults of the Recently Formed Massachusett's Abolition, and the American and Foreign Anti-Slavery Societies,* introductory letter by Martineau (Glasgow: Gallie, 1841);

Charles Knight, ed., *Mind amongst the Spindles: A Miscellany, Wholly Composed by the Factory Girls,* includes a letter by Martineau (Boston: Jordan, Swift & Wiley, 1845); republished as *Mind amongst the Spindles: A Selection from the Lowell Offering, a Miscellany; Wholly Composed by the Factory Girls of an American City* (London: Knight, 1845);

The Positive Philosophy of Auguste Comte, Freely Translated and Condensed, 2 volumes (London: Chapman, 1853; New York: Appleton, 1854);

Reinhold Pauli, *Simon de Montfort, Earl of Leicester, the Creator of the House of Commons,* introduction by Martineau (London: Trübner, 1876).

In the obituary she wrote for herself, Harriet Martineau claimed that her powers as a writer derived merely from "earnestness and intellectual clearness within a certain range," that she had "small imaginative and suggestive powers," and that she could only "popularise, while she could neither discover nor invent." These words both summarize her reputation among her readers and reveal the tactics of self-representation that allowed her to maintain the unusual and controversial place she held as a public figure for almost half a century. Among a generation of prominent intellectual reformers, Martineau was one of the few women. She wrote not only on causes that women improvers had championed before–education, the antislavery movement, and the position of women–but also on an astonishingly wide range of political topics, from political economy to foreign policy. Given Victorian definitions of femininity as inherently domestic, private, and protected from a corrupt public world, her activities as a female political writer made her public role a paradoxical one.

Martineau successfully integrated herself into Victorian public affairs and letters to a certain extent. She was celebrated for her intelligence, her industry, and her morality. However, her reputation was never free of the ambivalence of Victorians about women who were publicly assertive. She managed to write about subjects that had been the exclusive preserve of male writers and won a degree of acceptance by presenting herself as a passive transmitter of knowledge produced by others. Her role as a public figure was twofold. She was an agent of reform through the effect her popular writings had on the minds of workers, and because of her womanhood and her physical disabilities, she also exemplified the supposedly subordinate members of society who were the focus of those reforms. In carrying out some of the most controversial of her career moves she portrayed herself as propelled by circumstances, by the needs of others, and by the limitations and frailties of her own body. Under cover of this passivity she exerted an unusual degree of control over her own affairs.

Martineau, the sixth of eight children, was born on 12 June 1802 to Thomas Martineau, a Norwich cloth manufacturer, and his wife, Elizabeth Rankin, the daughter of a sugar refiner at Newcastle. Norwich was one of the more sophisticated and culturally diverse provincial towns in the early nineteenth century, and it had a large community of religious Dissenters, those who deliberately kept outside the established Anglican Church. This setting, in combination with the liberal politics and manufacturing interests in which Martineau was raised, helped shape her early interests.

The continuing interests of Martineau's social reform campaigns–the abolition of slavery, the "Woman Question," and popular and national education–emerged naturally from traditional Unitarian concerns. She claimed to have become a political economist at the tender age of fourteen, and if so, it is likely that her early enthusiasm for this new social science was particularly indebted to the studies of Unitarian philosophy that she was undertaking when she attended a Bristol school in the 1810s. One of her younger brothers, James, later a highly influential Unitarian divine, was studying there under Unitarian Lant Carpenter, who also became a mentor to Martineau. Preoccupied with human improvement and mental development, Martineau approached her tasks with an extraordinary tenacity and an unusually methodical turn of mind. She was introduced to classic works by philosophers such as Joseph Priestley and David Hartley, and she enthu-

Martineau's birthplace on Magdalen Street, Norwich

siastically embraced the doctrine of Necessity, the notion that each human action is made necessary by the constraints of circumstances.

Martineau came to reject the notion of free will and to regard people as agents through which forces were manifest in the world. One had only a choice between "resigned submission" and "enthusiastic compliance." Her conception of Necessity taught that the latter of these choices was most likely to bring personal fulfillment. This view gave her a philosophical grounding hospitable to the Philosophic Radicalism that she came to champion in the late 1820s and 1830s as well as with a clear motivation for proselytizing. As she put it in a letter to Carpenter, "the greatest service w^h can be rendered to our population is to familiarize them with the principles which regulate their own interests."

Throughout her early career Martineau believed in an omnipotent God orchestrating the orderly progress of civilization through the action of simple natural and spiritual laws. Though she later abandoned this notion for a more agnostic definition of natural law, during the 1820s and 1830s her early belief supplied the assumptions for her pedagogical writings that taught readers the nature of those laws. Her earliest works, such as "Female Practical Writers" and "Devotional Exercises," focus on Unitarian religious concerns. A few other works confirmed her vocation as a writer; however, it is unlikely that she would have become a writer as a means of financial support had not a series of family tragedies in the 1820s propelled her into a writing career.

Thomas Martineau, one of her brothers, died in 1826, and the family business was soon after severely damaged by the stock market crash that year. Meanwhile, she had become engaged to a young man who became insane and died of "brain fever"—a tragedy that Martineau later represented as a lucky escape for her. The family was finally bankrupted in 1829, and, as she writes in *Harriet Martineau's Autobiography, with Memorials by Maria Westman Chapman* (1877), the loss of their respectability left her free to sell her writing in a way that would have been unacceptable for a "respectable" lady of society.

Another "fortunate" difficulty catalyzed Martineau's writing career: her own ill health. Throughout her childhood she had been thought to be "nervous" and "morbid," and in fact her intellectual development had been marked by bodily infirmity. Her nervousness provoked her family's decision to send her to Bristol and therefore indirectly effected her exposure to Unitarian philosophy and her first published writing. In the late 1820s she suffered a long illness that she later attributed to her family difficulties during those years. By this time her childhood hearing disabilities had become so marked that she could hear only what was spoken directly into an ear trumpet. Her physical frailty and especially her deafness made it impossible for her to adopt a position as governess, the standard occupation of impoverished ladies. She was therefore free to take up the far more controversial choice of a writing career.

In the later 1820s she supported herself by needlework while struggling to publish her essays. She edited and published *Traditions of Palestine,* a strongly Unitarian account of the historical context from which early Christianity emerged, in 1830. She entered all three categories in a writing competition sponsored by the Unitarian Association, who published her works in 1831 and 1832 after she won prizes in each category for *The Essential Faith of the Universal Church Deduced from the Sacred Records* (1831), *The Faith as Unfolded by Many Prophets: An Essay . . . Addressed to the Disciples of Mohammed* (1832), and *Providence as Manifested through Israel* (1832). She was then commissioned to write a "Life of Howard" for the Society for the Diffusion of Useful Knowledge; she completed this essay, but the society never published it. During these years she wrote many other essays on various subjects, from the newly founded Hanwell Lunatic Asylum to the genius of Sir Walter Scott, and these were collected in her *Miscellanies* (1836).

While these works were making her known among the Unitarian community and among metropolitan education reformers, her real break came when she read Jane Marcet's *Conversations on Political Economy* (1816) and decided to produce a volume on the same subject and with a similar educational purpose. Martineau, however, planned to use the vehicle of fiction rather than the didactic style that Marcet and most other educational writers employed. Many reformers—certainly the Philosophic Radicals whom Martineau admired—regarded popular educational literature as a chief ensurer of social stability. The flood of literature intended to "improve" its readers was supposed to distract workers from subversive literature that was becoming increasingly accessible following the advent of the steam press; it was also supposed to align the social perceptions of the working classes with those of the ruling classes.

Martineau's project would capitalize on both the economics of cheap print and the ideological aims of bodies such as the Society for the Diffusion of Useful Knowledge, with which she was already involved. Her *Illustrations of Political Economy* (1832–1834) popularizes claims that James Mill, Jeremy Bentham, Adam Smith, Thomas Malthus, and David Ricardo make about the free market, the dangers of protectionism, and the principles of population growth.

Since didactic or epistolary styles provided the current mode of instructional writing, Martineau had to struggle to persuade W. J. Fox, editor of the *Monthly Repository,* the journal that had published much of her early work, to publish the tales. But her *Illustrations,* first serialized in twenty-five monthly parts, became a tremendous success. As many as ten thousand copies were sold each month. Martineau's idiom and timing were the reasons for her success. By 1832 doctrines associated with political economy were profoundly influencing legislation, but despite the fashionable enthusiasm for literature aimed at improving its readers, no one had thought to package such works in fiction. The first run of Martineau's stories sold out and was reprinted in the first month of publication; the other stories proved to be equally popular, and she wrote a story each month until the first series was finished in 1834. In that year she also wrote *Poor Laws and Paupers, Illustrated* (1833–1834), a series to ease the passage of the New Poor Law, and *Illustrations of Taxation* (1834), a series to support Lord Chancellor Henry Brougham's proposed tax reforms.

Illustrations of Taxation contained features of what became known as the "Condition of England" novel, and each narrative covered a distinct topic and delivered practical solutions to the social problems of England. "Demerara" attacked slavery; "Weal and Woe in Garveloch" summarized Malthus's population theory; "A Manchester Strike" told both factory owners and operatives that their interests coincided in the accumulation of capital, and "Homes Abroad" encouraged emigration. Generally *Illustrations of Taxation* taught readers that rigid natural laws explicable by principles of political economy determined the course of human affairs whether or not the people whose affairs were so directed could perceive this.

Self-help in becoming familiar with these laws was therefore necessary, and Martineau's service to the working classes was that of making them aware of how their actions were shaped by the force of Necessity. According to the theory workers who understood these doctrines became the most diligent and confident ones. Moreover, Martineau's preach-

Martineau in 1849 (portrait by George Richmond; National Portrait Gallery, London)

ing to these readers, the subordinates of society, was done from a position of empathy because her own role as a popularizer was one of subordinate, "auxiliary usefulness" to the political leaders whom she served. Martineau was in no way a modern liberal. She was uncompromisingly optimistic about the beneficial effects of the New Poor Law on the lives of the poor, and she foresaw a simple solution to the problem of the erosion of the mass workforce by industrial technology: in sympathy with suffering factory operatives she anticipated that "the race will die out in two or three generations, by which time machinery may be found to do their work better than their miserable selves."

As author of these tales Martineau cast herself in the role of the teacher or nurse of the workers, as someone disseminating a therapeutic dose of knowledge to an ailing body politic according to the prescription written by the economic physicians of the time. Her work was received as apologetic rather than original and assertive, and, deferring to the authority of political economists, she claimed to have no pretensions to originality. Although many readers took Martineau at her word, historians recognize that by representing herself as a popularizer she was certainly able to deflect the criticism that women should not be involved in producing knowledge, especially political knowledge.

Her stories were reviewed in major journals, and overall their reception established for her a conspicuous, if ambivalent, reputation. G. P. Scrope's review in the *Quarterly Review* was one of the most hostile, claiming that Martineau betrayed the sanctity of the home and of children. She was attacked for being a *"female Malthusian"* propounding "unfeminine and mischievous doctrines on the principles of social welfare." The radical *Poor Man's Guardian* was less concerned with Martineau's feminine propriety than with what it considered the first clear evidence of the evil intentions of political economists: "The juggle of the Political Economists . . . is now seen through; when translated into plain English, [it reads,] . . . Give up the whole produce of your labour–fill everybody's cupboard but your own–and then starve quietly!!!"

Between the positions adopted by these two attacks, published in journals that represented the extremes of the political spectrum, lay a middle ground where Martineau found strong support. This approval was most enthusiastically delivered by the *Edinburgh Review,* although the anonymous reviewer in this Whig journal also finds it necessary to establish some ground rules for supporting a project such as Martineau's:

> Women have long reigned supreme over both the learning and practice of domestic economy. They are the proper legislators for, as well as ministers of, the interior. But the province of Political Economy, although it may begin with home, is so vast and complicated, that these two departments cannot have much in common beyond the approximation of a name.

Ultimately the reviewer decides that Martineau's work does not contravene these limits since she is disseminating rather than creating original knowledge. Martineau's work could be considered "domestic" because it was philanthropic and because her audience was the working classes rather than the political economists and politicians. As a disseminator rather than an originator, and as a philanthropist rather than a political figure, she could be acceptable to the most sympathetic of reviewers.

Illustrations of Taxation catapulted Martineau from the financial constraints and social obscurity she had endured and into bustling London society circles, where she was lionized in the 1830s. Within months of publishing the first volume of *Illustrations of Taxation* Martineau was socializing with literary figures such as Henry Hallam, Sydney Smith, Thomas Babington Macaulay, Henry Milman, Richard Monckton Milnes, Thomas Carlyle, Thomas Campbell, and Edward Bulwer-Lytton, not to mention personal heroes such as Malthus. Her intimate social circle included the Darwins and the Wedgwoods, and in the late 1830s there was talk that she and Erasmus Darwin, brother of Charles Darwin, might marry; but this came to nothing. She also acquired new political influence—even, she claimed, to have "direct access to the cabinet," as Robert Kiefer Webb records. Thomas Drummond, private secretary to John Charles Spencer (Viscount Althorp), visited her frequently. Brougham gave her access to private papers, and she collaborated with John George Lambton, first Earl of Durham, and Francis Place on responses to labor unrest.

Yet Martineau was not an ideologically committed ally of liberal Whigs. She described herself as a radical and in a letter to Place writes that she thought she was "known to be so wherever I go." However, she linked herself only loosely with leaders of middle-class radicalism such as Brougham and certainly did not link herself with Owenite circles. She supported Whig legislation in the 1830s but claimed to have done so because she considered the legislation progressive, not because she was allied with the party. Martineau preferred what she called "radical reformers"—individuals who might be of any or of no party but who were firmly committed to understanding and complying with the inexorable laws of social progress as she construed them.

For a few years following publication of *Illustrations of Political Economy* Martineau—sensitive yet objective, femininely deferential yet firm in her support of the most extreme reforms—became known as one of the most mannish women in England. Martineau's "Letter to the Deaf" (1834) exemplifies her technique of casting her own experiences in broad social generalizations or discussions of social policy. All the paradoxes and contradictions attendant upon such a reputation sharpened as her fame increased during the 1830s. For example, she described how her partial deafness has sharpened her other senses even as it isolates her from the world. The letter successfully reached a mass audience similarly confined by the limitations of its senses, and, indeed, Martineau eventually gained access to these groups directly when "all deaf people and their friends [were] brought to me wherever I went"—following publication of her letter.

A portrait of Martineau of 1833 linked her deafness to her public identity. Her hand cupped near her ear marked the famousness of her infirmity, but also suggested the notion that her sex and her deafness made her unusually sensitive to the problems of the vulnerable members of society. Even as her works gained for her a reputation of feminine sensitivity and fine moral values, other writings established her among middle-class audiences as a prototype of the precise observer and reliable reporter. Throughout the 1830s the subjects of her written work gained more public attention and encompassed greater public dimensions. While her *Devotional Exercises, Consisting of Reflections and Prayers, for the Use of Young Persons, to Which Is Added a Treatise on the Lord's Supper* (1823) had been written and published for consumption in a private domain, Martineau's *Society in America* (1837) was an ambitious treatment of a national community.

Martineau visited America in 1834–1835 partly as a break from the intense cycle of writing she had maintained for the previous two years, but, as was her habit, she turned the voyage into a working vacation. On the voyage to the United States she wrote a volume for the How to Observe series, *Morals and Manners* (1838), in which, using the ship as a laboratory of human phenomena, she abstracted a series of rules for those wishing to embark on an inductive study of other societies. Her methods were sometimes drastic: once, during a violent storm, Martineau insisted on staying on deck, being strapped to the ship so she would not be swept overboard, in order to observe the storm and the terror it produced in the other passengers.

She used her visit to America as another occasion for disciplined observation, a means of broadening her field of evidence regarding the principles of political economy at work in different social environments. *Society in America* was written as a sociological work that attempted to evaluate American society according to the ability of the people to fulfill the promise of the founding constitutional principles of the nation, especially those principles of egalitarianism and human rights. Martineau was supremely optimistic about the future of the United States once certain inconsistencies are righted. Two of the most important of these are slavery and the position of women. During her visit she championed the cause of the abolitionists at some personal risk, and in *Society in America* she presented a strong antislavery argument, which she developed from strictly economic arguments rather than from principles of human rights. She made a similar argument about marriage as it was conducted in many households: she argued that women technically held the status of slaves, in terms of their ability to make active and informed contributions to society.

Society in America and to a lesser extent *A Retrospect of Western Travel* (1838), the more personal account of her journey, confirmed Martineau's reputation as a powerful British journalist. By the late 1830s she had become firmly established as a popular moral and scientific writer, especially for middle-

The Knoll, Ambleside, the house in the Lake District where Martineau spent the last thirty years of her life (drawing by Claude Harrison)

class readers. Her work embodied the ideals of precise observation and subtlety on the one hand and fine moral values on the other. She advertised herself as applying to human affairs a new rationality and scientific method. Her admirers considered her to be the epitome of observational purity informed by sound morals; her critics acknowledged the strength of her popularity even as they condemned it.

In 1837 she was offered the opportunity to edit the *Economic Magazine,* the publication of which was to begin in 1839. But Martineau was also considering writing a novel, and the two projects were incompatible. She had to choose between the powerful role of a journal editor, controlling the public form taken by others' work, and the more private role of the woman novelist, whose writing was subject to the whims of publishers and editors in the process of becoming public. She was acutely conscious of choosing between what she saw as a public, male route and a private, womanly one. Were she to edit the *Economic Magazine,* she wrote in her *Autobiography,* "I must brace myself up to do and suffer like a man. No more waywardness, precipitation and reliance on others! Undertaking a man's duty, I must brave a man's fate."

Eventually she rejected the offer to become editor of the magazine, and in her *Autobiography* she attributed her decision entirely to the influence of her brother James, who was more politically conservative than Martineau and who strongly disapproved of the project. In any event, after turning down the *Economic Magazine* Martineau wrote her first novel, *Deerbrook* (1838), which had many features of what came to be known as the "novels of community." *Deerbrook* is the story of the unfulfilled love between a country physician and his sister-in-law in a rural village. In both plot and structure it illustrates Martineau's guiding principle of "reason over passion" as her characters' rationality and moral fortitude conquer their feelings for each other.

During a journey to Venice in 1839 Martineau collapsed and had to be rushed home to England for medical treatment. She retired to the home of her brother-in-law, the physician Thomas Michael Greenhow, and placed herself under his care in a domestic situation eerily reminiscent of the recently published *Deerbrook*. Greenhow's diagnosis was that Martineau was suffering from an extreme ovarian tumor.

When Martineau became an invalid, her independence—financial, physical, and intellectual—was immediately threatened. On one hand she became the epitome of the Victorian woman, ruled over by her reproductive system and languishing delicately on a couch. Ironically she found it easy to maintain a reputation as a heroic public figure in the relative isolation of the sickroom. The ambivalence that had marked her career was ameliorated by the sight of Martineau in the most feminine of Victorian scenarios: the invalid in her sickroom. Friends and admirers met to provide for her well-being; she was offered financial help of various kinds; and admirers made pilgrimages to her room.

However, Martineau was no ordinary invalid as she did not give up her public life and the control she had exercised over her affairs. Instead she redefined the sickroom by transforming it into a quasi-public space—one which, unlike the ordinary Victorian sickroom, was firmly under the control of its inmate. She refused offers of civil pensions from the government as she worried that they would compromise her intellectual independence. She moved from her comfortable but dependent room in her brother-in-law's house to her own apartment, and she entered into a series of acrimonious exchanges with correspondents over what was to be done with her letters after her imminent death. Martineau was alarmed at the prospect that her letters might be published, without her supervision or control, after her death, and she taxed the patience of many friends with her demands for privacy beyond the grave.

Her condition did make it difficult for her to maintain the pace of writing she had sustained. In 1841 she published *The Hour and the Man: A Historical Romance*—a three-volume, rather unsuccessful historical romance about Toussaint L'Ouverture, the Haitian leader—and in the same year *The Playfellow*, a collection of four children's novels that includes *The Crofton Boys, Feats on the Fiord, Settlers at Home,* and *The Peasant and the Prince. Feats on the Fiord* and *The Crofton Boys* became the most widely read of this collection. In the latter work Martineau presented a child's psychological development being inspired by physical infirmity in a manner that prefigured the most successful work of her convalescent years, *Life in the Sick-Room: Essays, by an Invalid* (1844).

In *Life in the Sick-Room* Martineau avowed most publicly the powers of authority that she and all invalids discover. Always the reformer, Martineau sought to revise the habits of all who are involved in the sickroom: nurses, doctors, family, and especially the invalid, whose authority was to be respected by all. Among many of her readers the collection established Martineau as a public martyr but above all as being terminally ill. Consequently, when she left her sickbed only months after publication of the book, attributing her miraculous cure to the controversial science of mesmerism, she caused a sensation.

Mesmerism, which was thought to affect a patient's state of mind or health by means of his or her physical proximity to another individual was a therapy that imparted authority to the unusual mental states of patients. It therefore lent the epistemological framework that justified Martineau's claim that the mental state of the invalid was not only to be taken seriously but was especially authoritative. She published an account of her extraordinary cure in the *Athenaeum* in November and December 1844, and she then engaged in a controversy over the efficacy of mesmerism as a science. The elite of the medical and surgical professions and many members of her family were involved.

Martineau's interest in mesmerism did not detract from her continued commitment to political economy, for even before she fully recovered, she resumed her participation in the liberal projects of the day. She published *Dawn Island* (1845) and *Forest and Game Law Tales* (1845-1846), both of which celebrated the free market, in aid of the Anti-Corn Law League. Both were crudely packaged as fiction; *Dawn Island,* for example, is the story of a tropical island on which the inhabitants are saved from disaster when a British ship brings "commerce to their shores." Neither book was successful.

Her most powerful exposition of utilitarianism was published in 1849, after she had used a commission to write *The History of England during the Thirty Years' Peace: 1816-1846* as a license to present arguably the most thoroughly utilitarian interpretation of that period in existence. Martineau argued that a stalwart middle class—by which she meant small tradesmen and skilled artisans from the industrial heartlands—rescued Britain from revolution in 1831. Moreover, Britain was saved again in 1848 during the recent Chartist demonstrations by these same groups, who spilled into the streets to reinforce the powers of the civic police. Generally the work sought to establish the necessity of extended suffrage as the only real mechanism for social improvement.

In 1845 Martineau moved to the Lake District, where she built The Knoll, the house in which she would reside for the rest of her life. There she held court to a stream of mesmerists, admirers, and members of the intellectual community who settled in the region. In administering both her household and the surrounding farm she tried to follow the principles

Martineau in 1867

she preached in her writings. Many of the educational works she published during the next two decades were informed in some ways by her domestic and farming projects. When she contributed to *Mind amongst the Spindles: A Miscellany, Wholly Composed by the Factory Girls* (1845), a group of essays by factory operatives of Lowell, Massachusetts, she took into her home several downtrodden servants to whom she planned to teach domestic science. This plan and its results inspired her *Household Education* (1849), which portrayed the orderly household as the orderly society in miniature, maintained by good systems of self-discipline. While *Household Education* was intended for artisan readers, her *Endowed Schools of Ireland* (1859), a collection of articles published in the London *Daily News*, discussed future provisions for the "rising middle classes." In this collection she argued for increased supervision of endowed schools and the extension of competitive examination systems that other reformers were urging many different kinds of educational institutions to adopt. In *Health, Husbandry and Handicraft* (1861) she described her farming projects and threaded arguments about education as the key to social progress throughout her exposition.

During the 1840s Martineau's religious and philosophical views were transformed. Her upbringing had given her a belief in an afterlife and a traditional Unitarian conception of God. He was a real figure who, though not constantly intervening in earthly affairs, sustained the laws of nature. In the mid 1840s she dismissed these two orthodoxies. The philosophical framework she discovered to be most hospitable to her new beliefs was that of positivism, a new perspective in which religious causation was rejected and history was seen as unfolding in a series of specific stages. Martineau felt that the movement of her own belief from religion to positivism followed a natural development of human belief. While it is difficult to pinpoint exactly when her beliefs shifted, by the 1850s she renounced Christianity altogether and adopted what would eventually be termed "agnosticism."

Clear signs of such a change appear in her *Eastern Life, Present and Past* (1848), a work in which she did not regard Christianity as the sole source of spiritual truth. In its final pages she concluded that human knowledge is as yet in its "infancy" and that as humans progress, the "reflective and substantiating powers which characterize the Western Mind [will] be brought into union with the Perceptive, Imaginative and Aspiring quality of the East, so as to create a new order of knowledge and wisdom."

However, nothing could have adequately prepared her Christian admirers for the publication of her correspondence with Henry George Atkinson in *Letters on the Laws of Man's Nature and Development* (1851). Reviewers of this rambling, sometimes contradictory collage of the more fashionable materialist views and debates of the day described a sensational declaration of atheism. It was forbidden reading in many families. Even writers for some of the most radical journals were hostile; George Jacob Holyoake's *Reasoner* was one of its few supporters. Its publication even divided Martineau from her family: she and her brother James, who reviewed the *Letters* as "Mesmeric atheism" in the *Prospective Review*, never spoke afterward.

Undaunted by the strong criticism she received, Martineau moved on to an ambitious project along the same lines when she translated Auguste Comte's *Positive Philosophy* in 1853. She had read the summary by Maximilien Littré, Comte's disciple, as well as the concluding chapter on the French philosopher in George Henry Lewes's *A Biographical History of Philosophy* (1845–1846). She found in Comte's views a welcoming philosophical framework for her developing views, especially in the notion that society passes through three evolutionary stages, and in Comte's optimistic portrayal of the natural laws by which civilization progresses. As she put it, "the positive philosophers have emerged upon the broad, airy, sunny common of nature with firm ground underneath, and unfathomable light overhead."

She considered translating Comte's full six volumes but eventually decided on a free translation and drastic condensation of those six into a single volume, *The Positive Philosophy of Auguste Comte, Freely Translated and Condensed* (1853). Her translation was well received by English positivists such as Lewes, Herbert Spencer, and Thomas Henry Huxley, and secularists such as Holyoake regarded it as a justification of their views. The one exception among Comtean sympathizers was Frederic Harrison, a leading disciple of Comte in Britain, who thought the translation was rather unpolished. Comte approved of the work and recommended it to students as a reliable summary of his system.

Even as she was making this translation, Martineau had become a prolific journalist. From the late 1840s she had begun to write for various periodicals, although her staples included the *Westminster Review*, the *Edinburgh Review*, and the *National Anti-Slavery Journal*. She published several articles in Charles Dickens's *Household Words* until disagreements about Martineau's portrayal of Catholicism in his popular journal ended their professional relations and a subsequent difference of opinion about factory legislation ended in an acrimonious pamphlet war in which Martineau participated with her *The Factory Controversy: A Warning against Meddling Legislation* (1855). Martineau contributed profusely to the London *Daily News*, a relatively new daily that had been founded as a liberal antidote to the London *Times*. Each week she wrote between two and six articles on a broad range of topics. She claimed to be able to write on more than fifty different topics as the occasion required, and these routinely covered not only her pet issues such as the position of women, education, and slavery but also political issues and events from foreign policy to free trade.

Like the campaigns of many reform agitators, Martineau's became international in the 1850s and 1860s. From the time of the Crimean War to the end of the Civil War in the United States she emphasized international issues more than she had in the past, while she continued to cover domestic ones. For Martineau the Crimean War was a major international conflict and a landmark in the evolution or devolution of government; she felt that it would determine whether the principle of government would be defined by eastern or western principles. A long-time pacifist, she supported the war only because the ultimate prize–a representative democracy–was at stake. When the war proved only to contain Russian aggression rather than to resolve the conflict, she felt that British involvement had not been worthwhile, and in 1859 she championed the struggle of "democracy against autocracy" in the conflict between Italy and Austria but did not agitate for Britain to become involved in the war.

In the Indian Mutiny of 1857 she saw the issues as concerning the nature of government and the nature of British colonial relations rather than a simple question of colonial discipline. In *British Rule in India: An Historical Sketch* (1857) and *Suggestions towards the Future Government of India* (1858), both based on articles in the *Daily News,* she provided a competent history of British government in India and a prescription for the future management of colonial affairs. She attacked what she saw as a typically dismissive attitude of the British toward the Indian population, and she argued that British rule in India could succeed only if British authorities took Indian culture and ideas seriously and integrated Indian people into the colonial government. She stressed the importance of understanding Indian culture and claimed that reforms in government could succeed only if they took seriously how deeply rooted existing Indian institutions were. Most important, she argued that colonial rule in India should aim ultimately at producing a society that would rule itself, albeit within a moral and political framework acceptable to Britain. She argued that India had stagnated until it had been electrified by the British Empire—literally, since international telegraphy was beginning at this time—and had been energized by the force of British imperialism, with its "methods of steaming by sea and land, and flashing our thoughts over 1000 miles in a second."

Better relations between Britain and colonial India also offered a possible solution to one of the major dilemmas England faced at the beginning of the Civil War in the United States. Martineau's tireless abolitionist campaigning had helped shape British sympathies with the North, but this political position was complicated by the fact that the British textile industry was economically almost entirely dependent on the cotton of the South. Martineau hoped that it would be possible to grow cotton in India and thereby reduce reliance on cotton produced by American slave labor. For Martineau the issue of slavery raised by the Civil War was the single most important issue in deciding the fate of the United States as a society. She felt that it was foolish for the South to struggle against the inexorable forces of social progress. As Webb reports, she wrote to one acquaintance that it was the "'manifest destiny' of justice and humanity to lead the world." She regarded the Civil War as an engine of progress in both the United States and Britain, in the latter of which it supported her campaign for an extended suffrage.

Martineau argued that the relatively quiescent behavior of the Lancashire working classes, who had suffered privations rather than rioted in support of the Southerners who produced cotton for Lancashire mills, proved them worthy of the franchise. She lived to see the abolition of American slavery and the extension of British suffrage in 1867, although she had little to say about the chaos of the Reconstruction years following the Civil War. This was primarily because her illness had become so pronounced by the mid 1860s that in 1866 she ended her writing career.

In 1854 Martineau had suffered renewed symptoms of illness although she had steadfastly maintained that this was a new malady unrelated to the tumor from which she had suffered in the 1840s and which she still believed had been cured by mesmerism. In 1855 she hurriedly wrote the two volumes of her *Autobiography* and had them privately printed for circulation after her death in order to preclude the possibility of a future editor or publisher altering the text. Although this illness had progressed steadily through the years until she was forced to abandon her writing in the 1860s, she produced works on positivism, the Crimea, India, and the United States, and through the 1850s and 1860s she had joined forces with reformers such as Florence Nightingale and Josephine Butler in various campaigns related to women's health and woman's rights. One of the most successful of these was their campaign for repealing the Contagious Diseases Acts of 1865 and 1867, which required prostitutes to be examined routinely for venereal diseases but did not require men also to be examined. The acts were eventually repealed in 1871.

Following her retirement from the *Daily News* and the end of her writing career in 1866, Martineau compiled a set of notes that her first biographer, Maria Westman Chapman, would subsequently put into narrative form as a third volume to the two-volume *Autobiography* that Martineau had begun writing in 1854 but never brought up to date. Her illness became markedly worse through the next decade, and she died on 27 June 1876.

Although Martineau had hoped to have the last word on her life in her obituary and *Autobiography,* this was not the case. Her brother-in-law performed a public postmortem and claimed to have been correct in his skepticism about mesmerism when he triumphantly revealed that she had a massive ovarian tumor. Other postmortems reached a wider audience. The frank discussion of her contemporaries that she had incorporated in her *Autobiography,* when it was published, caused a sensation, and hagiographers and historians have continued to redefine her place in Victorian culture. Martineau has figured in histories of sociology, economics, education, and the women's movement, and her place as a historiographer and a reform writer of Victorian England is as multifaceted and filled with contradictions as was her reputation among her Victorian contemporaries.

Letters:

Elisabeth Sanders Arbuckle, ed., *Harriet Martineau's Letters to Fanny Wedgwood* (Stanford, Cal.: Stanford University Press, 1983).

Bibliography:

Joseph Barry Rivlin, *Harriet Martineau: A Bibliography of Her Separately Printed Books* (New York: New York Public Library, 1947).

References:

Theodora Bosanquet, *Harriet Martineau: An Essay in Comprehension* (London: Etchells & Macdonald, 1927);

Deirdre David, *Intellectual Women and Victorian Patriarchy: Harriet Martineau, Elizabeth Barrett Browning, George Eliot* (Ithaca, N.Y.: Cornell University Press, 1987);

Florence Fenwick Miller, *Harriet Martineau* (London: W. H. Allen, 1884; Boston: Roberts, 1885);

Valerie Kossew Pichanick, *Harriet Martineau: The Woman and Her Work, 1802-1876* (Ann Arbor: University of Michigan Press, 1980);

Valerie Sanders, *Reason over Passion: Harriet Martineau and the Victorian Novel* (Sussex: Harvester/ New York: St. Martin's Press, 1986);

Gillian Thomas, *Harriet Martineau* (Boston: Twayne, 1985);

Robert Kiefer Webb, *Harriet Martineau, A Radical Victorian* (London: Heinemann, 1960; New York: Columbia University Press, 1960);

Vera Wheatley, *Life and Work of Harriet Martineau* (London: Secker & Warburg, 1957; New York: Essential Books, 1957).

Papers:

The main holdings of the Martineau papers are at Birmingham University Library. Other collections of papers are scattered among repositories such as Dr. Williams's Library, Gordon Square, London; the British Library; the Devon Records Office; and Trinity College, Cambridge.

Henry Mayhew
(25 November 1812 - 25 July 1887)

Lynn MacKay
Trent University

See also the Mayhew entries in *DLB 18: Victorian Novelists After 1885* and *DLB 55: Victorian Prose Writers Before 1867.*

BOOKS: *The Wandering Minstrel: A Farce, in One Act* (London: Miller, 1834; Philadelphia: Turner / New York: Turner & Fisher, 1836);

"But However—": A Farce, in One Act, by Mayhew and Henry Baylis (London: Chapman & Hall, 1838);

What to Teach, and How to Teach It: So That the Child May Become a Wise and Good Man (London: Smith, 1842);

The Prince of Wales Library, No. 1—The Primer (London: Illuminated Magazine, 1844);

The Greatest Plague of Life; or, The Adventures of a Lady in Search of a Good Servant, by Mayhew and Augustus Mayhew (London: Bogue, 1847; London & New York: Routledge, 1859);

The Good Genius That Turned Everything into Gold; or, The Queen Bee and the Magic Dress: A Christmas Fairy Tale, by Mayhew and Augustus Mayhew (London: Bogue, 1847; New York: Harper, 1848?);

Whom to Marry and How to Get Married; or, The Adventures of a Lady in Search of a Good Husband, by Mayhew and Augustus Mayhew (London: Bogue, 1848; New York: Office of the "New World," 1848);

The Image of His Father; or, One Boy Is More Trouble Than a Dozen Girls: Being a Tale of a "Young Monkey," by Mayhew and Augustus Mayhew (London: Hurst, 1848; New York: Harper, 1848);

The Magic of Kindness; or, The Wondrous Story of the Good Huan, by Mayhew and Augustus Mayhew (London: Darton, 1848; New York: Harper, 1849);

Acting Charades; or, Deeds Not Words: A Christmas Game to Make a Long Evening Short, by Mayhew and Augustus Mayhew (London: Bogue, 1850);

The Fear of the World; or, Living for Appearances, by Mayhew and Augustus Mayhew (New York:

Henry Mayhew

Harper, 1850); republished as *Living for Appearances: A Tale* (London: Blackwell, 1855);

London Labour and the London Poor, no. 1–63 (London, 1850–1851); volume 1 and parts of volumes 2 and 3 (London: Woodfall, 1851–1852; 4 volumes [volume 4 by Mayhew and others], London: Griffin, Bohn, 1861–1862);

Low Wages: Their Causes, Consequences and Remedies, 4 parts (London: Woodfall, 1851);

1851; or, The Adventures of Mr. and Mrs. Sandboys and Family, Who Came up to London to "Enjoy Themselves," and to See the Great Exhibition, by Mayhew, George Cruikshank, and John Binny (London: Bogue, 1851); republished as *The World's Show, 1851; or, The Adventures of Mr. and Mrs. Sandboys and Family, Who Came up to London to "Enjoy Themselves," and to See the Great Exhibition* (London: Bogue, 1851); republished as *1851; or, The Adventures of Mr. and Mrs. Sandboys, Their Son and Daughter, Who Came up to London to Enjoy Themselves and to See the Great Exhibition* (New York: Stringer & Townsend, 1851);

The Mormons; or, Latter-Day Saints: With Memories of the Life and Death of Joseph Smith, the "American Mahomet," anonymous (London: Office of the National Illustrated Library, 1851); republished as *History of the Mormons; or, Latter-Day Saints: With Memories of the Life and Death of Joseph Smith, the "American Mahomet"* (Auburn, N.Y.: Derby & Miller, 1852; revised and corrected edition, London: Ward & Lock, 1856); enlarged as *The Religious, Social, and Political History of the Mormons, or Latter-Day Saints, from Their Origin to the Present Time: Containing Full Statements of Their Doctrines, Government and Condition, and Memoirs of Their Founder, Joseph Smith* (New York & Auburn: Miller, Orton & Mulligan, 1856); enlarged again as *Life among the Mormons; or, The Religious, Social, and Political History of the Mormons, from Their Origin to the Present Time: Containing Full Statements of Their Doctrines, Government and Condition, and Memoirs of Their Founder, Joseph Smith* (New York: Hurst, 1860);

The Story of the Peasant-Boy Philosopher; or, "A Child Gathering Pebbles on the Sea Shore" (London: Bogue, 1854; New York: Harper, 1855);

The Wonders of Science; or, Young Humphrey Davy (the Cornish Apothecary's Boy, Who Taught Himself Natural Philosophy, and Eventually Became President of the Royal Society): The Life of a Wonderful Boy, Written for Boys (London: Routledge, 1854; New York: Harper, 1854);

The Rhine and Its Picturesque Scenery (London: Bogue / New York: Bangs, 1856); republished as *The Lower Rhine and Its Picturesque Scenery* (London & New York: Routledge, Warne & Routledge, 1860);

The Great World of London, parts 1-9 (London: Bogue, 1856); completed by Mayhew and Binny as *The Criminal Prisons of London and Scenes of Prison Life* (London: Griffin, Bohn, 1862);

The Upper Rhine and Its Picturesque Scenery (London: Routledge, 1858; London & New York: Routledge, Warne & Routledge, 1860);

Young Benjamin Franklin (London: Griffin, Bohn, 1861; New York: Harper, 1862);

The Boyhood of Martin Luther; or, The Sufferings of the Heroic Little Beggar-Boy Who Afterwards Became the Great German Reformer (London: Sampson Low, 1863; New York: Harper, 1864; New York: Whittaker, 1891);

German Life and Manners as Seen in Saxony at the Present Day: With an Account of Village Life–Town Life–Fashionable Life–Domestic Life–Married Life–School and University Life, &c., of Germany at the Present Time, 2 volumes (London: W. H. Allen, 1864);

Lon on Characters and the Humorous Side of London Life, by Mayhew and others (London: Rivers, 1870);

Report Concerning the Trade and Hours of Closing Usual among the Unlicensed Victualing Establishments Now Open for the Unrestricted Sale of Beer, Wine and Spirits at Certain So-Called "Working Men's Clubs," Distributed throughout the Metropolis (London: Judd, 1871);

London Characters: Illustrations of the Humour, Pathos, and Peculiarities of London Life, by Mayhew and others (London: Chatto & Windus, 1874);

Mont Blanc: A Comedy, in Three Acts, by Mayhew and Athol Mayhew (London: Privately printed, 1874);

The Morning Chronicle Survey of Labour and the Poor (Horsham, U.K.: Caliban Books, 1981)–comprises "Labour and the Poor," letters 1-82, *Morning Chronicle* (London), 19 October 1849-12 December 1850.

PLAY PRODUCTIONS: *The Wandering Minstrel*, London, Royal Fitzroy Theatre, 16 January 1834;

"But However–," London, Theatre Royal, Hay-Market, 30 October 1838.

OTHER: *Figaro in London*, volumes 4-8, edited by Mayhew, January 1835-August 1839;

Punch; or, The London Charivari, edited by Mayhew, 17 July 1841-1842;

The Comic Almanac: An Ephemeris in Jest and Earnest, Containing Merry Tales, Humorous Poetry, Quips, and Oddities, edited by Mayhew (London: Bogue, 1850-1851);

"Home Is Home, Be It Never So Homely," in *Meliora; or, Better Times to Come*, edited by Charles John Talbot, nineteenth Earl of Shrewsbury, as Viscount Ingestre (London: Parker, 1852);

"On Capital Punishments," in *Three Papers on Capital Punishment* (London: Cox & Wyman, 1856), pp. 32-61;

Cover for a weekly part of Mayhew's study of London workers

Morning News, edited by Mayhew, January 1859;
The Shops and Companies of London, and the Grades and Manufactories of Great Britain, edited by Mayhew, parts 1-7 (London: Strand, 1865);
Only Once a Year, edited by Mayhew (London: Stevens & Richardson, 1870).

SELECTED PERIODICAL PUBLICATION–
UNCOLLECTED: "The Great Exhibition," parts 1-9, *News and Literary Chronicle* (Edinburgh), May 1851–July 1851.

Henry Mayhew was both a founder of *Punch; or, The London Charivari* (1841) and a preeminent investigator of poverty in nineteenth-century London. While his association with this humorous magazine was brief, Mayhew's interviews with the poor provide historians with a rich source of information into the attitudes, beliefs, and problems of working-class Londoners. Although his work was not free from bias, he was the first social investigator to attempt to let the poor tell their stories in their own words. His investigation for the London *Morning Chronicle,* in particular, was popular, and his work also sheds light on upper-class attitudes toward poverty during the mid nineteenth century.

Henry Mayhew was the fourth son of Joshua Dorset Joseph Mayhew, a prosperous London solicitor, and Mary Ann Fenn Mayhew, his wife–a couple who were parents of seventeen children. Joshua Mayhew was the archetypal straight-laced Victorian father, and Mayhew spent much of his life rebelling against but never quite escaping from the bourgeois respectability that his father represented. Mayhew was sent to school at Westminster, but he ran away from there at age fifteen in order to escape a beating that he regarded as unfair. His first ambition was to conduct research in chemistry, an unheard-of profession and a vocational choice that his father staunchly opposed. Joshua Mayhew apprenticed his son as a midshipman bound for India, but for unknown reasons this career was also not successful; by the late 1820s young Mayhew was back in London. Hoping that his son would ultimately follow in his footsteps and become a solicitor, Joshua Mayhew apprenticed his son in his own law office in the 1830s, but this attempt to establish Henry as a solicitor also proved to be spectacularly unsuccessful: young Mayhew forgot to file some papers, and as a result his father was nearly arrested during dinner one evening. During this period Mayhew began to conduct many chemistry experiments and to move in literary and journalistic circles.

Having reached the end of his legal career, Mayhew–bolstered by an allowance of one pound a week from his father–began to devote his energies to science and literature. He set up a laboratory in the house of his older brother Alfred and continued to conduct chemistry experiments, one of which exploded and greatly damaged the kitchen. Mayhew also became part of a bohemian circle that included the young Charles Dickens and William Makepeace Thackeray. With Mark Lemon and Stirling Coyne, Mayhew founded *Punch* magazine and became its first editor, but around one year later the magazine was sold to new owners, and Mayhew was eased out as editor. In part, Mayhew's removal as editor probably resulted from his erratic nature: he alternated between bouts of intense energy and indolence, a pattern of behavior that persisted throughout his life and, in conjunction with his optimistic but irresponsible temperament, caused him rarely to realize his potential.

In 1844 he married Jane Jerrold, the daughter of Douglas Jerrold, a fellow contributor to *Punch,* and the Mayhews eventually had two children, Amy and Athol. Mayhew spent large sums decorating the new house in which he and his family settled at Fulham, and he helped found *Iron Times* (1846), a newspaper attempting to capitalize on the rapid growth of railways. When the paper failed that same year, late in 1846 Mayhew petitioned for bankruptcy, which seems to have permanently ruptured his relationship with his father. When Joshua Mayhew died in 1858, he left an estate worth £50,000—but of this total Henry received only an allowance of £1 a week; Jane, his wife, received £2 a week.

Immediately after the bankruptcy Mayhew began writing novels to reestablish his financial position, and in October 1849 he took a job with the *Morning Chronicle,* a London daily newspaper that supported free trade and that hired him to investigate the state of the London poor. Mayhew wrote a total of eighty-two articles for the *Morning Chronicle,* which published these between 19 October 1849 and 12 December 1850. This series of articles, which Mayhew called letters, formed part of a much larger *Morning Chronicle* project that included reports from the mining and manufacturing centers as well as the rural districts of England. Being published in the aftermath of the Chartist agitations, the political uprisings on the Continent in 1848, and a cholera epidemic that had killed thirteen thousand people in London alone during the summer of 1849, these studies were conducted in an atmosphere of concern for social stability.

In these letters Mayhew set out to document the living and working conditions of the London poor, whom he defined as those whose incomes were insufficient to provide for the necessities of life. He divided these poor into three groups: those who were willing to work, those who were unwilling to do so, and those who could not work. He intended to consider all of the metropolitan poor, but various disputes and his own waning energy prevented him from ever doing so.

His articles investigate the lives and working conditions of those employed in many trades and occupations. The manufacturing trades, which are covered in thirty-two of the letters, occupy a large proportion of Mayhew's attention, and of these articles, twenty-five concern the clothing, footwear, and woodworking trades. He also broadly classifies the trades he investigated as honorable and dishonorable: workers in honorable trades were protected by strong trade societies, were paid by the hour, and were more or less permanently employed by one firm. Workers in the dishonorable trades were highly exploited, were poorly paid (based on the number of pieces they produced), had no trade societies to protect their interests, and worked for various employers as jobs became available.

Unskilled laborers and service workers are treated in fewer letters than are manufacturing workers, with dock and transit workers figuring prominently. Devoting seven letters to the study of the costermongers, a group whose honesty Mayhew doubted, he also examines the lives of some of those who would not work. With most of his attention given to the manufacturing laborers, Mayhew thus presents a highly selective examination of certain segments of the London poor in his *Morning Chronicle* letters.

Mayhew continued this project until December 1850, by which time his comments on free trade had become increasingly critical. Claiming that his comments were being censored, Mayhew left the paper but continued his investigations independently through 1851 by publishing a weekly series, *London Labour and the London Poor,* from 14 December 1850 to 21 February 1852, when a legal dispute between Mayhew and his printer halted his studies permanently. This dispute, which might have been easily resolved, seems to have provided Mayhew with an excuse to abandon the project, and despite several desultory attempts to revive these studies in later years, the project was never completed.

Some of the material that Mayhew incorporated in *London Labour and the London Poor: A Cyclopaedia of the Condition and Earnings of Those That Will Work, Those That Cannot Work, and Those That Will Not Work* (1851), especially that on street traders, was reprinted or expanded from his *Morning Chronicle* articles. All of these parts were bound in volume form and were subsequently published as the first two volumes of the 1851–1862 edition of *London Labour and the London Poor*. All of the first volume and part of the second focus on street sellers. The second also considers street buyers and finders, the latter of which include workers such as rubbish collectors and chimney and crossing sweeps. A study of prostitutes as well as a comparative study of various laboring societies and a classification of workers and nonworkers formed a third volume added to the 1851 edition. This added volume was only 192 pages, and an expanded third volume was created for the 1861 edition when new material (which Augustus Mayhew contributed) on exterminators and street performers as well as reprinted pieces from the *Morning Chronicle* series on cabinetmakers, dock and transit workers, and vagrants was added. In 1862 a fourth volume, dealing with those who refused to work, was added, and to this volume Mayhew contributed only a piece that he had published earlier on prostitution. Other investigators wrote articles on beggars, thieves, and swindlers for this final volume.

Thus, while the *Morning Chronicle* letters concentrate on manufacturing trades, the *London Labour and the London Poor* investigation emphasizes the lives of street folk and those who will not work. This change in emphasis, however, does not constitute a major change in the way Mayhew saw the problem of poverty, for his understanding of poverty and the solutions he proposed were developed during his surveys for the *Morning Chronicle* and *London Labour and the London Poor* and remained consistent throughout the two investigations. Given the amount of reprinting and borrowing from the newspaper series that Mayhew did in compiling *London Labour and the London Poor,* it would be surprising to find otherwise: he reproduced sixteen letters in somewhat rearranged form in the second investigation, and parts of many other letters appeared in *London Labour and the London Poor.*

Mayhew's views of poverty reveal in part how he understood social relations. He believed that all social classes had obligations and responsibilities to each other, and this belief underlay his understanding of the plight of the poor. He saw two causes for poverty, and the first of these included the economic system, which was beyond the control of the poor. He believed that skilled workers and laborers were poverty stricken because of the sweated-labor system, not through any fault of their own. Workers in the sweated trades were employed–at very low wages, for long hours, and under poor conditions–to produce items for consumers who wanted cheap, ready-made products. Mayhew greatly admired the courage and perseverance of workers caught in the trammels of this system, and he blamed their difficulties on the greed of large middlemen and contractors who built their own profits by forcing down wages. He faulted these middlemen and contractors precisely because they were not meeting what he saw as their social responsibilities to ensure that workers in their trades could earn decent and fair wages for their labor.

Mayhew came to realize that wage levels were not being set by the free market forces of supply and demand as proponents of political economy supposed. Instead, he discovered, when wages were cut by contractors and middlemen, workers responded by working longer hours in an attempt to maintain their previous income levels. When workers labored for longer hours, this in effect established an artificial surplus of labor and kept wages permanently at increasingly lower levels. Mayhew summed up the situation by observing that underpayment led to overwork, and overwork brought further underpayment. He also believed that the social environment was an important cause of poverty, for children born to the criminal or semi-criminal poor would never have known a better way of life and consequently would not seek to struggle to better themselves.

Mayhew did not think that the poor were free from blame for their condition, however, and this belief was the basis for what he saw as a second cause of poverty: individual choice. He thought that many of the poor–especially those who would not work–had freely chosen to live in morally degraded ways, and those poor who had been born to respectable parents but who chose to become beggars, vagrants, and criminals because they disliked steady work earned his strongest censure. He believed that such people were incorrigible and all but irreclaimable, and he thought them dangerous because they corrupted the honest and respectable poor with whom they interacted. Indeed, he disapproved of any association between those whom he considered upright and those whom he thought were morally depraved, whether from choice or ignorance of any other way of life. He opposed the "ragged schools" of Anthony Ashley Cooper, Lord Ashley, for instance, because their existence forced honest children to mix with young thieves and thereby be led astray. Mayhew quoted a policeman who opined that, by teaching the children to read, these schools simply enabled them to steal items with the highest price tags and did not effect any kind of moral reformation.

Because of such beliefs, Mayhew's attitudes toward the poor varied, depending on whom he was interviewing. In the *Morning Chronicle* series, with its emphasis on those who were willing to work but had difficulties doing so because of the London labor market, Mayhew is therefore sympathetic and admiring. In the second series, which focuses more on the disreputable street folk than on those willing laborers, Mayhew is much more critical of his subjects although he is also clearly fascinated with them. In both series those subjects of his interviews emerge as real people, and their discussions of their lives and problems were a revelation to upper-class readers.

If Mayhew's understanding of poverty is remarkably sensitive, his solutions are more problematic. Desiring a society in which all classes meet their social responsibilities, Mayhew is especially concerned that the rich accept their responsibilities toward the poor, and he proposes many programs to effect this. One proposal is for employers to see that workers are paid a fair wage and are ensured decent working conditions. He also wants free edu-

Illustrations from Mayhew's London Labour and the London Poor *(1851)*

cation provided to cultivate moral virtue in the reclaimable poor, and he favors sanitary legislation to force cheap lodging houses, which he believes are breeding grounds for vagrancy, prostitution, thievery, and mendicancy, to be cleaned up. Generally he approves of upper-class activities that help the poor to attain economic independence and disapproves of activities that demoralize the poor by encouraging ôhem to live off charity rather than through their own honest labor.

Mayhew hopes that by shouldering their social responsibilities toward the poor the upper classes will lead the working class to respectability, which he conceives as the familiar Victorian constellation of values. He wants hardworking, sober, thrifty, honest, and knowledgeable working class. Mayhew is never happy, however, with the notion that these people should try to better themselves through organized actions such as strikes. He occasionally espouses such activities, but only as a last resort—when it is clear that the upper classes have no intention of meeting their obligations. Thus, while Mayhew does not question the values of middle-class England, he is critical of how the upper classes implement these values in fulfilling (or failing to fulfill) their obligations to society.

The great problem with the solutions Mayhew proposes for poverty is his inability to explain how they can be achieved. He can never say, for example, how employers can be forced to pay their workers a fair wage, or how this fair wage is to be determined. It is generally unclear how the upper classes can be brought to accept their social responsibilities as Mayhew understood such obligations.

The methodology he uses in conducting his social investigations differs markedly from that of twentieth-century social scientists. One of the most striking things about his investigations is his penchant for classification. He has an immense, complex subject—the London poor—and his investigations have to be divided into manageable sections; some overall framework must also be established. Problems arise with his methodology, however, for two reasons. First, throughout his investigations he keeps developing new classification systems, which sometimes conflict with earlier ones. Second, he does not follow any of his organizational schemes in any systematic way. Instead, Mayhew jumps from trade to trade, or wherever his clues lead him, in conducting his investigations. Thus, he begins a *Morning Chronicle* investigation by examining silk weavers, and when he learns that in slack times they turn to dock work, he immediately begins to explore this occupation. During an interview with some dockworkers he learns that they live in cheap lodging houses where the conditions are deplorable, and he at once turns to an examination of these residences. This pattern of investigation recurs throughout his work.

His classification is systematic, however, within his discussion of each trade or group that he examines. Mayhew begins to study a trade by giving a brief history of it and then sets out the divisions within it. Thus, for the footwear trade he discusses shoemakers and bootmakers and subdivides each of these vocations into those who make these forms of footwear for women and those who make each for men. He also discusses separately the various footwear makers in the West End of London (principally the honorable sector) and those in the East End, who are for the most part sweated workers. Once he has established the necessary divisions, Mayhew then interviews workers in each category and reports their statements in the first person although he removes his questions from the published interview.

Mayhew tries to ensure that the interview information is reliable and typical of the workers he examines, but he does not do this on the basis of modern statistical techniques. Consistently seeking out gentlemen who are familiar with the trades and groups he is examining, Mayhew asks them to recommend names of reliable and knowledgeable candidates for interviews. He also asks workers within a trade to recommend knowledgeable colleagues. From his interviewees he tries to elicit information about many past and present conditions: wage levels, hours and regularity of employment, and working conditions. He also inquires about living conditions; costs of rent, food, and other expenses; and the family profile (details such as the number of children in the family and the identity of those who are working, for example). He ascertains his subjects' levels of formal education, their religious affiliations, and the kinds of amusements their families enjoy. Mayhew is concerned not merely with the jobs that the poor hold or try to hold; rather, he tries to explore their whole way of life.

Where possible, Mayhew supports his interview information with statistical data. He had a mania for statistics, and sometimes his figures do not support anything at all but are given purely for their own sake. One can learn all manner of things from Mayhew's investigations—everything from his estimate of the amount of horse dung annually deposited on London streets (36,662 tons) to crime rates throughout the country. Whereas twentieth-century social scientists use interview evidence to illustrate statistically based data and allow statistics to determine what interview information is used, this is not

Mayhew's procedure. His statistics do not determine whom he interviews. Because statistical science was just being developed during this time in the nineteenth century, to demand of Mayhew what later social-science methodology considers to be orthodox is patently unfair.

Mayhew's investigations engendered controversy in his own day and among historians. His increasingly critical comments about political economy aroused the wrath of *Economist* magazine even before he left his position with the *Morning Chronicle* over this same issue. The *Economist* accused him of displaying an excessive sentimentality that cast a slur on the commercial prosperity of England. To this defense of political economy the *Economist* added a somewhat unfair criticism of Mayhew's letters on the needlewomen: the magazine accepted at face value the statements that one of the most notorious of the ready-made clothing contractors gave about how much the clothing workers earned.

A second controversy erupted over Mayhew's criticisms of the ragged schools. He attacked these schools by reporting many critical interviews and failing to allow their proponents to provide any information. When the secretary of the ragged schools attacked Mayhew's accuracy, Mayhew was forced to include statements from witnesses to his interviews, who denied that he had manipulated his subjects or suppressed information.

Mayhew's investigations of the lives of the metropolitan poor caused a great sensation in upper-class London, where their publication brought praise from Thackeray, Thomas Hughes, and Frederick Denison Maurice. Charles Kingsley drew on Mayhew's material in writing his novel *Alton Locke, Tailor and Poet: An Autobiography* (1850) and in writing *Cheap Clothes and Nasty* (1850), his anonymous pamphlet condemning the ready-made-clothing market. Mayhew's articles on the needlewomen, whose low pay forced them into prostitution, evoked the most powerful responses to any of his investigations. For these poor needlewomen Sidney Herbert and Lord Ashley proposed an emigration scheme that was supported by William Ewart Gladstone and the provincial press, although not by Mayhew, who did not believe that emigration was an adequate response to the problem. Horrified by Mayhew's revelations about sweated workers, readers of the *Morning Chronicle* sent the newspaper donations that at one time totaled £800.

Between 1852 and 1855 Mayhew seems to have left England. He went to Germany, possibly to live cheaply, for at least part of the period. After he returned to England he became active once more in journalism and in the theater. His last in-

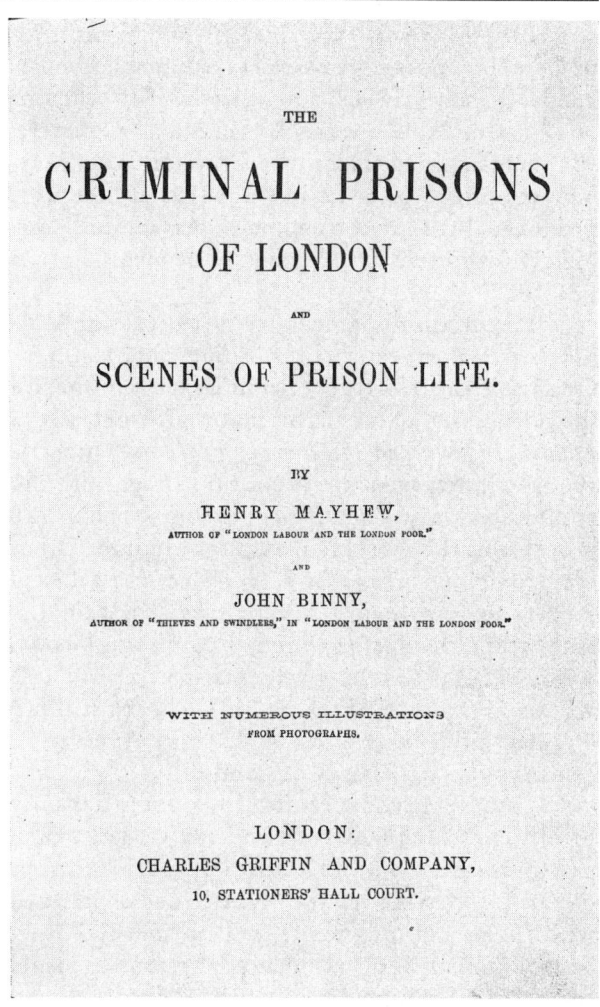

Title page for the exposé that Mayhew began publishing serially in 1856 as The Great World of London *and completed with the help of John Binny in 1862*

vestigation of the lower classes, *The Great World of London,* less innovative than his earlier surveys of the London poor, was published serially in nine parts through much of 1856 before it ended in midsentence when Mayhew's publisher, David Bogue, suddenly died. It was eventually completed in collaboration with John Binny and published in 1862 as *The Criminal Prisons of London and Scenes of Prison Life*. In this investigation of London criminals Mayhew was not permitted to interview any convicts, but he provided detailed descriptions of how the inmates of each prison spent their days.

Contemporaries do not record Mayhew's activities after the mid 1850s. He seemed to suffer continued financial difficulties and possibly marital problems also. The remarkable energy he had shown in conducting his social surveys between 1849 and 1852 dissipated, and by the late 1850s he was resuming a bohemian way of life. He produced scientific books for children, and he returned to Germany, possibly to escape creditors, in the late 1850s, the early 1860s, and again in 1870 when he and his son Athol apparently served as war correspondents during the Franco-Prussian War. Mayhew continued to write in the 1870s although he produced little of consequence. An almost completely forgotten man, he died of bronchitis on 25 July 1887.

Historians disagree in trying to evaluate Mayhew's social investigations. Some, such as Peter Quennell and Gertrude Himmelfarb, emphasize the sensational nature of his material, especially in *London Labour and the London Poor,* in which he spent so much time on the colorful street folk who comprised only a small proportion—perhaps 20 percent—of the working classes of London. Other historians, most notably Eileen Yeo and Edward P. Thompson, regard Mayhew as a systematic, empirical investigator whose attempts at objectivity have been seriously underestimated. What is certain is that Mayhew and his work are still frequently cited in studies of the mid-nineteenth-century working classes of London.

Henry Mayhew realized his potential only briefly, between late 1849 and early 1852, when he conducted two of the most important surveys of the London poor. While his work is imbued with his moral judgments and his methodology does not meet twentieth-century canons of social scientific investigation, his studies are a rich and illuminating exploration of working-class life and conditions during the mid nineteenth century. They also reveal much about upper-class attitudes to the problem of poverty. While his work has always engendered controversy, it will undoubtedly continue to be a valued resource.

Biography:
Anne Humpherys, *Travels into the Poor Man's Country* (Athens: University of Georgia Press, 1977).

References:
John L. Bradley, Introduction to *Selections from "London Labour and The London Poor"* (London: Oxford University Press, 1965);

Henry Sutherland Edwards, *Personal Recollections* (London: Cassell, 1900);

Gertrude Himmelfarb, "The Culture of Poverty," in *The Victorian City: Images and Realities,* 2 volumes, edited by H. J. Dyos and Michael Wolff (London: Routledge & Kegan Paul, 1973), II: 707-736;

Himmelfarb, *The Idea of Poverty* (New York: Vintage, 1985);

Himmelfarb, "Mayhew's Poor: A Problem of Identity," *Victorian Studies,* 14 (1971): 307-320;

Anne Humpherys, *Henry Mayhew* (Boston: Twayne, 1984);

Peter Quennell, ed., *Mayhew's London* (London: Kimber, 1951);

P. E. Razzell and R. W. Wainwright, *The Victorian Working Class: Selections from the Morning Chronicle* (London: Cass, 1974);

John D. Rosenberg, Introduction to *London Labour and the London Poor,* 4 volumes (New York: Dover, 1968);

F. B. Smith, "Mayhew's Convict," *Victorian Studies,* 21 (1979): 431-445;

Edward P. Thompson, "Mayhew and the *Morning Chronicle,*" in *The Unknown Mayhew,* edited by Thompson and Eileen Yeo (Harmondsworth: Penguin, 1973), pp. 9-55;

Thompson, "The Political Education of Henry Mayhew," *Victorian Studies,* 11 (1967): 41-62;

Karel Williams, *From Pauperism to Poverty* (London: Routledge & Kegan Paul, 1981);

Eileen Yeo, "Mayhew as a Social Investigator," in *The Unknown Mayhew,* edited by Thompson and Yeo (Harmondsworth: Penguin, 1973), pp. 56-109.

John Stuart Mill
(20 May 1806 - 7 May 1873)

Eugene R. August
University of Dayton

See also the Mill entry in *DLB 55: Victorian Prose Writers Before 1867.*

BOOKS: *A System of Logic, Ratiocinative and Inductive, Being a Connected View of the Principles of Evidence, and the Methods of Scientific Investigation* (2 volumes, London: Parker, 1843; revised, 1846; 1 volume, New York: Harper, 1846; revised again, 1851, 1856, 1862, 1865, 1868, 1872);

Essays on Some Unsettled Questions of Political Economy (London: Parker, 1844);

Principles of Political Economy, with Some of Their Applications to Social Philosophy, 2 volumes (London: Parker, 1848; Boston: Little & Brown, 1848; revised, 1849, 1852, 1857, 1862, 1865, 1868, 1872);

On Liberty (London: Parker, 1859; Boston: Ticknor & Fields, 1863);

Thoughts on Parliamentary Reform (London: Parker, 1859; enlarged, 1859);

Dissertations and Discussions: Political, Philosophical, and Historical; Reprinted Chiefly from the Edinburgh and Westminster Reviews (4 volumes: volumes 1–2, London: Parker, 1859; volume 3, London: Longmans, Green, Reader & Dyer, 1867; volume 4, London: Parker, 1875; 5 volumes, Boston: Spencer, 1865–1875);

Considerations on Representative Government (London: Parker, Son & Bourn, 1861; New York: Harper, 1862);

Utilitarianism (London: Parker, Son & Bourn, 1863; revised, 1864, 1867, 1871; Boston: Small, 1887);

Auguste Comte and Positivism (London: Trübner, 1865; Philadelphia: Lippincott, 1866);

An Examination of Sir William Hamilton's Philosophy, and of the Principal Philosophical Questions Discussed in His Writings (1 volume, London: Longmans, Green, Longmans, Roberts & Green, 1865; 2 volumes, Boston: Spencer, 1865; revised, 1867, 1872);

John Stuart Mill (Radio Times Hulton Picture Library)

Speech of John Stuart Mill, M.P., on the Admission of Women to the Electoral Franchise (London: Trübner, 1867);

Personal Representation: Speech . . . Delivered in the House of Commons (London: Henderson, Rait & Fenton, 1867);

Inaugural Address Delivered to the University of St. Andrews, Feb. 1st, 1867 (London: Longmans, Green, Reader & Dyer, 1867; Boston: Littell & Gay, 1867);

England and Ireland (London: Longmans, Green, Reader & Dyer, 1868);

The Subjection of Women (London: Longmans, Green, Reader & Dyer, 1869; Philadelphia: Lippincott, 1869);

Chapters and Speeches on the Irish Land Question (London: Longmans, Green, Reader & Dyer, 1870);

Autobiography (London: Longmans, Green, Reader & Dyer, 1873; New York: Holt, 1873);

Nature, The Utility of Religion, and Theism (London: Longmans, Green, Reader & Dyer, 1874); republished as *Three Essays on Religion* (New York: Holt, 1874);

Early Essays by John Stuart Mill, edited by J. W. M. Gibbs (London: Bell, 1897);

The Spirit of the Age, edited by Frederick A. von Hayek (Chicago: University of Chicago Press, 1942);

Mill on Bentham and Coleridge, edited by F. R. Leavis (London: Chatto & Windus, 1950; New York: Stewart, 1951);

Prefaces to Liberty: Selected Writings of John Stuart Mill, edited by Bernard Wishy (Boston: Beacon, 1959);

John Mill's Boyhood Visit to France: Being a Journal and Notebook Written by John Stuart Mill in France, 1820-21, edited by Anna Jean Mill (Toronto: University of Toronto Press, 1960);

The Early Draft of John Stuart Mill's Autobiography, edited by Jack Stillinger (Urbana: University of Illinois Press, 1961);

Essays on Literature and Society, edited by J. B. Schneewind (New York: Collier, 1965);

Literary Essays, edited by Edward Alexander (Indianapolis: Bobbs-Merrill, 1967);

The Nigger Question, by Thomas Carlyle, and *The Negro Question,* by Mill, edited by Eugene R. August (New York: Appleton-Century-Crofts, 1971);

Essays on Poetry, edited by F. Parvin Sharpless (Columbia: University of South Carolina Press, 1976);

J. S. Mill and the Irish Land Question, with an essay by Richard Ned Lebour (Philadelphia: Institute for the Study of Human Issues, 1979).

Collection: *Collected Works of John Stuart Mill,* edited by John M. Robson and others, 33 volumes (Toronto: University of Toronto Press, 1963-1991).

OTHER: Jeremy Bentham, *The Rationale of Judicial Evidence, Specially Applied to English Practice,* edited, with a preface, by Mill, 5 volumes (London: Hunt & Clarke, 1827);

Public Agency or Trading Companies: Memorials on Sanitary Reform, and on the Economical and Administrative Principles of Water-Supply for the Metropolis, Including Correspondence between John Stuart Mill and the Metropolitan Sanitary Association (London: Gadsby, 1851);

Henry Romilly, *Public Responsibility and Vote by Ballot,* letter appended by Mill (London, 1867);

James Mill, *Analysis of the Phenomenon of the Human Mind, with Notes Illustrative and Critical by Alexander Bain, Andrew Findlater, and George Grote,* edited, with additional notes, by John Stuart Mill, 2 volumes (London: Longmans, Green, Reader & Dyer, 1869);

Programme of the Land Tenure Reform Association, explanatory statement by Mill (London: Longmans, Green, Reader & Dyer, 1871);

Henry Aimé Ouvry, *Stein and His Reforms in Prussia,* appendix with advice by Mill to land reformers (London: Kerby & Endean, 1873);

Plato, *Four Dialogues of Plato, Including the "Apology of Socrates,"* translated and annotated by Mill (London: Watts, 1946).

In his *Autobiography* (1873) John Stuart Mill reports that in 1821 he discovered that his mission in life was to be "a reformer of the world." Mill was only fourteen years old at the time, and his later intellectual development expanded and modified many of his youthful enthusiasms. But he never abandoned his choice to be an improver of the human lot. Throughout his lifetime Mill used his impressive reasoning and rhetorical skills to support various reforms—philosophical, legal, ethical, educational, and social—and many of his writings are widely recognized as classics of the liberal reform tradition.

Mill was bred, quite literally, to be a social reformer. Born in London, he was the son of James Mill, a disciple of Jeremy Bentham, the brilliant and eccentric Utilitarian philosopher. Bentham advocated many social reforms, most notably in prisons, government, and the law. James and his wife, Harriet Burrow Mill, moved next door to Bentham's house in Westminster, where James gave his eldest son one of the world's most remarkable educations. Young Mill began learning Greek at the age of three, and during the next eleven years he also learned Latin, political economy, logic, history, mathematics, and philosophy, along with a smattering of literature. By the time he was fourteen years old he had acquired the equivalent of a university education as well as an ability to question and to think for himself. But his tutelage had drawbacks. The lack of physical play stunted Mill's motor development; his father's sternness withered Mill's spontaneity; and the lack of love in the Mill household left psychosexual scars on Mill's personality.

Mill's education succeeded brilliantly, however, in its main objective—to turn the boy's mind into a model of Utilitarian logic and social awareness. In 1821 when the boy read a French version of Bentham's *Introduction to the Principles of Morals and Legislation* (1789), the book capped his entire education by inspiring young Mill to become a "reformer of the world," exactly as his father had planned.

Benthamite philosophy was based on the principle of utility, or the greatest happiness principle. Bentham gauged the morality of any social action by whether or not it fostered the greatest happiness of the greatest number of people. Such a principle allowed the Utilitarian reformer to advocate many political, legal, and social reforms, and young Mill proceeded to do just that. He formed the Utilitarian Society. He distributed birth-control information to workers, and for his efforts he apparently was arrested for disseminating "obscene" literature. He began writing articles for periodicals such as the *Westminster Review* and became actively involved with the Philosophical Radicals, a group of reformers seeking to acquire political influence in Parliament. Mill's social activism was only moderately restrained (at least initially) when he started to work at the East India Office in 1823.

What sidetracked his reform enthusiasm was a "mental crisis" in 1826. Feeling was building in England for a reform bill that would widen the voting franchise, but Mill was prevented from fully participating in such reform activities when he suffered an emotional breakdown that lasted about a year. His malaise has been the subject of endless speculation by biographers, and in his *Autobiography* Mill attributes his crisis to the fact that his education tended to drain away the feelings and to leave him, instead, disposed to respond to people and human events with rational calculation. Gradually Mill recovered from his crisis by rediscovering his feelings, but his process of recovery forced him to begin questioning Benthamite ideology and led him to discover value in the conservative social thought of Samuel Taylor Coleridge and in the lyrical jeremiads of Thomas Carlyle, the Scottish "mystic."

When an 1829 article by Thomas Babington Macaulay in the *Edinburgh Review* attacked James Mill's philosophical method as too narrow, young Mill was forced to admit that some of Macaulay's strictures were valid. Mill began to recognize that an understanding of human behavior cannot, and should not, be reduced to crude calculations of pleasure and pain. He began to see that any attempt to reform society would have to be based on a con-

Harriet Taylor, circa 1834 (courtesy of F. A. Hayek)

cept of happiness founded on human development, both personal and social.

Mill was further distracted in the early 1830s by a relationship that profoundly shaped the rest of his life. In 1830 he met Harriet Hardy Taylor, the wife of John Taylor, a London merchant, and within a year Mill had fallen in love with her. The resulting triangle was painful for all involved. Eventually Harriet chose to remain as Taylor's wife in name only, while she and Mill shared an intimate but platonic friendship. After Taylor's death in 1849, Harriet and Mill married in 1851 and remained so until her death in 1858.

The nature and value of Harriet Taylor's influence on Mill is a matter of great disagreement among scholars. Mill regarded her as a model of human excellence, and she most likely increased his awareness of the disabilities of women in nineteenth-century England and encouraged his tolerance for socialist reform experiments. The gossip and social pressure that Mill and she experienced sensitized them to how vulnerable individual freedom is when threatened by society's intolerance, which became a major theme in Mill's *On Liberty* (1859).

In the 1830s Mill continued to be ambivalent about parliamentary reform. On the one hand he

Mill, circa 1840 (British Library of Political and Economic Science)

strove mightily to capitalize on the opportunity promised by passage of the 1832 Reform Bill and the subsequent election of several Philosophical Radicals to Parliament. In 1835 he founded and edited the *London Review,* which, after a year, became the *London and Westminster Review,* which he operated as a showplace of enlightened radical views. On the other hand, Mill was beset by personal and intellectual turmoil. His relationship with Harriet Taylor and, in 1836, the death of his father took their toll on Mill's emotions. He was also struggling confusedly to supplement the narrow Benthamism of his youth with philosophical "manysidedness."

However much he speculated about immediate, practical reform measures such as universal manhood suffrage, annual Parliaments, and voting by ballot, he continued to feel that larger issues were at stake. At the heart of his discontent was his sense that Bentham's greatest happiness principle enshrined the ordinary pleasures of the ordinary person as an ultimate standard. This principle did not allow for the possibility of human moral development, and it did not encourage growth toward an ideal concept of humanity. Although in supernatural matters Mill is perhaps best described as an agnostic, he held to a religion of humanity—one that revered as "saints" figures such as Socrates, Jesus (regarded as a human moralist), and George Washington, who were models whom humans should emulate. Instead of aiming to pursue a simplistic "greatest happiness" principle, Mill placed ultimate value on "the improvement of mankind," and the improvement that he sought was not just material but moral. As he wrote in *Utilitarianism* (1863), first published in *Fraser's Magazine* (October–December 1861), "It is better to be a human being dissatisfied than a pig satisfied; better to be Socrates dissatisfied than a fool satisfied."

In 1840 Mill abandoned the *London and Westminster Review* and his hopes for the Philosophical Radical venture in Parliament, but he did not abandon his commitment to reform. He began a lifelong, two-pronged campaign for the transformation of society. In his books he addressed long-term changes needed for human improvement; in his shorter works, most notably in his periodical articles and letters to journals, he passionately addressed immediate social needs.

Viewed as expressions of Mill's overriding goals of human improvement, even extensive technical books such as *A System of Logic, Ratiocinative and Inductive, Being a Connected View of the Principles of Evidence, and the Methods of Scientific Investigation* (1843) and *Principles of Political Economy, with Some of Their Applications to Social Philosophy* (1848) can be seen as reform literature. Despite their surface objectivity, both works contribute to the renewal of character and society.

A System of Logic is the first step in Mill's campaign to regenerate the human mind. Before people could decide what political and social changes were wise, Mill believed that they had to know how to think straight. In his view the great enemy of clear thought was an "Idealist" philosophy that exalted one's intuitions (which often turned out to be one's prejudices) into natural laws. Mill found the antidote to such idealism in a form of empiricism, or "experience philosophy," in which one applied systematic logic to his or her experiences. Mill devotes the bulk of *A System of Logic* to clarifications of language and thought, deductive and inductive logic, common fallacies, methodology in the social sciences, and the logic of the moral sciences. At the end of *A System of Logic* he endorses the Utilitarian greatest happiness principle, but he subordinates it to another: "the cultivation of an ideal nobleness of will and conduct." In this way *A System of Logic* outlines a vision of human progress in which the ultimate goal is individual and social moral improvement.

In *Principles of Political Economy* the significant reforms Mill envisions are in his argument that, while the materials of production are fixed, the methods of distributing those materials and products are not. Consequently, Mill argues throughout the book for a series of reforms that will distribute wealth more equitably and provide increasing economic independence for larger numbers of people than the present socioeconomic system does. He supports capitalist freedom but urges some restraints on it for the public good. In one chapter, "On the Probable Futurity of the Labouring Classes," he insists that paternalism toward workers is no longer valid and that laborers should and will organize to seek their own advancement. In the first edition of *Principles of Political Economy* Mill was skeptical about utopian socialist experiments, which he saw as inimical to individual liberty. But in later editions he was apparently influenced by Harriet Taylor and endorsed more favorably some of these schemes, if only as experiments in alternative social organizations. Throughout the book he applies the principles of political economy to specific social problems. In particular, he urges the British government to seize the "waste lands" of Ireland, parcel them out to independent farmers, and thereby rescue Irish peasants from the "rack rent" of British landowners.

During the 1840s while Mill was theorizing on the comparatively rarefied topics of logic and political economy, he and Harriet Taylor did not forget more-immediate matters. In a series of articles and letters in journals they addressed many pressing social problems. After a potato famine struck Ireland in 1845, Mill wrote a series of forty-three articles for the London *Morning Chronicle* in which he proposed ways for the British government to meet the crisis and achieve land reform. Other articles, many written mostly by Taylor, denounced widely accepted forms of social brutality such as the flogging of soldiers and boys, the laxity of the legal system toward domestic violence, and the maltreatment of servants.

Between 1853 and 1858 Mill also devoted himself to another reform, albeit with much caution. His father, an important official in the East India Company, had secured a position for the seventeen-year-old Mill in the company, and through the years the younger Mill rose to a position of some authority there. Although his influence on events in India was always subject to considerable modification by other officials, Mill became a reformer-at-a-distance in Indian affairs. Because he regarded India as a nation unprepared for representative government, he justified British imperialism there only if it nurtured the people for self-rule sometime in the future, and his Indian reforms were aimed at ensuring self-determination for those people.

He resisted the efforts of officials who, without regard for Indian customs and beliefs, tried to impose English language and culture on Indians. He supported efforts, however, to stamp out Indian practices that he regarded as barbaric—for example, human sacrifice, infanticide, and suttee. He supported Indian land reform that he hoped would create a class of independent farmers. When the British government withdrew rule of India from the company in 1858, Mill fought tenaciously to retain a system of governmental checks and balances that he believed would foster the progress of India toward representative self-rule. His *Memorandum of the Improvements in the Administration of India during the Last Thirty Years, and the Petition of the East-India Company to Parliament* (1858) significantly surveys the reform in India that had been achieved during his tenure with the East India Office.

When Taylor and Mill married in 1851, they settled at Blackheath, where they jointly planned and drafted a series of works for future publication. In 1858, just after Mill retired from his employment with the East India Company, he was devastated by the sudden death of his wife. His sorrow moved him to publish the first and perhaps most important of these "joint productions"—*On Liberty*.

On Liberty is a splendid defense of individualism in the age of democratic mass conformity. As Mill saw it, "the tyranny of the majority" was as inimical to individual freedom as the older monarchical and oligarchic tyrannies had been. The argument of the book is built on a single principle: "the sole end for which mankind are warranted, individually or collectively, in interfering with the liberty of action of any of their number, is self-protection." That is, unless an individual's behavior causes "harm to others," it should be permitted by law. Most of *On Liberty* exalts the value of individuality and freedom as a means of advancing the improvement of humanity. In the final chapter Mill considers specific applications of his principle and weighs the demands of individual freedom against those of the public good. By distinguishing between the authority of society and government, on the one hand, and the liberty of the individual, on the other, Mill provides a blueprint for legal and social changes that still underlie the democratic theory of Western society. His principle in *On Liberty* echoes in debates on matters such as abortion, sexual relations between consenting adults, compulsory education, assisted suicide, and other controversies.

In 1861 Mill serially published in *Fraser's Magazine* the essays that were collected two years later as *Utilitarianism,* a small work with the ambitious goal of overhauling Benthamite ethics. The

MILL'S LOGIC; OR, FRANCHISE FOR FEMALES.
"PRAY CLEAR THE WAY, THERE, FOR THESE—A—PERSONS."

*Editorial cartoon on Mill's campaign to extend voting rights to women (*Punch, *30 March 1867)*

old principle of utility had stressed the attainment of pleasure and the avoidance of pain. In *Utilitarianism* Mill links the old principle to a new concept of happiness—that is, to happiness as understood by a highly developed human being. Mill thereby yokes utility with the moral growth of the human species. Among the many debates that *Utilitarianism* has sparked is whether Mill succeeds in grafting his own ethos of human growth onto the old Benthamite stock.

Mill's most extensive discussion of voting reform, *Considerations on Representative Government,* was also published in 1861, and it superseded his earlier work, *Thoughts on Parliamentary Reform* (1859). During the 1850s social pressure had been building for another reform bill, and Mill was eager to endorse the idea of wider representation in Parliament and to assuage opponents' fears of a larger electorate.

Some of Mill's suggestions look almost reactionary from a twentieth-century perspective. For example, he endorses literacy tests for voters and multiple votes for people who are more highly educated than others; he rejects the secret ballot, and he refuses to extend voting rights to nontaxpayers. But many of his other suggestions are well ahead of their time—for example, extending the franchise to women, eliminating indirect voting mechanisms such as the electoral college, and limiting campaign spending.

In 1865 Mill had an opportunity to demonstrate his commitment to reform in a direct manner. Through a series of improbable events he was elected as a member of Parliament for Westminster. During the three years of his political career he focused primarily on five issues: a new electoral reform bill, an extradition bill, Irish land reform, an

Mill and his stepdaughter, Helen Taylor, circa 1865 (Radio Times Hulton Picture Library)

abuse of power by the governor of Jamaica, and reform of certain corrupt election practices. Although he proved to be an adroit politician, his success in achieving social reforms or correcting political problems on these issues was uneven.

When Liberal Party leaders were unable to get a reform bill through Parliament, Conservative leaders decided to capitalize on the fever for reform and presented a bill of their own. In the political maneuvering over this new reform bill, Mill advocated extending voting rights to workers and women, and he pushed for a measure to ensure that minorities would be represented. Although the 1867 Reform Bill did not contain all that Mill desired as a Radical, he voted for its passage.

In other ways he attempted to preserve enlightened reform aims from the vagaries of political expediency. He helped to block an extradition bill that would have enabled the British government to hand over political refugees to the foreign governments pursuing them. When an uprising of blacks in Jamaica was brutally suppressed by the British colonial governor there, Mill sought unsuccessfully to have him prosecuted for murder. He also failed in his efforts to extend the coverage of a bill restricting corrupt election practices, although he supported the final bill and rejoiced in getting it passed. Despite his long efforts, Mill had no success in mustering parliamentary support for Irish land reform.

During his parliamentary years Mill published his most important statement on education, the *Inaugural Address Delivered to the University of St. Andrews, Feb. 1st, 1867* (1867). Composed in his loftiest style, the address describes an ideal university education that includes studies in both the arts and the sciences while it fosters freedom of speculation. His

"A Feminine Philosopher," caricature of Mill published in the 29 March 1873 issue of Vanity Fair

defense of genuine liberal education remains pertinent and compelling.

After being defeated as an incumbent in the election of 1868, Mill set about publishing his most controversial work, *The Subjection of Women* (1869). The inception of the book owed much to Helen Taylor, Mill's stepdaughter and the daughter of Harriet and John Taylor. As in *On Liberty* Mill argues in *The Subjection of Women* for a single principle: the perfect legal and social equality of the sexes. For better or for worse Mill does not argue the case temperately, and *The Subjection of Women* has always provoked strong reactions, both positive and negative. The book opens by denouncing men as malignant oppressors throughout history and by depicting women as slaves; the second chapter contains a heated indictment of male evil and female subjugation in the family. In chapter 3 Mill's argument debunking the idea of female inferiority is more temperate than these opening sections. The final chapter presents the benefits to be derived from sexual equality.

Arguing against maintaining the legal and social inequalities of women to men, *The Subjection of Women* is both humane and prophetic, but by ignoring the legal and social inequalities experienced by men and by reigniting the war between the sexes, the book seems strangely reactionary and self-defeating. Moreover, Mill's chivalry keeps getting in the way of his quest for sexual equality, as it does when he argues that, under ordinary circumstances, wives should not work outside the home.

During the remaining years of his life Mill continued his reform activities; he and Helen Taylor committed themselves to the cause of woman suffrage. Mill's last major reform publication, *Chapters and Speeches on the Irish Land Question* (1870), was another attempt to alleviate problems in Ireland through land reform.

His posthumously published *Autobiography* and *Nature, The Utility of Religion, and Theism* (1874) are important works in the Mill canon. Because they also foster "the improvement of mankind," they may be considered at least marginally as examples of reform literature. In the *Autobiography* Mill depicts himself as a secular Everyman striving toward a human perfection that Harriet Taylor Mill represents. In two of the three essays on religion in the 1874 volume, "Nature" and "The Utility of Religion," Mill debunks the beliefs, then fashionable, that nature is beneficent and that supernatural faith and moral behavior are connected. The final essay, "Theism," cautiously affirms belief in a divine being while sanctioning the "imaginative hope" of an afterlife.

As a prose writer Mill at first seems at the opposite end of the spectrum from other great Victorian sages such as Carlyle, Cardinal John Henry Newman, and John Ruskin. In contrast to their elaborately imaginative prose, Mill's style initially seems stark and almost depersonalized. To be sure, its systematic logic eminently distinguishes a writer who is urging the use of reason to solve the problems of humanity. Beneath the calm surface of Mill's writing, however, surges an intense tide of emotion. His commitment to many-sidedness and his tolerance of others' views never stopped him from being a vigorously partisan writer for his own viewpoint. In his most famous works Mill the reformer quickly enlists the reader's sympathies in a crusade to abolish some long-standing wrong or some current social mischief. Few authors have been able to match his ability to enliven an intellectual issue by assigning to it a crucial role in fostering the progress of humanity.

In the best of Mill's mature writing, logic and passion combine to create an image of the author as a reasonable reformer, a crusader with his feet on the ground. When the logician dominates the reformer, as in large stretches of *A System of Logic* and *Principles of Political Economy,* the general reader's interest may flag. When the passionate reformer is unchecked by the reasonable thinker, as in the opening chapters of *The Subjection of Women* and parts of "Nature," the general reader is likely to discount the author as a zealot. But at its best—as in *On Liberty* and *Utilitarianism*—Mill's prose combines the rational thinker with the public moralist, and the combination creates a work of such power that it can alter people's lives. Charles Kingsley, for example, discovered *On Liberty* at a publisher's shop, read it then and there, and reported that it made him "a clearer-headed, braver-minded man on the spot." Mill's inaugural address at St. Andrews argues the case for liberal education so grandly that it has been mined for quotations by college presidents ever since it was published. When reason and feeling balance each other in Mill's writings, the result is a prose style that addresses mind and heart with unforgettable force.

Mill's influence on reform philosophy has been, and continues to be, considerable. The single principle that *On Liberty* presents has become a touchstone in the West for deciding questions in which individual liberty is pitted against the interests of society. Mill argues that individual adults should be free to do as they see fit, as long as they do not unjustifiably harm anyone else, and legal and legislative bodies continue to invoke this argument. As an advocate of sexual equality, Mill still influences modern feminism, although that influence is sometimes problematic. In "The Negro Question" (1850) and "The Contest in America" (1862) he mounts vigorously thoughtful defenses for racial equality.

The St. Andrews address, with its eloquent argument for including both the humanities and the sciences in the formal education of students, anticipates modern university curricula. Although Mill respected educational reform, his glowing tribute to traditional humanities studies provides a valuable counterstatement to some experiments in academic curricula. Even in his *Autobiography* Mill can be seen as an educational reformer. In recounting his own early education, Mill demonstrates that children, starting at age three, possess an ability to learn many subjects, especially languages; in this respect, he can be seen as a forerunner of educational re-

Mill in 1873 (portrait by G. F. Watts; National Portrait Gallery, London)

formers such as Maria Montessori. The negative features of the education that young Mill was given—the lack of physical play he was permitted, the repression of imagination and feeling he suffered, the love he failed to receive—define problems that educators have tried, with varying success, to correct.

In *Principles of Political Economy* Mill's argument that the methods of distribution are not fixed by immutable laws of economics kept the door open for rethinking the ways in which wealth is allocated in society. He identified means by which capitalism can be modified to maximize its benefits to humanity. For instance, his sense that society benefits by the existence of a class of independent farmers resembles the thinking of Wendell Berry and other advocates of small farming. Although Mill fulminates against the natural world in "Nature," many ecologists look to his chapter "Of the Stationary State" in *The Principles of Political Economy* as an early statement of the need to preserve wilderness. In writing on social problems Mill and Harriet Taylor called attention to the need for social and legal reform of matters such as child abuse and domestic violence. Above all, Mill's argument that reform philosophy must consider the nature of human beings as a species that is evolving historically and morally has shaped much thought on human progress.

As Mill lay dying in Avignon in 1873, he murmured half-deliriously to Helen Taylor, "You know that I have done my work." If he were thinking of his efforts to better humanity in both immediate and far-reaching matters, he had indeed done his work. Few reformers of any century can claim such an impressive body of literature devoted to the improvement of the human race.

Letters:

Earlier Letters, 1812–1848, edited by Francis E. Mineka, 2 volumes (Toronto: University of Toronto Press, 1963);

Later Letters, 1849–1873, edited by Mineka and Dwight N. Lindley, 4 volumes (Toronto: University of Toronto Press, 1972);

Additional Letters of John Stuart Mill, edited by Marion Filipiuk, Michael Laine, and John M. Robson (Toronto: University of Toronto Press, 1991).

Bibliographies:

Ney MacMinn, J. R. Hainds, and James McNab McCrimmon, eds., *Bibliography of the Published Writings of John Stuart Mill: Edited from His Manuscript, with Corrections and Notes* (Evanston, Ill.: Northwestern University Press, 1945);

John M. Robson, "John Stuart Mill," in *Victorian Prose: A Guide to Research,* edited by David J. DeLaura (New York: Modern Language Association, 1973), pp. 187–218;

Robert Goehlert, *John Stuart Mill: A Bibliography* (Monticello, Ill.: Vance Bibliographies, 1982);

Michael Laine, *Bibliography of Works on John Stuart Mill* (Toronto: University of Toronto Press, 1982).

Biographies:

Alexander Bain, *John Stuart Mill: A Criticism, with Personal Recollections* (London: Holt, 1882);

F. A. Hayek, *John Stuart Mill and Harriet Taylor: Their Friendship and Subsequent Marriage* (London: Routledge & Kegan Paul, 1951; Chicago: University of Chicago Press, 1951);

Michael St. John Packe, *The Life of John Stuart Mill* (London: Secker & Warburg, 1954; New York: Macmillan, 1954);

H. O. Pappe, *John Stuart Mill and the Harriet Taylor Myth* (Melbourne: Melbourne University Press, 1960);

Bruce Mazlish, *James and John Stuart Mill: Father and Son in the Nineteenth Century* (New York: Basic Books, 1975);

Josephine Kamm, *John Stuart Mill in Love* (London: Gordon & Cremone, 1977);

Bruce L. Kinzer, Ann P. Robson, and John Robson, *A Moralist in and out of Parliament: John Stuart Mill at Westminster, 1865–1868* (Toronto: University of Toronto Press, 1992).

References:

Edward Alexander, "John Stuart Mill: A Post-Holocaust Retrospective," in *The Victorian Experience: The Prose Writers,* edited by Richard A. Levine (Athens: Ohio University Press, 1982), pp. 83–111;

Alexander, *Matthew Arnold and John Stuart Mill* (New York: Columbia University Press, 1965);

Eugene August, *John Stuart Mill: A Mind at Large* (New York: Scribners, 1975);

Fred R. Berger, *Happiness, Justice, and Freedom: The Moral and Political Philosophy of John Stuart Mill* (Berkeley: University of California Press, 1984);

Janice Carlisle, *John Stuart Mill and the Writing of Character* (Athens: University of Georgia Press, 1991);

Graeme Duncan, *Marx and Mill: Two Views of Social Conflict and Social Harmony* (Cambridge: Cambridge University Press, 1973);

John B. Ellery, *John Stuart Mill* (New York: Twayne, 1964);

Francis W. Garforth, *Educative Democracy: John Stuart Mill on Education in Society* (Oxford: Oxford University Press, for the University of Hull, 1980);

Garforth, *John Stuart Mill's Theory of Education* (Oxford: Robertson, 1979; New York: Barnes & Noble, 1979);

John Gray and G. W. Smith, eds., *J. S. Mill: On Liberty in Focus* (London & New York: Routledge, 1991);

Joseph Hamberger, *Intellectuals in Politics: John Stuart Mill and the Philosophical Radicals* (New Haven: Yale University Press, 1965);

Gertrude Himmelfarb, *On Liberty and Liberalism: The Case of John Stuart Mill* (New York: Knopf, 1974);

Steward Justman, *The Hidden Text of Mill's Liberty* (Savage, Md.: Rowman & Littlefield, 1991);

Oskar Kurer, *John Stuart Mill: The Politics of Progress* (New York: Garland, 1991);

Michael Laine, ed., *A Cultivated Mind: Essays on J. S. Mill Presented to John M. Robson* (Toronto: University of Toronto Press, 1991);

David Lyons, *Rights, Welfare, and Mill's Moral Theory* (New York: Oxford University Press, 1994);

Emery Neff, *Carlyle and Mill: An Introduction to Victorian Thought,* revised edition (New York: Columbia University Press, 1952);

Jonathan Riley, *Liberal Utilitarianism: Social Choice Theory and J. S. Mill's Philosophy* (Cambridge: Cambridge University Press, 1988);

John M. Robson, *The Improvement of Mankind: The Social and Political Thought of John Stuart Mill* (Toronto: University of Toronto Press, 1968);

Robson and Michael Laine, eds., *James and John Stuart Mill: Papers of the Centenary Conference* (Toronto: University of Toronto Press, 1976);

Alan Ryan, *John Stuart Mill* (New York: Pantheon, 1970);

Bernard Semmel, *John Stuart Mill and the Pursuit of Virtue* (New Haven: Yale University Press, 1984);

J. B. Schneewind, ed., *Mill: A Collection of Critical Essays* (Garden City, N.Y.: Doubleday-Anchor, 1968);

Paul Smart, *Mill and Marx: Individual Liberty and the Roads to Freedom* (Manchester: Manchester University Press / New York: St. Martin's Press, 1991);

William Thomas, *Mill* (Oxford & New York: Oxford University Press, 1985);

Thomas, *The Philosophical Radical: Nine Studies in Theory and Practice, 1817–1841* (Oxford: Oxford University Press, 1979);

Gail Tulloch, *Mill and Sexual Equality* (Hertfordshire, England: Harvester Wheatsheaf / Boulder, Colo.: Rienner, 1989);

Fred Wilson, *Psychological Analysis and the Philosophy of John Stuart Mill* (Toronto: University of Toronto Press, 1990);

Lynn Zastoupil, John Stuart Mill and India (Stanford, Cal.: Stanford University Press, 1994).

Papers:

Important collections of Mill's letters and papers can be found in the Mill-Taylor Collection, British Library of Political and Economic Science, London School of Economics; the National Library of Scotland; the Keynes Library, King's College, Cambridge; and the John Stuart Mill Collection in the Yale University Library, New Haven, Connecticut. Official copies of dispatches drafted by Mill for the East India Company are located in the archival series of the India Office Library and Records, British Library, London. The manuscript of the *Autobiography* is located in the Columbia University Library, and the early draft of the *Autobiography* is in the library of the University of Illinois, Urbana-Champaign. The copy of Robert Browning's *Pauline* with Mill's annotations is in the Forster and Dyce Collection at the Victoria and Albert Museum, London. The early draft of *A System of Logic* and the only known manuscript of *The Principles of Political Economy* are located at the J. Pierpont Morgan Library, New York. The press-copy manuscript of *A System of Logic* is in the British Library. Mill's will is located at Somerset House, London.

Hugh Miller

(10 October 1802 – 24 December 1856)

Douglas S. Campbell
Lock Haven University

BOOKS: *Poems, Written in the Leisure Hours of a Journeyman Mason* (Inverness: Carruthers, 1829);

Letters on the Herring Fishing in the Moray Firth, anonymous (Inverness: Carruthers, 1829);

Scenes and Legends of the North of Scotland; or, The Traditional History of Cromarty (Edinburgh: Black, 1835; Boston: Gould & Lincoln, 1851);

Letter from One of the Scotch People to the Right Hon. Lord Brougham & Vaux, on the Opinions Expressed by His Lordship in the Auchterarder Case (Edinburgh: Johnstone, 1839);

The Whiggism of the Old School, as Exemplified by the Past History and Present Policies of the Church of Scotland (Edinburgh: Johnstone, 1839);

Memoir of William Forsyth, Esq., a Scotch Merchant of the Eighteenth Century (London: Stewart & Murray, 1839);

The Old Red Sandstone; or, New Walks in an Old Field (Edinburgh: Johnstone, 1841; Boston: Gould & Lincoln, 1851); enlarged as *The Old Red Sandstone; or, New Walks in an Old Field, to Which Is Appended a Series of Geological Papers Read before the Royal Physical Society of Edinburgh* (Edinburgh: Constable, 1858; Boston: Gould & Lincoln / New York: Sheldon, 1858);

The Two Parties in the Church of Scotland, Exhibited as Missionary and Anti-Missionary (Edinburgh: Johnstone, 1841);

Sutherland as It Was and Is; or, How a Country May Be Ruined, anonymous (Edinburgh: Johnstone, 1843);

Words of Warning to the People of Scotland, on Sir Robert Peels' Scotch Currency Scheme (Edinburgh: J. Johnstone, 1844);

First Impressions of England and Its People (London: Johnstone, 1847; Boston: Gould & Lincoln, 1851);

Foot-prints of the Creator; or, The Asterolepis of Stromness (London: Johnstone & Hunter, 1849; Boston: Gould & Lincoln, 1850);

Thoughts on the Educational Question; or, "The Battle of Scotland" (Edinburgh, 1850);

Hugh Miller, circa 1844 (calotype by D. O. Hill and Robert Adamson; Scottish National Portrait Gallery)

The Two Records: The Mosaic and the Geological. A Lecture Delivered before the Young Men's Christian Association, in Exeter Hall, London (London: Nisbet, 1854; Boston: Gould & Lincoln, 1854);

The Fossiliferous Deposits of Scotland: Being an Address to the Royal Physical Society, Delivered on the 22d November 1854 (Edinburgh: Shepherd, 1854);

My Schools and Schoolmasters; or, The Story of My Education (Edinburgh, 1854); republished as *An Autobiography: My Schools and Schoolmasters; or, The Story of My Education* (Boston: Gould & Lincoln,

1854); republished as *My Schools and Schoolmasters; or, The Story of My Education: An Autobiography* (Boston: Gould & Lincoln, 1864);

Geology Versus Astronomy; or, The Conditions and the Periods: Being a View of the Modifying Effects of Geological Discovery on the Old Astronomic Inferences Respecting the Plurality of Inhabited Worlds (Glasgow, 1855);

Strange but True: Incidents in the Life of J. Kitto (Edinburgh, 1856);

Macaulay on Scotland: A Critique (Boston: Gould & Lincoln / New York: Sheldon, Blakeman, 1857);

The Testimony of the Rocks; or, Geology and Its Bearings on the Two Theologies, Natural and Revealed (Edinburgh: Constable, 1857; Boston: Gould & Lincoln / New York: Sheldon, Blakeman, 1857);

The Cruise of the Betsey; or, A Summer Ramble among the Fossiliferous Deposits of the Hebrides, with Rambles of a Geologist; or, Ten Thousand Miles over the Fossiliferous Deposits of Scotland (Boston: Gould & Lincoln, 1858; Edinburgh: Constable, 1858);

Sketch-book of Popular Geology: Being a Series of Lectures Delivered before the Philosophical Institution of Edinburgh (Edinburgh, 1859); republished as *Sketch Book of Popular Geology. Popular Geology: A Series of Lectures Read before the Philosophical Institution of Edinburgh, with Descriptive Sketches from a Geologist's Portfolio* (Boston: Gould & Lincoln, 1859; Edinburgh: Constable, 1859); expanded as *Popular Geology: A Series of Lectures Read before the Philosophical Institution of Edinburgh, with Descriptive Sketches from a Geologist's Portfolio* (Boston: Gould & Lincoln / New York: Sheldon, 1860);

The Headship of Christ, and the Rights of the Christian People (Edinburgh, 1861); republished as *The Witness Papers: The Headship of Christ, and the Rights of Christian People, a Collection of Essays, Historical and Descriptive Sketches, and Personal Portraitures* (New York: Hurst, 1863);

Essays: Historical and Biographical, Political and Social, Literary and Scientific, edited by Peter Bayne (Edinburgh: Black, 1862; Boston: Gould & Lincoln, 1865);

The Witness Papers: Headship of Christ and the Rights of Christian People, A Collection of Essays, Historical and Descriptive Sketches, and Personal Portraitures, edited by Peter Bayne (New York: Hurst, 1863; Edinburgh: A. & C. Black, 1865);

Tales and Sketches, edited by Lydia Miller (Edinburgh: Black, 1863; Boston: Gould & Lincoln / New York: Sheldon, 1863);

Edinburgh and Its Neighbourhood, Geological and Historical, with the Geology of the Bass Rock, edited by Lydia Miller (Edinburgh: Black, 1864);

Leading Articles on Various Subjects, edited by John Davidson (Edinburgh, 1870; New York: Virtue & Yorston, 1870);

The Geology of the Country around Otterburn and Elsdon (London: Eyre & Spottiswoode, 1887).

Collections: *Works* (10 volumes, Boston, 1867; 13 volumes, Edinburgh: Nimmo, 1870–1879);

Life and Works, 6 volumes (New York: Carter, 1882).

OTHER: John MacDonald, *Memoirs and Manuscript of Isabel Hood,* introductory notice by Miller (Edinburgh, 1844);

Sermons for Sabbath Evenings, by Ministers of the Free Church of Scotland, introductory remarks by Miller (Edinburgh, 1848);

"Geology of the Bass," in *The Bass Rock: Its Civil and Ecclesiastic History, Geology, Martyrology, Zoology and Botany,* by Thomas MacCrie and others (Edinburgh: Grieg, 1848);

"Thomas of Chartres," in *Tales of the Borders and of Scotland,* edited by Wilson (Edinburgh, 1869), XVIII: 1-32;

"The Scottish Hunters of Hudson's Bay," in *Tales of the Borders and of Scotland,* edited by Wilson (Edinburgh, 1885), XII: 1-29;

"Sandy Wood's Sepulchre," in *Little Classics: Laughter* (Boston, 189-?), V: 127-134.

Deeply religious and sincerely humble, Hugh Miller was a reluctant reformer who is most widely known for his writings on geology and the Scottish Kirk. His strong will, described by some as stubbornness, and his unrelenting opposition to evil and pursuit of truth made Miller determined not to ignore important sociopolitical issues of early nineteenth-century Scotland. His ideas on trade unions, education, poverty, and the franchise received the most attention in his political writing.

Although mildly in favor of general reforms such as those in the Reform Bill of 1832, which gave him the franchise, Miller vigorously opposed many types of radical reformers and reformation schemes such as Chartism. He opposed state-sponsored schemes to help the working class, for example, because he was a self-taught and self-made man who, as a stonemason, wrote poetry, closely observed his natural environment, and studied religion. Other working men, he noticed, were poor and unhappy because they were lazy and uninterested in intellectual matters. He opposed grand schemes of reformation because he believed that many of the matters discussed in Parliament were simply not relevant to

Miller's birthplace in Cromarty, built by his great-grandfather John Feddes in 1711

the local communities in Scotland. Even when he expressed his first thoughts on reform in three issues of *The Village Observer*, a journal he and a few friends published from January through March 1820, these articles criticized the motives of the British reformers, whom he called tyrants duping the masses.

Born into a long line of seafaring men, Miller was only five years old when his father, also named Hugh, perished at sea. He was raised by his father's second wife, Harriet Roy, a fervently religious and superstitious mother. In addition to her fascination with fairies and demons, his mother passed to Miller the memory of her great-grandfather, Donald Roy of Nigg. Roy achieved some fame for his soccer achievements and his courage in standing alone to oppose the intrusion of an unpopular pastor. The memory of his ancestor's courageous stand may account in part for Miller's commitment to nonintrusionist principles.

Miller's commitment to the principle of establishment can likewise be traced to his childhood. In his autobiography, *My Schools and Schoolmasters; or, The Story of My Education* (1854), he recounts one occasion during which a visiting Baptist tried to convince his uncle Alexander (Sandy), who Miller said "held stiffly to the Establishment scheme of [John] Knox," of the virtues of volunteerism. When the Baptist said that he thought the established Church would sink to hell after everyone left, Miller's uncle deemed it a "bold blasphemy."

In addition to reinforcing the religious values of Miller's mother, Sandy and another uncle, James, introduced Miller to books and encouraged him to seek a university education. One influential book he read as a youth is Blind Harry's *Wallace; or, The Life and Acts of Sir William Wallace* (c. 1488), the Scottish epic that Robert Burns said "poured Scottish prejudice" into his veins. Reading this poem made Miller an avid Scottish patriot, with an unwavering commitment to his notions of the 1690 Constitution and its provision establishing his beloved Scottish Kirk. Mediocre teachers bored him, however, and he reacted by skipping school, writing poems, telling stories that he had read or made up to other students during class, and challenging some of his teachers' assertions. At the age of fifteen Miller was forced to leave school permanently after fighting with his teacher.

To earn a living he worked from February 1820 to November 1822 as an apprentice stonemason to David Wright, his mother's brother-in-law. At first he continued the wild life of his childhood, roaming about at night and joining other workers in wild drinking parties. One night he came home after imbibing much liquor and tried to read Francis Bacon's *The Essays; or Counsels, Civill and Morall* (1597–1625). When he could not focus his eyes clearly enough to read the words, he became frightened and vowed never again to waste his life in such carousing.

Working in the southern town of Niddrie, Miller suffered from the prejudice of the local masons against Highlanders. There he acquired a profound distrust and contempt for strikes, labor unions, and the working class in general. Peter Bayne writes that Miller remembered one of the rougher laborers warning an evangelical companion that he would break the face of anyone who tried to convert him. Observing the unending toil of young men who labored as hired hands on the farms, Miller called their lives a "ruinous process of brute-making," and he concluded that such persons were incapable of promoting their own best interests through joining a union or participating in government.

Yet touching evidence of his genuine concern for the welfare of others occurred when he finished his apprenticeship and became a journeyman stonemason. His first job was to take a portion of the small plot of land that he had inherited from his father and build on it a house for his aunt, Jenny, so that she would no longer have to worry about paying rent from the meager money she earned by sewing.

The first strike he experienced ended in the dismal failure he had told his colleagues it would become. Because the strike resulted from wages being cut almost in half, Miller was convinced that the goals of strikes were just and that workers indeed had a right to demand a fair wage, but at bottom striking was simply impractical and would worsen, not improve, the economic condition of laborers.

His observation of the lives of his fellow workers led him not only to reject their style of living but also to consider the meaning of his own existence. Bayne reports that in an 1827 letter to William Ross, a childhood friend, Miller wrote: "From seeing the connection which the passing time and my wasting life have together, I was insensibly led to think of time and eternity, life and death," and his reflection on these matters made him determined "to make the doctrines of Christianity the rule of my belief."

His rediscovered faith–first inculcated by his mother and his well-meaning, pious uncles–pointed him away from the need for governmental reforms. In 1828 he wrote to Ross that he believed earth would become heaven if only the New Testament scheme of morals would be followed by every human being. He believed that hard work and faith in Christ, not government reforms, were solutions to the pains and ills inherent in the poverty of common Scottish laborers.

True to his beliefs, Miller began to devote his free time to literature. When a prestigious literary journal rejected an ode that he had submitted for publication, he began to develop a friendship with Robert Carruthers, editor of the *Inverness Courier*. In 1829 for a small price Carruthers published Miller's first book, *Poems, Written in the Leisure Hours of a Journeyman Mason*. Although the volume was generally politely received, Miller admitted that he did not have the talent to become another Robert Burns.

His prose works, however, were more highly regarded and eagerly read by the newspaper subscribers than was his poetry, and later that year Carruthers published as a pamphlet *Letters on the Herring Fishing in the Moray Firth,* a series of articles Miller had written on fishing. For the first time in this writing appeared evidence of his talent for precise observation of fine details, a talent that later served him well in his scientific, religious, and political pieces. A short newspaper article on crabbing may, in fact, have marked the beginning of his interest in writing on scientific matters. His descriptions of objects are extremely precise and lucid, and he devotes much more attention to these descriptions than does a literary stylist or a typical anecdotal writer such as a sportswriter.

Miller's chance to wield political influence occurred in 1833 after being elected to a three-year term as a Cromarty burgh councillor. At the first meeting the council's only transaction was to discuss the shortage of town funds to pay postage for official business. Miller never returned. He justified his three-year absence by saying that since there was nothing to do at the meetings, nothing is what he did.

Unlike Miller's interest in local political affairs, his interest in literature continued to develop, and in time he was introduced to one of the younger members of the Cromarty women's literary society. Lydia Mackenzie Fraser, ten years younger than Miller, soon found him to be an unusually kind and gentle stonemason and fell in love with him. Although he was also in love with Fraser, because he shared social-class prejudices against laborers, Miller refused to marry her as long as he earned a living as a workingman. He redoubled his efforts at becoming a writer so that he could consider himself worthy of her attentions, and he worked hard on what was to become *Scenes and Legends of the North of Scotland; or, The Traditional History of Cromarty* (1835).

At the end of 1834 Robert Ross, recently appointed agent of the newly established Commercial Bank in Cromarty, offered Miller a position as accountant. Bayne writes that Miller was at first inclined to refuse the post, but he reconsidered, saying, "I remembered that no man has ever been born an accountant; and that the practice and perseverance, which did so much for others, might do a little for me." In a short time Miller became a superior accountant and married Fraser on 7 January 1837. Possessing a bright mind and no small writing talent herself, she later served as Miller's best critic and published many children's stories with a religious theme between 1845 and 1877. One child, Liza, died in infancy, but the Millers raised four other children: Harriet, Bessie, William, and Hugh.

The dreary routine of a bank clerkship tired Miller, and for a short while he lost interest in writing during his free time. Instead he renewed his interest in observing geological phenomena and began to correspond with well-known geologists such as Sir Roderick Murchison and Louis Agassiz. In one letter Murchison advised Miller to stop wasting his talent writing for newspapers and to develop instead a permanent work of reference synthesizing the best of his geological observations.

Before he could write such a work Miller was offered another opportunity to change his vocation when the congregation of the Auchterarder parish rejected, by a vote of three hundred to three, the pastor presented by its patron, Thomas Robert Hay Drummond, Lord Kinnoull. The civil courts ordered the pastor installed, and an appeal by the church was taken ultimately to the House of Lords, where Prime Minister Henry Brougham gave a speech rather cavalierly dismissing the proposition that the congregations of the Church of Scotland have a right to choose their own pastors.

Enraged, Miller wrote a letter to Brougham and sent it to a fellow nonintrusionist and the manager of the Commercial Bank, Robert Paul, who in turn gave it to the Reverend Robert A. Candlish. Upon reading the entire letter Candlish was determined that he had found a candidate for the editorship of *The Witness*, a new church newspaper that he planned to establish. Late in 1839 Miller left his wife in Cromarty and moved to Edinburgh to become editor of this paper. Although he was a kindhearted man, Miller became in the pages of *The Witness* a tenacious defender of any person or cause that he believed to be just. He did not write much on everyday politics because he believed such matters to be mostly petty and uninteresting, and he looked with disdain on fast-paced journalism. He liked to write on what he felt were weightier subjects that merited much thought. Thomas Chamblers said that Miller took a long time to reload, but when he went off, he was a great gun, and the reverberation of his shot was long audible.

Miller made it clear from the start that *The Witness* would be not simply a house organ for the Free Church but a periodical of general interest. Bayne writes that Miller was determined that it "should have a high character as an intellectual newspaper, by no means confining itself to ecclesiastical topics, but making wide incursions into the realms of literature and still more into those of science." A typical issue of *The Witness* consequently included news from foreign countries including Russia and America, marriages and obituaries, concert reviews, weather reports, much police news, and even stock market reports.

Indeed, one of Miller's first series of articles was devoted to geology, and these were published in 1841 as *The Old Red Sandstone; or, New Walks in an Old Field*, a collection that assured him a place in the history of geology and gave him the nickname of "Old Red." French geologist Agassiz was so impressed with Miller's work that he proposed naming a species of flying fish *Pterichthys milleri*.

Much to the consternation of Candlish and other evangelical Presbyterians, Miller refused to adhere to the opinions of the Free Church clergy on ecclesiastical matters. As time passed, Candlish became sufficiently disillusioned with Miller's independence and outspokenness on religious issues and tried to have him replaced. Although Miller decried this as censorship and was able to retain his position as editor, the battle took much out of him. He began to avoid writing about his beloved Scottish Kirk, confined his interests to literature and science, and left others to carry on the battles of the Free Church of Scotland.

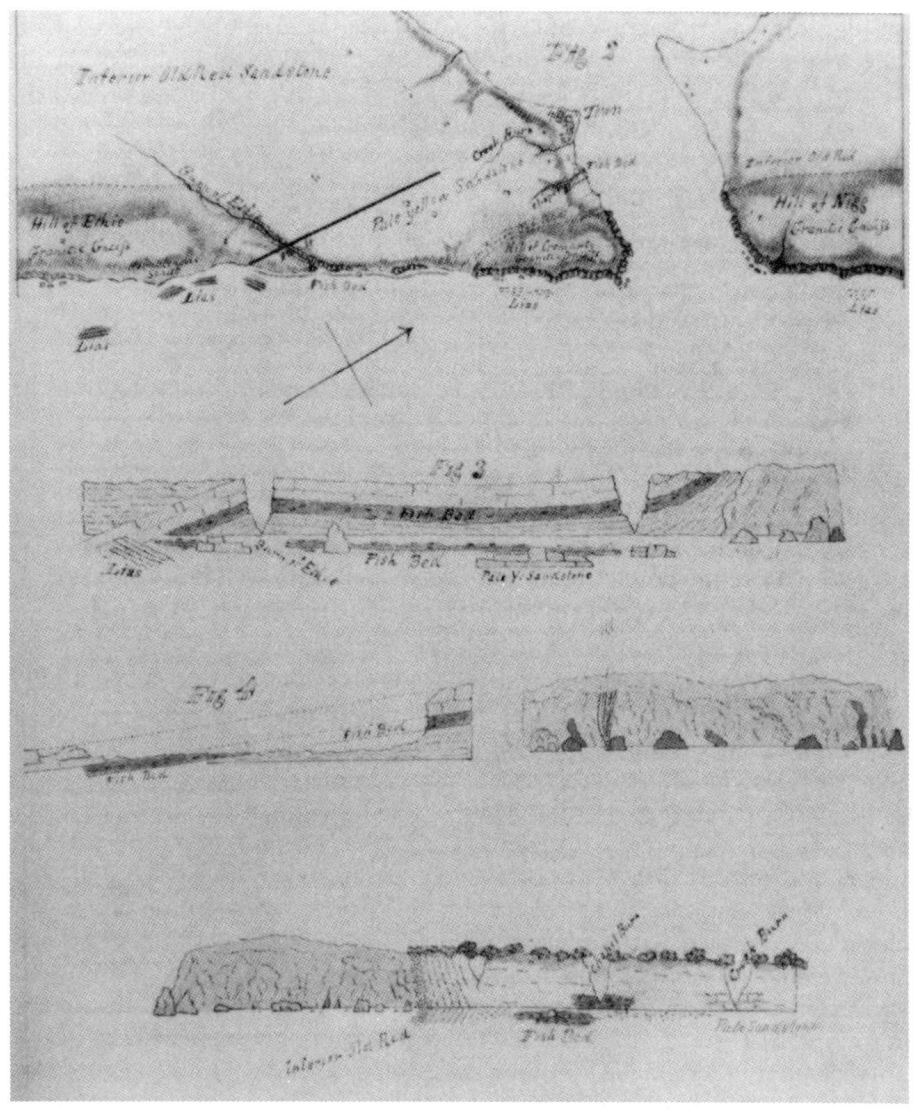

Geological map and sections of the Cromarty area, drawn by Miller in 1839 (New College Library, University of Edinburgh)

His reputation as a reformer rests for the most part on disjunctive articles rather whimsically published during his sixteen-year editorship. Some of these articles were collected and published as books (those geological or political in nature) and pamphlets (mainly on religious matters). A glance at his political writings reveals that, like his scientific works, his political notions were based more on personal observations than on ideas he gained from books.

An examination of his newspaper writings on some of the important issues of the day gives a representative view of Miller's attitudes toward reform, which in the main developed from his experiences with the working class. To Miller the goal of reform is not merely that of establishing a more comfortable social existence but also a higher moral one.

One social reform that Miller supported strongly was the improvement of Scottish housing as he insisted that "sufficiency of the dwelling" was a cornerstone of societal well-being. His essay on the bothy system illustrates well his ideas on housing. Having lived in a bothy during his early twenties, Miller uses his powers of observation to describe them. They included only a few stools for furniture, bowls of tin or earthenware, a water pail, and a pot for eight to ten workers. His criticism of these barracks is directed not at their physical discomfort but at the intellectual and religious shortcomings that these sparse materials and close living conditions nurture. He notes that such crowded environs discourage cultivation of the mind and observance of the Sabbath.

A political reform that interests Miller is the franchise. He admits that, theoretically, a tenant can be a more knowledgeable voter than a property owner, but in *Essays: Historical and Biographical, Political and Social, Literary and Scientific* (1862) Miller points out that, as a class, tenants are "more unsteady and unbalanced in their views and opinions." He unabashedly asserts that his fears of universal suffrage are based on his "long and intimate acquaintance" with the working class, and these experiences have shown him that the poor are unjust and cruel to others who are poor, just as the aristocracy are. Perhaps remembering his days as a stonemason, he asserts he has not seen a workman rightly use his wages. In *My Schools and Schoolmasters* Miller recalls that the fortnightly wages that highly paid workmen had received on Saturday were spent over the weekend in Edinburgh on "drinking and debauchery," and on Monday or Tuesday these workmen, "pale, dirty, disconsolate-looking," would return to their jobs with a sickness they called "the horrors."

His opposition to the Poor Law of 1845 was based on the threat that this law presented to the established Church, for if the State were to care for the poor, then his beloved Kirk would lose opportunities to evangelize the destitute. Miller says that the poor should be helped only if their poverty is the result of misfortune, and he fears that the Poor Law will result in the state rewarding indolence. As a nonintrusionist he believed that self-determination by the poor is closely connected with the formation of their moral character, and the nurture of such self-determination along with the assistance of the Church will enable the poor to pull themselves out of their poverty. Having escaped poverty by hard work alone, Miller asserts that by instilling the "working habit" in the poor, not by building poor houses, will poverty be resolved.

Seeing his erstwhile fellow laborers imprisoned for what he felt was their immoral but relatively harmless pleasures, Miller opposed the game laws. To him these laws perpetuated an inescapable cycle: the poor poach game to find food, are caught and imprisoned, and, when released, the only way in which they are able to obtain food is by resuming their poaching, and so the cycle beings anew. He felt that game was not property which the rich owned and which the poor could be denied.

Another reform that interested Miller was education. Candlish and others in the Free Church began to side with religious dissenters on this issue and asserted that the business of schools should be divorced from religion altogether. Such a position was anathema to Miller, whose understanding of what it meant to be a true Scotsman was rooted in the Constitution of 1689, in which Presbyterianism is established as the Church of Scotland.

In a series of *Witness* articles Miller collected and published as *Thoughts on the Educational Question; or, "The Battle of Scotland"* (1850), Miller advocated excluding narrow, sectarian views from the schools, but he refused to exclude the teaching of religion from the classroom. He also did not feel that the State should fail to support schools that provided religious instruction, and he proposed a compromise in which the State would build and maintain the schools, control the secular curriculum, and pay most of the teachers' salaries. Local school committees would supplement these teacher salaries with monies from tuition charged to support religious instruction. Although a committee would employ and discharge teachers, it could not do so on the basis of sectarian beliefs of the teachers. Yet Miller felt that teachers should be disciplined for inculcating in students religious beliefs different from those of the hereditary faith of the parents of those students.

Ultimately the stonemason's malady—bits of stone and stone dust residing in the lungs—weakened Miller, who became delirious and suffered terrible nightmares like those of the childhood fantasies that his mother's superstition had induced in him. He also resumed sleepwalking, a condition he had periodically suffered when he was most severely depressed throughout his life. On Christmas Eve 1856 he died from a wound self-inflicted by a pistol that he had carried since he began writing personal criticisms published in *The Witness*. According to a suicide note, Miller believed that he had walked in his sleep the night before, and this confirmed his fears that his mind was diseased and he was becoming insane.

Biographies:

Thomas Brown, *The Life and Times of Hugh Miller* (New York: Rudd & Carleton, 1858);

Peter Bayne, *The Life and Letters of Hugh Miller* (Boston: Gould & Lincoln, 1871);

W. Keith Leask, *Hugh Miller* (New York: Scribners, 1896).

References:

Hugh Miller Centenary Celebration Committee, *The Centenary of Hugh Miller: Being an Account of the Celebration Held at Cromarty on 22nd August 1902* (Glasgow: Maclehose, 1902);

Hugh Miller Institute Dedication Speech (Dunfermline: Journal Print Works, 1904).

John Morley

(24 December 1838 - 23 September 1923)

Christopher A. Kent
University of Saskatchewan

See also the Morley entries in *DLB 57: Victorian Prose Writers After 1867* and *DLB 144: Nineteenth-Century British Literary Biographers*.

BOOKS: *Modern Characteristics: A Series of Short Essays From the "Saturday Review,"* anonymous (London: Tinsley, 1865);

Studies in Conduct: Short Essays from the "Saturday Review," anonymous (London: Chapman & Hall, 1867);

Edmund Burke: A Historical Study (London: Macmillan, 1867; New York: Knopf, 1924);

Critical Miscellanies, 4 series (volumes 1 and 2, London: Chapman & Hall, 1871, 1877; volume 1, New York: Scribner & Welford, 1879; volumes 1 and 2 revised and published with volume 3, London & New York: Macmillan, 1886; volume 4, London & New York: Macmillan, 1908); volume 4 also published as *Miscellanies, Fourth Series* (London: Macmillan, 1908);

Voltaire (London: Chapman & Hall, 1872; revised edition, London: Chapman & Hall, 1872; New York: Appleton, 1872);

Rousseau, 2 volumes (London: Chapman & Hall, 1873; New York: Scribner & Welford, 1878);

The Struggle for National Education (London: Chapman & Hall, 1873);

On Compromise (London: Chapman & Hall, 1874; revised edition, 1877; London & New York: Macmillan, 1903);

Diderot and the Encyclopaedists, 2 volumes (London: Chapman & Hall, 1878; New York: Scribner & Welford, 1878);

Burke (London: Macmillan, 1879; New York: Harper, 1879?);

The Life of Richard Cobden (2 volumes, London: Chapman & Hall, 1881; 1 volume, Boston: Roberts, 1881);

Ralph Waldo Emerson: An Essay (New York: Macmillan, 1884);

John Morley

Walpole (London: Macmillan, 1889; London & New York: Macmillan, 1889);

Studies in Literature (London & New York: Macmillan, 1891);

Machiavelli: The Romanes Lecture Delivered in the Sheldonian Theatre, June 2, 1897 (London: Macmillan / New York: Macmillan, 1897);

Macaulay: An Essay (London & New York: Macmillan, 1898);

Oliver Cromwell (London: Macmillan, 1900; New York: Century, 1900);

The Life of William Ewart Gladstone, 3 volumes (London: Macmillan / New York: Macmillan,

1903); republished as *The Life of Gladstone* (London: Hodder & Stoughton, 1927);

Literary Essays (London: Humphreys, 1906);

Speeches on Indian Affairs (Madras: Natesan, 1908; revised and enlarged, 1917);

Indian Speeches (1907-1909) (London: Macmillan, 1909);

Science and Literature (Oxford: Oxford University Press, 1911);

Notes on Politics & History: A University Address (London: Macmillan, 1913; New York: Macmillan, 1914);

Recollections, 2 volumes (London: Macmillan, 1917; New York: Macmillan, 1917);

Memorandum on Resignation, August 1914 (London: Macmillan, 1928; New York: Macmillan, 1928).

Collection: *The Works of John Morley*, 15 volumes (London: Macmillan, 1921).

OTHER: *The Fortnightly Review*, edited by Morley (1867-1882);

English Men of Letters, edited by Morley, 67 volumes (London: Macmillan, 1878-1919);

The Pall Mall Gazette, edited by Morley (1880-1883);

Ralph Waldo Emerson, *The Works of Ralph Waldo Emerson*, edited by Morley, 6 volumes (London: Macmillan, 1883);

Macmillan's Magazine, edited by Morley (1883-1885);

William Wordsworth, *The Complete Poetical Works of William Wordsworth*, introduction by Morley (London: Macmillan, 1888; London: Macmillan / New York: Macmillan, 1903);

"The Rt. Hon. John Morley on Home Rule," in *Both Sides of the Home Rule Question* (Oxford: Blackwell, 1888);

"The Study of Literature," in *Aspects of Modern Study*, edited by Robert Davies Roberts (London & New York: Macmillan, 1894);

François-Marie Arouet de Voltaire, *The Works of Voltaire*, critique and biography by Morley (Paris & New York: Du Mont, 1901).

SELECTED PERIODICAL PUBLICATIONS—
UNCOLLECTED: "England and the Annexation of Mysore," *Fortnightly Review*, 6 (1866): 257-271;

"Young England and the Political Future," *Fortnightly Review*, 7 (1867): 491-496;

"England and the European Crisis," *Fortnightly Review*, 7 (1867): 621-629;

"Anonymous Journalism," *Fortnightly Review*, 8 (1867): 287-292;

"The Liberal Programme," *Fortnightly Review*, 8 (1867): 359-369;

"The Political Prelude," *Fortnightly Review*, 10 (1868): 103-114;

"Old Parties and New Policy," *Fortnightly Review*, 10 (1868): 320-336;

"The Chamber of Mediocrity," *Fortnightly Review*, 10 (1868): 681-694;

"The *Fortnightly Review* and Positivism: A Note," *Fortnightly Review*, 14 (1870): 118-120;

"The Five Gas Stokers," *Fortnightly Review*, 19 (1873): 138-141;

"The Liberal Eclipse," *Fortnightly Review*, 23 (1875): 295-304;

"An Address to Some Miners," *Fortnightly Review*, 27 (1877): 392-409;

"Lancashire," *Fortnightly Review*, 30 (1878): 1-25;

"A Political Epilogue," *Fortnightly Review*, 30 (1878): 313-333;

"An Economic Address: With Some Notes," *Fortnightly Review*, 30 (1878): 547-567;

"The Impoverishment of India Not Proven," *Fortnightly Review*, 30 (1878): 867-881;

"The Plain Story of the Zulu War," *Fortnightly Review*, 31 (1879): 329-352;

"Further Remarks on Zulu Affairs," *Fortnightly Review*, 31 (1879): 546-562;

"The House of Commons," *Fortnightly Review*, 32 (1879): 186-196;

"A Word with Some Critics," *Fortnightly Review*, 32 (1879): 577-584;

"England and Ireland," *Fortnightly Review*, 35 (1881): 407-425;

"Conciliation with Ireland," *Fortnightly Review*, 36 (1881): 1-25;

"Egyptian Policy: A Retrospect," *Fortnightly Review*, 38 (1882): 94-123;

"Irish Revolution and English Liberalism," *Nineteenth Century*, 12 (1882): 647-666;

"The Radical Programme (No. VI): Religious Equality," *Fortnightly Review*, 41 (1884): 569-592.

John Morley's claim to a prominent place among British reform writers of the later nineteenth century rests mainly on his position as editor of and chief contributor to the *Fortnightly Review* between 1867 and 1882, its period of greatest influence as the leading radical intellectual journal in England.

He was born in Blackburn, Lancashire, in the heart of the cotton-manufacturing region. His father, an ambitious Yorkshire-born surgeon who left Methodism for the Church of England, intended that his son become a clergyman. Morley won a scholarship to Lincoln College, Oxford, but had to graduate without an honors degree because his father withdrew all support on learning that Morley had decided he could not take holy orders. Forced to support himself, Morley came to London and soon found a well-paid journalistic position as a contributor of sententious, politically innocuous editorials for the conservative, intellectual *Saturday Review*. Ambitious, energetic, and personable, he quickly became well connected in the intellectual community, which included luminaries such as John Stuart Mill and George Eliot.

His college friendship with James Cotter Morison, a well-to-do follower of Auguste Comte and a financial backer of the *Fortnightly Review*, helped Morley gain the editorship of that journal following the resignation of G. H. Lewes as its editor in December 1866. Founded in May 1865 as an intellectual "open house" for writers of all shades of opinion, the journal under Morley's hand quickly attracted the attention of advanced liberals, rationalists, and freethinkers. Writing nearly one-eighth of its articles, some two hundred of them, during his term as editor, Morley set its tone of strenuous progressivism. Almost every issue included something he had written.

The keynote of his reform writing is explicit intellectual elitism. Like many Victorian intellectuals, Morley was concerned about what he perceived to be a condition of intellectual anarchy attributable largely to the dissolution of religious doctrines by the influence of scientific rationalism, particularly the idea of evolution, and the growing relativism generated by historicism, with its skeptical premise that each era shapes its criteria for what constitutes truth. He was deeply committed to the possibility, though not the inevitability, of social progress. He believed that what the nation needed most was intellectual leadership, for, as John Stuart Mill's *On Liberty* (1859) taught, only the unimpeded flow of new ideas could ensure social progress. The *Fortnightly Review* was to be a channel for these ideas, and under Morley it attracted many leading British intellectuals: Mill, Thomas Henry Huxley, Matthew Arnold, Leslie Stephen, Frederic Harrison, William Kingdon Clifford, and Walter Bagehot—all skilled essayists in political and cultural criticism.

Morley's arrival as editor of the *Fortnightly Review* occurred at the same time as the social ferment accompanying the Second Reform Act of 1867, when Parliament rewarded members of the skilled working class for their responsible conduct and their contribution to mid-Victorian prosperity by extending the franchise to them. Strong working-class support for the election of John Stuart Mill as a member of Parliament for Westminster in

"The Fortnightly Review," caricature of Morley published in the 30 November 1878 issue of Vanity Fair

1865 signaled to Morley and other young radicals that the working classes respected the leadership of progressive intellectuals more than the upper classes did. The long thralldom to pragmatism and practicality and a suspicion of intellectuals and political ideas that had characterized England seemed about to be broken. In "Young England and the Political Future" (April 1867), one of Morley's earliest *Fortnightly Review* essays, he celebrated the imminent consummation of the political alliance of "brains and numbers." In "The Liberal Programme" (September 1867) he wrote that the passing of the Second Reform Bill marked the beginning of "the New Revolution," as political power had been transferred "from a class to the nation." He expected that newly enfranchised voters, outnumbering the old electorate, would respond to guidance from "courageous and instructed men who know what policy means," and he saw the passing of this reform bill as an unprecedented opportunity for the elite to seize the day. He wrote in "The Political Prelude" in July 1868 that "the result will depend upon the number of men who can be found with the will and faculty to help, in the press and on the platform, in the creation of a virtuous public opinion."

At the time of writing these hortatory essays Morley was strongly attracted to the ideas of Comte, whose ideology of Positivism drew much attention from British intellectual circles in the 1860s and 1870s, thanks to the skillful propagandizing of Comte's English disciples. In the French philosopher's ideal society, through the power of public opinion a morally virtuous proletariat, instructed by an intellectual elite who comprised the spiritual power of that nation, would exercise a sublimated authority over a managerial elite of capitalists who would manage the practical conduct of affairs. Comte's confident and precise definition of the political power that intellectuals were to acquire in the ultimate and imminent stage of social evolution attracted great interest among progressive intellectuals such as Morley. Comte's ideal regime abolished class society and the politics of reconciling class interests by ordaining that there would only be a proletariat (Morley's "nation") altruistically served by two elites whose interests would always coincide with public opinion. Comte's ideology decisively answered the central question of intellectuals in that society: what is their relationship with the masses? Morley never formally enrolled in the Church of Humanity, the organized body of the British Comtist movement, but he was certainly an ardent supporter. At this time the *Fortnightly Review* was the favorite journalistic platform of Comte's followers, and Frederic Harrison, Morley's friend and the most articulate of them, became a leading contributor. Most of *Order and Progress* (1875), Harrison's Comtist manifesto, appeared first in the form of articles in the *Fortnightly Review*.

Morley was deeply interested in the French Revolution, and his historical thinking was most explicitly influenced by Comte. Unlike many British intellectuals Morley did not regard the Revolution as an ideological demon to be exorcized but as the event that had brought the world into its current epoch, the intellectually and socially anarchic age of transition which indicated that the Revolution was not yet ended. To understand it was therefore essential in order to understand the world in which one lived.

Most of Morley's writings during his editorship of the *Fortnightly Review* can be seen as contributions to a history of the intellectual background of the French Revolution. Largely biographical studies, they start with two of the most able critics of the Revolution–Edmund Burke and Count Joseph-Marie de Maistre–and are followed by a series on its intellectual progenitors: Marie-Jean-Antoine-Nicholas de Caritat, Marquis de Condorcet; Anne-Robert-Jacques Turgot, Baron de l'Aulne; François-Marie Arouet de Voltaire; Jean-Jacques Rousseau, and Denis Diderot. This series ended with a study of Maximilien-François-Marie-Isidore de Robespierre, which was intended to be the first in a series, never completed, on the Revolution. These studies are an antidote to the works of Thomas Carlyle, whose hostile attitude to the philosophes and the Revolution prevented their proper appreciation in Britain. These works also enabled Morley to explore how ideas shape history, a question that continued to fascinate him, and it is significant that he adopted a biographical approach to this question. Rather than view ideas as disembodied influences or as parts of some spiritual entity such as a spirit of the age, Morley saw them as embodied in men of ideas, men whose words and deeds shaped history. In this he was adopting something of Carlyle's idea of the hero as a man of letters, for Morley was far from repudiating Carlyle entirely.

Morley's French essays were intended to combat the English prejudice against ideas as a political force, that prevailing anti-intellectualism in the English tradition of political thought that contrasts theory and system, the supposedly characteristic vices of the French mind to the healthy English genius for common sense and experience. To combat the English stereotype of the philosophes as metaphysicians and impractical theory-mongers Morley emphasized their deeds: Voltaire's courageous public campaigns against specific cases of injustice, Diderot's entrepreneurial direction of the *Encyclopédie, ou Dictionnaire raisonné des sciences, des arts et des métiers* (1751–1772; Encyclopedia, or Detailed Dictionary of the Sciences, Arts, and Crafts), and especially Turgot's heroic, if ill-fated, attempt to reform the financial administration of the ancien régime.

In *Edmund Burke: A Historical Study* (1867) Morley attempts almost to anglicize the French Revolution that Burke had stigmatized so compellingly. What, Morley asks, was that fearsome bogey, "Liberty, Equality and Fraternity"? Judiciously redefined by Morley, Liberty means only popular sovereignty, which ultimately denotes the state of general happiness, the reassuring touchstone of English utilitarianism. Equality, stripped of its metaphysical excrescences, means simply equality of opportunity, and Fraternity, "the generous and sublime sentiment of the brotherhood of man," is a cardinal principle of Christianity. What is a "right," if not virtually the same thing as an "interest"? What is a principle, if not expediency writ large? What is "society"? "Only a name for other people." What should British readers fear in the ideas of the French Revolution? Not much, according to Morley, if only they understand the Revolution properly.

He subscribes to the Liberal view that the French Revolution went wrong when it fell into the hands of the Jacobins, and therefore Rousseau and Robespierre, his disciple, do not undergo Morley's anglicizing rehabilitation. Recognizing the emotional power of Rousseau's writings that attracted disciples, Morley tries hard to be just to him, although Morley is deeply unsympathetic toward the ideas and personality of the French revolutionary. But the social contract is a revolutionary idea that Morley makes no attempt to domesticate, stigmatizing it essentially as Comte does—as a deeply regressive idea, a dangerously emotional abstraction that corresponds to no social reality. The social contract, Morley acknowledges, is a politically dangerous idea. Unfortunately it was not confined to the safety of a hypothetical study but was taken up by Robespierre, the doctrinaire Jacobin whose attempt to put Rousseau's ideas into practice fatally turned the Revolution into the Reign of Terror.

Morley's essays on figures from French history implicitly, and sometimes explicitly, engage a traditional problem of intellectual history: what difference does the individual make in the origin, formulation, and transmission of ideas? Morley's choice of biography as his format affirms the importance of the individual. This is an option that readily encourages popular treatment. Morley's guide was again Comte, who celebrates individual genius to the point of having every month and day of his Comtist calendar named after a great thinker. In his three-stage scheme for understanding history—which he subdivides into the theological era, the metaphysical era, and the positive era—any thinker, even a genius, is constrained by the limits of thinkability imposed by the intellectual era he inhabits. As an intellectual schema for dealing with Enlightenment thinkers, those at the end of the metaphysical era, such a conception of constraints appealed to Morley. It was a progressive, teleological schema that assisted him in evaluating how those thinkers were related to the French Revolution, but it was not as satisfactory in assessing social and political thought after the Revolutionary period, in Morley's own time. According to Comte, intellectuals must think within the positivist paradigm, which essentially meant subscribing to Comtist ideology.

Morley was instead attracted to the views of John Stuart Mill, who criticized Comte's elaborate ideology as excessively prescriptive and authoritarian, foreclosing on intellectual options and forcing a final intellectual synthesis—in effect, an "end of History" in the Hegelian sense—that Mill believed was at best premature. Morley admired Mill's *On Liberty,* which argues that thought must be as free as possible because it is impossible to be certain which ideas will ultimately contribute to progress and that society needs an open intellectual marketplace in which conflicting ideas can be freely tested in competition with one another. For Morley this view also emphasized the importance of personal qualities such as character, integrity, and "manliness"—the last of which denoted a readiness to stand up for one's ideas even when they oppose popular prejudice or conventional wisdom.

On Compromise (1874), first published as a series of *Fortnightly Review* articles, stands as Morley's central work of this period. With Mill's *The Subjection of Women* (1869) and Leslie Stephen's *Essays on Freethinking and Plainspeaking* (1873), it belongs in the canon of nineteenth-century radical texts. As Morley remarked to Joseph Chamberlain, *On Compromise* was intended to "exalt the importance of Principles, and show what a beggarly mood England was in because she had none." It is a manifesto of elitist rationalism addressed specifically to those who should be giving the nation its intellectual leadership—those who constituted the select readership of the *Fortnightly Review*. The volume can be read as an attempt to map the terrain that lies between thought and action and to get free of Comtist doctrine on this problem.

A central article of Comte's ideology is the separation of powers in the social order, the principle that intellectuals, who embody the spiritual power, should not be involved in practical political matters, which belong to the temporal power. When thought and action overlap, disorder ensues and progress suffers. One of Comte's main criticisms of the French Enlightenment philosophes is that they had been drawn into political action and that this merging of thought and action, as embodied in Robespierre above all, perverted the French Revolution when the ideologue-dictator tried to force untidy reality to conform to tidy theory. Morley claims that Comte is generalizing from French experience and that Comte's concern is not a problem in England, where, on the contrary, the besetting vice of English intellectuals is their undue deference to practical considerations. Consequently, as Morley saw it, English intellectuals have too little influence in British so-

MEMORANDUM
ON
RESIGNATION

August 1914

by

JOHN VISCOUNT MORLEY

NEW YORK
THE MACMILLAN COMPANY
1928
All rights reserved

Title page for the American edition of Morley's last book, his explanation of why he resigned as lord president of the Council when the British entered World War I

ciety: a "profound distrust of all general principles" was endemic among the English.

This tendency was particularly evident in the British press. As an example, Morley cited the censure that the London *Times* had imposed on Charles Darwin for having published his *The Descent of Man, and Selection in Relation to Sex* (1871) "while the sky of Paris was red with flames of the Commune." English intellectuals were far too prone to submit their ideas to a form of political self-censorship, to abandon their duty of providing the unadulterated flow of higher ideas necessary to political and intellectual progress, and to acquiesce in the "leaden tyranny of the man of the world." Building on Mill's *On Liberty* by arguing that there was really no need for reservations or compromise in the formation and expression of one's ideas, Morley tried to establish for intellec-

tuals a practical formula that specified the proper degree of separation between political speculation and political action. He believed that the new ideas of an intellectual elite, properly schooled in the principles of such a formula, would almost of necessity serve the cause of progress and that the only serious problem in effecting such progress was that of timing. Deciding when the time was ripe for acting on an idea was properly to be left to the politician's sense of practicalities.

In the aftermath of the 1867 Reform Act, Morley talked eagerly yet vaguely about the "demolition of privileged orders and creeds." The first of these targets was a coded reference to the republicanism that was briefly fashionable among intellectual radicals in the early 1870s. Morley and others believed that the irrational institution of the monarchy would eventually wither in the heat of democracy but that this change could be left to develop and need not be forced. Morley regarded the established Church as equally vulnerable to the inexorable progress of democracy. Religion was a source of uneasiness for him. He had suffered personally from having renounced the ambitions his parents had imposed on him, and many of his rationalist friends had also known the anguish of breaking away from the faith of their fathers. He won notoriety as an editor by printing the word *God* with a small *g*, and he devoted one chapter of *On Compromise* to refuting the suggestion—which to Morley's dismay Mill had made in "The Utility of Religion," one of three essays in his posthumously published collection *Nature, The Utility of Religion, and Theism* (1874)—that religion might be "morally useful" even if not intellectually sustainable.

This concession struck at the heart of Morley's reformist creed, that the cause of progress was essentially the cause of truth overcoming error. To say that an error might be useful seemed tantamount to saying that truth could be harmful, an even greater heresy. The obstacles of error were roadblocks on the path of progress and had to be cleared away. In the spirit of Victorian liberalism Morley's whole reformist credo was essentially negative; the magic word was *free*. Just as free trade had seemingly cleared the roadblock to economic prosperity, so education had to be freed from the sectarian and clerical influences enshrined in William Edward Forster's Education Act of 1870. This was the target of "The Struggle for National Education," a series of blistering *Fortnightly Review* articles Morley wrote in 1873 and collected as a book in that year. Disappointed by William Ewart Gladstone's government of 1868–1874, Morley aligned his journal to the radical program of Joseph Chamberlain, who was calling for a "Free Church, Free Land, Free Schools and Free Labour," a program that, if it were realized, would essentially eliminate obstructive legislation in these areas.

Although Morley attained a position of considerable prestige as editor of the *Fortnightly Review,* his ambitions increasingly chafed under the restrictive conditions of his editorship. He had been proud to style himself a professional journalist; Carlyle had called journalists the "true kings and clergy" of the modern world. Yet the policy of requiring all contributors to publish their names with their articles somewhat impaired the traditional power of the editor. Writing under their own names and claiming authority on the strength of those names, his contributors—who grew in number as Morley attracted the most eminent intellectuals to contribute to his journal—could not easily be brought under editorial discipline. So many of the Comtists contributed, and contributed so frequently, that he had to mitigate the public impression that his journal was a Comtist organ, especially after he had decided to end his own flirtation with Comtism. He liked to compare himself to Diderot, editor of the *Encyclopédie,* by calling himself the "entrepreneur of the spiritual power," the coordinator of the intellectual forces of progress. But Morley grew disenchanted with his inability to focus his journal on the political issues that interested him. A note of disappointment is evident in his valedictory article as editor of the *Fortnightly Review* in 1882, when he noted that its policies of being open to various ideas and publishing only signed articles prevented it from becoming "the organ of a systematic policy." From 1880 to 1883 he also edited the *Pall Mall Gazette,* a politically influential daily, and in its editorial pages (which published anonymous essays) he was able to offer more-systematic support than he had previously for the policies of Gladstone, who became his new hero.

Morley's fascination with the two powers, the spiritual and temporal, stemmed from his uncertainty about his own proper milieu. As early as 1868 he had stood unsuccessfully for Parliament, and the temptation to become a man of deeds rather than words, of action rather than contemplation, was with him until he finally left journalism and entered politics as an M.P. for Newcastle-upon-Tyne in 1883. Some writers have viewed his subsequent political career as a disappointment. He quickly rose to cabinet rank as chief secretary for Ireland in 1886 and 1892–1895, secretary of state for India in 1905–1910, and lord president of the council in 1910–1914. Though he filled these offices conscientiously and competently, he did not prove to be a dynamic intellectual force for reform.

In fact Morley seemed conscious of being an intellectual in politics and often attempted to overcome this label by trying to project an image as a tough-minded man of action, especially in Parliament. His concern with Home Rule for Ireland was long-standing and has been interpreted, particularly by David A. Hamer, as keeping with his negativist creed of reform. Insofar as he came to see the Irish issue as an obstruction to the cause of reform in England, it was an obstacle from which his country could be freed only by Irish Home Rule. His critical attitude toward resurgent imperialism in late-Victorian England can be interpreted as an attempt to free his country from the thralldom of empire, yet another obstacle to reform. But if these obstacles were removed, what reforms Morley might have taken up are by no means clear because he was suspicious of state intervention in social issues.

Once he was engaged in politics his writing was largely confined to political biographies, which he wrote mostly during periods when his party was not in power. These include lives of Richard Cobden (1881), the great apostle of free trade; of Robert Walpole (1889); of Oliver Cromwell (1900), the saint in politics; and above all his official biography of Gladstone (1903). Perhaps with the exception of *Walpole* these can be seen as displaced studies in reform, with the emphasis on action rather than on thought.

Morley was also a very influential literary broker, as under his editorship the *Fortnightly Review* was a major publisher of the works of Dante Gabriel Rossetti, A. C. Swinburne, George Meredith, Walter Pater, and John Addington Symonds at times when their works presented somewhat radical voices. Despite an early, anonymous attack on Swinburne's poetry in the *Saturday Review,* Morley was largely sympathetic to their writings. As a reader and chief literary adviser to the Macmillan publishing house as well as editor of *Macmillan's Magazine* from May 1883 to September 1885, he exercised further behind-the-scenes power. Most significant was his founding and editing of the influential English Men of Letters series, which did much to establish a literary canon and a distinctive style of literary criticism at a time when the study of English literature was just becoming established as an academic discipline.

He was much concerned with promoting good literature among the working classes, whose access to education, culture, and leisure was growing significantly. If his published addresses to members of these classes seem somewhat patronizing, in the context of his time Morley deserves credit for addressing them directly and seriously on cultural matters.

John Morley

As Edward Alexander has noted, Morley avoided the conventional bromides about the moral value of literature. Although he was a reformer, he did not believe that it was the duty of literature to advance the cause of reform in any didactic way. In fact, he applied to literature his doctrine of the separation between the spiritual and temporal power. No more than for other intellectuals was it "the business of an artist to form judgments in the sphere of practical politics." From this perspective Morley subscribed to the doctrine of art for art's sake most explicitly in an essay where—without entirely agreeing with Pater's ideas—he nevertheless commends Pater's "intellectual play" for being more effective and valuable than John Ruskin's presumptuous political and social prescriptions in promoting a climate from which social change might eventually emerge.

Morley's critics might claim that *eventually* is the crucial word in this qualification, as it might be of so much of his reformism. His progressivism was a product of mid Victorianism, an intellectual climate in which appropriate reforms could be trusted to "ripen," but he lived to see that optimism blighted by World War I. He was one of the two members of the Liberal cabinet in 1914 who opposed Britain's decision to enter the war, and he publicly but silently resigned his office because of this decision. As he remarked to a friend at the time, "I've run my course and kept the faith. That's enough." He retreated into writing his *Recollections* (1917), which are not very helpful in understanding young John Morley, the ardent reformer with whom even the older Morley had apparently lost touch. His recollections concern mainly the life and career of the politician and man of action rather than those of the earlier writer and man of ideas.

He died in 1923, but his last work—*Memorandum on Resignation, August 1914,* in which he finally explained his reasons for resigning political office in 1914—was not published until 1928, in a posthumous manner somewhat at odds with the principles of *On Compromise*. Essentially, he resigned because he could not accept that it was necessary for England to become an ally of Russia, a dangerous empire that was one of the greatest obstacles to the progress of civilization, and go to war against Germany, a nation that was on the side of progress.

Bibliography:

John W. Bicknell, "The Unbelievers: IV, John Morley," in *Victorian Prose: A Guide to Research,* edited by David J. DeLaura (New York: Modern Language Association of America, 1973), pp. 506-515.

Biographies:

John Morgan, *John, Viscount Morley* (London: John Murray, 1925);

Francis W. Hirst, *The Early Life and Letters of John Morley,* 2 volumes (London: Macmillan, 1927).

References:

Edward Alexander, *John Morley* (New York: Twayne, 1972);

Merle M. Bevington, *The Saturday Review, 1855-1868: Representative Educated Opinion in Victorian England* (New York: Columbia University Press, 1941);

Winston S. Churchill, "John Morley," in his *Great Contemporaries* (London: Macmillan, 1942), pp. 71-84;

Edwin M. Everett, *The Party of Humanity* (Chapel Hill: University of North Carolina Press, 1939);

John Gross, *The Rise and Fall of the Man of Letters* (London: Weidenfeld & Nicolson, 1969);

David A. Hamer, *John Morley: Liberal Intellectual in Politics* (Oxford: Clarendon Press, 1968);

Christopher A. Kent, *Brains and Numbers: Elitism, Comtism and Democracy in Mid-Victorian England* (Toronto: University of Toronto Press, 1978);

John L. Kijinski, "John Morley's 'English Men of Letters' Series and the Politics of Reading," *Victorian Studies,* 34 (1991): 205–226;

Frances W. Knickerbocker, *Free Minds: John Morley and His Friends* (Cambridge, Mass.: Harvard University Press, 1943);

Stephen Koss, *John Morley at the India Office, 1905–1910* (New Haven: Yale University Press, 1969);

Koss, *The Rise and Fall of the Political Press in Britain: The Nineteenth Century* (Chapel Hill: University of North Carolina Press, 1981);

Molly C. Poulter, *A Catalogue of the Morley Collection* (London: India Office Library, Commonwealth Relations Office, 1965);

James W. Robertson Scott, *The Life and Death of a Great Newspaper* (London: Methuen, 1952);

Richard T. Shannon, *Gladstone and the Bulgarian Agitation* (London: Nelson, 1963);

Warren Staebler, *The Liberal Mind of John Morley* (Princeton: Princeton University Press, 1943);

Peter Stansky, *Ambitions and Strategies: The Struggle for Leadership of the Liberal Party in the 1890s* (Oxford: Oxford University Press, 1964);

Lytton Strachey, "A Statesman: John Morley," in his *Characters and Commentaries* (London: Chatto & Windus, 1933), pp. 227–231;

Basil Willey, "John Morley," in his *More Nineteenth Century Studies: A Group of Honest Doubters* (London: Chatto & Windus, 1956), pp. 248–301;

Stanley Wolpert, *Morley and India, 1906–1910* (Berkeley: University of California Press, 1967).

Papers:

The major collections containing substantial correspondence from Morley include the John Morley Papers, India Office Library and Wadham College, Oxford; the Joseph Chamberlain Papers, Birmingham University Library; the William Ewart Gladstone Papers, British Library; the Frederic Harrison Papers, British Library of Political and Economic Science; and the John Stuart Mill Papers, British Library of Political and Economic Science.

Frederic W. H. Myers
(6 February 1843 – 17 January 1901)

Barbara Frey Waxman
University of North Carolina at Wilmington

BOOKS: *The Distress in Lancashire: A Poem Which Obtained the Chancellor's Medal at the Cambridge Commencement* (Cambridge, 1863);

Saint Paul (London: Macmillan, 1867; New York: Randolph, 1868; corrected edition, London: Macmillan / New York: Macmillan, 1905);

Poems (London & Cambridge: Macmillan, 1870);

Wordsworth (London: Macmillan, 1881; New York: Harper, 1881);

The Renewal of Youth, and Other Poems (London: Macmillan, 1882);

Essays–Classical (London: Macmillan, 1883; London: Macmillan / New York: Macmillan, 1897);

Essays–Modern (London: Macmillan, 1883; London: Macmillan / New York: Macmillan, 1897);

Phantasms of the Living, by Myers, Edmund Gurney, and Frank Podmore (London: Society for Psychical Research, 1886);

Science and a Future Life, with Other Essays (London & New York: Macmillan, 1893);

Human Personality and Its Survival of Bodily Death, edited by Richard Hodgson and Alice Johnson, 2 volumes (London: Green, 1903; New York: Longmans & Green, 1903);

Fragments of Prose & Poetry, edited by Eveleen Myers (London, New York & Bombay: Longmans, Green, 1904);

Collected Poems, with Autobiographical and Critical Fragments, edited by Eveleen Myers (London: Macmillan, 1921);

Saint John the Baptist (London: Allenson, 1927);

Fragments of Inner Life: An Autobiographical Sketch (London: Society for Psychical Research, 1961).

OTHER: "Greek Oracles," in *Hellenica: A Collection of Essays on Greek Poetry, Philosophy, History, and Religion,* edited by Evelyn Abbott (London: Rivingtons, 1880), pp. 425–492;

Frederic Myers, *Catholic Thoughts on the Church of Christ and the Church of England,* introduction by Frederic W. H. Myers (London: Isbister, 1883);

Frederic W. H. Myers

Richard Chenevix Trench, *In Time of War: Poems,* preface by Myers (London: Kegan Paul, 1900).

SELECTED PERIODICAL PUBLICATIONS–
UNCOLLECTED: "Local Lectures for Women," *Macmillan's Magazine,* 19 (1868): 159–163;

"Mr. Jebb's Translations," *Fortnightly Review,* old series 20, new series 14 (1873): 645–655;

"Thought Reading," by Myers, W. F. Barrett, and Edmund Gurney, *Nineteenth Century,* 11 (1882): 890–900;

"Transferred Impressions and Telepathy," by Myers and Gurney, *Fortnightly Review,* old series 39, new series 33 (1883): 437-452;

"Mesmerism," by Myers and Gurney, *Nineteenth Century,* 14 (1883): 695-719;

"Apparitions," by Myers and Gurney, *Nineteenth Century,* 15 (1884): 791-815;

"Automatic Writing," *Contemporary Review,* 47 (1885): 233-249;

"Some Higher Aspects of Mesmerism," by Myers and Gurney, *National Review,* 5 (1885): 681-703;

"Human Personality," *Fortnightly Review,* old series 44, new series 38 (1885): 637-655;

"Multiplex Personality," *Nineteenth Century,* 20 (1886): 648-666;

"Matthew Arnold," *Fortnightly Review,* old series 49, new series 43 (1888): 719-728;

"Noticeable Books: Janet's *Psychical Automatism*," *Nineteenth Century,* 26 (1889): 341-343;

"The Drift of Psychical Research," *National Review,* 24 (1894): 190-209;

"On Some Fresh Facts Indicating Man's Survival of Death," *National Review,* 32 (1898): 230-242;

"Rossetti and the Religion of Beauty," *Bibelot,* 8 (1902): 337-367.

Frederic William Henry Myers was a British poet, literary critic, essayist, social observer, mystic, philosopher, and scientific researcher into the human mind and soul. While he modestly characterizes himself in *Fragments of Inner Life: An Autobiographical Sketch* (1961) as "a fusion of a minor poet and an amateur *savant*," Myers is also a significant British reform writer. As a literary critic and a biographer of William Wordsworth, he wrote a balanced reassessment of the poet, whom he designated as an "epoch-maker" in literary history. Myers also pointed out the literary merits of writings by the poet's sister, Dorothy, and he worked to reform women's limited cultural roles in Britain by writing essays supporting higher education for women, praising women writers such as Dorothy Wordsworth and George Eliot, and celebrating enlightened literary depictions of women. Myers also pursued a quite radical reform in attempting to fuse scientific with religious inquiry: in 1882 he founded–with Edmund Gurney, the Reverend W. Moses Stainton, Sir William F. Barrett, and the husband and wife Henry and Eleanor Sidgwick–the Society for Psychical Research and began psychological and physiological studies to gather evidence for the immortality of the soul. Myers questioned prevailing deterministic notions such as that psychic life is shaped entirely by heredity. He formulated a concept of mental evolution that extended Charles Darwin's theory of evolution into the psychic and spiritual realms. Myers's spiritual questing, scientific studies of the human mind and hypnosis, and development of the concept of the subliminal self offered powerful alternatives to both the faltering Christianity and the philosophical materialism of his day.

Born in Keswick, Cumberland, Myers was the eldest of three sons of the Reverend Frederic Myers, a man of Yorkshire yeoman stock and vicar of Keswick from 1838 until his death in 1851. The Reverend Myers was a Broad Church clergyman, among the first to express liberal speculative tendencies. His wife, also descended from several Yorkshire families, was the daughter of John Marshall, a member of Parliament from Leeds. Both parents were religious, and in *Fragments of Inner Life* Myers claims to have inherited their religious feelings and preoccupation with the unseen, feelings that he experienced early in his childhood and recorded both in his writings on psychic phenomena and in his emphasis on religious themes in discussing the poetry of Virgil, Wordsworth, and Matthew Arnold. He also inherited his mother's love of poetry and natural scenery, an influence apparent in his own verse and in his panegyrics to Virgil, Wordsworth, Arnold, and Alfred Tennyson.

An anecdote from his early boyhood, as reported in *Fragments of Inner Life,* illustrates Myers's early and persistent fascination with death and the immortality of the soul. He recalls seeing a dead mole and asking his mother whether its soul has gone to heaven. Her reply that the mole had no soul and would not be reborn strikes him with "the first horror of a death without resurrection." Just after the death of his father and when Frederic was eight years old, he had another conversation with his mother, this one about the possibility that evil men might not go to hell but might be annihilated at death; again he was shocked at the thought of death without resurrection. Myers's sensitivity to death and uncertainties about an afterlife combined with a mature, tender, and generous nature to make the boy an able comforter of his mother when the Reverend Myers died. Arthur Christopher Benson, who heard and remembered Myers's "thrilling" voice as the boy spoke with "solemn and noble eloquence" at Eton and who later met Myers when he was a student at Cambridge, characterizes Myers as possessing from childhood "loyal affection, . . . [the capacity to face] great issues, a vitality of spirit, . . . almost feminine tenderness, . . . sympathy, [and] a preoccupation with the needs and sorrows of others." Although Myers was quite reserved in company, he was an impassioned man—noble, refined, and dignified, yet courteous and unintimidating.

In boyhood when his father taught him Latin and gave him a copy of Virgil's *Aeneid,* Myers developed a passion for the works of Plato and ancient Greek and Roman poets, which deepened when Myers went to Trinity College, Cambridge, at age seventeen. Between the ages of sixteen and twenty-three he embraced Hellenism as his "religion." He recalled reading Plato's *Phaedo* as the moment of his conversion to this religion, and while his religious belief subsequently changed many times, he always considered the teachings of Plato, Virgil, and Marcus Aurelius to be the mainstays of his faith. In 1865 he became a fellow and classical lecturer at Cambridge, and this appointment enabled him to focus his energies on classical materials.

A dimension of Myers's passion for the past was his attention to gender issues in Greece during the sixth century B.C., the heyday of the Hellenic spirit. He notes in his autobiography that in that era women played "their due part with men," and he speculates: "What might the Greeks have made of the female sex had they continued to care for it!" Myers's interest in reforms of women's roles included his own times, and in 1869 he left his Cambridge lectureship to help start the new movement for the higher education of women. "Local Lectures for Women," which he published in *Macmillan's Magazine* in December 1868, reflects his enthusiasm for this new movement to remedy the cultural isolation of British women by cultivating their "eager, receptive minds." He answers parents' objections to the education of their daughters by explaining that both males and females have God-given intelligence that it is society's duty to cultivate and then employ. He also notes that men want clever wives as companions and as intelligent, liberally educated mothers who can effectively educate their children and introduce them to concepts of truth. He concludes that it takes wisdom for people to help each other and glorify God and that God would be pleased that humanity is seeking to acquire this wisdom.

Following his Hellenic period of belief, Myers for a brief time was suspended between religious faiths before he passionately reconverted to Christianity under the influence of Josephine Butler, the Salvation Army philanthropist and feminist author whose *Women's Work and Women's Culture* (1869) may have helped to raise Myers's consciousness of the social status of women. His Christian fervor is evident in his two poems *Saint Paul* (1867) and *Saint John the Baptist* (1927). The latter poem was especially praised by John Ruskin, but Benson, writing his biographical sketch of Myers in 1911, asserts instead that *Saint Paul* "has won a secure place in English literature" because it is experimental and original in form and meter.

During this period of renewed Christian faith Myers also added history and science to his store of knowledge, which gradually moved him into a period of painful agnosticism that he strove to escape through seeking evidence for religious faith. Some of his spiritual struggles are recorded in a collection of his poems published in 1870, and this collection was followed in 1882 by *The Renewal of Youth, and Other Poems,* which signaled his growing interests in psychical studies after he had met Henry Sidgwick in 1871. All of Myers's poems were collected after his death by his wife, Eveleen Tennant, whom he married in 1880; with some of his prose pieces and his autobiographical essay she published these poems as *Fragments of Prose & Poetry* in 1904. One of these poems, "A Child of the Age," expresses Myers's yearning for a voice that can reveal the spiritual secret of life and "the bliss to be." The poem also describes his dream that he will provide the "marching music" for his skeptical era of "doubtful fighting-men" whom he hoped to awaken to a new faith.

Noting that Virgil is Myers's intellectual and aesthetic mentor, John Addington Symonds also compares the attention Myers gives to the emotional associations of sound and sense in his poetry to those in the poetry of Edgar Allan Poe. Myers's insistent rhythms also show his affinities to the poetry of A. C. Swinburne, and Symonds observes that Myers's style assures his place in literary history. Symonds also acknowledges two main themes of Myers's verses, one evident in his early commitment to the higher education of women and the second in his interests in psychical studies, and he writes that "If we seek the leading ideas which animate him as a poet, I think that we shall find them to be the aspiration after personal immortality and the influence of women in human affairs. . . . He has given musical utterance to these two factors of man's spiritual life."

Symonds's observation about Myers's attitude toward women was evident in Myers's positive relationships with his mother and his wife. His marriage was an especially happy one, and his intense love for his wife and three children reinforced his longing to prove the existence of the afterlife of the soul, because he could not bear the thought of being separated from them at death. In his autobiography he embraces as his premise Plato's definition of the highest love as "'a desire for the eternal possession' of the beloved object," and he argues that "removal by death, if no reunion be looked for, at once reduces this life to an act of endurance alone." Myers refused to think that God would torture his creatures in this way, and soon after he married he began his spiritual quest with "patient ardour," as Benson writes in referring to Myers's posthumously published *Human Personality and Its Survival of Bodily Death* (1903). But through the early 1880s Myers was also writing essays and literary criticism and working as an inspector of schools, a post that he had assumed in 1872 and retained until his death.

In 1881 Myers's *Wordsworth* was published, and a review in the *Spectator* hailed it as the gem of the English Men of Letters Series. In *Academy* another reviewer emphasized the excellence of all the chapters, and in the *Saturday Review* still another praised its account of the poet's life and concluded that most readers would find it a good book. Benson characterizes *Wordsworth* and Myers's essay on Virgil, which was collected in *Essays–Classical* (1883), as songs of praise rather than objective literary analyses. In preaching the Wordsworthian faith, Myers's book on the poet contains chapters on his childhood and education; his years at Cambridge; his residence in London and France; the publication of his major poems; the role of Grasmere and the English Lake District in Wordsworth's life and work; his relationships with Dorothy, his brother John, Samuel Taylor Coleridge, and others; his tours of Scotland and Italy; his poetic diction; his natural religion; and his political views.

Benson's claim that Myers's biography praises Wordsworth excessively may be too severe. Myers acknowledges that *The Prelude; or, Growth of a Poet's Mind: An Autobiographical Poem* (1850) is initially "tedious and insipid," egoistic, and inappropriate in form, but he then appreciatively describes its cumulative effect, its use of personal experience for general moral lessons, and its ability to capture hardy young English readers. Myers calls it a work "of good augury for human nature" and praises its tribute to the power of the soul. He also challenges critics' antagonism toward Wordsworth's blissful calm and perennial felicity, and in indicating that the poet felt sorrow and did indeed suffer, especially at the deaths of his children, Myers shows that passion underlies Wordsworth's deliberately stoic philosophy. He concedes that Wordsworth's poetry lacks humor, but he attributes this lack to the fact that the poet had to endure the consistent attacks of critics. He praises Wordsworth's 1800 preface to *Lyrical Ballads* for its theory of the literary creative process, but he notes the inadequacy of Wordsworth's theory to explain the merits of his own poetry and acknowledges how the poet's insight, melody, and

Myers and his son

magic atrophies in later poems, such as his patriotic sonnets, which include no new lessons about British heroism and represent a "summary of patriotism, a manual of national honour." Myers also sympathetically explains how Wordsworth's growing political conservatism in his old age stems from what the poet observes as a vanishing ideal of national happiness. In these respects Myers is quite fair as a literary biographer. He summarizes Wordsworth's spiritual and literary achievement as follows: "the true epoch-maker in the history of the human soul is the man who educes from this bewildering universe a new and elevating joy." Myers thinks that Wordsworth has done this, and readers may surmise that Myers hoped to do the same in establishing the existence of the soul's afterlife.

Myers's concern for gender issues in *Wordsworth* is also apparent in his attention to Dorothy Wordsworth's letters and journals and in his tribute to her sensitivity and eloquence. He claims that the poetic abilities of the Wordsworths were "almost more dominant and conspicuous in Dorothy Wordsworth than in the poet himself," especially in her appreciation of nature, although not in her intellectual capacities.

Myers's interest in antiquity and historical figures as well as in the contemporary literary scene is reflected in his *Essays—Classical* and *Essays—Modern*, both published in 1883. These two volumes cover a range of topics, from Greek oracles and Virgil to Mazzini, George Sand, Victor Hugo, George Eliot, and Dante Gabriel Rossetti's religion of beauty. Critics praised the volumes for their erudition, their power to create ideas, and their range of interesting subjects, and critics in the United States also agreed. Melville B. Anderson liked the collection's thoroughness, quality of instructive thought, and eloquence of tone and style. He notes Myers's unifying theme—the issue of life after death—and summarizes his ever-hopeful agnosticism by writing: "His thought is that . . . God simply subordinates laws known to science to more potent laws, as yet unknown, but perhaps ascertainable."

Myers's fascination with unseen forces is articulated in "Greek Oracles," in which he analyzes the evolution of the Greeks' conception of oracles from magical spirits into moral teachers. Myers describes the oracles' inspired trances as instances of possession by spirits similar to those that the biblical prophets experienced, and he discusses the scientific explanations—delirium, hysteria, or epilepsy—that have been given for the behavior of these oracles. His methods of analyzing the oracles that he surveys are those of the comparative mythologist and anthropologist as well as the philologist interpreting the texts of the oracles, their gift of revelation. Myers's erudition is evident as he discusses the interactions of the oracles with Herodotus, Plato, Socrates, Porphyry, and Plotinus; compares Greek religion with its philosophy; and traces other influences of the oracles on public and private lives. He theorizes about the gradual demise of the oracles' power as the concept of a comprehensive supreme power became popular. His mysticism is apparent in the attention he gives throughout the essay to the conditions necessary for possession by spirits and in his examination of the Greek religion for ways of achieving union with the unseen. Myers intended that the insights this essay provides into human beings' spiritual needs would serve as a powerful alternative to the philosophical materialism current in his day.

In his literary criticism, especially of Virgil, Myers retains the mystic's appreciation of the emotional force and music of poetry. He is antagonistic toward German "scientific" literary criticism and its analytical methods, which betray an impulse to "degrade every masterpiece of human genius into the mere pabulum of hungry professors" and value a literary text "only as a field for the rivalries of sterile pedantry." Myers praises the musical and mystical intensity of Virgil's poetry, which enables readers to glimpse the eternal in the passionate soul. He analyzes Virgil's place within the Roman religion and discusses Virgil's spiritual yearnings and prescience of Christianity. Myers's attention to gender issues in this essay is evident in his discussion of the poet's characterization of Dido in the *Aeneid*. He praises Virgil for having insight into the female heart, and Myers pays tribute to what he sees as woman's range of feelings and behavior, her passion and moral fiber.

In his essay on Eliot, Myers stresses the spiritual struggles of Marian Evans and her prophetic utterances and places her alongside two other great Victorian prophets, Thomas Carlyle and John Ruskin. Myers chronologically recounts the development of her spiritual education, including her Evangelical period and her turning from belief in Jesus. Unlike some Victorian writers on Eliot, Myers both respects the privacy of her life and defends the morality of her decision to live with G. H. Lewes, who was living apart from but was still married to another woman: "[I]f ever her intimate history is made more fully known to the world it will be found to contain nothing at variance with her own unselfish teaching; no postponement of principle to passion, no personal happiness based upon others' pain." Myers depicts Eliot as serious, wise, intellectually vital, and an influence for good. He does not idealize her; he sees her faults as vanity, resentment, and envy, but he suggests that she struggles against them and achieves moral dignity. He feels profound sorrow at her stoic resignation to the absence of a God and the mortality of the soul, but he praises her religion of humanity and her courage for insisting on virtue, duty, and moral striving while being unable to envision the rewards of an afterlife. In analyzing the moral crises in her novels he admires the inspiring way she portrays human fellowship.

Myers's treatment of Eliot's life and work is balanced and clear, but his message about Dante Gabriel Rossetti's art and moral influence is not stated so effectively in "Rossetti and the Religion of Beauty," the final work in *Essays—Modern*. He seems intent on defending Rossetti's paintings from criticism of their dangerous sensuality by explaining that the artist's aestheticism opposes materialism and commonplace passions, presents mystical passions, and presents through material things a higher spiritual significance. He claims that Rossetti's means of apprehending higher spiritual states is not through ethical feelings but through love. While the artist's aestheticism thus may not elicit elevating virtues, it intensifies and exalts the emotions and sensory powers of people and thereby enriches their lives. In trying to defend Rossetti's aestheticism, Myers betrays his own discomfort with what he perceives to be Rossetti's amorality, and his essay concludes by suggesting that love is Rossetti's means of uniting moral agency, beauty, and joy. Anderson complains of Myers's lack of clarity in this essay, an obscurity that he attributes not to Myers's lack of skill but to the nature of the task Myers adopts in seeking to explain the tenets of a religion of beauty.

Myers's *Science and a Future Life, with Other Essays* (1893) had been preceded by *Phantasms of the Living* (1886), a collection written in collaboration with Edmund Gurney and Frank Podmore, his fellow researchers in psychic phenomena. "Science and a Future Life" offers some fruits of Myers's labors through the 1880s to prove the existence of a life after death by using scientific, psychological, and physiological discoveries about the personality and phenomena such as automatism. The essay rejects a conception of humans as purely material beings and argues against ruling out the possibility of an afterlife by claiming that no one knows all the answers to the questions that science poses and that this question of whether an afterlife exists should be posed from a scientific perspective. His essay also places this question in the context of the history of philosophy and theology. Myers illustrates his point through the scenario of two larvae analyzing themselves on a cabbage leaf: as insects, they consider their future and see their aerial origins in their construction, from which their butterfly destiny might be deduced. From man's spiritual construction, Myers intimates, his "transcendental energy," the future life of his soul, might be similarly deduced. Myers would thus extend the theoretical implications of evolution to spiritual states of being, to progressive stages of "life, consciousness, thought."

In "Charles Darwin and Agnosticism," another essay in his 1893 collection, Myers responds to *The Life and Letters of Charles Darwin, Including an Autobiographical Chapter* (1887) by discussing Darwin's agnosticism without attacking it. Myers explains how Darwin's theory weakens one's belief in Providence and one's conception of sin, which human beings had based on a conception of their relationship to a Supreme Being. He regrets that humanity has lost a sense of divine aid and forgiveness and consequently depends on laws of heredity to work out human destiny. Much of the essay concerns different theories on the origin of the human soul, which Myers places beside Darwin's studies. Characterizing Darwin's agnosticism as modest and gentle-hearted rather than combative or joyful, Myers observes Darwin's contentment with life on

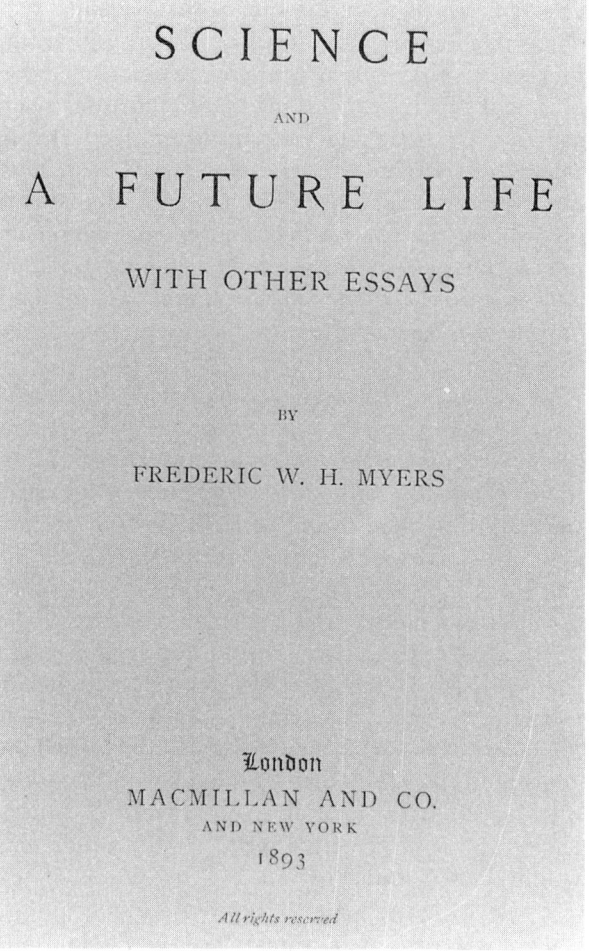

Title page for one of the collections that includes Myers's attempts to reconcile science and religion

earth despite his weakening religious instincts and attributes to the scientist an enviable temperament, a moral nature free from conflicts and "from our self-questioning complexities—from the *Welt-Schmerz* which . . . has paralyzed or saddened so many of the best lives of our time." Myers fights this weltschmerz by arguing that the theory of evolution should be extended into psychic and spiritual realms, to enable humanity to witness the "more than corporeal descent and destiny of man."

In a third essay of this collection, "The Disenchantment of France," Myers analyzes sociohistorically and philosophically the malaise of France in the 1890s. He examines four kinds of illusions that have been dispelled in France: religious, political, sexual, and personal. He reports that the loss of belief has reduced the population growth in France, as the people adjust to living in a universe without hope. Myers emphasizes how the French have lost personal illusions, those ideas of the individual's free will and psychical unity, and he resists the prevailing fatalistic notion in France that psychic life is determined entirely by heredity. He urges that further study, especially psychophysiological observations and experiments, be made with the human personality, and he suggests that the disengaged, skeptical, but alert minds of the French may contribute discoveries in experimental psychology. His essay is perceptive, systematically organized, and rationally argued, but as is the case with most of his essays that address the issue of the afterlife, it is infused with his impassioned commitment to the immortality of the soul.

Myers never lived to see the publication of *Human Personality and Its Survival of Bodily Death,* his great work on the human personality and the afterlife of the soul, but his data, appendices, and preliminary text were compiled by Richard Hodgson and Alice Johnson, who published the two-volume work in 1903. William James, professor of experimental psychology, pays perhaps the greatest tribute to Myers for his contributions to psychology. In reviewing Myers's book in the *Proceedings* of the Society for Psychical Research, James hails Myers as the father of a new science for having developed the concept of the subliminal self (that part of the mind dissociated from forgotten or repressed experiences) and for having mapped two different levels within the subliminal region.

He validates Myers's exploration of hypnotic phenomena and of "automatisms"—hallucinations or unmotivated impulses to act—connected to hypnotic trances. He does say that Myers reaches overgeneralized conclusions about human nature based on his limited observations of subliminal life, and James registers some skepticism when Myers discusses "automatisms of the sensory order" (phantasms and spirit messages). Although he respects Myers's scientific reasoning about and sorting of data, James suggests that Myers's emotional attachment to the idea of immortality and his literary skill work against persuading scientific readers to accept his theory. Still, James concludes by praising Myers's map of the subliminal as "the only scientifically serious investigation that has yet been offered."

James presented an even greater tribute when he spoke to the Society for Psychical Research on "Frederic Myers's services to psychology." He credited Myers with being the first to formulate the problem of the constituents of the subliminal self and the methods for ascertaining those constituents. He praised Myers for his ability to create analogies, to collect and classify data, and to hypothesize. He hailed Myers for his brilliant conception of hysteria and for his imaginative idea of mental evolution, which he called "a hypothesis of first-rate philosophic importance . . . [and] one of those sweeping ideas by which the scientific researches of an entire generation are often moulded." He concluded that Myers's place in the history of psychology was secure "as the pioneer who staked out a vast tract of mental wilderness and planted the flag of genuine science upon it."

Some reviewers of *Human Personality* were more cautious than James in assessing Myers's scientific method and reasoning. J. H. Muirhead praises Myers's brilliant investigative and organizing abilities as well as his intellectual sincerity and the practical applications of his ideas about the relationship between mind and matter, but Muirhead notes that these qualities conflict with Myers's mystical nature and his intense longing for an intuitive apprehension of the soul's afterlife. Muirhead also suggests that the facts Myers offers to prove the existence of an afterlife do not establish a faith but act only as an aid to faith, at best; at worst, they may confuse readers with religious doubts about the spiritual nature of their world. Muirhead acknowledges the tenuousness of Myers's argument but appreciates his efforts: "In an age where old faiths seem to many to be crumbling about us, our sympathy is claimed for any genuine attempt to regain a foothold on the old peace and confidence."

Muirhead's criticisms are gentler than those of W. H. Mallock, who calls Myers's book "an astounding monument of misapplied talents and speculation." He criticizes Myers's premise that the part of the personality removed from consciousness is an entirely separate self, and Mallock claims that the two independent selves are really the same self under different conditions. He protests the removal of the subliminal from the conscious self, because to do so leaves the latter as a "meaningless moral vacuum" and makes the former too vulnerable to external forces such as hypnotism. Like many of Myers's other readers, Mallock is uncomfortable with Myers's vacillation between the scientific and the mystical, which he characterizes as "a kind of Buddhism harmonised with scientific fact." The responses of these three reviewers reflect the conflicted yet rich, provocative nature of Myers's book, as well as the religious and philosophical turmoil of an era of British reform in which men and women of faith felt the pressures of an increasingly skeptical influence from men and women of science.

The reforming spirit of Frederic W. H. Myers, who began his career as a poet, essayist, and literary critic, was apparent in his early reassessments of the literary giants of his century and of antiquity, in his celebration of women's contributions to literature and to British culture generally, and in his support for higher education for women, a means that he saw to end women's cultural isolation and relegation to domesticity. Under the influence of his intensely mystical and inquiring spirituality, in the middle of Myers's career he rechanneled his energies into research in the human sciences, investigations of the human personality, and philosophical explorations of the meaning of human life. His contributions to the fledgling field of psychology were noteworthy and are still praised in the twentieth century. He has been honored in particular for mapping levels of the subliminal self well before Sigmund Freud's theory of the unconscious was published.

What is most important in understanding his work as a British reform writer is that Myers attempted to reverse the growing fragmentation of his era, the dichotomizing of scientific and religious inquiry, through his synthesizing investigations into the psyche and the immortality of the soul. His collection and organization of voluminous data on psychic phenomena in support of an afterlife culminated in his last, greatest, and most controversial work, *Human Personality and Its Survival of Bodily Death*. With this work Myers may not have successfully established a new faith for an increasingly skeptical British public, but he entered provocatively into the turbulent dialogue about science, religion, and human potential that characterized an era of British reform.

References:

Melville B. Anderson, Review of *Essays, Classical and Modern, Dial,* 4 (1883): 108–110;

Arthur Christopher Benson, "Frederic Myers," in his *The Leaves of the Tree: Studies in Biography* (New York & London: Putnam, 1911), pp. 222–254;

William James, "Frederic Myers' Services to Psychology," in his *Memories and Studies* (New York: Longmans, Green, 1911), pp. 145–170;

W. H. Mallock, "The Gospel of Mr. F. W. H. Myers," *Nineteenth Century,* 53 (1903): 628–644;

J. H. Muirhead, "The Survival of the Soul," *Contemporary Review,* 84 (1903): 112–121;

Gardner Murphy, Introduction to Myers's *Human Personality and Its Survival of Bodily Death* (New York & London: Longmans, Green, 1903);

W. H. Salter, "Our Pioneers II: Frederic W. H. Myers," *Journal of the Society for Psychical Research,* 39 (1958): 261–266;

Susy Smith, preface to Myers's *Human Personality and Its Survival of Bodily Death,* edited by Smith (New Hyde Park, N.Y.: University Books, 1961);

John Addington Symonds, "Frederic Myers," in *The Poets and the Poetry of the Nineteenth Century,* 12 volumes, edited by Alfred H. Miles (London: Hutchinson, 1905–1907), VII: 61–66.

Francis William Newman
(27 June 1805 – 4 October 1897)

Sidney Coulling

BOOKS: *Lectures on Logic, or on the Science of Evidence Generally, Embracing Both Demonstrative and Probable Reasonings, with the Doctrine of Causation, Delivered at Bristol College in the Year 1836* (Oxford: J. H. Parker, 1838);

The Difficulties of Elementary Geometry, Especially Those which Concern the Straight Line, the Plane, and the Theory of Parallels (London: W. Ball, 1841);

On the Illiberality of Sentiment and Practice Apprehended from Separating Church and State (London, 1846);

A State Church Not Defensible on the Theory Espoused by Liberal Episcopalians (London: British Anti-State-Church Association, 1846);

Four Lectures on the Contrasts of Ancient and Modern History: Delivered at the Manchester Athenaeum, Michaelmas 1846 (London: Taylor & Walton, 1847);

A History of the Hebrew Monarchy, from the Administration of Samuel to the Babylonish Captivity (London: J. Chapman, 1847);

On the Relations of Free Knowledge to Moral Sentiment: A Lecture Delivered in University College, London, on the 13th Oct. 1846 (London, 1847);

An Appeal to the Middle Classes on the Urgent Necessity of Numerous Radical Reforms, Financial and Organic (London: Taylor & Walton, 1848);

On the Constitutional and Moral Right or Wrong of Our National Debt (London: Taylor, Walton & Maberly, 1849);

The Soul, Her Sorrows and Her Aspirations: An Essay towards the Natural History of the Soul, as the True Basis of Theology (London: J. Chapman, 1849);

Phases of Faith; or, Passages from the History of My Creed (London: J. Chapman, 1850; augmented, 1853);

Lectures on Political Economy (London: J. Chapman, 1851);

Regal Rome: An Introduction to Roman History (London: Taylor, Walton & Maberly, 1852);

The Crimes of the House of Hapsburg against Its Own Liege Subjects (London: J. Chapman, 1853);

Catholic Union: Essays towards a Church of the Future, as the Organization of Philanthropy (London: J. Chapman, 1854);

The Prospects of England (Leeds: Green, 1855);

Personal Narrative; in Letters, Principally from Turkey, in the Years 1830–3 (London: Holyoake, 1856);

Theism, Doctrinal and Practical; or, Didactic Religious Utterances (London: J. Chapman, 1858); revised and enlarged as *Hebrew Theism: The Common Basis of Judaism, Christianity, and Mohammedism* (London: Trübner, 1874);

The Relations of Professional to Liberal Knowledge: A Lecture Delivered in University College, London, October 12, 1859, Introductory to the Session of the Faculty of

Arts and Laws, 1859–60 (London: Walton & Maberly, 1859);

Homeric Translation in Theory and Practice: A Reply to Matthew Arnold, Esq., Professor of Poetry, Oxford (London & Edinburgh: Williams & Norgate, 1861);

Character of the Southern States of America: Letter to a Friend who had Joined the Southern Independence Association (Manchester: Union & Emancipation Society's Depot, 1863);

The Good Cause of President Lincoln (London: Emancipation Society, 1863);

A Discourse against Hero-Making in Religion, Delivered in South Place Chapel, Finsbury, April 24th, 1864 (London: Trübner, 1864);

English Institutions and Their Most Necessary Reforms: A Contribution of Thought (London: Trübner, 1865);

The Permissive Bill More Urgent than any Extension of the Franchise: Address at Ramsgate, February 17th, 1865 (Manchester: A. Heywood, 1865);

A Handbook of Modern Arabic: Consisting of a Practical Grammar, with Numerous Examples, Dialogues, and Newspaper Extracts; in a European Type (London: Trübner, 1866);

The Religious Weakness of Protestantism (Ramsgate: T. Scott, 1866);

On the Defective Morality of the New Testament (Ramsgate: T. Scott, 1867);

On the Philosophical Classification of National Institutions: A Lecture Delivered at the Bristol Institution for the Advancement of Science, Literature and the Arts, March 4th, 1867 (London: Trübner, 1867);

Thoughts on a Free and Comprehensive Christianity (Ramsgate: T. Scott, 1868);

The Bigot and the Sceptic: What Is Their Euthanasia? (Ramsgate: T. Scott, 1869);

The Cure of the Great Social Evil, with Special Reference to Recent Laws Delusively Called Contagious Diseases' Acts (London: Trübner / Bristol: Arrowsmith, 1869);

James and Paul: A Tract (Ramsgate: T. Scott, 1869);

A Lecture on Women's Suffrage (Bristol: I. Arrowsmith, 1869);

Orthoëpy: or, A Simple Mode of Accenting English, for the Advantage of Foreigners, and of All Learners (London: Trübner, 1869);

A Reply to the Question, "What Have We Got to Rely On, If We Cannot on the Bible?" (Ramsgate: T. Scott, 1869);

Miscellanies, 5 volumes (London: Trübner, 1869–1891);

Anthropomorphism: A Comment by F. W. Newman on Some Poetry Sent Him by a Lady (Ramsgate: T. Scott, 1870);

Divergence of Calvinism from Pauline Doctrine (Ramsgate: T. Scott, 1871);

Europe of the Near Future, with Three Letters on the Franco-German War (London: Trübner, 1871);

Lecture on Vegetarianism Delivered at Gloucester, Dec. 20, 1870 (London, 1871);

On the Causes of Atheism: A Lecture Delivered at Bristol, on February 7, 1871 (Ramsgate: T. Scott, 1871);

The True Temptation of Jesus (Ramsgate: T. Scott, 1871);

Is Romanism Real Christianity?, by Newman and Francis E. Abbot (Toledo: Index Association, 1872);

On the Relations of Theism to Pantheism, and on the Galla Religion (Ramsgate: T. Scott, 1872);

Thoughts on the Existence of Evil (Ramsgate: T. Scott, 1872);

The Controversy about Prayer (London: T. Scott, 1873);

On the Historical Depravation of Christianity (London: T. Scott, 1873);

Ancient Sacrifice (London: T. Scott, 1874);

On Religious Endowments, Read to the Members of the Reform Club, Manchester, 12th October, 1874 (Manchester: A. Ireland, 1874);

The Two Theisms (London: T. Scott, 1874);

A Discourse on the Presence of God (London, 1875);

A Discourse on the Service of God . . . at the Free Christian Church, Croydon, London (London, 1875);

On This and the Other World (London: T. Scott, 1875);

Re-Organization of English Institutions: A Lecture Delivered in the Manchester Athenaeum, on Friday, October 15, 1875 (Manchester: J. Heywood, 1875);

Religion, Not History (London: Trübner, 1877);

Morning Prayers in the Household of a Believer in God (London: Trübner, 1878);

What Is Christianity without Christ? (London: Trübner, 1881);

The Coming Revolution (Nottingham: Stevenson, Bailey & Smith, 1882);

Libyan Vocabulary: An Essay Towards Reproducing the Ancient Numidian Language, out of Four Modern Tongues (London: Trübner, 1882);

The Right and Duty of Every State to Enforce Sobriety on Its Citizens (Nottingham: Stevenson, Bailey & Smith, 1882);

A Christian Commonwealth (London: Trübner, 1883);

Essays on Diet (London: Kegan Paul, Trench, 1883);

The Land as National Property: With Special View to the Scheme of Reclaiming It for the Nation Proposed by Alfred Russel Wallace (London: W. Reeves, 1883);

Christianity in Its Cradle (London: Trübner, 1884);

Comments on the Text of Aeschylus (London: Trübner, 1884);

Life after Death? Palinōdia (London: Trübner, 1886);

The New Crusades; or, Duty of the Church to the World: Addressed Especially to Ministers of Religion (Nottingham: Stevenson, Bailey & Smith, 1886);

Kabail Vocabulary, Supplemented by Aid of a New Source (London: Trübner, 1887);

Mathematical Tracts (Cambridge, U.K.: Macmillan & Bowes, 1888);

Reminiscences of Two Exiles (Kossuth and Pulszky) and Two Wars (Crimean and Franco-Austrian) (London: K. Paul, Trench, 1888);

Anglo-Saxon Abolition of Negro Slavery (London: K. Paul, Trench, 1889);

The Corruption Now Called Neo-Malthusianism . . . (London: Moral Reform Union, 1889);

Elliptic Integrals (Cambridge, U.K.: Macmillan & Bowes, 1889);

Supplement to Studies in Aeschylus and Notes on Euripides (London: Kegan Paul, 1890);

Contributions Chiefly to the Early History of the Late Cardinal Newman (London: K. Paul, Trench, Trübner, 1891);

First Steps in Etruscan (London, 1892);

The Higher Trigonometry, Superrationals of Second Order (Cambridge: Macmillan & Bowes, 1892);

The Gospel of Paul of Tarsus, and of His Opponent, James the Just (Nottingham: Stevenson, Bailey & Smith, 1893);

Hebrew Jesus: His True Creed; from Canonical Texts of the Anglicans, before Paul of Tarsus Was a Christian, with the Cardinal Prayer of Jesus as Our Sole Sufficient Creed (Nottingham: Stevenson, Bailey & Smith, 1895).

TRANSLATIONS: *The Odes of Horace Translated into Unrhymed Metres, with Introductions and Notes* (London: Walton & Maberly, 1853);

The Iliad of Homer Faithfully Translated into Unrhymed English Metre (London: Walton & Maberly, 1856);

Henry Wadsworth Longfellow, *Hiawatha: Rendered into Latin, with Abridgment* (London: Walton & Maberly, 1862);

The Text of the Iguvine Inscriptions, with Interlinear Latin Translation, and Notes (London: A. Asher, 1864);

Translations of English Poetry into Latin Verse: Designed as Part of a New Method of Instructing in Latin (London, 1868);

Daniel Defoe, *Rebilius Cruso: Robinson Crusoe, in Latin: A Book to Lighten Tedium to a Learner* (London: Trübner, 1884).

OTHER: Lajos Kossuth, *Select Speeches of Kossuth, Condensed and Abridged, with Kossuth's Express Sanction*, edited by Newman (London: Trübner, 1853);

A Dictionary of Modern Arabic, 2 volumes, compiled by Newman (London: Trübner, 1871);

Secret Hymns, edited by Newman (Nottingham: Stevenson, Bailey & Smith, 1892).

In the concluding chapter of his *Apologia pro Vita Sua* (1864), John Henry Newman contrasts the serenity he experienced upon being received into the Roman Catholic Church with the self-destructive skepticism that eventually subverts all religious truth. The contrast might well have been suggested by his brilliant younger brother, Francis William, who in his own spiritual autobiography, *Phases of Faith; or, Passages from the History of My Creed* (1850), had recounted his painful journey from unconditional faith to complete rejection of the fundamental tenets of Christianity. Unlike the elder Newman, Francis regarded distrust of authority as inseparably related to the pursuit of truth. Accordingly he became, in his own words, "anti-everything," adamantly opposed to "things as they are." His "sharp-cutting, restlessly advancing intellect," as Thomas Carlyle admiringly described it in his *Life of John Sterling* (1851), led him to challenge received opinions in virtually every area of Victorian life and, until he fell into obscurity, brought him both adulation and notoriety as one of the most liberal thinkers of his time.

Born in London on 27 June 1805, Francis William Newman was the third son and fourth child of John and Jemima Fourdrinier Newman. His father was a banker whom his son later characterized in *Contributions Chiefly to the Early History of the Late Cardinal Newman* (1891) as "an admirer of Benjamin Franklin and Thomas Jefferson" and a worldly man without religious pretensions. His mother, of Huguenot descent, belonged to a family of paper manufacturers. These parents, members of the Church of England, practiced a religion that emphasized the Bible rather than creeds and nurtured in two of the sons an intimate knowledge of Scripture and a lifelong delight in reading it.

Newman began his formal education at the private school of Dr. George Nicholas, in nearby Ealing, Middlesex, where he had been preceded by his two brothers. In 1821, at the age of sixteen, he went up to Oxford to prepare for entering Worcester College the following year. His father's bank had closed, creating a financial crisis for the family, so Newman lived with John Henry, who was then at Trinity College and who supported him with money earned from tutoring. The elder brother's confidence in the boy's future was not misplaced, for in 1826, with seemingly effortless ease, Newman achieved first-class honors in classics and mathematics and was elected to a fellowship in Balliol College.

During these years, however, Newman had suffered religious doubts that nearly caused him to refuse his degree. In order to gain admission to Oxford he had willingly subscribed to the Thirty-nine Articles of faith of the Anglican Church, but after witnessing the religious apathy of his fellow students he concluded that subscription was a meaningless and even corrupting requirement. Meanwhile he had developed unconventional views of the Trinity, atonement, infant baptism, and strict observance of the Sabbath. In his difficulties he could not turn for help to his brother, whom he considered a Catholic in Anglican disguise and who had caused an open breach by ordering a picture of the Virgin Mary for Newman's room. By the time he took his degree Newman was aware that he could never become a clergyman in the Church of England, but he nevertheless felt spiritual longings that he hoped to realize as a Christian missionary in a heathen land.

In 1827 Newman went to Dublin to serve as tutor in the household of Henry Brooke Parnell, first Baron Congleton and thereby entered a decisive period of his life. At the time he was experiencing the pangs of unrequited love, having unsuccessfully proposed marriage to a beautiful young woman named Maria Rosina Giberne. Overtaxed emotionally as well as intellectually, he was easily susceptible to the influences that now pressed on him. The strongest of these was exerted by a relative of Lord Congleton, John Nelson Darby, later the founder of a branch of the Plymouth Brethren, whose stark asceticism seemed to Newman the true embodiment of Christianity. His desire to become a missionary reawakened by Darby, Newman found himself in the congenial company of two other zealous men who shared his ambition–Lord Congleton's son, John Vesey Parnell, and a dentist named Anthony Norris Groves, who together had undergone a religious conversion. Thus began the strange episode that provided Newman with the subject for his *Personal Narrative; in Letters, Principally from Turkey, in the Years 1830-3* (1856).

The quixotic plan of the group–to bring Christ to Baghdad–proved to be a disastrous affair. With Newman in the party were Parnell, who had given his entire fortune to the mission; Edward Cronin, a doctor, and his mother, sister (whom Parnell married), and infant child (whose mother had just died and whom the father did not wish to leave behind); and a man named Hamilton, who returned early to England, his health broken. Groves and his wife had gone ahead and were to be joined in Baghdad by the others. In September 1830 the party left Dublin by steamer with a staggering amount of luggage that included, in addition to the usual bags and trunks, a small library of books and a press for printing tracts. But comedy turned to tragedy before they could establish themselves at their destination. Many of their pos-

Maria Kennaway, whom Newman married in 1835

sessions were stolen or lost, and they were stoned by fanatics and beset by the plague; the men barely escaped with their lives, and all of the women died. Despite untold hardships, moreover, they accomplished almost nothing as missionaries beyond distributing a few Bibles. In *Phases of Faith* Newman implicitly conceded defeat as he recalled a conversation with an Islamic carpenter who told him that "God has given you English a great many good gifts" but has withheld the most important–"knowledge of the true religion by which one may be saved."

In September 1832, exactly two years after his departure from Dublin, Newman set out on his return trip to England. He arrived the following June on the very day John Henry reached home from Sicily, a coincidence of prophetic significance. Newman had returned to England with the purpose of gaining fresh recruits for the work in Baghdad, but his arrival coincided with not only the beginning of the Oxford Movement and the increasing estrangement from his brother, but also the questioning of his faith by Darby and other friends. "Where is union? Where is the Church, which was to convert the heathen?" Newman asked himself, answering that to return to Baghdad to preach a Christianity divided against itself was absurd. As a result he abandoned all plans of continuing missionary work and settled instead into a life he was later to describe as "eminently uneventful."

That life began with his appointment in 1834 as classical tutor and lecturer in mathematics at the newly established and short-lived Bristol College, a nonsectarian institution. There he also delivered a series of lectures that became his first published book, *Lectures on Logic, or on the Science of Evidence Generally, Embracing Both Demonstrative and Probable Reasonings, with the Doctrine of Causation, Delivered at Bristol College in the Year 1836* (1838). In the year following his appointment he married Maria Kennaway, daughter of Sir John Kennaway, recently retired from the East India Company after meritorious service in India. According to biographer William Robbins, she was a beautiful young woman, simple and devout in her faith, and "given to good works among the poor and to religious instruction in neighboring village schools." The marriage, although childless, brought Newman more than forty years of happiness until her death in July 1876.

In the meantime Newman had been made classical professor in Manchester New College, where he began a long and close friendship with James Martineau, the influential Unitarian who joined the faculty that same year (1840) as professor of mental and moral philosophy. Six years later Newman was appointed to the chair of Latin in University College, London, a position he held until 1863. During this period of his professorships he became widely known among his detractors for eccentricities in dress and manner, literal-mindedness, and complete absence of a sense of humor, and among his admirers for stimulating lectures and especially for piety. In an 1849 letter Elizabeth Gaskell, novelist and wife of a Unitarian minister in Manchester, praised him as "high, and noble, and child-like," and George Eliot, who referred to him in a letter of 1 February 1853 to Mrs. Peter Alfred Taylor as "Saint Francis," declared that he was such a "very pure, noble being" that it was "good only to look at" him.

But Newman soon reached a larger audience through the press than in person or from the lectern. He became a prolific contributor to journals such as the *Westminster Review* and *Fraser's Magazine* and the author of a steady stream of pamphlets and books on a broad range of religious, social, and political questions. The first work of importance was *A History of the Hebrew Monarchy, from the Administration of Samuel to the Babylonish Captivity* (1847), in which he subjected the Old Testament to a "free, critical inquiry" that distressed many of his readers and, in the view of scholar Alfred William Benn, initiated rationalistic criticism of popular religious belief in Victorian England. Having plunged with this book into the theological controversies of his age, Newman followed it two years later with *The Soul, Her Sorrows and Her Aspirations: An Essay towards the Natural History of the Soul, as the True Basis of Theology*. It became his most widely read and admired work, appearing in a ninth edition by 1874, and was for Martineau a "milestone" in his "spiritual life."

Newman's dual purpose in *The Soul* was first to restore religious belief to a skeptical century by showing that the individual soul can commune directly with God; and second to argue that contemporary theology, with its insistence on external authority and the need for mediation between God and the individual, could never reach the unbelieving. The soul requires no outside aid, Newman contends, for it is the sense or organ by which one can come to know God and thus is to the spiritual what the conscience is to the moral. Its development begins early in life with a growing sense of awe and wonder toward the infinite and sublime, which in turn is followed by a perception of order, design, and wisdom that brings reverence for the eternal mind we call God. Here, Newman says, is the true beginning of religion, as the soul aspires to infinite love and goodness, and desires union with it.

Hindering this religious growth, however, are various forms of what Newman terms idolatry: surrender of reason and understanding to the soul, a sacrifice that leads to fanaticism; worship of authority, that of the Church for the Catholic, and of the Bible for the Protestant; and pursuit of spiritual enrichment through mechanical means such as fasting and prayer meetings. Making light of its historical and miraculous side, Newman declares that Christianity can again be a living force only by becoming spiritual, as in apostolic times, and appealing to the soul rather than to the critical faculties; for the kingdom of God, he concludes in a peroration many readers have found eloquent and moving, consists not of sermons and exegesis and belief in biblical infallibility but of "righteousness and peace and joy in the Holy Spirit."

The positive response to *The Soul* encouraged Newman the following year (1850) to publish a book that radically extended his views and met with a different reception. An account of his spiritual pilgrimage, *Phases of Faith* has been described by Benn as "the most formidable direct attack ever made against Christianity in England," and it was violently denounced by its critics. Newman begins with his initial "unhesitating" acceptance of everything in the Bible and traces, through a series of crises, the gradual but inexorable repudiation of his early faith. Rejection of dogma, starting with difficulties over the question of infant baptism, was followed by loss of belief in scriptural infallibility. The claims of creed and canon destroyed, Newman next rested his faith on the moral teachings of the New Testament. But again he experienced disillusionment, for he found biblical morality to be gravely impaired by its

Portions of an 1855 letter from Newman to his friend, scholar John Nicholson (from Isabel Giberne Sieveking, Memoir and Letters of Francis W. Newman, *1909)*

failure to condemn such evils as sexual inequality, slavery, and religious intolerance. Turning finally to the historical Jesus as the bedrock of his faith, Newman became disenchanted once more, explaining in a chapter added in 1853 that he was unable to see in Jesus more than a mere man, and a clearly imperfect one at that—a teacher who deliberately adopted an enigmatic way of teaching, and at the end "a conscious and wilful imposter" who flouted authority in order to provoke his execution and thereby conceal his messianic pretensions.

James Anthony Froude, who the previous year had depicted his own spiritual travail in *The Nemesis of Faith,* was "repelled" by Newman's "unimaginative" treatment of Jesus, and Martineau complained that his "rigorously logical" method precluded "judicial largeness of view." But more recently Basil Willey has praised Newman as an "honest doubter" and *Phases of Faith* as the "touching" record of his painful search after truth.

Newman never again attracted the attention given to *The Soul* and *Phases of Faith,* but, driven to controversy by a sense of being in "direct conflict with current opinion," he became during the next decades one of the most copious and versatile writers of his time. No summary can do justice to the scope of his work or attempt to do more than suggest the number and variety of articles, pamphlets, books, and translations that he produced.

Many of these works continued and in some cases modified the religious views Newman had earlier expressed. In *Catholic Union: Essays towards a Church of the Future, as the Organization of Philanthropy* (1854), one of the clearest statements of his moral theism, he outlined a plan for a universal and undogmatic church based on the common needs and aspirations of humanity. It was followed four years later by *Theism, Doctrinal and Practical; or, Didactic Religious Utterances,* which Martineau found "curious" and "eccentric" but which Newman called "in some sense the work of my life." Later revised and enlarged as *Hebrew Theism: The Common Basis of Judaism,*

Francis William Newman

Christianity, and Mohammedism (1874), it includes inspirational and reflective passages of a moral and spiritual nature. In several publications, including *A Discourse against Hero-Making in Religion* (1864), *The Religious Weakness of Protestantism* (1866), and *On the Defective Morality of the New Testament* (1867), Newman returned to the subject of Jesus and biblical morality, but in his final years he significantly revised his previous position. *James and Paul* (1869) makes Pauline doctrine responsible for the divisions within Christianity; *What Is Christianity without Christ?* (1881) distinguishes between the real and the gospel Jesus; and *Hebrew Jesus: His True Creed* (1895) corrects the errors surrounding Jesus and identifies the Lord's Prayer as the essence of his teaching. Perhaps the most characteristic of Newman's productions during this period is *Life after Death? Palinōdia* (1886), in which he counters the Victorians' obsessive concern with the question of immortality by urging his readers to work instead for mercy and justice in this life.

Meanwhile, Newman had entered the arena of political and social controversy, typically writing from the position of a moral reformer and uncompromising idealist but capable also of being a pragmatist in search of real solutions to human problems. He most frequently played an oppositional role, criticizing what he thought to be injustices and abuses that cried out for protest. He was an outspoken opponent of slavery and was outraged by English mistreatment of India and Ireland and incompetence in the Crimean War. He opposed vivisection and venereal-diseases legislation on the respective grounds of their cruelty to animals and callousness toward defenseless prostitutes, and conversely he supported causes promoting human welfare, among them vegetarianism, temperance, liberalized divorce laws, and woman suffrage.

Newman could speak at times as an orthodox laissez-faire economist, as in the lectures delivered at Bedford College for Women and published as *Lectures on Political Economy* (1851), but he could not altogether suppress his humanitarian impulses, and in *Religion, Not History* (1877) he explicitly warned that England could never look for moral improvement until it had eliminated poverty. He called for political reforms in *An Appeal to the Middle Classes on the Urgent Necessity of Numerous Radical Reforms, Financial and Organic* (1848) and again in *English Institutions and Their Most Necessary Reforms: A Contribution of Thought* (1865), in which he supported an expanded suffrage and decentralization of political power. Later, in *Europe of the Near Future* (1871), written after the Franco-Prussian War, he dealt with still larger issues as he sought ways of preventing wars of aggression through international cooperation.

During these years Newman had largely neglected one of the subjects in which he had won honors at Oxford–mathematics–although near the end of his life he returned to it in two treatises, *Elliptic Integrals* (1889) and *The Higher Trigonometry, Superrationals of Second Order* (1892). But he had not ignored the other subject–classics. He was in fact a linguist of awesome powers, with a commanding knowledge of more than a dozen ancient and modern languages (among them Arabic, of which he compiled a two-volume dictionary in 1871), and he was recognized as one of the finest Latinists of his time. He brought a new method to the teaching of language, attempting more to arouse interest than to demand exactness, and illustrated it with Latin translations of English poetry, Henry Wadsworth Longfellow's *Hiawatha,* and Daniel Defoe's *Robinson Crusoe*. In addition he published textual notes on Aeschylus and Euripides and translations of Horace's odes and Homer's *Iliad*. The only one of these works to attract much notice was the translation of Homer, which Matthew Arnold, in his Homeric lectures at Oxford, ridiculed as "ignoble." Newman indignantly replied in *Homeric Translation in Theory and Practice* (1861), reiterating his belief that Homer was a quaint poet of a barbaric age and must be so rendered into modern English. The exchange, though in some respects inconclusive, demonstrated that although Newman had the greater erudition, Arnold had the greater gift for poetry.

Despite his many achievements few honors came to Newman. He was made emeritus professor on his retirement from Manchester College and in 1883 was elected honorary fellow of his old college at Oxford, Worcester. He held minor positions with the British and Foreign Unitarian Association and the Land Nationalization Society. But for the most part he became increasingly forgotten by the world. After the death of his first wife he married a Miss Williams, who had been his wife's companion and with whom he lived during his remaining years in relative seclusion at Weston-super-Mare, near Bristol.

There Newman wrote the book that dismayed even his admirers, *Contributions Chiefly to the Early History of the Late Cardinal Newman,* which gave a startlingly unflattering account of the recently deceased John Henry. Ostensibly published to inform those who believed otherwise that his brother had despised Protestantism and had sought as his divine mission to supplant it with Catholicism, the book was in reality the public airing of grievances against John Henry that long had festered in Newman. It was among his last publications, for within a few years blindness and failing health made it impossible for him to continue writing. But at the age of ninety-two he made clear in a final letter to an old friend that he wished "once again definitely to take the name of Christian."

During his lifetime the attention given to Newman's religious thought obscured his more significant work as a social reformer. Here, especially, he showed the courage, intellectual integrity, and passion for justice that form his chief legacy. No real change for the better could occur, he believed, without a relentless challenging of entrenched power, of conventional thinking, and of "things as they are." Both a pragmatist and a visionary, he devoted much of his long and prolific career to speaking out against inequities and abuses, and at the very least he gained for unpopular causes a hearing they otherwise might not have received. He was a strong advocate of women's rights and an eloquent spokesman for the poor. He protested against crowded prisons and the exportation of criminals and proposed more-humane punishment. He sought political reform through an expanded suffrage and a decentralized government. He actively supported the struggles for independence in Italy and Hungary and urged international cooperation as a means of preventing war. He repeatedly condemned religious intolerance and argued for a practical and ecumenical Christianity that placed greater emphasis on mercy and justice than on dogma and creeds. An essentially simple and self-effacing crusader, he had earned, well before his death on 4 October 1897, the tribute of the Congregationalist minister who eulogized him as "a true philanthropist," a champion of "the cause of the oppressed everywhere," and above all "a truth seeker."

Biographies:
Isabel Giberne Sieveking, *Memoir and Letters of Francis W. Newman* (London: Kegan Paul, Trench, Trübner, 1909);

William Robbins, *The Newman Brothers: An Essay in Comparative Intellectual Biography* (Cambridge, Mass.: Harvard University Press, 1966).

References:
Matthew Arnold, "On Translating Homer," in *The Complete Prose Works,* 11 volumes, edited by R. H. Super (Ann Arbor: University of Michigan Press, 1960–1977), I: 97–216;

Alfred William Benn, *The History of English Rationalism in the Nineteenth Century,* 2 volumes (London: Longmans, Green, 1906);

James R. Bennett, "Francis W. Newman and Religious Liberalism in Nineteenth Century England," dissertation, Stanford University, 1960;

W. M. W. Call, "F. W. Newman and His Evangelical Critics," *Westminster Review,* new series 14 (October 1858): 376–435;

Francis Gribble, "Francis William Newman," *Fortnightly Review,* 78 (July 1905): 151–161;

James Martineau, "New Passage from Professor Newman's Creed," *Prospective Review,* 9 (1853): 534–559; reprinted in his *Essays, Reviews and Addresses,* 4 volumes (London: Longmans, Green, 1890–1891), III: 1–82;

Martineau, "*Phases of Faith,*" *Prospective Review,* 6 (1850): 359–403;

John Rickards Mozley, "Francis William Newman," *Hibbert Journal,* 23 (January 1925): 345–360;

Thomas Mozley, *Reminiscences Chiefly of Oriel College and the Oxford Movement,* 2 volumes (London: Longmans, Green / Boston: Houghton, Mifflin, 1882);

Bernard M. G. Reardon, *From Coleridge to Gore: A Century of Religious Thought in Britain* (London: Longman, 1971);

Kenneth N. Ross, "Francis William Newman," *Church Quarterly Review,* 118 (July 1934): 231–244;

Robert Vaughan, "Newman's *Phases of Faith,*" *British Quarterly Review,* 12 (August 1850): 1–56;

Basil Willey, *More Nineteenth Century Studies: A Group of Honest Doubters* (London: Chatto & Windus / New York: Columbia University Press, 1956).

Papers:
Letters by Francis William Newman to John Henry Newman are at the Birmingham Oratory. Other letters are at the University of London and in the Bodleian Library, Oxford.

Margaret Oliphant
(4 April 1828 - 25 June 1897)

Rhonda Batchelor
University of Alberta

See also the Oliphant entry in *DLB 18: Victorian Novelists After 1885.*

BOOKS: *Passages in the Life of Mrs. Margaret Maitland, of Sunnyside, Written by Herself* (3 volumes, London: Colburn, 1849; 1 volume, New York: Appleton, 1851);

Merkland: A Story of Scottish Life, 3 volumes (London: Colburn, 1851 [i.e., 1850]); republished as *Merkland; or, Self Sacrifice,* 1 volume (New York: Stringer & Townsend, 1854);

Caleb Field: A Tale of the Puritans (London: Colburn, 1851; New York: Harper, 1851);

John Drayton, the Liverpool Engineer, as William Wilson (2 volumes, London: Bentley, 1851);

The Melvilles, attributed to William Wilson, 3 volumes (London: Bentley, 1852);

Memoirs and Resolutions of Adam Graeme, of Mossgray (3 volumes, London: Colburn, 1852; 1 volume, New York: Munro, 1885);

Katie Stewart: A True Story (New York: Harper, 1852; Edinburgh & London: Blackwood, 1853);

Aileford. A Family History, attributed to William Wilson (3 volumes, London: Hurst & Blackett, 1853; 1 volume, New York: Stringer & Townsend, 1855); republished as *The Lost Love* (Philadelphia: T. B. Peterson, 1865?);

Harry Muir: A Story of Scottish Life (3 volumes, London: Hurst & Blackett, 1853; 1 volume, New York: Appleton, 1853);

The Quiet Heart (Edinburgh & London: Blackwood, 1854; New York: Harper, 1854);

Magdalen Hepburn: A Story of the Scottish Reformation (3 volumes, London: Hurst & Blackett, 1854; 1 volume, New York: Riker, Thorne, 1854);

Lilliesleaf: Being a Concluding Series of Passages in the Life of Mrs. Margaret Maitland, of Sunnyside, Written by Herself (3 volumes, London: Hurst & Blackett, 1855; 1 volume, Boston: Burnham, 1862);

Christian Melville, as William Wilson (London: Bogue, 1856);

Margaret Oliphant (photograph by H. L. Mendelssohn)

Zaidee: A Romance (3 volumes, Edinburgh & London: Blackwood, 1856; 1 volume, Boston: Jewett, 1856);

Adam Graeme of Mossgray: A Novel (New York: Garrett, Dick & Fitzgerald, 1857; London: Hurst & Blackett, 188?);

The Athelings; or, The Three Gifts (3 volumes, Edinburgh & London: Blackwood, 1857; 1 volume, New York: Harper, 1857);

The Days of My Life: An Autobiography (3 volumes, London: Hurst & Blackett, 1857; 1 volume, New York: Harper, 1857);

Sundays (London: Nisbet, 1858);

Orphans: A Chapter in a Life (London: Hurst & Blackett, 1858; New York: Munro, 1880);

The Laird of Norlaw: A Scottish Story (3 volumes, London: Hurst & Blackett, 1858; 1 volume, New York: Harper, 1859);

Agnes Hopetoun's Schools and Holidays (Cambridge: Macmillan, 1859; Boston: Gould & Lincoln, 1859);

Lucy Crofton (London: Hurst & Blackett, 1860 [i.e., 1859]; New York: Harper, 1860);

The House on the Moor (3 volumes, London: Hurst & Blackett, 1861; 1 volume, New York: Harper, 1861);

The Last of the Mortimers: A Story in Two Voices (3 volumes, London: Hurst & Blackett, 1862; 1 volume, New York: Harper, 1862);

The Life of Edward Irving, Minister of the National Scotch Church (2 volumes, London: Hurst & Blackett, 1862; 1 volume, New York: Harper, 1862);

The Chronicles of Carlingford (Boston: Littell, 1862?; enlarged edition, New York: Harper, 1863);

Salem Chapel, 2 volumes (Edinburgh & London: Blackwood, 1863);

Heart and Cross (London: Hurst & Blackett, 1863; New York: Gregory, 1863);

The Rector and The Doctor's Family (Edinburgh & London: Blackwood, 1863);

The Perpetual Curate (3 volumes, Edinburgh & London: Blackwood, 1864; 1 volume, New York: Harper, 1865);

A Son of the Soil (1 volume, New York: Harper, 1865; 2 volumes, London: Macmillan, 1866);

Agnes (3 volumes, London: Hurst & Blackett, 1866 [i.e., 1865]; 1 volume, New York: Harper, 1866);

Madonna Mary: A Novel (3 volumes, London: Hurst & Blackett, 1867 [i.e., 1866]; 1 volume, New York: Harper, 1866);

Miss Marjoribanks (3 volumes, Edinburgh & London: Blackwood, 1866; 1 volume, New York: Harper, 1867);

Brownlows (3 volumes, Edinburgh & London: Blackwood, 1868; 1 volume, New York: Harper, 1868);

The Minister's Wife (3 volumes, London: Hurst & Blackett, 1869; 1 volume, New York: Harper, 1869);

Historical Sketches of the Reign of George Second (2 volumes, Edinburgh & London: Blackwood, 1869; 1 volume, Boston: Littell & Gay, 1869);

John: A Love Story (2 volumes, Edinburgh & London: Blackwood, 1870; 1 volume, New York: Harper, 1870);

The Three Brothers (3 volumes, London: Hurst & Blackett, 1870; 1 volume, New York: Appleton, 1870);

Francis of Assisi (London: Macmillan, 1870; London & New York: Macmillan, 1888);

Squire Arden (3 volumes, London: Hurst & Blackett, 1871; 1 volume, New York: Harper, 1874);

Memoir of Count de Montalembert, 2 volumes (Edinburgh & London: Blackwood, 1872);

Ombra (3 volumes, London: Hurst & Blackett, 1872; 1 volume, New York: Harper, 1872);

At His Gates: A Novel (3 volumes, London: Tinsley, 1872; 1 volume, New York: Scribner, Armstrong, 1873);

Innocent: A Tale of Modern Life (3 volumes, London: Low, Marston, Low & Searle, 1873; 1 volume, New York: Harper, 1873);

May (3 volumes, London: Hurst & Blackett, 1873; 1 volume, New York: Scribners, 1873);

A Rose in June (2 volumes, London: Hurst & Blackett, 1874; 1 volume, Boston: Osgood, 1874);

For Love and Life (3 volumes, London: Hurst & Blackett, 1874; 1 volume, New York: Munro, 1879);

The Story of Valentine and His Brother (3 volumes, Edinburgh & London: Blackwood, 1875; 1 volume, New York: Harper, 1875);

Whiteladies (3 volumes, London: Tinsley, 1875; 1 volume, New York: Holt, 1875);

The Curate in Charge (2 volumes, London: Macmillan, 1876; 1 volume, New York: Harper, 1876);

An Odd Couple (Philadelphia: Porter & Coates, 1876);

Phoebe Junior: A Last Chronicle of Carlingford (3 volumes, London: Hurst & Blackett, 1876; 1 volume, New York: Harper, 1876);

The Makers of Florence: Dante, Giotto, Savonarola; and Their City (London: Macmillan, 1876; London & New York: Macmillan, 1881);

Carita (3 volumes, London: Smith, Elder, 1877; 1 volume, New York: Harper, 1877);

Dante (Edinburgh & London: Blackwood, 1877; Philadelphia: Lippincott, 1877);

Mrs. Arthur (3 volumes, London: Hurst & Blackett, 1877; 1 volume, New York: Harper, 1877);

Young Musgrave (3 volumes, London: Macmillan, 1877; 1 volume, New York: Harper, 1878);

The Primrose Path: A Chapter in the Annals of the Kingdom of Fife (3 volumes, London: Hurst & Blackett, 1878; 1 volume, New York: Harper, 1878);

Dress (London: Macmillan, 1878; Philadelphia: Porter & Coates, 1879);

Within the Precincts (3 volumes, London: Smith, Elder, 1879; 1 volume, New York: Harper, 1879);

Molière, by Oliphant and F. Tarver (Edinburgh & London: Blackwood, 1879; Philadelphia: Lippincott, 1879);

A Beleaguered City: Being a Narrative of Certain Recent Events in the City of Semur, in the Department of the Haute Bourgogne. A Story of the Seen and the Unseen (New York: Munro, 1879; London: Macmillan, 1880 [i.e., 1879]);

The Greatest Heiress in England: A Novel (3 volumes, London: Hurst & Blackett, 1879; 1 volume, New York: Harper, 1880);

The Fugitives (New York: Munro, 1979); republished in *The Duke's Daughter and The Fugitives,* 3 volumes (Edinburgh & London: Blackwood, 1890);

Cervantes (Edinburgh & London: Blackwood, 1880; Philadelphia: Lippincott, 1881);

No. 3 Grove Road (New York: Munro, 1880);

The Queen (New York: Harper, 1880);

He That Will Not When He May: A Novel (3 volumes, London: Macmillan, 1880; 1 volume, New York: Harper, 1880);

Harry Joscelyn (3 volumes, London: Hurst & Blackett, 1881; 1 volume, New York: Harper, 1881);

In Trust: The Story of a Lady and Her Lover (1 volume, New York: Munro, 1881; 3 volumes, London: Longmans, Green, 1882);

Lady Jane (New York: Munro, 1882); republished as *The Duke's Daughter* in *The Duke's Daughter and The Fugitives,* 3 volumes (Edinburgh & London: Blackwood, 1890);

The Literary History of England in the End of the Eighteenth and Beginning of the Nineteenth Century (3 volumes, London: Macmillan, 1882; 1 volume, New York: Macmillan, 1882);

A Little Pilgrim in the Unseen (London: Macmillan, 1882; Boston: Roberts, 1882); enlarged as *The Little Pilgrim and Further Experiences of a Little Pilgrim* (Boston: Little, Brown, 1882?);

It Was a Lover and His Lass (3 volumes, London: Hurst & Blackett, 1883; 1 volume, New York: Harper, 1883);

Sir Tom (New York: Harper, 1883; London: Macmillan, 1884);

The Ladies Lindores: A Novel (3 volumes, Edinburgh & London: Blackwood, 1883; 1 volume, New York: Harper, 1883);

Hester: A Story of Contemporary Life (3 volumes, London: Macmillan, 1883; 1 volume, New York: Harper, 1884);

Sheridan, in the English Men of Letters series (London: Macmillan, 1883; New York: Harper, 1883);

The Lady's Walk (New York: Munro, 1883; London: Methuen, 1897);

The Wizard's Son (London: Macmillan, 1884; New York: Lovell, 1884?);

Old Lady Mary: A Story of the Seen and the Unseen (Boston: Roberts, 1884)

Madam: A Novel (1 volume, New York: Harper, 1884; 3 volumes, London: Longmans, Green, 1885 [i.e., 1884]);

Two Stories of the Seen and Unseen: The Open Door, Old Lady Mary (Edinburgh & London: Blackwood, 1885);

The Open Door. The Portrait. Two Stories of the Seen and the Unseen (Boston: Roberts, 1885);

Oliver's Bride: A New Novel (New York: Lovell, 1885); revised as *Oliver's Bride: A True Story* (London: Ward & Downey, 1886);

The Prodigals and Their Inheritance (New York: Munro, 1885; 2 volumes, London: Methuen, 1894);

A Country Gentleman and His Family (3 volumes, London: Macmillan, 1886; 1 volume, New York: Harper, 1886);

The Son of His Father (1 volume, New York: Harper, 1886; 3 volumes, London: Hurst & Blackett, 1887);

Effie Ogilvie: The Story of a Young Life (2 volumes, Glasgow: Maclehose, 1886; 1 volume, New York: Harper, 1886);

A House Divided against Itself (3 volumes, Edinburgh & London: Blackwood, 1886; 1 volume, New York: Harper, 1886);

A Poor Gentleman (2 volumes, New York: Munro, 1886; 3 volumes, London: Hurst & Blackett, 1889);

The Makers of Venice: Doges, Conquerors, Painters, and Men of Letters (London & New York: Macmillan, 1887);

Cousin Mary (London: Partridge, 1888);

A Memoir of the Life of John Tulloch, D.D., L.L.D., Principal and Primarius Professor of St. Mary's College (Edinburgh & London: Blackwood, 1888);

The Land of Darkness, Along with Some Further Chapters in the Experiences of the Little Pilgrim (London & New York: Macmillan, 1888);

Joyce (3 volumes, London & New York: Macmillan, 1888; 1 volume, New York: Harper, 1888);

The Second Son (3 volumes, London & New York: Macmillan, 1888; 1 volume, Boston & New York: Houghton, Mifflin, 1888);

Lady Car: The Sequel of a Life (London: Longmans, Green, 1889; New York: Harper, 1889);

Neighbours on the Green (3 volumes, London & New York: Macmillan, 1889);

Stories of the Seen and the Unseen (Boston: Roberts, 1889; abridged, Edinburgh: Blackwood, 1902);

The Mystery of Mrs Blencarrow (London: Blackett, 1890?; Chicago: Donohue, Henneberry, 1894);

Kirsteen: The Story of a Scotch Family Seventy Years Ago (3 volumes, London & New York: Macmillan, 1890; 1 volume, New York: Harper, 1890);

Sons and Daughters (Edinburgh & London: Blackwood, 1890);

Royal Edinburgh: Her Saints, Kings, Prophets and Poets (London & New York: Macmillan, 1890);

The Railway Man and His Children (3 volumes, London & New York: Macmillan, 1891; 1 volume, New York: Lovell, 1891);

Janet, 3 volumes (London: Hurst & Blackett, 1891); republished as *The Story of a Governess,* 1 volume (New York: Fenno, 1895);

Jerusalem: Its History and Hope (London: Macmillan, 1891); republished as *Jerusalem, the Holy City: Its History and Hope* (London & New York: Macmillan, 1891);

The Heir Presumptive and the Heir Apparent (1 volume, New York: Lovell, 1891; 3 volumes, London: Macmillan, 1892);

Memoir of the Life of Laurence Oliphant and of Alice Oliphant, His Wife (2 volumes, Edinburgh: Blackwood, 1891; New York: Harper, 1891);

The Marriage of Elinor (New York: United States Book Company, 1891; London & New York: Macmillan, 1892);

The Cuckoo in the Nest (3 volumes, London: Hutchinson, 1892; 1 volume, New York & Chicago: United States Book Company, 1892);

The Victorian Age of English Literature (2 volumes, London: Percival, 1892; New York: Dodd, Mead, 1892);

Diana Trelawny: The History of a Great Mistake, 2 volumes (Edinburgh & London: Blackwood, 1892); republished as *Diana: The History of a Great Mistake,* 1 volume (New York & Chicago: United States Book Company, 1892);

Lady William, 3 volumes (London & New York: Macmillan, 1893);

The Sorceress (3 volumes, London: White, 1893; 1 volume, New York: Taylor, 1893);

Thomas Chalmers: Preacher, Philosopher, and Statesman (London: Methuen, 1893; Boston & New York: Houghton, Mifflin, 1893);

Historical Characters of the Reign of Queen Anne (New York: Century, 1894);

Sir Robert's Fortune (New York: Harper, 1894; London: Methuen, 1895);

Historical Sketches of the Reign of Queen Anne (London: Macmillan, 1894);

A House in Bloomsbury: A Novel (2 volumes, London: Hutchinson, 1894; 1 volume, New York: Dodd, Mead, 1894);

Two Strangers (London: Unwin, 1894; New York: Fenno, 1895);

Who Was Lost and Is Found (Edinburgh & London: Blackwood, 1894; New York: Harper, 1895);

The Makers of Modern Rome (London & New York: Macmillan, 1895);

The Story of a Governess (New York: Fenno, 1895);

Old Mr. Tredgold (New York: Longmans, Green, 1895; London: Longmans, Green, 1896);

Jeanne d'Arc: Her Life and Death (London & New York: Putnam, 1896);

The Two Marys (London: Methuen, 1896);

The Unjust Steward; or, The Minister's Debt (London & Edinburgh: Chambers, 1896; Philadelphia: Lippincott, 1896);

A History of Scotland for the Young (London: Fisher, 1896; New York: Mansfield, 1898);

The Ways of Life: Two Stories (London: Smith, Elder, 1897; New York & London: Putnam, 1897);

Annals of a Publishing House: William Blackwood and His Sons, Their Magazine and Friends (2 volumes, Edinburgh & London: Blackwood, 1897; 3 volumes, New York: Scribners, 1897-1898);

The Little Cutty. Dr. Barrere. Isabel Dysart. (London & New York: Macmillan, 1898);

A Widow's Tale and Other Stories (Edinburgh & London: Blackwood, 1898; New York: Fenno, 1899);

The Autobiography and Letters of Mrs. M. O. W. Oliphant, edited by Mrs. H. Coghill (Edinburgh & London: Blackwood, 1899; New York: Dodd, Mead, 1899);

Queen Victoria: A Personal Sketch (London: Cassell, 1901).

SELECTED PERIODICAL PUBLICATIONS–UNCOLLECTED: "Mary Russel Mitford," *Blackwood's Magazine,* 75 (June 1854): 658-670;

"Thackeray and His Novels," *Blackwood's Magazine,* 77 (January 1855): 86-96;

"Bulwer," *Blackwood's Magazine,* 77 (February 1855): 221-232;

"Charles Dickens," *Blackwood's Magazine,* 77 (April 1855): 451-466;

"Modern Novelists," *Blackwood's Magazine,* 77 (May 1855): 554-568;

"Modern Light Literature: Theology," *Blackwood's Magazine,* 78 (July 1855): 72-86;

"Modern Light Literature: Science," *Blackwood's Magazine,* 78 (August 1855): 215-230;

"Modern Light Literature: History," *Blackwood's Magazine*, 78 (September 1855): 437-451;

"Modern Light Literature: Travellers' Tales," *Blackwood's Magazine*, 78 (November 1855): 586-599;

"Modern Light Literature: Art," *Blackwood's Magazine*, 78 (December 1855): 702-717;

"Modern Light Literature: Poetry," *Blackwood's Magazine*, 79 (February 1856): 125-138;

"Laws Concerning Women," *Blackwood's Magazine*, 79 (April 1856): 379-387;

"A New Una," *Blackwood's Magazine*, 80 (October 1856): 485-488;

"The Art of Cavilling," *Blackwood's Magazine*, 80 (November 1856): 613-628;

"Picture Books," *Blackwood's Magazine*, 81 (March 1857): 309-318;

"Modern Light Literature: Society," *Blackwood's Magazine*, 82 (October 1857): 423-437;

"The Condition of Women," *Blackwood's Magazine*, 83 (February 1858): 139-154;

"The Missionary Explorer," *Blackwood's Magazine*, 83 (April 1858): 392-401;

"Religious Memoirs," *Blackwood's Magazine*, 83 (June 1858): 702-718;

"The Byways of Literature," *Blackwood's Magazine*, 84 (August 1858): 200-216;

"Edward Irving," *Blackwood's Magazine*, 84 (November 1858): 567-586;

"Poetry," *Blackwood's Magazine*, 88 (July 1860): 37-53;

"Social Science," *Blackwood's Magazine*, 88 (December 1860): 698-715;

"The Lives of Two Ladies," *Blackwood's Magazine*, 91 (April 1862): 401-423;

"Sensation Novels," *Blackwood's Magazine*, 91 (May 1862): 564-584;

"The Great Unrepresented," *Blackwood's Magazine*, 98 (September 1866): 603-621;

"The Latest Lawgiver," *Blackwood's Magazine*, 103 (June 1868): 675-691;

"Mill's *The Subjection of Women*," *Edinburgh Review*, 130 (October 1869): 572-602;

"Miss Austen and Miss Mitford," *Blackwood's Magazine*, 107 (March 1870): 290-313;

"Epic of Arthur," *Edinburgh Review*, 131 (April 1870): 502-539;

"Charles Dickens," *Blackwood's Magazine*, 109 (February 1871): 673-695;

"Browning's *Balaustion*," *Edinburgh Review*, 135 (January 1872): 221-249;

"The Scientific Gentleman," *Cornhill Magazine*, 26 (November 1872): 618-640, 737-760;

"The Indian Mutiny," *Blackwood's Magazine*, 115 (January 1874): 102-120;

"The Ancient Classics," *Blackwood's Magazine*, 116 (September 1874): 365-386;

"The Classics: Latin Literature," *Blackwood's Magazine*, 116 (November 1874): 599-620;

"Lace and Bric-a-brac," *Blackwood's Magazine*, 119 (January 1876): 59-78;

"Thackeray's Sketches," *Blackwood's Magazine*, 119 (February 1876): 232-243;

"The Opium-Eater," *Blackwood's Magazine*, 122 (December 1877): 717-741;

"Englishmen and Frenchmen," *Blackwood's Magazine*, 124 (August 1878): 219-237;

"Russia and Nihilism in Tourgenief," *Blackwood's Magazine*, 127 (May 1880): 623-647;

"The Grievances of Women," *Fraser's Magazine*, 101 (May 1880): 698-710;

"Thomas Carlyle," *Macmillan's Magazine*, 43 (April 1881): 482-496;

"American Literature in England," *Blackwood's Magazine*, 133 (January 1883): 136-161;

"Mrs. Carlyle," *Contemporary Review*, 43 (May 1883): 609-628;

"The Ethics of Biography," *Contemporary Review*, 44 (July 1883): 76-93;

"The Life of George Eliot," *Edinburgh Review*, 161 (April 1885): 514-553;

"Mrs. Craik," *Macmillan's Magazine*, 57 (December 1887): 81-85;

"Tennyson," *Blackwood's Magazine*, 152 (November 1892): 748-766;

"Letters of Sir Walter Scott," *Blackwood's Magazine*, 155 (January 1894): 15-26;

"Men and Women," *Blackwood's Magazine*, 157 (April 1895): 620-650;

"The Anti-Marriage League," *Blackwood's Magazine*, 159 (January 1896): 135-149;

"The Verdict of Old Age," *Blackwood's Magazine*, 160 (October 1896): 555-571;

"'Tis Sixty Years Since," *Blackwood's Magazine*, 161 (May 1897): 599-624.

Few women represent the issues that surrounded Victorian England's "woman question" as literally and literarily as Margaret Oliphant Wilson Oliphant, whose odd full name was the result of her marrying a cousin on her mother's side of the family. By the end of her life Oliphant had been a daughter, a sister, a wife, a mother, and a widow. She was also a professional writer and worked hard throughout her long career as a novelist, literary critic, social commentator, and historical writer in order to support her family. Thus, she had both a personal and professional stake in the changing definitions of roles for women in Victorian society. As a woman of letters, she was able to participate in the cultural debate with a measure of authority, offering her own constructions of moral and relatively autonomous womanhood to stand in implicit and potentially reformative contrast to her society's dichotomous vision of women as either dependent domestic angels or independent public whores.

Whether because she actually adhered to traditional conceptions of womanhood or because she did not want to alarm and alienate her predominantly conservative, middle-class readers, Oliphant does not openly contest the received attributes of femininity. But while in much of her fiction and nonfiction Oliphant explores the seeming naturalness of such attributes, she yet carefully demonstrates that woman is not naturally inferior to man but in most respects is his equal.

The only exceptions to Oliphant's perception of the equality of the sexes, as she wrote in "The Condition of Women" for the February 1858 issue of *Blackwood's Magazine,* are the discrepancies between men and women in their physical abilities and in their degree of interest in participating in political institutions. Convinced of the fundamental importance of a woman's roles as mother and first teacher of children, Oliphant did not believe that women needed to hold either the vote or political office, although she qualified this position in a May 1880 article for *Fraser's Magazine* titled "The Grievances of Women" by remarking that women should not be barred from these "official" proofs of citizenship because of their sex. To her way of thinking, though, women could realize themselves more meaningfully and beneficially if the range of their "natural" domestic sphere was fully recognized and occupied.

When Margaret Oliphant Wilson was born on 4 April 1828 in Wallyford, Midlothian, Scotland, her parents, Francis and Margaret Wilson, were about forty years old. Frank, her oldest brother, was twelve, and Willie, the second oldest, was nine. Her early domestic life revolved around the needs of her withdrawn, antisocial father, a clerk, and his sons. In *The Autobiography and Letters of Mrs. M. O. W. Oliphant* (1899) she recalls that one of her clearest memories of childhood is of her mother hovering around the kitchen table at which Frank sat, catering blissfully to his every need. In spite of the attention that Margaret Wilson devoted to her sons, she also doted on her daughter, who the mother felt "had brought back life" to a heart numbed by the loss of three children between Willie's birth and her daughter's.

Although Oliphant makes no mention of formal education in her *Autobiography and Letters,* it is probable that she attended the parish school that

Oliphant in her early thirties

was available to most children of the lower and lower-middle classes of Scotland. Her informal education, though, was far more important as her mother passed on an abiding love for the printed word. Margaret Wilson's early introduction of literature to her children opened their minds while helping to preserve the quiet domestic environment that her husband demanded. Both before and after Oliphant learned to read on her own at six years of age she was, according to biographer and critic Merryn Williams, regularly entertained by her mother with "Bible stories, bits of family history, ballads, tales of the saintly Queen Margaret who had brought the arts of civilisation to Scotland, Shakespeare, Pope, Wordsworth, Burns, and Scott." Oliphant became a regular visitor to the circulating library in Glasgow, where the family had moved in 1834 to accommodate her father's new job as a clerk at the Royal Bank. Williams notes that the only restrictions placed upon Oliphant's reading were those of the librarian, who stopped short of lending Edward Bulwer-Lytton's "immoral novel" *Ernest Maltravers* (1837) to the nine-year-old.

The Wilsons moved to Liverpool in 1838 so that the father could take up yet another clerical position, this time with the export department of the Customs House. The city then embodied the stereotypical urban nightmare of working-class poverty that underwrote the industrial dream of middle-class wealth and genteel living. Oliphant speaks of "the great distress" of fellow rural immigrants in her *Autobiography and Letters* and tells how she came to understand the potential for general social improvement inherent in individual or private charity. She recalls being intellectually challenged by the "political and Radical" conversations that passed between her mother and her brother Frank.

Another important influence in the shaping of Oliphant's mind and character was her family's membership in the Free Church of Scotland. This denomination was a radical sect of the state religion, Presbyterianism, that in 1843 separated from the main body during Oliphant's childhood. The sect believed that congregations should choose their own leaders rather than having them chosen by authorities who wished to consolidate their institutionalized control over local worship and private moral practice. The Wilson family was fully committed to this progressive tenet and participated in the agitation that led to its realization.

Oliphant was active in her family's efforts to redress the domestic and social injustices that were everywhere around them in Liverpool. At the personal level she remembers her mother repairing a dress for a charwoman whose old one had been torn from her back by her husband's mistress. As Oliphant recalls in her autobiography, the Wilsons were also involved in collecting signatures for an anti–Corn Law petition:

> There was a great deal of talk in the papers, which were full of [Anti-Corn law] agitation, about a petition from women to Parliament upon that subject, with instructions to get sheets ruled for signatures, and an appeal to ladies to help in procuring them. It was just after or about the time of our great charity, and I was in the way of going thus from house to house [collecting orders for needed provisions and coal which Willie would then assemble and deliver]. Accordingly I got a number of these sheets, or probably Frank got them for me, and set to work.

Oliphant's involvement in this protest is important because it indicates her early ideological alliance with the middle-class women whose domestic values necessitated and justified their moral intervention in the public domain. In *Autobiography and Letters* Oliphant sees both personal and public acts of charity as originating in the values of the home.

Oliphant's participation in such public movements as the anti–Corn Law effort were her first real interactions with the world. She remembers them in her autobiography as "breaks . . . in [her] most singularly secluded" early life and as the only interruptions of her family's usual "pleasures" which typically consisted of

> books of all and every kind, newspapers and magazines, . . . form[ing] the staple of our conversation, as well as our amusement. In the time of my depression and sadness [over a vaguely recounted near-marriage to "a good, simple, pious, domestic, kind-hearted fellow, fair-haired, not good-looking, not ideal at all"] my mother had a bad illness, and I was her nurse, or at least attendant. I had no liking for needlework, a taste which I developed afterwards, so I took to writing.

As with the other literature, Oliphant's writing became a source of entertainment for the family, with evening readings and critiques of her daily production forming a prominent part of the nightly after-supper assemblies.

Oliphant's writing became a source of income when the prominent publisher Henry Colburn inaugurated her remarkable professional career by accepting *Passages in the Life of Mrs. Margaret Maitland, of Sunnyside, Written by Herself* (1849). During the next forty-eight years Oliphant produced nearly one hundred novels, more than one hundred nonfiction books, and some three hundred periodical pieces. Her success elevated her to what her first modern biographers, Vineta and Robert Colby, call the social eminence of being "the favorite novelist" of Queen Victoria.

Passages in the Life of Mrs. Margaret Maitland sets the tone and themes that inform Oliphant's fiction and much of her nonfiction. According to the reviewer for the 24 November 1849 *Athenaeum* it is a realistic portrayal of quotidian existence in a Scottish community rendered without "exaggeration in the sayings and doings of the character." The influence of the domestic, social, political, and religious ideas that shaped Oliphant's intellect is clear as the novel features as its narrator and central character Margaret Maitland, a woman of independent thought and self-determined moral philosophy. She observes and considers the domestic relations between men and women, the subordinate place of women within a patriarchal social and economic system, and realizes the moral need for each individual to question the right of institutionalized authority to wholly determine private existence. The work thus displays Oliphant's recognition that she could through her writing participate in her culture's debate about what it meant to be both a woman and a citizen.

Oliphant with her sons Cecco (lower left) and Cyril (upper right) and her nephew Frank Wilson (lower right)

The plot of *Passages in the Life of Mrs. Margaret Maitland* eventually confirms the soundness of the heroine's original principles. On the way to that determination, however, her testing suggests that the woman who adheres to these standards is as vulnerable to economic injustice and personal oppression at the hands of men—her curiously dependent social and domestic superiors—as are those women who fall away from these principles. Critics such as Williams who see Oliphant as "disparaging of the feminist movement" fail to note that the novel contains the then unheard-of suggestion that women were capable of doing more than just domestic labor. Oliphant's novel shows that autonomous women who refuse to hand over their lives and properties to their male superiors are valuable members of society because their relative freedom enables them to exert a beneficial feminine influence beyond the limited domestic sphere.

Three years and five novels after the publication of *Passages in the Life of Mrs. Margaret Maitland* Oliphant on 4 May 1852 married her first cousin Frank Oliphant, whom she had met in London in 1850 when she was there to care for her alcoholic brother Willie. They were married on the same day that Oliphant received the galley proofs of *Katie Stewart* (1852) from her new publisher, William Blackwood and Sons. Of the two relationships begun that day, the professional one was to last the longest and bring Oliphant the most stability. Frank was a painter at heart but by trade a designer of Gothic-style stained-glass windows, for which there was little demand and less recognition. Oliphant discovered within a year of their marriage that the economic maintenance of their slightly bohemian lifestyle was to fall to her. Frank was not a capable businessman, and he was unable to manage profitably the artisans who worked for him in his small workshop studio.

The Quiet Heart, the serialized novel that Oliphant published in book form in 1854, reflects many of the domestic upheavals she experienced early in her marriage. In the novel a young heroine falls in love with a promising but eventually unsuccessful artist—a writer rather than a painter or a glazier—who is constantly insolvent and often at odds with the heroine's mother. The pending marriage is deemed unsuitable, and the writer remains unworthy until he reconciles with the mother and recognizes his dependence on the domestic place maintained by the heroine, who has become financially secure through her career as an illustrator. As the Colbys remark, although Oliphant insisted that she did not use her life in her fiction, *The Quiet Heart* is "so personal that one wonders how she could have allowed her husband to read it."

Although Oliphant looks back in *Autobiography and Letters* to reveal many disappointed expectations, she also suggests that such experiences forced her to mature and allowed her to see her role as both breadwinner and wife in realistic terms:

> The glimpse of society I had during my married life in London was not of a very elevating kind; or perhaps I—with my shyness and complete unacquaintance with the ways of people who gave parties and paid incessant visits—was only unable to take any pleasure in it, or get beyond the outside petty view, and the same strange disappointment and disillusion with which the pictures and the stage had filled me, bringing down my ridiculous impossible ideal to the ground.... I had expected everything that was superlative,—beautiful conversation, all about books and the finest subjects, great people whose notice would be an honour, poets and painters, and all the sympathy of congenial minds, and the feast of reason and the flow of soul.... I found everything commonplace and poor, not at all what I expected.

Despite her disappointment in society Oliphant did expand her social circle during this period. She met Dinah Mulock, who was later to become a popular novelist and to marry George Craik of Macmillan's publishing house, which would become a useful connection for the author. Her other acquaintances included Mary Howitt; Grace Greenwood, an American author whose real name was Sara Jane Clarke Lippincott; Mr. and Mrs. Samuel Carter Hall; Stephen Fullom, a renowned literary and social critic; Frank Smedley, author of *Frank Farleigh* and *Harry Coverdale's Courtship;* George Lovell, a playwright; and Rosa Bonheur. She also continued and deepened the friendship with photographer Geddie Macpherson that she had formed during her first trip to London to care for Willie.

Oliphant's greatest joy during the early years of her marriage was the birth of her daughter Maggie on 21 May 1853. A year and a day later her second child, Marjorie, was born. These births were followed by two deaths, as Oliphant's mother died on 17 September 1854 and Marjorie died before her first birthday on 8 February 1855. Oliphant's autobiography barely refers to her father throughout this period, and he seems to have all but disappeared from her life after the death of Margaret Wilson. Oliphant was devastated by these deaths, particularly the unexpected passing of her daughter. She also lost her first son, who died a day after he was born in November 1855. Only the birth on 16 November 1856 of her beloved son Cyril (who nicknamed himself Tiddy) assuaged her sense of loss.

Tiddy's birth marks the beginning of one of the few prolonged periods of contentment that Oliphant was ever to know. During the next three years she published eight moderately successful novels and twenty-six pieces in *Blackwood's Magazine*. Her journalism continued to reflect Oliphant's early concerns about the changing nature of society, the place and role of woman, and the function of literature. In *The Woman Question: Society and Literature in Britain and America, 1837–1883* (1983) her "distinctive concern" is seen as "the nature and destiny of woman." Her titles included "Religion in Common Life," "Laws Concerning Women," "Modern Light Literature: Society," and "The Byways of Literature." Oliphant's domestic life was also fairly tranquil despite the death of her six-week-old son Stephen Thomas on 28 May 1858 from a "defective valve in the heart, which [Howitt] said was somehow connected with too much mental work on the part of the mother." Oliphant recalls this period in her autobiography:

> among the happy moments which I can recollect is one which is so curiously common and homely, with nothing in it, that it is strange even to record such a recollection, and yet it embodied more happiness to me than almost any real occasion as might be supposed for happiness. It was the moment after dinner when I used to run up-stairs to see that all was well in the nursery.... [M]y heart [was] full of joy and peace—for what?—for nothing—that there was no harm anywhere, the children well above stairs and their father below. I had few of the pleasures of society, no gaiety at all.... I can feel now the sensation of that sweet calm and ease and peace.

This peace ended on 20 October 1859 when her husband died while the family was visiting Rome in the hope that a change of climate would alleviate the symptoms of his tuberculosis. Oliphant buried her husband in Italy and then remained there to await the birth of her son Francis (nicknamed Cecco), who was born on 12 December.

Oliphant's remarkably candid account of her time in Rome reveals her resentment over Frank's

Oliphant's drawing room and study

irresponsibility in taking her, pregnant at the time, and their two children away from the shores of home when he knew that in all likelihood his death was near:

> Frank died quite conscious, kissing me when his lips were already cold, and quite, quite free from anxiety, though he left me with two helpless children and one unborn, and very little money, and no friends but the Macphersons [the photographers], who were as good to me as brother and sister; but had no power to help beyond that, if anything could have been beyond that.... When I thus began the world anew I had for all my fortune about £1000 of debt, a small insurance of, I think, £200 on Frank's life, our furniture laid up in a warehouse [back in England], and my own faculties, such as they were, to make our living and pay off our burdens by.

Oliphant's dependence on her writing, and thus on her publishers' approval of her work, was complete.

In the next five years Oliphant established herself as a popular professional writer. She produced close to thirty-five periodical pieces on diverse subjects. Her titles included "Social Science," "Scotland and Her Accusers," "Sensation Novels," and "The Life of Jesus." She also wrote regular reviews of popular fiction, becoming the foremost female reviewer of the period, and eight books. One of these books was the unremunerative but lovingly undertaken *The Life of Edward Irving, Minister of the National Scotch Church* (1862). Four other pieces—*The Rector and The Doctor's Family* (1863), *Salem Chapel* (1863), and *The Perpetual Curate* (1864)—were installments in a series that was to become the tremendously popular Chronicles of Carlingford series, which, in Michael Wheeler's view, "offers a sarcastic but moderate view of the pettiness of mid-Victorian religious life in the dullest of towns . . . that has a rather awful ring of truth." Owing to the success of her Carlingford work, Oliphant was able to demand and receive large sums both on speculation and for completion of her novels. For *The Perpetual Curate* she received £1,500.

Oliphant's financial success enabled her to take her family on a return trip to Rome in 1864. This trip was made in the company of her friend Mrs. Tulloch and her five children as well as Oliphant's redoubtable maid, Jane. The party of women and children had traveled to Italy "with the sense of holiday, a little outburst of freedom, no man interfering, keeping [them] to rule or formality." The trip home was made without Oliphant's beloved daughter, who died in Rome and was buried beside her father. With only a brief interlude for mourning, Oliphant's writing continued to be published at a phenomenal rate.

Oliphant's work continued to be popular, especially the next novel in the Carlingford series, *Miss Marjoribanks* (1866), an unrelated novel titled *A Son of the Soil* (1865), the nonfictional *Historical Sketches of the Reign of George Second* (1869), and *The Story of Valentine and His Brother* (1875). Nevertheless, she was hard-pressed to meet her family's increased demands for money. In her autobiography she reports that in 1870 her brother Frank after the death of his wife "came to me like a child glad to get home, not much disturbed about anything that could happen." Frank brought his children with him and relinquished all responsibility for his and their well-being to Oliphant. Her writing supported eight children, two adults—she was also financing her drunken brother Willie's life in Italy—and at least two servants.

Oliphant's periodical output during the years from 1864 to 1875 was extraordinary. Her writing remained in high demand even though she was often her own greatest competitor, with books and articles often being published simultaneously by rival houses. She wrote forcefully and thoughtfully about topical subjects without taking refuge in the complex intellectualism that so alienated readers. Her articles were distributed to five magazines: ninety-one in *Blackwood's Magazine*, including an article on women titled "The Great Unrepresented"; nine short-fiction pieces in *Cornhill Magazine;* four short stories in *Macmillan's Magazine;* three pieces in the *Edinburgh Review,* including a response to Mill's *The Subjection of Women* in 1869; and a serialized novel, *The Three Brothers,* that was published as a book in 1870.

Oliphant is typically understated in her recollection of the burden she carried in these years:

> Of course I had to face a prospect considerably changed by this great addition to my family. I had been obliged to work pretty hard before to meet all the too great expenses of the house.... I remember making a kind of pretense to myself that I had to think it over, to make a decision, to give up what hope I might have had of doing now my very best, and to set myself steadily to make as much money as I could for the three boys. I think that in some pages of my old book I have put this down with a little half-sincere attempt at a heroical attitude. I don't think, however, that there was any reality in it. I never did nor could, of course, hesitate for a moment as to what had to be done. It had to be done, and that was enough, and there is no doubt that it was much more congenial to me to drive on and keep everything going, with a certain scorn of the increased work . . . than it ever would have been to labour with an artist's fervour and concentration to produce a masterpiece. One can't be two things or serve two masters. Which was God and which was mammon in that individual case it would be hard to say.

By the time her brother died in 1875, Oliphant had educated his son Frank and was preparing to send him off to a post in India. She had installed her own two boys at Eton. She had also taken into her home another young female relative, Annie Coghill, who would edit *Autobiography and Letters.*

Oliphant wrote many articles that were rejected, and unless she could produce what was wanted, insolvency was throughout her life only a month or so away. She recalls in her autobiography how she came to regard as almost unethical her ability to conquer all difficulties and live rather well despite her precarious livelihood:

> It was always a struggle to get safely through every year and make my ends meet. Indeed I fear they never did quite meet; there was always a tugging together, which cost me a great deal of work and much anxiety. The wonder was that the much was never too much. . . . If I had not had unbroken health, and a spirit almost criminally elastic I could not have done it. I ought to have been worn out by work, and crushed by care, half a hundred times by all rules, but I never was so. . . . [I]t was in its way an immoral, or at least an un-moral, mode of life, dashing forward in the face of all obstacles and taking up all burdens with a kind of levity, as if my strength and resources could never fail. If they failed, I should have been left in the direst bankruptcy; and I had no right to reckon upon being delivered at the critical moment. . . . I persuaded myself then that I could not help it, that no better way was practicable, and indeed did live by faith, whether it was or was not exercised in a legitimate way. I might say now that another woman doing the same thing was tempting Providence. To tempt Providence or to trust God, which was it?

The money from her work may have seemed so providential that her family took it for granted. From hints in Oliphant's autobiography it seems that her sons neither comprehended nor appreciated their mother's enormous labor on their behalf. Williams in his *Margaret Oliphant: A Critical Biography* (1986) asserts that the boys responded to any wishes of hers that curtailed their "gentlemanly" pursuits with contempt, discourtesy, and increasingly petulant demands for more money and freedom.

In the last twelve years of her life Oliphant published at an unprecedented rate. Seventy-four books made it into print, and five more were published posthumously. She also wrote 114 pieces for periodicals. Many in this periodical group appeared in two regular columns Oliphant wrote for *Blackwood's Magazine:* "The Old Saloon," which ran from January 1887 to December 1892, and "The Looker-On," which appeared from August 1894 to October

1896. The subjects of her nonfiction submissions were divided among critical biographies and literary and social critiques. The latter group included papers such as "The Grievances of Women," "Men and Women," and "The Anti-Marriage League."

Many of the short stories from this time reflect Oliphant's awakened interest in the effects of social existence on authentic selfhood, which she posits in these works as a comprehensible truth of moral being that is able to communicate itself across the barriers between spiritual and material existence. These stories include "A Little Pilgrim in the Unseen," which was collected with another story in *A Little Pilgrim in the Unseen* (1882); "The Open Door" and "Old Lady Mary," which were collected in *Two Stories of the Seen and Unseen: The Open Door, Old Lady Mary* (1885); "The Portrait" and "The Land of Darkness," which were included in *Stories of the Seen and the Unseen* (1889); "The Library Window," which appeared in the British version of the collection titled *Stories of the Seen and the Unseen* (1902); and "The Land of Suspense," an uncollected story that appeared in the January 1897 issue of *Blackwood's Magazine*. Oliphant's intense attention in her supernatural fiction work seems to have had two motivations: first, stories of this type had become popular; second, many of her friends and nearly all of her family were now dead.

Oliphant's health had begun to fail as early as 1890, when rheumatism occasionally curtailed her activity, and 1894 marked the beginning of her final decline. At least part of this slow collapse was owing to the loss of purpose and identity she felt once all of her children had died. Her letters from this time speak of her grief and her bewilderment:

> When God called upon me to give up what was the half of my being [she refers here to Tiddy], I could speak a little and express the anguish that was in me; for then I had still my Cecco, his ever-ready arm to lean on, and a motive and object for every self-denial. But now I have lost all, everything on this earth that came from me and was wholly mine. . . . God only knows, who has not spared, what Cecco was to me—my child still, though a man, my dearest friend and closest companion. . . . [N]ature is very weak and humanity very short-sighted, and the distance that is between him and me and the silence seem more than flesh and blood can bear. . . . I know that I ought to bear it better, only that my prayers are all silent—I seem to have so little to ask for, nothing but that I may soon be reunited again to my dearest boys . . . in that above, which is dim, of which we know so little.

As had always been the case, however, Oliphant's work went steadily onward. Shortly before Cecco died in 1894, the Blackwood family commissioned

Oliphant, circa 1895 (portrait by Janet Mary Oliphant; from Mrs. Harry Coghill, ed., The Autobiography and Letters of Mrs. M. O. W. Oliphant, *1899)*

Oliphant to write a history of their publishing house. Because she regarded the house as representing "a most important piece of the recent history of literature, as well as many extremely interesting figures" and also because the Blackwoods were offering £500 per year until the work's completion, Oliphant happily took on the project, which she "would very fain make . . . [her] last work." The writing of *Annals of a Publishing House: William Blackwood and His Sons, Their Magazine and Friends* (1897) was in an important sense the writing of her own memoirs, a fact that she notes in a letter to the last Blackwood who would ever employ her: "I began my married life by my first story in 'Maga' the proofs of which ('Katie Stewart') I received on my wedding day: I should like to wind up the long laborious record (which seems to me now to have been so vain, so vain, my life all coming to nothing) with this."

Still, Oliphant wrote—in or out of the sickbed that she took to more and more often during the last year of her life. At one point she observes, with detached interest, the toll that her incessant labor was finally taking on her body: "I have worked a hole in my right forefinger—with the pen I suppose!—and can't get it to heal,—also from excessive use of that little implement." As the editor of Oliphant's autobiography notes, "Work, which had been her comfort and stimulant, was beginning to be evidently burdensome. Even the crippling of her finger, where the pen seemed to have really worn through the skin by long usage, was both a symptom and an aggravation of her depressed physical condition." To her great relief Oliphant in late April 1897 entered the final stages of her illness. When she could no longer write, she dictated. On 25 June she "softly passed away. The names of her boys were on her lips almost at the last though she had said repeatedly, 'I seem to see nothing but God and our Lord.'"

Although Margaret Oliphant left little material wealth to those who survived her, she did bequeath a large cultural and literary legacy. At Christmas in 1894 Oliphant happened to compare her work to that of Charlotte Brontë:

> I was reading of Charlotte Brontë the other day, and could not help comparing myself with the picture more or less as I read. I don't suppose my powers are equal to hers—my work to myself looks perfectly pale and colourless beside hers—but yet I have had far more experience and, I think, a fuller conception of life. I have learned to take perhaps a man's view of mortal affairs,—to feel that the love between men and women, the marrying and giving in marriage, occupy in fact so small a portion of either existence or thought. When I die I know what people will say of me: they will give me credit for courage (which I almost think is not courage but insensibility), and for honesty and honourable dealing; they will say I did my duty with a kind of steadiness, not knowing how I have rebelled and groaned under the rod.

Oliphant was right in her assessment of what her experience, conception of life, and view of mortal affairs contributed to her work and certainly correct in believing that she would be admired for courage and honesty. She was wrong, though, in the evaluation of her work. At her best Oliphant was a formidable writer who sought the redefinition of "woman" and her "place" in Victorian culture.

Letters:

Autobiography and Letters of Mrs. Margaret Oliphant, edited by Annie Coghill (Edinburgh: Blackwood, 1899; Leicester University Press, 1974).

Biography:

Vineta and Robert Colby, *The Equivocal Virtue: Mrs. Oliphant and the Victorian Literary Market Place* (New York: Archon, 1966).

References:

Elizabeth Helsinger, Robin Lauterbach Sheets, and William Veeder, *The Woman Question: Literary Issues, 1837–1883,* volume 3 of *The Woman Question: Society and Literature in Britain and America, 1837–1883,* 3 volumes (New York: Garland, 1983);

Michael Wheeler, *English Fiction of the Victorian Period: 1830–1890* (London: Longman, 1985);

Merryn Williams, *Margaret Oliphant: A Critical Biography* (New York: St. Martin's Press, 1986);

Robert Lee Wolff, *Gains and Losses: Novels of Faith and Doubt in Victorian England* (New York: Garland, 1977).

Sir Arthur Quiller-Couch

(21 November 1863 – 12 May 1944)

John Ferns
McMaster University

See also the Quiller-Couch entries in *DLB 135: Victorian Poets After 1850* and *DLB 153: Late-Victorian and Edwardian British Novelists, First Series.*

BOOKS: *Athens: A Poem* (Bodmin: Liddell, 1881);
Dead Man's Rock: A Romance (London: Cassell, 1887; New York: Cassell, 1887);
The Astonishing History of Troy Town (London & New York: Cassell, 1888);
The Splendid Spur: Being Memoirs of the Adventures of Mr. John Marvel, a Servant of His Late Majesty King Charles I, in the Years 1642–3 (London & New York: Cassell, 1889);
The Blue Pavilions (New York & London: Cassell, 1891);
Noughts and Crosses: Stories, Studies, and Sketches (London: Cassell, 1891; New York: Scribners, 1898);
The Warwickshire Avon (London: Osgood, 1892; New York: Harper, 1892);
I Saw Three Ships, and Other Winter's Tales (London & New York: Cassell, 1892);
The Delectable Duchy: Stories, Studies, and Sketches (London: Cassell, 1893; New York & London: Macmillan, 1893);
Green Bays: Verses and Parodies (London: Methuen, 1893; enlarged edition, London: Oxford University Press, 1930);
Wandering Heath: Stories, Studies, and Sketches (London: Cassell, 1895; New York: Scribners, 1895);
Fairy Tales, Far and Near (London & Paris: Cassell, 1895; New York: Hurst, 1895);
Ia: A Love Story (New York: Scribners, 1895; London: Cassell, 1896);
Poems and Ballads (London: Methuen, 1896);
Adventures in Criticism (London: Cassell, 1896; New York: Scribners, 1896);
The Ship of Stars (London: Cassell, 1899; New York: Scribners, 1899);
Historical Tales from Shakespeare (London: Arnold, 1899; New York: Scribners, 1900);

Arthur Quiller-Couch (The Hulton-Deutsch Collection)

A Fowey Garland (London: Cassell, 1899);
Old Fires and Profitable Ghosts: A Book of Stories (London: Cassell, 1900; New York: Scribners, 1900);
The Laird's Luck, and Other Fireside Tales (London: Cassell, 1901; New York: Scribners 1901);
The Westcotes (Philadelphia: Coates, 1902; Bristol: Arrowsmith / London: Simpkin, Marshall, Hamilton, Kent, 1907);
The White Wolf and Other Fireside Tales (London: Methuen, 1902; New York: Scribners, 1902);

The Adventures of Harry Revel (London: Cassell, 1903; New York: Scribners, 1903);

Hetty Wesley (London & New York: Harper, 1903);

Two Sides of the Face: Midwinter Tales (New York: Scribners, 1903; Bristol: Arrowsmith / London: Simpkin, Marshall, Hamilton, Kent, 1903);

Fort Amity (London: John Murray, 1904; New York: Scribners, 1904);

Shining Ferry (London: Hodder & Stoughton, 1905; New York: Scribners, 1905);

Shakespeare's Christmas and Other Stories (London: Smith, Elder, 1905; New York: Longmans, Green, 1905);

From a Cornish Window (Bristol: Arrowsmith / London: Simpkin, Marshall, Hamilton, Kent, 1906; New York: Dutton, 1906);

Sir John Constantine: Memoirs of His Adventures at Home and Abroad, and Particularly in the Island of Corsica, Beginning with the Year 1756 (New York: Scribners, 1905; London: Smith, Elder, 1906);

The Mayor of Troy (New York: Scribners, 1905; London: Methuen, 1906);

Poison Island (New York: Scribners, 1906; London: Smith, Elder, 1907);

Major Vigoureux (London: Methuen, 1907; New York: Scribners, 1907);

Merry-Garden, and Other Stories (London: Methuen, 1907; London: Dent / New York: Dutton, 1929);

True Tilda (Bristol: Arrowsmith, 1909; New York: Scribners, 1909);

Lady Good-for-Nothing (London, Edinburgh, Dublin, Leeds & New York: Nelson, 1910; New York: Scribners, 1910);

Corporal Sam, and Other Stories (London: Smith, Elder, 1910);

The Sleeping Beauty and Other Fairy Tales from the Old French (London: Hodder & Stoughton, 1910; New York: Hodder & Stoughton, 1910);

Brother Copas (Bristol: Arrowsmith / London: Simpkin, Marshall, Hamilton, Kent, 1911; New York: Scribners, 1911);

The Roll Call of Honour: A New Book of Golden Deeds (London & New York: Nelson, 1911);

The Vigil of Venus, and Other Poems (London: Methuen, 1912);

Hocken and Hunken: A Tale of Troy (Edinburgh: Blackwood, 1912; New York: Appleton, 1913);

In Powder & Crinoline: Old Fairy Tales Retold (London: Hodder & Stoughton, 1913); republished as *The Twelve Dancing Princesses, and Other Fairy Tales* (New York: Doran, 1923);

News from the Duchy (Bristol: Arrowsmith / London: Simpkin, Marshall, Hamilton, Kent, 1913; Boston: Badger, 1914);

An Appeal to Cornishwomen (Plymouth: Bowering, 1914);

Poetry (London: Batsford, 1914; New York: Dutton, 1914);

Nicky-Nan, Reservist (Edinburgh & London: Blackwood, 1915; New York: Appleton, 1915);

On the Art of Writing: Lectures Delivered in the University of Cambridge, 1913–1914 (Cambridge: Cambridge University Press, 1916; New York: Putnam, 1916);

Memoir of Arthur John Butler (London: Smith, Elder, 1917);

Mortallone and Aunt Trinidad: Tales of the Spanish Main (Bristol: Arrowsmith, 1917);

Notes on Shakespeare's Workmanship (New York: Holt, 1917); republished as *Shakespeare's Workmanship* (London: Unwin, 1918);

Foe-Farrell (London: Collins, 1918; New York: Macmillan, 1918);

Studies in Literature, First Series (Cambridge: Cambridge University Press / New York: Putnam, 1918);

On the Art of Reading: Lectures Delivered in the University of Cambridge, 1916–1917 (Cambridge: Cambridge University Press, 1920; New York & London: Putnam, 1920);

Studies in Literature, Second Series (Cambridge: Cambridge University Press / New York: Putnam, 1922);

Charles Dickens and Other Victorians (London: Cambridge University Press, 1925; New York & London: Putnam, 1925);

The Age of Chaucer (London & Toronto: Dent, 1926);

A Lecture on Lectures, Introductory Volume (London: Leonard & Virginia Woolf, 1927; New York: Harcourt, Brace, 1928);

Studies in Literature, Third Series (Cambridge: Cambridge University Press, 1929; New York: Putnam / Cambridge: Cambridge University Press, 1930);

Poems (London: Oxford University Press, 1929);

The Poet as Citizen, and Other Papers (Cambridge: Cambridge University Press, 1934; New York: Macmillan / Cambridge: Cambridge University Press, 1935);

Cambridge Lectures (London: Dent / New York: Dutton, 1943);

Shorter Stories (London: Dent, 1944);

Memories & Opinions: An Unfinished Autobiography (Cambridge: Cambridge University Press, 1944; Cambridge: Cambridge University Press / New York: Macmillan, 1945).

Collection: *The Duchy Edition of Tales & Romances,* 30 volumes (London & Toronto: Dent / New York: Dutton, 1928-1929).

OTHER: René Bazin, *A Blot of Ink,* translated by Quiller-Couch and Paul M. Francke (New York: Cassell, 1892);

"Dead Man's Rock," in *My First Book,* by Quiller-Couch, Jerome K. Jerome, and others (London: Chatto & Windus, 1894), pp. 269-282;

The Golden Pomp: A Procession of English Lyrics from Surrey to Shirley, edited by Quiller-Couch (London: Methuen, 1895);

The Story of the Sea, edited by Quiller-Couch, 2 volumes (London: Cassell, 1895-1896);

English Sonnets, edited, with an introduction, by Quiller-Couch (London: Chapman & Hall, 1897; New York: Crowell, 1936);

Robert Louis Stevenson, *St. Ives: Being the Adventures of a French Prisoner in England,* completed by Quiller-Couch (New York: Scribners, 1897; London: Heinemann, 1898);

The Cornish Magazine, edited by Quiller-Couch (July 1898-May 1899);

The Oxford Book of English Verse, 1250-1900, edited by Quiller-Couch (Oxford: Clarendon Press, 1900; enlarged, 1939);

The World of Adventure: A Collection of Stirring Scenes and Moving Accidents, edited by Quiller-Couch, 6 volumes (London & New York: Cassell, 1904-1905);

The Pilgrims' Way: A Little Scrip of Good Counsel for Travellers, compiled by Quiller-Couch (London: Seeley, 1906; New York: Dutton, 1907);

The Oxford Book of Ballads, edited by Quiller-Couch (Oxford: Clarendon Press, 1910);

The Oxford Book of Victorian Verse, edited by Quiller-Couch (Oxford: Clarendon Press, 1912);

Shakespeare, *The Works of Shakespeare,* New Cambridge Edition, comedies edited by Quiller-Couch and John Dover Wilson, 13 volumes (Cambridge: Cambridge University Press, 1921-1931);

A Bible Anthology, edited by Quiller-Couch (London & Toronto: Dent / New York: Dutton, 1922);

The Children's Bible, edited by Quiller-Couch, A. Nairne, and T. R. Glover (Cambridge: Cambridge University Press, 1924);

The Little Children's Bible, edited by Quiller-Couch, Nairne, and Glover (Cambridge: Cambridge University Press, 1924);

The Oxford Book of English Prose, edited by Quiller-Couch (Oxford: Clarendon Press, 1925);

The Englishman, edited by Quiller-Couch, 4 volumes (London & Toronto: Dent, 1926-1927);

The Cambridge Shorter Bible, edited by Quiller-Couch, Nairne, and Glover (Cambridge: Cambridge University Press, 1928);

Pages of English Prose, 1390-1930, edited by Quiller-Couch (Oxford: Clarendon Press, 1930);

Thomas Edward Brown: A Memorial Volume, 1830-1930, includes a memoir by Quiller-Couch (Cambridge: Cambridge University Press, 1930);

Thomas Traherne, *Felicities of Thomas Traherne,* edited, with an introduction, by Quiller-Couch (London: Dobell, 1934);

Matthew Arnold, *The Poetical Works of Matthew Arnold,* edited, with an introduction, by Quiller-Couch (London & New York: Oxford University Press, 1945).

Sir Arthur Quiller-Couch, commonly known as "Q," the initial with which he signed many of his works, was a reformer and reform writer primarily in working to improve secondary education in Cornwall and in contributing to the reform of the study of English at Cambridge University in the 1910s and 1920s. "Cambridge English," a movement in literary criticism associated with William Empson, Mansfield Forbes, I. A. Richards, and F. R. and Q. D. Leavis, was partly Q's creation. It strongly influenced the study of English in universities throughout the world. Quiller-Couch was an anthologist, educationist, critic, scholar, and poet who initially made his reputation as a short-story writer and novelist in the 1890s and the early twentieth century.

Born in Bodmin, Cornwall, in 1863, Q was the eldest of five children of Mary Ford and Dr. Thomas Quiller-Couch, the local physician. From Q's father and paternal grandfather, Jonathan Couch, author of the four-volume *A History of the Fishes of the British Islands* (1862-1865) and the leading ichthyologist of his day, Q acquired his interest in writing. He began his schooling at Newton Abbot College, Devon, in 1873 and completed it at Clifton College, Bristol, in 1882. Shaw Sparrow, a fellow student, described Q as absorbing "Greek and Latin as a sponge drinks water." From Clifton, Q won an entrance scholarship in classics to Trinity College, Oxford, where he studied from 1882 to 1887. As a scholar he earned a first class in Classical Moderations in 1884, and he contributed verse parodies to *The Oxford Magazine.* He also enjoyed boating, rowed in the Trinity first boat, and became captain of the college boat club.

Unfortunately, his university career was almost ended by the death of his father in October 1884. Q's father left considerable debts, but the intervention of his maternal grandfather permitted him to complete his university education. He re-

The Haven, Quiller-Couch's house in Fowey

ceived only a second class in his final examinations in summer 1886, but he was appointed to a college lecturership in 1886–1887.

By 1887 Q's grandfather could no longer support him, so in order to assist his mother, two brothers, and two sisters Q began writing novels. His first novel, *Dead Man's Rock: A Romance* (1887), is an adventure story in the manner of Robert Louis Stevenson and H. Rider Haggard. During the next thirty years Q published twenty novels and thirteen volumes of short stories, and these were collected in thirty volumes as *The Duchy Edition of Tales & Romances* in 1928–1929.

Leaving Oxford in 1887, Q settled in London, where he worked as a freelance writer in addition to writing for the Cassell publishing house, which had published his first novel. In London, Q knew many contemporary artists, actors, and writers, such as John Sargent, Ellen Terry, and Henry James, and from there Q frequently visited Fowey (pronounced "Foy"), the Cornwall home of Louisa Hicks, his fiancée, whom he married at Fowey parish church on 22 August 1888. Fowey became the Troy of his Cornish novels, the first of which—*The Astonishing History of Troy Town*—was published by Cassell in 1888. His third novel, *The Splendid Spur: Being Memoirs of the Adventures of Mr. John Marvel, a Servant of His Late Majesty King Charles I, in the Years 1642–3*, was also published by Cassell the following year.

At this time Q was also writing for Cassell's weekly paper, *The Speaker,* and many of his early stories were published there. Its editor, Thomas Wemyss Reid, who had been general manager of Cassell's since 1887, was a radical Liberal, and Q, despite his love of tradition, shared Reid's political convictions. Writers for *The Speaker* included J. M. Barrie, who became a lifelong friend of Q; George Moore; John Morley; Sidney Webb; Henry James; William Butler Yeats; and John Davidson. The chief rival of *The Speaker* was the Conservative *National Observer* edited by William Ernest Henley and Charley Whibley, but the staffs of both papers were on friendly terms, and some of the writers, such as Barrie and Yeats, contributed to both papers.

Q and Louisa's first child—a boy, Bevil Bryan—was born in October 1890. Life as a Fleet Street journalist did not suit Q, and in autumn 1891 Q, who had been overworking, had a serious breakdown. In 1892 he bought The Haven at Fowey, a site he loved; he eventually became commodore of the Royal Fowey Yacht Club and helped to organize the local celebrations of Queen Victoria's Diamond Jubilee in 1897. The Haven became his family home until his death in 1944.

Q's early fiction had been composed primarily of adventure and humor, and following Robert Louis Stevenson's death in 1894, Q was invited by Sidney Colvin, Stevenson's literary executor, to complete *St. Ives: Being the Adventures of a French Prisoner in England*, Stevenson's unfinished novel. Q finished this novel and published it in 1897; two years earlier he had published *Ia: A Love Story,* his first novel of character. This book was not as successful with the public as his adventure writing had been;

nevertheless, in 1899 Q published another novel of character, *The Ship of Stars*. This novel is autobiographical as Taffy Raymond, its central character, is based heavily on Q and expresses much of his philosophy of independence.

Q's growing popularity with the Fowey inhabitants received a setback during the South African War (1899-1902). As a Liberal Q opposed the war, and while speaking at one local meeting he received a note indicating that a member of the audience intended to shoot David Lloyd George, who was to be the principal speaker that evening. Q was able to finish his speech, but he was jostled as the meeting broke up.

In 1900 his best-known anthology, *The Oxford Book of English Verse, 1250-1900,* was published. Nearly half a million copies were sold, and it was reprinted twelve times before an enlarged edition was published as *The Oxford Book of English Verse, 1250-1918* (1939). Q later edited other anthologies such as *The Oxford Book of Ballads* (1910), *The Oxford Book of Victorian Verse* (1912), and *The Oxford Book of English Prose* (1925).

The human interest in Q's novels deepened in *The Westcotes* (1902), which concerns the love of a middle-aged spinster for a younger man. He then published *Hetty Wesley* (1903), a controversial novel that exposes the severe treatment that its heroine receives at the hands of her father, the Reverend Samuel Wesley, and her famous brothers, John and Charles. Many Methodists were angered by Q's presentation of the founders of their church. *Lady Good-for-Nothing* (1910) was later published as a third novel about the sufferings of women.

Q's novels and stories frequently have historical settings and often display his knowledge of Cornish history, but *Fort Amity* (1904) is set in North America during the Seven Years' War and concerns the effect of war on the nerves of a young officer. Q's twelfth novel, *Sir John Constantine: Memoirs of His Adventures at Home and Abroad, and Particularly in the Island of Corsica, Beginning with the Year 1756* (1905), became his favorite. Set in eighteenth-century Corsica and influenced by Miguel de Cervantes, one of Q's favorite authors, the novel recounts the adventures of Sir John Constantine, the Cornish knight. As does Taffy Raymond in *The Ship of Stars*, Constantine expresses many of Q's chivalrous concerns.

Some of Q's most important work as a reformer occurred during this period. In 1902 at Fowey he participated in celebrations of the coronation of Edward VII. This was also the year in which the Balfour Education Act, which gave wide powers to county councils for the conduct of elementary and secondary education, was passed. Before this legislation was passed, public bodies had no power to provide secondary education, and under the provisions of this act the Cornwall county education committee was convened in September 1903. Q became a member of the committee in 1904, and with R. G. Rows, a farmer and Methodist preacher who was chairman of the committee, and F. R. Pascoe, its secretary, Q worked to build secondary schools throughout Cornwall. He also served as chairman of the school management committee, and he spent much time visiting elementary schools throughout Cornwall. For this work as well as for his literary and political services he was knighted on the recommendation of the government of Herbert Henry Asquith, Lord Asquith, in 1910. Q's work in Cornish education anticipated by ten years his reform work to establish a new Cambridge English tripos. In his preface to *On the Art of Reading: Lectures Delivered in the University of Cambridge, 1916-1917* (1920) from his vantage point as a university professor Q wrote:

> The real battle for English lies in our Elementary Schools, and in the training of our Elementary Teachers. . . . My thoughts have too often strayed from my audience in a University theatre away to remote rural class-rooms where the hungry sheep look up and are not fed; to piteous groups of urchins standing at attention and chanting *The Wreck of the Hesperus* [(1842) by Henry Wadsworth Longfellow] in unison.

Frederick Brittain writes that after the passage of the Balfour Act "Q had the great satisfaction of seeing numbers of children go from Cornish elementary schools to the secondary schools and on to the universities, one of them (A. L. Rowse) becoming a fellow of All Souls."

During 1902-1910 Q was also trying to return Liberal candidates to Parliament to represent southeast Cornwall. However, although Q was president of the Liberal Association for his constituency, in 1912 he wrote letters opposing the Mental Deficiency Bill that the Liberal government supported, and these letters were sent to Hilaire Belloc's weekly, *The Eye-Witness*. This bill sought to retain the weak-minded and the insane in government-controlled institutions. Before a third parliamentary reading the bill was withdrawn. Despite differences with his party over this issue and although he occasionally voted for the Labour Party if no Liberal candidate was standing, Q remained a Liberal throughout his life.

Following the death in June 1912 of Arthur Verrall, the first King Edward VII Professor of English Literature at Cambridge University, Q's life of Liberal politics and educational and literary work

Quiller-Couch in 1937 (The Hulton-Deutsch Collection)

took a new turn. He was invited to replace Verrall in the professorship and was appointed on 31 October 1912, at which time he also became a fellow of Jesus College. In January 1913 he took up residence in Cambridge, and his inaugural lecture was delivered at the end of that month. His first dozen lectures were collected in *On the Art of Writing: Lectures Delivered in the University of Cambridge, 1913–1914* (1916). His lectures were well attended–often by more women than men–and Q always began these lectures by addressing his audience as "Gentlemen." This called attention to the fact that the women's colleges were not yet formally included in the university.

As well as giving lectures Q offered classes on Aristotle's *Poetics* and on "The Background of the English Moralists: Aristotle's *Ethics*." Because he was a professor, Q was not required to give individual instruction to undergraduates, but he directed doctoral students–including F. R. Leavis–when a doctoral program in English was instituted after World War I.

During that war Q began the reform work that was his most important, after that of establishing secondary schools in Cornwall: developing a new English course at Cambridge University. In 1916 he began a course of lectures that were collected as *On the Art of Reading*. This was dedicated to his two Cambridge colleagues, H. F. Stewart and H. M. Chadwick, his closest supporters in establishing the new English program. These three proposed their reforms to the special board for medieval and modern languages at the university and received its support in spring 1917. The board recommended to the university that the medieval and modern languages tripos be replaced by two triposes, one in modern and medieval languages and the other in English. The most important part of the proposal was that in the new English tripos the study of philology, Anglo-Saxon and Middle English, was to become optional and that candidates could offer literary criticism and comparative literature instead.

Although the English Association and the senate of the university opposed the proposal, it eventually succeeded, and the new tripos flourished after the end of the war. Mansfield Forbes and I. A. Richards seized the opportunity that Q, Stewart, and Chadwick provided. Their work prepared the way for the original work of William Empson and F. R. and Q. D. Leavises. Q's place in the making of Cambridge English is perhaps less central than in establishing secondary education in Cornwall, but these two achievements are his most important educational reforms.

As well as reforming the study of English at Cambridge during the war, Q was active in the British war effort. At the beginning of the war he wrote *An Appeal to Cornishwomen* (1914) for the Cornwall parliamentary recruiting committee, and he helped to raise and train men for the light infantry of the duke of Cornwall. On one occasion he and his wife entertained an entire company of men for tea at The Haven. He ended his novel writing during this period. In 1915 he published *Nicky-Nan, Reservist*, which is based on his experiences in recruiting. In 1918 he published *Foe-Farrell*, a novel about two enemies who pursue each other around the world. It can be interpreted as an allegory of the Anglo-German conflict during the war. His son, Bevil, fought in and survived the war only to die of pneumonia in occupied Germany in February 1919. This was the great sadness of Q's and Louisa's lives.

Bevil's death shadowed the last twenty-five years of Q's life. Brittain quotes from a letter that expresses Q's sense of loss and illustrates his effort to bury his loss in his work, a letter Q wrote more than a year after Bevil's death:

> I have been rather heavily overworking–at Cambridge and, later, at Oxford–on examination work. It

deadens pain. But I begin to see that it were better–and braver–to face the pain and "have it out": for by shirking it, one's whole mind gets deadened. Really I don't care, half my time, what happens in a world that has killed my dearest and most natural hope.

Unlike Rudyard Kipling, who also lost a son in the war, Q was unable to write about the experience. Instead he threw himself increasingly into his work at the university and his civic work in Cornwall, where he continued to serve on the education committee. He was also a magistrate, commodore of the Royal Fowey Yacht Club and principal organizer of its annual regatta, and mayor of Fowey in 1937-1938.

The responsibilities that Q assumed in trying to deaden the pain of losing his son included becoming general editor of The King's Treasuries of Literature, a new series of English school texts for the Dent publishing house. More than 250 volumes of this series, begun in 1920, were published during Q's life. In 1921 he began his collaboration with John Dover Wilson to edit the plays of William Shakespeare for the Cambridge University Press, and between 1921 and 1931 fourteen comedies appeared, each with an introduction by Q. He also helped form a Cambridge branch of the British Empire Shakespeare Society in 1921, and at this time he became president of the Village Drama Society, which held meetings in various parts of England. He was also reading extensively in preparing for his editorial work on *The Oxford Book of English Prose*.

After the war the number of students entering the university increased greatly, and the English tripos proved to be popular: the number of those who took it in a given year during Q's time at the university rose from 20 to 150. Q felt that the tripos should be divided into two parts, and during summer 1922 he wrote:

> What I'm groping after is a second Part of the Tripos which shall (1) mainly concern itself with English *thought,* and (2) be a stiff test of our men's capacity to *write* (which includes thinking). What we want is a Part II that will turn out men provided with some useful principles for statesmanship, the better journalism, etc., and some knowledge of what Englishmen have thought from time to time. For my part, I believe that nowadays the true mission of the English Tripos is to preach the spirit of Greece.

The tripos was not divided, however, until 1928.

Q became increasingly involved in Cambridge social life. From 1919 until his death he was president of the Cambridge University Cruising Club. He was also a member of two dining clubs, the Ad Eundem and The Society. His work was divided between Cambridge and Cornwall, where the county council in summer 1919 invited him to draw up the resolution that was cut into the wall of the county hall in Truro following the signing of the international treaties after the war. He was also vice chairman of the county education committee and later became its chairman. Of his Cornish work he wrote in July 1922:

> All the back-end of the week is filled up with the sort of committee work (local) that makes up an alleged vacation. All yesterday I spent at Truro on a School Building and Furnishing committee. This morning I spent on agenda of full Education Committee, at which I must take the chair to-morrow: and this very afternoon I've (1) presided at Harbour Commission, and (2) attended meeting for winding up accounts of local War Memorial.

Christmas was a celebration that Q greatly enjoyed. He loved decorating The Haven, and on Christmas Day he always spent some time reading the fairy tales of Hans Christian Andersen. A few days after Christmas in 1920 he and Louisa were invited to dine "with a few friends" at the Fowey Hotel. At this surprise celebration were fifty-four friends who were dressed as characters from Q's novels, friends both honoring and seeking to lift him and Louisa from the pain of having lost Bevil. Q bought his son's mare from the War Office, looked after her until her death, and then in his keeping room at Cambridge hung her photograph under a photograph of his son in military uniform.

From 1923 to 1933 Q published two volumes of collected lectures and essays, an anthology of English prose, a share in three Bible anthologies, and a thirty-volume edition of his fiction. In addition he frequently wrote introductions to books by other writers. Q dedicated *The Oxford Book of English Prose* to the Oxford and Cambridge colleges with which he had been associated–"To two houses of learning and hospitality, Trinity College, Oxford, and Jesus College, Cambridge, and to friendship."

Q began to suffer from eye trouble at this time, but he began a new novel, "Castle d'Or," his first since *Foe-Farrell*. This work, however, remained unfinished at his death. In 1923 he became chairman of the Cornwall county education committee, an office he held for the next eight years. In 1927 when the committee held a special Education Week to celebrate the twenty-fifth anniversary of the passing of the Balfour Education Act, Q wrote a preface for the handbook of the celebration. It summarizes well his educational views as he discusses the central place of education in human life, of education as an invisible force and spirit, and as a gift–sometimes the remembered word of a cherished teacher–that permits a creative and vital redirection. The final paragraph of Q's preface recapitulates what had inspired him, Rows and Pascoe, and had shaped the aims they had undertaken in the times following the passing of the Education Act:

> [I]f we [of the Local Education Authority] in our turn would look into our hearts for a rebuke to self-complacency, [we] should admit that in the beginning we wasted many months over bitter and barren sectarian debates, until the mute appeal of the children somehow became audible, and the reproach shook us together into a body with one strong purpose—I can even recall the day and hour when this miracle happened. It was the children who wrought it, the children who taught us; and it must be the children who, in Education Week, will reward us with our visible justification, all unconsciously pleading for us to the public with their healthy frames, refined movements, graceful rivalries, happy faces.

This passage reveals the warm, Christian heart of Q's liberalism. The son of a father who died in debt because he "forgot" to collect payments from his patients for their medical bills, Q recognized his privileged place and helped those less privileged in Cornish society. This is what inspired Q's work as a reformer. He continued the work that he began as a member of the Cornwall county council education committee into the design of a new English tripos at Cambridge University.

In 1931 he resigned as chairman of the education committee although he continued to serve as vice chairman until 1934. He remained a governor of the Fowey Grammar School and was for twelve years president of the Workers' Educational Association. In 1926 Trinity College made him an Honorary Fellow, and in 1927 and 1930 he received honorary degrees from the universities of Aberdeen and Edinburgh, respectively. Groups such as the Dickens Fellowship and the British Academy sought him as a public speaker.

Q was on hand in Fowey to help organize the royal celebration of the Silver Jubilee of George V in May 1935 and of the coronation of George VI two years later. In 1936 he was made a freeman of his native Bodmin; in 1937, of Fowey; and during 1937–1938, of Truro, the county town. A portrait by Henry Lamb was commissioned by Q's Cornish friends, and Q presented this to the Royal Institution of Cornwall. Four years earlier Sir William Nicholson had painted Q's portrait for Jesus College. *The Poet as Citizen, and Other Papers* (1934), Q's last collected volume of lectures and essays, includes Q's answer to T. S. Eliot's "Tradition and Orthodoxy," an attack on Liberalism in *After Strange Gods: A Primer of Modern Heresy* (1934). Q argues that "this 'Liberalism' which Mr. Eliot arraigns as a worm eating into the traditions of our society, reveals itself rather as Tradition itself, throughout Literature (which is Thought worth setting down and recording), the organic spirit persisting, aerating, preserving, the liberties our ancestors won and we inherit."

As the Allies' invasion of France was being prepared in hopes of ending World War II, Q died in Fowey on 12 May 1944. Three days later six naval men carried his coffin into the parish church where he had been married and where his son and his daughter, Foy Felicia, had been christened. As a reformer Q is remembered primarily for his work on behalf of secondary education in Cornwall beginning in 1902 and for his efforts in establishing the English tripos at Cambridge University during and after World War I. As a literary figure he is also remembered as an anthologist, short-story writer, novelist, critic, and scholar. He was a man of many accomplishments, and the liberal spirit that he displayed as a reforming educationist helped to expand educational opportunities for his fellow Cornishmen and women and to design a Cambridge University English program in which some of the finest literary critics of the twentieth century were educated.

Bibliography:

Frederick Brittain, "Chronological List of Q's Publications," in his *Arthur Quiller-Couch: A Biographical Study of "Q"* (Cambridge: Cambridge University Press, 1947; New York: Macmillan, 1948), pp. 159–166.

Biographies:

Frederick Brittain, *Arthur Quiller-Couch: A Biographical Study of "Q"* (Cambridge: Cambridge University Press, 1947; New York: Macmillan, 1948);

A. L. Rowse, *Quiller Couch: A Portrait of "Q"* (London: Methuen, 1988).

References:

Helene Hanff, *Q's Legacy* (Boston: Little, Brown, 1985);

Ian MacKillop, *F. R. Leavis: A Life in Criticism* (London: Allen Lane, 1995);

S. Gorley Putt, "Technique and Culture: Three Cambridge Portraits," *Essays & Studies,* 14 (1960): 17–34;

R. J. Schork, "The Holy Word," *Studies in Short Fiction,* 27 (1990): 603–604;

Basil Willey, *The 'Q' Tradition: An Inaugural Lecture* (Cambridge: Cambridge University Press, 1946).

John Ruskin
(8 February 1819 - 20 January 1900)

Gregory Claeys
Royal Holloway College

See also the Ruskin entries in *DLB 55: Victorian Prose Writers Before 1867* and *DLB 163: British Children's Writers, 1800-1880*.

BOOKS*: *Salsette and Elephanta: A Prize Poem* (Oxford: Vincent, 1839);

Modern Painters (5 volumes, London: Smith, Elder, 1843-1860; volumes 1-2, New York: Wiley & Putnam, 1847-1848; volumes 3-5, New York: Wiley, 1856-1860);

The Seven Lamps of Architecture (London: Smith, Elder, 1849; New York: Wiley, 1849);

The King of the Golden River; or, The Black Brothers: A Legend of Stiria (London: Smith, Elder, 1851; New York: Wiley, 1860);

Notes on the Construction of Sheepfolds (London: Smith, Elder, 1851; New York: Wiley, 1851);

The Stones of Venice, 3 volumes (London: Smith, Elder, 1851-1853; New York: Wiley, 1860);

Pre-Raphaelitism (London: Smith, Elder, 1851; New York: Wiley, 1851);

Giotto and His Works in Padua (3 parts, London: Printed for the Arundel Society, 1853-1860; 1 volume, New York: Scribners, 1899);

Lectures on Architecture and Painting, Delivered at Edinburgh in November 1853 (London: Smith, Elder, 1854; New York: Wiley, 1854);

The Opening of the Crystal Palace, Considered in Some of Its Relations to the Prospects of Art (London: Smith, Elder, 1854; New York: Alden, 1885);

Notes on Some of the Principal Pictures Exhibited in the Rooms of the Royal Academy: 1855 (London: Smith, Elder, 1855);

Notes on Some of the Principal Pictures Exhibited in the Rooms of the Royal Academy, and the Society of Painters in Water Colours, No. II-1856 (London: Smith, Elder, 1856);

The Harbours of England (London: Gambart, 1856);

Notes on the Turner Gallery at Marlborough House, 1856 (London: Smith, Elder, 1857);

*This list excludes revised and enlarged editions.

John Ruskin

The Political Economy of Art: Being the Substance (with Additions) of Two Lectures Delivered at Manchester, July 10th and 13th, 1857 (London: Smith, Elder, 1857; New York: Wiley & Halsted, 1858); republished as *"A Joy Forever" (and Its Price in the Market): Being the Substance (with Additions) of Two Lectures on the Political Economy of Art, Delivered at Manchester, July 10th and 13th, 1857* (Orpington, Kent: George Allen, 1880); republished as *The Political Economy of Art; or, "A Joy Forever" (and Its Price in the Market)* (New York: Wiley, 1888);

Notes on Some of the Principal Pictures Exhibited in the Rooms of the Royal Academy and the Society of Painters in Water Colours, No. III-1857 (London: Smith, Elder, 1857);

The Elements of Drawing in Three Letters to Beginners (London: Smith, Elder, 1857; New York: Wiley & Halsted, 1857);

Notes on Some of the Principal Pictures Exhibited in the Rooms of the Royal Academy, the Old and New Society of Painters in Water Colours, the Society of British Artists, and the French Exhibition, No. IV–1858 (London: Smith, Elder, 1858);

Cambridge School of Art: Mr. Ruskin's Inaugural Address Delivered at Cambridge, Oct. 29, 1858 (Cambridge: Deighton, Bell / London: Bell & Daldy, 1858);

The Oxford Museum, by Ruskin and Henry W. Acland (London: Smith, Elder / Oxford: Parker, 1859);

The Unity of Art . . ., Delivered at the Annual Meeting of the Manchester School of Art, February 22nd, 1859 (Manchester: Sowler, 1859);

The Two Paths: Being Lectures on Art, and Its Application to Decoration and Manufacture, Delivered in 1858-9 (London: Smith, Elder, 1859; New York: Wiley, 1859);

The Elements of Perspective Arranged for the Use of the Schools and Intended to Be Read in Connexion with the First Three Books of Euclid (London: Smith, Elder, 1859; New York: Wiley, 1860);

Notes on Some of the Principal Pictures Exhibited in the Royal Academy, the Old and New Societies of Painters in Water Colours, the Society of British Artists, and the French Exhibition, No. V–1859 (London: Smith, Elder, 1859);

"Unto This Last": Four Essays on the First Principles of Political Economy (London: Smith, Elder, 1862; New York: Wiley, 1866);

Sesame and Lilies: Two Lectures Delivered at Manchester in 1864 (London: Smith, Elder, 1865; New York: Wiley, 1865);

The Ethics of the Dust: Ten Lectures to Little Housewives on the Elements of Crystallisation (London: Smith, Elder, 1866; New York: Wiley, 1866);

An Inquiry into Some of the Conditions at Present Affecting "the Study of Architecture" in Our Schools (New York: Wiley, 1866);

The Crown of Wild Olive: Three Lectures on Work, Traffic, and War (London: Smith, Elder, 1866; New York: Wiley, 1866);

Time and Tide, by Weare and Tyne: Twenty-Five Letters to a Working Man of Sunderland on the Laws of Work (London: Smith, Elder, 1867; New York: Wiley, 1868);

First Notes on the General Principles of Employment for the Destitute and Criminal Classes (London: For private circulation, 1868);

The Queen of the Air: Being a Study of the Greek Myths of Cloud and Storm (London: Smith, Elder, 1869; New York: Home Book, 1869);

Catalogue of Examples Arranged for Elementary Study in the University Galleries (Oxford: Clarendon Press, 1870);

Lectures on Art Delivered before the University of Oxford in Hilary Term, 1870 (London & New York: Macmillan / Oxford: Clarendon Press, 1870);

Fors Clavigera: Letters to the Workmen and Labourers of Great Britain, 96 letters (London: Printed for the author by Smith, Elder, 1871–1884; New York: Wiley, 1871–1878, 1880, 1884–1886);

Munera Pulveris: Six Essays on the Elements of Political Economy (London: Printed for the author by Smith, Elder, 1872; New York: Wiley, 1872);

Aratra Pentelici: Six Lectures on the Elements of Sculpture, Given before the University of Oxford in Michaelmas Term, 1870 (London: Printed for the author by Smith, Elder, 1872; New York: Wiley, 1872);

The Relation between Michael Angelo and Tintoret: Seventh of the Course of Lectures on Sculpture Delivered at Oxford, 1870-71 (London: Printed for the author by Smith, Elder, 1872; New York: Alden, 1885);

The Eagle's Nest: Ten Lectures on the Relation of Natural Science to Art, Given before the University of Oxford in Lent Term, 1872 (London: Printed for the author by Smith, Elder, 1872; New York: Wiley, 1873);

The Sepulchral Monuments of Italy: Monuments of the Cavalli Family in the Church of Santa Anastasia, Verona (London: Arundel Society, 1872);

Love's Meinie: Lectures on Greek and English Birds, 3 parts (lectures 1-2, Keston, Kent: George Allen, 1873; New York: Wiley, 1873; lecture 3, Orpington, Kent: George Allen, 1881); republished in 1 volume (Orpington, Kent: George Allen, 1881);

Ariadne Florentina: Six Lectures on Wood and Metal Engraving, with Appendix, Given before the University of Oxford, in Michaelmas Term, 1872, 7 parts (lecture 1, Keston, Kent: George Allen, 1873; lectures 2-6 & appendix, Orpington, Kent: George Allen, 1874–1876); republished in 2 volumes (New York: Wiley, 1874–1875); republished in 1 volume (Orpington, Kent: George Allen, 1876);

The Poetry of Architecture: Cottage, Villa, Etc., to Which Is Added Suggestions on Works of Art, as Kata Phusin (New York: Wiley, 1873); republished as *The Poetry of Architecture; or, The Architecture of the Nations of Europe Considered in Its Association with Natural Scenery and National Character* (Orpington, Kent: George Allen, 1893);

Val d'Arno: Ten Lectures on the Tuscan Art Directly Antecedent to the Florentine Year of Victories, Given before the University of Oxford in Michaelmas Term, 1873 (Orpington, Kent: George Allen, 1874; New York: Lovell, 1885);

Notes on Some of the Principal Pictures Exhibited in the Rooms of the Royal Academy: 1875 (Orpington, Kent: George Allen / London: Ellis & Bond, 1875);

Mornings in Florence: Being Simple Studies of Christian Art, for English Travellers (6 parts, Orpington, Kent: George Allen, 1875-1877; 1 volume, New York: Wiley, 1876);

Deucalion: Collected Studies of the Lapse of Waves, and Life of Stones (6 parts, Orpington, Kent: George Allen, 1875-1879; 1 volume, Orpington, Kent: George Allen, 1879; New York: Lovell, 1885);

Proserpina: Studies of Wayside Flowers, While the Air Was Yet Pure among the Alps, and in the Scotland and England Which My Father Knew (10 parts, Orpington, Kent: George Allen, 1875-1879, 1882-1886); parts 1-6 republished in 1 volume (Orpington, Kent: George Allen, 1879; New York: Lovell, 1885);

Guide to the Principal Pictures in the Academy of Fine Arts at Venice, Arranged for English Travellers, 2 parts (Venice, 1877; Orpington, Kent: George Allen, 1882, 1883);

The Laws of Fésole: A Familiar Treatise on the Elementary Principles and Practice of Drawing and Painting, as Determined by the Tuscan Masters, Arranged for the Use of Schools (4 parts, Orpington, Kent: George Allen, 1877-1878; 1 volume, Orpington, Kent: George Allen, 1879; New York: Wiley, 1879);

St. Mark's Rest: The History of Venice, Written for the Help of the Few Travellers Who Still Care about Her Monuments (6 parts, Orpington, Kent: George Allen, 1877-1884); republished in 1 volume (Orpington, Kent: George Allen, 1884; New York: Wiley, 1884);

Notes by Mr. Ruskin on His Drawings by the Late J. M. W. Turner, R. A. (London: Fine Art Society, 1878);

Notes by Mr. Ruskin on Samuel Prout and William Hunt, Illustrated by a Loan Collection of Drawings Exhibited at the Fine Art Society's Galleries (London, 1879-1880);

Letters Addressed by Professor Ruskin, D.C.L., to the Clergy on the Lord's Prayer and the Church, edited by F. A. Malleson (N.p.: Privately printed, 1879);

Elements of English Prosody for Use in St. George's Schools (Orpington, Kent: George Allen, 1880);

Arrows of the Chace: Being a Collection of Scattered Letters Published chiefly in the Daily Newspapers, 1840-1880, 2 volumes (Orpington, Kent: George Allen, 1880; New York: Wiley, 1881);

"Our Fathers Have Told Us." Sketches of the History of Christendom for Boys and Girls Who Have Been Held at Its Fonts, Part I: The Bible of Amiens (5 parts, Orpington, Kent: George Allen, 1880-1885; 1 volume, New York: Alden, 1885);

Catalogue of the Collection of Siliceous Minerals Given to and Arranged for St. David's School, Reigate (Brantwood: Privately printed, 1883);

The Art of England: Lectures Given in Oxford (7 parts, Orpington, Kent: George Allen, 1883-1884; 1 volume, New York: Wiley, 1884);

The Storm Cloud of the Nineteenth Century: Two Lectures Delivered at the London Institution, February 4th and 11th, 1884 (2 parts, Orpington, Kent: George Allen, 1884; 1 volume, New York: Wiley, 1884);

The Pleasures of England: Lectures Given in Oxford (4 parts, Orpington, Kent: George Allen, 1884-1885; 1 volume, New York: Wiley, 1885);

On the Old Road: A Collection of Miscellaneous Essays, Pamphlets, &c., &c., Published 1834-1885, 2 volumes, edited by Alexander D. O. Wedderburn (Orpington, Kent: George Allen, 1885);

Praeterita: Outlines of Scenes and Thoughts Perhaps Worthy of Memory in My Past Life (28 parts, Orpington, Kent: George Allen, 1885-1889; 3 volumes, Orpington, Kent: George Allen, 1886-1889; New York: Wiley, 1886-1889);

Dilecta: Correspondence, Diary Notes, and Extracts from Books, Illustrating Praeterita, 3 parts (Orpington, Kent: George Allen, 1886-1889);

Hortus Inclusus: Messages from the Wood to the Garden, Sent in Happy Days to the Sister Ladies of the Thwaite, Coniston (Orpington, Kent: George Allen, 1887);

The Poems of John Ruskin: Now First Collected from Original Manuscript and Printed Sources, and Edited in Chronological Order, with Notes, Biographical and Critical, 2 volumes, edited by William Gershom Collingwood (Orpington, Kent: George Allen, 1891; New York: Merrill / London & Orpington, Kent: George Allen, 1891);

Verona, and Other Lectures, edited by Collingwood (Orpington, Kent: George Allen, 1894; New York & London: Macmillan, 1894);

The Diaries of John Ruskin, 3 volumes, edited by Joan Evans and John Howard Whitehouse (Oxford: Clarendon Press, 1956-1959);

The Brantwood Diary of John Ruskin, Together with Selected Related Letters and Sketches of Persons Mentioned, edited by Helen Gill Viljoen (New Haven: Yale University Press, 1971).

Collection: *The Works of John Ruskin,* 39 volumes, edited by Edward Tyas Cook and Alexander Wedderburn (London: George Allen / New York: Longmans, Green, 1903-1912).

OTHER: *Bibliotheca Pastorum,* 4 volumes, edited by Ruskin (London, 1876-1885);

A. Gordon Crawford [Alexander Gordon Hay Wise], *Notes on Some of the Principal Pictures of Sir J. E. Millais, Exhibited at the Grosvenor Gallery, 1886,* preface and criticisms by Ruskin (London: Reeves, 1886).

John Ruskin attained his reputation as an art historian and architectural critic with the publication of three works: *Modern Painters* (1843-1860), *The Seven Lamps of Architecture* (1849), and *The Stones of Venice* (1851-1853). His central social theme in the last two works in particular concerns the relation of architecture to society, and he argues that the degeneration of society is reflected in its architecture. Building on this theme, Ruskin became one of the most important Victorian critics of the effects of competition, utilitarianism, industrialism, and the subserviency of all higher values to mere money-getting. His chief mature work of social theory is *"Unto This Last": Four Essays on the First Principles of Political Economy* (1862), first published in the *Cornhill Magazine.* Later important works include *Fors Clavigera: Letters to the Workmen and Labourers of Great Britain* (1871-1884) and his uncompleted autobiography, *Praeterita: Outlines of Scenes and Thoughts Perhaps Worthy of Memory in My Past Life* (1885-1889). A survey of literary influences on early Labour Party members done in 1906 showed Ruskin to have been one of the more important writers for his early twentieth-century British social criticism, especially through *Unto This Last.*

Ruskin, the grandson of an Edinburgh wine merchant and son of John James Ruskin, cofounder of the sherry business of Ruskin, Telford and Domencq, was born at Brunswick Square, London. His mother, Margaret Ruskin, was a stern Calvinist who deprived her son of toys, frequently whipped him, and enforced the methodical reading of the Bible on him. The young Ruskin was, however, early trained in music, drawing, reading, and the observation of nature. When he was four years old the family moved to Herne Hill. During the next ten years he traveled frequently with his mother, father, and nurse on business trips to Flanders, Germany, and Switzerland. He was deeply impressed with the Alps in particular, and by the age of fifteen he began to publish short notes on the color of the Rhine River and the strata of Mont Blanc, notes illustrated with his own drawings. His father encouraged him to read the works of William Shakespeare; Alexander Pope; George Gordon, Lord Byron; and other English writers in particular, and young Ruskin soon began to compose poetry, dramas, and romances in imitation.

Though his precocious talents were everywhere evident, his schooling was irregular and consisted largely of two years of day school under the Reverend T. Dale at Peckham as well as a few courses in literature at age seventeen at King's College, London. At that time he fell desperately in love with a Parisian beauty, Adèle Domencq, the daughter of his father's partner. After three years of slavish worship on his part and somewhat malignant neglect on hers, she married Baron Duquesne. Ruskin went to Oxford in 1837, but his career as a student was interrupted by two years of poor health, much of which he spent on the Continent. He did, however, succeed in winning the Newdigate Prize for a poem, "Salsette and Elephanta," which he recited at the Sheldonian Theatre in June 1839. By then he had abandoned his mother's plan to enroll him in the ministry.

Instead he embarked on a career as an historian and critic of art and architecture. Though the first volume of *Modern Painters* in May 1843 received little praise from either painters or critics, Ruskin's reputation increased with the appearance of volume two in 1846. By the time *The Seven Lamps of Architecture* appeared, the focus of his critical interest had shifted to architecture, and with the first volume of *The Stones of Venice* he was already established as one of the leading critics and architectural historians of his day. He was also the champion of artistic rebels—William Holman Hunt, Dante Gabriel Rossetti, John Everett Millais, and other members of the Pre-Raphaelite Brotherhood, who sought to recapture the spirit of painting before Raphael—against the prevailing ethos of utilitarianism. They began exhibiting their pictures in 1849 and shared with Ruskin a strong interest in both the Gothic Revival and the close imitation of nature in painting.

Ruskin quickly became regarded as something of a prophet and high moralist, for his central interests—in the relationships between the art and architecture, on one hand, and the religion, morality, and customs of people of different cultures, on the other—caught the mood of those not infected with the vapid optimism of the Great Exhibition in London in 1851. That year Ruskin met his great teacher

William Bell Scott, Ruskin, and Dante Gabriel Rossetti, 1863

in moral philosophy, Thomas Carlyle, whose waning reputation as a critic of industrialism and utilitarianism and as a prophet of philo-medievalist paternalism Ruskin largely inherited. In 1842 he had read Carlyle's *On Heroes, Hero Worship, and the Heroic in Poetry* (1841), and at that time Ruskin, following Carlyle in seeing sincerity as the mainspring of artistic energy, had begun to apply its principles to the defense of great art and its heroes.

The rest of Ruskin's life was largely devoted to developing his ideas on the relationship between social and industrial upheaval; on the necessity for upholding morality and religion against the spread of Benthamism, secularism, and unbelief; and on ways art might both restore an aesthetic component to production and induce an appreciation of higher values. His production until the early 1870s, consisting largely of lectures, articles, and pamphlet series, was enormous. Ruskin also began to put his ideas into practice, aiding Christian Socialists such as Frederick Denison Maurice and Thomas Hughes in the Working Men's College in 1854 and teaching art to working-class students.

Ruskin's reputation as a social theorist hinged on his first serious attack on the dogmas of classical political economy in *"Unto This Last,"* arguably the most influential work of British radical criticism of the second half of the nineteenth century. The principal works in which Ruskin subsequently developed its themes were *Sesame and Lilies: Two Lectures Delivered at Manchester in 1864* (1865), of which some forty-four thousand copies were sold by 1900; *The Crown of Wild Olive: Three Lectures on Work, Traffic, and War* (1866); and *Time and Tide, by Weare and Tyne: Twenty-Five Letters to a Working Man of Sunderland on the Laws of Work* (1867). In the early 1860s he spent much of his time assisting at a girls' school in Winnington; *The Ethics of the Dust: Ten Lectures to Little Housewives on the Elements of Crystallisation* (1866) was a series of children's stories that grew out of this experience.

In his later years Ruskin was also much concerned with giving his ideas practical form through the Guild of St. George, an organization begun in May 1871 with the aim of forming cooperative industrial and agricultural establishments along the lines of those suggested by Robert Owen and the Owenites from 1820 to 1850. These were to be funded by a lay guild that would donate a tenth of its income to the common good, buy land, resolve to build no railways or steam engines, and produce only beautiful articles. Ruskin began the guild with £7,000 of his own funds, but by the end of 1874 twenty-four other members had added only £370. 7s., and by 1875 they had donated only an acre of land with cottages. Ruskin planned to expand the estate, govern its cottagers benevolently, decide how best to spend rents, and regulate the inhabitants' clothing by sumptuary laws. An aristocracy of brains and talent was to run the estate, with laborers being permitted to rise within their own class but being devoted chiefly to intensive agricultural cultivation while preserving natural beauty and providing parks for harmless animals.

Though the guild failed to flourish, Ruskin societies were founded throughout Britain in the last decades of Ruskin's life, and these did much to disseminate his ideals and works. Elected Slade Professor of Art at the University of Oxford in 1869, he lectured there for ten years, attracting a new generation of disciples such as Arnold Toynbee and Oscar Wilde until disease of the brain forced him to resign in 1879. Having exhausted an inherited fortune estimated at some £200,000 and having become dependent on his literary income, Ruskin continued to write sporadically through the 1880s. His last decade was spent in retirement at the cottage he had acquired at Brantwood, Coniston, in 1871.

Ruskin's personal life was not particularly happy. On 10 April 1848, at the height of the great Chartist march on London, he married Euphemia Gray but was unable to consummate the marriage; he later claimed that his religious motives, hatred of children, desire to preserve his wife's beauty, and shock at seeing her nakedness contributed to this failure. In fact, he remained fixated on prepubescent girls throughout his life, particularly on Rose LaTouche, whom he met when she was the ten-year-old acquaintance of a friend and offered to marry in 1866 although she was almost thirty years younger than he. Ruskin's wife Euphemia had fallen in love with John Everett Millais, but she had refused to provide Ruskin with a divorce on the grounds of adultery. Their marriage finally was annulled in 1854, and when Rose LaTouche learned the truth about Ruskin's first marriage, she turned against him.

Despite suffering such personal dissatisfactions, Ruskin remained "the greatest social teacher of his age" to disciples such as J. A. Hobson. Ruskin's ideas are best understood as "socialist" if one accepts a sufficiently broad meaning of the term, for only through William Morris's adaptation of the aesthetic theories of *The Stones of Venice* is Ruskin wedded to the Marxian tradition. Ruskin's socialism entails his rejection of classical political economy and his support for a cooperative ideal in which a more equitable distribution of wealth might not only alleviate poverty but also improve the mental and spiritual lives of the majority. He was not, however, an egalitarian in the mold of Owen; Ruskin's socialism owes more to the hierarchical and traditionalist if nonetheless meritocratic paternalism of Carlyle. His proposals for a dual economy of public-sector manufacturing alongside private enterprise continue ideas similar to those mooted by the Owenite John Gray in particular (*The Social System,* 1831), and such ideas were continued most notably by Hobson.

Ruskin's ideas evolved from the idea, first elaborated in *Modern Painters,* that the perception of beauty was neither sensuous nor intellectual but essentially moral. Beauty was thus both an external quality in things that reflected divine attributes ("Typical Beauty") and "the appearance of felicitous fulfillment and right exertion of perfect life in man" ("Vital Beauty"). This pious aesthetic was threatened, however, by the overwhelming devotion of modern civilization to manufacturers and commerce and the denigration of any higher moral ideals. *The Seven Lamps of Architecture,* which is concerned with the "spirit" that brings about one's passionate appreciation of beauty, emphasizes that the aim of the beautiful is to enhance mankind's intellectual life, all activities being "noble" in proportion to how much they contribute to this end. Ruskin stresses that things of beauty should be built before those of utility—churches and beautiful houses before railways, for instance. He also emphasizes that workers should find employment that is not only healthy and well-paid but will, like stone carving, assist in cultivating "certain qualities of mind." Thus, architectural standards can be preserved by continuing to produce things by hand, while the individual artisan is mentally advanced by contributing to the productive process in a creative, imaginative fashion.

In *The Stones of Venice* Ruskin first outlined these concerns on a grand scale in his argument that Venetian Gothic architecture arose from "a state of pure national faith, and of domestic virtue." Vol-

Page from the manuscript for Fors Clavigera *(1871–1884), ninety-six "letters" from Ruskin to the workingmen of England (from W. G. Collingwood,* The Life and Work of John Ruskin, *1893)* ume two contains "The Nature of Gothic," the famous chapter often separately reprinted and containing Ruskin's most concise account of the wellbeing of workmen as an integral feature of the production of art. His plea that the "thoughtful" element in all laborers must be developed underlies the view that this could occur only by building in a Gothic style, which allows much irregularity, detail, and fancy. The existing division of labor in modern manufactures, the principle upon which Adam Smith and subsequent classical political economists had claimed that the progress of civilization depended, is thus for Ruskin wholly unsuited to human life because it degrades the individual workman. Instead the progress of creation must stress invention, originality, and creativity. Gothic workmen, Ruskin contends, had possessed a sense of savageness, a love of change and nature, a sense of the grotesque, and qualities such as obstinacy and generosity. English workmen, too, might possess "some powers for better things" that ought to be prized and honored "above the best and most perfect manual skill." Far from the workman being "only a machine . . . an animated tool," what was necessary "with all our labourers" was "to look for the thoughtful part of them, and get that out of them."

Industrial techniques of production, by contrast, had brought the "degradation of the operative into a machine" and had led "the mass of nations everywhere into a vain, incoherent, destructive struggling for a freedom of which they cannot explain the nature to themselves." Work had become no pleasure in itself, and the workman's hatred of the wealthy and the nobility stemmed from this fact. The influence of Carlyle is evident in Ruskin's assertion that "right freedom" meant that it was not slavery to labor for another or to yield reverence to him. This was, indeed, "often the best form of liberty,—liberty from care," not a servile but a noble reverence, "reasonable and loving," to a caring and worthy employer. To consider how best to expand the volume of production is thus to assign the wrong priority to material goods; the true question to consider is only "what kinds of labour are good for men, raising them, and making them happy; by a determined sacrifice of such convenience; or beauty, or cheapness as is to be got only by the degradation of the workman; and by equally determined demand for the products and results of healthy and ennobling labour."

This ennobling of the worker, Ruskin contends, can be accomplished by following some simple principles. First, never encourage the manufacture of any article that is not absolutely necessary and that requires no invention; for example, glass beads require no art to manufacture and are useless, while glass cups and vessels may require great invention. Second, never demand an exact finish for its own sake, but only for some practical or noble end, the rudeness of an article being better if no genius is available for finishing it. Thus, Ruskin wishes to blunt the division of labor between manual and mental as much as possible, so that

> it would be well if all of us were good handicraftsmen in some kind, and the dishonour of manual labour done away with altogether; so that though there should still be a trenchant distinction of race between nobles and commoners, there should not, among the latter, be a trenchant distinction of employment, as between idle and working men, or between men of liberal and illiberal professions. All professions should be liberal, and there should be less pride felt in peculiarity of employment, and more in excellence of achievement. And yet more, in each several profession, no master should be too proud to do its hardest work."

In practice, thus, a painter may grind his or her own colors while a master-manufacturer will be distinguished from his workmen "only in expertise and skill, and the authority and wealth which there must naturally and justly obtain." Imitation or copying should never be encouraged except to preserve the records of great works. Clearly the most important qualities in Gothic construction, from the viewpoint of the independence and creativity of the workman, were changefulness and variety. Where the worker is enslaved, buildings are strikingly similar in appearance; where even inferior workmen are given a degree of independence, "the perpetual variety of every feature of the building" becomes evident. Other qualities of the Gothic mind—such as naturalism, or the imitation of nature, and a sense of the grotesque—might well inform such innovations. But within established aesthetic parameters, Ruskin argues, workmen are to be free to impress upon their products the force of their own personalities.

The Stones of Venice did not provide a political context for reconstituting the relationship between the laborer and the product of labor. Like Carlyle, Ruskin had little faith in political reform or democracy. His ethos was imbued with a sense of noblesse oblige that required some elite class to implement. Ruskin's importance as a social theorist thus rests on his outlining the moral case for state interference in the age of Victorian laissez-faire rather than on his providing a sketch of the structures and mechanisms by which the state is to care for its less fortunate members.

Nonetheless, Ruskin outlined a program of sorts in a series of letters to the *Times* (London) written in March 1852 but not published because of objections by his Tory father. In these letters Ruskin advocated free trade, a graduated income tax, universal suffrage with variable voting power, and state education for all children—including, especially, vocational training as well as instruction in politics and religion. He argued in a Carlylean vein that "the first duty of a State is to see that every child born therein shall be well housed, clothed, fed and educated until it attains years of discretion. But in order to the effecting of this, the government must have authority over the people which we do not now so much as dream." Following this series of letters Ruskin's practical proposals frequently stress education, with the government being urged to provide trade schools for all unemployed workers and to attempt to give workers the best artistic and literary education possible.

If "The Nature of Gothic" provided a practical critique of the doctrine of the division of labor, Ruskin's most important mature social work, *"Unto This Last,"* was a full-scale assault on the central doctrines of political economy. Though Ruskin termed its points among "the best . . . the truest, rightest worded, and most servicable things I have ever written," the work was so unpopular when it first appeared as essays in *Cornhill Magazine* that the editor stopped publication of the series.

"Unto This Last" presents a set of practical proposals that incorporate four ideas: (1) the provision of government-run training schools for the young, to teach health, gentleness, and justice as well as particular callings; (2) the creation of government-run workshops and factories that would not compete with private enterprise (Ruskin did not explain how this would be avoided) but would produce well-made, unadulterated goods such as bread and ale; (3) the provision of education and training for all the unemployed except "shirkers," who were to be sent into the mines or other forms of strict labor; (4) the ensuring of a sufficient provision, possibly in the form of parish pensions, for old age.

The chief aim of the book was to give a "logical definition of wealth," thus wresting from political economy its central concept by arguing that the acquisition of wealth was "finally possible only under certain moral conditions of society," especially a belief in the attainability of honesty. Ruskin's note to the second edition indicated that the appeal of the work was primarily to the "Christian reader," and the reception of *"Unto This Last"* can be assessed in light of a tradition of radical Christian criticism of laissez-faire proponents who, earlier in the century, had included Samuel Taylor Coleridge, Robert

Self-portrait by Ruskin, circa 1870 (Education Trust, Bembridge)

Southey, Richard Oastler, Joseph Rayner Stephens, and the Christian Socialists.

Like such thinkers, Ruskin was deeply disturbed at the erosion of social ties among individual members of society. Political economy depended upon competition between individuals and assumed that avarice was a primary and constant motivation for most people. Ruskin contested this point in arguing that both master and man shared a common interest in performing good work at a just price, and justice and right relations between them thus depended on an affection between them that Ruskin thought should be the basis of a wider bond of social affection. Servants worked best in the family when such affection was evident. Factories were different from families, but even among factory workers the regulation of wages (so that demand for labor did not unduly affect wage rates) and a measure of employment security might, Ruskin argued, create a sense of common endeavor and mutual advantage that was largely lacking. Wages generally might be regulated by modeling factory labor on a professional ethos—with all labor being paid at a fixed rate and with bad laborers simply not being "chosen" to work and thus being forced to undergo further training. To maintain a fixed number of laborers in a given enterprise despite fluctuations in trade and demand presented different problems, but Ruskin insisted that an unselfish attitude in commerce would countenance an occasional loss and permit workers to remain at their post during industrial downturns. "Honour" would thus govern relations between employer and employed, with a reciprocal devotion to duty ensuring loyalty on both sides through good times and bad.

In "The Veins of Wealth," the second essay of *Unto This Last,* Ruskin argues that the existing motives for increasing both individual and national wealth are to increase inequality and to gain power over others. He contends that such inequality, however, is justified only if wealth is justly established and nobly used. The core question about the creation of wealth is thus one of abstract justice and entails considering the welfare of all, especially as seen in terms of manufacturing "Souls of a good quality" and producing a happy and healthy people. "Buying cheap and selling dear," the summum bonum of political economy, took no account of the type of society that the extension of such principles would produce. Like Owen, Coleridge, Carlyle, John Stuart Mill, Matthew Arnold, and many other liberal, socialist, and conservative critics, Ruskin is clearly concerned with the inferiority of "commercial character" to that which incorporates some higher moral ideals of human development and culture.

In the third essay, "Qui Judicatis Terram" (Ye Who Judge the Earth), he focused on the provision of wages, the basis of economic relationships. Building on an Owenite idea, and in particular on the justice of rewarding labor according to the time devoted to work rather than to what the market establishes as the wage rate, Ruskin stresses that Solomon's view of political economy emphasized honesty and justice in the acquisition of wealth and precluded taking advantage of the poor merely because they were poor. To pay a wage justly, Ruskin argues, is to offer an equivalent in time and labor for that which is offered; to give less labor in return is thus an underpayment. Justice consists solely in "absolute exchange." Though Ruskin acknowledges that calculating different levels of skill, for example, is difficult, he insists that good and bad work should be paid the same since all work has a worth that needs to be recognized. The just payment of wages in this fashion, he argues, will also diminish the power of wealth over individuals by enforcing a partial redistribution of it, and such wage payment will further assist in diminishing luxury and reducing the moral influence held by employers over their employees. Ruskin's model is essentially the military profession: the army and navy, he contends, are paid on socialist principles. What is required is not absolute social equality, which is impossible, but "government and co-operation . . . Soldiers of the Ploughshare as well as Soldiers of the Sword."

The fourth essay, "Ad Valorem" (Of Value), extends this argument by focusing on the question of how equivalents of labor can be exchanged justly. Taking as his target the orthodox Ricardian political economy of John Stuart Mill, Ruskin insists that while value depends on utility, an adequate account of utility in turn requires considering whether a thing can "avail towards life . . . with its whole strength." Possessing wealth does not entail having a large stock of useful things as Mill proposes, but instead means having things one can use. But use in turn depends on applying commodities to a correct end; wine, for example, is useful in small quantities and harmful in large. Usefulness thus depends on knowing correct uses, and "usefulness is value in the hands of the valiant"—or those, chiefly, who know how to use goods in the common interest. Wealth is thus "the possession of the valuable by the valiant," and it can be acquired only through a just science of exchange, or "catallactics," as Ruskin terms it, in which price is essentially embodied labor time.

The moral qualities in human relationships—which, political economists insisted, must be excluded from the first principles of economic theory if "scientific" criteria were to be met—were thus for Ruskin at the core of any humane account of economic relationships. Political economy had to assist in "developing manly character to deal with material wealth" while recognizing at the same time that material wealth tended to undermine this character. Production could accordingly be divided into two types, positive and negative, according to whether or not it tended to realize this end of producing "life." Prosperity did not entail production alone but encompassed the wise distribution and consumption of the produce of labor. Capital was capable of destroying life as well as supporting it, and its accumulation was not an end in itself but was something to be measured against what was "good for life." The final aim of political economy was thus to achieve a good method of consumption as well as a great quantity of consumption: to use everything as far as possible but also to use it nobly. The question for the nation was thus

> not how much labour it employs, but how much life it produces. For as consumption is the end and aim of production, so life is the end and aim of production. . . . THERE IS NO WEALTH BUT LIFE. . . . That country is the richest which nourishes the greatest number of noble and happy human beings; that man is richest who, having perfected the functions of his own life to the utmost, has also the widest helpful influence, both personal, and by means of his possessions, over the lives of others.

Ruskin defending the "Lady of the Lake District" against the incursion of the railroads, a cartoon published in the 5 February 1875 issue of Punch

The goal of political economy was no less than the creation of the greatest number of noble and happy human beings, but this was not to be achieved by expropriating landed wealth or the possessions of the rich. Ruskin denied that he was a socialist in the sense of being one who accepts some division of property; this he termed "the destruction of all hope, all industry, and all justice." Regulatory legislation might be required, but what was essential was an advancement by individual effort. For the rich this effort was focused not on greater wealth "but [on] simpler pleasures, not higher fortune, but deeper felicity." For the poor this individual effort was focused on justice, honesty, moral restraint, and the application of duty to employment relations. All classes needed to engage in moral restraint, to avoid wasteful production and consumption, and to reconstruct economic relations along human lines.

This demanded a social revolution, but one along lines that were more Christian than radically political, such as those of Chartist reformers. Ruskin's cooperative ideal, though not fleshed out with much practical detail, is the most important socialist contribution to late-Victorian social and economic theory, and his pleas for intervening in favor of the poor and for bringing about just labor relations profoundly influenced late-nineteenth-century social reformers. Though his contribution to the notion of the "alienation" of the worker from the product of labor in industrial society was enormous, Ruskin failed to prove that a large body of workmen could successfully escape the clutches of an ever-expanding system of mass production. From a Christian and humanist viewpoint he challenged with great force the intellectual predominance of laissez-faire theorists in Victorian Britain and the justifications of "getting wealth" and "buying cheap and selling dear." Through his opposition to a narrow division of labor Ruskin thus remains–with Owen, Morris, and Karl Marx–one of the greatest of Victorian anticapitalist prophets.

Letters:

Letters upon Subjects of General Interest to Various Correspondents (London, 1892);

Stray Letters from Professor Ruskin to a London Bibliophile, edited by Thomas J. Wise (London: Privately printed, 1892);

Letters Addressed to a College Friend during the Years 1840–1845 (New York: Macmillan / London: George Allen, 1894);

Letters to Ernest Chesneau (London, 1894);

Ruskin in 1882

Letters to the Clergy on the Lord's Prayer and the Church, edited by F. A. Malleson (London: George Allen, 1896);

Letters to M. G. & H. G. (Edinburgh: Ballantyne, Hanson, 1903; New York: Harper, 1903);

Letters of John Ruskin to Charles Eliot Norton, 2 volumes, edited by Charles Eliot Norton (Boston & New York: Houghton, Mifflin, 1904);

John Ruskin's Letters to William Ward (Boston: Marshall Jones, 1922);

John Ruskin's Letters to Francesca and Memoirs of the Alexanders, compiled by Lucia Gray Swett (Boston: Lothrop, Lee & Shepard, 1931);

Letters of John Ruskin to Bernard Quaritch, 1867–1888 (London: Quaritch, 1938);

The Gulf of Years: Letters from John Ruskin to Kathleen Olander (London: Allen & Unwin, 1953);

Ruskin's Letters from Venice, 1851–1852, edited by John Lewis Bradley (New Haven: Yale University Press, 1955);

The Letters of John Ruskin to Lord and Lady Mount-Temple, edited by John Lewis Bradley (Columbus: Ohio State University Press, 1964);

The Winnington Letters: John Ruskin's Correspondence with Margaret Alexis Bell and the Children at Winnington Hall, edited by Van Akin Burd (London: Allen & Unwin, 1969);

Ruskin in Italy: Letters to His Parents, 1845, edited by Harold I. Shapiro (Oxford: Clarendon Press, 1972);

Sublime & Instructive: Letters from John Ruskin to Louisa, Marchioness of Waterford, Anna Blunden and Ellen Heaton, edited by Virginia Surtees (London: Joseph, 1972);

The Ruskin Family Letters: The Correspondence of John James Ruskin, His Wife, and Their Son, John, 1801–1843, 2 volumes, edited by Burd (Ithaca, N.Y. & London: Cornell University Press, 1973);

John Ruskin and Alfred Hunt, edited by Robert Secor (Victoria, B.C.: University of Victoria Press, 1982);

The Correspondence of Thomas Carlyle and John Ruskin, edited by George Allan Cate (Stanford, Cal.: Stanford University Press, 1982);

My Dearest Dora: Letters to Dora Livesey, Her Family and Friends, 1860–1900 (Kendal, U.K.: Privately printed, 1984).

Bibliographies:

Thomas J. Wise and James P. Smart, *A Complete Bibliography of the Writings in Prose and Verse of John Ruskin, LL.D.,* 2 volumes (London: Privately printed, 1893);

Kirk H. Beetz, *John Ruskin: A Bibliography, 1900–1974* (Metuchen, N.J.: Scarecrow Press, 1976).

Biographies:

William Gershom Collingwood, *The Life of John Ruskin* (London: Methuen, 1900);

A. C. Benson, *Ruskin: A Study in Personality* (London: Smith, Elder, 1911; New York & London: Putnam, 1911);

Edward Tyas Cook, *The Life of John Ruskin* (2 volumes, London: Routledge & Kegan Paul, 1911; 1 volume, New York: Haskell House, 1968);

Derrick Leon, *Ruskin: The Great Victorian* (London: Routledge & Kegan Paul, 1949);

Peter Quennell, *John Ruskin: The Portrait of a Prophet* (London: Collins, 1949; New York: Viking, 1949);

Joan Evans, *John Ruskin* (New York: Oxford University Press, 1954);

John D. Rosenberg, *The Darkening Glass: A Portrait of Ruskin's Genius* (New York: Columbia University Press, 1961);

Patrick Conner, *Savage Ruskin* (Detroit: Wayne State University Press, 1979);

Joan Abse, *John Ruskin: The Passionate Moralist* (New York: Knopf, 1981);

John Dixon Hunt, *The Wider Sea: A Life of John Ruskin* (New York: Viking, 1982);

Tim Hilton, *John Ruskin: The Early Years* (New Haven: Yale University Press, 1985).

References:

Quentin Bell, *Ruskin* (Edinburgh: Oliver & Boyd, 1963);

William Gershom Collingwood, *The Life and Work of John Ruskin* (Boston & New York: Houghton, Mifflin, 1893);

Edward Tyas Cook, *Studies in Ruskin: Some Aspects of the Work and Teaching of John Ruskin* (Orpington, Kent & London: George Allen, 1891);

Frederic Harrison, *John Ruskin* (New York: Macmillan / London: Macmillan, 1902);

John Atkinson Hobson, *John Ruskin, Social Reformer* (Boston: Estes, 1898);

Benjamin Evans Lippincott, *Victorian Critics of Democracy: Carlyle, Ruskin, Arnold, Stephen, Maine, Lecky* (London: Milford, Oxford University Press / Minneapolis: University of Minnesota Press, 1938);

Marshall Mather, *John Ruskin: His Life and Teaching* (London & New York: Warne, 1898);

Edith Julia Morley, *John Ruskin and Social Ethics* (Westminster: Fabian Society, 1917?);

James Clark Sherburne, *John Ruskin; or, The Ambiguities of Abundance: A Study in Social and Economic Criticism* (Cambridge, Mass.: Harvard University Press, 1972);

John Howard Whitehouse, ed., *Ruskin the Prophet and Other Centenary Studies* (London: George Allen / New York: Dutton, 1920);

Whitehouse, *To the Memory of Ruskin* (Cambridge: Printed at the University Press for the Ruskin Society, 1934);

Reginald Howard Wilenski, *John Ruskin: An Introduction to the Further Study of His Life and Work* (London: Faber & Faber, 1933).

Papers:

Repositories of Ruskin's papers include the Pierpont Morgan Library, New York City; the Beinecke Library, Yale University; the Ruskin Gallery at Bembridge School, Isle of Wight; and the John Rylands Library, Manchester.

Olive Schreiner
(24 March 1855 - 11 December 1920)

Sylvia Vance
Oxford University

See also the Schreiner entries in *DLB 18: Victorian Novelists After 1885* and *DLB 156: British Short-Fiction Writers, 1880–1914: The Romantic Tradition.*

BOOKS: *The Story of an African Farm: A Novel,* as Ralph Iron (2 volumes, London: Chapman & Hall, 1883; Boston: Little, Brown, 1883);

Dreams (London: Unwin, 1891; Boston: Roberts, 1891);

Dream Life and Real Life: A Little African Story, as Ralph Iron (London: Unwin, 1893; Boston: Roberts, 1893);

The Political Situation, by Schreiner and Samuel Cron Cronwright-Schreiner (London: Unwin, 1896);

Trooper Peter Halket of Mashonaland (London: Unwin, 1897; Boston: Roberts, 1897);

An English South African's View of the Situation: Words in Season (London: Hodder & Stoughton, 1899);

Closer Union: A Letter on the South African Union and the Principles of Government (London: Fifield, 1909);

Woman and Labour (London: Unwin, 1911; New York: Stokes, 1911);

Stories, Dreams and Allegories (London: Unwin, 1923; New York: Stokes, 1923);

Thoughts on South Africa (London: Unwin, 1923; New York: Stokes, 1923);

From Man to Man; or, Perhaps Only . . . (London: Unwin, 1926; New York & London: Harper, 1927);

Undine (New York & London: Harper, 1928; London: Benn, 1929).

OTHER: "African Moonshine," as Ralph Iron, in *In a Good Cause: A Collection of Stories, Poems, and Illustrations,* edited by Margaret Susan Mitford Tyssen-Amherst (London: Gardner, Darton, 1885), pp. 85–99;

"Waste Land in Mashonaland," in *Big Game Shooting and Travel in South-East Africa,* by Frederick Roderick Noble Findlay (London: Unwin, 1903), pp. 261–268;

Olive Schreiner, 1879 (photograph by Emery Walker)

Veldsingers Verse: A Compilation of the Works of the Members of the Veldsingers' Club, foreword by Schreiner (London: Dent, 1910).

SELECTED PERIODICAL PUBLICATIONS–
UNCOLLECTED: "Stray Thoughts on South Africa," *Fortnightly Review,* new series 59 (1896): 510; new series 60 (1896): 225;

"The Policy in Favour of Protection," *Bibelot,* 17 (1911): 359–372;

"Lyndall," *Bibelot,* 20 (1914): 123–159.

Born at the Wittenbergen mission station near Basutoland in the Cape Colony of South Africa, Olive Schreiner was the ninth of twelve children of Gottlob and Rebecca Schreiner, a missionary couple. Gottlob had a simple Christianity but limited skills at converting, and after he was eventually let go as a missionary, he became an unsuccessful storekeeper. He was an unusually kind and sympathetic man, and his sympathy for black Africans influenced Schreiner and her siblings.

Schreiner's mother was noted for her quick wit and intelligence, and she fiercely defended British culture in the wilderness. When Schreiner used a Dutch word after her mother had forbidden the children to use it, the young girl received one of the two whippings of her life. She said that this experience convinced her of the horror of whipping anyone, especially the Bantu, and her broken friendship with Cecil Rhodes was exacerbated by his support of the Flogging Bill, which was introduced in the Cape Parliament in 1890 and 1891. Known as the Strop Bill, it defined the number of lashes that could be used on Africans for minor offences, which included disobeying an order or being absent from work.

Schreiner was outraged, and that bill embroiled her in South African politics, her profile having been heightened after the success of *The Story of an African Farm* (1883). The book, a challenge to Christianity, racism, and sexism, was written when she was a governess on the outback. Her desk was her bed, and her light was a small candle since her employers would not provide a big one. The novel was first sent to friends in England, who sent it on to a publisher in Scotland. It showed talent but required cutting and was sent back to her.

Schreiner left the Cape for England in 1881, not to pursue her writing career but to try to enter medical school. In her later years she said that all she had really wanted to do was to be a doctor. Realizing the financial impossibility of attending medical school, she registered in a nursing school in Edinburgh but stayed there only three days. She spent some time that summer studying for the entrance exams to medical school, but since her limited education made it unlikely that she could pass these exams, she did not take them and went instead to Women's Hospital in London. What she intended to do there is not clear as the hospital did not have a nursing school, but in any case she lasted there only five days. She left when she became seriously ill with a lung infection; however, during those five days she had been immersed in the lives of the poor, especially women, and she never forgot that experience.

Some writers have found Schreiner's asthma, lung inflammations and infections, and the effect her asthma had on her heart to be only psychosomatic while other writers have found both psychological and physical causes for these. Whatever the cause might have been, the onset of asthma in her teenage years affected her the rest of her life. The biography written by her husband, Samuel Cron Cronwright-Schreiner, is full of references to places, houses, and even rooms where Schreiner could not live because of wind or ventilation problems. She constantly moved, both in Africa and Europe, and the physical manifestations of asthma continued to strain her heart. Her asthma and her temperament filled her with wanderlust. Often she would settle into a house comfortably only to find within two weeks or two months that this room or location made her asthma particularly bad. Although her asthma often disabled her, at the same time she was known to walk the floor at all hours, and only the most tolerant of landladies and the most patient of friends were able to have her in their homes. Her condition made her incapable of meeting the physical demands that would have been placed on her as a member of the medical profession, as a doctor or as a nurse. She seems to have been fit only to be a writer.

She began taking the reworked manuscript of *The Story of an African Farm* to publishers in 1882, and it was published in two volumes in early 1883. The first two editions of it were published by Chapman and Hall under the pseudonym Ralph Iron, but the third edition (also published in 1883) was published under Schreiner's name. Virginia Woolf read it and was astounded. Nadine Gordimer, because of it, called Schreiner that "amazing woman." In Schreiner's time it was considered anti-Christian by some and a most religious book by others. Her narrative treated the Boers sympathetically when they were despised by most English. She took the issue of owning someone, whether a woman or a black, to a philosophical plane that had not been previously reached. In one character, Waldo, she presented the idea of an inner grace and beauty and articulated what that might mean to the inarticulate. The complexity of the issues that Schreiner addressed in her first book made her at the same time a villain and an international hero, and although she continued writing, she never again wrote anything as fine as this book.

Two of the many themes traced in *The Story of an African Farm* have made it a lasting text: the movement from a deep Christian belief to a loss of faith and the examination of the position of women in a patriarchal culture. At the time of its publication the

Schreiner and her husband, Samuel Cron Cronwright-Schreiner at The Homestead, their farm in Kimberley, South Africa, circa 1895–1898

narrative of lost Christian faith gained the most attention, and Schreiner was considered a heretic and anti-Christian. Her own loss of faith, an experience that the book recounts in a part that is almost purely autobiographical, had been heartbreaking to her and seemed particularly to betray her much-loved father's deep belief. The resultant examinations that Schreiner makes of other modes of religion seem somewhat tedious to a twentieth-century reader, but contemporary readers saw these alternatively as honest and revealing or as outrageous.

The reputation of the book would not have survived were it not for Schreiner's exploration of the position of women and her treatment of Lyndall, her major character. Sent from the farm to a boarding school, which Schreiner describes as using every negative practice of education to destroy a woman's soul, Lyndall subverts the intentions of the school and gains both the education she wants and an understanding of her position in her culture. As a result, when she becomes pregnant, she refuses to marry the father of her child. After the child has been born and has died, another man who loves her and dresses as a female nurse in order to remain anonymous devotedly cares for her, and in his willingness to adopt such a nurturing position Schreiner challenges sex-role definitions. This reduction of the plot to its bare, sentimental outlines unfairly diminishes Schreiner's accomplishment. Powerfully written, the novel examines issues in a provocative and convincing manner, and its descriptive passages defy repetition.

With her insight into the role of women and the position of the downtrodden, Schreiner became a political rather than simply an aesthetic writer. Both in England and the Cape she wrote frequently about and tirelessly campaigned against the Boer War and for suffrage. The war made her into a pacifist, and she wrote two particularly interesting antiwar works–*Trooper Peter Halket of Mashonaland* (1897), a novel, and "The Dawn of Civilization," a treatise which remained uncompleted at her death. Although *The Story of an African Farm* had been published first, in *Woman and Labour* (1911) Schreiner tried to develop themes of that novel in a more cognitive, systematic manner.

Woman and Labour is a collection of Schreiner's positions on "the woman question," on women and sex. She started collecting pieces for this book years before it was published, and she claimed that she had a hefty manuscript written by the time of the Boer War although Cronwright-Schreiner questions this. When war broke out, she was living in Johannesburg but was away from the city, and the imposition of martial law at that time kept her from returning there. After someone, perhaps British troops, broke into her home, the contents of her desk—including the manuscript, which contained the results of many years of her thinking on women—were burned. After the war she started rewriting the book.

Schreiner believed that throughout history women had been taken away from valued work and that without that work they were becoming "sex parasites." She was sympathetic to and almost worshiped the state of motherhood, but she felt that it did not and should not exclude women from other kinds of labor. Domestic labor, which she valued, was decreasing from the days when women took care of all the physical needs of the family, including tasks such as making clothes and candles. Schreiner saw that women's virtues and abilities were being neglected because women did not have work.

In her writing on the role of prostitutes in Victorian society Schreiner's construction of women as sex objects and her vision of women as needing to be sexually responsive and responsible were largely influenced by Havelock Ellis, whom she met in May 1884, after Ellis had read *The Story of an African Farm*. She and Ellis corresponded for three months before their meeting in London, and they remained friends until her death. His research on and examination of female sexuality powerfully influenced his times although that influence was somewhat obscured by revelations of his preference for curious sexual practices. In a time when the issues involving sex and women were neither discussed nor recognized, Ellis's greatest contribution was in recognizing that women had sexual natures. As a man of his time he was too highly influenced by Darwinism and notions that there was a simple biological basis for sexuality. There seemed to be little notion of women and men as equals. Through some years in which Schreiner and Ellis wrote to each other daily, they explored notions of women's sexuality that helped form the basis of *Woman and Labour*.

A combination of ideas about women's sexuality and women's labor grounds Schreiner's concerns in this collection. She also argues that by taking a part in governing, women can prevent war, for women are the makers of the men who die in wars. Although her exploration of women's sexuality was interesting in her time, her determination that women have a right to labor and govern continues to influence readers, particularly feminists. Vera Brittain and her entire generation of woman's rights activists were dramatically influenced by Schreiner and *Woman and Labour* as Brittain claimed that World War I made her a pacifist while *Woman and Labour* made her a feminist. Feminists before Brittain were also influenced by Schreiner: the suffragettes passed around compositions such as "Three Dreams in a Desert"—one of the pieces Schreiner had collected in her second book, *Dreams* (1891)—to convince women how necessary it was to continue the struggle.

Schreiner's concerns about the woman question were never far from the forefront. Although she often identified childhood experiences such as being whipped as rationales for her adult interests, she knew that women were treated as second-class citizens. She thought of being married as no more meaningful than obeying a general law about walking on sidewalks, but she also believed that marriage should be the result of deep passion. She portrayed Lyndall in *The Story of an African Farm* as someone quite heroic because she refused to marry without such passionate love. Schreiner's views were complicated and could be contradictory, but she had a vision of a truth and maintained a quest for it, as her interpolated story in *The Story of an African Farm* so poignantly demonstrates when Waldo dies without having found the truth for which he has been searching but knows that he has laid the steps for someone else to climb closer to it. This conception of truth, especially in South Africa, often placed Schreiner in conflict with those toward whom she was most sympathetic, as when she resigned from the Cape Women's Enfranchisement League in 1913—because they would not agree to support a concept of universal suffrage that included Africans.

Returning to South Africa in 1889, she left an England that treated her as a celebrity, but she wanted additional time to write. England also had provided an inhospitable climate for her asthma, and her physical condition had deteriorated. She had left *Dreams,* a book of allegories, with Ellis, who was to find a publisher for it. She hoped that this collection might make enough money to support her for some time in Africa while she recovered her health and dedicated herself to writing. Her first writings were political, and many of these articles—later collected in *Thoughts on South Africa* (1923)—took up what it meant to her to return to Africa and to support the Boers. Her articles on the Boers were not published in South Africa but in American and British journals, and she led a quiet life in a small town outside Cape Town for three years.

Schreiner's body being carried to its final resting place at the top of Buffel's Kop, 13 August 1921 (photograph by S.C.C.S.)

In 1890 she met Cecil Rhodes. Although the two were full of admiration for each other and continued meeting formally and informally, their political differences became increasingly apparent. Powerful and charismatic, Rhodes in 1890 became prime minister of the Cape. He controlled mining interests and was head of the Chartered Company, which could annex territory and even engage in war. Will Schreiner, one of Schreiner's brothers, was devoted to Rhodes and became his attorney general. Although she continued to admire Rhodes, it became apparent that their political differences would never be reconciled.

Samuel Cron Cronwright was a neighbor of old friends whom Schreiner was visiting in December 1892. After reading *The Story of an African Farm*, he had decided that if he ever met Lyndall he would marry her, and Cronwright insisted on meeting Schreiner. The two were immediately attracted to one another, and on 24 February 1894 they were married, with Cronwright adding her surname to his. They moved to his ostrich farm, but he soon had to sell his portion of the farm when her asthma became worse than it had been.

Shortly after settling in Kimberley, Schreiner became pregnant, and on 30 April 1895 her baby, a healthy girl, was born. Schreiner, who had a difficult period of labor, was given the night to sleep, and a nurse was to care for the baby. When Schreiner awoke the next morning, the baby was dead, after having lived only sixteen hours. Schreiner had at least four miscarriages during the next few years and felt a great yearning for a child, and the death of this first daughter haunted her. Following Schreiner's death, the baby's remains were eventually transported to Schreiner's burial place and interred with her.

Cronwright-Schreiner became involved in politics in Kimberley and in 1895 delivered a paper that was published in England as *The Political Situation* (1896), with him and Schreiner listed as coauthors. They became politically involved when Rhodes maneuvered the Jameson Raid, an attempt to annex the Transvaal Republic by claiming to put down a revolt within it. When Rhodes and his company and troops moved into Rhodesia, Schreiner wrote her powerful allegory, *Trooper Peter Halket of Mashonaland* (1897), in which Christ talks with an English soldier sent there to put down the Mashonaland rebellion. The book harshly portrays the unconcerned brutality of an imperial army, and Schreiner was directing its message toward British readers. She and her husband were in England when Rhodes's action occurred, and although it received wide coverage in the English press, she could not persuade people that his activities in South Africa were leading to war.

In 1898 Schreiner and her husband moved to Johannesburg, where Cronwright-Schreiner became articled to an attorney, and in 1899 Schreiner published *An English South African's View of the Situation,* another appeal to English readers to stop what Schreiner saw as an inevitable war. The work was sold out in days in England. The Boer War began in November of that year, and during the war years Schreiner and her husband lived under martial law in the small town of Hanover. Schreiner could not even go for a walk without getting permission to do so, but the war years became one of the few periods when her political writings and activities were compatible with her times. She supported the Boers and was considered their champion, but after the war ended in 1902 she recognized that the Africans were being left out in the reassignment of political power to the all-white settlers. Schreiner and her husband, who was elected as M.P. for Colesburg in 1902 and for Beaufort West in 1903, remained in Hanover for seven years, and there he also opened a business.

When they moved to De Aar in 1907, it was because of the success of Cronwright-Schreiner's business interests as he was valuer for the government land bank, secretary to the municipality, and deputy sheriff to the Supreme Court. Her brother Will had broken his allegiance with Rhodes, and Schreiner and her brother fought for what they saw as "native issues." The Zulu nation had been destroyed, and Will Schreiner was the defense lawyer in the trial of Dinusulu, a Zulu chief charged with murder, sedition, and other crimes following appropriation of Zulu lands by whites. Although acquitted of serious charges, he was found guilty of harboring rebels and was sentenced to a five-year term of imprisonment. It was a bitter defeat. At the same time Schreiner had been working with the Women's Enfranchisement League, from which she felt forced to resign because the organization was unwilling to support the enfranchisement of Africans.

By 1913 Schreiner's health was so precarious that she felt she must leave South Africa, and she sought treatment for her worsening heart condition in Italy, London, and Germany. She was in Germany when World War I broke out in August 1914, and after returning to London she had difficulty renting a room because of her German surname and felt isolated politically because of her pacifism and anti-imperialism. Being chronically ill, she did what she could for peace and for the women's movement, but her writing days were finished. Rousing herself only for meetings with old friends, she lived alone, ill and debilitated most of the time. Her husband arrived in London five years after she had returned there, and they spent a short time together before she returned to South Africa, the home that had formed her and whose landscape she loved, to die alone.

Following all her struggles in life, her death during the night of 10 to 11 December 1920 was a quiet one. She was found sitting up in bed, where she had been reading, with her glasses still on the end of her nose. She was buried in a large sarcophagus on Buffels Kop, the summit of Buffels Hoek, with her only daughter, a favorite dog, and, following the death of her husband years later, Cronwright-Schreiner.

Schreiner's life and art influenced generations of women. Despite her failings—for example, she never lost her paternalistic view of Africans—her work articulates the call of women for a full life, one dedicated, as hers was, to work and choice and challenge.

Letters:

The Letters of Olive Schreiner 1876-1920, edited by Samuel Cron Cronwright-Schreiner (London: Unwin, 1924; Boston: Little, Brown, 1924);

Olive Schreiner: Letters—Volume I, 1871-1899, edited by Richard Rive (Oxford: Oxford University Press, 1988);

"My Other Self": The Letters of Olive Schreiner and Havelock Ellis, 1894-1920, edited by Yaffa Claire Draznin (New York: Peter Lang, 1992).

Bibliographies:

Evelyn Verster, *Olive Emilie Albertina Schreiner, 1855-1920: Bibliography* (Cape Town: University of Cape Town, School of Librarianship, 1946);

Roslyn Davis, *Olive Schreiner (1920-1971)* (Johannesburg: University of Witwatersrand, Department of Bibliography, Librarianship and Typography, 1972);

Douglas Ridley Beeton, *Olive Schreiner: A Short Guide to Her Writings* (Cape Town: Timmons, 1974).

Biographies:

Samuel Cron Cronwright-Schreiner, *The Life of Olive Schreiner* (London: Unwin, 1924);

Vera Buchanan-Gould, *Not Without Honour: The Life and Writings of Olive Schreiner* (London: Hutchinson, 1948);

D. L. Hobman, *Olive Schreiner: Her Friends and Times* (London: Watts, 1955);

Johannes Meintjes, *Olive Schreiner: Portrait of a South African Woman* (Johannesburg: Keartland, 1965);

Ruth First and Ann Scott, *Olive Schreiner: A Biography* (London: Deutsch, 1980; New York: Schocken, 1980).

References:

Joyce Avrech Berkman, *The Healing Imagination of Olive Schreiner: Beyond South African Colonialism* (Amherst: University of Massachusetts Press, 1989);

Marion V. Friedmann, *Olive Schreiner: A Study in Latent Meanings* (Johannesburg: Witwatersrand University Press, 1954);

Lyndall Gregg, *Memories of Olive Schreiner* (London: Chambers, 1957);

Michael Harmel, *Olive Schreiner 1855–1955* (Cape Town: Real Printing & Publishing, 1955);

Gerald Monsman, *Olive Schreiner's Fiction: Landscape and Power* (New Jersey: Rutgers University Press, 1991).

Papers:

Most of Schreiner's papers are at the Department of Manuscripts, South African Library, Cape Town. The Olive Schreiner–Havelock Ellis correspondence is in the Harry Ransom Humanities Research Center at the University of Texas, Austin.

Bernard Shaw
(26 July 1856 – 2 November 1950)

Sos Eltis
Oxford University

See also the Shaw entries in *DLB 10: Modern British Dramatists, 1900–1945,* and *DLB 57: Victorian Prose Writers After 1867.*

BOOKS: *A Manifesto,* Fabian Tracts 2 (London: Standring, 1884);

Cashel Byron's Profession (London: Modern Press, 1886; unauthorized edition, New York: Munro, 1886; revised edition, London: Scott, 1889); revised again, including *The Admirable Bashville* (London: Richards, 1901; Chicago: Stone, 1901);

An Unsocial Socialist (London: Sonnenschein, Lowrey, 1887; unauthorized edition, New York: Brentano's, 1900; authorized edition, New York: Brentano's, 1908);

The Legal Eight Hours Question: A Public Debate between Mr. Geo. Bernard Shaw and Mr. G. W. Foote at the Hall of Science, London, Jan. 14 & 15, 1891 (London: Forder, 1891);

The Quintessence of Ibsenism (London: Scott, 1891; unauthorized edition, Boston: Tucker, 1891; revised and enlarged edition, London: Constable, 1913; New York: Brentano's, 1913);

Widowers' Houses (London: Henry, 1893);

Plays: Pleasant and Unpleasant, 2 volumes (London: Richards, 1898; Chicago: Stone, 1898);

The Perfect Wagnerite: A Commentary on the Ring of the Niblungs (London: Richards, 1898; Chicago & New York: Stone, 1899; revised edition, London: Richards, 1902; New York: Brentano's, 1909);

Love among the Artists (unauthorized edition, Chicago: Stone, 1900; authorized, revised edition, London: Constable, 1914);

Three Plays for Puritans: The Devil's Disciple, Caesar and Cleopatra, & Captain Brassbound's Conversion (London: Richards, 1901; Chicago & New York: Stone, 1901);

Man and Superman: A Comedy and a Philosophy (Westminster: Constable, 1903; New York: Brentano's, 1904);

Bernard Shaw, 1891 (photograph by Elliott & Fry, London)

The Common Sense of Municipal Trading (Westminster: Constable, 1904; New York: John Lane, 1911);

Fabianism and the Fiscal Question: An Alternative Policy (London: Fabian Society, 1904);

The Irrational Knot (New York: Brentano's, 1905; London: Constable, 1905);

Dramatic Opinions and Essays, 2 volumes (unauthorized edition, New York: Brentano's, 1906; authorized, 1907; London: Constable, 1907);

Wie er ihren Mann belog: Eine Warnung für Theaterbesucher, translation by Siegfried Trebitsch of *How He Lied to Her Husband* (Berlin: Fischer, 1906);

John Bull's Other Island and Major Barbara, also includes *How He Lied to Her Husband* (New York: Brentano's, 1907; London: Constable, 1907);

The Sanity of Art: An Exposure of the Current Nonsense about Artists Being Degenerate (London: New Age Press, 1908; New York: Tucker, 1908);

Der Arzt am Scheideweg: Komödie in fünf Akten, translation by Trebitsch of *The Doctor's Dilemma* (Berlin: Fischer, 1908);

Press Cuttings (London: Constable, 1909; New York: Brentano's, 1913);

Kleine Dramen, translation by Trebitsch of *How He Lied to Her Husband, The Shewing-Up of Blanco Posnet,* and *Press Cuttings* (Berlin: Fischer, 1910);

Die Ehe: Eine Diskussion, translation by Trebitsch of *Getting Married* (Berlin: Fischer, 1910);

The Doctor's Dilemma, Getting Married, and The Shewing-Up of Blanco Posnet (London: Constable, 1911; New York: Brentano's, 1911);

Mesallianz, translation by Trebitsch of *Misalliance* (Berlin: Fischer, 1911);

Fanny's erstes Stück: Komödie in drei Akten, einem Vorspiel und einem Nachspiel, translation by Trebitsch of *Fanny's First Play* (Berlin: Fischer, 1911);

Pygmalion: Komödie in fünf Akten, translation by Trebitsch of *Pygmalion* (Berlin: Fischer, 1913);

Androklus und der Löwe: Ein Märchenspiel in drei Akten, translation by Trebitsch of *Androcles and the Lion* (Berlin: Fischer, 1913);

Misalliance, The Dark Lady of Sonnets, and Fanny's First Play, with a Treatise on Parents and Children (London: Constable, 1914; New York: Brentano's, 1914);

Common Sense about the War (London: Statesman, 1914);

Androcles and the Lion, Overruled, Pygmalion (New York: Brentano's, 1916; London: Constable, 1916);

How to Settle the Irish Question (Dublin: Talbot Press / London: Constable, 1917);

Peace Conference Hints (London: Constable, 1919);

Heartbreak House, Great Catherine, and Playlets of the War (New York: Brentano's, 1919; London: Constable, 1919);

Die Geliebte Shakespeares und andere Essays: Erstes bis drittes Tausend, translations by Trebitsch (Zurich: Rascher, 1919);

Back to Methuselah: A Metabiological Pentateuch (New York: Brentano's, 1921; London: Constable, 1921);

Saint Joan (London: Constable, 1924; New York: Brentano's, 1924);

Table-Talk of G. B. S.: Conversations on Things in General between George Bernard Shaw and His Biographer, by Shaw (uncredited) and Archibald Henderson (New York & London: Harper, 1925; revised edition, London: Chapman & Hall, 1925);

Translations and Tomfooleries (London: Constable, 1926; New York: Brentano's, 1926);

The Socialism of Shaw, edited by James Fuchs (unauthorized edition, New York: Vanguard Press, 1926);

The Intelligent Woman's Guide to Socialism and Capitalism (London: Constable / New York: Brentano's, 1928); enlarged and republished as *The Intelligent Woman's Guide to Socialism, Capitalism, Sovietism and Fascism,* 2 volumes (London: Penguin, 1937);

Der Kaiser von America: Eine politische Komödie in drei Akten, translation by Trebitsch of *The Apple Cart: A Political Extravaganza* (Berlin: Fischer, 1929);

Bernard Shaw & Karl Marx: A Symposium, 1884–1889 (unauthorized edition, New York: Random House, 1930);

Immaturity (London: Constable, 1930);

Saint Joan and The Apple Cart (London: Constable, 1930);

What I Really Wrote about the War (London: Constable, 1930; first American trade edition, New York: Brentano's, 1932);

Our Theatres in the Nineties (London: Constable, 1931; New York: Wise, 1931);

Music in London, 1890–1894 (London: Constable, 1931; New York: Wise, 1931);

Short Stories, Scraps and Shavings (London: Constable, 1932; first trade edition, London: Constable, 1934; New York: Dodd, Mead, 1934);

Zu Wahr um schön zu sein: Komödie in drei Akten, translation by Trebitsch of *Too True to Be Good* (Berlin: Fischer, 1932);

The Adventures of the Black Girl in Her Search for God (London: Constable, 1932; New York: Dodd, Mead, 1933);

Ländliche Werbung: Komödie in drei Zwiegesprächen, translation by Trebitsch of *Village Wooing* (Berlin: Fischer, 1933);

Too True to Be Good, Village Wooing & On the Rocks: Three Plays (London: Constable, 1934; New York: Dodd, Mead, 1934);

Die Sechs von Calais: Eine mittelalterliche Kriegsgeschichte in einem Akt, translation by Trebitsch of *The Six of Calais* (Berlin: Fischer, 1934);

Die Insel der Überraschungen: Ein Spiel in zwei Akten und einem Prolog, translation by Trebitsch of *The Simpleton of the Unexpected Isles* (Berlin: Fischer, 1935);

Die Millionärin: Eine turbulente Komödie in vier Akten, translation by Trebitsch of *The Millionaress* (Berlin: Fischer, 1935);

The Simpleton, The Six, and The Millionairess (London: Constable, 1936); republished as *The Simpleton of the Unexpected Isles, The Six of Calais & The Millionairess* (New York: Dodd, Mead, 1936);

London Music in 1888–89 As Heard by Corno di Bassetto (Later Known as Bernard Shaw), with Some Further Autobiographical Particulars (London: Constable, 1937; New York: Dodd, Mead, 1937);

Geneva: A Fancied Page of History in Three Acts (London: Constable, 1939; enlarged, 1940);

Shaw Gives Himself Away: An Autobiographical Miscellany (Newtown, Montgomeryshire: Gregynog Press, 1939);

In Good King Charles's Golden Days (London: Constable, 1939);

Everybody's Political What's What? (London: Constable, 1944; New York: Dodd, Mead, 1944);

Major Barbara: A Screen Version (New York: Penguin, 1946; Harmondsworth: Penguin, 1946);

Geneva, Cymbeline Refinished, & Good King Charles (London: Constable, 1947; New York: Dodd, Mead, 1947);

Zu viel Geld: Eine unmanierliche Komödie in vier Akten, translation by Trebitsch of *Buoyant Billions* (Zurich: Artemis, 1948);

Shaw on Vivisection, compiled and edited by G. H. Bowker for the National Antivivisection Society (London: Allen & Unwin, 1949);

Sixteen Self Sketches (London: Constable, 1949; New York: Dodd, Mead, 1949);

Buoyant Billions: A Comedy of No Manners in Prose (London: Constable, 1950);

Buoyant Billions, Farfetched Fables, & Shakes versus Shav (London: Constable, 1951; New York: Dodd, Mead, 1951);

My Dear Dorothea: A Practical System of Moral Education for Females, Embodied in a Letter to a Young Person of That Sex, edited by Stephen Winsten (London: Phoenix House, 1956; New York: Vanguard, 1957);

An Unfinished Novel, edited by Stanley Weintraub (London: Constable / New York: Dodd, Mead, 1958);

Shaw on Theatre, edited by E. J. West (New York: Hill & Wang, 1958; London: MacGibbon & Kee, 1960);

How to Become a Musical Critic, edited by Dan H. Laurence (London: Hart-Davis, 1960; New York: Hill & Wang, 1961);

Shaw on Shakespeare, edited by Edwin Wilson (New York: Dutton, 1961; London: Cassell, 1962);

Platform and Pulpit, edited by Laurence (New York: Hill & Wang, 1961; London: Hart-Davis, 1962);

The Matter with Ireland, edited by Laurence and David H. Greene (New York: Hill & Wang, 1962; London: Hart-Davis, 1962);

The Religious Speeches of Bernard Shaw, edited by Warren Sylvester Smith (University Park: Pennsylvania State University Press, 1963);

George Bernard Shaw on Language, edited by Abraham Tauber (New York: Philosophical Library, 1963; London: Owen, 1965);

The Rationalization of Russia, edited by Harry M. Geduld (Bloomington: Indiana University Press, 1964);

Shaw on Religion, edited by Smith (London: Constable, 1967; New York: Dodd, Mead, 1967);

Saint Joan: A Screenplay, edited by Bernard F. Dukore (Seattle & London: University of Washington Press, 1968);

Shaw–"The Chucker-Out": A Biographical Exposition and Critique, compiled by Allan Chappelow (London: Allen & Unwin, 1969);

Shaw: An Autobiography, 1856–1898, compiled and edited by Weintraub (New York: Weybright & Talley, 1969; London, Sydney & Toronto: Reinhardt, 1970);

Shaw: An Autobiography, 1898–1950. The Playwright Years, compiled and edited by Weintraub (New York: Weybright & Talley, 1970; London, Sydney & Toronto: Reinhardt, 1970);

Passion Play: A Dramatic Fragment, 1878, edited by Jerald E. Bringle (Iowa City: University of Iowa at the Windhover Press, 1971);

The Road to Equality: Ten Unpublished Lectures and Essays, 1884–1918, edited by Louis Crompton and Hilayne Cavanaugh (Boston: Beacon Press, 1971);

Bernard Shaw's Nondramatic Literary Criticism, edited by Weintraub (Lincoln: University of Nebraska Press, 1972);

Practical Politics: Twentieth-Century Views on Politics and Economics, edited by Lloyd J. Hubenka (Lincoln & London: University of Nebraska Press, 1976);

Flyleaves, edited by Laurence and Daniel J. Leary (Austin, Tex.: W. Thomas Taylor, 1977);

Shaw and Ibsen: Bernard Shaw's The Quintessence of Ibsenism and Related Writings, edited by J. L. Wisenthal (Toronto, Buffalo & London: University of Toronto Press, 1979);

The Collected Screenplays of Bernard Shaw, edited by Dukore (London: Prior, 1980; Athens: University of Georgia Press, 1980);

Early Texts: Play Manuscripts in Facsimile, 12 volumes, edited by Laurence and others (New York: Garland, 1981);

Shaw's Music, 3 volumes, edited by Laurence (London: Reinhardt/Bodley Head, 1981; New York: Dodd, Mead, 1981);

Shaw on Dickens, edited by Laurence and Martin Quinn (New York: Ungar, 1985);

Bernard Shaw: The Diaries 1885-1897, 2 volumes, edited by Weintraub (University Park & London: Pennsylvania State University Press, 1986);

Bernard Shaw on Photography: Essays and Photographs, edited by Bill Jay and Margaret Moore (Wellingborough: Equation, 1989; Salt Lake City: P. Smith Books, 1989).

Collections: *The Works of Bernard Shaw: Collected Edition,* volumes 1-30 (London: Constable, 1930-1932); republished as the *Ayot St. Lawrence Edition of the Collected Works of Bernard Shaw* (New York: Wise, 1930-1932); volumes 31-33 (London: Constable, 1934-1938); enlarged and republished as *The Works of Bernard Shaw: Standard Edition,* 37 volumes (London: Constable, 1931-1951);

The Bodley Head Bernard Shaw: Collected Plays with Their Prefaces, 7 volumes (London, Sydney & Toronto: Reinhardt/Bodley Head, 1970-1974); republished as *Collected Plays with Their Prefaces* (New York: Dodd, Mead, 1975).

OTHER: "The Basis of Socialism: Economic" and "The Transition to Social Democracy," in *Fabian Essays in Socialism,* edited, with an introduction, by Shaw (London: Fabian Society, 1889); unauthorized edition, edited by H. G. Wilshire (New York: Humboldt, 1891)»

Fabianism and the Empire: A Manifesto by the Fabian Society, drafted and edited by Shaw (London: Richards, 1900).

Bernard Shaw was one of the most important, and certainly the most prolific, reform writers of the twentieth century. In provocative, trenchant, and humorous style he tried to formulate a constructive alternative to the sham ideals of the Victorian age. His ideal vision was of a classless society based on equality of income and opportunity regardless of sex, creed, race, or birth, and he attempted to combine this vision with a realistic assessment of the facts of social and political life.

George Bernard Shaw was born on 26 July 1856 in Upper Synge Street, Dublin, the third child and only son of George Carr and Lucinda Elizabeth Gurly Shaw. His father was an unsuccessful grain merchant whose addiction to alcohol was the inspiration behind Shaw's lifelong teetotalism. His mother, a ladylike, highly educated young woman from the Protestant gentry, compensated for her disappointment in her husband by concentrating her attentions on her singing teacher and music master, George John Vandaleur Lee. Shaw received little maternal affection but a considerable love of music from her.

Shaw attended a succession of schools until at the age of fifteen he started work as a rent collector for a Dublin land agent; he kept the job for five years, and his dislike of it was later channeled into his first play, *Widowers' Houses* (1893). Shaw's mother and two sisters followed Lee to London in 1873, where the younger sister died. Three years later, just short of his twentieth birthday, Shaw completed the family desertion and left his father in Dublin, joining his mother and remaining sister in London. For the next ten years Shaw scraped a living with his writing, first ghostwriting articles for Lee as music critic for *The Hornet,* then writing book reviews, drama reviews, and music and art criticism for various magazines. At the same time Shaw tried to establish himself as a novelist, but his first four attempts—*Immaturity* (written in 1879 but not published until 1930), *The Irrational Knot* (written in 1880), *Love among the Artists* (written in 1881), and *Cashel Byron's Profession* (written in 1882)—were all initially rejected by a succession of publishers. In a 1946 preface added to the manuscript of his fifth novel Shaw explained this early lack of success by his unconventional choice of subject matter:

> A clerk for a hero (my first) was not a recommendation but at least he accepted the world as it was and wore a white linen collar in its social eddies. I was perhaps to be encouraged. But my second, a working electrical engineer crashing through the castes and mastering them: that was distasteful and incorrect. I was going wrong. Then a British Beethoven, careless of his clothes, ungovernable, incomprehensible, poor, living in mean lodgings at an unfashionable address: this was absurd. The next, a prize-fighter, wooing and marrying a priggishly refined lady of property, made a bit of romance, without a dying child in it but with a fight or two. But a Socialist! A Red, an enemy of civilization, a universal thief, atheist, adulterer, anarchist, and apostle of the Satan he disbelieved in!! And presented as a rich young gentleman, eccentric but not socially unpresentable. Too bad.

The political content of the fifth novel Shaw mentions, *An Unsocial Socialist* (1887), may have discounted it in the eyes of commercial publishers, but the subject gained Shaw a select readership for its se-

Cover designs for the first British edition (left, by Walter Crane) and first American edition of a volume edited by Shaw

rialization in 1884 in Annie Besant's new socialist magazine, *To-Day*.

Shaw's interest in socialism, which was to become the driving force behind his work, dated from his attending a lecture on land nationalization by the American reformer Henry George on 5 September 1882. George impressed upon Shaw the importance of the economic basis of society, a conviction that was further reinforced by Shaw's reading of Karl Marx's *Das Kapital* (1867) in French translation in 1883, a book which he was later to refer to as "a revelation" that provided him with "a purpose and a mission in life." In 1884 he joined the Fabian Society, whose policy was one of socialist permeation by a process of rational argument and persuasion founded on research, to convince the leaders of all political parties to accept the need for basic reform and a new structure for society and the economy. Shaw went on to write many tracts for the society, including his first contribution, *A Manifesto*, in 1884. A year later Shaw was elected to the executive committee of the society, and in 1889 he edited *Fabian Essays in Socialism*, also contributing a long introduction and two additional essays on the economic basis of, and the transition to, socialism.

On 18 July 1890, as part of a series of lectures on socialism in literature, Shaw gave a talk on Henrik Ibsen, which was expanded and published the following year as *The Quintessence of Ibsenism*. Shaw greeted Ibsen as the apostle of individualism, welcoming his plays as a much-needed change from the conventional well-made plays of the contemporary English stage. Ibsen, he argued, had transformed the drama, bringing social problems and moral issues to the fore instead of sensational incidents and sentimental resolutions. Describing the drama he himself wished to write as much as the plays Ibsen had written, Shaw declared that the question was no longer whether the hero would triumph over the villain onstage but a more subtle moral dilemma as to which was the hero and which was the villain. In the theater Shaw found a medium through which to present his criticism of the hypocrisies, inequalities, and injustices of late-Victorian capitalism, stripping off false ideals to reveal the social realities beneath.

Shaw's first three plays, as he described them

in a 10 June 1896 letter to R. Golding Bright, "were what people call realistic. They were dramatic pictures of middle-class society from the point of view of a Socialist who regards the basis of that society as thoroughly rotten economically and morally.... All three plays were criticisms of a special phase, the capitalist phase, of modern social organization, and their purpose was to make people thoroughly uncomfortable whilst entertaining them artistically."

The first of these plays, *Widowers' Houses,* completed in 1892, reveals the horrendous conditions of slum housing while demonstrating how the landlord class depends for its wealth on the ruthless exploitation of the poor. Shaw's young hero is horrified to discover that his fiancée's wealth derives from slum rents and indignantly refuses to accept any of this tainted money as part of her dowry. His prospective father-in-law thereupon reveals that the young man's income, derived from interest on his unearned capital, is made for him by men exactly like himself, forced to squeeze the poor harder in order to pay the interest the rich investors demand. The young man then promptly abandons his ideals and marries his fiancée, resigning himself to living comfortably on their tainted wealth. Shaw thus sought not only to highlight the ills of the slum system but also to implicate the audience themselves. The villains of his play are not the landlord or the rent collector but capitalist society as a whole; the audiences are as much the villains as the characters they survey. Shaw also fulfilled his ambition of leaving the audience uncomfortable by failing to offer any satisfactory ending to his play. A happy solution to *Widowers' Houses,* he implies, cannot be encompassed onstage, for it would involve a reform of the entire Victorian economic system.

Shaw's next play, *The Philanderer,* written in 1893, is a critical examination of the relation between the sexes, upholding Shaw's belief that there is no essential difference between the way men and women think and feel, only unequal social pressures and artificial social structures. In his third play, *Mrs Warren's Profession,* also completed in 1893, he extends his critique of capitalist society, condemning its failure to offer women a reasonable living wage for decent work. Mrs. Warren's profession is revealed to be prostitution, but Shaw reverses theatrical conventions; his fallen heroine does not apologize for her business but indignantly justifies herself, laying the blame on society at large. Given the degrading and dangerous conditions of factory work, she asserts, prostitution was the only work available that allowed her to preserve the self-respect which more "respectable" labor denied. Shaw once again pointed the finger at his audience: prostitution was not a matter of female vice or virtue but of social economics.

All three of these plays were refused a license for the public stage and were confined to private theater-club performances. Shaw sought to address a larger audience by publishing the plays together as the "unpleasant" works in *Plays: Pleasant and Unpleasant* in 1898, complete with long authorial prefaces and extended stage directions (a format he preserved in all his published plays). In the preface to *Mrs Warren's Profession* Shaw attacks the system of theatrical censorship that he believed worked to exclude serious thought from the stage while sanctioning licentiousness, sensationalism, and sentimentality. Plays such as Arthur Wing Pinero's *The Second Mrs Tanqueray* (produced in 1893) and Alexandre Dumas *fils' La Dame aux Camélias* (first published as a novel in 1848) which, he argued, offer a romanticized and falsely idealized picture of prostitution, had received licenses while his own more realistic and starkly unpalatable version of the facts was kept from the public. Shaw was energetic in his demand for reform of the theatrical licensing system, amassing a huge body of evidence to present to the 1909 Parliamentary Select Committee Enquiry into stage censorship. In the same year his play *The Shewing-Up of Blanco Posnet* was refused a license, a difficulty which Shaw overcame by securing its performance at the Abbey Theatre in Dublin, in spite of English disapproval. In his 1911 preface to the play Shaw explains his lifelong battle with the censor:

> I regard much current morality as to economic and sexual relations as disastrously wrong; and I regard certain doctrines of the Christian religion as understood in England today with abhorrence. I write plays with the deliberate object of converting the nation to my opinion in these matters.... If I were prevented from producing immoral and heretical plays, I should cease to write for the theatre, and propagate my views from the platform and through books.

After facing the failure of his outspoken "unpleasant" plays to reach the public stage, Shaw recognized the necessity of compromising his dramatic method and combining more entertainment with his educational intentions. *Arms and the Man* (produced in 1894) is "An Anti-Romantic Comedy" in which Shaw attacks the romantic myths of warfare, simultaneously emphasizing the barbarity and the ridiculousness of war. The play was his first commercial success, but it remained a failure in Shaw's eyes, for though audiences were delighted with his jokes, they missed his serious intent. This was to remain an enduring problem for Shaw as a reform writer. His argumentative technique, a mixture of paradox,

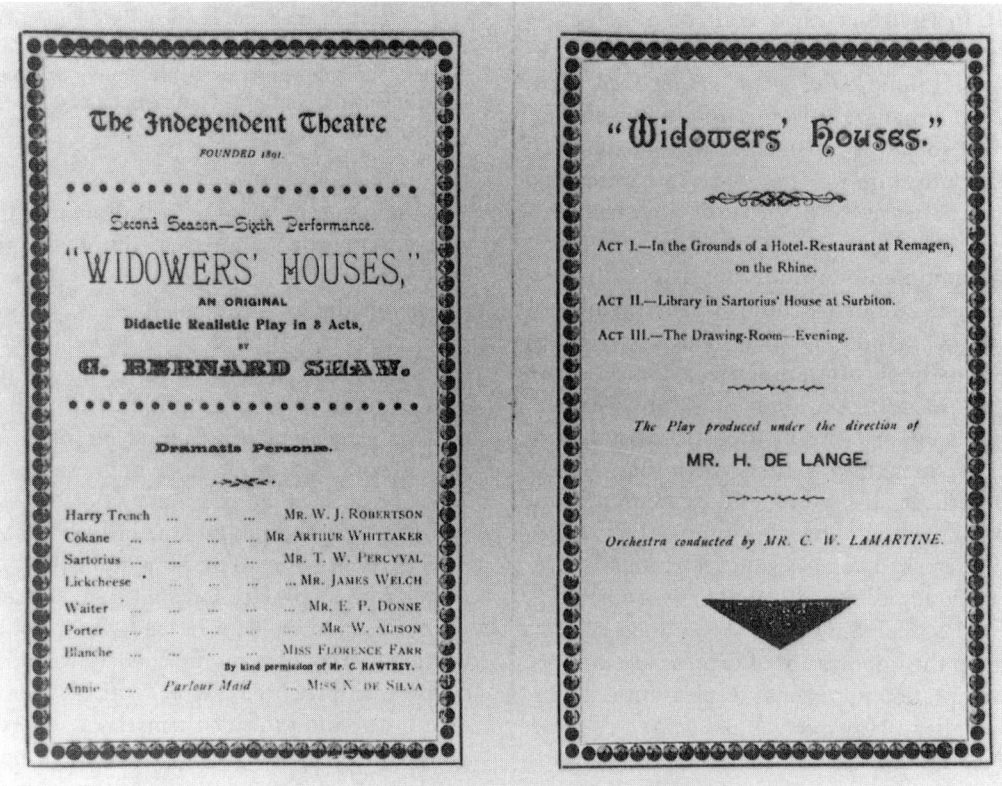

Program for a production of Shaw's first play

humor, exaggeration, and forthright common sense, secured the attention of the public but also enabled them to dismiss what they found uncomfortable as simply the product of Shavian extravagance. As he comments with wry humor in his preface to the standard edition of *The Intelligent Woman's Guide to Socialism and Capitalism:*

> When the spirit drives me to tell the truth, and the flesh reminds me of the police and of the fate of those who have yielded to that temptation in the past, I screw my courage up by reflecting on the extreme improbability of anybody seeing anything in my treatise but a paradoxical joke.

Arms and the Man was published in the "pleasant" volume of *Plays: Pleasant and Unpleasant,* together with three other plays: *Candida,* a domestic drama in which a wife does not leave her husband for her lover because, unconventionally, the husband is the pampered, childlike doll in need of her protection; *The Man of Destiny,* a comic battle of wits between a Strange Lady and Napoleon Bonaparte; and *You Never Can Tell,* Shaw's version of a popular West End farce, complete with seaside resort and comic waiter but also with a strong injection of Shavian realism that renders the farcical situation as tragic as it is comic. With the success of these plays Shaw resigned his post as drama critic of the *Saturday Review* and married Charlotte Payne-Townshend, a fellow socialist, described by Beatrice Webb as "sympathetic and genuinely anxious to increase the world's enjoyment and diminish the world's pain." The marriage was happy, long-lasting, and celibate.

Shaw's nonliterary activities for reform included aiding Sidney Webb to establish the London School of Economics in 1894. Three years later he was elected vestryman of a ward of Saint Pancras, campaigning vigorously on sanitation, public health, and living conditions for the poor. He was reelected in 1900, but in 1904 he stood unsuccessfully as a Progressive candidate for the London County Council in South Saint Pancras and retired from local government.

From this point onward the stage became Shaw's main forum for debating social and political issues. His dramatic technique successfully combined elements of theatrical entertainment with discussion of serious subjects. For example, in *Captain Brassbound's Conversion* (written in 1899 and performed in 1900) brigands, pirates, and sheikhs provide the backdrop to Shaw's examination of British imperialism. In 1900 Shaw had drafted and edited a new manifesto declaring the Fabian Society's position on imperial policy, *Fabianism and the Empire,* in which he argued that the existence of the British empire was a fact socialists must acknowledge and that the important question was how best to administer it. He was fiercely critical of patriotic jingoism and imperial hypocrisy that attempted to present commercial expansion and exploitation as missionary zeal and the defense of freedom. In his theatrical heroine, Lady Cicely Wayneflete, Shaw presented the superior power of common sense, sympathy, humanitarian consideration, morality, and simple good manners against the brutal and brutalizing methods of the male imperialists, with their rifles, pistols, vengeful legal system, and dependence on physical force, which Shaw denounced in an 8 August 1899 letter to actress Ellen Terry as "mere cowardice masquerading as 'resolute government.'"

During the 1890s Shaw's emphasis in his reform writing was on the importance of facing facts and resisting the temptation to disguise unpleasant realities with false idealism. However, *Man and Superman: A Comedy and a Philosophy* (1903), written between 1901 and 1902, marks a change in Shaw's thought as it presents the necessity of progressing beyond realism in the pursuit of human and social improvement. In the third act of the play, a dream sequence set in hell, Don Juan enters into a long philosophical discussion with the Devil over the future of humankind. Shaw, according to his custom, reverses the expectations of the audience: hell is the home of idealism, a place where there are no solid facts to contradict the abstract concepts of beauty, heroism, and virtue; in heaven, by contrast, there are only realities, questions of sanitation, education, health, and politics. Held in isolation, both stagnate, for the realism of heaven needs some vision of a better world in order to progress while hell is a static world of abstract dreams. The Devil offers a pessimistic view of human nature and history, pointing out how much better humans are at inventing weapons of murder and destruction than of creation, but Shaw counters this threat of despair with his newfound belief in creative evolution. Don Juan offers a creed of philosophical optimism based on the concept of the Life Force, a vision of Nature imbued with intelligence and foresight, guiding the overall evolutionary progress of mankind. Shaw's enduring faith in the power of the Life Force supported his confidence in the ability of society to change and adapt, reforming itself of its ills, as he commented in an undated letter to Norman Clark:

> my creed of creative evolution means in practice that man can change himself to meet every vital need, and that however long the trials and frequent the failures may be, we can put up a soul as an athlete puts up a muscle. Thus to men who are themselves cynical I am a pessimist; but to genuinely religious men I am an optimist, and even a fantastic and extravagant one.

Shaw's reputation both as dramatist and political thinker had grown immensely during this time, securing a hearing for his ideas not only from the public but also from the government itself. London performances of his play on Ireland, *John Bull's Other Island,* at the Court Theatre in 1904 were attended not only by the Conservative prime minister, Arthur Balfour, and by two leaders of the Liberal opposition, Herbert Asquith and Henry Campbell-Bannerman, but also by King Edward VII at a command performance during which he laughed so much he broke the chair specifically hired for him. The play, published in 1907 together with a "preface for politicians," unequivocally advocates home rule for Ireland. Shaw challenges conventional prejudices on the childishness and impracticality of the Irish character, which supposedly rendered them unfit to rule themselves, by reversing traditional stereotypes. He paints the Englishman as sentimental, unrealistic, and unintellectual in contrast to the Irishman, who is politically clear-sighted, having a strong hold on the realities of life. In Shaw's play the problems of Ireland are rooted in the ignorance and cultural poverty suffered by the wage laborer in a system of ownership dominated by peasants' proprietorship and a system of worship dominated by an archaic and corrupt church. The most urgent reforms needed in Ireland are therefore an injection of capital investment, a transformation of landownership, a standard wage, and an established church.

In 1917 Shaw extended his argument for Irish self-government in *How to Settle the Irish Question,* a series of articles that appeared first in the *Daily Express* and were subsequently published in pamphlet form in England and Ireland. Shaw proposed the federation of the United Kingdom into three or four distinct national parliaments. Federalism was the only solution that would offer a partnership that did not obliterate the individuality of the nation which entered into it, whereas the denial of home rule, Shaw warned, led inevitably to a military style of government with all its resultant history of atrocities, panic, and cowardice.

Major Barbara, a play in which Shaw demonstrates the degrading effects of poverty and unemployment, secured a similarly prestigious audience; its first performance on 28 November 1905 was attended by a box full of Salvation Army commissioners and Prime Minister Balfour, accompanied by Beatrice Webb, whom five days earlier he had appointed to the new Royal Commission on the Poor

Stained-glass window by Caroline Townshend depicting E. R. Pease, Sidney Webb, and Shaw (the three figures at top) and other Fabians (Beatrice Webb House, Leith Hill, Surrey)

Law. The play examines the priorities for reform, arguing that feeding, clothing, and housing the poor must be the first and most important step since spiritual values cannot exist for hungry, ill-clothed, and roofless people. The heroine, Barbara, abandons her idealism, understanding the need to accept her father's wealth, made from his munitions factory empire, in order to alleviate the suffering of the poor in the city; religion must be preached to full stomachs, she concludes. In political terms the play suggests the need for reform before revolution, for a compromise with capitalist wealth rather than the absolute idealism of the theoretical purist. It ends with a triumvirate of Barbara, her rich father, and her fiancé, a professor of ancient Greek, taking over the munitions factory. It is Shaw's vision of the alliance of the future, a trinity of spirit, body, and mind: idealism, realism, and intelligence.

Shaw's success as a commercial dramatist in the early years of the twentieth century did not distract him from his educational and reformist purpose. Indeed, confident in being guaranteed a hearing for his ideas, he allowed the discursive element of his dramas to become even more dominant. So, for example, *Getting Married* (performed in 1908), first subtitled "A Conversation" and later "A Disquisitory Play," consists of an extended examination of the disadvantages of marriage, and *Misalliance* (performed in 1910) is subtitled "A Debate in One Sitting," combining sensational incidents such as a plane crash-landing in a country house with extended discussion on the relationship between parents and children.

Shaw's newly established popularity was entirely exploded, however, with the outbreak of World War I. A monumental twenty-eight-page pamphlet supplement to the *New Statesman* published in November 1914, Shaw's *Common Sense about the War* argues that the motives behind the war were not heroic but economic, having their roots in the immense wealth that had built up in Europe unaccompanied by any corresponding equitable distribution. He refuses to build any illusion of nobility, purity, or patriotism around the war and finds his only consolation in the hope that some of the aims of socialism will be advanced when the enormous demands for coal, army rations, weapons, transport vehicles, and all the other accessories of war arrest the huge exports of capital and transform them into wages and when taxation of unearned incomes is doubled. Though he had previously written articles in the papers urging soldiers on both sides to shoot their officers and return home, he now reluctantly recognizes the need for social solidarity but urges that while socialists must fight in the trenches they should also question their own belligerent governments as to what they are fighting for. *Common Sense* brought down a storm of protest on Shaw's head: libraries and bookshops removed his works from their shelves; newspapers urged their readers to boycott his plays; and he was forced to resign from the Society of Authors and the Dramatists Club. In April 1916 he wrote "The German Case against Germany" for *The New York Times* (and later collected it in *What I Really Wrote about the War,* 1930), but by that time he was widely regarded in England as a German sympathizer.

Though his reputation had sufficiently recovered by 1917 for Douglas Haig, commander in chief of the British army, to invite him to visit the front, by the end of the war Shaw was once again at loggerheads with public opinion. Strongly opposed to the popular demand for revenge and heavy reparation from Germany, in March 1919 Shaw published ten thousand copies of *Peace Conference Hints* (which had first appeared in the *New York American* weekly from 19 January to 23 March 1919), in which he admonished Britain against exploiting her self-righteousness at the Versailles Peace Conference. His recommendations for peace were based on the idea of a League of Nations that was to play a central role in preventing future conflicts with the combined powers of conscience and an international police force. The accuracy of Shaw's gloomy predictions that vindictive settlements at Versailles would sow the seeds for future wars did nothing to increase his popularity.

Composed between 1916 and 1917, Shaw's next major play, *Heartbreak House,* added another dimension to his analysis of the causes and effects of the war. It is an apocalyptic work that belongs with similar works of the period such as W. B. Yeats's "The Second Coming" (1920), D. H. Lawrence's *Women in Love* (1921), and T. S. Eliot's *The Waste Land* (1922). Subtitled "A Fantasia in the Russian Manner on English Themes," the play was strongly influenced by Anton Chekhov, offering a vision of the English ruling class slipping dreamily and irresponsibly into decline. The house of the title is built like a ship, hinting at allegorical representations of the ship of state drifting toward ruin. The head of the household is a drunken former sailor, Captain Shotover, who is now forced to earn money by devising weapons of destruction since society will not pay him for his more life-enhancing creations. The captain's daughters and their husbands are artistic bohemians, possibly modeled on the Bloomsbury group, who float through the play in unreal dreams of love and heroism. The play ends with them ecstatically greeting the danger of death; a bomb misses them but kills the rich, philistine industrialist who is visiting them, leaving the bohemians to look forward eagerly to the thrills of the next night's bombing raid. The thesis of the play is conveyed by atmosphere rather than overt allegory or discussion, but it is nonetheless clear: the indifference of the cultured class to the political concerns of the nation is largely responsible for the self-destructive malaise of the country. The play did not premiere in England but in New York in November 1920, where it was well received. The first English production, at the Court Theatre in 1921, was greeted with predictably abusive reviews.

The only hope for the future in *Heartbreak House* is offered by the young houseguest Ellie, who rejects a financially rich but emotionally impoverished alliance to the industrialist and instead enters into a spiritual alliance with Captain Shotover. But the glimmer of hope is a faint one; Ellie's experience of heartbreak may have given her a more realistic outlook on life, but it has also sapped her youthful energy and enthusiasm, while Shotover's age brings both wisdom and a tired resignation. In his ambitious series of plays, *Back to Methuselah: A Metabiological Pentateuch* (written in 1918–1920), Shaw found an optimistic antidote to this dilemma. The cycle of five acts, each a play in itself, is Shaw's answer to Richard Wagner's *Der Ring des Nibelungen* (1869–1876); it presents a metaphysical inquiry into the causes of pessimism in the development of thought since Darwin and a search for a legitimate philosophical basis for hope in the future. Pinning his faith on the Life Force and the powers of creative evolution, Shaw presents a biological utopia in which human beings learn to live for two hundred years just by willing themselves to do so. The five acts span across time from the Garden of Eden in the first act to the year 31,920 A.D. in the last act, which depicts humankind nearing perfection, having attained such high levels of self-mastery that by the age of four the sensual life gives way entirely to the intellect. It is thus, Shaw suggests, that real improvement is possible for mankind; whereas "short-livers" only attain real knowledge and understanding at an age when they are too old to have an investment in the future, the new race of "long-livers" finally adopt the long-term view rather than wasting life in childish quarrels, love affairs, and other selfish pettiness. Performances of the entire cycle in the United States and England in 1922 and 1924 ran at a loss, but sales of the published version complete with preface were huge.

Shaw's reinstatement in English public opinion was secured by *Saint Joan* (written and performed in 1923), a play which was accepted internationally as a masterpiece of dramatic literature and for which he was awarded the Nobel Prize for literature in 1925. Shaw used the prize money to establish an Anglo-Swedish Foundation to make Swedish works, in particular those of August Strindberg, available in English translation. In Shaw's play Saint Joan becomes an embodiment of the Life Force, a genius filled with a vision of the future who falls victim to the forces of reaction. Joan becomes a Shavian saint, a rebel who fights against the established order, and her martyrdom presents the agony of the individual whose need to advance the species transcends the need for self-preservation. She is a champion of nationalism; her ambition to unite France brings her into conflict with the interests of feudal barons and the universal church. The tragedy is not hers alone but is the tragedy of a world which, Shaw suggests, will never be ready for its saints. Shaw's sympathy with Joan as a nationalist was predictable as he was an advocate of the Marxist theory that it is necessary for social organizations to pass through a nationalist phase on the way to world socialism. In the preface to the play he also provocatively links medieval France to modern-day Ireland, declaring that contemporary Irish Joans would be given an even more cursory trial under the Defence of the Realm Act and condemning modern English tyranny as more oppressive than its earlier manifestation.

On 1 June 1928 some 90,000 copies of *The Intelligent Woman's Guide to Socialism and Capitalism* were published simultaneously in Britain and America. It was Shaw's greatest attempt to demystify the subject of economics, to denounce capitalist society as it stood, and to set out his guidelines for future reform. According to Siegfried Trebitsch's *Chronicle of a Life* (1953), it inspired the first Labour Party prime minister, Ramsay MacDonald, to declare, "After the Bible this is in my eyes the most important book that humanity possesses." The timing of its publication was significant, for six weeks previously an act had been passed in Parliament lowering the voting age for women from thirty to twenty-one and giving them the same residence qualifications as men. This extension of the franchise added five million women to the electorate. In the subsequent 1929 election the

Editorial cartoon published in Punch *after the appearance of* The Intelligent Woman's Guide to Socialism and Capitalism *(1928)*

Labour Party enlarged its following by three million votes, many of which were assumed to be from newly enfranchised women. Shaw was a lifelong supporter of sexual equality and women's rights and had consistently supported the woman suffrage campaign though he never spoke for it in public, believing women should be left to prove they could speak for themselves. In *The Quintessence of Ibsenism* he had attacked the Victorian ideal of the self-sacrificing "womanly woman," arguing that a woman's first duty was to herself and that she must learn to help herself before she could know how to help others. His writings from *Mrs Warren's Profession* onward advocate moral, intellectual, and financial independence for women, and *The Intelligent Woman's Guide* is concerned with securing such opportunities not just for women but for all individuals.

The basic principles behind *The Intelligent Woman's Guide* are moral fairness and equality of income: the entitlement of everyone to an equal share of the wealth of the nation regardless of occupation. Capitalism, Shaw maintains, diminishes the collective well-being of the community by expending so much energy in supporting the parasitic rich who live by owning land and consume without producing. Shaw recommends that the land and basic industries of the nation be managed for the benefit of all; for example, the railways, mines, cotton industry, and banks should be made community property. Compulsion is an important ingredient in his scheme: his future society is based on quality of leisure and the imposition on all serviceable citizens of mandatory social service, together with a reform of the democratic system of election and rule, including more rigorous testing of candidates' qualifications before allowing them to seek election and possible compulsion of the best potential candidates to undertake the responsibilities of government against their own inclination. *The Intelligent Woman's Guide* was immensely successful, and in 1937 it was republished in a new paperback series with two new chapters dealing with events of the last decade and with its title extended to *The Intelligent Woman's Guide to Socialism, Capitalism, Sovietism and Fascism*.

Shaw's disillusionment with the parliamentary party system found further expression in *The Apple Cart*, first performed in Warsaw in June 1929. In the 1930 preface to the play he likens democracy to a hot-air balloon that diverts the attention of the public while its pockets are being picked. Parliamentary elections, the play suggests, are dominated by the huge mass of ignorant voters, who in turn are dominated by a corrupt press and by the personal appeal of candidates who win votes with such frivolous amusements as comic songs and mimicry. Furthermore, there is a divorce between real power and the functions of government, for while the elected representatives of the people spend the play making speeches and squabbling over constitutional issues, the country is dominated by the unchallenged power of Breakages Limited, the corrupt capitalist business that makes private profit from public loss. Nor is hope for reform to be found in the younger generation, which, in Shaw's view, is squandering its energies in a pointless and unrewarding pursuit of pleasure. *Too True to Be Good*, completed in 1931, dramatizes a widespread crisis of belief, portraying a group of young people who come into the possession of considerable riches and embark on an ultimately unsuccessful search for a good time. As Shaw wrote to a friend, "Its main theme is the dissolution of established morals by the shock of war."

It was this combination of disillusionment and impatience with the ignorance and inherent conservatism of the public that led Shaw to abandon hope in his long-held belief in the principles of Fabian socialism, which advocated a waiting game in which reform was secured through gradual modification of existing systems. "There is no use in waiting," he declared in 1920. Despairing of democracy and the masses, Shaw was impressed by the early achievements of the new dictators of the 1920s and in an undated letter to a friend he defended his enthusiasm: "All dictators begin as reformers and are encouraged by all sensible people until they find that their subjects do not understand their reforms and respond to nothing but military glory . . . I applauded both Hitler and Musso while they were in their reform phase, just as Churchill did." His admiration for the individual achievements of these dictators made him all too ready to overlook their methods and the price paid for them in human suffering. He continued to support Benito Mussolini's regime in spite of being aware of his having murdered his socialist opponent Giacomo Matteoti in June 1924 and having established a campaign of beating up his opponents. Shaw's support of Joseph Stalin was, perhaps unsurprisingly, even more forgiving and far longer lasting.

Shaw had greeted the Russian Revolution with enthusiasm, and in July 1931 he paid a visit to Russia and had an audience with Stalin. He recognized Stalin's ruthless opportunism and argued to Beatrice Webb that Soviet brutalities were manifestations of a backward country with a barbarous history; Stalin's methods were nothing remarkable after the czarist regime. Shaw's readiness to dismiss tales of atrocities as the fabrications of a hostile press is more understandable in the light of his need to believe in the success of the new communist order. So he declared in an impromptu speech at a film studio in Leningrad:

> if this great communistic experiment spreads over the whole world, we shall have a new era in history. We shall not have the old collapse and failure, the beginning again, the going through the whole miserable story to the same miserable end. . . . If the future is the future as Lenin foresaw it, then we may all smile and look forward to the future without fear. But if the experiment is overthrown and fails . . . then I shall have to take a very melancholy farewell of you, my friends.

Shaw may have been lenient toward Stalinist Russia, but his condemnation of South African society was wholehearted. He visited South Africa in 1932 and was disgusted by the poverty, by the extreme inequality of wealth, and above all by the injustices of apartheid. As he declared in an 8 February 1932 *Cape Times* article, "One of the first things I noticed when I landed was that I had immediately become dependent on the services of men and women who are not of my colour. I felt that I was in a Slave State, and that, too, the very worst sort of

Photograph used on the jacket of Shaw on Vivisection *(1949)*

Slave State." To the end of his life he continued to believe and assert that apartheid was "flat persecution like that of the Jews by the Nazis." *The Adventures of the Black Girl in Her Search for God* (1932), a tale begun by Shaw during his stay in South Africa, ends with the black heroine marrying a red-haired socialist Irishman and producing "charmingly coffee-coloured" children, following the policy of interracial marriage and breeding that Shaw believed was the best solution to the problem of race. The tale is also highly critical of missionary Christianity, which Shaw characterizes as "Crostianity." His rejection of any form of established religion and extreme distaste for the iconography of Christianity endured throughout his life. In his will he directed that,

> As my religious convictions and scientific views cannot at present be more specifically defined than those of a believer in Creative Evolution I desire that no public monument or work of art or inscription or sermon or ritual service commemorating me shall suggest that I accepted the tenets peculiar to any established church or denomination nor take the form of a cross or any other instrument of torture or symbol of blood sacrifice.

He returned to the problem of reforming British society and politics in *On the Rocks,* written and performed in 1933, a play in which a harassed prime minister reads the works of Marx, Lenin, and Leon Trotsky and offers a plan to lift the country out of the depression into which it has plunged. His plan of regeneration is similar to that advocated in *The Intelligent Woman's Guide,* including the nationalization of banks, transport, and ground rents, a doubling of surtax on unearned income, and compulsory civilian or military service irrespective of income. The plan is defeated, however, by combined forces of the extreme right and left. Members of a Labour deputation from the Isle of Cats object to the idea of compulsory labor, the no-strike agreement, and the offer of compensation for land nationalization. They are addicted to class war because they believe they will win and gain control of the country. On the opposite side, the prime minister is faced with outraged opposition from the leader of the Conservatives, who believes that his duty is to prevent any reform or change ever being implemented.

During the 1930s, as the hold of fascism with all its attendant horrors tightened on Europe, Shaw clung desperately to his optimistic belief in the enduring power of common sense and common standards of decency and sanity. Thus, as the extent of Adolf Hitler's anti-Semitic campaign became clear, Shaw offered a typically Shavian solution in the 26 November 1938 *Time and Tide:*

> The League of Nations should at once appoint a com-

mittee, assisted by an international staff of expert psychiatrists, to determine whether the anti-Semite measures taken by Germany and Italy are legitimate legislation or pathological phobia. If the report of the Committee and the subsequent decision of the League is for phobia, the Führer and the Duce will have either to cancel the measures or stand before Europe as certified lunatics.

Shaw's response to 1930s fascism was largely determined by his fiercely maintained faith in essential human reason and the power of public opinion, and by the hopes he pinned on the League of Nations as a source of rationality and control in Europe. His revulsion and horror at the persecution of the Jews and the other victims of fascist aggression were undeniable, though his solutions occasionally seemed sadly out of proportion. *Geneva* (performed in 1938), a play whose centerpiece is a fictional trial of Hitler, Mussolini, and Francisco Franco before the International Court of the Hague, displays exactly this uneasy balance. The characteristic jokes and tomfoolery seem even more inappropriate with hindsight, but the Judge's concluding address to the dictators offers a clear articulation of Shaw's outrage and reveals how close world events brought him to despair:

> Your objective is domination: your weapons fire and poison, starvation and ruin, extermination by every means known to science. You have reduced one another to such a condition of terror that no atrocity makes you recoil and say that you will die rather than commit it. You call this patriotism, courage, glory. There are a thousand good things to be done in your countries. They remain undone for hundreds of years; but the fire and the poison are always up to date. If this be not scoundrelism what is scoundrelism? I give you up as hopeless. Man is a failure as a political animal. The creative forces which produce him must produce something better.

Shaw's condemnation was sufficient for all publication or performances of *Geneva* to be banned in Germany in 1939. In October 1939 Shaw wrote an article that appeared in the *New York Journal-American* with the title "'War Is Over,' Shaw Says" and in the *New Statesman* with the title "Uncommon Sense about the War." In the article he proposes that Britain enter truce negotiations with Germany in a last-ditch attempt to determine if a second world war is inevitable. "If it is, we can fight as easily after a conference as before it," he advises, believing that at least that much is owed to those who had known the heartbreak of the last war. Shavian diplomacy was in this case entirely impotent.

Shaw's main work during the war was the composition of *Everybody's Political What's What?* (1944), an amalgam of autobiography, sociology, history, and political economy. Initially subtitled "Machiavelli Modernised," the book is Shaw's attempt to lay out a plan for organizing society so as to achieve the fairest distribution of wealth, service, leisure, and opportunities for self-development. It was intended to be an elementary textbook on politics, comprising everything an informed voter should know in a parliamentary democracy. Published in September 1944, it sold eighty-five thousand hardback copies in Britain within a year.

On Shaw's ninetieth birthday Penguin brought out the "Shaw Million," a simultaneous publication of ten of Shaw's works in editions of one hundred thousand copies each. They sold out in six weeks. He continued to write, producing several small plays, fantasies, and conversation pieces, including a puppet play, *Shakes versus Shav* (written and performed in 1949), in which, with typically provocative humor, he pits himself against William Shakespeare. He also continued his support for various causes; for example, he helped the National Antivivisection Society select several of his articles and speeches, which he then revised, to be published as *Shaw on Vivisection* (1949).

Shaw's wife, Charlotte, had died in 1943, and he felt her loss deeply. He grew gradually weaker, and on 2 November 1950 he died at the age of ninety-four. According to his instructions, he was cremated, and his ashes were then mixed with those of his wife and scattered in the garden of their house at Ayot Saint Lawrence.

Shaw wrote in the preface to *Buoyant Billions: A Comedy of No Manners in Prose* (1950): "I cannot hold my tongue nor my pen. As long as I live I must write. If I stopped writing I should die for want of something to do." He left behind him an immense body of work, including plays, pamphlets, reviews, articles, and several volumes of letters, through all of which shines his indefatigable desire to educate, enlighten, and inform his audience. So he wrote in the preface to *Geneva*:

> A little knowledge is a dangerous thing; but we must take that risk because a little is as much as our biggest heads can hold; and a citizen who knows that the earth is round and older than six thousand years is less dangerous than one of equal capacity who believes it is a flat ground between a first floor heaven and a basement hell.

As a political thinker and sage he was both influential and respected, meeting and talking with world leaders from Stalin to Mahatma Gandhi. His socialist beliefs, as he explains in *Everybody's Political What's What?*, provided the central inspiration behind his efforts toward reform: "Socialism is not charity nor loving-kindness, nor sympathy with the poor, nor popular philanthropy . . . but the economist's hatred of waste and disorder, the aesthete's hatred of ugliness and dirt, the lawyer's hatred of injustice, the doctor's hatred of disease, the saint's hatred of the seven deadly sins." In spite of all the suffering, waste, brutality, and stupidity he witnessed and railed against, his faith in the potential for human progress, social reform, and creative evolution remained undimmed.

Letters:

Ellen Terry and Bernard Shaw: A Correspondence, edited by Christopher St. John (New York: Fountain Press / London: Constable, 1931);

Bernard Shaw and Mrs. Patrick Campbell: Their Correspondence, edited by Alan Dent (London: Gollancz, 1952; New York: Knopf, 1952);

Advice to a Young Critic and Other Letters, edited by E. J. West (New York: Crown, 1955); republished as *Advice to a Young Critic: Letters 1894-1928* (London: Owen, 1956);

Bernard Shaw's Letters to Granville Barker, edited by C. B. Purdom (New York: Theatre Arts Books, 1957; London: Phoenix House, 1957);

To a Young Actress: The Letters of Bernard Shaw to Molly Tompkins, edited by Peter Tompkins (New York: Potter, 1960; London: Constable, 1961);

Collected Letters, 1856-1950, 4 volumes, edited by Dan H. Laurence (London: Reinhardt, 1965-1988);

Bernard Shaw and Alfred Douglas: A Correspondence, edited by Mary Hyde (London: John Murray, 1982; New Haven: Ticknor & Fields, 1982);

The Playwright and the Pirate: Bernard Shaw and Frank Harris: A Correspondence, edited by Stanley Weintraub (University Park: Pennsylvania State University Press, 1982);

Agitations: Letters to the Press 1875-1950, edited by Laurence and James Rambeau (New York: Ungar, 1985);

Bernard Shaw's Letters to Siegfried Trebitsch, edited by Samuel A. Weiss (Stanford, Cal.: Stanford University Press, 1986);

Letters from Margaret: Correspondence between Bernard Shaw and Margaret Wheeler, 1944-1950, edited by Rebecca Swift (London: Chatto & Windus, 1992);

Shaw, Lady Gregory and the Abbey: A Correspondence and a Record, edited by Laurence and Nicholas Grene (Gerrards Cross: Colin Smythe, 1993);

Theatrics: Selected Correspondence of Bernard Shaw, edited by Laurence (Toronto & London: University of Toronto Press, 1995).

Interviews:

Shaw: Interviews and Recollections, edited by A. M. Gibbs (Basingstoke: Macmillan, 1990; Iowa City: University of Iowa Press, 1990).

Bibliographies:

Dan H. Laurence, *Bernard Shaw: A Bibliography,* 2 volumes (Oxford: Clarendon Press / New York: Oxford University Press, 1983);

Stanley Weintraub, *Bernard Shaw: A Guide to Research* (University Park: Pennsylvania State University Press, 1992).

Biographies:

Archibald Henderson, *George Bernard Shaw: His Life and Works* (London: Hurst & Blackett, 1911; Cincinnati: Stewart & Kidd, 1911);

Hesketh Pearson, *Bernard Shaw: His Life and Personality* (London: Collins, 1942); republished as *Bernard Shaw: A Full-Length Portrait* (New York: Harper, 1942; revised edition, London: Methuen, 1951; New York: Atheneum, 1963);

Michael Holroyd, *Bernard Shaw, 1856-1950,* 5 volumes (London: Chatto & Windus, 1988-1992).

References:

Alan P. Barr, *Victorian Stage Pulpiteer: Bernard Shaw's Crusade* (Athens: University of Georgia Press, 1973);

Eric Bentley, *Bernard Shaw, 1856-1950* (New York: New Directions, 1957);

Tracy C. Davis, *George Bernard Shaw and the Socialist Theatre* (Westport, Conn.: Greenwood Press, 1994);

T. F. Evans, ed., *Shaw and Politics* (University Park: Pennsylvania State University Press, 1991);

A. M. Gibbs, *The Art and Mind of Shaw: Essays in Criticism* (New York: St. Martin's Press, 1983);

Gareth Griffith, *Socialism and Superior Brains: The Political Thought of Bernard Shaw* (London: Routledge, 1993);

Leon Hugo, *Bernard Shaw: Playwright and Preacher* (London: Methuen, 1971);

Paul A. Hummert, *Bernard Shaw's Marxian Romance* (Lincoln: University of Nebraska Press, 1973);

Norman MacKenzie and Jeanne MacKenzie, *The Fabians* (New York: Simon & Schuster, 1977);

Keith May, *Ibsen and Shaw* (London: Macmillan, 1985);

Harry Morrison, *The Socialism of Bernard Shaw* (Jefferson, N.C.: McFarland, 1989);

J. Percy Smith, *The Unrepentant Pilgrim: A Study of the Development of George Bernard Shaw* (Boston: Houghton Mifflin, 1965);

E. Strauss, *Bernard Shaw: Art and Socialism* (London: Gollancz, 1942);

Alfred Turco, *Shaw's Moral Vision: The Self and Salvation* (Ithaca: Cornell University Press, 1976);

Maurice Valency, *The Cart and the Trumpet: The Plays of George Bernard Shaw* (New York: Oxford University Press, 1973);

Barbara Bellow Watson, *A Shavian Guide to the Intelligent Woman* (New York: Norton, 1964);

Robert F. Whitman, *Shaw and the Play of Ideas* (Ithaca: Cornell University Press, 1977);

J. L. Wisenthal, *Shaw's Sense of History* (Oxford: Clarendon Press, 1988).

Papers:
The major repositories of Shaw correspondence and manuscripts are the Shaw Archive at the British Library, London, and the Hanley Collection at the Harry Ransom Humanities Research Center, University of Texas at Austin. Other important collections are at the National Library of Ireland, the New York Public Library (Berg Collection), the University of North Carolina (Henderson Collection), Cornell University (Burgunder Collection), Bucknell University (Butler Collection), and the Houghton Library of Harvard University. The libraries of Boston University, Yale University, and Hofstra University have significant holdings as well.

Edith Jemima Simcox
(21 August 1844 – 15 September 1901)

James Diedrick
Albion College

BOOKS: *Natural Law: An Essay in Ethics* (London: Trübner, 1877; Boston: Osgood, 1877);

Episodes in the Lives of Men, Women, and Lovers (London: Trübner, 1882; Boston: Osgood, 1882);

Primitive Civilizations; or, Outlines of the History of Ownership in Archaic Communities, 2 volumes (London: Sonnenschein / New York: Macmillan, 1894);

A Monument to the Memory of George Eliot: Edith Jemima Simcox's Autobiography of a Shirtmaker, edited by Constance M. Fulmer & Margaret E. Barfield (New York: Garland, 1998).

OTHER: Review of *Middlemarch,* as H. Lawrenny (1873), in *A Century of George Eliot Criticism,* edited by Gordon Haight (Boston: Houghton Mifflin, 1965), pp. 73-80;

"Autobiographies" (1870), "Women's Work and Women' Wages" (1887), and "The Capacity of Women" (1887), in *Prose by Victorian Women,* edited by Andrea Broomfield and Sally Mitchell (New York: Garland, 1996).

SELECTED PERIODICAL PUBLICATIONS–UNCOLLECTED: "Custom and Sex," as H. Lawrenny, *Fortnightly Review,* 17 (1872): 310-323;

"On the Influence of John Stuart Mill's Writings," *Contemporary Review,* 22 (1873): 297-317;

Review of *Personal Recollections of Mary Somerville, Fortnightly Review,* 15 (1874): 109-120;

"The Present Trade Depression," *Times* (London), 8 January 1878, p. 4;

"The Organization of Unremunerative Industry," *Fraser's Magazine,* 18 (1878): 609-621;

"Technical Education for Women," *Times* (London), 21 November 1878, p. 7;

"The Employment of Women," *Times* (London), 8 October 1879, p. 12;

"Ideals of Feminine Usefulness," *Fortnightly Review,* 27 (1880): 656-671;

"Elementary Education and the Code of 1880," *Times* (London), 4 May 1880, p. 10;

"George Eliot," *Nineteenth Century,* 9 (1881): 778-801;

"St. Paul's Industrial School," *Times* (London), 16 November 1881, p. 7; 19 November 1881, p. 7;

"The New Education Code," *Times* (London), 7 April 1882, p. 4;

"Mr. Morris' Hopes and Fears for Art," *Fortnightly Review,* 31 (1882): 771-779;

"A Turning Point in the History of Cooperation," *Fraser's Magazine,* 26 (1882): 222-235;

"The Housing of the Poor," *Times* (London), 7 January 1884, p. 4;

"The Extension of the Franchise," *Times* (London), 26 May 1884, p. 8;

"Eight Years of Cooperative Shirtmaking," *Nineteenth Century,* 15 (1884): 1037-1054;

"The Penny Dinner System," *Times* (London), 19 December 1884, p. 13.

Best known as one of the several worshipers who literally sat at the feet of George Eliot during the last decade of the novelist's life, Edith Simcox deserves recognition for her own substantial contributions to reform in Victorian England. Diffident by nature and denied the Oxford education that purchased distinguished careers for her two brothers, she nonetheless achieved distinction in her lifetime as a writer and woman of action. She wrote influential essays and reviews on a range of topics for many leading Victorian periodicals; she published three books, including two volumes of a projected multivolume history of ownership; she demonstrated the feasibility of labor cooperatives by jointly operating a shirtmaking enterprise; she lectured widely on trade unionism, socialism, and women's suffrage; and she won wide praise for her work on the London School Board and on behalf of the international labor movement. As her essays and books demonstrate, she was a capable theorist of reform in the tradition of Jeremy Bentham and John Stuart Mill, to whom speculation meant nothing unless it formed the basis for action. Her praise of Mill in her essay "On the Influence of John Stuart

Mill's Writings" (1873) applies with equal relevance to her own career:

> Nearly the first of the many prejudices which he helped to undermine was the belief that all theories were "visionary" and unpractical; comparatively few people would now venture to question that a sound theory is the best rule of action, but he himself went a degree further than this, and carried his confidence in the results of candid speculation to the point of being willing to act upon his own convictions.

Edith Jemima Simcox was born into a middle-class Victorian family on 21 August 1844. Her father, George Price Simcox, was a merchant prosperous enough to send his two sons to Oxford University, where both became brilliant scholars and fellows. George Augustus, born 18 July 1841, edited Greek and Latin texts and wrote poems, essays, and *A History of Latin Literature from Ennius to Boethius* (1883). William Henry, born 6 March 1843, took religious orders and published books on church history, theology, and biblical commentary. Like her brothers, Edith was intellectually precocious, but Oxford did not admit women as degree candidates until 1920, and her formal education did not extend beyond grammar school. Her subsequent writings indicate, however, that she pursued a rigorous course of self-education after her formal schooling had ended.

While at school she learned Latin, French, and German and read widely in English literature. In "Autobiography of a Shirtmaker," her unpublished memoir, she describes herself at school as being shy, rebellious, eager for approval from her professors, and decidedly uninterested in the opposite sex. One entry in that autobiography records her dawning sense of sexual difference by noting that "when I was eight or nine my dreams were of some discovery that should prove me to be a boy." Simcox declares repeatedly in this autobiography that she never wished to marry, and while she attributes what she calls her "own bad case" of melancholia to her solitary life, she also characteristically rejects the notion that marriage is the sole "remedy" for such loneliness. At odds with social and sexual conventions from an early age and barred from educational opportunities because of her gender, Simcox became acutely sensitive to all marginalized members of society. Much of her best writing, in fact, is fueled by her indignation at restrictive social and economic systems.

Volumes eight and nine of Gordon Haight's *The George Eliot Letters* and the discovery in 1951 of "Autobiography of a Shirtmaker," liberally excerpted in K. A. McKenzie's *Edith Simcox and George Eliot* (1961), helped to reclaim Edith Simcox for twentieth-century readers. But these works have also unfortunately focused excessive attention on her unrequited love for George Eliot and distracted attention from her achievements as a writer and activist. Simcox first met George Eliot in 1872, when she was twenty-eight years old and the novelist was fifty-three. Having just completed *Middlemarch* (1871–1872), Eliot was living in London, and Sunday gatherings at her home attracted most of the leading intellectuals and writers of the day—Robert Browning, Henry James, Alfred Tennyson, Anthony Trollope, Herbert Spencer, and Leslie Stephen. For the next eight years until Eliot's death on 22 December 1880, Simcox visited her often, encouraged in part by Eliot's common-law husband George Henry Lewes, who believed that the presence of fervent admirers was an effective antidote to his wife's diffidence.

Simcox's rationalism and radicalism were well established by the time she met Eliot, and Simcox had been writing reviews for *The Academy* for three years, yet such was her devotion to the woman whom she called her "idol" that she attributed all her subsequent accomplishments to Eliot's influence. The "Autobiography of a Shirtmaker" is an invaluable record of Simcox's tireless efforts on behalf of reform as well as a frank chronicle of the history of what she called "the love passion of my life." Eliot was receptive to Simcox's friendship and welcomed her into her home, but the novelist was clearly uncomfortable in the face of Simcox's ardent and physical professions of devotion. Nonetheless, Simcox continued to derive inspiration from this unequal relationship; the "Autobiography of a Shirtmaker" contains many references to discussions between the two women concerning ideas that both explored in their respective work.

While Simcox's love for George Eliot may have inspired much of her writing, her reading of Bentham, Mill, and August Comte, which preceded her acquaintance with Eliot by many years, provided its philosophical underpinnings. Indeed, Simcox's major writings might be seen as both extending and modifying (especially in terms of class and gender) Mill's arguments on political economy, ethics, and the woman question. Simcox's "On the Influence of John Stuart Mill's Writings," which appeared in the *Contemporary Review* less than two months after Mill's death, demonstrates her thorough grounding in the writings of the major philosophical radicals of the nineteenth century. It also reveals her own discriminating judgment. Acknowledging Comte's genius and the influence of his early writings on Mill's thought, Simcox consistently contrasts his dogmatic and dictatorial tendencies to Mill's consensual approach. In one of her many felicitous expressions Simcox calls Comte a "soldier of fortune" who is willing to effect the new social order he envisions through authority and force. Mill, on the other hand, envisions "the reorganization of society . . . as an impending natural necessity, not as something arbitrary or authoritative."

Given her lifelong concern for social justice, it is not surprising that Simcox singles out Mill's *Principles of Political Economy* (1848) and *The Subjection of Women* (1869) for special mention. She praises the former for its enlightened, antipaternalistic attitude toward the laboring classes, and she writes of the "generous courage" that characterizes *The Subjection of Women*. At the same time, she disagrees with some of the terms of Mill's argument in the latter work. She faults Mill for focusing exclusively on how prevailing social structures constrain women and failing to consider how these structures affect men, and she notes that at times Mill speaks of the "nature of women" as if this were "a fixed and ascertainable quantity." Simcox proposes a more fluid model:

> The "original qualities" of a species or a sex, are something like the archetypal skeleton of the Vertebrates; a type fixed by abstraction and idealization for convenience of mental reference, but not seriously supposed to have a real existence in nature. Practically, human nature is always conceived as that corrected copy of the real men and women of the day, which each generation proposes to itself as a desirable model for imitation.

Simcox wrote several distinguished essays for the *Contemporary Review,* but her longest association with a Victorian periodical began on 9 October 1869, when she published her first review in *The Academy* under the pseudonym "H. Lawrenny." *The Academy* was founded in 1869 by a group of young university liberals, and it eventually included Matthew Arnold, George Saintsbury, and Walter Pater among its contributors. Its first editor was an Oxford fellow and Hegelian philosopher whose scientific rationalism informed the scope and focus of the journal. Both of Simcox's brothers were regular contributors and doubtless helped her get her start with the journal. Most of its writers were Oxford dons or graduates, and this helps explain why Simcox's gender was concealed for several years under a pseudonym.

Reviewing French, German, and English fiction, studies of literature, and treatises on ethics and economics, she wrote for *The Academy* for more than twenty-five years. The quality of her writing for *The Academy* can be gauged by her review of *Middlemarch,* which remains one of the more perceptive evalua-

Title page for the American edition of Simcox's first book, which reveals the influences of Benedict de Spinoza, Auguste Comte, and John Stuart Mill

tions of the novel. It appeared in the 1 January 1873 issue, just one month after the novel had completed its serial publication and less than a month after Simcox had met Eliot. Simcox ranks *Middlemarch* as the greatest of Eliot's novels and one of the supreme achievements in English fiction. She praises Eliot's characterization, use of parallel plots, and mastery of figurative language, and she anticipates future evaluations by identifying one of its distinctive achievements:

> *Middlemarch* marks an epoch in the history of fiction in so far as its incidents are taken from the inner life, as the action is developed by the direct influence of mind on mind and character on character, as the material circumstances of the outer world are made subordinate and accessory to the artistic presentation of a definite passage of mental experience, but chiefly as giving a background of perfect realistic truth to a profoundly imaginative psychological study.

At the same time, Simcox notes, this psychological emphasis is linked to the theme of reform in the novel, as it illuminates the complex and necessary interrelationship between personal and political change.

In addition to her reviews for the *Contemporary Review* and *The Academy*, Simcox wrote essays and reviews for the *Fortnightly Review*, *Fraser's Magazine*, *Nineteenth Century*, the *North British Review*, and *Longman's Magazine*. She also contributed to the *Co-operative News*, *Women's Union Journal*, the *Labour Tribune*, and the *Manchester Guardian*. Her publications in the *Fortnightly Review* and *Nineteenth Century* included four important feminist essays, the most important of which, "The Capacity of Women," appeared in the September 1887 issue of *Nineteenth Century*. In this essay Simcox brings a class analysis to bear on the issue of women's status. Pointedly rejecting what she calls "vague metaphysical notions" about the essential nature and capacity of women and taking a long historical view, Simcox notes that "the first thinkers of the first ages were taken from the class of gentlemen of leisure, rulers of men, possessed of whatever experience life then could teach; their leisure was secured by the industry of wives and slaves, and any latent aptitude their sisters might have had for religion or philosophy was sacrificed to the necessity for grinding corn or looking after the maids."

Simcox militantly rejects the prevalent Victorian ideology of separate spheres for men and women. She argues that women have the right to pursue careers outside the home and that thwarting these pursuits threatens social and intellectual progress. She concludes that "we must look forward, not to a continued difference between the functions and ideals of the sexes, but to the evolution of an ideal of human character and duty combining the best elements in the two detached and incomplete ideals." In this essay she develops a conception of the social construction of gender roles that she later expressed fully in *Primitive Civilizations; or, Outlines of the History of Ownership in Archaic Communities* (1894).

In contrast to many Victorian feminists, Simcox extended her concerns beyond those difficulties faced by middle-class women. In 1875 she became involved in the trade union movement through her acquaintance with Emma Paterson, who had been secretary of the Women's Suffrage Association from 1872 to 1873 and in 1874 had founded the Women's Protective and Provident League. League members were men and women of the upper middle class who helped working women form trade unions, and the first women's union formed through the efforts of this league was the London Women Bookbinders Union, established in 1874. At a public meeting on 1 July 1875 Paterson and Simcox joined together to form the Shirt and Collar Makers' Union. As a result of their efforts Patterson and Simcox became the first women admitted as delegates to a Trade Union Congress—the eighth annual congress, held in Glasgow from 11 October to 16 October 1875.

While both women were warmly welcomed by the membership, Simcox immediately distinguished herself by her quick wit and her superior understanding of economic principles. She spoke on the inadequacy of factory inspections and on the needs for reduced hours and for parliamentary representation, and she noted that parliamentary representatives of the working classes would be effective only if they exercised their power on behalf of the governed rather than the ruling class. At the penultimate session of the congress Simcox presented a paper on the organization of women's labor, a paper in which she supported equal pay for women and men and attacked class as well as gender divisions. She ended her remarks with praise for the congress, which,

> by including the fortunes of women among the objects of its care and admitting their representatives to its deliberations, . . . had set a most valuable example of disinterested liberality to other public bodies which was not likely to be thrown away; and by recognizing the natural identity of interest of all members of the family without distinction of sex they had led the way to a recognition of that neglected and still more important truth, the natural identity of interest of all members of society without distinction of class.

During the same meeting at which the Shirt and Collar Makers' Union was established, Simcox also suggested the creation of a cooperative shirt-making workshop. This scheme was well received, and in 1875 she and Mary Hamilton became partners in a firm they named Hamilton and Company. Her experiences comanaging this enterprise are detailed in "Eight Years of Cooperative Shirtmaking," published in *Nineteenth Century* in June 1884, the same year that she resigned her part in the business. The article describes in careful detail the administrative and organizational steps that went into creating the cooperative and making it a success. It also contains much powerful social criticism, which was all the more persuasive in coming from the pen of a middle-class woman who worked alongside working women for nearly ten years. Like Charles Dickens's attacks on "telescopic philanthropy" in *Bleak House* (1852–1853), "Eight Years of Cooperative Shirtmaking" unmasks the ignorance and condescension that often underlie charitable schemes:

For the moment the religious and charitable world is interested in the denizens of the slums; but will that world bear to be told that the slums are peopled by those whom they themselves help to send there? What about the shilling bibles and sixpenny or penny testaments which it is supposed to be a good work to disseminate? The women that fold and sew these books must live in slums, with the rest of the vast army whose life amongst us is a slow death upon starvation wages. Are the Bible societies or they to blame if they take to drinking? Ladies who "work among the poor" think it right to save their money for charity, and buy cheap costumes, made far off by the same sisterhood; and who can tell the ladies that their so-called charity is a theft, and they themselves parties to more oppression than the district visiting of a lifetime can atone?

Simcox insists on an economic solution to an economic problem: "underpayment of honest industry . . . does more than drink, more than vice, more than improvidence to people our slums, and is itself the most fertile mother of all these three."

In 1877 Simcox published her first book, *Natural Law: An Essay in Ethics*. Revealing all of the major influences on her thinking, *Natural Law* is an amalgam of Spinozan ethics, Comtean Positivism, and Utilitarianism—all leavened by a sympathetic awareness of human frailty inspired by Eliot's novels. Like Mill and Comte before her, Simcox attempts to identify the "laws" that underlie human relations in order to contribute to a "science" of society. As a thoroughgoing rationalist, Simcox is concerned "with the duties of men to each other. . . . [i]t is still a new and somewhat startling conception that the claims from this quarter may be as infinite as the demands of any imaginary creator."

After distinguishing between natural, customary, and positive law in her first two chapters, Simcox compares theological, naturalistic, utilitarian, and sentimental "systems" of morality, her central concern. Chapter 3 demythologizes religious explanations of human life, while chapters 4 and 5 make a case for the superiority of "natural," "practical" morality to "theistic" morality. Simcox views theistic morality as antithetical to moral responsibility and social progress: it posits a God who forgives sins and thereby annuls individual responsibility. Moreover, Simcox argues, appeals to a supernatural agent who will right all earthly wrongs allow the rich to evade social responsibility, for the rich can claim that God will ultimately take care of the unfortunate. In a system of practical morality there is no supernatural remission: "the evil is evil all the same, and though it is well for sin to be atoned for, it is better for it not to be committed; no unimaginable eventualities hatching under the brooding wings of the unknowable can turn its commission into a good in disguise."

In her concluding chapter Simcox argues against despair in the face of the disappearance of God; she insists that the search for perfection and the fulfillment of duty are worthy goals, whether God does or does not exist. Both the language and the substance of Simcox's arguments on religion in *Natural Law* contain echoes of Eliot's religious humanism, and Simcox notes in "Autobiography of a Shirtmaker" that, "barring the somewhat too impersonal, unconcerned or hypothetical way of saying it," Eliot approved of the discussion of religion in the book.

Simcox's venture into moral philosophy did not mark a move away from her practical concerns. In January 1878 she debated with Sir Edmund Beckett in the pages of the London *Times* concerning the current trade depression and resultant disputes between labor and management. Beckett insisted that strikes and trade unionism in general were to blame for the current economic slump; Simcox replied by defending the workers and insisted that unionism and cooperation strengthen and supplement one another. She also suggested that the international organization of labor would help alleviate many of the workers' difficulties. In the November issue of *Fraser's Magazine* that year she published "The Organization of Unremunerative Industry," which considers the problem of structural unemployment and the plight of working mothers. Simcox acknowledges that it is difficult to object to the increasing prosperity that economic expansion has made possible, but she writes that no amount of affluence can obscure the fact that many people are continuing to suffer, especially during downturns in the economic cycle such as that which occurred in 1878, a year of severe trade depression. She notes that present schemes of charitable relief, such as those she later attacked in "Eight Years of Cooperative Shirtmaking," do nothing to meliorate conditions that bring about poverty.

Simcox identifies four "unproductive classes" in her essay—the criminal class, invalids, the "criminally idle," and those who are victims of "economic incapacity"—and she notes that this last class could be productive if opportunities were available. But she remarks that the philanthropist merely wants to hand out charity to this class, and the "rigid economist" blames the victim by accusing him of laziness. Simcox takes a broader view and claims that the existence of these victims of economic incapacity challenges prevailing economic theories and the current system of competi-

Title page for the book in which Simcox used historical analysis for the purpose of social criticism

tive industry. She claims that rational, collective efforts could aid these "victims of economic ineptitude," and she suggests how this might be done. She proposes pooling the resources of the various charity groups in order to create a kind of "job bank" for those who desire work and training. She offers two examples of needful work that "competitive industry" does not see fit to fund: the cleaning of city streets and the staffing of a "day boarding school" where children of working mothers can go after the schoolday ends and before those mothers finish work for the day. Simcox is proposing a Victorian version of "day care," and her arguments for its importance to both mothers and children sound surprisingly modern.

Just one year after publishing this essay, while Simcox was still jointly managing Hamilton and Company, she stood for election to the London School Board for the Westminster district. The board was established as a result of the Education Act of 1870 and was to administer all the schools in greater London. The election pitted the Conservatives, who wished to keep the schools under the jurisdiction of the Church of England, against the Radicals, who desired compulsory education—free from the control of the Church—for all children. Simcox stood as the Radical candidate and won the three-year term by a large majority. She worked diligently on the board, as she visited classes and talked with teachers, set and enforced school policies, and traveled throughout England to observe the workings of other school boards. Her fellow board members praised her for her rare combination of speculative and practical abilities.

Compared to the anguish she expresses in "Autobiography of a Shirtmaker" following the death of Eliot, the commemorative article that Simcox published on the novelist in the May 1881 issue of *Nineteenth Century* is subdued and understated. She discusses the love Eliot inspired in those who knew her, the crucial role that George Henry Lewes had played in encouraging Eliot's writing, and the quality of her fiction. Simcox obliquely refers to herself as one of Eliot's "worshippers" and notes that Lewes had encouraged others such as she in this devotion. But most of her essay attempts to evaluate Eliot's vision—the novelist's imaginative sympathy, her meliorism, her quasi-scientific analysis of the laws governing human life.

Simcox also asks rhetorically whether Eliot's "constant exaltation of the domestic relations" in her novels is a sign that she takes a narrow view of women's capacities and roles, whether she is "out of sympathy with any phase of social aspiration or reform." Simcox acknowledges that Eliot's sympathies "went out more readily towards enthusiasm for the discharge of duties than for the assertion of rights," which might create an impression that she had been opposed to agitation for reform, but Simcox insists that Eliot held the most advanced opinions on the subject of women. As one example of Eliot's underlying feminism, Simcox notes the novelist's gift of £100 toward the founding of Girton College, a commitment to the improvement of educational opportunities for women that was a prerequisite to future reforms.

A full year before publication of this essay on Eliot, Simcox had begun work on what became her second book, *Episodes in the Lives of Men, Women, and Lovers* (1882). Similar in some ways to Walter Pater's *Imaginary Portraits* (1887), Simcox's book began as a series of "Vignettes," five of which were published anonymously in *Fraser's*

Magazine during 1881. The eleven loosely connected fables that are collected in *Episodes* obliquely explore Simcox's love for Eliot in fictional terms. Although contemporary readers never guessed at the highly personal nature of the vignettes, one can use "Autobiography of a Shirtmaker" as a key to interpret what the tales reveal about Simcox's emotional responses to the death of Lewes in 1878, to Eliot's grieving at his death, and to Eliot's subsequent marriage to John Walter Cross in 1880.

For readers interested in Simcox's perspective on reform, only two of the vignettes—"Men Our Brothers" and the last *Episode,* "Sat est vixisse"—hold serious interest. "Men Our Brothers," which includes a dialogue between a trade union sympathizer and a plasterer, reveals Simcox's firsthand knowledge of workingmen and working conditions, and it includes a debate on the desirability of a socialist future. In "Sat est vixisse" Philo, a sixty-year-old philosopher, celebrates the efforts of those who work in obscurity to ameliorate social conditions. Clearly reflecting Simcox's low-profile work on behalf of trade unions, the cooperative movement, and educational reform, "Sat est vixisse" envisions an enlightened society achieved by "the co-operation of countless lives, disciplined each in action and forbearance, and all alike gloriously indispensable to the final triumph of the race."

Simcox's public efforts on behalf of reform continued during this and other writing projects. In 1879 she gave a series of lectures to workingmen's societies in London; in early 1880 she delivered an address titled "Common Ground" to a group of fellow Radicals. Later that year she spoke to the Democratic Club, and in 1881 she addressed the Free Thinkers of Walworth, the Hatcham Liberals, and an unnamed group who gathered to hear her discuss unfair rents. Also in 1881 she attended the London Trade Union Congress. In October 1883 she traveled to Paris for the Workmen's International Conference, where she made several well-received speeches. After returning to England she made a short speech at a suffrage meeting at St. James Hall in 1884 and then lectured on China at Toynbee Hall and delivered a paper to the Fabian Society in 1885. She attended the International Workmen's Congress held in London in November 1888 and wrote about the event for the *Manchester Guardian.* When British Trade Union leaders withdrew their support for international organizing in 1889, Simcox joined with the Socialist Trade Unionists to keep the international movement alive through writing letters in French, German, Flemish, and Dutch to socialists on the Continent. In July 1889 she attended the Paris Trade Union Congress, which split into two separate congresses as a result of infighting, and she helped organize a Miners' International Conference held the week after these two convocations.

"Women's Work and Women's Wages," published in the July 1887 issue of *Longman's Magazine,* is a reminder that Simcox's solidarity with the laboring classes was rooted in her own work experiences—and those of other working women. The essay also reveals how interrelated were Simcox's feminist, labor, and literary commitments. Noting that Walter Besant's popular novels generated sympathy for the East End poor and encouraged the social regeneration of their neighborhood, in this article she calls on readers and critics to support literature that engages rather than evades social problems—and to engage their imaginations in the service of reform:

> it takes a robust imagination like Mr. Besant's to conceive so radical a reconstruction of the social order as would be involved in halving the work and doubling the wages [of women workers]. Yet such a reconstruction is in the nature of things quite possible; and not more difficult than the complete revolution in our industrial economy affected by the introduction of the factory system.

Drawing on her experience in trade union organizing, Simcox sketches the careers of Emma Paterson and two other union activists and urges women of all classes to reform an unjust economic system by supporting the rights of their sisters to receive living wages and humane work hours and to form trade unions alongside men.

Simcox pursued all of her union activity while she was conducting her research for *Primitive Civilizations; or, Outlines of the History of Ownership in Archaic Communities,* which was the product of nearly sixteen years of intermittent effort. Simcox first recorded her intention to attempt such a work in a 16 January 1878 entry in her "Autobiography." Encouraged by the generally favorable reception of *Natural Law,* she writes that she discussed other possible book projects, including a history of property, with Eliot. By August 1878 Simcox was studying Greek in order to facilitate her research, and though the entire project was thrown in doubt when Eliot died that December, Simcox devoted much of the subsequent decade to the enormous task of research and synthesis that her approach demanded.

Although the study is confined to the period of written history, its scope is impressive. Volume one encompasses "Ownership in Egypt," "Ancient Babylonia," and "From Massalia to Malabar"; volume two surveys "Ownership in China" and also contains a lengthy conclusion drawing lessons from the social and economic history of these civilizations. These volumes analyze the influence of geography, agriculture, political structures, religious traditions, domestic arrangements, and economic circumstances, and both volumes draw from a range of contemporary scholarship. Historical reclamation is not Simcox's only aim, however.

Like John Ruskin's *The Stones of Venice* (1851–1853), *Primitive Civilizations* appropriates the past for purposes of social criticism. Just as Ruskin discovers in Gothic architecture the signs of a culture that honored the efforts of its workers in contrast to what he observes as the dehumanization of the worker in industrial England, Simcox finds that the social and economic systems of ancient Egypt and China reveal the shortcomings of contemporary English society. By showing readers that earlier, non-Western cultures often distributed wealth, power, and status more equitably than does contemporary European culture, she hoped to dispel their chauvinism and make them aware of needed reforms.

Formally dedicated to her mother, with whom Simcox lived for much of her adult life, *Primitive Civilizations* particularly addresses how social expectations and legal structures shape the lives of women and mothers. "Ownership in Egypt" contains a long chapter on marriage and domestic relations, and it notes that Egyptian marriage law established between husband and wife a fundamental equality that sharply contrasts to present English practices. Domestic relations in ancient Egypt were closely interwoven with proprietary considerations, Simcox notes, and the wife became joint ruler and mistress of the family heritage. She writes that the antagonism between love and money, which is a commonplace of domestic romance, was unknown in Egypt. In "Ownership in China" she adds that although ancient China was far more patriarchal than ancient Egypt was and granted fewer legal rights to wives than Egypt had granted, Chinese custom extended considerable status and authority to the mother. Furthermore, even in China "the legal position of the mother is higher than in Western Europe," and "primitive Chinese custom causes every lawful wife to become, on marriage, a partner in her husband's estate."

Simcox also finds less acquisitiveness, greed, and class division in ancient Egypt and China than in contemporary England. Acknowledging that ancient Chinese society was "addicted beyond all others to the avocations of industry and trade," she notes that custom and legal constraints prevented this addiction from increasing "the natural inequality of men to reflect and exaggerate itself in the inequality of their possessions." Simcox writes that such cultural influences demonstrate a potential for humane regulation of the economic order that contemporary "economists of the *a priori* school have been apt to contest." Much of her conclusion is in fact given to attacking those political economists who argue that the natural evolution of the present economic order means that it is also the necessary one.

Having demonstrated how superior certain practices and assumptions, both social and economic, were in ancient Egypt and China to those of contemporary England, Simcox urges reformative intervention:

> if the uncontrolled liberty of the swift and strong to push and jostle their neighbours in the industrial race results in the accidental overthrow and maiming of the feebler competitors, there is nothing to prevent the common sense of the majority, who are neither athletes nor cripples, from laying down rules to make the game less dangerous while leaving it still sufficiently interesting to call out the skill of the players. Energy and enterprise are not necessarily paralyzed because they are forbidden to produce suffering.

These sections of *Primitive Civilizations* reveal Simcox as a forceful critic of laissez-faire economics and a strong proponent of state-regulated industry.

By the time *Primitive Civilizations* was published in 1894, Simcox's career as an activist and writer was ending. She had continued to work on behalf of the miners' international organization until 1892, facilitating meetings between the British union and those on the Continent. But she confided in "Autobiography of a Shirtmaker" that she was becoming more and more disillusioned by the infighting within the trade union movement. She was no longer contributing to journals with any regularity, although one last essay, on the marriage rules of the Australian Aborigines, appeared in the July 1899 issue of *Nineteenth Century*. The few entries in "Autobiography of a Shirtmaker" during the last decade of her life chronicle the pain of her mother's last illness and death, her own repeated bouts with respiratory illness, and anxiety about her failing eyesight.

When Simcox died on 15 September 1901, she was buried with her mother at Aspley Guise near Bedford, far from Highgate Cemetery, where she had once hoped to lie near Eliot. Neither in life nor in death could Edith Simcox remain merely in the shadow of her "idol," even though she often expressed this desire. Her energy, eloquence, and effectiveness as an agitator for reform created a legacy of lasting significance.

Biography:

K. A. McKenzie, *Edith Simcox and George Eliot* (London: Oxford University Press, 1961; Westport, Conn.: Greenwood Press, 1978).

References:

Gillian Beer, "Middlemarch and the Woman Question," in her *George Eliot* (Bloomington: Indiana University Press, 1986), pp. 147-199;

Gordon Haight, *George Eliot: A Biography* (London: Oxford University Press, 1968);

Haight, ed., *The George Eliot Letters* (New Haven: Yale University Press, 1978), VIII: xviii-xix; IX: 190-324;

Patricia Hollis, *Women in Public 1850-1900: Documents of the Victorian Women's Movement* (London: Allen & Unwin, 1979);

Diderick Rolle-Hansen, *The Academy, 1869-1879: Intellectuals in Revolt* (Copenhagen: Rosenkilde & Bagger, 1957);

Geoffrey Tillotson, *A View of Victorian Literature* (Oxford: Oxford University Press, 1978);

Laurie Zierer, "Edith Jemima Simcox," in *Prose by Victorian Women: An Anthology,* edited by Andrea Broomfield and Sally Mitchell (London & New York: Garland, 1996), pp. 523-525.

Papers:

The Bodleian Library at Oxford University has the only known surviving Simcox manuscript, that of "Autobiography of a Shirtmaker."

Sir Leslie Stephen
(28 November 1832 – 22 February 1904)

Kathryn Harvey
University of Alberta

See also the Stephen entries in *DLB 57: Victorian Prose Writers After 1867* and *DLB 144: Nineteenth-Century British Literary Biographers.*

BOOKS: *The Poll Degree from a Third Point of View* (Cambridge & London: Macmillan, 1863);

Sketches from Cambridge (London & Cambridge: Macmillan, 1865);

The "Times" on the American War: A Historical Study, as L. S. (London: Ridgeway, 1865; New York: Abbatt, 1915);

The Playground of Europe (London: Longmans, Green, 1871; London & New York: Longmans, Green, 1894);

Essays on Freethinking and Plainspeaking (London: Longmans, Green, 1873; New York: Putnam, 1877);

Hours in a Library, three series (London: Smith, Elder, 1874–1879); first series (New York: Scribner, Armstrong, 1875); third series, enlarged edition (3 volumes, London: Smith, Elder, 1892; New York: Putnam, 1894; enlarged again, 4 volumes, New York: Putnam, 1904; London: Smith, Elder / Duckworth, 1907);

History of English Thought in the Eighteenth Century, 2 volumes (London: Smith, Elder, 1876; New York: Putnam, 1876);

Samuel Johnson (London: Macmillan, 1878; New York: Harper, 1878);

Alexander Pope (London: Macmillan, 1880; New York: Harper, 1880);

Swift (London: Macmillan, 1882; New York: Harper, 1882);

The Science of Ethics (London: Smith, Elder, 1882; New York: Putnam, 1882);

Life of Henry Fawcett (London: Smith, Elder, 1885; New York: Putnam, 1886);

An Agnostic's Apology, and Other Essays (London: Smith, Elder, 1893; New York: Putnam, 1893);

Leslie Stephen, 1860

The Life of Sir James Fitzjames Stephen, Bart., K.C.S.I., a Judge of the High Court of Justice (London: Smith, Elder, 1895; New York: Putnam, 1895);

Social Rights and Duties: Addresses to Ethical Societies, 2 volumes (London: Sonnenschein / New York: Macmillan, 1896);

Studies of a Biographer, 4 volumes (London: Duckworth, 1898–1902; New York: Putnam, 1898–1902);

The English Utilitarians, 3 volumes (London: Duckworth, 1900; New York: Putnam, 1900);

George Eliot (London: Macmillan, 1902; New York: Macmillan, 1902);

Robert Louis Stevenson: An Essay (New York & London: Putnam, 1903);

English Literature and Society in the Eighteenth Century (London: Duckworth, 1904; New York & London: Putnam, 1907);

Hobbes (New York & London: Macmillan, 1904);

Some Early Impressions (London: Leonard & Virginia Woolf at the Hogarth Press, 1924);

Men, Books, and Mountains: Essays, edited by S. O. A. Ullman (London: Hogarth Press, 1956; Minneapolis: University of Minnesota Press, 1956);

Sir Leslie Stephen's Mausoleum Book, edited by Alan Bell (Oxford: Clarendon Press, 1977).

OTHER: Hermann von Alexander Berlepsch, *The Alps; or, Sketches of Life and Nature in the Mountains,* translated by Stephen (London: Longman, Green, Longman & Roberts, 1861);

"The Allelein-Horn," in *Vacation Tourists and Notes of Travel in 1860,* edited by Francis Galton, 3 volumes (London: Macmillan, 1861-1864), I: 264-281;

"The Ascent of the Schreckhorn" and "The Eiger Joch," in *Peaks, Passes, and Glaciers,* second series, edited by E. S. Kennedy, 2 volumes (London: Longman, Green, Longman & Green, 1862), II: 3-14, 15-32;

Brighton Election Reporter, edited by Stephen, numbers 1-6 (10 February 1864-25 February 1864);

"On the Choice of Representatives by Popular Constituencies," in *Essays on Reform* (London: Macmillan, 1867), pp. 85-125;

Cornhill Magazine, edited by Stephen (April 1871 - December 1882);

"The Writings of W. M. Thackeray," in *The Works of William Makepeace Thackeray,* 24 volumes (London: Smith, Elder, 1878-1879), XXIV: 315-378;

William Kingdon Clifford, *Lectures and Essays,* edited by Stephen and Frederick Pollock, 2 volumes (London: Macmillan, 1879; London & New York: Macmillan, 1886);

The Works of Henry Fielding, Esq., edited, with a biographical essay, by Stephen, 10 volumes (London: Smith, Elder, 1882);

Samuel Richardson, *The Works of Samuel Richardson,* prefatory chapter of biographical criticism by Stephen, 12 volumes (London: Sotheran, 1883-1884);

The Dictionary of National Biography, 66 volumes, volumes 1-21 edited by Stephen; volumes 22-26 edited by Stephen and Sidney Lee; volumes 27-36 include contributions by Stephen (London: Smith, Elder, 1885-1901);

Margaret Veley, *A Marriage of Shadows, and Other Poems,* preface by Stephen (London: Smith, Elder, 1888; Philadelphia: Lippincott, 1889);

James Dykes Campbell, *Samuel Taylor Coleridge: A Narrative of the Events of His Life,* memoir of Campbell by Stephen (London: Macmillan, 1896; New York: Macmillan, 1896);

Emile Legouis, *The Early Life of William Wordsworth, 1770-1798,* prefatory note by Stephen (London: Dent, 1897);

James Payn, *The Backwater of Life; or, Essays by a Literary Veteran,* introduction by Stephen (London: Smith, Elder, 1899);

"Evolution and Religious Conceptions," in *The 19th Century: A Review of Progress* (London & New York: Putnam, 1901), pp. 370-383;

John Richard Green, *Letters,* edited by Stephen (London & New York: Macmillan, 1901);

"In Memoriam," in *George Smith: A Memoir,* by Sidney Lee (London: For private circulation, 1902);

"Robert Browning" and "Thomas Carlyle," in *Encyclopaedia Britannica,* eleventh edition, 29 volumes (Cambridge & New York: Cambridge University Press, 1910), IV: 670-674; V: 349-354.

SELECTED PERIODICAL PUBLICATIONS–
UNCOLLECTED: "Reform," *Macmillan's Magazine,* 15 (1867): 529-536;

"University Organization," *Fraser's Magazine,* 77 (1868): 135-153;

"The Political Situation in England," *North American Review,* 107 (1868): 543-567;

"Some Remarks upon Travelling in America," *Cornhill Magazine,* 19 (1869): 321-339;

"The Redundancy of Women," *Saturday Review,* 67 (1869): 545-546;

"Our Rulers–Public Opinion," *Cornhill Magazine,* 21 (1870): 288-298;

"Social Slavery," *Cornhill Magazine,* 21 (1870): 566-577;

"Athletic Sports and University Studies," *Fraser's Magazine,* new series 2 (1870): 691-704;

"The Future of University Reform," *Fraser's Magazine,* new series 4 (1871): 269-281;

"Thoughts of an Outsider: Public Schools," *Cornhill Magazine,* 27 (1873): 281-292;

"Thoughts of an Outsider: The Public Schools Again," *Cornhill Magazine,* 28 (1873): 605-615;

Minnie and Leslie Stephen soon after their marriage in June 1867

"Housekeeping," *Cornhill Magazine,* 29 (1874): 69-79;

"Thoughts of an Outsider: The Ethics of Vivisection," *Cornhill Magazine,* 33 (1876): 468-478.

Leslie Stephen was born five months after British Parliament passed the First Reform Bill extending the male franchise—an auspicious birth year for one of the eminent reform writers of the Victorian period. During his lifetime Stephen was a noted man of letters, first editor of *The Dictionary of National Biography* (from 1885 to 1891), and a passionate mountain climber. Shortly after his death in 1904 Stephen was relegated to critical obscurity; however, he has slowly regained recognition beyond that accorded him as the father of one of the twentieth century's greatest writers, Virginia Woolf. Today Stephen has become known also for his militant agnosticism and his contributions to the major religious, social, ethical, and political controversies of his day.

As a reformer he argued for the admission of Dissenters to universities and for parliamentary reform, though he opposed women's suffrage; he discoursed on British-American relations and the American Civil War, intervened in vivisection debates, and even wrote about changes in domestic service. Stephen's life may be traced through three overlapping periods: the early years (1832-1862), in which he was immersed in a family tradition of evangelicalism and gained experiences at Eton and Cambridge University that colored his later beliefs; the middle years (1850s-1875), in which he became a committed agnostic and political radical; and the later years (1870-1902), during which he turned from practical politics toward literary criticism, social theory, and the history of ideas. Noel Annan's *Leslie Stephen: The Godless Victorian* (1984), an expanded version of his *Leslie Stephen: His Thought and Character in Relation to His Time* (1951), has brought the essayist, historian, literary critic, biographer, and outdoors enthusiast back into prominence on his own account.

Stephen was born on 28 November 1832 in London, the third of four children to reach adulthood. One child, born prior to Stephen, died in infancy. His parents descended from Clapham evangelicals, followers of a sect known (like the Quakers) for their social and political engagement. His mother, Jane Catherine Venn, daughter of the Clapham rector, was a devout, good-natured woman who guided her children's early education. Her journals depict Stephen, her favorite child, as a sensitive boy with a passion for reading and painting but prone to ill health. Sir James, Stephen's father, became a colonial undersecretary largely in order to influence the development of British policy on the slave trade. He garnered from colleagues the nicknames "King Stephen" and "Mr. Over-Secretary Stephen" for his tireless work—most notably for drafting legislation to abolish slavery throughout the British Empire. From both parents Stephen learned devotion free from austerity and ostentation, and he gained an appreciation of literature and an awareness of broad social and political issues.

Stephen's delicacy became a concern in the early 1840s, so his doctor prescribed a regimen of vigorous exercise and discouraged both reading poetry (which was deemed to upset him) and associating with adults. His father therefore enrolled Stephen and his brother Fitzjames at Eton in 1842. His four years as a day student were spent in what he remembered bitterly and vividly sixty years later as an almost endless stream of psychological stress and physical bullying. Fitzjames, the stronger of the two, often had to defend his younger brother, and Stephen's public-school experiences made an indelible mark. In the *Cornhill Magazine*, thirty years after his public school days, Stephen must have recalled these experiences when he criticized "the theory that our public schools are perfect."

He refuted the widespread belief that thrashing of younger boys by older ones was a healthy disciplinary practice. "At worst," he wrote about sending boys to public school, "we say it is only for a year or two; but a child's year is equivalent to a generation with an adult.... The little victims imbibe unconsciously the peculiar code of morality which justifies their sufferings. They sympathise more with their tyrants than with themselves." Such abuses had to stop, he argued, and they would only with the help of "an amount of pressure from the outside." Ten months after this article was published, Stephen, then editor of the *Cornhill Magazine*, again discoursed on reforms in the status of the schoolmaster, a subject prompted by scandals publicized in the newspapers. He maintained in November 1873 that "The domestic influence, carefully as we endeavour to neutralize it in our system of public school education, still remains incomparably the most important" influence in the education of boys, and its importance was followed only by "The healthy influence of good masters [which] is the salt of the system." Boys should receive humane, judicious treatment and not be subjected to barbarity at the hands of schoolmates or schoolmasters.

After leaving Eton, Stephen studied under private tutors and at King's College, London, before entering Trinity College, Cambridge, in October 1850 at the age of seventeen. As an undergraduate he obtained first-class standing and a scholarship at the end of his first year, and in 1854 he was offered a fellowship. However, during this period he is remembered less for his academic achievements than for his participation in all manner of political debate and his accomplishments in athletics. His parents were originally worried that he wanted to read for an honors degree because many far healthier men barely completed the physically and intellectually demanding program. Indeed, Stephen's father had chosen to study law instead of reading for honors, and Fitzjames failed twice to obtain a Trinity scholarship, finishing with a pass degree. As if reading for honors were not enough, Stephen was also keen on holding office in the Union Debating Society. But under the advice of his tutor Isaac Todhunter, Stephen abandoned the latter ambition and contented himself with delivering only nine orations. These, his 1906 biographer Frederic William Maitland recounts, firmly established him as "a young Liberal of the fifties. He was for the ballot, for 'an extensive measure of parliamentary reform,' for the education of the people, and for 'the proposed admission of dissenters to universities.'"

In accordance with the requirements of his fellowship, Stephen, in 1855, was ordained a deacon, in spite of doubts expressed by friends and family as to the wisdom of his decision. At that time Stephen thought the idea of ordination was a good one; he wanted to spare his father the burden of supporting him, and he found university life exceedingly agreeable. Most of his memorable times arose from his participation in athletics: the once-delicate boy had transformed himself into an athletic young man with a passion for rowing, walking, and cross-country running. So he stayed at the university, and in 1859 Stephen, a presbyter fellow and tutor at Trinity, went the next step and was ordained a priest. Over the years his feats of endurance became the stuff of legends: striding along the riverbank and keeping pace with the rowers whom he coached; challenging a friend to run three miles while he walked two (Stephen won); or walking fifty miles from Cambridge to London in twelve hours to attend a dinner of the Alpine Club, of which he had become a member in 1859.

In the summer of 1862, however, Stephen realized what his sister, Caroline, had suspected all along. To say that he suffered a crisis in faith would be too strong; rather, as he put it in *Some Early Impressions* (1924), a collection republished from articles which first appeared in 1903 in the *National Review*, he slowly realized that he no longer believed in "Noah's Ark": he ceased viewing biblical events as historically veracious and found rationalist and scientific challenges to Christianity to be unanswerable. He promptly informed his dean that he could no longer conduct services; however, he did not completely sever his ties with Cambridge University until his marriage in 1867.

Although the first phase of Stephen's life may be said to have ended with this spiritual break, a second phase had really begun with his enrollment at Cambridge, which came at a time when major educational reforms were the subject of both academic and public debate. Henry Fawcett, the young radical new to Trinity Hall in 1853, soon formed a close, lasting friendship with Stephen and influenced his thinking about university reform and parliamentary politics. Fawcett,

Stephen with his second wife, Julia Duckworth Stephen, and children: Adrian Stephen (at his mother's right) and (standing) Gerald Duckworth, Virginia Stephen, Thoby Stephen, Vanessa Stephen, and George Duckworth

who became Stephen's closest friend, introduced him to the writings of John Stuart Mill and Auguste Comte, and Stephen went on to read the works of Thomas Hobbes, John Locke, George Berkeley, David Hume, Jeremy Bentham, economists Adam Smith and David Ricardo, Utilitarian historians George Grote and Thomas Buckle, and most of the important contemporary works in intellectual history. He also enjoyed reading literature—particularly William Makepeace Thackeray's works—in addition to the works required by his program. The breadth of knowledge he gained from such reading prompted Stephen to argue for broadening the university curriculum to include studies that, as he wrote in *Fraser's Magazine* (December 1870), "had more direct bearing upon the active work of life" than did reading only for narrow examinations. Much to the surprise of his colleagues, who had no idea of the scholarly diversity of the rowing coach's interests, Stephen was appointed as examiner in the newly established moral science tripos in 1861.

Stephen and Fawcett agreed on the need for university reform; they disagreed about precisely what was wrong. Fawcett strenuously opposed the establishment of the new tripos and valorized the intellectual discipline required by the competition for places in the math and classical tripos examinations; Stephen, on the other hand, favored a broad education for all students—both the tripos (honors-degree) and poll (pass-degree) students. *The Poll Degree from a Third Point of View* (1863) records his strong objections to the view, implicit in the university system's design, of poll-men as "intellectual pariahs." Stephen held no great hope that a majority of the poll-men would ever be stunning scholars; however, he was genuinely concerned that they receive decent and useful educations. His students who were poll-men, in turn, sincerely appreciated his regard for their welfare and his refusal to treat them in the condescending manner to which they had grown so accustomed. On the subject of university reform Stephen moved close to the views of radical reformers led by John Robert Seeley at Cambridge and Mark Pattison at Oxford.

In the 1870s Stephen wrote a series of articles for *Fraser's Magazine* that identified several practices that universities would do well to improve. He observed that the independent college system severely thwarted meaningful university reform, that the university did not have enough adequately paid professorships to attract good men, that honors students read too narrowly as a result of intense competition for prizes and fellowships, and that many good students were ignored for taking pass-degrees. In "Athletic Sports and University Studies" (*Fraser's Magazine,* December 1870), for example, Stephen objects to the way Wilkie Collins in *Man and Wife* (1870) represents the university athlete as a man whose "moral and intellectual nature has been atrophied." Stephen faces Collins's "onslaught" against muscular Christianity, a movement that Stephen (at least as much as Charles Kingsley) helped popularize at Cambridge. Always a great admirer of the athletic university man, Stephen argues for restoring educational balance "by elevating the intellectual standard . . . rather than depressing [students'] physical energies."

In 1856 the British government had established a commission to study university reform. Though the commission visited Trinity College in 1859, Cambridge, like other universities, continued to resist reform. Stephen's fruitless attempts to effect change within the university and his growing religious skepticism became intimately related, as Jeffrey Paul von Arx has noted: "The resistance of the universities to reform . . . became a symbol of the entrenched power of the Church, which Stephen gradually came to see as pervading English life." Since the mid 1850s Stephen had supported the removal of religious restrictions on fellowships, a position that still only a minority at Cambridge supported by 1867. Only in 1869 did dons begin to take seriously the charge that their inflexibility might, in fact, have been responsible for turning good students away, and religious tests for fellowships were finally repealed two years later.

Stephen and Fawcett were interested in reforms of voting rights and of Parliament as much as they were in reforms of the university. Early on, Stephen campaigned on behalf of Fawcett, who ran unsuccessfully for a professorship in political economy at Cambridge (1863) and for Parliament in Brighton (1864). Stephen also supported John Stuart Mill's election bid in 1865. Stephen's interest in the experiment of democracy in America informed his theorizing about a reformed British franchise. His contribution to *Essays on Reform* (1867), "On the Choice of Representatives by Popular Constituencies," published during the same year in which the Second Reform Bill passed, supported extending the vote to more working-class men and was clearly aimed at an audience that included his cousin, jurist A. V. Dicey, and fellow Alpinist James Bryce. This audience, hostile to an American-style Parliament of "ungentlemanly" men, feared the destruction of their quality of life and an overnight revolution in the composition of Parliament in England. Stephen was not in favor of the working classes "taking over" the government, nor did he believe that it was likely to happen. He challenged the appropriateness of any comparison of British and American political bodies on the grounds of the great differences in culture and in educational and political systems. He conjectured that British voters would elect responsible men from "the most highly educated classes" who would guard the interests of the whole country rather than the interests of only their own class.

Despite his desire for reforms of Parliament and the franchise, Stephen was not cheered by the passage of the Second Reform Bill—not because he entirely disapproved of the bill but because the political maneuvering "sickened" him. In the article "The Political Situation in England" in the *North American Review* (October 1868) Stephen questioned the sincerity and motivation of the Disraeli government and saw Gladstone as a "bad tactician" about whom "no one can feel quite certain of his principles." Yet the sight of such political disarray did not quell Stephen's hope that soon "a peaceful revolution" would sweep the nation and "unsettle man of the firmest foundations of the established order of things" (especially the Anglican Church); it did, however, quell his enthusiasm for and confidence in practical politics.

Stephen's interest in American politics arose not simply from the democratic experiment in the United States but also from the controversy over slavery there. Born into a family of abolitionists, he followed British press reports of struggles in the United States and aligned himself with the abolitionists in the North. Supporters of the South at Cambridge—most of whom had never set foot in America—aggravated Stephen to no end with their constant reiteration of the biased reports they read. He therefore decided to make a tour of the United States to give himself an edge. His visit in 1863, at the height of the war, put Stephen in touch with several men whom he considered close friends throughout his life: Charles Eliot Norton of Harvard University; Oliver Wendell Holmes Jr., later a Supreme Court justice; and James Russell Lowell of Cambridge, Massachusetts. He alludes to these friendships in "Some Remarks upon Travelling in America," a *Cornhill Magazine* article written on his return from a second trip to the United States and published in March 1869.

During his first trip Stephen wrote to his mother, whom he asked to forward the letters to Fawcett, voicing his opinions about politics and the Civil War. In one of these letters (21 July

Leslie Stephen and James Russell Lowell at Elmwood, Lowell's house in Cambridge, Massachusetts, summer 1890 (Harvard University Archives)

1863) on the war Stephen confided: "It matters very little what people mean now or what they meant when they began.... The North are destroying slavery, not because they are abolitionists, but because the South depends on slavery. That seems to me as plain as two and two makes four." Pursuing this bold line might easily have offended his hosts; instead, it won many new friends. In their eyes Stephen had what any good journalist should have: honesty and integrity. As he wrote in "The Duties of Authors," collected in *Social Rights and Duties: Addresses to Ethical Societies* (1896), "Till you can tell men of their faults without being suspected of spite or bad temper—till you can praise them without being suspected of unworthy flattery—you are not really in a position to be called independent." This Stephen proved to be, especially when Fawcett tried to persuade him to produce a book on the United States.

Stephen knew well that his understanding, based on little more than a five-month tour, would not adequately support a claim that he had intimate knowledge of American life or politics, so he focused on what he believed was useful to British readers—an indictment of reporting on American issues in *The Times* of London, the most widely read newspaper in England. *The "Times" on the American War: A Historical Study* (1865) argues that "human nature on both sides of the Atlantic is tolerably alike, and that in both countries angry men use strong language." However, the newspaper has a duty to rise above prejudices and present a balanced view of controversies, he writes, and Stephen has harsh words for its failings: "I contend that I have proved simultaneously that it was guilty of 'foolish vituperation,' and ... of a public crime. It was, I admit, due to gross ignorance, and not to malice; ... but I still think its conduct criminal."

Stephen published the pamphlet with only his initials to identify him as author, a decision dictated not by shame but by prudence. He received good advice warning him that a person newly embarking on a journalistic career should not incite the wrath of *The Times*. Yet even after he was an established and respected writer, Stephen produced many more unsigned articles or pieces signed with an alias such as "A Don" or "A Cynic," although he kept to beliefs he later stated in "The Duties of Authors"—that the journalist "should never say anything anonymously to which he would be ashamed to sign his name" and should not use anonymity as a license "to spin words out of mental vacuity." The press, Stephen wrote both in the *Cornhill Magazine* (March 1870) and later in "The Duties of Authors," functioned as a secular priesthood; it set out to "enlighten and encourage and purify public opinion." It therefore had a responsibility to report the "truth." His hundred-page pamphlet on *The Times* established Stephen as a leading political radical.

Believing that a career in either politics or the law was impossible because he had taken orders, Stephen put his hope in journalism. His father had died in 1859, and Stephen moved to London to live with his mother and only sister, Caroline. Fitzjames, who had already become a successful journalist, introduced Stephen to the editor of the *Saturday Review,* and Stephen soon began writing two articles a week—one a review, the other a topical essay. He continued this hectic pace throughout the 1860s, and other work came his way: he published in the newly established *Pall Mall Gazette* alongside writers such as Matthew Arnold, Anthony Trollope, Charles Kingsley, James Anthony Froude, and George Henry Lewes, and by 1866 he was writing for *The Nation* (New York) and for the *Cornhill Magazine.*

Stephen's talent was quickly recognized, and by the mid 1870s he was publishing in the *National Review, Fraser's Magazine,* the *Fortnightly Review,* the *North American Review, Macmillan's Magazine, Nineteenth Century,* and the *Contemporary Review.* He also wrote for the *Alpine Journal,* which he edited from January 1868 to May 1872 after serving his term as Alpine Club president. One publisher in particular took great interest in Stephen, and in 1871 George Smith offered him the editorship of the *Cornhill Magazine,* whose founding editor, in 1860, had been Thackeray. Stephen welcomed the opportunity. Not only had he been an admirer of Thackeray, but also of his daughter. Stephen married Harriet Marian (Minny) on 19 June 1867 and quickly whisked her off for an Alpine honeymoon.

Minny did not share his love of mountain climbing and worried while her husband went on his long excursions. Stephen, however, regarded the mountains as sublime, true monuments of nature, and of the twenty-five trips he eventually made to the Alps, many of these early adventures formed the basis of his first major work, *The Playground of Europe* (1871). These Alpine experiences also figured prominently in his boldest attack on religion, *Essays on Freethinking and Plainspeaking* (1873). Of all the essays in this latter volume, the most elegant, "A Bad Five Minutes in the Alps," clearly identifies Stephen as a committed agnostic. Unlike Benjamin Jowett, Kingsley, or Arthur Penrhyn Stanley, Stephen did not turn to the liberalism of the Broad Church movement when his Anglicanism faced serious rationalistic and scientific challenges, nor did he follow the steps of Frederick Denison Maurice, his old mentor, in retaining his belief but shunning all "parties" within the Church. Stephen gave up his faith, and "A Bad Five Minutes" provides an interesting analogue of his struggle.

The narrator, hanging precipitously from a rock face, is figuratively disinclined toward materialist, pantheist, and positivist views of life. He recognizes that he cannot hold on to such bases of belief forever, so he attempts to stabilize his footing and yet falls—only a short distance and onto firm ground. In hindsight, the narrator concludes,

> The sudden alarm produced by the slip, whilst reviving so much else, had expunged this one practically useful memory [of the ledge below] completely and instantaneously. But now, as it came back to me, I easily convinced myself not only that I had never been in danger, and thus that all my agony had been thrown away, but that I had never even done anything rash.

Minny could not share her husband's enthusiasm for mountains and did miss going to church, but this did not dampen Stephen's ardor for her. She brought Stephen out of his painfully shy manner, and he proved to be a loving father following the birth of their first child. To Oliver Wendell Holmes, Stephen wrote on 4 January 1871: "Did you ever remark what a beautiful object a small baby is? I never did before, but I see it now. As for a mother and child in the attitude of a Madonna, I can only say that the sight goes a long way to reconcile me to papists." His wife's first pregnancy had ended in a miscarriage, so when Laura, a sickly baby, was born, the Stephens doted on her. Minny's third pregnancy was even more devastating than the first: she became ill and died on 28 November 1875, Stephen's forty-third birthday. He did not celebrate his birthday again.

His eight years of security in marriage had also come with a live-in sister-in-law, Anne Isabella "Anny" Thackeray. The arrangement was surprisingly happy, and Anny proved genuinely supportive to Stephen and especially to five-year-old Laura after Minny's death. Even so, Stephen withdrew almost completely from public life. His only other main source of support came from Julia Duckworth (née Jackson), a widow and close friend who had visited the Stephens the day before Minny's death. Julia provided reasoned counsel when Stephen and Anny quarreled—over finances, over Laura's care, over Anny's marriage to Richmond Ritchie. (Stephen objected to her marrying a man approximately seventeen years her junior, and a second cousin at that.) Stephen began to rely on Julia's good sense and slowly realized that he had fallen in love. He proposed in April 1877, but she refused him, asking that they simply remain friends. She finally relented, and they married on 26 March 1878. Julia, who had three children when she married Stephen, provided an anchor for Stephen's life, both domestically and ideologically. She shared her husband's agnosticism just as she shared his views on women's proper role in society.

In an article in the *Saturday Review* on 24 April 1869 Stephen had argued that the "considerable excess of unmarried women" in England was "certain to produce some very serious evils." The expansion of women's social roles was one of these evils, and he attributed this expansion of roles to the "simple fact that the supply of the female sex greatly exceeds the demand." Although he believed that a gradual evolution of the structure and values of society was inevitable, he was not enthusiastic at the prospect of women acquiring new roles. Women, he argued in the *Cornhill Magazine* in January 1874, should not put "all the[ir] freed energy to purely selfish purposes" in aiming to become "lawyers, physicians, and professors." Instead they should increase their charity work.

Women's agitation for the right to enter professions was not the only "great evil" that Stephen and his second wife opposed. They also objected to women's suffrage: women, they argued, did not have the benefit of a proper education and were hardly in a position to make informed voting decisions. Stephen was also afraid that the inclination of women toward religion would make it even more difficult to diminish the influence of the Church of England on British politics and education. According to biographer/critic Noel Annan, Stephen became infuriated after hearing friends agree over dinner that women should be given the vote. One witness, C. B. Clarke, recalled Stephen's response: "it makes one wild to listen to you fellows drivelling radicalism.... To give women votes—why, it might save the Church of England for a quarter of a century."

In the 1870s Stephen's interest in the rough-and-tumble of politics waned, and his interests turned to the history of ideas. Yet at least twice in the 1880s Stephen offered public support to two men whom he believed had been unjustly treated, even persecuted, because of their atheism—Charles Bradlaugh, who tried to take his seat in the House of Commons in 1880, and G. W. Foote, editor of the *Freethinker,* who was imprisoned in 1883 for blasphemy.

Stephen's transition from a political radical to a historian, literary critic, and biographer marks the final phase of his career, a phase distinguished by the publication of his monumental *History of English Thought in the Eighteenth Century* (1876) a year after the death of Minny Stephen. In spite of its mistakes and omissions this work has remained a classic, and it is Stephen's most important contribution to intellectual history. Influenced by the works of Comte, Buckle, William Edward Hartpole Lecky, and Charles Darwin, Stephen's book placed great faith in "the

Stephen in 1902

intellectual activity of the acuter intellects." Such revolutionaries, "however feeble may be [their] immediate influence," he claimed, helped usher in "periods of moral earthquakes, which destroy the existing order." Three of these revolutionaries, Stephen believed, were Hume, "by far the greatest interpreter" of his age; Adam Smith, the economist whose social theories Stephen invoked to justify the divisions of labor and social class; and Bishop Joseph Butler, whom Stephen admired for his belief that conscience is the best antidote for world evil.

The ink had barely dried on Stephen's two-volume *History of English Thought* before he began writing what became *The Science of Ethics* (1882), which he considered to be his finest work. Few critics then or now have shared his opinion. This work presents Stephen's thesis that the family is the basis of the moral health of society, but Annan calls the book "worthless as ethics" and notes that even as sociology its scientific claims lack empirical evidence. Stephen's synthesis of the ideas of Comte, Darwin, and the utilitarians is not a satisfactory one, as critics from Henry Sidgwick and George Edward Moore to Annan and John Bicknell have noted.

In 1882 Stephen's daughter Virginia was born, and he began his editorship of *The Dictionary of National Biography* (1885-1901). George Smith saw that sales figures for his *Cornhill Magazine* had dropped by almost 50 percent, to a total of about twelve thousand copies since Stephen had become its editor in 1871. The decline resulted partly from the appearance of other, more-radical journals, but Smith and Stephen agreed that the magazine would benefit from a new editorial perspective, and Smith put him at the helm of the massive *Dictionary of National Biography* (DNB) project. Stephen was kept busy—too busy—in the 1870s and 1880s. He had no sooner finished collecting his literary criticism from the *Cornhill Magazine* in his three-series *Hours in a Library* (1874-1879) and writing *Samuel Johnson* (1878), *Alexander Pope* (1880), and *Swift* (1882) than he accepted the DNB editorship as well as a request from Fawcett's widow to write the *Life of Henry Fawcett* (1885). In all this time Stephen took barely a moment's rest.

His wife recognized how greatly Stephen was suffering from mounting pressures; so did his doctor. In 1887 Stephen took his prescribed short rest in the Alps. His health continued to deteriorate from overwork (just as his father's had at the end of his life), and he almost never got a full night's sleep. In 1889 mounting pressures on the sixty-six-year-old Stephen resulted in two attacks of nervous exhaustion. After another Alpine rest in the winter of 1890 he caught influenza and finally gave in to the persistent pleas of Julia and his doctors to retire.

Yet this did not mean that he stopped writing. In fact most of the articles that he contributed to the DNB were composed after his "retirement." He was also reworking previously published essays from the *Fortnightly Review, Nineteenth Century,* and the *North American Review* for publication as *An Agnostic's Apology, and Other Essays* (1893); preparing *The Life of Sir James Fitzjames Stephen, Bart., K.C.S.I., a Judge of the High Court of Justice* (1895), a biography of his brother; and compiling, by request, his lectures to the Ethical Societies of London for publication as the two-volume *Social Rights and Duties: Addresses to Ethical Societies* (1896). Although Stephen may not have thought highly of these lectures, they contain the historically interesting essays "Social Equality" and "The Duties of Authors." His four-volume *Studies of a Biographer,* containing articles collected from the *National Review,* was published between 1898 and 1902.

The publication of the four volumes in this series was interrupted in 1900 by that of *The English Utilitarians,* Stephen's sequel to *History of English Thought in the Eighteenth Century.* This three-volume overview of British Utilitarians was published by Duckworth and Company, the new publishing house of his stepson, Gerald. These two series, Phyllis Grosskurth notes, "are still regarded as unexcelled in their field." Stephen had been thinking about the idea for *The English Utilitarians* for about eighteen years, and it took eight years to complete because, as Maitland explains, "it was always being pushed aside by disaster, by sickness, or by the loss of friends whose lives were at once to be written." In addition to the full biographies Stephen wrote he contributed obituary notes for many friends, such as James Payn, George Smith, and Sidgwick.

Most distracting of all was his wife's impending death from rheumatic fever in 1895, after her resistance was lowered by a spell of influenza. After the death of his first wife Stephen had withdrawn almost completely from society and had plunged into his work. Julia had provided his lifeline back to the world; she had been able to mitigate the effects of Stephen's hot temper, had consoled him in his loss and set him back on course. Stella, Stephen's stepdaughter, felt duty-bound to provide what comfort and stability she could following Julia's death, but her own marriage in 1897 and her early death in July that year removed another of Stephen's emotional crutches. To Vanessa, the eldest of Stephen's daughters, fell the thankless task of maintaining the household and seeing that finances were always in order so that her father would not have one of his familiar tantrums. Even before Julia died, finances plagued Stephen's thoughts to the extent that many times he was convinced the family would plunge into economic ruin.

As harsh and unpredictable as Stephen was at times, he cared deeply about his children—in particular about the education of his sons and his daughters. Thoby and Adrian were sent off to Cambridge University; Vanessa received the artistic training she desired; and Virginia was tutored by Clara Pater and Janet Case and allowed free use of her father's library. Shortly after Julia's death Stephen began a book for his children that recorded his life with their mother, and the book included another story as well. Dubbed the "Mausoleum Book" by Stephen's children for its concluding chronology of friends' deaths, this work played a sad strain: it constantly reminded Stephen how many old friends were gone. Yet he was also forming new friendships with people such as Alice Green, widow of historian John Richard Green, whose letters Stephen edited in 1901; Mrs. Humphry Ward, whose Christian preaching Stephen overlooked because of her kindness; and Maitland, who became Stephen's biographer.

In the last twenty years before Stephen's death, honors poured in, and these helped rebuild his confidence: he received honorary doctorates from universities at Edinburgh, Harvard, Cambridge, and Oxford (1885, 1890, 1892, 1901) and was elected president of the London Library following Alfred Tennyson's tenure. Stephen was also offered, and gladly accepted, the 1903 Ford Lectureship at Oxford. However, he was too weak to deliver the lectures, so his nephew Herbert Fisher read them. Shortly before Stephen died, he was given a copy of these lectures, which were published as *English Literature and Society in the Eighteenth Century* (1904).

This highly praised work incorporated his wide reading in philosophy and history and his concern with politics, society, and literary analysis, and his sociological approach was a new departure in literary criticism. As Stephen was finishing his work on these lectures, word arrived that he was to be knighted—predominantly for his service to the nation as editor of the DNB series. His characteristic modesty made him hesitate in deciding whether to accept, but his family insisted, and in February 1903 he became a Knight-Commander of the Order of Bath (KCB).

As Stephen's health rendered him too weak to write, he turned heartily to reading. Works by François-René de Chateaubriand, Harriet Martineau, Walter Pater, Fyodor Dostoyevsky, and Emile Zola were among those that Stephen requested from the London Library shortly before his death. In his final weeks he wrote many letters to friends and received visits from friends, and he receiver well-wishers until the day before he died.

His doctors expected he would not live past Christmastime; however, Stephen clung tenaciously to life until 21 February 1904. After seeing a visitor that day, "his mind," Maitland records, "began to wander." Stephen passed a restful night but lapsed into a coma early the next morning. With his family by his side, he died without awakening early on 22 February. His funeral was held two days later in Golder's Green, and for his service the Anglican funeral rites were revised to include the beatitudes in place of the traditional passage from Saint Paul's first letter to the Corinthians.

Stephen's place in the annals of British reform writing is not to be underestimated. He made his suggestions about university reforms at least twenty years too early for them to receive proper consideration. His hopes for reforms of Parliament and of the franchise revealed his desire for politicians to be more honest and sincere, less concerned with their own vested interests and more concerned about governing fairly. As Annan has observed of Stephen's character, "If in his early middle age [Stephen] was somewhat too fierce a radical and too sardonic and silent in manner, his achievements and character changed men's opinion of him and he ended revered by many and respected by all his peers." He did not believe that one could make a clean break with the established order of society, nor did he believe that all change was progress: he could not countenance a society in which women could serve in public affairs as freely as men could. But he was consistent. What Stephen said of revolutionaries in the introduction to his magnum opus, *History of English Thought in the Eighteenth Century,* might be said of him: "even . . . the most vehement reformers generally retain more than they know of the old spirit."

Biography:

Frederic William Maitland, *The Life and Letters of Leslie Stephen* (London: Duckworth, 1906).

References:

Noel Annan, *Leslie Stephen: The Godless Victorian* (New York: Random House, 1984);

Annan, *Leslie Stephen: His Thought and Character in Relation to His Time* (London: MacGibbon & Kee, 1951);

Jeffrey Paul von Arx, "Leslie Stephen: Inventing the Progressive Tradition," in his *Progress and Pessimism: Religion, Politics, and History in Late Nineteenth-Century Britain* (Cambridge, Mass.: Harvard University Press, 1987), pp. 11–63;

Quentin Bell, "The Mausoleum Book," *Review of English Literature,* 6 (1965): 9–18;

Bell, *Virginia Woolf,* volume 1 (London: Triad/Paladin, 1976), pp. 1–21;

John W. Bicknell, "Leslie Stephen as an Intellectual Historian," dissertation, Cornell University, 1950;

Bicknell, "Leslie Stephen's *English Thought in the Eighteenth Century*: A Tract for the Times," *Victorian Studies,* 6 (1962): 103–120;

Bicknell, "Mr. Ramsey Was Young Once," in *Virginia Woolf and Bloomsbury: A Centenary Celebration,* edited by Jane Marcus (Bloomington: Indiana University Press, 1987), pp. 52–67;

Bicknell, "The Unbelievers, V: Leslie Stephen," in *Victorian Prose: A Guide to Research,* edited by David J. DeLaura (New York: Modern Language Association, 1973), pp. 516–527;

Ronald William Clark, *The Victorian Mountaineers* (London: Batsford, 1953);

Phyllis Grosskurth, *Leslie Stephen* (Harlow, Essex: Longmans, Green, 1968);

Katherine Hill, "Virginia Woolf and Leslie Stephen: History and Revolution," *PMLA*, 96 (1981): 351-362;

Virginia Hyman, "Concealment and Disclosure in Sir Leslie Stephen's *Mausoleum Book*," *Biography*, 3 (1980): 121-131;

Hyman, "Reflections in the Looking Glass: Leslie Stephen and Virginia Woolf," *Journal of Modern Literature*, 10 (1983): 197-216;

Desmond MacCarthy, *Leslie Stephen* (Cambridge: Cambridge University Press, 1937);

Oscar Maurer, "Leslie Stephen and the *Cornhill Magazine*," *University of Texas Studies in English*, 32 (1953): 67-95;

Harold Orel, *Victorian Literary Critics: George Henry Lewes, Walter Bagehot, Richard Holt Hutton, Leslie Stephen, Andrew Lang, George Saintsbury, and Edmund Gosse* (New York: St. Martin's Press, 1984);

Mark Allen Reger, *Leslie Stephen and the Victorian Crisis of Faith*, dissertation, University of Missouri, 1989;

S. P. Rosenbaum, "An Educated Man's Daughter: Leslie Stephen, Virginia Woolf and the Bloomsbury Group," in *Virginia Woolf: New Critical Essays*, edited by Patricia Clements and Isobel Grundy (Totowa, N.J.: Barnes & Noble, 1983), pp. 32-56;

Barbara Ann Schmidt, "In the Shadow of Thackeray: Leslie Stephen as the Editor of the *Cornhill Magazine*," in *Innovators and Preachers: The Role of Editor in Victorian England*, edited by Joel Wiener (Westport, Conn.: Greenwood Press, 1985), pp. 77-96;

John Dover Wilson, *Leslie Stephen and Matthew Arnold as Critics of Wordsworth* (Cambridge: Cambridge University Press, 1939);

Virginia Woolf, "Leslie Stephen, the Philosopher at Home," in her *The Captain's Deathbed and Other Essays* (New York: Harcourt, Brace, 1950);

Woolf, "Reminiscences" and "A Sketch of the Past," in her *Moments of Being*, edited by Jeanne Schulkind (London: Chatto & Windus for Sussex University Press, 1976), pp. 28-59, 64-131;

David Zinck, *Leslie Stephen* (New York: Twayne, 1972).

Papers:

The major repositories holding Stephen's letters are the Houghton Library, Harvard University; Perkins Library, Duke University; Henry W. and Albert Berg Collection, New York Public Library; National Library of Scotland; J. Pierpont Morgan Library, New York; Bodleian Library, Oxford; Brotherton Library, University of Leeds; and Macmillan Archives, British Library. Forty manuscripts of articles by Stephen for the *Cornhill Magazine* are held by the Perkins Library at Duke University; the manuscript of *History of English Thought in the Eighteenth Century* is held by the J. Pierpont Morgan Library; the manuscript of *The Science of Ethics* is held by the Berg Collection; the first draft and a bound manuscript of *Sir Leslie Stephen's Mausoleum Book*, as well as a "Book of Extracts" from letters that Stephen and Julia Duckworth wrote before their marriage, and a "Calendar of Correspondence" by Stephen are held by the British Library. Rose Memorial Library, Drew University, holds two of Stephen's reading notebooks and the draft of an unfinished and unpublished philosophical treatise.

Hesba Stretton
(Sarah Smith)
(27 July 1832 - 8 October 1911)

Patricia Demers
University of Alberta

See also the Stretton entry in *DLB 163: British Children's Writers, 1800–1880.*

BOOKS: *Fern's Hollow* (London: Religious Tract Society, 1864);

Enoch Roden's Training (London: Religious Tract Society, 1865);

The Children of Cloverley (London: Religious Tract Society, 1865);

The Fishers of Derby Haven (London: Religious Tract Society, 1866); republished as *Peter Killip's King; or, The Fishers of Derby Haven* (Boston: Bradley, 1880?);

The Clives of Burcot: A Novel (3 volumes, London: Tinsley, 1867 [i.e., 1866]; 1 volume, London & New York: Routledge, 1867);

Jessica's First Prayer (London: Religious Tract Society, 1867; Boston: Hoyt, 1867);

Paul's Courtship: A Novel, 3 volumes (London: Wood, 1867);

Pilgrim Street: A Story of Manchester Life (London: Religious Tract Society, 1867; Philadelphia: American Sunday-School Union, 1883);

Little Meg's Children (London: Religious Tract Society, 1868?; Boston: Hoyt, 1869?);

Alone in London (London: Religious Tract Society, 1869; New York: American Tract Society, 1869);

David Lloyd's Last Will (2 volumes, London, 1869; anonymous, 1 volume, New York: Dodd, Mead, 188–?);

Nelly's Dark Days (Glasgow: Scottish Temperance League, 1870; New York: Dodd & Mead, 1870);

Max Krömer: A Story of the Siege of Strasbourg, anonymous (London: Religious Tract Society, 1871; New York: Dodd & Mead, 1871);

Bede's Charity (London: Religious Tract Society, 1872; New York: Dodd & Mead, 1872);

The Doctor's Dilemma: A Novel, 3 volumes (London & Edinburgh, 1872; New York: Appleton, 1872);

Hesba Stretton in the 1890s

Ally Transome; or, Faithful in Little (New York: Dodd & Mead, 1873);

The King's Servants (London: King, 1873; New York: Dodd & Mead, 1873?);

Hester Morley's Promise, 3 volumes (London: H. S. King, 1873; New York: Dodd & Mead, 1873);

Lost Gip (London: Religious Tract Society, 1873; New York: Dodd & Mead, 1873?);

Michel Lorio's Cross (London: H. S. King, 1873; New York: Dodd & Mead, 1873);

Cassy (London: Religious Tract Society, 1874; New York: Dodd & Mead, 1874);

Brought Home (Edinburgh: Scottish Temperance League, 1875; New York: Dodd & Mead, 1875);

No Work, No Bread!, as H. Smith (London: Religious Tract Society, 1875);

The Wonderful Life (London: Religious Tract Society, 1875; New York: Dodd & Mead, 1875); republished as *The Life of Christ; or, The Wonderful Life* (Chicago & Philadelphia: Monarch, 1895); republished as *The Wonderful Story of Christ and His Apostles* (Philadelphia & Chicago: Winston, 1896); republished as *The Wonderful Life of Christ* (London: Religious Tract Society, 1899); republished as *The Story of Jesus and the Lives of His Apostles,* anonymous (Philadelphia: World Bible House, 1902); republished as *The Teachings of Jesus and the Lives of His Apostles* (Philadelphia, 1902); republished as *The Beautiful Story of Jesus and the Lives of His Apostles* (Philadelphia: World Bible House, 1906);

The Crew of the Dolphin (London: King, 1876; New York: Dodd, Mead, 1876);

Friends till Death (London, 1876);

Old Transome (London: Religious Tract Society, 1876);

The Storm of Life (London: Religious Tract Society, 1876);

Two Christmas Stories: Sam Franklin's Savings-Bank; A Miserable Christmas and a Happy New Year (London: King, 1876);

The Worth of a Baby, and How Apple-Tree Court Was Won (London: Religious Tract Society, 1876);

A Man of His Word (London: Religious Tract Society, 1878);

Through a Needle's Eye (New York: Dodd, Mead, 1878; 2 volumes, London: Paul, 1879);

A Thorny Path (London: Religious Tract Society, 1879; New York: American Tract Society, 1879);

A Night and a Day (London: Religious Tract Society, 1879);

"Facts on a Thread of Fiction": In Prison and Out (London: Isbister, 1880 [i.e., 1879]); republished as *In Prison and Out* (New York: Dodd, Mead, 1879; London: Religious Tract Society, 1906);

Cobwebs and Cables (London: Religious Tract Society, 1881; New York: Dodd, Mead, 1881);

"No Place Like Home" (London: Religious Tract Society, 1881);

Two Secrets and A Man of His Word (London: Religious Tract Society, 1882);

Under the Old Roof (London: Religious Tract Society, 1882);

The Lord's Purse-Bearers (Boston: Lothrop, 1882; London: Nisbet, 1883);

Carola (London: Religious Tract Society, 1884; New York: Dodd, Mead, 1874);

The Sweet Story of Old: A Sunday Book for the Little Ones, as Sarah Smith (London: Religious Tract Society, 1884);

A Green Bay Tree (London, 1887);

Her Only Son (Glasgow: Scottish Temperance League, 1887; New York: Dodd, Mead, 1887);

The Ray of Sunlight; or, Jack Sanford's Resolve, and Other Readings for Working Men's Homes, by Stretton and others (London: Religious Tract Society, 1887);

The Christmas Child (London: Religious Tract Society, 1888; New York: Crowell, 1909);

Only a Dog: A Story (London: Religious Tract Society, 1888);

Papers on the Parables (London: Religious Tract Society, 1888);

Sam Franklin's Savings Bank (London: Religious Tract Society, 1888);

An Acrobat's Girlhood (London: SPCK, 1889);

Mrs. Burton's Best Bedroom, and Other Stories (London: Religious Tract Society, 188-?);

Half Brothers (London: Religious Tract Society, 1892; New York: Cassell, 1892);

The Highway of Sorrow at the Close of the Nineteenth Century, by Stretton and Sergei Mikhailovich Kravchinski (London: Cassell, 1894; New York: Dodd, Mead, 1894);

Paul Rodents, by Stretton and Sergius Stepniak (London: Cassell, 1894);

In the Hollow of His Hand: A Story of the Stundists (London: Religious Tract Society, 1897);

Jessica's Mother (Philadelphia: Altemus, 1898; London: Religious Tract Society, 1904);

The Soul of Honour (London: Isbister, 1898);

The Parables of Our Lord (London: Religious Tract Society, 1903);

Left Alone, and Other Stories (London: Religious Tract Society, 1905).

OTHER: Thomas John Barnardo, *Children Reclaimed for Life: The Story of Dr. Barnardo's Work in London,* introduction by Stretton (London: Hodder & Stoughton, 1875);

Good Words from the Apocrypha, selected and arranged by Stretton and H. L. Synnot (London: Skeffington, 1903);

Thoughts on Old Age: Good Words from Many Minds, edited by Stretton (London: Religious Tract Society, 1906).

In 1911 *The Sunday at Home* eulogized Sarah Smith, who had used the name Hesba Stretton, for much of her "long, happy, useful and noble life." It

Illustration from The Fishers of Derby Haven *(1866)*

was fitting that this tribute appeared in the periodical that in 1866 had published "Jessica's First Prayer," the work that was subsequently published in book form in 1867, translated into Braille and fifteen European and Asiatic languages, depicted on colored slides for Band of Hope temperance programs, and placed in all Russian schools by order of Czar Alexander II. This memoir left the impression that Smith had led a placid, tranquil life, but in fact she was no plaster saint.

The third daughter of Benjamin Smith, a printer, bookseller, and the first postmaster of Wellington, Shropshire, and Anne Bakewell Smith, a strict and notably intelligent Methodist, Sarah Smith was a best-selling Religious Tract Society author whose pseudonym became a byword for Evangelical fiction for children and the newly literate. She was a strong-willed businesswoman in Paternoster Row, a reformer-activist who was one of the founding members of the National Society for the Prevention of Cruelty to Children and who associated with Angela Burdett-Coutts, Dr. Thomas J. Barnardo, Octavia Hill, and Henrietta Synnot. A Christian Dissenter at heart, Smith was expert at crafting spare, engaging, and accurately detailed stories of neglected street arabs, slum children, and servant girls whose scavenging for food, shelter, and security leads them to an unconventional knowledge of grace and heaven. In her writing she exposed the hypocrisy of mercantile plutocrats and purse-proud churchgoers of all denominations. She also wrote dramatic, often sensational short fiction in various periodicals and triple-decker novels about the trials of courtship, inheritances, and loveless marriages. She was sympathetic and acerbic, a tart and censorious yet effective champion of reform. She literally translated into action the directive of the Reverend Alexander Maclaren, one of the few preachers of whom she approved, who enjoined his followers to pursue the "Christian duty of vigorous protest."

At the age of twenty-six Smith began her career as a journalist, using the pseudonym Hesba Stretton, which she derived from the initials of her name and the names of her siblings—Hannah, Elizabeth, Sarah, Benjamin, and Anna—and from the Shropshire village of All Stretton, where her younger sister, Anna, was bequeathed property. Smith and Elizabeth, her older sister who became her constant companion, attended the Old Hall, a girls' day school in Wellington, but they gained most of their education from the books in their father's shop. Both qualified as governesses, and neither of them married.

In March 1859 Charles Dickens, editor of *Household Words,* published Stretton's first story, "The Lucky Leg," a bizarre tale of a widower who proposes to women with wooden legs. She was invited to contribute "The Ghost in the Clock Room" to the first Christmas number of *All the Year Round* in 1859, and her Christmas contributions were successful again in 1864, 1865, and 1866. Although Dickens did not accept all of Stretton's submissions and never met her, he was unfailingly helpful and encouraging. "The Postmaster's Daughter," "A Provincial Post Office," and "The Travelling Post-Office" reflect many of her own and her family's experiences. Stretton published stories, from the authentic and factual to the lurid and romantic, in *Chambers's Edinburgh Journal, The Welcome Guest, Temple Bar, Tinsley's Magazine,* and Charles Woods's *Argosy.*

Her logbooks—records of her continental travels (mainly in France and Switzerland), frequent moves in Manchester and London, and dealings with publishers from 1859 to 1871–1872—and journals for 1875 and 1884–1896 show Stretton to have been prickly in negotiations about payment, fully aware of her own worth, impatient with servants, and driven by the detection of "BUGS" from one lodging house to another. (One entry for 11 September 1865 records that "Bugs had a glorious time in the cracks all around: they were not to be defeated.") She writes that she likes "simple countrified pleasures" and "detests London," and she is disappointed with the "awful state of all the churches." Ronald Webb writes in his manuscript "Notes Regarding the Life of Hesba Stretton" that "My great aunt Sarah *was* rather pernickety, & demanded *much* more from frail humans than one can possibly get" (MS 6891v.f., Shropshire Records and Research Unit).

In September 1863 Stretton and Elizabeth left home for Manchester, where Elizabeth worked as a governess until 1870 and Stretton published a stream of children's books drawing on family histories and experiences. *Fern's Hollow* (1864) deals with the enclosure movement (the fencing of common land, thereby converting it to private property and forcing farming people into urban settings) and the standards of mining safety that were being flouted in areas surrounding Shropshire; *Enoch Roden's Training* (1865) deals with printing apprentices; and *The Children of Cloverley* (1865) concerns two children sent to England from their farm on the shores of Lake Huron while their father serves in the American Civil War. Stretton's brother, Benjamin, had run away from home at age seventeen and had immigrated to Canada, married in Edmonton, and raised a family in southern Ontario before moving to Kansas.

The huge success that launched Stretton's long writing career with the Religious Tract Society was *Jessica's First Prayer* (1867), a novel about a London waif neglected by her mother, a drunken actress. "No man could have composed a page of it," declared Anthony Ashley Cooper, seventh Earl of Shaftesbury, in praising the "simplicity, pathos and depth of Christian feeling" in the story. Jessica reveals the prejudice of the Methodist congregation that initially shuns her and the miserliness of the coffee-stall keeper who eventually adopts her. Sailors who read the novel were reduced to tears, and its "pathetic simplicity" made E. Nesbit's "throat go lumpy."

Stretton takes pains to convey the dehumanizing nature of Jessica's existence in "a single room . . . over the stable of an old inn," a room accessible only by "a wooden ladder whose rungs were crazy and broken" and consisting of "only a litter of straw for the bedding, and a few bricks and boards for the furniture." Stretton comments on the desolation of goods and spirit there: "Everything that could be pawned had disappeared long ago, and Jessica's mother often lamented that she could not thus dispose of her child." Notwithstanding the congregation's phariseism, Stretton is also explicit about the haven the church affords

Illustration from Alone in London *(1869)*

her "drudge and errand girl" as early as Jessica's first visit there: "Thinking sadly of the light, and warmth, and music that were within the closed doors, she stepped into the cold and darkness of the streets, and loitered homewards with a heavy heart."

Stretton's firsthand observations make her pictures of slum poverty accurate and compelling. *Little Meg's Children* (1868?), set in a dismal yard in East London, features a ten-year-old coping with abandonment, destitution, the deaths of her mother and an infant sibling, and teenage prostitution. Through Meg's faith in the Bible and some narrative twists the story also presents reconciliation and reformation. Stretton makes this precocious, stunted, and impoverished child a credible, ingenuous character whose grim surroundings in "Angel Court," a setting based on Stretton's visit to "Cherubim Court," an East London alley, are immediate and palpable. In "Three Hours with the Boys' Beadle" Stretton remarks on the irony of the name of this place, where "there was a flagged pavement thick with old mud . . . and about it were

Illustration from The Doctor's Dilemma *(1872)*

crawling half-naked children of all ages and sizes . . . while their drunken mothers lolled in the doorways, or upon the window-sills, gossiping and quarelling." A meliorist who deliberately throws "a cloak over her father's faults," Meg silences her brother's reference to their father's wickedness "when he's drunk," but her trust in Providence and her ignorance of sex make her a genuine innocent. When Kitty, the teenage prostitute whom Meg has befriended, intervenes to help Meg bargain with the pawnbroker (one of Kitty's clients), Stretton allows the vulnerable and the knowing to complement one another. Without sermons or metaphors, the girls' candid exchanges reverberate with innuendo.

The crowded industrial slums of London and Manchester were not Stretton's only sources of inspiration. As she explains in the preface to *Max Krömer: A Story of the Siege of Strasbourg* (1871), this novel was prompted by her experiences while returning from Switzerland at the time of the siege of Strasbourg, when she saw "how children were involved in the keen suffering of the war." The adolescent boy-narrator who, with his sister, is sent from London to live with their paternal grandmother while their explorer-father is busy in Africa, arrives in the old walled city shortly before the German siege. The contrast between the opening descriptions of the beauty of Strasbourg and the surrounding countryside and the war-torn remnants frames Max's account. Two of Madame Krömer's lodgers are killed, and the narrator notes "an agony of grief and terror such as [he] had never felt before." The model on whom Max draws to hint at the indescribable bombardment is the prophet Zephaniah: "That day is a day of wrath, a day of clouds and thick darkness, a day of the trumpet and alarm against the fenced cities and against the high towers." His exegesis reinforces Stretton's antiwar stance: "If the old prophet could only come back again, and if the words had been put into his lips, he might have so told it, that people hearing of it, who had never seen the horrors or felt the terrors, would have vowed, with a solemn vow, that there should be no war like that again in a Christian country."

Stretton underscored the often tragic truthfulness of her child characters, usually waifs or orphans. In *The Fishers of Derby Haven* (1866) Peter merits only flogging for his honesty; the heroic Tom Haslam in *Pilgrim Street: A Story of Manchester Life* (1867) dies while rescuing his father, an abusive convict trapped in the fire that the reprobate himself has set; and the unreclaimed, unchurched Tony in *Alone in London* (1869) tries to get Dolly, a dying child, admitted to an overcrowded hospital. Stretton's adult characters also argue forcibly for the maligned child. In *In Prison and Out* (1879) the counsel appointed to defend the wrongly accused David Fell addresses both the jury and the middle-class reader:

> Would you send those thoughtless, passionate lads of yours, who are to come after you in life, as citizens standing in the places you win for them, would you send them for such crimes as David Fell committed, begging for his dying mother and defending her good name, to the black shadow of a gaol, and the deep brand of imprisonment? Would you bind your boys hand and foot, and cast them into a gulf, and if they crawled out of it, crush them down again because they brought with them the mire and clay of the pit? Yet this is what we do with our juvenile criminals.

Stretton's fiction for the young was succinct and focused, always hitting hard at social issues such as alcoholism and parental neglect (*Nelly's Dark Days*, 1870; *Lost Gip*, 1873; and *Brought Home*, 1875), streetwalkers and rescue missions (*The King's Servants*, 1873), the abuse of domestics (*Cassy*, 1874), and the starving of children to make them effective beggars (*The Lord's Purse-Bearers*, 1882).

Her three-volume novels for adult readers also display her detailed accuracy in presenting locale and dialect and add, as in *The Doctor's Dilemma* (1872), sentimental conflicts between love and duty along with factual explanations of the legal rights of a wife—in advance of the passage of the Married Woman's Property Act. As a detective mystery and the story of a protracted affair, the novel uses the alternate narration of Oliva, a young runaway wife, and Martin Dobrée, a doctor, in moving from scenes in London and the Channel Islands to France. Stretton's characters have a nobility that transcends mere letter-of-the-law observance. When Olivia finds refuge in a small French village, the curé does not throw any barriers between Protestant and Catholic but welcomes her and the child with whom she has fled "as if they were good Catholics." Olivia risks her life in agreeing to nurse her dying, fever-racked husband, the man who has tormented and hounded her. The twentieth-century reader finds that the coincidences and convenient deaths of characters in the complex plots of Stretton's entangled adult novels stretch one's patience.

Stretton was a champion of causes free of narrow or restrictive denominational affiliations. In her belief system practical considerations such as food, shelter, and emotional warmth not only guided faith but took precedence over any allegiance to denomination or creed. With the Reverend Banjamin Waugh, editor of the *Sunday Magazine*, she lobbied for the establishment of the National Society for the Prevention of Cruelty to Children in 1884 and served on its executive board for a decade before she resigned because of the society's financial mismanagement. She also collected more than £900 and wrote books to support the cause of Russian Evangelicals (Stundists) who were famine victims in the early 1890s.

At the age of sixty in 1892 Stretton settled with Elizabeth in their first permanent residence, Ivycroft on Ham Common, Richmond-on-Thames, where they founded a branch of the Popular Book Club to circulate good books among the working classes. The two spent their last nineteen years living together here, Stretton dying eight months after her sister.

Stretton's career and immense productivity illuminate the development of nineteenth-century Evangelical and print culture. Questions remain about her ease with like-minded women activists and her pugnacity with publishers, even the likable William Henry Wills of *All the Year Round* and Edmund Routledge. Although Stretton was really not "the Evangelical dove" that Margaret Maison presents, Stretton's stories provide an immediate visceral reality that allows her, as Robert Lee Wolff notes, to strike "a new note in Evangelical fiction" and to be, as Margaret Cutt describes her, "a genuine social reformer."

References:

Jacqueline Banerjee, *Through the Northern Gate: Childhood and Growing Up in British Fiction, 1719–1901* (New York: Peter Lang, 1996);

J. S. Bratton, "Hesba Stretton's Journalism," *Victorian Periodicals Review*, 21 (1979): 60–70;

Margaret Nancy Cutt, *Ministering Angels: A Study of Nineteenth-century Evangelical Writing for Children* (Broxburne, Herts: Five Owls, 1979);

Patricia Demers, "Mrs. Sherwood and Hesba Stretton," in *Romanticism and Children's Literature in Nineteenth-Century England*, edited by J. H. McGavran Jr. (Athens: University of Georgia Press, 1991), pp. 129–149;

Hulda Friederichs, "Hesba Stretton at Home," *Young Woman*, 22 (1894): 327–333;

"Hesba Stretton," *Sunday at Home*, 58 (1911): 121–127;

Margaret Maison, *Search Your Soul, Eustace: A Survey of the Religious Novel in the Victorian Age* (London: Sheed & Ward, 1961);

Lance Salway, "Pathetic Simplicity: Hesba Stretton and Her Books for Children," in *The Signal Approach to Children's Books*, edited by Nancy Chambers (Middlesex: Kestrel, 1980), pp. 34–45;

Hesba D. Webb, "A Personal Note," *Sunday at Home*, 58 (1911): 124–125;

Robert Lee Wolff, *Gains and Losses; Novels of Faith and Doubt in Victorian England* (New York: Garland, 1977).

Charlotte Maria Tucker (A.L.O.E.)
(8 May 1821 – 2 December 1893)

Erika Rothwell
University of Alberta

See also the Tucker entry in *DLB 163: British Children's Writers, 1800–1880*.

BOOKS: *The Claremont Tales; or, Illustrations of the Beatitudes* (London & Edinburgh: Gall & Inglis, 1852; enlarged, 1858);

Abbeokuta; or, Sunrise within the Tropics: An Outline of the Origin and Progress of the Yoruba Mission (New York: Carter, 1853; London: Nisbet, 1854);

Glimpses of the Unseen: Poems (London & Edinburgh: Gall & Inglis, 1853);

Angus Tarlton; or, Illustrations of the Fruits of the Spirit (London: Nelson, 1853-1856?; New York: Carter, 1862);

Life of Luther . . . Taken Chiefly from D'Aubigné's History of the Reformation (London, 1853-1856?);

True Heroism (London, 1853-1856?; New York: Carter, 1856);

Wings and Stings: A Tale for the Young (London, Edinburgh & New York: Gall & Inglis, 1855; New York: Carter, 1856);

The Giant-Killer; or, The Battle Which All Must Fight (London & New York: Nelson, 1856; New York: Carter, 1862);

New Year's Address for 1857: As Ye Sow, So Shall Ye Reap (Edinburgh, 1856);

Upwards and Downwards; or, The Sluggard and the Diligent: A Story for Boys (London, Edinburgh & New York: Gall & Inglis, 1856);

Walter Binning, the Adopted Son; or, Illustrations of the Lord's Prayer (New York: Carter, 1856; London: Gall & Inglis, 186-?); republished as *The Adopted Son; or, Illustrations of the Lord's Prayer* (London & Edinburgh, 1877);

The Rambles of a Rat (London, Edinburgh & New York: Gall & Inglis, 1857; New York: Carter, 1858);

The Roby Family; or, Battling with the World: A Sequel to "The Giant-Killer" (London: Nelson, 1857; New York: Carter, 1859);

From a Photograph taken at Toronto in 1875.

The Young Pilgrim: A Tale Illustrative of "The Pilgrim's Progress" (London: Nelson, 1857; New York: Carter, 1860);

Flora; or, Self-deception, and The Great Reformer (London: Nelson, 1858; New York: Carter, 1867);

Futteypoor; or, The City of Victory (London, 1858);

Harry Dangerfield, the Poacher (London: Nelson, 1858; New York: Carter, 1864);

The Mine; or, Darkness and Light (London & Edinburgh: Nelson, 1858; New York: General Protestant Episcopal Sunday School Union and Church Book Society, 1859);

Ned Manton; or, The Cottage by the Stream (London: Nelson, 1858; New York: Carter, 1867);

Old Friends with New Faces (London: Nelson, 1858; Boston: Lothrop, 1870); also published as *Eddie Ellerslie; or, Old Friends with New Faces* (New York: General Protestant Episcopal Sunday School Union and Church Book Society, 1859);

Precepts in Practice; or, Stories Illustrating the Proverbs (London: Gall & Inglis 1858; New York, 1859);

The Story of a Needle (London: Nelson, 1858; New York: Carter, 1862);

The Christian's Mirror; or, Words in Season (London, 1859; New York: Carter, 1872);

Idols in the Heart: A Tale (London: Nelson, 1859; New York: Carter, 1863);

Invited Guests: A Religious Tract for Children (London, 1860);

The Lost Jewel: A Tale (London, 1860);

Pride and His Prisoners (London: Nelson, 1860);

The Convict's Child; or The Helmet of Hope; Friend and Foe; or The Breastplate of Righteousness; A Hasty Blow; or The Sandals of Peace; Proved in Peril; or The Shield of Faith; The Sailor's Home; or The Girdle of Truth; Son of Israel; or the Sword of the Spirit, 6 tracts in 1 volume (London: Gall & Inglis, 186–?); republished as *Ned Franks, or The Christian's Panoply* (London: Nelson, 1864); republished as *Red Cross Knight, or The Christian's Panoply* (New York: Carter, 1867); republished as *The Christian's Panoply* (Edinburgh, 1870);

Illustrations of the Parables (London, 1861);

Parliament in the Play-Room (London: Nelson, 1861; New York: Carter, 1864);

The Two Paths and Other Stories (New York: Carter, 1861);

My Neighbour's Shoes; or, Feeling for Others: A Tale (London & New York: Nelson, 1861; New York: Carter, 1867);

The Shepherd of Bethlehem, King of Israel (London: Nelson, 1862; New York: Carter, 1864);

War and Peace: A Tale of the Retreat from Caubul (London: Nelson, 1862; New York: Carter, 1863);

The Light in the Robber's Cave (London: Nelson, 1862); republished as *The Robber's Cave: A Story of Italy* (London & New York: Nelson, 1863);

Christian Love and Loyalty; or, The Rebel Reclaimed (London: Nelson, 1862; New York: Carter, 1864); republished as *Grace Vernon; or, Christian Love and Loyalty* (London: Gall & Inglis, n.d.; London: Nelson, n.d.);

Falsely Accused; or, Christian Conquests (London: Nelson, 1862; New York: Carter, 1864);

Imogen; or, Daybreak in Britain (New York: General Protestant Episcopal Sunday School Union and Church Book Society; 1862); also published as *The Chief's Daughter; or, Daybreak in Britain* (London: Nelson, n.d.; New York: Carter, 1866); republished as *Daybreak in Britain* (London: Nelson, 1870);

The Broken Chain, and Other Stories on the Parables (New York: Carter, 1863);

The Crown of Success; or, Four Heads to Furnish: A Tale (London: Nelson, 1863; New York: Carter, 1863);

New Stories (London & Edinburgh, 1863; New York: General Protestant Episcopal Sunday School Union and Church Book Society, 1865);

Picture Reward Cards, Illustrating the Life of Christ, two series (London & Edinburgh, 1863);

Poetry by A.L.O.E. (London, 1863);

A.L.O.E.'s Pretty Present for the Pets (London, 1863);

The Silver Casket (London & Edinburgh: Nelson, 1863; New York: Carter, 1876);

Sketches of the History of the Jews (London, 1863);

Stories from Jewish History, from the Babylonish Captivity to the Destruction of Jerusalem by Titus (London, 1863; New York: Carter, 1864);

Exiles in Babylon; or, Children of Light (London: Nelson, 1864);

Esther Parsons; or, Try Again, and Other Stories (New York: Carter, 1864); republished as *Try Again, and Other Stories* (London & Edinburgh, 1872);

Fanny Aiken; or, The Village Home (New York: Carter, 1864);

Missing Links in Jewish History (Philadelphia: A.B.P.S., 1864);

Paying Dear, and Other Stories (New York: Carter, 1864);

Stories for the Young (London, 1864);

Tit, Tiny, and Tittens, the Three White Kittens: Rhymes (London, 1864);

Our Sympathizing High Priest: Meditations on the Daily Sorrows of the Saviour (London: Nelson, 1865; Boston & New York: American Tract Society, n.d.);

The Wanderer in Africa: A Tale Illustrating the Thirty-Second Psalm (London: Nelson, 1866); republished as *David Aspinall; or, The Wanderer in Africa: A Tale Illustrating the Thirty-Second Psalm* (New York: Carter, 1869);

Fairy Know-a-Bit (London & New York: Nelson, 1866);

Rescued from Egypt (London, Edinburgh & New York: Nelson, 1866);

The Straight Road Is Shortest and Surest (London: Nelson, 1866); republished as *Cortley Hall; or, The Straight Road Is Shortest and Surest* (New York: Carter, 1869);

The Children's Treasury (London: Nelson, 1867); republished as *The Children's Tabernacle; or, Hand-Work and Heart-Work* (London, 1871; New York: Carter, 1872);

The Holiday Chaplet of Stories (London, Edinburgh & New York: Nelson, 1867);

The Lake of the Woods: A Tale Illustrative of the Twelfth Chapter of Romans (London: Gall & Inglis, 1867); republished as *The Lake of the Woods: A Story of the Backwoods* (Chicago & New York: Revell, n.d.);

Sheer Off (Edinburgh: Gall & Inglis, 1867; New York: Carter, 1870);

The Sunday Chaplet of Stories (London & Edinburgh: Nelson, 1867; New York: Carter, 1869);

Thoughtful Alice, and Other Stories (London: Nelson, 1867);

The Triumph over Midian (London, Edinburgh & New York: Nelson, 1867);

Zaida's Nursery Note-Book: For the Use of Mothers (London, Edinburgh & New York: Nelson, 1867);

Hymns and Poems (London: Nelson, 1868 [i.e., 1867]);

Castle of Carlsmont (London, 1868);

House Beautiful; or, The Bible Museum (London & Edinburgh, 1868; New York: Carter, 1868);

Living Jewels: Diversities of Christian Character Suggested by Precious Stones, with Biographical Examples (London: Nelson, 1868);

Miracles of Heavenly Love in Daily Life (London: Nelson, 1868);

On the Way; or, Places Passed by Pilgrims (New York: Nelson, 1868); republished as *Places Passed by Pilgrims: Twelve Tales Illustrating the Pilgrim's Progress* (London: Nelson, 1869);

The Golden Fleece (London, 1869 [i.e., 1868]; New York & Boston: Dutton, 1869);

A Braid of Cords (London & Edinburgh: Gall & Inglis, 1869; New York: Routledge, 187-?);

The Children's Treasury of New Stories (New York: Carter, 1869);

Claudia: A Tale (London & Edinburgh: Nelson, 1869; New York: Carter, 1870);

Hebrew Heroes: A Tale Founded on Jewish History (London, 1869; New York: Carter, 1869);

New Year's Hymn for 1870 (London, 1870);

Be on Your Guard: A New Year's Address to Sunday Scholars (London: Sunday School Union, 1870);

Bought With a Price (New York: American Tract Society, 1870);

The Cord of Love (London: Gall & Inglis, 1870);

Cyril Ashley: A Tale (London: Nelson, 1870);

A Gift Book for the New-Year (London, 1870);

Is There Heart in It? A New Year's Address for 1871 (London, 1871);

New Year's Hymn for 1871 (London, 1871);

A.L.O.E.'s Picture Story Book (London & New York: Nelson, 1871);

Dora's Mistake; or, The Children's Tabernacle (London, 1871);

Freedom: A Tale of the Early Christians (London, 1871);

The Hymn My Mother Taught Me, and Other Stories (London, Edinburgh & New York: Nelson, 1871);

A Lady of Provence; or, Humbled and Healed: A Tale of the First French Revolution (London & New York: Nelson, 1871);

A.L.O.E.'s Sunday Picture Book: Illustrating the Life of . . . Christ, in a Series of Short Poems (London, 1871);

A Wreath of Smoke (London & Edinburgh, 1871);

Guy Dalesford; or, A Wreath of Smoke (New York: Carter, 1872);

The Black Cliff, and Other Stories on the Parables (New York: Carter, 1872);

Edith and Her Ayah, and Other Stories (London & New York: Nelson, 1872);

New-Year's Story for 1873: Trusty and Truthful (London, 1872);

The Olive-Branch, and Other Stories (London, 1872);

The Silver Keys: A Tale (London & Edinburgh: Gall & Inglis, 1872);

The City of Nocross and Its Famous Physician (London: Nelson, 1873; New York: Carter, 1873);

A Friend in Need, and Other Stories (London & New York: Nelson, 1873);

Good for Evil, and Other Stories (London, 1873; New York: Carter, 1883);

The Father's Letter: A New Year's Story (London: Sunday School Union, 1874);

An Eden in England: A Tale (London: Nelson, 1874; New York: Carter, 1879);

Fairy Frisket; or, Peeps at Insect Life (London: Nelson, 1874; New York: Carter, 1875);

The Little Maid (London, 1874);

Nora's Trial: A Tale (London & Edinburgh: Gall & Inglis, 1874);

The Backward Swing, and Other Stories (London, 1875);

The Beautiful Villa, and Other Stories (London: Nelson, 1875);

The Brother's Return, and Other Stories (London, 1875);

The Children's Garland: A Picture Story Book (London, 1875);

Every Cloud Has a Silver Lining and Five Other Little Books (London, 1875); republished as *Every Cloud Has a Silver Lining and Other Stories* (London & New York: Nelson, 1881);

The Little Maid and Living Jewels (New York: Carter, 1875);

Little Bullets from Batala (London: Nelson, 1875-1876);

The Message of Hope, and Other Stories (London, 1875);

Only a Little, and Other Stories (London, 1875);

The Spanish Cavalier: A Story of Seville (London, Edinburgh & New York: Nelson, 1875);

The Thorn in the Conscience, and Other Stories (London: Nelson, 1875);

The Truant Kitten and Other Stories (London, 1875);

The Victory, and Other Stories (London, 1875);

Haunted Rooms: A Tale (London, Edinburgh & New York: Nelson, 1876);

The Tiny Red Night-Cap, and Other Stories (London, 1876);

A Wreath of Indian Stories (London: Nelson, 1876);

Blind Alice and Her Benefactress (London, 1877);

Fritz's Victory and Other Stories (New York: Carter, 1877);

Jai Singh, the Brave Sikh (Madras: Christian Vernacular Education Society, 1877);

Victory Stories (New York: Carter, 1877);

Christ and the Soul: Texts Selected and Spiritual Songs Written (London, 1878);

Pomegranates from the Punjab: Indian Stories (London & Edinburgh: Gall & Inglis, 1878; Chicago: Revell, n.d.);

The Zenana Reader (Madras: Christian Vernacular Education Society, 1880; London, 1880);

The Brother's Return and Other Stories by A.L.O.E. (London, Edinburgh & New York: Nelson, 1881);

Hours with Orientals (London: Gall & Inglis, 1881);

Seven Perils Passed (London: Gall & Inglis, 1882);

Life in the Eagle's Nest: A Tale of Afghanistan (London: Gall & Inglis, 1883);

Little Bullets from Batala and Seven Perils Passed (New York: Carter, 1883);

Mahala, The Jewish Slave: A Story of Early Christianity (London: Religious Tract Society, 1883);

Fred's Whisper; or, The Promise Kept (London: Nelson, 1884);

Life in the Eagle's Nest and Mahala, The Jewish Slave (New York: Carter, 1884);

Life in the White Bear's Den: A Tale of Labrador (London: Gall & Inglis, 1884);

Harold Hartley; or, Pictures Drawn in an English Home (London, 1885);

Pictures of St. Paul, Drawn in an English Home (London: Gall & Inglis, 1885);

Pictures of St. Peter in an English Home (London, 1886);

Fairy in the Spider's Web (London: Gall & Inglis, 1887);

In the Spider's Web: The Story of the Indian Mutiny (London, 1887);

Percival's Picture Gallery (London: Morgan & Scott, 1887);

The Battle of Life; or, What Is a Christian? (London: Gall & Inglis, 1888);

Driven into Exile: A Story of the Huguenots (London & New York: Nelson, 1888);

Harold's Bride: A Tale (London: Nelson, 1889);

The Hartley Brothers; or, The Knights of Saint John (London: Gall & Inglis, 1889);

Ben Stone (London, 1890?);

Beyond the Black Waters: A Tale (London, Edinburgh & New York: Nelson, 1890);

Sophie Claymore (London, 1890?);

The Teacher Taught (London, 1890?);

The Whirlpool (London, 1890?);

The Wondrous Sickle and Other Stories (London, 1890?);

The Blacksmith of Boniface Lane (London, Edinburgh & New York: Nelson, 1891);

Black Yarn and Blue, . . . and Other Stories (London: Nelson, 1891);

The Little Brother . . . and Other Stories (London: Nelson, 1891);

The Rope Cable Cut, and Other Stories (London: Nelson, 1891);

The Two Crutches (London: Nelson, 1891);

The Two Dinners (London: Nelson, 1891);

The Iron Chain and the Golden (London, Edinburgh & New York: Nelson, 1892);

The Forlorn Hope (London: Nelson, 1893);

The Story of Dr. Duff (London, 1896);

The Two Pilgrims of Kashi and Other Stories (London & Madras: Christian Literature Society for India, 1901);

The Pearl and Other Stories (Rock Island, Ill.: Augustana Book Concern, 1926);

The Beautiful Garment and Other Stories (Rock Island, Ill.: Augustana Book Concern, 1927);

Grannie's Love Proof; or, Words without Deeds Are like Husks without Seeds (London: Pickering & Inglis, 1932).

Charlotte Maria Tucker belongs to the tradition of women reformers writing Sunday-school and missionary literature in eighteenth- and nineteenth-century Britain. Such literature focused on various social and religious causes and disseminated much useful knowledge. She was influenced by predeces-

Tucker, circa 1882

sors such as Mary Martha Sherwood and Hannah More and can be compared to contemporaries such as Maria Louisa Charlesworth and Hesba Stretton.

Born into a large, middle-class Victorian family with strong ties to the British Empire in India, Tucker was the sixth child and third daughter of Henry St. George Tucker and Jane Boswell. Her father was born on the Isle of St. George in Bermuda, was educated in England, and at the age of fourteen was sent to India, where he entered the Bengal Civil Service in 1792 and eventually became a chairman in the East India Company. After twenty-five years in India he returned to England and, in 1811, married twenty-one-year-old Jane Boswell, who was distantly related to James Boswell, the famous biographer of Samuel Johnson.

After their marriage the Tuckers returned briefly to India, but the climate did not agree with either Jane Tucker or her young family. Returning to England, the family lived first in Edinburgh, then in Barnet (where Charlotte Maria was born), and in 1822 settled in London at number 3. Upper Portland Place, where they remained for more than forty-five years. The family eventually included ten children. Like their father, Charlotte Tucker's five brothers were educated at English public schools and were employed in India in civil and military capacities.

Tucker was not destined for either a public school or a public career. Her father deplored girls' schools, so she and her sisters were educated at home, as were many Victorian daughters, by governesses and special masters. She was especially close to Robert, her older brother, and Dorothea Laura, a younger sister. Her older sisters, Sibella and Frances, were graceful and elegant, but according to Agnes Giberne, Tucker was described within the family as "the clever heroic sister." This was an ambivalent compliment recognizing that she was lively, merry, and good-humored but also tall, thin, and outspoken. She was also ginger-haired (rather than pretty), modest, and not "gifted in the art of dressing well." Her father encouraged literary and dramatic accomplishments within the family circle, and Tucker wrote several historical plays during her teenage years and the following decade. She also participated in many family theatricals and began a family magazine.

As a young girl she seems to have been expected to remain a stay-at-home, unmarried daughter devoted to the interests of her family. She received at least one offer of marriage, but her parents disapproved, and she acquiesced with their decision. Her father, feeling that the domestic circle should suffice in fulfilling all the social, intellectual, and emotional needs of his daughters, saw little need for them to socialize outside the family, and Tucker accordingly devoted herself to her family. In her late teens or early twenties she began teaching her younger brothers and sisters; she later devoted herself to her parents and then cared for various nieces and nephews sent to stay at the family home while their parents took up various posts in India. From 1847 she had exclusive charge of Robert's three children, Louis, Charley, and Letitia.

Around this time Tucker also became increasingly eager to do additional work outside the family circle, to serve the cause of social reform more actively than as a benevolent almsgiver. She could see that much social work was needed among the London poor. Under her father's guidance Tucker had been raised in the Church of England, but rationalistic, eighteenth-century morality and duty were more prominent than evangelical devotion in his religious scheme. She seems, however, always to have thought carefully and deeply on spiritual matters, and one of her younger brothers described her as always being religious. As an adult in the 1840s Tucker, along with Frances, underwent a conversion, became a practicing Evangelical, and felt her duty was that of performing good works beyond the family circle.

She particularly wished to volunteer at the Marylebone Workhouse, but her father resisted this idea strenuously and objected that she would be exposed to infectious diseases. Feeling that such work was her religious duty, however, she persisted, and in 1851 her parents reluctantly gave their permission; Tucker became a regular charity visitor at the Workhouse, where she met with London's poor and gained an awareness of social problems in Victorian London. In 1851 her life was also dramatically altered by two other events: the death of her father and the engagement of her sister Laura. Her home circle was drastically altered.

After the age of thirty Charlotte Tucker suddenly sought to become a writer with her first book, *The Claremont Tales; or, Illustrations of the Beatitudes* (1852), a collection of didactic and religious stories stressing the need for religious devotion, self-control, education, and charity. Precisely when she began and finished writing these tales is not clear. It seems likely, however, that she had refrained from writing and hoping to publish while her father lived, for she was certain that he would disapprove. It is also likely that, faced with losing both her father and her sister Laura, Tucker felt a need for new interests.

Tucker began her career in a most unprofessional manner by sending her manuscript to publishers William and Robert Chambers with an unsigned letter and no return address. Giberne writes that Tucker's letter stressed her "anxious desire to add [her] mite to the Treasury of useful literature . . . opened to the young as well as the old" and made clear her lack of interest in "earthly remuneration." She explained that her most pressing interest was to obtain "God's blessing upon my attempts to instruct His lambs in the things which concern their everlasting welfare." The publishers did not find the volume to be suitable and passed the manuscript along to Gall and Inglis, another publishing house, which printed *The Claremont Tales*. When Tucker saw her stories in print, she wrote to Gall and Inglis to ask how they had come to publish her work.

Tucker's letter also showed that she had given some thought to her identity and purpose as an author: for the first time she referred to herself by using the pseudonym A.L.O.E., or A Lady of England. This name identified her as a woman who discreetly and properly concealed her name from public view; underlined her conception of herself as a member of the upper, educated classes who saw little possibility of change in the class system but plenty of opportunity for individual reform, education, and betterment; and stressed her belief in the superiority of the English Empire and the new English industrial age. Tucker, who was fond of allegorical and representational effects, may also have considered the traditional soothing and healing properties of the aloe plant and intended to present her work as administering intellectual and educational balm to the minds and souls of her readers. She had also begun to think about the possibilities involved in authorship, for Giberne writes that Tucker asked Gall and Inglis if they might consider "adopting her suggestion of printing some or all of *The Claremont Tales* in a *very cheap* form, for distribution amongst poor children, Ragged Schools etc." Throughout her career Tucker published her works as tracts printed by cheap presses as well as in the more decorative and formal styles suitable for Sunday-school reward books and middle- and upper-class children. She found the opportunity to reach and influence a large public to be attractive.

Her letter also offered Gall and Inglis an opportunity to publish a collection of her verse, and this was published as *Glimpses of the Unseen: Poems* in 1853. She thus began a career as a prolific author of books for children, young adults, and beginning adult readers, and by the end of her life in 1893 she had published more than 140 works. The exact number is difficult to document because she destroyed most of her records and personal papers before leaving England for India. In addition her works were published by many small presses and societies as well as by her usual British publishers—Gall and Inglis and Thomas Nelson—and by Robert Carter in the United States. Confusion about changes in titles and subtitles of her books and other practices of publishers, who often produced "new" collections of previously published short stories, also makes it difficult to determine accurately the size of her canon.

Her work shows the influence of earlier didactic and reformist women writers for children—Hannah More, Dorothy Kilner, Mary Martha Sherwood, and Maria Edgeworth. Drawing on these predecessors, Tucker's stories include domestic family tales, animal stories, histories of inanimate objects, adventure stories, symbolic and allegorical tales, retellings of Bible stories, educational treatises, religious tracts, social critiques, sermons, fairy tales, dream visions, and presentations of useful knowledge about history, biology, and industry. She also combines these forms. *The Story of a Needle* (1858) is told from the point of view of a needle and interweaves useful knowledge with a family story that includes an impending financial crisis (averted

The last page of Tucker's diary (from Agnes Giberne, A Lady of England: The Life and Letters of Charlotte Maria Tucker, *1895)*

by the selfless behavior of the eldest son) and discussion of the education and duties of children.

Unlike her predecessors Tucker never contemplated a return to a preindustrial England. She began writing in the shadow of the Great Exhibition of 1851 and was committed to an industrialized England. Set in industrial London, *The Story of a Needle* is designed to educate readers about the production of various material goods and explain how the empire yields raw materials that are transformed into material goods that bring the English comfort, convenience, and profit.

Yet despite her dedication to an ethos of work and progress Tucker was distressed by the side effects of industrialization and urbanization, and many of her works graphically depict the London poor and urge readers to act to relieve the sufferings of their fellow human beings. Her solutions do not entail any radical social restructuring but are rooted in individual responsibility, charity, and widespread education–both religious and secular. *The Rambles of a Rat* (1857), for example, presents readers with useful information about rats, their habits, and habitats, but it is also a fanciful history of anthropomorphized rats, Whiskerandros and Ratto, interwoven with the adventures of two London waifs who are eventually rescued and sent to a ragged school by a philanthropic gentleman and his son.

Ragged schools designed to educate the lower working classes were a favorite charity of Tucker and a new philanthropic aim. Nine-year-old Neddy in this story is taught about theories and circumstances surrounding the foundation of ragged schools and exclaims, "What a glorious thing it is to have ragged schools and reformatories, to give the poor and the ignorant, and the wicked a chance of becoming honest and happy." Neddy also forms philanthropic ambitions of his own as he exclaims, "How I should like to build a ragged school myself!" Tucker wrote never merely to amuse her readers but to present useful information, urge social action that might improve living conditions, and foster

Evangelical charity that would bring individuals closer to God. She assumed that all classes and all age groups needed the encouragement to be more hardworking, more charitable, than they were. Nor were children exempt. In *Rambles* Tucker points out that "were all the children of the middle classes in England to give each but one penny a week, no wretched boy need wander about desolate London, to perish both here and hereafter because no one cared for his soul!"

For nearly twenty-five years Tucker continued to write such stories from her London home and to feel that she was doing useful work and contributing to the reformation of society by urging her public to devote themselves to work, charity, and self-betterment for the glorification of God and the improvement of England. Tucker followed her teachings by donating all of the considerable profits from her writing to educational and religious charities. Her books were popular among young middle-class readers and readers of all ages in villages, Sunday schools, missionary societies, and ragged schools. Her work easily found publishers. Emma Marshall notes that Tucker's stories "were deservedly popular, and bore the crucial test of being read aloud to an attentive audience several times." Marshall adds that critics typically tended to praise Tucker's humor and ability to create whimsical characters and stirring action, but they deplored her tendency toward "the moral" and "long and discursive 'preachments.'" Yet Tucker saw herself as a reform writer, and her books were sold as serious moral works for children and given as Sunday-school gift books for more than four decades.

While she wrote, Tucker remained devoted to family needs. Robert's children were orphaned after his death in the Indian Mutiny in 1857; the health of her elder sister Frances began to fail seriously in 1864; and Leila, Robert's daughter, died suddenly while visiting family in India in the same year. In 1869 Tucker's mother died, and the Tucker family home at Portsmouth Place was broken up. In September, Frances and Tucker went to live in Sutton with their brother's family. After Frances died there in November, Tucker spent six years living with her brother and sister-in-law, educating their children and continuing to write, visit the poor, and teach a class of boys in night school.

From the time of her mother's death Tucker had begun to contemplate going to India as a missionary. Against all advice she studied Hindustani, investigated missionary institutions, and in 1875 finally became a missionary in India. Her writing presents the need for missionaries and Christian witnesses that she subsequently found there in collections such as *Edith and Her Ayah, and Other Stories* (1872), the title story of which draws heavily on Sherwood's *The History of Little Henry and His Bearer* (1814). In Tucker's story fair-haired Edith tries to convert Motte Ayah, her beloved ayah, or nursemaid, to Christianity. After much prayer and a scene in which Edith's prayers avert the attack of a Bengal tiger, her ayah is saved, and Tucker closes by exhorting to her young readers to pray for the heathen:

> Oh, if, in our dear land, all the little ones who have no money to give to the missionary cause, who have never even seen an idolater, would lift up their hands and hearts to the Lord, saying, "Teach the poor heathen to love thee!" how rich a harvest of blessings would be drawn down by such a prayer on those who know not the truth, and still sit in darkness and the shadow of death!

Becoming a missionary at the age of fifty-four was a most unusual step for a Victorian woman to take, and in a letter to her sister Tucker identified her reasons for becoming one. These included the need for Christian workers in the Indian subcontinent, her ability to bear heat, her freedom from home ties, and the great need that Indian women had for suitable Christian literature. Duty, she felt, called her to India. She worked first with the Indian Female Normal School and Instruction Society and then at a boys' school in Batala. Her official position was that of Zenana visitor—the female missionary who visited and instructed Indian women in Christian belief.

In becoming a missionary she did not abandon her writing; she merely readjusted her focus. She wrote familiar allegorical tales and stories to be translated into the vernacular for educational use in India and fictionalized her experiences for English readers, to whom those tales stressed how much the missions needed contributions. The profits she received from these stories were reinvested in missionary work as her writing remained an extension of her need to feel useful and to bring about reforms. In collections such as *A Wreath of Indian Stories* (1876) and *Pomegranates from the Punjab: Indian Stories* (1878) she sought to reach and teach a large audience, as she explains in the preface to *Little Bullets from Batala and Seven Perils Passed* (1883), where she notes that even a secular education allows the natives to be influenced through the press.

Her stories were used with such educational aims both in English and in translation. Published by the Christian Literary Society and the Punjab Religious Book Society, her works were among the most widely sought and sold publications of those organizations. Coworkers and students in India, like those in England, admired her energy and determination and responded to her good nature and generosity—although, like her family members, they noted that she was often tactless and could be narrow-minded in her appreciation of Indian culture. Margaret Nancy Cutt, however, believes that Tucker

> represented something very much larger than her strongly opinionated self. She publicized; she was one of many women, who by their single-hearted devotion to the work of school and hospital first opened the doors of opportunity to the women of India, Africa, and China. With the establishment of mission schools and hospitals came the training of thousands of women of the Orient who have helped to bring their own people into the twentieth century.

Tucker never returned to England. After an illness lasting several months she died in 1893 and was buried in Batala.

Biography:

Agnes Giberne, *A Lady of England: The Life and Letters of Charlotte Maria Tucker* (London: Hodder & Stoughton, 1895).

References:

Jacqueline S. Bratton, *The Impact of Victorian Children's Fiction* (London: Croom Helm, 1981);

Margaret Nancy Cutt, *Ministering Angels: A Study of Nineteenth Century Evangelical Writing for Children* (Wormley, U.K.: Five Owls, 1979);

Emma Marshall, "'A.L.O.E.' (Miss Tucker) and Mrs. Ewing," in *Women Novelists of Queen Victoria's Reign: A Book of Appreciations,* edited by Margaret Oliphant (London: Hurst & Blackett, 1897), pp. 293–297.

Alfred Russel Wallace
(8 January 1823 – 7 November 1913)

Charles Blinderman
Clark University

BOOKS: *A Dissertation on the True Age of the World, in which is Determined the Chronology of the Period from the Creation to the Christian Era* (London: Smith, 1844);

A Narrative of Travels on the Amazon and Rio Negro, with an Account of the Native Tribes, and Observations on the Climate, Geology, and Natural History of the Amazon Valley (London: Reeve, 1853); republished as *Travels on the Amazon* (New York: Harper, 1889; London & New York: Ward, Lock, 1889);

Palm Trees of the Amazon and Their Uses (London: Van Voorst, 1853);

The Scientific Aspect of the Supernatural: Indicating the Desirableness of an Experimental Enquiry by Men of Science in the Alleged Powers of Clairvoyants and Mediums (London: Austin, 1866);

The Malay Archipelago, the Land of the Orang-utan and the Bird of Paradise: A Narrative of Travel, with Studies of Man and Nature (2 volumes, London: Macmillan, 1869; 1 volume, New York: Harper, 1869);

Contributions to the Theory of Natural Selection: A Series of Essays (London & New York: Macmillan, 1870);

The Action of Natural Selection on Man (New Haven, Conn.: Chatfield, 1871);

A Defence of Modern Spiritualism (Boston: Colby & Rich, 1874);

On Miracles and Modern Spiritualism: Three Essays (London: Burns, 1875); revised as *Miracles and Modern Spiritualism* (London: Nichols, 1895);

The Geographical Distribution of Animals, with a Study of the Relations of Living and Extinct Faunas as Elucidating the Past Changes of the Earth's Surface, 2 volumes (London: Macmillan, 1876; New York: Harper, 1876);

Tropical Nature and Other Essays (London: Macmillan, 1878);

Island Life; or, The Phenomena and Causes of Insular Faunas and Floras, including a Revision and Attempted Solution of the Problem of Geological Climates (London: Macmillan, 1880; New York: Harper, 1881);

Land Nationalization, Its Necessity and Its Aims: Being a Comparison of the System of Landlord and Tenant with that of Occupying Ownership in Their Influence on the Well-Being of the People (London: Tribune, 1882; New York: Scribners, 1902);

The "Why" and "How" of Land Nationalisation (London: Land Nationalisation Society, 1883);

Bad Times: An Essay on the Present Depression of Trade, Tracing It to Its Sources in Enormous Foreign Loans, Excessive War Expenditure, the Increase of Specula-

tion and Millionaires, and the Depopulation of the Rural Districts; with Suggested Remedies (London: Macmillan, 1885);

The Distribution of Life, by Wallace and W. T. Thiselton Dyer (New York: Fitzgerald, 1885);

Forty-Five Years of Registration Statistics, Proving Vaccination to Be Both Useless and Dangerous (London: E. W. Allen, 1885);

Darwinism: An Exposition of the Theory of Natural Selection, with Some of Its Applications (London & New York: Macmillan, 1889; New York: Humboldt, 1889);

Australia and New Zealand (London: Stanford, 1893); revised by John Walter Gregory (London: Stanford, 1907);

Vaccination a Delusion, Its Penal Enforcement a Crime; Proved by the Official Evidence in the Reports of the Royal Commission (London: Sonnenschein, 1898);

The Wonderful Century: Its Successes and Its Failures (London: Sonnenschein / New York: Dodd, Mead, 1898; revised edition, London: Sonnenschein, 1903);

Studies Scientific and Social, 2 volumes (London & New York: Macmillan, 1900);

The Wonderful Century Reader (London: Sonnenschein, 1901);

Man's Place in the Universe: A Study of the Results of Scientific Research in Relation to the Unity of Plurality of Worlds (New York: McClure, Phillips, 1903; enlarged edition, London: Chapman & Hall, 1904);

My Life: A Record of Events and Opinions (London: Chapman & Hall, 1905; New York: Dodd, Mead, 1905; condensed and revised edition, London: Chapman & Hall, 1908);

Is Mars Habitable? A Critical Examination of Professor Percival Lowell's Book "Mars and Its Canals," with an Alternative Explanation (London: Macmillan, 1907);

The World of Life: A Manifestation of Creative Power, Directive Mind and Ultimate Purpose (London: Chapman & Hall, 1910; New York: Moffat, Yard, 1911);

Social Environment and Moral Progress (London & New York: Cassell, 1913);

The Revolt of Democracy (London & New York: Cassell, 1913).

OTHER: "Dr. Carpenter on Spiritualism," in *The Psycho-Physiological Sciences, and Their Assailants* (Boston: Colly & Rich, 1878);

Australasia, edited by Wallace (London: Stanford, 1879);

Richard Spruce, *Notes of a Botanist on the Amazon and Andes,* edited by Wallace (London: Macmillan, 1908);

Percy Parker Livingstone, ed., *Character & Life: A Symposium,* by Wallace, John A. Hobson, Walter Crane, and Emil Reich (London: Williams & Norgate, 1912).

During his long career Alfred Russel Wallace wrote more than four hundred articles and reviews as well as more than twenty-five books and is best remembered for his biological and ethnological investigations. Like Charles Darwin, Thomas Huxley, and Joseph Dalton Hooker, Wallace sailed strange seas in pursuit of knowledge, which in his case took him to the Amazon and to the Malay Archipelago. Like them, he also undertook journeys over strange seas of thought, sharing with his contemporaries a belief in evolution, but unlike them his interests carried him from the exotic to the erratic, to a defense of spiritualism as an empirically authenticated practice. In the realm of reform he became an advocate for socialism as the cure for a culture wounded by capitalistic spoliation.

Wallace is credited with conceiving the idea of natural selection independently of Darwin and was evidently the first to commit a complete version of the concept to paper, but his legacy as a cofounder of the theory of natural selection was somewhat undercut by his advocacy of discredited ideas. He believed that such a theory could not account for the development of the human intellect—a contention related to his belief in spiritualism. One of the most ardent collectors of biota, he was also an avid collector of accounts of ghosts, and although a declared agnostic, he wrote enthusiastically of a supernatural world, affirming that spirits could communicate with human beings. While he argued against the efficacy of vaccination as a means to prevent disease, he was sure that "phreno-mesmerism" (touching certain areas of the skull of a hypnotized subject) could arouse desired behaviors. In his autobiography, *My Life: A Record of Events and Opinions* (1905), Wallace relates the story of a subject whose organ of generation was touched, upon which the subject "fell upon his knees, closed his palms together, and gazed upwards, with the facial expression of a saint in the ecstasy of adoration."

Wallace's major contribution to the literature of reform is his corrosive criticism of nineteenth-century society, through which he offered a humane vision of social reformation. He advocated recognizing racial equality, nationalizing land, giving women equal opportunity for education and employment, decreasing military expenditure, and saving the environment. His friend James Marchant wrote in *Alfred Russel Wallace: Letters and Reminiscences* (1916) that "his greatest ambition was to improve the cruel conditions under which thousands of his fellow-creatures suffered and died, and to make their lives sweeter and happier."

The eighth of nine children, Wallace was born on 8 January 1823 in the town of Usk in Monmouthshire to Thomas Vere Wallace and Mary Anne Greenell Wallace. In 1828 the family moved to Hertford, where Wallace attended grammar school. More important than his studies at school, however, was his informal education gained through reading, which was much encouraged by his father, who for a time served as the librarian of the town. In the biographical sketch by Marchant included in *The Revolt of Democracy* (1913) Wallace is critical of the rote learning of the provincial school: "I cannot but think that the same amount of mental exertion, wisely directed, might have produced far greater and more generally useful results.... Whatever little knowledge of history I have ever acquired has been derived more from Shakespeare's plays and from good historical novels than from anything I learned at school."

Wallace's family was unable to afford his continued schooling and sent the fourteen-year-old to London to become an apprentice to his nineteen-year-old brother John, a carpenter. In the evenings Wallace attended lectures at the Hall of Science, a workingman's club in Tottenham Court Road. In addition to scientific lectures he also went to lectures on Owenite socialism and read Thomas Paine's subversive deistic work *The Age of Reason* (1794–1795). His exposure to such ideas had a profound effect on Wallace and led to his deep skepticism regarding Christianity. He would later find that Christianity was faulty in its attempt to reconcile the Scriptures with geology and would reject what he regarded as its pernicious notion of eternal punishment in hell for sinners. Wallace the reformer would also criticize the justification Christianity provided for the rich robbing the poor, who, it was maintained on scriptural authority, would always exist.

After a few months in London, Wallace found work assisting his brother William in surveying land, his occupation for four years. Traveling about the English countryside introduced him to botany, zoology, geology, and cartography. He was also introduced to an epidemic of despair because their surveying was a stage in the process of effecting the General Inclosure Act, which abolished the commons and thus prohibited peasants from using that land to graze livestock, grow vegetables, or dig up

Wallace in 1848

peat. Young Wallace was disturbed more by aesthetic than ethical concerns, for he found it a pity to fence in the picturesque countryside. Wallace's first papers, written when he was twenty years old, were on botany; half a century later his papers promoted land nationalization.

In 1844, with the surveying trade depressed, Wallace found a job as a teacher at Leicester Collegiate School. He taught English, reading, writing, and arithmetic, reading mostly books on science but also Thomas Malthus's *Essay on the Principle of Population* (1798), which would turn out to be the key for him as well as for Darwin in suggesting the mechanism of evolution. Inspired by Darwin's *Journal of Researches into the Geology and Natural History of the Various Countries Visited by H.M.S. Beagle* (1839) and Alexander von Humboldt's *Voyage de Humboldt et Bonpland aux régions équinoxiales du nouveau continent, fait en 1799–1804* (1805–1834; translated as *Personal Narrative of Travels to the Equinoctial Regions of the New Continent During the Years 1799–1804*, 1814–1829), Wallace suggested to a friend, entomologist Henry

Bates, that they explore the Amazon. They sailed from Liverpool in April 1848 on a journey that would last more than four years. When Wallace later reflected on reading Malthus and the travelogues and on meeting Bates, he chose the year he spent at Leicester as the most important of his early life.

Wallace had earned a pittance as assistant surveyor and as teacher, so his financial prospects were a little improved by his collecting animals and plants from the Amazon for shipment to biologists. His professional prospects were much brightened by the articles and books he wrote on the geographical distribution of Amazonian plants and animals, especially *Palm Trees of the Amazon and Their Uses* and *A Narrative of Travels on the Amazon and Rio Negro, with an Account of the Native Tribes, and Observations on the Climate, Geology, and Natural History of the Amazon Valley*, both published in 1853.

In March 1854 Wallace undertook a voyage to the Malay Archipelago. During the eight years devoted to this exploration he garnered an extensive collection of more than 125,000 specimens and considered the question of how species originate. In the September 1855 issue of the *Annals and Magazine of Natural History* he published "On the Law which Has Regulated the Introduction of New Species," in which he argued that "Every species has come into existence coincident both in time and space with a preexisting closely allied species." In a flash of insight while recovering from a fever in 1858, he grasped the mechanism of evolution and sent a letter summarizing his ideas to Darwin, who was then working along a similar line of thought. The letter provoked Charles Lyell and Hooker to recommend that a joint Darwin-Wallace paper be read at the Linnean Society in 1858. When Darwin published *On the Origin of Species* a year later, Wallace was satisfied with his status as coinventor of the hypothesis of natural selection.

Wallace's later disagreement with Darwinists about the applicability of natural selection to humanity provides insight into the fundamental perspective that led to his dedication to social reform. Natural selection for Wallace was a satisfactory explanation of how all living beings evolved except the human being. He came to believe that the theory could not explain the unique human capacity for thinking, for making tools, and for distinguishing right from wrong.

Wallace's "The Origin of the Human Races and the Antiquity of Man deduced from Natural Selection," which appeared in 1864 in the *Anthropological Society Journal*, shows that he for a time shared in the conventional Victorian thinking about race. He assumed that the races of tropical regions were inferior to northern races because their eternal summer-warm weather, easy shelter, abundant food-did not inspire ingenuity or cunning. Races of northern regions, however, were supposedly honed to superiority by having to exercise their intelligence in coping with wintry weather. To support this proposition Wallace offered evidence of the great invasions of history, always from north to south, the "bold and adventurous" northern tribes easily subduing lax southern competitors. At this time he believed that natural selection dictated the preservation of favored races in the struggle for life among human beings as well as among beetles.

But Wallace soon discarded this jingoistic assumption for a new, non-Darwinian view of racial equality. In Borneo he had observed that the Dayaks not only learned how to play cat's cradle, but could beat him at it. Wallace was struck that while the mental requirements for survival of primitive people are not much above that for animals-the Dyaks could survive excellently without a brain competent to play cat's cradle or agile enough to allow for bi-lingualism-the brain of even the most primitive people had a potential far in excess of what was needed. "[N]atural selection," he wrote in an April 1869 review in *Quarterly Review* titled "Geological Climates and the Origin of Species," could only have endowed the savage with a brain a little superior to that of an ape, whereas he actually possesses one but little inferior to that of the average member of our learned societies." The Darwinian perspective held natural selection as accountable for the evolution of the human mind as well as for the evolution of the finch beak and for racial ranking. But Wallace did not believe that natural selection explained Dyak intelligence and sought another explanation.

Wallace's dissatisfaction with natural selection as the complete answer to the evolutionary puzzle was doubtless a major reason for his growing interest in spiritualism in the early 1860s. In July 1865 he attended the first of many séances in which spirits disported themselves and chatted. He invited Huxley to attend a demonstration of this "new branch of anthropology," but Huxley declined the opportunity to eavesdrop upon "disembodied gossip." In *The Scientific Aspect of the Supernatural: Indicating the Desirableness of an Experimental Enquiry by Men of Science in the Alleged Powers of Clairvoyants and Mediums* (1866) Wallace explained such validated phenomena as spirits rapping, playing music, and relaying messages as the manifestation of a Great Mind, an Intelligence, unseen, superior, supreme.

A September 1858 letter from Wallace to the secretary of the Royal Geographical Society (Royal Geographical Society of London)

While natural selection led to the evolution of the mentalities of animals, Wallace believed that an Intelligence designed the human mind. Wallace wrote to E. B. Poulton: "I (think I) *know* that non-human intelligences exist–that there are *minds* disconnected from a physical brain–that there is, therefore, a *spiritual world*. This is not, for me a *belief* merely, but *knowledge* founded on the long-continued observation of facts–and such *knowledge* must modify my views as to the origin and nature of human faculty." He held to this belief throughout his life. In 1891 he wrote to a friend, "a superior intelligence has guided the development of man in a definite direction, and for a special purpose, just as man guides the development of many animal and vegetable forms."

Spiritualism not only explained something natural selection was deficient at explaining but also took the place of conventional religion for Wallace. He recounted in *My Life* that as a child he liked to listen to hymns that inspired "religious fervour," but the experience was transitory: "As, however, there was no sufficient basis of intelligible fact or connected reasoning to satisfy my intellect, this feeling soon left me, and has never returned." Despite his affection for spirits he considered himself a lifelong agnostic. From Delli, on the island of Timor, he had written to his brother-in-law in 1861: "In my solitude I have often pondered much on the incomprehensible subjects of space, eternity, life and death. I think I have fairly heard and fairly weighed the evidence on both sides, and I remain an *utter unbeliever* in almost all that you consider the most sacred truths." Wallace believed that orthodox belief is "more a matter of blind faith than intelligent conviction."

Upon his return from the Amazon, Wallace wrote *The Malay Archipelago, the Land of the Orang-utan and the Bird of Paradise: A Narrative of Travel, with Studies of Man and Nature* (1869). This presentation of Malayan culture concluded with a harsh critique of Victorian progress. The English, Wallace argued, had succeeded in developing a technology that led to much wealth for some and much more poverty for most, to cities which "support and continually renew a mass of human misery and crime *absolutely* greater than has ever existed before."

Wallace was amazed at the high civilization of the Malayans, who enjoyed a compassionate social state that held no distinctions between the educated and ignorant, wealthy and poor, or master and servant. Contrasted to such benign egalitarianism was the malign circumstance in his own country:

> We permit absolute possession of the soil of our country, with no legal rights of existence on the soil, to the vast majority who do not possess it. A great landholder may legally convert his whole property into a forest or a hunting-ground, and expel every human being who has hitherto lived upon it. In a thickly-populated country like England, where every acre has its owner and occupier, this is a power of legally destroying his fellow-creatures, and that such a power should exist, and be exercised by individuals, in however small a degree, indicates that, as regards true social science, we are still in a state of barbarism.

Malay Archipelago, his most popular book, vividly indicated a new direction in Wallace's labors. In 1871 he joined the Land Tenure Reform Association.

In 1882 Wallace was invited to be president of the Society for Psychical Research and also of the newly formed Land Nationalization Society. He rejected the first of these honors, while accepting the second. That same year he published *Land Nationalization, Its Necessity and Its Aims: Being a Comparison of the System of Landlord and Tenant with that of Occupying Ownership in Their Influence on the Well-Being of the People,* which was dedicated to "the working men of England." Wallace argued that a person could "own land only so long as he occupies it personally, that is, he must be a perpetual *holder* of the land, not its absolute *owner.*" In 1890, after reading Henry George's *Progress and Poverty* (1879) and Edward Bellamy's *Looking Backward: 2000–1887* (1888), Wallace converted to socialism.

With other socialists Wallace believed that neither genetic endowment nor divine prescription was responsible for the behavior of men and women, that instead the prime agent of social discord was bad government. He argued that the state ought to provide equality of opportunity and that no one should get a head start through inheritance: "To secure equality of opportunity there must be no inequality of initial wealth. To allow one child to be born a millionaire and another a pauper is a crime against humanity." Andrew Carnegie would later share this view on the inheritance of wealth. Wallace further argued that the state ought to own and manage the railways and pay the doctors. He envisioned a Ministry of Public Health, its doctors acting as servants of the state, that is, of the people—and he added, perhaps mischievously, "they should be paid according as they kept people well and not ill." Wallace's model of the beneficent state is evident in his homage to Robert Owen included in *My Life.* For Wallace, Owen's New Lanark experiment showed that sympathetic treatment of people, especially of children, and an emphasis on cooperation rather than competition among adult workers will cultivate decent citizens.

In *My Life* Wallace was especially incensed by the General Inclosure Act, which prohibited use of the commons by those who needed the land for survival and distributed it to the rich landowners who used it for play: "To those that had much, much was to be given, while from the poor their rights were taken away.... [It] was simple robbery ... a legalized robbery of the poor for the aggrandizement of the rich, who were the lawmakers." For the poor, Wallace saw the result as a transmigration from "comfort to penury," a forced emigration from their homes in healthy rural districts to hovels in miserable, overcrowded cities, the elderly among them driven to workhouses or worse: homelessness, disease, and death. For the rich, the result was finer gold cuff links. The rich could destroy antiquities, deplete the land of its minerals, and commit whatever rape they were inclined to. And to this injury was added an outrageous insult:

> it is the advocates and beneficiaries of this inhuman system who, when a partial restitution of their unholy gains is proposed, are the loudest in their cries of 'robbery'! But all the robbery, all the spoilation, all the legal and illegal filching, has been on *their* side, and they still hold the stolen property. *They* make laws to legalize their actions, and, some day, we, the people, will make laws which will not only legalize but justify our process

of restitution . . . to restore to the whole people their birthright in their native soil.

In essays such as "Human Progress: Past and Future," which was collected in *Studies Scientific and Social* (1900), Wallace consistently argued for the equal treatment of the sexes and asserted that women especially suffered in the capitalistic system. Deprived of equality of opportunity in education and employment, women were forced into marriage just to survive: the ideal mate under the capitalistic system was a man of wealth and power, someone adroit at succeeding in the social struggle for survival. Wallace told his friend Marchant that the first step to improving humanity was to ensure that women were free to choose their mates: "Clear up, change the environment so that all may have an adequate opportunity of living a useful and happy life, and give women a free choice in marriage, and when that has been going on for some generations you may be in a better position to apply whatever has been discovered about heredity and human breeding, and you may then known which are the better stocks."

If society were reorganized to give women equality of opportunity so that they could be well educated, have well-paying jobs, and become as active as men in the service of their country, Wallace contended that they would be sufficiently independent so that they need not marry at all or could choose to marry late. In either case the high birth rate would be lowered. And if women preferred marriage, they could choose a mate based on his moral and intellectual features, such as his sense of humor, his ability to speak eloquently, his kindness, or his courage. Wallace's view of sexual selection differed from Darwin's, for Wallace believed that free, independent women would be swayed by a man's nobility of personality rather than his physical strength or his ability to succeed economically. By exercising sexual selection wisely women would become "the regenerators of the entire human race."

Just as Wallace's views on race changed dramatically as he matured, so did his view of international relations and militarism. Early in his career Wallace supported the Crimean War. Russia, he noted, was an imperialist power poised to take Constantinople and move from there into the Mediterranean, with its ultimate goal being the subjugation of Europe. In a letter written in Singapore in 1856, he argued that Russia built "tremendous fortresses" to protect itself from attacks brought on by its imperialistic projects. "Russia is perpetually increasing her means both of defense and of aggression." Wallace believed the Crimean War was "absolutely neces-

THE WONDERFUL CENTURY

ITS SUCCESSES AND ITS FAILURES

BY
ALFRED RUSSEL WALLACE
AUTHOR OF "THE MALAY ARCHIPELAGO,"
"DARWINISM," ETC., ETC.

NEW YORK
DODD, MEAD AND COMPANY
1899

Title page for Wallace's 1899 book, more than half of which is devoted to the failures of the nineteenth century because they "are either ignored or denied, and therefore required to be proved"

sary as the only means of teaching Russia that Europe will not submit to the indefinite increase of her territory and power, and the constant menace of her thousands of cannons and millions of men."

When Wallace reread this later in life, he found truth in it, but he no longer believed the Russian government to be any worse than the German or French or English governments. In *My Life* he argued that all imperialist nations were guilty: "All have the same insatiable craving for extending their territories and ruling subject peoples for the benefit of their own upper classes." He attacked the United States for its annexing Puerto Rico and the Philippines; he attacked Russia for its persecution of Jews and its taking liberty away from the Finns; and he attacked Germany and France for their invasions of China.

Wallace's wrath was directed mainly against the imperialism of Great Britain. Our rulers and our teachers, he wrote bitterly, the legislature, the press, and the church, unite in "compelling other peoples, against their will, to submit to our ignorant and often disastrous rule." In the dealings of his government with other nations Wallace saw great hypocrisy:

> In disputes with the powerful we often give way; with the weak and helpless, or those we think so, we are—allowing for advance in civilization—bloody, bold, and ruthless as any conqueror of the Middle Ages. And with it all we are sanctimonious. We profess religion. We claim to be more moral than other nations, and to conquer, and govern, and tax, and plunder weaker people for *their* good! While robbing them we actually claim to be benefactors! And then we wonder, or profess to wonder, why other Governments hate us!

He advocated that Great Britain demolish its empire, give Gibraltar to Spain, allow Crete and Cyprus to join Greece, let Malta and India decide their own futures, and above all give home rule to Ireland.

Wallace was especially critical of the military establishment, which he argued drained the wealth of the nation to no good purpose. Military organizations, he wrote in "Anticipations and Hopes for the Immediate Future," an article published in the 1 January 1904 issue of the *Clarion,* "are a permanent menace to liberty, to national morality, and to all real progress towards a rational social evolution." They commit "crimes against liberty and humanity—to say nothing of Christianity—almost unequalled in the whole course of modern history."

In a letter to the *Clarion* in 1904, "A Substitute for Militarism," he observed that advocates of a strong military complain of "our pitiable military situation" compared to that of Russia or Germany. He noted that the military constantly claims that it needs more money for "adequate and efficient defense." According to the militarists, "We must increase army, navy, and home defenses, and be prepared to fight all the world." While the ostensible argument for increased military spending is to defend "the greatness or safety of the empire, the extension of commerce or the advance of civilisation," Wallace suggests the real reason is to "distract attention" from domestic wretchedness and exploitation of foreign lands so that the rich can get richer.

In *My Life* Wallace argued that if armaments are reduced, a "principle of arbitration in the settlement of national difficulties" could emerge. But he maintained that it is hopeless to "expect any real improvement from the existing governments of the great civilized nations, supported and controlled as they are by the ever-increasing power of vast military and official organizations." The first order of business for a united group of workers of the world is "to weaken and ultimately to abolish militarism": "They will therefore be guilty of folly as well as crime if they much longer permit their rulers to drill them into armies, and force them to invade, and rob, and kill each other."

Wallace was as passionate in his environmentalism as he was in his attack on militarism. An early expression of Wallace the ecologist is found in "On the Physical Geography of the Malay Archipelago," which was published in the June 1863 issue of the *Royal Geographical Society*. He recommends a formal policy of preservation for natural-history collections. Without this the age would be charged "with having culpably allowed the destruction of some of those records of Creation which we had in our power to preserve; and while professing to regard every living thing as the direct handiwork and best evidence of a Creator, yet, with a strange inconsistency seeing many of them perish irrecoverably from the face of the earth, uncared for and unknown." Wallace had in mind not only fossils but also living species of animals and plants, thousands of which have disappeared in the century since he sounded his warning.

In *The Wonderful Century: Its Successes and Its Failures* (1898) Wallace urges his readers to pity the "plunder of the earth." He deplores the way coffee is cultivated through the obliteration of Brazilian rain forests. He explains that when the steep slopes in India were denuded rich topsoil "was quickly washed away by the tropical rains, leaving great areas of bare rock or furrowed clay, absolutely sterile, and which will probably not regain its former fertility for hundreds, perhaps thousands, of years." He found further evidence of "the reckless destruction of the stored-up products of nature" in the search for natural gas, coal, and oil. He also cites how factories expose workers to toxic chemicals such as yellow phosphorus. In Wallace's view poor people as well as plants and the land suffer from the barrage of ecological exploitation.

Wallace became increasingly caustic in his condemnation of governments and social organization. In *The Wonderful Century* he writes:

> These governments do not exist for the good of humanity or civilisation, but for the aggrandisement and greed and lust of power of the ruling classes—kings and kaisers, ministers and generals, nobles and millionaires—the true vampires of our civilisation ever seeking fresh dominions from whose people they may suck the very life-blood. . . . The welfare of the people is little

cared for except so far as to make them submissive tax payers, enabling the ruling and moneyed classes to extend their sway over new territories, and to create well-paid places and exciting work for their sons and relatives.

Fifteen years later in *Social Environment and Moral Progress* (1913) he is even harsher in his assessment: "It is not too much to say that our whole system of Society is rotten from top to bottom, and that the social environment as a whole in relation to our possibilities and our claims is the worst that the world has ever seen." Wallace was indefatigable until the end. *Social Environment and Moral Progress* is the first of two books he published in the year of his death.

During his career Wallace tended to write too optimistically of the hoped-for implementation of his favorite ideas. He asserted that spiritualism "affords the only sure foundation for improvement of society." He predicted that in the twentieth century phrenology would "gain general acceptance" as one of the highest sciences. He maintained that women would redeem the human species or that the socialists would: "They already influence public opinion, and will soon influence the legislatures." He thought that the United States would open the window into utopia: "It is to America that the world looks to lead the way towards a just and peaceful modification of the social organism, based upon a recognition of the principle of Equality of Opportunity, and by means of the Organization of the Labour of all for the Equal Good of all." In *My Life* he put his faith in the people: "The people are always better than their rulers. But the rulers have power, wealth, tradition, and the insatiable love of conquest and of governing others against their will. It is, then, in the People alone that I have any hope for the future of humanity."

Much of Wallace's agenda of course has been discredited. Spiritualism and phrenology are held no higher today than they were in the Victorian period; socialists have not cured the ills of the world nor have women redeemed the human species. But some of his ideas are so current that they could have been written last week rather than last century. His program for social reform is still the liberal agenda, its targets including genocide, ecocide, racism, militarism, the gross disparity of wealth, the political control exercised by the wealthy, and the restriction of women's rights. Undeniably Wallace had a prophetic talent for identifying problems that the world would continue to face long after his death.

Letters:

James Marchant, *Alfred Russel Wallace: Letters and Reminiscences*, 2 volumes (London: Cassell, 1916).

Bibliography:

H. Lewis McKinney, *Wallace and Natural Selection* (New Haven: Yale University Press, 1972).

Biographies:

Lancelot T. Hogben, *Alfred Russel Wallace: The Story of a Great Discoverer* (London: Society for Promoting Christian Knowledge, 1918);

E. B. Moulton, "Alfred Russel Wallace," *Proceedings of the Royal Society of London,* series B, 95 (January 1924): 1–35;

Loren C. Eiseley, "Alfred Russel Wallace," *Scientific American,* 200 (1959): 70–84;

Wilma George, *Biologist Philosopher. A Study of the Life and Writings of Alfred Russel Wallace* (London, 1964).

References:

John R. Durant, "Scientific Naturalism and Social Reform in the Thought of Alfred Russel Wallace," *British Journal for the History of Science,* 12 (1979): 31–58;

Martin Fichman, *Alfred Russel Wallace* (Boston: Twayne, 1981);

Bernard Lightman, ed., *Victorian Science in Context* (Chicago & London: University of Chicago Press, 1997);

Roger Smith, "Alfred Russel Wallace–Philosophy of Nature and Man," *British Journal for the History of Science,* 6 (1972): 177–199.

Samuel Warren
(23 May 1807 – 29 July 1877)

Bege K. Bowers
Youngstown State University

BOOKS: *Affecting Scenes; Being Passages from the Diary of a Physician,* anonymous, 2 volumes (New York: Harper, 1831); complete, authorized edition published as *Passages from the Diary of a Late Physician,* 3 volumes (Edinburgh & London: Blackwood, 1832-1838);

More Light on the Radcliffe Affair; or, The Gratitude of 1829 & 1831, Contrasted with the Ingratitude of 1834, in Letters from Samuel Warren, Esq., Barrister, and Son of the Rev. Samuel Warren (Manchester: J. E. Storey, 1834);

A Popular and Practical Introduction to Law Studies (London: Maxwell, 1835; Philadelphia: J. S. Littell, 1836); revised and enlarged as *A Popular and Practical Introduction to Law Studies, and to Every Department of the Legal Profession, Civil, Criminal, and Ecclesiastical: With an Account of the State of the Law in Ireland, and Scotland, and Occasional Illustrations from American Law* (London: Maxwell, 1845; Boston: Little, Brown, 1845); revised and enlarged again, 2 volumes (London: Maxwell, 1863);

The Merchant's Clerk, and Other Tales (New York: Harper, 1836);

Ten Thousand a-Year (6 volumes, Philadelphia: Carey & Hart, 1840-1841; 3 volumes, Edinburgh & London: Blackwood, 1841; Boston: Little, Brown, 1841; revised edition, 2 volumes, Paris: Baudry's European Library, 1842; revised edition, 3 volumes, Edinburgh & London: Blackwood, 1851); abridged by Cyrus Townsend Brady as *Tittlebat Titmouse* (New York & London: Funk & Wagnalls, 1903);

The Opium Question (London: J. Ridgway, 1840);

The Destroyer: A Tale of Guilt and Sorrow (Boston: Brainard, 1843);

Now and Then.—Through a Glass, Darkly (2 volumes, Edinburgh & London: Blackwood, 1847; 1 volume, New York: Harper, 1848);

The Moral, Social, and Professional Duties of Attornies and Solicitors (Edinburgh & London: Blackwood, 1848; New York: Harper, 1849);

Samuel Warren

Correspondence Between Samuel Warren, Esq., Barrister-at-Law, and Charles Phillips, Esq., Relative to the Trial of Courvoisier (London: King, 1849);

A Letter to the Queen on a Late Court Martial (Edinburgh & London: Blackwood, 1850);

The Queen, or the Pope? The Question Considered in Its Political, Legal, and Religious Aspects: In a Letter to Spencer H. Walpole, Esq., Q.C., M.P. (Edinburgh & London: Blackwood, 1850);

The Lily and the Bee, an Apologue of the Crystal Palace (Edinburgh & London: Blackwood, 1851; New York: Harper, 1851; revised edition, Edinburgh & London: Blackwood, 1854);

The Confessions of an Attorney: By Gustavus Sharp, Esq., of the Late Firm of Flint & Sharp; To Which Are Added Several Papers on English Law and Lawyers, by Charles Dickens (New York: Cornish, Lamport, 1852);

The Experiences of a Barrister, as Warren Warner, Esq., of the Inner Temple (New York: Cornish, Lamport, 1852); as S*** ****** ******, D. C. L. (London: J. & C. Brown, 1856);

A Manual of the Parliamentary Election Law of the United Kingdom of Great Britain and Ireland (London, 1852); enlarged as *A Manual of the Parliamentary Election Law of the United Kingdom of Great Britain and Ireland; with the Addition of the Statutes and Decisions of the Court of Common Pleas to the Present Time* (London: Butterworths, 1857);

The Intellectual and Moral Development of the Present Age (Edinburgh: Blackwood, 1853);

The Law and Practice of Election Committees; Being the Completion of A Manual of Parliamentary Election Law (London: Butterworths, 1853);

Miscellanies, Critical, Imaginative, and Juridical; Contributed to Blackwood's Magazine, 2 volumes (Edinburgh & London: Blackwood, 1855);

Labour: Its Rights, Difficulties, Dignity and Consolations. A Paper Read before the Hull Mechanics' Institute on Thursday, January 3, 1856 (London: Longman, 1856).

Collections: *Works of Samuel Warren* (5 volumes, Edinburgh & London: Blackwood, 1854–1855; revised edition, 4 volumes, Edinburgh: Blackwood, 1871–1874);

The Experiences of a Barrister and Other Tales (London & Edinburgh: W. & R. Chambers, 1878).

OTHER: Sir William Blackstone, *Select Extracts from Blackstone's Commentaries, Carefully Adapted to the Use of Schools and Young Persons,* edited by Warren (London: Maxwell, 1837).

Samuel Warren, a staunch conservative, takes his place among British reform writers not because he raised the call for reform in the 1820s and 1830s but because he *opposed* it—most notably in his best-selling legal novel, *Ten Thousand a-Year* (1840–1841). But while the novel and other works by Warren attack large-scale political reforms such as Catholic emancipation, disestablishment of the Church of England, and what Warren called the "great BILL FOR GIVING EVERY BODY EVERY THING," they advocate reform of a different kind: the moral regeneration of corrupt and self-serving individuals in all classes of society, all branches of government, all trades and professions.

In sales and popularity Warren's works threatened for a while to surpass those of Charles Dickens. However, as Warren soon learned, "greatness" is relative, and fame may be as fleeting as it is hard-won. Today little is known about the early life of Samuel Warren, who was born 23 May 1807 in Denbighshire, Wales, to a Wesleyan minister of the same name and his wife, Anne Williams Warren. Contemporary accounts indicate only that he studied medicine from 1821 through 1827; pursued law at the University of Edinburgh in 1827–1828; moved to London and entered the Inns of Court in 1828; served as a special pleader from 1831 to 1837; became a fellow of the Royal Society in 1835; and was called to the bar in 1837. He married a daughter of James Ballinger in 1831 and had three children: two sons, Samuel Lilckendy and Edward Walpole; and a daughter, Emily.

Early on, Warren showed both audacity and an interest in writing: at age seventeen, in the midst of medical training, he wrote to Sir Walter Scott asking advice on how to get published. Scott, denying authorship of the Waverley novels, replied that he could not "be useful in the way you propose." Later, while studying law at Edinburgh, Warren won a prize for poetry and also exposed his conservative political leanings in a pamphlet opposing Catholic emancipation.

Warren's bittersweet literary career and long association with the politically conservative *Blackwood's Magazine* began in August 1830, when William Blackwood printed a work three other publishers had rejected: the first installment of *Passages from the Diary of a Late Physician.* Throughout its serial publication (which ended in August 1837) and subsequently in book form the *Diary* enjoyed tremendous popularity with the general public both in England and abroad. Nevertheless, while it went through multiple editions and was translated into French and German, it set a precedent for the mixed reception that would haunt Warren throughout much of his literary career.

In many respects the fictional *Diary* was a candid and realistic picture of the newly professionalizing medical practice in nineteenth-century Britain; however, it was also a series of tales attributing physical and emotional illnesses to patients' *moral* indiscretions. Thus, doctors—who assumed that the work was a chronicle of actual medical cases—complained that its explicit details compromised patient confidentiality, while respected literary reviewers found its graphic scenes too "lurid," its sentiment too pronounced, and its moral lessons strained. The comments of one critic writing in the *London Quarterly Review* after the republication of the *Diary* in *Works of Samuel Warren* (1854–1855) suggest both the nature of the individual tales and the typical critical response:

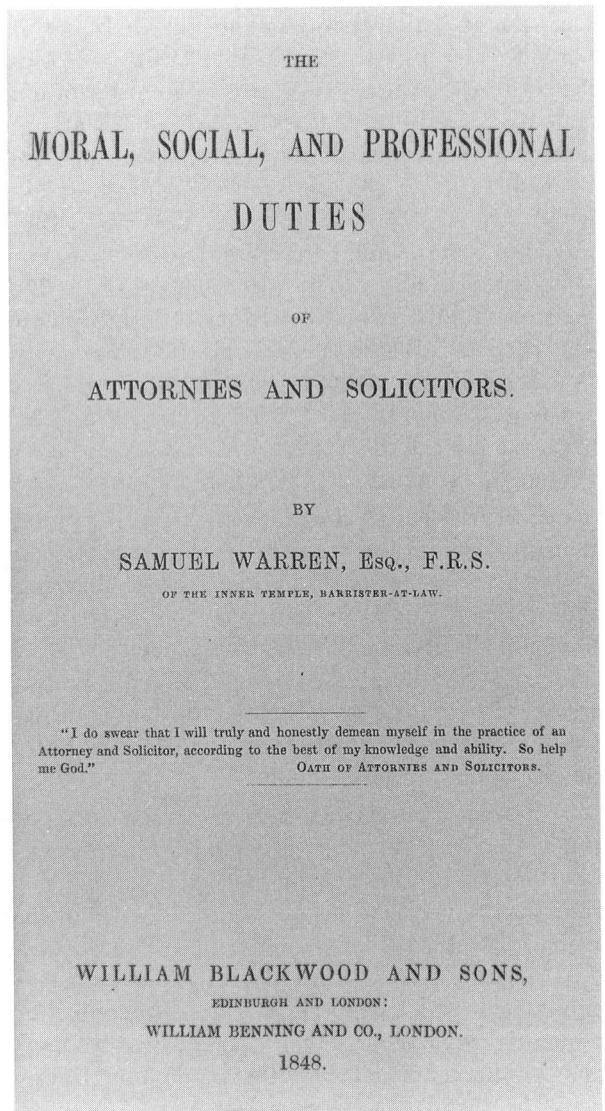

Title page for one of Warren's handbooks for aspiring lawyers

> To make the flesh creep and the roots of the hair strike cold, is not by any means the legitimate effect of art. A picture of some miserable object, racked by physical anguish, or writhing under the influence of some inexplicable remorse, is very easily produced by the aid of the coarsest brush and the strongest colors; but when done, what is it better than worthless and revolting?

All agreed, however, that the *Diary* was destined to sell: its morbid sensationalism was, as Francis Watt points out, clearly "a gem of the first water," at least "from the book-seller's point of view" if not the critic's.

Although Warren published the *Diary* anonymously, its enormous popularity, his deep-seated longing for public recognition, and the 1831 pirating of some early installments by an American publisher soon led him to acknowledge authorship. Thereafter he always imagined, whether rightly or not, that his success in literary endeavors lessened his credibility as a lawyer. Less-than-sympathetic commentators argued that Warren was surprisingly "dull, prosy, sententious" as a barrister, while kinder ones suggested that his imagination was simply more suited to literary pursuits.

Like many other lawyers of the period whose practices were less than spectacular, Warren tried his hand at legal publications, beginning with *A Popular and Practical Introduction to Law Studies* in 1835. Designed for aspiring lawyers in an age in which the formal education and moral training of would-be lawyers in England were poor at best, the *Introduction* outlined a course of study and professional development that, particularly in the revised and enlarged editions of 1845 and 1863, was more ambitious than most could achieve. Nevertheless, this publication, along with others such as *The Moral, Social, and Professional Duties of Attornies and Solicitors* (1848), helped to demystify the "learned" profession and set forth a clear program of study open to anyone with the discipline and means to follow it. At the same time—and probably equally important, given his need for public approval—the legal publications bolstered Warren's reputation when his performance as a barrister went unheralded.

Following the completed publication of the *Diary* in 1838, Warren embarked on the most successful—and controversial—of his literary endeavors: the novel *Ten Thousand a-Year,* serialized anonymously in *Blackwood's Magazine* from October 1839 through August 1841. After magazine publication it too went through several editions and translations, establishing itself as "one of the best, as it certainly was one of the most popular" novels of the century. According to Margaret Oliphant, with characteristic vanity Warren compared himself to Dickens, boasting that "some very able judges" and members of the legal profession had pronounced "a single page" of *Ten Thousand a-Year* "worth all that Dickens had ever written."

Combining humor, sentiment, and a heavy dose of the ludicrous, the novel both attacks the political Reform movement of the early 1830s and calls for widespread moral reform. It focuses on the efforts of Oily Gammon, a scheming, unscrupulous solicitor, to divest Charles Aubrey, a true "Christian gentleman" and rising Tory, of his property and seat in Parliament—a feat calling for considerable orchestration since Gammon has neither a viable case nor a legitimate client. The client he summons up is an odious little drapery clerk named Tittlebat Titmouse, who aspires to a much higher rank in society and whom Gammon convinces to sue Aubrey in an entirely manufactured suit of ejectment.

Reform politics underlie the plot of the novel and often come to the fore as, almost simultaneously, Titmouse wins the suit and the "great BILL FOR GIVING EVERY BODY EVERY THING" passes into law, precipitating a "prodigious flight of Titmice into the House of Commons." Warren depicts the fate of Aubrey and the future of the country as equally dire when the drunken and foolish Titmouse, aided by Gammon's machinations, usurps not only Aubrey's home but also his seat in the House. Espousing "good old whig principles," "papacy," and "the greatest happiness to the greatest number," Titmouse and his fellow miscreants threaten the structure of society itself:

> The first glance which John Bull caught of his new House of Commons, under the *Bill for Giving Everybody Everything*, almost turned his stomach, strong as it was, inside out; and he stood for some time staring with feelings of alternate disgust and dismay. Really ... there seemed scarcely fifty gentlemen among them; and those appeared ashamed and afraid of their position. 'Twas, indeed, as though the scum that had risen to the simmering surface of the caldron placed over the fierce fires of revolutionary ardour, had been ladled off and flung upon the floor of the House of Commons. The shock and mortification produced such an effect upon John, that he took for some time to his bed.

Ultimately, however, Gammon destroys himself; Aubrey exposes the illegitimacy of Titmouse's claim; and order is restored, whereupon the "Liberal party at Yatton" is "completely paralysed and crushed."

The story, both in novel form and in an 1841 dramatic version, brought Warren considerable fame and an extensive following, although, as Alexander Allardyce and John Blackwood point out, "The public was not slow to find many faults with 'Ten Thousand a-Year.' Some cavilled at the characters, many at the political bias, a good few at the plot." Some felt the characters were too thinly drawn—Titmouse too ridiculous, the Aubreys too pure and good (so good, in fact, that William Makepeace Thackeray included them in his *Book of Snobs*, 1848), and the lawyers and politicians too stereotypical.

In the face of such allegations Warren's admirers, and *Blackwood's Magazine* in particular, found themselves in the awkward position of reconciling the popularity of the novel with Warren's conservative political bias. Allardyce and Blackwood argue:

> A very natural objection has been taken to 'Ten Thousand a-Year,' that its art is all of a partisan character—that the Tories are all demi-gods and angels, and the Whigs for the most part incarnations of vice and vulgarity. There may be some justice in this allegation, but the complaint has not lowered the place of the novel among the classics of English fiction. To form a just estimate of this charge, we must consider the society which 'Ten Thousand a-Year' seeks to portray. The estate of Yatton is lost and won amid the furious agitations which preceded the first Reform Bill. The stirring politics of the day penetrated everywhere, and leavened the tone and feelings of society to an extent which the present generation has some difficulty in conceiving possible.

Whether posterity would concur that Warren's work is a "classic of English fiction" remains to be seen, but the novel stands as one of the most vocal literary proponents of maintaining the status quo in an age of encroaching reform.

After *Ten Thousand a-Year* Warren wrote one other successful novel, *Now and Then.—Through a Glass, Darkly* (1847), the story of a young man unjustly convicted of murder on the basis of circumstantial evidence. With his sharp sense of what would sell, Warren composed this new novel for the Christmas trade of 1847, beginning work near midnight on 20 November and delivering the completed manuscript to the printer the morning of 9 December. Like *Ten Thousand a-Year*, *Now and Then* (as its allusive title suggests) advocates submission to God's inscrutable will. It lacks the humor and satire of the earlier novel and is by far the most "preachy" of Warren's works, yet it enjoyed enormous—though short-lived—popularity, selling out the first edition in only two days.

Following *Now and Then*, however, Warren's literary fame slowly declined. His long poem, *The Lily and the Bee, an Apologue of the Crystal Palace,* was published by Blackwood in 1851 and was generally acknowledged a fiasco. Variously described as "one of the curiosities of English literature" and "the greatest abortion of the muse of which we have any knowledge," this poem celebrating the Great Exhibition did little to further Warren's literary career.

That career, in fact, slowly took second place to his legal and political career, which culminated in his appointment as recorder of Hull from 1852 to 1874, a position offered by the Conservative M.P. Spencer Walpole. He was also appointed Master of Lunacy, presiding over inquiries into the sanity of alleged lunatics and persons accused of criminal behavior; he held this post from 1859 until his death on 29 July 1877.

During the 1850s Warren attempted to renew his literary fame by republishing his earlier works in a five-volume series, *Works of Samuel Warren*, and the two-volume *Miscellanies, Critical, Imaginative, and Juridical; Contributed to Blackwood's Magazine* (1855). But critics argued that many of his works had hardly deserved their initial publication, and they accused him of initiating and indulging in "one of the most objectionable arts of puffery" known to the literary world: the publication of collected works during an author's lifetime.

Much to his personal gratification, however, Warren was elected to Parliament for a short stint from 1856 to 1859, though he failed to distinguish himself as he might have hoped. Known politically for his efforts to reform legal procedure, he also unfortunately retained his old social and religious prejudices, arguing vociferously against such measures as extending the franchise, admitting Jews to Parliament, and altering the parliamentary oath so that Jews would not have to swear on "the true faith of a Christian." His pronounced Tory and Church-of-England sentiments were in fact highly reminiscent of *Ten Thousand a-Year* (without the humor) and of *The Queen, or the Pope?*, a popular booklet he had published in 1850. In the latter Warren attacks the "political power of the papacy" as a "venomous serpent" threatening the sovereignty of "Her Majesty, the sole Source of honour and dignity" in a country that continued to change despite the reactionary spirit of Warren and other political conservatives.

In the end, the story of Warren's career—literary, legal, and political—is a story of struggle: an intense effort to win, and then to maintain, the public esteem he so desperately sought. Despite his otherwise-amiable nature, his vanity, one critic acknowledged, "almost amounted to disease." Some claimed that whenever obscurity threatened, Warren wrote another "shilling shocker," produced a new political pamphlet, or republished his collected works. His ultimate reception, personal and literary, was almost invariably mixed. In 1857 a reviewer for *Fraser's Magazine* wrote:

> if we can trace in [Warren] such failings as a disposition to hang on to the skirts of great men; a good deal of snobbishness and flunkeyism; a tendency to clap-trap and horrors; much indulgence in philosophy of the old-woman mark; great lack of taste, and occasionally of sense; a strong bias towards moral and religious reflections which remind us of the very washiest lessons of the pulpit;—why, no man is wholly without faults; and his real merits, acknowledged by none more cheerfully than by ourselves, may well outweigh much greater faults than those of Mr. Samuel Warren.

"With all his oddities," concludes J. B. Atlay, Warren "had more than a dash of genius," and according to John H. Wigmore's legal bibliography *Ten Thousand a-Year* was still "*the* book for lawyers by a lawyer" as late as 1908. But Warren never gained the unmitigated respect for which he longed.

Warren is known today, when he is known at all, only for the novel *Ten Thousand a-Year*. Even this, his greatest triumph, strikes a chord of ambivalence. Politically the novel drew sharp reactions in Warren's own time, primarily for its one-sided depiction of the 1830s Reform movement. In retrospect modern historians might say that the political sentiments of the novel lie somewhere between the outright attack on reform launched by Warren's narrator and the more moderate "Tory paternalism" represented by Charles Aubrey, who in his benevolence and Christian ethics is the most "liberal . . . landlord" in the country. But even this revisionist political reading says something of the artistic weaknesses of the novel. Though of enduring literary value, its artistry, consensus suggests, is unconscious; its achievement–ironically subverting the "narrowly conservative values" its author so strongly espoused–that of a writer notably, regrettably, inferior to Dickens.

References:

Alexander Allardyce and John Blackwood, "Samuel Warren," *Blackwood's*, 122 (September 1877): 381–390;

J. B. Atlay, "The Author of 'Ten Thousand a Year,'" *Cornhill*, new series 23 (October 1907): 476–488;

David Duncan, "Samuel Warren," *Appleton's Journal of Popular Literature, Science, and Art*, 4 (22 October 1870): 492–494;

R. B. McDowell, *British Conservatism, 1832–1914* (London: Faber & Faber, 1959);

"Mr. Warren's 'Miscellanies,'" *Fraser's*, 55 (May 1857): 590–601;

Bege Bowers Neel, "Lawyers on Trial: Attitudes Toward the Lawyer's Use and Abuse of Rhetoric in Nineteenth-Century England," dissertation, University of Tennessee, 1984, pp. 70–73, 89, 183–193;

Margaret Oliphant, *Annals of a Publishing House: William Blackwood and His Sons,* volume 2 (New York: Scribners, 1897);

Jonathan Parry, *The Rise and Fall of Liberal Government in Victorian Britain* (New Haven & London: Yale University Press, 1993);

"Popular Authorship–Samuel Warren," *London Quarterly Review*, 5 (January 1856): 464–480;

Michael Steig, "Subversive Grotesque in Samuel Warren's *Ten Thousand a-Year*," *Nineteenth-Century Fiction*, 24 (September 1969): 154–168;

Francis Watt, "Samuel Warren," *Juridical Review*, 30 (June 1918): 85–98;

John H. Wigmore, "A List of Legal Novels," *Illinois Law Review*, 2 (1908): 574–593;

Samuel A. Yorks, "Samuel Warren: An Early Contributor to Victorian Literature," dissertation, University of Washington, 1956.

Beatrice Webb
(22 January 1858 – 30 April 1943)

and

Sidney Webb
(13 July 1859 – 13 October 1947)

Sylvia Vance
St. Edmund Hall, Oxford University

BOOKS: *Facts for Socialists,* by Sidney Webb (London: Privately printed, 1887);

Wanted, A Programme: An Appeal to the Liberal Party, by Sidney Webb (London: Privately printed, 1888);

Socialism in England, by Sidney Webb (London: Sonnenschein, 1890; London: Sonnenschein / New York: Scribners, 1893);

The Co-operative Movement in Great Britain, by Beatrice Webb (London: Sonnenschein, 1891; London: Sonnenschein / New York: Scribners, 1895);

The London Programme, by Sidney Webb (London: Sonnenschein, 1891);

The Eight Hour Day, by Sidney Webb and Harold Cox (London: W. Scott, 1891);

The Reform of London, by Sidney Webb (London: Eighty Club, 1892);

The History of Trade Unionism, by Sidney Webb and Beatrice Webb (London & New York: Longmans, Green, 1894; revised and enlarged, 1920);

Industrial Democracy, 2 volumes, by Sidney Webb and Beatrice Webb (London & New York: Longmans, Green, 1897);

Labour in the Longest Reign, by Sidney Webb (London: Richards, 1897);

Problems of Modern Industry, by Sidney Webb and Beatrice Webb (London & New York: Longmans, Green, 1898);

The History of Liquor Licensing in England, Principally from 1700 to 1830, by Sidney Webb and Beatrice Webb (London & New York: Longmans, Green, 1903);

London Education, by Sidney Webb (London & New York: Longmans, Green, 1904);

English Local Government from the Revolution to the Municipal Corporations Act, 11 volumes, by Sidney Webb and Beatrice Webb (London & New York: Longmans, Green, 1906–1929);

Bibliography of Road Making and Maintenance in Great Britain, by Sidney Webb and Beatrice Webb (London: Roads Improvement Association, 1906);

The Basis and Policy of Socialism, by Sidney Webb and the Fabian Society (London: Fifield, 1908);

Socialism and Individualism, by Sidney Webb, Sidney Ball, Oliver Lodge, and Bernard Shaw (London: Fifield, 1908);

Socialism and National Minimum, by Beatrice Webb (London: Fifield, 1909);

The State and the Doctor, by Sidney Webb and Beatrice Webb (London & New York: Longmans, Green, 1910);

Grants in Aid: A Criticism and a Proposal, by Sidney Webb (London & New York: Longmans, Green, 1911; revised and enlarged, 1920);

The Prevention of Destitution, by Sidney Webb and Beatrice Webb (London & New York: Longmans, Green, 1911);

Complete National Provision for Sickness: How to Amend the Insurance Act, by Beatrice Webb (London: Standing Joint Committee of the Independent Labour Party and the Fabian Society, 1912);

Towards Social Democracy? A Study of Social Evolution During the Past Three-Quarters of a Century, by Sidney Webb (London: Fabian Society/Allen & Unwin, 1916);

Great Britain After the War, by Sidney Webb and Arnold Freeman (London: Allen & Unwin, 1916);

Sidney and Beatrice Webb in the early 1890s

The Restoration of Trade Union Conditions, by Sidney Webb (London: Nisbet, 1917; New York: Huebsch, 1917);

The Works Manager To-Day, by Sidney Webb (London & New York: Longmans, Green, 1917);

The Wages of Men and Women: Should They Be Equal?, by Beatrice Webb (London: Fabian Society, 1919);

A Constitution for the Socialist Commonwealth of Great Britain, by Sidney Webb and Beatrice Webb (London & New York: Longmans, Green, 1920);

The Story of the Durham Miners (1662–1921), by Sidney Webb (London: Fabian Society/Labour Publishing, 1921);

The Consumers' Co-operative Movement, by Sidney Webb and Beatrice Webb (London & New York: Longmans, Green, 1921);

The Decay of Capitalist Civilisation, by Sidney Webb and Beatrice Webb (London: Fabian Society/Allen & Unwin, 1923; New York: Harcourt, Brace, 1923);

My Apprenticeship, by Beatrice Webb (London & New York: Longmans, Green, 1926);

The English Poor-Law, Will It Endure?, by Beatrice Webb (London: Oxford University Press, 1928);

Methods of Social Study, by Sidney Webb and Beatrice Webb (London & New York: Longmans, Green, 1932);

Soviet Communism: A New Civilisation?, 2 volumes, by Sidney Webb and Beatrice Webb (London & New York: Longmans, Green, 1935; New York: Scribners, 1936); republished, with a new introduction by Beatrice Webb (London & New York: Longmans, Green, 1941); introduction revised as *The Truth about Soviet Russia* (London & New York: Longmans, Green, 1942);

Our Partnership, by Beatrice Webb, edited by Barbara Drake and Margaret I. Cole (London: Longmans, Green, 1948; New York: Longmans, Green, 1948);

The Evolution of Local Government, by Sidney Webb (London: Municipal Journal, 1951);

Beatrice Webb's Diaries, 1912–1924, 2 volumes, by Beatrice Webb, edited by Cole (London & New York: Longmans, Green, 1952);

Visit to New Zealand in 1898: Beatrice Webb's Diary, with Entries by Sidney Webb, by Beatrice Webb and Sidney Webb (Wellington, N.Z.: Price, Milburn, 1959);

The Webbs' Australian Diary, 1898, edited by A. G. Austin (Melbourne: Pitman, 1965);

The Diary of Beatrice Webb, edited by Norman Ian MacKenzie and Jeanne Daisy MacKenzie, 4 volumes (London: Virago in association with the London School of Economics and Political Science, 1982–1984; Cambridge, Mass.: Belknap Press of Harvard University Press, 1982–1985);

The Webbs in Asia: The 1911–12 Travel Diary, edited by George Feaver (Basingstoke, U.K.: Macmillan, 1992).

OTHER: *The Case for the Factory Acts,* edited by Beatrice Webb (London: Richards, 1901; New York: Dutton, 1901);

The Break-up of the Poor Law: Being Part One of the Minority Report of the Poor Law Commission, edited by Sidney Webb and Beatrice Webb (London & New York: Longmans, Green, 1909);

The Public Organisation of the Labour Market: Being Part Two of the Minority Report of the Poor Law Commission, edited by Sidney Webb and Beatrice Webb (London & New York: Longmans, Green, 1909);

Seasonal Trades, edited by Sidney Webb and Arnold Freeman (London: Constable, 1912);

National Committee for the Prevention of Destitution, *The Case for the National Minimum,* preface by Beatrice Webb (London: National Committee for the Prevention of Destitution, 1913);

How to Pay for the War: Being Ideas Offered to the Chancellor of the Exchequer, edited by Sidney Webb (Westminster: Fabian Society / London: Allen & Unwin, 1916);

Agnes Edith Metcalfe, *Woman: A Citizen,* preface by Beatrice Webb (London: Allen & Unwin, 1918).

A canon of nearly five hundred books, pamphlets, articles, introductions, and edited volumes by Beatrice and Sidney Webb lends some understanding to the lives of two of the most important and prolific British Socialists. But they did not merely write. They gave speeches, conducted demanding research, ran for office (and won), worked on royal commissions, and sustained a happy marriage.

When Beatrice Potter and Sidney Webb met and, after a strained courtship, married, they were dubbed somewhat unfairly the beauty and the beast. They were an unlikely couple: they came from different educational and social backgrounds, and she was one of the beautiful Potter sisters. But by the time they met, each of them was committed to socialism, and together they believed that they could make a considerable contribution to the Socialist cause. Their marriage was one more of commitment than passion, but it became one of great love.

Beatrice Potter, the eighth of nine sisters, was born 22 January 1858. Having given birth to seven girls, her mother had been wishing for a boy, and, as a somewhat unwelcome new baby girl, Potter was barely tolerated by her mother throughout her life. Her childhood was uneventful and unhappy. Although her father did not stint his emotions, as a wealthy timber entrepreneur he was often away, and the child found most of her consolation and comfort with Martha Jackson, a poor relation living with the Potters, and with her favorite domestic servant in the laundry room of the household.

Poorly educated, as Victorian girls were, Potter nevertheless read widely and was burdened with a temperament that forced her to think deeply. By her teenage years she was already feeling the conflict between the privileged society into which she had been born and her need to answer a greater calling. Religion, however, did not hold answers for her. A deeply spiritual woman, she was influenced by scientific ideas and was eventually persuaded that one could apply scientific method to the management of human lives and social problems. Herbert Spencer was a friend of the family and was particularly fond of Potter. His "scientific method" influenced her throughout her life.

One of the ideal roles of the Victorian woman was that of succorer to the poor. Potter was not immune to the cultural ideals of her time, and she joined the Charity Organisation Society in 1883, less to serve its rationale of relieving the poor from charity (which members of the organization saw as a demoralization of character) than to serve her own purposes of creating a way to observe humanity scientifically. She visited the poor and indigent to judge whether a request for financial aid was legitimate or, more important, whether the person making the request was worthy. Middle-class values such as those personified in social worker Octavia Hill, for whom Potter's sister Kate worked, were imposed on the poor, and Potter soon became disillusioned with conventional views of the poor and with her ability to help them, in part because she perceived that the problems of the poor were more intransigent than remediable through a forced shift of their values. She also met Joseph Chamberlain, a striking Progressive Party politician who took Birmingham by storm with his Four Fs program: Free Schools, Free Land, Free Church, and Free Labour.

Beatrice and Sidney Webb with fellow Fabian Bernard Shaw (center) at the Webbs' house at Passfield

Remorselessly handsome and charismatic, he was looking for a third wife, and it looked as if Potter might be she.

After much heartbreak Potter realized that a marriage to Chamberlain would result only if she were willing to reduce herself to being his adoring helpmate. She did adore him, but she was strong enough in her opinions to know that she could never be only a man's mirror. During their up-and-down courtship Potter was developing her own ideas about social science and her own role as a social investigator, and as a farmer's daughter she went to a small working-class mill town to look at what were considered to be functional working-class people and compare them with those living in poverty in London. She was one of the first researchers to understand the possibility that there were underlying causes of poverty in a time when most members of the middle class believed that poverty was an earned and deserved state. Her visit to Bacup, Lancashire, left a lasting impression on her and created the basis for both her belief in social investigation and the cooperative movement. For Potter this experience marked a significant move toward socialism.

In 1885 her philanthropic work took her to managing Katherine Buildings, a new housing project for the poor in which she and Ella Pycroft chose the tenants for around three hundred rooms. Never conscious of the intrusiveness of their mission, they investigated prospective tenants' incomes, lifestyles, and personal habits. Potter's work there led her gradually to a revulsion with capitalism, and her experiences moved her to write a letter to the *Pall Mall Gazette,* which published it as "A Lady's View of the Unemployed." Her work at Katherine Buildings had turned her into a rent collector, and she was beginning to distrust the efficacy of philanthropic work. When her father suddenly suffered a severe stroke, Potter had to leave her work and move him to lodgings in Bournemouth to care for him. On the whole it was a difficult time, but her experience allowed her, still interested in housing for the poor, seriously to study English economics, history, and law.

Relieved by her sisters from some responsibilities of caring for her father, she returned to London and apprenticed herself to Charles Booth, doing research for his investigations into the lives of working-class people that eventually was incorporated into seventeen volumes of his *The Life and Labour of the People in London* (1902–1903). Living in the East End, she spent months investigating the lives of people who lived there and in October 1887 published her first article, "Dock Life," in *Nineteenth Century*. It was well received, and Potter, disguising herself as a worker, was encouraged to investigate the "sweating system," by which laborers in the garment industry served as subcontracted manufacturers of cheap goods.

She went to the garment district, hired on as a seamstress, and published her experiences in "Pages from a Work-Girl's Diary." Disguising herself in order to observe through firsthand experience was her preferred method of working all her life. She wanted to investigate how people lived by living and working alongside them, however briefly; she realized that no theorizing by anyone of her class would mean anything without a thorough understanding of the realities of people's lives. Through publishing "Pages from a Work-Girl's Diary" she achieved some notoriety and was called before the House of Lords Select Committee on Sweating in May 1888. Turning away from the ethos of Victorian society, which members of her class expected her to support, and from Spencer's faith in capitalism, she turned toward socialism.

THE WEBB OF DESTINY

"Mr. Sidney Webb: 'I am waving this red flag not provocatively, but to signalise what I have so happily called the "Inevitability of Gradualness" which marks our roller's advance.'"

Cartoon by Frank Reynolds published in Punch (4 July 1923) after Sidney Webb heralded the gradual and inevitable advance of socialism in his presidential address at the Labour Party Conference

Born on 13 July 1859, Sidney Webb became a Socialist by a more direct route. His father, an admirer of John Stuart Mill, was an infrequently employed accountant who, as a Radical, devoted much time and labor to unpaid work. The mainstay of the Webb family income was his mother's hairdressing business, and her evangelical Christianity was the mainstay of the family spiritual life. Webb taught himself to read early and started to win prizes at school. In spite of the limits of the family income, Webb's mother sent him and Charles, his older brother, to Europe to learn French and German. Leaving school at sixteen to contribute to the family finances, Webb acquired a facility in those languages that helped him get a job. In the evenings he attended London University, and in 1878 he entered the civil service. Working his way up the ranks through sheer hard work, he studied the law and by 1886 earned a law degree from London University. At the same time he supplemented his income by freelance journalism.

In 1879 Webb met Bernard Shaw, who recognized Webb's intellectual qualities and devoted himself to a profound, lifelong friendship with Webb. They became the nucleus of the Fabian Society, which Shaw joined in September 1884 and Webb in May 1885. The Society developed in the late nineteenth century from the milieu of clubs that were dedicated to spiritual discovery. Edward Pease wanted to include social as well as spiritual interests, and with Frank Podmore he became an early member of the Fabian Society in January 1884. At first the kind of Socialist values they wanted to promote were unclear and remained unclear even after

Webb wrote a document defining the basis for membership. It was so vague that almost every variety of Socialist would qualify for membership, and in a way this breadth became the strength of the society. The membership was small, growing from forty members in 1885 to sixty-seven in 1886. But the Fabians' influence was substantial after Webb in 1887 wrote *Facts for Socialists,* a pamphlet of which twenty thousand copies were sold, and after seven of the Fabians wrote *Fabian Essays in Socialism* (1889), of which forty-six thousand copies were sold.

Beatrice Potter met Webb following publication of his essay, which she thought the most interesting of those in the 1889 collection. By this time she was traveling the country and interviewing people in the cooperative movement. Staying with working-class families and eating with cooperators, she was preparing the ground for her first book, *The Co-operative Movement in Great Britain* (1891). She was drawn to the idea of cooperativism when she was working in some of the Jewish-run sweatshops in London. Never a racist, Potter decided that the basis for London Jews to survive in conditions as bad as those of other poor was their close community and social ties. If those ties could not be provided culturally, she thought, they could be provided through social organizations, and she traveled to see how those organizations functioned. When she was ready to write her book, however, she realized that her historical information was thin, and she asked Maggie Harkness, her friend, for the name of someone to whom she might turn for help. Webb was the man, and Potter met him in January 1890.

Webb had a large head and a handsome profile, but physically he was otherwise singularly unattractive. His body was small; he was unkempt, usually wearing a shiny suit; and his accent was decidedly Cockney. Potter might have left the glamour of Victorian society behind in deciding to become a social investigator, but she was still a social snob. Her longings for Chamberlain may have subsided, especially after he had married an American woman, but his physical magnetism still haunted her. Webb was not going to be a replacement. She and Webb continued meeting, however, and soon their intellectual compatibility became apparent. Their courtship was rocky, with Webb deeply in love with a Beatrice Potter who had no intentions of taking him seriously as a romantic interest, although he was constantly persuading her that they could work together.

Twentieth-century portraits of the Webbs, especially those by H. G. Wells and Virginia Woolf, do little to explore what they were like in the 1890s. Sidney Webb became more and more like a civil servant, dry and full of facts. Beatrice Webb traveled an equally cerebral path and eventually became a cold beauty. But in the 1890s Sidney Webb was probably at his intellectual zenith, combining his amazing grasp of facts and information with a still youthful curiosity. Beatrice Potter in the 1890s was still very much a member of her class as well as a beautiful woman spiritually hungry and intellectually commanding. They were, for all their differences, exciting people.

Having published her book, Potter began lecturing on the cooperative movement. At the same time Webb, having published *Socialism in England* (1890), was traveling in the north of England to speak on Fabianism and was working on *The London Programme* (1891). He was a prolific if dry writer, continuing to produce his newspaper articles and pamphlets for the Fabian Society. For reasons that remain unclear, in early January 1891 Potter changed her mind and decided to marry Webb, but the engagement had to remain secret while her father remained alive but still ailing. When he died on 1 January 1892 they were free to marry, and the two were married on 23 July 1892. Webb had won election to Parliament as the Progressive candidate for Deptford in the London county-council elections in March 1892, and Potter's anticipated inheritance allowed Webb to leave the civil service in 1891. The Webbs' first book they wrote together was *The History of Trade Unionism* (1894), which Shaw helpfully edited, and it was the beginning of a prolific writing relationship. Together they wrote on multitudinous subjects from a socialist perspective, and although their prose became drier as they aged, the influence of what they wrote and the effects they had on government policies are still felt in Britain.

One of the most important of their publications was the two-volume *The Minority Report of the Poor Law Commission* (1909), a study they began working on after Prime Minister Arthur Balfour had appointed Beatrice Webb to the Royal Commission on the Poor Law and Relief of Distress in 1905. Led by a Conservative, the commission was peopled with politically and socially disparate individuals who spent little time in agreement, even on the principles of research. As a result, Webb set up her own research team with the intention of investigating the root causes of poverty—when it was supposed that the commission was to support the Poor Law, which was designed to send the most impoverished of the poor to the workhouse. Her inspiration came in 1907 when she realized that the Poor Law should be broken up, that individual services for the poor should be handled by appropriate government departments under the rubric of that service. At the

Portrait of the Webbs painted in 1928 by Sir William Nicholson (London School of Economics)

heart of her plans was a national health service. She also devised a scheme of labor exchanges to remedy the problems of the unemployed. It was clear that the commission was not going to agree with her plans, and she and Sidney Webb published a minority report, a revolutionary document that established the foundation of the social-services system for which Britain came to be well known.

During the time she served on the commission both she and Sidney Webb worked on the English Local Government series (1906–1929), eventually an eleven-volume study examining the process of governing at the local level. More important, however, they watched the growth of the London School of Economics and Political Science, a school founded as a result of a bequest by Henry Hutchinson, a Fabian solicitor, to the Fabian Society. The Webbs decided that a research school of the social sciences should be established, and William Albert Samuel Hewins was hired as its first director. Sidney Webb found housing for the school, and both he and Beatrice raised funds for the library. In October 1896 the school opened.

Sidney Webb's interest in education, which he regarded as a source of salvation for the working poor, never abated, and in 1902 he worked with Robert Laurie Morant to draft the 1902 Education Act. Called "Webb's Act," it established a scholarship system and provided that schools be financially supported by ratepayers. The act displeased the educational reform wishes of every party, and the Webbs' minority report on the Poor Law was being poorly received in spite of Beatrice Webb's speaking tour throughout the country in an attempt to drum up support for it. As a result of hostility to the Webb Act, the Conservative David Lloyd George mustered enough votes to pass his employment insurance bill, inspired by fears of the Webbs' socialism.

The Webbs had traveled to Australia in 1898, and in 1911, exhausted and defeated, they embarked on a world tour, including visits to Canada, Japan, China, and India. The failures of imperialism were most apparent in India; the successes of an appropriate school system were most apparent in Japan. When they returned, they were probably as uncommitted to projects as they had ever been during their married life, although Sidney Webb was an honorary professor of public administration at the University of London from 1912 to 1927. The *New Statesman* was founded in 1913, however, and the

Webbs began to write for it regularly. After a shaky start it became the voice of Fabian socialism and was successful, but World War I began in 1914, and the Webbs' belief in a new society of peaceful workers ended. Though the Webbs were anti-war, they were not pacifists and scorned those who were, as they believed that their world had returned to more-barbaric times.

By 1916 Beatrice Webb was asked to join the Reconstruction Committee and was soon sitting on many more. In 1918 Sidney Webb ran for the University of London seat and lost, but the Labour Party formed the opposition for the first time. Prime Minister Lloyd George appointed him to a commission that was investigating the demands of miners for more pay and fewer working hours. Back in political harness, Sidney Webb ran for and won the seat representing the mining constituency of Seaham in Durham. Fulfilling the expectations that had been held for him decades earlier, he entered Parliament at the age of sixty-three. Having a quiet voice and manner, he was not very successful as an M.P., but with the 1924 election the Labour Party formed its first minority government, and Sidney Webb was made president of the board of trade by Premier Ramsay MacDonald. That government fell in 1924, and although he was not a member of Parliament in the new government in 1929, Sidney Webb was offered a peerage as First Baron Passfield and a position as minister for the colonies with the Colonial Office. He was delighted to be a minister in the office where he had been a clerk, and he accepted the peerage with alacrity. Beatrice Webb, on the other hand, always refused to be recognized as Lady Passfield.

That government was the last served by Sidney Webb, and when it failed, the Webbs turned their eyes to the East. Having always believed that the growth of socialism was an evolutionary process, they became seduced by the results of the Soviet revolution. They traveled to Russia in 1932 and returned to England to write *Soviet Communism: A New Civilisation?* (1935) at a time when the enthusiasm of some early Russian Socialists was already cooling. In failing health by the beginning of World War II, both of the Webbs seemed unable to change their minds about the Soviet Union and Joseph Stalin, its leader, even in the face of evidence that would have swayed them to do so when they were younger.

Beatrice Webb died on 30 April 1943, Sidney Webb on 13 October 1947. They are the only married couple to have been interred in Westminster Abbey.

Letters:

The Letters of Sidney and Beatrice Webb, edited by Norman MacKenzie (London: London School of Economics and Political Science / Cambridge: Cambridge University Press, 1978).

References:

Barbara Caine, *Destined to Be Wives: The Sisters of Beatrice Webb* (Oxford: Clarendon Press / New York: Oxford University Press, 1986);

Margaret I. Cole, *Beatrice Webb* (London, New York & Toronto: Longmans, 1945);

Cole, ed., *The Webbs and Their Work* (London: Muller, 1949);

Brian Lee Crowley, *The Self, The Individual and The Community: Liberalism in the Political Thought of F. A. Hayek and Sidney and Beatrice Webb* (Oxford: Clarendon Press, 1987);

Robert G. Gregory, *Sidney Webb and East Africa: Labour's Experiment with the Doctrine of Native Paramountcy* (Berkeley: University of California Publications in History, 1962);

Mary Agnes Hamilton, *Sidney and Beatrice Webb: A Study in Contemporary Biography* (London: Sampson Low, Marston, 1933);

Jeanne Daisy MacKenzie, *A Victorian Courtship: The Story of Beatrice Potter and Sidney Webb* (London: Weidenfeld & Nicolson, 1979);

Norman Ian MacKenzie, *Socialism and Society: A New View of the Webb Partnership* (London: London School of Economics, 1978);

Alan M. McBriar, *An Edwardian Mixed Doubles: The Bosanquets versus the Webbs, A Study in British Social Policy 1890–1929* (Oxford: Clarendon Press, 1987);

Deborah Epstein Nord, *The Apprenticeship of Beatrice Webb* (London: Macmillan, 1985; Amherst: University of Massachusetts Press, 1985);

Lisanne Radice, *Beatrice and Sidney Webb: Fabian Socialists* (London: Macmillan, 1984);

Carole Seymour-Jones, *Beatrice Webb: Woman of Conflict* (London: Allison & Busby, 1992);

Richard Henry Tawney, *The Webbs in Perspective* (London: Athlone Press, 1953).

Papers:

Most of the Webbs' papers are held by the London School of Economics and Political Science.

Richard Whately
(1 February 1787 – 8 October 1863)

William F. Naufftus
Winthrop University

BOOKS: *Historic Doubts Relative to Napoleon Buonaparte,* anonymous (London: J. Hatchard, 1819; Cambridge, Mass.: Brown, Shattuck, 1832);

The Use and Abuse of Party Feeling in Matters of Religion, Considered in Eight Sermons Preached before the University of Oxford, in the Year MDCCCXXII (Oxford: Printed for the author by Oxford University Press, 1822);

Five Sermons on Several Occasions Preached before the University of Oxford (Oxford: Oxford University Press, 1823);

Essays on Some of the Peculiarities of the Christian Religion (London: J. Parker, 1825; Andover, Mass: Warren F. Draper, 1870);

Elements of Logic, Comprising the Substance of the Article in the Encyclopaedia Metropolitana, with Additions (London: J. Mawman, 1826; New York: William Jackson, 1832; revised edition, London: B. Fellowes, 1844; New York: Harper, 1845?);

Miscellanea (London: B. Fellowes, 1831);

Letters on the Church by an Episcopalian, anonymous (London, 1826; New York: Harper, 1837);

Elements of Rhetoric, Comprising the Substance of the Article in the Encyclopaedia Metropolitana, with Additions (Oxford: John Murray, 1828; Cambridge, Mass.: Brown, Shattuck / Boston: Hilliard, Gray, 1832); revised as *Elements of Rhetoric, comprising an analysis of the Laws of Moral Evidence and of Persuasion, with Rules for Argumentative Composition and Elocution* (London: B. Fellowes, 1841; New York: W. H. Colyer, 1846);

Essays on Some Difficulties in the Writings of St. Paul, and in Other Parts of the New Testament (London: B. Fellowes, 1828; New York: Protestant Episcopal Press, 1831);

A View of the Scripture Revelations Concerning a Future State: Laid before his Parishioners by a Country Pastor, anonymous (London: B. Fellowes, 1829; Philadelphia: Lindsay & Blakiston, 1855);

Essays on the Errors of Romanism Traced to their Origin in Human Nature (London: B. Fellowes, 1830; Philadelphia: J. M. Campbell, 1843);

Richard Whately

An Essay on the Omission of Creeds, Liturgies and Codes of Ecclesiastical Canons, in the New Testament (London: B. Fellowes, 1831);

Introductory Lectures on Political Economy, Being Part of a Course Delivered in Easter Term MDCCCXXXI (London: B. Fellowes, 1831; enlarged edition, 1832);

The Evidence of His Grace, the Archbishop of Dublin as Taken before the Select Committee of the House of Lords, Appointed to Inquire into the Collection and Payment of Tithes in Ireland and the State of the Laws Relating Thereto (London: B. Fellowes, 1832);

Thoughts on Secondary Punishments, in a Letter to Earl Grey, to which are Added, Two Articles on Transpor-

tation to New South Wales, and on Secondary Punishments, and Some Observations on Colonization (London: B. Fellowes, 1832);

Scripture Lessons, adapted for the Use of Schools: Old Testament, No. 1, anonymous, by Whately, James Carlile, and others (Dublin: Hardy, 1832);

Easy Lessons on Money Matters for the Use of Young People anonymous (London: J. W. Parker, 1833);

A Speech in the House of Lords, August 1, 1833, on a Bill for the Removal of Certain Disabilities from His Majesty's Subjects of the Jewish Persuasion, with Additional Remarks on Some of the Objections Urged Against That Measure (London: B. Fellowes, 1833);

Considerations on the Law of Libel, as Relating to Publications on the Subject of Religion, as John Search (London: J. Ridgway, 1833);

Scripture Lessons: New Testament, No. 1 for the Use of the Irish National Schools, anonymous, by Whately, Carlile, and others (Dublin: Hardy, 1834);

Remarks on Transportation, and on a Recent Defense of the System; in a Second Letter to Earl Grey (London: B. Fellowes, 1834);

Scripture Lessons: New Testament, No. II, for the Irish National Schools, anonymous, by Whately, Carlile, and others (Dublin: Hardy, 1835);

Sermons on Various Subjects, Delivered in Several Churches in the City of Dublin, and in Other Parts of the Diocese (London: B. Fellowes, 1835; enlarged edition, London: J. W. Parker, 1849);

Charges and Other Tracts (London: J. W. Parker/B. Fellowes, 1836);

Christianity Independent of the Civil Government, anonymous (New York: Harper, 1837);

Introductory Lessons on Christian Evidences (London: J. W. Parker, 1838; Boston: W. S. Crosby and H. P. Nichols, 1850); republished as *Lessons on the Truth of Christianity; being an Appendix to the Fourth Book of Lessons for the Use of the Schools* (Dublin: Published by direction of the Commissioners of National Education, 1838);

Essays on Some of the Dangers to Christian Faith, which May Arise from the Teaching or the Conduct of Its Professors; to which are Subjoined Three Discourses Delivered on Several Occasions (London: B. Fellowes, 1839);

Substance of a Speech on Transportation, Delivered in the House of Lords, on the 19th of May, 1840 (London: B. Fellowes, 1840);

The Kingdom of Christ Delineated in Two Essays, on Our Lord's own Account of His Person and of the Nature of His Kingdom and on the Constitution, Powers and Ministry of a Christian Church as Appointed by Himself (London: B. Fellowes, 1841; New York: Wiley & Putnam, 1842; revised edition, London: B. Fellowes, 1842; New York: Wiley & Putnam, 1843); abridged as *Apostolical Succession Considered: or, the Constitution of a Christian Church, Its Powers and Ministry,* edited by Elizabeth Jane Whately (London: Longman, 1877; New York: Longman, Green, 1912);

Religion and Her Name, a Metrical Tract with Notes, as John Search (London: J. Ridgway, 1841);

Kingdom of Christ and the Errors of Romanism (New York: Wiley, 1842);

Easy Lessons on Reasoning (London, 1843; Boston: J. Monroe, 1845);

Sequel to the Second Book of Lessons for the Use of the Schools, anonymous (Dublin, 1844);

Reflections of a Grant to a Roman Catholic Seminary; being a Charge Delivered at the Visitation of the Dioceses of Dublin and Glandalough, 26 June, 1845, Comprising the Substance of a Speech delivered in the House or Lords, 3 June 1845 (London: B. Fellowes, 1845);

Scripture Lessons for the Use of Schools: Old Testament, No. II, anonymous, by Whately, Carlile, and others (Dublin: Hardy, 1846);

Address to the Clergy and other Members of the Established Church on the Use and Abuse of the Present Occasion for the Exercise of Beneficence (Dublin: Hodges & Smith, 1847; London: B. Fellowes, 1847);

Charge to the Clergy of the Dioceses of Dublin and Kildare, Delivered at the Visitations of those Dioceses Respectively in July, 1847 (Dublin: Hodges & Smith, 1847);

Lectures on the Characters of Our Lord's Apostles, and Especially Their Conduct at the Time of His Apprehension and Trial, by a Country Pastor (London: J. W. Parker, 1851; enlarged edition, 1853);

Cautions for the Times: Addressed to the Parishioners of a Parish in England, by Their Former Rector, anonymous, by Whately and William Fitzgerald (London: J. W. Parker, 1851; New York: Stanford & Swords, 1853);

English Synonyms (1851); republished as *English Synonyms Discriminated by Richard Whately* (Boston: Lee & Shepard, 1887);

Historic Certainties Respecting the Early History of America, Developed in a Critical Examination of the Book of Chronicles of the Land of Ecnarf, by the Rev. Aristarchus Newlight, by Whately and William Fitzgerald (London: J. W. Parker, 1851; New York: Robert Carter, 1867);

Lectures on the Scripture Revelations Respecting Good and Evil Angels, by a Country Pastor, anonymous (London: J. W. Parker, 1851);

Protective Measures in Behalf of the Established Church, Considered in a Charge, to the Dioceses of Dublin,

Glandalagh, and Kildare, Delivered August, 1851 (London: J. W. Parker, 1851);

Detached Thoughts and Apophthegms Extracted from Some of the Writings of Archbishop Whately (London: Blackader, 1854);

Introductory Lessons on the British Constitution, anonymous (London: J. W. Parker, 1854);

Introductory Lessons on Morals (London, 1855);

Thoughts on the New Dogma of the Church of Rome. A Charge Delivered to the Clergy of the Dioceses of Dublin, Glandalagh, and Kildare, at the Visitation in June 1855 (London: J. W. Parker / Dublin: Hodges & Smith, 1855);

Introductory Lessons on Morals and Christian Evidences (Cambridge, Mass.: J. Bartlett, 1856);

Selections from the Writings of Dr. Whately, Archbishop of Dublin (London: R. Bentley, 1856); republished as *Thoughts and Apophthegms from the Writings of Archbishop Whately* (Philadelphia: Lindsay & Blakiston, 1856);

Christian Evidences, Intended Chiefly for the Young (London, 1857);

The Scripture Doctrine Concerning the Sacraments and the Points Connected Therewith (London: J. W. Parker, 1857);

Introductory Lessons on Mind (Boston: James Munroe, 1859);

Lectures on Some of the Scripture Parables, by a Country Pastor (London: J. W. Parker, 1859);

A General View of the Rise, Progress, and Corruptions of Christianity (New York: W. Gowans, 1860);

Lectures on Prayer, by a Country Pastor, (London: J. W. Parker, 1860);

The Parish Pastor (London: Parker, 1860);

Miscellaneous Lectures and Reviews (London: Parker & Bourn, 1861);

The Judgment of Conscience, and Other Sermons, edited by E. Jane Whately (London: Longman, Green, Longman, Roberts & Green, 1864);

Miscellaneous Remains from the Commonplace Book of Richard Whately, D.D., edited by E. Jane Whately (London: Longman, Green, Longman, Roberts & Green, 1864).

OTHER: "In What Arts have the Moderns been Less Successful than the Ancients?," 1810 Oxford English Prize Essay, published in *The Oxford English Prize Essays II* (Oxford: Oxford University Press, 1830), pp. 253–273;

"Emigration to Canada," *Quarterly Review,* 23 (July 1820): 373–408;

"Modern Novels," *Quarterly Review,* 24 (January 1821): 352–376;

William McDermott, *Third Book of Lessons for the Use of Schools,* revised by Whately (Dublin, 1846);

"Notes on Tar as a Preservative against Potatoe Disease," *Proceedings of the Royal Irish Academy,* first series 4 (1847–1850): 119;

"A Few Words of Remonstrance and Advice Addressed to the Farming and Labouring Classes of Ireland by a Sincere Friend" (Dublin, 1848);

Edward Copleston, *Remains of the Late Edward Copleston,* introduction by Whately (London: J. W. Parker, 1854);

Francis Bacon, *Bacon's Essays, with Annotations,* annotated by Whately (London, 1856; Boston: Lee & Shepard, 1856);

"The Song of the Butcher-Bird," *Proceedings of the Natural History Society of Dublin* (December 1856): 4–5;

William Paley, *A View of the Evidences of Christianity, with Annotations,* annotations by Whately (London, 1859; New York: J. Miller, 1860);

Paley, *Paley's Moral Philosophy: with Annotations,* annotated by Whately (London: J. W. Parker, 1859).

Richard Whately is now best remembered as the author of a brilliant satire on David Hume and an extraordinarily durable rhetoric textbook that went through seven editions in his lifetime and is still in print today. In the first half of the nineteenth century he was a formidable figure in the educational and religious life of England and Ireland. As tutor, lecturer, and administrator at Oxford, he did much to revive the intellectual life of the university after a period of academic decline. To John Stuart Mill in his posthumous *Autobiography* (1873) he was the man who had "rehabilitated" the study of logic; to his younger colleague John Henry Newman in *Apologia Pro Vita Sua* (1864) he was the man "who opened my mind and taught me to think and to use reason." After leaving Oxford he became Anglican archbishop of Dublin, where he worked until his death in the difficult task of finding a role for an established Protestant Church in a predominantly Roman Catholic country. To his friend Thomas Arnold he was "a truly great man–in the highest sense of the word," who was more likely than any man "in the whole empire" to succeed in saving Irish Protestantism. Both as Oxford don and as Irish archbishop Whately was a prolific writer who consistently sought to advance reform measures that he thought were essential if Oxford and Anglicanism were to survive.

The future archbishop was born in London on 1 February 1787. His family was eminent and prosperous, his maternal grandfather and two of his uncles being members of Parliament and his father being vicar of Widfield in Hertfordshire and later

Title page for Whately's second book, which according to a friend represented an attempt to find "a via media between indifference and intolerance"

canon of Bristol Cathedral. Richard was the youngest of nine children and physically quite fragile in his early years, and he led a rather lonely childhood. By the time his father died in 1797, however, he had been enrolled in a private school near Bristol, where his health improved and where he began to develop the social confidence and bluff manner that were to remain with him for the rest of his life. In 1805 the eighteen-year-old Whately went up to Oxford; he matriculated at Oriel College, then generally considered the most intellectually stimulating of the Oxford colleges.

Oriel was the focus of Whately's life until his departure for Ireland in 1831. Even in his student days the college was the center of efforts to reform the university's curriculum and raise its academic standards. One step in this process had been the institution of a comprehensive oral examination in classics and mathematics for the B.A. degree, and while Whately was regarded as a promising student, he earned only a second class in each subject when he took his B.A. in 1808. After this he stayed on at the university, winning the English Essay Prize in 1811 and receiving the M.A. in 1812. His great achievement, however, was being elected a fellow of Oriel College in 1811. This election brought him into a senior common room that included some of the most impressive men at Oxford. Edward Copleston and Edward Hawkins were the leaders of this society, but other Oriel fellows achieved more-lasting reputations: Thomas Arnold, John Henry Newman, John Keble, Edward Pusey, and Mark Pattison. Several of these men were later to be the central figures in the Tractarian, or Anglo-Catholic, movement, but Whately, Copleston, Hawkins, and Arnold constituted a quite different group, the Oriel "Noetics."

The term *noetics* is the Greek equivalent of "intellectuals," and the men who were so described were united by seriousness of purpose, devotion to logical argument, and reforming zeal. The Oriel common room served tea rather than port, but the Noetics needed no stronger stimulant, and the evening conversation was disputatious, rigorous, and competitive. England and Ireland were moving toward an era of sweeping reforms, and these reforms were sure to have an impact on Oxford and the Anglican Church. The university and the clergy generally opposed many proposed reforms as being anti-Anglican and often anti-Christian, but the Noetics took a different attitude. They sought to preserve what was good in the university and the Church by reforming these institutions before genuinely destructive reforms could be forced on them by their enemies. Also in these years—partly as a result of reform pressures—the Church of England saw the final formation of the three parties that would struggle with each other throughout the nineteenth and twentieth centuries to define the nature of Anglicanism: the Low Church Evangelicals, who were strong at Cambridge but less prominent at Oxford; the High Church Tractarians, or Anglo-Catholics; and the Broad Church, or liberal party, to which Whately and most of the Noetics belonged.

Between his election to the Oriel fellowship and his temporary departure from Oxford following his marriage in 1821, Whately enjoyed the life of an Oxford don, arguing with his colleagues, pursuing his studies, teaching undergraduates, and cultivating his eccentricities. "The first time I saw Whately," Hawkins remembered, "he wore a pea-green coat, white waistcoat, stone-colored shorts, flesh-colored silk stockings. His hair was powdered." A little later Whately began to wear a white beaver hat and a long, white coat—instead of the expected cap and gown—and to walk around flamboyantly in Christ Church Meadow with his dog Sailor, whom he had taught to climb up the trees by the River Cherwell and then jump down into the water. Sailor gained a considerable audience, and Whately began to be known as the White Bear. His bearlike manner was also apparent in his teaching, which was based on his own aggressive version of the Socratic method.

Like Socrates, Whately preferred the spoken to the written word; Mill later offered the view that Whately was one of the two modern philosophers whose reading was scantiest in proportion to intellectual abilities. He read and reread a few favorite authors— Aristotle, Francis Bacon, and such Augustan controversialists as Bishop Joseph Butler, Bishop William Warburton, Adam Smith, and Archdeacon William Paley—but he made no effort to be acquainted with a great range of authors. "My own learning," he once said, "is of a very singular kind, being more purely elementary than anyone's I know. I am acquainted with the elements of most things, and that more accurately than many who are much versed in them, but I know nothing thoroughly, except such studies as are intrinsically of an elementary character, viz. grammar, logic, metaphysics, ethics, and rhetoric." This was not a reluctant confession; Whately regarded his "elementary" subjects as the tools that led to an accurate understanding of the "elements" of all other subjects. For him the medium of instruction was combative, argumentative talk—either in the Oriel common room or on walks with students or colleagues who would serve as the anvil for Whately's conversational hammer—the exchange ultimately leading both participants toward reliable opinions on the subject under discussion.

It was during these years that Whately wrote his most successful argumentative work, *Historic Doubts Relative to Napoleon Buonaparte,* first published anonymously in 1819. The basic premise of the book is that skepticism is often irrational and that many people apply a level of skepticism to the Christian religion that they would never think of applying to anything else. Whately adopted an authorial persona who professes to believe that Napoleon Bonaparte (who was still alive in 1819 on Saint Helena) never really existed and was invented by the British government to justify high taxes and defense expenditures. The satiric target is David Hume, who in his essay on miracles in *Philosophical Essays Concerning Human Understanding* (1748) had argued that miracles were so inherently improbable that one could not accept them on the basis of supposed eyewitness accounts. Hume also argued that testimony in such cases tends to be contradictory and to advance the interests of the witnesses.

Whately's approach is to show that the same principles would oblige one to deny Napoleon's existence as well. His rise from Corsican nobody to become the emperor of the French and arbiter of the destinies of Europe was improbable and completely without precedent. Newspaper accounts of Napoleon's exploits were certainly contradictory, and both the journalists and politicians could be shown to have interested motives for saying whatever they said on the subject. Throughout the book Whately refers the reader to "the celebrated Hume," whose "Essay on Miracles" should warn us against believing such a bizarre story. At one point he summarizes Napoleon's Egyptian expedition in the style of the Old Testament histories as presented in the King James version of the Bible. Napoleon's story when told this way does sound completely implausible, but Whately's readers nevertheless all believe it to be true. By what reasonable standard, he asks, are they then so sure that extraordinary stories from the Bible are to be dismissed as fabrications?

Historic Doubts Relative to Napoleon Buonaparte was a clever, popular work that was reprinted as late as 1886, but already in 1819 it was an old-fashioned work, having more in common with the eighteenth century than the nineteenth. An attack on David Hume in the style of Jonathan Swift or John Arbuthnot could still have considerable appeal in 1819, but it suggests one reason why Whately never quite became a major writer: in his best works he always seemed to be looking back to the previous century, a more rational, less emotional world in which he felt more at home intellectually. Whately and his secretary William Fitzgerald (later bishop of Cork) tried to use the same technique of ironic skepticism many years later in *Historic Certainties Respecting the Early History of America, Developed in a Critical Examination of the Book of Chronicles of the Land of Ecnarf, by the Rev. Aristarchus Newlight* (1851) to attack biblical critics, particularly F. D. Strauss. This work never enjoyed the success of the earlier satire, and E. Jane Whately claims that it was entirely the work of Bishop Fitzgerald.

Because fellows of Oxford colleges were then required to be bachelors, Whately had to resign from Oriel when he married Elizabeth Pope. In 1822 he became rector of Hebsworth in Suffolk, where he was a conscientious but not particularly successful parish priest for three years. During this time he maintained his connection with the university, serving as an occasional preacher and delivering the 1822 Bampton Lectures, published as *The Use and Abuse of Party Feeling in Matters of Religion, Considered in Eight Sermons Preached before the University of Oxford, in the Year MDCCCXXII* (1822). According to Whately's friend W. Tuckwell the lectures were an attempt to find "a *via media* between indifference and intolerance." Two volumes of Whately's sermons were published while he was still at Hebsworth: *Five Sermons on Several Occasions Preached before the University of Oxford* (1823) and *Essays on Some of the Peculiarities of the Christian Religion* (1825).

The Whatelys soon began a family–Elizabeth Jane Whately, her father's future biographer, was born on 1 June 1822 and was followed by daughters born in 1823 and 1824 as well as a fourth daughter and a son later–and became close friends of the family of Thomas Arnold, who had married and left Oriel in 1820 and whose son Matthew Arnold was born in 1822. The two families vacationed together for many years. Whately taught Dr. Arnold's young sons Tom and Matthew to carve Australian boomerangs. Tom eventually became an unsuccessful suitor for the hand of Whately's daughter Henrietta, and Matthew eventually asked Whately to be godfather to one of his daughters.

Meanwhile, Whately was developing a less durable friendship with Thomas Arnold's future antagonist, John Henry Newman. In 1825 Whately received the degrees of bachelor of divinity and doctor of divinity from Oxford and returned to the university as principal of St. Alban Hall. This institution was perhaps the weakest branch of the university, enrolling only a dozen students and having gained for itself a reputation as the last resort for young men who could not gain acceptance at other halls or colleges. In 1826 Whately installed John Henry Newman as vice principal, and together these two men began the process of improving the academic reputation of St. Alban Hall.

Before leaving Oxford in 1822, Whately had been given the task of drawing Newman out when the latter was a shy probationary fellow of Oriel College because the other fellows were beginning to worry that his election had been a mistake. Whately's boisterous manner had overcome Newman's shyness, and Whately had assured his colleagues that Newman was an able man who would be an ornament to the college. At St. Alban Hall these two extremely different men got along well for a time, and their association bore fruit in Whately's second important book, *Elements of Logic, Comprising the Substance of the Article in the Encyclopaedia Metropolitana, with Additions* (1826), which was first published as a long article in Samuel Taylor Coleridge's encyclopedia in 1825 and then expanded as a separate volume in the following year, eventually going through nine editions by 1872. It grew out of Whately's many conversations with Copleston, to whom it was dedicated, and young Newman, who wrote several pages himself, edited other sections, and was handsomely acknowledged in the preface.

Like so much of what Whately wrote, *Elements of Logic* is both conservative and reforming. It is conservative in that it basically restates in clear and engaging language the principles of Aristotelian, deductive, syllogistic logic. Whately's consideration of connotative meaning, his classification of fallacies, and his discussion of "the drift of propositions" have all been cited as modest innovations, but few of his ideas about logic were genuinely new. The later history of logic in the nineteenth century was to be an expansion of its province to emphasize induction–a development begun by Francis Bacon and John Locke and considerably advanced by Mill's *System of Logic* (1843)–and mathematical applications, as in the work of Sir William Hamilton, Augustus DeMorgan, and George Boole. Whately implicitly denied the validity of induction and ignored the relation of logic to mathematics, saying that logic was "entirely a matter of language." Yet both Mill and DeMorgan held Whately's work in high regard. DeMorgan said that to Whately "is due the title of restorer of logical study in England," and Mill, who had reviewed the *Elements of Logic* favorably in the *Westminster Review* in 1833, declared in his *Autobiography* that "Archbishop Whately had, indeed, rehabilitated the name of Logic, and the study of the forms, rules and fallacies of Ratiocination."

To rehabilitate an ancient discipline and make it a living part of the university curriculum after generations of neglect is a reforming act, and indeed Whately's was the first significant book on logic published in England since Dean Henry Aldrich's *Artis Logicae Compendium* (1691), which was in use as a logic text at Oxford until the appearance of Whately's book. In his book he tried to show that logic is a practical subject, arguing that "the contempt with which logical studies are usually treated may be traced, in part, to a notion, that the science is incapable of useful application to any matters of real importance" being restricted to "syllogisms to prove that a horse is an animal." The primary usefulness of logic, as Whately saw it, was in assisting argument, particularly argument on the truths of the Christian religion. "Among the enemies of the Gospel now," he says in his preface, "are to be found men not only of learning and ingenuity, but of *cultivated argumentative powers,* and not unversed in the principles of logic. If the advocates of our religion think proper to disregard this help, they will find, on careful inquiry, that *their opponents do not.*"

The examples chosen by Whately in the body of his book are frequently religious. For instance, his initial example of a syllogism deals with the Christian problem of pain: "Every dispensation of Providence is beneficial; Afflictions are dispensations of Providence, Therefore they are beneficial." His discussions of fallacies and of ambiguous terms are similarly full of examples chosen to illustrate or advance his own theological views, but he also draws examples from Homer, the table talk of Charles II, and testimony before parliamentary committees on secular subjects. Throughout the book his basic assumption is that all reasoning is syllogistic, even though most people who reason have never studied formal logic, just as all speech is grammatical, even though most speakers cannot grammatically parse their sentences. *Elements of Logic* immediately became the standard textbook on the subject and was widely used for half a century. By the 1880s, however, it was becoming a forgotten book, and modern historians of logic do not regard Whately as an important figure.

Whately's habit of anonymous publication makes it difficult to attribute some books to him with complete certainty, but he was generally regarded as the author of *Letters on the Church by an Episcopalian* (1826). Newman and others at Oxford believed Whately to be the author; Whately never denied authorship; and nobody else ever claimed it. The authorial persona is a Scottish Episcopalian—an Anglican resident of the one part of the British Isles where Anglicanism was not the established church—and his thesis is that the Church of England should also be disestablished. This would prevent the Church from meddling in political matters, but more significantly it would prevent politicians from meddling in the Church. The author argues that the church derives its authority from God, not from the state, and that a disestablished church should both retain its property and be given an endowment to replace the present right to collect tithes. The church should not be dependent on either taxes voted by government nor donations contributed by the laity because neither politicians nor parishioners should be able to control the church. In the *Apologia Pro Vita Sua* Newman says that this book "had a gradual, but a deep effect on my mind" and taught him to see the church as a "substantive body or corporation" rather than simply a composite group of individual believers. Whately later advocated disestablishment of the Church of Ireland on substantially this basis.

In 1828 Whately published his most influential book, *Elements of Rhetoric, Comprising the Substance*

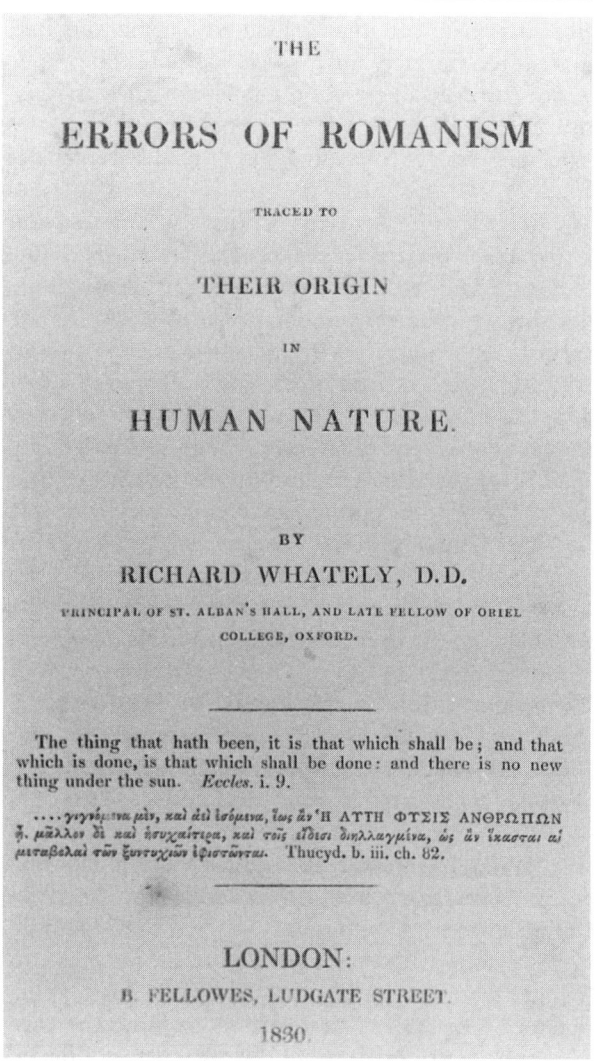

Title page for Whately's 1830 book, published a year before he was named the Anglican archbishop of Dublin in heavily Catholic Ireland

of the Article in the Encyclopaedia Metropolitana, with Additions, which he clearly intended to be read together with his logic text. In the introduction to *Elements of Rhetoric* Whately proposes "to treat of 'Argumentative Composition' *generally* and *exclusively;* considering Rhetoric (in conformity with the very just and philosophical view of Aristotle) as an off-shoot of Logic." In chapter 2 he clarifies the relationship of rhetoric and logic by declaring that "the finding of suitable arguments to prove a given point, and the skillful arrangement of them, may be considered as the immediate and proper province of Rhetoric, and of that alone. The business of Logic is, as Cicero complains, to judge arguments, not to invent them." This question of the proper province of rhetoric is more significant than it might at first seem since Whately is here engaging in a debate already several centuries old and still rumbling in the twentieth century. Rhetoric and logic (along with grammar) had constituted the "trivium" which was the subject matter for the B.A. degree in the medieval universities, and even as late as the early nineteenth century "rhetoric" was still widely taught but differently defined.

As George Kennedy points out in *Classical Rhetoric and Its Christian and Secular Tradition* (1980), rhetoric throughout its history has gone through periods of what he calls *literazazione,* his name for the process by which rhetoric becomes the study and criticism of belletristic literature. In Whately's day this tendency was represented by Hugh Blair's *Lectures on Rhetoric and Belles Lettres* (1783), a text widely used throughout Britain and the United States into the 1820s. Another important rival rhetorician was George Campbell, whose *Philosophy of Rhetoric* (1776) dismissed the syllogism as a tautology, derided the Aristotelian emphasis on rhetoric as the study of the available means of persuasion, and focused instead on an examination of the psychological faculties of the human mind. For Whately, as for Aristotle, rhetoric was primarily the study of argument.

Elements of Rhetoric is divided into four sections: argument, persuasion, style, and delivery, the first of which is generally considered the most impressive. Whately's most recent editor, Douglas Ehninger, introduces the book as an "ecclesiastical rhetoric" because its most obvious use was to prepare divinity students to deliver effective sermons, but it would be almost equally helpful to an aspiring politician or lawyer. The first section classifies the various kinds of arguments that the preacher, politician, or advocate might find useful, and many of these arguments are such as can only establish a sense of probability rather than certainty. As in *Elements of Logic,* Whately chooses examples from ancient history, current politics, and the natural sciences, but religious examples of arguments predominate, and the rhetorical effect of reading the section on argument is the impression that Whately's Broad Church Anglicanism is the most plausible view of life that could be imagined.

As in *Elements of Logic,* Whately is fundamentally concerned with establishing rational grounds for belief, specifically Christian belief, and his approach to skepticism is not to attack it directly but to give it a dose of its own medicine:

> It is most important to keep in mind the self-evident, but often forgotten maxim that *Disbelief is Belief:* only they have reference to *opposite conclusions.* E.G. to disbelieve the real existence of the City of Troy is to believe that it was feigned: and which conclusion implies the greater credulity is the question to be decided. . . . So also, though the terms "infidel" and "unbeliever" are commonly applied to one who rejects Christianity, it is plain that to disbelieve its divine origin is to believe its human origin: and which belief requires the more credulous mind, is the very question and issue.

As in *Historic Doubts Relative to Napoleon Buonaparte,* Whately here suggests that religious skeptics are capable of great credulity, and he is not willing to give skepticism an advantage in debate by allowing it to attack Christianity without having to defend a position itself.

The most frequently discussed idea in *Elements of Rhetoric* is one by which Whately sought to give Christianity a certain advantage in debate. This idea, the burden of proof, basically holds that an idea already having general acceptance—the doctrines of the Christian religion, for example—need not itself be argued because the obligation to prove is on whoever seeks to revise current opinion. This conservative concept gives an advantage in debate to whatever in a particular time and place is the established doctrine—Christianity in early-nineteenth-century Britain, but also religious skepticism in late twentieth-century Britain, or Islam in Saudi Arabia.

The second section of *Elements of Rhetoric* on persuasion differs from the first section on argument in that it considers nonlogical elements—emotional appeal, or what Whately calls "the influence of the passions." The section on style emphasizes clarity but adds little that could not be found in comparable sections of Blair or Campbell. The final section on delivery contains a celebrated passage on stage fright and argues for a restrained and natural oratorical manner—setting Whately apart from the writers of the then-popular elocutionary school who suggested elaborate and rather mechanical bodily movements that supposedly communicated particular emotions most effectively.

Both *Elements of Logic* and *Elements of Rhetoric* were reforming works in the sense that they encouraged changes in the course of studies at Oxford and elsewhere, but they were also essentially revivalist and conservative. In each case Whately dusted off Aristotle's ideas and repackaged them in a form appropriate for the early nineteenth century, showing them to be intellectually stimulating and practically useful and then answering stock objections that had been leveled against the Aristotelian approach or the discipline as a whole. Such ideas as the rejection of induction in *Elements of Logic* and the burden of proof in *Elements of Rhetoric* show Whately standing for what is established and turning his back on the most innovative ideas of the Renaissance and the Enlightenment in favor of a return to Aristotle.

Thomas De Quincey's review of *Elements of Rhetoric* in *Blackwood's Magazine,* although generally favorable, saw the whole idea of the revival of the study of rhetoric as a quixotic and antiquarian enterprise: "No; the age of Rhetoric, like that of Chivalry, has passed amongst forgotten things; and the rhetorician can have no more chance of returning than the rhapsodist of early Greece or the troubadour of romance." De Quincey was eloquent but mistaken. Whately's *Elements of Rhetoric* went through seven editions by 1846 and was widely used in both British and North American colleges and universities for a generation. One of the indirect influences of the book was almost certainly on Newman. Though Dean Richard William Church in his *The Oxford Movement: Twelve Years, 1833–45* (1892) says that the Tractarians generally reacted against "Whately's hard and barren dialectics," Newman's *An Essay in Aid of a Grammar of Assent* (1845) and *Apologia Pro Vita Sua* repeat many of Whately's ideas about the nature of belief and use arguments found earlier in *Elements of Rhetoric.*

The impact of Whately's rhetoric has also been felt in the twentieth century. In *The Philosophy of Rhetoric* (1936) I. A. Richards condemns Whately's lessons on argument by saying that "no one ever learned about them from a treatise who did not know about them already" and dismisses Whately's ideas on style as "the usual postcard's work of crude common sense." This condescending attitude came from the fact that Richards had given rhetoric yet another definition as the "study of misunderstanding and its remedies," and Whately's Aristotelian study of argument did not fit this new definition. But as Ehninger points out in his introduction, Whately's work continued to exert a considerable influence throughout most of the twentieth century. When departments of speech began to separate from American departments of English at about the time of World War I, the founders of the new discipline of speech communication tended to accept Whately's ideas on rhetoric and to develop new textbooks on the lines that his book suggested. So *Elements of Rhetoric,* Ehninger concludes, "while not to be numbered among the great creative works on the subject, is certainly to be ranked among the most influential."

In his last years at Oxford Whately wrote several more books, the most important of which was *Essays on Some of the Difficulties in the Writings of St. Paul, and in Other Parts of the New Testament* (1828), which sought to distinguish Saint Paul's thoughts from his language. The premise is that Saint Paul's terminology did not have for him the precise theo-

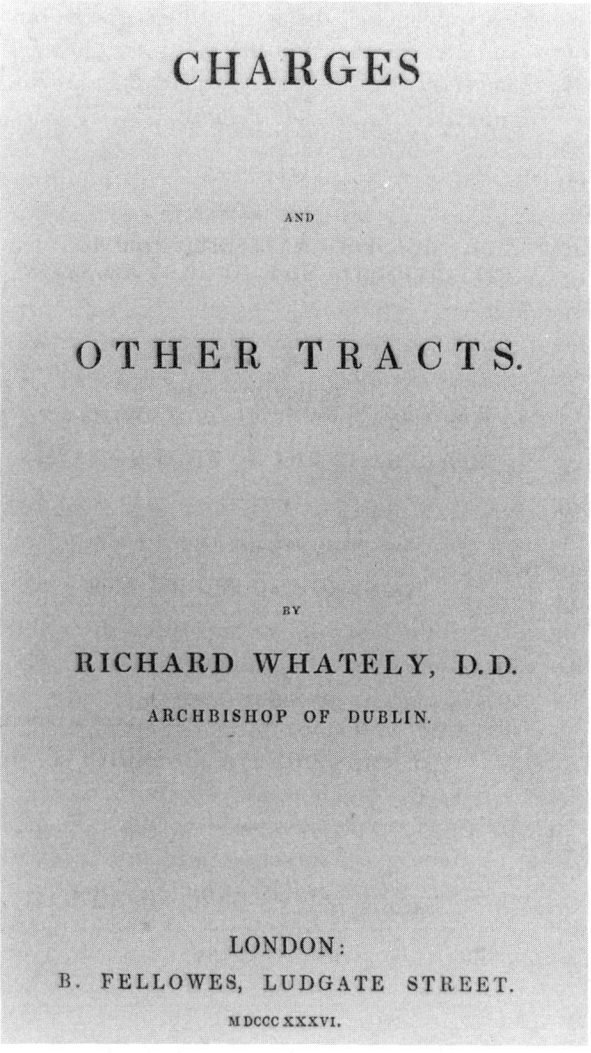

Title page for Whately's 1836 book, which includes some of his sermons to the clergy and people of Dublin

logical meanings that it has for us. Words such as *grace* or *election* have acquired all sorts of encrusted meanings since the first century A.D. as a result of theological commentary, but Saint Paul used these terms in what was their popular meaning in his own time, and one must try to recapture the original sense of his words.

How the Bible should be read was to become a central concern of nineteenth-century religious writers, and Whately makes an early contribution to the debate. Like Samuel Taylor Coleridge in *Confessions of an Inquiring Spirit* (1840), he sought to persuade Christians to read the Scriptures in a flexible spirit both because he thought this was the best way to understand the biblical texts and also because crude literalism led Christians into untenable positions. As late as 1870 Matthew Arnold's *St. Paul and Protestantism* shows signs of Whately's influence, and Whately's basic approach of differentiating between language and meaning became central in Arnold's *Literature and Dogma* (1873) and *God and the Bible* (1875).

Introductory Lectures on Political Economy, Being Part of a Course Delivered in Easter Term MDCCCXXXI, published in 1831 and 1832, is also worth noting. Whately's last appointment at Oxford was as Drummond Professor of Political Economy, and these lectures were the result. They are, as the title suggests, introductory, both because the audience was fairly new to the discipline and because the author was just beginning to come to terms with it himself. In fact he sought the appointment so that he would be obligated to learn about so important a subject. The lectures are largely a plea for the study of economics and a defense of the subject against charges that it is immoral, un-Christian, or superfluous. While before he had worked for the revival of the neglected but venerable disciplines of logic and rhetoric, Whately here champions an important discipline that was genuinely new.

In 1831 Whately's life was dramatically changed by his being named Anglican archbishop of Dublin by the new Whig prime minister, Lord Grey, whose government was determined to advance liberal clergymen and reduce Tory influence within the Church of England and the Church of Ireland. Whately later remarked that "I never knew what absolute distress was till I became archbishop," but this appointment gave him a seat in the House of Lords, an enormous salary of £7,786 per year, and a princely station in life. He lived in a palace, was surrounded by secretaries and chaplains who addressed him as "your grace," and was consulted by the lord lieutenant for Ireland and even by British prime minister Lord Melbourne. For a while in the 1830s it even seemed possible that Melbourne might make him the next archbishop of York or archbishop of Canterbury.

But he was to end his days in Ireland, often longing—like Jonathan Swift in the previous century—to leave his ecclesiastical dignities in Dublin and return to more-congenial English surroundings. "It was an evil hour," Thomas Arnold later wrote, "which took Whately from Oxford, where he was doing great and certain good, to exhaust his powers in what is an attempt to raise corn out of the sea sand." The problems Whately faced were daunting. Only one out of eight Irish people belonged to the Church of Ireland, and the era of reform, which was now in full swing, was bound to be hostile to an established church that seemed to embody so many of the undemocratic and archaic principles under which the Tories had been governing the United Kingdom for a generation. In 1801 William Pitt had brought about the union of Great Britain and Ireland, abolishing the Irish Parliament, granting Irish representation in the House of Commons and the House of Lords in Westminster, and joining the Church of Ireland and the Church of England into one united church. By 1829 the threat of civil war in Ireland persuaded the Duke of Wellington's Tory government to push through Parliament the Catholic Emancipation Bill, giving Roman Catholics the vote and the right to hold almost all civil offices under the Crown, with the result that the Irish members of the House of Commons soon became overwhelmingly Roman Catholic.

By the time Whately arrived in Ireland the burning issue was the legal right of the Anglican clergy to collect tithes from the non-Anglican residents of their parishes. The Roman Catholic majority and the Presbyterian minority were waging a "tithe war" that ranged from passive refusal of payment to frequent acts of violence. In his 1832 testimony before the select committee on tithes of the House of Lords, Whately contended that the existing system could only be maintained by military force and that the right to collect tithes should be bought from the Anglican clergy, who would then be supported by the investment of the resulting funds. Something like this proposal was eventually enacted after Whately's death, when William Gladstone forced his Irish Disestablishment Bill through the British Parliament in 1869.

During Whately's tenure a series of compromises, beginning with the Irish Church Temporalities Bill of 1833, changed the basis for funding the Church of Ireland but did not effectively solve the problem. The compromises left the critics unsatisfied but tended to alarm the Anglican clergy and their supporters. Whately consistently maintained the positions stated in the *Letters on the Church by an Episcopalian:* the Church should not be a political institution but should keep its inherited property and be compensated for lost sources of revenue. While these views were far from being radical, Whately's support or acceptance of various Whig ecclesiastical reforms alienated many members of his own denomination.

In 1831 there were four Anglican archbishops in Ireland (two more than in England), and the senior one was not Whately but Lord John George Beresford, archbishop of Armagh. The Church of Ireland tended to be more evangelical than the Church of England and more hostile to Roman Catholicism, and the aristocratic, conservative Archbishop Beresford was far more congenial to clergy and laity then the rather boorish and liberal Archbishop Whately. Beginning in the

1830s and continuing into the 1840s, the number of Church of Ireland dioceses was reduced by the government as incumbent bishops and archbishops died off, so that the Province of Tuam was joined to Beresford's Province of Armagh, and the Province of Cashel became part of Whately's Province of Dublin. While Whately took little part in these reforms, he was identified with them by his general support of Whig measures, and he caused great resentment by his attempts, beginning in the 1830s, to reform the Anglican Trinity College, Dublin, in ways similar to those he had worked for at Oxford during his time there. Most Church of Ireland clergy were graduates of Trinity College and resented what they saw as the meddling of an Oxford-bred foreigner.

Throughout his years as archbishop Whately continued to write tirelessly and publish his work energetically, but most of it consists of sermons, charges to his clergy, and tracts concerning the religious politics of Ireland. Most of these works were not widely read when they appeared, and few if any are read today. In *The Victorian Church* (1966) Owen Chadwick flatly asserts, "Whately left no sermon which posterity cared to preserve." His only important publications during his Irish years are a series of school texts that he helped supervise and to which he contributed. The heart of this series was a group of six graded readers (similar in basic plan and approximately contemporaneous with McGuffey's *Eclectic Readers* in America). "Quaint as the books now strike us," says Donald Akenson, Whately's most recent biographer, "in their time they were the best set of school texts in the British Isles," and, "in the middle years of the nineteenth century, the Irish readers were the most popular and widely used set of books in England." Akenson's estimate is that by 1859 nearly one million of these books were being used in England and more than half a million in Ireland.

Whately alone wrote the *Sequel to Second Book of Lessons for the Use of the Schools* (1844) when it was found that the gap between the second and third readers was too challenging, and he completely revised the *Third Book of Lessons for the Use of Schools* (1846). He also contributed several supplementary texts to the series. *Easy Lessons on Money Matters for the Use of Young People* (1833) sought to introduce schoolchildren to the basics of political economy and was eventually split into two sections and incorporated into the *Third Book of Lessons* and *Fourth Book of Lessons*. Whately's other textbooks, *Introductory Lessons on Christian Evidences* (1838) and four volumes of *Scripture Lessons* (1832, 1834, 1835, and 1846) were widely used for several years but were to become the occasion of his greatest defeat in Irish political life.

The major event of Irish history in the period of Whately's residence was the great Potato Famine of the 1840s, which led to widespread starvation, massive emigration, and an enormous increase in bitterness on the part of Roman Catholics. While Whately was not popular with Anglicans, he had tried hard to have cordial relations with Roman Catholics. In 1845 he supported a controversial parliamentary bill to grant funds to the Roman Catholic Seminary at Maynooth, and during the famine he tried to discourage "souperism," efforts by Protestant proselytizing societies to provide hunger relief only to those Roman Catholics who were willing to abandon their religion. His daughter Elizabeth Jane Whately estimates that during the height of the famine in 1849 the archbishop gave approximately £8,000 of his own money to the poor, and he tried to advocate remedies for Ireland's agricultural problems.

Certainly one of Whately's strangest publications was an 1845 paper, "Notes on Tar as a Preservative against Potato Disease," published in the *Proceedings of the Royal Irish Academy,* but what he saw as his best contribution, economic advice, was the one that gave the greatest offense. As a former professor of political economy Whately had been studying the Irish economic picture since arriving in that country, and in the years 1833 through 1836 he chaired the Royal Commission on the condition of the Irish poor, which resulted in a six-volume report. He acknowledged the Christian duty to provide for the poor but, in keeping with his economic theories, thought that the poor had to be discouraged from taking advantage of charitable institutions. This was standard Manchester economic theory, but it is a little shocking to have Archbishop Whately suggesting that female paupers should be required to have their hair cut off as a condition of admission to the workhouse. On the other hand, he thought the Irish situation so different from England's that the English New Poor Law of 1834 would not work in Ireland; rather he recommended that government encourage emigration to Canada and Australia and find employment for the rest of the Irish labor surplus in public-works projects that would give Ireland needed infrastructure.

During the famine he published *A Few Words of Remonstrance and Advice Addressed to the Farming and Labouring Classes of Ireland by a Sincere Friend* (1848), in which he tells the starving Irish that their own slovenly farming and violent assaults on property have contributed heavily to the lack of capital that ultimately caused the famine. While this pamphlet was published anonymously and was both well meant and largely accurate in its analysis, it shows a bluntness and condescension not likely to commend

Whately to an angry Catholic population or its leaders.

In 1852 Whately's friend Daniel Murray, Roman Catholic archbishop of Dublin, died and was replaced by Paul Cullen, who was hostile to Protestants and Englishmen in general and had already condemned several of Whately's writings, going so far as to place *Elements of Logic* on the index of prohibited books. Cullen seems to have believed that all of Whately's books were part of a devious plot to turn Roman Catholics into Protestants. The two archbishops served as national education commissioners, and in 1853 Cullen persuaded the other commissioners to join him in voting to withdraw their approval from Whately's *Introductory Lessons on Christian Evidences*. This seemingly minor matter hit Whately hard. He had been in the habit of working together with Archbishop Murray to dominate the Commission, and he was shocked both by the new Roman Catholic militance personified in Archbishop Cullen and by the failure of the British authorities at Dublin Castle to help him in his battle with Cullen. He resigned from the Education Commission and began to withdraw from Irish public life.

During the time when Whately was contending with Archbishop Cullen, Newman was in Dublin attempting unsuccessfully to establish a Catholic University of Ireland. Whately and Newman had begun to drift apart as early as 1829, as Newman began to move from Broad Church liberalism toward the emerging ideas of the Tractarian movement. In 1834 they had exchanged some letters that revealed the extent of their disagreements, and Newman's attacks on some of Whately's Broad Church friends had led to a total break between the two old friends. When Newman appeared in Dublin as part of Cullen's entourage, it is not surprising to find that Whately refused to see him. Whately was beginning to be hostile to Roman Catholics, and he had always been hostile to Tractarians. In 1856 he suffered a stroke which reduced his ability to be active, but he continued to administer his diocese and to produce books. The most notable of these are a series of editions of his favorite authors: *Remains of the Late Edward Copleston, D. D., Bishop of Llandaff* (1854), *Bacon's Essays, with Annotations* (1856), *Paley's Moral Philosophy: with Annotations* (1859); and Paley's *A View of the Evidences of Christianity, with Annotations* (1859).

Whately's own muse was not silent in these last years either, and he produced a long list of religious books, several of which went through more than one edition: *Lectures on the Characters of Our Lord's Apostles, and Especially Their Conduct at the Time of His Apprehension and Trial* (1851), *Cautions for the Times: Addressed to the Parishioners of a Parish in England, by Their Former Pastor* (1851), *Lectures on the Scripture Revelations Respecting Good and Evil Angels* (1851), *Scripture Doctrine Concerning the Sacraments* (1857), *Lectures on Some of the Scripture Parables* (1859), *Lectures on Prayer* (1860), *The Parish Pastor* (1860), and *Miscellaneous Lectures and Reviews* (1861). In many of these late works one can see the harassed and often frustrated archbishop turning from questions of ecclesiastical policy to devotional and pastoral concerns and frequently assuming the persona of the rural English rector that he once briefly had been and perhaps now wished to be again. In his later years Whately suffered from a series of illnesses, which he treated with homeopathic remedies because he distrusted medical doctors; he died in his palace on St. Stephen's Green, Dublin, on 8 October 1863 and was buried in Christ Church Cathedral.

Most of Richard Whately's books are today forgotten, and his name is most frequently encountered in general studies of Oxford or the Church of England in the nineteenth century or in works dealing with Newman, Arnold, or the Oxford movement. He is not a major figure for contemporary Irish historians; for example, Robert F. Foster's massive 1988 volume, *Modern Ireland: 1600-1972*, mentions Whately in only two footnotes among its six hundred pages. Anglicanism is far more embattled in both Ireland and England than it was when Whately set out to save it by salutary reforms; there have been plenty of reforms, but they have not accomplished what Whately had hoped for in church revival. And while his academic reforms at Oxford were fruitful, he probably would not find the modern secular university a congenial environment.

The one area where Whately continues to be taken seriously today is as a rhetorician. Scholarly studies of his *Elements of Rhetoric* appear regularly, and this interest has led to several recent discussions of *Elements of Logic* and *Historic Doubts Relative to Napoleon Buonaparte*. In the past most of these studies have come from departments of speech communication, but English departments are now also becoming seriously interested in the history of rhetoric. The new importance of writing instruction and the growth of political literary criticism have both generated a new enthusiasm for the study of rhetoric, a field in which Whately's status as a major figure seems clearly established.

Bibliographies:

Peter E. Kane, "Richard Whately in the United States: A Partial Bibliography," *Bulletin of Bibliography*, 23 (1961): 87-88;

Donald Harmon Akenson, "Bibliographic Comments," in *A Protestant in Purgatory: Richard*

Whately, Archbishop of Dublin (Hamden, Conn.: Archon, 1981), pp. 253–269.

Biographies:

William J. Fitzpatrick, *Memoirs of Richard Whately, Archbishop of Dublin, with a Glance at His Contemporaries and Times* (London: Bentley, 1864);

Elizabeth Jane Whately and Herman Merivale, *Life and Correspondence of Richard Whately, D.D., Late Archbishop of Dublin* (London: Longmans, Green, 1866);

Donald Harmon Akenson, *A Protestant in Purgatory: Richard Whately, Archbishop of Dublin* (Hamden, Conn.: Archon, 1981).

References:

James Berlin, "Richard Whately and Current-Traditional Rhetoric," *College English,* 42 (September 1980): 10–17;

Owen Chadwick, *The Victorian Church* (New York: Oxford University Press, 1966);

R. W. Church, *The Oxford Movement: Twelve Years, 1833–45,* edited by Geoffrey Best (Chicago: University of Chicago Press, 1970);

A. Dwight Culler, *The Imperial Intellect: A Study of Newman's Educational Ideal* (New Haven: Yale University Press, 1955);

Douglas Ehninger, "Cambell, Blair and Whately: Old Friends in a New Light," *Western Speech,* 19 (October 1955): 263–269;

Ehninger, "Campbell, Blair and Whately Revisited," *Southern Speech Communication Journal,* 28 (Spring 1963): 169–182;

Ehninger, "Introduction," in *Elements of Rhetoric,* by Richard Whately (Carbondale: University of Southern Illinois Press, 1963);

Lois J. Einhorn, "Consistency in Richard Whately: The Scope of His Rhetoric," *Philosophy and Rhetoric,* 14 (Spring 1981): 89–99;

Einhorn, "Did Napoleon Live? Presumption and Burden of Proof in Richard Whately's *Historic Doubts Relative to Napoleon Buonaparte,*" *Rhetoric Society Quarterly,* 16 (Fall 1986): 285–297;

Einhorn, "Richard Whately's Public Persuasion: The Relationship between His Rhetorical Theory and His Rhetorical Practice," *Rhetorica,* 4 (Winter 1986): 47–63;

Wilbur Samuel Howell, *Eighteenth Century British Logic and Rhetoric* (Princeton: Princeton University Press, 1971);

George Kennedy, *Classical Rhetoric and Its Christian and Secular Tradition* (Chapel Hill: University of North Carolina Press, 1980);

Raymie E. McKerrow, "Campbell and Whately on the Utility of Syllogistic Logic," *Western Journal of Speech Communication,* 40 (Winter 1976): 3–13;

McKerrow, "'Method of Composition': Whately's Earliest 'Rhetoric,'" *Philosophy and Rhetoric,* 11 (Winter 1978): 43–58;

McKerrow, "Probable Argument and Proof in Whately's Theory of Rhetoric," *Central States Speech Journal,* 36 (Winter 1975): 259–266;

McKerrow, "Richard Whately and the Revival of Logic in Nineteenth-Century England," *Rhetorica,* 5 (Spring 1987): 163–185;

John Henry Newman, *Apologia Pro Vita Sua,* edited by A. Dwight Culler (Boston: Houghton Mifflin, 1956).

Papers:

There are substantial collections of Whately's papers at the British Library, the Lambeth Palace Library, the National Library of Ireland, the Library of Oriel College, Oxford, and the Library of Trinity College, Dublin.

Oscar Wilde
(16 October 1854 - 30 November 1900)

Jennifer Kelly
Birbeck College, London University

See also the Wilde entries in *DLB 10: Modern British Dramatists, 1900-1945; DLB 19: British Poets, 1880-1914; DLB 34: British Novelists, 1890-1929: Traditionalists; DLB 57: Victorian Prose Writers After 1867; DLB 141: British Children's Writers, 1880-1914;* and *DLB 156: British Short-Fiction Writers, 1880-1914: The Romantic Tradition.*

BOOKS: *Newdigate Prize Poem: Ravenna, Recited in the Theatre, Oxford, 27 June 1878* (Oxford: Shrimpton, 1878);

Vera; or, The Nihilists: A Drama in Four Acts (London: Privately printed, 1880);

Poems (London: Bogue, 1881; Boston: Roberts, 1881);

The Duchess of Padua: A Tragedy of the XVI Century, Written in Paris in the XIX Century (New York: Privately printed, 1883);

The Happy Prince and Other Tales (London: Nutt, 1888; Boston: Roberts, 1888);

The Picture of Dorian Gray (London, New York & Melbourne: Ward, Lock, 1891);

Intentions (London: Osgood, McIlvaine, 1891; New York: Dodd, Mead, 1891);

Lord Arthur Savile's Crime & Other Stories (London: Osgood, McIlvaine, 1891; New York: Dodd, Mead, 1891);

A House of Pomegranates (London: Osgood, McIlvaine; 1891; New York: Dodd, Mead, 1892);

Salomé: Drame en un acte (Paris: Librairie de l'Art Indépendant / London: Elkin Mathews & John Lane, Bodley Head, 1893); republished as *Salomé: A Tragedy ins One Act,* translated by Alfred Douglas (London: Elkin Mathews & John Lane / Boston: Copeland & Day, 1894);

Lady Windermere's Fan: A Play about a Good Woman (London: Elkin Mathews & John Lane, Bodley Head, 1893);

Phrases and Philosophies for the Use of the Young (London: Privately printed, 1894);

The Sphinx (London: Elkin Mathews & John Lane, Bodley Head / Boston: Copeland & Day, 1894);

Oscar Wilde (Gale International Portrait Gallery)

A Woman of No Importance (London: John Lane, Bodley Head, 1894);

The Soul of Man (London: Privately printed, 1895); republished as *The Soul of Man under Socialism* (London: Privately printed, 1904);

The Ballad of Reading Gaol, as C.3.3. (London: Smithers, 1898);

The Importance of Being Earnest: A Trivial Comedy for Serious People (London: Smithers, 1899);

An Ideal Husband (London: Smithers, 1899);

Essays, Criticisms, and Reviews (London: Privately printed, 1901);

The Portrait of Mr. W. H. (Portland, Maine: Mosher, 1901; London: Privately printed, 1904);

De Profundis (London: Methuen, 1905; New York & London: Putnam, 1905);

Poems in Prose (Paris: Privately printed, 1905);

Impressions of America, edited by Stuart Mason (Sunderland, U.K.: Keystone Press, 1906);

Decorative Art in America: A Lecture . . . Together with Letters, Reviews and Interviews, edited by R. B. Glaenzer (New York: Brentano's, 1906);

A Florentine Tragedy (Boston: Luce, 1908);

The Suppressed Portion of "De Profundis" (New York: Reynolds, 1913);

To M.B.J., edited by Mason as C. S. Millard (London: Privately printed, 1920);

For Love of the King: A Burmese Masque (London: Methuen, 1922);

Essays of Oscar Wilde, edited by Hesketh Pearson (London: Methuen, 1950);

The Literary Criticism of Oscar Wilde, edited by Stanley Weintraub (Lincoln: University of Nebraska Press, 1968);

The Artist as Critic: Critical Writings of Oscar Wilde, edited by Richard Ellmann (New York: Random House, 1969);

Oscar Wilde: Complete Shorter Fiction, edited by Isobel Murray (Oxford: Oxford University Press, 1979);

Oscar Wilde's Oxford Notebooks: A Portrait of Mind in the Making, edited by Philip E. Smith II and Michael Helfand (New York: Oxford University Press, 1989).

Editions and Collections: *First Collected Edition of the Works of Oscar Wilde,* edited by Robert Ross (volumes 1–11, 13–14, London: Methuen, 1908; Boston: Luce, 1910; volume 12, Paris: Carrington, 1908);

Second Collected Edition of the Works of Oscar Wilde, edited by Ross (volumes 1–12, London: Methuen, 1909; volume 13, Paris: Carrington, 1910; volume 14, London: John Lane, 1912);

The Complete Works of Oscar Wilde, edited by Vyvyan Holland (London: Collins, 1948);

PLAY PRODUCTIONS: *Vera; or, the Nihilists,* New York, Union Square Theatre, 20 August 1883;

Guido Ferranti: A Tragedy of the XVI Century, New York, Broadway Theatre, 26 January 1891;

Lady Windermere's Fan, London, St. James's Theatre, 20 February 1892;

A Woman of No Importance, London, Haymarket Theatre, 19 April 1893;

An Ideal Husband, London, Haymarket Theatre, 3 January 1895;

The Importance of Being Earnest, London, St. James's Theatre, 14 February 1895;

Salomé, Paris, Théâtre de l'Oeuvre, 11 February 1895; London, Bijou, 10 May 1905;

A Florentine Tragedy, by Wilde, with opening scene by T. Sturge Moore, London, King's Hall, 10 June 1906.

Oscar Wilde was a reform writer through the trenchant moral and social criticism in his works. Famous for his public speaking and wit, Wilde has often been accused of merely reproducing witty repartee in his plays, and the temptation to treat his work lightly is in large part due to his flamboyant and notorious lifestyle, which is often better known than his writings. He posed as an Aesthete and a Decadent, which were movements of the late-Victorian age whose followers believed in "art for art's sake." Wilde himself stated in *The Picture of Dorian Gray* (1891) that "All art is at once surface and symbol." Nevertheless, Wilde advocated reform through social critique in his plays, short stories, novel, essays, and poems, and he challenged Victorian morality with his work and his lifestyle. There is much more to Wilde than "surface and symbol."

Oscar Fingall O'Flahertie Wills Wilde was born in Dublin on 16 October 1854 into a family of middle-class professionals. His paternal great-great-grandfather had been a Dublin merchant, his great-grandfather a farmer, and his grandfather a doctor. His father, Sir William Wilde, followed his father's profession and became a renowned ear and eye specialist. His success led to his appointment as Surgeon Oculist to the Queen in Ireland in 1863, and he received a knighthood the following year, thus completing the family's rise from mercantile middle classes to gentry status. Sir William, as a man with a prominent position, was bound to distance himself from the republican Fenianism of the late 1860s, yet he was a nationalist with kind feelings for the peasant population of Ireland. Oscar may well have learned sympathy for the poor from his father, who would collect folklore instead of fees from the peasants he treated. In 1852 Sir William published *Irish Popular Superstitions,* which he dedicated to Speranza, the pen name used by Oscar's mother, Jane Francesca Elgee Wilde.

She also came from a professional middle-class background, and, like Sir William, she was a staunch Irish nationalist. Her grandfather was a rector and archdeacon in the Protestant Church of Ireland; her father was a lawyer; and she was the great-niece of Charles Robert Maturin, the author

Lord Alfred Douglas, whose affair with Wilde led to Wilde's imprisonment

of several extravagant Gothic novels. During his years of exile at the end of his life Oscar Wilde took the name of Sebastian Melmoth, perhaps identifying with the isolated and satanic hero of Maturin's best-known novel, *Melmoth the Wanderer* (1820). Jane Wilde was a writer and poet with a flair for the dramatic not only in her writing but also in her appearance. She dressed up in increasingly outlandish costumes, with headdresses and bizarre jewelry. Oscar shared her flamboyance in dress and her literary tastes. Writers whom they both admired include John Keats, Percy Bysshe Shelley, Benjamin Disraeli, and Honoré de Balzac. Jane Wilde created a salon society in Dublin, and her large Saturday-afternoon receptions included writers, government officials, professors, actors, and musicians. After the death of her husband in 1876 she moved her salon to London. Her poetry was inflammatory and pro-nationalist, and in 1849 during the trial for sedition of Gavan Duffy, editor of *The Nation,* she stood up in court and claimed authorship of the offending articles. She became famous for this incident and many years later encouraged Wilde to stand trial rather than run away, no doubt imagining another famous court victory for the Wilde family.

Having famous and eccentric parents, Wilde realized from a young age the importance of cutting a figure in order to be noticed in his family. A fragment of a letter written by Wilde when he was thirteen demonstrates his desire to impress his mother with his dress sense and humor: "The flannel shirts you sent in the hamper are both Willie's, mine are one quite scarlet and the other lilac but it is too hot to wear them yet.... And have you written to Aunt Warren on the green note paper?" Wilde obviously shared his mother's humor, since the aunt in question was a staunch unionist who did not approve of her younger sister's nationalist politics. Richard Ellmann, in his definitive biography of Wilde, suggests that Aunt Warren may have provided some of the material for the character of Lady Augusta Bracknell in *The Importance of Being Earnest* (1899).

Wilde's childhood appears to have been happy, if unconventional. He had an older brother, Willie, whom he considered a rival for his mother's attention, but it was not a bitter rivalry in childhood. He also had a younger sister, Isola, who died at the age of eight in 1867. The family was devastated by Isola's death, and Wilde, who regularly visited her grave, wrote the poem "Requiescat" in her memory. Sir William Wilde's three illegitimate children, fathered before he married Jane, were also included in the family, and all of the children spent their holidays together. Mysterious births and problems of legitimacy are recurrent themes in Wilde's work: Guido Ferranti in *The Duchess of Padua* (1883) has his illustrious parentage kept secret and is raised by a peasant; Jack Worthing in *The Importance of Being Earnest* is a foundling; Lady Windermere in *Lady Windermere's Fan* (1893) was abandoned by her unconventional mother; Arbuthnot's mother in *A Woman of No Importance* (1894) is unmarried; and Dorian Gray falls in love with an illegitimate young woman.

Wilde soon supplanted his brother Willie as his mother's favorite by distinguishing himself at the Portora Royal School. In 1870 he won the Carpenter Prize for the Greek Testament, and in 1871 he was one of three pupils awarded a Royal School scholarship to Trinity College, Dublin. His excellence as a classical scholar was evident at Trinity, where he received one of ten foundation scholarships awarded in 1873. The pinnacle of his success as a classicist came when he won the Berkeley gold medal for Greek. At Trinity he was also renowned for his pose as an Aesthete; the college offered a course in aesthetics, and its Philosophical Society discussed Dante Gabriel Rossetti and A. C. Swinburne. Wilde also flirted with the more aesthetic side of Catholicism while at Trinity; for this reason his father agreed he should go to Oxford, in the hope that England would keep him a Protestant. Wilde was himself keen to go to Oxford, for he had become interested in the English movement of the Pre-Raphaelites. In 1874 he was awarded one of two scholarships in classics at Magdalen College, but despite the financial aid he was always short of money. His pose as an Aesthete involved him in expenses that he could not really afford. He dressed flamboyantly and furnished his rooms extravagantly because cutting a figure was of the utmost importance to an Aesthete. He also achieved renown as a scholar. In 1878 Wilde won the Newdigate Prize for his poem *Ravenna*, and he finished his university career with an Oxford double first.

Already a celebrity, Wilde published his first collection of poetry in 1881. He left Oxford for London and quickly made a name for himself as a wit, critic, and public speaker. Wilde's pose as an Aesthete caused him to be featured prominently in the satirical cartoons of *Punch* magazine. There was more to this pose than frivolity, however. In order to set themselves apart from the dominant ideology of the professional middle classes, self-professed Aesthetes and Decadents transgressed against middle-class Victorian morality in their works and lifestyles, even though they were of the upper and middle classes themselves. Aesthetes and Decadents were countercultures operating from within the ruling classes. Art and literature were supposed by Aesthetes and Decadents to be morally neutral, while form and effect were all-important. The one movement led into the other. Walter Pater's and John Ruskin's works were crucial to these movements, and Wilde had met them both while at Oxford.

Wilde's classical expertise is much in evidence in *Poems* (1881), along with the influences of Swinburne, Matthew Arnold, Rossetti, Alfred Tennyson, Pater, and Ruskin. The general critical reaction at the time of publication was condemning and dismissive. Most reviewers were eager to denounce Wilde on the grounds of imitation of various writers and on his ornate language. Cambridge don Oscar Browning was almost a lone voice in his appreciation of the volume, but even he had reservations.

Browning treats *Poems* as a first collection by a new poet, which in fact it is. But Browning feels Wilde should be encouraged because he has the makings of a great poet. The audacity of Wilde, an unknown in the literary world, perhaps triggered the critical attack when he published a collection of poetry. He published *Poems* at his own expense, and in spite of the generally hostile reaction, within a year five editions had been sold.

In *Poems* Wilde experiments with form and touches on many of the themes he would develop in his later works as a social and cultural reformer. Cumulatively these poems represent a conscious experiment of spiritual and imaginative odyssey and social critique. Wilde displays his cultural, literary, and philosophical heritage and links them using the idea of physical journey based on his actual travels in Italy and Greece. He comments on what he regards as the decline of civilization from the ancient Greeks to modern-day Europe. Decline is a recurrent theme in Wilde's later work and a theme he uses to attack Victorian ruling-class values. "Theoretikos" is typical of his attitude to the Victorian world. In this poem he refers to Britain as an empire with "feet of clay," a "vile traffic-house, where day by day / Wisdom and reverence are sold at mart." It is this refusal to see the Victorian age as one of glory, along with his portrayal of the seedy, usually unmentioned side of Victorian life and sympathy for the poor, that makes Wilde a reform writer. In this early work Wilde also sees the artist standing aloof from society, which becomes yet another recurrent theme.

By 1882 Wilde's fame as a personality and poet had spread to the United States and Canada. His lecture tour there attracted a great deal of attention in the popular press on both sides of the Atlantic. Wilde gave two principal lectures, "The English Renaissance of Art" and "Decorative Art in America," which were a continuation of ideas he explored in *Poems*. Walter Hamilton included a lengthy chapter on Wilde in *The Aesthetic Movement in England* (1882) that effectively ranked Wilde with such figures as Rossetti, Ruskin, and William Morris. Wilde's tour was a huge success, if controversial, and he spent the better part of a year in the United States and Canada. He spent the most time in New York negotiating terms for *The Duchess of Padua* and trying to promote his play, *Vera; or, The Nihilists* (1880). On his return to Europe he went first to London and then to Paris, where he was able to live off the proceeds of his lecture tour for three months.

The following year, in August 1883, *Vera* was performed in New York. The play is a vehicle to express what Ellman terms Wilde's "aristocratic socialism." Wilde insists that socialism is beautiful and enjoyable, and he denounces tyranny and injustice. *Vera* is based loosely on Russian history, with the notorious cruelty of the czars serving as a backdrop to Wilde's message of liberation and reform. In July 1883 Wilde wrote to Marie Prescott, who took the title role in *Vera:* "I have tried in it to express within the limits of art that Titan cry of the peoples for liberty, which in the Europe of our day is threatening thrones, and making governments unstable from Spain to Russia.... But it is a play not of politics but of passion." He was later to say to Constance Lloyd, his future wife, that he wrote *Vera* to show how an abstract idea, such as liberty, could be as powerful a passion as love. Wilde's hopes of success for the play were dashed by the almost universally damning reviews. *Vera* closed within a week, and its failure meant that Wilde was forced to go on lecturing.

Jane Wilde had suggested to her sons that they marry heiresses as a way out of financial difficulty after the death of their father in 1876. Wilde seems to have resolved upon marriage as early as 1880 but was rejected by Violet Hunt and Charlotte Montefiore. After these setbacks he met Lloyd in June 1881, and they were married on 29 May 1884. Constance was not exactly an heiress; she had £250 a year that would increase to £900 when her grandfather died. This amount was not enough for Wilde's extravagance, and financial problems plagued him throughout his life. When he was in funds, however, Wilde was generous to his friends and to the poor. Two sons born in rapid succession, Cyril on 5 June 1885 and Vyvyan on 5 November 1886, placed further strain on the Wildes' relationship. Wilde is reputed to have been disgusted by Constance's changed body during her pregnancies. Nevertheless, they remained good friends, and Wilde was devoted to his children. He encouraged Constance's involvement in women's liberation movements and political activity. She edited the *Gazette* of the Rational Dress Society in 1888-1889 and gave a speech on 6 November 1888 advocating lighter clothing and divided skirts instead of petticoats. Wilde accompanied her to a demonstration in Hyde Park in support of the dock strike on 1 September 1889.

Wilde was also a reformer in support of women's liberation. He took over the editorship of *The Lady's World: A Magazine of Fashion and Society* in 1887 and reconstituted it. Discussion of fashion was relegated to the end of each issue, and articles on serious topics, including the education of women, as well as serial fiction were substituted. Wilde also insisted the magazine be renamed *The Woman's World*, since he regarded "lady" as a pejorative term. In November 1887 the first issue under his leadership appeared. Wilde remained editor for two years, but his involvement quickly flagged, in part because of his other interests.

Wilde saw art as moral and social reform; what was not beautiful was not good, including poverty. But Wilde's views on the immorality of poverty were opposed to those of Victorian middle-class morality. The idea of poverty as dehumanizing ran counter to accepted middle-class views, both secular and religious, for by implication the ruling classes were responsible for this oppression. The value of domesticity and the ennobling quality of poverty were popular Victorian literary themes. Religion preached patience and tolerance of one's lot in this life: reward for the virtuous poor would come in heaven. In his lectures and essays Wilde preached a new Aestheticism and social reform through art. Like Ruskin, Wilde criticized the false glamour of Victorian upper-class society, but Wilde was also attracted to this world. He viewed Victorian ideals of art, reflected in the ornate and orderly decor of upper- and middle-class homes, as a sham. He disapproved of the idea that every picture should tell a story—a notion that dominated the mainstream Victorian art world. During his Aesthetic phase he set about to reform rigid notions of art and decorated his home and his person as exhibits of this new modern art.

In May 1888 Wilde published *The Happy Prince and Other Tales,* comprised of the title story, "The Nightingale and the Rose," "The Selfish Giant," "The Devoted Friends," and "The Remarkable Rocket." Implicit in the social criticism of these tales is the notion of reform from within the ruling classes. Wilde was influenced by a great many sources, traditions, and authors in these tales, most obviously Hans Christian Andersen, in both technique and theme. The stories explore the price paid in human suffering for beauty, art, power, and wealth, with the hope of salvation offered by sacrificial love. The critical reaction to the volume was positive; Wilde also received a letter of praise from Walter Pater.

Wilde first told the title story of "The Happy Prince" to entertain his friends during a visit to Cambridge in November 1885. The story opens with a description of the Happy Prince—a splendid and imposing statue covered in gold leaf, with sapphires for eyes and a large ruby in his sword pommel. Placed on a large column, he looks down over the city. Almost immediately the Victorian middle-class dilemma over the usefulness of art is raised by one of the town councillors. In opposition to the councillor's view is that of a child who sees the "use" of the statue in inspiring dreams. The story

The first page of the manuscript for De Profundis, *the letter Wilde wrote to Douglas from Reading Gaol (British Library)* also presents unrequited love between a swallow and a reed. The swallow, who has remained behind after all the other birds have migrated, finally decides to leave for warmer climes. Its courtship of the reed has proved unsuccessful when she refuses to travel with him. She is not prepared to make a sacrifice for the swallow because she does not love it. The swallow seeks a place to rest in the city before continuing its journey to Egypt. He alights on the Prince's column delighted at having found such a splendid resting place.

Although the Prince had spent his entire life on earth in the palace of Sans-Souci, he was sympathetic to the poor, and his spirit lives on in his memorial statue. From his pedestal high above the city he sees the wretchedness and misery of the poor and laments their condition. The Prince enlists the swallow's aid in relieving the worst cases of poverty. The swallow agrees and delays its plan to migrate south, gradually picking away the valuable decorations of the statue to give to various members of the deserving poor. Winter progresses, and the swallow realizes that it is going to die from the cold. It informs the Prince, kisses him goodbye, and falls dead at his feet. At that moment the Prince's lead heart breaks in two. Soon after, the local dignitaries gather in the town square and decide that as the statue "is no longer beautiful" it "is no longer useful." The statue is melted down, but the lead heart will not melt, so it is thrown on a rubbish pile alongside the body of the swallow. God then enters the story: "'Bring me the two most precious things in the city,' said God to one of His Angels; and the Angel brought Him the leaden heart and the dead bird." By elevating the broken heart of a statue and the body of a bird over the wealth of an industrial city, Wilde criticizes industrial society and its ruling elites, arguing for reform through Christian ethics.

The second tale, "The Nightingale and the Rose," shows the pointlessness of self-sacrifice in an industrial age. The spirit of commerce is shown to be all-powerful, while man's spiritual nature has been lost. In "The Selfish Giant," which Pater describes in his 12 June 1888 letter to Wilde as "perfect in its kind," Wilde comments on the erosion of public spaces and the effects of land enclosure. Using the by-now-familiar device of a giant to represent the ruling classes and children to represent the poor, Wilde calls for social reform from within the ruling classes. During the giant's absence children play in his garden. The garden flourishes; the birds sing; and the children are happy. When the giant returns, he banishes the children and builds a high wall to exclude them. The giant is punished for his selfishness because spring and summer never come to his garden after he has sent the children away; the garden is trapped in eternal winter. But the children discover a hole in the wall and creep back into the garden. The giant is awakened to the sound of birds, and he looks out to see the children sitting in the branches of the now-blossoming trees. Then the giant notices a little child crying because he is too small to reach the branches, and "the Giant's heart melted." He goes out and places the little boy in the tree. From then on he allows the children to play in his garden. But he does not see the little boy again until the day of his death. The child is transformed into the figure of Christ and says to the giant, "You let me play once in your garden, to-day you shall come with me to my garden, which is Paradise."

"The Devoted Friend" is akin to "The Nightingale and the Rose" as a tale of unappreciated self-sacrifice. Little Hans is the victim of the rich miller's false friendship, betrayed and destroyed by greed. An animal framework gives the tale a comic effect which is heightened by matching the miller with an equally egotistical and smug water rat. Nevertheless, underlying the comedy is serious social criticism. For while "The Devoted Friend" borrows its animal framework from Andersen, the title is reminiscent of the kind of moral tale printed by the Cheap Repository Tract Society, which produced middle-class propaganda for the poor, and it is clearly a satire on those tales. Rather than depicting the ennobling quality of poverty, "The Devoted Friend" comments on the exploitation of the poor by the wealthy.

"The Remarkable Rocket" deals with the subject of vanity. Although Wilde was himself often accused of vanity, he did not approve of it. In this story Wilde again uses satire for social critique, but the depiction of the remarkable rocket is also a personal attack on the painter James McNeill Whistler. Wilde had been a great admirer of Whistler's for many years, during which time Wilde overlooked Whistler's vanity. But here Wilde turns the tables on Whistler by putting some of Whistler's own witticisms into the mouth of the Rocket in such a way as to make the Rocket ridiculous.

Wilde continued to experiment with literary form, and in July 1889 "The Portrait of Mr. W. H." was published in *Blackwood's Magazine*. Here Wilde creates fiction within a fiction that is part story, part critical essay, and part confessional. He was advised not to publish it because it includes allusions to homosexual practices. Wilde puts forward an old theory that William Shakespeare was attracted to a young boy; but he does so in a story that is original. The story is, however, dangerously autobiographical. Wilde imagines Shakespeare, a married man with two children like himself, attracted to a young boy, just as Wilde had been captivated by Robert Ross sometime in 1886.

In November 1891 Wilde published *A House of Pomegranates,* a collection of stories in fairy-tale form. But these stories are more deliberately aimed at an adult readership than *The Happy Prince* was. The first story, "The Young King," is a development of "The Happy Prince" from the earlier collection. Like "The Happy Prince," it is a social critique with a clear Christian and socialist message. The second story, "The Birthday of the Infanta," differs from the other stories and centers around the antithesis of Art and Nature. The surface beauty and the cruelty of the Infanta, a product of the civilized and cultured ruling classes, is opposed to the inner spiritual beauty of the ugly but kindhearted dwarf, who dies of a broken heart. Wilde again uses the figure of size to represent class. The dwarf is lower-class and lacking in culture but is also therefore closer to nature. The third story, "The Fisherman and His Soul," deals with the opposition of the body and soul, but Wilde makes an interesting distinction between heart and soul. And the last, "The Star Child," again explores the theme of outward beauty and cruelty in opposition to inner beauty. The Star Child must learn pity, but after suffering and transformation he only rules for three years: "And he who came after him ruled evilly." Again the story ends on a negative note.

The years 1889 to 1895 were prolific ones for Wilde, but during these years he led an increasingly double life, which ended in his imprisonment in 1895. This secret life was also featured increasingly in his work. *The Picture of Dorian Gray,* published as a novel in 1891, first appeared as a story in *Lippincott's Magazine* in July 1890. Joris-Karl Huysmans's *A rebours* (1884), known as the guidebook of Decadence, was a great influence on *The Picture of Dorian Gray.* Wilde had read Huysmans's novel on his honeymoon. The earlier version of *The Picture of Dorian Gray* included stronger suggestions of a homosexual relationship between Basil Hallward and Dorian Gray. Because of the adverse critical reaction and his own then-illegal homosexual relations, Wilde revised and expanded his novel and added the preface in response to the critics. But there is little doubt that he named the hero of his work "Gray" as a compliment to his friend John Gray, and that Wilde and Gray became lovers. During this period Wilde's popularity soared, and the number of young men who attached themselves to him, including Aubrey Beardsley and Max Beerbohm, increased with his success.

In the novel Wilde stresses the importance of the artistic relationship between Basil and Dorian. In the preface Wilde questions whether art can corrupt and defends his work on artistic grounds. Yet he also goes against what he states in the preface, for there is a moral in the book. *The Picture of Dorian Gray* is not only a psychological exploration but also a critique of the emphasis placed on surface in Victorian middle-class life and an attack on the ruling classes that produce the kind of young man who seeks sensation for the sake of it. It is also a return to the theme of human decline under industrialization and the loss of the spiritual in the face of a material age. Dorian shuts the portrait away, thereby divorcing himself from his soul. He epitomizes the fragmentation of the individual when body is divorced from soul, and as a result he becomes incapable of good and the contemplation of beauty.

The impact of *The Picture of Dorian Gray* was considerable. Wilde's circle of followers was delighted with it, but in general it caused contradictory sentiments in its readers. The success also led to Wilde's first meeting with Lord Alfred Douglas. Wilde was smitten with Douglas's beauty, and the young man's praise of the novel prompted Wilde to give him a deluxe copy. Wilde also offered to coach Douglas when he heard Douglas was studying classics at Oxford.

Wilde published another collection of short stories, *Lord Arthur Savile's Crime & Other Stories,* and a collection of essays, *Intentions,* in 1891. *Intentions* includes the essay "The Critic as Artist," in which Wilde presents a defense of Aestheticism as an antidote to the negative portrayal of it in *The Picture of Dorian Gray.* Also in 1891 Wilde's article "The Soul of Man under Socialism," aimed at radical social reform, appeared in the *Fortnightly Review;* it was published in book form in 1895. It is a continuation and broadening of the argument he sets out in "The Critic as Artist" but looks to the future rather than dwelling on the past and present. In "The Soul of Man under Socialism" Wilde deals with Aestheticism in political and social terms. He argues that socialism is the only way to individual freedom by freeing mankind from the necessity of living for others. He believes charity institutionalizes poverty and degrades the poor, who are right to steal rather than receive alms. To insist that the poor be thrifty is insulting, and to praise the dignity of manual labor is ridiculous when all know it is degrading. Wilde opposes any authoritarian socialism but acknowledges that his is a utopian ideal.

Already a sensation in London, Wilde again turned his attention to Paris. He felt the French were of a more artistic temperament than the En-

Wilde's tomb in Père Lachaise cemetery, Paris

glish and more generous to artists. His friends there included Marcel Schwob, Pierre Louÿs, and André Gide. It was during the closing months of 1891 in Paris that Wilde started work on his play *Salomé* (1893). Huysmans's description of Gustave Moreau's painting of Salome in *A rebours* was the inspiration for Wilde's play. He wrote it in French and later gave this explanation to Ross in an interview for the *Pall Mall Budget:* "I have one instrument I know I can command, and that is the English language. There was another instrument to which I had listened all my life, and I wanted once to touch this new instrument to see whether I could make any beautiful thing out of it." *Salomé* dramatizes the power struggle between the opposing forces of patriarchy, which represents control and authority, and women, who represent nature or the flesh. There is a fear of the natural, but Wilde demonstrates the blurring of gender in the struggle for power. Salomé describes Jokanaan in exactly the same terms as she herself has been described. This point is reflected in the illustrations by Beardsley, which make Jokanaan a mirror image of Salomé. They represent desire and repression. Herod is enfeebled by his desire for Salomé and can only reassert his patriarchal authority when she is dead.

Wilde's most popular plays are comedies, but they are also social satires aimed at reform. The condition of woman in Victorian society was a major concern for Wilde, and, like his mother, he took a feminist line. In *Lady Windermere's Fan, A Woman of No Importance,* and *An Ideal Husband* (1899) Wilde comments on the moral double standard imposed on women by patriarchal society. He shows how the Victorian "lady," a vestige of eighteenth-century courtly society, reinforces this double standard. Women are forced to conform or seek underhanded means to achieve their ends. There is no question that seventeenth-century Restoration comedy was an influence on these comedies, but Wilde owes just as much to his contemporaries Henrik Ibsen and Anton Chekhov. Like Ibsen and Chekhov, Wilde gives detailed stage directions and attaches symbolic significance to the detail in setting. Costume, gesture, language, and vocal nuance are all-important to Wilde. His plays hold a mirror to contemporary society and reflect the polished social surface he then undercuts. In spite of making light of his work to some, Wilde took his plays seriously. He involved himself during rehearsals and was always ready with suggestions and revisions.

Lady Windermere's Fan was first performed at St. James's Theatre on 20 February 1892. Wilde had begun work on the play in the autumn of 1891 at the instigation of actor-manager George Alexander. The play opened to a full house with a glittering array of celebrities in attendance. Arthur Walter and Henry James disliked the play, and most other critics were against it, but Frank Harris and Bernard Shaw admired it, as did most of the audience. It launched Wilde's success as a playwright; crowds came to see it, and the Prince of Wales gave it his approval. The play is more complex than it seems; it is not just the case of a "fallen woman," Mrs. Erlynne, rescuing her daughter, Lady Windermere, from a similar situation. Lady Windermere is prompted by her puritan and moral ideals to behave in a way alien to her nature and in opposition to morality. In order to be a "good woman" she must learn to be less severe in moral judgment and recognize that not everything is black and white. Mrs. Erlynne, although censured by society for her past transgression, is a good woman. She is prepared to sacrifice herself in order to spare her daughter. Wilde exposes the hypocrisy and ridiculous standards of the fashionable world of the elite. The social structure encourages seduction while appearing to condemn it, and women are judged by a moral double standard: when a woman commits a sexual transgression, she is damned forever in the eyes of society, but the man is blameless. Mrs. Erlynne is compelled by the moral hypocrisy of society to employ corrupt methods. In addition to the social criticism Wilde was radical in his ending of the play: instead of the conventional dénouement, at the end of this comedy three secrets are left undisclosed.

By now the relationship between Douglas and Wilde had intensified, with Wilde spending more and more time away from his family. Wilde allowed Douglas to translate *Salomé*, which had been banned from performance by the Lord Chamberlain but was published in French in Paris and London in 1893. The translation appeared a year later. The success of *Lady Windermere's Fan* served as a consolation for Wilde's frustration over *Salomé*, and he was already at work on his next play. *A Woman of No Importance* opened at the Haymarket Theatre on 19 April 1893, and Wilde had another hit. *An Ideal Husband* was first performed on 3 January 1895 and was also a huge success.

The Importance of Being Earnest, Wilde's last and most brilliant play, went into rehearsal soon after the opening of *An Ideal Husband*. In spite of the subtitle, *A Trivial Comedy for Serious People*, Wilde's play is a serious critique of Victorian society. Wilde anticipates modern writers such as Samuel Beckett in his use of farce to comment upon serious issues. But Wilde is subversive in his criticism of Victorian institutions. The Victorian upper classes are presented as enclosed characters more intent on social surface in a world where form replaces emotion. The language of the play is simple and straightforward, but the characters speak epigrammatically, thereby preventing real exchange of ideas. Marriage, education, and religion are all critiqued in Wilde's satirical handling. He comments on the subservient role of women by comically inverting gender roles—the women in the play are dominating and controlling. The hypocrisy and heartlessness of the characters reflect Wilde's own view of Victorian society.

Wilde's dazzling success came swiftly to an end with his ill-judged libel action against Douglas's father, the marquess of Queensberry. The case resulted in success for the marquess and the arrest, trial, and imprisonment of Wilde on charges of offenses to minors. The society Wilde had satirized in his works as hypocritical and shallow turned its back on him, and his plays were taken off the stage. Wilde's last works, *The Ballad of Reading Gaol* (1898) and *De Profundis* (1905), were written in Reading Gaol. Wilde entrusted the manuscript of *De Profundis* to Ross, one of his few loyal friends, who published it after Wilde's death.

Wilde's achievement as a reform writer in his own day was overshadowed by his disgrace and imprisonment. Wilde saw himself as "a man who stood in symbolic relations to the art and culture of [his] age," but he paid a terrible price. He suffered two years hard labor and bankruptcy. Victorian England was unforgiving, and upon his release from prison on 19 May 1897 he went into exile, staying first in Dieppe and later in Paris. Although *The Ballad of Reading Gaol* sold well beyond expectations, it did not make enough money for Wilde to live on. During his last years he relied on friends, including Douglas, for financial support. Reginald Turner and Ross were with Wilde at the end; he died on 30 November 1900 in Paris. After his death came a renewed critical interest in him, but it is only within the last thirty years that his work has received serious scholarly attention.

Letters:

The Letters of Oscar Wilde, edited by Rupert Hart-Davis (New York: Harcourt, Brace & World, 1962);

Selected Letters of Oscar Wilde, edited by Hart-Davis (Oxford: Oxford University Press, 1979);

More Letters of Oscar Wilde, edited by Hart-Davis (New York: Vanguard, 1985).

Interviews:

Oscar Wilde: Interviews and Recollections, edited by E. H. Mikhail, 2 volumes (London: Macmillan, 1979);

Bibliographies:

Stuart Mason (Christopher Millard), *Bibliography of Oscar Wilde* (London: Laurie, 1914);

Donald L. Lawler, "Oscar Wilde in the *New Cambridge Bibliography of English Literature,*" *Papers of the Bibliographical Society of America,* 67 (1973): 172–188;

Ian Fletcher and John Stokes, "Oscar Wilde," in *Anglo-Irish Literature: A Review of Research,* edited by Richard Finneran (New York: Modern Language Association, 1976), pp. 48–137;

E. H. Mikhail, *Oscar Wilde; An Annotated Bibliography of Criticism* (London: Macmillan, 1978; Totowa, N.J.: Rowman & Littlefield, 1978);

Fletcher and Stokes, "Oscar Wilde," in *Recent Research on Anglo-Irish Writers,* edited by Finneran (New York: Modern Language Association, 1983), pp. 21–47;

Ian Small, *Oscar Wilde Revalued: An Essay on New Materials and Methods of Research* (Greensboro, N.C.: ELT Press, 1993);

Thomas A. Mikolyzk, *Oscar Wilde: An Annotated Bibliography* (Westport, Conn.: Greenwood Press, 1993).

Biographies:

Robert H. Sherard, *The Life of Oscar Wilde* (London: Laurie, 1906; New York: Kennerley, 1907);

Arthur Symons, *A Study of Oscar Wilde* (London: Sawyer, 1930);

Hesketh Pearson, *The Life of Oscar Wilde* (London: Methuen, 1946); republished as *Oscar Wilde: His Life and Wit* (New York: Harper, 1946);

Vyvyan Holland, *Son of Oscar Wilde* (London: Hart-Davis, 1954; New York: Dutton, 1954);

Lewis Broad, *The Friendships and Follies of Oscar Wilde* (London: Hutchinson, 1954; New York: Crowell, 1955);

Holland, *Oscar Wilde: A Pictorial Biography* (London: Thames & Hudson, 1960);

Phillippe Julian, *Oscar Wilde,* translated by Violet Wyndham (London: Constable, 1969);

Rubert Croft-Cooke, *The Unrecorded Life of Oscar Wilde* (London & New York: W. H. Allen, 1972);

H. Montgomery Hyde, *Oscar Wilde: A Biography* (New York: Farrar, Straus & Giroux, 1975);

Sheridan Morley, *Oscar Wilde: An Illustrated Biography* (London: Weidenfeld & Nicolson, 1976);

Louis Kronenberger, *Oscar Wilde* (Boston: Little, Brown, 1976);

Richard Ellmann, *Oscar Wilde* (London: Hamilton, 1987; New York: Knopf, 1988);

Peter Raby, *Oscar Wilde* (Cambridge: Cambridge University Press, 1988);

Horst Schroeder, *Additions and Corrections to Richard Ellmann's "Oscar Wilde"* (Braunschweig, Germany: Privately printed, 1989).

References:

Karl Beckson, ed., *Oscar Wilde: The Critical Heritage* (New York: Barnes & Noble, 1970);

Joyce Bentley, *The Importance of Being Constance* (London: Hale, 1983);

J. E. Chamberlin, *Ripe Was the Drowsy Hour: The Age of Oscar Wilde* (New York: Seabury, 1977);

Barbara Charlesworth, *Dark Passages: Decadent Consciousness in Victorian Literature* (Madison: University of Wisconsin Press, 1965);

Philip Cohen, *The Moral Vision of Oscar Wilde* (Rutherford, N.J.: Fairleigh Dickinson University Press, 1976);

Richard Dellamora, *Masculine Desire: The Sexual Politics of Victorian Aestheticism* (Chapel Hill: University of North Carolina Press, 1990);

Richard Ellmann, ed., *Oscar Wilde: A Collection of Critical Essays* (Englewood Cliffs, N.J.: Prentice-Hall, 1969);

Ian Fletcher and Malcolm Bradbury, eds., *Decadence and the 1890s* (London: Arnold, 1979);

Regenia A. Gagnier, *Idylls of the Marketplace: Oscar Wilde and the Victorian Public* (Stanford: Stanford University Press, 1986);

Jonathan Goodman, *The Oscar Wilde File* (London: Allison, 1989);

H. Montgomery Hyde, ed., *The Trials of Oscar Wilde* (London: Hodge, 1948); republished as *The Three Trials of Oscar Wilde* (New York: University Books, 1956); enlarged as *Famous Trials,* seventh series: *Oscar Wilde* (Baltimore: Penguin, 1963);

Gerhard Joseph, "Framing Wilde," *Victorian Newsletter,* 72 (Fall 1987): 61–63;

Michael C. Kotzin, "'The Selfish Giant' as Literary Fairy Tale," *Studies in Short Fiction,* 16 (Fall 1979): 301–309;

Robert K. Martin, "Oscar Wilde and the Fairy Tale: 'The Happy Prince' as Self-Dramatization," *Studies in Short Fiction,* 16 (Winter 1979): 74–77;

Stuart Mason (Christopher Millard), ed., *Oscar Wilde: Art and Morality, A Defence of "The Picture of Dorian Gray"* (London: Jacobs, 1907);

John Allen Quintus, "The Moral Prerogative in Oscar Wilde: A Look at the Fairy Tales," *Virginia Quarterly Review,* 53 (Autumn 1977): 708–717;

Epifanio San Juan Jr., *The Art of Oscar Wilde* (Princeton: Princeton University Press, 1967);

Gary Schmidgall, *The Stranger Wilde: Interpreting Oscar* (New York: Dutton, 1994);

Frances Winwar, *Oscar Wilde and the Yellow Nineties* (New York: Harper, 1940).

Papers:

The William Andrews Clark Memorial Library, University of California, Los Angeles, has the most extensive collection of Wilde's papers. Additional collections are held by the New York Public Library; the Pierpont Morgan Library; the Beinecke Library, Yale University; the British Library; the Harry Ransom Humanities Research Center, University of Texas at Austin; the Houghton Library, Harvard University; the University of Edinburgh Library; the Rosenbach Museum, Philadelphia; and Magdalen College, Oxford University.

Books for Further Reading

Baylen, Joseph O., and Norbert J. Gossman, eds. *Biographical Dictionary of Modern British Radicals.* Volume 2, *1830–1870*; Volume 3: *1870–1914*. Hassocks, Sussex: Harvester Press / Atlantic Highlands, N.J.: Humanities Press, 1979.

Benn, Alfred William. *The History of English Rationalism in the Nineteenth Century.* 2 volumes. London: Longmans Green, 1906.

Brand, Jack. *Local Government Reform in England, 1888–1974.* London: Croom Helm, 1974.

Brantlinger, Patrick. *The Spirit of Reform: British Literature and Politics, 1832–1867.* Cambridge, Mass.: Harvard University Press, 1977.

Breisach, Ernst. *Historiography: Ancient, Medieval, and Modern.* Chicago & London: University of Chicago Press, 1983.

Brinton, Crane. *English Political Thought in the Nineteenth Century.* London: Benn, 1949.

Bristow, Edward J. *Vice and Vigilance: Social Purity Movements in Britain since 1700.* Dublin: Gill & Macmillan, 1977.

Bullock, Alan, and Maurice Shock, eds. *The Liberal Tradition from Fox to Keynes.* London: Black, 1956.

Caine, Barbara. *Victorian Feminists.* Oxford: Oxford University Press, 1992.

Cazamian, Louis. *The Social Novel in England, 1830–1850.* Translated by Martin Fido. London: Routledge & Kegan Paul, 1973.

Chadwick, Owen. *The Mind of the Oxford Movement.* Stanford: Stanford University Press, 1961.

Chadwick. *The Victorian Church.* 2 volumes. London: Black, 1966–1970. New York: Oxford University Press, 1966–1970.

Claeys, Gregory. *Machinery, Money and the Millennium: From Moral Economy to Socialism, 1815–1860.* Princeton: Princeton University Press, 1987.

Conacher, J. B. *The Emergence of British Parliamentary Democracy in the Nineteenth Century.* New York: Wiley, 1971.

Corrigan, Philip, and Derek Sayer. *The Great Arch: English State Formation as Cultural Revolution.* Oxford & New York: Blackwell, 1985.

Davidoff, Leonore, and Catherine Hall. *Family Fortunes: Men and Women of the English Middle Class, 1780–1850.* London: Hutchinson, 1987.

Dorson, Richard M. *The British Folklorists: A History.* London: Routledge & Kegan Paul / Chicago: University of Chicago Press, 1968.

Evans, Eric J. *The Forging of the Modern State: Early Industrial Britain, 1783–1870.* London & New York: Longman, 1983.

Books for Further Reading

Everett, Edwin M. *The Party of Humanity*. Chapel Hill: University of North Carolina Press, 1939.

Fairweather, Eugene R., ed. *The Oxford Movement*. New York: Oxford University Press, 1964.

Gallagher, Catherine. *The Industrial Reformation of English Fiction: Social Discourse and Narrative Form, 1832-1867*. Chicago & London: University of Chicago Press, 1985.

Gilbert, Alan D. *Religion and Society in Industrial England: Church, Chapel and Social Change, 1740-1914*. London & New York: Longman, 1976.

Hammond, J. L., and Barbara Hammond. *The Bleak Age*. Revised edition. Middlesex, U.K. & New York: Penguin, 1947.

Himmelfarb, Gertrude. *The Idea of Poverty: England in the Early Industrial Age*. New York: Vintage, 1985.

Holton, Sandra Stanley. *Feminism and Democracy: Women's Suffrage and Reform Politics in Britain, 1900-1918*. Cambridge: Cambridge University Press, 1986.

Jahn, Rosemary. *The Art and Science of Victorian History*. Columbus: Ohio State University Press, 1985.

Kent, Christopher. *Brains and Numbers: Elitism, Comtism and Democracy in Mid-Victorian England*. Toronto: University of Toronto Press, 1978.

Levine, Philippa. *Victorian Feminism, 1850-1900*. London: Hutchinson, 1987.

Maccoby, Simon, ed. *The British Political Tradition: The English Radical Tradition, 1763-1914*. London: Kaye, 1952.

Midwinter, E. C. *Victorian Social Reform*. London: Longman, 1968.

Morazé, Charles. *The Triumph of the Middle Classes: A Study of European Values in the Nineteenth Century*. Translated by Peter Wait and Barbara Ferryan. London: Weidenfeld & Nicolson, 1966.

Perkin, Harold. *The Origins of Modern English Society, 1780-1880*. London: Routledge & Kegan Paul, 1969.

Polanyi, Karl. *The Great Transformation: The Political and Economic Origins of Our Time*. Boston: Beacon, 1957.

Radzinowicz, Leon. *A History of Criminal Law and Its Administration*. 2 volumes. London: Stevens, 1956.

Reardon, Bernard M. G. *From Coleridge to Gore: A Century of Religious Thought in Britain*. London: Longman, 1971.

Rendall, Jane. *The Origins of Modern Feminism: Women in Britain, France and the United States, 1780-1860*. Basingstoke & London: Macmillan, 1985.

Robbins, Keith. *The Eclipse of a Great Power: Modern Britain, 1870-1975*. London & New York: Longman, 1983.

Schilling, Bernard. *Human Dignity and the Great Victorians*. New York: Columbia University Press, 1946.

Semmel, Bernard. *Imperialism and Social Reform: English Social-Imperial Thought, 1895-1914*. London: Allen & Unwin, 1960.

Stewart, Alexander P., and Edward Jenkins. *The Medical and Legal Aspects of Sanitary Reform*. Leicester: Leicester University Press, 1969.

Thomas, William. *The Philosophical Radicals: Nine Studies in Theory and Practice, 1817–1841.* Oxford: Oxford University Press, 1979.

Vicinus, Martha. *The Industrial Muse.* London: Croom Helm, 1974.

Vidler, Alec R. *The Church in an Age of Revolution: 1789 to the Present.* Revised edition. Harmondsworth: Penguin, 1974.

Vincent, David. *Bread, Knowledge and Freedom: A Study of Nineteenth-Century Working Class Autobiography.* London: Europa, 1981.

Williams, Karel. *From Pauperism to Poverty.* London: Routledge & Kegan Paul, 1981.

Williams, Raymond. *Culture and Society, 1780–1950.* London: Chatto & Windus / New York: Columbia University Press, 1958.

Woodward, Ernest L. *The Age of Reform, 1815–1870.* Second edition. Oxford: Clarendon Press, 1962.

Young, George M. *Portrait of an Age: Victorian England.* Second edition, corrected. Oxford & New York: Oxford University Press, 1977.

Contributors

Donald S. Armentrout	*University of the South*
Paul G. Ashdown	*University of Tennessee, Knoxville*
Eugene R. August	*University of Dayton*
Rhonda Batchelor	*University of Alberta*
Charles Blinderman	*Clark University*
Bege K. Bowers	*Youngstown State University*
Douglas S. Campbell	*Lock Haven University*
Gregory Claeys	*Royal Holloway College*
Sidney Coulling	*Lexington, Virginia*
Patricia Demers	*University of Alberta*
James Diedrick	*Albion College*
Sos Eltis	*St. John's College*
Kirsten Escobar	*Baylor University*
Timothy J. Evans	*William Bland College of the College of William and Mary*
John Ferns	*McMaster University*
Isobel M. Findlay	*University of Saskatchewan*
Susan Hamilton	*University of Alberta*
Kathryn Harvey	*University of Alberta*
Jennifer Kelly	*Birbeck College, London University*
Christopher A. Kent	*University of Saskatchewan*
Lynn MacKay	*Trent University*
Susan Mumm	*York University*
William Naufftus	*Winthrop University*
Sandra den Otter	*Queen's University*
Timothy Randall	*London, England*
Terrie M. Romano	*Queen's University*
Erika Rothwell	*University of Alberta*
Pamela Shorrocks	*Colchester, England*
Max Keith Sutton	*University of Kansas*
Ronald Tetreault	*Dalhousie University*
Sylvia Vance	*St. Edmund Hall, Oxford University*
Hayden Ward	*West Virginia University*
Barbara Frey Waxman	*University of North Carolina at Wilmington*
Alison Winter	*California Institute of Technology*

Cumulative Index

Dictionary of Literary Biography, Volumes 1-190
Dictionary of Literary Biography Yearbook, 1980-1996
Dictionary of Literary Biography Documentary Series, Volumes 1-16

Cumulative Index

DLB before number: *Dictionary of Literary Biography,* Volumes 1-190
Y before number: *Dictionary of Literary Biography Yearbook,* 1980-1996
DS before number: *Dictionary of Literary Biography Documentary Series,* Volumes 1-16

A

Abbey, Edwin Austin 1852–1911 .... DLB-188
Abbey Press DLB-49
The Abbey Theatre and Irish Drama, 1900-1945 .... DLB-10
Abbot, Willis J. 1863-1934 .... DLB-29
Abbott, Jacob 1803-1879 .... DLB-1
Abbott, Lee K. 1947- DLB-130
Abbott, Lyman 1835-1922 .... DLB-79
Abbott, Robert S. 1868-1940 .... DLB-29, 91
Abe, Kōbō 1924-1993 .... DLB-182
Abelard, Peter circa 1079-1142 ..... DLB-115
Abelard-Schuman DLB-46
Abell, Arunah S. 1806-1888 ...... DLB-43
Abercrombie, Lascelles 1881-1938 ... DLB-19
Aberdeen University Press Limited DLB-106
Abish, Walter 1931- DLB-130
Ablesimov, Aleksandr Onisimovich 1742-1783 .... DLB-150
Abraham à Sancta Clara 1644-1709 .... DLB-168
Abrahams, Peter 1919- DLB-117
Abrams, M. H. 1912- DLB-67
Abrogans circa 790-800 .... DLB-148
Abschatz, Hans Aßmann von 1646-1699 .... DLB-168
Abse, Dannie 1923- DLB-27
Academy Chicago Publishers DLB-46
Accrocca, Elio Filippo 1923- DLB-128
Ace Books DLB-46
Achebe, Chinua 1930- DLB-117
Achtenberg, Herbert 1938- DLB-124
Ackerman, Diane 1948- DLB-120
Ackroyd, Peter 1949- DLB-155
Acorn, Milton 1923-1986 .... DLB-53
Acosta, Oscar Zeta 1935?- DLB-82
Actors Theatre of Louisville DLB-7
Adair, James 1709?-1783? DLB-30
Adam, Graeme Mercer 1839-1912 ... DLB-99
Adam, Robert Borthwick II 1863-1940 .... DLB-187

Adame, Leonard 1947- DLB-82
Adamic, Louis 1898-1951 .... DLB-9
Adams, Alice 1926- Y-86
Adams, Brooks 1848-1927 .... DLB-47
Adams, Charles Francis, Jr. 1835-1915 .... DLB-47
Adams, Douglas 1952- Y-83
Adams, Franklin P. 1881-1960 ..... DLB-29
Adams, Henry 1838-1918 ... DLB-12, 47, 189
Adams, Herbert Baxter 1850-1901 .... DLB-47
Adams, J. S. and C. [publishing house] DLB-49
Adams, James Truslow 1878-1949 .... DLB-17
Adams, John 1735-1826 ...... DLB-31, 183
Adams, John 1735-1826 and Adams, Abigail 1744-1818 ..... DLB-183
Adams, John Quincy 1767-1848 ..... DLB-37
Adams, Léonie 1899-1988 .... DLB-48
Adams, Levi 1802-1832 .... DLB-99
Adams, Samuel 1722-1803 ..... DLB-31, 43
Adams, Thomas 1582 or 1583-1652 .... DLB-151
Adams, William Taylor 1822-1897 ... DLB-42
Adamson, Sir John 1867-1950 ..... DLB-98
Adcock, Arthur St. John 1864-1930 .... DLB-135
Adcock, Betty 1938- DLB-105
Adcock, Betty, Certain Gifts DLB-105
Adcock, Fleur 1934- DLB-40
Addison, Joseph 1672-1719 ...... DLB-101
Ade, George 1866-1944 ...... DLB-11, 25
Adeler, Max (see Clark, Charles Heber)
Adonias Filho 1915-1990 .... DLB-145
Advance Publishing Company DLB-49
AE 1867-1935 .... DLB-19
Ælfric circa 955-circa 1010 ...... DLB-146
Aeschines circa 390 B.C.-circa 320 B.C. DLB-176
Aeschylus 525-524 B.C.-456-455 B.C. DLB-176
Aesthetic Poetry (1873), by Walter Pater DLB-35
After Dinner Opera Company Y-92

Afro-American Literary Critics: An Introduction DLB-33
Agassiz, Elizabeth Cary 1822-1907 ... DLB-189
Agassiz, Jean Louis Rodolphe 1807-1873 .... DLB-1
Agee, James 1909-1955 ..... DLB-2, 26, 152
The Agee Legacy: A Conference at the University of Tennessee at Knoxville Y-89
Aguilera Malta, Demetrio 1909-1981 .... DLB-145
Ai 1947- DLB-120
Aichinger, Ilse 1921- DLB-85
Aidoo, Ama Ata 1942- DLB-117
Aiken, Conrad 1889-1973 ..... DLB-9, 45, 102
Aiken, Joan 1924- DLB-161
Aikin, Lucy 1781-1864 .... DLB-144, 163
Ainsworth, William Harrison 1805-1882 .... DLB-21
Aitken, George A. 1860-1917 ..... DLB-149
Aitken, Robert [publishing house] DLB-49
Akenside, Mark 1721-1770 .... DLB-109
Akins, Zoë 1886-1958 .... DLB-26
Akutagawa, Ryūnsuke 1892-1927 .... DLB-180
Alabaster, William 1568-1640 ..... DLB-132
Alain-Fournier 1886-1914 .... DLB-65
Alarcón, Francisco X. 1954- DLB-122
Alba, Nanina 1915-1968 .... DLB-41
Albee, Edward 1928- DLB-7
Albert the Great circa 1200-1280 ..... DLB-115
Alberti, Rafael 1902- DLB-108
Albertinus, Aegidius circa 1560-1620 .... DLB-164
Alcaeus born circa 620 B.C. DLB-176
Alcott, Amos Bronson 1799-1888 ..... DLB-1
Alcott, Louisa May 1832-1888 ...... DLB-1, 42, 79; DS-14
Alcott, William Andrus 1798-1859 .... DLB-1
Alcuin circa 732-804 .... DLB-148
Alden, Henry Mills 1836-1919 ..... DLB-79
Alden, Isabella 1841-1930 .... DLB-42
Alden, John B. [publishing house] DLB-49

377

Alden, Beardsley and Company.....DLB-49
Aldington, Richard
  1892-1962.......DLB-20, 36, 100, 149
Aldis, Dorothy 1896-1966.........DLB-22
Aldis, H. G. 1863-1919...........DLB-184
Aldiss, Brian W. 1925-............DLB-14
Aldrich, Thomas Bailey
  1836-1907........DLB-42, 71, 74, 79
Alegría, Ciro 1909-1967..........DLB-113
Alegría, Claribel 1924-..........DLB-145
Aleixandre, Vicente 1898-1984.....DLB-108
Aleramo, Sibilla 1876-1960........DLB-114
Alexander, Charles 1868-1923......DLB-91
Alexander, Charles Wesley
  [publishing house]............DLB-49
Alexander, James 1691-1756.......DLB-24
Alexander, Lloyd 1924-...........DLB-52
Alexander, Sir William, Earl of Stirling
  1577?-1640..................DLB-121
Alexie, Sherman 1966-............DLB-175
Alexis, Willibald 1798-1871.......DLB-133
Alfred, King 849-899.............DLB-146
Alger, Horatio, Jr. 1832-1899......DLB-42
Algonquin Books of Chapel Hill....DLB-46
Algren, Nelson 1909-1981.....DLB-9; Y-81, 82
Allan, Andrew 1907-1974..........DLB-88
Allan, Ted 1916-.................DLB-68
Allbeury, Ted 1917-..............DLB-87
Alldritt, Keith 1935-..............DLB-14
Allen, Ethan 1738-1789...........DLB-31
Allen, Frederick Lewis 1890-1954...DLB-137
Allen, Gay Wilson
  1903-1995............DLB-103; Y-95
Allen, George 1808-1876..........DLB-59
Allen, George [publishing house]....DLB-106
Allen, George, and Unwin
  Limited......................DLB-112
Allen, Grant 1848-1899.....DLB-70, 92, 178
Allen, Henry W. 1912-...............Y-85
Allen, Hervey 1889-1949.........DLB-9, 45
Allen, James 1739-1808............DLB-31
Allen, James Lane 1849-1925......DLB-71
Allen, Jay Presson 1922-..........DLB-26
Allen, John, and Company.........DLB-49
Allen, Paula Gunn 1939-..........DLB-175
Allen, Samuel W. 1917-............DLB-41
Allen, Woody 1935-................DLB-44
Allende, Isabel 1942-.............DLB-145
Alline, Henri 1748-1784............DLB-99
Allingham, Margery 1904-1966.....DLB-77
Allingham, William 1824-1889......DLB-35
Allison, W. L.
  [publishing house]............DLB-49

The *Alliterative Morte Arthure* and
  the *Stanzaic Morte Arthur*
  circa 1350-1400..............DLB-146
Allott, Kenneth 1912-1973..........DLB-20
Allston, Washington 1779-1843......DLB-1
Almon, John [publishing house].....DLB-154
Alonzo, Dámaso 1898-1990........DLB-108
Alsop, George 1636-post 1673......DLB-24
Alsop, Richard 1761-1815..........DLB-37
Altemus, Henry, and Company......DLB-49
Altenberg, Peter 1885-1919........DLB-81
Altolaguirre, Manuel 1905-1959....DLB-108
Aluko, T. M. 1918-................DLB-117
Alurista 1947-....................DLB-82
Alvarez, A. 1929-..............DLB-14, 40
Amadi, Elechi 1934-..............DLB-117
Amado, Jorge 1912-...............DLB-113
Ambler, Eric 1909-................DLB-77
*America: or, a Poem on the Settlement of the
  British Colonies* (1780?), by Timothy
  Dwight......................DLB-37
American Conservatory Theatre......DLB-7
American Fiction and the 1930s.....DLB-9
American Humor: A Historical Survey
  East and Northeast
  South and Southwest
  Midwest
  West........................DLB-11
The American Library in Paris......Y-93
American News Company...........DLB-49
The American Poets' Corner: The First
  Three Years (1983-1986)..........Y-86
American Proletarian Culture:
  The 1930s....................DS-11
American Publishing Company......DLB-49
American Stationers' Company.....DLB-49
American Sunday-School Union.....DLB-49
American Temperance Union.......DLB-49
American Tract Society...........DLB-49
The American Trust for the
  British Library..................Y-96
The American Writers Congress
  (9-12 October 1981)............Y-81
The American Writers Congress: A Report
  on Continuing Business..........Y-81
Ames, Fisher 1758-1808............DLB-37
Ames, Mary Clemmer 1831-1884.....DLB-23
Amini, Johari M. 1935-............DLB-41
Amis, Kingsley 1922-1995
  ....DLB-15, 27, 100, 139, Y-96
Amis, Martin 1949-................DLB-14
Ammons, A. R. 1926-...........DLB-5, 165
Amory, Thomas 1691?-1788.........DLB-39
Anaya, Rudolfo A. 1937-...........DLB-82
Ancrene Riwle circa 1200-1225....DLB-146

Andersch, Alfred 1914-1980........DLB-69
Anderson, Alexander 1775-1870....DLB-188
Anderson, Margaret 1886-1973...DLB-4, 91
Anderson, Maxwell 1888-1959.......DLB-7
Anderson, Patrick 1915-1979.......DLB-68
Anderson, Paul Y. 1893-1938......DLB-29
Anderson, Poul 1926-...............DLB-8
Anderson, Robert 1750-1830.......DLB-142
Anderson, Robert 1917-.............DLB-7
Anderson, Sherwood
  1876-1941........DLB-4, 9, 86; DS-1
Andreae, Johann Valentin
  1586-1654...................DLB-164
Andreas-Salomé, Lou 1861-1937.....DLB-66
Andres, Stefan 1906-1970..........DLB-69
Andreu, Blanca 1959-.............DLB-134
Andrewes, Lancelot
  1555-1626...............DLB-151, 172
Andrews, Charles M. 1863-1943.....DLB-17
Andrews, Miles Peter ?-1814.......DLB-89
Andrian, Leopold von 1875-1951....DLB-81
Andrić, Ivo 1892-1975............DLB-147
Andrieux, Louis (see Aragon, Louis)
Andrus, Silas, and Son............DLB-49
Angell, James Burrill 1829-1916....DLB-64
Angell, Roger 1920-..........DLB-171, 185
Angelou, Maya 1928-...............DLB-38
Anger, Jane flourished 1589.......DLB-136
Angers, Félicité (see Conan, Laure)
Anglo-Norman Literature in the
  Development of Middle English
  Literature...................DLB-146
The *Anglo-Saxon Chronicle*
  circa 890-1154...............DLB-146
The "Angry Young Men"...........DLB-15
Angus and Robertson (UK)
  Limited......................DLB-112
Anhalt, Edward 1914-..............DLB-26
Anners, Henry F.
  [publishing house]............DLB-49
Annolied between 1077
  and 1081....................DLB-148
Anselm of Canterbury
  1033-1109...................DLB-115
Anstey, F. 1856-1934.........DLB-141, 178
Anthony, Michael 1932-...........DLB-125
Anthony, Piers 1934-...............DLB-8
Anthony Burgess's *99 Novels*:
  An Opinion Poll.................Y-84
Antin, David 1932-...............DLB-169
Antin, Mary 1881-1949..............Y-84
Anton Ulrich, Duke of Brunswick-Lüneburg
  1633-1714...................DLB-168
Antschel, Paul (see Celan, Paul)

Anyidoho, Kofi 1947- DLB-157

Anzaldúa, Gloria 1942- DLB-122

Anzengruber, Ludwig
    1839-1889 . . . . DLB-129

Apess, William 1798-1839 . . . . DLB-175

Apodaca, Rudy S. 1939- DLB-82

Apollonius Rhodius third century B.C.
    . . . . DLB-176

Apple, Max 1941- DLB-130

Appleton, D., and Company DLB-49

Appleton-Century-Crofts DLB-46

Applewhite, James 1935- DLB-105

Apple-wood Books DLB-46

Aquin, Hubert 1929-1977 . . . . DLB-53

Aquinas, Thomas 1224 or
    1225-1274 . . . . DLB-115

Aragon, Louis 1897-1982 . . . . DLB-72

Aralica, Ivan 1930- DLB-181

Aratus of Soli circa 315 B.C.-circa 239 B.C.
    . . . . DLB-176

Arbor House Publishing
    Company DLB-46

Arbuthnot, John 1667-1735 . . . . . . DLB-101

Arcadia House DLB-46

Arce, Julio G. (see Ulica, Jorge)

Archer, William 1856-1924 . . . . . . DLB-10

Archilochhus mid seventh century B.C.E.
    . . . . DLB-176

The Archpoet circa 1130?-? DLB-148

Archpriest Avvakum (Petrovich)
    1620?-1682 . . . . DLB-150

Arden, John 1930- DLB-13

Arden of Faversham DLB-62

Ardis Publishers Y-89

Ardizzone, Edward 1900-1979 . . . . DLB-160

Arellano, Juan Estevan 1947- DLB-122

The Arena Publishing Company . . . DLB-49

Arena Stage DLB-7

Arenas, Reinaldo 1943-1990 . . . . . DLB-145

Arensberg, Ann 1937- Y-82

Arguedas, José María 1911-1969 . . . DLB-113

Argueta, Manlio 1936- DLB-145

Arias, Ron 1941- DLB-82

Arishima, Takeo 1878-1923 . . . . . . DLB-180

Aristophanes circa 446 B.C.-circa 446 B.C.-
    circa 386 B.C. DLB-176

Aristotle 384 B.C.-322 B.C. DLB-176

Ariyoshi, Sawako 1931-1984 . . . . . DLB-182

Arland, Marcel 1899-1986 . . . . DLB-72

Arlen, Michael
    1895-1956 . . . . . . DLB-36, 77, 162

Armah, Ayi Kwei 1939- DLB-117

Der arme Hartmann
    ?-after 1150 . . . . DLB-148

Armed Services Editions DLB-46

Armstrong, Richard 1903- DLB-160

Arndt, Ernst Moritz 1769-1860 . . . . DLB-90

Arnim, Achim von 1781-1831 . . . . . DLB-90

Arnim, Bettina von 1785-1859 . . . . DLB-90

Arno Press DLB-46

Arnold, Edwin 1832-1904 . . . . DLB-35

Arnold, Edwin L. 1857-1935 . . . . . DLB-178

Arnold, Matthew 1822-1888 . . . DLB-32, 57

Arnold, Thomas 1795-1842 . . . . . . DLB-55

Arnold, Edward
    [publishing house] DLB-112

Arnow, Harriette Simpson
    1908-1986 . . . . DLB-6

Arp, Bill (see Smith, Charles Henry)

Arpino, Giovanni 1927-1987 . . . . . DLB-177

Arreola, Juan José 1918- DLB-113

Arrian circa 89-circa 155 . . . . DLB-176

Arrowsmith, J. W.
    [publishing house] DLB-106

Arthur, Timothy Shay
    1809-1885 . . . . . . DLB-3, 42, 79; DS-13

The Arthurian Tradition and Its European
    Context DLB-138

Artmann, H. C. 1921- DLB-85

Arvin, Newton 1900-1963 . . . . DLB-103

As I See It, by
    Carolyn Cassady DLB-16

Asch, Nathan 1902-1964 . . . . . DLB-4, 28

Ash, John 1948- DLB-40

Ashbery, John 1927- DLB-5, 165; Y-81

Ashburnham, Bertram Lord
    1797-1878 . . . . DLB-184

Ashendene Press DLB-112

Asher, Sandy 1942- Y-83

Ashton, Winifred (see Dane, Clemence)

Asimov, Isaac 1920-1992 . . . . . DLB-8; Y-92

Askew, Anne circa 1521-1546 . . . . . DLB-136

Asselin, Olivar 1874-1937 . . . . DLB-92

Asturias, Miguel Angel
    1899-1974 . . . . DLB-113

Atheneum Publishers DLB-46

Atherton, Gertrude 1857-1948 . . DLB-9, 78, 186

Athlone Press DLB-112

Atkins, Josiah circa 1755-1781 . . . . . DLB-31

Atkins, Russell 1926- DLB-41

The Atlantic Monthly Press DLB-46

Attaway, William 1911-1986 . . . . . . DLB-76

Atwood, Margaret 1939- DLB-53

Aubert, Alvin 1930- DLB-41

Aubert de Gaspé, Phillipe-Ignace-François
    1814-1841 . . . . DLB-99

Aubert de Gaspé, Phillipe-Joseph
    1786-1871 . . . . DLB-99

Aubin, Napoléon 1812-1890 . . . . . . DLB-99

Aubin, Penelope 1685-circa 1731 . . . DLB-39

Aubrey-Fletcher, Henry Lancelot
    (see Wade, Henry)

Auchincloss, Louis 1917- DLB-2; Y-80

Auden, W. H. 1907-1973 . . . . . DLB-10, 20

Audio Art in America: A Personal
    Memoir Y-85

Audubon, John Woodhouse
    1812-1862 . . . . DLB-183

Auerbach, Berthold 1812-1882 . . . . DLB-133

Auernheimer, Raoul 1876-1948 . . . . DLB-81

Augustine 354-430 . . . . DLB-115

Austen, Jane 1775-1817 . . . . DLB-116

Austin, Alfred 1835-1913 . . . . DLB-35

Austin, Mary 1868-1934 . . . . . . DLB-9, 78

Austin, William 1778-1841 . . . . . . DLB-74

Author-Printers, 1476–1599 . . . . . . DLB-167

The Author's Apology for His Book
    (1684), by John Bunyan DLB-39

An Author's Response, by
    Ronald Sukenick Y-82

Authors and Newspapers
    Association DLB-46

Authors' Publishing Company DLB-49

Avalon Books DLB-46

Avancini, Nicolaus 1611-1686 . . . . . DLB-164

Avendaño, Fausto 1941- DLB-82

Averroëö 1126-1198 . . . . DLB-115

Avery, Gillian 1926- DLB-161

Avicenna 980-1037 . . . . DLB-115

Avison, Margaret 1918- DLB-53

Avon Books DLB-46

Awdry, Wilbert Vere 1911- DLB-160

Awoonor, Kofi 1935- DLB-117

Ayckbourn, Alan 1939- DLB-13

Aymé, Marcel 1902-1967 . . . . DLB-72

Aytoun, Sir Robert 1570-1638 . . . . . DLB-121

Aytoun, William Edmondstoune
    1813-1865 . . . . DLB-32, 159

B

B. V. (see Thomson, James)

Babbitt, Irving 1865-1933 . . . . DLB-63

Babbitt, Natalie 1932- DLB-52

Babcock, John [publishing house] . . . DLB-49

Babrius circa 150-200 . . . . DLB-176

Baca, Jimmy Santiago 1952- DLB-122

Bache, Benjamin Franklin 1769-1798 . . . . DLB-43

Bachmann, Ingeborg 1926-1973 . . . . . DLB-85

Bacon, Delia 1811-1859 . . . . DLB-1

Bacon, Francis 1561-1626 . . . . DLB-151

Bacon, Roger circa 1214/1220-1292 . . . . DLB-115

Bacon, Sir Nicholas circa 1510-1579 . . . . DLB-132

Bacon, Thomas circa 1700-1768 . . . . DLB-31

Badger, Richard G., and Company DLB-49

Bage, Robert 1728-1801. . . . . DLB-39

Bagehot, Walter 1826-1877. . . . . DLB-55

Bagley, Desmond 1923-1983 . . . . DLB-87

Bagnold, Enid 1889-1981 . . . . . DLB-13, 160

Bagryana, Elisaveta 1893-1991 . . . . . DLB-147

Bahr, Hermann 1863-1934 . . . . . DLB-81, 118

Bailey, Alfred Goldsworthy 1905- DLB-68

Bailey, Francis [publishing house] DLB-49

Bailey, H. C. 1878-1961 . . . . DLB-77

Bailey, Jacob 1731-1808 . . . . DLB-99

Bailey, Paul 1937- DLB-14

Bailey, Philip James 1816-1902 . . . . . . DLB-32

Baillargeon, Pierre 1916-1967 . . . . DLB-88

Baillie, Hugh 1890-1966 . . . . DLB-29

Baillie, Joanna 1762-1851 . . . . DLB-93

Bailyn, Bernard 1922- DLB-17

Bainbridge, Beryl 1933- DLB-14

Baird, Irene 1901-1981 . . . . DLB-68

Baker, Augustine 1575-1641 . . . . DLB-151

Baker, Carlos 1909-1987 . . . . DLB-103

Baker, David 1954- DLB-120

Baker, Herschel C. 1914-1990 . . . . . . DLB-111

Baker, Houston A., Jr. 1943- DLB-67

Baker, Samuel White 1821-1893 . . . . DLB-166

Baker, Walter H., Company ("Baker's Plays") DLB-49

The Baker and Taylor Company DLB-49

Balaban, John 1943- DLB-120

Bald, Wambly 1902- DLB-4

Balde, Jacob 1604-1668 . . . . DLB-164

Balderston, John 1889-1954 . . . . DLB-26

Baldwin, James 1924-1987 . . . . DLB-2, 7, 33; Y-87

Baldwin, Joseph Glover 1815-1864 . . . . DLB-3, 11

Baldwin, Richard and Anne [publishing house] DLB-170

Baldwin, William circa 1515-1563 . . . . DLB-132

Bale, John 1495-1563 . . . . DLB-132

Balestrini, Nanni 1935- DLB-128

Balfour, Arthur James 1848-1930 . . . . DLB-190

Ballantine Books DLB-46

Ballantyne, R. M. 1825-1894 . . . . . . DLB-163

Ballard, J. G. 1930- DLB-14

Ballerini, Luigi 1940- DLB-128

Ballou, Maturin Murray 1820-1895 . . . . DLB-79, 189

Ballou, Robert O. [publishing house] DLB-46

Balzac, Honoré de 1799-1855 . . . . . . DLB-119

Bambara, Toni Cade 1939- DLB-38

Bamford, Samuel 1788-1872 . . . . DLB-190

Bancroft, A. L., and Company DLB-49

Bancroft, George 1800-1891 . . . . DLB-1, 30, 59

Bancroft, Hubert Howe 1832-1918 . . . . DLB-47, 140

Bandelier, Adolph F. 1840-1914 . . . . DLB-186

Bangs, John Kendrick 1862-1922 . . . . DLB-11, 79

Banim, John 1798-1842 . . . . DLB-116, 158, 159

Banim, Michael 1796-1874 . . . . . DLB-158, 159

Banks, John circa 1653-1706 . . . . . . DLB-80

Banks, Russell 1940- DLB-130

Bannerman, Helen 1862-1946 . . . . . . DLB-141

Bantam Books DLB-46

Banti, Anna 1895-1985 . . . . DLB-177

Banville, John 1945- DLB-14

Baraka, Amiri 1934- DLB-5, 7, 16, 38; DS-8

Barbauld, Anna Laetitia 1743-1825 . . . . . DLB-107, 109, 142, 158

Barbeau, Marius 1883-1969 . . . . DLB-92

Barber, John Warner 1798-1885 . . . . . DLB-30

Bàrberi Squarotti, Giorgio 1929- DLB-128

Barbey d'Aurevilly, Jules-Amédée 1808-1889 . . . . DLB-119

Barbour, John circa 1316-1395 . . . . . DLB-146

Barbour, Ralph Henry 1870-1944 . . . . DLB-22

Barbusse, Henri 1873-1935 . . . . DLB-65

Barclay, Alexander circa 1475-1552 . . . . DLB-132

Barclay, E. E., and Company DLB-49

Bardeen, C. W. [publishing house] DLB-49

Barham, Richard Harris 1788-1845 . . . . DLB-159

Barich, Bill 1943- DLB-185

Baring, Maurice 1874-1945 . . . . DLB-34

Baring-Gould, Sabine 1834-1924. . . . . DLB-156, 190

Barker, A. L. 1918- DLB-14, 139

Barker, George 1913-1991 . . . . DLB-20

Barker, Harley Granville 1877-1946 . . . . DLB-10

Barker, Howard 1946- DLB-13

Barker, James Nelson 1784-1858 . . . . . DLB-37

Barker, Jane 1652-1727 . . . . DLB-39, 131

Barker, Lady Mary Anne 1831-1911 . . . . DLB-166

Barker, William circa 1520-after 1576 . . . . DLB-132

Barker, Arthur, Limited DLB-112

Barkov, Ivan Semenovich 1732-1768 . . . . DLB-150

Barks, Coleman 1937- DLB-5

Barlach, Ernst 1870-1938 . . . . . DLB-56, 118

Barlow, Joel 1754-1812 . . . . DLB-37

Barnard, John 1681-1770 . . . . DLB-24

Barne, Kitty (Mary Catherine Barne) 1883-1957 . . . . DLB-160

Barnes, Barnabe 1571-1609 . . . . DLB-132

Barnes, Djuna 1892-1982 . . . . . DLB-4, 9, 45

Barnes, Jim 1933- DLB-175

Barnes, Julian 1946- Y-93

Barnes, Margaret Ayer 1886-1967 . . . . . DLB-9

Barnes, Peter 1931- DLB-13

Barnes, William 1801-1886 . . . . DLB-32

Barnes, A. S., and Company DLB-49

Barnes and Noble Books DLB-46

Barnet, Miguel 1940- DLB-145

Barney, Natalie 1876-1972 . . . . DLB-4

Barnfield, Richard 1574-1627 . . . . . . DLB-172

Baron, Richard W., Publishing Company DLB-46

Barr, Robert 1850-1912 . . . . DLB-70, 92

Barral, Carlos 1928-1989 . . . . DLB-134

Barrax, Gerald William 1933- DLB-41, 120

Barrès, Maurice 1862-1923 . . . . DLB-123

Barrett, Eaton Stannard 1786-1820 . . . . DLB-116

Barrie, J. M. 1860-1937 . . . . DLB-10, 141, 156

Barrie and Jenkins DLB-112

Barrio, Raymond 1921- DLB-82

Barrios, Gregg 1945- DLB-122

Barry, Philip 1896-1949 . . . . DLB-7

Barry, Robertine (see Françoise)

Barse and Hopkins DLB-46

Barstow, Stan 1928- DLB-14, 139

Barth, John 1930- DLB-2

Barthelme, Donald 1931-1989 . . . . DLB-2; Y-80, 89
Barthelme, Frederick 1943- Y-85
Bartholomew, Frank 1898-1985 . . . . . DLB-127
Bartlett, John 1820-1905 . . . . DLB-1
Bartol, Cyrus Augustus 1813-1900 . . . . DLB-1
Barton, Bernard 1784-1849 . . . . DLB-96
Barton, Thomas Pennant 1803-1869 . . . . DLB-140
Bartram, John 1699-1777 . . . . DLB-31
Bartram, William 1739-1823 . . . . DLB-37
Basic Books DLB-46
Basille, Theodore (see Becon, Thomas)
Bass, T. J. 1932- Y-81
Bassani, Giorgio 1916- DLB-128, 177
Basse, William circa 1583-1653 . . . . . DLB-121
Bassett, John Spencer 1867-1928 . . . . . DLB-17
Bassler, Thomas Joseph (see Bass, T. J.)
Bate, Walter Jackson 1918- DLB-67, 103
Bateman, Christopher [publishing house] DLB-170
Bateman, Stephen circa 1510-1584 . . . . DLB-136
Bates, H. E. 1905-1974 . . . . DLB-162
Bates, Katharine Lee 1859-1929 . . . . . DLB-71
Batsford, B. T. [publishing house] DLB-106
Battiscombe, Georgina 1905- DLB-155
The Battle of Maldon circa 1000 . . . . . DLB-146
Bauer, Bruno 1809-1882 . . . . DLB-133
Bauer, Wolfgang 1941- DLB-124
Baum, L. Frank 1856-1919 . . . . DLB-22
Baum, Vicki 1888-1960 . . . . DLB-85
Baumbach, Jonathan 1933- Y-80
Bausch, Richard 1945- DLB-130
Bawden, Nina 1925- DLB-14, 161
Bax, Clifford 1886-1962 . . . . . . DLB-10, 100
Baxter, Charles 1947- DLB-130
Bayer, Eleanor (see Perry, Eleanor)
Bayer, Konrad 1932-1964 . . . . DLB-85
Baynes, Pauline 1922- DLB-160
Bazin, Hervé 1911- DLB-83
Beach, Sylvia 1887-1962 . . . . . DLB-4; DS-15
Beacon Press DLB-49
Beadle and Adams DLB-49
Beagle, Peter S. 1939- Y-80
Beal, M. F. 1937- Y-81
Beale, Howard K. 1899-1959 . . . . . . DLB-17
Beard, Charles A. 1874-1948 . . . . . . DLB-17
A Beat Chronology: The First Twenty-five Years, 1944-1969 . . . . DLB-16
Beattie, Ann 1947- Y-82

Beattie, James 1735-1803 . . . . DLB-109
Beauchemin, Nérée 1850-1931 . . . . . DLB-92
Beauchemin, Yves 1941- DLB-60
Beaugrand, Honoré 1848-1906 . . . . . DLB-99
Beaulieu, Victor-Lévy 1945- DLB-53
Beaumont, Francis circa 1584-1616 and Fletcher, John 1579-1625 . . . . DLB-58
Beaumont, Sir John 1583?-1627 . . . . . DLB-121
Beaumont, Joseph 1616–1699 . . . . . . DLB-126
Beauvoir, Simone de 1908-1986. . . . . DLB-72; Y-86
Becher, Ulrich 1910- DLB-69
Becker, Carl 1873-1945 . . . . DLB-17
Becker, Jurek 1937- DLB-75
Becker, Jurgen 1932- DLB-75
Beckett, Samuel 1906-1989 . . . . DLB-13, 15; Y-90
Beckford, William 1760-1844 . . . . . . DLB-39
Beckham, Barry 1944- DLB-33
Becon, Thomas circa 1512-1567 . . . . DLB-136
Bećković, Matija 1939- DLB-181
Beddoes, Thomas 1760-1808 . . . . . . DLB-158
Beddoes, Thomas Lovell 1803-1849 . . . . DLB-96
Bede circa 673-735 . . . . DLB-146
Beecher, Catharine Esther 1800-1878 . . . . DLB-1
Beecher, Henry Ward 1813-1887 . . . . DLB-3, 43
Beer, George L. 1872-1920 . . . . DLB-47
Beer, Johann 1655-1700 . . . . DLB-168
Beer, Patricia 1919- DLB-40
Beerbohm, Max 1872-1956 . . . . . DLB-34, 100
Beer-Hofmann, Richard 1866-1945 . . . . DLB-81
Beers, Henry A. 1847-1926 . . . . DLB-71
Beeton, S. O. [publishing house] DLB-106
Bégon, Elisabeth 1696-1755 . . . . DLB-99
Behan, Brendan 1923-1964 . . . . DLB-13
Behn, Aphra 1640?-1689 . . . . DLB-39, 80, 131
Behn, Harry 1898-1973 . . . . DLB-61
Behrman, S. N. 1893-1973 . . . . . . DLB-7, 44
Belaney, Archibald Stansfeld (see Grey Owl)
Belasco, David 1853-1931 . . . . DLB-7
Belford, Clarke and Company DLB-49
Belitt, Ben 1911- DLB-5
Belknap, Jeremy 1744-1798 . . . . . DLB-30, 37
Bell, Clive 1881-1964 . . . . DS-10
Bell, Gertrude Margaret Lowthian 1868-1926 . . . . DLB-174
Bell, James Madison 1826-1902 . . . . . DLB-50

Bell, Marvin 1937- DLB-5
Bell, Millicent 1919- DLB-111
Bell, Quentin 1910- DLB-155
Bell, Vanessa 1879-1961 . . . . DS-10
Bell, George, and Sons DLB-106
Bell, Robert [publishing house] DLB-49
Bellamy, Edward 1850-1898 . . . . DLB-12
Bellamy, John [publishing house] DLB-170
Bellamy, Joseph 1719-1790 . . . . DLB-31
Bellezza, Dario 1944- DLB-128
La Belle Assemblée 1806-1837 . . . . . . DLB-110
Belloc, Hilaire 1870-1953 . . . . . DLB-19, 100, 141, 174
Bellow, Saul 1915- DLB-2, 28; Y-82; DS-3
Belmont Productions DLB-46
Bemelmans, Ludwig 1898-1962 . . . . . DLB-22
Bemis, Samuel Flagg 1891-1973 . . . . . DLB-17
Bemrose, William [publishing house] DLB-106
Benchley, Robert 1889-1945 . . . . DLB-11
Benedetti, Mario 1920- DLB-113
Benedictus, David 1938- DLB-14
Benedikt, Michael 1935- DLB-5
Benét, Stephen Vincent 1898-1943. . . . . DLB-4, 48, 102
Benét, William Rose 1886-1950 . . . . . DLB-45
Benford, Gregory 1941- Y-82
Benjamin, Park 1809-1864 . . . . DLB-3, 59, 73
Benjamin, S. G. W. 1837-1914 . . . . . DLB-189
Benlowes, Edward 1602-1676 . . . . . DLB-126
Benn, Gottfried 1886-1956 . . . . DLB-56
Benn Brothers Limited DLB-106
Bennett, Arnold 1867-1931 . . . . DLB-10, 34, 98, 135
Bennett, Charles 1899- DLB-44
Bennett, Gwendolyn 1902- DLB-51
Bennett, Hal 1930- DLB-33
Bennett, James Gordon 1795-1872 . . . DLB-43
Bennett, James Gordon, Jr. 1841-1918 . . . . DLB-23
Bennett, John 1865-1956 . . . . DLB-42
Bennett, Louise 1919- DLB-117
Benoit, Jacques 1941- DLB-60
Benson, A. C. 1862-1925 . . . . DLB-98
Benson, E. F. 1867-1940 . . . . . DLB-135, 153
Benson, Jackson J. 1930- DLB-111
Benson, Robert Hugh 1871-1914 . . . . DLB-153
Benson, Stella 1892-1933 . . . . . DLB-36, 162
Bent, James Theodore 1852-1897 . . . . DLB-174
Bent, Mabel Virginia Anna ?-? DLB-174

Bentham, Jeremy
   1748-1832. . . . . DLB-107, 158

Bentley, E. C. 1875-1956. . . . . DLB-70

Bentley, Richard
   [publishing house]. DLB-106

Benton, Robert 1932- and Newman,
   David 1937-. DLB-44

Benziger Brothers DLB-49

Beowulf circa 900-1000
   or 790-825. . . . . DLB-146

Beresford, Anne 1929- DLB-40

Beresford, John Davys
   1873-1947 . . . . DLB-162; 178

Beresford-Howe, Constance
   1922- DLB-88

Berford, R. G., Company DLB-49

Berg, Stephen 1934- DLB-5

Bergengruen, Werner 1892-1964. . . . DLB-56

Berger, John 1926- DLB-14

Berger, Meyer 1898-1959. . . . . DLB-29

Berger, Thomas 1924- DLB-2; Y-80

Berkeley, Anthony 1893-1971 . . . . . DLB-77

Berkeley, George 1685-1753 . . . DLB-31, 101

The Berkley Publishing
   Corporation. DLB-46

Berlin, Lucia 1936- DLB-130

Bernal, Vicente J. 1888-1915 . . . . . . DLB-82

Bernanos, Georges 1888-1948 . . . . . DLB-72

Bernard, Harry 1898-1979 . . . . DLB-92

Bernard, John 1756-1828. . . . . DLB-37

Bernard of Chartres
   circa 1060-1124?. DLB-115

Bernari, Carlo 1909-1992 . . . . DLB-177

Bernhard, Thomas
   1931-1989 . . . . DLB-85, 124

Bernstein, Charles 1950- DLB-169

Berriault, Gina 1926- DLB-130

Berrigan, Daniel 1921- DLB-5

Berrigan, Ted 1934-1983. . . . . . DLB-5, 169

Berry, Wendell 1934- DLB-5, 6

Berryman, John 1914-1972 . . . . DLB-48

Bersianik, Louky 1930- DLB-60

Berthelet, Thomas
   [publishing house]. DLB-170

Berto, Giuseppe 1914-1978 . . . . DLB-177

Bertolucci, Attilio 1911- DLB-128

Berton, Pierre 1920- DLB-68

Besant, Sir Walter 1836-1901 . . . DLB-135, 190

Bessette, Gerard 1920- DLB-53

Bessie, Alvah 1904-1985 . . . . DLB-26

Bester, Alfred 1913-1987. . . . . DLB-8

The Bestseller Lists: An Assessment Y-84

Betham-Edwards, Matilda Barbara (see Edwards,
   Matilda Barbara Betham-)

Betjeman, John 1906-1984 . . . . DLB-20; Y-84

Betocchi, Carlo 1899-1986. . . . . . . DLB-128

Bettarini, Mariella 1942- DLB-128

Betts, Doris 1932- Y-82

Beveridge, Albert J. 1862-1927. . . . . DLB-17

Beverley, Robert
   circa 1673-1722. . . . . DLB-24, 30

Beyle, Marie-Henri (see Stendhal)

Bianco, Margery Williams
   1881-1944 . . . . DLB-160

Bibaud, Adèle 1854-1941. . . . . DLB-92

Bibaud, Michel 1782-1857 . . . . DLB-99

Bibliographical and Textual Scholarship
   Since World War II. Y-89

The Bicentennial of James Fenimore
   Cooper: An International
   Celebration Y-89

Bichsel, Peter 1935- DLB-75

Bickerstaff, Isaac John
   1733-circa 1808. . . . . DLB-89

Biddle, Drexel [publishing house] DLB-49

Bidermann, Jacob
   1577 or 1578-1639 . . . . DLB-164

Bidwell, Walter Hilliard
   1798-1881. . . . . DLB-79

Bienek, Horst 1930- DLB-75

Bierbaum, Otto Julius 1865-1910. . . . DLB-66

Bierce, Ambrose
   1842-1914?. . . DLB-11, 12, 23, 71, 74, 186

Bigelow, William F. 1879-1966. . . . . DLB-91

Biggle, Lloyd, Jr. 1923- DLB-8

Bigiaretti, Libero 1905-1993 . . . . . . DLB-177

Biglow, Hosea (see Lowell, James Russell)

Bigongiari, Piero 1914- DLB-128

Billinger, Richard 1890-1965 . . . . . . DLB-124

Billings, Hammatt 1818-1874 . . . . . . DLB-188

Billings, John Shaw 1898-1975 . . . . . DLB-137

Billings, Josh (see Shaw, Henry Wheeler)

Binding, Rudolf G. 1867-1938 . . . . . DLB-66

Bingham, Caleb 1757-1817. . . . . . . DLB-42

Bingham, George Barry
   1906-1988 . . . . DLB-127

Bingley, William
   [publishing house]. DLB-154

Binyon, Laurence 1869-1943 . . . . . . DLB-19

Biographia Brittanica DLB-142

Biographical Documents I Y-84

Biographical Documents II. Y-85

Bioren, John [publishing house] DLB-49

Bioy Casares, Adolfo 1914- DLB-113

Bird, Isabella Lucy 1831-1904. . . . . . DLB-166

Bird, William 1888-1963. . . . . DLB-4; DS-15

Birken, Sigmund von 1626-1681 . . . . DLB-164

Birney, Earle 1904- DLB-88

Birrell, Augustine 1850-1933 . . . . . . DLB-98

Bisher, Furman 1918- DLB-171

Bishop, Elizabeth 1911-1979 . . . . DLB-5, 169

Bishop, John Peale 1892-1944 . . . DLB-4, 9, 45

Bismarck, Otto von 1815-1898 . . . . . DLB-129

Bisset, Robert 1759-1805 . . . . DLB-142

Bissett, Bill 1939- DLB-53

Bitzius, Albert (see Gotthelf, Jeremias)

Black, David (D. M.) 1941- DLB-40

Black, Winifred 1863-1936 . . . . DLB-25

Black, Walter J.
   [publishing house]. DLB-46

The Black Aesthetic: Background DS-8

The Black Arts Movement, by
   Larry Neal DLB-38

Black Theaters and Theater Organizations in
   America, 1961-1982:
   A Research List. DLB-38

Black Theatre: A Forum
   [excerpts] DLB-38

Blackamore, Arthur 1679-? DLB-24, 39

Blackburn, Alexander L. 1929- Y-85

Blackburn, Paul 1926-1971 . . . . DLB-16; Y-81

Blackburn, Thomas 1916-1977 . . . . . DLB-27

Blackmore, R. D. 1825-1900 . . . . . . DLB-18

Blackmore, Sir Richard
   1654-1729 . . . . DLB-131

Blackmur, R. P. 1904-1965. . . . . . . DLB-63

Blackwell, Basil, Publisher. DLB-106

Blackwood, Algernon Henry
   1869-1951 . . . . DLB-153, 156, 178

Blackwood, Caroline 1931- DLB-14

Blackwood, William, and
   Sons, Ltd. DLB-154

Blackwood's Edinburgh Magazine
   1817-1980 . . . . DLB-110

Blades, William 1824-1890 . . . . DLB-184

Blair, Eric Arthur (see Orwell, George)

Blair, Francis Preston 1791-1876. . . . . DLB-43

Blair, James circa 1655-1743 . . . . . . DLB-24

Blair, John Durburrow 1759-1823 . . . . DLB-37

Blais, Marie-Claire 1939- DLB-53

Blaise, Clark 1940- DLB-53

Blake, Nicholas 1904-1972 . . . . DLB-77
   (see Day Lewis, C.)

Blake, William
   1757-1827 . . . . DLB-93, 154, 163

The Blakiston Company DLB-49

Blanchot, Maurice 1907- DLB-72

Blanckenburg, Christian Friedrich von
   1744-1796 . . . . DLB-94

Blaser, Robin 1925- DLB-165

Bledsoe, Albert Taylor
   1809-1877 . . . . DLB-3, 79

Blelock and Company DLB-49
Blennerhassett, Margaret Agnew
    1773-1842 .... DLB-99
Bles, Geoffrey
    [publishing house] DLB-112
Blessington, Marguerite, Countess of
    1789-1849 .... DLB-166
The Blickling Homilies
    circa 971 .... DLB-146
Blish, James 1921-1975 .... DLB-8
Bliss, E., and E. White
    [publishing house] DLB-49
Bliven, Bruce 1889-1977 .... DLB-137
Bloch, Robert 1917-1994 .... DLB-44
Block, Rudolph (see Lessing, Bruno)
Blondal, Patricia 1926-1959 .... DLB-88
Bloom, Harold 1930- DLB-67
Bloomer, Amelia 1818-1894 .... DLB-79
Bloomfield, Robert 1766-1823 ..... DLB-93
Bloomsbury Group DS-10
Blotner, Joseph 1923- DLB-111
Bloy, Léon 1846-1917 .... DLB-123
Blume, Judy 1938- DLB-52
Blunck, Hans Friedrich 1888-1961 .... DLB-66
Blunden, Edmund
    1896-1974 .... DLB-20, 100, 155
Blunt, Lady Anne Isabella Noel
    1837-1917 .... DLB-174
Blunt, Wilfrid Scawen
    1840-1922 .... DLB-19, 174
Bly, Nellie (see Cochrane, Elizabeth)
Bly, Robert 1926- DLB-5
Blyton, Enid 1897-1968 .... DLB-160
Boaden, James 1762-1839 .... DLB-89
Boas, Frederick S. 1862-1957 ...... DLB-149
The Bobbs-Merrill Archive at the
    Lilly Library, Indiana University Y-90
The Bobbs-Merrill Company DLB-46
Bobrov, Semen Sergeevich
    1763?-1810 .... DLB-150
Bobrowski, Johannes 1917-1965 .... DLB-75
Bodenheim, Maxwell 1892-1954 ... DLB-9, 45
Bodenstedt, Friedrich von
    1819-1892 .... DLB-129
Bodini, Vittorio 1914-1970 .... DLB-128
Bodkin, M. McDonnell
    1850-1933 .... DLB-70
Bodley Head DLB-112
Bodmer, Johann Jakob 1698-1783 .... DLB-97
Bodmershof, Imma von 1895-1982 ... DLB-85
Bodsworth, Fred 1918- DLB-68
Boehm, Sydney 1908- DLB-44
Boer, Charles 1939- DLB-5
Boethius circa 480-circa 524 .... DLB-115

Boethius of Dacia circa 1240-? DLB-115
Bogan, Louise 1897-1970 ...... DLB-45, 169
Bogarde, Dirk 1921- DLB-14
Bogdanovich, Ippolit Fedorovich
    circa 1743-1803 .... DLB-150
Bogue, David [publishing house] DLB-106
Böhme, Jakob 1575-1624 .... DLB-164
Bohn, H. G. [publishing house] DLB-106
Bohse, August 1661-1742 .... DLB-168
Boie, Heinrich Christian
    1744-1806 .... DLB-94
Bok, Edward W. 1863-1930 ... DLB-91; DS-16
Boland, Eavan 1944- DLB-40
Bolingbroke, Henry St. John, Viscount
    1678-1751 .... DLB-101
Böll, Heinrich 1917-1985 ...... Y-85, DLB-69
Bolling, Robert 1738-1775 .... DLB-31
Bolotov, Andrei Timofeevich
    1738-1833 .... DLB-150
Bolt, Carol 1941- DLB-60
Bolt, Robert 1924- DLB-13
Bolton, Herbert E. 1870-1953 ..... DLB-17
Bonaventura DLB-90
Bonaventure circa 1217-1274 ..... DLB-115
Bonaviri, Giuseppe 1924- DLB-177
Bond, Edward 1934- DLB-13
Bond, Michael 1926- DLB-161
Bonnin, Gertrude Simmons (see Zitkala-Ša)
Boni, Albert and Charles
    [publishing house] DLB-46
Boni and Liveright DLB-46
Robert Bonner's Sons DLB-49
Bonsanti, Alessandro 1904-1984 .... DLB-177
Bontemps, Arna 1902-1973 ..... DLB-48, 51
The Book Arts Press at the University
    of Virginia Y-96
The Book League of America DLB-46
Book Reviewing in America: I Y-87
Book Reviewing in America: II Y-88
Book Reviewing in America: III Y-89
Book Reviewing in America: IV Y-90
Book Reviewing in America: V Y-91
Book Reviewing in America: VI Y-92
Book Reviewing in America: VII ... Y-93
Book Reviewing in America: VIII .. Y-94
Book Reviewing in America and the
    Literary Scene Y-95
Book Reviewing and the
    Literary Scene Y-96
Book Supply Company DLB-49
The Book Trade History Group Y-93
The Booker Prize Y-96

The Booker Prize
    Address by Anthony Thwaite,
    Chairman of the Booker Prize Judges
    Comments from Former Booker
    Prize Winners Y-86
Boorde, Andrew circa 1490-1549 .... DLB-136
Boorstin, Daniel J. 1914- DLB-17
Booth, Mary L. 1831-1889 .... DLB-79
Booth, Franklin 1874-1948 ...... DLB-188
Booth, Philip 1925- Y-82
Booth, Wayne C. 1921- DLB-67
Booth, William 1829-1912 .... DLB-190
Borchardt, Rudolf 1877-1945 ..... DLB-66
Borchert, Wolfgang
    1921-1947 .... DLB-69, 124
Borel, Pétrus 1809-1859 .... DLB-119
Borges, Jorge Luis
    1899-1986 .... DLB-113; Y-86
Börne, Ludwig 1786-1837 .... DLB-90
Borrow, George
    1803-1881 .... DLB-21, 55, 166
Bosch, Juan 1909- DLB-145
Bosco, Henri 1888-1976 .... DLB-72
Bosco, Monique 1927- DLB-53
Boston, Lucy M. 1892-1990 ...... DLB-161
Boswell, James 1740-1795 .... DLB-104, 142
Botev, Khristo 1847-1876 .... DLB-147
Bote, Hermann
    circa 1460-circa 1520 .... DLB-179
Botta, Anne C. Lynch 1815-1891 .... DLB-3
Bottomley, Gordon 1874-1948 ..... DLB-10
Bottoms, David 1949- DLB-120; Y-83
Bottrall, Ronald 1906- DLB-20
Boucher, Anthony 1911-1968 ...... DLB-8
Boucher, Jonathan 1738-1804 ..... DLB-31
Boucher de Boucherville, George
    1814-1894 .... DLB-99
Boudreau, Daniel (see Coste, Donat)
Bourassa, Napoléon 1827-1916 .... DLB-99
Bourget, Paul 1852-1935 .... DLB-123
Bourinot, John George 1837-1902 ... DLB-99
Bourjaily, Vance 1922- DLB-2, 143
Bourne, Edward Gaylord
    1860-1908 .... DLB-47
Bourne, Randolph 1886-1918 ..... DLB-63
Bousoño, Carlos 1923- DLB-108
Bousquet, Joë 1897-1950 .... DLB-72
Bova, Ben 1932- Y-81
Bovard, Oliver K. 1872-1945 ..... DLB-25
Bove, Emmanuel 1898-1945 ...... DLB-72
Bowen, Elizabeth 1899-1973 ... DLB-15, 162
Bowen, Francis 1811-1890 ..... DLB-1, 59
Bowen, John 1924- DLB-13

Cumulative Index

Bowen, Marjorie 1886-1952 . . . . DLB-153
Bowen-Merrill Company DLB-49
Bowering, George 1935- DLB-53
Bowers, Claude G. 1878-1958 . . . . . DLB-17
Bowers, Edgar 1924- DLB-5
Bowers, Fredson Thayer
  1905-1991 . . . . DLB-140; Y-91
Bowles, Paul 1910- DLB-5, 6
Bowles, Samuel III 1826-1878 . . . . . DLB-43
Bowles, William Lisles 1762-1850 . . . . DLB-93
Bowman, Louise Morey
  1882-1944 . . . . DLB-68
Boyd, James 1888-1944 . . . . . . DLB-9; DS-16
Boyd, John 1919- DLB-8
Boyd, Thomas 1898-1935 . . . . . DLB-9; DS-16
Boyesen, Hjalmar Hjorth
  1848-1895. . . . . DLB-12, 71; DS-13
Boyle, Kay
  1902-1992 . . . . . DLB-4, 9, 48, 86; Y-93
Boyle, Roger, Earl of Orrery
  1621-1679 . . . . DLB-80
Boyle, T. Coraghessan 1948- Y-86
Božić, Mirko 1919- DLB-181
Brackenbury, Alison 1953- DLB-40
Brackenridge, Hugh Henry
  1748-1816. . . . . DLB-11, 37
Brackett, Charles 1892-1969 . . . . . . DLB-26
Brackett, Leigh 1915-1978 . . . . . . DLB-8, 26
Bradburn, John
  [publishing house]. DLB-49
Bradbury, Malcolm 1932- DLB-14
Bradbury, Ray 1920- DLB-2, 8
Bradbury and Evans. DLB-106
Braddon, Mary Elizabeth
  1835-1915 . . . . DLB-18, 70, 156
Bradford, Andrew 1686-1742 . . . . DLB-43, 73
Bradford, Gamaliel 1863-1932 . . . . . DLB-17
Bradford, John 1749-1830. . . . . DLB-43
Bradford, Roark 1896-1948. . . . . . . DLB-86
Bradford, William 1590-1657 . . . . DLB-24, 30
Bradford, William III
  1719-1791 . . . . DLB-43, 73
Bradlaugh, Charles 1833-1891 . . . . . DLB-57
Bradley, David 1950- DLB-33
Bradley, Marion Zimmer 1930- DLB-8
Bradley, William Aspenwall
  1878-1939. . . . . DLB-4
Bradley, Ira, and Company DLB-49
Bradley, J. W., and Company DLB-49
Bradshaw, Henry 1831-1886 . . . . . . DLB-184
Bradstreet, Anne
  1612 or 1613-1672 . . . . DLB-24
Bradwardine, Thomas circa
  1295-1349 . . . . DLB-115

Brady, Frank 1924-1986. . . . . DLB-111
Brady, Frederic A.
  [publishing house]. DLB-49
Bragg, Melvyn 1939- DLB-14
Brainard, Charles H.
  [publishing house]. DLB-49
Braine, John 1922-1986 . . . . . DLB-15; Y-86
Braithwait, Richard 1588-1673 . . . . . DLB-151
Braithwaite, William Stanley
  1878-1962. . . . . DLB-50, 54
Braker, Ulrich 1735-1798. . . . . DLB-94
Bramah, Ernest 1868-1942 . . . . DLB-70
Branagan, Thomas 1774-1843 . . . . . DLB-37
Branch, William Blackwell
  1927- DLB-76
Branden Press. DLB-46
Brant, Sebastian 1457-1521 . . . . . . DLB-179
Brassey, Lady Annie (Allnutt)
  1839-1887 . . . . DLB-166
Brathwaite, Edward Kamau
  1930- DLB-125
Brault, Jacques 1933- DLB-53
Braun, Volker 1939- DLB-75
Brautigan, Richard
  1935-1984 . . . . DLB-2, 5; Y-80, 84
Braxton, Joanne M. 1950- DLB-41
Bray, Anne Eliza 1790-1883. . . . . . . DLB-116
Bray, Thomas 1656-1730. . . . . DLB-24
Braziller, George
  [publishing house] DLB-46
The Bread Loaf Writers'
  Conference 1983 . . . . Y-84
The Break-Up of the Novel (1922),
  by John Middleton Murry. DLB-36
Breasted, James Henry 1865-1935 . . . . DLB-47
Brecht, Bertolt 1898-1956 . . . . . DLB-56, 124
Bredel, Willi 1901-1964 . . . . DLB-56
Breitinger, Johann Jakob
  1701-1776 . . . . DLB-97
Bremser, Bonnie 1939- DLB-16
Bremser, Ray 1934- DLB-16
Brentano, Bernard von
  1901-1964 . . . . DLB-56
Brentano, Clemens 1778-1842 . . . . . DLB-90
Brentano's DLB-49
Brenton, Howard 1942- DLB-13
Breslin, Jimmy 1929- DLB-185
Breton, André 1896-1966 . . . . DLB-65
Breton, Nicholas
  circa 1555-circa 1626 . . . . DLB-136
The Breton Lays
  1300-early fifteenth century DLB-146
Brewer, Luther A. 1858-1933 . . . . . DLB-187
Brewer, Warren and Putnam DLB-46
Brewster, Elizabeth 1922- DLB-60

Bridge, Horatio 1806-1893 . . . . DLB-183
Bridgers, Sue Ellen 1942- DLB-52
Bridges, Robert 1844-1930 . . . . . DLB-19, 98
Bridie, James 1888-1951 . . . . DLB-10
Bright, Mary Chavelita Dunne
  (see Egerton, George)
Brimmer, B. J., Company DLB-46
Brines, Francisco 1932- DLB-134
Brinley, George, Jr. 1817-1875 . . . . DLB-140
Brinnin, John Malcolm 1916- DLB-48
Brisbane, Albert 1809-1890 . . . . DLB-3
Brisbane, Arthur 1864-1936. . . . . . . DLB-25
British Academy DLB-112
The British Library and the Regular
  Readers' Group Y-91
The British Critic 1793-1843 . . . . . . DLB-110
*The British Review and London
  Critical Journal* 1811-1825 . . . . . . DLB-110
Brito, Aristeo 1942- DLB-122
Broadway Publishing Company DLB-46
Broch, Hermann 1886-1951. . . . DLB-85, 124
Brochu, André 1942- DLB-53
Brock, Edwin 1927- DLB-40
Brockes, Barthold Heinrich
  1680-1747 . . . . DLB-168
Brod, Max 1884-1968. . . . . DLB-81
Brodber, Erna 1940- DLB-157
Brodhead, John R. 1814-1873 . . . . . DLB-30
Brodkey, Harold 1930- DLB-130
Broeg, Bob 1918- DLB-171
Brome, Richard circa 1590-1652 . . . . DLB-58
Brome, Vincent 1910- DLB-155
Bromfield, Louis 1896-1956 . . . DLB-4, 9, 86
Broner, E. M. 1930- DLB-28
Bronk, William 1918- DLB-165
Bronnen, Arnolt 1895-1959 . . . . . . DLB-124
Brontë, Anne 1820-1849 . . . . DLB-21
Brontë, Charlotte 1816-1855 . . . . DLB-21, 159
Brontë, Emily 1818-1848 . . . . . . DLB-21, 32
Brooke, Frances 1724-1789 . . . . . DLB-39, 99
Brooke, Henry 1703?-1783 . . . . DLB-39
Brooke, L. Leslie 1862-1940 . . . . . . DLB-141
Brooke, Margaret, Ranee of Sarawak
  1849-1936 . . . . DLB-174
Brooke, Rupert 1887-1915 . . . . DLB-19
Brooker, Bertram 1888-1955 . . . . . . DLB-88
Brooke-Rose, Christine 1926- DLB-14
Brookner, Anita 1928- Y-87
Brooks, Charles Timothy
  1813-1883. . . . . DLB-1
Brooks, Cleanth 1906-1994 . . . DLB-63; Y-94
Brooks, Gwendolyn
  1917- DLB-5, 76, 165

Brooks, Jeremy 1926- DLB-14
Brooks, Mel 1926- DLB-26
Brooks, Noah 1830-1903..... DLB-42; DS-13
Brooks, Richard 1912-1992........ DLB-44
Brooks, Van Wyck
 1886-1963.......... DLB-45, 63, 103
Brophy, Brigid 1929- DLB-14
Brossard, Chandler 1922-1993 ..... DLB-16
Brossard, Nicole 1943- DLB-53
Broster, Dorothy Kathleen
 1877-1950 .... DLB-160
Brother Antoninus (see Everson, William)
Brotherton, Lord 1856-1930........ DLB-184
Brougham and Vaux, Henry Peter
 Brougham, Baron
 1778-1868........ DLB-110, 158
Brougham, John 1810-1880........ DLB-11
Broughton, James 1913- DLB-5
Broughton, Rhoda 1840-1920 ..... DLB-18
Broun, Heywood 1888-1939 .... DLB-29, 171
Brown, Alice 1856-1948.......... DLB-78
Brown, Bob 1886-1959 .... DLB-4, 45
Brown, Cecil 1943- DLB-33
Brown, Charles Brockden
 1771-1810........... DLB-37, 59, 73
Brown, Christy 1932-1981 .... DLB-14
Brown, Dee 1908- Y-80
Brown, Frank London 1927-1962 .... DLB-76
Brown, Fredric 1906-1972 .... DLB-8
Brown, George Mackay
 1921- DLB-14, 27, 139
Brown, Harry 1917-1986 .... DLB-26
Brown, Marcia 1918- DLB-61
Brown, Margaret Wise
 1910-1952............... DLB-22
Brown, Morna Doris (see Ferrars, Elizabeth)
Brown, Oliver Madox
 1855-1874 .... DLB-21
Brown, Sterling
 1901-1989........... DLB-48, 51, 63
Brown, T. E. 1830-1897......... DLB-35
Brown, William Hill 1765-1793 ..... DLB-37
Brown, William Wells
 1814-1884........... DLB-3, 50, 183
Browne, Charles Farrar
 1834-1867 .... DLB-11
Browne, Francis Fisher
 1843-1913 .... DLB-79
Browne, Michael Dennis
 1940- DLB-40
Browne, Sir Thomas 1605-1682 .... DLB-151
Browne, William, of Tavistock
 1590-1645 .... DLB-121
Browne, Wynyard 1911-1964 ..... DLB-13
Browne and Nolan DLB-106

Brownell, W. C. 1851-1928 .... DLB-71
Browning, Elizabeth Barrett
 1806-1861 .... DLB-32
Browning, Robert
 1812-1889 .... DLB-32, 163
Brownjohn, Allan 1931- DLB-40
Brownson, Orestes Augustus
 1803-1876 .... DLB-1, 59, 73
Bruccoli, Matthew J. 1931- DLB-103
Bruce, Charles 1906-1971......... DLB-68
Bruce, Leo 1903-1979........... DLB-77
Bruce, Philip Alexander
 1856-1933 .... DLB-47
Bruce Humphries
 [publishing house] DLB-46
Bruce-Novoa, Juan 1944- DLB-82
Bruckman, Clyde 1894-1955....... DLB-26
Bruckner, Ferdinand 1891-1958....... DLB-118
Brundage, John Herbert (see Herbert, John)
Brutus, Dennis 1924-............ DLB-117
Bryan, C. D. B. 1936- DLB-185
Bryant, Arthur 1899-1985........ DLB-149
Bryant, William Cullen
 1794-1878 .... DLB-3, 43, 59, 189
Bryce Echenique, Alfredo
 1939- DLB-145
Bryce, James 1838-1922 ..... DLB-166, 190
Brydges, Sir Samuel Egerton
 1762-1837 .... DLB-107
Bryskett, Lodowick 1546?-1612 ..... DLB-167
Buchan, John 1875-1940 ... DLB-34, 70, 156
Buchanan, George 1506-1582...... DLB-132
Buchanan, Robert 1841-1901..... DLB-18, 35
Buchman, Sidney 1902-1975 .... DLB-26
Buchner, Augustus 1591-1661...... DLB-164
Büchner, Georg 1813-1837....... DLB-133
Bucholtz, Andreas Heinrich
 1607-1671 .... DLB-168
Buck, Pearl S. 1892-1973....... DLB-9, 102
Bucke, Charles 1781-1846 .... DLB-110
Bucke, Richard Maurice
 1837-1902 .... DLB-99
Buckingham, Joseph Tinker 1779-1861 and
 Buckingham, Edwin
 1810-1833 .... DLB-73
Buckler, Ernest 1908-1984 .... DLB-68
Buckley, William F., Jr.
 1925- DLB-137; Y-80
Buckminster, Joseph Stevens
 1784-1812 .... DLB-37
Buckner, Robert 1906- DLB-26
Budd, Thomas ?-1698 .... DLB-24
Budrys, A. J. 1931- DLB-8
Buechner, Frederick 1926- Y-80
Buell, John 1927- DLB-53

Buffum, Job [publishing house]...... DLB-49
Bugnet, Georges 1879-1981........ DLB-92
Buies, Arthur 1840-1901 .... DLB-99
Building the New British Library
 at St Pancras............... Y-94
Bukowski, Charles
 1920-1994.......... DLB-5, 130, 169
Bulatović, Miodrag 1930-1991...... DLB-181
Bulger, Bozeman 1877-1932....... DLB-171
Bullein, William
 between 1520 and 1530-1576.... DLB-167
Bullins, Ed 1935- DLB-7, 38
Bulwer-Lytton, Edward (also Edward Bulwer)
 1803-1873 .... DLB-21
Bumpus, Jerry 1937- Y-81
Bunce and Brother DLB-49
Bunner, H. C. 1855-1896 ..... DLB-78, 79
Bunting, Basil 1900-1985 .... DLB-20
Buntline, Ned (Edward Zane Carroll Judson)
 1821-1886 .... DLB-186
Bunyan, John 1628-1688 .... DLB-39
Burch, Robert 1925- DLB-52
Burciaga, José Antonio 1940- DLB-82
Bürger, Gottfried August
 1747-1794 .... DLB-94
Burgess, Anthony 1917-1993....... DLB-14
Burgess, Gelett 1866-1951 .... DLB-11
Burgess, John W. 1844-1931....... DLB-47
Burgess, Thornton W.
 1874-1965 .... DLB-22
Burgess, Stringer and Company DLB-49
Burick, Si 1909-1986........... DLB-171
Burk, John Daly circa 1772-1808 .... DLB-37
Burke, Edmund 1729?-1797....... DLB-104
Burke, Kenneth 1897-1993...... DLB-45, 63
Burlingame, Edward Livermore
 1848-1922 .... DLB-79
Burnet, Gilbert 1643-1715 .... DLB-101
Burnett, Frances Hodgson
 1849-1924...... DLB-42, 141; DS-13, 14
Burnett, W. R. 1899-1982......... DLB-9
Burnett, Whit 1899-1973 and
 Martha Foley 1897-1977 ...... DLB-137
Burney, Fanny 1752-1840 .... DLB-39
Burns, Alan 1929- DLB-14
Burns, John Horne 1916-1953....... Y-85
Burns, Robert 1759-1796 .... DLB-109
Burns and Oates............... DLB-106
Burnshaw, Stanley 1906- DLB-48
Burr, C. Chauncey 1815?-1883 ..... DLB-79
Burroughs, Edgar Rice 1875-1950..... DLB-8
Burroughs, John 1837-1921........ DLB-64
Burroughs, Margaret T. G.
 1917- DLB-41

Burroughs, William S., Jr.
1947-1981 . . . . DLB-16

Burroughs, William Seward
1914- DLB-2, 8, 16, 152; Y-81

Burroway, Janet 1936- DLB-6

Burt, Maxwell Struthers
1882-1954 . . . . DLB-86; DS-16

Burt, A. L., and Company DLB-49

Burton, Hester 1913- DLB-161

Burton, Isabel Arundell
1831-1896 . . . . DLB-166

Burton, Miles (see Rhode, John)

Burton, Richard Francis
1821-1890 . . . . DLB-55, 166, 184

Burton, Robert 1577-1640 . . . . DLB-151

Burton, Virginia Lee 1909-1968 . . . . . DLB-22

Burton, William Evans
1804-1860 . . . . DLB-73

Burwell, Adam Hood 1790-1849 . . . . . DLB-99

Bury, Lady Charlotte
1775-1861 . . . . DLB-116

Busch, Frederick 1941- DLB-6

Busch, Niven 1903-1991 . . . . DLB-44

Bushnell, Horace 1802-1876 . . . . DS-13

Bussieres, Arthur de 1877-1913 . . . . . DLB-92

Butler, Josephine Elizabeth
1828-1906 . . . . DLB-190

Butler, Juan 1942-1981 . . . . DLB-53

Butler, Octavia E. 1947- DLB-33

Butler, Pierce 1884-1953 . . . . DLB-187

Butler, Robert Olen 1945- DLB-173

Butler, Samuel 1613-1680 . . . . . DLB-101, 126

Butler, Samuel 1835-1902 . . . DLB-18, 57, 174

Butler, William Francis
1838-1910 . . . . DLB-166

Butler, E. H., and Company DLB-49

Butor, Michel 1926- DLB-83

Butter, Nathaniel
[publishing house] DLB-170

Butterworth, Hezekiah 1839-1905 . . . . DLB-42

Buttitta, Ignazio 1899- DLB-114

Buzzati, Dino 1906-1972 . . . . DLB-177

Byars, Betsy 1928- DLB-52

Byatt, A. S. 1936- DLB-14

Byles, Mather 1707-1788 . . . . DLB-24

Bynneman, Henry
[publishing house] DLB-170

Bynner, Witter 1881-1968 . . . . DLB-54

Byrd, William circa 1543-1623 . . . . . DLB-172

Byrd, William II 1674-1744 . . . . DLB-24, 140

Byrne, John Keyes (see Leonard, Hugh)

Byron, George Gordon, Lord
1788-1824 . . . . DLB-96, 110

C

Caballero Bonald, José Manuel
1926- DLB-108

Cabañero, Eladio 1930- DLB-134

Cabell, James Branch
1879-1958 . . . . DLB-9, 78

Cabeza de Baca, Manuel
1853-1915 . . . . DLB-122

Cabeza de Baca Gilbert, Fabiola
1898- DLB-122

Cable, George Washington
1844-1925 . . . . DLB-12, 74; DS-13

Cabrera, Lydia 1900-1991 . . . . DLB-145

Cabrera Infante, Guillermo
1929- DLB-113

Cadell [publishing house] DLB-154

Cady, Edwin H. 1917- DLB-103

Caedmon flourished 658-680 . . . . . . DLB-146

Caedmon School circa 660-899 . . . . DLB-146

Cafés, Brasseries, and Bistros DS-15

Cahan, Abraham
1860-1951 . . . . DLB-9, 25, 28

Cain, George 1943- DLB-33

Caldecott, Randolph 1846-1886 . . . . . DLB-163

Calder, John
(Publishers), Limited DLB-112

Calderón de la Barca, Fanny
1804-1882 . . . . DLB-183

Caldwell, Ben 1937- DLB-38

Caldwell, Erskine 1903-1987 . . . . . DLB-9, 86

Caldwell, H. M., Company DLB-49

Calhoun, John C. 1782-1850 . . . . DLB-3

Calisher, Hortense 1911- DLB-2

A Call to Letters and an Invitation
to the Electric Chair,
by Siegfried Mandel DLB-75

Callaghan, Morley 1903-1990 . . . . . . DLB-68

Callahan, S. Alice 1868-1894 . . . . . . DLB-175

Callaloo Y-87

Callimachus circa 305 B.C.-240 B.C.
. . . . DLB-176

Calmer, Edgar 1907- DLB-4

Calverley, C. S. 1831-1884 . . . . DLB-35

Calvert, George Henry
1803-1889 . . . . DLB-1, 64

Cambridge Press DLB-49

Cambridge Songs (Carmina Cantabrigensia)
circa 1050 . . . . DLB-148

Cambridge University Press DLB-170

Camden, William 1551-1623 . . . . . . DLB-172

Camden House: An Interview with
James Hardin Y-92

Cameron, Eleanor 1912- DLB-52

Cameron, George Frederick
1854-1885 . . . . DLB-99

Cameron, Lucy Lyttelton
1781-1858 . . . . DLB-163

Cameron, William Bleasdell
1862-1951 . . . . DLB-99

Camm, John 1718-1778 . . . . DLB-31

Campana, Dino 1885-1932 . . . . DLB-114

Campbell, Gabrielle Margaret Vere
(see Shearing, Joseph, and Bowen, Marjorie)

Campbell, James Dykes
1838-1895 . . . . DLB-144

Campbell, James Edwin
1867-1896 . . . . DLB-50

Campbell, John 1653-1728 . . . . DLB-43

Campbell, John W., Jr.
1910-1971 . . . . DLB-8

Campbell, Roy 1901-1957 . . . . DLB-20

Campbell, Thomas
1777-1844 . . . . DLB-93, 144

Campbell, William Wilfred
1858-1918 . . . . DLB-92

Campion, Edmund 1539-1581 . . . . . DLB-167

Campion, Thomas
1567-1620 . . . . DLB-58, 172

Camus, Albert 1913-1960 . . . . DLB-72

The Canadian Publishers' Records
Database Y-96

Canby, Henry Seidel 1878-1961 . . . . . DLB-91

Candelaria, Cordelia 1943- DLB-82

Candelaria, Nash 1928- DLB-82

Candour in English Fiction (1890),
by Thomas Hardy DLB-18

Canetti, Elias 1905-1994 . . . . . . DLB-85, 124

Canham, Erwin Dain
1904-1982 . . . . DLB-127

Canitz, Friedrich Rudolph Ludwig von
1654-1699 . . . . DLB-168

Cankar, Ivan 1876-1918 . . . . DLB-147

Cannan, Gilbert 1884-1955 . . . . DLB-10

Cannell, Kathleen 1891-1974 . . . . . . DLB-4

Cannell, Skipwith 1887-1957 . . . . . . DLB-45

Canning, George 1770-1827 . . . . . . DLB-158

Cannon, Jimmy 1910-1973 . . . . DLB-171

Cantwell, Robert 1908-1978 . . . . DLB-9

Cape, Jonathan, and Harrison Smith
[publishing house] DLB-46

Cape, Jonathan, Limited DLB-112

Capen, Joseph 1658-1725 . . . . DLB-24

Capes, Bernard 1854-1918 . . . . DLB-156

Capote, Truman
1924-1984 . . . . . . DLB-2, 185; Y-80, 84

Caproni, Giorgio 1912-1990 . . . . . . DLB-128

Cardarelli, Vincenzo 1887-1959 . . . . . DLB-114

Cárdenas, Reyes 1948- DLB-122

Cardinal, Marie 1929- DLB-83	Cary, Joyce 1888-1957 ...... DLB-15, 100	The Center for the Book in the Library of Congress. Y-93
Carew, Jan 1920- DLB-157	Cary, Patrick 1623?-1657 .... DLB-131	Center for the Book Research. Y-84
Carew, Thomas 1594 or 1595-1640 .... DLB-126	Casey, Juanita 1925- DLB-14	Centlivre, Susanna 1669?-1723 ..... DLB-84
Carey, Henry circa 1687-1689-1743 .... DLB-84	Casey, Michael 1947- DLB-5	The Century Company. DLB-49
Carey, Mathew 1760-1839 ...... DLB-37, 73	Cassady, Carolyn 1923- DLB-16	Cernuda, Luis 1902-1963 .... DLB-134
Carey and Hart. DLB-49	Cassady, Neal 1926-1968. .... DLB-16	Cervantes, Lorna Dee 1954- DLB-82
Carey, M., and Company DLB-49	Cassell and Company DLB-106	Chacel, Rosa 1898- DLB-134
Carlell, Lodowick 1602-1675 ...... DLB-58	Cassell Publishing Company DLB-49	Chacón, Eusebio 1869-1948 .... DLB-82
Carleton, William 1794-1869 ...... DLB-159	Cassill, R. V. 1919- DLB-6	Chacón, Felipe Maximiliano 1873-? DLB-82
Carleton, G. W. [publishing house]. DLB-49	Cassity, Turner 1929- DLB-105	Chadwyck-Healey's Full-Text Literary Data-bases: Editing Commercial Databases of Primary Literary Texts Y-95
Carlile, Richard 1790-1843 .... DLB-110, 158	Cassius Dio circa 155/164-post 229 .... DLB-176	
Carlyle, Jane Welsh 1801-1866. ..... DLB-55	Cassola, Carlo 1917-1987 .... DLB-177	Challans, Eileen Mary (see Renault, Mary)
Carlyle, Thomas 1795-1881. .... DLB-55, 144	*The Castle of Perseverance* circa 1400-1425 .... DLB-146	Chalmers, George 1742-1825. ...... DLB-30
Carman, Bliss 1861-1929 .... DLB-92	Castellano, Olivia 1944- DLB-122	Chaloner, Sir Thomas 1520-1565 .... DLB-167
Carmina Burana circa 1230. ...... DLB-138	Castellanos, Rosario 1925-1974 ..... DLB-113	Chamberlain, Samuel S. 1851-1916. .... DLB-25
Carnero, Guillermo 1947- DLB-108	Castillo, Ana 1953- DLB-122	Chamberland, Paul 1939- DLB-60
Carossa, Hans 1878-1956. .... DLB-66	Castlemon, Harry (see Fosdick, Charles Austin)	Chamberlin, William Henry 1897-1969 .... DLB-29
Carpenter, Humphrey 1946- DLB-155	Čašule, Kole 1921- DLB-181	
Carpenter, Stephen Cullen ?-1820? ... DLB-73	Caswall, Edward 1814-1878 ...... DLB-32	Chambers, Charles Haddon 1860-1921 .... DLB-10
Carpentier, Alejo 1904-1980. ...... DLB-113	Catacalos, Rosemary 1944- DLB-122	Chambers, W. and R. [publishing house]. DLB-106
Carrier, Roch 1937- DLB-53	Cather, Willa 1873-1947. .... DLB-9, 54, 78; DS-1	
Carrillo, Adolfo 1855-1926 ...... DLB-122		Chamisso, Albert von 1781-1838 .... DLB-90
Carroll, Gladys Hasty 1904- DLB-9	Catherine II (Ekaterina Alekseevna), "The Great," Empress of Russia 1729-1796 .... DLB-150	
Carroll, John 1735-1815 .... DLB-37		Champfleury 1821-1889 .... DLB-119
Carroll, John 1809-1884 .... DLB-99	Catherwood, Mary Hartwell 1847-1902. .... DLB-78	Chandler, Harry 1864-1944 ...... DLB-29
Carroll, Lewis 1832-1898 .... DLB-18, 163, 178		Chandler, Norman 1899-1973. ..... DLB-127
Carroll, Paul 1927- DLB-16	Catledge, Turner 1901-1983. ...... DLB-127	Chandler, Otis 1927- DLB-127
Carroll, Paul Vincent 1900-1968. .... DLB-10	Catlin, George 1796-1872 ..... DLB-186, 189	Chandler, Raymond 1888-1959 .... DS-6
Carroll and Graf Publishers DLB-46	Cattafi, Bartolo 1922-1979. .... DLB-128	Channing, Edward 1856-1931 ...... DLB-17
Carruth, Hayden 1921- DLB-5, 165	Catton, Bruce 1899-1978 .... DLB-17	Channing, Edward Tyrrell 1790-1856 .... DLB-1, 59
Carryl, Charles E. 1841-1920 ...... DLB-42	Causley, Charles 1917- DLB-27	
Carswell, Catherine 1879-1946. ..... DLB-36	Caute, David 1936- DLB-14	Channing, William Ellery 1780-1842 .... DLB-1, 59
Carter, Angela 1940-1992. .... DLB-14	Cavendish, Duchess of Newcastle, Margaret Lucas 1623-1673 .... DLB-131	
Carter, Elizabeth 1717-1806. ...... DLB-109		Channing, William Ellery, II 1817-1901. .... DLB-1
Carter, Henry (see Leslie, Frank)	Cawein, Madison 1865-1914 .... DLB-54	
Carter, Hodding, Jr. 1907-1972. .... DLB-127	The Caxton Printers, Limited DLB-46	Channing, William Henry 1810-1884 .... DLB-1, 59
Carter, Landon 1710-1778 .... DLB-31	Caxton, William [publishing house] DLB-170	
Carter, Lin 1930- Y-81		Chaplin, Charlie 1889-1977. .... DLB-44
Carter, Martin 1927- DLB-117	Cayrol, Jean 1911- DLB-83	Chapman, George 1559 or 1560 - 1634. ..... DLB-62, 121
Carter and Hendee DLB-49	Cecil, Lord David 1902-1986. ...... DLB-155	
Carter, Robert, and Brothers. DLB-49	Celan, Paul 1920-1970. .... DLB-69	Chapman, John DLB-106
Cartwright, John 1740-1824 ...... DLB-158	Celaya, Gabriel 1911-1991. .... DLB-108	Chapman, William 1850-1917 ..... DLB-99
Cartwright, William circa 1611-1643 .... DLB-126	Céline, Louis-Ferdinand 1894-1961. .... DLB-72	Chapman and Hall DLB-106
Caruthers, William Alexander 1802-1846. .... DLB-3	The Celtic Background to Medieval English Literature. DLB-146	Chappell, Fred 1936- DLB-6, 105
		Chappell, Fred, A Detail in a Poem DLB-105
Carver, Jonathan 1710-1780 ...... DLB-31	Celtis, Conrad 1459-1508 .... DLB-179	Charbonneau, Jean 1875-1960 ..... DLB-92
Carver, Raymond 1938-1988. .... DLB-130; Y-84, 88	Center for Bibliographical Studies and Research at the University of California, Riverside Y-91	Charbonneau, Robert 1911-1967. .... DLB-68
		Charles, Gerda 1914- DLB-14

Charles, William
 [publishing house]..........DLB-49

The Charles Wood Affair:
 A Playwright Revived........Y-83

Charlotte Forten: Pages from
 her Diary..............DLB-50

Charteris, Leslie 1907-1993........DLB-77

Charyn, Jerome 1937-............Y-83

Chase, Borden 1900-1971..........DLB-26

Chase, Edna Woolman
 1877-1957..............DLB-91

Chase-Riboud, Barbara 1936-.....DLB-33

Chateaubriand, François-René de
 1768-1848..............DLB-119

Chatterton, Thomas 1752-1770.....DLB-109

Chatto and Windus............DLB-106

Chaucer, Geoffrey 1340?-1400......DLB-146

Chauncy, Charles 1705-1787.......DLB-24

Chauveau, Pierre-Joseph-Olivier
 1820-1890..............DLB-99

Chávez, Denise 1948-...........DLB-122

Chávez, Fray Angélico 1910-......DLB-82

Chayefsky, Paddy
 1923-1981........DLB-7, 44; Y-81

Cheever, Ezekiel 1615-1708........DLB-24

Cheever, George Barrell
 1807-1890..............DLB-59

Cheever, John
 1912-1982.......DLB-2, 102; Y-80, 82

Cheever, Susan 1943-............Y-82

Cheke, Sir John 1514-1557.......DLB-132

Chelsea House..............DLB-46

Cheney, Ednah Dow (Littlehale)
 1824-1904..............DLB-1

Cheney, Harriet Vaughn
 1796-1889..............DLB-99

Cherry, Kelly 1940............Y-83

Cherryh, C. J. 1942-...........Y-80

Chesnutt, Charles Waddell
 1858-1932..........DLB-12, 50, 78

Chesney, Sir George Tomkyns
 1830-1895..............DLB-190

Chester, Alfred 1928-1971.........DLB-130

Chester, George Randolph
 1869-1924..............DLB-78

The Chester Plays circa 1505-1532;
 revisions until 1575..........DLB-146

Chesterfield, Philip Dormer Stanhope,
 Fourth Earl of 1694-1773......DLB-104

Chesterton, G. K. 1874-1936
 .....DLB-10, 19, 34, 70, 98, 149, 178

Chettle, Henry
 circa 1560-circa 1607.........DLB-136

Chew, Ada Nield 1870-1945.......DLB-135

Cheyney, Edward P. 1861-1947.....DLB-47

Chiara, Piero 1913-1986..........DLB-177

Chicano History..............DLB-82

Chicano Language.............DLB-82

Child, Francis James
 1825-1896.............DLB-1, 64

Child, Lydia Maria
 1802-1880.............DLB-1, 74

Child, Philip 1898-1978..........DLB-68

Childers, Erskine 1870-1922.......DLB-70

Children's Book Awards
 and Prizes..............DLB-61

Children's Illustrators,
 1800-1880..............DLB-163

Childress, Alice 1920-1994......DLB-7, 38

Childs, George W. 1829-1894......DLB-23

Chilton Book Company..........DLB-46

Chinweizu 1943-..............DLB-157

Chitham, Edward 1932-.........DLB-155

Chittenden, Hiram Martin
 1858-1917..............DLB-47

Chivers, Thomas Holley
 1809-1858..............DLB-3

Chopin, Kate 1850-1904.......DLB-12, 78

Chopin, Rene 1885-1953.........DLB-92

Choquette, Adrienne 1915-1973.....DLB-68

Choquette, Robert 1905-.........DLB-68

The Christian Publishing
 Company...............DLB-49

Christie, Agatha 1890-1976.....DLB-13, 77

Christus und die Samariterin
 circa 950..............DLB-148

Christy, Howard Chandler 1873-1952. DLB-188

Chulkov, Mikhail Dmitrievich
 1743?-1792..............DLB-150

Church, Benjamin 1734-1778.......DLB-31

Church, Francis Pharcellus
 1839-1906..............DLB-79

Church, William Conant
 1836-1917..............DLB-79

Churchill, Caryl 1938-...........DLB-13

Churchill, Charles 1731-1764......DLB-109

Churchill, Sir Winston
 1874-1965..........DLB-100; DS-16

Churchyard, Thomas
 1520?-1604.............DLB-132

Churton, E., and Company.......DLB-106

Chute, Marchette 1909-1994......DLB-103

Ciardi, John 1916-1986........DLB-5; Y-86

Cibber, Colley 1671-1757.........DLB-84

Cima, Annalisa 1941-...........DLB-128

Čingo, Živko 1935-1987.........DLB-181

Cirese, Eugenio 1884-1955........DLB-114

Cisneros, Sandra 1954-......DLB-122, 152

City Lights Books.............DLB-46

Cixous, Hélène 1937-...........DLB-83

Clampitt, Amy 1920-1994.........DLB-105

Clapper, Raymond 1892-1944......DLB-29

Clare, John 1793-1864........DLB-55, 96

Clarendon, Edward Hyde, Earl of
 1609-1674..............DLB-101

Clark, Alfred Alexander Gordon
 (see Hare, Cyril)

Clark, Ann Nolan 1896-..........DLB-52

Clark, C. E. Frazer Jr. 1925-......DLB-187

Clark, C. M., Publishing
 Company...............DLB-46

Clark, Catherine Anthony
 1892-1977..............DLB-68

Clark, Charles Heber
 1841-1915..............DLB-11

Clark, Davis Wasgatt 1812-1871.....DLB-79

Clark, Eleanor 1913-............DLB-6

Clark, J. P. 1935-.............DLB-117

Clark, Lewis Gaylord
 1808-1873...........DLB-3, 64, 73

Clark, Walter Van Tilburg
 1909-1971..............DLB-9

Clark, William (see Lewis, Meriwether)

Clark, William Andrews Jr.
 1877-1934..............DLB-187

Clarke, Austin 1896-1974......DLB-10, 20

Clarke, Austin C. 1934-......DLB-53, 125

Clarke, Gillian 1937-...........DLB-40

Clarke, James Freeman
 1810-1888.............DLB-1, 59

Clarke, Pauline 1921-..........DLB-161

Clarke, Rebecca Sophia
 1833-1906..............DLB-42

Clarke, Robert, and Company......DLB-49

Clarkson, Thomas 1760-1846......DLB-158

Claudius, Matthias 1740-1815......DLB-97

Clausen, Andy 1943-............DLB-16

Clawson, John L. 1865-1933......DLB-187

Claxton, Remsen and
 Haffelfinger..............DLB-49

Clay, Cassius Marcellus
 1810-1903..............DLB-43

Cleary, Beverly 1916-...........DLB-52

Cleaver, Vera 1919- and
 Cleaver, Bill 1920-1981........DLB-52

Cleland, John 1710-1789.........DLB-39

Clemens, Samuel Langhorne (Mark Twain) 1835-1910
 .....DLB-11, 12, 23, 64, 74, 186, 189

Clement, Hal 1922-.............DLB-8

Clemo, Jack 1916-.............DLB-27

Cleveland, John 1613-1658.......DLB-126

Cliff, Michelle 1946-...........DLB-157

Clifford, Lady Anne 1590-1676....DLB-151

Clifford, James L. 1901-1978.....DLB-103

Clifford, Lucy 1853?-1929....DLB-135, 141

Clifton, Lucille 1936- DLB-5, 41
Clines, Francis X. 1938- DLB-185
Clode, Edward J.
  [publishing house]. DLB-46
Clough, Arthur Hugh 1819-1861 . . . . DLB-32
Cloutier, Cécile 1930- DLB-60
Clutton-Brock, Arthur
  1868-1924 . . . . DLB-98
Coates, Robert M.
  1897-1973 . . . . DLB-4, 9, 102
Coatsworth, Elizabeth 1893- DLB-22
Cobb, Charles E., Jr. 1943- DLB-41
Cobb, Frank I. 1869-1923 . . . . DLB-25
Cobb, Irvin S.
  1876-1944. . . . . DLB-11, 25, 86
Cobbe, Frances Power 1822-1904 . . . DLB-190
Cobbett, William 1763-1835 . . . . DLB-43, 107
Cobbledick, Gordon 1898-1969 . . . . . DLB-171
Cochran, Thomas C. 1902- DLB-17
Cochrane, Elizabeth 1867-1922 . . . DLB-25, 189
Cockerill, John A. 1845-1896. . . . . . DLB-23
Cocteau, Jean 1889-1963 . . . . DLB-65
Coderre, Emile (see Jean Narrache)
Coffee, Lenore J. 1900?-1984. . . . . . DLB-44
Coffin, Robert P. Tristram
  1892-1955 . . . . DLB-45
Cogswell, Fred 1917- DLB-60
Cogswell, Mason Fitch
  1761-1830 . . . . DLB-37
Cohen, Arthur A. 1928-1986. . . . . . DLB-28
Cohen, Leonard 1934- DLB-53
Cohen, Matt 1942- DLB-53
Colden, Cadwallader
  1688-1776. . . . . DLB-24, 30
Cole, Barry 1936- DLB-14
Cole, George Watson
  1850-1939 . . . . DLB-140
Colegate, Isabel 1931- DLB-14
Coleman, Emily Holmes
  1899-1974. . . . . DLB-4
Coleman, Wanda 1946- DLB-130
Coleridge, Hartley 1796-1849. . . . . . DLB-96
Coleridge, Mary 1861-1907 . . . . DLB-19, 98
Coleridge, Samuel Taylor
  1772-1834 . . . . DLB-93, 107
Colet, John 1467-1519 . . . . DLB-132
Colette 1873-1954 . . . . DLB-65
Colette, Sidonie Gabrielle (see Colette)
Colinas, Antonio 1946- DLB-134
Coll, Joseph Clement 1881-1921 . . . . DLB-188
Collier, John 1901-1980 . . . . DLB-77
Collier, John Payne 1789-1883 . . . . . DLB-184
Collier, Mary 1690-1762 . . . . DLB-95

Collier, Robert J. 1876-1918 . . . . . . DLB-91
Collier, P. F. [publishing house] DLB-49
Collin and Small DLB-49
Collingwood, W. G. 1854-1932. . . . . DLB-149
Collins, An floruit circa 1653. . . . . . DLB-131
Collins, Merle 1950- DLB-157
Collins, Mortimer 1827-1876. . . . . DLB-21, 35
Collins, Wilkie 1824-1889 . . . DLB-18, 70, 159
Collins, William 1721-1759 . . . . . . DLB-109
Collins, William, Sons and
  Company DLB-154
Collins, Isaac [publishing house] DLB-49
Collyer, Mary 1716?-1763? DLB-39
Colman, Benjamin 1673-1747 . . . . . DLB-24
Colman, George, the Elder
  1732-1794 . . . . DLB-89
Colman, George, the Younger
  1762-1836 . . . . DLB-89
Colman, S. [publishing house] DLB-49
Colombo, John Robert 1936- DLB-53
Colquhoun, Patrick 1745-1820 . . . . DLB-158
Colter, Cyrus 1910- DLB-33
Colum, Padraic 1881-1972 . . . . . . DLB-19
Colvin, Sir Sidney 1845-1927 . . . . . DLB-149
Colwin, Laurie 1944-1992 . . . . Y-80
Comden, Betty 1919- and Green,
  Adolph 1918- DLB-44
Comi, Girolamo 1890-1968 . . . . . . DLB-114
The Comic Tradition Continued
  [in the British Novel]. DLB-15
Commager, Henry Steele
  1902- DLB-17
The Commercialization of the Image of
  Revolt, by Kenneth Rexroth. DLB-16
Community and Commentators: Black
  Theatre and Its Critics. DLB-38
Compton-Burnett, Ivy
  1884?-1969 . . . . DLB-36
Conan, Laure 1845-1924 . . . . DLB-99
Conde, Carmen 1901- DLB-108
Conference on Modern Biography Y-85
Congreve, William
  1670-1729 . . . . DLB-39, 84
Conkey, W. B., Company DLB-49
Connell, Evan S., Jr. 1924- DLB-2; Y-81
Connelly, Marc 1890-1980 . . . . DLB-7; Y-80
Connolly, Cyril 1903-1974 . . . . DLB-98
Connolly, James B. 1868-1957 . . . . . DLB-78
Connor, Ralph 1860-1937 . . . . DLB-92
Connor, Tony 1930- DLB-40
Conquest, Robert 1917- DLB-27
Conrad, Joseph
  1857-1924. . . . . . . DLB-10, 34, 98, 156
Conrad, John, and Company DLB-49

Conroy, Jack 1899-1990 . . . . Y-81
Conroy, Pat 1945- DLB-6
The Consolidation of Opinion: Critical
  Responses to the Modernists DLB-36
Constable, Henry 1562-1613 . . . . . . DLB-136
Constable and Company
  Limited. DLB-112
Constable, Archibald, and
  Company DLB-154
Constant, Benjamin 1767-1830 . . . . . DLB-119
Constant de Rebecque, Henri-Benjamin de
  (see Constant, Benjamin)
Constantine, David 1944- DLB-40
Constantin-Weyer, Maurice
  1881-1964 . . . . DLB-92
Contempo Caravan: Kites in
  a Windstorm. Y-85
A Contemporary Flourescence of Chicano
  Literature Y-84
The Continental Publishing
  Company DLB-49
A Conversation with Chaim Potok Y-84
Conversations with Editors. Y-95
Conversations with Publishers I: An Interview
  with Patrick O'Connor Y-84
Conversations with Publishers II: An Interview
  with Charles Scribner III Y-94
Conversations with Publishers III: An Interview
  with Donald Lamm Y-95
Conversations with Publishers IV: An Interview
  with James Laughlin Y-96
Conversations with Rare Book Dealers I: An
  Interview with Glenn Horowitz Y-90
Conversations with Rare Book Dealers II: An
  Interview with Ralph Sipper Y-94
Conversations with Rare Book Dealers
  (Publishers) III: An Interview with
  Otto Penzler Y-96
The Conversion of an Unpolitical Man,
  by W. H. Bruford DLB-66
Conway, Moncure Daniel
  1832-1907. . . . . DLB-1
Cook, Ebenezer
  circa 1667-circa 1732 . . . . . . DLB-24
Cook, Edward Tyas 1857-1919 . . . . DLB-149
Cook, Michael 1933- DLB-53
Cook, David C., Publishing
  Company DLB-49
Cooke, George Willis 1848-1923 . . . . DLB-71
Cooke, Increase, and Company DLB-49
Cooke, John Esten 1830-1886 . . . . . DLB-3
Cooke, Philip Pendleton
  1816-1850 . . . . DLB-3, 59
Cooke, Rose Terry
  1827-1892 . . . . DLB-12, 74
Cook-Lynn, Elizabeth 1930- DLB-175
Coolbrith, Ina 1841-1928 . . . . . . DLB-54, 186

Cooley, Peter 1940- DLB-105

Cooley, Peter, Into the Mirror DLB-105

Coolidge, Susan (see Woolsey, Sarah Chauncy)

Coolidge, George
[publishing house]........... DLB-49

Cooper, Giles 1918-1966 .... DLB-13

Cooper, James Fenimore
1789-1851.............. DLB-3, 183

Cooper, Kent 1880-1965 .... DLB-29

Cooper, Susan 1935- DLB-161

Cooper, William
[publishing house].......... DLB-170

Coote, J. [publishing house]....... DLB-154

Coover, Robert 1932- DLB-2; Y-81

Copeland and Day DLB-49

Ćopić, Branko 1915-1984 .... DLB-181

Copland, Robert 1470?-1548 ..... DLB-136

Coppard, A. E. 1878-1957 .... DLB-162

Coppel, Alfred 1921- Y-83

Coppola, Francis Ford 1939- DLB-44

Copway, George (Kah-ge-ga-gah-bowh)
1818-1869............ DLB-175, 183

Corazzini, Sergio 1886-1907....... DLB-114

Corbett, Richard 1582-1635........ DLB-121

Corcoran, Barbara 1911- DLB-52

Corelli, Marie 1855-1924 ..... DLB-34, 156

Corle, Edwin 1906-1956 .... Y-85

Corman, Cid 1924- DLB-5

Cormier, Robert 1925- DLB-52

Corn, Alfred 1943- DLB-120; Y-80

Cornish, Sam 1935- DLB-41

Cornish, William
circa 1465-circa 1524 .... DLB-132

Cornwall, Barry (see Procter, Bryan Waller)

Cornwallis, Sir William, the Younger
circa 1579-1614 .... DLB-151

Cornwell, David John Moore
(see le Carré, John)

Corpi, Lucha 1945- DLB-82

Corrington, John William 1932- DLB-6

Corrothers, James D. 1869-1917..... DLB-50

Corso, Gregory 1930- DLB-5, 16

Cortázar, Julio 1914-1984 .... DLB-113

Cortez, Jayne 1936- DLB-41

Corvinus, Gottlieb Siegmund
1677-1746 .... DLB-168

Corvo, Baron (see Rolfe, Frederick William)

Cory, Annie Sophie (see Cross, Victoria)

Cory, William Johnson
1823-1892................. DLB-35

Coryate, Thomas
1577?-1617............ DLB-151, 172

Ćosić, Dobrica 1921- DLB-181

Cosin, John 1595-1672........... DLB-151

Cosmopolitan Book Corporation..... DLB-46

Costain, Thomas B. 1885-1965 ...... DLB-9

Coste, Donat 1912-1957 .... DLB-88

Costello, Louisa Stuart 1799-1870 ... DLB-166

Cota-Cárdenas, Margarita
1941- DLB-122

Cotten, Bruce 1873-1954 .... DLB-187

Cotter, Joseph Seamon, Sr.
1861-1949 .... DLB-50

Cotter, Joseph Seamon, Jr.
1895-1919 .... DLB-50

Cottle, Joseph [publishing house] DLB-154

Cotton, Charles 1630-1687 .... DLB-131

Cotton, John 1584-1652.......... DLB-24

Coulter, John 1888-1980 .... DLB-68

Cournos, John 1881-1966......... DLB-54

Cousins, Margaret 1905- DLB-137

Cousins, Norman 1915-1990 ..... DLB-137

Coventry, Francis 1725-1754 ...... DLB-39

Coverdale, Miles
1487 or 1488-1569 .... DLB-167

Coverly, N. [publishing house]...... DLB-49

Covici-Friede................ DLB-46

Coward, Noel 1899-1973......... DLB-10

Coward, McCann and
Geoghegan DLB-46

Cowles, Gardner 1861-1946 .... DLB-29

Cowles, Gardner ("Mike"), Jr.
1903-1985............ DLB-127, 137

Cowley, Abraham
1618-1667............. DLB-131, 151

Cowley, Hannah 1743-1809 .... DLB-89

Cowley, Malcolm
1898-1989 .... DLB-4, 48; Y-81, 89

Cowper, William
1731-1800............. DLB-104, 109

Cox, A. B. (see Berkeley, Anthony)

Cox, James McMahon
1903-1974 .... DLB-127

Cox, James Middleton
1870-1957 .... DLB-127

Cox, Palmer 1840-1924.......... DLB-42

Coxe, Louis 1918-1993........... DLB-5

Coxe, Tench 1755-1824 .... DLB-37

Cozzens, James Gould
1903-1978.......... DLB-9; Y-84; DS-2

Crabbe, George 1754-1832 .... DLB-93

Crackanthorpe, Hubert
1870-1896 .... DLB-135

Craddock, Charles Egbert
(see Murfree, Mary N.)

Cradock, Thomas 1718-1770...... DLB-31

Craig, Daniel H. 1811-1895 .... DLB-43

Craik, Dinah Maria
1826-1887 .... DLB-35, 136

Cramer, Richard Ben 1950- DLB-185

Cranch, Christopher Pearse
1813-1892 .... DLB-1, 42

Crane, Hart 1899-1932 .... DLB-4, 48

Crane, R. S. 1886-1967.......... DLB-63

Crane, Stephen 1871-1900.... DLB-12, 54, 78

Crane, Walter 1845-1915 .... DLB-163

Cranmer, Thomas 1489-1556 ..... DLB-132

Crapsey, Adelaide 1878-1914...... DLB-54

Crashaw, Richard
1612 or 1613-1649 .... DLB-126

Craven, Avery 1885-1980 .... DLB-17

Crawford, Charles
1752-circa 1815.............. DLB-31

Crawford, F. Marion 1854-1909 ..... DLB-71

Crawford, Isabel Valancy
1850-1887................. DLB-92

Crawley, Alan 1887-1975......... DLB-68

Crayon, Geoffrey (see Irving, Washington)

Creamer, Robert W. 1922- DLB-171

Creasey, John 1908-1973 .... DLB-77

Creative Age Press DLB-46

Creech, William
[publishing house] DLB-154

Creede, Thomas
[publishing house] DLB-170

Creel, George 1876-1953 .... DLB-25

Creeley, Robert 1926- DLB-5, 16, 169

Creelman, James 1859-1915 ...... DLB-23

Cregan, David 1931- DLB-13

Creighton, Donald Grant
1902-1979 .... DLB-88

Cremazie, Octave 1827-1879 ...... DLB-99

Crémer, Victoriano 1909?- DLB-108

Crescas, Hasdai
circa 1340-1412?............ DLB-115

Crespo, Angel 1926- DLB-134

Cresset Press................ DLB-112

Cresswell, Helen 1934- DLB-161

Crèvecoeur, Michel Guillaume Jean de
1735-1813 .... DLB-37

Crews, Harry 1935- DLB-6, 143, 185

Crichton, Michael 1942- Y-81

A Crisis of Culture: The Changing Role
of Religion in the New Republic
.... DLB-37

Crispin, Edmund 1921-1978 ...... DLB-87

Cristofer, Michael 1946- DLB-7

"The Critic as Artist" (1891), by
Oscar Wilde DLB-57

"Criticism In Relation To Novels" (1863),
by G. H. Lewes DLB-21

Crnjanski, Miloš 1893-1977 ...... DLB-147

Crockett, David (Davy)
1786-1836.......... DLB-3, 11, 183

Croft-Cooke, Rupert (see Bruce, Leo)

Crofts, Freeman Wills
1879-1957................ DLB-77

Croker, John Wilson
1780-1857............... DLB-110

Croly, George 1780-1860....... DLB-159

Croly, Herbert 1869-1930...... DLB-91

Croly, Jane Cunningham
1829-1901................ DLB-23

Crompton, Richmal 1890-1969..... DLB-160

Crosby, Caresse 1892-1970....... DLB-48

Crosby, Caresse 1892-1970 and Crosby,
Harry 1898-1929........ DLB-4; DS-15

Crosby, Harry 1898-1929....... DLB-48

Cross, Gillian 1945-........... DLB-161

Cross, Victoria 1868-1952...... DLB-135

Crossley-Holland, Kevin
1941-.............. DLB-40, 161

Crothers, Rachel 1878-1958...... DLB-7

Crowell, Thomas Y., Company..... DLB-49

Crowley, John 1942-............. Y-82

Crowley, Mart 1935-........... DLB-7

Crown Publishers............. DLB-46

Crowne, John 1641-1712........ DLB-80

Crowninshield, Edward Augustus
1817-1859............... DLB-140

Crowninshield, Frank 1872-1947..... DLB-91

Croy, Homer 1883-1965........ DLB-4

Crumley, James 1939-............. Y-84

Cruz, Victor Hernández 1949-..... DLB-41

Csokor, Franz Theodor
1885-1969................ DLB-81

Cuala Press................ DLB-112

Cullen, Countee
1903-1946.......... DLB-4, 48, 51

Culler, Jonathan D. 1944-........ DLB-67

The Cult of Biography
Excerpts from the Second Folio Debate:
"Biographies are generally a disease of
English Literature" – Germaine Greer,
Victoria Glendinning, Auberon Waugh,
and Richard Holmes........ Y-86

Cumberland, Richard 1732-1811..... DLB-89

Cummings, Constance Gordon
1837-1924............... DLB-174

Cummings, E. E. 1894-1962..... DLB-4, 48

Cummings, Ray 1887-1957....... DLB-8

Cummings and Hilliard......... DLB-49

Cummins, Maria Susanna
1827-1866................ DLB-42

Cundall, Joseph
[publishing house]........... DLB-106

Cuney, Waring 1906-1976....... DLB-51

Cuney-Hare, Maude 1874-1936..... DLB-52

Cunningham, Allan 1784-1842... DLB-116, 144

Cunningham, J. V. 1911-........ DLB-5

Cunningham, Peter F.
[publishing house]........... DLB-49

Cunquiero, Alvaro 1911-1981...... DLB-134

Cuomo, George 1929-............ Y-80

Cupples and Leon............. DLB-46

Cupples, Upham and Company..... DLB-49

Cuppy, Will 1884-1949......... DLB-11

Curll, Edmund
[publishing house]........... DLB-154

Currie, James 1756-1805........ DLB-142

Currie, Mary Montgomerie Lamb Singleton,
Lady Currie (see Fane, Violet)

Cursor Mundi circa 1300........ DLB-146

Curti, Merle E. 1897-........... DLB-17

Curtis, Anthony 1926-.......... DLB-155

Curtis, Cyrus H. K. 1850-1933..... DLB-91

Curtis, George William
1824-1892............. DLB-1, 43

Curzon, Robert 1810-1873....... DLB-166

Curzon, Sarah Anne
1833-1898................ DLB-99

Cushing, Harvey 1869-1939...... DLB-187

Cynewulf circa 770-840......... DLB-146

Czepko, Daniel 1605-1660....... DLB-164

D

D. M. Thomas: The Plagiarism
Controversy................ Y-82

Dabit, Eugène 1898-1936........ DLB-65

Daborne, Robert circa 1580-1628.... DLB-58

Dacey, Philip 1939-............ DLB-105

Dacey, Philip, Eyes Across Centuries:
Contemporary Poetry and "That
Vision Thing"............ DLB-105

Dach, Simon 1605-1659......... DLB-164

Daggett, Rollin M. 1831-1901..... DLB-79

D'Aguiar, Fred 1960-........... DLB-157

Dahl, Roald 1916-1990......... DLB-139

Dahlberg, Edward 1900-1977..... DLB-48

Dahn, Felix 1834-1912......... DLB-129

Dale, Peter 1938-............. DLB-40

Daley, Arthur 1904-1974....... DLB-171

Dall, Caroline Wells (Healey)
1822-1912................ DLB-1

Dallas, E. S. 1828-1879........ DLB-55

The Dallas Theater Center...... DLB-7

D'Alton, Louis 1900-1951....... DLB-10

Daly, T. A. 1871-1948.......... DLB-11

Damon, S. Foster 1893-1971..... DLB-45

Damrell, William S.
[publishing house]........... DLB-49

Dana, Charles A. 1819-1897..... DLB-3, 23

Dana, Richard Henry, Jr.
1815-1882............. DLB-1, 183

Dandridge, Ray Garfield........ DLB-51

Dane, Clemence 1887-1965...... DLB-10

Danforth, John 1660-1730....... DLB-24

Danforth, Samuel, I 1626-1674..... DLB-24

Danforth, Samuel, II 1666-1727..... DLB-24

Dangerous Years: London Theater,
1939-1945................ DLB-10

Daniel, John M. 1825-1865...... DLB-43

Daniel, Samuel
1562 or 1563-1619......... DLB-62

Daniel Press................ DLB-106

Daniells, Roy 1902-1979........ DLB-68

Daniels, Jim 1956-............ DLB-120

Daniels, Jonathan 1902-1981..... DLB-127

Daniels, Josephus 1862-1948..... DLB-29

Dannay, Frederic 1905-1982 and
Manfred B. Lee 1905-1971..... DLB-137

Danner, Margaret Esse 1915-..... DLB-41

Danter, John [publishing house]..... DLB-170

Dantin, Louis 1865-1945........ DLB-92

Danzig, Allison 1898-1987...... DLB-171

D'Arcy, Ella circa 1857-1937..... DLB-135

Darley, Felix Octavious Carr 1822-1888 DLB-188

Darley, George 1795-1846....... DLB-96

Darwin, Charles 1809-1882..... DLB-57, 166

Darwin, Erasmus 1731-1802..... DLB-93

Daryush, Elizabeth 1887-1977..... DLB-20

Dashkova, Ekaterina Romanovna
(née Vorontsova) 1743-1810..... DLB-150

Dashwood, Edmée Elizabeth Monica
de la Pasture (see Delafield, E. M.)

Daudet, Alphonse 1840-1897..... DLB-123

d'Aulaire, Edgar Parin 1898- and
d'Aulaire, Ingri 1904-........ DLB-22

Davenant, Sir William
1606-1668............. DLB-58, 126

Davenport, Guy 1927-.......... DLB-130

Davenport, Robert ?-?.......... DLB-58

Daves, Delmer 1904-1977....... DLB-26

Davey, Frank 1940-............ DLB-53

Davidson, Avram 1923-1993..... DLB-8

Davidson, Donald 1893-1968..... DLB-45

Davidson, John 1857-1909...... DLB-19

Davidson, Lionel 1922-......... DLB-14

Davidson, Sara 1943-.......... DLB-185

Davie, Donald 1922-........... DLB-27

Davie, Elspeth 1919-........... DLB-139

Davies, Sir John 1569-1626..... DLB-172

Cumulative Index

Davies, John, of Hereford
1565?-1618. . . . . DLB-121

Davies, Rhys 1901-1978. . . . . DLB-139

Davies, Robertson 1913- DLB-68

Davies, Samuel 1723-1761. . . . . . . DLB-31

Davies, Thomas 1712?-1785. . . . DLB-142, 154

Davies, W. H. 1871-1940. . . . . . DLB-19, 174

Davies, Peter, Limited. DLB-112

Daviot, Gordon 1896?-1952. . . . . . DLB-10
(see also Tey, Josephine)

Davis, Charles A. 1795-1867. . . . . . DLB-11

Davis, Clyde Brion 1894-1962. . . . . DLB-9

Davis, Dick 1945- DLB-40

Davis, Frank Marshall 1905-? DLB-51

Davis, H. L. 1894-1960 . . . . DLB-9

Davis, John 1774-1854 . . . . DLB-37

Davis, Lydia 1947- DLB-130

Davis, Margaret Thomson 1926- DLB-14

Davis, Ossie 1917- DLB-7, 38

Davis, Paxton 1925-1994. . . . . Y-94

Davis, Rebecca Harding
1831-1910 . . . . DLB-74

Davis, Richard Harding 1864-1916
. . . . . . DLB-12, 23, 78, 79, 189; DS-13

Davis, Samuel Cole 1764-1809. . . . . DLB-37

Davison, Peter 1928- DLB-5

Davys, Mary 1674-1732 . . . . DLB-39

DAW Books DLB-46

Dawson, Ernest 1882-1947 . . . . . . DLB-140

Dawson, Fielding 1930- DLB-130

Dawson, William 1704-1752 . . . . . . DLB-31

Day, Angel flourished 1586 . . . . . . DLB-167

Day, Benjamin Henry 1810-1889 . . . . DLB-43

Day, Clarence 1874-1935. . . . . . . DLB-11

Day, Dorothy 1897-1980. . . . . . . DLB-29

Day, Frank Parker 1881-1950 . . . . . DLB-92

Day, John circa 1574-circa 1640. . . . . DLB-62

Day, John [publishing house]. DLB-170

Day Lewis, C. 1904-1972 . . . . . DLB-15, 20
(see also Blake, Nicholas)

Day, Thomas 1748-1789 . . . . DLB-39

Day, The John, Company DLB-46

Day, Mahlon [publishing house]. DLB-49

Dazai, Osamu 1909-1948 . . . . . . DLB-182

Deacon, William Arthur
1890-1977 . . . . DLB-68

Deal, Borden 1922-1985 . . . . DLB-6

de Angeli, Marguerite 1889-1987. . . . DLB-22

De Angelis, Milo 1951- DLB-128

De Bow, James Dunwoody Brownson
1820-1867 . . . . DLB-3, 79

de Bruyn, Günter 1926- DLB-75

de Camp, L. Sprague 1907- DLB-8

The Decay of Lying (1889),
by Oscar Wilde [excerpt] DLB-18

Dechert, Robert 1895-1975 . . . . . . DLB-187

Dedication, *Ferdinand Count Fathom* (1753),
by Tobias Smollett DLB-39

Dedication, *The History of Pompey the Little*
(1751), by Francis Coventry. DLB-39

Dedication, *Lasselia* (1723), by Eliza
Haywood [excerpt] DLB-39

Dedication, *The Wanderer* (1814),
by Fanny Burney. DLB-39

Dee, John 1527-1609. . . . . DLB-136

Deeping, George Warwick
1877-1950 . . . . DLB 153

Defense of *Amelia* (1752), by
Henry Fielding DLB-39

Defoe, Daniel 1660-1731 . . . . DLB-39, 95, 101

de Fontaine, Felix Gregory
1834-1896 . . . . DLB-43

De Forest, John William
1826-1906 . . . . DLB-12, 189

DeFrees, Madeline 1919- DLB-105

DeFrees, Madeline, The Poet's Kaleidoscope:
The Element of Surprise in the Making
of the Poem DLB-105

DeGolyer, Everette Lee 1886-1956 . . . DLB-187

de Graff, Robert 1895-1981 . . . . Y-81

de Graft, Joe 1924-1978 . . . . DLB-117

De Heinrico circa 980? DLB-148

Deighton, Len 1929- DLB-87

DeJong, Meindert 1906-1991 . . . . . DLB-52

Dekker, Thomas
circa 1572-1632 . . . . DLB-62, 172

Delacorte, Jr., George T.
1894-1991 . . . . DLB-91

Delafield, E. M. 1890-1943. . . . . . . DLB-34

Delahaye, Guy 1888-1969 . . . . DLB-92

de la Mare, Walter
1873-1956 . . . . DLB-19, 153, 162

Deland, Margaret 1857-1945 . . . . . . DLB-78

Delaney, Shelagh 1939- DLB-13

Delano, Amasa 1763-1823 . . . . DLB-183

Delany, Martin Robinson
1812-1885 . . . . DLB-50

Delany, Samuel R. 1942- DLB-8, 33

de la Roche, Mazo 1879-1961 . . . . . DLB-68

Delbanco, Nicholas 1942- DLB-6

De León, Nephtal 1945- DLB-82

Delgado, Abelardo Barrientos
1931- DLB-82

De Libero, Libero 1906-1981 . . . . . . DLB-114

DeLillo, Don 1936- DLB-6, 173

de Lisser H. G. 1878-1944 . . . . DLB-117

Dell, Floyd 1887-1969 . . . . DLB-9

Dell Publishing Company DLB-46

delle Grazie, Marie Eugene
1864-1931 . . . . DLB-81

Deloney, Thomas died 1600 . . . . . DLB-167

Deloria, Ella C. 1889-1971 . . . . . . DLB-175

Deloria, Vine, Jr. 1933- DLB-175

del Rey, Lester 1915-1993. . . . . . . DLB-8

Del Vecchio, John M. 1947- DS-9

de Man, Paul 1919-1983 . . . . DLB-67

Demby, William 1922- DLB-33

Deming, Philander 1829-1915 . . . . . DLB-74

Demorest, William Jennings
1822-1895 . . . . DLB-79

De Morgan, William 1839-1917 . . . . DLB-153

Demosthenes 384 B.C.-322 B.C. DLB-176

Denham, Henry
[publishing house] DLB-170

Denham, Sir John
1615-1669 . . . . DLB-58, 126

Denison, Merrill 1893-1975. . . . . . . DLB-92

Denison, T. S., and Company. DLB-49

Dennie, Joseph
1768-1812 . . . . . . DLB-37, 43, 59, 73

Dennis, John 1658-1734 . . . . DLB-101

Dennis, Nigel 1912-1989 . . . . . DLB-13, 15

Denslow, W. W. 1856-1915 . . . . . DLB-188

Dent, Tom 1932- DLB-38

Dent, J. M., and Sons. DLB-112

Denton, Daniel circa 1626-1703 . . . . DLB-24

DePaola, Tomie 1934- DLB-61

De Quille, Dan 1829-1898 . . . . . . DLB-186

De Quincey, Thomas
1785-1859. . . . . DLB-110, 144

Derby, George Horatio
1823-1861 . . . . DLB-11

Derby, J. C., and Company DLB-49

Derby and Miller DLB-49

Derleth, August 1909-1971 . . . . . . DLB-9

The Derrydale Press DLB-46

Derzhavin, Gavriil Romanovich
1743-1816 . . . . DLB-150

Desaulniers, Gonsalve
1863-1934 . . . . DLB-92

Desbiens, Jean-Paul 1927- DLB-53

des Forêts, Louis-Rene 1918- DLB-83

Desnica, Vladan 1905-1967 . . . . . . DLB-181

DesRochers, Alfred 1901-1978 . . . . . DLB-68

Desrosiers, Léo-Paul 1896-1967. . . . . DLB-68

Dessì, Giuseppe 1909-1977 . . . . . . DLB-177

Destouches, Louis-Ferdinand
(see Céline, Louis-Ferdinand)

De Tabley, Lord 1835-1895 . . . . . . DLB-35

Deutsch, Babette 1895-1982. . . . . . DLB-45

Deutsch, Niklaus Manuel (see Manuel, Niklaus)

Deutsch, André, Limited DLB-112
Deveaux, Alexis 1948- DLB-38
The Development of the Author's Copyright
    in Britain. DLB-154
The Development of Lighting in the Staging
    of Drama, 1900-1945 . . . . DLB-10
The Development of Meiji Japan. . . . DLB-180
de Vere, Aubrey 1814-1902 . . . . . . DLB-35
Devereux, second Earl of Essex, Robert
    1565-1601 . . . . DLB-136
The Devin-Adair Company DLB-46
De Vinne, Theodore Low
    1828-1914 . . . . DLB-187
De Voto, Bernard 1897-1955 . . . . . . DLB-9
De Vries, Peter 1910-1993 . . . . . DLB-6; Y-82
Dewdney, Christopher 1951- DLB-60
Dewdney, Selwyn 1909-1979 . . . . . . DLB-68
DeWitt, Robert M., Publisher DLB-49
DeWolfe, Fiske and Company. DLB-49
Dexter, Colin 1930- DLB-87
de Young, M. H. 1849-1925. . . . . . . DLB-25
Dhlomo, H. I. E. 1903-1956 . . . . . DLB-157
Dhuoda circa 803-after 843 . . . . . . DLB-148
The Dial Press DLB-46
Diamond, I. A. L. 1920-1988 . . . . . . DLB-26
Dibdin, Thomas Frognall
    1776-1847 . . . . DLB-184
Di Cicco, Pier Giorgio 1949- DLB-60
Dick, Philip K. 1928-1982 . . . . DLB-8
Dick and Fitzgerald DLB-49
Dickens, Charles
    1812-1870 . . . . . DLB-21, 55, 70, 159, 166
Dickinson, Peter 1927- DLB-161
Dickey, James
    1923-1997 . . . . . . DLB-5; Y-82, 93; DS-7
James Dickey, American Poet Y-96
Dickey, William 1928-1994 . . . . DLB-5
Dickinson, Emily 1830-1886 . . . . . . DLB-1
Dickinson, John 1732-1808 . . . . DLB-31
Dickinson, Jonathan 1688-1747. . . . . DLB-24
Dickinson, Patric 1914- DLB-27
Dickinson, Peter 1927- DLB-87
Dicks, John [publishing house] DLB-106
Dickson, Gordon R. 1923- DLB-8
*Dictionary of Literary Biography
    Yearbook* Awards Y-92, 93
The Dictionary of National Biography
    . . . . DLB-144
Didion, Joan
    1934- DLB-2, 173, 185; Y-81, 86
Di Donato, Pietro 1911- DLB-9
Die Fürstliche Bibliothek Corvey Y-96
Diego, Gerardo 1896-1987 . . . . . . DLB-134

Digges, Thomas circa 1546-1595 . . . . DLB-136
Dillard, Annie 1945- Y-80
Dillard, R. H. W. 1937- DLB-5
Dillingham, Charles T.,
    Company DLB-49
The Dillingham, G. W.,
    Company DLB-49
Dilly, Edward and Charles
    [publishing house] DLB-154
Dilthey, Wilhelm 1833-1911. . . . . . DLB-129
Dimitrova, Blaga 1922- DLB-181
Dimov, Dimitŭr 1909-1966 . . . . . . DLB-181
Dimsdale, Thomas J. 1831?-1866. . . . DLB-186
Dingelstedt, Franz von
    1814-1881 . . . . DLB-133
Dintenfass, Mark 1941- Y-84
Diogenes, Jr. (see Brougham, John)
Diogenes Laertius circa 200. . . . . . DLB-176
DiPrima, Diane 1934- DLB-5, 16
Disch, Thomas M. 1940- DLB-8
Disney, Walt 1901-1966 . . . . DLB-22
Disraeli, Benjamin 1804-1881 . . . . DLB-21, 55
D'Israeli, Isaac 1766-1848 . . . . DLB-107
Ditzen, Rudolf (see Fallada, Hans)
Dix, Dorothea Lynde 1802-1887 . . . . . DLB-1
Dix, Dorothy (see Gilmer,
    Elizabeth Meriwether)
Dix, Edwards and Company. DLB-49
Dixie, Florence Douglas
    1857-1905 . . . . DLB-174
Dixon, Paige (see Corcoran, Barbara)
Dixon, Richard Watson
    1833-1900 . . . . DLB-19
Dixon, Stephen 1936- DLB-130
Dmitriev, Ivan Ivanovich
    1760-1837 . . . . DLB-150
Dobell, Bertram 1842-1914 . . . . . . DLB-184
Dobell, Sydney 1824-1874 . . . . DLB-32
Döblin, Alfred 1878-1957 . . . . DLB-66
Dobson, Austin
    1840-1921 . . . . DLB-35, 144
Doctorow, E. L.
    1931- DLB-2, 28, 173; Y-80
Documents on Sixteenth-Century
    Literature. DLB-167, 172
Dodd, William E. 1869-1940. . . . . . DLB-17
Dodd, Anne [publishing house]. . . . DLB-154
Dodd, Mead and Company DLB-49
Doderer, Heimito von 1896-1968 . . . . DLB-85
Dodge, Mary Mapes
    1831?-1905 . . . . DLB-42, 79; DS-13
Dodge, B. W., and Company DLB-46
Dodge Publishing Company DLB-49

Dodgson, Charles Lutwidge
    (see Carroll, Lewis)
Dodsley, Robert 1703-1764. . . . . . . DLB-95
Dodsley, R. [publishing house] DLB-154
Dodson, Owen 1914-1983 . . . . DLB-76
Doesticks, Q. K. Philander, P. B.
    (see Thomson, Mortimer)
Doheny, Carrie Estelle
    1875-1958 . . . . DLB-140
Doherty, John 1798?-1854. . . . . . . DLB-190
Domínguez, Sylvia Maida
    1935- DLB-122
Donahoe, Patrick
    [publishing house]. DLB-49
Donald, David H. 1920- DLB-17
Donaldson, Scott 1928- DLB-111
Doni, Rodolfo 1919- DLB-177
Donleavy, J. P. 1926- DLB-6, 173
Donnadieu, Marguerite (see Duras,
    Marguerite)
Donne, John 1572-1631 . . . . . DLB-121, 151
Donnelley, R. R., and Sons
    Company DLB-49
Donnelly, Ignatius 1831-1901. . . . . . DLB-12
Donohue and Henneberry DLB-49
Donoso, José 1924- DLB-113
Doolady, M. [publishing house] DLB-49
Dooley, Ebon (see Ebon)
Doolittle, Hilda 1886-1961. . . . . . DLB-4, 45
Doplicher, Fabio 1938- DLB-128
Dor, Milo 1923- DLB-85
Doran, George H., Company DLB-46
Dorgelès, Roland 1886-1973 . . . . . . DLB-65
Dorn, Edward 1929- DLB-5
Dorr, Rheta Childe 1866-1948. . . . . DLB-25
Dorris, Michael 1945-1997 . . . . . . DLB-175
Dorset and Middlesex, Charles Sackville,
    Lord Buckhurst,
    Earl of 1643-1706 . . . . DLB-131
Dorst, Tankred 1925- DLB-75, 124
Dos Passos, John
    1896-1970 . . . . DLB-4, 9; DS-1, 15
John Dos Passos: A Centennial
    Commemoration Y-96
Doubleday and Company DLB-49
Dougall, Lily 1858-1923 . . . . DLB-92
Doughty, Charles M.
    1843-1926. . . . . DLB-19, 57, 174
Douglas, Gavin 1476-1522 . . . . . . DLB-132
Douglas, Keith 1920-1944. . . . . . . DLB-27
Douglas, Norman 1868-1952 . . . . . . DLB-34
Douglass, Frederick
    1817?-1895 . . . . DLB-1, 43, 50, 79
Douglass, William circa
    1691-1752 . . . . DLB-24

Dourado, Autran 1926- DLB-145

Dove, Arthur G. 1880-1946. . . . . . DLB-188

Dove, Rita 1952- DLB-120

Dover Publications DLB-46

Doves Press DLB-112

Dowden, Edward 1843-1913 . . . . DLB-35, 149

Dowell, Coleman 1925-1985 . . . . . DLB-130

Dowland, John 1563-1626. . . . . . . DLB-172

Downes, Gwladys 1915- DLB-88

Downing, J., Major (see Davis, Charles A.)

Downing, Major Jack (see Smith, Seba)

Dowriche, Anne
 before 1560-after 1613 . . . . . . DLB-172

Dowson, Ernest 1867-1900 . . . . DLB-19, 135

Doxey, William
 [publishing house]. DLB-49

Doyle, Sir Arthur Conan
 1859-1930 . . . . . . DLB-18, 70, 156, 178

Doyle, Kirby 1932- DLB-16

Drabble, Margaret 1939- DLB-14, 155

Drach, Albert 1902- DLB-85

Dragojević, Danijel 1934- DLB-181

Drake, Samuel Gardner 1798-1875 . . . DLB-187

The Dramatic Publishing
 Company DLB-49

Dramatists Play Service DLB-46

Drant, Thomas
 early 1540s?-1578 . . . . DLB-167

Draper, John W. 1811-1882 . . . . . . DLB-30

Draper, Lyman C. 1815-1891 . . . . . DLB-30

Drayton, Michael 1563-1631 . . . . . DLB-121

Dreiser, Theodore
 1871-1945 . . . . DLB-9, 12, 102, 137; DS-1

Drewitz, Ingeborg 1923-1986 . . . . . DLB-75

Drieu La Rochelle, Pierre
 1893-1945 . . . . DLB-72

Drinkwater, John 1882-1937
 . . . . DLB-10, 19, 149

Droste-Hülshoff, Annette von
 1797-1848 . . . . DLB-133

The Drue Heinz Literature Prize
 Excerpt from "Excerpts from a Report
 of the Commission," in David
 Bosworth's *The Death of Descartes*
 An Interview with David
 Bosworth Y-82

Drummond, William Henry
 1854-1907 . . . . DLB-92

Drummond, William, of Hawthornden
 1585-1649 . . . . DLB-121

Dryden, Charles 1860?-1931 . . . . . DLB-171

Dryden, John 1631-1700 . . . DLB-80, 101, 131

Držić, Marin circa 1508-1567 . . . . . DLB-147

Duane, William 1760-1835 . . . . . . DLB-43

Dubé, Marcel 1930- DLB-53

Dubé, Rodolphe (see Hertel, François)

Dubie, Norman 1945- DLB-120

Du Bois, W. E. B.
 1868-1963. . . . . DLB-47, 50, 91

Du Bois, William Pène 1916- DLB-61

Dubus, Andre 1936- DLB-130

Du Chaillu, Paul Belloni
 1831?-1903 . . . . DLB-189

Ducharme, Réjean 1941- DLB-60

Dučić, Jovan 1871-1943 . . . . DLB-147

Duck, Stephen 1705?-1756 . . . . . . DLB-95

Duckworth, Gerald, and
 Company Limited. DLB-112

Dudek, Louis 1918- DLB-88

Duell, Sloan and Pearce DLB-46

Duerer, Albrecht 1471-1528 . . . . . . DLB-179

Dufief, Nicholas Gouin 1776-1834 . . . DLB-187

Duff Gordon, Lucie 1821-1869 . . . . . DLB-166

Duffield and Green DLB-46

Duffy, Maureen 1933- DLB-14

Dugan, Alan 1923- DLB-5

Dugard, William
 [publishing house] DLB-170

Dugas, Marcel 1883-1947 . . . . DLB-92

Dugdale, William
 [publishing house] DLB-106

Duhamel, Georges 1884-1966 . . . . . DLB-65

Dujardin, Edouard 1861-1949 . . . . . DLB-123

Dukes, Ashley 1885-1959 . . . . DLB-10

Du Maurier, George
 1834-1896. . . . . DLB-153, 178

Dumas, Alexandre, *père*
 1802-1870 . . . . DLB-119

Dumas, Henry 1934-1968 . . . . DLB-41

Dunbar, Paul Laurence
 1872-1906. . . . . DLB-50, 54, 78

Dunbar, William
 circa 1460-circa 1522 . . . . . DLB-132, 146

Duncan, Norman 1871-1916 . . . . . . DLB-92

Duncan, Quince 1940- DLB-145

Duncan, Robert 1919-1988 . . . . . DLB-5, 16

Duncan, Ronald 1914-1982 . . . . . . DLB-13

Duncan, Sara Jeannette
 1861-1922 . . . . DLB-92

Dunigan, Edward, and Brother DLB-49

Dunlap, John 1747-1812 . . . . DLB-43

Dunlap, William
 1766-1839. . . . . DLB-30, 37, 59

Dunn, Douglas 1942- DLB-40

Dunn, Harvey Thomas 1884-1952 . . . DLB-188

Dunn, Stephen 1939- DLB-105

Dunn, Stephen, The Good,
 The Not So Good DLB-105

Dunne, Finley Peter
 1867-1936. . . . . DLB-11, 23

Dunne, John Gregory 1932- Y-80

Dunne, Philip 1908-1992 . . . . DLB-26

Dunning, Ralph Cheever
 1878-1930. . . . . DLB-4

Dunning, William A. 1857-1922 . . . . DLB-17

Duns Scotus, John
 circa 1266-1308 . . . . DLB-115

Dunsany, Lord (Edward John Moreton
 Drax Plunkett, Baron Dunsany)
 1878-1957 . . . . . . DLB-10, 77, 153, 156

Dunton, John [publishing house] DLB-170

Dunton, W. Herbert 1878-1936 . . . . DLB-188

Dupin, Amantine-Aurore-Lucile (see Sand, George)

Durand, Lucile (see Bersianik, Louky)

Duranty, Walter 1884-1957. . . . . . . DLB-29

Duras, Marguerite 1914- DLB-83

Durfey, Thomas 1653-1723. . . . . . . DLB-80

Durrell, Lawrence
 1912-1990 . . . . DLB-15, 27; Y-90

Durrell, William
 [publishing house]. DLB-49

Dürrenmatt, Friedrich
 1921-1990 . . . . DLB-69, 124

Dutton, E. P., and Company DLB-49

Duvoisin, Roger 1904-1980. . . . . . . DLB-61

Duyckinck, Evert Augustus
 1816-1878 . . . . DLB-3, 64

Duyckinck, George L. 1823-1863 . . . . DLB-3

Duyckinck and Company DLB-49

Dwight, John Sullivan 1813-1893 . . . . DLB-1

Dwight, Timothy 1752-1817 . . . . . . DLB-37

Dybek, Stuart 1942- DLB-130

Dyer, Charles 1928- DLB-13

Dyer, George 1755-1841 . . . . DLB-93

Dyer, John 1699-1757 . . . . DLB-95

Dyer, Sir Edward 1543-1607 . . . . . . DLB-136

Dylan, Bob 1941- DLB-16

E

Eager, Edward 1911-1964 . . . . DLB-22

Eames, Wilberforce 1855-1937 . . . . . DLB-140

Earle, James H., and Company DLB-49

Earle, John 1600 or 1601-1665 . . . . . DLB-151

Early American Book Illustration,
 by Sinclair Hamilton DLB-49

Eastlake, William 1917- DLB-6

Eastman, Carol ?- DLB-44

Eastman, Charles A. (Ohiyesa)
 1858-1939 . . . . DLB-175

Eastman, Max 1883-1969. . . . . DLB-91

Eaton, Daniel Isaac 1753-1814 . . . . . DLB-158	Eisenreich, Herbert 1925-1986 . . . . . . DLB-85	Empson, William 1906-1984 . . . . DLB-20
Eberhart, Richard 1904- DLB-48	Eisner, Kurt 1867-1919 . . . . DLB-66	Enchi, Fumiko 1905-1986 . . . . DLB-182
Ebner, Jeannie 1918- DLB-85	Eklund, Gordon 1945- Y-83	Encounter with the West DLB-180
Ebner-Eschenbach, Marie von 1830-1916 . . . . DLB-81	Ekwensi, Cyprian 1921- DLB-117	The End of English Stage Censorship, 1945-1968 . . . . DLB-13
Ebon 1942- DLB-41	Eld, George [publishing house] DLB-170	Ende, Michael 1929- DLB-75
Ecbasis Captivi circa 1045. . . . . DLB-148	Elder, Lonne III 1931- DLB-7, 38, 44	Endō, Shūsaku 1923-1996 . . . . DLB-182
Ecco Press DLB-46	Elder, Paul, and Company DLB-49	Engel, Marian 1933-1985 . . . . DLB-53
Eckhart, Meister circa 1260-circa 1328 . . . . DLB-115	*Elements of Rhetoric* (1828; revised, 1846), by Richard Whately [excerpt] DLB-57	Engels, Friedrich 1820-1895 . . . . . . DLB-129
The Eclectic Review 1805-1868 . . . . . . DLB-110	Elie, Robert 1915-1973 . . . . DLB-88	Engle, Paul 1908- DLB-48
Edel, Leon 1907- DLB-103	Elin Pelin 1877-1949. . . . . DLB-147	*English Composition and Rhetoric* (1866), by Alexander Bain [excerpt] DLB-57
Edes, Benjamin 1732-1803 . . . . DLB-43	Eliot, George 1819-1880 . . . . . DLB-21, 35, 55	The English Language: 410 to 1500 . . . . DLB-146
Edgar, David 1948- DLB-13	Eliot, John 1604-1690 . . . . DLB-24	The English Renaissance of Art (1908), by Oscar Wilde DLB-35
Edgeworth, Maria 1768-1849 . . . . DLB-116, 159, 163	Eliot, T. S. 1888-1965 . . . . DLB-7, 10, 45, 63	Enright, D. J. 1920- DLB-27
The Edinburgh Review 1802-1929 . . . . DLB-110	Eliot's Court Press DLB-170	Enright, Elizabeth 1909-1968 . . . . . . DLB-22
Edinburgh University Press DLB-112	Elizabeth I 1533-1603 . . . . DLB-136	L'Envoi (1882), by Oscar Wilde DLB-35
The Editor Publishing Company DLB-49	Elizabeth of Nassau-Saarbrücken after 1393-1456 . . . . DLB-179	Epictetus circa 55-circa 125-130 . . . . DLB-176
Editorial Statements DLB-137	Elizondo, Salvador 1932- DLB-145	Epicurus 342/341 B.C.-271/270 B.C. DLB-176
Edmonds, Randolph 1900- DLB-51	Elizondo, Sergio 1930- DLB-82	
Edmonds, Walter D. 1903- DLB-9	Elkin, Stanley 1930- DLB-2, 28; Y-80	Epps, Bernard 1936- DLB-53
Edschmid, Kasimir 1890-1966 . . . . . DLB-56	Elles, Dora Amy (see Wentworth, Patricia)	Epstein, Julius 1909- and Epstein, Philip 1909-1952 . . . . . . DLB-26
Edwards, Amelia Anne Blandford 1831-1892 . . . . DLB-174	Ellet, Elizabeth F. 1818?-1877 . . . . . DLB-30	Equiano, Olaudah circa 1745-1797 . . . . DLB-37, 50
Edwards, Edward 1812-1886 . . . . . . DLB-184	Elliot, Ebenezer 1781-1849 . . . . . DLB-96, 190	Eragny Press DLB-112
Edwards, Jonathan 1703-1758 . . . . . DLB-24	Elliot, Frances Minto (Dickinson) 1820-1898 . . . . DLB-166	Erasmus, Desiderius 1467-1536 . . . . . DLB-136
Edwards, Jonathan, Jr. 1745-1801 . . . . DLB-37	Elliott, George 1923- DLB-68	Erba, Luciano 1922- DLB-128
Edwards, Junius 1929- DLB-33	Elliott, Janice 1931- DLB-14	Erdrich, Louise 1954- DLB-152, 178
Edwards, Matilda Barbara Betham- 1836-1919 . . . . DLB-174	Elliott, William 1788-1863 . . . . DLB-3	Erichsen-Brown, Gwethalyn Graham (see Graham, Gwethalyn)
Edwards, Richard 1524-1566 . . . . . . DLB-62	Elliott, Thomes and Talbot DLB-49	Eriugena, John Scottus circa 810-877 . . . . DLB-115
Edwards, James [publishing house] DLB-154	Ellis, Edward S. 1840-1916 . . . . DLB-42	Ernest Hemingway's Toronto Journalism Revisited: With Three Previously Unrecorded Stories Y-92
Effinger, George Alec 1947- DLB-8	Ellis, Frederick Staridge [publishing house] DLB-106	
Egerton, George 1859-1945 . . . . . . DLB-135	The George H. Ellis Company DLB-49	Ernst, Paul 1866-1933 . . . . DLB-66, 118
Eggleston, Edward 1837-1902 . . . . . DLB-12	Ellis, Havelock 1859-1939 . . . . DLB-190	Erskine, Albert 1911-1993 . . . . Y-93
Eggleston, Wilfred 1901-1986 . . . . . . DLB-92	Ellison, Harlan 1934- DLB-8	Erskine, John 1879-1951 . . . . DLB-9, 102
Ehrenstein, Albert 1886-1950 . . . . . . DLB-81	Ellison, Ralph Waldo 1914-1994 . . . . DLB-2, 76; Y-94	Ervine, St. John Greer 1883-1971 . . . . DLB-10
Ehrhart, W. D. 1948- DS-9	Ellmann, Richard 1918-1987 . . . . DLB-103; Y-87	Eschenburg, Johann Joachim 1743-c820 . . . DLB-97
Eich, Günter 1907-1972 . . . . . . DLB-69, 124		Escoto, Julio 1944- DLB-145
Eichendorff, Joseph Freiherr von 1788-1857 . . . . DLB-90	The Elmer Holmes Bobst Awards in Arts and Letters Y-87	Eshleman, Clayton 1935- DLB-5
1873 Publishers' Catalogues DLB-49	Elyot, Thomas 1490?-1546 . . . . DLB-136	Espriu, Salvador 1913-1985 . . . . . . DLB-134
Eighteenth-Century Aesthetic Theories DLB-31	Emanuel, James Andrew 1921- DLB-41	Ess Ess Publishing Company DLB-49
Eighteenth-Century Philosophical Background DLB-31	Emecheta, Buchi 1944- DLB-117	Essay on Chatterton (1842), by Robert Browning DLB-32
Eigner, Larry 1927- DLB-5	The Emergence of Black Women Writers DS-8	Essex House Press DLB-112
Eikon Basilike 1649 . . . . DLB-151	Emerson, Ralph Waldo 1803-1882 . . . . . . DLB-1, 59, 73, 183	Estes, Eleanor 1906-1988 . . . . DLB-22
Eilhart von Oberge circa 1140-circa 1195 . . . . DLB-148	Emerson, William 1769-1811 . . . . . . DLB-37	Eszterhas, Joe 1944- DLB-185
Einhard circa 770-840 . . . . DLB-148	Emin, Fedor Aleksandrovich circa 1735-1770 . . . . DLB-150	Estes and Lauriat DLB-49
	Empedocles fifth century B.C. DLB-176	Etherege, George 1636-circa 1692 . . . . DLB-80

395

Ethridge, Mark, Sr. 1896-1981 . . . . . DLB-127
Ets, Marie Hall 1893- DLB-22
Etter, David 1928- DLB-105
Ettner, Johann Christoph
   1654-1724 . . . . DLB-168
Eudora Welty: Eye of the Storyteller Y-87
Eugene O'Neill Memorial Theater
   Center DLB-7
Eugene O'Neill's Letters: A Review. Y-88
Eupolemius
   flourished circa 1095 . . . . DLB-148
Euripides circa 484 B.C.-407/406 B.C.
   . . . . DLB-176
Evans, Caradoc 1878-1945 . . . . DLB-162
Evans, Charles 1850-1935 . . . . DLB-187
Evans, Donald 1884-1921 . . . . DLB-54
Evans, George Henry 1805-1856 . . . . DLB-43
Evans, Hubert 1892-1986 . . . . DLB-92
Evans, Mari 1923- DLB-41
Evans, Mary Ann (see Eliot, George)
Evans, Nathaniel 1742-1767 . . . . DLB-31
Evans, Sebastian 1830-1909 . . . . DLB-35
Evans, M., and Company DLB-46
Everett, Alexander Hill 1790-1847 . . . . DLB-59
Everett, Edward 1794-1865 . . . . . . DLB-1, 59
Everson, R. G. 1903- DLB-88
Everson, William 1912-1994 . . . . . . DLB-5, 16
Every Man His Own Poet; or, The
   Inspired Singer's Recipe Book (1877),
   by W. H. Mallock DLB-35
Ewart, Gavin 1916- DLB-40
Ewing, Juliana Horatia
   1841-1885 . . . . DLB-21, 163
The Examiner 1808-1881 . . . . DLB-110
Exley, Frederick
   1929-1992 . . . . DLB-143; Y-81
Experiment in the Novel (1929),
   by John D. Beresford DLB-36
von Eyb, Albrecht 1420-1475 . . . . . . DLB-179
Eyre and Spottiswoode DLB-106
Ezzo ?-after 1065 . . . . DLB-148

F

"F. Scott Fitzgerald: St. Paul's Native Son
   and Distinguished American Writer":
   University of Minnesota Conference,
   29-31 October 1982 . . . . Y-82
Faber, Frederick William
   1814-1863 . . . . DLB-32
Faber and Faber Limited DLB-112
Faccio, Rena (see Aleramo, Sibilla)
Fagundo, Ana María 1938- DLB-134
Fair, Ronald L. 1932- DLB-33

Fairfax, Beatrice (see Manning, Marie)
Fairlie, Gerard 1899-1983 . . . . DLB-77
Fallada, Hans 1893-1947 . . . . DLB-56
Falsifying Hemingway Y-96
Fancher, Betsy 1928- Y-83
Fane, Violet 1843-1905 . . . . DLB-35
Fanfrolico Press DLB-112
Fanning, Katherine 1927 . . . . DLB-127
Fanshawe, Sir Richard
   1608-1666 . . . . DLB-126
Fantasy Press Publishers DLB-46
Fante, John 1909-1983 . . . . . DLB-130; Y-83
Al-Farabi circa 870-950 . . . . DLB-115
Farah, Nuruddin 1945- DLB-125
Farber, Norma 1909-1984 . . . . DLB-61
Farigoule, Louis (see Romains, Jules)
Farjeon, Eleanor 1881-1965 . . . . . . DLB-160
Farley, Walter 1920-1989 . . . . DLB-22
Farmer, Penelope 1939- DLB-161
Farmer, Philip José 1918- DLB-8
Farquhar, George circa 1677-1707 . . . DLB-84
Farquharson, Martha (see Finley, Martha)
Farrar, Frederic William
   1831-1903 . . . . DLB-163
Farrar and Rinehart DLB-46
Farrar, Straus and Giroux DLB-46
Farrell, James T.
   1904-1979 . . . . DLB-4, 9, 86; DS-2
Farrell, J. G. 1935-1979 . . . . DLB-14
Fast, Howard 1914- DLB-9
Faulkner, William 1897-1962
   . . . . . . DLB-9, 11, 44, 102; DS-2; Y-86
Faulkner, George
   [publishing house] DLB-154
Fauset, Jessie Redmon 1882-1961 . . . DLB-51
Faust, Irvin 1924- DLB-2, 28; Y-80
Fawcett Books DLB-46
Fawcett, Millicent Garrett 1847-1929 . . DLB-190
Fearing, Kenneth 1902-1961 . . . . . . DLB-9
Federal Writers' Project DLB-46
Federman, Raymond 1928- Y-80
Feiffer, Jules 1929- DLB-7, 44
Feinberg, Charles E.
   1899-1988 . . . . DLB-187; Y-88
Feind, Barthold 1678-1721 . . . . DLB-168
Feinstein, Elaine 1930- DLB-14, 40
Feiss, Paul Louis 1875-1952 . . . . . . DLB-187
Feldman, Irving 1928- DLB-169
Felipe, Léon 1884-1968 . . . . DLB-108
Fell, Frederick, Publishers DLB-46
Felltham, Owen 1602?-1668 . . . . DLB-126, 151
Fels, Ludwig 1946- DLB-75

Felton, Cornelius Conway
   1807-1862 . . . . DLB-1
Fenn, Harry 1837-1911 . . . . DLB-188
Fennario, David 1947- DLB-60
Fenno, John 1751-1798 . . . . DLB-43
Fenno, R. F., and Company DLB-49
Fenoglio, Beppe 1922-1963 . . . . . . DLB-177
Fenton, Geoffrey 1539?-1608 . . . . . DLB-136
Fenton, James 1949- DLB-40
Ferber, Edna 1885-1968 . . . . . DLB-9, 28, 86
Ferdinand, Vallery III (see Salaam, Kalamu ya)
Ferguson, Sir Samuel 1810-1886 . . . . DLB-32
Ferguson, William Scott
   1875-1954 . . . . DLB-47
Fergusson, Robert 1750-1774 . . . . . DLB-109
Ferland, Albert 1872-1943 . . . . DLB-92
Ferlinghetti, Lawrence 1919- DLB-5, 16
Fern, Fanny (see Parton, Sara Payson Willis)
Ferrars, Elizabeth 1907- DLB-87
Ferré, Rosario 1942- DLB-145
Ferret, E., and Company DLB-49
Ferrier, Susan 1782-1854 . . . . DLB-116
Ferrini, Vincent 1913- DLB-48
Ferron, Jacques 1921-1985 . . . . DLB-60
Ferron, Madeleine 1922- DLB-53
Fetridge and Company DLB-49
Feuchtersleben, Ernst Freiherr von
   1806-1849 . . . . DLB-133
Feuchtwanger, Lion 1884-1958 . . . . . DLB-66
Feuerbach, Ludwig 1804-1872 . . . . . DLB-133
Fichte, Johann Gottlieb
   1762-1814 . . . . DLB-90
Ficke, Arthur Davison 1883-1945 . . . . DLB-54
Fiction Best-Sellers, 1910-1945 . . . . . . DLB-9
Fiction into Film, 1928-1975: A List of Movies
   Based on the Works of Authors in
   British Novelists, 1930-1959 . . . . . DLB-15
Fiedler, Leslie A. 1917- DLB-28, 67
Field, Edward 1924- DLB-105
Field, Edward, The Poetry File DLB-105
Field, Eugene
   1850-1895 . . . . . . DLB-23, 42, 140; DS-13
Field, John 1545?-1588 . . . . DLB-167
Field, Marshall, III 1893-1956 . . . . . DLB-127
Field, Marshall, IV 1916-1965 . . . . . DLB-127
Field, Marshall, V 1941- DLB-127
Field, Nathan 1587-1619 or 1620 . . . . DLB-58
Field, Rachel 1894-1942 . . . . DLB-9, 22
A Field Guide to Recent Schools of American
   Poetry Y-86
Fielding, Henry
   1707-1754 . . . . DLB-39, 84, 101
Fielding, Sarah 1710-1768 . . . . DLB-39

Fields, James Thomas 1817-1881 . . . . . DLB-1	Fitzgerald, Robert 1910-1985. . . . . Y-80	Foote, Samuel 1721-1777 . . . . DLB-89
Fields, Julia 1938- DLB-41	Fitzgerald, Thomas 1819-1891 . . . . . . DLB-23	Foote, Shelby 1916- DLB-2, 17
Fields, W. C. 1880-1946 . . . . DLB-44	Fitzgerald, Zelda Sayre 1900-1948 . . . . . . Y-84	Forbes, Calvin 1945- DLB-41
Fields, Osgood and Company DLB-49	Fitzhugh, Louise 1928-1974 . . . . DLB-52	Forbes, Ester 1891-1967 . . . . DLB-22
Fifty Penguin Years Y-85	Fitzhugh, William circa 1651-1701 . . . . DLB-24	Forbes and Company DLB-49
Figes, Eva 1932- DLB-14	Flagg, James Montgomery 1877-1960. . DLB-188	Force, Peter 1790-1868 . . . . DLB-30
Figuera, Angela 1902-1984 . . . . DLB-108	Flanagan, Thomas 1923- Y-80	Forché, Carolyn 1950- DLB-5
Filmer, Sir Robert 1586-1653 . . . . . . DLB-151	Flanner, Hildegarde 1899-1987 . . . . . . DLB-48	Ford, Charles Henri 1913- DLB-4, 48
Filson, John circa 1753-1788 . . . . DLB-37	Flanner, Janet 1892-1978 . . . . DLB-4	Ford, Corey 1902-1969 . . . . DLB-11
Finch, Anne, Countess of Winchilsea 1661-1720 . . . . DLB-95	Flaubert, Gustave 1821-1880 . . . . . . DLB-119	Ford, Ford Madox 1873-1939 . . . . DLB-34, 98, 162
Finch, Robert 1900- DLB-88	Flavin, Martin 1883-1967 . . . . DLB-9	Ford, Jesse Hill 1928- DLB-6
Findley, Timothy 1930- DLB-53	Fleck, Konrad (flourished circa 1220) DLB-138	Ford, John 1586-? DLB-58
Finlay, Ian Hamilton 1925- DLB-40	Flecker, James Elroy 1884-1915 . . . DLB-10, 19	Ford, R. A. D. 1915- DLB-88
Finley, Martha 1828-1909 . . . . DLB-42	Fleeson, Doris 1901-1970 . . . . DLB-29	Ford, Worthington C. 1858-1941 . . . . DLB-47
Finn, Elizabeth Anne (McCaul) 1825-1921 . . . . DLB-166	Fleißer, Marieluise 1901-1974 . . . . DLB-56, 124	Ford, J. B., and Company DLB-49
Finney, Jack 1911- DLB-8	Fleming, Ian 1908-1964 . . . . DLB-87	Fords, Howard, and Hulbert DLB-49
Finney, Walter Braden (see Finney, Jack)	Fleming, Paul 1609-1640 . . . . DLB-164	Foreman, Carl 1914-1984 . . . . DLB-26
Firbank, Ronald 1886-1926 . . . . DLB-36	The Fleshly School of Poetry and Other Phenomena of the Day (1872), by Robert Buchanan DLB-35	Forester, Frank (see Herbert, Henry William)
Firmin, Giles 1615-1697 . . . . DLB-24		Forman, Harry Buxton 1842-1917 . . . DLB-184
Fischart, Johann 1546 or 1547-1590 or 1591 . . . . DLB-179	The Fleshly School of Poetry: Mr. D. G. Rossetti (1871), by Thomas Maitland (Robert Buchanan) DLB-35	Fornés, María Irene 1930- DLB-7
First Edition Library/Collectors' Reprints, Inc Y-91		Forrest, Leon 1937- DLB-33
First International F. Scott Fitzgerald Conference Y-92	Fletcher, Giles, the Elder 1546-1611 . . . . DLB-136	Forster, E. M. 1879-1970 . . . DLB-34, 98, 162, 178; DS-10
First Strauss "Livings" Awarded to Cynthia Ozick and Raymond Carver An Interview with Cynthia Ozick An Interview with Raymond Carver Y-83	Fletcher, Giles, the Younger 1585 or 1586-1623 . . . . DLB-121	Forster, Georg 1754-1794 . . . . DLB-94
	Fletcher, J. S. 1863-1935 . . . . DLB-70	Forster, John 1812-1876 . . . . DLB-144
	Fletcher, John (see Beaumont, Francis)	Forster, Margaret 1938- DLB-155
	Fletcher, John Gould 1886-1950 . . . DLB-4, 45	Forsyth, Frederick 1938- DLB-87
Fischer, Karoline Auguste Fernandine 1764-1842 . . . . DLB-94	Fletcher, Phineas 1582-1650 . . . . . . DLB-121	Forten, Charlotte L. 1837-1914 . . . . . . DLB-50
Fish, Stanley 1938- DLB-67	Flieg, Helmut (see Heym, Stefan)	Fortini, Franco 1917- DLB-128
Fishacre, Richard 1205-1248 . . . . . . DLB-115	Flint, F. S. 1885-1960 . . . . DLB-19	Fortune, T. Thomas 1856-1928 . . . . . DLB-23
Fisher, Clay (see Allen, Henry W.)	Flint, Timothy 1780-1840 . . . . . . DLB-73, 186	Fosdick, Charles Austin 1842-1915 . . . . DLB-42
Fisher, Dorothy Canfield 1879-1958 . . . . DLB-9, 102	Florio, John 1553?-1625 . . . . DLB-172	Foster, Genevieve 1893-1979 . . . . DLB-61
Fisher, Leonard Everett 1924- DLB-61	Foix, J. V. 1893-1987 . . . . DLB-134	Foster, Hannah Webster 1758-1840 . . . . DLB-37
Fisher, Roy 1930- DLB-40	Foley, Martha (see Burnett, Whit, and Martha Foley)	
Fisher, Rudolph 1897-1934 . . . . . DLB-51, 102		Foster, John 1648-1681 . . . . DLB-24
Fisher, Sydney George 1856-1927 . . . . DLB-47	Folger, Henry Clay 1857-1930 . . . . . DLB-140	Foster, Michael 1904-1956 . . . . DLB-9
Fisher, Vardis 1895-1968 . . . . DLB-9	Folio Society DLB-112	Foster, Myles Birket 1825-1899 . . . . . DLB-184
Fiske, John 1608-1677 . . . . DLB-24	Follen, Eliza Lee (Cabot) 1787-1860 . . . DLB-1	Foulis, Robert and Andrew / R. and A. [publishing house] DLB-154
Fiske, John 1842-1901 . . . . DLB-47, 64	Follett, Ken 1949- Y-81, DLB-87	
Fitch, Thomas circa 1700-1774 . . . . . . DLB-31	Follett Publishing Company DLB-46	Fouqué, Caroline de la Motte 1774-1831 . . . . DLB-90
Fitch, William Clyde 1865-1909 . . . . . . DLB-7	Folsom, John West [publishing house] DLB-49	
FitzGerald, Edward 1809-1883 . . . . . . DLB-32		Fouqué, Friedrich de la Motte 1777-1843 . . . . DLB-90
Fitzgerald, F. Scott 1896-1940 . . . . . DLB-4, 9, 86; Y-81; DS-1, 15, 16	Folz, Hans between 1435 and 1440-1513 . . . DLB-179	Four Essays on the Beat Generation, by John Clellon Holmes DLB-16
	Fontane, Theodor 1819-1898 . . . . . . DLB-129	Four Seas Company DLB-46
F. Scott Fitzgerald Centenary Celebrations Y-96	Fonvisin, Denis Ivanovich 1744 or 1745-1792 . . . . DLB-150	Four Winds Press DLB-46
		Fournier, Henri Alban (see Alain-Fournier)
Fitzgerald, Penelope 1916- DLB-14	Foote, Horton 1916- DLB-26	Fowler and Wells Company DLB-49
		Fowles, John 1926- DLB-14, 139
	Foote, Mary Hallock 1847-1938 . . DLB-186, 188	Fox, John, Jr. 1862 or 1863-1919 DLB-9; DS-13

397

Fox, Paula 1923- DLB-52	Samuel French, Limited DLB-106	Furness, Horace Howard 1833-1912 .... DLB-64
Fox, Richard Kyle 1846-1922 ..... DLB-79	Freneau, Philip 1752-1832 ...... DLB-37, 43	Furness, William Henry 1802-1896 .... DLB-1
Fox, William Price 1926- DLB-2; Y-81	Freni, Melo 1934- DLB-128	Furnivall, Frederick James 1825-1910 .... DLB-184
Fox, Richard K. [publishing house]........... DLB-49	Freshfield, Douglas W. 1845-1934 .... DLB-174	Furthman, Jules 1888-1966 .... DLB-26
Foxe, John 1517-1587 .... DLB-132	Freytag, Gustav 1816-1895 ...... DLB-129	Furui, Yoshikichi 1937- DLB-182
Fraenkel, Michael 1896-1957....... DLB-4	Fried, Erich 1921-1988 .... DLB-85	Futabatei, Shimei (Hasegawa Tatsunosuke) 1864-1909 .... DLB-180
France, Anatole 1844-1924 .... DLB-123	Friedman, Bruce Jay 1930- DLB-2, 28	The Future of the Novel (1899), by Henry James DLB-18
France, Richard 1938- DLB-7	Friedrich von Hausen circa 1171-1190 .... DLB-138	
Francis, Convers 1795-1863 .... DLB-1	Friel, Brian 1929- DLB-13	Fyleman, Rose 1877-1957 .... DLB-160
Francis, Dick 1920- DLB-87	Friend, Krebs 1895?-1967?......... DLB-4	
Francis, Jeffrey, Lord 1773-1850 .... DLB-107	Fries, Fritz Rudolf 1935- DLB-75	**G**
Francis, C. S. [publishing house]..... DLB-49	Fringe and Alternative Theater in Great Britain........... DLB-13	
François 1863-1910 .... DLB-92	Frisch, Max 1911-1991 .... DLB-69, 124	The G. Ross Roy Scottish Poetry Collection at the University of South Carolina Y-89
François, Louise von 1817-1893 ... DLB-129	Frischlin, Nicodemus 1547-1590..... DLB-179	
Franck, Sebastian 1499-1542...... DLB-179	Frischmuth, Barbara 1941- DLB-85	Gadda, Carlo Emilio 1893-1973 .... DLB-177
Francke, Kuno 1855-1930......... DLB-71	Fritz, Jean 1915- DLB-52	Gaddis, William 1922- DLB-2
Frank, Bruno 1887-1945......... DLB-118	Fromentin, Eugene 1820-1876...... DLB-123	Gág, Wanda 1893-1946.......... DLB-22
Frank, Leonhard 1882-1961..... DLB-56, 118	From *The Gay Science,* by E. S. Dallas DLB-21	Gagnon, Madeleine 1938- DLB-60
Frank, Melvin (see Panama, Norman)		Gaine, Hugh 1726-1807.......... DLB-43
Frank, Waldo 1889-1967 .... DLB-9, 63	Frost, A. B. 1851-1928 ..... DLB-188; DS-13	Gaine, Hugh [publishing house] DLB-49
Franken, Rose 1895?-1988 .... Y-84	Frost, Robert 1874-1963 ...... DLB-54; DS-7	Gaines, Ernest J. 1933- DLB-2, 33, 152; Y-80
Franklin, Benjamin 1706-1790....... DLB-24, 43, 73, 183	Frothingham, Octavius Brooks 1822-1895................ DLB-1	Gaiser, Gerd 1908-1976.......... DLB-69
Franklin, James 1697-1735 .... DLB-43	Froude, James Anthony 1818-1894 .... DLB-18, 57, 144	Galarza, Ernesto 1905-1984 .... DLB-122
Franklin Library............... DLB-46	Fry, Christopher 1907- DLB-13	Galaxy Science Fiction Novels DLB-46
Frantz, Ralph Jules 1902-1979....... DLB-4	Fry, Roger 1866-1934............ DS-10	Gale, Zona 1874-1938.......... DLB-9, 78
Franzos, Karl Emil 1848-1904...... DLB-129	Frye, Northrop 1912-1991 ...... DLB-67, 68	Galen of Pergamon 129-after 210 ... DLB-176
Fraser, G. S. 1915-1980.......... DLB-27	Fuchs, Daniel 1909-1993......... DLB-9, 26, 28; Y-93	Gall, Louise von 1815-1855....... DLB-133
Fraser, Kathleen 1935- DLB-169		Gallagher, Tess 1943- DLB-120
Frattini, Alberto 1922-........... DLB-128	Fuentes, Carlos 1928- DLB-113	Gallagher, Wes 1911- DLB-127
Frau Ava ?-1127.............. DLB-148	Fuertes, Gloria 1918- DLB-108	Gallagher, William Davis 1808-1894 .... DLB-73
Frayn, Michael 1933- DLB-13, 14	The Fugitives and the Agrarians: The First Exhibition Y-85	
Frederic, Harold 1856-1898......... DLB-12, 23; DS-13	Fulbecke, William 1560-1603?...... DLB-172	Gallant, Mavis 1922- DLB-53
Freeling, Nicolas 1927- DLB-87	Fuller, Charles H., Jr. 1939- DLB-38	Gallico, Paul 1897-1976 .... DLB-9, 171
Freeman, Douglas Southall 1886-1953 .... DLB-17	Fuller, Henry Blake 1857-1929...... DLB-12	Gallup, Donald 1913- DLB-187
Freeman, Legh Richmond 1842-1915 .... DLB-23	Fuller, John 1937- DLB-40	Galsworthy, John 1867-1933 ... DLB-10, 34, 98, 162; DS-16
Freeman, Mary E. Wilkins 1852-1930................ DLB-12, 78	Fuller, Margaret (see Fuller, Sarah Margaret, Marchesa D'Ossoli)	Galt, John 1779-1839 .... DLB-99, 116
Freeman, R. Austin 1862-1943...... DLB-70	Fuller, Roy 1912-1991 .... DLB-15, 20	Galton, Sir Francis 1822-1911...... DLB-166
Freidank circa 1176-circa 1233 ..... DLB-138	Fuller, Samuel 1912- DLB-26	Galvin, Brendan 1938- DLB-5
Freiligrath, Ferdinand 1810-1876 .... DLB-133	Fuller, Sarah Margaret, Marchesa D'Ossoli 1810-1850 ... DLB-1, 59, 73, 183	Gambit DLB-46
Frémont, John Charles 1813-1890 ... DLB-186		Gamboa, Reymundo 1948- DLB-122
Frémont, John Charles 1813-1890 and Frémont, Jessie Benton 1834-1902 .... DLB-183	Fuller, Thomas 1608-1661........ DLB-151	*Gammer Gurton's Needle*............. DLB-62
	Fullerton, Hugh 1873-1945 ...... DLB-171	Gannett, Frank E. 1876-1957 .... DLB-29
	Fulton, Len 1934- Y-86	Gaos, Vicente 1919-1980 .... DLB-134
French, Alice 1850-1934 ..... DLB-74; DS-13	Fulton, Robin 1937- DLB-40	García, Lionel G. 1935- DLB-82
French, David 1939- DLB-53	Furbank, P. N. 1920- DLB-155	García Lorca, Federico 1898-1936 .... DLB-108
French, James [publishing house]..... DLB-49	Furman, Laura 1945- Y-86	
French, Samuel [publishing house]... DLB-49		

García Márquez, Gabriel 1928- DLB-113
Gardam, Jane 1928- DLB-14, 161
Garden, Alexander circa 1685-1756 .... DLB-31
Gardiner, Margaret Power Farmer (see Blessington, Marguerite, Countess of)
Gardner, John 1933-1982 ...... DLB-2; Y-82
Garfield, Leon 1921- DLB-161
Garis, Howard R. 1873-1962 .... DLB-22
Garland, Hamlin 1860-1940 .... DLB-12, 71, 78, 186
Garneau, Francis-Xavier 1809-1866 .... DLB-99
Garneau, Hector de Saint-Denys 1912-1943 .... DLB-88
Garneau, Michel 1939- DLB-53
Garner, Alan 1934- DLB-161
Garner, Hugh 1913-1979 .... DLB-68
Garnett, David 1892-1981 .... DLB-34
Garnett, Eve 1900-1991 .... DLB-160
Garnett, Richard 1835-1906 .... DLB-184
Garrard, Lewis H. 1829-1887 .... DLB-186
Garraty, John A. 1920- DLB-17
Garrett, George 1929- DLB-2, 5, 130, 152; Y-83
Garrett, John Work 1872-1942 ..... DLB-187
Garrick, David 1717-1779 .... DLB-84
Garrison, William Lloyd 1805-1879 .... DLB-1, 43
Garro, Elena 1920- DLB-145
Garth, Samuel 1661-1719 .... DLB-95
Garve, Andrew 1908- DLB-87
Gary, Romain 1914-1980 .... DLB-83
Gascoigne, George 1539?-1577 ..... DLB-136
Gascoyne, David 1916- DLB-20
Gaskell, Elizabeth Cleghorn 1810-1865 .... DLB-21, 144, 159
Gaspey, Thomas 1788-1871 .... DLB-116
Gass, William Howard 1924- DLB-2
Gates, Doris 1901- DLB-22
Gates, Henry Louis, Jr. 1950- DLB-67
Gates, Lewis E. 1860-1924 .... DLB-71
Gatto, Alfonso 1909-1976 .... DLB-114
Gaunt, Mary 1861-1942 .... DLB-174
Gautier, Théophile 1811-1872 ..... DLB-119
Gauvreau, Claude 1925-1971 ...... DLB 88
The *Gawain*-Poet flourished circa 1350-1400 .... DLB-146
Gay, Ebenezer 1696-1787 .... DLB-24
Gay, John 1685-1732 .... DLB-84, 95
The Gay Science (1866), by E. S. Dallas [excerpt] DLB-21
Gayarré, Charles E. A. 1805-1895 .... DLB-30

Gaylord, Edward King 1873-1974 .... DLB-127
Gaylord, Edward Lewis 1919- DLB-127
Gaylord, Charles [publishing house] DLB-49
Geddes, Gary 1940- DLB-60
Geddes, Virgil 1897- DLB-4
Gedeon (Georgii Andreevich Krinovsky) circa 1730-1763 .... DLB-150
Geibel, Emanuel 1815-1884 ...... DLB-129
Geiogamah, Hanay 1945- DLB-175
Geis, Bernard, Associates DLB-46
Geisel, Theodor Seuss 1904-1991 .... DLB-61; Y-91
Gelb, Arthur 1924- DLB-103
Gelb, Barbara 1926- DLB-103
Gelber, Jack 1932- DLB-7
Gelinas, Gratien 1909- DLB-88
Gellert, Christian Füerchtegott 1715-1769 .... DLB-97
Gellhorn, Martha 1908- Y-82
Gems, Pam 1925- DLB-13
A General Idea of the College of Mirania (1753), by William Smith [excerpts] DLB-31
Genet, Jean 1910-1986 .... DLB-72; Y-86
Genevoix, Maurice 1890-1980 ..... DLB-65
Genovese, Eugene D. 1930- DLB-17
Gent, Peter 1942- Y-82
Geoffrey of Monmouth circa 1100-1155 .... DLB-146
George, Henry 1839-1897 .... DLB-23
George, Jean Craighead 1919- DLB-52
Georgslied 896? DLB-148
Gerhardie, William 1895-1977 ...... DLB-36
Gerhardt, Paul 1607-1676 .... DLB-164
Gérin, Winifred 1901-1981 ...... DLB-155
Gérin-Lajoie, Antoine 1824-1882 ... DLB-99
German Drama 800-1280 .... DLB-138
German Drama from Naturalism to Fascism: 1889-1933 ...... DLB-118
German Literature and Culture from Charlemagne to the Early Courtly Period DLB-148
German Radio Play, The DLB-124
German Transformation from the Baroque to the Enlightenment, The DLB-97
The Germanic Epic and Old English Heroic Poetry: *Widseth*, *Waldere*, and *The Fight at Finnsburg* DLB-146
Germanophilism, by Hans Kohn DLB-66
Gernsback, Hugo 1884-1967 ..... DLB-8, 137
Gerould, Katharine Fullerton 1879-1944 .... DLB-78
Gerrish, Samuel [publishing house] ... DLB-49
Gerrold, David 1944- DLB-8

The Ira Gershwin Centenary Y-96
Gersonides 1288-1344 .... DLB-115
Gerstäcker, Friedrich 1816-1872 .... DLB-129
Gerstenberg, Heinrich Wilhelm von 1737-1823 .... DLB-97
Gervinus, Georg Gottfried 1805-1871 .... DLB-133
Geßner, Salomon 1730-1788 .... DLB-97
Geston, Mark S. 1946- DLB-8
Al-Ghazali 1058-1111 .... DLB-115
Gibbon, Edward 1737-1794 .... DLB-104
Gibbon, John Murray 1875-1952 .... DLB-92
Gibbon, Lewis Grassic (see Mitchell, James Leslie)
Gibbons, Floyd 1887-1939 .... DLB-25
Gibbons, Reginald 1947- DLB-120
Gibbons, William ?-? DLB-73
Gibson, Charles Dana 1867-1944 .... DS-13
Gibson, Charles Dana 1867-1944 .... DLB-188; DS-13
Gibson, Graeme 1934- DLB-53
Gibson, Margaret 1944- DLB-120
Gibson, Margaret Dunlop 1843-1920 .... DLB-174
Gibson, Wilfrid 1878-1962 .... DLB-19
Gibson, William 1914- DLB-7
Gide, André 1869-1951 .... DLB-65
Giguère, Diane 1937- DLB-53
Giguère, Roland 1929- DLB-60
Gil de Biedma, Jaime 1929-1990 .... DLB-108
Gil-Albert, Juan 1906- DLB-134
Gilbert, Anthony 1899-1973 ...... DLB-77
Gilbert, Michael 1912- DLB-87
Gilbert, Sandra M. 1936- DLB-120
Gilbert, Sir Humphrey 1537-1583 .... DLB-136
Gilchrist, Alexander 1828-1861 .... DLB-144
Gilchrist, Ellen 1935- DLB-130
Gilder, Jeannette L. 1849-1916 ..... DLB-79
Gilder, Richard Watson 1844-1909 .... DLB-64, 79
Gildersleeve, Basil 1831-1924 ...... DLB-71
Giles, Henry 1809-1882 .... DLB-64
Giles of Rome circa 1243-1316 ..... DLB-115
Gilfillan, George 1813-1878 ...... DLB-144
Gill, Eric 1882-1940 .... DLB-98
Gill, William F., Company DLB-49
Gillespie, A. Lincoln, Jr. 1895-1950 .... DLB-4
Gilliam, Florence ?-? DLB-4
Gilliatt, Penelope 1932-1993 ...... DLB-14
Gillott, Jacky 1939-1980 .... DLB-14

Gilman, Caroline H. 1794-1888.... DLB-3, 73

Gilman, W. and J.
[publishing house]............. DLB-49

Gilmer, Elizabeth Meriwether
1861-1951 .... DLB-29

Gilmer, Francis Walker
1790-1826 .... DLB-37

Gilroy, Frank D. 1925- DLB-7

Gimferrer, Pere (Pedro) 1945- DLB-134

Gingrich, Arnold 1903-1976....... DLB-137

Ginsberg, Allen 1926- DLB-5, 16, 169

Ginzburg, Natalia 1916-1991 ...... DLB-177

Ginzkey, Franz Karl 1871-1963 ..... DLB-81

Gioia, Dana 1950- DLB-120

Giono, Jean 1895-1970 .... DLB-72

Giotti, Virgilio 1885-1957 .... DLB-114

Giovanni, Nikki 1943- DLB-5, 41

Gipson, Lawrence Henry
1880-1971 .... DLB-17

Girard, Rodolphe 1879-1956 ...... DLB-92

Giraudoux, Jean 1882-1944 .... DLB-65

Gissing, George 1857-1903 .. DLB-18, 135, 184

Giudici, Giovanni 1924-.......... DLB-128

Giuliani, Alfredo 1924- DLB-128

Glackens, William J. 1870-1938..... DLB-188

Gladstone, William Ewart
1809-1898 .... DLB-57, 184

Glaeser, Ernst 1902-1963 .... DLB-69

Glancy, Diane 1941- DLB-175

Glanville, Brian 1931- DLB-15, 139

Glapthorne, Henry 1610-1643?..... DLB-58

Glasgow, Ellen 1873-1945 .... DLB-9, 12

Glasier, Katharine Bruce 1867-1950 .. DLB-190

Glaspell, Susan 1876-1948 ..... DLB-7, 9, 78

Glass, Montague 1877-1934 ...... DLB-11

The Glass Key and Other Dashiell Hammett
Mysteries Y-96

Glassco, John 1909-1981 .... DLB-68

Glauser, Friedrich 1896-1938...... DLB-56

F. Gleason's Publishing Hall DLB-49

Gleim, Johann Wilhelm Ludwig
1719-1803 .... DLB-97

Glendinning, Victoria 1937- DLB-155

Glover, Richard 1712-1785........ DLB-95

Glück, Louise 1943- DLB-5

Glyn, Elinor 1864-1943 .... DLB-153

Gobineau, Joseph-Arthur de
1816-1882 .... DLB-123

Godbout, Jacques 1933- DLB-53

Goddard, Morrill 1865-1937 ...... DLB-25

Goddard, William 1740-1817...... DLB-43

Godden, Rumer 1907- DLB-161

Godey, Louis A. 1804-1878 .... DLB-73

Godey and McMichael.......... DLB-49

Godfrey, Dave 1938- DLB-60

Godfrey, Thomas 1736-1763....... DLB-31

Godine, David R., Publisher....... DLB-46

Godkin, E. L. 1831-1902......... DLB-79

Godolphin, Sidney 1610-1643 ..... DLB-126

Godwin, Gail 1937- DLB-6

Godwin, Mary Jane Clairmont
1766-1841 .... DLB-163

Godwin, Parke 1816-1904....... DLB-3, 64

Godwin, William
1756-1836.... DLB-39, 104, 142, 158, 163

Godwin, M. J., and Company DLB-154

Goering, Reinhard 1887-1936...... DLB-118

Goes, Albrecht 1908- DLB-69

Goethe, Johann Wolfgang von
1749-1832 .... DLB-94

Goetz, Curt 1888-1960 .... DLB-124

Goffe, Thomas circa 1592-1629 ..... DLB-58

Goffstein, M. B. 1940- DLB-61

Gogarty, Oliver St. John
1878-1957 .... DLB-15, 19

Goines, Donald 1937-1974 .... DLB-33

Gold, Herbert 1924- DLB-2; Y-81

Gold, Michael 1893-1967 .... DLB-9, 28

Goldbarth, Albert 1948- DLB-120

Goldberg, Dick 1947- DLB-7

Golden Cockerel Press DLB-112

Golding, Arthur 1536-1606 ...... DLB-136

Golding, William 1911-1993 .... DLB-15, 100

Goldman, William 1931- DLB-44

Goldsmith, Oliver
1730?-1774.... DLB-39, 89, 104, 109, 142

Goldsmith, Oliver 1794-1861....... DLB-99

Goldsmith Publishing Company DLB-46

Goldstein, Richard 1944- DLB-185

Gollancz, Victor, Limited DLB-112

Gómez-Quiñones, Juan 1942- DLB-122

Gomme, Laurence James
[publishing house]............ DLB-46

Goncourt, Edmond de 1822-1896 ... DLB-123

Goncourt, Jules de 1830-1870...... DLB-123

Gonzales, Rodolfo "Corky"
1928- DLB-122

González, Angel 1925- DLB-108

Gonzalez, Genaro 1949- DLB-122

Gonzalez, Ray 1952- DLB-122

González de Mireles, Jovita
1899-1983 .... DLB-122

González-T., César A. 1931- DLB-82

Goodbye, Gutenberg? A Lecture at
the New York Public Library,
18 April 1995 .... Y-95

Goodison, Lorna 1947- DLB-157

Goodman, Paul 1911-1972 .... DLB-130

The Goodman Theatre DLB-7

Goodrich, Frances 1891-1984 and
Hackett, Albert 1900- DLB-26

Goodrich, Samuel Griswold
1793-1860 .... DLB-1, 42, 73

Goodrich, S. G. [publishing house] ... DLB-49

Goodspeed, C. E., and Company.... DLB-49

Goodwin, Stephen 1943- Y-82

Googe, Barnabe 1540-1594 ...... DLB-132

Gookin, Daniel 1612-1687 .... DLB-24

Gordon, Caroline
1895-1981........ DLB-4, 9, 102; Y-81

Gordon, Giles 1940- DLB-14, 139

Gordon, Lyndall 1941- DLB-155

Gordon, Mary 1949- DLB-6; Y-81

Gordone, Charles 1925- DLB-7

Gore, Catherine 1800-1861 ...... DLB-116

Gorey, Edward 1925- DLB-61

Gorgias of Leontini circa 485 B.C.-376 B.C.
.... DLB-176

Görres, Joseph 1776-1848......... DLB-90

Gosse, Edmund 1849-1928 .. DLB-57, 144, 184

Gosson, Stephen 1554-1624 ...... DLB-172

Gotlieb, Phyllis 1926- DLB-88

Gottfried von Straßburg
died before 1230 .... DLB-138

Gotthelf, Jeremias 1797-1854 ...... DLB-133

Gottschalk circa 804/808-869 ...... DLB-148

Gottsched, Johann Christoph
1700-1766 .... DLB-97

Götz, Johann Nikolaus
1721-1781 .... DLB-97

Gould, Wallace 1882-1940 .... DLB-54

Govoni, Corrado 1884-1965....... DLB-114

Gower, John circa 1330-1408 ...... DLB-146

Goyen, William 1915-1983 ..... DLB-2; Y-83

Goytisolo, José Augustín 1928- DLB-134

Gozzano, Guido 1883-1916 ...... DLB-114

Grabbe, Christian Dietrich
1801-1836 .... DLB-133

Gracq, Julien 1910- DLB-83

Grady, Henry W. 1850-1889....... DLB-23

Graf, Oskar Maria 1894-1967 ..... DLB-56

Graf Rudolf between circa 1170
and circa 1185............. DLB-148

Grafton, Richard
[publishing house].......... DLB-170

Graham, George Rex
1813-1894 .... DLB-73

Graham, Gwethalyn 1913-1965..... DLB-88

Graham, Jorie 1951- DLB-120

Graham, Katharine 1917- DLB-127

Graham, Lorenz 1902-1989 . . . . DLB-76	Greenaway, Kate 1846-1901 . . . . . . DLB-141	Griggs, S. C., and Company DLB-49
Graham, Philip 1915-1963 . . . . DLB-127	Greenberg: Publisher DLB-46	Griggs, Sutton Elbert 1872-1930 . . . . DLB-50
Graham, R. B. Cunninghame 1852-1936 . . . . DLB-98, 135, 174	Green Tiger Press DLB-46	Grignon, Claude-Henri 1894-1976 . . . . DLB-68
Graham, Shirley 1896-1977 . . . . DLB-76	Greene, Asa 1789-1838 . . . . DLB-11	Grigson, Geoffrey 1905- DLB-27
Graham, W. S. 1918- DLB-20	Greene, Belle da Costa 1883-1950 . . . DLB-187	Grillparzer, Franz 1791-1872 . . . . . DLB-133
Graham, William H. [publishing house] DLB-49	Greene, Benjamin H. [publishing house] DLB-49	Grimald, Nicholas circa 1519-circa 1562 . . . . DLB-136
Graham, Winston 1910- DLB-77	Greene, Graham 1904-1991 . . . DLB-13, 15, 77, 100, 162; Y-85, Y-91	Grimké, Angelina Weld 1880-1958 . . . . DLB-50, 54
Grahame, Kenneth 1859-1932 . . . . DLB-34, 141, 178	Greene, Robert 1558-1592 . . . . . DLB-62, 167	Grimm, Hans 1875-1959 . . . . DLB-66
Grainger, Martin Allerdale 1874-1941 . . . . DLB-92	Greene Jr., Robert Bernard (Bob) 1947- DLB-185	Grimm, Jacob 1785-1863 . . . . DLB-90
Gramatky, Hardie 1907-1979 . . . . . . DLB-22	Greenhow, Robert 1800-1854 . . . . . DLB-30	Grimm, Wilhelm 1786-1859 . . . . . . DLB-90
Grand, Sarah 1854-1943 . . . . DLB-135	Greenlee, William B. 1872-1953 . . . . DLB-187	Grimmelshausen, Johann Jacob Christoffel von 1621 or 1622-1676 . . . . DLB-168
Grandbois, Alain 1900-1975 . . . . . . DLB-92	Greenough, Horatio 1805-1852 . . . . . DLB-1	Grimshaw, Beatrice Ethel 1871-1953 . . . . DLB-174
Grange, John circa 1556-? DLB-136	Greenwell, Dora 1821-1882 . . . . DLB-35	Grindal, Edmund 1519 or 1520-1583 . . . . DLB-132
Granich, Irwin (see Gold, Michael)	Greenwillow Books DLB-46	Griswold, Rufus Wilmot 1815-1857 . . . . DLB-3, 59
Grant, Duncan 1885-1978 . . . . DS-10	Greenwood, Grace (see Lippincott, Sara Jane Clarke)	Grosart, Alexander Balloch 1827-1899 . . . . DLB-184
Grant, George 1918-1988 . . . . DLB-88	Greenwood, Walter 1903-1974 . . . . . DLB-10	Gross, Milt 1895-1953 . . . . DLB-11
Grant, George Monro 1835-1902 . . . . DLB-99	Greer, Ben 1948- DLB-6	Grosset and Dunlap DLB-49
Grant, Harry J. 1881-1963 . . . . DLB-29	Greflinger, Georg 1620?-1677 . . . . . DLB-164	Grossman Publishers DLB-46
Grant, James Edward 1905-1966 . . . . DLB-26	Greg, W. R. 1809-1881 . . . . DLB-55	Grosseteste, Robert circa 1160-1253 . . . . DLB-115
Grass, Günter 1927- DLB-75, 124	Gregg, Josiah 1806-1850 . . . . . . DLB-183, 186	Grosvenor, Gilbert H. 1875-1966 . . . . DLB-91
Grasty, Charles H. 1863-1924 . . . . . DLB-25	Gregg Press DLB-46	Groth, Klaus 1819-1899 . . . . DLB-129
Grau, Shirley Ann 1929- DLB-2	Gregory, Isabella Augusta Persse, Lady 1852-1932 . . . . DLB-10	Groulx, Lionel 1878-1967 . . . . DLB-68
Graves, John 1920- Y-83	Gregory, Horace 1898-1982 . . . . . . DLB-48	Grove, Frederick Philip 1879-1949 . . . . DLB-92
Graves, Richard 1715-1804 . . . . DLB-39	Gregory of Rimini circa 1300-1358 . . . . DLB-115	Grove Press DLB-46
Graves, Robert 1895-1985 . . . . DLB-20, 100; Y-85	Gregynog Press DLB-112	Grubb, Davis 1919-1980 . . . . DLB-6
Gray, Asa 1810-1888 . . . . DLB-1	Greiffenberg, Catharina Regina von 1633-1694 . . . . DLB-168	Gruelle, Johnny 1880-1938 . . . . DLB-22
Gray, David 1838-1861 . . . . DLB-32	Grenfell, Wilfred Thomason 1865-1940 . . . . DLB-92	von Grumbach, Argula 1492-after 1563? DLB-179
Gray, Simon 1936- DLB-13	Greve, Felix Paul (see Grove, Frederick Philip)	Grymeston, Elizabeth before 1563-before 1604 . . . . . . DLB-136
Gray, Thomas 1716-1771 . . . . DLB-109	Greville, Fulke, First Lord Brooke 1554-1628 . . . . DLB-62, 172	Gryphius, Andreas 1616-1664 . . . . . DLB-164
Grayson, William J. 1788-1863 . . . . DLB-3, 64	Grey, Sir George, K.C.B. 1812-1898 . . . . DLB-184	Gryphius, Christian 1649-1706 . . . . . DLB-168
The Great Bibliographers Series Y-93	Grey, Lady Jane 1537-1554 . . . . . . DLB-132	Guare, John 1938- DLB-7
The Great War and the Theater, 1914-1918 [Great Britain] DLB-10	Grey Owl 1888-1938 . . . . DLB-92	Guerra, Tonino 1920- DLB-128
Greeley, Horace 1811-1872 . . . DLB-3, 43, 189	Grey, Zane 1872-1939 . . . . DLB-9	Guest, Barbara 1920- DLB-5
Green, Adolph (see Comden, Betty)	Grey Walls Press DLB-112	Guèvremont, Germaine 1893-1968 . . . . DLB-68
Green, Duff 1791-1875 . . . . DLB-43	Grier, Eldon 1917- DLB-88	Guidacci, Margherita 1921-1992 . . . . DLB-128
Green, Elizabeth Shippen 1871-1954 . . DLB-188	Grieve, C. M. (see MacDiarmid, Hugh)	Guide to the Archives of Publishers, Journals, and Literary Agents in North American Libraries Y-93
Green, Gerald 1922- DLB-28	Griffin, Bartholomew flourished 1596 . . . . DLB-172	
Green, Henry 1905-1973 . . . . DLB-15	Griffin, Gerald 1803-1840 . . . . DLB-159	Guillén, Jorge 1893-1984 . . . . DLB-108
Green, Jonas 1712-1767 . . . . DLB-31	Griffith, Elizabeth 1727?-1793 . . . . DLB-39, 89	Guilloux, Louis 1899-1980 . . . . DLB-72
Green, Joseph 1706-1780 . . . . DLB-31	Griffith, George 1857-1906 . . . . . . DLB-178	Guilpin, Everard circa 1572-after 1608? DLB-136
Green, Julien 1900- DLB-4, 72	Griffiths, Trevor 1935- DLB-13	
Green, Paul 1894-1981 . . . . . . DLB-7, 9; Y-81	Griffiths, Ralph [publishing house] DLB-154	Guiney, Louise Imogen 1861-1920 . . . . DLB-54
Green, T. and S. [publishing house] DLB-49		
Green, Thomas Hill 1836-1882 . . . . . DLB-190		
Green, Timothy [publishing house] DLB-49		

Guiterman, Arthur 1871-1943 . . . . . . DLB-11
Günderrode, Caroline von
   1780-1806 . . . . DLB-90
Gundulić, Ivan 1589-1638 . . . . DLB-147
Gunn, Bill 1934-1989 . . . . DLB-38
Gunn, James E. 1923- DLB-8
Gunn, Neil M. 1891-1973 . . . . DLB-15
Gunn, Thom 1929- DLB-27
Gunnars, Kristjana 1948- DLB-60
Günther, Johann Christian
   1695-1723 . . . . DLB-168
Gurik, Robert 1932- DLB-60
Gustafson, Ralph 1909- DLB-88
Gütersloh, Albert Paris 1887-1973 . . . . DLB-81
Guthrie, A. B., Jr. 1901- DLB-6
Guthrie, Ramon 1896-1973 . . . . DLB-4
The Guthrie Theater DLB-7
Guthrie, Thomas Anstey (see Anstey, FC)
Gutzkow, Karl 1811-1878 . . . . DLB-133
Guy, Ray 1939- DLB-60
Guy, Rosa 1925- DLB-33
Guyot, Arnold 1807-1884 . . . . DS-13
Gwynne, Erskine 1898-1948 . . . . DLB-4
Gyles, John 1680-1755 . . . . DLB-99
Gysin, Brion 1916- DLB-16

H

H. D. (see Doolittle, Hilda)
Habington, William 1605-1654 . . . . . DLB-126
Hacker, Marilyn 1942- DLB-120
Hackett, Albert (see Goodrich, Frances)
Hacks, Peter 1928- DLB-124
Hadas, Rachel 1948- DLB-120
Hadden, Briton 1898-1929 . . . . DLB-91
Hagedorn, Friedrich von
   1708-1754 . . . . DLB-168
Hagelstange, Rudolf 1912-1984 . . . . . DLB-69
Haggard, H. Rider
   1856-1925 . . . . . . DLB-70, 156, 174, 178
Haggard, William 1907-1993 . . . . . . Y-93
Hahn-Hahn, Ida Gräfin von
   1805-1880 . . . . DLB-133
Haig-Brown, Roderick 1908-1976 . . . . DLB-88
Haight, Gordon S. 1901-1985 . . . . . . DLB-103
Hailey, Arthur 1920- DLB-88; Y-82
Haines, John 1924- DLB-5
Hake, Edward
   flourished 1566-1604 . . . . DLB-136
Hake, Thomas Gordon 1809-1895 . . . . DLB-32
Hakluyt, Richard 1552?-1616 . . . . . . DLB-136
Halbe, Max 1865-1944 . . . . DLB-118

Haldane, J. B. S. 1892-1964 . . . . DLB-160
Haldeman, Joe 1943- DLB-8
Haldeman-Julius Company DLB-46
Hale, E. J., and Son DLB-49
Hale, Edward Everett
   1822-1909 . . . . DLB-1, 42, 74
Hale, Janet Campbell 1946- DLB-175
Hale, Kathleen 1898- DLB-160
Hale, Leo Thomas (see Ebon)
Hale, Lucretia Peabody
   1820-1900 . . . . DLB-42
Hale, Nancy 1908-1988 . . . . DLB-86; Y-80, 88
Hale, Sarah Josepha (Buell)
   1788-1879 . . . . DLB-1, 42, 73
Hales, John 1584-1656 . . . . DLB-151
Haley, Alex 1921-1992 . . . . DLB-38
Haliburton, Thomas Chandler
   1796-1865 . . . . DLB-11, 99
Hall, Anna Maria 1800-1881 . . . . DLB-159
Hall, Donald 1928- DLB-5
Hall, Edward 1497-1547 . . . . DLB-132
Hall, James 1793-1868 . . . . DLB-73, 74
Hall, Joseph 1574-1656 . . . . . . DLB-121, 151
Hall, Samuel [publishing house] DLB-49
Hallam, Arthur Henry 1811-1833 . . . . DLB-32
Halleck, Fitz-Greene 1790-1867 . . . . . DLB-3
Haller, Albrecht von 1708-1777 . . . . . DLB-168
Halliwell-Phillipps, James Orchard
   1820-1889 . . . . DLB-184
Hallmann, Johann Christian
   1640-1704 or 1716? DLB-168
Hallmark Editions DLB-46
Halper, Albert 1904-1984 . . . . DLB-9
Halperin, John William 1941- DLB-111
Halstead, Murat 1829-1908 . . . . DLB-23
Hamann, Johann Georg 1730-1788 . . . DLB-97
Hamburger, Michael 1924- DLB-27
Hamilton, Alexander 1712-1756 . . . . . DLB-31
Hamilton, Alexander 1755?-1804 . . . . DLB-37
Hamilton, Cicely 1872-1952 . . . . DLB-10
Hamilton, Edmond 1904-1977 . . . . . . DLB-8
Hamilton, Elizabeth 1758-1816 . . . DLB-116, 158
Hamilton, Gail (see Corcoran, Barbara)
Hamilton, Ian 1938- DLB-40, 155
Hamilton, Patrick 1904-1962 . . . . . . DLB-10
Hamilton, Virginia 1936- DLB-33, 52
Hamilton, Hamish, Limited DLB-112
Hammett, Dashiell 1894-1961 . . . . . . DS-6
Dashiell Hammett:
   An Appeal in TAC Y-91
Hammon, Jupiter 1711-died between
   1790 and 1806 . . . . DLB-31, 50
Hammond, John ?-1663 . . . . DLB-24

Hamner, Earl 1923- DLB-6
Hampton, Christopher 1946- DLB-13
Handel-Mazzetti, Enrica von
   1871-1955 . . . . DLB-81
Handke, Peter 1942- DLB-85, 124
Handlin, Oscar 1915- DLB-17
Hankin, St. John 1869-1909 . . . . DLB-10
Hanley, Clifford 1922- DLB-14
Hannah, Barry 1942- DLB-6
Hannay, James 1827-1873 . . . . DLB-21
Hansberry, Lorraine 1930-1965 . . . . DLB-7, 38
Hapgood, Norman 1868-1937 . . . . . . DLB-91
Happel, Eberhard Werner
   1647-1690 . . . . DLB-168
Harcourt Brace Jovanovich DLB-46
Hardenberg, Friedrich von (see Novalis)
Harding, Walter 1917- DLB-111
Hardwick, Elizabeth 1916- DLB-6
Hardy, Thomas 1840-1928 . . . . DLB-18, 19, 135
Hare, Cyril 1900-1958 . . . . DLB-77
Hare, David 1947- DLB-13
Hargrove, Marion 1919- DLB-11
Häring, Georg Wilhelm Heinrich (see Alexis, Willibald)
Harington, Donald 1935- DLB-152
Harington, Sir John 1560-1612 . . . . . DLB-136
Harjo, Joy 1951- DLB-120, 175
Harlow, Robert 1923- DLB-60
Harman, Thomas
   flourished 1566-1573 . . . . DLB-136
Harness, Charles L. 1915- DLB-8
Harnett, Cynthia 1893-1981 . . . . DLB-161
Harper, Fletcher 1806-1877 . . . . DLB-79
Harper, Frances Ellen Watkins
   1825-1911 . . . . DLB-50
Harper, Michael S. 1938- DLB-41
Harper and Brothers DLB-49
Harraden, Beatrice 1864-1943 . . . . . . DLB-153
Harrap, George G., and Company
   Limited DLB-112
Harriot, Thomas 1560-1621 . . . . DLB-136
Harris, Benjamin ?-circa 1720 . . . . DLB-42, 43
Harris, Christie 1907- DLB-88
Harris, Frank 1856-1931 . . . . DLB-156
Harris, George Washington
   1814-1869 . . . . DLB-3, 11
Harris, Joel Chandler
   1848-1908 . . . . . . DLB-11, 23, 42, 78, 91
Harris, Mark 1922- DLB-2; Y-80
Harris, Wilson 1921- DLB-117
Harrison, Charles Yale
   1898-1954 . . . . DLB-68
Harrison, Frederic 1831-1923 . . . . DLB-57, 190

Harrison, Harry 1925- DLB-8

Harrison, Jim 1937- Y-82

Harrison, Mary St. Leger Kingsley
(see Malet, Lucas)

Harrison, Paul Carter 1936- DLB-38

Harrison, Susan Frances
1859-1935 . . . . DLB-99

Harrison, Tony 1937- DLB-40

Harrison, William 1535-1593 . . . . . DLB-136

Harrison, James P., Company DLB-49

Harrisse, Henry 1829-1910 . . . . DLB-47

Harsdörffer, Georg Philipp
1607-1658 . . . . DLB-164

Harsent, David 1942- DLB-40

Hart, Albert Bushnell 1854-1943 . . . . DLB-17

Hart, Julia Catherine 1796-1867 . . . . DLB-99

The Lorenz Hart Centenary Y-95

Hart, Moss 1904-1961 . . . . DLB-7

Hart, Oliver 1723-1795 . . . . DLB-31

Hart-Davis, Rupert, Limited DLB-112

Harte, Bret
1836-1902 . . . . . DLB-12, 64, 74, 79, 186

Harte, Edward Holmead 1922- DLB-127

Harte, Houston Harriman 1927- . . . DLB-127

Hartlaub, Felix 1913-1945 . . . . DLB-56

Hartlebon, Otto Erich
1864-1905 . . . . DLB-118

Hartley, L. P. 1895-1972 . . . . . . DLB-15, 139

Hartley, Marsden 1877-1943 . . . . . . DLB-54

Hartling, Peter 1933- DLB-75

Hartman, Geoffrey H. 1929- DLB-67

Hartmann, Sadakichi 1867-1944 . . . . DLB-54

Hartmann von Aue
circa 1160-circa 1205 . . . . DLB-138

Harvey, Gabriel 1550?-1631 . . . . . . DLB-167

Harvey, Jean-Charles 1891-1967 . . . . DLB-88

Harvill Press Limited DLB-112

Harwood, Lee 1939- DLB-40

Harwood, Ronald 1934- DLB-13

Haskins, Charles Homer
1870-1937 . . . . DLB-47

Hass, Robert 1941- DLB-105

The Hatch-Billops Collection DLB-76

Hathaway, William 1944- DLB-120

Hauff, Wilhelm 1802-1827 . . . . DLB-90

A Haughty and Proud Generation (1922),
by Ford Madox Hueffer DLB-36

Haugwitz, August Adolph von
1647-1706 . . . . DLB-168

Hauptmann, Carl
1858-1921 . . . . DLB-66, 118

Hauptmann, Gerhart
1862-1946 . . . . DLB-66, 118

Hauser, Marianne 1910- Y-83

Hawes, Stephen
1475?-before 1529 . . . . DLB-132

Hawker, Robert Stephen
1803-1875 . . . . DLB-32

Hawkes, John 1925- DLB-2, 7; Y-80

Hawkesworth, John 1720-1773 . . . . . DLB-142

Hawkins, Sir Anthony Hope (see Hope, Anthony)

Hawkins, Sir John
1719-1789 . . . . DLB-104, 142

Hawkins, Walter Everette 1883-? DLB-50

Hawthorne, Nathaniel
1804-1864 . . . . DLB-1, 74, 183

Hawthorne, Nathaniel 1804-1864 and
Hawthorne, Sophia Peabody
1809-1871 . . . . DLB-183

Hay, John 1835-1905 . . . . . DLB-12, 47, 189

Hayashi, Fumiko 1903-1951 . . . . . . DLB-180

Hayden, Robert 1913-1980 . . . . . DLB-5, 76

Haydon, Benjamin Robert
1786-1846 . . . . DLB-110

Hayes, John Michael 1919- DLB-26

Hayley, William 1745-1820 . . . . . DLB-93, 142

Haym, Rudolf 1821-1901 . . . . DLB-129

Hayman, Robert 1575-1629 . . . . DLB-99

Hayman, Ronald 1932- DLB-155

Hayne, Paul Hamilton
1830-1886 . . . . DLB-3, 64, 79

Hays, Mary 1760-1843 . . . . . DLB-142, 158

Haywood, Eliza 1693?-1756 . . . . DLB-39

Hazard, Willis P. [publishing house] DLB-49

Hazlitt, William 1778-1830 . . . . DLB-110, 158

Hazzard, Shirley 1931- Y-82

Head, Bessie 1937-1986 . . . . DLB-117

Headley, Joel T.
1813-1897 . . . . DLB-30, 183; DS-13

Heaney, Seamus 1939- DLB-40

Heard, Nathan C. 1936- DLB-33

Hearn, Lafcadio 1850-1904 . . . DLB-12, 78, 189

Hearne, John 1926- DLB-117

Hearne, Samuel 1745-1792 . . . . DLB-99

Hearst, William Randolph
1863-1951 . . . . DLB-25

Hearst, William Randolph, Jr
1908-1993 . . . . DLB-127

Heartman, Charles Frederick
1883-1953 . . . . DLB-187

Heath, Catherine 1924- DLB-14

Heath, Roy A. K. 1926- DLB-117

Heath-Stubbs, John 1918- DLB-27

Heavysege, Charles 1816-1876 . . . . . DLB-99

Hebbel, Friedrich 1813-1863 . . . . . . DLB-129

Hebel, Johann Peter 1760-1826 . . . . . DLB-90

Heber, Richard 1774-1833 . . . . DLB-184

Hébert, Anne 1916- DLB-68

Hébert, Jacques 1923- DLB-53

Hecht, Anthony 1923- DLB-5, 169

Hecht, Ben 1894-1964
. . . . DLB-7, 9, 25, 26, 28, 86

Hecker, Isaac Thomas 1819-1888 . . . . DLB-1

Hedge, Frederic Henry
1805-1890 . . . . DLB-1, 59

Hefner, Hugh M. 1926- DLB-137

Hegel, Georg Wilhelm Friedrich
1770-1831 . . . . DLB-90

Heidish, Marcy 1947- Y-82

Heißenbüttel 1921- DLB-75

Hein, Christoph 1944- DLB-124

Heine, Heinrich 1797-1856 . . . . DLB-90

Heinemann, Larry 1944- DS-9

Heinemann, William, Limited DLB-112

Heinlein, Robert A. 1907-1988 . . . . . DLB-8

Heinrich Julius of Brunswick
1564-1613 . . . . DLB-164

Heinrich von dem Türlîn
flourished circa 1230 . . . . DLB-138

Heinrich von Melk
flourished after 1160 . . . . DLB-148

Heinrich von Veldeke
circa 1145-circa 1190 . . . . DLB-138

Heinrich, Willi 1920- DLB-75

Heiskell, John 1872-1972 . . . . DLB-127

Heinse, Wilhelm 1746-1803 . . . . DLB-94

Heinz, W. C. 1915- DLB-171

Hejinian, Lyn 1941- DLB-165

Heliand circa 850 . . . . DLB-148

Heller, Joseph 1923- DLB-2, 28; Y-80

Heller, Michael 1937- DLB-165

Hellman, Lillian 1906-1984 . . . . . DLB-7; Y-84

Hellwig, Johann 1609-1674 . . . . DLB-164

Helprin, Mark 1947- Y-85

Helwig, David 1938- DLB-60

Hemans, Felicia 1793-1835 . . . . DLB-96

Hemingway, Ernest 1899-1961
. . . DLB-4, 9, 102; Y-81, 87; DS-1, 15, 16

Hemingway: Twenty-Five Years
Later Y-85

Hémon, Louis 1880-1913 . . . . DLB-92

Hemphill, Paul 1936- Y-87

Hénault, Gilles 1920- DLB-88

Henchman, Daniel 1689-1761 . . . . . . DLB-24

Henderson, Alice Corbin
1881-1949 . . . . DLB-54

Henderson, Archibald
1877-1963 . . . . DLB-103

Henderson, David 1942- DLB-41

Henderson, George Wylie
1904- DLB-51

Henderson, Zenna 1917-1983 . . . . . . DLB-8

Henisch, Peter 1943- DLB-85

Henley, Beth 1952- Y-86

Henley, William Ernest
1849-1903 .... DLB-19

Henniker, Florence 1855-1923...... DLB-135

Henry, Alexander 1739-1824 .... DLB-99

Henry, Buck 1930- DLB-26

Henry VIII of England
1491-1547 .... DLB-132

Henry, Marguerite 1902- DLB-22

Henry, O. (see Porter, William Sydney)

Henry of Ghent
circa 1217-1229 - 1293 .... DLB-115

Henry, Robert Selph 1889-1970 .... DLB-17

Henry, Will (see Allen, Henry W.)

Henryson, Robert
1420s or 1430s-circa 1505 .... DLB-146

Henschke, Alfred (see Klabund)

Hensley, Sophie Almon 1866-1946.... DLB-99

Henson, Lance 1944- DLB-175

Henty, G. A. 1832?-1902...... DLB-18, 141

Hentz, Caroline Lee 1800-1856 ..... DLB-3

Heraclitus flourished circa 500 B.C.
.... DLB-176

Herbert, Agnes circa 1880-1960..... DLB-174

Herbert, Alan Patrick 1890-1971..... DLB-10

Herbert, Edward, Lord, of Cherbury
1582-1648. .... DLB-121, 151

Herbert, Frank 1920-1986 .... DLB-8

Herbert, George 1593-1633 .... DLB-126

Herbert, Henry William
1807-1858 .... DLB-3, 73

Herbert, John 1926- DLB-53

Herbert, Mary Sidney, Countess of Pembroke
(see Sidney, Mary)

Herbst, Josephine 1892-1969....... DLB-9

Herburger, Gunter 1932- DLB-75, 124

Èercules, Frank E. M. 1917- DLB-33

Herder, Johann Gottfried
1744-1803 .... DLB-97

Herder, B., Book Company DLB-49

Herford, Charles Harold
1853-1931 .... DLB-149

Hergesheimer, Joseph
1880-1954............ DLB-9, 102

Heritage Press............ DLB-46

Hermann the Lame 1013-1054 ..... DLB-148

Hermes, Johann Timotheus
1738-1821 .... DLB-97

Hermlin, Stephan 1915- DLB-69

Hernández, Alfonso C. 1938- DLB-122

Hernández, Inés 1947- DLB-122

Hernández, Miguel 1910-1942..... DLB-134

Hernton, Calvin C. 1932- DLB-38

"The Hero as Man of Letters: Johnson,
Rousseau, Burns" (1841), by Thomas
Carlyle [excerpt] DLB-57

The Hero as Poet. Dante; Shakspeare (1841),
by Thomas Carlyle. DLB-32

Herodotus circa 484 B.C.-circa 420 B.C.
.... DLB-176

Heron, Robert 1764-1807 .... DLB-142

Herr, Michael 1940- DLB-185

Herrera, Juan Felipe 1948- DLB-122

Herrick, Robert 1591-1674 .... DLB-126

Herrick, Robert 1868-1938 .... DLB-9, 12, 78

Herrick, William 1915- Y-83

Herrick, E. R., and Company DLB-49

Herrmann, John 1900-1959 .... DLB-4

Hersey, John 1914-1993 ..... DLB-6, 185

Hertel, François 1905-1985 .... DLB-68

Hervé-Bazin, Jean Pierre Marie (see Bazin, Hervé)

Hervey, John, Lord 1696-1743 .... DLB-101

Herwig, Georg 1817-1875........ DLB-133

Herzog, Emile Salomon Wilhelm (see Maurois,
André)

Hesiod eighth century B.C........ DLB-176

Hesse, Hermann 1877-1962 .... DLB-66

Hessus, Helius Eobanus
1488-1540 .... DLB-179

Hewat, Alexander
circa 1743-circa 1824 .... DLB-30

Hewitt, John 1907- DLB-27

Hewlett, Maurice 1861-1923 .... DLB-34, 156

Heyen, William 1940- DLB-5

Heyer, Georgette 1902-1974 ...... DLB-77

Heym, Stefan 1913- DLB-69

Heyse, Paul 1830-1914 .... DLB-129

Heytesbury, William
circa 1310-1372 or 1373 ...... DLB-115

Heyward, Dorothy 1890-1961....... DLB-7

Heyward, DuBose
1885-1940. .... DLB-7, 9, 45

Heywood, John 1497?-1580? DLB-136

Heywood, Thomas
1573 or 1574-1641 .... DLB-62

Hibbs, Ben 1901-1975.......... DLB-137

Hichens, Robert S. 1864-1950..... DLB-153

Hickman, William Albert
1877-1957 .... DLB-92

Hidalgo, José Luis 1919-1947...... DLB-108

Hiebert, Paul 1892-1987 .... DLB-68

Hieng, Andrej 1925- DLB-181

Hierro, José 1922- DLB-108

Higgins, Aidan 1927- DLB-14

Higgins, Colin 1941-1988 .... DLB-26

Higgins, George V. 1939- DLB-2; Y-81

Higginson, Thomas Wentworth
1823-1911 .... DLB-1, 64

Highwater, Jamake 1942?- DLB-52; Y-85

Hijuelos, Oscar 1951- DLB-145

Hildegard von Bingen
1098-1179 .... DLB-148

Das Hildesbrandslied circa 820 ..... DLB-148

Hildesheimer, Wolfgang
1916-1991 .... DLB-69, 124

Hildreth, Richard
1807-1865 .... DLB-1, 30, 59

Hill, Aaron 1685-1750 .... DLB-84

Hill, Geoffrey 1932- DLB-40

Hill, "Sir" John 1714?-1775 .... DLB-39

Hill, Leslie 1880-1960........... DLB-51

Hill, Susan 1942- DLB-14, 139

Hill, Walter 1942- DLB-44

Hill and Wang DLB-46

Hill, George M., Company........ DLB-49

Hill, Lawrence, and Company,
Publishers DLB-46

Hillberry, Conrad 1928- DLB-120

Hilliard, Gray and Company DLB-49

Hills, Lee 1906- DLB-127

Hillyer, Robert 1895-1961 .... DLB-54

Hilton, James 1900-1954 ...... DLB-34, 77

Hilton, Walter died 1396 .... DLB-146

Hilton and Company DLB-49

Himes, Chester
1909-1984........... DLB-2, 76, 143

Hindmarsh, Joseph
[publishing house] DLB-170

Hine, Daryl 1936- DLB-60

Hingley, Ronald 1920- DLB-155

Hinojosa-Smith, Rolando
1929- DLB-82

Hippel, Theodor Gottlieb von
1741-1796 .... DLB-97

Hippocrates of Cos flourished circa 425 B.C.
.... DLB-176

Hirabayashi, Taiko 1905-1972...... DLB-180

Hirsch, E. D., Jr. 1928- DLB-67

Hirsch, Edward 1950- DLB-120

The History of the Adventures of Joseph Andrews
(1742), by Henry Fielding
[excerpt] DLB-39

Hoagland, Edward 1932- DLB-6

Hoagland, Everett H., III 1942- DLB-41

Hoban, Russell 1925- DLB-52

Hobbes, Thomas 1588-1679....... DLB-151

Hobby, Oveta 1905- DLB-127

Hobby, William 1878-1964 ...... DLB-127

Hobsbaum, Philip 1932- DLB-40

Hobson, Laura Z. 1900- DLB-28

Hoby, Thomas 1530-1566 . . . . DLB-132

Hoccleve, Thomas
   circa 1368-circa 1437 . . . . DLB-146

Hochhuth, Rolf 1931- DLB-124

Hochman, Sandra 1936- DLB-5

Hocken, Thomas Morland
   1836-1910 . . . . DLB-184

Hodder and Stoughton, Limited DLB-106

Hodgins, Jack 1938- DLB-60

Hodgman, Helen 1945- DLB-14

Hodgskin, Thomas 1787-1869 . . . . . DLB-158

Hodgson, Ralph 1871-1962 . . . . . . DLB-19

Hodgson, William Hope
   1877-1918 . . . . . DLB-70, 153, 156, 178

Hoe, Robert III 1839-1909 . . . . . . DLB-187

Hoffenstein, Samuel 1890-1947 . . . . . DLB-11

Hoffman, Charles Fenno
   1806-1884 . . . . DLB-3

Hoffman, Daniel 1923- DLB-5

Hoffmann, E. T. A. 1776-1822 . . . . . DLB-90

Hoffman, Frank B. 1888-1958 . . . . . DLB-188

Hoffmanswaldau, Christian Hoffman von
   1616-1679 . . . . DLB-168

Hofmann, Michael 1957- DLB-40

Hofmannsthal, Hugo von
   1874-1929 . . . . DLB-81, 118

Hofstadter, Richard 1916-1970 . . . . . DLB-17

Hogan, Desmond 1950- DLB-14

Hogan, Linda 1947- DLB-175

Hogan and Thompson DLB-49

Hogarth Press DLB-112

Hogg, James 1770-1835 . . . . DLB-93, 116, 159

Hohberg, Wolfgang Helmhard Freiherr von
   1612-1688 . . . . DLB-168

von Hohenheim, Philippus Aureolus
   Theophrastus Bombastus (see Paracelsus)

Hohl, Ludwig 1904-1980 . . . . DLB-56

Holbrook, David 1923- DLB-14, 40

Holcroft, Thomas
   1745-1809 . . . . DLB-39, 89, 158

Holden, Jonathan 1941- DLB-105

Holden, Jonathan, Contemporary
   Verse Story-telling DLB-105

Holden, Molly 1927-1981 . . . . DLB-40

Hölderlin, Friedrich 1770-1843 . . . . . DLB-90

Holiday House DLB-46

Holinshed, Raphael died 1580 . . . . . DLB-167

Holland, J. G. 1819-1881 . . . . DS-13

Holland, Norman N. 1927- DLB-67

Hollander, John 1929- DLB-5

Holley, Marietta 1836-1926 . . . . . . DLB-11

Hollingsworth, Margaret 1940- DLB-60

Hollo, Anselm 1934- DLB-40

Holloway, Emory 1885-1977 . . . . . . DLB-103

Holloway, John 1920- DLB-27

Holloway House Publishing
   Company DLB-46

Holme, Constance 1880-1955 . . . . . DLB-34

Holmes, Abraham S. 1821?-1908 . . . . DLB-99

Holmes, John Clellon 1926-1988 . . . . DLB-16

Holmes, Oliver Wendell
   1809-1894 . . . . DLB-1, 189

Holmes, Richard 1945- DLB-155

Holmes, Thomas James 1874-1959 . . . DLB-187

Holroyd, Michael 1935- DLB-155

Holst, Hermann E. von
   1841-1904 . . . . DLB-47

Holt, John 1721-1784 . . . . DLB-43

Holt, Henry, and Company DLB-49

Holt, Rinehart and Winston DLB-46

Holthusen, Hans Egon 1913- DLB-69

Hölty, Ludwig Christoph Heinrich
   1748-1776 . . . . DLB-94

Holz, Arno 1863-1929 . . . . DLB-118

Home, Henry, Lord Kames (see Kames, Henry
   Home, Lord)

Home, John 1722-1808 . . . . DLB-84

Home, William Douglas 1912- DLB-13

Home Publishing Company DLB-49

Homer circa eighth-seventh centuries B.C.
   . . . . DLB-176

Homer, Winslow 1836-1910 . . . . . . DLB-188

Homes, Geoffrey (see Mainwaring, Daniel)

Honan, Park 1928- DLB-111

Hone, William 1780-1842 . . . . DLB-110, 158

Hongo, Garrett Kaoru 1951- DLB-120

Honig, Edwin 1919- DLB-5

Hood, Hugh 1928- DLB-53

Hood, Thomas 1799-1845 . . . . DLB-96

Hook, Theodore 1788-1841 . . . . . . DLB-116

Hooker, Jeremy 1941- DLB-40

Hooker, Richard 1554-1600 . . . . . . DLB-132

Hooker, Thomas 1586-1647 . . . . . . DLB-24

Hooper, Johnson Jones
   1815-1862 . . . . DLB-3, 11

Hope, Anthony 1863-1933 . . . . DLB-153, 156

Hopkins, Ellice 1836-1904 . . . . DLB-190

Hopkins, Gerard Manley
   1844-1889 . . . . DLB-35, 57

Hopkins, John (see Sternhold, Thomas)

Hopkins, Lemuel 1750-1801 . . . . . . DLB-37

Hopkins, Pauline Elizabeth
   1859-1930 . . . . DLB-50

Hopkins, Samuel 1721-1803 . . . . . . DLB-31

Hopkins, John H., and Son DLB-46

Hopkinson, Francis 1737-1791 . . . . . DLB-31

Hoppin, Augustus 1828-1896 . . . . . DLB-188

Horgan, Paul 1903- DLB-102; Y-85

Horizon Press DLB-46

Horne, Frank 1899-1974 . . . . DLB-51

Horne, Richard Henry (Hengist)
   1802 or 1803-1884 . . . . DLB-32

Hornung, E. W. 1866-1921 . . . . . . DLB-70

Horovitz, Israel 1939- DLB-7

Horton, George Moses
   1797?-1883? DLB-50

Horváth, Ödön von
   1901-1938 . . . . DLB-85, 124

Horwood, Harold 1923- DLB-60

Hosford, E. and E.
   [publishing house] DLB-49

Hoskyns, John 1566-1638 . . . . DLB-121

Hotchkiss and Company DLB-49

Hough, Emerson 1857-1923 . . . . . . DLB-9

Houghton Mifflin Company DLB-49

Houghton, Stanley 1881-1913 . . . . . DLB-10

Household, Geoffrey 1900-1988 . . . . DLB-87

Housman, A. E. 1859-1936 . . . . . . DLB-19

Housman, Laurence 1865-1959 . . . . DLB-10

Houwald, Ernst von 1778-1845 . . . . . DLB-90

Hovey, Richard 1864-1900 . . . . . . DLB-54

Howard, Donald R. 1927-1987 . . . . . DLB-111

Howard, Maureen 1930- Y-83

Howard, Richard 1929- DLB-5

Howard, Roy W. 1883-1964 . . . . . . DLB-29

Howard, Sidney 1891-1939 . . . . . DLB-7, 26

Howe, E. W. 1853-1937 . . . . . . DLB-12, 25

Howe, Henry 1816-1893 . . . . DLB-30

Howe, Irving 1920-1993 . . . . DLB-67

Howe, Joseph 1804-1873 . . . . DLB-99

Howe, Julia Ward 1819-1910 . . . . DLB-1, 189

Howe, Percival Presland
   1886-1944 . . . . DLB-149

Howe, Susan 1937- DLB-120

Howell, Clark, Sr. 1863-1936 . . . . . . DLB-25

Howell, Evan P. 1839-1905 . . . . . . DLB-23

Howell, James 1594?-1666 . . . . DLB-151

Howell, Warren Richardson
   1912-1984 . . . . DLB-140

Howell, Soskin and Company DLB-46

Howells, William Dean
   1837-1920 . . . . . DLB-12, 64, 74, 79, 189

Howitt, William 1792-1879 and
   Howitt, Mary 1799-1888 . . . . . . DLB-110

Hoyem, Andrew 1935- DLB-5

Hoyers, Anna Ovena 1584-1655 . . . . DLB-164

Hoyos, Angela de 1940- DLB-82

Hoyt, Palmer 1897-1979 . . . . DLB-127

Hoyt, Henry [publishing house] DLB-49

Hrabanus Maurus 776?-856 . . . . DLB-148

Hrotsvit of Gandersheim
  circa 935-circa 1000 . . . . DLB-148

Hubbard, Elbert 1856-1915 . . . . DLB-91

Hubbard, Kin 1868-1930 . . . . DLB-11

Hubbard, William circa 1621-1704 . . . . DLB-24

Huber, Therese 1764-1829 . . . . DLB-90

Huch, Friedrich 1873-1913 . . . . DLB-66

Huch, Ricarda 1864-1947 . . . . DLB-66

Huck at 100: How Old Is
  Huckleberry Finn? Y-85

Huddle, David 1942- DLB-130

Hudgins, Andrew 1951- DLB-120

Hudson, Henry Norman
  1814-1886 . . . . DLB-64

Hudson, W. H.
  1841-1922 . . . . DLB-98, 153, 174

Hudson and Goodwin DLB-49

Huebsch, B. W.
  [publishing house] DLB-46

Hughes, David 1930- DLB-14

Hughes, John 1677-1720 . . . . DLB-84

Hughes, Langston
  1902-1967 . . . . . . DLB-4, 7, 48, 51, 86

Hughes, Richard 1900-1976 . . . . DLB-15, 161

Hughes, Ted 1930- DLB-40, 161

Hughes, Thomas 1822-1896 . . . . DLB-18, 163

Hugo, Richard 1923-1982 . . . . DLB-5

Hugo, Victor 1802-1885 . . . . DLB-119

Hugo Awards and Nebula Awards DLB-8

Hull, Richard 1896-1973 . . . . DLB-77

Hulme, T. E. 1883-1917 . . . . DLB-19

Humboldt, Alexander von
  1769-1859 . . . . DLB-90

Humboldt, Wilhelm von
  1767-1835 . . . . DLB-90

Hume, David 1711-1776 . . . . DLB-104

Hume, Fergus 1859-1932 . . . . DLB-70

Hummer, T. R. 1950- DLB-120

Humorous Book Illustration DLB-11

Humphrey, William 1924- DLB-6

Humphreys, David 1752-1818 . . . . . . DLB-37

Humphreys, Emyr 1919- DLB-15

Huncke, Herbert 1915- DLB-16

Huneker, James Gibbons
  1857-1921 . . . . DLB-71

Hunold, Christian Friedrich
  1681-1721 . . . . DLB-168

Hunt, Irene 1907- DLB-52

Hunt, Leigh 1784-1859 . . . . DLB-96, 110, 144

Hunt, Violet 1862-1942 . . . . DLB-162

Hunt, William Gibbes 1791-1833 . . . . DLB-73

Hunter, Evan 1926- Y-82

Hunter, Jim 1939- DLB-14

Hunter, Kristin 1931- DLB-33

Hunter, Mollie 1922- DLB-161

Hunter, N. C. 1908-1971 . . . . DLB-10

Hunter-Duvar, John 1821-1899 . . . . . DLB-99

Huntington, Henry E.
  1850-1927 . . . . DLB-140

Hurd and Houghton DLB-49

Hurst, Fannie 1889-1968 . . . . DLB-86

Hurst and Blackett DLB-106

Hurst and Company DLB-49

Hurston, Zora Neale
  1901?-1960 . . . . DLB-51, 86

Husson, Jules-François-Félix (see Champfleury)

Huston, John 1906-1987 . . . . DLB-26

Hutcheson, Francis 1694-1746 . . . . . . DLB-31

Hutchinson, Thomas
  1711-1780 . . . . DLB-30, 31

Hutchinson and Company
  (Publishers) Limited DLB-112

von Hutton, Ulrich 1488-1523 . . . . . DLB-179

Hutton, Richard Holt 1826-1897 . . . . . DLB-57

Huxley, Aldous
  1894-1963 . . . . DLB-36, 100, 162

Huxley, Elspeth Josceline 1907- DLB-77

Huxley, T. H. 1825-1895 . . . . DLB-57

Huyghue, Douglas Smith
  1816-1891 . . . . DLB-99

Huysmans, Joris-Karl 1848-1907 . . . . DLB-123

Hyde, Donald 1909-1966 and
  Hyde, Mary 1912- DLB-187

Hyman, Trina Schart 1939- DLB-61

I

Iavorsky, Stefan 1658-1722 . . . . . . DLB-150

Ibn Bajja circa 1077-1138 . . . . DLB-115

Ibn Gabirol, Solomon
  circa 1021-circa 1058 . . . . DLB-115

Ibuse, Masuji 1898-1993 . . . . DLB-180

The Iconography of Science-Fiction
  Art DLB-8

Iffland, August Wilhelm
  1759-1814 . . . . DLB-94

Ignatow, David 1914- DLB-5

Ike, Chukwuemeka 1931- DLB-157

Iles, Francis (see Berkeley, Anthony)

The Illustration of Early German
  Literary Manuscripts,
  circa 1150-circa 1300 . . . . DLB-148

Imbs, Bravig 1904-1946 . . . . DLB-4

Imbuga, Francis D. 1947- DLB-157

Immermann, Karl 1796-1840 . . . . . . DLB-133

Inchbald, Elizabeth 1753-1821 . . . DLB-39, 89

Inge, William 1913-1973 . . . . DLB-7

Ingelow, Jean 1820-1897 . . . . . DLB-35, 163

Ingersoll, Ralph 1900-1985 . . . . DLB-127

The Ingersoll Prizes Y-84

Ingoldsby, Thomas (see Barham, Richard
  Harris)

Ingraham, Joseph Holt 1809-1860 . . . . DLB-3

Inman, John 1805-1850 . . . . DLB-73

Innerhofer, Franz 1944- DLB-85

Innis, Harold Adams 1894-1952 . . . . DLB-88

Innis, Mary Quayle 1899-1972 . . . . . DLB-88

Inoue, Yasushi 1907-1991 . . . . DLB-181

International Publishers Company DLB-46

An Interview with David Rabe Y-91

An Interview with George Greenfield,
  Literary Agent Y-91

An Interview with James Ellroy Y-91

An Interview with Peter S. Prescott . . . Y-86

An Interview with Russell Hoban Y-90

An Interview with Tom Jenks Y-86

Introduction to Paul Laurence Dunbar,
  Lyrics of Lowly Life (1896),
  by William Dean Howells DLB-50

Introductory Essay: *Letters of Percy Bysshe
  Shelley* (1852), by Robert
  Browning DLB-32

Introductory Letters from the Second Edition
  of *Pamela* (1741), by Samuel
  Richardson DLB-39

Irving, John 1942- DLB-6; Y-82

Irving, Washington 1783-1859
  . . . . DLB-3, 11, 30, 59, 73, 74, 183, 186

Irwin, Grace 1907- DLB-68

Irwin, Will 1873-1948 . . . . DLB-25

Isherwood, Christopher
  1904-1986 . . . . DLB-15; Y-86

Ishikawa, Jun 1899-1987 . . . . DLB-182

The Island Trees Case: A Symposium on
  School Library Censorship
    An Interview with Judith Krug
    An Interview with Phyllis Schlafly
    An Interview with Edward B. Jenkinson
    An Interview with Lamarr Mooneyham
    An Interview with Harriet
      Bernstein Y-82

Islas, Arturo 1938-1991 . . . . DLB-122

Ivanišević, Drago 1907-1981 . . . . . . DLB-181

Ivers, M. J., and Company DLB-49

Iwano, Hōmei 1873-1920 . . . . DLB-180

Iyayi, Festus 1947- DLB-157

Izumi, Kyōka 1873-1939 . . . . DLB-180

J

Jackmon, Marvin E. (see Marvin X)

Jacks, L. P. 1860-1955. . . . . DLB-135
Jackson, Angela 1951- DLB-41
Jackson, Helen Hunt
    1830-1885 . . . . . . DLB-42, 47, 186, 189
Jackson, Holbrook 1874-1948. . . . . . DLB-98
Jackson, Laura Riding 1901-1991 . . . DLB-48
Jackson, Shirley 1919-1965. . . . . . . DLB-6
Jacob, Piers Anthony Dillingham (see Anthony, Piers)
Jacobi, Friedrich Heinrich
    1743-1819 . . . . DLB-94
Jacobi, Johann Georg 1740-1841 . . . . DLB-97
Jacobs, Joseph 1854-1916 . . . . DLB-141
Jacobs, W. W. 1863-1943. . . . . DLB-135
Jacobs, George W., and Company . . . DLB-49
Jacobson, Dan 1929- DLB-14
Jaggard, William
    [publishing house] DLB-170
Jahier, Piero 1884-1966 . . . . DLB-114
Jahnn, Hans Henny
    1894-1959 . . . . DLB-56, 124
Jakes, John 1932- Y-83
James, C. L. R. 1901-1989 . . . . DLB-125
James, George P. R. 1801-1860. . . . . DLB-116
James, Henry
    1843-1916 . . . DLB-12, 71, 74, 189; DS-13
James, John circa 1633-1729 . . . . . . DLB-24
The James Jones Society Y-92
James, M. R. 1862-1936. . . . . DLB-156
James, P. D. 1920- DLB-87
James, Will 1892-1942 . . . . DS-16
James Joyce Centenary: Dublin, 1982. . . . Y-82
James Joyce Conference Y-85
James VI of Scotland, I of England
    1566-1625. . . . . DLB-151, 172
James, U. P. [publishing house] DLB-49
Jameson, Anna 1794-1860. . . . . . DLB-99, 166
Jameson, Fredric 1934- DLB-67
Jameson, J. Franklin 1859-1937. . . . . DLB-17
Jameson, Storm 1891-1986. . . . . DLB-36
Jančar, Drago 1948- DLB-181
Janés, Clara 1940- DLB-134
Janevski, Slavko 1920- DLB-181
Jaramillo, Cleofas M. 1878-1956 . . . . DLB-122
Jarman, Mark 1952- DLB-120
Jarrell, Randall 1914-1965 . . . . . DLB-48, 52
Jarrold and Sons. DLB-106
Jarves, James Jackson 1818-1888 . . . . DLB-189
Jasmin, Claude 1930- DLB-60
Jay, John 1745-1829. . . . . DLB-31
Jefferies, Richard 1848-1887. . . . . DLB-98, 141
Jeffers, Lance 1919-1985 . . . . DLB-41
Jeffers, Robinson 1887-1962 . . . . DLB-45

Jefferson, Thomas 1743-1826 . . . . DLB-31, 183
Jelinek, Elfriede 1946- DLB-85
Jellicoe, Ann 1927- DLB-13
Jenkins, Elizabeth 1905- DLB-155
Jenkins, Robin 1912- DLB-14
Jenkins, William Fitzgerald (see Leinster, Murray)
Jenkins, Herbert, Limited DLB-112
Jennings, Elizabeth 1926- DLB-27
Jens, Walter 1923- DLB-69
Jensen, Merrill 1905-1980. . . . . DLB-17
Jephson, Robert 1736-1803 . . . . DLB-89
Jerome, Jerome K.
    1859-1927 . . . . DLB-10, 34, 135
Jerome, Judson 1927-1991 . . . . DLB-105
Jerome, Judson, Reflections: After a
    Tornado DLB-105
Jerrold, Douglas 1803-1857 . . . . DLB-158, 159
Jesse, F. Tennyson 1888-1958 . . . . . . DLB-77
Jewett, Sarah Orne 1849-1909 . . . . DLB-12, 74
Jewett, John P., and Company. DLB-49
The Jewish Publication Society. DLB-49
Jewitt, John Rodgers 1783-1821 . . . . . DLB-99
Jewsbury, Geraldine 1812-1880. . . . . . DLB-21
Jhabvala, Ruth Prawer 1927- DLB-139
Jiménez, Juan Ramón 1881-1958 . . . . DLB-134
Joans, Ted 1928- DLB-16, 41
John, Eugenie (see Marlitt, E.)
John of Dumbleton
    circa 1310-circa 1349 . . . . DLB-115
John Edward Bruce: Three
    Documents DLB-50
John O'Hara's Pottsville Journalism Y-88
John Steinbeck Research Center. Y-85
John Webster: The Melbourne
    Manuscript Y-86
Johns, Captain W. E. 1893-1968 . . . . DLB-160
Johnson, B. S. 1933-1973 . . . . . . DLB-14, 40
Johnson, Charles 1679-1748 . . . . DLB-84
Johnson, Charles R. 1948- DLB-33
Johnson, Charles S. 1893-1956. . . . DLB-51, 91
Johnson, Denis 1949- DLB-120
Johnson, Diane 1934- Y-80
Johnson, Edgar 1901- DLB-103
Johnson, Edward 1598-1672 . . . . DLB-24
Johnson E. Pauline (Tekahionwake)
    1861-1913 . . . . DLB-175
Johnson, Fenton 1888-1958 . . . . . DLB-45, 50
Johnson, Georgia Douglas
    1886-1966 . . . . DLB-51
Johnson, Gerald W. 1890-1980 . . . . . DLB-29
Johnson, Helene 1907- DLB-51

Johnson, James Weldon
    1871-1938 . . . . DLB-51
Johnson, John H. 1918- DLB-137
Johnson, Linton Kwesi 1952- DLB-157
Johnson, Lionel 1867-1902 . . . . DLB-19
Johnson, Nunnally 1897-1977 . . . . . DLB-26
Johnson, Owen 1878-1952 . . . . Y-87
Johnson, Pamela Hansford
    1912- DLB-15
Johnson, Pauline 1861-1913. . . . . . . DLB-92
Johnson, Ronald 1935- DLB-169
Johnson, Samuel 1696-1772. . . . . . . DLB-24
Johnson, Samuel
    1709-1784 . . . . . . DLB-39, 95, 104, 142
Johnson, Samuel 1822-1882 . . . . DLB-1
Johnson, Uwe 1934-1984 . . . . DLB-75
Johnson, Benjamin
    [publishing house] DLB-49
Johnson, Benjamin, Jacob, and
    Robert [publishing house] DLB-49
Johnson, Jacob, and Company DLB-49
Johnson, Joseph [publishing house] . . . DLB-154
Johnston, Annie Fellows 1863-1931 . . . DLB-42
Johnston, David Claypole 1798?-1865 . DLB-188
Johnston, Basil H. 1929- DLB-60
Johnston, Denis 1901-1984 . . . . DLB-10
Johnston, George 1913- DLB-88
Johnston, Sir Harry 1858-1927 . . . . . DLB-174
Johnston, Jennifer 1930- DLB-14
Johnston, Mary 1870-1936. . . . . DLB-9
Johnston, Richard Malcolm
    1822-1898 . . . . DLB-74
Johnstone, Charles 1719?-1800? DLB-39
Johst, Hanns 1890-1978 . . . . DLB-124
Jolas, Eugene 1894-1952. . . . . DLB-4, 45
Jones, Alice C. 1853-1933 . . . . DLB-92
Jones, Charles C., Jr. 1831-1893 . . . . . DLB-30
Jones, D. G. 1929- DLB-53
Jones, David 1895-1974 . . . . DLB-20, 100
Jones, Diana Wynne 1934- DLB-161
Jones, Ebenezer 1820-1860 . . . . DLB-32
Jones, Ernest 1819-1868. . . . . DLB-32
Jones, Gayl 1949- DLB-33
Jones, George 1800-1870 . . . . DLB-183
Jones, Glyn 1905- DLB-15
Jones, Gwyn 1907- DLB-15, 139
Jones, Henry Arthur 1851-1929 . . . . . DLB-10
Jones, Hugh circa 1692-1760 . . . . . . DLB-24
Jones, James 1921-1977 . . . . DLB-2, 143
Jones, Jenkin Lloyd 1911- DLB-127
Jones, LeRoi (see Baraka, Amiri)
Jones, Lewis 1897-1939 . . . . DLB-15

Jones, Madison 1925- DLB-152

Jones, Major Joseph (see Thompson, William Tappan)

Jones, Preston 1936-1979. .... DLB-7

Jones, Rodney 1950- DLB-120

Jones, Sir William 1746-1794 ..... DLB-109

Jones, William Alfred 1817-1900..... DLB-59

Jones's Publishing House DLB-49

Jong, Erica 1942- DLB-2, 5, 28, 152

Jonke, Gert F. 1946- DLB-85

Jonson, Ben 1572?-1637....... DLB-62, 121

Jordan, June 1936- DLB-38

Joseph, Jenny 1932- DLB-40

Joseph, Michael, Limited DLB-112

Josephson, Matthew 1899-1978 ..... DLB-4

Josephus, Flavius 37-100. .... DLB-176

Josiah Allen's Wife (see Holley, Marietta)

Josipovici, Gabriel 1940- DLB-14

Josselyn, John ?-1675 .... DLB-24

Joudry, Patricia 1921- DLB-88

Jovine, Giuseppe 1922- DLB-128

Joyaux, Philippe (see Sollers, Philippe)

Joyce, Adrien (see Eastman, Carol)

Joyce, James
1882-1941........ DLB-10, 19, 36, 162

Judd, Sylvester 1813-1853 .... DLB-1

Judd, Orange, Publishing
Company DLB-49

Judith circa 930 .... DLB-146

Julian of Norwich
1342-circa 1420. .... DLB-1146

Julian Symons at Eighty Y-92

June, Jennie (see Croly, Jane Cunningham)

Jung, Franz 1888-1963........ DLB-118

Jünger, Ernst 1895- DLB-56

Der jüngere Titurel circa 1275 ..... DLB-138

Jung-Stilling, Johann Heinrich
1740-1817 .... DLB-94

Justice, Donald 1925- Y-83

The Juvenile Library (see Godwin, M. J., and Company)

K

Kacew, Romain (see Gary, Romain)

Kafka, Franz 1883-1924. .... DLB-81

Kahn, Roger 1927. .... DLB-171

Kaikō, Takeshi 1939-1989. .... DLB-182

Kaiser, Georg 1878-1945 .... DLB-124

Kaiserchronik circca 1147 .... DLB-148

Kaleb, Vjekoslav 1905- DLB-181

Kalechofsky, Roberta 1931- DLB-28

Kaler, James Otis 1848-1912 .... DLB-12

Kames, Henry Home, Lord
1696-1782 .... DLB-31, 104

Kandel, Lenore 1932- DLB-16

Kanin, Garson 1912- DLB-7

Kant, Hermann 1926- DLB-75

Kant, Immanuel 1724-1804........ DLB-94

Kantemir, Antiokh Dmitrievich
1708-1744 .... DLB-150

Kantor, Mackinlay 1904-1977 .... DLB-9, 102

Kaplan, Fred 1937- DLB-111

Kaplan, Johanna 1942- DLB-28

Kaplan, Justin 1925- DLB-111

Kapnist, Vasilii Vasilevich
1758?-1823........ DLB-150

Karadžić, Vuk Stefanović
1787-1864 .... DLB-147

Karamzin, Nikolai Mikhailovich
1766-1826 .... DLB-150

Karsch, Anna Louisa 1722-1791 ..... DLB-97

Kasack, Hermann 1896-1966........ DLB-69

Kasai, Zenzō 1887-1927 .... DLB-180

Kaschnitz, Marie Luise 1901-1974 .... DLB-69

Kaštelan, Jure 1919-1990 .... DLB-147

Kästner, Erich 1899-1974. .... DLB-56

Kattan, Naim 1928- DLB-53

Katz, Steve 1935- Y-83

Kauffman, Janet 1945- Y-86

Kauffmann, Samuel 1898-1971 ..... DLB-127

Kaufman, Bob 1925- DLB-16, 41

Kaufman, George S. 1889-1961 ..... DLB-7

Kavanagh, P. J. 1931- DLB-40

Kavanagh, Patrick 1904-1967 ..... DLB-15, 20

Kawabata, Yasunari 1899-1972 ..... DLB-180

Kaye-Smith, Sheila 1887-1956. .... DLB-36

Kazin, Alfred 1915- DLB-67

Keane, John B. 1928- DLB-13

Keary, Annie 1825-1879........ DLB-163

Keating, H. R. F. 1926- DLB-87

Keats, Ezra Jack 1916-1983........ DLB-61

Keats, John 1795-1821 .... DLB-96, 110

Keble, John 1792-1866 .... DLB-32, 55

Keeble, John 1944- Y-83

Keeffe, Barrie 1945- DLB-13

Keeley, James 1867-1934 .... DLB-25

W. B. Keen, Cooke
and Company. DLB-49

Keillor, Garrison 1942- Y-87

Keith, Marian 1874?-1961 .... DLB-92

Keller, Gary D. 1943- DLB-82

Keller, Gottfried 1819-1890 .... DLB-129

Kelley, Edith Summers 1884-1956..... DLB-9

Kelley, William Melvin 1937- DLB-33

Kellogg, Ansel Nash 1832-1886 ..... DLB-23

Kellogg, Steven 1941- DLB-61

Kelly, George 1887-1974........ DLB-7

Kelly, Hugh 1739-1777 .... DLB-89

Kelly, Robert 1935- DLB-5, 130, 165

Kelly, Piet and Company DLB-49

Kelmscott Press DLB-112

Kemble, E. W. 1861-1933........ DLB-188

Kemble, Fanny 1809-1893 .... DLB-32

Kemelman, Harry 1908- DLB-28

Kempe, Margery circa 1373-1438.... DLB-146

Kempner, Friederike 1836-1904..... DLB-129

Kempowski, Walter 1929- DLB-75

Kendall, Claude [publishing company].. DLB-46

Kendell, George 1809-1867........ DLB-43

Kenedy, P. J., and Sons DLB-49

Kennan, George 1845-1924 .... DLB-189

Kennedy, Adrienne 1931- DLB-38

Kennedy, John Pendleton 1795-1870 .... DLB-3

Kennedy, Leo 1907- DLB-88

Kennedy, Margaret 1896-1967 ..... DLB-36

Kennedy, Patrick 1801-1873........ DLB-159

Kennedy, Richard S. 1920- DLB-111

Kennedy, William 1928- DLB-143; Y-85

Kennedy, X. J. 1929- DLB-5

Kennelly, Brendan 1936- DLB-40

Kenner, Hugh 1923- DLB-67

Kennerley, Mitchell
[publishing house]. DLB-46

Kenny, Maurice 1929- DLB-175

Kent, Frank R. 1877-1958 .... DLB-29

Kenyon, Jane 1947- DLB-120

Keough, Hugh Edmund 1864-1912... DLB-171

Keppler and Schwartzmann. DLB-49

Kerlan, Irvin 1912-1963........ DLB-187

Kern, Jerome 1885-1945........ DLB-187

Kerner, Justinus 1776-1862 .... DLB-90

Kerouac, Jack 1922-1969 .... DLB-2, 16; DS-3

The Jack Kerouac Revival........ Y-95

Kerouac, Jan 1952- DLB-16

Kerr, Orpheus C. (see Newell, Robert Henry)

Kerr, Charles H., and Company DLB-49

Kesey, Ken 1935- DLB-2, 16

Kessel, Joseph 1898-1979........ DLB-72

Kessel, Martin 1901- DLB-56

Kesten, Hermann 1900- DLB-56

Keun, Irmgard 1905-1982. .... DLB-69

Key and Biddle DLB-49

Keynes, John Maynard 1883-1946..... DS-10

Keyserling, Eduard von 1855-1918 ... DLB-66

Khan, Ismith 1925- DLB-125

Khaytov, Nikolay 1919- DLB-181

Khemnitser, Ivan Ivanovich
1745-1784 . . . . DLB-150

Kheraskov, Mikhail Matveevich
1733-1807 . . . . DLB-150

Khristov, Boris 1945- DLB-181

Khvostov, Dmitrii Ivanovich
1757-1835 . . . . DLB-150

Kidd, Adam 1802?-1831 . . . . DLB-99

Kidd, William
[publishing house] DLB-106

Kidder, Tracy 1945- DLB-185

Kiely, Benedict 1919- DLB-15

Kieran, John 1892-1981 . . . . DLB-171

Kiggins and Kellogg. DLB-49

Kiley, Jed 1889-1962 . . . . DLB-4

Kilgore, Bernard 1908-1967 . . . . . . DLB-127

Killens, John Oliver 1916- DLB-33

Killigrew, Anne 1660-1685 . . . . DLB-131

Killigrew, Thomas 1612-1683 . . . . . . DLB-58

Kilmer, Joyce 1886-1918 . . . . DLB-45

Kilwardby, Robert
circa 1215-1279 . . . . DLB-115

Kincaid, Jamaica 1949- DLB-157

King, Charles 1844-1933 . . . . DLB-186

King, Clarence 1842-1901 . . . . DLB-12

King, Florence 1936 . . . . Y-85

King, Francis 1923- DLB-15, 139

King, Grace 1852-1932 . . . . DLB-12, 78

King, Henry 1592-1669 . . . . DLB-126

King, Stephen 1947- DLB-143; Y-80

King, Thomas 1943- DLB-175

King, Woodie, Jr. 1937- DLB-38

King, Solomon [publishing house] DLB-49

Kinglake, Alexander William
1809-1891 . . . . DLB-55, 166

Kingsley, Charles
1819-1875 . . . . DLB-21, 32, 163, 178, 190

Kingsley, Mary Henrietta
1862-1900 . . . . DLB-174

Kingsley, Henry 1830-1876 . . . . DLB-21

Kingsley, Sidney 1906- DLB-7

Kingsmill, Hugh 1889-1949 . . . . DLB-149

Kingston, Maxine Hong
1940- DLB-173; Y-80

Kingston, William Henry Giles
1814-1880 . . . . DLB-163

Kinnell, Galway 1927- DLB-5; Y-87

Kinsella, Thomas 1928- DLB-27

Kipling, Rudyard
1865-1936 . . . . . DLB-19, 34, 141, 156

Kipphardt, Heinar 1922-1982 . . . . . . DLB-124

Kirby, William 1817-1906 . . . . DLB-99

Kircher, Athanasius 1602-1680 . . . . . DLB-164

Kirk, John Foster 1824-1904 . . . . . . DLB-79

Kirkconnell, Watson 1895-1977 . . . . . DLB-68

Kirkland, Caroline M.
1801-1864 . . . . . . DLB-3, 73, 74; DS-13

Kirkland, Joseph 1830-1893 . . . . DLB-12

Kirkman, Francis
[publishing house] DLB-170

Kirkpatrick, Clayton 1915- DLB-127

Kirkup, James 1918- DLB-27

Kirouac, Conrad (see Marie-Victorin, Frère)

Kirsch, Sarah 1935- DLB-75

Kirst, Hans Hellmut 1914-1989 . . . . . DLB-69

Kiš, Danilo 1935-1989 . . . . DLB-181

Kita, Morio 1927- DLB-182

Kitcat, Mabel Greenhow
1859-1922 . . . . DLB-135

Kitchin, C. H. B. 1895-1967 . . . . DLB-77

Kizer, Carolyn 1925- DLB-5, 169

Klabund 1890-1928 . . . . DLB-66

Klaj, Johann 1616-1656 . . . . DLB-164

Klappert, Peter 1942- DLB-5

Klass, Philip (see Tenn, William)

Klein, A. M. 1909-1972 . . . . DLB-68

Kleist, Ewald von 1715-1759 . . . . . . DLB-97

Kleist, Heinrich von 1777-1811 . . . . . DLB-90

Klinger, Friedrich Maximilian
1752-1831 . . . . DLB-94

Klopstock, Friedrich Gottlieb
1724-1803 . . . . DLB-97

Klopstock, Meta 1728-1758 . . . . DLB-97

Kluge, Alexander 1932- DLB-75

Knapp, Joseph Palmer 1864-1951 . . . . DLB-91

Knapp, Samuel Lorenzo
1783-1838 . . . . DLB-59

Knapton, J. J. and P.
[publishing house] DLB-154

Kniazhnin, Iakov Borisovich
1740-1791 . . . . DLB-150

Knickerbocker, Diedrich (see Irving,
Washington)

Knigge, Adolph Franz Friedrich Ludwig,
Freiherr von 1752-1796 . . . . DLB-94

Knight, Damon 1922- DLB-8

Knight, Etheridge 1931-1992 . . . . . . DLB-41

Knight, John S. 1894-1981 . . . . DLB-29

Knight, Sarah Kemble 1666-1727 . . . . DLB-24

Knight, Charles, and Company DLB-106

Knight-Bruce, G. W. H.
1852-1896 . . . . DLB-174

Knister, Raymond 1899-1932 . . . . . . DLB-68

Knoblock, Edward 1874-1945 . . . . . . DLB-10

Knopf, Alfred A. 1892-1984 . . . . Y-84

Knopf, Alfred A.
[publishing house] DLB-46

Knorr von Rosenroth, Christian
1636-1689 . . . . DLB-168

Knowles, John 1926- DLB-6

Knox, Frank 1874-1944 . . . . DLB-29

Knox, John circa 1514-1572 . . . . . . DLB-132

Knox, John Armoy 1850-1906 . . . . . . DLB-23

Knox, Ronald Arbuthnott
1888-1957 . . . . DLB-77

Knox, Thomas Wallace 1835-1896 . . . DLB-189

Kobayashi, Takiji 1903-1933 . . . . . . DLB-180

Kober, Arthur 1900-1975 . . . . DLB-11

Kocbek, Edvard 1904-1981 . . . . DLB-147

Koch, Howard 1902- DLB-26

Koch, Kenneth 1925- DLB-5

Kōda, Rohan 1867-1947 . . . . DLB-180

Koenigsberg, Moses 1879-1945 . . . . . DLB-25

Koeppen, Wolfgang 1906- DLB-69

Koertge, Ronald 1940- DLB-105

Koestler, Arthur 1905-1983 . . . . Y-83

Kohn, John S. Van E. 1906-1976 and
Papantonio, Michael 1907-1978 . . . DLB-187

Kokoschka, Oskar 1886-1980 . . . . . . DLB-124

Kolb, Annette 1870-1967 . . . . DLB-66

Kolbenheyer, Erwin Guido
1878-1962 . . . . DLB-66, 124

Kolleritsch, Alfred 1931- DLB-85

Kolodny, Annette 1941- DLB-67

Komarov, Matvei
circa 1730-1812 . . . . DLB-150

Komroff, Manuel 1890-1974 . . . . DLB-4

Komunyakaa, Yusef 1947- DLB-120

Koneski, Blaže 1921-1993 . . . . DLB-181

Konigsburg, E. L. 1930- DLB-52

Konrad von Würzburg
circa 1230-1287 . . . . DLB-138

Konstantinov, Aleko 1863-1897 . . . . . DLB-147

Kooser, Ted 1939- DLB-105

Kopit, Arthur 1937- DLB-7

Kops, Bernard 1926?- DLB-13

Kornbluth, C. M. 1923-1958 . . . . DLB-8

Körner, Theodor 1791-1813 . . . . DLB-90

Kornfeld, Paul 1889-1942 . . . . DLB-118

Kosinski, Jerzy 1933-1991 . . . . . DLB-2; Y-82

Kosmač, Ciril 1910-1980 . . . . DLB-181

Kosovel, Srečko 1904-1926 . . . . DLB-147

Kostrov, Ermil Ivanovich
1755-1796 . . . . DLB-150

Kotzebue, August von 1761-1819 . . . . DLB-94

Kotzwinkle, William 1938- DLB-173

Kovačić, Ante 1854-1889 . . . . DLB-147

Kovič, Kajetan 1931- DLB-181

Kraf, Elaine 1946- Y-81

Kramer, Jane 1938- DLB-185

Kramer, Mark 1944- DLB-185

Kranjčević, Silvije Strahimir
  1865-1908 .... DLB-147

Krasna, Norman 1909-1984 ..... DLB-26

Kraus, Hans Peter 1907-1988 ..... DLB-187

Kraus, Karl 1874-1936 .... DLB-118

Krauss, Ruth 1911-1993 .... DLB-52

Kreisel, Henry 1922- DLB-88

Kreuder, Ernst 1903-1972 .... DLB-69

Kreymborg, Alfred 1883-1966 ..... DLB-4, 54

Krieger, Murray 1923- DLB-67

Krim, Seymour 1922-1989 .... DLB-16

Krleža, Miroslav 1893-1981 ...... DLB-147

Krock, Arthur 1886-1974 .... DLB-29

Kroetsch, Robert 1927- ‰DLB-53

Krutch, Joseph Wood 1893-1970 .... DLB-63

Krylov, Ivan Andreevich
  1769-1844 .... DLB-150

Kubin, Alfred 1877-1959 .... DLB-81

Kubrick, Stanley 1928- DLB-26

Kudrun circa 1230-1240 .... DLB-138

Kuffstein, Hans Ludwig von
  1582-1656 .... DLB-164

Kuhlmann, Quirinus 1651-1689 .... DLB-168

Kuhnau, Johann 1660-1722 .... DLB-168

Kumin, Maxine 1925- DLB-5

Kunene, Mazisi 1930- DLB-117

Kunikida, Doppo 1869-1908 ...... DLB-180

Kunitz, Stanley 1905- DLB-48

Kunjufu, Johari M. (see Amini, Johari M.)

Kunnert, Gunter 1929- DLB-75

Kunze, Reiner 1933- DLB-75

Kupferberg, Tuli 1923- DLB-16

Kurahashi, Yumiko 1935- DLB-182

Kürnberger, Ferdinand
  1821-1879 .... DLB-129

Kurz, Isolde 1853-1944 .... DLB-66

Kusenberg, Kurt 1904-1983 ...... DLB-69

Kuttner, Henry 1915-1958 .... DLB-8

Kyd, Thomas 1558-1594 .... DLB-62

Kyffin, Maurice
  circa 1560?-1598 .... DLB-136

Kyger, Joanne 1934- DLB-16

Kyne, Peter B. 1880-1957 .... DLB-78

L

L. E. L. (see Landon, Letitia Elizabeth)

Laberge, Albert 1871-1960 .... DLB-68

Laberge, Marie 1950- DLB-60

Lacombe, Patrice (see Trullier-Lacombe, Joseph Patrice)

Lacretelle, Jacques de 1888-1985 .... DLB-65

Lacy, Sam 1903- DLB-171

Ladd, Joseph Brown 1764-1786 .... DLB-37

La Farge, Oliver 1901-1963 .... DLB-9

Lafferty, R. A. 1914- DLB-8

La Flesche, Francis 1857-1932 ..... DLB-175

La Guma, Alex 1925-1985 .... DLB-117

Lahaise, Guillaume (see Delahaye, Guy)

Lahontan, Louis-Armand de Lom d'Arce,
  Baron de 1666-1715? DLB-99

Laing, Kojo 1946- DLB-157

Laird, Caroberth 1895- Y-82

Laird and Lee DLB-49

Lalić, Ivan V. 1931-1996 .... DLB-181

Lalić, Mihailo 1914-1992 .... DLB-181

Lalonde, Michèle 1937- DLB-60

Lamantia, Philip 1927- DLB-16

Lamb, Charles
  1775-1834 .... DLB-93, 107, 163

Lamb, Lady Caroline 1785-1828 .... DLB-116

Lamb, Mary 1764-1874 .... DLB-163

Lambert, Betty 1933-1983 .... DLB-60

Lamming, George 1927- DLB-125

L'Amour, Louis 1908?- Y-80

Lampman, Archibald 1861-1899 .... DLB-92

Lamson, Wolffe and Company DLB-49

Lancer Books DLB-46

Landesman, Jay 1919- and
  Landesman, Fran 1927- DLB-16

Landolfi, Tommaso 1908-1979 ..... DLB-177

Landon, Letitia Elizabeth 1802-1838 ... DLB-96

Landor, Walter Savage
  1775-1864 .... DLB-93, 107

Landry, Napoléon-P. 1884-1956 .... DLB-92

Lane, Charles 1800-1870 .... DLB-1

Lane, Laurence W. 1890-1967 ..... DLB-91

Lane, M. Travis 1934- DLB-60

Lane, Patrick 1939- DLB-53

Lane, Pinkie Gordon 1923- DLB-41

Lane, John, Company DLB-49

Laney, Al 1896-1988 .... DLB-4, 171

Lang, Andrew 1844-1912 .... DLB-98, 141, 184

Langevin, André 1927- DLB-60

Langgässer, Elisabeth 1899-1950 .... DLB-69

Langhorne, John 1735-1779 ...... DLB-109

Langland, William
  circa 1330-circa 1400 .... DLB-146

Langton, Anna 1804-1893 .... DLB-99

Lanham, Edwin 1904-1979 .... DLB-4

Lanier, Sidney 1842-1881 .... DLB-64; DS-13

Lanyer, Aemilia 1569-1645 .... DLB-121

Lapointe, Gatien 1931-1983 .... DLB-88

Lapointe, Paul-Marie 1929- DLB-88

Lardner, John 1912-1960 .... DLB-171

Lardner, Ring
  1885-1933 ... DLB-11, 25, 86, 171; DS-16

Lardner, Ring, Jr. 1915- DLB-26

Lardner 100: Ring Lardner
  Centennial Symposium Y-85

Larkin, Philip 1922-1985 .... DLB-27

La Roche, Sophie von 1730-1807 .... DLB-94

La Rocque, Gilbert 1943-1984 ..... DLB-60

Laroque de Roquebrune, Robert (see Roquebrune, Robert de)

Larrick, Nancy 1910- DLB-61

Larsen, Nella 1893-1964 .... DLB-51

Lasker-Schüler, Else
  1869-1945 .... DLB-66, 124

Lasnier, Rina 1915- DLB-88

Lassalle, Ferdinand 1825-1864 ..... DLB-129

Lathrop, Dorothy P. 1891-1980 .... DLB-22

Lathrop, George Parsons
  1851-1898 .... DLB-71

Lathrop, John, Jr. 1772-1820 ...... DLB-37

Latimer, Hugh 1492?-1555 .... DLB-136

Latimore, Jewel Christine McLawler
  (see Amini, Johari M.)

Latymer, William 1498-1583 ..... DLB-132

Laube, Heinrich 1806-1884 ...... DLB-133

Laughlin, James 1914- DLB-48

Laumer, Keith 1925- DLB-8

Lauremberg, Johann 1590-1658 ... DLB-164

Laurence, Margaret 1926-1987 ... DLB-53

Laurentius von Schnüffis
  1633-1702 .... DLB-168

Laurents, Arthur 1918- DLB-26

Laurie, Annie (see Black, Winifred)

Laut, Agnes Christiana 1871-1936 .... DLB-92

Lavater, Johann Kaspar 1741-1801 ... DLB-97

Lavin, Mary 1912- DLB-15

Lawes, Henry 1596-1662 .... DLB-126

Lawless, Anthony (see MacDonald, Philip)

Lawrence, D. H.
  1885-1930 ..... DLB-10, 19, 36, 98, 162

Lawrence, David 1888-1973 ...... DLB-29

Lawrence, Seymour 1926-1994 .... Y-94

Lawson, John ?-1711 .... DLB-24

Lawson, Robert 1892-1957 .... DLB-22

Lawson, Victor F. 1850-1925 ...... DLB-25

Layard, Sir Austen Henry
  1817-1894 .... DLB-166

Layton, Irving 1912- DLB-88

LaZamon flourished circa 1200 ... DLB-146

Lazarević, Laza K. 1851-1890......DLB-147
Lea, Henry Charles 1825-1909......DLB-47
Lea, Sydney 1942-......DLB-120
Lea, Tom 1907-......DLB-6
Leacock, John 1729-1802......DLB-31
Leacock, Stephen 1869-1944......DLB-92
Lead, Jane Ward 1623-1704......DLB-131
Leadenhall Press......DLB-106
Leapor, Mary 1722-1746......DLB-109
Lear, Edward 1812-1888......DLB-32, 163, 166
Leary, Timothy 1920-1996......DLB-16
Leary, W. A., and Company......DLB-49
Léautaud, Paul 1872-1956......DLB-65
Leavitt, David 1961-......DLB-130
Leavitt and Allen......DLB-49
Le Blond, Mrs. Aubrey 1861-1934......DLB-174
le Carré, John 1931-......DLB-87
Lécavelé, Roland (see Dorgeles, Roland)
Lechlitner, Ruth 1901-......DLB-48
Leclerc, Félix 1914-......DLB-60
Le Clézio, J. M. G. 1940-......DLB-83
Lectures on Rhetoric and Belles Lettres (1783), by Hugh Blair [excerpts]......DLB-31
Leder, Rudolf (see Hermlin, Stephan)
Lederer, Charles 1910-1976......DLB-26
Ledwidge, Francis 1887-1917......DLB-20
Lee, Dennis 1939-......DLB-53
Lee, Don L. (see Madhubuti, Haki R.)
Lee, George W. 1894-1976......DLB-51
Lee, Harper 1926-......DLB-6
Lee, Harriet (1757-1851) and Lee, Sophia (1750-1824)......DLB-39
Lee, Laurie 1914-......DLB-27
Lee, Li-Young 1957-......DLB-165
Lee, Manfred B. (see Dannay, Frederic, and Manfred B. Lee)
Lee, Nathaniel circa 1645 - 1692......DLB-80
Lee, Sir Sidney 1859-1926......DLB-149, 184
Lee, Sir Sidney, "Principles of Biography," in *Elizabethan and Other Essays*......DLB-149
Lee, Vernon 1856-1935......DLB-57, 153, 156, 174, 178
Lee and Shepard......DLB-49
Le Fanu, Joseph Sheridan 1814-1873......DLB-21, 70, 159, 178
Leffland, Ella 1931-......Y-84
le Fort, Gertrud von 1876-1971......DLB-66
Le Gallienne, Richard 1866-1947......DLB-4
Legaré, Hugh Swinton 1797-1843......DLB-3, 59, 73
Legaré, James M. 1823-1859......DLB-3

The Legends of the Saints and a Medieval Christian Worldview......DLB-148
Léger, Antoine-J. 1880-1950......DLB-88
Le Guin, Ursula K. 1929-......DLB-8, 52
Lehman, Ernest 1920-......DLB-44
Lehmann, John 1907-......DLB-27, 100
Lehmann, Rosamond 1901-1990......DLB-15
Lehmann, Wilhelm 1882-1968......DLB-56
Lehmann, John, Limited......DLB-112
Leiber, Fritz 1910-1992......DLB-8
Leibniz, Gottfried Wilhelm 1646-1716......DLB-168
Leicester University Press......DLB-112
Leigh, W. R. 1866-1955......DLB-188
Leinster, Murray 1896-1975......DLB-8
Leisewitz, Johann Anton 1752-1806......DLB-94
Leitch, Maurice 1933-......DLB-14
Leithauser, Brad 1943-......DLB-120
Leland, Charles G. 1824-1903......DLB-11
Leland, John 1503?-1552......DLB-136
Lemay, Pamphile 1837-1918......DLB-99
Lemelin, Roger 1919-......DLB-88
Lemon, Mark 1809-1870......DLB-163
Le Moine, James MacPherson 1825-1912......DLB-99
Le Moyne, Jean 1913-......DLB-88
Lemperly, Paul 1858-1939......DLB-187
L'Engle, Madeleine 1918-......DLB-52
Lennart, Isobel 1915-1971......DLB-44
Lennox, Charlotte 1729 or 1730-1804......DLB-39
Lenox, James 1800-1880......DLB-140
Lenski, Lois 1893-1974......DLB-22
Lenz, Hermann 1913-......DLB-69
Lenz, J. M. R. 1751-1792......DLB-94
Lenz, Siegfried 1926-......DLB-75
Leonard, Elmore 1925-......DLB-173
Leonard, Hugh 1926-......DLB-13
Leonard, William Ellery 1876-1944......DLB-54
Leonowens, Anna 1834-1914......DLB-99, 166
LePan, Douglas 1914-......DLB-88
Leprohon, Rosanna Eleanor 1829-1879......DLB-99
Le Queux, William 1864-1927......DLB-70
Lerner, Max 1902-1992......DLB-29
Lernet-Holenia, Alexander 1897-1976......DLB-85
Le Rossignol, James 1866-1969......DLB-92
Lescarbot, Marc circa 1570-1642......DLB-99
LeSeur, William Dawson 1840-1917......DLB-92

LeSieg, Theo. (see Geisel, Theodor Seuss)
Leslie, Frank 1821-1880......DLB-43, 79
Leslie, Frank, Publishing House......DLB-49
Lesperance, John 1835?-1891......DLB-99
Lessing, Bruno 1870-1940......DLB-28
Lessing, Doris 1919-......DLB-15, 139; Y-85
Lessing, Gotthold Ephraim 1729-1781......DLB-97
Lettau, Reinhard 1929-......DLB-75
Letter from Japan......Y-94
Letter from London......Y-96
Letter to [Samuel] Richardson on *Clarissa* (1748), by Henry Fielding......DLB-39
Lever, Charles 1806-1872......DLB-21
Leverson, Ada 1862-1933......DLB-153
Levertov, Denise 1923-......DLB-5, 165
Levi, Peter 1931-......DLB-40
Levi, Primo 1919-1987......DLB-177
Levien, Sonya 1888-1960......DLB-44
Levin, Meyer 1905-1981......DLB-9, 28; Y-81
Levine, Norman 1923-......DLB-88
Levine, Philip 1928-......DLB-5
Levis, Larry 1946-......DLB-120
Levy, Amy 1861-1889......DLB-156
Levy, Benn Wolfe 1900-1973......DLB-13; Y-81
Lewald, Fanny 1811-1889......DLB-129
Lewes, George Henry 1817-1878......DLB-55, 144
Lewis, Agnes Smith 1843-1926......DLB-174
Lewis, Alfred H. 1857-1914......DLB-25, 186
Lewis, Alun 1915-1944......DLB-20, 162
Lewis, C. Day (see Day Lewis, C.)
Lewis, C. S. 1898-1963......DLB-15, 100, 160
Lewis, Charles B. 1842-1924......DLB-11
Lewis, Henry Clay 1825-1850......DLB-3
Lewis, Janet 1899-......Y-87
Lewis, Matthew Gregory 1775-1818......DLB-39, 158, 178
Lewis, Meriwether 1774-1809 and Clark, William 1770-1838......DLB-183, 186
Lewis, R. W. B. 1917-......DLB-111
Lewis, Richard circa 1700-1734......DLB-24
Lewis, Sinclair 1885-1951......DLB-9, 102; DS-1
Lewis, Wilmarth Sheldon 1895-1979......DLB-140
Lewis, Wyndham 1882-1957......DLB-15
Lewisohn, Ludwig 1882-1955......DLB-4, 9, 28, 102
Leyendecker, J. C. 1874-1951......DLB-188
Lezama Lima, José 1910-1976......DLB-113
The Library of America......DLB-46

The Licensing Act of 1737 . . . . DLB-84

Lichfield, Leonard I
[publishing house] DLB-170

Lichtenberg, Georg Christoph
1742-1799 . . . . DLB-94

Lieb, Fred 1888-1980 . . . . DLB-171

Liebling, A. J. 1904-1963 . . . . . . DLB-4, 171

Lieutenant Murray (see Ballou, Maturin Murray)

Lighthall, William Douw
1857-1954 . . . . DLB-92

Lilar, Françoise (see Mallet-Joris, Françoise)

Lillo, George 1691-1739 . . . . DLB-84

Lilly, J. K., Jr. 1893-1966 . . . . DLB-140

Lilly, Wait and Company DLB-49

Lily, William circa 1468-1522 . . . . . DLB-132

Limited Editions Club DLB-46

Lincoln and Edmands DLB-49

Lindsay, Alexander William, Twenty-fifth Earl of Crawford 1812-1880 . . . . . . DLB-184

Lindsay, Jack 1900- Y-84

Lindsay, Sir David
circa 1485-1555 . . . . DLB-132

Lindsay, Vachel 1879-1931 . . . . DLB-54

Linebarger, Paul Myron Anthony (see Smith, Cordwainer)

Link, Arthur S. 1920- DLB-17

Linn, John Blair 1777-1804 . . . . DLB-37

Lins, Osman 1924-1978 . . . . DLB-145

Linton, Eliza Lynn 1822-1898 . . . . . DLB-18

Linton, William James 1812-1897 . . . DLB-32

Lintot, Barnaby Bernard
[publishing house] DLB-170

Lion Books DLB-46

Lionni, Leo 1910- DLB-61

Lippincott, Sara Jane Clarke
1823-1904 . . . . DLB-43

Lippincott, J. B., Company DLB-49

Lippmann, Walter 1889-1974 . . . . . DLB-29

Lipton, Lawrence 1898-1975 . . . . . DLB-16

Liscow, Christian Ludwig
1701-1760 . . . . DLB-97

Lish, Gordon 1934- DLB-130

Lispector, Clarice 1925-1977 . . . . . DLB-113

The Literary Chronicle and Weekly Review
1819-1828 . . . . DLB-110

Literary Documents: William Faulkner and the People-to-People Program Y-86

Literary Documents II: Library Journal Statements and Questionnaires from First Novelists Y-87

Literary Effects of World War II
[British novel] DLB-15

Literary Prizes [British] DLB-15

Literary Research Archives: The Humanities Research Center, University of Texas Y-82

Literary Research Archives II: Berg Collection of English and American Literature of the New York Public Library Y-83

Literary Research Archives III:
The Lilly Library Y-84

Literary Research Archives IV:
The John Carter Brown Library Y-85

Literary Research Archives V:
Kent State Special Collections Y-86

Literary Research Archives VI: The Modern Literary Manuscripts Collection in the Special Collections of the Washington University Libraries Y-87

Literary Research Archives VII:
The University of Virginia Libraries Y-91

Literary Research Archives VIII:
The Henry E. Huntington Library Y-92

"Literary Style" (1857), by William Forsyth [excerpt] DLB-57

Literatura Chicanesca: The View From Without DLB-82

Literature at Nurse, or Circulating Morals (1885), by George Moore DLB-18

Littell, Eliakim 1797-1870 . . . . DLB-79

Littell, Robert S. 1831-1896 . . . . . . DLB-79

Little, Brown and Company DLB-49

Little Magazines and Newspapers DS-15

The Little Review 1914-1929 . . . . . . DS-15

Littlewood, Joan 1914- DLB-13

Lively, Penelope 1933- DLB-14, 161

Liverpool University Press DLB-112

The Lives of the Poets DLB-142

Livesay, Dorothy 1909- DLB-68

Livesay, Florence Randal
1874-1953 . . . . DLB-92

Livings, Henry 1929- DLB-13

Livingston, Anne Howe
1763-1841 . . . . DLB-37

Livingston, Myra Cohn 1926- DLB-61

Livingston, William 1723-1790 . . . . . DLB-31

Livingstone, David 1813-1873 . . . . . DLB-166

Liyong, Taban lo (see Taban lo Liyong)

Lizárraga, Sylvia S. 1925- DLB-82

Llewellyn, Richard 1906-1983 . . . . . DLB-15

Lloyd, Edward
[publishing house] DLB-106

Lobel, Arnold 1933- DLB-61

Lochridge, Betsy Hopkins (see Fancher, Betsy)

Locke, David Ross 1833-1888 . . . DLB-11, 23

Locke, John 1632-1704 . . . . . . DLB-31, 101

Locke, Richard Adams 1800-1871 . . . DLB-43

Locker-Lampson, Frederick
1821-1895 . . . . DLB-35, 184

Lockhart, John Gibson
1794-1854 . . . . DLB-110, 116 144

Lockridge, Ross, Jr.
1914-1948 . . . . DLB-143; Y-80

Locrine and *Selimus* DLB-62

Lodge, David 1935- DLB-14

Lodge, George Cabot 1873-1909 . . . . DLB-54

Lodge, Henry Cabot 1850-1924 . . . . . DLB-47

Lodge, Thomas 1558-1625 . . . . DLB-172

Loeb, Harold 1891-1974 . . . . DLB-4

Loeb, William 1905-1981 . . . . DLB-127

Lofting, Hugh 1886-1947 . . . . DLB-160

Logan, James 1674-1751 . . . . . DLB-24, 140

Logan, John 1923- DLB-5

Logan, William 1950- DLB-120

Logau, Friedrich von 1605-1655 . . . . DLB-164

Logue, Christopher 1926- DLB-27

Lohenstein, Daniel Casper von
1635-1683 . . . . DLB-168

Lomonosov, Mikhail Vasil'evich
1711-1765 . . . . DLB-150

London, Jack 1876-1916 . . . . . DLB-8, 12, 78

The London Magazine 1820-1829 . . . . DLB-110

Long, Haniel 1888-1956 . . . . DLB-45

Long, Ray 1878-1935 . . . . DLB-137

Long, H., and Brother DLB-49

Longfellow, Henry Wadsworth
1807-1882 . . . . DLB-1, 59

Longfellow, Samuel 1819-1892 . . . . . DLB-1

Longford, Elizabeth 1906- DLB-155

Longinus circa first century DLB-176

Longley, Michael 1939- DLB-40

Longman, T. [publishing house] DLB-154

Longmans, Green and Company DLB-49

Longmore, George 1793?-1867 . . . . . DLB-99

Longstreet, Augustus Baldwin
1790-1870 . . . . DLB-3, 11, 74

Longworth, D. [publishing house] . . . DLB-49

Lonsdale, Frederick 1881-1954 . . . . . DLB-10

A Look at the Contemporary Black Theatre Movement DLB-38

Loos, Anita 1893-1981 . . . . . DLB-11, 26; Y-81

Lopate, Phillip 1943- Y-80

López, Diana (see Isabella, Ríos)

Loranger, Jean-Aubert 1896-1942 . . . . DLB-92

Lorca, Federico García 1898-1936 . . . DLB-108

Lord, John Keast 1818-1872 . . . . . . DLB-99

The Lord Chamberlain's Office and Stage Censorship in England DLB-10

Lorde, Audre 1934-1992 . . . . DLB-41

Lorimer, George Horace 1867-1939 . . . . DLB-91
Loring, A. K. [publishing house] DLB-49
Loring and Mussey DLB-46
Lossing, Benson J. 1813-1891 . . . . . . DLB-30
Lothar, Ernst 1890-1974 . . . . DLB-81
Lothrop, Harriet M. 1844-1924 . . . . . DLB-42
Lothrop, D., and Company DLB-49
Loti, Pierre 1850-1923 . . . . DLB-123
Lotichius Secundus, Petrus 1528-1560 . . . . DLB-179
Lott, Emeline ?-? DLB-166
The Lounger, no. 20 (1785), by Henry Mackenzie DLB-39
Lounsbury, Thomas R. 1838-1915 . . . . DLB-71
Louÿs, Pierre 1870-1925 . . . . DLB-123
Lovelace, Earl 1935- DLB-125
Lovelace, Richard 1618-1657 . . . . . . DLB-131
Lovell, Coryell and Company DLB-49
Lovell, John W., Company DLB-49
Lover, Samuel 1797-1868 . . . . DLB-159, 190
Lovesey, Peter 1936- DLB-87
Lovingood, Sut (see Harris, George Washington)
Low, Samuel 1765-? DLB-37
Lowell, Amy 1874-1925 . . . . . . DLB-54, 140
Lowell, James Russell 1819-1891 . . . . . DLB-1, 11, 64, 79, 189
Lowell, Robert 1917-1977 . . . . . DLB-5, 169
Lowenfels, Walter 1897-1976 . . . . . . DLB-4
Lowndes, Marie Belloc 1868-1947 . . . . DLB-70
Lowndes, William Thomas 1798-1843 . . . . DLB-184
Lownes, Humphrey [publishing house] DLB-170
Lowry, Lois 1937- DLB-52
Lowry, Malcolm 1909-1957 . . . . DLB-15
Lowther, Pat 1935-1975 . . . . DLB-53
Loy, Mina 1882-1966 . . . . DLB-4, 54
Lozeau, Albert 1878-1924 . . . . DLB-92
Lubbock, Percy 1879-1965 . . . . DLB-149
Lucas, E. V. 1868-1938 . . . . DLB-98, 149, 153
Lucas, Fielding, Jr. [publishing house] DLB-49
Luce, Henry R. 1898-1967 . . . . DLB-91
Luce, John W., and Company DLB-46
Lucian circa 120-180 . . . . DLB-176
Lucie-Smith, Edward 1933- DLB-40
Lucini, Gian Pietro 1867-1914 . . . . . DLB-114
Luder, Peter circa 1415-1472 . . . . . . DLB-179
Ludlum, Robert 1927- Y-82
Ludus de Antichristo circa 1160 . . . . . DLB-148
Ludvigson, Susan 1942- DLB-120

Ludwig, Jack 1922- DLB-60
Ludwig, Otto 1813-1865 . . . . DLB-129
Ludwigslied 881 or 882 . . . . DLB-148
Luera, Yolanda 1953- DLB-122
Luft, Lya 1938- DLB-145
Luke, Peter 1919- DLB-13
Lummis, Charles F. 1859-1928 . . . . . DLB-186
Lupton, F. M., Company DLB-49
Lupus of Ferrières circa 805-circa 862 . . . . DLB-148
Lurie, Alison 1926- DLB-2
Luther, Martin 1483-1546 . . . . DLB-179
Luzi, Mario 1914- DLB-128
L'vov, Nikolai Aleksandrovich 1751-1803 . . . . DLB-150
Lyall, Gavin 1932- DLB-87
Lydgate, John circa 1370-1450 . . . . . DLB-146
Lyly, John circa 1554-1606 . . . . DLB-62, 167
Lynch, Patricia 1898-1972 . . . . DLB-160
Lynch, Richard flourished 1596-1601 . . . . DLB-172
Lynd, Robert 1879-1949 . . . . DLB-98
Lyon, Matthew 1749-1822 . . . . DLB-43
Lysias circa 459 B.C.-circa 380 B.C. DLB-176
Lytle, Andrew 1902-1995 . . . . . DLB-6; Y-95
Lytton, Edward (see Bulwer-Lytton, Edward)
Lytton, Edward Robert Bulwer 1831-1891 . . . . DLB-32

M

Maass, Joachim 1901-1972 . . . . DLB-69
Mabie, Hamilton Wright 1845-1916 . . . . DLB-71
Mac A'Ghobhainn, Iain (see Smith, Iain Crichton)
MacArthur, Charles 1895-1956 . . . . DLB-7, 25, 44
Macaulay, Catherine 1731-1791 . . . . . DLB-104
Macaulay, David 1945- DLB-61
Macaulay, Rose 1881-1958 . . . . DLB-36
Macaulay, Thomas Babington 1800-1859 . . . . DLB-32, 55
Macaulay Company DLB-46
MacBeth, George 1932- DLB-40
Macbeth, Madge 1880-1965 . . . . . . DLB-92
MacCaig, Norman 1910- DLB-27
MacDiarmid, Hugh 1892-1978 . . . . . DLB-20
MacDonald, Cynthia 1928- DLB-105
MacDonald, George 1824-1905 . . . . DLB-18, 163, 178

MacDonald, John D. 1916-1986 . . . . DLB-8; Y-86
MacDonald, Philip 1899?-1980 . . . . . DLB-77
Macdonald, Ross (see Millar, Kenneth)
MacDonald, Wilson 1880-1967 . . . . . DLB-92
Macdonald and Company (Publishers) DLB-112
MacEwen, Gwendolyn 1941- DLB-53
Macfadden, Bernarr 1868-1955 . . . . DLB-25, 91
MacGregor, John 1825-1892 . . . . . . DLB-166
MacGregor, Mary Esther (see Keith, Marian)
Machado, Antonio 1875-1939 . . . . . DLB-108
Machado, Manuel 1874-1947 . . . . . DLB-108
Machar, Agnes Maule 1837-1927 . . . . DLB-92
Machen, Arthur Llewelyn Jones 1863-1947 . . . . DLB-36, 156, 178
MacInnes, Colin 1914-1976 . . . . DLB-14
MacInnes, Helen 1907-1985 . . . . . . DLB-87
Mack, Maynard 1909- DLB-111
Mackall, Leonard L. 1879-1937 . . . . . DLB-140
MacKaye, Percy 1875-1956 . . . . DLB-54
Macken, Walter 1915-1967 . . . . DLB-13
Mackenzie, Alexander 1763-1820 . . . . . DLB-99
Mackenzie, Alexander Slidell 1803-1848 . . . . DLB-183
Mackenzie, Compton 1883-1972 . . . . DLB-34, 100
Mackenzie, Henry 1745-1831 . . . . . . DLB-39
Mackenzie, William 1758-1828 . . . . . DLB-187
Mackey, Nathaniel 1947- DLB-169
Mackey, William Wellington 1937- DLB-38
Mackintosh, Elizabeth (see Tey, Josephine)
Mackintosh, Sir James 1765-1832 . . . . DLB-158
Maclaren, Ian (see Watson, John)
Macklin, Charles 1699-1797 . . . . DLB-89
MacLean, Katherine Anne 1925- DLB-8
MacLeish, Archibald 1892-1982 . . . . DLB-4, 7, 45; Y-82
MacLennan, Hugh 1907-1990 . . . . . DLB-68
Macleod, Fiona (see Sharp, William)
MacLeod, Alistair 1936- DLB-60
Macleod, Norman 1906-1985 . . . . . . DLB-4
Macmillan and Company DLB-106
The Macmillan Company DLB-49
Macmillan's English Men of Letters, First Series (1878-1892) DLB-144
MacNamara, Brinsley 1890-1963 . . . . DLB-10
MacNeice, Louis 1907-1963 . . . . DLB-10, 20
MacPhail, Andrew 1864-1938 . . . . . DLB-92
Macpherson, James 1736-1796 . . . . . DLB-109

Macpherson, Jay 1931- DLB-53
Macpherson, Jeanie 1884-1946 . . . . . . DLB-44
Macrae Smith Company DLB-46
Macrone, John
  [publishing house] DLB-106
MacShane, Frank 1927- DLB-111
Macy-Masius DLB-46
Madden, David 1933- DLB-6
Madden, Sir Frederic 1801-1873 . . . . DLB-184
Maddow, Ben 1909-1992 . . . . DLB-44
Maddux, Rachel 1912-1983 . . . . Y-93
Madgett, Naomi Long 1923- DLB-76
Madhubuti, Haki R.
  1942- DLB-5, 41; DS-8
Madison, James 1751-1836 . . . . DLB-37
Magee, David 1905-1977 . . . . DLB-187
Maginn, William 1794-1842 . . . . DLB-110, 159
Mahan, Alfred Thayer 1840-1914 . . . . DLB-47
Maheux-Forcier, Louise 1929- DLB-60
Mahin, John Lee 1902-1984 . . . . DLB-44
Mahon, Derek 1941- DLB-40
Maikov, Vasilii Ivanovich
  1728-1778 . . . . DLB-150
Mailer, Norman
  1923- . . DLB-2, 16, 28, 185; Y-80, 83; DS-3
Maillet, Adrienne 1885-1963 . . . . . . DLB-68
Maimonides, Moses 1138-1204 . . . . DLB-115
Maillet, Antonine 1929- DLB-60
Maillu, David G. 1939- DLB-157
Main Selections of the Book-of-the-Month
  Club, 1926-1945 . . . . DLB-9
Main Trends in Twentieth-Century Book Clubs
  . . . . DLB-46
Mainwaring, Daniel 1902-1977 . . . . . DLB-44
Mair, Charles 1838-1927 . . . . DLB-99
Mais, Roger 1905-1955 . . . . DLB-125
Major, Andre 1942- DLB-60
Major, Clarence 1936- DLB-33
Major, Kevin 1949- DLB-60
Major Books DLB-46
Makemie, Francis circa 1658-1708 . . . . DLB-24
The Making of a People, by
  J. M. Ritchie DLB-66
Maksimović, Desanka 1898-1993 . . . . DLB-147
Malamud, Bernard
  1914-1986 . . . . . DLB-2, 28, 152; Y-80, 86
Malet, Lucas 1852-1931 . . . . DLB-153
Malleson, Lucy Beatrice (see Gilbert, Anthony)
Mallet-Joris, Françoise 1930- DLB-83
Mallock, W. H. 1849-1923 . . . . . . DLB-18, 57
Malone, Dumas 1892-1986 . . . . DLB-17
Malone, Edmond 1741-1812 . . . . . . DLB-142

Malory, Sir Thomas
  circa 1400-1410 - 1471 . . . . DLB-146
Malraux, André 1901-1976 . . . . DLB-72
Malthus, Thomas Robert
  1766-1834 . . . . DLB-107, 158
Maltz, Albert 1908-1985 . . . . DLB-102
Malzberg, Barry N. 1939- DLB-8
Mamet, David 1947- DLB-7
Manaka, Matsemela 1956- DLB-157
Manchester University Press DLB-112
Mandel, Eli 1922- DLB-53
Mandeville, Bernard 1670-1733 . . . . . DLB-101
Mandeville, Sir John
  mid fourteenth century DLB-146
Mandiargues, André Pieyre de
  1909- DLB-83
Manfred, Frederick 1912-1994 . . . . . . DLB-6
Mangan, Sherry 1904-1961 . . . . DLB-4
Mankiewicz, Herman 1897-1953 . . . . . DLB-26
Mankiewicz, Joseph L. 1909-1993 . . . . DLB-44
Mankowitz, Wolf 1924- DLB-15
Manley, Delarivière
  1672?-1724 . . . . DLB-39, 80
Mann, Abby 1927- DLB-44
Mann, Heinrich 1871-1950 . . . . DLB-66, 118
Mann, Horace 1796-1859 . . . . DLB-1
Mann, Klaus 1906-1949 . . . . DLB-56
Mann, Thomas 1875-1955 . . . . DLB-66
Mann, William D'Alton
  1839-1920 . . . . DLB-137
Manning, Marie 1873?-1945 . . . . DLB-29
Manning and Loring DLB-49
Mannyng, Robert
  flourished 1303-1338 . . . . DLB-146
Mano, D. Keith 1942- DLB-6
Manor Books DLB-46
Mansfield, Katherine 1888-1923 . . . . . DLB-162
Manuel, Niklaus circa 1484-1530 . . . . DLB-179
Manzini, Gianna 1896-1974 . . . . DLB-177
Mapanje, Jack 1944- DLB-157
March, William 1893-1954 . . . . . . DLB-9, 86
Marchand, Leslie A. 1900- DLB-103
Marchant, Bessie 1862-1941 . . . . . . DLB-160
Marchessault, Jovette 1938- DLB-60
Marcus, Frank 1928- DLB-13
Marden, Orison Swett
  1850-1924 . . . . DLB-137
Marechera, Dambudzo
  1952-1987 . . . . DLB-157
Marek, Richard, Books DLB-46
Mares, E. A. 1938- DLB-122
Mariani, Paul 1940- DLB-111
Marie-Victorin, Frère 1885-1944 . . . . . DLB-92

Marin, Biagio 1891-1985 . . . . DLB-128
Marincović, Ranko 1913- DLB-147
Marinetti, Filippo Tommaso
  1876-1944 . . . . DLB-114
Marion, Frances 1886-1973 . . . . DLB-44
Marius, Richard C. 1933- Y-85
The Mark Taper Forum DLB-7
Mark Twain on Perpetual Copyright Y-92
Markfield, Wallace 1926- DLB-2, 28
Markham, Edwin 1852-1940 . . . . DLB-54, 186
Markle, Fletcher 1921-1991 . . . DLB-68; Y-91
Marlatt, Daphne 1942- DLB-60
Marlitt, E. 1825-1887 . . . . DLB-129
Marlowe, Christopher 1564-1593 . . . . DLB-62
Marlyn, John 1912- DLB-88
Marmion, Shakerley 1603-1639 . . . . . DLB-58
Der Marner
  before 1230-circa 1287 . . . . DLB-138
The *Marprelate* Tracts 1588-1589 . . . . DLB-132
Marquand, John P. 1893-1960 . . . DLB-9, 102
Marqués, René 1919-1979 . . . . DLB-113
Marquis, Don 1878-1937 . . . . . . DLB-11, 25
Marriott, Anne 1913- DLB-68
Marryat, Frederick 1792-1848 . . . . DLB-21, 163
Marsh, George Perkins
  1801-1882 . . . . DLB-1, 64
Marsh, James 1794-1842 . . . . DLB-1, 59
Marsh, Capen, Lyon and Webb DLB-49
Marsh, Ngaio 1899-1982 . . . . DLB-77
Marshall, Edison 1894-1967 . . . . DLB-102
Marshall, Edward 1932- DLB-16
Marshall, Emma 1828-1899 . . . . DLB-163
Marshall, James 1942-1992 . . . . DLB-61
Marshall, Joyce 1913- DLB-88
Marshall, Paule 1929- DLB-33, 157
Marshall, Tom 1938- DLB-60
Marsilius of Padua
  circa 1275-circa 1342 . . . . DLB-115
Marson, Una 1905-1965 . . . . DLB-157
Marston, John 1576-1634 . . . . . . DLB-58, 172
Marston, Philip Bourke 1850-1887 . . . . DLB-35
Martens, Kurt 1870-1945 . . . . DLB-66
Martien, William S.
  [publishing house] DLB-49
Martin, Abe (see Hubbard, Kin)
Martin, Charles 1942- DLB-120
Martin, Claire 1914- DLB-60
Martin, Jay 1935- DLB-111
Martin, Johann (see Laurentius von Schnüffis)
Martin, Violet Florence (see Ross, Martin)
Martin du Gard, Roger 1881-1958 . . . DLB-65

Martineau, Harriet 1802-1876
...... DLB-21, 55, 159, 163, 166, 190

Martínez, Eliud 1935- DLB-122

Martínez, Max 1943- DLB-82

Martyn, Edward 1859-1923....... DLB-10

Marvell, Andrew 1621-1678...... DLB-131

Marvin X 1944- DLB-38

Marx, Karl 1818-1883.......... DLB-129

Marzials, Theo 1850-1920 .... DLB-35

Masefield, John
1878-1967 ...... DLB-10, 19, 153, 160

Mason, A. E. W. 1865-1948. ... DLB-70

Mason, Bobbie Ann
1940- DLB-173; Y-87

Mason, William 1725-1797 ...... DLB-142

Mason Brothers DLB-49

Massey, Gerald 1828-1907....... DLB-32

Massey, Linton R. 1900-1974...... DLB-187

Massinger, Philip 1583-1640 ..... DLB-58

Masson, David 1822-1907........ DLB-144

Masters, Edgar Lee 1868-1950..... DLB-54

Mastronardi, Lucio 1930-1979..... DLB-177

Matevski, Mateja 1929- DLB-181

Mather, Cotton
1663-1728.......... DLB-24, 30, 140

Mather, Increase 1639-1723. .... DLB-24

Mather, Richard 1596-1669....... DLB-24

Matheson, Richard 1926- DLB-8, 44

Matheus, John F. 1887- DLB-51

Mathews, Cornelius
1817?-1889............. DLB-3, 64

Mathews, John Joseph
1894-1979 .... DLB-175

Mathews, Elkin
[publishing house] DLB-112

Mathias, Roland 1915- DLB-27

Mathis, June 1892-1927......... DLB-44

Mathis, Sharon Bell 1937- DLB-33

Matković, Marijan 1915-1985 ..... DLB-181

Matúš, Anton Gustav 1873-1914 .... DLB-147

Matsumoto, Seichō 1909-1992...... DLB-182

The Matter of England
1240-1400 .... DLB-146

The Matter of Rome
early twelfth to late fifteenth
century.................. DLB-146

Matthews, Brander
1852-1929......... DLB-71, 78; DS-13

Matthews, Jack 1925- DLB-6

Matthews, William 1942- DLB-5

Matthiessen, F. O. 1902-1950 ...... DLB-63

Maturin, Charles Robert
1780-1824 .... DLB-178

Matthiessen, Peter 1927- DLB-6, 173

Maugham, W. Somerset
1874-1965..... DLB-10, 36, 77, 100, 162

Maupassant, Guy de 1850-1893 .... DLB-123

Mauriac, Claude 1914- DLB-83

Mauriac, François 1885-1970....... DLB-65

Maurice, Frederick Denison
1805-1872.............. DLB-55

Maurois, André 1885-1967........ DLB-65

Maury, James 1718-1769 .... DLB-31

Mavor, Elizabeth 1927- DLB-14

Mavor, Osborne Henry (see Bridie, James)

Maxwell, William 1908- Y-80

Maxwell, H. [publishing house] DLB-49

Maxwell, John [publishing house].... DLB-106

May, Elaine 1932- DLB-44

May, Karl 1842-1912 .... DLB-129

May, Thomas 1595 or 1596-1650.... DLB-58

Mayer, Bernadette 1945- DLB-165

Mayer, Mercer 1943- DLB-61

Mayer, O. B. 1818-1891.......... DLB-3

Mayes, Herbert R. 1900-1987...... DLB-137

Mayes, Wendell 1919-1992........ DLB-26

Mayfield, Julian 1928-1984..... DLB-33; Y-84

Mayhew, Henry 1812-1887 .. DLB-18, 55, 190

Mayhew, Jonathan 1720-1766 ...... DLB-31

Mayne, Jasper 1604-1672 .... DLB-126

Mayne, Seymour 1944- DLB-60

Mayor, Flora Macdonald
1872-1932 .... DLB-36

Mayrocker, Friederike 1924- DLB-85

Mazrui, Ali A. 1933- DLB-125

Mažuranić, Ivan 1814-1890 .... DLB-147

Mazursky, Paul 1930- DLB-44

McAlmon, Robert
1896-1956......... DLB-4, 45; DS-15

McArthur, Peter 1866-1924........ DLB-92

McBride, Robert M., and
Company DLB-46

McCaffrey, Anne 1926- DLB-8

McCarthy, Cormac 1933- DLB-6, 143

McCarthy, Mary 1912-1989 .... DLB-2; Y-81

McCay, Winsor 1871-1934........ DLB-22

McClane, Albert Jules 1922-1991.... DLB-171

McClatchy, C. K. 1858-1936....... DLB-25

McClellan, George Marion
1860-1934 .... DLB-50

McCloskey, Robert 1914- DLB-22

McClung, Nellie Letitia 1873-1951.... DLB-92

McClure, Joanna 1930- DLB-16

McClure, Michael 1932- DLB-16

McClure, Phillips and Company..... DLB-46

McClure, S. S. 1857-1949 .... DLB-91

McClurg, A. C., and Company DLB-49

McCluskey, John A., Jr. 1944- DLB-33

McCollum, Michael A. 1946......... Y-87

McConnell, William C. 1917- DLB-88

McCord, David 1897- DLB-61

McCorkle, Jill 1958- Y-87

McCorkle, Samuel Eusebius
1746-1811............... DLB-37

McCormick, Anne O'Hare
1880-1954............... DLB-29

McCormick, Robert R. 1880-1955.... DLB-29

McCourt, Edward 1907-1972....... DLB-88

McCoy, Horace 1897-1955 .... DLB-9

McCrae, John 1872-1918......... DLB-92

McCullagh, Joseph B. 1842-1896..... DLB-23

McCullers, Carson
1917-1967 .... DLB-2, 7, 173

McCulloch, Thomas 1776-1843 ..... DLB-99

McDonald, Forrest 1927- DLB-17

McDonald, Walter
1934- DLB-105, DS-9

McDonald, Walter, Getting Started:
Accepting the Regions You Own—
or Which Own You DLB-105

McDougall, Colin 1917-1984....... DLB-68

McDowell, Obolensky DLB-46

McEwan, Ian 1948- DLB-14

McFadden, David 1940- DLB-60

McFall, Frances Elizabeth Clarke
(see Grand, Sarah)

McFarlane, Leslie 1902-1977 .... DLB-88

McFee, William 1881-1966 .... DLB-153

McGahern, John 1934- DLB-14

McGee, Thomas D'Arcy
1825-1868 .... DLB-99

McGeehan, W. O. 1879-1933 ... DLB-25, 171

McGill, Ralph 1898-1969......... DLB-29

McGinley, Phyllis 1905-1978..... DLB-11, 48

McGinniss, Joe 1942- DLB-185

McGirt, James E. 1874-1930 .... DLB-50

McGlashan and Gill............. DLB-106

McGough, Roger 1937- DLB-40

McGraw-Hill................ DLB-46

McGuane, Thomas 1939- DLB-2; Y-80

McGuckian, Medbh 1950- DLB-40

McGuffey, William Holmes
1800-1873............... DLB-42

McIlvanney, William 1936- DLB-14

McIlwraith, Jean Newton
1859-1938............... DLB-92

McIntyre, James 1827-1906........ DLB-99

McIntyre, O. O. 1884-1938 .... DLB-25

McKay, Claude
1889-1948 .... DLB-4, 45, 51, 117

The David McKay Company DLB-49
McKean, William V. 1820-1903 . . . . . DLB-23
The McKenzie Trust. Y-96
McKinley, Robin 1952- DLB-52
McLachlan, Alexander 1818-1896 . . . . DLB-99
McLaren, Floris Clark 1904-1978 . . . . DLB-68
McLaverty, Michael 1907- DLB-15
McLean, John R. 1848-1916 . . . . DLB-23
McLean, William L. 1852-1931 . . . . . DLB-25
McLennan, William 1856-1904 . . . . . DLB-92
McLoughlin Brothers DLB-49
McLuhan, Marshall 1911-1980 . . . . . DLB-88
McMaster, John Bach 1852-1932 . . . . DLB-47
McMurtry, Larry
   1936- DLB-2, 143; Y-80, 87
McNally, Terrence 1939- DLB-7
McNeil, Florence 1937- DLB-60
McNeile, Herman Cyril
   1888-1937 . . . . DLB-77
McNickle, D'Arcy 1904-1977 . . . . . . DLB-175
McPhee, John 1931- DLB-185
McPherson, James Alan 1943- DLB-38
McPherson, Sandra 1943- Y-86
McWhirter, George 1939- DLB-60
McWilliams, Carey 1905-1980 . . . . . DLB-137
Mead, L. T. 1844-1914 . . . . DLB-141
Mead, Matthew 1924- DLB-40
Mead, Taylor ?- DLB-16
Meany, Tom 1903-1964 . . . . DLB-171
Mechthild von Magdeburg
   circa 1207-circa 1282 . . . . DLB-138
Medill, Joseph 1823-1899 . . . . DLB-43
Medoff, Mark 1940- DLB-7
Meek, Alexander Beaufort
   1814-1865. . . . . DLB-3
Meeke, Mary ?-1816? DLB-116
Meinke, Peter 1932- DLB-5
Mejia Vallejo, Manuel 1923- DLB-113
Melanchthon, Philipp 1497-1560 . . . . DLB-179
Melançon, Robert 1947- DLB-60
Mell, Max 1882-1971 . . . . DLB-81, 124
Mellow, James R. 1926- DLB-111
Meltzer, David 1937- DLB-16
Meltzer, Milton 1915- DLB-61
Melville, Elizabeth, Lady Culross
   circa 1585-1640 . . . . DLB-172
Melville, Herman 1819-1891 . . . . DLB-3, 74
Memoirs of Life and Literature (1920),
   by W. H. Mallock [excerpt] DLB-57
Menander 342-341 B.C.-circa 292-291 B.C.
   . . . . DLB-176
Menantes (see Hunold, Christian Friedrich)

Mencke, Johann Burckhard
   1674-1732 . . . . DLB-168
Mencken, H. L.
   1880-1956. . . . . . . DLB-11, 29, 63, 137
Mencken and Nietzsche: An Unpublished Excerpt
   from H. L. Mencken's *My Life
   as Author and Editor*. Y-93
Mendelssohn, Moses 1729-1786 . . . . DLB-97
Méndez M., Miguel 1930- DLB-82
The Mercantile Library of
   New York Y-96
Mercer, Cecil William (see Yates, Dornford)
Mercer, David 1928-1980 . . . . DLB-13
Mercer, John 1704-1768 . . . . DLB-31
Meredith, George
   1828-1909 . . . . . . DLB-18, 35, 57, 159
Meredith, Louisa Anne
   1812-1895 . . . . DLB-166
Meredith, Owen (see Lytton, Edward Robert Bulwer)
Meredith, William 1919- DLB-5
Mergerle, Johann Ulrich
   (see Abraham ä Sancta Clara)
Mérimée, Prosper 1803-1870 . . . . . . DLB-119
Merivale, John Herman
   1779-1844. . . . . DLB-96
Meriwether, Louise 1923- DLB-33
Merlin Press DLB-112
Merriam, Eve 1916-1992 . . . . DLB-61
The Merriam Company DLB-49
Merrill, James
   1926-1995 . . . . DLB-5, 165; Y-85
Merrill and Baker DLB-49
The Mershon Company DLB-49
Merton, Thomas 1915-1968 . . . . DLB-48; Y-81
Merwin, W. S. 1927- DLB-5, 169
Messner, Julian [publishing house] DLB-46
Metcalf, J. [publishing house] DLB-49
Metcalf, John 1938- DLB-60
The Methodist Book Concern DLB-49
Methuen and Company DLB-112
Mew, Charlotte 1869-1928 . . . . . DLB-19, 135
Mewshaw, Michael 1943- Y-80
Meyer, Conrad Ferdinand 1825-1898 . . . DLB-129
Meyer, E. Y. 1946- DLB-75
Meyer, Eugene 1875-1959 . . . . DLB-29
Meyer, Michael 1921- DLB-155
Meyers, Jeffrey 1939- DLB-111
Meynell, Alice 1847-1922 . . . . . . DLB-19, 98
Meynell, Viola 1885-1956 . . . . DLB-153
Meyrink, Gustav 1868-1932 . . . . DLB-81
Michaels, Leonard 1933- DLB-130
Micheaux, Oscar 1884-1951 . . . . DLB-50

Michel of Northgate, Dan
   circa 1265-circa 1340 . . . . DLB-146
Micheline, Jack 1929- DLB-16
Michener, James A. 1907?- DLB-6
Micklejohn, George
   circa 1717-1818 . . . . DLB-31
Middle English Literature:
   An Introduction DLB-146
The Middle English Lyric DLB-146
Middle Hill Press DLB-106
Middleton, Christopher 1926- DLB-40
Middleton, Richard 1882-1911 . . . . . DLB-156
Middleton, Stanley 1919- DLB-14
Middleton, Thomas 1580-1627 . . . . . DLB-58
Miegel, Agnes 1879-1964 . . . . DLB-56
Mihailović, Dragoslav 1930- DLB-181
Mihalić, Slavko 1928- DLB-181
Miles, Josephine 1911-1985 . . . . DLB-48
Miliković, Branko 1934-1961 . . . . . . DLB-181
Milius, John 1944- DLB-44
Mill, James 1773-1836 . . . . DLB-107, 158
Mill, John Stuart 1806-1873 . . . . DLB-55, 190
Millar, Kenneth
   1915-1983. . . . . DLB-2; Y-83; DS-6
Millar, Andrew
   [publishing house] DLB-154
Millay, Edna St. Vincent
   1892-1950 . . . . DLB-45
Miller, Arthur 1915- DLB-7
Miller, Caroline 1903-1992 . . . . DLB-9
Miller, Eugene Ethelbert 1950- DLB-41
Miller, Heather Ross 1939- DLB-120
Miller, Henry 1891-1980 . . . . . DLB-4, 9; Y-80
Miller, Hugh 1802-1856 . . . . DLB-190
Miller, J. Hillis 1928- DLB-67
Miller, James [publishing house] DLB-49
Miller, Jason 1939- DLB-7
Miller, Joaquin 1839-1913 . . . . DLB-186
Miller, May 1899- DLB-41
Miller, Paul 1906-1991 . . . . DLB-127
Miller, Perry 1905-1963 . . . . DLB-17, 63
Miller, Sue 1943- DLB-143
Miller, Vassar 1924- DLB-105
Miller, Walter M., Jr. 1923- DLB-8
Miller, Webb 1892-1940 . . . . DLB-29
Millhauser, Steven 1943- DLB-2
Millican, Arthenia J. Bates
   1920- DLB-38
Mills and Boon DLB-112
Milman, Henry Hart 1796-1868 . . . . DLB-96
Milne, A. A.
   1882-1956 . . . . . . DLB-10, 77, 100, 160
Milner, Ron 1938- DLB-38

Milner, William
  [publishing house] DLB-106
Milnes, Richard Monckton (Lord Houghton)
  1809-1885 . . . . DLB-32, 184
Milton, John 1608-1674 . . . . . DLB-131, 151
Minakami, Tsutomu 1919- DLB-182
The Minerva Press DLB-154
Minnesang circa 1150-1280 . . . . DLB-138
Minns, Susan 1839-1938. . . . . DLB-140
Minor Illustrators, 1880-1914 . . . . DLB-141
Minor Poets of the Earlier Seventeenth
  Century DLB-121
Minton, Balch and Company DLB-46
Mirbeau, Octave 1848-1917 . . . . DLB-123
Mirk, John died after 1414? DLB-146
Miron, Gaston 1928- DLB-60
A Mirror for Magistrates DLB-167
Mishima, Yukio 1925-1970 . . . . DLB-182
Mitchel, Jonathan 1624-1668 . . . . DLB-24
Mitchell, Adrian 1932- DLB-40
Mitchell, Donald Grant
  1822-1908 . . . . DLB-1; DS-13
Mitchell, Gladys 1901-1983 . . . . DLB-77
Mitchell, James Leslie 1901-1935 . . . . . DLB-15
Mitchell, John (see Slater, Patrick)
Mitchell, John Ames 1845-1918 . . . . . DLB-79
Mitchell, Joseph 1908-1996 . . . . DLB-185; Y-96
Mitchell, Julian 1935- DLB-14
Mitchell, Ken 1940- DLB-60
Mitchell, Langdon 1862-1935 . . . . DLB-7
Mitchell, Loften 1919- DLB-38
Mitchell, Margaret 1900-1949 . . . . DLB-9
Mitchell, W. O. 1914- DLB-88
Mitchison, Naomi Margaret (Haldane)
  1897- DLB-160
Mitford, Mary Russell
  1787-1855 . . . . DLB-110, 116
Mittelholzer, Edgar 1909-1965 . . . . . . DLB-117
Mitterer, Erika 1906- DLB-85
Mitterer, Felix 1948- DLB-124
Mitternacht, Johann Sebastian
  1613-1679 . . . . DLB-168
Miyamoto, Yuriko 1899-1951 . . . . . . DLB-180
Mizener, Arthur 1907-1988 . . . . DLB-103
Modern Age Books DLB-46
"Modern English Prose" (1876),
  by George Saintsbury DLB-57
The Modern Language Association of America
  Celebrates Its Centennial Y-84
The Modern Library DLB-46
"Modern Novelists – Great and Small" (1855), by
  Margaret Oliphant DLB-21
"Modern Style" (1857), by Cockburn
  Thomson [excerpt] DLB-57

The Modernists (1932),
  by Joseph Warren Beach DLB-36
Modiano, Patrick 1945- DLB-83
Moffat, Yard and Company DLB-46
Moffet, Thomas 1553-1604 . . . . . . DLB-136
Mohr, Nicholasa 1938- DLB-145
Moix, Ana María 1947- DLB-134
Molesworth, Louisa 1839-1921 . . . . . DLB-135
Möllhausen, Balduin 1825-1905 . . . . DLB-129
Momaday, N. Scott 1934- . . . DLB-143, 175
Monkhouse, Allan 1858-1936 . . . . . . DLB-10
Monro, Harold 1879-1932 . . . . DLB-19
Monroe, Harriet 1860-1936 . . . . DLB-54, 91
Monsarrat, Nicholas 1910-1979 . . . . . DLB-15
Montagu, Lady Mary Wortley
  1689-1762 . . . . DLB-95, 101
Montague, John 1929- DLB-40
Montale, Eugenio 1896-1981 . . . . . DLB-114
Monterroso, Augusto 1921- DLB-145
Montgomerie, Alexander
  circa 1550?-1598 . . . . DLB-167
Montgomery, James
  1771-1854 . . . . DLB-93, 158
Montgomery, John 1919- DLB-16
Montgomery, Lucy Maud
  1874-1942 . . . . DLB-92; DS-14
Montgomery, Marion 1925- DLB-6
Montgomery, Robert Bruce (see Crispin, Edmund)
Montherlant, Henry de 1896-1972 . . . DLB-72
The Monthly Review 1749-1844 . . . . . DLB-110
Montigny, Louvigny de 1876-1955 . . . DLB-92
Montoya, José 1932- DLB-122
Moodie, John Wedderburn Dunbar
  1797-1869 . . . . DLB-99
Moodie, Susanna 1803-1885 . . . . . . DLB-99
Moody, Joshua circa 1633-1697 . . . . . DLB-24
Moody, William Vaughn
  1869-1910 . . . . DLB-7, 54
Moorcock, Michael 1939- DLB-14
Moore, Catherine L. 1911- DLB-8
Moore, Clement Clarke 1779-1863 . . . DLB-42
Moore, Dora Mavor 1888-1979 . . . . DLB-92
Moore, George
  1852-1933 . . . . . DLB-10, 18, 57, 135
Moore, Marianne
  1887-1972 . . . . DLB-45; DS-7
Moore, Mavor 1919- DLB-88
Moore, Richard 1927- DLB-105
Moore, Richard, The No Self, the Little Self,
  and the Poets DLB-105
Moore, T. Sturge 1870-1944 . . . . . . DLB-19
Moore, Thomas 1779-1852 . . . . DLB-96, 144
Moore, Ward 1903-1978 . . . . DLB-8

Moore, Wilstach, Keys and
  Company DLB-49
The Moorland-Spingarn Research
  Center DLB-76
Moorman, Mary C. 1905-1994 . . . . . DLB-155
Moraga, Cherríe 1952- DLB-82
Morales, Alejandro 1944- DLB-82
Morales, Mario Roberto 1947- DLB-145
Morales, Rafael 1919- DLB-108
Morality Plays: *Mankind* circa 1450-1500 and
  Everyman circa 1500 . . . . DLB-146
Morante, Elsa 1912-1985 . . . . DLB-177
Morata, Olympia Fulvia
  1526-1555 . . . . DLB-179
Moravia, Alberto 1907-1990 . . . . . . DLB-177
Mordaunt, Elinor 1872-1942 . . . . . . DLB-174
More, Hannah
  1745-1833 . . . . . DLB-107, 109, 116, 158
More, Henry 1614-1687 . . . . DLB-126
More, Sir Thomas
  1477 or 1478-1535 . . . . DLB-136
Moreno, Dorinda 1939- DLB-122
Morency, Pierre 1942- DLB-60
Moretti, Marino 1885-1979 . . . . . . DLB-114
Morgan, Berry 1919- DLB-6
Morgan, Charles 1894-1958 . . . . DLB-34, 100
Morgan, Edmund S. 1916- DLB-17
Morgan, Edwin 1920- DLB-27
Morgan, John Pierpont
  1837-1913 . . . . DLB-140
Morgan, John Pierpont, Jr.
  1867-1943 . . . . DLB-140
Morgan, Robert 1944- DLB-120
Morgan, Sydney Owenson, Lady
  1776?-1859 . . . . DLB-116, 158
Morgner, Irmtraud 1933- DLB-75
Morhof, Daniel Georg
  1639-1691 . . . . DLB-164
Mori, Ōgai 1862-1922 . . . . DLB-180
Morier, James Justinian
  1782 or 1783?-1849 . . . . DLB-116
Mörike, Eduard 1804-1875 . . . . . . DLB-133
Morin, Paul 1889-1963 . . . . DLB-92
Morison, Richard 1514?-1556 . . . . . DLB-136
Morison, Samuel Eliot 1887-1976 . . . DLB-17
Moritz, Karl Philipp 1756-1793 . . . . . DLB-94
Moriz von Craûn
  circa 1220-1230 . . . . DLB-138
Morley, Christopher 1890-1957 . . . . . DLB-9
Morley, John 1838-1923 . . . . DLB-57, 144, 190
Morris, George Pope 1802-1864 . . . . DLB-73
Morris, Lewis 1833-1907 . . . . DLB-35
Morris, Richard B. 1904-1989 . . . . . DLB-17

Morris, William
  1834-1896 . . DLB-18, 35, 57, 156, 178, 184
Morris, Willie 1934- Y-80
Morris, Wright 1910- DLB-2; Y-81
Morrison, Arthur 1863-1945 . . . . DLB-70, 135
Morrison, Charles Clayton
  1874-1966 . . . . DLB-91
Morrison, Toni
  1931- DLB-6, 33, 143; Y-81
Morrow, William, and Company DLB-46
Morse, James Herbert 1841-1923 . . . . DLB-71
Morse, Jedidiah 1761-1826 . . . . DLB-37
Morse, John T., Jr. 1840-1937 . . . . . . DLB-47
Morselli, Guido 1912-1973 . . . . DLB-177
Mortimer, Favell Lee 1802-1878 . . . . DLB-163
Mortimer, John 1923- DLB-13
Morton, Carlos 1942- DLB-122
Morton, John P., and Company DLB-49
Morton, Nathaniel 1613-1685 . . . . . . DLB-24
Morton, Sarah Wentworth
  1759-1846 . . . . DLB-37
Morton, Thomas
  circa 1579-circa 1647 . . . . DLB-24
Moscherosch, Johann Michael
  1601-1669 . . . . DLB-164
Moseley, Humphrey
  [publishing house] DLB-170
Möser, Justus 1720-1794 . . . . DLB-97
Mosley, Nicholas 1923- DLB-14
Moss, Arthur 1889-1969 . . . . DLB-4
Moss, Howard 1922-1987 . . . . DLB-5
Moss, Thylias 1954- DLB-120
The Most Powerful Book Review in America
  [*New York Times Book Review*] Y-82
Motion, Andrew 1952- DLB-40
Motley, John Lothrop
  1814-1877 . . . . DLB-1, 30, 59
Motley, Willard 1909-1965 . . . . DLB-76, 143
Motte, Benjamin Jr.
  [publishing house] DLB-154
Motteux, Peter Anthony
  1663-1718 . . . . DLB-80
Mottram, R. H. 1883-1971 . . . . DLB-36
Mouré, Erin 1955- DLB-60
Mourning Dove (Humishuma)
  between 1882 and 1888?-1936 . . . . DLB-175
Movies from Books, 1920-1974 . . . . . DLB-9
Mowat, Farley 1921- DLB-68
Mowbray, A. R., and Company,
  Limited DLB-106
Mowrer, Edgar Ansel 1892-1977 . . . . . DLB-29
Mowrer, Paul Scott 1887-1971 . . . . . DLB-29
Moxon, Edward
  [publishing house] DLB-106

Moxon, Joseph
  [publishing house] DLB-170
Mphahlele, Es'kia (Ezekiel)
  1919- DLB-125
Mtshali, Oswald Mbuyiseni
  1940- DLB-125
Mucedorus DLB-62
Mudford, William 1782-1848 . . . . . . DLB-159
Mueller, Lisel 1924- DLB-105
Muhajir, El (see Marvin X)
Muhajir, Nazzam Al Fitnah (see Marvin X)
Mühlbach, Luise 1814-1873 . . . . DLB-133
Muir, Edwin 1887-1959 . . . . . . DLB-20, 100
Muir, Helen 1937- DLB-14
Muir, John 1838-1914 . . . . DLB-186
Mukherjee, Bharati 1940- DLB-60
Mulcaster, Richard
  1531 or 1532-1611 . . . . DLB-167
Muldoon, Paul 1951- DLB-40
Müller, Friedrich (see Müller, Maler)
Müller, Heiner 1929- DLB-124
Müller, Maler 1749-1825 . . . . DLB-94
Müller, Wilhelm 1794-1827 . . . . DLB-90
Mumford, Lewis 1895-1990 . . . . DLB-63
Munby, Arthur Joseph 1828-1910 . . . . DLB-35
Munday, Anthony 1560-1633 . . . . DLB-62, 172
Mundt, Clara (see Mühlbach, Luise)
Mundt, Theodore 1808-1861 . . . . . . DLB-133
Munford, Robert circa 1737-1783 . . . . DLB-31
Mungoshi, Charles 1947- DLB-157
Munonye, John 1929- DLB-117
Munro, Alice 1931- DLB-53
Munro, H. H. 1870-1916 . . . . . DLB-34, 162
Munro, Neil 1864-1930 . . . . DLB-156
Munro, George
  [publishing house] DLB-49
Munro, Norman L.
  [publishing house] DLB-49
Munroe, James, and Company DLB-49
Munroe, Kirk 1850-1930 . . . . DLB-42
Munroe and Francis DLB-49
Munsell, Joel [publishing house] DLB-49
Munsey, Frank A. 1854-1925 . . . . DLB-25, 91
Murakami, Haruki 1949- DLB-182
Munsey, Frank A., and
  Company DLB-49
Murav'ev, Mikhail Nikitich
  1757-1807 . . . . DLB-150
Murdoch, Iris 1919- DLB-14
Murdoch, Rupert 1931- DLB-127
Murfree, Mary N. 1850-1922 . . . . DLB-12, 74
Murger, Henry 1822-1861 . . . . DLB-119
Murger, Louis-Henri (see Murger, Henry)

Murner, Thomas 1475-1537 . . . . DLB-179
Muro, Amado 1915-1971 . . . . DLB-82
Murphy, Arthur 1727-1805 . . . . . DLB-89, 142
Murphy, Beatrice M. 1908- DLB-76
Murphy, Emily 1868-1933 . . . . DLB-99
Murphy, John H., III 1916- DLB-127
Murphy, John, and Company DLB-49
Murphy, Richard 1927-1993 . . . . . . DLB-40
Murray, Albert L. 1916- DLB-38
Murray, Gilbert 1866-1957 . . . . DLB-10
Murray, Judith Sargent 1751-1820 . . . . DLB-37
Murray, Pauli 1910-1985 . . . . DLB-41
Murray, John [publishing house] DLB-154
Murry, John Middleton
  1889-1957 . . . . DLB-149
Musäus, Johann Karl August
  1735-1787 . . . . DLB-97
Muschg, Adolf 1934- DLB-75
The Music of *Minnesang* DLB-138
Musil, Robert 1880-1942 . . . . . DLB-81, 124
Muspilli circa 790-circa 850 . . . . . . DLB-148
Mussey, Benjamin B., and
  Company DLB-49
Mutafchieva, Vera 1929- DLB-181
Mwangi, Meja 1948- DLB-125
Myers, Frederic W. H. 1843-1901 . . . DLB-190
Myers, Gustavus 1872-1942 . . . . DLB-47
Myers, L. H. 1881-1944 . . . . DLB-15
Myers, Walter Dean 1937- DLB-33

N

Nabl, Franz 1883-1974 . . . . DLB-81
Nabokov, Vladimir
  1899-1977 . . . . DLB-2; Y-80, Y-91; DS-3
Nabokov Festival at Cornell Y-83
The Vladimir Nabokov Archive
  in the Berg Collection Y-91
Nafis and Cornish DLB-49
Nagai, Kafū 1879-1959 . . . . DLB-180
Naipaul, Shiva 1945-1985 . . . . . DLB-157; Y-85
Naipaul, V. S. 1932- DLB-125; Y-85
Nakagami, Kenji 1946-1992 . . . . DLB-182
Nancrede, Joseph
  [publishing house] DLB-49
Naranjo, Carmen 1930- DLB-145
Narrache, Jean 1893-1970 . . . . DLB-92
Nasby, Petroleum Vesuvius (see Locke, David
  Ross)
Nash, Ogden 1902-1971 . . . . DLB-11
Nash, Eveleigh
  [publishing house] DLB-112

Nashe, Thomas 1567-1601?	DLB-167	
Nast, Conde 1873-1942	DLB-91	
Nast, Thomas 1840-1902	DLB-188	
Nastasijević, Momčilo 1894-1938	DLB-147	
Nathan, George Jean 1882-1958	DLB-137	
Nathan, Robert 1894-1985	DLB-9	
The National Jewish Book Awards	Y-85	
The National Theatre and the Royal Shakespeare Company: The National Companies	DLB-13	
Natsume, Sōseki 1867-1916	DLB-180	
Naughton, Bill 1910-	DLB-13	
Naylor, Gloria 1950-	DLB-173	
Nazor, Vladimir 1876-1949	DLB-147	
Ndebele, Njabulo 1948-	DLB-157	
Neagoe, Peter 1881-1960	DLB-4	
Neal, John 1793-1876	DLB-1, 59	
Neal, Joseph C. 1807-1847	DLB-11	
Neal, Larry 1937-1981	DLB-38	
The Neale Publishing Company	DLB-49	
Neely, F. Tennyson [publishing house]	DLB-49	
Negri, Ada 1870-1945	DLB-114	
"The Negro as a Writer," by G. M. McClellan	DLB-50	
"Negro Poets and Their Poetry," by Wallace Thurman	DLB-50	
Neidhart von Reuental circa 1185-circa 1240	DLB-138	
Neihardt, John G. 1881-1973	DLB-9, 54	
Neledinsky-Meletsky, Iurii Aleksandrovich 1752-1828	DLB-150	
Nelligan, Emile 1879-1941	DLB-92	
Nelson, Alice Moore Dunbar 1875-1935	DLB-50	
Nelson, Thomas, and Sons [U.S.]	DLB-49	
Nelson, Thomas, and Sons [U.K.]	DLB-106	
Nelson, William 1908-1978	DLB-103	
Nelson, William Rockhill 1841-1915	DLB-23	
Nemerov, Howard 1920-1991	DLB-5, 6; Y-83	
Nesbit, E. 1858-1924	DLB-141, 153, 178	
Ness, Evaline 1911-1986	DLB-61	
Nestroy, Johann 1801-1862	DLB-133	
Neukirch, Benjamin 1655-1729	DLB-168	
Neugeboren, Jay 1938-	DLB-28	
Neumann, Alfred 1895-1952	DLB-56	
Neumark, Georg 1621-1681	DLB-164	
Neumeister, Erdmann 1671-1756	DLB-168	
Nevins, Allan 1890-1971	DLB-17	
Nevinson, Henry Woodd 1856-1941	DLB-135	
The New American Library	DLB-46	
New Approaches to Biography: Challenges from Critical Theory, USC Conference on Literary Studies, 1990	Y-90	
New Directions Publishing Corporation	DLB-46	
A New Edition of *Huck Finn*	Y-85	
New Forces at Work in the American Theatre: 1915-1925	DLB-7	
New Literary Periodicals: A Report for 1987	Y-87	
New Literary Periodicals: A Report for 1988	Y-88	
New Literary Periodicals: A Report for 1989	Y-89	
New Literary Periodicals: A Report for 1990	Y-90	
New Literary Periodicals: A Report for 1991	Y-91	
New Literary Periodicals: A Report for 1992	Y-92	
New Literary Periodicals: A Report for 1993	Y-93	
The New Monthly Magazine 1814-1884	DLB-110	
The New *Ulysses*	Y-84	
The New Variorum Shakespeare	Y-85	
A New Voice: The Center for the Book's First Five Years	Y-83	
The New Wave [Science Fiction]	DLB-8	
New York City Bookshops in the 1930s and 1940s: The Recollections of Walter Goldwater	Y-93	
Newbery, John [publishing house]	DLB-154	
Newbolt, Henry 1862-1938	DLB-19	
Newbound, Bernard Slade (see Slade, Bernard)		
Newby, P. H. 1918-	DLB-15	
Newby, Thomas Cautley [publishing house]	DLB-106	
Newcomb, Charles King 1820-1894	DLB-1	
Newell, Peter 1862-1924	DLB-42	
Newell, Robert Henry 1836-1901	DLB-11	
Newhouse, Samuel I. 1895-1979	DLB-127	
Newman, Cecil Earl 1903-1976	DLB-127	
Newman, David (see Benton, Robert)		
Newman, Frances 1883-1928	Y-80	
Newman, Francis William 1805-1897	DLB-190	
Newman, John Henry 1801-1890	DLB-18, 32, 55	
Newman, Mark [publishing house]	DLB-49	
Newnes, George, Limited	DLB-112	
Newsome, Effie Lee 1885-1979	DLB-76	
Newspaper Syndication of American Humor	DLB-11	
Newton, A. Edward 1864-1940	DLB-140	
Ngugi wa Thiong'o 1938-	DLB-125	
Niatum, Duane 1938-	DLB-175	
The *Nibelungenlied* and the *Klage* circa 1200	DLB-138	
Nichol, B. P. 1944-	DLB-53	
Nicholas of Cusa 1401-1464	DLB-115	
Nichols, Dudley 1895-1960	DLB-26	
Nichols, Grace 1950-	DLB-157	
Nichols, John 1940-	Y-82	
Nichols, Mary Sargeant (Neal) Gove 1810-1884	DLB-1	
Nichols, Peter 1927-	DLB-13	
Nichols, Roy F. 1896-1973	DLB-17	
Nichols, Ruth 1948-	DLB-60	
Nicholson, Edward Williams Byron 1849-1912	DLB-184	
Nicholson, Norman 1914-	DLB-27	
Nicholson, William 1872-1949	DLB-141	
Ní Chuilleanáin, Eiléan 1942-	DLB-40	
Nicol, Eric 1919-	DLB-68	
Nicolai, Friedrich 1733-1811	DLB-97	
Nicolay, John G. 1832-1901 and Hay, John 1838-1905	DLB-47	
Nicolson, Harold 1886-1968	DLB-100, 149	
Nicolson, Nigel 1917-	DLB-155	
Niebuhr, Reinhold 1892-1971	DLB-17	
Niedecker, Lorine 1903-1970	DLB-48	
Nieman, Lucius W. 1857-1935	DLB-25	
Nietzsche, Friedrich 1844-1900	DLB-129	
Niggli, Josefina 1910-	Y-80	
Nightingale, Florence 1820-1910	DLB-166	
Nikolev, Nikolai Petrovich 1758-1815	DLB-150	
Niles, Hezekiah 1777-1839	DLB-43	
Nims, John Frederick 1913-	DLB-5	
Nin, Anaïs 1903-1977	DLB-2, 4, 152	
1985: The Year of the Mystery: A Symposium	Y-85	
Nissenson, Hugh 1933-	DLB-28	
Niven, Frederick John 1878-1944	DLB-92	
Niven, Larry 1938-	DLB-8	
Nizan, Paul 1905-1940	DLB-72	
Njegoš, Petar II Petrović 1813-1851	DLB-147	
Nkosi, Lewis 1936-	DLB-157	
Nobel Peace Prize		
The 1986 Nobel Peace Prize Nobel Lecture 1986: Hope, Despair and Memory Tributes from Abraham Bernstein, Norman Lamm, and John R. Silber	Y-86	
The Nobel Prize and Literary Politics	Y-86	
Nobel Prize in Literature		

The 1982 Nobel Prize in Literature
   Announcement by the Swedish Academy
   of the Nobel Prize Nobel Lecture 1982:
   The Solitude of Latin America Excerpt
   from *One Hundred Years of Solitude* The
   Magical World of Macondo A Tribute
   to Gabriel García Márquez Y-82

The 1983 Nobel Prize in Literature
   Announcement by the Swedish Academy No-
   bel Lecture 1983 The Stature of
   William Golding Y-83

The 1984 Nobel Prize in Literature
   Announcement by the Swedish Academy
   Jaroslav Seifert Through the Eyes of the
   English-Speaking Reader
   Three Poems by Jaroslav Seifert Y-84

The 1985 Nobel Prize in Literature
   Announcement by the Swedish Academy
   Nobel Lecture 1985 . . . . Y-85

The 1986 Nobel Prize in Literature
   Nobel Lecture 1986: This Past Must Address
   Its Present Y-86

The 1987 Nobel Prize in Literature
   Nobel Lecture 1987 . . . . Y-87

The 1988 Nobel Prize in Literature
   Nobel Lecture 1988 . . . . Y-88

The 1989 Nobel Prize in Literature
   Nobel Lecture 1989 . . . . Y-89

The 1990 Nobel Prize in Literature
   Nobel Lecture 1990 . . . . Y-90

The 1991 Nobel Prize in Literature
   Nobel Lecture 1991 . . . . Y-91

The 1992 Nobel Prize in Literature
   Nobel Lecture 1992 . . . . Y-92

The 1993 Nobel Prize in Literature
   Nobel Lecture 1993 . . . . Y-93

The 1994 Nobel Prize in Literature
   Nobel Lecture 1994 . . . . Y-94

The 1995 Nobel Prize in Literature
   Nobel Lecture 1995 . . . . Y-95

Nodier, Charles 1780-1844 . . . . DLB-119
Noel, Roden 1834-1894 . . . . DLB-35
Nogami, Yaeko 1885-1985 . . . . DLB-180
Nogo, Rajko Petrov 1945- DLB-181
Nolan, William F. 1928- DLB-8
Noland, C. F. M. 1810?-1858 . . . . . . DLB-11
Noma, Hiroshi 1915-1991 . . . . DLB-182
Nonesuch Press DLB-112
Noonday Press DLB-46
Noone, John 1936- DLB-14
Nora, Eugenio de 1923- DLB-134
Nordhoff, Charles 1887-1947 . . . . . . DLB-9
Norman, Charles 1904- DLB-111
Norman, Marsha 1947- Y-84
Norris, Charles G. 1881-1945 . . . . . . DLB-9
Norris, Frank 1870-1902 . . . . DLB-12, 71, 186
Norris, Leslie 1921- DLB-27
Norse, Harold 1916- DLB-16

North, Marianne 1830-1890 . . . . DLB-174
North Point Press DLB-46
Nortje, Arthur 1942-1970 . . . . DLB-125
Norton, Alice Mary (see Norton, Andre)
Norton, Andre 1912- DLB-8, 52
Norton, Andrews 1786-1853 . . . . DLB-1
Norton, Caroline 1808-1877 . . . . DLB-21, 159
Norton, Charles Eliot 1827-1908 . . . DLB-1, 64
Norton, John 1606-1663 . . . . DLB-24
Norton, Mary 1903-1992 . . . . DLB-160
Norton, Thomas (see Sackville, Thomas)
Norton, W. W., and Company DLB-46
Norwood, Robert 1874-1932 . . . . . . DLB-92
Nosaka, Akiyuki 1930- DLB-182
Nossack, Hans Erich 1901-1977 . . . . . DLB-69
Notker Balbulus circa 840-912 . . . . . DLB-148
Notker III of Saint Gall
   circa 950-1022 . . . . DLB-148
Notker von Zweifalten ?-1095 . . . . . DLB-148
A Note on Technique (1926), by
   Elizabeth A. Drew [excerpts] DLB-36
Nourse, Alan E. 1928- DLB-8
Novak, Slobodan 1924- DLB-181
Novak, Vjenceslav 1859-1905 . . . . . . DLB-147
Novalis 1772-1801 . . . . DLB-90
Novaro, Mario 1868-1944 . . . . DLB-114
Novás Calvo, Lino 1903-1983 . . . . . . DLB-145
"The Novel in [Robert Browning's] 'The Ring
   and the Book'" (1912), by
   Henry James DLB-32
The Novel of Impressionism,
   by Jethro Bithell DLB-66
Novel-Reading: *The Works of Charles Dickens,
   The Works of W. Makepeace Thackeray*
   (1879), by Anthony Trollope DLB-21
The Novels of Dorothy Richardson (1918),
   by May Sinclair DLB-36
Novels with a Purpose (1864), by
   Justin M'Carthy DLB-21
Noventa, Giacomo 1898-1960 . . . . . DLB-114
Novikov, Nikolai Ivanovich
   1744-1818 . . . . DLB-150
Nowlan, Alden 1933-1983 . . . . DLB-53
Noyes, Alfred 1880-1958 . . . . DLB-20
Noyes, Crosby S. 1825-1908 . . . . . . DLB-23
Noyes, Nicholas 1647-1717 . . . . DLB-24
Noyes, Theodore W. 1858-1946 . . . . DLB-29
N-Town Plays circa 1468 to early
   sixteenth century DLB-146
Nugent, Frank 1908-1965 . . . . DLB-44
Nugent, Richard Bruce 1906- DLB-151
Nušić, Branislav 1864-1938 . . . . DLB-147
Nutt, David [publishing house] DLB-106
Nwapa, Flora 1931- DLB-125

Nye, Bill 1850-1896 . . . . DLB-186
Nye, Edgar Wilson (Bill)
   1850-1896 . . . . DLB-11, 23
Nye, Naomi Shihab 1952- DLB-120
Nye, Robert 1939- DLB-14

O

Oakes, Urian circa 1631-1681 . . . . . DLB-24
Oakley, Violet 1874-1961 . . . . DLB-188
Oates, Joyce Carol
   1938- DLB-2, 5, 130; Y-81
Ōba, Minako 1930- DLB-182
Ober, Frederick Albion 1849-1913 . . . DLB-189
Ober, William 1920-1993 . . . . Y-93
Oberholtzer, Ellis Paxson
   1868-1936 . . . . DLB-47
Obradović, Dositej 1740?-1811 . . . . . DLB-147
O'Brien, Edna 1932- DLB-14
O'Brien, Fitz-James 1828-1862 . . . . . DLB-74
O'Brien, Kate 1897-1974 . . . . DLB-15
O'Brien, Tim
   1946- DLB-152; Y-80; DS-9
O'Casey, Sean 1880-1964 . . . . DLB-10
Occom, Samson 1723-1792 . . . . DLB-175
Ochs, Adolph S. 1858-1935 . . . . DLB-25
Ochs-Oakes, George Washington
   1861-1931 . . . . DLB-137
O'Connor, Flannery
   1925-1964 . . . . . DLB-2, 152; Y-80; DS-12
O'Connor, Frank 1903-1966 . . . . DLB-162
Octopus Publishing Group DLB-112
Oda, Sakunosuke 1913-1947 . . . . . . DLB-182
Odell, Jonathan 1737-1818 . . . . DLB-31, 99
O'Dell, Scott 1903-1989 . . . . DLB-52
Odets, Clifford 1906-1963 . . . . DLB-7, 26
Odhams Press Limited DLB-112
O'Donnell, Peter 1920- DLB-87
O'Donovan, Michael (see O'Connor, Frank)
Ōe, Kenzaburō 1935- DLB-182
O'Faolain, Julia 1932- DLB-14
O'Faolain, Sean 1900- DLB-15, 162
Off Broadway and Off-Off Broadway . . DLB-7
Off-Loop Theatres DLB-7
Offord, Carl Ruthven 1910- DLB-76
O'Flaherty, Liam
   1896-1984 . . . . DLB-36, 162; Y-84
Ogilvie, J. S., and Company DLB-49
Ogot, Grace 1930- DLB-125
O'Grady, Desmond 1935- DLB-40
Ogunyemi, Wale 1939- DLB-157
O'Hagan, Howard 1902-1982 . . . . . . DLB-68

O'Hara, Frank 1926-1966 . . . . . . DLB-5, 16

O'Hara, John 1905-1970 . . . . DLB-9, 86; DS-2

Okara, Gabriel 1921- DLB-125

O'Keeffe, John 1747-1833 . . . . DLB-89

Okes, Nicholas
[publishing house] DLB-170

Okigbo, Christopher 1930-1967 . . . . DLB-125

Okot p'Bitek 1931-1982 . . . . DLB-125

Okpewho, Isidore 1941- DLB-157

Okri, Ben 1959- DLB-157

Olaudah Equiano and Unfinished Journeys:
The Slave-Narrative Tradition and
Twentieth-Century Continuities, by
Paul Edwards and Pauline T.
Wangman DLB-117

Old English Literature:
An Introduction DLB-146

Old English Riddles
eighth to tenth centuries DLB-146

Old Franklin Publishing House DLB-49

Old German Genesis and *Old German Exodus*
circa 1050-circa 1130 . . . . DLB-148

Old High German Charms and
Blessings DLB-148

The *Old High German Isidor*
circa 790-800 . . . . DLB-148

Older, Fremont 1856-1935 . . . . DLB-25

Oldham, John 1653-1683 . . . . DLB-131

Olds, Sharon 1942- DLB-120

Olearius, Adam 1599-1671 . . . . DLB-164

Oliphant, Laurence
1829?-1888 . . . . DLB-18, 166

Oliphant, Margaret 1828-1897 . . . DLB-18, 190

Oliver, Chad 1928- DLB-8

Oliver, Mary 1935- DLB-5

Ollier, Claude 1922- DLB-83

Olsen, Tillie 1913?- DLB-28; Y-80

Olson, Charles 1910-1970 . . . . . . DLB-5, 16

Olson, Elder 1909- DLB-48, 63

Omotoso, Kole 1943- DLB-125

"On Art in Fiction "(1838),
by Edward Bulwer DLB-21

On Learning to Write Y-88

On Some of the Characteristics of Modern
Poetry and On the Lyrical Poems of
Alfred Tennyson (1831), by Arthur
Henry Hallam DLB-32

"On Style in English Prose" (1898), by
Frederic Harrison DLB-57

"On Style in Literature: Its Technical
Elements" (1885), by Robert Louis
Stevenson DLB-57

"On the Writing of Essays" (1862),
by Alexander Smith DLB-57

Ondaatje, Michael 1943- DLB-60

O'Neill, Eugene 1888-1953 . . . . DLB-7

Onetti, Juan Carlos 1909-1994 . . . . . DLB-113

Onions, George Oliver
1872-1961 . . . . DLB-153

Onofri, Arturo 1885-1928 . . . . DLB-114

Opie, Amelia 1769-1853 . . . . . DLB-116, 159

Opitz, Martin 1597-1639 . . . . DLB-164

Oppen, George 1908-1984 . . . . . . DLB-5, 165

Oppenheim, E. Phillips 1866-1946 . . . . DLB-70

Oppenheim, James 1882-1932 . . . . . . DLB-28

Oppenheimer, Joel 1930- DLB-5

Optic, Oliver (see Adams, William Taylor)

Orczy, Emma, Baroness
1865-1947 . . . . DLB-70

Origo, Iris 1902-1988 . . . . DLB-155

Orlovitz, Gil 1918-1973 . . . . DLB-2, 5

Orlovsky, Peter 1933- DLB-16

Ormond, John 1923- DLB-27

Ornitz, Samuel 1890-1957 . . . . . DLB-28, 44

O'Rourke, P. J. 1947- DLB-185

Ortese, Anna Maria 1914- DLB-177

Ortiz, Simon J. 1941- DLB-120, 175

Ortnit and *Wolfdietrich*
circa 1225-1250 . . . . DLB-138

Orton, Joe 1933-1967 . . . . DLB-13

Orwell, George 1903-1950 . . . . . DLB-15, 98

The Orwell Year Y-84

Ory, Carlos Edmundo de 1923- . . . DLB-134

Osbey, Brenda Marie 1957- DLB-120

Osbon, B. S. 1827-1912 . . . . DLB-43

Osborne, John 1929-1994 . . . . DLB-13

Osgood, Herbert L. 1855-1918 . . . . . . DLB-47

Osgood, James R., and
Company DLB-49

Osgood, McIlvaine and
Company DLB-112

O'Shaughnessy, Arthur
1844-1881 . . . . DLB-35

O'Shea, Patrick
[publishing house] DLB-49

Osipov, Nikolai Petrovich
1751-1799 . . . . DLB-150

Oskison, John Milton 1879-1947 . . . . DLB-175

Osler, Sir William 1849-1919 . . . . . . DLB-184

Osofisan, Femi 1946- DLB-125

Ostenso, Martha 1900-1963 . . . . DLB-92

Ostriker, Alicia 1937- DLB-120

Osundare, Niyi 1947- DLB-157

Oswald, Eleazer 1755-1795 . . . . DLB-43

Oswald von Wolkenstein
1376 or 1377-1445 . . . . DLB-179

Otero, Blas de 1916-1979 . . . . DLB-134

Otero, Miguel Antonio
1859-1944 . . . . DLB-82

Otero Silva, Miguel 1908-1985 . . . . . DLB-145

Otfried von Weißenburg
circa 800-circa 875? DLB-148

Otis, James (see Kaler, James Otis)

Otis, James, Jr. 1725-1783 . . . . DLB-31

Otis, Broaders and Company DLB-49

Ottaway, James 1911- DLB-127

Ottendorfer, Oswald 1826-1900 . . . . . DLB-23

Ottieri, Ottiero 1924- DLB-177

Otto-Peters, Louise 1819-1895 . . . . . DLB-129

Otway, Thomas 1652-1685 . . . . DLB-80

Ouellette, Fernand 1930- DLB-60

Ouida 1839-1908 . . . . DLB-18, 156

Outing Publishing Company DLB-46

Outlaw Days, by Joyce Johnson DLB-16

Overbury, Sir Thomas
circa 1581-1613 . . . . DLB-151

The Overlook Press DLB-46

Overview of U.S. Book Publishing,
1910-1945 . . . . DLB-9

Owen, Guy 1925- DLB-5

Owen, John 1564-1622 . . . . DLB-121

Owen, John [publishing house] DLB-49

Owen, Robert 1771-1858 . . . . . DLB-107, 158

Owen, Wilfred 1893-1918 . . . . DLB-20

Owen, Peter, Limited DLB-112

The Owl and the Nightingale
circa 1189-1199 . . . . DLB-146

Owsley, Frank L. 1890-1956 . . . . . . DLB-17

Oxford, Seventeenth Earl of, Edward de Vere
1550-1604 . . . . DLB-172

Ozerov, Vladislav Aleksandrovich
1769-1816 . . . . DLB-150

Ozick, Cynthia 1928- DLB-28, 152; Y-82

P

Pace, Richard 1482?-1536 . . . . DLB-167

Pacey, Desmond 1917-1975 . . . . DLB-88

Pack, Robert 1929- DLB-5

Packaging Papa: *The Garden of Eden* Y-86

Padell Publishing Company DLB-46

Padgett, Ron 1942- DLB-5

Padilla, Ernesto Chávez 1944- DLB-122

Page, L. C., and Company DLB-49

Page, P. K. 1916- DLB-68

Page, Thomas Nelson
1853-1922 . . . . DLB-12, 78; DS-13

Page, Walter Hines 1855-1918 . . . DLB-71, 91

Paget, Francis Edward
1806-1882 . . . . DLB-163

Paget, Violet (see Lee, Vernon)

Pagliarani, Elio 1927- DLB-128

Pain, Barry 1864-1928. .... DLB-135

Pain, Philip ?-circa 1666 .... DLB-24

Paine, Robert Treat, Jr. 1773-1811 ... DLB-37

Paine, Thomas
1737-1809. .... DLB-31, 43, 73, 158

Painter, George D. 1914- DLB-155

Painter, William 1540?-1594. ...... DLB-136

Palazzeschi, Aldo 1885-1974. ...... DLB-114

Paley, Grace 1922- DLB-28

Palfrey, John Gorham
1796-1881 .... DLB-1, 30

Palgrave, Francis Turner
1824-1897 .... DLB-35

Palmer, Joe H. 1904-1952. .... DLB-171

Palmer, Michael 1943- DLB-169

Paltock, Robert 1697-1767 .... DLB-39

Pan Books Limited DLB-112

Panama, Norman 1914- and
Frank, Melvin 1913-1988. ...... DLB-26

Pancake, Breece D'J 1952-1979 ..... DLB-130

Panero, Leopoldo 1909-1962 ...... DLB-108

Pangborn, Edgar 1909-1976 .... DLB-8

"Panic Among the Philistines": A Postscript,
An Interview with Bryan Griffin Y-81

Panizzi, Sir Anthony 1797-1879. .... DLB-184

Panneton, Philippe (see Ringuet)

Panshin, Alexei 1940- DLB-8

Pansy (see Alden, Isabella)

Pantheon Books DLB-46

Papantonio, Michael (see Kohn, John S. Van E.)

Paperback Library. DLB-46

Paperback Science Fiction DLB-8

Paquet, Alfons 1881-1944. .... DLB-66

Paracelsus 1493-1541. .... DLB-179

Paradis, Suzanne 1936- DLB-53

Pareja Diezcanseco, Alfredo
1908-1993 .... DLB-145

Pardoe, Julia 1804-1862 .... DLB-166

Parents' Magazine Press DLB-46

Parise, Goffredo 1929-1986 .... DLB-177

Parisian Theater, Fall 1984: Toward
A New Baroque Y-85

Parizeau, Alice 1930- DLB-60

Parke, John 1754-1789 .... DLB-31

Parker, Dorothy
1893-1967. .... DLB-11, 45, 86

Parker, Gilbert 1860-1932. .... DLB-99

Parker, James 1714-1770 .... DLB-43

Parker, Theodore 1810-1860. .... DLB-1

Parker, William Riley 1906-1968. .... DLB-103

Parker, J. H. [publishing house] DLB-106

Parker, John [publishing house]. DLB-106

Parkman, Francis, Jr.
1823-1893. ...... DLB-1, 30, 183, 186

Parks, Gordon 1912- DLB-33

Parks, William 1698-1750. .... DLB-43

Parks, William [publishing house] DLB-49

Parley, Peter (see Goodrich, Samuel Griswold)

Parmenides late sixth-fifth century B.C.
.... DLB-176

Parnell, Thomas 1679-1718. .... DLB-95

Parr, Catherine 1513?-1548. .... DLB-136

Parrington, Vernon L.
1871-1929. .... DLB-17, 63

Parrish, Maxfield 1870-1966. ...... DLB-188

Parronchi, Alessandro 1914- DLB-128

Partridge, S. W., and Company DLB-106

Parton, James 1822-1891 .... DLB-30

Parton, Sara Payson Willis
1811-1872. .... DLB-43, 74

Parun, Vesna 1922- DLB-181

Pasinetti, Pier Maria 1913- DLB-177

Pasolini, Pier Paolo 1922- DLB-128, 177

Pastan, Linda 1932- DLB-5

Paston, George 1860-1936. .... DLB-149

The Paston Letters 1422-1509. ...... DLB-146

Pastorius, Francis Daniel
1651-circa 1720 .... DLB-24

Patchen, Kenneth 1911-1972 .... DLB-16, 48

Pater, Walter 1839-1894 ..... DLB-57, 156

Paterson, Katherine 1932- DLB-52

Patmore, Coventry 1823-1896. .... DLB-35, 98

Paton, Joseph Noel 1821-1901 ..... DLB-35

Paton Walsh, Jill 1937- DLB-161

Patrick, Edwin Hill ("Ted")
1901-1964 .... DLB-137

Patrick, John 1906- DLB-7

Pattee, Fred Lewis 1863-1950 ..... DLB-71

Pattern and Paradigm: History as
Design, by Judith Ryan DLB-75

Patterson, Alicia 1906-1963 ...... DLB-127

Patterson, Eleanor Medill
1881-1948 .... DLB-29

Patterson, Eugene 1923- DLB-127

Patterson, Joseph Medill
1879-1946 .... DLB-29

Pattillo, Henry 1726-1801. .... DLB-37

Paul, Elliot 1891-1958 .... DLB-4

Paul, Jean (see Richter, Johann Paul Friedrich)

Paul, Kegan, Trench, Trubner and Company
Limited. DLB-106

Paul, Peter, Book Company DLB-49

Paul, Stanley, and Company
Limited. DLB-112

Paulding, James Kirke
1778-1860 .... DLB-3, 59, 74

Paulin, Tom 1949- DLB-40

Pauper, Peter, Press. DLB-46

Pavese, Cesare 1908-1950 ..... DLB-128, 177

Pavić, Milorad 1929- DLB-181

Pavlov, Konstantin 1933- DLB-181

Pavlović, Miodrag 1928- DLB-181

Paxton, John 1911-1985. .... DLB-44

Payn, James 1830-1898 .... DLB-18

Payne, John 1842-1916 .... DLB-35

Payne, John Howard 1791-1852 .... DLB-37

Payson and Clarke DLB-46

Peabody, Elizabeth Palmer
1804-1894. .... DLB-1

Peabody, Elizabeth Palmer
[publishing house]. DLB-49

Peabody, Oliver William Bourn
1799-1848 .... DLB-59

Peace, Roger 1899-1968 .... DLB-127

Peacham, Henry 1578-1644? DLB-151

Peacham, Henry, the Elder
1547-1634 .... DLB-172

Peachtree Publishers, Limited. DLB-46

Peacock, Molly 1947- DLB-120

Peacock, Thomas Love
1785-1866 .... DLB-96, 116

Pead, Deuel ?-1727 .... DLB-24

Peake, Mervyn 1911-1968 ..... DLB-15, 160

Peale, Rembrandt 1778-1860 ...... DLB-183

Pear Tree Press DLB-112

Pearce, Philippa 1920- DLB-161

Pearson, H. B. [publishing house] DLB-49

Pearson, Hesketh 1887-1964. ...... DLB-149

Peck, George W. 1840-1916. .... DLB-23, 42

Peck, H. C., and Theo. Bliss
[publishing house]. DLB-49

Peck, Harry Thurston
1856-1914. .... DLB-71, 91

Peele, George 1556-1596 ..... DLB-62, 167

Pegler, Westbrook 1894-1969 ..... DLB-171

Pekić, Borislav 1930-1992 .... DLB-181

Pellegrini and Cudahy DLB-46

Pelletier, Aimé (see Vac, Bertrand)

Pemberton, Sir Max 1863-1950 .... DLB-70

Penfield, Edward 1866-1925. ...... DLB-188

Penguin Books [U.S.]. DLB-46

Penguin Books [U.K.]. DLB-112

Penn Publishing Company DLB-49

Penn, William 1644-1718. .... DLB-24

Penna, Sandro 1906-1977 .... DLB-114

Pennell, Joseph 1857-1926. .... DLB-188

Penner, Jonathan 1940- Y-83

Pennington, Lee 1939- Y-82

Pepys, Samuel 1633-1703 .... DLB-101

Percy, Thomas 1729-1811 . . . . DLB-104	Pforzheimer, Carl H. 1879-1957 . . . . DLB-140	Pinckney, Josephine 1895-1957 . . . . . . DLB-6
Percy, Walker 1916-1990 . . . . DLB-2; Y-80, 90	Phaer, Thomas 1510?-1560 . . . . DLB-167	Pindar circa 518 B.C.-circa 438 B.C. DLB-176
Percy, William 1575-1648 . . . . DLB-172	Phaidon Press Limited DLB-112	
Perec, Georges 1936-1982 . . . . DLB-83	Pharr, Robert Deane 1916-1992 . . . . . DLB-33	Pindar, Peter (see Wolcot, John)
Perelman, S. J. 1904-1979 . . . . . DLB-11, 44	Phelps, Elizabeth Stuart 1844-1911 . . . . DLB-74	Pinero, Arthur Wing 1855-1934 . . . . . DLB-10
Perez, Raymundo "Tigre" 1946- DLB-122		Pinget, Robert 1919- DLB-83
	Philander von der Linde (see Mencke, Johann Burckhard)	Pinnacle Books DLB-46
Peri Rossi, Cristina 1941- DLB-145		Piñon, Nélida 1935- DLB-145
Periodicals of the Beat Generation DLB-16	Philip, Marlene Nourbese 1947- DLB-157	Pinsky, Robert 1940- Y-82
Perkins, Eugene 1932- DLB-41	Philippe, Charles-Louis 1874-1909 . . . . DLB-65	Pinter, Harold 1930- DLB-13
Perkoff, Stuart Z. 1930-1974 . . . . . . DLB-16		Piontek, Heinz 1925- DLB-75
Perley, Moses Henry 1804-1862 . . . . . DLB-99	Phillipps, Sir Thomas 1792-1872 . . . . DLB-184	Piozzi, Hester Lynch [Thrale] 1741-1821 . . . . DLB-104, 142
Permabooks DLB-46	Philips, John 1676-1708 . . . . DLB-95	
Perrin, Alice 1867-1934 . . . . DLB-156	Philips, Katherine 1632-1664 . . . . . . DLB-131	Piper, H. Beam 1904-1964 . . . . DLB-8
Perry, Bliss 1860-1954 . . . . DLB-71	Phillips, Caryl 1958- DLB-157	Piper, Watty DLB-22
Perry, Eleanor 1915-1981 . . . . DLB-44	Phillips, David Graham 1867-1911 . . . . DLB-9, 12	Pirckheimer, Caritas 1467-1532 . . . . . DLB-179
Perry, Matthew 1794-1858 . . . . DLB-183		Pirckheimer, Willibald 1470-1530 . . . . DLB-179
Perry, Sampson 1747-1823 . . . . DLB-158	Phillips, Jayne Anne 1952- Y-80	
"Personal Style" (1890), by John Addington Symonds DLB-57	Phillips, Robert 1938- DLB-105	Pisar, Samuel 1929- Y-83
	Phillips, Robert, Finding, Losing, Reclaiming: A Note on My Poems DLB-105	Pitkin, Timothy 1766-1847 . . . . DLB-30
Perutz, Leo 1882-1957 . . . . DLB-81		The Pitt Poetry Series: Poetry Publishing Today Y-85
Pesetsky, Bette 1932- DLB-130		
Pestalozzi, Johann Heinrich 1746-1827 . . . . DLB-94	Phillips, Stephen 1864-1915 . . . . DLB-10	Pitter, Ruth 1897- DLB-20
	Phillips, Ulrich B. 1877-1934 . . . . . . DLB-17	Pix, Mary 1666-1709 . . . . DLB-80
Peter, Laurence J. 1919-1990 . . . . . . DLB-53	Phillips, Willard 1784-1873 . . . . DLB-59	Plaatje, Sol T. 1876-1932 . . . . DLB-125
Peter of Spain circa 1205-1277 . . . . . DLB-115	Phillips, William 1907- DLB-137	The Place of Realism in Fiction (1895), by George Gissing DLB-18
Peterkin, Julia 1880-1961 . . . . DLB-9	Phillips, Sampson and Company DLB-49	
Peters, Lenrie 1932- DLB-117	Phillpotts, Eden 1862-1960 . . . . . . DLB-10, 70, 135, 153	Plante, David 1940- Y-83
Peters, Robert 1924- DLB-105		Platen, August von 1796-1835 . . . . . . DLB-90
Peters, Robert, Foreword to Ludwig of Bavaria DLB-105	Philo circa 20-15 B.C.-circa A.D. 50 . . . . DLB-176	Plath, Sylvia 1932-1963 . . . . . DLB-5, 6, 152
		Plato circa 428 B.C.-348-347 B.C. DLB-176
Petersham, Maud 1889-1971 and Petersham, Miska 1888-1960 . . . . . DLB-22	Philosophical Library DLB-46	
	"The Philosophy of Style" (1852), by Herbert Spencer DLB-57	Platon 1737-1812 . . . . DLB-150
Peterson, Charles Jacobs 1819-1887 . . . . DLB-79		Platt and Munk Company DLB-46
	Phinney, Elihu [publishing house] DLB-49	Playboy Press DLB-46
Peterson, Len 1917- DLB-88	Phoenix, John (see Derby, George Horatio)	Playford, John [publishing house] DLB-170
Peterson, Louis 1922- DLB-76	PHYLON (Fourth Quarter, 1950), The Negro in Literature: The Current Scene DLB-76	
Peterson, T. B., and Brothers DLB-49		Plays, Playwrights, and Playgoers DLB-84
Petitclair, Pierre 1813-1860 . . . . DLB-99		Playwrights and Professors, by Tom Stoppard DLB-13
	Physiologus circa 1070-circa 1150 . . . . DLB-148	
Petrov, Aleksandar 1938- DLB-181		Playwrights on the Theater DLB-80
Petrov, Gavriil 1730-1801 . . . . DLB-150	Piccolo, Lucio 1903-1969 . . . . DLB-114	Der Pleier flourished circa 1250 . . . . DLB-138
Petrov, Vasilii Petrovich 1736-1799 . . . . DLB-150	Pickard, Tom 1946- DLB-40	Plenzdorf, Ulrich 1934- DLB-75
	Pickering, William [publishing house] DLB-106	Plessen, Elizabeth 1944- DLB-75
Petrov, Valeri 1920- DLB-181		Plievier, Theodor 1892-1955 . . . . . . DLB-69
Petrović, Rastko 1898-1949 . . . . . . DLB-147	Pickthall, Marjorie 1883-1922 . . . . . . DLB-92	Plimpton, George 1927- DLB-185
Petruslied circa 854? DLB-148	Pictorial Printing Company DLB-49	Plomer, William 1903-1973 . . . . DLB-20, 162
Petry, Ann 1908- DLB-76	Piel, Gerard 1915- DLB-137	Plotinus 204-270 . . . . DLB-176
Pettie, George circa 1548-1589 . . . . . DLB-136	Piercy, Marge 1936- DLB-120	Plumly, Stanley 1939- DLB-5
Peyton, K. M. 1929- DLB-161	Pierro, Albino 1916- DLB-128	Plumpp, Sterling D. 1940- DLB-41
Pfaffe Konrad flourished circa 1172 . . . . DLB-148	Pignotti, Lamberto 1926- DLB-128	Plunkett, James 1920- DLB-14
	Pike, Albert 1809-1891 . . . . DLB-74	Plutarch circa 46-circa 120 . . . . DLB-176
Pfaffe Lamprecht flourished circa 1150 . . . . DLB-148	Pike, Zebulon Montgomery 1779-1813 . . DLB-183	
	Pilon, Jean-Guy 1930- DLB-60	Plymell, Charles 1935- DLB-16

Pocket Books DLB-46

Poe, Edgar Allan
 1809-1849 . . . . DLB-3, 59, 73, 74

Poe, James 1921-1980. . . . . DLB-44

The Poet Laureate of the United States
 Statements from Former Consultants
 in Poetry Y-86

Pohl, Frederik 1919- DLB-8

Poirier, Louis (see Gracq, Julien)

Polanyi, Michael 1891-1976 . . . . DLB-100

Pole, Reginald 1500-1558 . . . . DLB-132

Poliakoff, Stephen 1952- DLB-13

Polidori, John William
 1795-1821 . . . . DLB-116

Polite, Carlene Hatcher 1932- DLB-33

Pollard, Edward A. 1832-1872 . . . . . . DLB-30

Pollard, Percival 1869-1911 . . . . DLB-71

Pollard and Moss DLB-49

Pollock, Sharon 1936- DLB-60

Polonsky, Abraham 1910- DLB-26

Polotsky, Simeon 1629-1680 . . . . DLB-150

Polybius circa 200 B.C.-118 B.C. DLB-176

Pomilio, Mario 1921-1990 . . . . DLB-177

Ponce, Mary Helen 1938- DLB-122

Ponce-Montoya, Juanita 1949- DLB-122

Ponet, John 1516?-1556 . . . . DLB-132

Poniatowski, Elena 1933- DLB-113

Ponsonby, William
 [publishing house] DLB-170

Pony Stories DLB-160

Poole, Ernest 1880-1950 . . . . DLB-9

Poole, Sophia 1804-1891 . . . . DLB-166

Poore, Benjamin Perley
 1820-1887 . . . . DLB-23

Popa, Vasko 1922-1991 . . . . DLB-181

Pope, Abbie Hanscom
 1858-1894 . . . . DLB-140

Pope, Alexander 1688-1744 . . . . DLB-95, 101

Popov, Mikhail Ivanovich
 1742-circa 1790 . . . . DLB-150

Popović, Aleksandar 1929-1996 . . . . . DLB-181

Popular Library DLB-46

Porlock, Martin (see MacDonald, Philip)

Porpoise Press DLB-112

Porta, Antonio 1935-1989 . . . . DLB-128

Porter, Anna Maria
 1780-1832 . . . . DLB-116, 159

Porter, David 1780-1843 . . . . DLB-183

Porter, Eleanor H. 1868-1920 . . . . . . DLB-9

Porter, Gene Stratton (see Stratton-Porter, Gene)

Porter, Henry ?-? DLB-62

Porter, Jane 1776-1850 . . . . . . DLB-116, 159

Porter, Katherine Anne
 1890-1980. . . . DLB-4, 9, 102; Y-80; DS-12

Porter, Peter 1929- DLB-40

Porter, William Sydney
 1862-1910 . . . . DLB-12, 78, 79

Porter, William T. 1809-1858 . . . . DLB-3, 43

Porter and Coates DLB-49

Portis, Charles 1933- DLB-6

Posey, Alexander 1873-1908 . . . . . . DLB-175

Postans, Marianne
 circa 1810-1865 . . . . DLB-166

Postl, Carl (see Sealsfield, Carl)

Poston, Ted 1906-1974 . . . . DLB-51

Postscript to [the Third Edition of] *Clarissa*
 (1751), by Samuel Richardson DLB-39

Potok, Chaim 1929- DLB-28, 152; Y-84

Potter, Beatrix 1866-1943 . . . . DLB-141

Potter, David M. 1910-1971 . . . . DLB-17

Potter, John E., and Company DLB-49

Pottle, Frederick A.
 1897-1987 . . . . DLB-103; Y-87

Poulin, Jacques 1937- DLB-60

Pound, Ezra 1885-1972 . . DLB-4, 45, 63; DS-15

Povich, Shirley 1905- DLB-171

Powell, Anthony 1905- DLB-15

Powell, John Wesley 1834-1902 . . . . . DLB-186

Powers, J. F. 1917- DLB-130

Pownall, David 1938- DLB-14

Powys, John Cowper 1872-1963 . . . . . DLB-15

Powys, Llewelyn 1884-1939 . . . . DLB-98

Powys, T. F. 1875-1953 . . . . . . DLB-36, 162

Poynter, Nelson 1903-1978 . . . . DLB-127

The Practice of Biography: An Interview
 with Stanley Weintraub Y-82

The Practice of Biography II: An Interview
 with B. L. Reid Y-83

The Practice of Biography III: An Interview
 with Humphrey Carpenter Y-84

The Practice of Biography IV: An Interview with
 William Manchester Y-85

The Practice of Biography V: An Interview
 with Justin Kaplan Y-86

The Practice of Biography VI: An Interview with
 David Herbert Donald Y-87

The Practice of Biography VII: An Interview with
 John Caldwell Guilds Y-92

The Practice of Biography VIII: An Interview
 with Joan Mellen Y-94

The Practice of Biography IX: An Interview
 with Michael Reynolds Y-95

Prados, Emilio 1899-1962 . . . . DLB-134

Praed, Winthrop Mackworth
 1802-1839 . . . . DLB-96

Praeger Publishers DLB-46

Praetorius, Johannes 1630-1680 . . . . . DLB-168

Pratolini, Vasco 1913-1991 . . . . DLB-177

Pratt, E. J. 1882-1964 . . . . DLB-92

Pratt, Samuel Jackson 1749-1814 . . . . DLB-39

Preface to *Alwyn* (1780), by
 Thomas Holcroft DLB-39

Preface to *Colonel Jack* (1722), by
 Daniel Defoe DLB-39

Preface to *Evelina* (1778), by
 Fanny Burney DLB-39

Preface to *Ferdinand Count Fathom* (1753), by
 Tobias Smollett DLB-39

Preface to *Incognita* (1692), by
 William Congreve DLB-39

Preface to *Joseph Andrews* (1742), by
 Henry Fielding DLB-39

Preface to *Moll Flanders* (1722), by
 Daniel Defoe DLB-39

Preface to *Poems* (1853), by
 Matthew Arnold DLB-32

Preface to *Robinson Crusoe* (1719), by
 Daniel Defoe DLB-39

Preface to *Roderick Random* (1748), by
 Tobias Smollett DLB-39

Preface to *Roxana* (1724), by
 Daniel Defoe DLB-39

Preface to *St. Leon* (1799), by
 William Godwin DLB-39

Preface to Sarah Fielding's *Familiar Letters*
 (1747), by Henry Fielding
 [excerpt] DLB-39

Preface to Sarah Fielding's *The Adventures of
 David Simple* (1744), by
 Henry Fielding DLB-39

Preface to *The Cry* (1754), by
 Sarah Fielding DLB-39

Preface to *The Delicate Distress* (1769), by
 Elizabeth Griffin DLB-39

Preface to *The Disguis'd Prince* (1733), by
 Eliza Haywood [excerpt] DLB-39

Preface to *The Farther Adventures of Robinson
 Crusoe* (1719), by Daniel Defoe . . . DLB-39

Preface to the First Edition of *Pamela* (1740), by
 Samuel Richardson DLB-39

Preface to the First Edition of *The Castle of
 Otranto* (1764), by
 Horace Walpole DLB-39

Preface to *The History of Romances* (1715), by
 Pierre Daniel Huet [excerpts] DLB-39

Preface to *The Life of Charlotta du Pont* (1723),
 by Penelope Aubin DLB-39

Preface to *The Old English Baron* (1778), by
 Clara Reeve DLB-39

Preface to the Second Edition of *The Castle of
 Otranto* (1765), by Horace
 Walpole DLB-39

Preface to *The Secret History, of Queen Zarah,
 and the Zarazians* (1705), by Delariviere
 Manley DLB-39

Preface to the Third Edition of *Clarissa* (1751), by Samuel Richardson [excerpt] DLB-39

Preface to *The Works of Mrs. Davys* (1725), by Mary Davys DLB-39

Preface to Volume 1 of *Clarissa* (1747), by Samuel Richardson DLB-39

Preface to Volume 3 of *Clarissa* (1748), by Samuel Richardson DLB-39

Préfontaine, Yves 1937- DLB-53

Prelutsky, Jack 1940- DLB-61

Premisses, by Michael Hamburger. . . . DLB-66

Prentice, George D. 1802-1870. . . . . . DLB-43

Prentice-Hall DLB-46

Prescott, Orville 1906-1996. . . . . Y-96

Prescott, William Hickling 1796-1859 . . . . DLB-1, 30, 59

The Present State of the English Novel (1892), by George Saintsbury DLB-18

Prešeren, Francè 1800-1849 . . . . . . DLB-147

Preston, May Wilson 1873-1949 . . . . DLB-188

Preston, Thomas 1537-1598 . . . . . . DLB-62

Price, Reynolds 1933- DLB-2

Price, Richard 1723-1791 . . . . DLB-158

Price, Richard 1949- Y-81

Priest, Christopher 1943- DLB-14

Priestley, J. B. 1894-1984
. . . . . . DLB-10, 34, 77, 100, 139; Y-84

Primary Bibliography: A Retrospective Y-95

Prime, Benjamin Young 1733-1791 . . . DLB-31

Primrose, Diana floruit circa 1630 . . . . DLB-126

Prince, F. T. 1912- DLB-20

Prince, Thomas 1687-1758 . . . . DLB-24, 140

The Principles of Success in Literature (1865), by George Henry Lewes [excerpt] . . . DLB-57

Printz, Wolfgang Casper 1641-1717 . . . . DLB-168

Prior, Matthew 1664-1721 . . . . DLB-95

Prisco, Michele 1920- DLB-177

Pritchard, William H. 1932- DLB-111

Pritchett, V. S. 1900- DLB-15, 139

Procter, Adelaide Anne 1825-1864 . . . . DLB-32

Procter, Bryan Waller 1787-1874 . . . . DLB-96, 144

Proctor, Robert 1868-1903. . . . . . . DLB-184

The Profession of Authorship: Scribblers for Bread Y-89

The Progress of Romance (1785), by Clara Reeve [excerpt] DLB-39

Prokopovich, Feofan 1681?-1736 . . . DLB-150

Prokosch, Frederic 1906-1989 . . . . . DLB-48

The Proletarian Novel DLB-9

Propper, Dan 1937- DLB-16

The Prospect of Peace (1778), by Joel Barlow DLB-37

Protagoras circa 490 B.C.-420 B.C. DLB-176

Proud, Robert 1728-1813. . . . . DLB-30

Proust, Marcel 1871-1922. . . . . DLB-65

Prynne, J. H. 1936- DLB-40

Przybyszewski, Stanislaw 1868-1927 . . . . DLB-66

Pseudo-Dionysius the Areopagite floruit circa 500 . . . . DLB-115

The Public Lending Right in America Statement by Sen. Charles McC. Mathias, Jr. PLR and the Meaning of Literary Property Statements on PLR by American Writers Y-83

The Public Lending Right in the United Kingdom Public Lending Right: The First Year in the United Kingdom Y-83

The Publication of English Renaissance Plays. DLB-62

Publications and Social Movements [Transcendentalism] DLB-1

Publishers and Agents: The Columbia Connection Y-87

A Publisher's Archives: G. P. Putnam . . . Y-92

Publishing Fiction at LSU Press. Y-87

Pückler-Muskau, Hermann von 1785-1871 . . . . DLB-133

Pufendorf, Samuel von 1632-1694 . . . . DLB-168

Pugh, Edwin William 1874-1930 . . . . DLB-135

Pugin, A. Welby 1812-1852 . . . . DLB-55

Puig, Manuel 1932-1990. . . . . DLB-113

Pulitzer, Joseph 1847-1911 . . . . DLB-23

Pulitzer, Joseph, Jr. 1885-1955 . . . . . DLB-29

Pulitzer Prizes for the Novel, 1917-1945. . . . . DLB-9

Pulliam, Eugene 1889-1975 . . . . . . DLB-127

Purchas, Samuel 1577?-1626 . . . . . . DLB-151

Purdy, Al 1918- DLB-88

Purdy, James 1923- DLB-2

Purdy, Ken W. 1913-1972 . . . . DLB-137

Pusey, Edward Bouverie 1800-1882 . . . . DLB-55

Putnam, George Palmer 1814-1872 . . . . DLB-3, 79

Putnam, Samuel 1892-1950 . . . . DLB-4

G. P. Putnam's Sons [U.S.] DLB-49

G. P. Putnam's Sons [U.K.] DLB-106

Puzo, Mario 1920- DLB-6

Pyle, Ernie 1900-1945. . . . . DLB-29

Pyle, Howard 1853-1911 . . . . DLB-42, 188; DS-13

Pym, Barbara 1913-1980. . . . . . DLB-14; Y-87

Pynchon, Thomas 1937- DLB-2, 173

Pyramid Books DLB-46

Pyrnelle, Louise-Clarke 1850-1907 . . . . DLB-42

Pythagoras circa 570 B.C.-? DLB-176

Q

Quad, M. (see Lewis, Charles B.)

Quaritch, Bernard 1819-1899 . . . . . DLB-184

Quarles, Francis 1592-1644 . . . . . . DLB-126

The Quarterly Review 1809-1967 . . . . DLB-110

Quasimodo, Salvatore 1901-1968 . . . . DLB-114

Queen, Ellery (see Dannay, Frederic, and Manfred B. Lee)

The Queen City Publishing House . . . DLB-49

Queneau, Raymond 1903-1976. . . . . DLB-72

Quennell, Sir Peter 1905-1993 . . . . . DLB-155

Quesnel, Joseph 1746-1809 . . . . DLB-99

The Question of American Copyright in the Nineteenth Century Headnote
Preface, by George Haven Putnam
The Evolution of Copyright, by Brander Matthews
Summary of Copyright Legislation in the United States, by R. R. Bowker
Analysis oæ the Provisions of the Copyright Law of 1891, by George Haven Putnam
The Contest for International Copyright, by George Haven Putnam
Cheap Books and Good Books, by Brander Matthews. DLB-49

Quiller-Couch, Sir Arthur Thomas 1863-1944. . . . . . DLB-135, 153, 190

Quin, Ann 1936-1973. . . . . DLB-14

Quincy, Samuel, of Georgia ?-? DLB-31

Quincy, Samuel, of Massachusetts 1734-1789 . . . . DLB-31

Quinn, Anthony 1915- DLB-122

Quinn, John 1870-1924 . . . . DLB-187

Quintana, Leroy V. 1944- DLB-82

Quintana, Miguel de 1671-1748 A Forerunner of Chicano Literature. DLB-122

Quist, Harlin, Books DLB-46

Quoirez, Françoise (see Sagan, Françoise)

R

Raabe, Wilhelm 1831-1910 . . . . DLB-129

Rabe, David 1940- DLB-7

Raboni, Giovanni 1932- DLB-128

Rachilde 1860-1953 . . . . DLB-123

Racin, Kočo 1908-1943 . . . . DLB-147

Rackham, Arthur 1867-1939 . . . . . . DLB-141

Radcliffe, Ann 1764-1823 . . . . . . DLB-39, 178
Raddall, Thomas 1903- DLB-68
Radichkov, Yordan 1929- DLB-181
Radiguet, Raymond 1903-1923. . . . . . DLB-65
Radishchev, Aleksandr Nikolaevich
  1749-1802 . . . . DLB-150
Radványi, Netty Reiling (see Seghers, Anna)
Rahv, Philip 1908-1973 . . . . DLB-137
Raičković, Stevan 1928- DLB-181
Raimund, Ferdinand Jakob
  1790-1836 . . . . DLB-90
Raine, Craig 1944- DLB-40
Raine, Kathleen 1908- DLB-20
Rainolde, Richard
  circa 1530-1606 . . . . DLB-136
Rakić, Milan 1876-1938 . . . . DLB-147
Ralegh, Sir Walter 1554?-1618 . . . . . DLB-172
Ralin, Radoy 1923- DLB-181
Ralph, Julian 1853-1903 . . . . DLB-23
Ralph Waldo Emerson in 1982 . . . . Y-82
Ramat, Silvio 1939- DLB-128
Rambler, no. 4 (1750), by Samuel Johnson
  [excerpt] DLB-39
Ramée, Marie Louise de la (see Ouida)
Ramírez, Sergío 1942- DLB-145
Ramke, Bin 1947- DLB-120
Ramler, Karl Wilhelm 1725-1798 . . . . DLB-97
Ramon Ribeyro, Julio 1929- DLB-145
Ramous, Mario 1924- DLB-128
Rampersad, Arnold 1941- DLB-111
Ramsay, Allan 1684 or 1685-1758 . . . . DLB-95
Ramsay, David 1749-1815 . . . . DLB-30
Ranck, Katherine Quintana
  1942- DLB-122
Rand, Avery and Company DLB-49
Rand McNally and Company DLB-49
Randall, David Anton
  1905-1975 . . . . DLB-140
Randall, Dudley 1914- DLB-41
Randall, Henry S. 1811-1876 . . . . . . DLB-30
Randall, James G. 1881-1953 . . . . . . DLB-17
The Randall Jarrell Symposium: A Small
  Collection of Randall Jarrells
  Excerpts From Papers Delivered at
  the Randall Jarrel Symposium Y-86
Randolph, A. Philip 1889-1979 . . . . . DLB-91
Randolph, Anson D. F.
  [publishing house] DLB-49
Randolph, Thomas 1605-1635 . . . DLB-58, 126
Random House DLB-46
Ranlet, Henry [publishing house] DLB-49
Ransom, Harry 1908-1976 . . . . . . DLB-187
Ransom, John Crowe
  1888-1974 . . . . DLB-45, 63

Ransome, Arthur 1884-1967 . . . . . . DLB-160
Raphael, Frederic 1931- DLB-14
Raphaelson, Samson 1896-1983 . . . . DLB-44
Raskin, Ellen 1928-1984 . . . . DLB-52
Rastell, John 1475?-1536 . . . . . . DLB-136, 170
Rattigan, Terence 1911-1977 . . . . . . DLB-13
Rawlings, Marjorie Kinnan
  1896-1953 . . . . DLB-9, 22, 102
Raworth, Tom 1938- DLB-40
Ray, David 1932- DLB-5
Ray, Gordon Norton
  1915-1986 . . . . DLB-103, 140
Ray, Henrietta Cordelia
  1849-1916 . . . . DLB-50
Raymond, Henry J. 1820-1869 . . . DLB-43, 79
Raymond Chandler Centenary Tributes
  from Michael Avallone, James Elroy, Joe
  Gores,
  and William F. Nolan Y-88
Reach, Angus 1821-1856 . . . . DLB-70
Read, Herbert 1893-1968 . . . . . DLB-20, 149
Read, Herbert, "The Practice of Biography," in
  *The English Sense of Humour and Other
  Essays* DLB-149
Read, Opie 1852-1939 . . . . DLB-23
Read, Piers Paul 1941- DLB-14
Reade, Charles 1814-1884 . . . . DLB-21
Reader's Digest Condensed
  Books DLB-46
Reading, Peter 1946- DLB-40
Reading Series in New York City Y-96
Reaney, James 1926- DLB-68
Rebhun, Paul 1500?-1546 . . . . . . DLB-179
Rèbora, Clemente 1885-1957 . . . . . DLB-114
Rechy, John 1934- DLB-122; Y-82
The Recovery of Literature: Criticism in the
  1990s: A Symposium Y-91
Redding, J. Saunders
  1906-1988 . . . . DLB-63, 76
Redfield, J. S. [publishing house] DLB-49
Redgrove, Peter 1932- DLB-40
Redmon, Anne 1943- Y-86
Redmond, Eugene B. 1937- DLB-41
Redpath, James [publishing house] . . . DLB-49
Reed, Henry 1808-1854 . . . . DLB-59
Reed, Henry 1914- DLB-27
Reed, Ishmael
  1938- DLB-2, 5, 33, 169; DS-8
Reed, Rex 1938- DLB-185
Reed, Sampson 1800-1880 . . . . . . DLB-1
Reed, Talbot Baines 1852-1893 . . . . DLB-141
Reedy, William Marion 1862-1920 . . . DLB-91
Reese, Lizette Woodworth
  1856-1935 . . . . DLB-54

Reese, Thomas 1742-1796 . . . . DLB-37
Reeve, Clara 1729-1807 . . . . DLB-39
Reeves, James 1909-1978 . . . . DLB-161
Reeves, John 1926- DLB-88
Regnery, Henry, Company DLB-46
Rehberg, Hans 1901-1963 . . . . DLB-124
Rehfisch, Hans José 1891-1960 . . . . DLB-124
Reid, Alastair 1926- DLB-27
Reid, B. L. 1918-1990 . . . . DLB-111
Reid, Christopher 1949- DLB-40
Reid, Forrest 1875-1947 . . . . DLB-153
Reid, Helen Rogers 1882-1970 . . . . . DLB-29
Reid, James ?-? DLB-31
Reid, Mayne 1818-1883 . . . . . . DLB-21, 163
Reid, Thomas 1710-1796 . . . . DLB-31
Reid, V. S. (Vic) 1913-1987 . . . . . . DLB-125
Reid, Whitelaw 1837-1912 . . . . . . DLB-23
Reilly and Lee Publishing
  Company DLB-46
Reimann, Brigitte 1933-1973 . . . . . . DLB-75
Reinmar der Alte
  circa 1165-circa 1205 . . . . DLB-138
Reinmar von Zweter
  circa 1200-circa 1250 . . . . DLB-138
Reisch, Walter 1903-1983 . . . . DLB-44
Remarque, Erich Maria 1898-1970 . . . DLB-56
"Re-meeting of Old Friends": The Jack
  Kerouac Conference Y-82
Remington, Frederic
  1861-1909 . . . . DLB-12, 186, 188
Renaud, Jacques 1943- DLB-60
Renault, Mary 1905-1983 . . . . Y-83
Rendell, Ruth 1930- DLB-87
Representative Men and Women: A Historical
  Perspective on the British Novel,
  1930-1960 . . . . DLB-15
(Re-)Publishing Orwell Y-86
Rettenbacher, Simon 1634-1706 . . . . DLB-168
Reuchlin, Johannes 1455-1522 . . . . . DLB-179
Reuter, Christian 1665-after 1712 . . . DLB-168
Reuter, Fritz 1810-1874 . . . . DLB-129
Reuter, Gabriele 1859-1941 . . . . . . DLB-66
Revell, Fleming H., Company DLB-49
Reventlow, Franziska Gräfin zu
  1871-1918 . . . . DLB-66
Review of Reviews Office DLB-112
Review of [Samuel Richardson's] *Clarissa* (1748),
  by Henry Fielding DLB-39
The Revolt (1937), by Mary Colum
  [excerpts] DLB-36
Rexroth, Kenneth
  1905-1982 . . . . . DLB-16, 48, 165; Y-82
Rey, H. A. 1898-1977 . . . . DLB-22
Reynal and Hitchcock DLB-46

Reynolds, G. W. M. 1814-1879 . . . . . DLB-21

Reynolds, John Hamilton
1794-1852 . . . . DLB-96

Reynolds, Mack 1917- DLB-8

Reynolds, Sir Joshua 1723-1792. . . . DLB-104

Reznikoff, Charles 1894-1976 . . . . DLB-28, 45

"Rhetoric" (1828; revised, 1859), by
Thomas de Quincey [excerpt] DLB-57

Rhett, Robert Barnwell 1800-1876 . . . . DLB-43

Rhode, John 1884-1964 . . . . DLB-77

Rhodes, James Ford 1848-1927 . . . . . DLB-47

Rhodes, Richard 1937- DLB-185

Rhys, Jean 1890-1979 . . . . . DLB-36, 117, 162

Ricardo, David 1772-1823 . . . . . DLB-107, 158

Ricardou, Jean 1932- DLB-83

Rice, Elmer 1892-1967 . . . . DLB-4, 7

Rice, Grantland 1880-1954 . . . . . DLB-29, 171

Rich, Adrienne 1929- DLB-5, 67

Richards, David Adams 1950- DLB-53

Richards, George circa 1760-1814 . . . . DLB-37

Richards, I. A. 1893-1979 . . . . DLB-27

Richards, Laura E. 1850-1943 . . . . . DLB-42

Richards, William Carey
1818-1892 . . . . DLB-73

Richards, Grant
[publishing house] DLB-112

Richardson, Charles F. 1851-1913 . . . . DLB-71

Richardson, Dorothy M.
1873-1957 . . . . DLB-36

Richardson, Jack 1935- DLB-7

Richardson, John 1796-1852 . . . . . . DLB-99

Richardson, Samuel
1689-1761 . . . . DLB-39, 154

Richardson, Willis 1889-1977. . . . . . DLB-51

Riche, Barnabe 1542-1617. . . . . . . DLB-136

Richler, Mordecai 1931- DLB-53

Richter, Conrad 1890-1968 . . . . DLB-9

Richter, Hans Werner 1908- DLB-69

Richter, Johann Paul Friedrich
1763-1825 . . . . DLB-94

Rickerby, Joseph
[publishing house] DLB-106

Rickword, Edgell 1898-1982 . . . . . . DLB-20

Riddell, Charlotte 1832-1906 . . . . . DLB-156

Riddell, John (see Ford, Corey)

Ridge, John Rollin 1827-1867 . . . . . DLB-175

Ridge, Lola 1873-1941 . . . . DLB-54

Ridge, William Pett 1859-1930 . . . . . DLB-135

Riding, Laura (see Jackson, Laura Riding)

Ridler, Anne 1912- DLB-27

Ridruejo, Dionisio 1912-1975. . . . . . DLB-108

Riel, Louis 1844-1885. . . . . DLB-99

Riemer, Johannes 1648-1714 . . . . . . DLB-168

Riffaterre, Michael 1924- DLB-67

Riggs, Lynn 1899-1954 . . . . DLB-175

Riis, Jacob 1849-1914 . . . . DLB-23

Riker, John C. [publishing house] DLB-49

Riley, James 1777-1840 . . . . DLB-183

Riley, John 1938-1978. . . . . DLB-40

Rilke, Rainer Maria 1875-1926. . . . . . DLB-81

Rimanelli, Giose 1926- DLB-177

Rinehart and Company. DLB-46

Ringuet 1895-1960. . . . . DLB-68

Ringwood, Gwen Pharis
1910-1984 . . . . DLB-88

Rinser, Luise 1911- DLB-69

Ríos, Alberto 1952- DLB-122

Ríos, Isabella 1948- DLB-82

Ripley, Arthur 1895-1961. . . . . DLB-44

Ripley, George 1802-1880. . . . . DLB-1, 64, 73

The Rising Glory of America:
Three Poems DLB-37

The Rising Glory of America: Written in 1771
(1786), by Hugh Henry Brackenridge and
Philip Freneau. DLB-37

Riskin, Robert 1897-1955 . . . . DLB-26

Risse, Heinz 1898- DLB-69

Rist, Johann 1607-1667 . . . . DLB-164

Ritchie, Anna Mowatt 1819-1870 . . . . DLB-3

Ritchie, Anne Thackeray
1837-1919 . . . . DLB-18

Ritchie, Thomas 1778-1854. . . . . . . DLB-43

Rites of Passage
[on William Saroyan] Y-83

The Ritz Paris Hemingway Award Y-85

Rivard, Adjutor 1868-1945 . . . . DLB-92

Rive, Richard 1931-1989 . . . . DLB-125

Rivera, Marina 1942- DLB-122

Rivera, Tomás 1935-1984 . . . . DLB-82

Rivers, Conrad Kent 1933-1968 . . . . . DLB-41

Riverside Press DLB-49

Rivington, James circa 1724-1802 . . . . DLB-43

Rivington, Charles
[publishing house] DLB-154

Rivkin, Allen 1903-1990 . . . . DLB-26

Roa Bastos, Augusto 1917- DLB-113

Robbe-Grillet, Alain 1922- DLB-83

Robbins, Tom 1936- Y-80

Roberts, Charles G. D. 1860-1943. . . . DLB-92

Roberts, Dorothy 1906-1993 . . . . . . DLB-88

Roberts, Elizabeth Madox
1881-1941. . . . . DLB-9, 54, 102

Roberts, Kenneth 1885-1957 . . . . . . DLB-9

Roberts, William 1767-1849 . . . . . . DLB-142

Roberts Brothers DLB-49

Roberts, James [publishing house] . . . DLB-154

Robertson, A. M., and Company DLB-49

Robertson, William 1721-1793 . . . . . DLB-104

Robinson, Casey 1903-1979 . . . . . . DLB-44

Robinson, Edwin Arlington
1869-1935 . . . . DLB-54

Robinson, Henry Crabb
1775-1867 . . . . DLB-107

Robinson, James Harvey
1863-1936 . . . . DLB-47

Robinson, Lennox 1886-1958. . . . . . DLB-10

Robinson, Mabel Louise
1874-1962 . . . . DLB-22

Robinson, Mary 1758-1800 . . . . . . DLB-158

Robinson, Richard
circa 1545-1607 . . . . DLB-167

Robinson, Therese
1797-1870 . . . . DLB-59, 133

Robison, Mary 1949- DLB-130

Roblès, Emmanuel 1914- DLB-83

Roccatagliata Ceccardi, Ceccardo
1871-1919 . . . . DLB-114

Rochester, John Wilmot, Earl of
1647-1680 . . . . DLB-131

Rock, Howard 1911-1976 . . . . DLB-127

Rockwell, Norman Perceval
1894-1978 . . . . DLB-188

Rodgers, Carolyn M. 1945- DLB-41

Rodgers, W. R. 1909-1969 . . . . DLB-20

Rodríguez, Claudio 1934- DLB-134

Rodriguez, Richard 1944- DLB-82

Rodríguez Julia, Edgardo
1946- DLB-145

Roethke, Theodore 1908-1963. . . . . . DLB-5

Rogers, Pattiann 1940- DLB-105

Rogers, Samuel 1763-1855 . . . . DLB-93

Rogers, Will 1879-1935 . . . . DLB-11

Rohmer, Sax 1883-1959 . . . . DLB-70

Roiphe, Anne 1935- Y-80

Rojas, Arnold R. 1896-1988 . . . . . . DLB-82

Rolfe, Frederick William
1860-1913 . . . . DLB-34, 156

Rolland, Romain 1866-1944 . . . . . . DLB-65

Rolle, Richard
circa 1290-1300 - 1340 . . . . DLB-146

Rölvaag, O. E. 1876-1931 . . . . DLB-9

Romains, Jules 1885-1972. . . . . DLB-65

Roman, A., and Company DLB-49

Romano, Lalla 1906- DLB-177

Romano, Octavio 1923- DLB-122

Romero, Leo 1950- DLB-122

Romero, Lin 1947- DLB-122

Romero, Orlando 1945- DLB-82

Rook, Clarence 1863-1915 . . . . DLB-135

Roosevelt, Theodore 1858-1919 . . DLB-47, 186

Root, Waverley 1903-1982. . . . . DLB-4
Root, William Pitt 1941- DLB-120
Roquebrune, Robert de 1889-1978. . . . DLB-68
Rosa, João Guimarães
   1908-1967 . . . . DLB-113
Rosales, Luis 1910-1992. . . . . DLB-134
Roscoe, William 1753-1831 . . . . DLB-163
Rose, Reginald 1920- DLB-26
Rose, Wendy 1948- DLB-175
Rosegger, Peter 1843-1918. . . . . DLB-129
Rosei, Peter 1946- DLB-85
Rosen, Norma 1925- DLB-28
Rosenbach, A. S. W. 1876-1952 . . . . DLB-140
Rosenbaum, Ron 1946- DLB-185
Rosenberg, Isaac 1890-1918. . . . . . . DLB-20
Rosenfeld, Isaac 1918-1956 . . . . DLB-28
Rosenthal, M. L. 1917- DLB-5
Rosenwald, Lessing J. 1891-1979 . . . . DLB-187
Ross, Alexander 1591-1654 . . . . DLB-151
Ross, Harold 1892-1951. . . . . DLB-137
Ross, Leonard Q. (see Rosten, Leo)
Ross, Lillian 1927- DLB-185
Ross, Martin 1862-1915 . . . . DLB-135
Ross, Sinclair 1908- DLB-88
Ross, W. W. E. 1894-1966 . . . . DLB-88
Rosselli, Amelia 1930- DLB-128
Rossen, Robert 1908-1966 . . . . DLB-26
Rossetti, Christina Georgina
   1830-1894 . . . . DLB-35, 163
Rossetti, Dante Gabriel 1828-1882 . . . . DLB-35
Rossner, Judith 1935- DLB-6
Rosten, Leo 1908- DLB-11
Rostenberg, Leona 1908- DLB-140
Rostovsky, Dimitrii 1651-1709 . . . . . DLB-150
Bertram Rota and His Bookshop Y-91
Roth, Gerhard 1942- DLB-85, 124
Roth, Henry 1906?- DLB-28
Roth, Joseph 1894-1939. . . . . DLB-85
Roth, Philip 1933- DLB-2, 28, 173; Y-82
Rothenberg, Jerome 1931- DLB-5
Rothschild Family DLB-184
Rotimi, Ola 1938- DLB-125
Routhier, Adolphe-Basile
   1839-1920 . . . . DLB-99
Routier, Simone 1901-1987 . . . . DLB-88
Routledge, George, and Sons DLB-106
Roversi, Roberto 1923- DLB-128
Rowe, Elizabeth Singer
   1674-1737 . . . . DLB-39, 95
Rowe, Nicholas 1674-1718 . . . . DLB-84
Rowlands, Samuel
   circa 1570-1630 . . . . DLB-121

Rowlandson, Mary
   circa 1635-circa 1678 . . . . DLB-24
Rowley, William circa 1585-1626 . . . . DLB-58
Rowse, A. L. 1903- DLB-155
Rowson, Susanna Haswell
   circa 1762-1824 . . . . DLB-37
Roy, Camille 1870-1943 . . . . DLB-92
Roy, Gabrielle 1909-1983 . . . . DLB-68
Roy, Jules 1907- DLB-83
The Royal Court Theatre and the English
   Stage Company DLB-13
The Royal Court Theatre and the New Drama
   . . . . DLB-10
The Royal Shakespeare Company
   at the Swan Y-88
Royall, Anne 1769-1854 . . . . DLB-43
The Roycroft Printing Shop DLB-49
Royster, Vermont 1914- DLB-127
Royston, Richard
   [publishing house] DLB-170
Ruark, Gibbons 1941- DLB-120
Ruban, Vasilii Grigorevich
   1742-1795 . . . . DLB-150
Rubens, Bernice 1928- DLB-14
Rudd and Carleton. DLB-49
Rudkin, David 1936- DLB-13
Rudolf von Ems
   circa 1200-circa 1254 . . . . DLB-138
Ruffin, Josephine St. Pierre
   1842-1924 . . . . DLB-79
Ruganda, John 1941- DLB-157
Ruggles, Henry Joseph 1813-1906 . . . . DLB-64
Rukeyser, Muriel 1913-1980 . . . . DLB-48
Rule, Jane 1931- DLB-60
Rulfo, Juan 1918-1986. . . . . DLB-113
Rumaker, Michael 1932- DLB-16
Rumens, Carol 1944- DLB-40
Runyon, Damon 1880-1946 . . DLB-11, 86, 171
Ruodlieb circa 1050-1075 . . . . DLB-148
Rush, Benjamin 1746-1813 . . . . DLB-37
Rusk, Ralph L. 1888-1962 . . . . DLB-103
Ruskin, John 1819-1900. . . . DLB-55, 163, 190
Russ, Joanna 1937- DLB-8
Russell, B. B., and Company DLB-49
Russell, Benjamin 1761-1845 . . . . . . DLB-43
Russell, Bertrand 1872-1970 . . . . DLB-100
Russell, Charles Edward
   1860-1941 . . . . DLB-25
Russell, Charles M. 1864-1926 . . . . . DLB-188
Russell, George William (see AE)
Russell, R. H., and Son DLB-49
Rutherford, Mark 1831-1913 . . . . . . DLB-18
Ruxton, George Frederick
   1821-1848 . . . . DLB-186

Ryan, Michael 1946- Y-82
Ryan, Oscar 1904- DLB-68
Ryga, George 1932- DLB-60
Rylands, Enriqueta Augustina Tennant
   1843-1908 . . . . DLB-184
Rylands, John 1801-1888 . . . . DLB-184
Rymer, Thomas 1643?-1713 . . . . . . DLB-101
Ryskind, Morrie 1895-1985. . . . . DLB-26
Rzhevsky, Aleksei Andreevich
   1737-1804 . . . . DLB-150

S

The Saalfield Publishing
   Company DLB-46
Saba, Umberto 1883-1957. . . . . DLB-114
Sábato, Ernesto 1911- DLB-145
Saberhagen, Fred 1930- DLB-8
Sabin, Joseph 1821-1881. . . . . DLB-187
Sacer, Gottfried Wilhelm
   1635-1699 . . . . DLB-168
Sachs, Hans 1494-1576 . . . . DLB-179
Sack, John 1930- DLB-185
Sackler, Howard 1929-1982 . . . . DLB-7
Sackville, Thomas 1536-1608 . . . . . . DLB-132
Sackville, Thomas 1536-1608
   and Norton, Thomas
   1532-1584 . . . . DLB-62
Sackville-West, V. 1892-1962. . . . . . . DLB-34
Sadlier, D. and J., and Company DLB-49
Sadlier, Mary Anne 1820-1903. . . . . . DLB-99
Sadoff, Ira 1945- DLB-120
Saenz, Jaime 1921-1986 . . . . DLB-145
Saffin, John circa 1626-1710 . . . . . . DLB-24
Sagan, Françoise 1935- DLB-83
Sage, Robert 1899-1962 . . . . DLB-4
Sagel, Jim 1947- DLB-82
Sagendorph, Robb Hansell
   1900-1970 . . . . DLB-137
Sahagún, Carlos 1938- DLB-108
Sahkomaapii, Piitai (see Highwater, Jamake)
Sahl, Hans 1902- DLB-69
Said, Edward W. 1935- DLB-67
Saiko, George 1892-1962 . . . . DLB-85
St. Dominic's Press DLB-112
Saint-Exupéry, Antoine de
   1900-1944 . . . . DLB-72
St. John, J. Allen 1872-1957. . . . . . . DLB-188
St. Johns, Adela Rogers 1894-1988 . . . DLB-29
The St. John's College Robert
   Graves Trust Y-96
St. Martin's Press DLB-46
St. Omer, Garth 1931- DLB-117

Saint Pierre, Michel de 1916-1987 . . . . DLB-83
Saintsbury, George
  1845-1933 . . . . DLB-57, 149
Saki (see Munro, H. H.)
Salaam, Kalamu ya 1947- DLB-38
Šalamun, Tomaž 1941- DLB-181
Salas, Floyd 1931- DLB-82
Sálaz-Marquez, Rubén 1935- DLB-122
Salemson, Harold J. 1910-1988 . . . . . . DLB-4
Salinas, Luis Omar 1937- DLB-82
Salinas, Pedro 1891-1951 . . . . DLB-134
Salinger, J. D. 1919- DLB-2, 102, 173
Salkey, Andrew 1928- DLB-125
Salt, Waldo 1914- DLB-44
Salter, James 1925- DLB-130
Salter, Mary Jo 1954- DLB-120
Salustri, Carlo Alberto (see Trilussa)
Salverson, Laura Goodman
  1890-1970 . . . . DLB-92
Sampson, Richard Henry (see Hull, Richard)
Samuels, Ernest 1903- DLB-111
Sanborn, Franklin Benjamin
  1831-1917 . . . . DLB-1
Sánchez, Luis Rafael 1936- DLB-145
Sánchez, Philomeno "Phil"
  1917- DLB-122
Sánchez, Ricardo 1941- DLB-82
Sanchez, Sonia 1934- DLB-41; DS-8
Sand, George 1804-1876 . . . . DLB-119
Sandburg, Carl 1878-1967 . . . . . DLB-17, 54
Sanders, Ed 1939- DLB-16
Sandoz, Mari 1896-1966 . . . . DLB-9
Sandwell, B. K. 1876-1954 . . . . DLB-92
Sandy, Stephen 1934- DLB-165
Sandys, George 1578-1644 . . . . DLB-24, 121
Sangster, Charles 1822-1893 . . . . DLB-99
Sanguineti, Edoardo 1930- DLB-128
Sansom, William 1912-1976 . . . . DLB-139
Santayana, George
  1863-1952 . . . . DLB-54, 71; DS-13
Santiago, Danny 1911-1988 . . . . DLB-122
Santmyer, Helen Hooven 1895-1986 . . . . Y-84
Sapidus, Joannes 1490-1561 . . . . DLB-179
Sapir, Edward 1884-1939 . . . . DLB-92
Sapper (see McNeile, Herman Cyril)
Sappho circa 620 B.C.-circa 550 B.C.
  . . . . DLB-176
Sarduy, Severo 1937- DLB-113
Sargent, Pamela 1948- DLB-8
Saro-Wiwa, Ken 1941- DLB-157
Saroyan, William
  1908-1981 . . . . DLB-7, 9, 86; Y-81
Sarraute, Nathalie 1900- DLB-83

Sarrazin, Albertine 1937-1967 . . . . . . DLB-83
Sarris, Greg 1952- DLB-175
Sarton, May 1912- DLB-48; Y-81
Sartre, Jean-Paul 1905-1980 . . . . DLB-72
Sassoon, Siegfried 1886-1967 . . . . . . DLB-20
Sata, Ineko 1904- DLB-180
Saturday Review Press DLB-46
Saunders, James 1925- DLB-13
Saunders, John Monk 1897-1940 . . . . . DLB-26
Saunders, Margaret Marshall
  1861-1947 . . . . DLB-92
Saunders and Otley DLB-106
Savage, James 1784-1873 . . . . DLB-30
Savage, Marmion W. 1803?-1872 . . . . DLB-21
Savage, Richard 1697?-1743 . . . . DLB-95
Savard, Félix-Antoine 1896-1982 . . . . . DLB-68
Saville, (Leonard) Malcolm
  1901-1982 . . . . DLB-160
Sawyer, Ruth 1880-1970 . . . . DLB-22
Sayers, Dorothy L.
  1893-1957 . . . . . . DLB-10, 36, 77, 100
Sayle, Charles Edward 1864-1924 . . . DLB-184
Sayles, John Thomas 1950- DLB-44
Sbarbaro, Camillo 1888-1967 . . . . . . DLB-114
Scannell, Vernon 1922- DLB-27
Scarry, Richard 1919-1994 . . . . DLB-61
Schaeffer, Albrecht 1885-1950 . . . . . . DLB-66
Schaeffer, Susan Fromberg 1941- DLB-28
Schaff, Philip 1819-1893 . . . . DS-13
Schaper, Edzard 1908-1984 . . . . DLB-69
Scharf, J. Thomas 1843-1898 . . . . DLB-47
Schede, Paul Melissus 1539-1602 . . . . DLB-179
Scheffel, Joseph Viktor von
  1826-1886 . . . . DLB-129
Scheffler, Johann 1624-1677 . . . . DLB-164
Schelling, Friedrich Wilhelm Joseph von
  1775-1854 . . . . DLB-90
Scherer, Wilhelm 1841-1886 . . . . DLB-129
Schickele, René 1883-1940 . . . . DLB-66
Schiff, Dorothy 1903-1989 . . . . DLB-127
Schiller, Friedrich 1759-1805 . . . . DLB-94
Schirmer, David 1623-1687 . . . . DLB-164
Schlaf, Johannes 1862-1941 . . . . DLB-118
Schlegel, August Wilhelm
  1767-1845 . . . . DLB-94
Schlegel, Dorothea 1763-1839 . . . . . . DLB-90
Schlegel, Friedrich 1772-1829 . . . . . . DLB-90
Schleiermacher, Friedrich
  1768-1834 . . . . DLB-90
Schlesinger, Arthur M., Jr. 1917- DLB-17
Schlumberger, Jean 1877-1968 . . . . . . DLB-65
Schmid, Eduard Hermann Wilhelm (see
  Edschmid, Kasimir)

Schmidt, Arno 1914-1979 . . . . DLB-69
Schmidt, Johann Kaspar (see Stirner, Max)
Schmidt, Michael 1947- DLB-40
Schmidtbonn, Wilhelm August
  1876-1952 . . . . DLB-118
Schmitz, James H. 1911- DLB-8
Schnabel, Johann Gottfried
  1692-1760 . . . . DLB-168
Schnackenberg, Gjertrud 1953- DLB-120
Schnitzler, Arthur 1862-1931 . . . . DLB-81, 118
Schnurre, Wolfdietrich 1920- DLB-69
Schocken Books DLB-46
Scholartis Press DLB-112
The Schomburg Center for Research
  in Black Culture DLB-76
Schönbeck, Virgilio (see Giotti, Virgilio)
Schönherr, Karl 1867-1943 . . . . DLB-118
Schoolcraft, Jane Johnston
  1800-1841 . . . . DLB-175
School Stories, 1914-1960 . . . . DLB-160
Schopenhauer, Arthur 1788-1860 . . . . DLB-90
Schopenhauer, Johanna 1766-1838 . . . . DLB-90
Schorer, Mark 1908-1977 . . . . DLB-103
Schottelius, Justus Georg
  1612-1676 . . . . DLB-164
Schouler, James 1839-1920 . . . . DLB-47
Schrader, Paul 1946- DLB-44
Schreiner, Olive 1855-1920 . . DLB-18, 156, 190
Schroeder, Andreas 1946- DLB-53
Schubart, Christian Friedrich Daniel
  1739-1791 . . . . DLB-97
Schubert, Gotthilf Heinrich
  1780-1860 . . . . DLB-90
Schücking, Levin 1814-1883 . . . . DLB-133
Schulberg, Budd 1914- . . DLB-6, 26, 28; Y-81
Schulte, F. J., and Company DLB-49
Schulze, Hans (see Praetorius, Johannes)
Schupp, Johann Balthasar
  1610-1661 . . . . DLB-164
Schurz, Carl 1829-1906 . . . . DLB-23
Schuyler, George S. 1895-1977 . . . DLB-29, 51
Schuyler, James 1923-1991 . . . . . . DLB-5, 169
Schwartz, Delmore 1913-1966 . . . . DLB-28, 48
Schwartz, Jonathan 1938- Y-82
Schwarz, Sibylle 1621-1638 . . . . DLB-164
Schwerner, Armand 1927- . . . . DLB 165
Schwob, Marcel 1867-1905 . . . . DLB-123
Sciascia, Leonardo 1921-1989 . . . . . . DLB-177
Science Fantasy DLB-8
Science-Fiction Fandom and
  Conventions DLB-8
Science-Fiction Fanzines: The Time
  Binders DLB-8

Science-Fiction Films DLB-8
Science Fiction Writers of America and the
    Nebula Awards. DLB-8
Scot, Reginald circa 1538-1599 . . . . . DLB-136
Scotellaro, Rocco 1923-1953 . . . . DLB-128
Scott, Dennis 1939-1991 . . . . DLB-125
Scott, Dixon 1881-1915 . . . . DLB-98
Scott, Duncan Campbell 1862-1947 . . . DLB-92
Scott, Evelyn 1893-1963 . . . . DLB-9, 48
Scott, F. R. 1899-1985 . . . . DLB-88
Scott, Frederick George 1861-1944 . . . . DLB-92
Scott, Geoffrey 1884-1929 . . . . DLB-149
Scott, Harvey W. 1838-1910 . . . . DLB-23
Scott, Paul 1920-1978 . . . . DLB-14
Scott, Sarah 1723-1795 . . . . DLB-39
Scott, Tom 1918- DLB-27
Scott, Sir Walter
    1771-1832 . . . . DLB-93, 107, 116, 144, 159
Scott, William Bell 1811-1890 . . . . . . DLB-32
Scott, Walter, Publishing
    Company Limited DLB-112
Scott, William R.
    [publishing house] DLB-46
Scott-Heron, Gil 1949- DLB-41
Scribner, Arthur Hawley
    1859-1932 . . . . DS-13, 16
Scribner, Charles 1854-1930 . . . . . . DS-13, 16
Scribner, Charles, Jr. 1921-1995 . . . . Y-95
Charles Scribner's Sons . . . DLB-49; DS-13, 16
Scripps, E. W. 1854-1926 . . . . DLB-25
Scudder, Horace Elisha
    1838-1902 . . . . DLB-42, 71
Scudder, Vida Dutton 1861-1954 . . . . DLB-71
Scupham, Peter 1933- DLB-40
Seabrook, William 1886-1945 . . . . . . DLB-4
Seabury, Samuel 1729-1796 . . . . DLB-31
Seacole, Mary Jane Grant
    1805-1881 . . . . DLB-166
The Seafarer circa 970 . . . . DLB-146
Sealsfield, Charles (Carl Postl)
    1793-1864 . . . . DLB-133, 186
Sears, Edward I. 1819?-1876 . . . . DLB-79
Sears Publishing Company DLB-46
Seaton, George 1911-1979 . . . . DLB-44
Seaton, William Winston
    1785-1866 . . . . DLB-43
Secker, Martin, and Warburg
    Limited DLB-112
Secker, Martin [publishing house] DLB-112
Second-Generation Minor Poets of the
    Seventeenth Century DLB-126
Sedgwick, Arthur George
    1844-1915 . . . . DLB-64

Sedgwick, Catharine Maria
    1789-1867 . . . . DLB-1, 74, 183
Sedgwick, Ellery 1872-1930 . . . . DLB-91
Sedley, Sir Charles 1639-1701 . . . . . . DLB-131
Seeger, Alan 1888-1916 . . . . DLB-45
Seers, Eugene (see Dantin, Louis)
Segal, Erich 1937- Y-86
Šegedin, Petar 1909- DLB-181
Seghers, Anna 1900-1983 . . . . DLB-69
Seid, Ruth (see Sinclair, Jo)
Seidel, Frederick Lewis 1936- Y-84
Seidel, Ina 1885-1974 . . . . DLB-56
Seigenthaler, John 1927- DLB-127
Seizin Press DLB-112
Séjour, Victor 1817-1874 . . . . DLB-50
Séjour Marcou et Ferrand, Juan Victor (see Séjour,
    Victor)
Selby, Hubert, Jr. 1928- DLB-2
Selden, George 1929-1989 . . . . DLB-52
Selected English-Language Little Magazines
    and Newspapers [France,
    1920-1939] DLB-4
Selected Humorous Magazines
    (1820-1950) DLB-11
Selected Science-Fiction Magazines and
    Anthologies DLB-8
Selenić, Slobodan 1933-1995 . . . . DLB-181
Self, Edwin F. 1920- DLB-137
Seligman, Edwin R. A. 1861-1939 . . . . DLB-47
Selimović, Meša 1910-1982 . . . . DLB-181
Selous, Frederick Courteney
    1851-1917 . . . . DLB-174
Seltzer, Chester E. (see Muro, Amado)
Seltzer, Thomas
    [publishing house] DLB-46
Selvon, Sam 1923-1994 . . . . DLB-125
Semmes, Raphael 1809-1877 . . . . . . DLB-189
Senancour, Etienne de 1770-1846 . . . . DLB-119
Sendak, Maurice 1928- DLB-61
Senécal, Eva 1905- DLB-92
Sengstacke, John 1912- DLB-127
Senior, Olive 1941- DLB-157
Šenoa, August 1838-1881 . . . . DLB-147
"Sensation Novels" (1863), by
    H. L. Manse DLB-21
Sepamla, Sipho 1932- DLB-157
Seredy, Kate 1899-1975 . . . . DLB-22
Sereni, Vittorio 1913-1983 . . . . DLB-128
Seres, William
    [publishing house] DLB-170
Serling, Rod 1924-1975 . . . . DLB-26
Serote, Mongane Wally 1944- DLB-125
Serraillier, Ian 1912-1994 . . . . DLB-161

Serrano, Nina 1934- DLB-122
Service, Robert 1874-1958 . . . . DLB-92
Sessler, Charles 1854-1935 . . . . DLB-187
Seth, Vikram 1952- DLB-120
Seton, Ernest Thompson
    1860-1942 . . . . DLB-92; DS-13
Setouchi, Harumi 1922- DLB-182
Settle, Mary Lee 1918- DLB-6
Seume, Johann Gottfried
    1763-1810 . . . . DLB-94
Seuse, Heinrich 1295?-1366 . . . . DLB-179
Seuss, Dr. (see Geisel, Theodor Seuss)
The Seventy-fifth Anniversary of the Armistice:
    The Wilfred Owen Centenary and the Great
    War Exhibit at the University of
    Virginia Y-93
Sewall, Joseph 1688-1769 . . . . DLB-24
Sewall, Richard B. 1908- DLB-111
Sewell, Anna 1820-1878 . . . . DLB-163
Sewell, Samuel 1652-1730 . . . . DLB-24
Sex, Class, Politics, and Religion [in the
    British Novel, 1930-1959] DLB-15
Sexton, Anne 1928-1974 . . . . DLB-5, 169
Seymour-Smith, Martin 1928- DLB-155
Shaara, Michael 1929-1988 . . . . Y-83
Shadwell, Thomas 1641?-1692 . . . . . . DLB-80
Shaffer, Anthony 1976- DLB-13
Shaffer, Peter 1926- DLB-13
Shaftesbury, Anthony Ashley Cooper,
    Third Earl of 1671-1713 . . . . DLB-101
Shairp, Mordaunt 1887-1939 . . . . . . DLB-10
Shakespeare, William
    1564-1616 . . . . DLB-62, 172
The Shakespeare Globe Trust Y-93
Shakespeare Head Press DLB-112
Shakhovskoi, Aleksandr Aleksandrovich
    1777-1846 . . . . DLB-150
Shange, Ntozake 1948- DLB-38
Shapiro, Karl 1913- DLB-48
Sharon Publications DLB-46
Sharp, Margery 1905-1991 . . . . DLB-161
Sharp, William 1855-1905 . . . . DLB-156
Sharpe, Tom 1928- DLB-14
Shaw, Albert 1857-1947 . . . . DLB-91
Shaw, Bernard 1856-1950 . . . DLB-10, 57, 190
Shaw, Henry Wheeler 1818-1885 . . . . DLB-11
Shaw, Joseph T. 1874-1952 . . . . DLB-137
Shaw, Irwin 1913-1984 . . . . DLB-6, 102; Y-84
Shaw, Robert 1927-1978 . . . . DLB-13, 14
Shaw, Robert B. 1947- DLB-120
Shawn, William 1907-1992 . . . . DLB-137
Shay, Frank [publishing house] DLB-46
Shea, John Gilmary 1824-1892 . . . . . DLB-30

Sheaffer, Louis 1912-1993 . . . . DLB-103
Shearing, Joseph 1886-1952. . . . . . . DLB-70
Shebbeare, John 1709-1788 . . . . DLB-39
Sheckley, Robert 1928- DLB-8
Shedd, William G. T. 1820-1894 . . . . DLB-64
Sheed, Wilfred 1930- DLB-6
Sheed and Ward [U.S.] DLB-46
Sheed and Ward Limited [U.K.] DLB-112
Sheldon, Alice B. (see Tiptree, James, Jr.)
Sheldon, Edward 1886-1946 . . . . DLB-7
Sheldon and Company DLB-49
Shelley, Mary Wollstonecraft
    1797-1851 . . . . . DLB-110, 116, 159, 178
Shelley, Percy Bysshe
    1792-1822 . . . . DLB-96, 110, 158
Shelnutt, Eve 1941- DLB-130
Shenstone, William 1714-1763 . . . . . DLB-95
Shepard, Ernest Howard
    1879-1976 . . . . DLB-160
Shepard, Sam 1943- DLB-7
Shepard, Thomas I,
    1604 or 1605-1649 . . . . DLB-24
Shepard, Thomas II, 1635-1677 . . . . DLB-24
Shepard, Clark and Brown DLB-49
Shepherd, Luke
    flourished 1547-1554 . . . . DLB-136
Sherburne, Edward 1616-1702 . . . . . DLB-131
Sheridan, Frances 1724-1766 . . . . DLB-39, 84
Sheridan, Richard Brinsley
    1751-1816 . . . . DLB-89
Sherman, Francis 1871-1926 . . . . . . DLB-92
Sherriff, R. C. 1896-1975 . . . . DLB-10
Sherry, Norman 1935- DLB-155
Sherwood, Mary Martha
    1775-1851 . . . . DLB-163
Sherwood, Robert 1896-1955 . . . . DLB-7, 26
Shiel, M. P. 1865-1947 . . . . DLB-153
Shiels, George 1886-1949 . . . . DLB-10
Shiga, Naoya 1883-1971 . . . . DLB-180
Shiina, Rinzō 1911-1973 . . . . DLB-182
Shillaber, B.[enjamin] P.[enhallow]
    1814-1890 . . . . DLB-1, 11
Shimao, Toshio 1917-1986 . . . . DLB-182
Shimazaki, Tōson 1872-1943 . . . . . . DLB-180
Shine, Ted 1931- DLB-38
Ship, Reuben 1915-1975 . . . . DLB-88
Shirer, William L. 1904-1993 . . . . . . DLB-4
Shirinsky-Shikhmatov, Sergii Aleksandrovich
    1783-1837 . . . . DLB-150
Shirley, James 1596-1666 . . . . DLB-58
Shishkov, Aleksandr Semenovich
    1753-1841 . . . . DLB-150
Shockley, Ann Allen 1927- DLB-33

Shōno, Junzō 1921- DLB-182
Short, Peter
    [publishing house] DLB-170
Shorthouse, Joseph Henry
    1834-1903 . . . . DLB-18
Showalter, Elaine 1941- DLB-67
Shulevitz, Uri 1935- DLB-61
Shulman, Max 1919-1988 . . . . DLB-11
Shute, Henry A. 1856-1943 . . . . DLB-9
Shuttle, Penelope 1947- DLB-14, 40
Sibbes, Richard 1577-1635 . . . . DLB-151
Sidgwick and Jackson Limited DLB-112
Sidney, Margaret (see Lothrop, Harriet M.)
Sidney, Mary 1561-1621 . . . . DLB-167
Sidney, Sir Philip 1554-1586 . . . . . . DLB-167
Sidney's Press DLB-49
Siegfried Loraine Sassoon: A Centenary Essay
    Tributes from Vivien F. Clarke and
    Michael Thorpe Y-86
Sierra, Rubén 1946- DLB-122
Sierra Club Books DLB-49
Siger of Brabant
    circa 1240-circa 1284 . . . . DLB-115
Sigourney, Lydia Howard (Huntley)
    1791-1865 . . . . DLB-1, 42, 73, 183
Silkin, Jon 1930- DLB-27
Silko, Leslie Marmon
    1948- DLB-143, 175
Silliman, Benjamin 1779-1864 . . . . . DLB-183
Silliman, Ron 1946- DLB-169
Silliphant, Stirling 1918- DLB-26
Sillitoe, Alan 1928- DLB-14, 139
Silman, Roberta 1934- DLB-28
Silva, Beverly 1930- DLB-122
Silverberg, Robert 1935- DLB-8
Silverman, Kenneth 1936- DLB-111
Simak, Clifford D. 1904-1988 . . . . . . DLB-8
Simcoe, Elizabeth 1762-1850 . . . . . . DLB-99
Simcox, Edith Jemima 1844-1901 . . . DLB-190
Simcox, George Augustus
    1841-1905 . . . . DLB-35
Sime, Jessie Georgina 1868-1958 . . . . DLB-92
Simenon, Georges
    1903-1989 . . . . DLB-72; Y-89
Simic, Charles 1938- DLB-105
Simic, Charles,
    Images and "Images" DLB-105
Simmel, Johannes Mario 1924- DLB-69
Simmes, Valentine
    [publishing house] DLB-170
Simmons, Ernest J. 1903-1972 . . . . . DLB-103
Simmons, Herbert Alfred 1930- DLB-33
Simmons, James 1933- DLB-40

Simms, William Gilmore
    1806-1870 . . . . . . DLB-3, 30, 59, 73
Simms and M'Intyre DLB-106
Simon, Claude 1913- DLB-83
Simon, Neil 1927- DLB-7
Simon and Schuster DLB-46
Simons, Katherine Drayton Mayrant
    1890-1969 . . . . Y-83
Simović, Ljubomir 1935- DLB-181
Simpkin and Marshall
    [publishing house] DLB-154
Simpson, Helen 1897-1940 . . . . DLB-77
Simpson, Louis 1923- DLB-5
Simpson, N. F. 1919- DLB-13
Sims, George 1923- DLB-87
Sims, George Robert
    1847-1922 . . . . DLB-35, 70, 135
Sinán, Rogelio 1904- DLB-145
Sinclair, Andrew 1935- DLB-14
Sinclair, Bertrand William
    1881-1972 . . . . DLB-92
Sinclair, Catherine
    1800-1864 . . . . DLB-163
Sinclair, Jo 1913- DLB-28
Sinclair Lewis Centennial
    Conference Y-85
Sinclair, Lister 1921- DLB-88
Sinclair, May 1863-1946 . . . . . . DLB-36, 135
Sinclair, Upton 1878-1968 . . . . DLB-9
Sinclair, Upton [publishing house] . . . DLB-46
Singer, Isaac Bashevis
    1904-1991 . . . . DLB-6, 28, 52; Y-91
Singer, Mark 1950- DLB-185
Singmaster, Elsie 1879-1958 . . . . . . DLB-9
Sinisgalli, Leonardo 1908-1981 . . . . . DLB-114
Siodmak, Curt 1902- DLB-44
Siringo, Charles A. 1855-1928 . . . . . DLB-186
Sissman, L. E. 1928-1976 . . . . DLB-5
Sisson, C. H. 1914- DLB-27
Sitwell, Edith 1887-1964 . . . . DLB-20
Sitwell, Osbert 1892-1969 . . . . DLB-100
Skármeta, Antonio 1940- DLB-145
Skeat, Walter W. 1835-1912 . . . . . . DLB-184
Skeffington, William
    [publishing house] DLB-106
Skelton, John 1463-1529 . . . . DLB-136
Skelton, Robin 1925- DLB-27, 53
Skinner, Constance Lindsay
    1877-1939 . . . . DLB-92
Skinner, John Stuart 1788-1851 . . . . . DLB-73
Skipsey, Joseph 1832-1903 . . . . DLB-35
Slade, Bernard 1930- DLB-53
Slamnig, Ivan 1930- DLB-181

Slater, Patrick 1880-1951 . . . . DLB-68
Slaveykov, Pencho 1866-1912 . . . . . DLB-147
Slaviček, Milivoj 1929- DLB-181
Slavitt, David 1935- DLB-5, 6
Sleigh, Burrows Willcocks Arthur
   1821-1869 . . . . DLB-99
A Slender Thread of Hope: The Kennedy
   Center Black Theatre Project DLB-38
Slesinger, Tess 1905-1945 . . . . DLB-102
Slick, Sam (see Haliburton, Thomas Chandler)
Sloan, John 1871-1951 . . . . DLB-188
Sloane, William, Associates DLB-46
Small, Maynard and Company DLB-49
Small Presses in Great Britain and Ireland,
   1960-1985 . . . . DLB-40
Small Presses I: Jargon Society Y-84
Small Presses II: The Spirit That Moves
   Us Press Y-85
Small Presses III: Pushcart Press Y-87
Smart, Christopher 1722-1771 . . . . . DLB-109
Smart, David A. 1892-1957 . . . . . . DLB-137
Smart, Elizabeth 1913-1986 . . . . DLB-88
Smellie, William
   [publishing house] DLB-154
Smiles, Samuel 1812-1904 . . . . DLB-55
Smith, A. J. M. 1902-1980 . . . . DLB-88
Smith, Adam 1723-1790 . . . . DLB-104
Smith, Adam (George Jerome Waldo Goodman)
   1930- DLB-185
Smith, Alexander 1829-1867 . . . . . DLB-32, 55
Smith, Betty 1896-1972 . . . . Y-82
Smith, Carol Sturm 1938- Y-81
Smith, Charles Henry 1826-1903 . . . . DLB-11
Smith, Charlotte 1749-1806 . . . . . DLB-39, 109
Smith, Chet 1899-1973 . . . . DLB-171
Smith, Cordwainer 1913-1966 . . . . . . DLB-8
Smith, Dave 1942- DLB-5
Smith, Dodie 1896- DLB-10
Smith, Doris Buchanan 1934- DLB-52
Smith, E. E. 1890-1965 . . . . DLB-8
Smith, Elihu Hubbard 1771-1798 . . . . DLB-37
Smith, Elizabeth Oakes (Prince)
   1806-1893 . . . . DLB-1
Smith, F. Hopkinson 1838-1915 . . . . . DS-13
Smith, George D. 1870-1920 . . . . . . DLB-140
Smith, George O. 1911-1981 . . . . DLB-8
Smith, Goldwin 1823-1910 . . . . DLB-99
Smith, H. Allen 1907-1976 . . . . . DLB-11, 29
Smith, Harry B. 1860-1936 . . . . DLB-187
Smith, Hazel Brannon 1914- DLB-127
Smith, Henry
   circa 1560-circa 1591 . . . . DLB-136

Smith, Horatio (Horace)
   1779-1849 . . . . DLB-116
Smith, Horatio (Horace) 1779-1849 and
   James Smith 1775-1839 . . . . DLB-96
Smith, Iain Crichton
   1928- DLB-40, 139
Smith, J. Allen 1860-1924 . . . . DLB-47
Smith, Jessie Willcox 1863-1935 . . . DLB-188
Smith, John 1580-1631 . . . . DLB-24, 30
Smith, Josiah 1704-1781 . . . . DLB-24
Smith, Ken 1938- DLB-40
Smith, Lee 1944- DLB-143; Y-83
Smith, Logan Pearsall 1865-1946 . . . . DLB-98
Smith, Mark 1935- Y-82
Smith, Michael 1698-circa 1771 . . . . . DLB-31
Smith, Red 1905-1982 . . . . DLB-29, 171
Smith, Roswell 1829-1892 . . . . DLB-79
Smith, Samuel Harrison
   1772-1845 . . . . DLB-43
Smith, Samuel Stanhope
   1751-1819 . . . . DLB-37
Smith, Sarah (see Stretton, Hesba)
Smith, Seba 1792-1868 . . . . DLB-1, 11
Smith, Sir Thomas 1513-1577 . . . . . . DLB-132
Smith, Stevie 1902-1971 . . . . DLB-20
Smith, Sydney 1771-1845 . . . . DLB-107
Smith, Sydney Goodsir 1915-1975 . . . . DLB-27
Smith, Wendell 1914-1972 . . . . DLB-171
Smith, William
   flourished 1595-1597 . . . . DLB-136
Smith, William 1727-1803 . . . . DLB-31
Smith, William 1728-1793 . . . . DLB-30
Smith, William Gardner
   1927-1974 . . . . DLB-76
Smith, William Henry
   1808-1872 . . . . DLB-159
Smith, William Jay 1918- DLB-5
Smith, Elder and Company DLB-154
Smith, Harrison, and Robert Haas
   [publishing house] DLB-46
Smith, J. Stilman, and Company DLB-49
Smith, W. B., and Company DLB-49
Smith, W. H., and Son DLB-106
Smithers, Leonard
   [publishing house] DLB-112
Smollett, Tobias 1721-1771 . . . . . DLB-39, 104
Snellings, Rolland (see Touré, Askia
   Muhammad)
Snodgrass, W. D. 1926- DLB-5
Snow, C. P. 1905-1980 . . . . DLB-15, 77
Snyder, Gary 1930- DLB-5, 16, 165
Sobiloff, Hy 1912-1970 . . . . DLB-48
The Society for Textual Scholarship and
   TEXT Y-87

The Society for the History of Authorship, Reading and Publishing Y-92
Soffici, Ardengo 1879-1964 . . . . . . DLB-114
Sofola, 'Zulu 1938- DLB-157
Solano, Solita 1888-1975 . . . . DLB-4
Soldati, Mario 1906- DLB-177
Šoljan, Antun 1932-1993 . . . . DLB-181
Sollers, Philippe 1936- DLB-83
Solmi, Sergio 1899-1981 . . . . DLB-114
Solomon, Carl 1928- DLB-16
Solway, David 1941- DLB-53
Solzhenitsyn and America Y-85
Somerville, Edith Œnone
   1858-1949 . . . . DLB-135
Song, Cathy 1955- DLB-169
Sono, Ayako 1931- DLB-182
Sontag, Susan 1933- DLB-2, 67
Sophocles 497/496 B.C.-406/405 B.C.
   . . . . DLB-176
Šopov, Aco 1923-1982 . . . . DLB-181
Sorge, Reinhard Johannes
   1892-1916 . . . . DLB-118
Sorrentino, Gilbert
   1929- DLB-5, 173; Y-80
Sotheby, William 1757-1833 . . . . . . DLB-93
Soto, Gary 1952- DLB-82
Sources for the Study of Tudor and Stuart Drama
   DLB-62
Souster, Raymond 1921- DLB-88
The *South English Legendary*
   circa thirteenth-fifteenth
   centuries DLB-146
Southerland, Ellease 1943- DLB-33
Southern Illinois University Press Y-95
Southern, Terry 1924- DLB-2
Southern Writers Between the
   Wars DLB-9
Southerne, Thomas 1659-1746 . . . . . DLB-80
Southey, Caroline Anne Bowles
   1786-1854 . . . . DLB-116
Southey, Robert
   1774-1843 . . . . DLB-93, 107, 142
Southwell, Robert 1561?-1595 . . . . . DLB-167
Sowande, Bode 1948- DLB-157
Sowle, Tace
   [publishing house] DLB-170
Soyfer, Jura 1912-1939 . . . . DLB-124
Soyinka, Wole 1934- DLB-125; Y-86, 87
Spacks, Barry 1931- DLB-105
Spalding, Frances 1950- DLB-155
Spark, Muriel 1918- DLB-15, 139
Sparke, Michael
   [publishing house] DLB-170
Sparks, Jared 1789-1866 . . . . DLB-1, 30

Sparshott, Francis 1926- DLB-60

Späth, Gerold 1939- DLB-75

Spatola, Adriano 1941-1988 .... DLB-128

Spaziani, Maria Luisa 1924- DLB-128

The Spectator 1828- DLB-110

Spedding, James 1808-1881 .... DLB-144

Spee von Langenfeld, Friedrich
    1591-1635 .... DLB-164

Speght, Rachel 1597-after 1630 ..... DLB-126

Speke, John Hanning 1827-1864 .... DLB-166

Spellman, A. B. 1935- DLB-41

Spence, Thomas 1750-1814 .... DLB-158

Spencer, Anne 1882-1975 .... DLB-51, 54

Spencer, Elizabeth 1921- DLB-6

Spencer, George John, Second Earl Spencer
    1758-1834 .... DLB-184

Spencer, Herbert 1820-1903 .... DLB-57

Spencer, Scott 1945- Y-86

Spender, J. A. 1862-1942 .... DLB-98

Spender, Stephen 1909- DLB-20

Spener, Philipp Jakob 1635-1705 .... DLB-164

Spenser, Edmund circa 1552-1599 ... DLB-167

Sperr, Martin 1944- DLB-124

Spicer, Jack 1925-1965 .... DLB-5, 16

Spielberg, Peter 1929- Y-81

Spielhagen, Friedrich 1829-1911 ..... DLB-129

"*Spielmannsepen*"
    (circa 1152-circa 1500) DLB-148

Spier, Peter 1927- DLB-61

Spinrad, Norman 1940- DLB-8

Spires, Elizabeth 1952- DLB-120

Spitteler, Carl 1845-1924 .... DLB-129

Spivak, Lawrence E. 1900- DLB-137

Spofford, Harriet Prescott
    1835-1921 .... DLB-74

Squier, E. G. 1821-1888 .... DLB-189

Squibob (see Derby, George Horatio)

Stacpoole, H. de Vere
    1863-1951 .... DLB-153

Staël, Germaine de 1766-1817 ...... DLB-119

Staël-Holstein, Anne-Louise Germaine de
    (see Staël, Germaine de)

Stafford, Jean 1915-1979 .... DLB-2, 173

Stafford, William 1914- DLB-5

Stage Censorship: "The Rejected Statement"
    (1911), by Bernard Shaw
    [excerpts] DLB-10

Stallings, Laurence 1894-1968 ..... DLB-7, 44

Stallworthy, Jon 1935- DLB-40

Stampp, Kenneth M. 1912- DLB-17

Stanev, Emiliyan 1907-1979 .... DLB-181

Stanford, Ann 1916- DLB-5

Stanković, Borisav ("Bora")
    1876-1927 .... DLB-147

Stanley, Henry M. 1841-1904 . DLB-189; DS-13

Stanley, Thomas 1625-1678 .... DLB-131

Stannard, Martin 1947- DLB-155

Stansby, William
    [publishing house] DLB-170

Stanton, Elizabeth Cady 1815-1902 ... DLB-79

Stanton, Frank L. 1857-1927 ...... DLB-25

Stanton, Maura 1946- DLB-120

Stapledon, Olaf 1886-1950 .... DLB-15

Star Spangled Banner Office DLB-49

Starkey, Thomas circa 1499-1538 .... DLB-132

Starkweather, David 1935- DLB-7

Starrett, Vincent 1886-1974 ...... DLB-187

Statements on the Art of Poetry DLB-54

Stationers' Company of
    London, The DLB-170

Stead, Robert J. C. 1880-1959 ..... DLB-92

Steadman, Mark 1930- DLB-6

The Stealthy School of Criticism (1871), by
    Dante Gabriel Rossetti DLB-35

Stearns, Harold E. 1891-1943 ...... DLB-4

Stedman, Edmund Clarence
    1833-1908 .... DLB-64

Steegmuller, Francis 1906-1994 .... DLB-111

Steel, Flora Annie 1847-1929 ... DLB-153, 156

Steele, Max 1922- Y-80

Steele, Richard 1672-1729 ...... DLB-84, 101

Steele, Timothy 1948- DLB-120

Steele, Wilbur Daniel 1886-1970 ..... DLB-86

Steere, Richard circa 1643-1721 ..... DLB-24

Stefanovski, Goran 1952- DLB-181

Stegner, Wallace 1909-1993 ..... DLB-9; Y-93

Stehr, Hermann 1864-1940 .... DLB-66

Steig, William 1907- DLB-61

Stein, Gertrude
    1874-1946 .... DLB-4, 54, 86; DS-15

Stein, Leo 1872-1947 .... DLB-4

Stein and Day Publishers DLB-46

Steinbeck, John 1902-1968 .... DLB-7, 9; DS-2

Steiner, George 1929- DLB-67

Steinhoewel, Heinrich
    1411/1412-1479 .... DLB-179

Steloff, Ida Frances 1887-1989 ..... DLB-187

Stendhal 1783-1842 .... DLB-119

Stephen Crane: A Revaluation Virginia
    Tech Conference, 1989 .... Y-89

Stephen, Leslie 1832-1904 ... DLB-57, 144, 190

Stephens, Alexander H. 1812-1883 .... DLB-47

Stephens, Alice Barber 1858-1932 ... DLB-188

Stephens, Ann 1810-1886 .... DLB-3, 73

Stephens, Charles Asbury
    1844?-1931 .... DLB-42

Stephens, James
    1882?-1950 .... DLB-19, 153, 162

Stephens, John Lloyd 1805-1852 .... DLB-183

Sterling, George 1869-1926 .... DLB-54

Sterling, James 1701-1763 .... DLB-24

Sterling, John 1806-1844 .... DLB-116

Stern, Gerald 1925- DLB-105

Stern, Madeleine B. 1912- ... DLB-111, 140

Stern, Gerald, Living in Ruin DLB-105

Stern, Richard 1928- Y-87

Stern, Stewart 1922- DLB-26

Sterne, Laurence 1713-1768 .... DLB-39

Sternheim, Carl 1878-1942 ..... DLB-56, 118

Sternhold, Thomas ?-1549 and
    John Hopkins ?-1570 .... DLB-132

Stevens, Henry 1819-1886 .... DLB-140

Stevens, Wallace 1879-1955 .... DLB-54

Stevenson, Anne 1933- DLB-40

Stevenson, Lionel 1902-1973 ...... DLB-155

Stevenson, Robert Louis 1850-1894
    ..... DLB-18, 57, 141, 156, 174; DS-13

Stewart, Donald Ogden
    1894-1980 .... DLB-4, 11, 26

Stewart, Dugald 1753-1828 .... DLB-31

Stewart, George, Jr. 1848-1906 ..... DLB-99

Stewart, George R. 1895-1980 .... DLB-8

Stewart and Kidd Company DLB-46

Stewart, Randall 1896-1964 .... DLB-103

Stickney, Trumbull 1874-1904 ...... DLB-54

Stieler, Caspar 1632-1707 .... DLB-164

Stifter, Adalbert 1805-1868 ...... DLB-133

Stiles, Ezra 1727-1795 .... DLB-31

Still, James 1906- DLB-9

Stirner, Max 1806-1856 .... DLB-129

Stith, William 1707-1755 .... DLB-31

Stock, Elliot [publishing house] DLB-106

Stockton, Frank R.
    1834-1902 .... DLB-42, 74; DS-13

Stoddard, Ashbel
    [publishing house] DLB-49

Stoddard, Charles Warren
    1843-1909 .... DLB-186

Stoddard, Richard Henry
    1825-1903 .... DLB-3, 64; DS-13

Stoddard, Solomon 1643-1729 ...... DLB-24

Stoker, Bram 1847-1912 .... DLB-36, 70, 178

Stokes, Frederick A., Company DLB-49

Stokes, Thomas L. 1898-1958 ...... DLB-29

Stokesbury, Leon 1945- DLB-120

Stolberg, Christian Graf zu
    1748-1821 .... DLB-94

Stolberg, Friedrich Leopold Graf zu
    1750-1819 . . . . DLB-94
Stone, Herbert S., and Company DLB-49
Stone, Lucy 1818-1893 . . . . DLB-79
Stone, Melville 1848-1929 . . . . DLB-25
Stone, Robert 1937- DLB-152
Stone, Ruth 1915- DLB-105
Stone, Samuel 1602-1663 . . . . DLB-24
Stone and Kimball DLB-49
Stoppard, Tom 1937- DLB-13; Y-85
Storey, Anthony 1928- DLB-14
Storey, David 1933- DLB-13, 14
Storm, Theodor 1817-1888 . . . . . . DLB-129
Story, Thomas circa 1670-1742 . . . . . DLB-31
Story, William Wetmore 1819-1895. . . . DLB-1
Storytelling: A Contemporary
    Renaissance Y-84
Stoughton, William 1631-1701 . . . . . DLB-24
Stow, John 1525-1605 . . . . DLB-132
Stowe, Harriet Beecher
    1811-1896 . . . . . . DLB-1, 12, 42, 74, 189
Stowe, Leland 1899- DLB-29
Stoyanov, Dimitŭr Ivanov (see Elin Pelin)
Strabo 64 or 63 B.C.-circa A.D. 25
    . . . . DLB-176
Strachey, Lytton
    1880-1932 . . . . DLB-149; DS-10
Strachey, Lytton, Preface to *Eminent
    Victorians* DLB-149
Strahan and Company DLB-106
Strahan, William
    [publishing house] DLB-154
Strand, Mark 1934- DLB-5
The Strasbourg Oaths 842 . . . . DLB-148
Stratemeyer, Edward 1862-1930 . . . . DLB-42
Strati, Saverio 1924- DLB-177
Stratton and Barnard DLB-49
Stratton-Porter, Gene 1863-1924 . . . . DS-14
Straub, Peter 1943- Y-84
Strauß, Botho 1944- DLB-124
Strauß, David Friedrich
    1808-1874 . . . . DLB-133
The Strawberry Hill Press DLB-154
Streatfeild, Noel 1895-1986 . . . . . . DLB-160
Street, Cecil John Charles (see Rhode, John)
Street, G. S. 1867-1936 . . . . DLB-135
Street and Smith DLB-49
Streeter, Edward 1891-1976. . . . . . . DLB-11
Streeter, Thomas Winthrop
    1883-1965 . . . . DLB-140
Stretton, Hesba 1832-1911 . . . . DLB-163, 190
Stribling, T. S. 1881-1965 . . . . DLB-9
Der Stricker circa 1190-circa 1250 . . . DLB-138

Strickland, Samuel 1804-1867. . . . . . DLB-99
Stringer and Townsend. DLB-49
Stringer, Arthur 1874-1950 . . . . DLB-92
Strittmatter, Erwin 1912- DLB-69
Strniša, Gregor 1930-1987 . . . . DLB-181
Strode, William 1630-1645 . . . . . . DLB-126
Strother, David Hunter 1816-1888 . . . . DLB-3
Strouse, Jean 1945- DLB-111
Stuart, Dabney 1937- DLB-105
Stuart, Dabney, Knots into Webs: Some Autobio-
    graphical Sources DLB-105
Stuart, Jesse
    1906-1984 . . . . . DLB-9, 48, 102; Y-84
Stuart, Lyle [publishing house] DLB-46
Stubbs, Harry Clement (see Clement, Hal)
Stubenberg, Johann Wilhelm von
    1619-1663 . . . . DLB-164
Studio DLB-112
The Study of Poetry (1880), by
    Matthew Arnold DLB-35
Sturgeon, Theodore
    1918-1985 . . . . DLB-8; Y-85
Sturges, Preston 1898-1959 . . . . DLB-26
"Style" (1840; revised, 1859), by
    Thomas de Quincey [excerpt] DLB-57
"Style" (1888), by Walter Pater DLB-57
Style (1897), by Walter Raleigh
    [excerpt] DLB-57
"Style" (1877), by T. H. Wright
    [excerpt] DLB-57
"Le Style c'est l'homme" (1892), by
    W. H. Mallock DLB-57
Styron, William 1925- DLB-2, 143; Y-80
Suárez, Mario 1925- DLB-82
Such, Peter 1939- DLB-60
Suckling, Sir John 1609-1641? . . . DLB-58, 126
Suckow, Ruth 1892-1960. . . . . DLB-9, 102
Sudermann, Hermann 1857-1928 . . . . DLB-118
Sue, Eugène 1804-1857 . . . . DLB-119
Sue, Marie-Joseph (see Sue, Eugène)
Suggs, Simon (see Hooper, Johnson Jones)
Sukenick, Ronald 1932- DLB-173; Y-81
Suknaski, Andrew 1942- DLB-53
Sullivan, Alan 1868-1947 . . . . DLB-92
Sullivan, C. Gardner 1886-1965 . . . . DLB-26
Sullivan, Frank 1892-1976 . . . . DLB-11
Sulte, Benjamin 1841-1923 . . . . DLB-99
Sulzberger, Arthur Hays
    1891-1968 . . . . DLB-127
Sulzberger, Arthur Ochs 1926- DLB-127
Sulzer, Johann Georg 1720-1779 . . . . DLB-97
Sumarokov, Aleksandr Petrovich
    1717-1777 . . . . DLB-150
Summers, Hollis 1916- DLB-6

Sumner, Henry A.
    [publishing house] DLB-49
Surtees, Robert Smith 1803-1864. . . . DLB-21
Surveys: Japanese Literature,
    1987-1995 . . . . DLB-182
A Survey of Poetry Anthologies,
    1879-1960 . . . . DLB-54
Surveys of the Year's Biographies
A Transit of Poets and Others: American
    Biography in 1982 . . . . Y-82
The Year in Literary Biography . . . Y-83–Y-96
Survey of the Year's Book Publishing
The Year in Book Publishing Y-86
Survey of the Year's Children's Books
The Year in Children's Books
    . . . . Y-92–Y-96
Surveys of the Year's Drama
The Year in Drama
    . . . . Y-82–Y-85, Y-87–Y-96
The Year in London Theatre Y-92
Surveys of the Year's Fiction
The Year's Work in Fiction:
    A Survey Y-82
The Year in Fiction: A Biased View Y-83
The Year in
    Fiction Y-84–Y-86, Y-89, Y-94–Y-96
The Year in the
    Novel Y-87, Y-88, Y-90–Y-93
The Year in Short Stories Y-87
The Year in the
    Short Story Y-88, Y-90–Y-93
Survey of the Year's Literary Theory
The Year in Literary Theory Y-92–Y-93
Surveys of the Year's Poetry
The Year's Work in American
    Poetry Y-82
The Year in Poetry Y-83–Y-92, Y-94–Y-96
Sutherland, Efua Theodora
    1924- DLB-117
Sutherland, John 1919-1956 . . . . DLB-68
Sutro, Alfred 1863-1933 . . . . DLB-10
Swados, Harvey 1920-1972 . . . . DLB-2
Swain, Charles 1801-1874 . . . . DLB-32
Swallow Press DLB-46
Swan Sonnenschein Limited DLB-106
Swanberg, W. A. 1907- DLB-103
Swenson, May 1919-1989 . . . . DLB-5
Swerling, Jo 1897- DLB-44
Swift, Jonathan 1667-1745 . . . DLB-39, 95, 101
Swinburne, A. C. 1837-1909 . . . . DLB-35, 57
Swineshead, Richard floruit
    circa 1350 . . . . DLB-115
Swinnerton, Frank 1884-1982 . . . . . . DLB-34
Swisshelm, Jane Grey 1815-1884 . . . . DLB-43

Swope, Herbert Bayard 1882-1958.... DLB-25
Swords, T. and J., and Company.... DLB-49
Swords, Thomas 1763-1843 and
　Swords, James ?-1844 .... DLB-73
Sykes, Ella C. ?-1939 .... DLB-174
Sylvester, Josuah
　1562 or 1563 - 1618 .... DLB-121
Symonds, Emily Morse (see Paston, George)
Symonds, John Addington
　1840-1893 .... DLB-57, 144
Symons, A. J. A. 1900-1941 .... DLB-149
Symons, Arthur 1865-1945... DLB-19, 57, 149
Symons, Julian 1912-1994 .. DLB-87, 155; Y-92
Symons, Scott 1933- DLB-53
A Symposium on *The Columbia History of
　the Novel* Y-92
Synge, John Millington
　1871-1909 .... DLB-10, 19
Synge Summer School: J. M. Synge and the Irish
　Theater, Rathdrum, County Wiclow, Ireland
　................................ Y-93
Syrett, Netta 1865-1943 .... DLB-135
Szymborska, Wisława 1923- Y-96

T

Taban lo Liyong 1939?- DLB-125
Taché, Joseph-Charles 1820-1894..... DLB-99
Tachihara, Masaaki 1926-1980 ..... DLB-182
Tadijanović, Dragutin 1905- DLB-181
Tafolla, Carmen 1951- DLB-82
Taggard, Genevieve 1894-1948...... DLB-45
Tagger, Theodor (see Bruckner, Ferdinand)
Tait, J. Selwin, and Sons DLB-49
Tait's Edinburgh Magazine
　1832-1861 .... DLB-110
The Takarazaka Revue Company Y-91
Talander (see Bohse, August)
Talese, Gay 1932- DLB-185
Talev, Dimitŭr 1898-1966 .... DLB-181
Tallent, Elizabeth 1954- DLB-130
Talvj 1797-1870 .... DLB-59, 133
Tan, Amy 1952- DLB-173
Tanizaki, Jun'ichirō 1886-1965 ..... DLB-180
Tapahonso, Luci 1953- DLB-175
Taradash, Daniel 1913- DLB-44
Tarbell, Ida M. 1857-1944 .... DLB-47
Tardivel, Jules-Paul 1851-1905 ..... DLB-99
Targan, Barry 1932- DLB-130
Tarkington, Booth 1869-1946 .... DLB-9, 102
Tashlin, Frank 1913-1972 .... DLB-44
Tate, Allen 1899-1979 ...... DLB-4, 45, 63

Tate, James 1943- DLB-5, 169
Tate, Nahum circa 1652-1715 ...... DLB-80
Tatian circa 830 .... DLB-148
Taufer, Veno 1933- DLB-181
Tauler, Johannes circa 1300-1361.... DLB-179
Tavčar, Ivan 1851-1923 .... DLB-147
Taylor, Ann 1782-1866 .... DLB-163
Taylor, Bayard 1825-1878 ...... DLB-3, 189
Taylor, Bert Leston 1866-1921..... DLB-25
Taylor, Charles H. 1846-1921 ..... DLB-25
Taylor, Edward circa 1642-1729..... DLB-24
Taylor, Elizabeth 1912-1975 .... DLB-139
Taylor, Henry 1942- DLB-5
Taylor, Sir Henry 1800-1886 ...... DLB-32
Taylor, Jane 1783-1824 .... DLB-163
Taylor, Jeremy circa 1613-1667 .... DLB-151
Taylor, John 1577 or 1578 - 1653... DLB-121
Taylor, Mildred D. ?- DLB-52
Taylor, Peter 1917-1994 .... Y-81, Y-94
Taylor, William, and Company DLB-49
Taylor-Made Shakespeare? Or Is
　"Shall I Die?" the Long-Lost Text
　of Bottom's Dream? Y-85
Teasdale, Sara 1884-1933 .... DLB-45
The Tea-Table (1725), by Eliza Haywood [excerpt]
　DLB-39
Telles, Lygia Fagundes 1924- DLB-113
Temple, Sir William 1628-1699 ..... DLB-101
Tenn, William 1919- DLB-8
Tennant, Emma 1937- DLB-14
Tenney, Tabitha Gilman 1762-1837... DLB-37
Tennyson, Alfred 1809-1892 .... DLB-32
Tennyson, Frederick 1807-1898 ..... DLB-32
Terhune, Albert Payson 1872-1942 ... DLB-9
Terhune, Mary Virginia 1830-1922 .. DS-13, 16
Terry, Megan 1932- DLB-7
Terson, Peter 1932- DLB-13
Tesich, Steve 1943- Y-83
Tessa, Delio 1886-1939 .... DLB-114
Testori, Giovanni 1923-1993 .... DLB-128, 177
Tey, Josephine 1896?-1952 .... DLB-77
Thacher, James 1754-1844 .... DLB-37
Thackeray, William Makepeace
　1811-1863 .... DLB-21, 55, 159, 163
Thames and Hudson Limited DLB-112
Thanet, Octave (see French, Alice)
Thatcher, John Boyd 1847-1909 .... DLB-187
The Theater in Shakespeare's Time... DLB-62
The Theatre Guild DLB-7
Thegan and the Astronomer
　flourished circa 850 .... DLB-148
Thelwall, John 1764-1834 ...... DLB-93, 158

Theocritus circa 300 B.C.-260 B.C.
　.......................... DLB-176
Theodulf circa 760-circa 821 ...... DLB-148
Theophrastus circa 371 B.C.-287 B.C.
　.......................... DLB-176
Theriault, Yves 1915-1983 .... DLB-88
Thério, Adrien 1925- DLB-53
Theroux, Paul 1941- DLB-2
They All Came to Paris DS-16
Thibaudeau, Colleen 1925- DLB-88
Thielen, Benedict 1903-1965 ...... DLB-102
Thiong'o Ngugi wa (see Ngugi wa Thiong'o)
Third-Generation Minor Poets of the
　Seventeenth Century DLB-131
This Quarter 1925-1927, 1929-1932 ..... DS-15
Thoma, Ludwig 1867-1921 .... DLB-66
Thoma, Richard 1902- DLB-4
Thomas, Audrey 1935- DLB-60
Thomas, D. M. 1935- DLB-40
Thomas, Dylan
　1914-1953 .... DLB-13, 20, 139
Thomas, Edward
　1878-1917 .... DLB-19, 98, 156
Thomas, Gwyn 1913-1981 .... DLB-15
Thomas, Isaiah 1750-1831 ... DLB-43, 73, 187
Thomas, Isaiah [publishing house].... DLB-49
Thomas, Johann 1624-1679 .... DLB-168
Thomas, John 1900-1932 .... DLB-4
Thomas, Joyce Carol 1938- DLB-33
Thomas, Lorenzo 1944- DLB-41
Thomas, R. S. 1915- DLB-27
Thomasîn von Zerclære
　circa 1186-circa 1259 .... DLB-138
Thomasius, Christian 1655-1728 .... DLB-168
Thompson, David 1770-1857 ...... DLB-99
Thompson, Dorothy 1893-1961 .... DLB-29
Thompson, Francis 1859-1907 ..... DLB-19
Thompson, George Selden (see Selden, George)
Thompson, Henry Yates 1838-1928 .. DLB-184
Thompson, Hunter S. 1939- DLB-185
Thompson, John 1938-1976 .... DLB-60
Thompson, John R. 1823-1873 .... DLB-3, 73
Thompson, Lawrance 1906-1973 .... DLB-103
Thompson, Maurice
　1844-1901 .... DLB-71, 74
Thompson, Ruth Plumly
　1891-1976 .... DLB-22
Thompson, Thomas Phillips
　1843-1933 .... DLB-99
Thompson, William 1775-1833..... DLB-158
Thompson, William Tappan
　1812-1882 .... DLB-3, 11
Thomson, Edward William
　1849-1924 .... DLB-92

Thomson, James 1700-1748 .... DLB-95

Thomson, James 1834-1882 .... DLB-35

Thomson, Joseph 1858-1895 ...... DLB-174

Thomson, Mortimer 1831-1875 ..... DLB-11

Thoreau, Henry David
1817-1862. . . . . DLB-1, 183

Thorpe, Thomas Bangs
1815-1878 . . . . DLB-3, 11

Thoughts on Poetry and Its Varieties (1833),
by John Stuart Mill DLB-32

Thrale, Hester Lynch (see Piozzi, Hester
Lynch [Thrale])

Thucydides circa 455 B.C.-circa 395 B.C.
. . . . DLB-176

Thulstrup, Thure de 1848-1930 .... DLB-188

Thümmel, Moritz August von
1738-1817 . . . . DLB-97

Thurber, James
1894-1961 .... DLB-4, 11, 22, 102

Thurman, Wallace 1902-1934 .... DLB-51

Thwaite, Anthony 1930- DLB-40

Thwaites, Reuben Gold
1853-1913 . . . . DLB-47

Ticknor, George
1791-1871. . . . . DLB-1, 59, 140

Ticknor and Fields DLB-49

Ticknor and Fields (revived)...... DLB-46

Tieck, Ludwig 1773-1853......... DLB-90

Tietjens, Eunice 1884-1944 .... DLB-54

Tilney, Edmund circa 1536-1610 .... DLB-136

Tilt, Charles [publishing house]..... DLB-106

Tilton, J. E., and Company DLB-49

Time and Western Man (1927), by Wyndham
Lewis [excerpts]............ DLB-36

Time-Life Books. DLB-46

Times Books DLB-46

Timothy, Peter circa 1725-1782 ..... DLB-43

Timrod, Henry 1828-1867........ DLB-3

Tinker, Chauncey Brewster
1876-1963 . . . . DLB-140

Tinsley Brothers DLB-106

Tiptree, James, Jr. 1915-1987 ..... DLB-8

Tišma, Aleksandar 1924- DLB-181

Titus, Edward William
1870-1952 . . . . DLB-4; DS-15

Tlali, Miriam 1933- DLB-157

Todd, Barbara Euphan
1890-1976 . . . . DLB-160

Tofte, Robert
1561 or 1562-1619 or 1620 .... DLB-172

Toklas, Alice B. 1877-1967 .... DLB-4

Tokuda, Shūsei 1872-1943 .... DLB-180

Tolkien, J. R. R. 1892-1973 ..... DLB-15, 160

Toller, Ernst 1893-1939 .... DLB-124

Tollet, Elizabeth 1694-1754 .... DLB-95

Tolson, Melvin B. 1898-1966 .... DLB-48, 76

Tom Jones (1749), by Henry Fielding
[excerpt]................ DLB-39

Tomalin, Claire 1933- DLB-155

Tomasi di Lampedusa,
Giuseppe 1896-1957......... DLB-177

Tomlinson, Charles 1927- DLB-40

Tomlinson, H. M. 1873-1958 ... DLB-36, 100

Tompkins, Abel [publishing house] ... DLB-49

Tompson, Benjamin 1642-1714...... DLB-24

Tonks, Rosemary 1932- DLB-14

Tonna, Charlotte Elizabeth
1790-1846 . . . . DLB-163

Tonson, Jacob the Elder
[publishing house] DLB-170

Toole, John Kennedy 1937-1969 ...... Y-81

Toomer, Jean 1894-1967....... DLB-45, 51

Tor Books. DLB-46

Torberg, Friedrich 1908-1979....... DLB-85

Torrence, Ridgely 1874-1950....... DLB-54

Torres-Metzger, Joseph V.
1933- DLB-122

Toth, Susan Allen 1940- Y-86

Tottell, Richard
[publishing house] DLB-170

Tough-Guy Literature DLB-9

Touré, Askia Muhammad 1938- DLB-41

Tourgée, Albion W. 1838-1905 ...... DLB-79

Tourneur, Cyril circa 1580-1626..... DLB-58

Tournier, Michel 1924- DLB-83

Tousey, Frank [publishing house] DLB-49

Tower Publications DLB-46

Towne, Benjamin circa 1740-1793.... DLB-43

Towne, Robert 1936- DLB-44

The Townely Plays
fifteenth and sixteenth
centuries DLB-146

Townshend, Aurelian
by 1583 - circa 1651 .... DLB-121

Tracy, Honor 1913- DLB-15

Traherne, Thomas 1637?-1674..... DLB-131

Traill, Catharine Parr 1802-1899..... DLB-99

Train, Arthur 1875-1945..... DLB-86; DS-16

The Transatlantic Publishing
Company DLB-49

The Transatlantic Review 1924-1925 ..... DS-15

Transcendentalists, American......... DS-5

transition 1927-1938. . . . . DS-15

Translators of the Twelfth Century:
Literary Issues Raised and Impact
Created. DLB-115

Travel Writing, 1837-1875 .... DLB-166

Travel Writing, 1876-1909 .... DLB-174

Traven, B.
1882? or 1890?-1969?........ DLB-9, 56

Travers, Ben 1886-1980 .... DLB-10

Travers, P. L. (Pamela Lyndon)
1899- DLB-160

Trediakovsky, Vasilii Kirillovich
1703-1769 . . . . DLB-150

Treece, Henry 1911-1966 .... DLB-160

Trejo, Ernesto 1950- DLB-122

Trelawny, Edward John
1792-1881. . . . . . . DLB-110, 116, 144

Tremain, Rose 1943- DLB-14

Tremblay, Michel 1942- DLB-60

Trends in Twentieth-Century
Mass Market Publishing DLB-46

Trent, William P. 1862-1939....... DLB-47

Trescot, William Henry
1822-1898 . . . . DLB-30

Trevelyan, Sir George Otto
1838-1928 . . . . DLB-144

Trevisa, John
circa 1342-circa 1402 .... DLB-146

Trevor, William 1928- DLB-14, 139

Trierer Floyris circa 1170-1180 ...... DLB-138

Trillin, Calvin 1935- DLB-185

Trilling, Lionel 1905-1975 ...... DLB-28, 63

Trilussa 1871-1950. . . . . DLB-114

Trimmer, Sarah 1741-1810 .... DLB-158

Triolet, Elsa 1896-1970 .... DLB-72

Tripp, John 1927- DLB-40

Trocchi, Alexander 1925- DLB-15

Trollope, Anthony
1815-1882. . . . . DLB-21, 57, 159

Trollope, Frances 1779-1863 .... DLB-21, 166

Troop, Elizabeth 1931- DLB-14

Trotter, Catharine 1679-1749....... DLB-84

Trotti, Lamar 1898-1952 .... DLB-44

Trottier, Pierre 1925- DLB-60

Troupe, Quincy Thomas, Jr.
1943- DLB-41

Trow, John F., and Company...... DLB-49

Truillier-Lacombe, Joseph-Patrice
1807-1863 . . . . DLB-99

Trumbo, Dalton 1905-1976........ DLB-26

Trumbull, Benjamin 1735-1820..... DLB-30

Trumbull, John 1750-1831 .... DLB-31

Trumbull, John 1756-1843 ...... DLB-183

Tscherning, Andreas 1611-1659..... DLB-164

T. S. Eliot Centennial Y-88

Tsubouchi, Shōyō 1859-1935 ...... DLB-180

Tucholsky, Kurt 1890-1935. . . . . DLB-56

Tucker, Charlotte Maria
1821-1893. . . . . DLB-163, 190

Tucker, George 1775-1861 ..... DLB-3, 30

Tucker, Nathaniel Beverley
 1784-1851................ DLB-3
Tucker, St. George 1752-1827...... DLB-37
Tuckerman, Henry Theodore
 1813-1871................ DLB-64
Tunis, John R. 1889-1975..... DLB-22, 171
Tunstall, Cuthbert 1474-1559...... DLB-132
Tuohy, Frank 1925-........ DLB-14, 139
Tupper, Martin F. 1810-1889...... DLB-32
Turbyfill, Mark 1896-.......... DLB-45
Turco, Lewis 1934-............. Y-84
Turnball, Alexander H. 1868-1918... DLB-184
Turnbull, Andrew 1921-1970...... DLB-103
Turnbull, Gael 1928-........... DLB-40
Turner, Arlin 1909-1980........ DLB-103
Turner, Charles (Tennyson)
 1808-1879................ DLB-32
Turner, Frederick 1943-......... DLB-40
Turner, Frederick Jackson
 1861-1932............ DLB-17, 186
Turner, Joseph Addison
 1826-1868................ DLB-79
Turpin, Waters Edward
 1910-1968................ DLB-51
Turrini, Peter 1944-........... DLB-124
Tutuola, Amos 1920-.......... DLB-125
Twain, Mark (see Clemens, Samuel Langhorne)
Tweedie, Ethel Brilliana
 circa 1860-1940........... DLB-174
The 'Twenties and Berlin, by
 Alex Natan............... DLB-66
Tyler, Anne 1941-..... DLB-6, 143; Y-82
Tyler, Moses Coit 1835-1900.... DLB-47, 64
Tyler, Royall 1757-1826......... DLB-37
Tylor, Edward Burnett 1832-1917.... DLB-57
Tynan, Katharine 1861-1931...... DLB-153
Tyndale, William
 circa 1494-1536........... DLB-132

U

Udall, Nicholas 1504-1556....... DLB-62
Ugrešić, Dubravka 1949-....... DLB-181
Uhland, Ludwig 1787-1862....... DLB-90
Uhse, Bodo 1904-1963.......... DLB-69
Ujević, Augustin ("Tin")
 1891-1955............... DLB-147
Ulenhart, Niclas
 flourished circa 1600........ DLB-164
Ulibarrí, Sabine R. 1919-........ DLB-82
Ulica, Jorge 1870-1926......... DLB-82
Ulizio, B. George 1889-1969..... DLB-140
Ulrich von Liechtenstein
 circa 1200-circa 1275....... DLB-138

Ulrich von Zatzikhoven
 before 1194-after 1214...... DLB-138
Unamuno, Miguel de 1864-1936.... DLB-108
Under the Microscope (1872), by
 A. C. Swinburne........... DLB-35
Unger, Friederike Helene
 1741-1813................ DLB-94
Ungaretti, Giuseppe 1888-1970..... DLB-114
United States Book Company...... DLB-49
Universal Publishing and Distributing
 Corporation............... DLB-46
The University of Iowa Writers' Workshop
 Golden Jubilee.............. Y-86
The University of South Carolina
 Press.................... Y-94
University of Wales Press........ DLB-112
"The Unknown Public" (1858), by
 Wilkie Collins [excerpt]...... DLB-57
Uno, Chiyo 1897-1996......... DLB-180
Unruh, Fritz von 1885-1970.... DLB-56, 118
Unspeakable Practices II: The Festival of
 Vanguard Narrative at Brown
 University.................. Y-93
Unwin, T. Fisher
 [publishing house].......... DLB-106
Upchurch, Boyd B. (see Boyd, John)
Updike, John
 1932-..... DLB-2, 5, 143; Y-80, 82; DS-3
Upton, Bertha 1849-1912....... DLB-141
Upton, Charles 1948-.......... DLB-16
Upton, Florence K. 1873-1922..... DLB-141
Upward, Allen 1863-1926........ DLB-36
Urista, Alberto Baltazar (see Alurista)
Urzidil, Johannes 1896-1976...... DLB-85
Urquhart, Fred 1912-.......... DLB-139
The Uses of Facsimile............ Y-90
Usk, Thomas died 1388........ DLB-146
Uslar Pietri, Arturo 1906-...... DLB-113
Ustinov, Peter 1921-........... DLB-13
Uttley, Alison 1884-1976....... DLB-160
Uz, Johann Peter 1720-1796...... DLB-97

V

Vac, Bertrand 1914-............ DLB-88
Vail, Laurence 1891-1968........ DLB-4
Vailland, Roger 1907-1965........ DLB-83
Vajda, Ernest 1887-1954........ DLB-44
Valdés, Gina 1943-............ DLB-122
Valdez, Luis Miguel 1940-...... DLB-122
Valduga, Patrizia 1953-........ DLB-128
Valente, José Angel 1929-...... DLB-108
Valenzuela, Luisa 1938-........ DLB-113

Valeri, Diego 1887-1976......... DLB-128
Valgardson, W. D. 1939-........ DLB-60
Valle, Víctor Manuel 1950-...... DLB-122
Valle-Inclán, Ramón del
 1866-1936............... DLB-134
Vallejo, Armando 1949-......... DLB-122
Vallès, Jules 1832-1885......... DLB-123
Vallette, Marguerite Eymery (see Rachilde)
Valverde, José María 1926-...... DLB-108
Van Allsburg, Chris 1949-....... DLB-61
Van Anda, Carr 1864-1945....... DLB-25
Van Dine, S. S. (see Wright, Williard Huntington)
Van Doren, Mark 1894-1972...... DLB-45
van Druten, John 1901-1957...... DLB-10
Van Duyn, Mona 1921-......... DLB-5
Van Dyke, Henry
 1852-1933.......... DLB-71; DS-13
Van Dyke, John C. 1856-1932..... DLB-186
Van Dyke, Henry 1928-........ DLB-33
van Itallie, Jean-Claude 1936-...... DLB-7
Van Loan, Charles E. 1876-1919.... DLB-171
Van Rensselaer, Mariana Griswold
 1851-1934................ DLB-47
Van Rensselaer, Mrs. Schuyler (see Van
 Rensselaer, Mariana Griswold)
Van Vechten, Carl 1880-1964..... DLB-4, 9
van Vogt, A. E. 1912-.......... DLB-8
Vanbrugh, Sir John 1664-1726..... DLB-80
Vance, Jack 1916?-............. DLB-8
Vane, Sutton 1888-1963......... DLB-10
Vanguard Press............... DLB-46
Vann, Robert L. 1879-1940...... DLB-29
Vargas, Llosa, Mario 1936-...... DLB-145
Varley, John 1947-............. Y-81
Varnhagen von Ense, Karl August
 1785-1858................ DLB-90
Varnhagen von Ense, Rahel
 1771-1833................ DLB-90
Vásquez Montalbán, Manuel
 1939-................... DLB-134
Vassa, Gustavus (see Equiano, Olaudah)
Vassalli, Sebastiano 1941-........ DLB-128
Vaughan, Henry 1621-1695....... DLB-131
Vaughan, Thomas 1621-1666..... DLB-131
Vaux, Thomas, Lord 1509-1556.... DLB-132
Vazov, Ivan 1850-1921......... DLB-147
Vega, Janine Pommy 1942-...... DLB-16
Veiller, Anthony 1903-1965....... DLB-44
Velásquez-Trevino, Gloria
 1949-................... DLB-122
Veloz Maggiolo, Marcio 1936-.... DLB-145
Venegas, Daniel ?-?............ DLB-82
Vergil, Polydore circa 1470-1555.... DLB-132

Veríssimo, Erico 1905-1975 . . . . DLB-145

Verne, Jules 1828-1905 . . . . DLB-123

Verplanck, Gulian C. 1786-1870. . . . . DLB-59

Very, Jones 1813-1880. . . . . DLB-1

Vian, Boris 1920-1959 . . . . DLB-72

Vickers, Roy 1888?-1965 . . . . DLB-77

Victoria 1819-1901 . . . . DLB-55

Victoria Press DLB-106

Vidal, Gore 1925- DLB-6, 152

Viebig, Clara 1860-1952 . . . . DLB-66

Viereck, George Sylvester
 1884-1962 . . . . DLB-54

Viereck, Peter 1916- DLB-5

Viets, Roger 1738-1811 . . . . DLB-99

Viewpoint: Politics and Performance, by
 David Edgar DLB-13

Vigil-Piñon, Evangelina 1949- DLB-122

Vigneault, Gilles 1928- DLB-60

Vigny, Alfred de 1797-1863. . . . . . . DLB-119

Vigolo, Giorgio 1894-1983 . . . . DLB-114

The Viking Press DLB-46

Villanueva, Alma Luz 1944- DLB-122

Villanueva, Tino 1941- DLB-82

Villard, Henry 1835-1900. . . . . DLB-23

Villard, Oswald Garrison
 1872-1949. . . . . DLB-25, 91

Villarreal, José Antonio 1924- DLB-82

Villegas de Magnón, Leonor
 1876-1955 . . . . DLB-122

Villemaire, Yolande 1949- DLB-60

Villena, Luis Antonio de 1951- DLB-134

Villiers de l'Isle-Adam, Jean-Marie
 Mathias Philippe-Auguste, Comte de
 1838-1889 . . . . DLB-123

Villiers, George, Second Duke
 of Buckingham 1628-1687 . . . . . . DLB-80

Vine Press DLB-112

Viorst, Judith ?- DLB-52

Vipont, Elfrida (Elfrida Vipont Foulds,
 Charles Vipont) 1902-1992 . . . . . DLB-160

Viramontes, Helena María
 1954- DLB-122

Vischer, Friedrich Theodor
 1807-1887 . . . . DLB-133

Vivanco, Luis Felipe 1907-1975. . . . . DLB-108

Viviani, Cesare 1947- DLB-128

Vizenor, Gerald 1934- DLB-175

Vizetelly and Company DLB-106

Voaden, Herman 1903- DLB-88

Voigt, Ellen Bryant 1943- DLB-120

Vojnović, Ivo 1857-1929. . . . . DLB-147

Volkoff, Vladimir 1932- DLB-83

Volland, P. F., Company. DLB-46

Vollbehr, Otto H. F. 1872?-
 1945 or 1946 . . . . DLB-187

Volponi, Paolo 1924- DLB-177

von der Grün, Max 1926- DLB-75

Vonnegut, Kurt
 1922- DLB-2, 8, 152; Y-80; DS-3

Voranc, Prežihov 1893-1950. . . . . . . DLB-147

Voß, Johann Heinrich 1751-1826 . . . . DLB-90

Vroman, Mary Elizabeth
 circa 1924-1967 . . . . DLB-33

W

Wace, Robert ("Maistre")
 circa 1100-circa 1175 . . . . DLB-146

Wackenroder, Wilhelm Heinrich
 1773-1798 . . . . DLB-90

Wackernagel, Wilhelm
 1806-1869 . . . . DLB-133

Waddington, Miriam 1917- DLB-68

Wade, Henry 1887-1969 . . . . DLB-77

Wagenknecht, Edward 1900- DLB-103

Wagner, Heinrich Leopold
 1747-1779 . . . . DLB-94

Wagner, Henry R. 1862-1957 . . . . . DLB-140

Wagner, Richard 1813-1883. . . . . . . DLB-129

Wagoner, David 1926- DLB-5

Wah, Fred 1939- DLB-60

Waiblinger, Wilhelm 1804-1830 . . . . . DLB-90

Wain, John
 1925-1994 . . . . . . DLB-15, 27, 139, 155

Wainwright, Jeffrey 1944- DLB-40

Waite, Peirce and Company DLB-49

Wakeman, Stephen H. 1859-1924 . . . DLB-187

Wakoski, Diane 1937- DLB-5

Walahfrid Strabo circa 808-849 . . . . . DLB-148

Walck, Henry Z. DLB-46

Walcott, Derek 1930- DLB-117; Y-81, 92

Waldegrave, Robert
 [publishing house] DLB-170

Waldman, Anne 1945- DLB-16

Waldrop, Rosmarie 1935- DLB-169

Walker, Alice 1944- DLB-6, 33, 143

Walker, George F. 1947- DLB-60

Walker, Joseph A. 1935- DLB-38

Walker, Margaret 1915- DLB-76, 152

Walker, Ted 1934- DLB-40

Walker and Company DLB-49

Walker, Evans and Cogswell
 Company DLB-49

Walker, John Brisben 1847-1931. . . . . DLB-79

Wallace, Alfred Russel 1823-1913 . . . DLB-190

Wallace, Dewitt 1889-1981 and
 Lila Acheson Wallace
 1889-1984 . . . . DLB-137

Wallace, Edgar 1875-1932 . . . . DLB-70

Wallace, Lila Acheson (see Wallace, Dewitt,
 and Lila Acheson Wallace)

Wallant, Edward Lewis
 1926-1962. . . . . DLB-2, 28, 143

Waller, Edmund 1606-1687. . . . . . . DLB-126

Walpole, Horace 1717-1797. . . . DLB-39, 104

Walpole, Hugh 1884-1941 . . . . DLB-34

Walrond, Eric 1898-1966. . . . . DLB-51

Walser, Martin 1927- DLB-75, 124

Walser, Robert 1878-1956 . . . . DLB-66

Walsh, Ernest 1895-1926 . . . . . . DLB-4, 45

Walsh, Robert 1784-1859. . . . . DLB-59

Waltharius circa 825 . . . . DLB-148

Walters, Henry 1848-1931 . . . . DLB-140

Walther von der Vogelweide
 circa 1170-circa 1230 . . . . DLB-138

Walton, Izaak 1593-1683 . . . . DLB-151

Wambaugh, Joseph 1937- DLB-6; Y-83

Waniek, Marilyn Nelson 1946- DLB-120

Warburton, William 1698-1779. . . . . DLB-104

Ward, Aileen 1919- DLB-111

Ward, Artemus (see Browne, Charles Farrar)

Ward, Arthur Henry Sarsfield
 (see Rohmer, Sax)

Ward, Douglas Turner 1930- DLB-7, 38

Ward, Lynd 1905-1985. . . . . DLB-22

Ward, Lock and Company DLB-106

Ward, Mrs. Humphry 1851-1920 . . . . DLB-18

Ward, Nathaniel circa 1578-1652 . . . . DLB-24

Ward, Theodore 1902-1983 . . . . DLB-76

Wardle, Ralph 1909-1988 . . . . DLB-103

Ware, William 1797-1852 . . . . DLB-1

Warne, Frederick, and
 Company [U.S.] DLB-49

Warne, Frederick, and
 Company [U.K.]. DLB-106

Warner, Charles Dudley
 1829-1900 . . . . DLB-64

Warner, Rex 1905- DLB-15

Warner, Susan Bogert
 1819-1885 . . . . DLB-3, 42

Warner, Sylvia Townsend
 1893-1978 . . . . DLB-34, 139

Warner, William 1558-1609. . . . . . . DLB-172

Warner Books. DLB-46

Warr, Bertram 1917-1943 . . . . DLB-88

Warren, John Byrne Leicester
 (see De Tabley, Lord)

Warren, Lella 1899-1982. . . . . Y-83

Warren, Mercy Otis 1728-1814 . . . . . DLB-31

Warren, Robert Penn
    1905-1989 . . . . . DLB-2, 48, 152; Y-80, 89
Warren, Samuel 1807-1877 . . . . DLB-190
Die Wartburgkrieg
    circa 1230-circa 1280 . . . . DLB-138
Warton, Joseph 1722-1800 . . . . DLB-104, 109
Warton, Thomas 1728-1790 . . . DLB-104, 109
Washington, George 1732-1799 . . . . . DLB-31
Wassermann, Jakob 1873-1934 . . . . . DLB-66
Wasson, David Atwood 1823-1887 . . . . DLB-1
Waterhouse, Keith 1929- DLB-13, 15
Waterman, Andrew 1940- DLB-40
Waters, Frank 1902- Y-86
Waters, Michael 1949- DLB-120
Watkins, Tobias 1780-1855 . . . . DLB-73
Watkins, Vernon 1906-1967 . . . . . . DLB-20
Watmough, David 1926- DLB-53
Watson, James Wreford (see Wreford, James)
Watson, John 1850-1907 . . . . DLB-156
Watson, Sheila 1909- DLB-60
Watson, Thomas 1545?-1592 . . . . . DLB-132
Watson, Wilfred 1911- DLB-60
Watt, W. J., and Company DLB-46
Watterson, Henry 1840-1921 . . . . . . DLB-25
Watts, Alan 1915-1973 . . . . DLB-16
Watts, Franklin [publishing house] DLB-46
Watts, Isaac 1674-1748 . . . . DLB-95
Wand, Alfred Rudolph 1828-1891 . . . DLB-188
Waugh, Auberon 1939- DLB-14
Waugh, Evelyn 1903-1966 . . . . . DLB-15, 162
Way and Williams DLB-49
Wayman, Tom 1945- DLB-53
Weatherly, Tom 1942- DLB-41
Weaver, Gordon 1937- DLB-130
Weaver, Robert 1921- DLB-88
Webb, Beatrice 1858-1943 and
    Webb, Sidney 1859-1947 . . . . . . DLB-190
Webb, Frank J. ?-? DLB-50
Webb, James Watson 1802-1884 . . . . DLB-43
Webb, Mary 1881-1927 . . . . DLB-34
Webb, Phyllis 1927- DLB-53
Webb, Walter Prescott 1888-1963 . . . . DLB-17
Webbe, William ?-1591 . . . . DLB-132
Webster, Augusta 1837-1894 . . . . . . DLB-35
Webster, Charles L.,
    and Company DLB-49
Webster, John
    1579 or 1580-1634? DLB-58
Webster, Noah
    1758-1843 . . . . . . DLB-1, 37, 42, 43, 73
Weckherlin, Georg Rodolf
    1584-1653 . . . . DLB-164
Wedekind, Frank 1864-1918 . . . . . . DLB-118

Weeks, Edward Augustus, Jr.
    1898-1989 . . . . DLB-137
Weeks, Stephen B. 1865-1918 . . . . . DLB-187
Weems, Mason Locke
    1759-1825 . . . . DLB-30, 37, 42
Weerth, Georg 1822-1856 . . . . DLB-129
Weidenfeld and Nicolson DLB-112
Weidman, Jerome 1913- DLB-28
Weigl, Bruce 1949- DLB-120
Weinbaum, Stanley Grauman
    1902-1935 . . . . DLB-8
Weintraub, Stanley 1929- DLB-111
Weise, Christian 1642-1708 . . . . . . DLB-168
Weisenborn, Gunther
    1902-1969 . . . . DLB-69, 124
Weiß, Ernst 1882-1940 . . . . DLB-81
Weiss, John 1818-1879 . . . . DLB-1
Weiss, Peter 1916-1982 . . . . DLB-69, 124
Weiss, Theodore 1916- DLB-5
Weisse, Christian Felix 1726-1804 . . . . DLB-97
Weitling, Wilhelm 1808-1871 . . . . . DLB-129
Welch, James 1940- DLB-175
Welch, Lew 1926-1971? DLB-16
Weldon, Fay 1931- DLB-14
Wellek, René 1903- DLB-63
Wells, Carolyn 1862-1942 . . . . DLB-11
Wells, Charles Jeremiah
    circa 1800-1879 . . . . DLB-32
Wells, Gabriel 1862-1946 . . . . DLB-140
Wells, H. G.
    1866-1946 . . . . . . DLB-34, 70, 156, 178
Wells, Robert 1947- DLB-40
Wells-Barnett, Ida B. 1862-1931 . . . . DLB-23
Welty, Eudora
    1909- DLB-2, 102, 143; Y-87; DS-12
Wendell, Barrett 1855-1921 . . . . . . DLB-71
Wentworth, Patricia 1878-1961 . . . . . DLB-77
Werder, Diederich von dem
    1584-1657 . . . . DLB-164
Werfel, Franz 1890-1945 . . . . . . DLB-81, 124
The Werner Company DLB-49
Werner, Zacharias 1768-1823 . . . . . . DLB-94
Wersba, Barbara 1932- DLB-52
Wescott, Glenway 1901- DLB-4, 9, 102
Wesker, Arnold 1932- DLB-13
Wesley, Charles 1707-1788 . . . . DLB-95
Wesley, John 1703-1791 . . . . DLB-104
Wesley, Richard 1945- DLB-38
Wessels, A., and Company DLB-46
Wessobrunner Gebet
    circa 787-815 . . . . DLB-148
West, Anthony 1914-1988 . . . . DLB-15
West, Dorothy 1907- DLB-76

West, Jessamyn 1902-1984 . . . . . DLB-6; Y-84
West, Mae 1892-1980 . . . . DLB-44
West, Nathanael 1903-1940 . . . DLB-4, 9, 28
West, Paul 1930- DLB-14
West, Rebecca 1892-1983 . . . . . DLB-36; Y-83
West, Richard 1941- DLB-185
West and Johnson DLB-49
Western Publishing Company DLB-46
The Westminster Review 1824-1914 . . . . DLB-110
Weston, Elizabeth Jane
    circa 1582-1612 . . . . DLB-172
Wetherald, Agnes Ethelwyn
    1857-1940 . . . . DLB-99
Wetherell, Elizabeth (see Warner, Susan Bogert)
Wetzel, Friedrich Gottlob
    1779-1819 . . . . DLB-90
Weyman, Stanley J. 1855-1928 . . DLB-141, 156
Wezel, Johann Karl 1747-1819 . . . . . DLB-94
Whalen, Philip 1923- DLB-16
Whalley, George 1915-1983 . . . . . . DLB-88
Wharton, Edith
    1862-1937 . . . DLB-4, 9, 12, 78, 189; DS-13
Wharton, William 1920s?- Y-80
Whately, Mary Louisa
    1824-1889 . . . . DLB-166
Whately, Richard 1787-1863 . . . . . . DLB-190
What's Really Wrong With Bestseller
    Lists Y-84
Wheatley, Dennis Yates
    1897-1977 . . . . DLB-77
Wheatley, Phillis
    circa 1754-1784 . . . . DLB-31, 50
Wheeler, Anna Doyle
    1785-1848? DLB-158
Wheeler, Charles Stearns
    1816-1843 . . . . DLB-1
Wheeler, Monroe 1900-1988 . . . . DLB-4
Wheelock, John Hall 1886-1978 . . . . . DLB-45
Wheelwright, John
    circa 1592-1679 . . . . DLB-24
Wheelwright, J. B. 1897-1940 . . . . . . DLB-45
Whetstone, Colonel Pete (see Noland, C. F. M.)
Whetstone, George 1550-1587 . . . . . DLB-136
Whicher, Stephen E. 1915-1961 . . . . DLB-111
Whipple, Edwin Percy 1819-1886 . . DLB-1, 64
Whitaker, Alexander 1585-1617 . . . . . DLB-24
Whitaker, Daniel K. 1801-1881 . . . . . DLB-73
Whitcher, Frances Miriam
    1814-1852 . . . . DLB-11
White, Andrew 1579-1656 . . . . DLB-24
White, Andrew Dickson
    1832-1918 . . . . DLB-47
White, E. B. 1899-1985 . . . . DLB-11, 22
White, Edgar B. 1947- DLB-38

439

White, Ethel Lina 1887-1944. . . . . . . DLB-77
White, Henry Kirke 1785-1806 . . . . . DLB-96
White, Horace 1834-1916. . . . . DLB-23
White, Phyllis Dorothy James
    (see James, P. D.)
White, Richard Grant 1821-1885 . . . . . DLB-64
White, T. H. 1906-1964. . . . . DLB-160
White, Walter 1893-1955. . . . . DLB-51
White, William, and Company DLB-49
White, William Allen 1868-1944 . . . DLB-9, 25
White, William Anthony Parker
    (see Boucher, Anthony)
White, William Hale (see Rutherford, Mark)
Whitechurch, Victor L. 1868-1933. . . . DLB-70
Whitehead, Alfred North
    1861-1947 . . . . DLB-100
Whitehead, James 1936- Y-81
Whitehead, William 1715-1785. . . DLB-84, 109
Whitfield, James Monroe 1822-1871. . . DLB-50
Whitgift, John circa 1533-1604 . . . . . DLB-132
Whiting, John 1917-1963 . . . . DLB-13
Whiting, Samuel 1597-1679. . . . . DLB-24
Whitlock, Brand 1869-1934. . . . . DLB-12
Whitman, Albert, and Company. DLB-46
Whitman, Albery Allson
    1851-1901 . . . . DLB-50
Whitman, Alden 1913-1990 . . . . Y-91
Whitman, Sarah Helen (Power)
    1803-1878. . . . . DLB-1
Whitman, Walt 1819-1892 . . . . . . DLB-3, 64
Whitman Publishing Company. DLB-46
Whitney, Geoffrey
    1548 or 1552?-1601. . . . . DLB-136
Whitney, Isabella
    flourished 1566-1573 . . . . DLB-136
Whitney, John Hay 1904-1982 . . . . . DLB-127
Whittemore, Reed 1919- DLB-5
Whittier, John Greenleaf 1807-1892. . . . DLB-1
Whittlesey House DLB-46
Who Runs American Literature? Y-94
Wideman, John Edgar 1941- . . . DLB-33, 143
Widener, Harry Elkins 1885-1912 . . . . DLB-140
Wiebe, Rudy 1934- DLB-60
Wiechert, Ernst 1887-1950 . . . . DLB-56
Wied, Martina 1882-1957. . . . . DLB-85
Wiehe, Evelyn May Clowes (see Mordaunt, Elinor)
Wieland, Christoph Martin
    1733-1813 . . . . DLB-97
Wienbarg, Ludolf 1802-1872 . . . . . . DLB-133
Wieners, John 1934- DLB-16
Wier, Ester 1910- DLB-52
Wiesel, Elie 1928- DLB-83; Y-87

Wiggin, Kate Douglas 1856-1923 . . . . DLB-42
Wigglesworth, Michael 1631-1705 . . . DLB-24
Wilberforce, William 1759-1833. . . . . DLB-158
Wilbrandt, Adolf 1837-1911. . . . . . . DLB-129
Wilbur, Richard 1921- DLB-5, 169
Wild, Peter 1940- DLB-5
Wilde, Oscar 1854-1900
    . . . . . DLB-10, 19, 34, 57, 141, 156, 190
Wilde, Richard Henry
    1789-1847 . . . . DLB-3, 59
Wilde, W. A., Company. DLB-49
Wilder, Billy 1906- DLB-26
Wilder, Laura Ingalls 1867-1957. . . . . DLB-22
Wilder, Thornton 1897-1975 . . . . DLB-4, 7, 9
Wildgans, Anton 1881-1932. . . . . . . DLB-118
Wiley, Bell Irvin 1906-1980 . . . . DLB-17
Wiley, John, and Sons DLB-49
Wilhelm, Kate 1928- DLB-8
Wilkes, Charles 1798-1877 . . . . DLB-183
Wilkes, George 1817-1885 . . . . DLB-79
Wilkinson, Anne 1910-1961 . . . . . . DLB-88
Wilkinson, Sylvia 1940- Y-86
Wilkinson, William Cleaver
    1833-1920 . . . . DLB-71
Willard, Barbara 1909-1994. . . . . . . DLB-161
Willard, L. [publishing house] DLB-49
Willard, Nancy 1936- DLB-5, 52
Willard, Samuel 1640-1707. . . . . DLB-24
William of Auvergne 1190-1249 . . . DLB-115
William of Conches
    circa 1090-circa 1154 . . . . DLB-115
William of Ockham
    circa 1285-1347 . . . . DLB-115
William of Sherwood
    1200/1205 - 1266/1271 . . . . . . DLB-115
The William Chavrat American Fiction
    Collection at the Ohio State University
    Libraries. Y-92
Williams, A., and Company DLB-49
Williams, Ben Ames 1889-1953. . . . . DLB-102
Williams, C. K. 1936- DLB-5
Williams, Chancellor 1905- DLB-76
Williams, Charles
    1886-1945. . . . . DLB-100, 153
Williams, Denis 1923- DLB-117
Williams, Emlyn 1905- DLB-10, 77
Williams, Garth 1912- DLB-22
Williams, George Washington
    1849-1891 . . . . DLB-47
Williams, Heathcote 1941- DLB-13
Williams, Helen Maria
    1761-1827 . . . . DLB-158
Williams, Hugo 1942- DLB-40
Williams, Isaac 1802-1865 . . . . DLB-32

Williams, Joan 1928- DLB-6
Williams, John A. 1925- DLB-2, 33
Williams, John E. 1922-1994 . . . . . . DLB-6
Williams, Jonathan 1929- DLB-5
Williams, Miller 1930- DLB-105
Williams, Raymond 1921- DLB-14
Williams, Roger circa 1603-1683. . . . . DLB-24
Williams, Rowland 1817-1870. . . . . . DLB-184
Williams, Samm-Art 1946- DLB-38
Williams, Sherley Anne 1944- DLB-41
Williams, T. Harry 1909-1979. . . . . . DLB-17
Williams, Tennessee
    1911-1983. . . . . . . DLB-7; Y-83; DS-4
Williams, Ursula Moray 1911- DLB-160
Williams, Valentine 1883-1946. . . . . . DLB-77
Williams, William Appleman
    1921- DLB-17
Williams, William Carlos
    1883-1963. . . . . . . DLB-4, 16, 54, 86
Williams, Wirt 1921- DLB-6
Williams Brothers. DLB-49
Williamson, Jack 1908- DLB-8
Willingham, Calder Baynard, Jr.
    1922- DLB-2, 44
Williram of Ebersberg
    circa 1020-1085 . . . . DLB-148
Willis, Nathaniel Parker
    1806-1867 . . . DLB-3, 59, 73, 74, 183; DS-13
Willkomm, Ernst 1810-1886. . . . . . . DLB-133
Wilmer, Clive 1945- DLB-40
Wilson, A. N. 1950- DLB-14, 155
Wilson, Angus
    1913-1991 . . . . . . DLB-15, 139, 155
Wilson, Arthur 1595-1652 . . . . DLB-58
Wilson, Augusta Jane Evans
    1835-1909 . . . . DLB-42
Wilson, Colin 1931- DLB-14
Wilson, Edmund 1895-1972 . . . . . . DLB-63
Wilson, Ethel 1888-1980 . . . . DLB-68
Wilson, Harriet E. Adams
    1828?-1863? DLB-50
Wilson, Harry Leon 1867-1939. . . . . . DLB-9
Wilson, John 1588-1667 . . . . DLB-24
Wilson, John 1785-1854. . . . . DLB-110
Wilson, Lanford 1937- DLB-7
Wilson, Margaret 1882-1973. . . . . . . DLB-9
Wilson, Michael 1914-1978. . . . . . . DLB-44
Wilson, Mona 1872-1954 . . . . DLB-149
Wilson, Thomas
    1523 or 1524-1581 . . . . DLB-132
Wilson, Woodrow 1856-1924 . . . . . . DLB-47
Wilson, Effingham
    [publishing house]. DLB-154

Wimsatt, William K., Jr. 1907-1975 .... DLB-63
Winchell, Walter 1897-1972 .... DLB-29
Winchester, J. [publishing house]..... DLB-49
Winckelmann, Johann Joachim 1717-1768 .... DLB-97
Winckler, Paul 1630-1686........ DLB-164
Wind, Herbert Warren 1916- DLB-171
Windet, John [publishing house] DLB-170
Windham, Donald 1920- DLB-6
Wing, Donald Goddard 1904-1972... DLB-187
Wing, John M. 1844-1917 .... DLB-187
Wingate, Allan [publishing house] ... DLB-112
Winnemucca, Sarah 1844-1921 ..... DLB-175
Winnifrith, Tom 1938- DLB-155
Winsloe, Christa 1888-1944 .... DLB-124
Winsor, Justin 1831-1897......... DLB-47
John C. Winston Company DLB-49
Winters, Yvor 1900-1968......... DLB-48
Winthrop, John 1588-1649...... DLB-24, 30
Winthrop, John, Jr. 1606-1676 ..... DLB-24
Wirt, William 1772-1834 .... DLB-37
Wise, John 1652-1725............ DLB-24
Wise, Thomas James 1859-1937 .... DLB-184
Wiseman, Adele 1928- DLB-88
Wishart and Company DLB-112
Wisner, George 1812-1849 .... DLB-43
Wister, Owen 1860-1938 .... DLB-9, 78, 186
Wither, George 1588-1667 .... DLB-121
Witherspoon, John 1723-1794 ..... DLB-31
Withrow, William Henry 1839-1908.... DLB-99
Wittig, Monique 1935- DLB-83
Wodehouse, P. G. 1881-1975 .... DLB-34, 162
Wohmann, Gabriele 1932- DLB-75
Woiwode, Larry 1941- DLB-6
Wolcot, John 1738-1819......... DLB-109
Wolcott, Roger 1679-1767 .... DLB-24
Wolf, Christa 1929- DLB-75
Wolf, Friedrich 1888-1953........ DLB-124
Wolfe, Gene 1931- DLB-8
Wolfe, John [publishing house]..... DLB-170
Wolfe, Reyner (Reginald) [publishing house] DLB-170
Wolfe, Thomas 1900-1938.... DLB-9, 102; Y-85; DS-2, 16
Wolfe, Tom 1931- DLB-152, 185
Wolff, Helen 1906-1994 .... Y-94
Wolff, Tobias 1945- DLB-130
Wolfram von Eschenbach circa 1170-after 1220 .... DLB-138
Wolfram von Eschenbach's *Parzival*: Prologue and Book 3........ DLB-138

Wollstonecraft, Mary 1759-1797 .... DLB-39, 104, 158
Wondratschek, Wolf 1943- DLB-75
Wood, Benjamin 1820-1900 ...... DLB-23
Wood, Charles 1932- DLB-13
Wood, Mrs. Henry 1814-1887...... DLB-18
Wood, Joanna E. 1867-1927 ...... DLB-92
Wood, Samuel [publishing house] DLB-49
Wood, William ?-? DLB-24
Woodberry, George Edward 1855-1930 .... DLB-71, 103
Woodbridge, Benjamin 1622-1684 .... DLB-24
Woodcock, George 1912- DLB-88
Woodhull, Victoria C. 1838-1927 .... DLB-79
Woodmason, Charles circa 1720-? ... DLB-31
Woodress, Jr., James Leslie 1916- ... DLB-111
Woodson, Carter G. 1875-1950 ..... DLB-17
Woodward, C. Vann 1908- DLB-17
Woodward, Stanley 1895-1965 ..... DLB-171
Wooler, Thomas 1785 or 1786-1853 .... DLB-158
Woolf, David (see Maddow, Ben)
Woolf, Leonard 1880-1969 .... DLB-100; DS-10
Woolf, Virginia 1882-1941 ..... DLB-36, 100, 162; DS-10
Woolf, Virginia, "The New Biography," *New York Herald Tribune*, 30 October 1927 .... DLB-149
Woollcott, Alexander 1887-1943 ..... DLB-29
Woolman, John 1720-1772 .... DLB-31
Woolner, Thomas 1825-1892....... DLB-35
Woolsey, Sarah Chauncy 1835-1905. .. DLB-42
Woolson, Constance Fenimore 1840-1894 .... DLB-12, 74, 189
Worcester, Joseph Emerson 1784-1865............ DLB-1
Worde, Wynkyn de [publishing house] DLB-170
Wordsworth, Christopher 1807-1885 .. DLB-166
Wordsworth, Dorothy 1771-1855.... DLB-107
Wordsworth, Elizabeth 1840-1932 .... DLB-98
Wordsworth, William 1770-1850.. DLB-93, 107
Workman, Fanny Bullock 1859-1925. .. DLB-189
The Works of the Rev. John Witherspoon (1800-1801) [excerpts]......... DLB-31
A World Chronology of Important Science Fiction Works (1818-1979) DLB-8
World Publishing Company DLB-46
World War II Writers Symposium at the University of South Carolina, 12–14 April 1995 .... Y-95
Worthington, R., and Company.... DLB-49
Wotton, Sir Henry 1568-1639 ..... DLB-121
Wouk, Herman 1915- Y-82

Wreford, James 1915- DLB-88
Wren, Percival Christopher 1885-1941... DLB-153
Wrenn, John Henry 1841-1911..... DLB-140
Wright, C. D. 1949- DLB-120
Wright, Charles 1935- DLB-165; Y-82
Wright, Charles Stevenson 1932- ... DLB-33
Wright, Frances 1795-1852........ DLB-73
Wright, Harold Bell 1872-1944 ...... DLB-9
Wright, James 1927-1980........ DLB-5, 169
Wright, Jay 1935- DLB-41
Wright, Louis B. 1899-1984 .... DLB-17
Wright, Richard 1908-1960 .. DLB-76, 102; DS-2
Wright, Richard B. 1937- DLB-53
Wright, Sarah Elizabeth 1928- DLB-33
Wright, Willard Huntington ("S. S. Van Dine") 1888-1939 .... DS-16
Writers and Politics: 1871-1918, by Ronald Gray DLB-66
Writers and their Copyright Holders: the WATCH Project Y-94
Writers' Forum Y-85
Writing for the Theatre, by Harold Pinter DLB-13
Wroth, Lady Mary 1587-1653 ..... DLB-121
Wroth, Lawrence C. 1884-1970 .... DLB-187
Wurlitzer, Rudolph 1937- DLB-173
Wyatt, Sir Thomas circa 1503-1542 .... DLB-132
Wycherley, William 1641-1715....... DLB-80
Wyclif, John circa 1335-31 December 1384 ... DLB-146
Wyeth, N. C. 1882-1945 .... DLB-188; DS-16
Wylie, Elinor 1885-1928........ DLB-9, 45
Wylie, Philip 1902-1971 .... DLB-9
Wyllie, John Cook 1908-1968 .... DLB-140

X

Xenophon circa 430 B.C.-circa 356 B.C. DLB-176

Y

Yasuoka, Shōtarō 1920- DLB-182
Yates, Dornford 1885-1960..... DLB-77, 153
Yates, J. Michael 1938- DLB-60
Yates, Richard 1926-1992.... DLB-2; Y-81, 92
Yavorov, Peyo 1878-1914........ DLB-147
Yearsley, Ann 1753-1806 .... DLB-109
Yeats, William Butler 1865-1939........ DLB-10, 19, 98, 156

Yep, Laurence 1948- DLB-52

Yerby, Frank 1916-1991 .... DLB-76

Yezierska, Anzia 1885-1970 .... DLB-28

Yolen, Jane 1939- DLB-52

Yonge, Charlotte Mary
  1823-1901 .... DLB-18, 163

The York Cycle
  circa 1376-circa 1569 .... DLB-146

A Yorkshire Tragedy DLB-58

Yoseloff, Thomas
  [publishing house] DLB-46

Young, Al 1939- DLB-33

Young, Arthur 1741-1820 .... DLB-158

Young, Dick
  1917 or 1918 - 1987 .... DLB-171

Young, Edward 1683-1765 .... DLB-95

Young, Stark 1881-1963 ... DLB-9, 102; DS-16

Young, Waldeman 1880-1938 ..... DLB-26

Young, William [publishing house] DLB-49

Young Bear, Ray A. 1950- DLB-175

Yourcenar, Marguerite
  1903-1987 .... DLB-72; Y-88

"You've Never Had It So Good," Gusted by "Winds of Change": British Fiction in the 1950s, 1960s, and After DLB-14

Yovkov, Yordan 1880-1937 .... DLB-147

Z

Zachariä, Friedrich Wilhelm
  1726-1777 .... DLB-97

Zajc, Dane 1929- DLB-181

Zamora, Bernice 1938- DLB-82

Zand, Herbert 1923-1970 .... DLB-85

Zangwill, Israel 1864-1926 ..... DLB-10, 135

Zanzotto, Andrea 1921- DLB-128

Zapata Olivella, Manuel 1920- DLB-113

Zebra Books DLB-46

Zebrowski, George 1945- DLB-8

Zech, Paul 1881-1946 .... DLB-56

Zepheria DLB-172

Zeidner, Lisa 1955- DLB-120

Zelazny, Roger 1937-1995 .... DLB-8

Zenger, John Peter 1697-1746 .... DLB-24, 43

Zesen, Philipp von 1619-1689 ..... DLB-164

Zieber, G. B., and Company DLB-49

Zieroth, Dale 1946- DLB-60

Zigler und Kliphausen, Heinrich Anshelm von
  1663-1697 .... DLB-168

Zimmer, Paul 1934- DLB-5

Zingref, Julius Wilhelm
  1591-1635 .... DLB-164

Zindel, Paul 1936- DLB-7, 52

Zinzendorf, Nikolaus Ludwig von
  1700-1760 .... DLB-168

Zitkala-Ša 1876-1938 .... DLB-175

Zola, Emile 1840-1902 .... DLB-123

Zolotow, Charlotte 1915- DLB-52

Zschokke, Heinrich 1771-1848 ..... DLB-94

Zubly, John Joachim 1724-1781 .... DLB-31

Zu-Bolton II, Ahmos 1936- DLB-41

Zuckmayer, Carl 1896-1977 .... DLB-56, 124

Zukofsky, Louis 1904-1978 ..... DLB-5, 165

Zupan, Vitomil 1914-1987 .... DLB-181

Župančič, Oton 1878-1949 ...... DLB-147

zur Mühlen, Hermynia 1883-1951 .... DLB-56

Zweig, Arnold 1887-1968 .... DLB-66

Zweig, Stefan 1881-1942 ...... DLB-81, 118

ISBN 0-7876-1845-4

90000